COMPOUND BODY

UNSANGDONG Architects Cooperation
JANG YOON GYOO, SHIN CHANG HOON

USD PUBLISHING CO.

Appendix	4	**Profile** UNSANGDONG Architects Cooperation
	6	**Epilogue** KiUnSangDong
	8	**Compound Body**
	602	**Credits**

Projects	54	**KRING** BEING A BRANDSCAPE
	92	**Gallery YEH** MAKING URBAN CANVAS
	114	**Yeosu Expo Thematic Pavillion** OCEAN IMAGINATION
	136	**Asian Culture Complex** INTERACTIVE CULTURE STAGE
	160	**Outdoor Amphitheater for Youth, Nodeul Island** INTERACTIVE MUSIC STAGE WITH EVENT BUBBLE
	170	**KTNG Complex Center** FLYING CITY

#	Title	Subtitle
184	**Design Center in GwangJu**	INTERACTIVE PROGRAM
198	**Flagship Tower**	INTERACTIVE FLAGSHIP VOID
214	**Life & Power Press in PaJu Book City**	CULTURAL TOPOGRAPHY - STACKING CONTOUR
238	**Theater Contour**	TOPOGRAPHY STAGE OF CONTOUR
248	**Prehistoric Museum**	INTERACTIVE TOPOGRAPHY
268	**Shanghai EXPO Industrial Pavilion**	GREEN IMAGINATION
296	**Gallery 303**	CRYSTAL SCULPTURE
308	**Gallery The Hill**	CRYSTAL MOUNTAIN
320	**Stacking Gallery in ChungJu**	FLOATING STONE
328	**Dream Art Hall in Sung Dong**	CULTURE FOREST
342	**Museum for NamJune Paik**	MEDIA DAM
352	**Pusan Tower**	INTERACTIVE PASSAGE
356	**City Tower in ChungLa**	LANDSCAPE STACKING WITH PASSAGE
372	**ChiChi Memorial**	QUAKE-SCAPE
378	**Thousand Palace**	URBAN CONNECTING SCULPTURE
396	**Design of Exhibition Space in GwangJu Biennale**	CITY SCAPE
410	**Paris Olympic Memorial**	NAVIGATION CELL
424	**Gallery JUNGMISO**	LOOKING THROUGH THE GLASS
430	**Actress ⟨YOONSUKHWA⟩ Space for Performance**	ACTRESS YOON SUK-HWA'S SPACE, THEATER JUNGMISO STORY
446	**Gallery JUNSOOCHUN**	VINYL HOUSE
450	**Plaza of GwangJu Biennale**	SCULPTURE OF THE EARTH
458	**Ravin Peace Plaza Vertical Interaction**	VOIDSCAPE FOR PEACE FORUM
462	**Dancing Apartment**	
468	**Kolon Theme Housing**	
474	**Prugio Labotega Officetel**	THOUSAND LIFE
486	**Headquater Office of SK Networks**	CREATIVE OFFICE
502	**Headquater Office of Evervill**	BRAND SPACE
506	**Campus Complex, University of Seoul**	COMPOUND LANDSCAPE
520	**School of Architecture, Seoul National University**	RESEARCH SCAPE
530	**CheongShim Elementary School**	GREEN RING
540	**Province Hall of ChungNam**	MULTI-LAYERED LOOP
556	**Kaleidoscope Gallery**	
562	**Atelier for Ceramic Artist**	PASSAGE FRAME HOUSE
568	**Eco Frame House**	PASSAGE FRAME HOUSE
572	**Kolon E+ Green Home**	ECO-ROOFTECTURE
580	**Eco Deck House**	PASSAGE DECK HOUSE
584	**Gallery CAMELLIA HILL**	PASSAGE MOUND
588	**Korea Town Complex**	MEMORY ACCUMULATION THRESHOLD
592	**Wall Garden**	PROGRAM WALL
596	**Office of UNSANGDONG Architects Cooperation**	STACKING PROGRAM

Profile
unsangdong architects cooperation

JANG YOON GYOO

SHIN CHANG HOON

Interview, KRING Space

COMPOUND BODY 5

JANG YOON GYOO

UNSANGDONG Architects, Principal, 2001 - present
JANG YOON GYOO Experimental Studio 1995 - 2001
Kookmin University, Professor, 2004 - present
Gallery JungMiSo, Principal, 2004- present
KACI Architects, Design Principal, 2001 - 2003
HEERIM Architects & Engineers, Director of Design Pool, 1997 - 2001
Artech Architects & Partners, Co-Principal, 1995 -1996
Seoul Architecture Consultants, Project Designer, 1990 -1994
Seoul National University, M.Arch., 1990
Seoul National University, B.S., 1987
Grand prize award of Korean Space & Culture Institute, 2009
Good Designer prize of Korean Good Design Award, 2009
Award of Korean Architects Institute, 2010, 2007
Architecture Award of Seoul Metropolitan City, 2010, 2007
Award of Korean Architecture & Culture, 2007
Architectural Review commended award, 2007
Architecture Record Vangauard Award, 2006
Shinkenchiku Takiron International Competition, Honorable Mention, 1994

韻生同

UNSANGDONG
Architects Cooperation

SHIN CHANG HOON

UNSANGDONG Architects, Co-Principal, 2003 - present
Hongik University, a Lecturor, 2008 - present
HIMMMA Architects, 2003
M.A.R.U2 Architects, 2001
BAUM Architects, Project Designer, 1999
Artech Architects & Partners ,1995
University of Seoul, M.Arch., 2006
Youngnam University, B.A., 1996
Award of Korean Architects Institute, 2010, 2007
Architecture Award of Seoul Metropolitan City, 2010, 2007
Award of Korean Architecture & Culture, 2007
Architectural Review commended award, 2007
Architecture Record Vangauard Award, 2006

Website address _ WWW.USDSPACE.COM

UNSANGDONG Architects Cooperation Project 2001 - 2010

Prugio Labotega Officetel, 2010 Competition Winner
3-Terrace Housing in GaPyung, 2010 Competition Winner
CheongShim Elementary School, 2010 Competition Winner
Kolon E+Green Home, 2010
Headquarter Office of SK network, 2010 Competition Winner
Office of UNSANGDONG Architects Cooperation, 2010
Yeosu EXPO Thematic Pavilion, 2010 International Competition Honorable Prize
SK Flagship Tower, 2009
Dancing Apartment, 2009
Kolon Theme Hosing, 2009
Shanghai EXPO Industrial Pavilion, 2009
Dream Art Hall in SungDong, Seoul, 2009 Competition Winner
Thousand Palace _ Hi Seoul Festival Stage Sculpture, 2009
Province Hall of ChungNam, 2008 Competition Winner
Civic Center for Education & Culture in SunChun, 2008 Competition Winner
City Tower in ChungLa, 2008
Kring_ Kumho Culture Complex, 2008 Competition Winner, Grand prize award of Korean Space & Culture Institute, 2nd Grand prize of Korean Good Design Award
Gallery 303, GwangJu city, 2008 Honorable Prize of Korean Good Design Award
Stacking Gallery of Housing Culture in ChungJu, Korea, 2008
Life & Power Press in PaJu Book City, 2007 Architecture Award of KyungKi Province
Atelier for Ceramic Artist, 2007
Design Center in DeaHak-Ro, HongIk University, Korea, 2007 Competition Winner
Gallery 〈YEH〉, Seoul, Korea, 2007 Architectural Review commended award, Architecture Record Vangauard Award, Award of Korean Architects Institute, Architecture Award of Seoul Metropolitan City, Award of Korean Architecture & Culture
Eco Housing Complex in PyungChang, KOREA, 2006
Prehistoric Museum, 2006
Extension of the City Hall, Seoul, Korea,2006 International Competition 2nd Prize
School of Architecture, Seoul National University, Seoul, 2006 Competition Winner, Architecture Award of Seoul Metropolitan City

Head Office of Froebel in Paju Book City, Korea, 2005
Korean Town Complex, Newyork, 2005
Media Organ, 2005
ECO Deck & Eco Frame House, 2005 Competition Winner
Asian Culture complex in GwangJu, 2005 International Competition 3rd Prize
Outdoor Amphitheater for Youth, Nodeul Island, Korea, 2005 International Competition Winner
Campus Complex, Seoul University, Korea, 2004 Architecture Award of Seoul Metropolitan City, Award of Korean Architecture & Culture
KTNG Complex Center in SuWon city, Korea, 2003-2004 Competition Winner
Gallery 〈Camellia Hill〉, Jeju Island, Korea, 2004
Design of Exhibition Space in GwangJu Biennale, Korea, 2004
Head Office of Residential Research in GwangJu, Korea, 2004 Competition Winner
Paris Olympic Memorial, Paris, France, 2004
Wall Garden, HanNamDong, YongSan, Korea, 2004
Design Center in GwangJu, Korea, 2004 Competition Winner
Gallery 〈JUNSOOCHUN〉, Seoul, Korea, 2004
Gallery 〈JUNGMISO〉, Seoul, Korea, 2003
Pusan Tower, 2003
Museum for Nam June Paik, 2003
Performance Stage of Pusan Film Festival Memorial Concert, Seoul, Korea, 2003
Actor 〈YOONSUKHWA〉 Space for Performance, Seoul, Korea, 2002 - 2003
Yoon's Residence 〈Paysage House〉, Seoul, Korea, 2003
International Passenger Terminal in Kunsan, Korea, 2002 Competition Winner
Embassy of Egypt, Seoul, Korea, 2002 International Competition Winner
Ravi n Peace Plaza, 2001 International Competition Finalist
Millennium Memorial in Seoul, Korea, 2000 International Competition 3rd Prize

Epilogue
KiUnSangDong

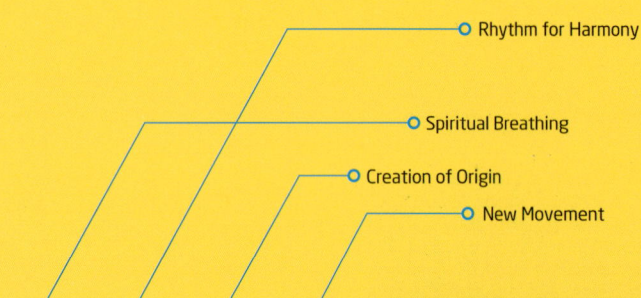
- Rhythm for Harmony
- Spiritual Breathing
- Creation of Origin
- New Movement

氣韻生動

KiUnSangDong
Effect

Jang Yoon Gyoo

UNSANGDONG ARCHITECTS

We all acknowledge that making culturally-viable space does not stop at the level of simple provision of physical space. The level goes further to a degree of inhabitation, through which its newly met operatives occupy and inhabit each other to generate new results and new creativity.

When we found the Group UnSangDong, our focus was forming a creative and interactive map of operative network that can embrace not just buildings, but all possible fields that can generate interesting feedbacks with architectural mode. These feedbacks play critical role in establishing cultural networks that surrounds the Group UnSangDong. Other groups included in the network are: Gallery JungMiSo - think-tank for young artists and designers, and Space Coordinator - a networking engine for the young professionals.

As active part of this group, architectural practice of UnSangDong has been carried out in similar manner in which the framework of projects are set up for continuous interaction between culture and architecture in fluidity. We call this attitude "working on cultural cracks". As if someone who is rediscovering the slit of air squeezing through the gap between the pieces in the armor, we seek architectural desires oozing through the cultural gap in-between the pieces of our society, or desires for finding ways to directly transcribe from physical space to cultural space. With major portion of our past efforts follow the hatch of theory called ⟨Compound Body⟩, various attempts were made to be included in the map - ⟨Skinscape⟩, ⟨Clip City⟩, ⟨Becoming Animal⟩, ⟨Floating Body⟩, ⟨Trans-Programming⟩, ⟨Reaction Body⟩, and etc.

Our works are based on how-to-construct a scenario of ⟨cultural interaction⟩ through architecture. One example, the story of ⟨Compound Body⟩ was described as a

GALLERY JUNGMISO

process of making interactive text through working in-betweenness among the territorial boundaries of various texts. Through the story I described - "It is an architectural framework where all texts can share, interact and create a new convergence. It transcends all visible crossings of texts, continuously encouraging reinterpretation, stress, abstraction and profundity - it posits itself above ⟨Reciprocal Text⟩". The background behind our hypothesis desires for architectural intervention to reinvent culture through ⟨interaction⟩.

There were several dialogues regarding the notion of architectural interaction with an analogy of a quality within ⟨armor⟩ in the past. The quality of armor depends on two things: one based on the strength of the skin as a whole composition; and the other the technology of fitting between pieces. Although different in scale and technology, the two can neither be rated individually nor partially. It can only be rated in its complete form and be measured for its readiness (for a battle) through a qualitative assembly of joints controlled by the cracks at the joint. We are particularly interested in the theme ⟨Crack in the Armor⟩. Not as the armor itself, but the code of "air" that infiltrates through the crack among the pieces seems analogous to the notion of cultural code which enables the interaction we have been discussing. The key moment here is to explore how the cultural opportunities are incorporated into architectural cracks and suggest specific strategies in making a 'scape' of cracks, of which its hidden spatial characteristics are revealed, enriched and connected with generation of new cultural programs. Through the lightness of air, the dense poetics are created. Skin sprouted by the air triumphs with cultural subtlety free from architectural authority. Architectural demeanor through ⟨Crack in the Armor⟩ has a critical linkage to the departure of perspective ⟨Orpheus's Gaze⟩. As I have described in the book ⟨Compound Body⟩, ⟨Orpheus's Gaze⟩ textualized new possibilities extracted out of a mythical code. It stands right on the borderline that connects new code and new mode of thinking. It is a new infiltration point, new crack through rearrangement of the conventional text. ⟨Crack in the Armor⟩ is decoded using mythical code, and the room is created for us to seek and capture perspectives and knowledge towards new possible outcomes. Our attempt to culturally combine the methodology and its material substances has generated several versions of mapping techniques that oscillate between the idea of ⟨Compoundization⟩ and ⟨Integration⟩. Both are in destability and have structure that is always in progress, possessing the cultural aspects which can displace and revise internally and creatively. In the age of information and media, ⟨Cultural Interaction⟩ created by the ⟨Crack in the Armor⟩ is inevitable demand. New maps will constantly be generated and organized with the progression of the crack's qualities and integrities. Making maps that corresponds with ⟨Crack in the Armor⟩ is a prerequisite for us to initiate new experimental possibilities. These maps are open-structure capable of accessing and engaging in any dimension, anytime, anywhere, in any form - like endless transforming device with infinite routes of accessibility always in hand. It is more than enough to explore the opportunity then, the spectrum that goes beyond mere the scale of ⟨Interaction⟩. Because cultural interaction is never achieved alone or by single means of fabrication, we as architects or artists are required to reach beyond our individuality and achieve new transformation. Architects intervene and challenge the territories of arts, and artists and young professionals infiltrate through slits of culture and provoke new questions with inquiries.

It is time to arm ourselves with new devices and strategies in envisioning society and culture before even thinking about doing something physical to transform and analyze. New perspectives are needed, to lead us towards mindset-shift, new programmatic innovations, and new social/cultural/urban transformations. In the middle of all this, interactions begin with ⟨Making Cultural Crack⟩.

Compound Body

Jang, Yoon Gyoo

Jang Yoon Gyoo + Lee Mee Young,
Orpheus's Gaze (1998)

Jang Yoon Gyoo's Writing
"Compound Body" (2005)

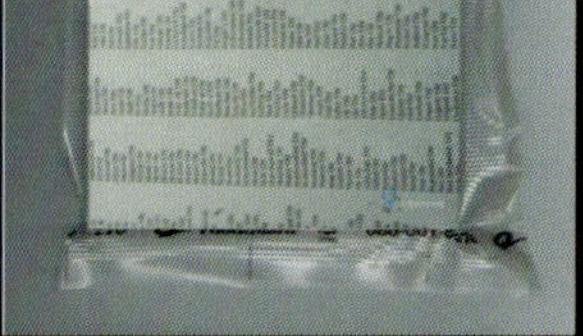

Peter Bruegel the Elder's, The Tower of Babel (1563)

⟨Writing Myth _ Beginning with Orpheus's Gaze⟩
What we try to capture. Even if it seems full of paradoxes and contradictions, I would like to explore all possible boundaries, one by one. The stories below are combinations of the past writings on architectural themes of my interest. If typical urban text takes rather analytical frameworks and approaches, the perspective here is focused on prescribing more integrated relationships among different texts.

⟨Orpheus's Gaze⟩   Disregarding the rule to not turn back and look at her, his desire finally concedes into looking at non-existent Eurydice. Just like the skin of which appeared as virtual, Eurydice was dead in reality. Orpheus sees her who is invisible. He touches her as Eurydice intact.

⟨Ulysses's Ear⟩   Having his men sealed their ears with wax, and himself tied to the ship's mast, Ulysses listened to beautiful, yet deadly songs of the Sirens - confronting another kinds of Orpheusian danger. His tricks earned the salvation out of hearing deadly songs. Ulyssesian space introduces new hypothesis of envisioning the new world by embracing experiments in and out of the virtual world.

It starts with ⟨Orpheus's Gaze⟩. We cannot pass by the Orpheus, the origin of mythical code that consistently lingers around us. With Orpheus's desire, we dare to see the new world even if it brings us disastrous consequences. We are aware of the risk of transposing the virtual text to the real. However, just as if Orpheus had to confront the second loss of Eurydice, the virtual must be actualized to the real and expose its limits, forcing us to see the risk and danger in it. What is more important is how to overcome these hypothesized danger in the process of transposition.

Ulysses's Ear means exploring the linkage possible for manipulating the text. A single text then does not exist as 'only one'. Manipulation required in modifying programs starts from rejecting the notion that space written only as a single text, and the space that exists as a single text. The meaning of our works lies along the transforming process, of how to transpose the skin and object of the space, into other meanings and values. Orpheus's Gaze connects with hypertextual space. Rather than constrained in its single meaning, the linkage of the text can be open to infinite trajectories, making it possible to express in multiple layers. I confront the moment to choose Orpheus's Gaze that generates continuous and creative linkages. At the crossroad between the danger and the new experimentation, to where shall we sail towards?

Taboos and violations possess Orpheusian Gaze. Against the stare towards him, Orpheus confidently takes off his medieval coat. Out of the text derived from bare reflection, we dream a feast of festivities. At the moment of festivity, taboos are accepted. Now needed are the new possibilities to reach extreme consciousness which breaks free from the convention and gaze. They form a direct linkage to exposing some of distorted and perverse codes that have been suppressed by social convention.

David Mach's, Babel Towers

Compound Body
01 Between Compound and Integration

It might be possible to achieve a complete integration beyond the boundaries. Wanted here is a complete ⟨Integration⟩ devoid of distinction between architecture and other territories. Our beginning was one world. Through noise and chaos, its essence must have been dispersed. Suppose we can re-trace our times as we keep integrating each other's territories, we might be close enough to the essence again.

⟨Compound Body⟩ is a virtual text written over the assumption that integrating the multiple layers of territorial elements invites the possibility of opening up question in producing the new outcome. The focus here should be how to examine a system as its unstable state before it becomes a complete, stabilized whole. It embodies the notion that a destabilized structure in fact could generate a series of opportunities which can lead to another creative displacement. Suppose the accomplishment of the ⟨Integrated Body⟩ is our final destination, we may regard the ⟨Compound Body⟩ as a set of classified system embracing all possibilities available through which its processes become a complete integration. This process then requires text-writing methods that can engage infinite variations existing in between compound and integration.

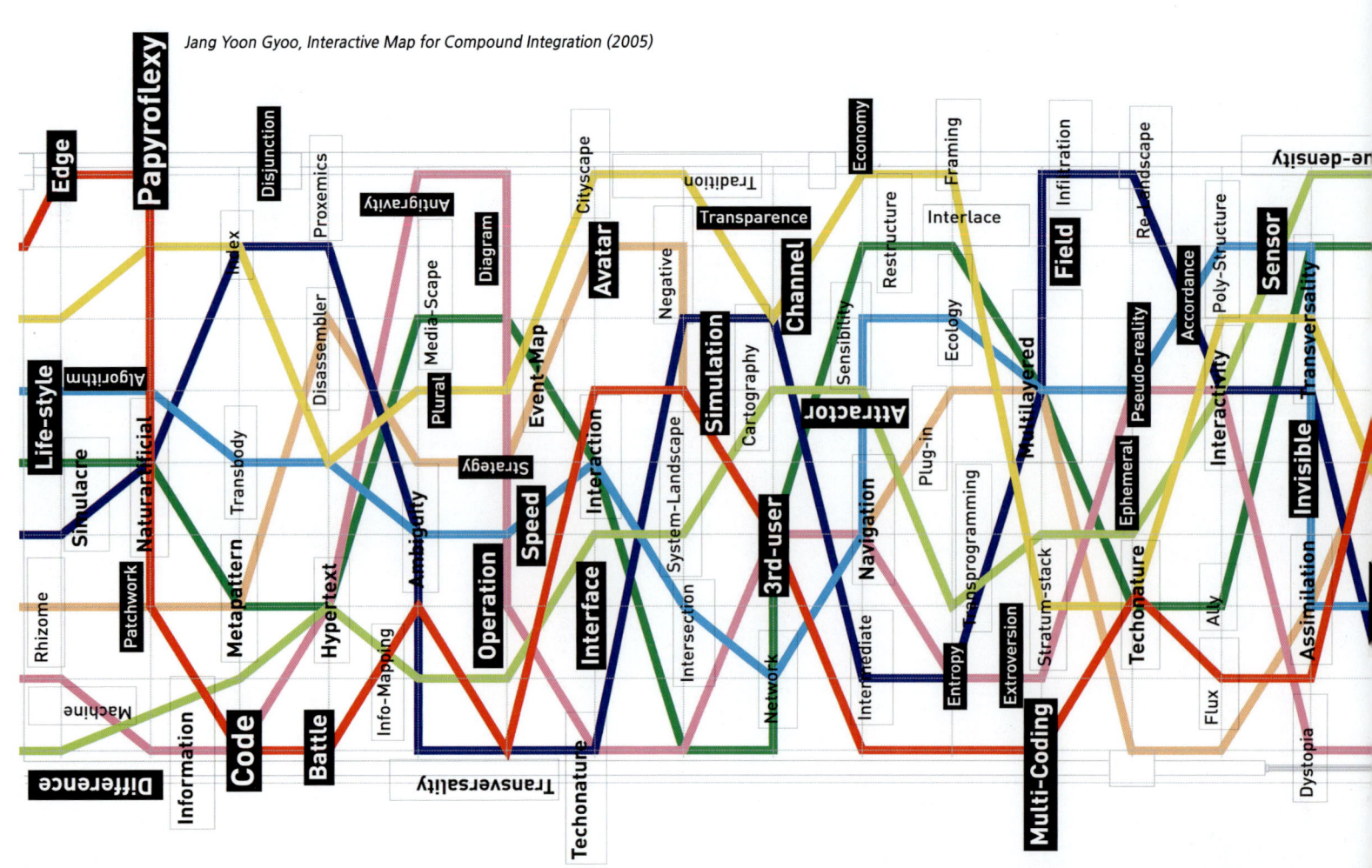

Jang Yoon Gyoo, Interactive Map for Compound Integration (2005)

COMPOUND BODY 11

Virtual text is one of many presuppositions that restructures the city and/or rewrites the space. Bearing in mind that the integration of the system's contents and logic can provide new linkage, and these linkages simultaneously engage various estranged territories within our urban and social landscape.

The new text considers integration in both material substances and organizations. It becomes a new loop that connects parts in different social and urban nature including its marginal areas. Sudden social jumps and swifts makes the preservation of the conventions as obsolete. The text is formed around errors and mixtures from the countless origins of things and matters instead. It continuously roams around the virtual network of online community and plays various roles in which new relationships can be formed. ⟨Compound Body⟩ never pursues for a complete singularization or unison of these linkages. Making progression towards the integration, it always posits itself in between its transformation and displacement state.

The boundaries among individual territories and its spatial demarcation no longer exist, replaced by the new text of Compound Body that continuously evolves by this in-betweenness. Thus, on one hand, ⟨Compound Body⟩ is the text generated from the interactions among boundaries. It is an architectural framework where all texts can share, interact and create a new convergence. It transcends all visible crossings of texts, continuously encouraging reinterpretation, stress, abstraction and profundity - it posits itself above ⟨Reciprocal Text⟩. Compound Body is reciprocal. The question regards to how to set up a framework for which these texts can be shared, and that its combination can generate endless branches of variety, taking different approaches and readings. Endless strings that keeps branching out, making its end with open, infinite variables. This question of "how to generate compoundization" resides along the potentials within infinite matrix of convergences - convergences among virtually-created hyper-real text and reproduced auras. The aura loses its meanings and values. Accordingly, in architecture, not only the architectural text takes its effect. Just as if the virtual text, possessed with endless possibility in duplication can take roles in cyberspace, virtual text in place of the original. Regardless of where and how the hyper-real text comes in play into architecture, the only factor to evaluate the ground of difference is its effects. Considering that this text-writing may be the most critical set-up for seeking the significance of the Compound Body, its methods become important yet open to many different approaches. One can disguise the false over the real as if Jorge Luis Borges is armed with hoaxes and forgeries to play and trick the real. Or agents and catalysts can be established in order to provoke and

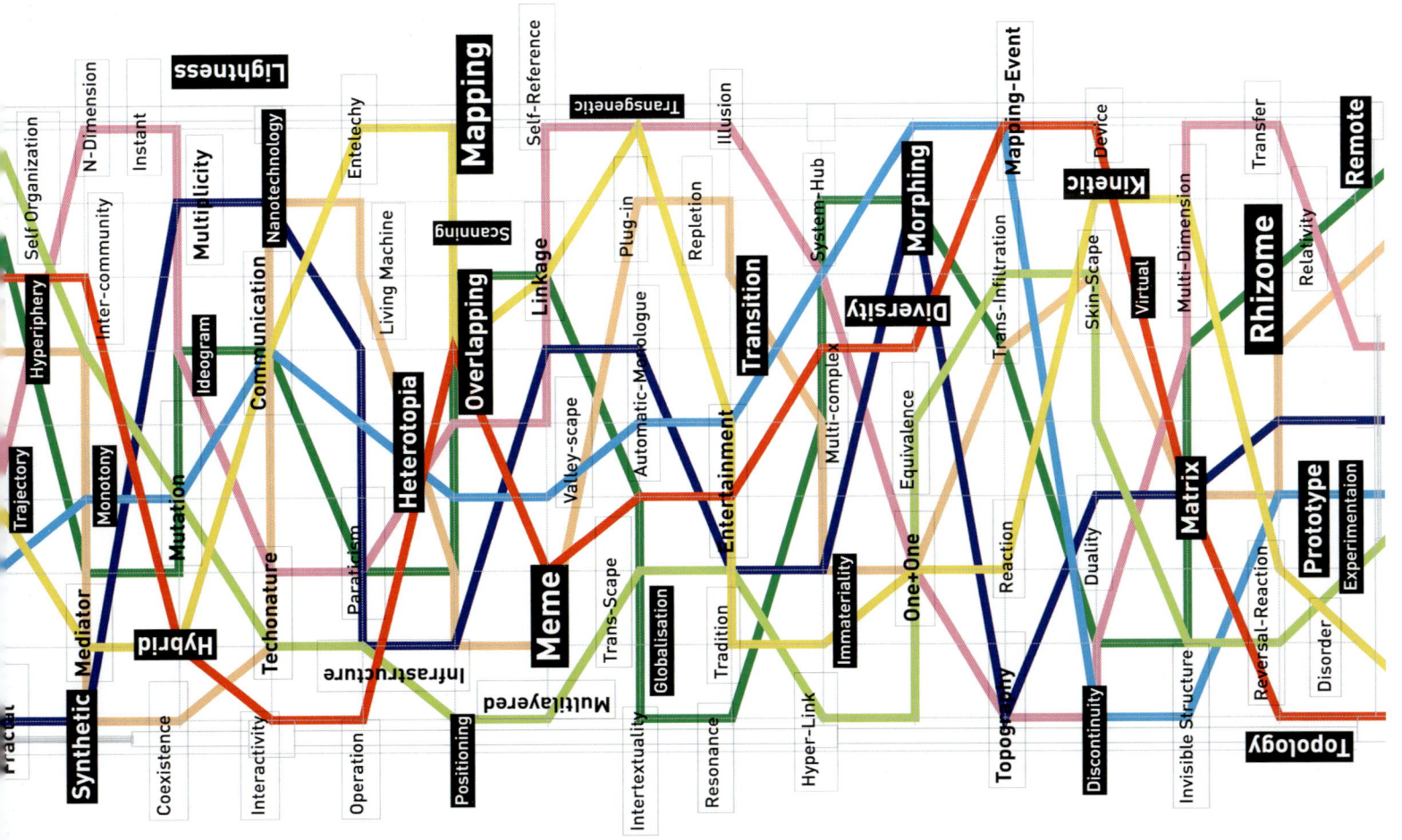

engage the feedbacks taking place in space in-between. These interstitial agents can either be visible or invisible. Whatever it may be, setting-up of these substances decides how "qualitative" the Compound Body might become.

Replication and formation, assembly and disassembly, transition and transformation,… The world moves in endless ranges of infinite displacements. Opportunity interestingly gained from the products of modernist architecture, I see, is that more or less it provided some aspects possible towards integration. One example would regard to architectural effort involved in interdisciplinary acts, as ways to blur the boundaries among disciplines and seeking for a new mixture. This intention of provoking new mix, also relates of the groundwork of the <Compound Body> - to bring new definitions and individuality out of newly-rephrased surface conditions. As if a great deal of information given through the media is almost encyclopedic in randomness and uncountable, new definition-generating probability goes endless, thus accelerates the characteristics of reciprocity to come and play among the texts.

In the age of information media, the workings of compound and integration may be our unavoidable task, yet can be a chaos. Defining new convergences generated though the Compound Body is merely one of many possible hypothesis to seek the new order from the newly perceived chaos. Architects who are bound to be driven by the physical and aesthetic space may escape their territories and take interest in immersing themselves into other spatial territories. They now play the role as mediators that allow architecture to communicate with other fields of disciplines, just as Hermes, the messenger of the gods and to the underworld. Architects no longer exist "only" as architects. Hermes becomes a new gender for the architects. Hermes-architect who is cultivated with diverse knowledge and wisdom, will maneuver disciplines and articulate his/her interest with architectural expression. The architect becomes the mediator blurring and mending the boundaries and concepts located in extreme distance. Architecture is only a medium to express self-identity, but does not have to be the only one anymore. Through online network of the Internet the world forms a single linkage. It is becoming less acceptable in discussing the values regarding individual activities and rationale. Even for those who pursues to stay individual is being forced now to acknowledge influences and ramifications from/to others. The compoundization only accelerates. What matters here the most is the question of quality, not quantity, in utilizing these networks to realize the Compound Body. Rather than acknowledging social compoundization, we have to understand the value in defining methods towards the Compound Body. This involves recognizing the world as a structure, a whole, the arrangement of encyclopedic information, and as a field of knowledge. We open our consciousness of knowledge in order to communicate with encyclopedia in front of us, and the space in-between disciplines.

For me the spirit of modernity is not so much based on its formal rebellion, but rather the attempt to materialize the aspects of compoundization and integration in technology and space. The final destination for the contemporary meaning behind the sprit of modernism, thus comprise a framework of integration among structure, space, material, skin, landscape, and etc. Now that the rapid development of technology providing even the clearer potential for us to approach to this destination, it is not difficult to imagine the world operated by technology, space and property in a single continuous flow. In architecture, such attempts are already being taken through works throughout the globe, illustrating the integration of skin and structure, or skin and landscape. Needless to say, these attempts are only parts of many countless attempts to be made. I have come to realization that even my past projects as far as

Jang Yoon Gyoo, Space of Interactive Map (2005)

COMPOUND BODY 13

10-years back, I may have been consciously and subconsciously laying out a groundwork around the notion of Compound Body, through making a series of architectural text that could locate somewhere "between the compound and integration".

Compound body possesses an irony that its structure as whole coexists with open and indeterminate spatial organization. This allows us explore architectural possibilities in the status of continuous open-endedness, with its characteristics that always generate progressive outputs towards integration. The premise of <Compound Body> is that this process would occur as a loop - the moment the integration achieved, its arrived-end-point at integration stage revert back to becomes yet another departure for a new process to start compounding again. Indeterminate integration allows us to construct the framework of new creativity.

The intention behind discussing the compound body and countless transformation of its linkages is to discover a hidden boundary condition we can reach. As one example, I often propose formats to establish <Search Machine>, to discover infinite edges surrounding boundaries and what exists in between them. This allows us to think about the in-betweenness of the form & deformed, as well as compound & integration. Then the question arises - how to generate maps in appropriate format, something that oscillates in between the <Compound & Integration>. The basic premise would be involving the mixing of the two different materials which starts primarily with exploration of its source of the mixture. Conventional method of urban research that we have been practicing also must be rethought to accommodate this approach. We must think about which materials and ingredients to begin with, before discussing mixing strategies. This reinforcement will help us to be assertive in elaborating new opportunity guided by the new mixture, rather than simply repeating the past exercise of claiming the city and architecture in superficial ways. Even if this mindset can cause inappropriate accidents and side effects, we must not fear for things to come in our time.

The <Search Machine> is for the sake of producing new images of the new reasoning ground. The opportunity within the Compound Body resides along its indeterminacy in defining clearly where and how the possible convergence might occur. This "ambiguity" raises and simultaneously accelerates the questioning of the true nature of things and matters. Boundaries between city structure, territories, people, interpretations, understanding,···are set to work ambiguously. Softening the characteristics of boundaries can be a beginning for new social groundwork with no differences regarded. As if we always tend to miss seeing certain part of an object when we see them, and others do not see what I see, architecture can be visualized in different ways when we start thinking outside-the-box, or leaving architecture. Although invisible by me, it can be visible by others. The notion of <Searching> would allow us to recognize things not yet known, possible, and in mediation with other fields of territories, and thus we may confront the worlds yet to be offered to architecture,

<Search Machine> is put to an endless journey along its infinite linkages. The countless categories of online information and substances form the virtual ocean, and the<Search Machine> is thrown in the middle to move with no guidance. It is left alone unexpected and unforeseeable in directions, lost in where to go next. Placing the machine with navigation has been obsolete for long time since the old sense of distance has been manipulated twisted to put out wrong and meaningless information. We need to establish a new guide that assists the navigation and generates the map accordingly. Today's Orpheus no longer dreams of returning home. If given a useful map that will be eternally provided, he would

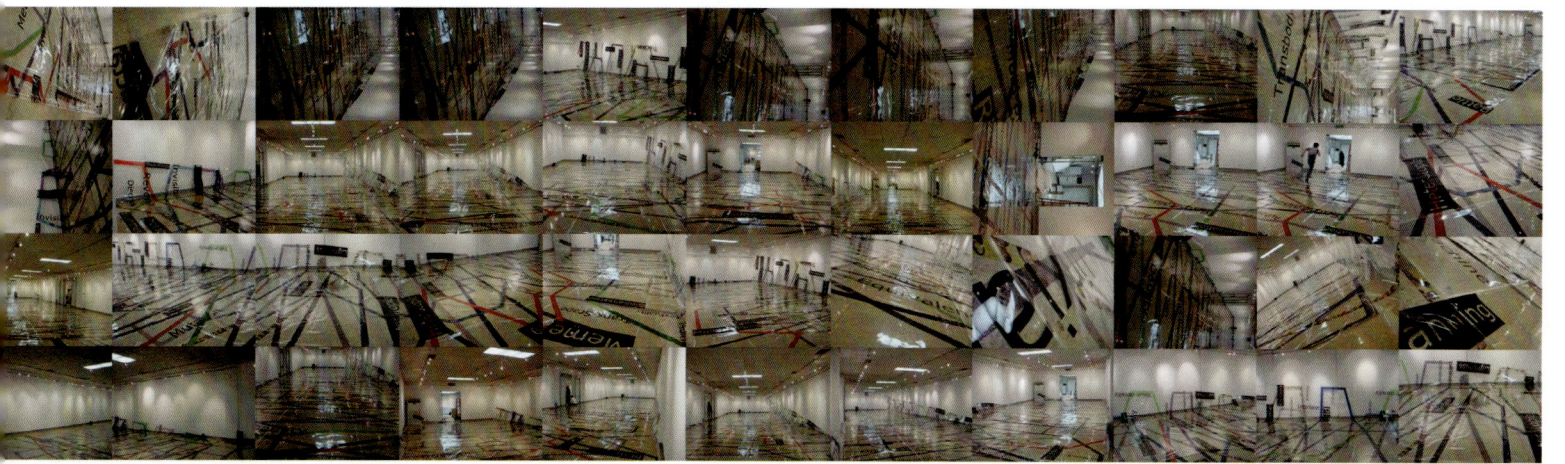

devote himself in exploring the world of his dream with the map forever. Home he needs to return is not the end of the reality, but the reality of the rest of journey. The new <Search Machine> does not practice random surfing, it searches parts with potential subject it desires to mix and match. Stories left in the infinite linkage generate another countless loops and their deformations. Escher was caught up in spatial delusions that take place endlessly and continuously. His mind leads us to kinds of space that expands in simultaneity - a continuous, imaginative, fantastic loop projected by various combinations. Cinematic organization and experience emerge. We can call working on continuous space such as Mobius-like space, an elimination process of distinction between inside and outside. Escher's loop physically substitutes double-coded conceptions, transposing the fictional code of the world into architectural articulation. A strange yet continuous framework of loop is achieved by the city and space. This continuity reminds us the Compound Body rooted in the idea of ceaseless moving structure, and maneuvering experience of city landscape.

We can generate different kinds of architecture through mixing two different substances, or two different programs. Starting from looking at social and urban phenomenon, we propose the method in which potential substances are selected, mixed and integrated. Architectural quality gained from the Compound Body originates from maximizing the limitations in these combinations of which today's technology can offer. The role of a poet is to call out those which are monotonous and chaotic, achieve their <Universal Balance>, and create the unique harmony from the new balance. Compound Body is based on the romantic chord of a poet. Countless romance displaced in new mode provides advantage of effect over utility. Possessing the alchemy and magical effect, the Compound Body contains a mystery and a danger.

Trick of the magic is based on the process of unveiling the god's law and secrets of its operation, and then exercising them towards the matter of interest. Heinrich Cornelius Agrippa was a physician and philosopher. Agrippa attempted to covet god's duty with combinations of medical practice, alchemy and philosophy, hoping he can govern all ills and transform all things to gold. Faust, who was still not satisfied with mastering all fields of study, discovered the secrets between the upper and the lower world with the devil's help. For a moment, with all arrogance, wealth and pleasure, he attempted to be a man equal to a god.

Plot by Goethe seems as if it sings along the process of a man who expands to reach into a god's territory. Plot in Compound Body may also bear this in mind - challenging today's limitations with contemporary alchemy. The ability to turn a piece of metal into gold may belong to a god, not to a man. But it is about the potential in man's effort, to ceaselessly pursue his unknown limits through the process of making combinations of different substances. Nanotechnology, DNA engineering,···. Efforts are there to create new outcomes of transformation, as if a man trying to covet god-like territories. Faustian encounter includes the framework of modifying the nature of a man. A man we know up to now is no longer the man we think he is. He provokes hidden sensibility within us and enforces ourselves to follow the trace of endless events unfolded by the new conceptual intervention. Things generated by the Compoundization can be said as a <Mixture> among the territories, as if the new breeds being made by DNA engineering. This <Mixture> may be the new breed, or the new architecture. It may offer us new territorial articulations ignored by the conventional architecture, and provides new architectural alternatives. The more strange <Mixture> we create, the newer displacement of architecture occurs. My flesh may not be a sole space, but posit in between many converging points of combinations, or along manifolds of thousands of spaces. Space of the Compound Body

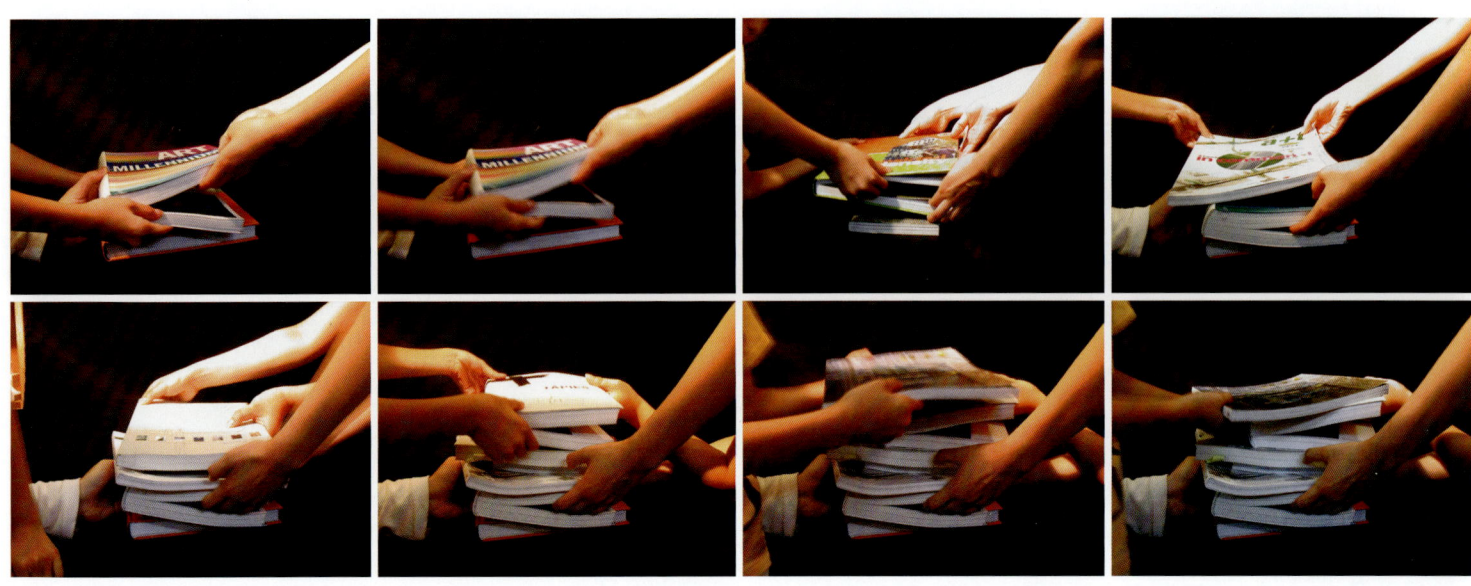

is comprised of structures that gain endless linearity and continuity. The endless line of void is lifted into three-dimensional form and space is generated. No distinctions are tolerated, only the tendencies of integration. Architectural compoundization, thus, can be generated as the pairs of the following:

City and architecture, art and architecture, architecture and product, architecture and science, architecture and Deleuze, Deleuze and skin, Hermes and Deleuze, man and animal, man and machine, architecture and machine, Lacan and architecture,⋯., space and space, space and skin, skin and skin, skin and structure, skin and program, program and structure, concept and space, skin and air, skin and landscape,⋯.

Through this process the integration takes place among the boundaries with ambiguity in architectural differentiation, including space, structure, wall, floor, column, light, and landscape. Coded transformation of spatial programs formulates even those in disability of encountering into Integration Body and Compound Body. Compound Body is constructed with codes not needed for any classification.

I have been exploring the idea of Compound Body through variety of projects. They are not complete as perfect set-up, but each of them can be seen as chapter in its own strategy. ⟨Reaction Body⟩, ⟨Skinscape⟩, ⟨Transcape⟩, ⟨Floating Body⟩,⋯and more, are the records of displacements led by different conceptual framework.

We attempted to generate urban reacting body through the idea of Compound Body by setting up reactions between city and architecture. The reaction of the boundary between city and architecture is explored when the relationship of what acts as foreground and background has been invalidated. Also there were other examples of Compound Body consisting of spatial and architectural factors - such as skin and others, skin and structure, or skin and space. ⟨Skinscape⟩ is the Compound Body made from program and skin, ⟨Transcape⟩ from program and others, ⟨Trans-user⟩ from commercial outline and architecture,⋯. Various factors and compounding substances are incorporated to explore their own versions of displacements.

One of major aspects in refining the compound body is to extract its comprising elements. As if we instigate cooking by mentioning its major ingredients first, the question should be what to select and use in order to comprise the body. The series of specific clarification follows, such as where to position those extracts, and so forth. As I peek around endless range of materials - cities, streets, alleys, media, space, novels, poems, music, art,⋯..and etc., the concept of "Clip City" embraces all of these, as one single flow of text. The materials scattered throughout the city are in fact associated very closely with the contents of the text in compound body. Although easy as one can say that the content and the method intertwine, the second part of structuring the compound body is how to mix and match those substances. This can be achieved by either interjecting a catalyst, literally mixing agents, or something in between the two to accidentally create 'another' reaction. Regardless of its method, the premise is that there must be a precise guide, to determine the properties of the compound body mutating in accordance with the model's process of 'becoming'. In the stage of such metamorphosis, various physical components intervene in the context of architectural space. Mixture of elements in the compound body includes both the mixture of existing architectural space, and the outcome resisting against such change. Metamorphosis promotes another metamorphosis as if a loop indicates no end but begins again as a new loop itself.

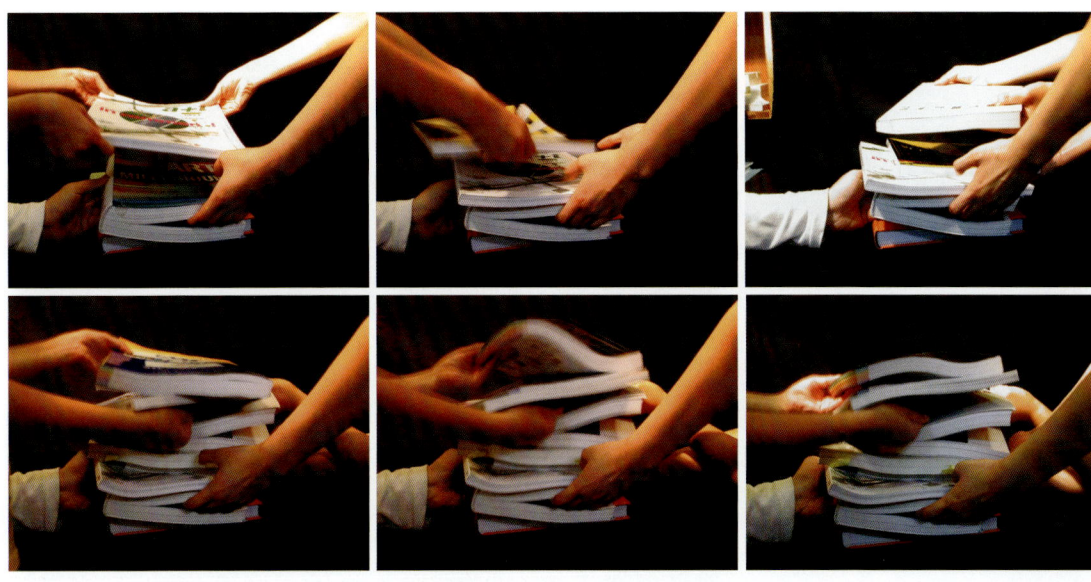

Jang Yoon Gyoo,
Hand's Performance for Communication

Abandoned City, All City, Abject City, Abstract City, Acme City, Actor-Network City, Actual City, Addictive City, Ad-hoc City, Affect City, Affirmative City, African City, Agglomeration City, Aggregative City, Agora City, Agricultural City, AIDS City, Air City, Air-Conditioning City, Airport City, Airship City, Airstrip City, Alarm City, Alert City, Alfa City, All-in-One City, Alpha City, Alternative City, Amazon City, Ambiguous City, American City, Amorphous City, Anal City, Analogue City, Analogous City, Anatomical City, And-so-on-City, Angel City, Angle City, Anticipatory City, Any City, Apocalyptic City, Apotheosized City, Arcade City, Archaic City, Archipelago City, ARKIPELAG City, Arty City, Artisanal City, Ash City

As-It-Could-Be City, Astral City, Asylum City, @ City, Atopic City, A-to-Z City, Automobile City, Autonomous City, Awkward City, Babylonian City, Bag City, Balance City, Bamboo City, Banal City, Bank City, Baroque City, Basic City, Bastard City, Bath City, Baton City, Be Yourself City, Beginning City, Beloved City, Best City, Better City, Beyond City, Big City, Bike City, Bio-City, Bioclimatic City, Bird City, Bird's-Eye City, Bit City, Bite City, Blasting City, Blind City, Blitz City, Blob City, Blood City, Blow City, Blow-Out City, Blur City, Body City, Bold City, Book City, Boom City, Box City, Brain City, Brand City, Brave City

Bridge City, Brilliant City, Broadacre City, Broken City, Browsing City, Bubble City, Bunker City, Bustling City, Button City, Cable City, Calibration City, Camp City, Camping City, Campus City, Canyon City, Capital City, Caprice City, Capsule City, Captive City, Car City, Card City, Cartoon City, Casino City, CompuCity, Cell City, Center City, Centerless City, Chaos City, Characteristic City, Charming City, Cheap City, Children's City, Choice City, Cinecittà, Cinema City, City on the Move, Clandestine City, Click City, Cliff City, Climax City, Clip City, Cloaca City, Cloud City, Club City, Cluster City, Coaxial City, Code City, Cohab City, Cold City

Collage City, Collapse City, Collective City, College City, Collision City, Color City, Combinational City, Coming City, Coming-to-Be City, Commercial City, Commodity City/ City-as-Commodity, Communal City, Commuter City, Compact City, Compassion City, Compatible City, Competition City, Complex City, Complex-Dynamic City, Comprehensive City, Compressed City, CompuCity, Computer City, Concentration City, Conclave City, Conclusive City, Concrete City, Confused City, Conglomerate City, Consolidated City, Constant City, Constellation City, Construction City, Container City, Contemporary City, Context City, Continent City, Continental City, Conversion City, Cool City, Cord City, Cordless City, Core City, Corporate City, Correspondence City, Corridor City, Cosmic City, Countless City

Crazy City, Cream City, Creative City, Creole City, Crime City, Crisscross City, Critical City, Cross City, Crossing City, Crowd City, Cruise City, Crumpled City, Crying City, Crystal City, Cult City, Cumulative City, Cut-and-Paste City, Cutting-Edge City, Cyber City, Cybernetic City, Cyborg City, Cynical City, Damned City, Dark City, Darrow City, Data City, Date City, Day City, Dead City, Dead-End City, Decentered City, Declining City, Deconstruction City, Decoy City, Defense City, Definite City, Delirious City, Demo City, Demon City, DenCity, Departure City, Derelict City, Deregulation City, Desert City, Detached City, Device City, Diamond City, Diaspora City, Diffuse City, Dilate City

Disaster City, Disc City, Discourse City, Discovery City, Disintegral City, Dismantled City, Disposal City, Distinctive City, Distorted City, Divercity, Dizzy City, DNA City, DNS City, Doc City, Dogma City, Do-It City, Do-It-Again City, Doll City, Doom City, Door City, Double City, Doubt City, Down City, Download City, Drag City, Drainage City, Dream City, Drive-By City, Drop City, Drug City, Drum City, Dull City, Dust City, Dust Cloud City, Dwelling City, Dynamo City, Dystopian City, Earth City, Earthbound City, Easy City, Ebola City, Echo City, E-City, Eco City, Eco-Media City, Ecstacity, Ecumenical City, Edge City, Edible City

Electric City, Electron City, Electronic City, Elementary City, Elusive City, Emergency City, Emergent City, Emotional City, Empty City, Enclave City, End City, Endless City, Endo City, Enhanced City, Enigmatic City, Entertainment City, Entropic City, Ephemeral City, Erosion City, Erotic City, Erratic City, Escalator City, Escaping City, Esoteric City, Etcetera City, Eternity City, Ether City, European City, Ever City, Every City, Everything-but-the-City, Everywhere City, Ex City, Exacerbated City, Exuberant City, Excuse City, Exhibition City, Expanding City, Expensive City, Experimental City, Exploding City, Exploration City, Exploding City, Export City, Extension City, Extra City, Extraterrestrial City, Fabulous City

Fair City, Falls City, Fame City, Fast City, Fax City, Feather City, Feed City, Finance City, Fire City, First City, Fist City, Flash City, Flat City, Floating City, Flood City, Flow City, Fluctuating City, Fluid City, Flux City, Fly City, Folly City, Footnote City, Forest City, Forever City, Formal City, Fort City, Fortress City, Fortune City, Fountain City, Fragile City, Free City, Free-City, Freefall City, Freeway City, Frenzy City, Fringe City, Frivolous City, Frontier City, Frozen City, Fuck City, Fuck-City, Function City, Funny City, Fuse City, Future City, Fuzzy City, Gallery City

---

Liquid City, Merge City, Neorealist City, Ought-to-Be-a-City, Port City, Ramified City, Rush City, Smart City
... City, Meta-City, Nerd City, Our City, Portable City, Ramp City, Sale City, Smiling City
... City, Metaphoric City, Nerve City, Ouss City, Portal City, Random City, Same City, Snow City
... City, Meteorite City, Nested City, Out City, Portfolio City, Ready City, Sand City, So What City
... City, Middle City, Net City, Outer City, Post City, Ready-Made City, Sandwich City, So-and-So City
... City, Migration City, Network City, Oxygen City, Postcard City, Real City, Scadenza City, So-Called City
... City, Milk City, Neural City, Oyster City, Posthuman City, Realized City, Scan City, Social City
... City, Millennium City, Neuro City, Ozone City, Post-Identity City, Realistic City, Scene City, Soft City
... City, Mini-City, Neuronal City, Paint City, Postindustrial City, Reconnection City, Schizophrenic City, Software City
... City, Minimal City, Never City, Palm City, Post-It City, Recreation City, Science City, So-Long City
... City, Minor City, New City, Pan City, Postmodern City, Refugee City, Sci-Fi City, Sonic City
... City, Micro-City, Niche City, Panoptic City, Postnational City, Regional City, Scoop City, Sore City
... City, Mitigated City, Night City, Panorama City, Posturban City, Regulation City, Scream City, Sorry City
Marine City, Mixing City, No City, Para City, Power City, Reject City, Screen City, Soul City
..ng City, Mobile City, No-Go City, Parallel City, Precinct City, Relational City, Sea City, Sound City
..ng City, Model City, Nodal City, Park City, Preemptive City, Remapping City, Season City, Space City
..ri City, Modern City, Node City, Passage City, Prefab City, Renaissance City, Secret City, Spacetime City
.. City, Modest City, Noise City, Passing City, Present City, Rent-a-City, Security City, Sparkling City
.et City, Modular City, Nomadic City, Patchwork City, Present-Day City, Repressive City, Sedative City, Spatial City
..ificent City, Module City, Nonlinear City, Pathological City, Pretext City, Reserve City, Seductive City, Speed City
.. City, Mobius City, Nonplace City, Patient City, Price City, Residential City, Self-Organized City, Sperm City
..rder City, Molecular City, Nonstop City, Pavilion City, Priceless City, Residual City, Semi-City, Sphere City
.. City, Monad City, No-Plan City, Pedestrian City, Private City, Resist City, Sequential City, Spider City
..ble City, Money City, Northern City, P-C City, Procedural City, Resistance City, Service City, Spiral City
.. City, Mono City, Nostalgic City, People's City, Process City, Resurrection City, Sewer City, Splace City
.. City, Monopoly City, Notable City, Performance City, Programmable City, Revolution City, Sex City, Splendid City
..sta City, Monumental City, Not-a-City, Performative City, Program City, Rhizomatic City, Shadow City, Sprawling City
..sto City, Moon City, No-Techno City, Periodic City, Project City, Rhizome City, Shaman City, Spreading City
.. City, More City, Nothing City, Peripatetic City, Promiscuous City, Rhizoming City, Shanty City, Stage City
.. City, More-than-All City, Now City, Peristaltic City, Prosperous City, Rich City, Sharp City, Star City
.. City, Morphing City, Number City, Pervasive City, Protein City, Rim City, Shifting City, Start-Up City
..nautical City, Mosaic City, Oasis City, Phantom City, Proto-City, Ring City, Shopping City, State City
..hka City, Multifunctional City, Oblique City, Piazza City, Proud City, Riot City, Sky City, State-of-the-Art City
.. City, Multinational City, Obsessive City, Pilot City, Proxy City, Rising City, Sick City, Stereo City
..m City, Mundane City, Obvious City, Piss City, Psychogeographic City, Rite City, Side-by-Side City, Still City
.. City, Museum City, Ocean City, Pixel City, Public City, River City, Sign City, Stir City
.. City, Must City, Odd City, Pizza City, Public Transportation City, Road City, Signal City, Stop City
.. City, Mutable City, Office City, Placard City, Pulse City, Roadless City, Sim City, Story City
.. City, Mutant City, OK City, Placebo City, Punch City, Rock City, Simple City, Strategic City
.. City, My City, Old City, Plan City, Pyramid City, Rogue City, Sin City, Street City
..cal City, Mythology City, 100 Percent City, Plant City, Quantum City, Romantic City, Sinking City, Stress City
.. City, Naked City, Only City, Play City, Quartz City, Roof City, Skin City, Stretched City
.. City, Nano-City, Open City, Pleasure City, Quasi-City, Rose City, Skinny City, String City
.. City, Narrow City, Open-to-Sky City, Plug-In City, Queen City, Rough City, Sky City, Stroll City
.. City, Natural City, Option City, Pneumatic City, ..een City, Row City, Skyline City, Strong City

Compound Body
02 Clip City

A city conceals the other city'. A building conceals the other building. A man conceals the other. The other man conceals the other city. ⟨Clip City / City Vision: Hans Ulrich Obrist: Describes the shock of experiencing Seoul through moving media, and state the possibility of translating the hidden urban codes into various media.⟩

What distinguishes the map from the tracing is that it is entirely oriented toward an experimentation in contact with the real. The map does not reproduce an unconscious closed in upon itself; it constructs the unconscious. If fosters connections between fields, the removal of blockages on bodies without organs, the maximum opening of bodies without organs onto a plane of consistency. It is itself a part of rhizome. The map is open and connectable in allof its dimensions; it is detachable, reversible, susceptible to constant modification. It can be torn, reversed, adapted to any kind of mounting, reworked by an individual, group, or social formation. It can be drawn on a wall, conceived of as a work of art, constructed as a political action or as a meditation⋯ A map has multiple entryways.. ⟨A Thousand Plateaus, Deleuze & Guattari⟩

⟨Seoul⟩ reveals itself as an urban prototype that oscillates between the past and the present. The reason that I would like to discuss architecture and city through the concept of Compound Body coincides with this phenomenon. Seoul offers peculiar simultaneity of old palaces and the latest contemporary productions. The city also possesses multiple layers that inhabits different eras and times. As society acts more sensitive than ever towards various urban issues, the western cities strive to dissolve and ease the over-saturated urban density within their city planning agenda, while the Third World cities focus to continuously generate new urban models that corresponds with their economic and political transitions. Time to conceive and practice the new researches, readings, and concepts has arrived.

As a way to create materials and contents for the Compound Body, I would like to suggest the concept of ⟨Clip City⟩. By broadening the gap between each text, it provides new process of making urban and architectural issues that have not been discussed before. Through the acts of 'searching' the city is endlessly disassembled and reinterpreted into displaced texts. We must explore this range of displacements in order to expand our urban approach into a way of making appropriation out of encyclopedic text, and further suggest a vision to construct cultural, artistic and architectural orientations to take place in the future. This attitude is similar in fashion of which we discover new standards and materials in respect to constituting other viewpoints and methods, so that they become fruitful investment to find new device for our city and environment.

⟨Clip City⟩ is proposed as the means to establish specific extraction methods towards the ⟨Compound Body⟩. Understanding certain needs and lacking urban requirements, it anticipates other kinds of mixtures and arrangements. ⟨Compound Body⟩ means extracting new programs or systems using newly arranged elements. By finding clues from the ⟨Clip City⟩ the city can embrace different set of interpretations and reiterations. It can also be said that this assists us to set up specific standards for the new apparatus being superimposed over the existing condition, environment, or urban context.

We are at the moment where the new transformations and explorations are needed for the endless conceptual opportunities. We must acknowledge that the concepts within artistic or cultural realms are constantly changing and transforming. In architecture, the agenda of ⟨New Fundamental Definitions for the Architecture⟩ is being reworked. From the conceptual range of stipulating space to articulation of the physical environment, the whole spectrum needs to be questioned and investigated. Experiments with spatial forms, transformation of architectural values, advancement

Abandoned City	As-It-Could-Be City	Bridge City	Collapse City	Cream City	Disc City	Electr...	Fame City	Gateway City
Abject City	Astral City	Brilliant City	Collective City	Creative City	Discourse City		Fast City	Gay City
Abstract City	Asylum City	Broadacre City	College City	Creole City	Discovery City		Fax City	Generic City
Acme City	Atopic City	Broken City	Collision City	Crime City	Disintegral City		Feather City	Genetic City
Actor-Network City	A-to-Z City	Browsing City	Color City	Crisscross City	Dismantled City		Feedback City	Geodesic City
Actual City	Automobile City	Bubble City	Combinational City	Critical City	Disposal City		Financial City	Ghetto City
Ad-hoc City	Autonomous City	Bunker City	Coming City	Cross City	Distinct...		Fire City	Ghost City
Adhesive City	Awkward City	Bustling City	Coming-to-Be City	Crossing City	Dis...	Enclave City	First City	Giant City
Affect City	Babylonian City	Busy City	Commercial City	Crowd City		End City	Fist City	Glam City
African City	Bag City	Button City	Commodity City /	Cruise City		Endless City	Flash City	Global City
Agglomeration City	Balance City	Cable City	City-as-Commodity	Crumpled City		Endo City	Flat City	Glocal City
Aggregative City	Bamboo City	Calibration City	Communal City	Crying City		Enhanced City	Floating City	Gl...
Agora City	Banal City	Camp City	Commuter City	Crystal City		Enigmatic City	Flood City	
Agricultural City	Baroque City	Camping City	Compact City	Cult City		Entertainment City		
AIDS City	Basic City	Campus City	Compassion City	Cumu...		Entropic City		
Air-Conditioning City	Bastard City	Canyon City	Compatible City	Cu...	Do-It-Again City	Ephemeral City		
Airport City	Bath City	Capital City	Competition City		Doll City	E...		
Airship City	Baton City	Caprice City	Complex City		Doom City		Erase City	Gray City
Alarm City	Be Yourself City	Capsule City	Complex-Dyna...		Door City		Escalator City	Gray Realm City
Alert City	Beginning City	Captive City	City		Double City		Escaping City	Gridlock City
Alfa City	...ed City	Car City	Comprehensive City	...ed City	Doubt City		Er...	Groundless City
All-in-One City		Card City	Compre...		Down City		Eternity City	Group City
Alpha City		Cartoon City	Com...	Data City	Download City		Formatted City	Growing City
Alternative City		Casino City	...glomerate City	Date City	Drag City		Fort City	Growth City
Am...		Cell City	Consolidated City	Day City	Drainage City	Ether City	Fortress City	Gula City
Amazon City		Center City	Constant City	Dead City	Dream City	European City	Fortune City	Gum City
American...		Centerless City	Constellation City	Dead-End City	Drive-By City	Ever City	Fountain City	Hang-on City
Amo...		Chaos City	Construction City	Decentered City		Every City	Fragile City	Happening City
Amb...		Characteristic...	Container City	Declining City	Dust City	Everything-but-the-... City	Free City	Happy City
A...		Claim...	Contemporary City	Deconstruction City	Dust Cloud City		Free-Flying City	Harbor City
Anal City			Context City	Decoy City	Dwelling City		Freedom City	Hard City
Analy...			Continent City	Defense City	Dynamo City		Freeway City	Harmony City
Ang...			Continental City	Definite City		Excuse City	Frenzy City	Heart City
Anti...			Conversion City	Delirious City	Dystopian City	Exhibition City		Heavy City
Anticip...			...	Demo City	Earth City	Expanding City		...ft City
Apocalyp...				Demon City	Earthbound City	Expensive City		
...othesized City				DenCity	Easy City	Experimental City		
Arcade City				Departure City	Ebola City	Exploding City		
Ar...			...ridor City	Derelict City	Echo City	Exploration City		
Archaic City				Deregulation City	E-City	Exploding City	Funnel City	
Archipelago City				Desert City	Eco City	Export City	Fuse City	
...KIPELAG City			...ndence City	Detached City	Eco-Media City	Extension City	Future City	
...ty City				Device City	Ecstacity	Extra City	Futurist City	
Artisanal City				Diamond City	Ecumenical City	Extraterrestrial City	Fuzzy City	Hitting City
...ch City		Brand City		Diaspora City	Edge City		Gallery City	Hoax City
...sh City		Brave City	Countless City	Diffuse City	Edible City	Fabulous City		
			Cosmic City	Dilate City				

City	Merge City	Neorealist City	Ought-to-Be-a-City	Port City	Ramified City	Rush City	Smart City	Success City	
City	Meta-City	Nerd City	Our City	Portable City	Ramp City	Sale City	Smiling City	Sudden City	
	Metaphoric City	Nerve City	Ouss City	Portal City	Random City	Same City	Snow City	Suicide City	
ty	Meteorite City	Nested City	Out City	Portfolio City	Ready City	Sand City	So What City	Sun City	
ty	Middle City	Net City	Outer City	Post City	Ready-Made City	Sandwich City	So-and-So City	Sunbelt City	
ty	Migration City	Network City	Oxygen City	Postcard City	Real City	Scadenza City	So-Called City	Super City	
	Milk City	Neural City	Oyster City	Posthuman City	Realized City	Scan City	Social City	Superblock City	
	Millennium City	Neuro City	Ozone City	Post-Identity City	Realistic City	Scene City	Soft City	Super-Fluid City	
y	Mini-City	Neuronal City	Paint City	Postindustrial City	Reconnection City	Schizophrenic City	Software City	Suprematist City	
y	Minimal City	Never City	Palm City	Post-It City	Recreation City	Science City	So-Long City	Surreal City	
	Minor City	New City	Pan City	Postmodern City	Refugee City	Sci-Fi City	Sonic City	Surrogate City	
y	Micro-City	Niche City	Panoptic City	Postnational City	Regional City	Scoop City	Sore City	Survival City	
	Mitigated City	Night City	Panorama City	Posturban City	Regulation City	Scream City	Sorry City	Sweet City	
	Mixing City	No City	Para City	Power City	Reject City	Screen City	Soul City	Syntax City	
ity	Mobile City	No-Go City	Parallel City	Precinct City	Relational City	Sea City	Sound City	System ...	
	Model City	Nodal City	Park City	Preemptive City	Remapping City	Season City	Space City	Tactile...	
ty	Modern City	Node City	Passage City	Prefab City	Renaissance City	Secret City	Spacetime City	Take-...	
ity	Modest City	Noise City	Passing City	Present City	Rent-a-City	Security City	Sparkling City	Tast...	
	Modular City	Nomadic City	Patchwork City	Present-Day City	Repressive City	Sedative City	Spatial City	Tek...	
t City	Module City	Nonlinear City	Pathological City	Pretext City	Reserve City	Seductive City	Speed City	T...	
r City	Mobius City	Nonplace City	Patient City	Price City	Residential City	Self-Organized City	Sperm City		
	Molecular City	Nonstop City	Pavilion City	Priceless City	Residual City	Semi-City	Sphere City	To...	
	Monad City	No-Plan City	Pedestrian City	Private City	Resist City	Sequential City	Spider City	Temp...	
r City	Money City	Northern City	People's City	Procedural City	Resistance City	Service City	Spiral City	Autono...	
	Mono City	Nostalgic City	P-C City	Process City	Resurrection City	Sewer City	Splace City	Temp...	
	Monopoly City	Notable City	Performance City	Programmable City	Revolution City	Sex City	Splendid City	T...	
ty	Monumental City	Not-a-City	Performative City	Program City	Rhizomatic City	Shadow City	Sprawling City	Tenac...	
	Moon City	No-Techno City	Periodic City	Project City	Rhizome City	Shaman City	Spreading City	Tenant City	
	More City	Nothing City	Peripatetic City	Promiscuous City	Rhizoming City	Shanty City	Stage City	Tender City	
	More-than-All City	Now City	Peristaltic City	Prosperous City	Rich City	Sharp City	Star City	T...	
	Morphing City	Number City	Pervasive City	Protein City	Rim City	Shifting City	Start-Up City		
al City	Mosaic City	Oasis City	Phantom City	Proto-City	Ring City	Shopping City	State C...		
al City	Multifunctional City	Oblique City	Plaza City	Proud City	Riot City	Shy City	State-...		
	Multinational City	Obsessive City	Pilot City	Proxy City	Rising City	Sick City	Step...		
	Mundane City	Obvious City	Piss City	Psychogeographic City	Rite City	Side-by-Side City	Stir...		
	Museum City	Ocean City	Pixel City	Public City	River City	Sign City	Stir...		
	Must City	Odd City	Pizza City	Public Transportation	Road City	Signal City	Stop City	Theme City	
	Mutable City	Office City	Placebo City	City	Roadless City	Sim City	Story City	Thick City	
	Mutant City	OK City	Placid City	Pulse City	Rock City	Simple City	Strategic City	Thin City	
	My City	Old City	Plan City	Punch City	Rogue City	Sin City	Street City	Think City	
	Mythology City	100 Percent City	Plant City	Pyramid City	Romantic City	Sinking City	Stress City	This-Way City	
	Naked City	Only City	Play City	Quantum City	Roof City	Skin City	Stretched City	3D City	
	Nano City	Open City	Pleasure City	Quartz City	Rose City	Skinny City	String City	Ticklish City	
	Narrow City	Open-to-Sky City	Plug-In City	Quasi-City	Rough City	Sky City	Stroll City	Time City	
	National City	Option City	Pneumatic City	Queen City	Row City	Skyline City	Strong City	Time-Warp...	
	Naval City	Oral City	Pocket City	Queer City	Royal City	Slacker City	Structural City	Tin City	
	Near City	Orchard City	Political City	Quiet City	Rubble City	Slam City	Studio City	Toast City	
	Negotiation City	Organ City	Pompous City	Radiant City	Ruin City	Sleepless City	Substitute City	Tool City	
	Neo City	Organic City	Poor City	Radio City	Rumor City	Slice-and-Dice City	Subtle City	Tool Top...	
		Original City	Pop-Up City		Running City	Slick City	Suburban City	Tool-K...	

in technology,⋯.are some of the examples for us to respond. As a starting subject to find some clues for these new opportunities, we can trace back to our ways of reading the city. The city provides us countless leads. There are always different interpretations towards cities and societies, while some of them are still hidden behind the screen for us to reveal them. We cannot resist our interest in these hidden codes, just as if the codes lying in ⟨Clip City⟩ provokes us to find infinite set of derivatives.

Clip city refers to the process of capturing city of countless gaps between the two binary digits of 0 and 1. It explores in-betweenness of gap already known for us in order to look for more. This can lead to arrange several possibility of city, where the typical urban programs are paired with invisible or overlooked codes. We need new research on capturing new urban DNA and set up reactions towards a city. The city we are aware of today, are acknowledged with things and matters of their physical attributes. As if we think we are touching the hand of an ant on an elephant, and the elephant will never be detected by us. Let us define the city as not a physical entity, but in other way of description. For example, culture, information, media, speed, movement, noise,⋯.can be interesting themes that needs different ways of description. Various numbers of urban episodes overlooked or invisible can be brought to our experience. Our perspective becomes not limited to mere physical coded maps and built spaces, but a different mode of practice based on exploring other aspects of urban experiences, like feeling the wind or aggressively wandering around the city.

⟨Clip City⟩ possesses methodological ways to disassemble, recombine and disintegrate bits of urban text. It intensifies already-chaotic-enough structure of the world, and provokes even more confusion by pushing the extreme at the level of indeterminacy. Endless disassemblies of cities from A to Z produce thousands of text. A city is not A city any more. Beyond its meaning, disassembled text awaits for the new transformation. Urban text desires to be captured, be mix-matched and move towards whimsical integration. Hans Obrist utilizes the encyclopedic text of A-Z and proposes mew words of text. I would like to superimpose few more over those texts. The series of superimposition is left out at the end, giving us something to ponder about.

⟨Clip City⟩ seeks to propose a new method in defining the city. We cannot earn new perspective through conventional practice of urban research. Many counts of branches regarding urban definitions must be reworked. List of texts is 'clipped', pulled out as a theme of analysis, programming and reassembling techniques. With the attitude of Clip City, we intend to generate a new urban map which consists of compound city and integrated city. Within the map, there will be hyperlinks among new combinations of words, which will then lead to story-makings of new city topography.

We focus invisibleness within the relationships among materials and substances, rather than their physical configurations. This is because we believe we can capture the essence of city and architecture out of those relationships. Various relationships such as - adaptation, confrontation, coexistence, self-organization, are concepts themselves. Despite the fact that we may feel frustrated and struggled with the gap between homogeneity and heterogeneity, facing of the two engages us towards proposal of new formulation. Urban flow corresponds to the path of relationships in guiding formless concept towards formal architecture. While themes such as water, air, and other natural elements were mainstreams of arranging urban flows in the past, the new conceptual elements of urban flows are discussed today. In order to respond to the tendency, architecture must not remain the object independent of its own, but the subject aggressive enough to create various relationships.

Making ⟨Clip City⟩ is very similar to making a version of a ⟨Encyclopedic Map⟩. A map embraces both method and substances. ⟨Map⟩ is also a presupposition that includes program, physical structure, and a manufactured strategy. Through processes and design projects, extracting an encyclopedic list of contents must be regarded as one step to establish a system for further utilization. Replacing a diagram with spatial metaphor, it is similar to discovering hidden maps from the corners of an empty space. One of these cases would be what I call hypertext map - presupposition in which architectural text is sprinkled around the space and create a system of movements that can progress toward another theme. This invisible text appears in the space and each subtext associate themselves to establish a web of linkages. Thus the text no longer exists as only one code or conveyed as singular interpretation. They constantly rearrange themselves in accordance with their changing relationships and linkages - a complex web of codes and networks. Maps are now ready and complete enough to be altered into a physical space.

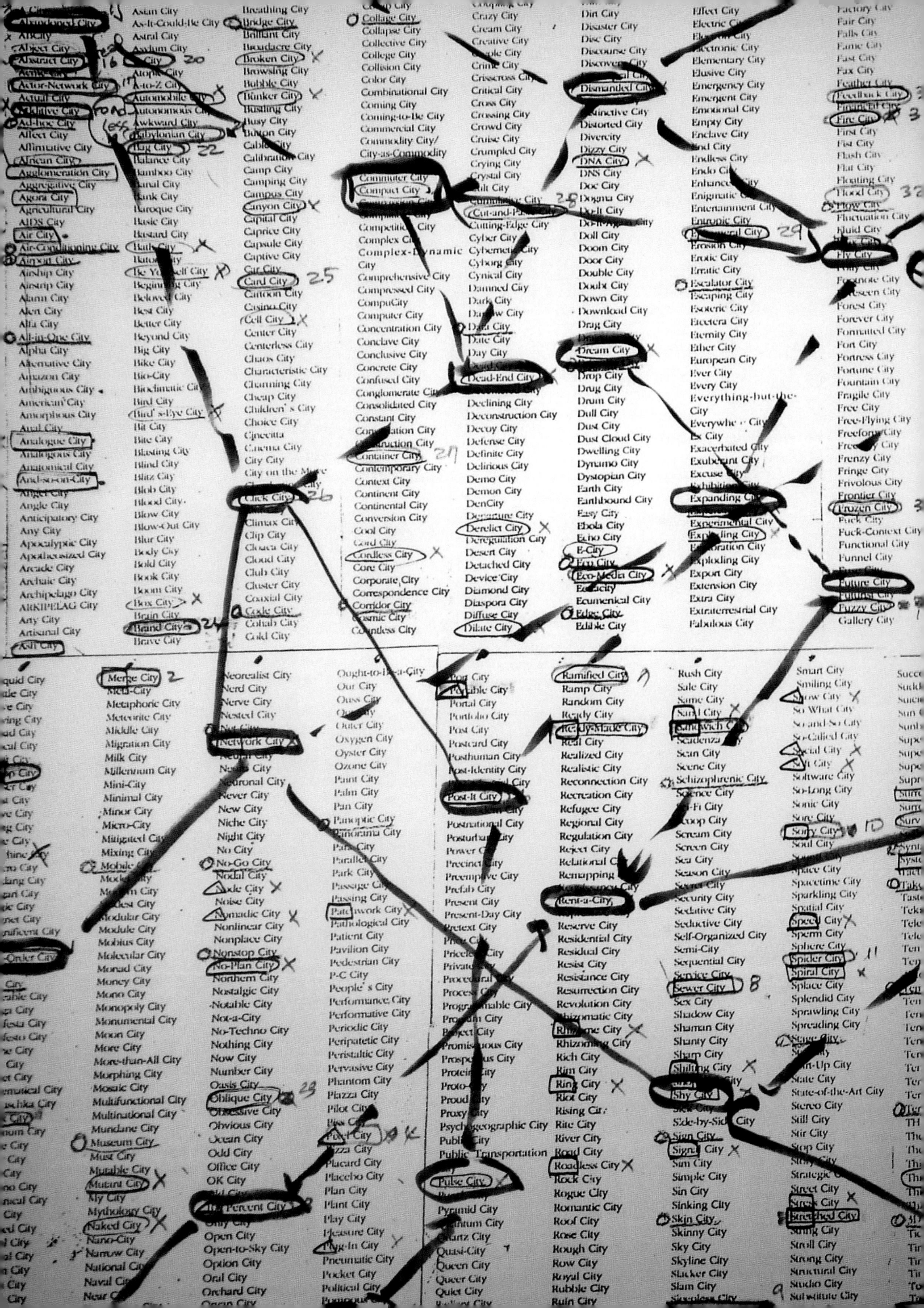
Abandoned City
ABCity
Abject City
Abstract City
Actor-Network City
Actual City
Additive City
Ad-hoc City
Affect City
Affirmative City
African City
Agglomeration City
Aggregative City
Agora City
Agricultural City
AIDS City
Air City
Air-Conditioning City
Airport City
Airship City
Airstrip City
Alarm City
Alert City
Alfa City
All-in-One City
Alpha City
Alternative City
Amazon City
Ambiguous City
American City
Amorphous City
Anal City
Analogue City
Analogous City
Anatomical City
And-so-on-City
Angel City
Angle City
Anticipatory City
Any City
Apocalyptic City
Apotheosized City
Arcade City
Archaic City
Archipelago City
ARKIPELAG City
Arty City
Artisanal City
Ash City
Asian City
As-It-Could-Be City
Astral City
Asylum City
Atopic City
A-to-Z City
Automobile City
Autonomous City
Awkward City
Babylonian City
Bag City
Balance City
Bamboo City
Banal City
Bank City
Baroque City
Basic City
Bastard City
Bath City
Baton City
Be Yourself City
Beginning City
Beloved City
Best City
Better City
Beyond City
Big City
Bike City
Bio-City
Bioclimatic City
Bird City
Bird's-Eye City
Bit City
Bite City
Blasting City
Blind City
Blitz City
Blob City
Blood City
Blow City
Blow-Out City
Blur City
Body City
Bold City
Book City
Boom City
Box City
Brain City
Brand City
Brave City
Breathing City
Bridge City
Brilliant City
Broadacre City
Broken City
Browsing City
Bubble City
Bunker City
Bustling City
Busy City
Button City
Cable City
Calibration City
Camp City
Camping City
Campus City
Canyon City
Capital City
Caprice City
Capsule City
Captive City
Car City
Card City
Cartoon City
Casino City
Cell City
Center City
Centerless City
Chaos City
Characteristic City
Charming City
Cheap City
Children's City
Choice City
Cinecitta
Cinema City
City City
City on the Move
Click City
Climax City
Clip City
Cloaca City
Cloud City
Club City
Cluster City
Coaxial City
Code City
Cohab City
Cold City
Collage City
Collapse City
Collective City
College City
Collision City
Color City
Combinational City
Coming City
Coming-to-Be City
Commercial City
Commodity City/ City-as-Commodity
Commuter City
Compact City
Competitive City
Complex City
Complex-Dynamic City
Comprehensive City
Compressed City
CompuCity
Computer City
Concentration City
Conclave City
Conclusive City
Concrete City
Confused City
Conglomerate City
Consolidated City
Constant City
Construction City
Container City
Contemporary City
Context City
Continent City
Continental City
Conversion City
Cool City
Cord City
Cordless City
Core City
Corporate City
Correspondence City
Corridor City
Cosmic City
Countless City
Crazy City
Cream City
Creative City
Crime City
Crisscross City
Critical City
Cross City
Crossing City
Crowd City
Cruise City
Crumpled City
Crying City
Crystal City
Cult City
Cut-and-Paste City
Cutting-Edge City
Cyber City
Cybernetic City
Cyborg City
Cynical City
Damned City
Dark City
Data City
Date City
Day City
Dead-End City
Declining City
Deconstruction City
Decoy City
Defense City
Definite City
Delirious City
Demo City
Demon City
DenCity
Departure City
Derelict City
Deregulation City
Desert City
Detached City
Device City
Diamond City
Diaspora City
Diffuse City
Dilate City
Dirt City
Disaster City
Disc City
Discourse City
Discovery City
Dismantled City
Distinctive City
Distorted City
Divercity
Dizzy City
DNA City
DNS City
Doc City
Dogma City
Do-It City
Doll City
Doom City
Door City
Double City
Doubt City
Down City
Download City
Drag City
Dream City
Drop City
Drug City
Drum City
Dull City
Dust City
Dust Cloud City
Dwelling City
Dynamo City
Dystopian City
Earth City
Earthbound City
Easy City
Ebola City
Echo City
E-City
Eco City
Eco-Media City
Ecumenical City
Edge City
Edible City
Effect City
Electric City
Electronic City
Elementary City
Elusive City
Emergency City
Emergent City
Emotional City
Empty City
Enclave City
End City
Endless City
Endo City
Enhanced City
Enigmatic City
Entertainment City
Entropic City
Ephemeral City
Erosion City
Erotic City
Erratic City
Escalator City
Escaping City
Esoteric City
Etcetera City
Eternity City
Ether City
European City
Ever City
Every City
Everything-but-the-City
Everywhere City
Ex City
Exacerbated City
Exuberant City
Excuse City
Exhibition City
Expanding City
Experimental City
Exploding City
Exploration City
Exploding City
Export City
Extension City
Extra City
Extraterrestrial City
Fabulous City
Factory City
Fair City
Falls City
Fame City
Fast City
Fax City
Feather City
Feedback City
Financial City
Fire City
First City
Fist City
Flash City
Flat City
Floating City
Flood City
Flow City
Fluctuation City
Fluid City
Fly City
Footnote City
Forest City
Forever City
Formatted City
Fort City
Fortress City
Fortune City
Fountain City
Fragile City
Free City
Free-Flying City
Freeform City
Frenzy City
Fringe City
Frivolous City
Frontier City
Frozen City
Fuck City
Fuck-Context City
Functional City
Funnel City
Future City
Fuzzy City
Gallery City
Merge City
Meta-City
Metaphoric City
Meteorite City
Middle City
Migration City
Milk City
Millennium City
Mini-City
Minimal City
Minor City
Micro-City
Mitigated City
Mixing City
Mobile City
Modular City
Module City
Mobius City
Molecular City
Monad City
Money City
Mono City
Monopoly City
Monumental City
Moon City
More City
More-than-All City
Morphing City
Mosaic City
Multifunctional City
Multinational City
Mundane City
Museum City
Must City
Mutable City
Mutant City
My City
Mythology City
Naked City
Nano-City
Narrow City
National City
Naval City
Near City
Neorealist City
Nerd City
Nerve City
Nested City
Network City
Neuronal City
Never City
New City
Niche City
Night City
No City
No-Go City
Nodal City
Node City
Noise City
Nomadic City
Nonlinear City
Nonplace City
Nonstop City
No-Plan City
Northern City
Nostalgic City
Notable City
Not-a-City
No-Techno City
Nothing City
Now City
Number City
Oasis City
Oblique City
Obsessive City
Obvious City
Ocean City
Odd City
Office City
OK City
One Percent City
Open City
Open-to-Sky City
Option City
Oral City
Orchard City
Ought-to-Be-a-City
Our City
Outer City
Oxygen City
Oyster City
Ozone City
Paint City
Palm City
Pan City
Panoptic City
Panorama City
Parallel City
Park City
Passage City
Passing City
Patchwork City
Pathological City
Patient City
Pavilion City
Pedestrian City
P-C City
People's City
Performance City
Performative City
Periodic City
Peripatetic City
Peristaltic City
Pervasive City
Phantom City
Piazza City
Pilot City
Pixel City
Pizza City
Placard City
Placebo City
Plan City
Plant City
Play City
Pleasure City
Plug-In City
Pneumatic City
Pocket City
Political City
Portable City
Portal City
Portfolio City
Post City
Postcard City
Posthuman City
Post-Identity City
Post-It City
Postnational City
Postsuburban City
Precinct City
Preemptive City
Prefab City
Present City
Present-Day City
Pretext City
Priceless City
Private City
Procedural City
Programmable City
Program City
Project City
Promiscuous City
Prosperous City
Protein City
Proto-City
Proud City
Proxy City
Psychogeographic City
Public City
Public Transportation City
Pulse City
Pyramid City
Quantum City
Quartz City
Quasi-City
Queen City
Queer City
Quiet City
Ramified City
Ramp City
Random City
Ready City
Ready-Made City
Real City
Realized City
Realistic City
Reconnection City
Recreation City
Refugee City
Regional City
Regulation City
Reject City
Relational City
Remapping City
Rent-a-City
Reserve City
Residential City
Residual City
Resist City
Resistance City
Resurrection City
Revolution City
Rhizomatic City
Rhizome City
Rhizoming City
Rich City
Rim City
Ring City
Riot City
Rising City
Rite City
River City
Road City
Roadless City
Rock City
Rogue City
Romantic City
Roof City
Rose City
Rough City
Row City
Royal City
Rubble City
Ruin City
Rush City
Sale City
Same City
Sand City
Sandwich City
Scan City
Scene City
Schizophrenic City
Science City
Sci-Fi City
Scoop City
Scream City
Screen City
Sea City
Season City
Secret City
Security City
Sedative City
Seductive City
Self-Organized City
Semi-City
Sequential City
Service City
Sewer City
Sex City
Shadow City
Shaman City
Shanty City
Sham City
Shifting City
Shy City
Side-by-Side City
Sign City
Signal City
Sim City
Simple City
Sin City
Sinking City
Skin City
Skinny City
Sky City
Skyline City
Slacker City
Slam City
Sleepless City
Smart City
Smiling City
Snow City
So What City
So-and-So City
So-Called City
Social City
Soft City
Software City
So-Long City
Sonic City
Sore City
Sorry City
Soul City
Space City
Spacetime City
Sparkling City
Spatial City
Speed City
Sperm City
Sphere City
Spider City
Spiral City
Splace City
Splendid City
Sprawling City
Spreading City
Stage City
State City
State-of-the-Art City
Stereo City
Still City
Stir City
Stop City
Story City
Strategic City
Street City
Streak City
Stretched City
String City
Stroll City
Strong City
Structural City
Studio City
Substitute City

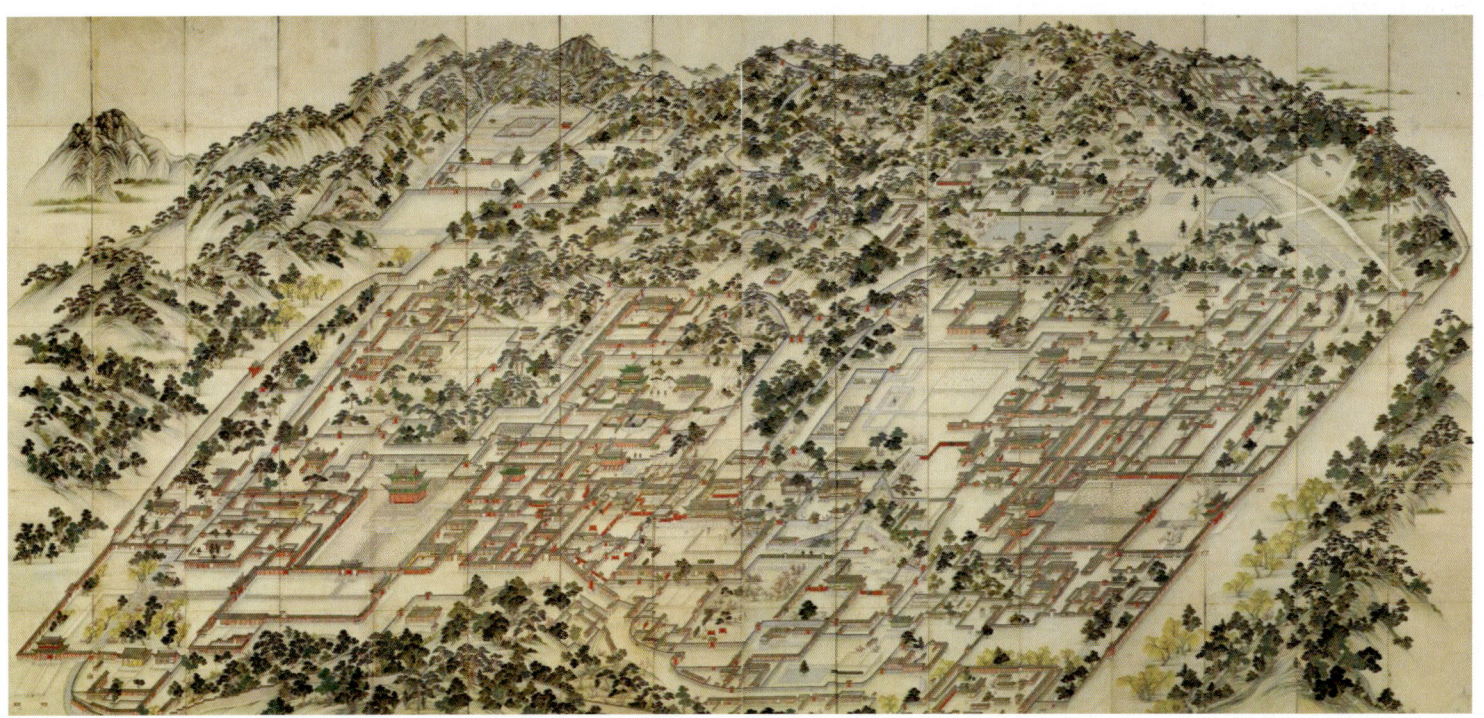
Compound City, The Royal Palace Plan, Compound Map Between City Structures & Nature

A city *The city that is not specifically defined, or specifically defined. It is the city wide open to infinite possibility including all possible definitions we must label the city as. It is a city as a departure, and for that the city of possibility. AB city with a nature of air.* **Abandoned city** *The city works as a living organism. It grows and lapse as the human does. In most cases cities are planned, grow, and prosper, but they become functionally discarded per proceedings of our civilization and cultural transformation. Despite the city operated normally with its functions, it will remain in its coma if the citizens do not sustain and mend it properly.* **Abject city** *Diseases, chaos, alienation, unconsciousness, crimes,…is there a device that can heal the urban lowdown? Is this device a destiny for the human, or the city?* **Abstract city** *The contemporary concept is comprised of the basis of all abstraction. Through urban abstraction we formulate cities that we never have imagined. This connects with creating virtual city that does not exist in actuality.* **Acme city** *Where shall we impose the peak of the city? Culture, science, technique, transportation,…must we orient ourselves through only physical attribute of these countless factors?* **Actor-Network city Actual city** *Means all cities that exist upon us, where we live at.* **Additive city** *In order to be take control of our new urban functions, we need to redefine some of the necessary urban factors. New system is articulated for the city, which must be given through projections and anticipations for the future.* **Ad-hoc city** *Where appropriate, we can construct an ad-hoc city. Not grounded on the continuous history or culture, the city responses in accordance with its specific needs and circumstances. It consists of devices that temporarily recover itself while reinforcing its flexibility and transformability.* **Affect city** *Some cities exert powerful implications to other cities.* **Affirmative city** *The city that reacts positive* **African city** *We go to Africa in search of the primitives.* **Agglomeration city Aggregative city** *The city of collectivity. It means the city generated by an assembly of individual characteristics. Some of the proposition would be - how to organize certain groups of mixture and to propose selections of certain factors. Thus it requires various explorations regarding both the factors and the way they are assembled.* **Agora city** *As it means a place of assembly, the city stands as central space. It also is a hub for religious, political, legislative, commercial, and social practices. Where can we enable our agora in the contemporary city?* **Agricultural city** *What it is needed for the contemporary urbanites may be the supply of space where they can cultivate their farms. It becomes the opportunity to regain the benefits of the nature and labor via agricultural lives.* **AIDS city Air city** *In terms of environmental issues, air became more important than ever. Controlling air and maintaining the comfort-levels of air enable environmental indices. Free from spatial limitation, the air adapts any form, sometimes becomes resistant or drifts away. The air contains myriads of drifts of the*

Seoul is Clip City: Foreground of Seoul

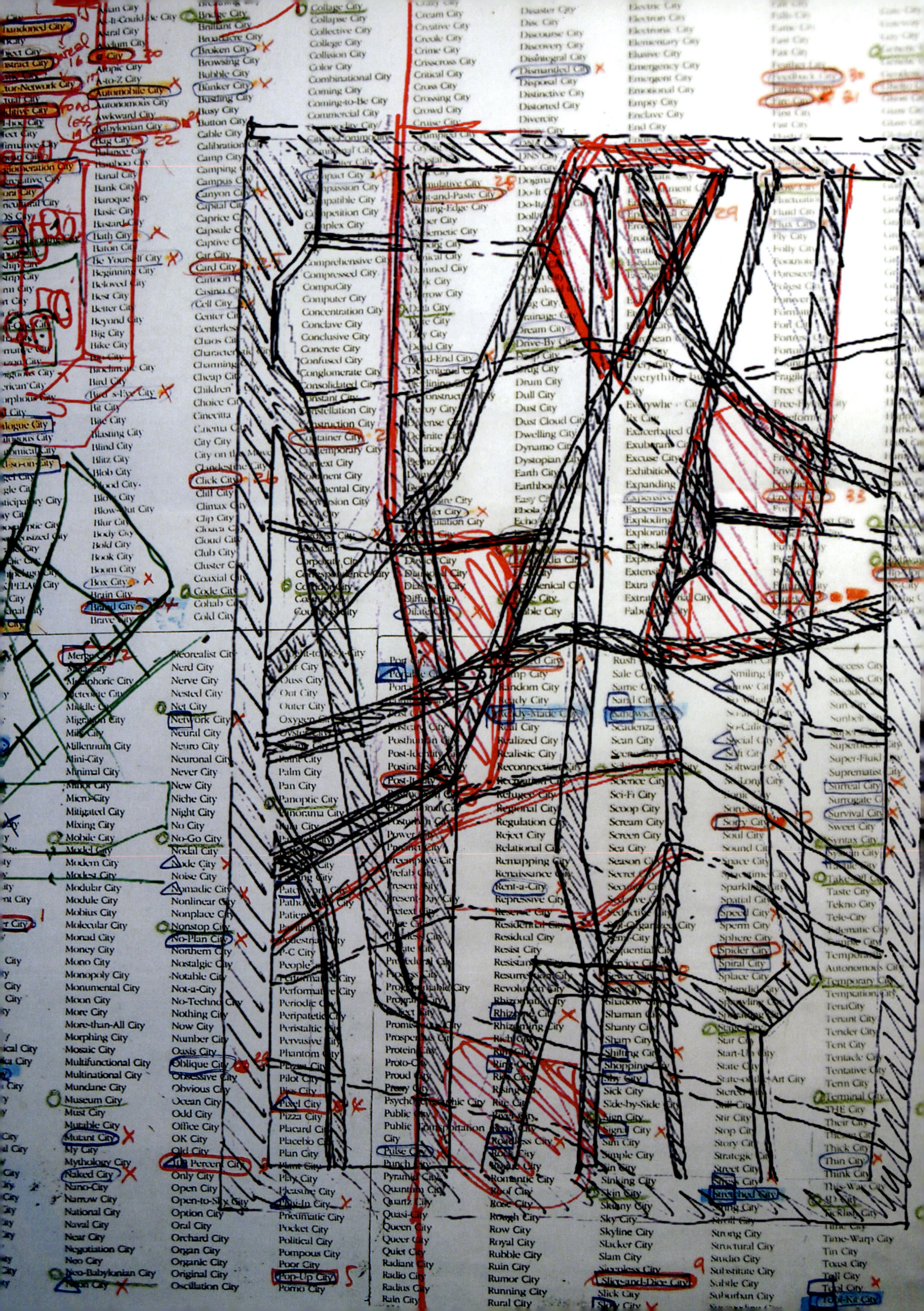

COMPOUND BODY 23

particles. The wind, produced by the pressure difference, circulates the air. The winds become the vehicle for the air. **Air-Conditioning city** *Would be applied for the purpose of air-control in the city. Not just the control of internal distribution of air within the buildings, but it means a complete system which considers the quality of both internal and external environment. By simply rethinking the way we control the air, we can come across the alternatives for new urban formation.* **Airport city Airship city Airstrip city Alarm city** *The city which provides alertness through fright and fear.* **Alert city Alfa city** *The most primitive and fundamental city is refocused and redefined.* **All-in-one city** *The city can be developed with putting out all possible modes of specialization and characterization. Although quite a risk in its success, the city possesses double-sided possibilities of extreme advancement and deterioration.* **Alpha city** *The first-ever city* **Alternative city** *The background behind pursuing the alternative city is to secure the existing city, in conjunction with drawing out the future map of the new potential. If we try to develop a type of city which never stops self-generating these alternatives, can we find the most appropriate city form?* **Amazon city** *Imagine the city only for the female, or the city that consists of single-gendered population. We may discover other urban positions never realized before.* **Ambiguous city** *It is true that today's cities have become more monotonous and ambiguous in individual characteristics. More and more the urban fabric and functions are becoming vague in the global networks of cities through the implications of digital information, rapid transportations and instant communications.* **American city Amorphous city** *The city that is formless, with no rules. Through the city that has no specific regulations provides new conceptual paradigm which can be self-prescribed.* **Anal city** *Most of cities today functions as discharging machine, rather than creating. With ruthless development that destroys the environment leaves only the enormous excretion instead of the city formed out of environmentally-linked relationships.* **Analogue city** *The city that appears analogue and humane, yet gives us the alternative attitudes in resolving the problematics of the digital, machinic character of a city.* **Analogous city Anatomical city** *'Anatomy' means, in biological term, investigating internal structure of parts of or whole organism by incision. It is also used as exploring through logical analysis on the system of the objects or disciplines.* **And-so-on city Angel city Angle city Anticipatory city** *New requirements are needed in producing contents and structure that can project and surpass the future. Transitions in consumptions, new city infrastructure, development strategies and making margins…. Through defining the changing urban stance and anticipations on developments, we can formulate more diverse range of city prototypes.* **Any city** *Any City?* **Apocalyptic city Apotheosized city Arcade city Archaic city Archipelago city ARKIPELAG city Arty city Artisanal city Ash city Asian city As-It-Could-Be city** *We dream of a city that realizes our imaginations and desires.* **Astral city Asylum city** *Imagine a city that has a structure of Pathos, a segregated asylum. Regardless of adjacent element, the city possesses clarity that enables to sustain its individuality. Where can there be programmatic requirements for the city which still remains like marbling and maintain its individuality even if it is mixed with other attributes?* **@city Atopic city A-to-Z city** *What possibility does a city have that comes as a complete gift set? The city exists under a system of complete set of equipments in which self-organization harbors urban integration, and is capable of handling all productions and consumptions.* **Automobile city** *The human inventions of new tools always have enormous impact, capable of changing the entire city. The automobile has changed the cities into a whole different level in terms of its moving speed and distance. Imagine unlimited urban transformations with just one change of tools.* **Autonomous city Awkward city Babylonian city Bag city** *Put a colossal city in your bag. Through a device called bag, we can articulate yet another urban culture. This bag can be viewed as the media bag that contains endless information and stories.* **Balance city Bamboo city Banal city Bank city Baroque city Basic city Bastard city Bath city** *There are several branches of methods to make a city structure that fills the water. Fun part is to generate a map of water being filled in a bathtub. Form of the water and space depends on its containers.* **Baton city Be Yourself city Beginning city** *Shifting our departure point of views carries the potential to lead us towards different latitudes. Just like our first gene, we can project the city that is possible to foresee the range of urban transformation. Our hopes may be the first city that can start from the beginning.* **Beloved city Best city Better city Beyond city Big city** *Architects today discuss exhaustion accompanied by the urban agglomeration. Traffic, population, environment, …. Maybe we might need to take pleasure in such a mess. The more cities of developing countries, I agree that they should pursue more 'big' in ambition. Maximum the ambition is, the power multiplies. For an extra-large city, even a little wobble or hesitance becomes part of its force.* **Bike city Bio-city** *The city that allows man and nature live in harmony and symbiosis. Throughout the globe, the city reconstitutes environmental*

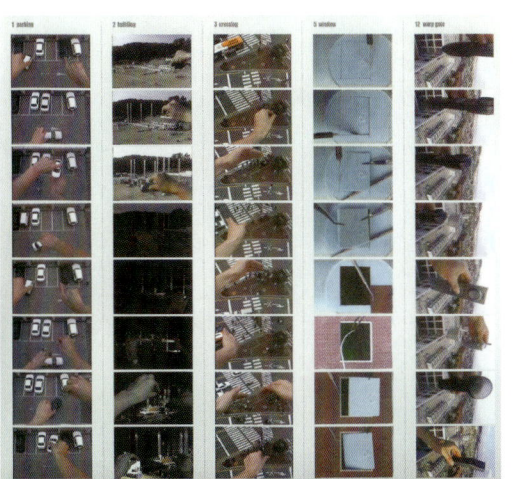

*Park Jun Bum,
Remote Control of City*

*Kim Jung Ju,
Stapler Clip City*

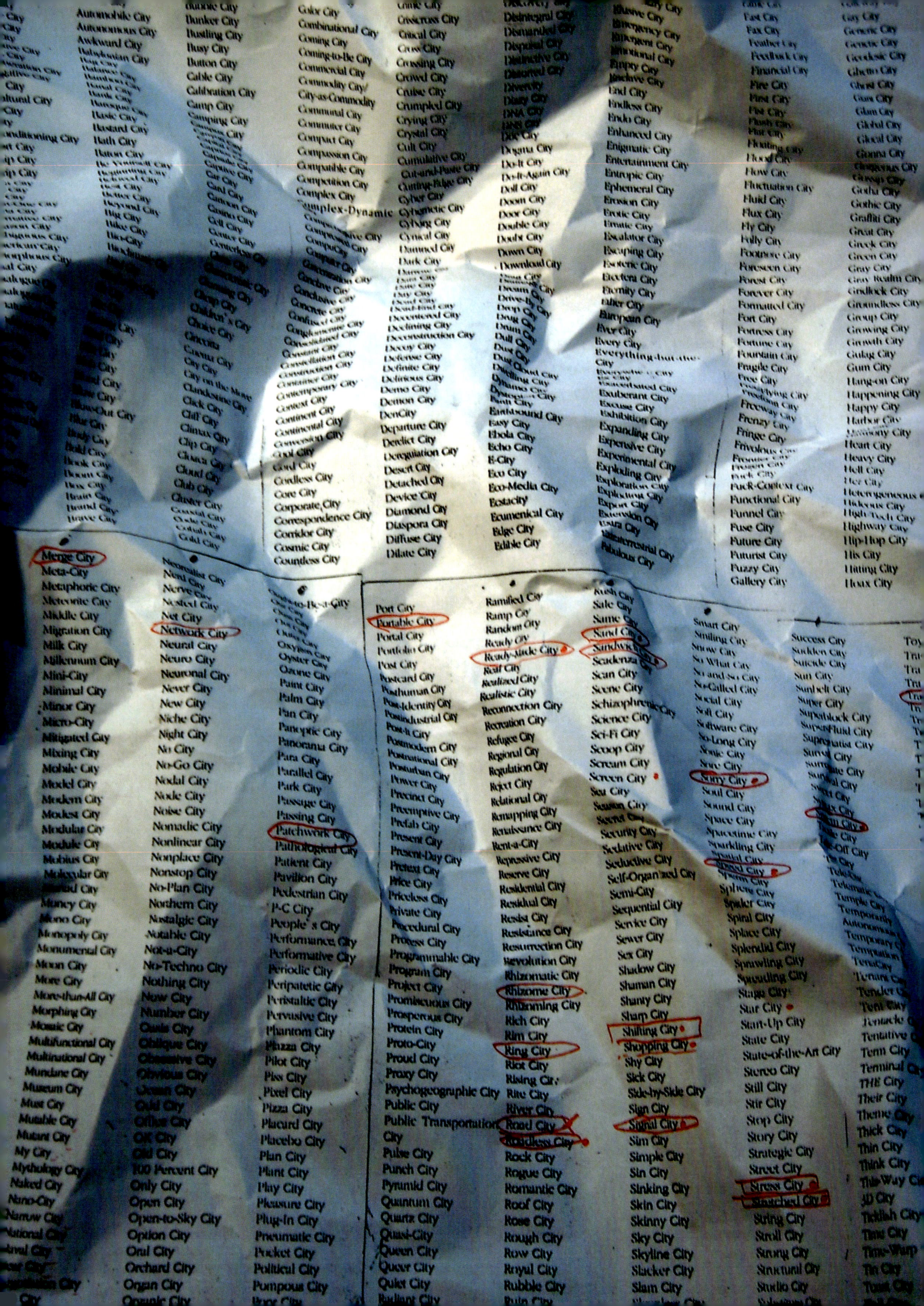

This page is a photograph of a crumpled printed list of "City" compound names arranged in many columns. The text is too distorted and partially obscured by shadows to transcribe reliably in full. Selected legible entries, with those circled or marked in red ink noted:

- Automobile City, Awkward City, Babylonian City, ... Basic City, Bastard City, Bath City, Button City ...
- Bunker City, Busting City, Busy City, Button City, Cable City, Calibration City, Camp City, Camping City ...
- Color City, Combinational City, Coming City, Coming-to-Be City, Commercial City, Commodity City, City-as-Commodity, Communal City, Commuter City, Compact City, Compassion City, Compatible City, Competition City, Complex City, Complex-Dynamic City ...
- Crisscross City, Crucial City, Crow City, Crossing City, Crowd City, Cruise City, Crumpled City, Crying City, Crystal City, Cult City, Cumulative City, Cut-and-Paste City, Cutting-Edge City, Cyber City, Cybernetic City, Cynical City, Damned City, Dark City ...
- Disintegral City, Dismantled City, Disposal City, Distinctive City, Distorted City, Diversity, Diary City, DNA City, Die City, Do-It City, Do-It-Again City, Doll City, Doom City, Door City, Double City, Doubt City, Down City, Download City ...
- Illusive City, Emergency City, Emergent City, Emotional City, Enclave City, End City, Endless City, Endo City, Enhanced City, Enigmatic City, Entertainment City, Entropic City, Ephemeral City, Erosion City, Erotic City, Ersatz City, Escalator City, Escaping City, Esoteric City, Esoteric City, Eternity City, Ether City, European City, Ever City, Everything-but-the-City ...
- East City, Fax City, Feather City, Feedback City, Financial City, Fire City, First City, Fist City, Flash City, Floating City, Flood City, Flow City, Fluctuation City, Fluid City, Flux City, Fly City, Folly City, Footbook City, Foreseen City, Forest City, Forever City, Formatted City, Fort City, Fortress City, Fortune City, Fountain City, Fragile City, Free City, Freedom City, Freeway City, Frenzy City, Fringe City, Frivolous City, Fuck-Context City, Functional City, Funnel City, Fuse City, Future City, Futurist City, Fuzzy City, Gallery City ...
- Gay City, Generic City, Geodesic City, Ghetto City, Giant City, Glam City, Global City, Global City, Gonna City, Gossip City, Gothic City, Graffiti City, Great City, Greek City, Green City, Gray City, Gray Realm City, Gridlock City, Groundless City, Group City, Growing City, Growth City, Gulag City, Gum City, Hang-on City, Happening City, Happy City, Harbor City, Heart City, Heavy City, Hell City, Her City, Heterogeneous City, Hideous City, High-Tech City, Highway City, Hip-Hop City, His City, Hitting City, Hoax City ...
- Merge City (circled), Meta-City, Metaphoric City, Meteoric City, Middle City, Migration City (circled: Network City), Milk City, Millennium City, Mini-City, Minimal City, Minor City, Micro-City, Mitigated City, Mixing City, Mobile City, Model City, Modern City, Modest City, Modular City, Module City, Möbius City, Molecular City, Money City, Mono City, Monopoly City, Monumental City, Moon City, More City, More-than-All City, Morphing City, Mosaic City, Multifunctional City, Multinational City, Mundane City, Museum City, Must City, Mutable City, Mutant City, My City, Mythology City, Naked City, Nano-City, Narrow City, National City ...
- Port City (circled), Portable City (circled), Portal City, Portfolio City, Post City, Postcard City, Posthuman City, Post-Identity City, Postindustrial City, Post-It, Postmodern City, Postnational City, Posturban City, Power City, Precinct City, Preemptive City, Prefab City, Present City, Present-Day City, Price City, Priceless City, Private City, Procedural City, Protest City, Programmable City, Project City, Promiscuous City, Prosperous City, Protein City, Proto-City, Proud City, Proxy City, Psychogeographic City, Public City, Public Transportation City, Pulse City, Punch City, Pyramid City, Quantum City, Quartz City, Quasi-City, Queen City, Queer City, Quiet City, Radiant City ...
- Ramified City, Ramp City, Random City, Ready City, Ready-Made City (circled), Reef City, Realized City, Realistic City, Reconnection City, Recreation City, Refugee City, Regional City, Regulation City, Reject City, Relational City, Remapping City, Renaissance City, Rent-a-City, Repressive City, Reserve City, Residential City, Residual City, Resist City, Resistance City, Resurrection City, Revolution City, Rhizomatic City, Rhizome City (circled), Rhizoming City, Rich City, Rim City, Ring City (circled), Riot City, Rising City, Rite City, River City, Road City (circled, crossed out), Roadless City, Rock City, Rogue City, Romantic City, Roof City, Rose City, Rough City, Row City, Royal City, Rubble City, Ruin City ...
- Rush City, Sale City, Same City, Sand City (circled), Sandwich City, Scadenza City, Scan City, Scene City, Schizophrenic City, Science City, Sci-Fi City, Scoop City, Scream City, Screen City, Sea City, Season City, Secret City, Security City, Sedative City, Seductive City, Self-Organized City, Semi-City, Sequential City, Service City, Sewer City, Sex City, Shadow City, Shaman City, Shanty City, Sharp City, Shifting City (circled), Shopping City (circled), Shy City, Sick City, Side-by-Side City, Sign City, Signal City (circled), Sim City, Simple City, Sin City, Sinking City, Skin City, Skinny City, Sky City, Skyline City, Slacker City, Slam City ...
- Smart City, Smiling City, Snow City, So What City, Sn-and-so City, So-Called City, Social City, Soft City, Software City, So-Long City, Sonic City, Sorry City (circled), Soul City, Sound City, Space City, Sparkling City, Spatial City, Speciated City, Sperm City (circled), Sphere City, Spider City, Spinal City, Space City, Splendid City, Sprawling City, Spreading City, Stage City, Star City, Start-Up City, State City, State-of-the-Art City, Stereo City, Still City, Stir City, Stop City, Story City, Strategic City, Street City, Stress City (circled, underlined), Starched City (crossed out), String City, Stroll City, Strong City, Structural City, Studio City ...
- Success City, Sudden City, Suicide City, Sun City, Sunbelt City, Super City, Superblock City, Superfluid City, Supernatural City, Surveil City, Surprise City, Survival City ...
- Toy City, This Way City, Think City, Thin City, Theme City, Their City, THE City, Terminal City, Term City, Tentative City, Tentacle City, Tent City, Tender City, Tenant City, Tenuous City, Temporary City, Temple City, Totemic City, 3D City, Ticklish City, Time City, Time-Warp City, Tin City ...

issues and balances the level of conservation and development. Being environmentally-conscious does not only mean going green. **Bioclimatic city Bird city Bird`s Eye city** *The city does not have to be viewed only by the human. Birds are also part of the city, surely the urban inhabitants.* **Bit city** *A bit is the minimum unit for the digital telecommunication, a binary digit that a computer can store. Imagine the city that explores the in-betweens of 0 and 1.* **Bite city** *There is a need for the city that is capable of its own internal revision through a self-examination process.* **Blasting city Blind city Blitz city Blob city Blood city Blow city Blow-Out city Blur city Body city Bold city Book city Boom city Borderless city** *The advancement of communication and transportation technology of the contemporary cities influences not only their own nation, but to other countries as well. Boundaries among the cities blurred, individual characteristics and identities of each city disappear, gradually possessing similar facades.* **Box city Brain city Brand city** *Through the way we make brand for the city, we can suggest possibilities to accelerate the urban growth. Just like the brand representing the product, the city is represented. Like we shop for the product, we navigate the city.* **Brave city Breathing city** *The city can be proposed as an living organism that breathes. In order to sustain their lives, cities must breathe. For the sake of urban wellness, we need to examine the city from the urban perspective, not from human perspective.* **Bridge city Brilliant city** *Retrospection of the Radiant City and Le Corbusier* **Broadacre city Broken city Browsing city Bubble city Bunker city Bustling city Busy city Button city Cable city** *Imagine the city filled with cables as portrayed in the film ⟨Brazil⟩. City connected with network of cables. Many cables exist in the city - for electrical use, telephones, the Internet, cable TV, and etc., - all connected in complexity. Having count of cables connected to a house in the city, there will be great number of cables throughout the city. The number probably counts beyond our imagination. The city is made with cables that control our body. Space and city seem to be manipulated these cables… If we revive all cables, including the ones that we don't see, we may not be able to move* **Calibration city Camp city Camping city** *Imagine the city of nomadic code. The entire city is an enormous field of nature. People move and migrate, and set up a great tent with all those who share their lives.* **Campus city Canyon city** *What happens if the deviation of urban topography is set at its maximum?* **Capital city Caprice city Capsule city** *Small units for the city might be defined as the size of spatial limitation people can share. Integrate the roles of the city over the unit called 'capsule', and let us carry our lives and our cities.* **Captive city Car city Card city** *Urban life is captured into a number of cards. Movement, shopping, food, living… Leave the details of their structural organization as the cards' share.* **Cartoon city Casino city Cell city Center city Centerless city** *Imagine the city structure where its center disturbed, making centerless, or multiple-centered city.* **Chaos city** *The city is comprised of complex, chaotic structure. We need to clarify the relationship between the urban diversity and lawful characteristics of the order.* **Characteristic city Charming city Channing city Cheap city Children`s city Choice city Cinecitta city Cinema city** *Create virtual city constructed upon the cinematic imagination. City city City within a city, space within space, time within time, …* **City on the Move** *Suppose we question the way space is organized. The city that responds itself to movements and transitions cannot be explained through the conventional description of making space.* **Clandestine city Click city** *The city is accumulation of mouse-click activities. People navigate the computer according to their needs. Simple ways of clicking their wishes transcend the concept of space, time and place. It becomes a great map of global navigation.* **Cliff city Climax city Clip city Cloaca city Cloud city** *"You can't build cloud. And that's why the future you dream of never comes" - Ludwig Wittgenstein* **Club city Cluster city Coaxial city Code city** *By articulating various urban codes, a different city can be established. Not by the typical urban apparatus, the new codes maximize the spectrum of transition possible in affect with other codes.* **Cohab city Cold city Collab city Collage city** *With different programmatic and contextual framework, cities collide and produce new programs and interpretations for the new urban codes.* **Collapse city Collective city** *For the representation of collective codes, the interpretation of a city shall not be based on its physical coordinates. Instead alternative attempts will be made by investigating relationship-based activities - such as reciprocity of programs and collaged texts. This will allow us to read programs and their linkages in utterly different context, thus generating new interpretations and feedbacks.* **College city Collision city Color city** *Colors of a city comprises of programmatic spectrums. City spectrum classifies its context into various categories, or leads us towards new alternatives and new urban codes.* **Combinational city Coming city Coming-to-Be city Commercial city Commodity city** *City-as-Commodity* **Communal city** *The quality of a city depends upon the way we control the public*

Jang Yoon Gyoo,
Trans-urban Program: Chunggyechun High Way Park (2003)

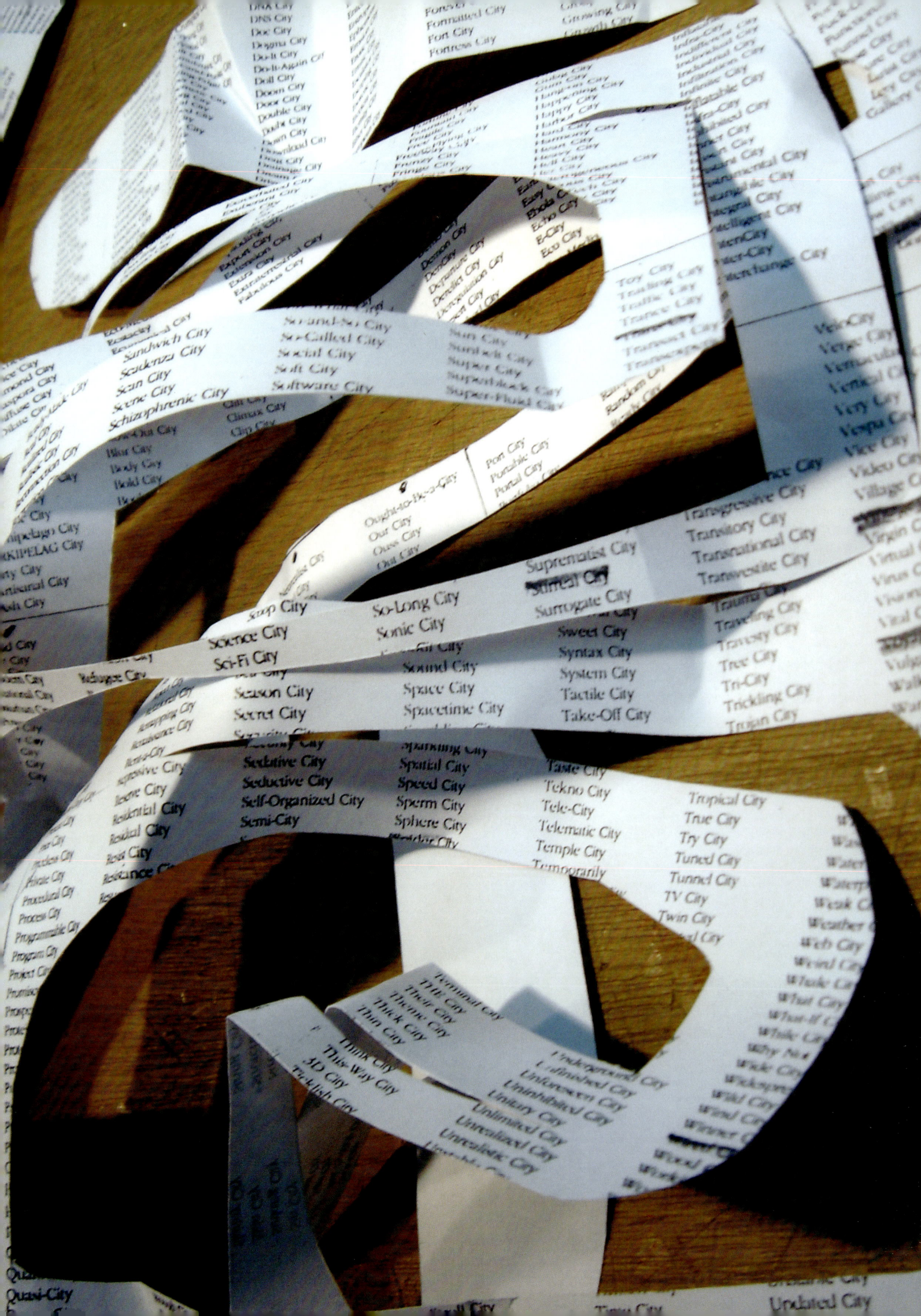

space. City infrastructure, landscape, plaza and so forth. We must seek appropriate ways to work space open to the public. **Compact city** *The city is an intricate organization which consists of various clusters of programs and substances. It can be called a network. Imagine the city as an intimate, systematic network formulated out of its self-organization process and its relationships with other cities. Infinite numbers of urban factors become closer in distance to result a dense, compact phenomenon.* **Compassion city Compatible city** *Discover a potential in rearrangements of the gap between incompatible urban elements. New compatibility is generated from those which could not coexist together and were not compatible to each other.* **Compassion city Competition city Complex city Complex-Dynamic city Comprehensive city Compressed city Computer city Concentration city Concrete city Confused city Conglomerate city Consolidated city Constant city Constellation city Construction city Container city** *City as a sectional container can be mobile and flexible in use - each section can be pulled out or plugged in to transport if desired. Thus the city becomes capable of being disassembled and reassembled.* **Contemporary city Context city Continent city Continental city Conversion city Concentration city Cool city Cord city Cordless city** *The advancement of technology enables a cordless city. From the moment of access, the city becomes free and reach the level of which can explore beyond the physical limitation of space.* **Core city** *City center means the area of a cultural, political, economical core working as a backbone. City infrastructure starts from its center to form a massive network of infrastructure throughout the city.* **Corporate city Correspondence city Corridor city** *If the city is looked as a system, we can imagine more intensified city. Let us map one of its physical feature called corridors. All city roads and pathway networks for access are reconfigured into multiple levels of urban connection network. The corridor no longer remains as one-dimensional path with a single orientation, but it becomes part of the three-dimensional complex network system.* **Cosmic city Countless city Coupling city Crazy city Cream city Creative city Creole city Crime city Crisscross city Critical city Cross city Crossing city Crowd city Cruise city Crumpled city Crying city Crystal city Cult city Cumulative city** *The city is not comprised of one layer - memories, culture, nature, technology,…multiple layers accumulate over time.* **Cut-and-Paste city** *Seek the ways to re-edit the city. Cut away some parts of the city, then insert new programs and urban topography.* **Cutting-Edge city Cyber city Cybernetic city Cyborg city Cynical city Damned city Dark city** *At midnight, the big city stops for a moment and takes a rest asleep. Skyscrapers disappear instantly, and reappear again. Moment where the clock's hour hand and minute hand cross, all those who were in sleep rise again as if nothing different. Chaos begins as the night becomes busy again in the city.* **Darrow city Data city** *We can bring various data from urban research into the new constitution of city. Yet the selection of data and its application shall be clear in substantiating alternative positions different from what has been discussed to the present. Provide a logical map for the new version of the city that convinces.* **Date city Day city Dead city Dead-End city Decentered city Declining city Deconstruction city Decoy city Defense city Definite city Delirious city** *City of schizophrenia* **Demo city Demon city Den city Departure city Derelict city Deregulation city Desert city Detached city Device city Diamond city Diaspora city Diffuse city Dilate city Dim city** *Imagine the city that works as dim fog - blurring the boundaries among the objects. City is organized as semi-landscape with dimmed borders.* **Dirt city Disaster city Discourse city Discovery city Disk city Disintegral city Dismantled city Disposal city Distinctive city** *Generate differences through displacing and interpreting the text, in order to discover the distinctive quality attained by displacements* **Distorted city** *Make distorted urban topography.* **Diver city Dizzy city DNA city** *Seek all outcomes through modifying urban DNA.* **DNS city Doc city Dogma city Do-It city Do-It-Again city Doll city** *An enormous framework is being manipulated by the controller - hidden hands that we cannot see.* **Doom city Door city Double city Doubt city Down city Download city Drag city** *Imagine the intervention as a way of modification, only if we can drag the city.* **Drainage city Dream city Drive-By city Drop city Drug city Drum city Dull city Duplication city** *Aura does not exist in the era of unlimited reproduction.* **Dust city Dwelling city Dynamo city Dystopian city Earth city Earthbound city Easy city Ebola city E-city Eco city Eco-Media city Ecsta city Ecumenical city Edge city Edible city Edo city Effect city Electric city Electron city Electronic city Elementary city Elusive city Emergency city Emergent city Emotional city Empty city Enclave city End city Endless city Endo city Enhanced city Enigmatic city Entertainment city Entropic city Ephemeral city** *Capitalist city consumes more products faster than ever, instigating more production. The trend cycles become ephemeral as the city changes its outfits like a mayfly, a chameleon. There is no such thing as eternal values in human desire. Only the ephemeral life exists.* **Erosion city Erotic city** *The city is located between the taboos and desire. Imagine a device that controls the cycles of consumption*

Jang Yoon Gyoo + Shin Chang Hoon, High Seoul Festival: Connection City

Jang Yoon Gyoo + Shin Chang Hoon, KT&G: Vertical Street City

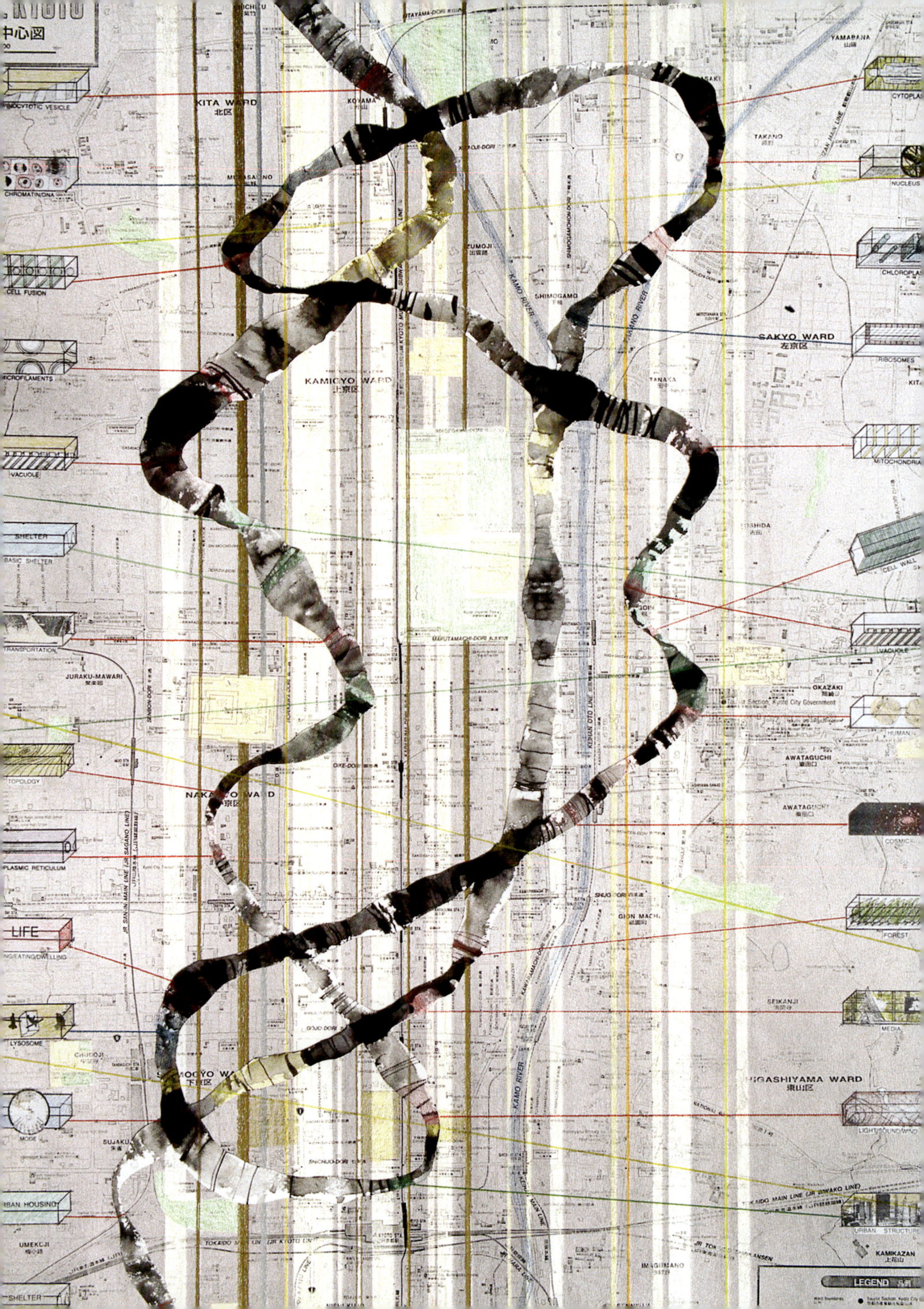

and production. Erratic city Escalator city Escaping city Esoteric city Etcetera city Eternity city Ether city European city Ever city Every city Everything-but-the-city Everywhere city Ex city Exacerbated city Exuberant city Excuse city Exhibition city Expanding city Expensive city Experimental city Exploding city Exploration city Exploding city Export city Extension city Extra city Extraterrestrial city Fabulous city Facade city Factory city Fair city Falls city Fame city Fast city *The city speed has changed. The city has become Mcdonalized. It wants fast, convenient and instant speed. We may need to control our psychological speed.* Fat city Fax city Feather city Feedback city Financial city Fire city First city Fist city Flash city Flat city Floating city Flood city Flow city Fluctuation city Fluid city Flux city Fly city Folly city Footnote city Foreseen city Forest city Forever city Formatted city Fort city Fortress city Fortune city Fragile city Free city Free-flying city Freedom city Freeway city Frenzy city Fringe city Frivolous city Frontier city Frozen city Fuck city Fuck-Contest city Functional city Funnel city Fuse city Future city Futurist city Fuzzy city Gallery city Game city *Both physical and non-physical elements for the city continue to revise itself and respond towards various catalysts. By blending different characteristics of urban prototypes we can generate diverse spectrum of urban models. It is becoming more difficult to project the responses and transformations of the mobile city. The stronger this game is in its variability, the more diverse outcomes in urban experiments.* Gap city *We cannot conclude that the city gap exists for the sake of being filled and packed. As the city grows, the gap takes the role of a buffer among the boundaries of different programs. It goes beyond its physical dimension, having economic, cultural influences.* Garden city *Garden possesses the programs of purification and filtration. The city has the characteristics of one big "Mega-Garden".* Gate city Gateway city Gay city Generic city Genetic city Geodesic city Ghetto city Ghost city Giant city Glam city Global city Glocal city Gonna city Gorgeous city Gossip city Gotha city Gothic city Graffiti city Gray city Gray Realm city Great city Greek city Green city Gridlock city Groundless city Group city Growing city Growth city Gulag city Gum city Hang-on city Happening city Happy city Harbor city Hard city Harmony city Heart city Heavy city Hell city Her city Heterogeneous city Hideous city High-Tech city Highway city Hip-Hop city His city Hitting city Hoax city Holistic city Holland city Holographic city Holy city Homogeneous city Horizontal city Hot city House city Hovering city Hub city Huge city Hurry city Hybrid city Hyper city Ice city Icon city Ideal city Illegal city Imaginary city Imagination city Immaterial city Immediate city Immersive city Imperfect city Inanimate city Indefinite city Indifferent city Individual city Industrial city Infiltration city Infinite city Inflatable city Infrastructure city Inhabited city Inner city Insert city Instant city Instrumental city Intangible city Integral city Intelligent city Inten-city Inter city Interchange city Interconnected city Interdisciplinary city Interest city Interface city Interfolded city Interior city Intermediate city International city Intertwined city Interval city Intra city Invisible city Island city Isotropic city Jealous city Jargon city Joint city Joy city Jumbo city Jump city Jump-cut city Jumping city Jungle city Junk city Just-in-Time city Kaleidoscope city Kid city King city Knowledge city Kool city Kraftwork city Lab city Label city Labor city Labyrinth city Laid-Back city Landmark city Landscape city Language city Large-scale city Last city Layered city Leaf city Learning city Lego city Leisure city Level city Life city Liminal city Limited city Linear city Lion city Liquid city Little city Live city Living city Load city Local city Loft city Loop city Loser city Lost city Love city Lung city Lure city Machine city Macro city Madang city Magic city Magari city Magnet city Magnificent city Mail city Mail-Order city Major city Mall city Malleable city Manga city Manifesta city Manifesto city Marine city Mark city Market city Mathematical city Matriuschka city Matrix city Maximum city Maybe city Mayor city Mean city Meccano city Mechanical city Media city Mediated city Medical city Medieval city Medium city Medusa city Meeting city Mega-city Megalo-city Memory city Mental city Merge city Meta-city Metaphonic city Metaphor city Meteorite city Middle city Migration city Milk city Millenium city Mini-city Minimal city Minor city Micro-city Mitigated city Mixing city Mobile city Mobius city Model city Modern city Modest city Modular city Module city Molecular city Monad city Money city Mono city Monopoly city Monumental city Moon city More city More-than-All city Morphing city Mosaic city Multifunctional city Multinational city Mundane city Museum city Must city Mutable city Mutant city My city *The city can be used as a machine for the bachelor who makes the useless forms and spaces, all in pursuit of his dream, fantasy, and illusion of memories.* Mythology city Naked city Nano-city Narrow city National city Naval city Near city Negotiation city Neo city Neo-Babylonian city Neon city Neorealist city Nerd city Nerve city Nested city Net city Network city Neural city Neuro city Neuronal city Never city New city Niche city Night city No city Nodal city No-Go city Node city Noise city Nomadic city Nonlinear city Nonplace city Nonstop city No-Plan city Northern city Nostalgic city Notable city

Jang Yoon Gyoo + Yoon Jung Hyun
Floating City for Urban Regeneration (1999)

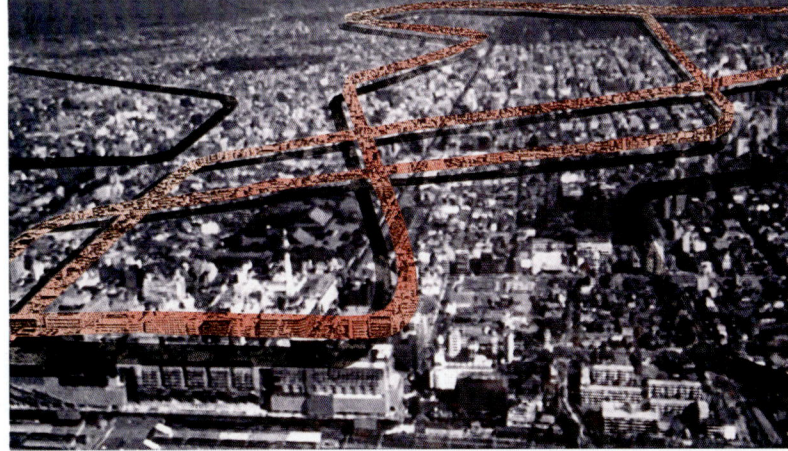

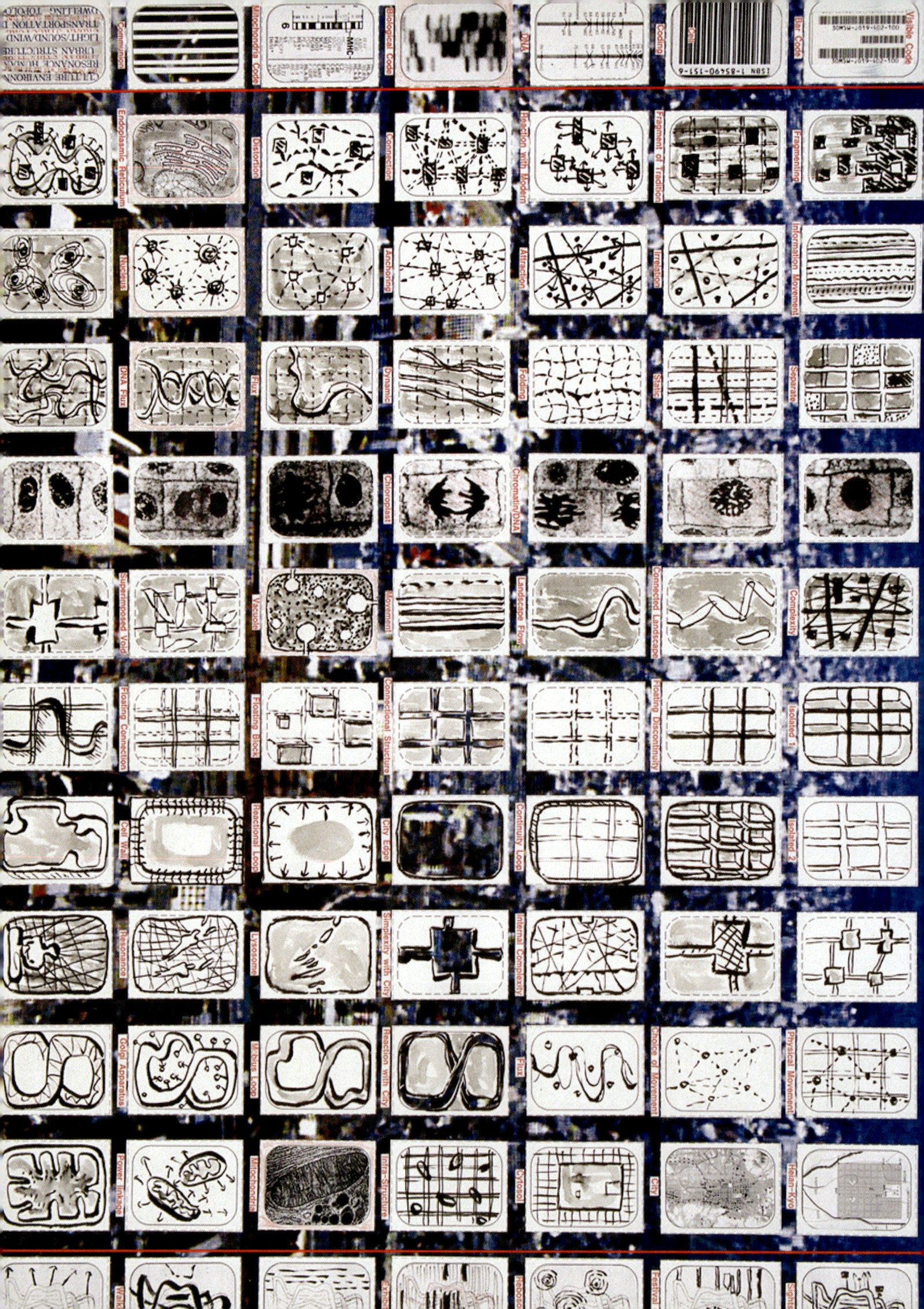

Not-a-city No-Techno city Nothing city Now city Number city Oasis city Oblique city Obsessive city Obvious city Ocean city Odd city Office city OK city Old city 100 Percent city Only city Open city Open-to-Sky city Option city Oral city Orchard city Organ city Organic city Original city Oscillation city Ought-to-Be-a-city Our city Ouss city Out city Outer city Oxygen city Oyster city Ozone city Paint city Palm city Pan city Panoptic city Panorama city Para city Parallel city Park city Passage city Passing city Patchwork city Pathological city Patient city Pavilion city P-C city Pedestrian city People's city People's city Performative city Periodic city Peripatetic city Peristaltic city Pervasive city Phantom city Piazza city Pilot city Piss city Pixel city Pizza city Placard city Placebo city Plan city Plant city Play city Pleasure city Plug-In city Pneumatic city Pocket city Political city Pompous city Poor city PoP-Up city Prono city Port city Portable city Portal city Portfolio city Post city Postcard city Posthuman city Post-Identity city Postindustrial city Post It city Postmodern city Postnational city Posturban city Power city Precinct city preemptive city Prefab city Pretext city Price city Present city Present-Day city Priceless city Private city Procedural city Process city Program city Programmable city Project city Promiscuous city Prosperous city Protein city Proto city Proud city Proxy city Psychogeographic city Public city Public Transportation city Pulse city Punch city Pyramid city Quantum city Quartz city Quasi city Queen city Queer city Quiet city Radiant city Radio city Radius city Rain city Ramified city Ramp city Random city Ready city Ready-made city Real city Realistic city Realized city Reconnection city Recreation city Refugee city Regional city Regulation city Reject city Relational city Remapping city Renaissance city Rent-a-city Repressive city Reserve city

Residential city Residual city Resist city Resistance city Resurrection city Revolution city Rhizomatic city Rhizoming city Rich city Rim city Ring city Riot city Rising city Rite city River city Road city Roadless city Rock city Rogue city Romantic city Roof city Rose city Rough city Row city Royal city Rubble city Ruin city Rumor city Running city Rural city Rush city Sale city Same city Sand city Sandwich city Scadenza city Scan city Scene city Schizophrenic city Science city Sci-Fi city Scoop city Scream city Screen city Sea city Season city Secret city Security city Sedative city Seductive city Self-Organized city Semi-city Sequential city Service city Sewer city Sex city Shadow city Shaman city Shanty city Sharp city Shifting city Shopping city Shy city Sick city Side-by-Side city Sign city Signal city Sim city Simple city Sin city Sinking city Skin city Skinny city Sky city Skyline city Slacker city Slam city Sleepless city Slice and Dice city Slick city Slow city Smart city Smiling city Snow city So Shat city So and So city So-called city Social city Soft city Software city So-Long city Sonic city Sore city Sorry city Soul city Sound city Space city Spacetime city Sparkling city Spatial city Speed city Sperm city Sphere city Spider city Spiral city Splace city Splendid city Sprawling city Spreading city Stage city Star city Start-Up city State-of-the-Art city Stereo city Still city Stir city Stop city Story city Strategic city Street city Stress city Stretched city String city Stroll city Strong city Structural city Studio city Substitute city Subtle city Suburban city Succeeding city Success city Sudden city Suicide city Sun city Sunbelt city Super city Super block city Super-fluid city Suprematist city Surreal city Surrogate city Survival city Sweet city Syntax city System city Tactile city Take—off city Taste city Tekno city Tele—city Telematic city Temple city Temporarily autonomous city Temporary city

Temptation city Tenacity Tenant city Tender city Tent city Tentacle city Tentative city Term city Terminal city The city Their city Theme city Thick city Thin city Think city This-way city 3D city Thicklish city Time city Time-Warp city Tin city Toast city Toll city Tool city Tool-kit city Tower city Toy city Trading city Traffic city Trance city Trans-city Transact city Transexperience city Transgressive city Transitory city Transnational city Transvestite city Trauma city Traveling city Travesty city Tree city Tri-city Trickling city Trojan city Tropical city True city Try city Tuned city TV city Twin city Twisted city Type city Typical city U city UFO city UN city Unbound city Uncertain city Un-city Underground city Unfinished city Unforeseen city Uninhibited city Unitary city Unlimited city Unrealized city Unrealistic city Unstable city Updated city Urban Mark city Utopian city Value city Vanishing city Vast city Vegan city Velcro city Velo city Verge city Vernacular city Vertical city Very city Vespa city Vice city Video city Village city Vintage city Virgin city Virtual city Virus city Visionary city Vital city Voyage city Vulgar city Walking city War city Wash city Waste city Waste city Water city Waterproof city Weak city Weather city Web city Weird city Whale city What city What-If city While city Why city Wide city Widespread city Wild city Wind city Winner city Wired city Wood city Working city World city Worldwide city Worm city Worse city Worst city Wrist city Wrong city www.city X city X-File city X-Ray city You city Your city Youth city Zap city Zero-Degree city Zip city Zombie city Zone city.........
More clips of texts to be continued.

The essence of making Clip City is not just to generate the encyclopedia of a city. It is the process of seeking appropriate programs for city's physical structure.

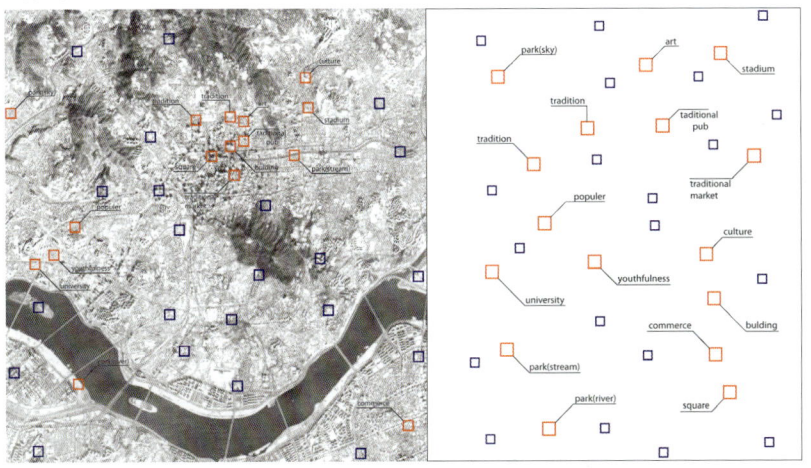

Clipping Urban Factor

Jang Yoon Gyoo Studio + Kim Kyung Hwan, Clip City

Compound Body
03 Becoming Animal

⟨Creation or Becoming⟩ is proposed as a paradox of what Deleuze discusses in his book ⟨A Thousand Plateaus⟩, where he questions the essence of becoming as the subject. This text questions the ways to deterritorialize one's self-being, completely free from the self to be rooted into others, or be free by becoming the root. ⟨Becoming⟩ will be explored to examine ways to rethink this matter.
False, the virtual text of mimesis. In order to actualize the falsity, we disguise them as reality, just like what Borges played hoaxes. One example would be a hypothesis that human species, the cultural core of this world, become newly modified, or different. A man is no longer the man from the past. He has become fussy and irritated species who desired for the new world. Suppose a new DNA _ between architecture and city a number of DNA's are manipulated and produce new species. A mutant lives in the city, proliferates its own kind, and start changing the city.

Alice in Wonderland is not a fiction any more. We live in a world where the White Rabbit is replaced by the computer. Not only we gaze through the looking-glass, we freely cross over the glass by just clicking keyboards. Hamlet groans in ⟨Alice in Wonderland⟩. "The time is out of joint" We live along the horizon in time of Hamlet's moan. We live in the society where all borders, along with time and space, disappear. The theme behind ⟨Becoming Animal⟩ also relates to how we can perceive our social milieu and form relationships with new breeds of space generated. Instead of reading these new breeds of space as single-shot of interest, the topic hopefully provokes us to acknowledge our space in new ways in order to anticipate them for the future. Just like a magical myth⋯.

⟨Compound Body⟩ necessarily goes through the process of displacement and transformation. Suppose we can imagine all possible conceptual spectrums of method and substance for the ⟨Compound Body⟩, and all of their transformations directly relate to the making of groundwork for ⟨Becoming Animal⟩. As we have seen in the previous chapter, the groundwork of ⟨Compound Body⟩ is also connected with urban narrative in the ⟨Clip City⟩. If we can assume that the text

Matthew Barney

Nam Ji, Between Human & Machine

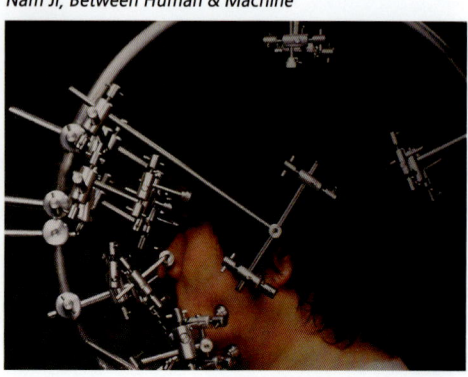

Being John Malkovich

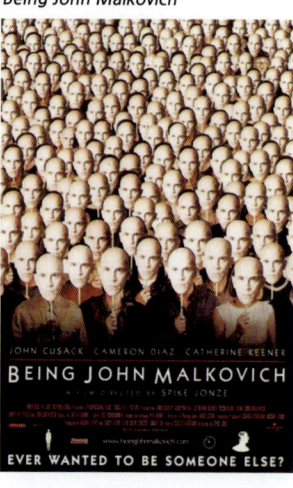

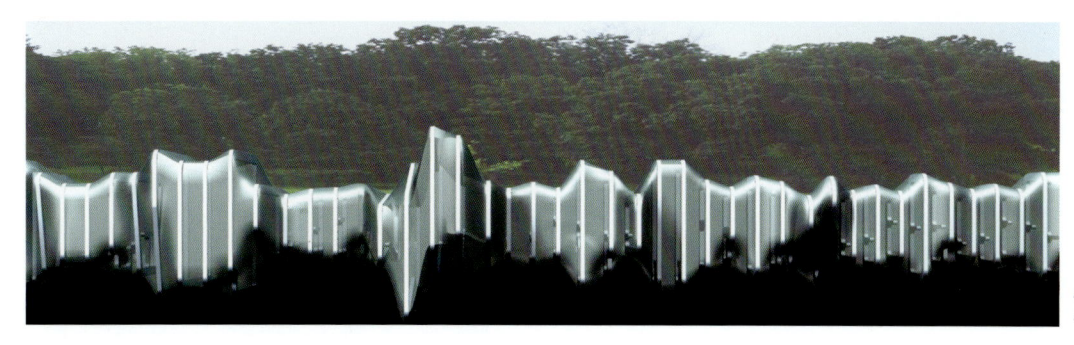

Jang Yoon Gyoo + Kim Min Tae,
Jun Soo Chun Atlier: Trans-morphing of Vinyl House

clips of ⟨Clip City⟩ are extracted materials and substances for making ⟨Compound Body⟩, ⟨Becoming Animal⟩ is closer to an acting device or tool which leads its ways of transformation towards constituting a new creative outline. Thus the story of ⟨Becoming Animal⟩ begins with a narrative of the outline which engages us to acknowledge invisible codes. We have to note that ⟨Becoming Animal⟩ is one of many accessible routes that we may able to find. In the midst of endless branches and strings, it instigates to promote the workings of new codes of paradox and myth. ⟨Becoming Animal⟩ can be viewed as an attitude of seeking future-oriented experiments and theorization regarding our current status. It is critical to catch up the modern by 'transcending' the modern. The framework of ⟨Becoming Animal⟩ posits itself as an alter-ego, standing in the borderline between the two acts of 'catching-up' and 'transcending'. Architectural requirement for the ⟨Becoming Animal⟩ is to seek new articulations in all possible approaches in architecture. Issues from urban perspective, practices, new articulations of architectural space, generating new spatial types,… The orientation of ⟨Becoming Animal⟩ exists somewhere that is not completely social, cultural, or architectural yet. Because of such ambiguous, in-between tendency, it generates new codes through its process. Important terms of the process are neither 'human' nor 'animal', it is ways of 'becoming' and substances that 'becomes'. Thus 'becoming' is based on framework of organization that allows new knowledge or creativity to occur. ⟨Organization of Becoming⟩ rejects all conventional subjectivity and differentiates itself from the core-conception of the western philosophy - eternity, universality, fundamentalism, essentialism, and etc. It desires for new exploration of mutation, displacement and creation.

The important aspect in 'becoming' is that it helps to refine individual characteristics of the new species as they proceed through a transformation. With respect to a city, the process begins with finding examples of space which promotes to form aggressive connection between architecture and social realm, followed by sorting out to modify their relationships. We need to acknowledge that the social transformation we experience is the outcomes intricately related to spatial deformation of which programs pair up with architecture. The process of 'becoming animal' is similar to generating clever framework between architecture and society. 'A man is hiding the other man' - is a question regarding the essence within the human kind and its continuity. The advancement of technology enables infinite mutation of things including the essence of a man. Not only we need to understand the criticality of transformations occurring to ourselves, but also the ways our urban space transforms with us. Putting aside of a dispute whether to sustain our essence in continuity, we need to acknowledge that the current social structure is becoming more prone to the acceleration of this trance.

The critical beginning of ⟨Becoming Animal⟩ connects with essence of aura. Essence is similar to a mobile thing rather than something transfixed. ⟨Becoming⟩ possesses potential to shift from the ordinary in us to the territory of transformation. It encourages different conception of criticism and perception towards 'the subject', for example, making possible to construct space like landscape, or inverting the relationship between the center and the periphery. The intention of 'becoming animal' is to introduce Deleuzian 'fold' into social and architectural realms - here the fold is no longer a form. Fold is a quality, pleat-producing

Richard Serra, Orchestra

Olafur Eliasson, Test Your Moblie Expectations (2006)

Jang Yoon Gyoo + Lee Mee Young, Space-sofa, Space Furniture (1999) reciprocal structure that mutates and offers random bends into continuity of a flat social structure. This newly-intervened, yet ambiguous social structure can be hypothesized as a framework of new creativity that also comes with various social ills and side effects. True that we may be uncomfortable and find ourselves criticizing about these new flaws and discontinuous proceeding, but these new cracks can offer us new opportunities. New flaws generate space of 'hyperreal text'. We ought to pay attention to this 'rhizomatic' structure which generates unlimited points of convergence in lieu of centralized space. From non-hierarchical and unlimited source of convergence, we arrive to recognize these new creative flaws in different angles. Our society does not consist of codes segmented by the media and digitalization, but a manifold with variety of substances as a whole. This manifold is a structure of 'hypertextual' codes. As a change is made in programs of the society and life, so does architectural programs.

Exploring a new framework even opens up spatial possibility that has been regarded as impossible in the past. 'Programmatic mutation' is one example. We must seek spatial transformation coming through revising our social and architectural programs. Time-transcending imagination of a man and scientific accomplishments changes the way we communicate, the distinction between the virtual and reality is being blurred. No longer is architecture interpreted only within physical dimension. The reciprocity of 'hyper-realization' and 'virtualization of the real' is no longer our fantasy. We enjoy penetrating into the world of cyber-network and navigate as if we maneuver through our physical space. Space desires to 'become architecture' even though it is not in architectural context. This is the same for a case of a city where we are about to make the first step towards putting our social desire out to its infinite spatial expansion. The fantasy of Alice in Wonderland is not a myth anymore. Computer in disguise of the White Rabbit, or 'the Rabbit becoming computer' is actually being implemented in our everyday life. We freely manipulate our keyboards, across the looking glass, a man becoming animal, to pursue 'boundarial transformation'. Like the hand of a magician, ⟨Becoming Animal⟩ mixes ⟨realization of the hyper⟩ and ⟨hyperization of the real⟩.

Through cyberspace architecture the ambiguity is expressed in multiple layers - like the boundaries between the real and virtual, and Sci-fi films' portrayal of confusion between the virtual and the reality.

A myth of man becoming animal is no longer a myth of magic. Technical transformation potentiates unlimited hybridization including human tendency. A mythical man and a cyborg are only few of examples of 'becoming animal'. There is a magician who manipulates the city. He who gives magical spells for a man ⟨becoming animal⟩, sometimes intensely, and sometimes with subtlety, responds to the needs of our social changes and requirements. One might think that a man becoming animal means a regression. However, we must acknowledge that the reality produced by ⟨becoming⟩ does not indicate an animal in completed form. It is a new factor made to generate new possibility which can inhabit the in-between space among social, cultural and architectural realms. ⟨Becoming Animal⟩ does not mean a man simply imitating a pig or wearing a pig mask, or becoming identical.

Rather than giving sarcasm or criticize the fact that reality not being able to engage society and architecture, we will begin by searching for possible spatial examples through ⟨becoming animal⟩ and rethink the linkage between the two more aggressively. Suppose a man become a dog for one day wandering around the city, the city and culture is viewed with completely different set of perspectives. In the city we live today, ⟨new hybrids⟩ are constantly being generated and mutated in conjunction with enormous social flux and cultural complexity. Urban spaces are formed to accommodate these hybrids, and transformed to spatial types which were not conceivable in the past. A bathroom does not stay as bathroom, while a house does not remain as a house for living. We already know that a bathroom becoming a café, or a house becoming as an office, is nothing new or unique idea. We should focus here that these hybridized space departs from everyday life rather than any specific accommodation. Despite of its ordinariness these spaces become hybrid in nature which quickly gets reshuffled in accordance with social demands and circumstances. The film ⟨Being John Malkovich⟩ throws

Jang Yoon Gyoo + Lee Mee Young, Transparent Chair with Lighting (1999)

Jang Yoon Gyoo, Cup Table

Jang Yoon Gyoo + Jang Yoon Sung, Media - Organ "Compound Morphing between Visual & Sound"

various propositions in respect to the notion of <Becoming>. Between 7th & 8th floor, on 7.5th floor, there is a pathway to enter into John Malkovich. Through this pathway the audience enters into a media of new experience - Malkovich, and come to realization of new life and thoughts. Through the space of 7.5th floor one does not <Becomes> Malkovich, or remains in himself/herself who experiences Malkovich's life, it is a newly-altered man. The pathway between man and Malkovich corresponds to creating the clever stage, just as what we have discussed in generating the <Becoming Animal> between architecture and society.

Essence is regarded as a fierce resistance towards thinking that it is not immutable. Human essence also transforms, like the ones of city and architecture, as well as our cultural and social essence. We must be aware that our urban space is being transformed as well. Transformation of essence potentiates <becoming intense> guided by <becoming animal>. <Becoming Animal> possesses hybridized codes generated by both a man and an animal. If the boundaries surrounding the disciplines collapse and the disciplines exchange influences reciprocally, all of them become part of one loop that circulates as a whole. In the society where things communicate and accelerate by crossing over one another, architecture would not deny the idea of <Becoming Hybrid>. Through <Becoming Hybrid> a strategy of inserting cultural code is being applied. There is a reason for putting importance on these question of 'how can the public spaces reach beyond its mere purpose of being shared by the public' and 'instead how to engage them culturally'. Society is implementing various projects in order to cultivate public spaces into cultural realm. Not only the space like bathrooms, but spaces of subways, parks, and streets are transformed into the new cultural code. When programs of social or everyday life transform, new architectural programs are generated in different characteristics. Even those which were socially forbid programs that generate secretive spaces, transforms into open-coded spaces. The shift of today's system from machine to digital was followed by the media called hyperreality, changing the way we recognize the real space. It is a paradigm shift that allowed yet another kind of hybrid space to appear.

The meaning behind <Becoming Animal> lies along the program's self-transforming capability rather than satisfying the demands, or changing itself per requirements of its externality - such as form or structure. It can organize & arrange its own sets of hybrid programs, or make attempts to create a manifold independent from formal or programmatic relationship. This manifold is not considered as a system that exercises single function, but rather a loose, flexible mechanism which accommodates transformative demands and mutating variables for the program. Embracing possibilities of programmatic transformation allows architectural models to be transformed, and therefore brings up a series of questions of its fundamental methodology of assembling programs. It also conveys possibilities of how the elements of incompatible codes can be mixed, and external data can be substituted into architectural spaces. In turn, this process is quite similar with substituting the Orpheus's Gaze with the Ulysses's Ear. The range of transformation depends on how to stretch the framework of <Becoming Animal>. More important issue, however, is to take the given framework and explore where we can reach in terms of creating new spatial possibilities or urban articulations. This can become especially powerful when these new definitions and characterizations penetrate the codes of everyday life. Everyday spaces we pass by not giving enough recognition - homes, bathroom in my house, several spaces scattered around a city, and etc., comes alive with altered interpretations and new spatial constitutions. This project is about rediscovering potential within us to create new interpretations and alternative perspectives, and then inserting new breed of programs and opportunities through the process of <Meaning Eraser> and <Providing New Meaning>. Just like constructing the meanings of the text, it is about removing all of the unnecessary extras and transforming the text in its essence into the text possible in other dimensions and contexts.

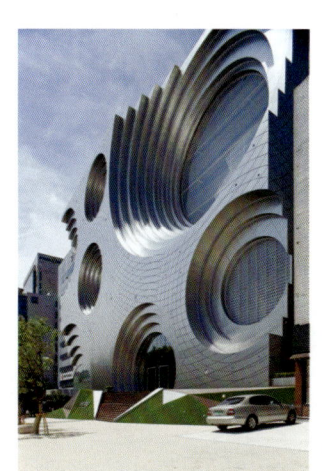

Jang Yoon Gyoo + Shin Chang Hoon,
GwangJu Biennale: Trans-map of Urban Structures (2004)

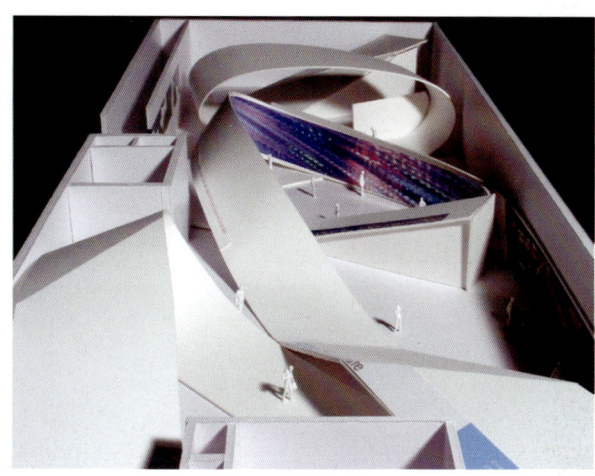

Jang Yoon Gyoo + Shin Chang Hoon,
Brand Space KRING

Jang Yoon Gyoo + Lee Mee Young, Zero - Gravity House

Gravity Space in Zero Gravity

Folding of the Earth Skin with Magnetic Gravity

Compound Body
04 Reaction- Interactive Map

"I used to dream what I only see. Sometimes I believed that even a fantasy visible. So did spirit. I realized that what I believed to be visible was only a simulacre. Essence exists where it is invisible. Even those visible do not remain as only visible. The visible things become invisible. I have dreamed the invisible as close to the essence. The moment invisible things are reborn, they are not invisible anymore. It is a new beginning for a knowledge that became close to essence capable of being visualized."

Reaction Body is superimposed over the invisibles. It becomes a device to recollect or rediscover things considered invisible. However the Reaction Body is not invisible substance like an 'invisible man'. It is a regenerating framework that strips away the curtains from blocking the light, and open to resonate with city and society.

One cannot read contemporary city simply with physical factors. City is now a massive chunk of complex system of which one minor shift brings the entire network to be reshuffled. We are in the era of compound - networks peculiarly and intricately mixed with information media. Architecture is also at a point where it is no longer about the production of buildings as it confronts reconstitution in the way we respond and react towards changing urban/social context. Compoundization of society, city, and human values demands an entity that can act as a new cultural container. Boundaries are blurred and physical world disappears. Physical world has turned into a large complex environment of digital, media and cyber community, penetrated and manipulated everyday with bountiful layers of information and culture. Architecture is now required to embrace unlimited potential of society as it attempts to react in various ways.

City does not cease to grow, develop and evolve. As darkness exists on the other side of the moon, growth of a city also accompanies certain degradation process with abandoned place in

Jang Yoon Gyoo + Park Byung Kyu,
Faust House "Fluid Void" (1999)

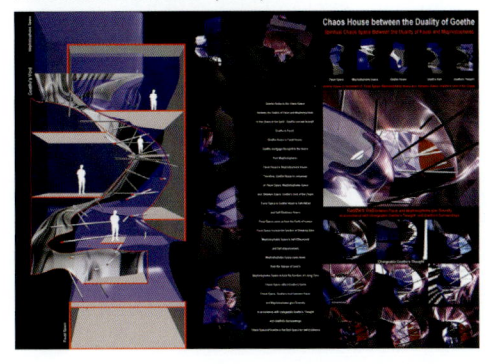

Jang Yoon Gyoo + Yoon Jung Hyun, Head Office of Barcelona Pavillion

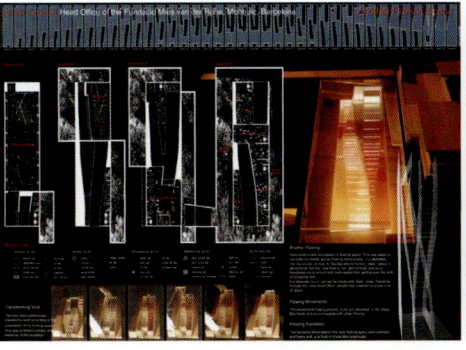

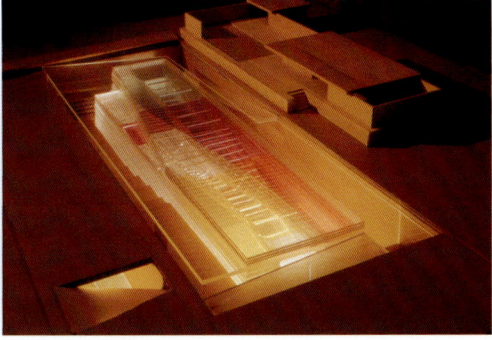

scales of both architecture and city structures. Cycles of civilization and ruins urge us to think the world as a circulation system. Especially, if the places being abandoned start to make direct connections with our public architecture and infrastructure, the issues become more than about makings of new buildings and developments. Concept of the <City Reaction Body> suggests to take active part in revitalizing overall environmental parameters of urban conventions - including urban environment, industry, economics, culture, and etc. By providing new programs and physical features that can promote new types of environmental shift than mere aesthetic fabrication, architecture demands rethinking in possibility of new circulation system.

<Reaction Body> attempts to bring out vital reactions similar to the techniques of eastern medicine, and takes interesting process of enabling the whole city to be reprogrammed. Architecture and city stimulated by the needle revive blood vessels and provoke urban regeneration. Through a new system inserted into the existing urban pattern, strange programmatic outcomes are constituted. Almost narcissistic, this process compels architecture to be reinstated as new urban value. Hence the architectural outcome generated by the <Reaction Body> is no longer passive urban character. It has become the main subject of making the city. In addition, the reaction that exists between urban subject and architectural object also demands for a change. Architecture becomes the urban subject by making such demand in aggression. If the acupuncture is the eastern means, let us take the western reaction techniques of transfusion and put into the context of reforming the city environment. It is not about completely erasing what has been deteriorated and refilling it with new contents. Rather it is transfusing the blood into bruises without removing them. New <Reaction Body> constituted over the city exists as additives of new life, thereby generating new blood. It is the same as creating 'techno-body' through reproduction and reimplantation, and implementing its life in the city/nature. Applied as a stimulating device between the city and environment, it brings new means of potential to the city. The value here is not having a physical structure of architecture itself, but as new ways to develop and promote our city infrastructure. Reaction Body is a living organism that accelerates urban filtration.

<Reaction Body> begins with the inquiry towards the depth of various values generated by the <Compound Body>. Criteria is set up for refining the framework of which these various compounds of urban factors mediate roles and implications for newly generated architectural space. <Reaction Body> goes far beyond the territorial boundaries and possesses necessary power to achieve total integration of territories. Not just existing along the boundaries, it accommodates new integrated roles as the city's infrastructural outset. The city now has its essential backbone of its organization.
<Compound Body> does not only mean sharing the space through which different territories are mixed. It finds numerous forms of coherence and communication among these territories. This process becomes more meaningful because it regenerates new communicative structure, not because it is a product of territories combined. Specific set up for the <Reaction> among the territories and its system comes in demand.
If the world is seen as a giant loop where the beginning and the end is closed with each other, all territories along the loop are interconnected. <Reaction Body> is one of devices to blur these territories along the loop. Boundaries are either connected or destroyed in order to prevent the

Jang Yoon Gyoo + Jang Yoon Sung,
Being Yun Suk Hwa Space "Clound Skin"

Jang Yoon Sung + Jang Yoon Gyoo,
Sponge Space: Exchange Between Exhibition Space & Exhibition Object

Jang Yoon Gyoo,
Gallery JungMiSo "Glass Floor"

COMPOUND BODY 41

system from reacting against physical circumstances. Furthermore, there is no stage of still-stance such as 'no-response', or 'no-work'. Instead it constantly potentiates movement like an organic body. Ambiguity in boundaries corresponds to the Reaction Body, while boundaries created by the movements are not transfixed.
Basis of the ⟨Reaction⟩ posits along making new organization by creating intricate relationships and confrontations among architectural and non-architectural attributes. Through various situations generated from these relationships, the process of making a mobile structure can be proposed. This is followed by making the device that actively engages the cycles of relationships. Movement of individual elements triggers subtlety of chemical reactions. As the cycles of these reactions persist, system sustains its function and is amalgamated into self-generating system of integration, similar to what keeps generating DNA. The fusion of these elements are the outcomes of countless mutual interference among each other, and its process harbors the new entity which transcends the idea of replication eventually riding along a great flow of changes.
Reaction Body shares texts. The relationship is the same as texts in reciprocal connection. Located above the converging points of various texts, it oversees a question of how to set up the text in new format. Spontaneous reactions coming from the various levels of exchange among the texts will certainly provide vibrancy we will never be able to project. Shared texts go through reciprocal reactions and will be translated to become a new type of text of which it will never repeat the same position and orientation. The crossover of these texts can be transformed into an infinite matrix. In the midst of combinations spitted by the matrix we confront the probability beyond our control and choice - type of reactions to the city, specific territory, variables, and etc. When the choices are made, this end of the road will mean yet another beginning.

Interactive _We may be aware of the fact that human race is not entity as a whole, but rather crystallized outcomes - of many connections or through connection made among countless branches of entities. Even for simply objects, we can take process of setting up its abyssal relationship between them, and articulate a kind of ⟨Interactive⟩ loop. This would include endless disassembly processes and interpretations of the city. Specifically this means devising factors for the new urban tools to superimpose over the existing city, condition or environment. We cannot obtain new perspective by simply repeating typical urban research. We need reinvestigations and redefinitions of the way the city makes endless series of branches of its growing paths. Various clips of text suggest

I do not believe that spatial organizations or urban fabrics are constructed as one specific framework. The structure of rhizome, an opposite structure of a tree, coincides more with the structure of the internet that reflects the way our society works these days. The issue here is making structure that resists such unified or standardized form or mode of thinking. It addresses for us to be against the notion that a society or a city is comprised as one singular code. Nothing in this world is not constructed in such way, and instead, continuous needs and desires for the transformation and change is hidden somewhere.

Jang Yoon Gyoo + Yoon Jung Hyun, Urban Threshold

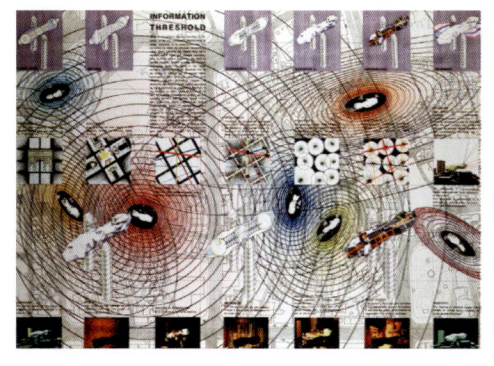

Jang Yoon Gyoo + Yoon Jung Hyun, Resonance Map

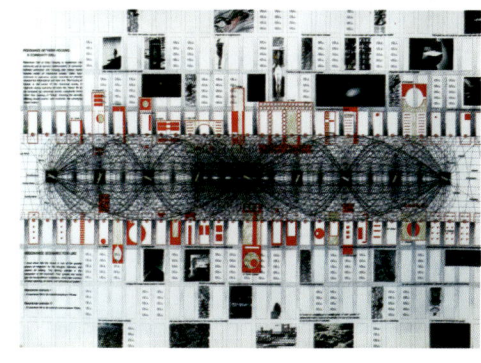

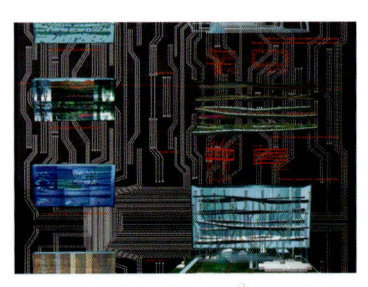

Jang Yoon Gyoo + Byun So Yun,
Urban Park for Purification

reconfigurations of - the outset that analyzes the city; the programs that comprise the city; and the methods that reassemble the city. Out of this enormous map of the text, we can create another map with another series of connections. Through the clip-city attitude, we wish for new possibility of making urban map, with its integration achieved in its means and contents. New combinations out of the text, along with combinations of new words made from them will lead us to connect yet another map of hyperlink.

Selective Reaction _ Reaction Body needs to potentiate selective reaction rather than all reactions. It requires reaction more than urban. It demands constituting stages of transformation in becoming useful urban device. It is a self-evaluation system for survival. It is a control device for accumulated energy, as well as an organic body which responds to the changing circumstance.

Adding _ Imagine agents that promote chemical reaction. They work as catalyst while controlling the speed of reaction. The process is similar to adding urban agent which is accessible in both directions to activate reactions to the city.

Releasing _ It is to define symbiotic relationships through mutual exchanges, not to mention the reinforcing architectural sustainability. It has universal impact, as if a window wide-open to the galaxy, towards the city and various subjects making relationships in the city. It becomes self-regulating entity, and forms a great loop to connect all relationships.

Substitution _ City is slowly responding to the change made by substituting elements that are developed in advance. Value in this is the notion of self-innovation and self-modification to reassure its self-consciousness. Elements replace themselves with more mature identity after breaking away from immature habits, causing overall advancement in relationships. Earlier stages may just be external modification on its skin or envelop, while later it reaches to a self-transformation as a whole and to an extreme revision, even changing its DNA and inherent properties.

Discharge _ All living things leave their traces, as to chemical reactions leave deposits. It is an evidence of life exists and has potential to perceive new life. Architecture and city produce endless discharges, from physical to non-physical. They become yet another group of agent to anticipate the future. They become products of reaction body through the process of production - reproduction.

Justification _ Reaction body becomes yet another 'justifying device' open to the world. It is a device of exchange between meditation which orients outside-in, and communion working inside-out. Through justification architecture amplifies its territories to - information, image, media, text, sound, entertainment, transportation, memory, light, culture, place and so forth. City transcending the present time, 'justification' allows for device to work in another dimension, capable of understanding and discovering.

Jang Yoon Gyoo + Shin Chang Hoon, Prehistoric Museum: Compound Map of Nature & Artificial

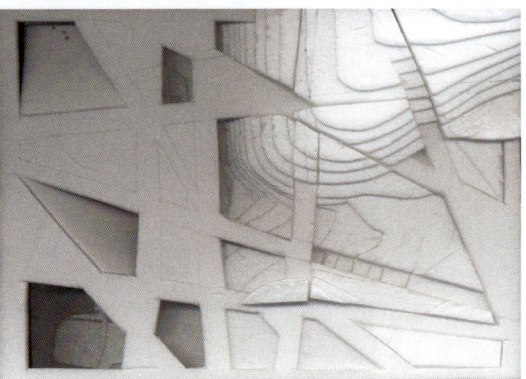

COMPOUND BODY 43

Compound Body
05 SkinScape

Take notice that our discussion is only the skin. As if the skin brushed off by,···or the bit of consciousness felt through, let us hypothesize that we can understand something in its entirety by only the partial experience of its skin. My body is no longer a body to touch, as it yearns for the digital flesh that does not exist in reality - as if Orpheus desires the fantasy of Eurydice.

What we propose the term 〈 _Scape〉 is a framework that sets up several branches of relationships residing along our landscape. It is also a part of our effort to create multiple entities of structures in the city. Critical in this notion, the agenda in 〈 _Scape〉 is to reach towards new articulation of spatial possibilities and/or urban requirements.

We ought to be aware that the nature of what designates architectural space is in process of revision, like body without organs. On the other hand, space in the digital age is maximizing the potential of the skin. No need to mention that the skin we are discussing here is not limited to a building skin. With refusal to acknowledge the skin in such a singular code, we must ask what kinds of skin we desire to generate through architecture today. Current architectural practice has several tendencies - to integrate differentiated programs; to generate a map that connects the trajectories of different status; or to produce continuity similar to organizing a new landscape or new landform. Regardless of all, we cannot let architecture to be read as merely a pattern or formal skin. Let us explore possible themes with the attitude of clarifying new definitions for our city structure. City can be recognized as a continuity of continuous skin. With a change in our attitude in looking at the city and new organizational framework for the city, we can pursue a continuous skin. The reality of skin, however, limits us within the boundaries by selecting easily accessible materials and programs, causing us to stay within and constrain ourselves. Let it transformed into

Hyun Bong Cil, Urban Folding

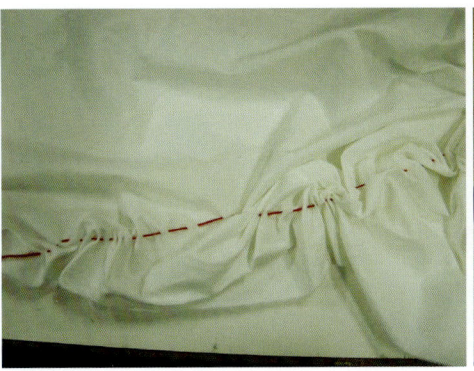

The Museum of Modern Art wrapped, Christoper & Jeanne-Claude

Jang Yoon Gyoo, JungMiSo Renovation "Being Space Skin"

the skin that is a new text - refusing to stay as overstated fashion or package that seduces us. As the boundaries between the virtual and the real blurs, and as if the ambiguous looking glass in front of Alice allowing us to enter into another dimension, skin is renewed in its reaction along the boundaries of double-sided reality.
The value of 〈SkinScape〉 amplifies at the moment we recognize the city infrastructure as skin-like structure. Gaze the city as a corrugated, pleated plate, which takes place in continuity. By looking at the city in its entirety as a continuous folded skin, we are able to realize that physical features in architecture such as columns, walls, floors are not individual elements, but part of a whole integration process.

Skin of the Compound Body is thought as integrated skin consisting of numerous codes. Hidden potential in these codes compels us to visualize a skin that makes physical codes unnecessary - no differentiation among the roof, floor and the wall, or other things that can act as any one of them. There is a level of freedom that can expand in infinity. The surfing earned by the SkinScape takes importance in consistent connectivity, like a surfer riding the waves. A structure of continuous surfing is achieved. The notion of differentiating the floors and walls are not needed here. 〈Spatial Surfing〉, 〈Skin Surfing〉, 〈Landscape Surfing〉, 〈Surfing between the structures〉,⋯.Codes crossover continuously and form compound space. Think of infinite unfolding of space conjectured from Escher's model, and then skin manipulates to form resistance towards gravitational governing of the space. Imagine non-gravitational space generated by the continuous skin, 〈Non-gravitational Skin〉, which removes any form of governance over our space. No longer there is a text differentiating the walls, floors, and ceilings. Only the continuous skin exists which later can be substituted for multiple skins to articulate building space.

From the continuity within the folded and smooth surface, Deleuze attempts to discover new creation of structure. Baroque contains unlimited possibility. Not to have architectural surface only as simple skin, but replacing its means as a fold instead. This allows us to accomplish spatial skin that repeats folding and unfolding. Architectural skin now contains multiple layers of space rather than being read as a single layer. Transposing the idea of skin from its physical limitation makes possible to work through the processes such as - 〈Skin Becoming Space〉; 〈Skin Becoming Media〉; 〈Skin Becoming Program〉; and 〈Skin Becoming Urban Organization〉, through which the framework of 〈SkinScape〉 is established.

Like the 〈Crack in the Armor〉 skin is not a surface for sealed limitation of space, it is a light, porous and ambiguous surface with aerial cracks. There is a metaphoric irony created by new spatialization achieved from the light materials and structure in contradiction to the word with heavy nuance - poetics in dense cast being created through the lightness.
The quality of skin relates to the potential of the cracks. We propose to generate a 'scape' of these cracks and draw its spatial richness hidden behind them.

Olafur Eliasson, Cystal Surface

Jang Yoon Gyoo + Lee Mee Young, Ravin Peace Plaza "Vertical Urban Plaza"

Jang Yoon Gyoo, SK Telecom Office "Program Skin"

Continuous line sweeps the air, overwhelming the void. It questions the purity of space constructed by the continuing surface which is neither more than a line nor less. One stroke of a brush. The line empties out all distractions and demands all its concentration - from head to toe, be at the tip of a brush. Space exists between the tightness of a psychological tension. Space and landscape exist between the trajectories of continuous line. Landscape of air between structures across the earth and air, earns continuity of poetic structure. Continuous line sweeping across the three-dimensional space transforms into bent and distorted surface. Potential of three-dimensional surface reaches at maximum when it alters to take a form of semi-structure. It is a multi-dimensional, linear space that transforms the continuity and looping system of civilization into poetic, physical structure.

〈SkinScape〉 is achieved by skin and other elements combined. Mixing skin and structure; skin and space; skin and program⋯We can imagine all probability in physical transformation by these combinations of various elements. 〈SkinScape〉 which corresponds with seeking new spatial model intends to maximize the range of mutation by minimizing process - removing excessive elements in space, or combining all extra chunks. The skin combined with a structure, or exterior surface combined with internal structure expands the level of spatial freedom. Structural modules (internal) relate to window-frame details (part of external façade), which acts as a 'frame' to bring the landscape in. Modification of form at the minute these combinations are achieved, a body without organ connects with spatial organization.growth of a city also accompanies certain degradation process with abandoned place in scales of both architecture and city structures. Cycles of civilization and ruins urge us to think the world as a circulation system. Especially, if the places being abandoned start to make direct connections with our public architecture and infrastructure, the issues become more than about makings of new buildings and developments. Concept of the 〈City Reaction Body〉 suggests to take active part in

Jang Yoon Gyoo,
Plaza of GwangJu Biennale "Sculpture of Plaza"

Jang Yoon Gyoo + Shin Chang Hoon + Kim Woo Il,
Evervill Head Office "Programmed Bubble"

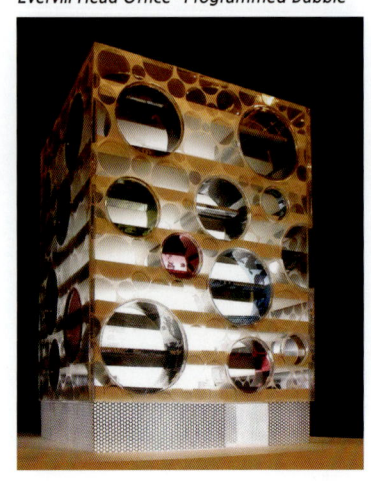

Jang Yoon Gyoo + Shin Chang Hoon,
Gallery Yeh "Skin Scape"

COMPOUND BODY 47

Compound Body
06 Floating + Floating

It must be us who needs to transform from the earthbound to something aerial. Then our transformation shall lighten the earth. The earth in us, a site within ourselves, will become something light. No sites or spaces of any kind shall be bound to anything, at last free from occupation. The new site which is free becomes a new foundation for architecture that can freely drift. Leaves are the wings that soar, ceaselessly flapping wings in the air. Tree full of leaves are fluttering as new dreams arouse by the air. No longer the air is bound by space, and dreams to become the wind traveling anywhere.

Floating is proposed here as an attitude in our attempts for new architecture. This can include number of meanings - social reflections, non-gravitational thinking, simultaneity of light architecture and heavy spiritual reaction. Once we soar up in the air, be free from physical restraint of gravity which governs the earth, we can take notice of things surrounding atmosphere as well as the social links we were unable to see. Rather than discussing the details regarding physical features, our center of focus are on those invisible and hidden. It means that the importance lies in more fundamental questioning in concept beyond merely proposing architectural resolutions.

This is a response towards urban flows. The most urban-sensitive architecture does not obstruct urban flows but adopt them. Let us float and adopt them into dreamy world of myth. Drift from the earth. Transfer from heaviness to lightness, from the visible to invisible. City and architecture is not merely the devices to hold up against the gravity, but the principal of its own to dominate over the law of physics. One strategy would be to separate the earth, the site from the city. The emptied-out block is converted into potential of activeness, abundance, connectivity and so forth. Not only as space for functions, but accelerating devices for various urban elements and attributes. Invisible layers, such as information, media, communication, and others, disintegrate urban boundaries and branches out in all possible directions. Architecture is worked to act as a device to capture these urban data.

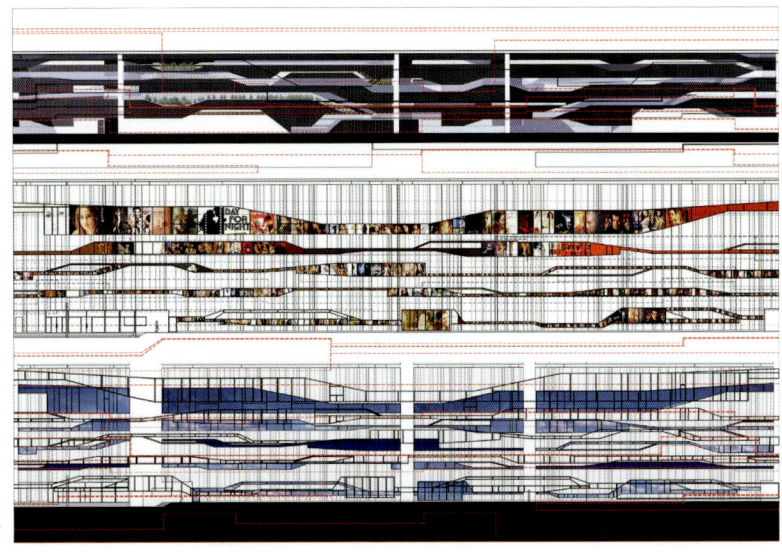

Jang Yoon Gyoo,
Floating Void, Floating Program, Floating Mass

Jang Yoon Gyoo + Heerim Architects & Partners, Egytian Embassy "Floating Stone"

The concept of floating does not proceed as a narrative of simply emptying out and altering. Focal point of this emptying-out process would be the perception of the freedom achieved by the urban skin, which heightens its level of freedom as the process intensifies. Escaping from the earth, the skin remains free. Accordingly these skins are superimposed upon each other, respond each case of urban requirement and form multiple layers. The further it escapes from the earth, the less potential the earth possesses. The emptied-out land of city block incorporates activity, abundance, and connectivity. Not just including functional means, but it would engage variety of urban characteristics and substances, and accelerates their mutual communications and dialogues - thus can be described as the Compound Body. Lifting up physical nature in subjects can hint us many meanings that we have yet to see, all concealed and hidden behind the physicality. How would you express in words, the meaning behind the moment of experiencing lifting a piece of cake?

Soaring is used as symbolic value as well. It is also a methodology of investigation. It is the same as if, in order to read precisely what has been entangled, one slightly picks up the knot. Another comparison would be to pick and choose what words and phrases to mix, match and structuralize for an appropriate use of a sentence. Architect reading architecture and city works for the same. Architect uses his/her words, phrases and languages to whom it is possible to communicate with. It is filling-up process. The earth is filled with these self-sustained, fully-charged 'skin device's which carry out various urban requirements. Tools for filling-up strategy can be understood as yet another experiment to provoke reversible actions over the existing city structure. Structure being filled here is not a parts or fragments of our physical city structure, it is a physical diversion off the spirit of gravity. In all, what is invisible and free-floating possesses the ideological force yet to be found, as its social, political, economic conceptions offer us a picture of more integrated vision in setting up new urban relationships.

The strength residing in the concept of Floating is that it offered a common ground of which city and architecture can understand and share each other - not distinguishing our structure as physical and social, and thus recognizing the two aspects as one reality. By not assuming architecture as physical entity or materialistic imperatives towards form or envelope, but instead seeking reactions from things that are architecturally invisible, the experimental mindset for the notion Floating offers a great potential for further development. (Prof. Youngbum Reigh, Gyeonggi University)

⟨Floating⟩ alters the lightness of our ordinary materials of everyday life into cultural and spatial characteristics. Through the lightness architecture as ⟨Cultural Contents⟩ is now constituted - a system which can be culturally occupiable than architecturally inhabitable. Let us begin with experiments. Fabric used for a bathing suit, vinyl…, materials of non-architectural character is used for making space. The outcome is space with freedom that is impossible to gain from rigid architecture. No structural rigidity, material cover-ups, and heavy philosophy. Only a poetic space with lightness. Non-constructive materials and disposable inhabitation of space offer us new experience. There is nothing grand in what I would like to discuss here, especially through these architectural outputs. Only few episodes and few texts and trajectories of thought in-between, while injecting few questions of essence lightly into the new text.

The project we are working on now involves layering of combinations - number of ideas combined, followed by combining with the general aspects of ⟨Floating⟩. In other words, the work regards to a generation of attributes combined with the ⟨Floating⟩. Presumed that there are countless manifold as described with the idea of ⟨Floating⟩, we tend to approach in atypical angle of perspective in examining the process. Establishing the notion of ⟨Floating⟩ relates to several questions and hypothesis differentiated from the basic range of what is expected. We began by disassembling the typical life patterns and various disciplinary territories, in which they start to be distorted into the characteristics of ⟨Floating⟩. ⟨Floating⟩ involves staying outside the frame of architecture. Instead it urges us to be devoted for experimenting with reactions towards city and environment. The nature of ⟨Floating⟩ is to find the gap in these reaction bodies which exists in between the frameworks of mutations.

Jang Yoon Gyoo + Shin Chang Hoon + Kim Woo Il, Asian Culture Complex "Floating Stage"

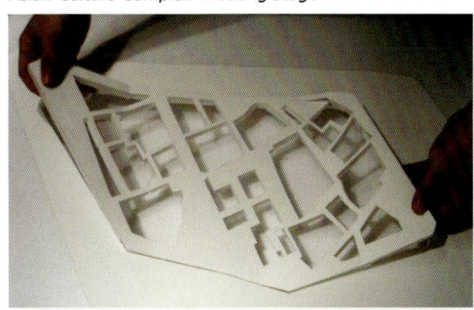

Jang Yoon Gyoo + Shin Chang Hoon, Extension of City Hall "Floating Plaza"

Jang Yoon Gyoo + Heerim Architects & Partners, Millenium Gate

Jang Yoon Gyoo & Lee Mee Young in Infinite Nets, Yayoi Kysama

Compound Body
07 Mythological Imagination

When I accidentally visited MoMA in San Francisco, I confronted very interesting exhibition of Olafur Eliasson, who completely destroyed the convention of exhibition and concept of space. In the project called ⟨Your Mobile Expectation⟩, he installed refrigerated space inside the museum space. Inside the fridge space, a luxury BMW was transformed into an ice car. It was experience of territorial transformation, conceived by the artist's imagination, of all possible elements - the exhibition concept, installation, experience, spatial concept, form, technology and so forth.

Why do I find myself going through my old bookshelves to talk ⟨Mythos⟩ again? Am I about to return to the risk of ⟨Orpheus's Gaze⟩ which I constantly emphasized all along, and attempt to repeat the circus again? The reason I suspect would be that there is a intricate similarity in the notion I would like to accomplish architecturally and the notion of ⟨Mythos⟩. Mythos, a Greek word, confronts Logos, meaning non-logical, nonsensical storytelling. What does Mythos mean today? With scientific leap and technological accomplishments, Mythos has been disintegrated, leaving only its fragments. More than anything these days, science plays the role of providing answers to questions and doubts that was done by Mythos in the past. Thus we live now in the era of mythical fragmentation, mythical dissolution. My intention behind bringing back Mythos is not to restore, or to make up strange stories. Rather I would like to revisit the meaning behind the potential in Mythos in order to explore new, imaginative narratives for defining things. The biggest of the effort in deploying Mythos is that scientific knowledge of contemporary society allows us to reach the level that we never have imagined in the past. Imagination through Mythos provides scientifically-improbable thesis of mixture and displacement. Including its rationale, we need to operate all possible cases of imaginations. We are experiencing cultural cinematic mixture not approachable by science. Like Barthes's infinitely-open paroles, endless elements in our current society become ingredients for Mythos.

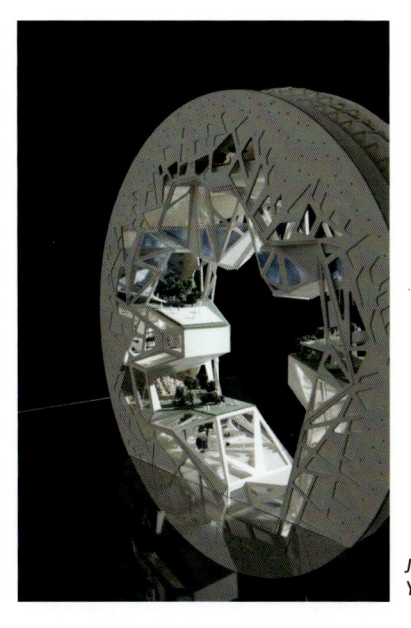

*Jang Yoon Gyoo + Shin Chang Hoon,
Yeosu EXPO "Imagination Nature"*

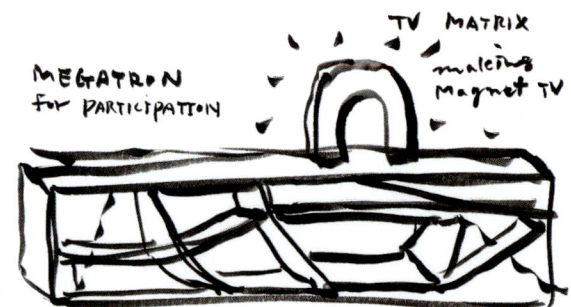

Jang Yoon Gyoo,
Paik Nam Jun Museum "Interactive Frame & Media Park"

The essence of imagination begins with defamiliarizing techniques towards objects. It links to acknowledging the codes which were not familiar to us. More diverse spectrums of transformations can be explored through these unfamiliar codes and their mixtures. Bertolt Brecht's distanciation can be appropriate here to describe defamiliarity. The distance is used as controlling device between a play and audience to bring consciousness within them. Using epic structure he manipulates the audience's understanding of the play by rupturing the flow between acts, montage-like scenes, and jumping stories. Such defamiliarizing structure awakens the audience's consciousness and reading. He rejects the conventional rules - such as linear plots, coherency of parts, reiteration of reality, and utilize defamiliarizing method instead, even with those which seem to be critical mistakes. We attempt to revisit Bertolt Brecht's challenge against traditional style and link our mindset to architectural space in the mode of avant-garde. Defamiliarizing technique destroys the concept of the work as coherence-in-entity and brings non-uniformity into recognition, thus creating self-contradiction for critical thoughts to enter. It is operated as new paradigm as if the avant-garde art based on freeing itself from all of its domination in order to seek new potential in art form.

Somewhere along the boundary between ⟨Defamiliarization⟩ and ⟨Estrangement⟩, ⟨Mythical⟩ imagination is located. With imaginative foundation of Escher and Magritte, ambiguous and surreal objects would be created. Creating a form and an object never existed in the past is what mythical code persuades. Mythical challenge means challenging the territories of god, and as the challenge becomes closer to a risk, strange scenes and objects will be provided to us. The moment is similar to a risk in confused ⟨Mermaid⟩ when she finds out her fantasy results in two different kinds of displacement - upper body as human, lower body as fish. Creating defamiliar space can be said as strengthening the structure of ⟨communication⟩. Desperation of achieving various possibility and flexibility through displacements must be recognized. The distance between defamiliarity and comprehension must be closer.

Only an imagination does not bring these imaginative spaces. The notion of ⟨Mythological Body⟩ transposes imagination into reality and promotes architectural space and materialization. Space of mythological imagination does not just remove logos and fill the space with absurd stories. Irrational aspects in logos must be also included. Integration of time, preference of multiplicity, resemblance and others included, mythos does not let go of rational dimension.
Reproduction and formation, assembly and disassembly, transformation and deformation,… we gaze towards Mythos through unlimited sources of potential in displacements. Mythological displacements correspond to enforcing structural articulation and its values. Thus coercive in language is used to bring out deliberate displacement. Once these categories are confronted with each other, group them to find magic beyond precluding their own limitations. Mythos requires exploration of seeking method. From perceiving society and urban phenomenon,

Jang Yoon Gyoo, Dancing Apartment

Jang Yoon Gyoo + Shin Chang Hoon, Paris Olympic Memorial "Navigation Cell"

some of mutual influences are to be found for us to mix them. We seek to provide mixtures leaping to its maximum limit that technology can accommodate.

Contemporary architecture and city posit themselves in seeking new models through making new framework of entity integrating structure, space, material, skin and landscape. The rapid advancement in technology only accelerates these movements even faster. Contemporary city today demands new experiments in architectural concepts and questions its fundamental values and meanings. From the ideas of traditional urban spaces to conceptual and physical demarcation of spaces, the time has arrived for which overall aspects in the field are to be tested and explored. Even those seemed to carry eternal values are being transformed and displaced. Architecture and city unfold over its time and era. Phenomenon of social speed, nomadic lifestyle, endless development in technology, and open-ended networks have generated unprecedented event by changing even the very inherent characteristics of architectural space. Now the time has become to anticipate more sources of imaginative urban narratives. Urban imagination tells us that architecture is not a concept that is fixed in single identity, but a territory of potentials that can incorporate newly evolved ideas and conceptions, including imaginations. Urban research will draw some of these conceptions, as we pursue to provide architectural displacements from the space of imagination to the actual space. Certainly the level of development is needed in order to embrace both imagination and the depth of actual materialization. Then imaginative city and its architectural proposition would not stop at the level of ridicule, instead would anticipate boundless roles in revitalizing the city and regenerate it into the new.

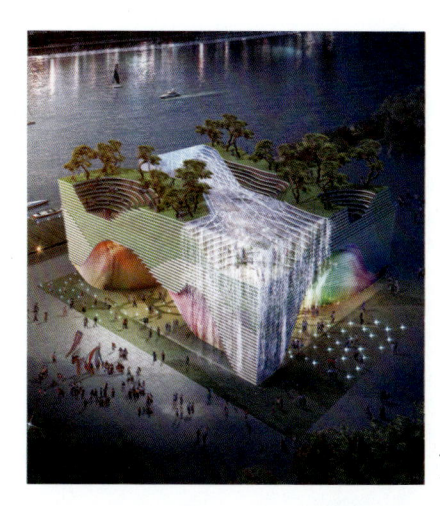

Jang Yoon Gyoo + Shin Chang Hoon,
Kolon Theme Housing "Floating Garden Housing"

Jang Yoon Gyoo + Shin Chang Hoon,
Sanghai EXPO "Nature Sculpture"

Brandscape

KRING
Kumho Compound Culture Complex

Competition Winner
Grand Prize Award of Korean Space & Culture Institute
2nd Grand Prize of Korean Good Design Award

Architects Jang Yoon Gyoo, Shin Chang Hoon, Kim Kyung Tae
Client Kumho Engineering & Construction.
Photographer Sergio Pirrone

COMPOUND BODY

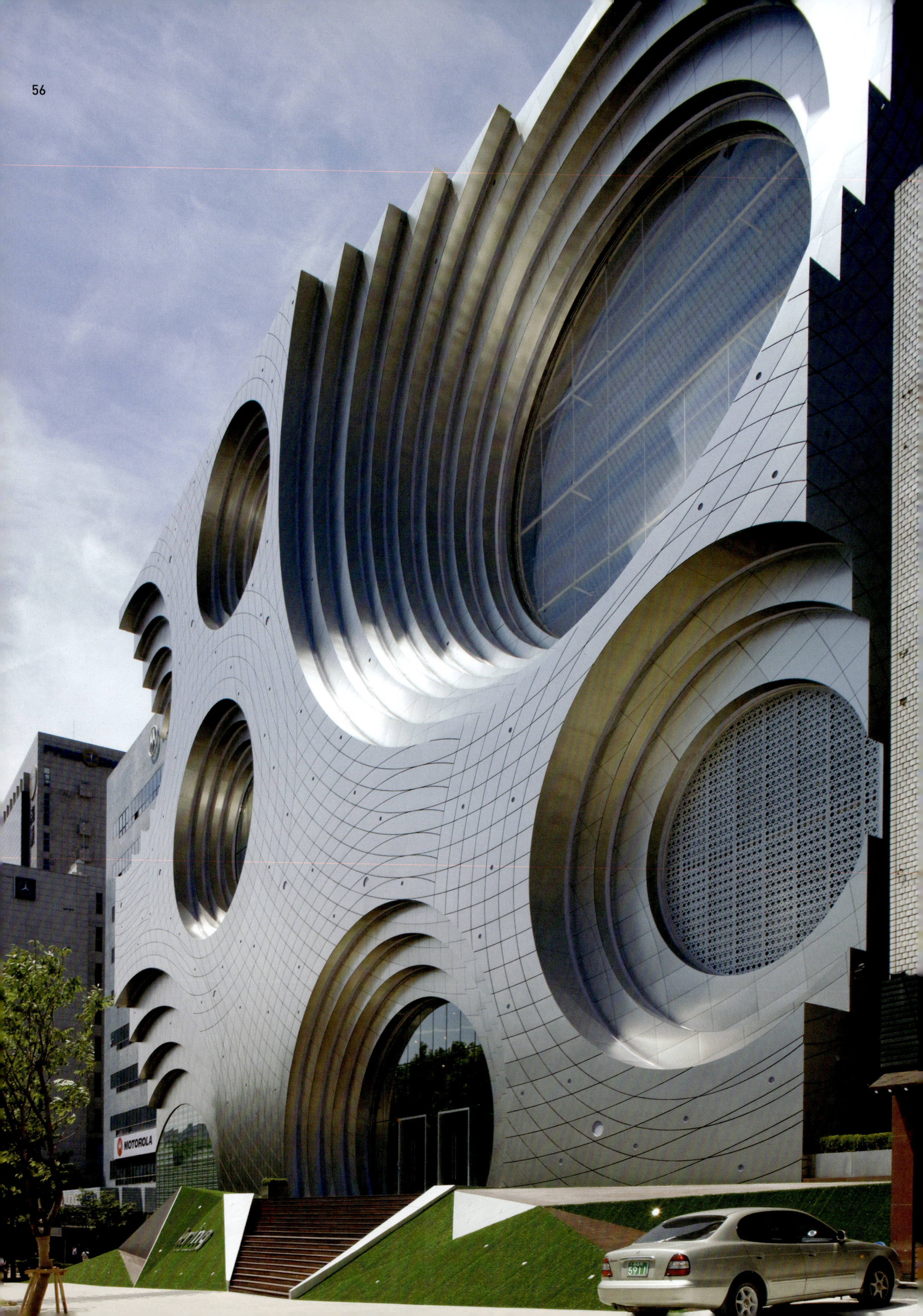
MOTOROLA

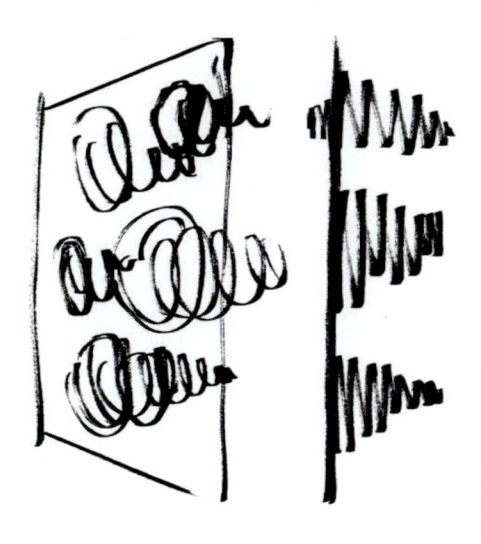

BEING A BRANDSCAPE

We, Unsangdong Architects, are proposing a rather unfamiliar approach to architecture, ⟨Making a brandspace⟩, which was exemplified in Kring_Kumho Compound Culture Space. Brand strategy, once used to be employed only by profit organizations as a means to create monetary assets, has evolved endlessly to reborn. Profit organizations are under more severe surveillance than ever before by public and required to demonstrate social responsibility of their own brand. Branding had been a useful tool for marketing, now it is re-categorized under brand new realm, which includes spatial concept. We would like to focus on new models of branding such as ⟨Concept of the third space⟩, or ⟨Spatial Design Marketing⟩. ⟨Spatial Design Marketing⟩ defines any and all marketing activities by profit organizations to provide a space as a direct means to satisfy customers' needs or desire, or offer a spatial experience to customers by making themselves reconsider a profit organization or the image of that particular brand with space.

Space, as well as spatial design, reinforces its image as a medium for facilitating communications between companies and consumers, as opposed to simply perform its previous role to provide a place for containing customer's human behavior. We can figure out that space design with brand identity, or design which symbolized brand identity can positively impact on customers by making them improve and reconsider a brand image.

The meaning of brandspace does not end at delivering brand images to consumers with the medium of a space or location. We live in a ⟨Society of Consumption⟩. Jean Baudrillard once mentioned that consumption of a product or commodity does not limit itself by suggesting consumption of usage value, the fundamentals of consumption is to satisfy human needs of social and cultural elements including happiness, comfort, success, abundance, power, authority, and modernity. People purchase and consume product or commodity to make themselves look better and gain social status or authority at the same time. Through these series of social process, consumption creates productive codes. The perspective of Baudrillard on consumption has notion of pessimistic point of view, although it is interesting that his idea on consumption as social meaning to be proliferated through the process of definition. The notion of brandspace can be proliferated with that kind of attitude. The impact on the meaning process of a brandspace does not end in simply consuming brand images, rather reinforcing and reproducing cultural influence and public sociality. It has to be shifted as ⟨Initiatives as cultural marketing⟩.

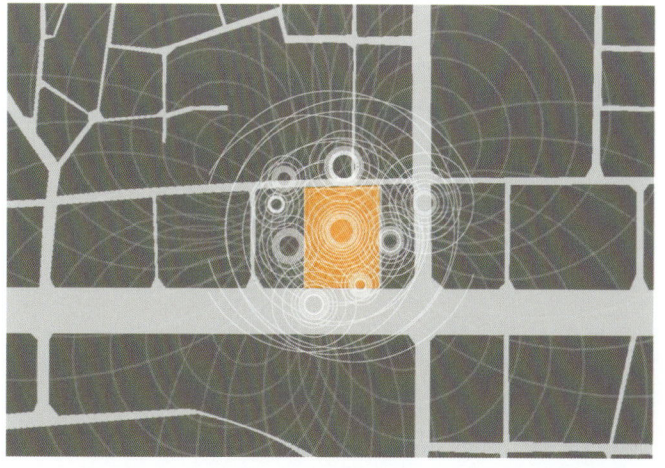

// **Container for Echo** We wanted to gather various elements of nature, life, and city harmoniously and that essence of harmony to rush out to the city creating echo and undulations, and that became the brand scenario of the project.

BEING A BRANDSCAPE

COMPOUND BODY   59

GEOMETRY FOR URBAN SCULPTURE

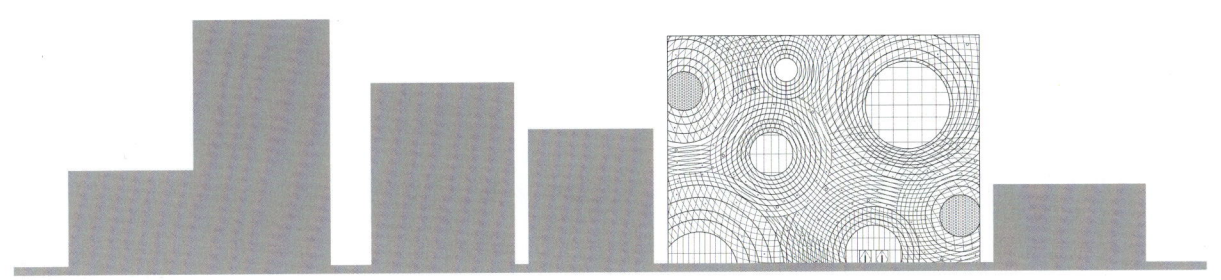

// **Brand Identity** Companies are using brand code and trademark as an architectural representation divide to be easily distinguished from one another. We need to recognize that demands of modern society are connected with architecture becoming a brand. Rather than being just customers, we tried to give identity to the building for complementary and reciprocal communication between the customer and companies.

// **Kring Multi** Complex established the identity of Uwoolim through figuration of architecture. GumHo's brand of Uwoolim starts from harmony, though our analysis was a deepening direction of harmony to connect and spread into the society. After harmonizing nature, life, and the city's various element, products of works compose scenarios that spread into the city and region. The big sounds hole connected with concept "dream." Cylinders penetrating into the space also ar elements of images to express dream, passion, and communication.

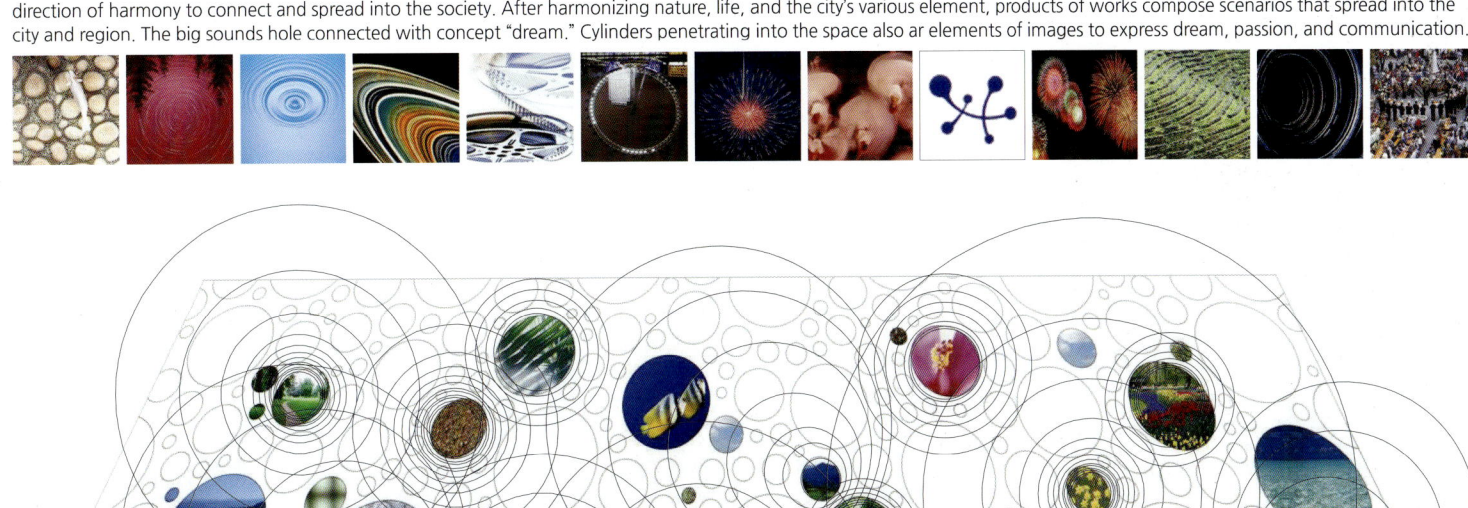

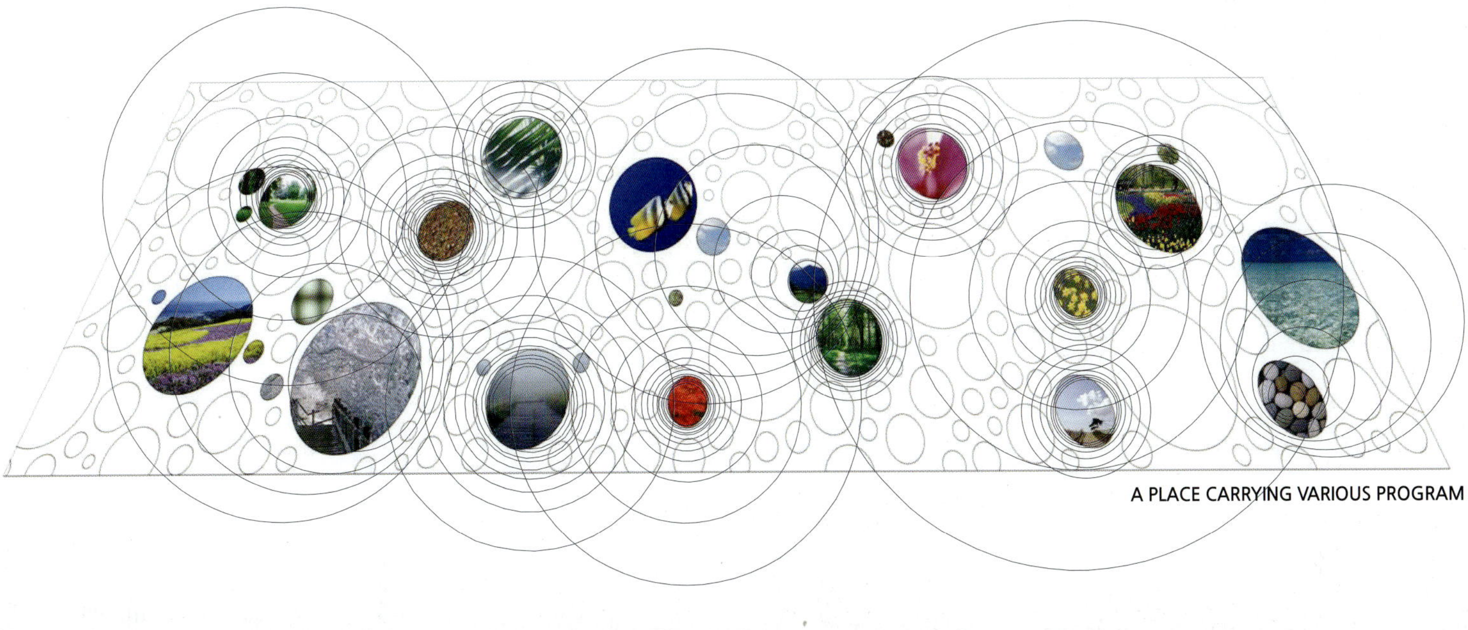

A PLACE CARRYING VARIOUS PROGRAM

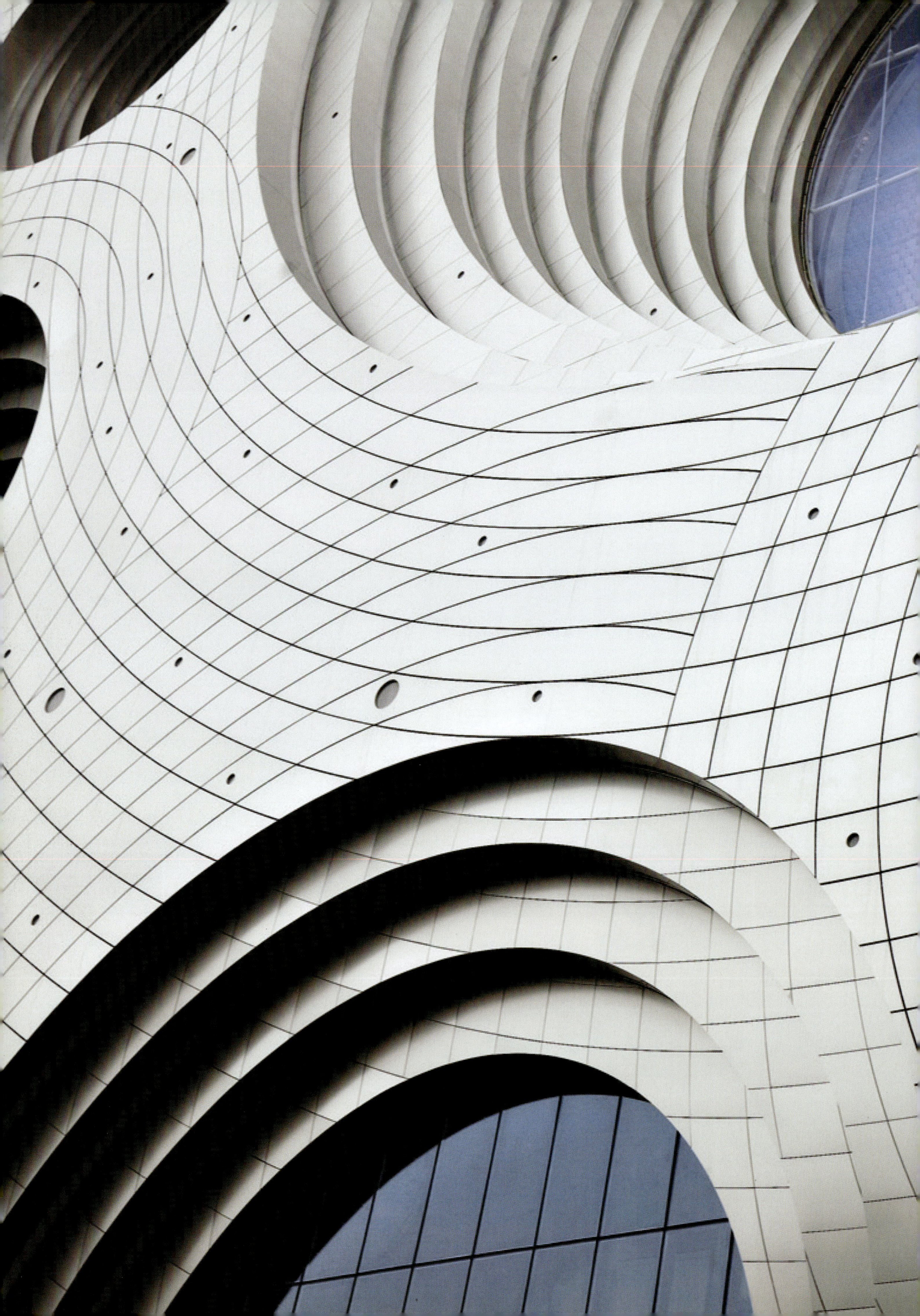

GEOMETRY FOR URBAN SCULPTURE

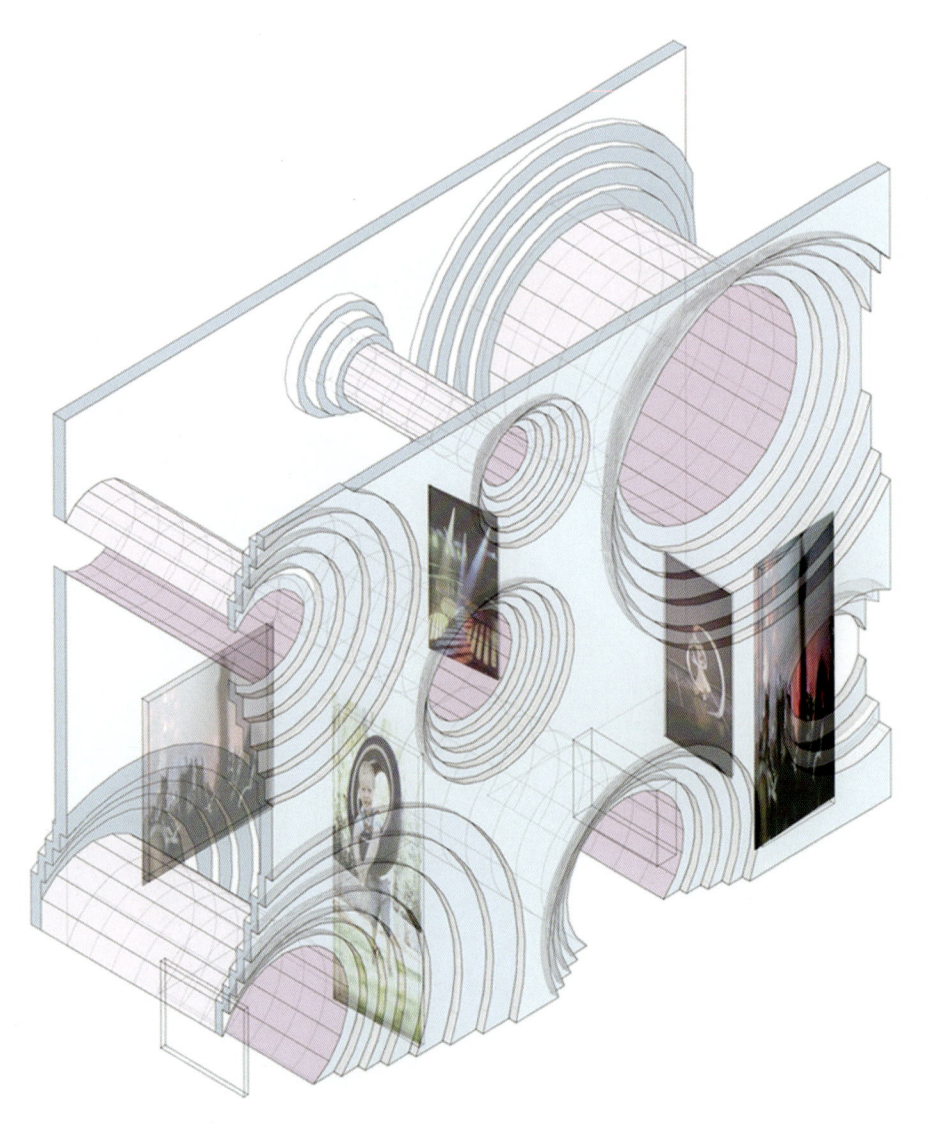

// **Culture Marketing** We recognized that architecture can be a tool of communication with a cultural code in addition to simply building construction. Designs have to escape from sale or publicity, as will as connect brand image with architecture. Furthermore, it is necessary to construct new cultural space that strengthens the cultural brand.

Our intention is to construct an architectural building to create codes for companies and consumers to facilitate communication, then embed an identity in that architecture. ⟨Urban Sculpture for Branding⟩ is the concept that we applied when we designed Kring_compound culture space to realize brand identity for the client. The way we approached to create this building was different from conventional method. It was about creating an urban sculpture, then compose a compound space in it. The innovative requests, which was made by Kumho E&C Co. and the conversion of conception on architectural design work which we proposed made it possible for us to approach to the project differently to create an unconventional brand icon.

⟨Uh-Ul-Lim; phonetic pronunciation of Korean word means 'harmony'⟩, the brand image of Kumho E&C was transformed as brand identity through the architectural shaping process. The starting point of Kumho brand was putting emphasis on 'harmony'. Through the architectural interpretation process, the phenomenon of harmony was connected and emphasized to the city and society with undulation, then the notion of undulation was deepened. We wanted to gather various elements of nature, life, and city harmoniously and that essence of harmony to rush out to the city creating echo and undulations, and that became the brand scenario of the project. Projecting images to the city and sucking up the energy of the city at the same time, gigantic ⟨container for echo⟩, was born that way, which leads to the concept of 'Dream' as well. We wanted this to be the monument of the city day and night, specifically, a lighting sculpture when it is dark. Moreover, it becomes a pure white space when entered into, and contains all and any types of cultural program. The pure white space which achieves spatial surrealism is acting as a stage for performance. Just like a stage changes itself to conform to the types and story of a play, this becomes a compound space to fit itself to diverse needs. Cultural art management program was conceptualized so that this space can be operated by professional curator(s) to offer something more significant than just temporary events. Compound space, a passageway to communication can be proposed through the innovation of internal program which contain diverse possibilities

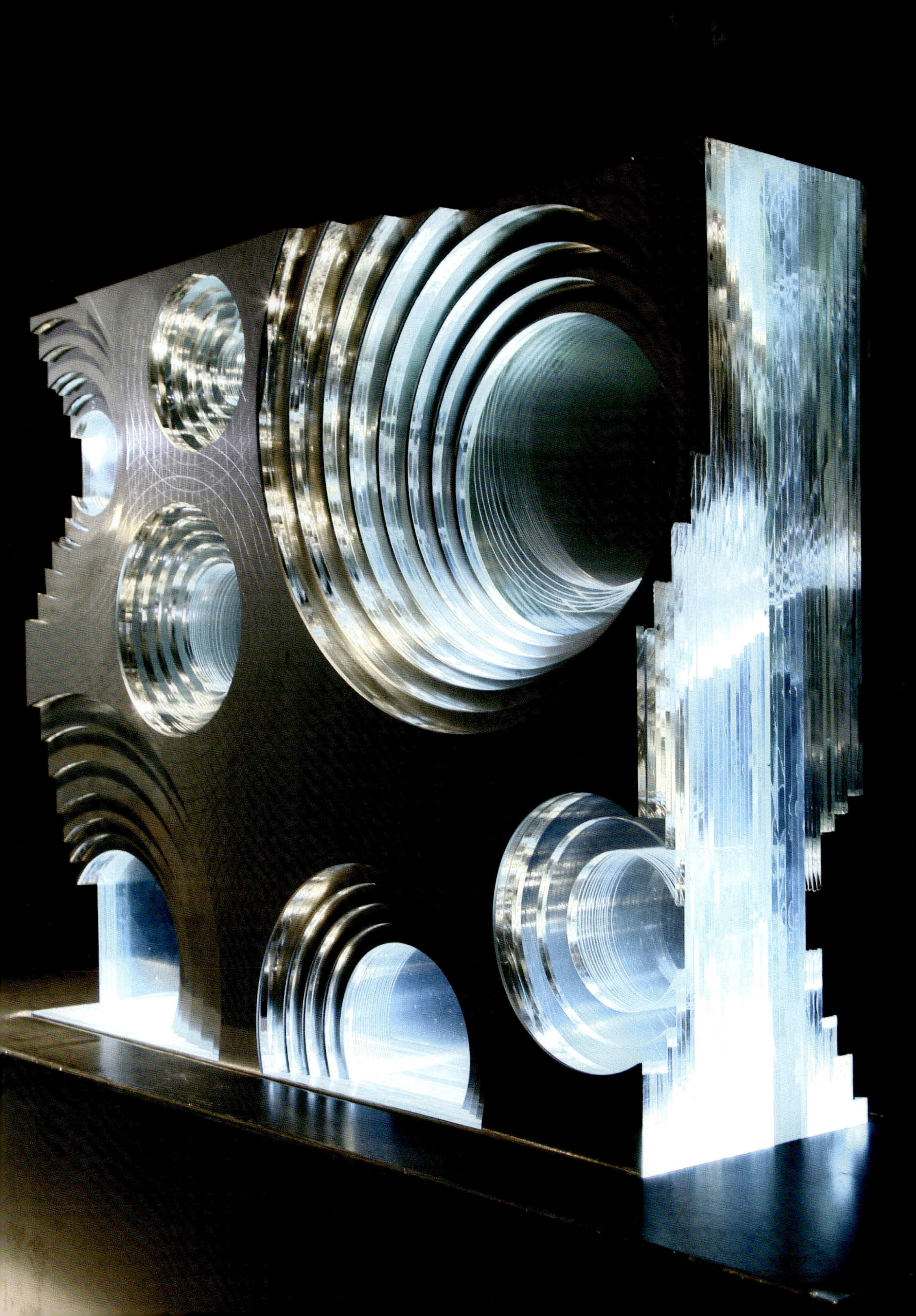

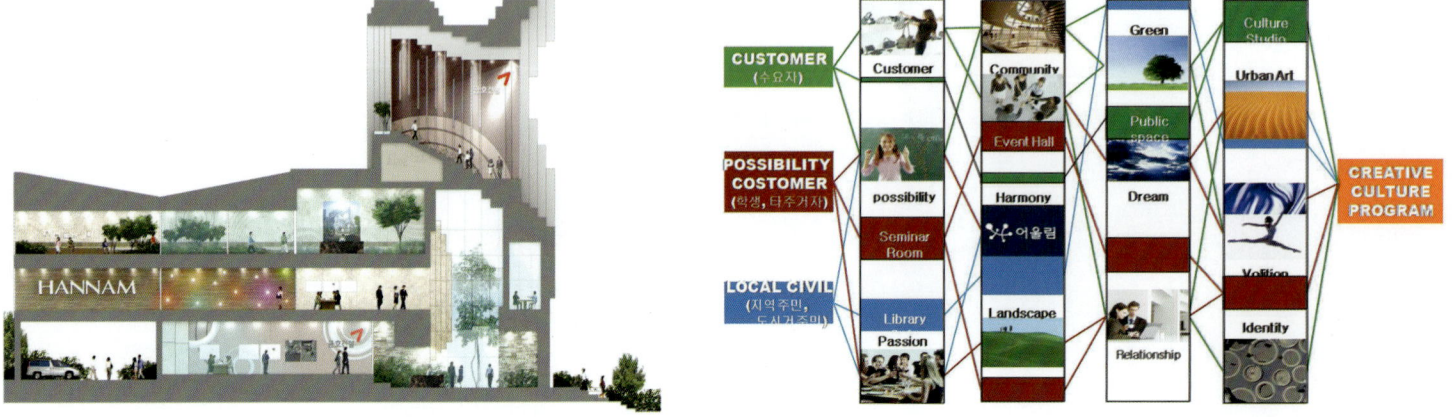

Fundamental understanding on methodologies to create a brand and sale is required. Selling a design does not stop at responding to consumers' needs, rather stimulate their emotion and then create new need for production.
The bases of societies were shifted from the product production to that of information as alchemy based society was changed to more of preference and image focused society before. It is more important than ever before for an architect to create his or her own brand and then convert that to a product armed with newly conceptualized brand value for the coming information age. It is critical to define where to put your coordinates to move around because there are no more boundaries existing between roles for architects, the scope of activities, concepts for architectural spaces, nor realm of it.
'Architecture as product' can be another way of expanding your horizons and work as an opportunity for you to create a cultural band along with new culture, society, and architectural market.

// **Creative Culture Space**   The main concept of cultural center is not only a simple model house but also to compose a multi-complex with past model houses. That accepts the intervention of professional art coordinators to experience the culture and art, not a one-time event. We propose the complex like a passage for communication with customers, through holding public performances, events, exhibitions, and competitions in the cultural complex.

URBAN LANDSCAPE PROGRAM

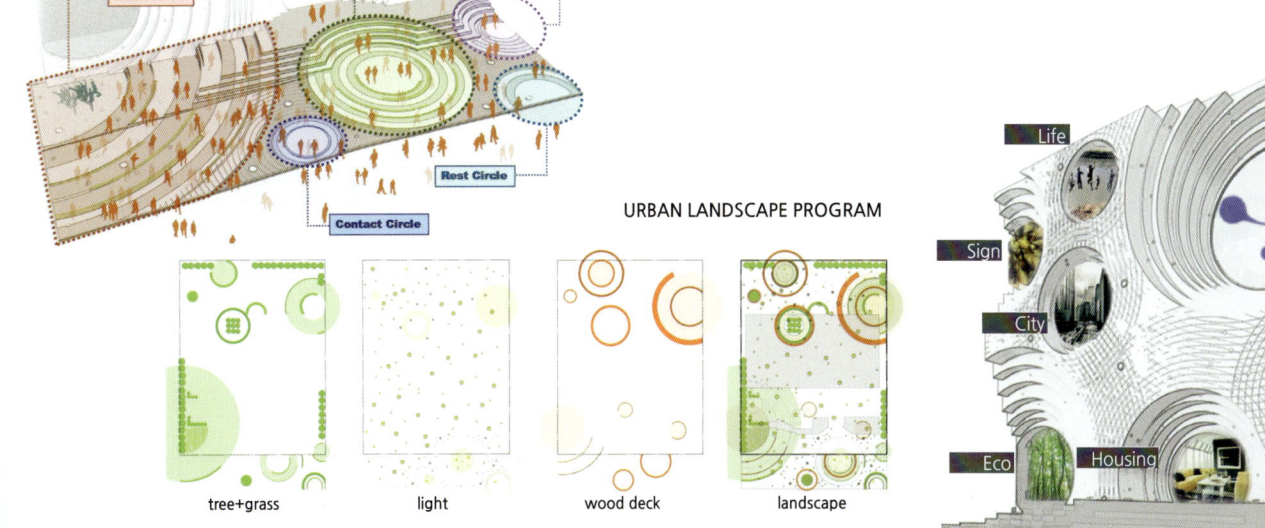

tree+grass | light | wood deck | landscape

Event Circle | Green Square | Play Circle | Rest Circle | Contact Circle

Life | Brand | Sign | City | Eco | Housing | Living

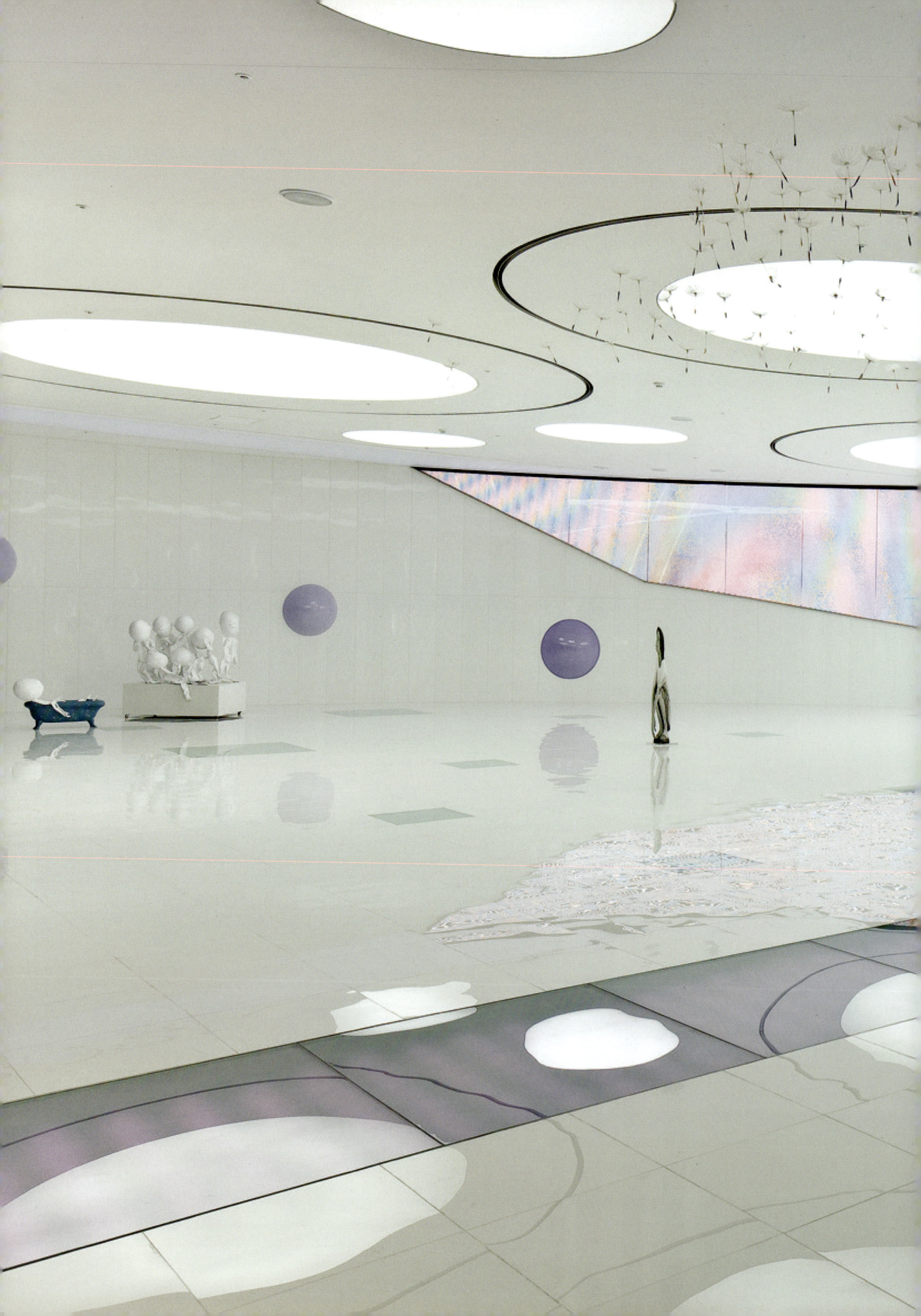

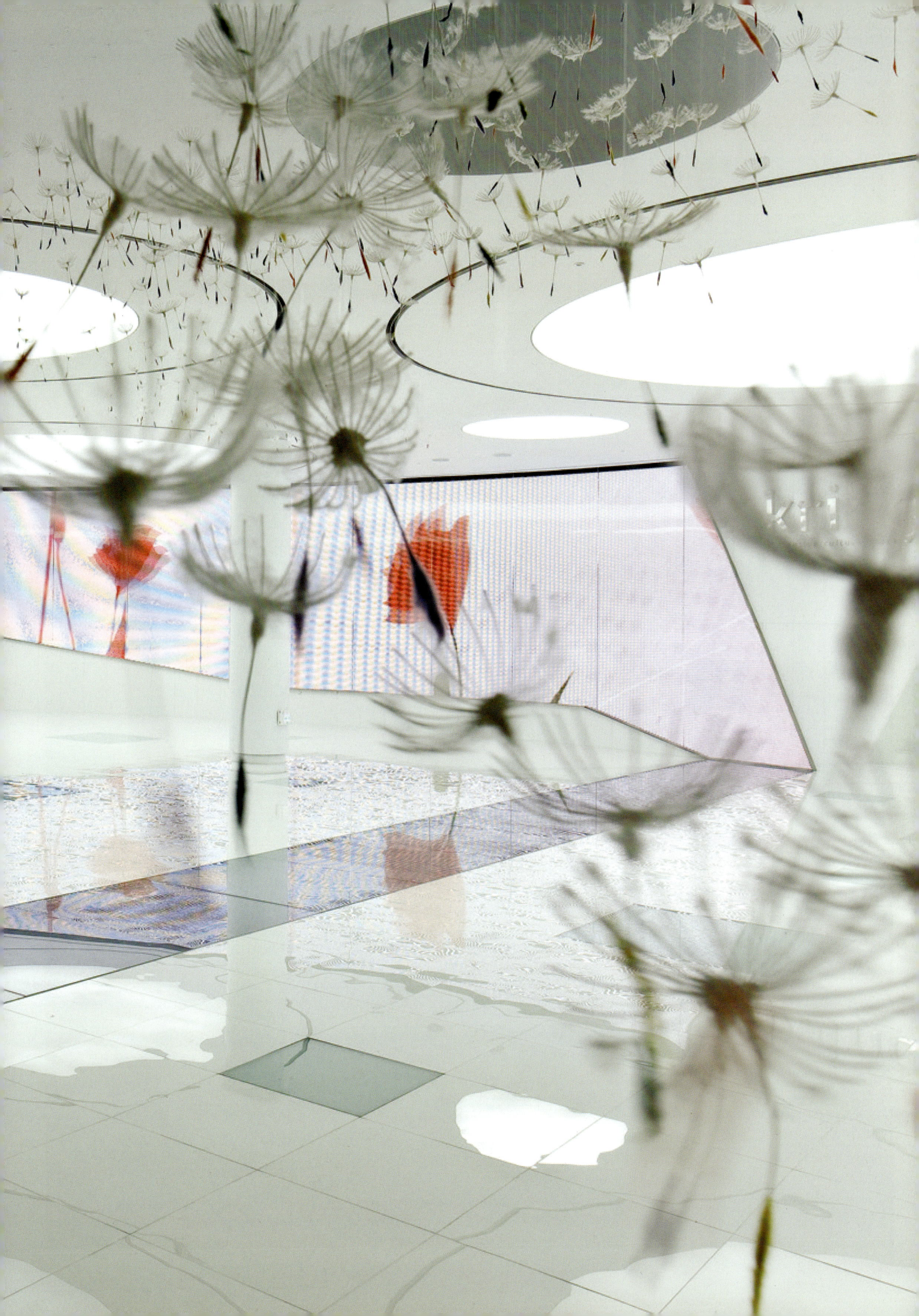

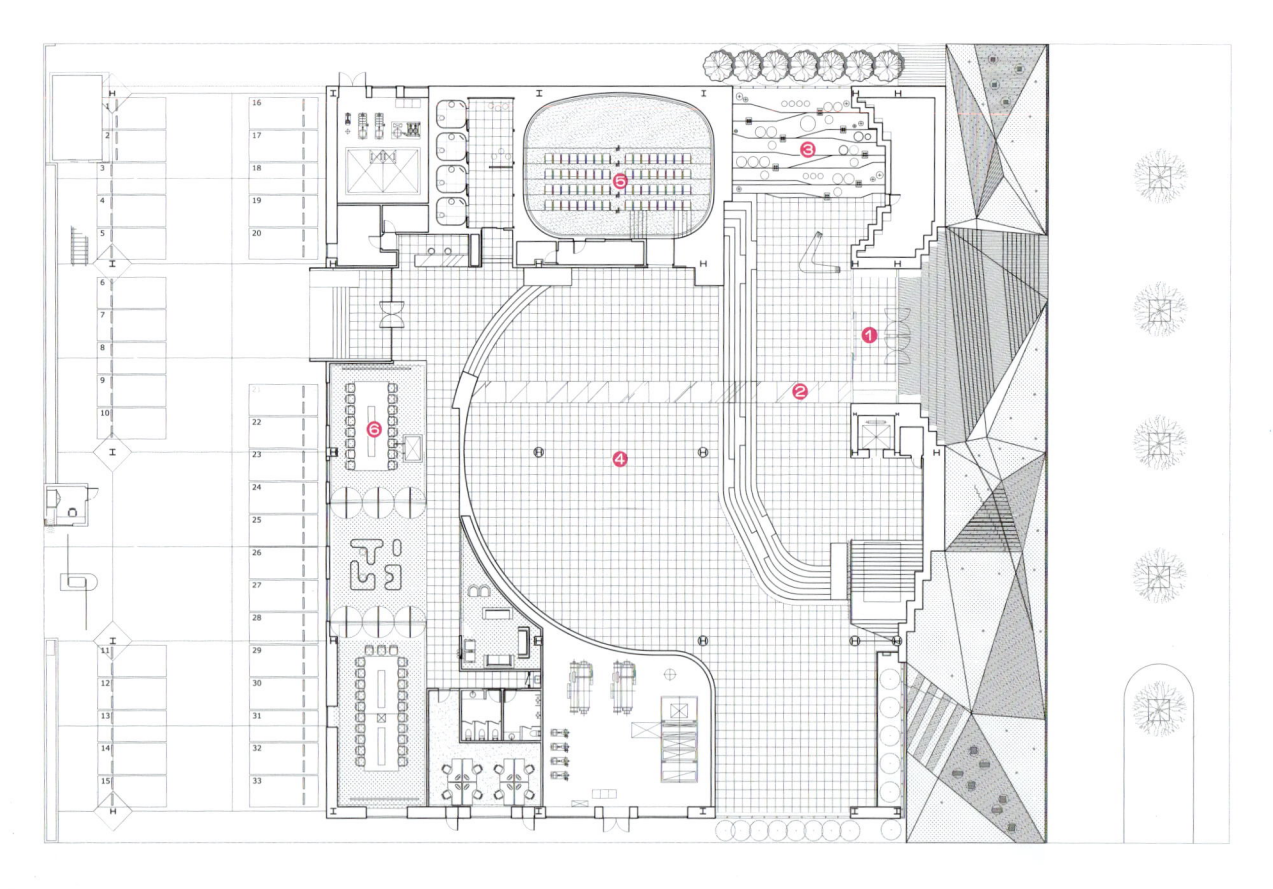

1ST FLOOR PLAN
1. Entrance
2. Entrance Hall
3. Information Terminals
4. Exhibition Hall
5. Theatre
6. Meeting Room

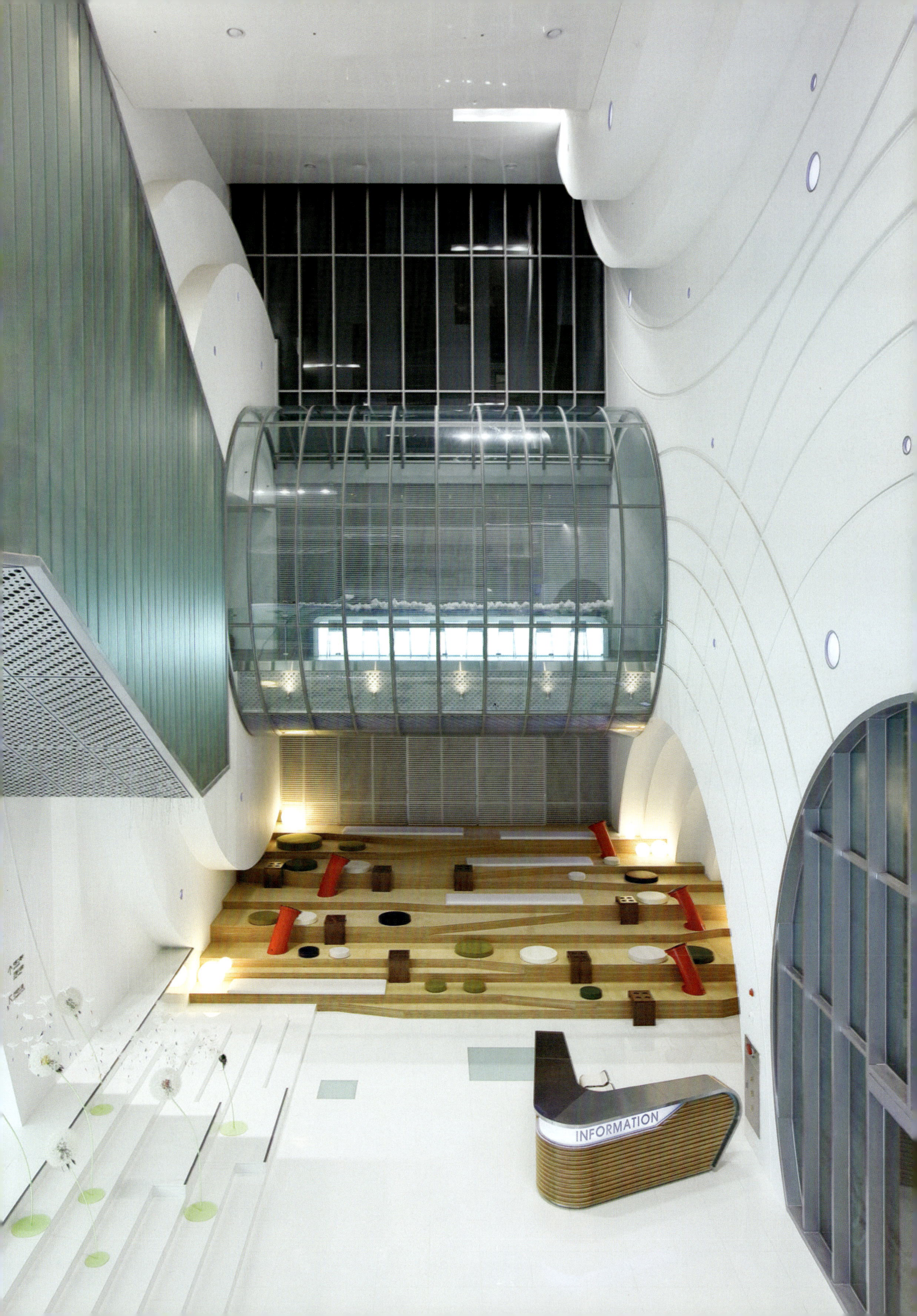
INFORMATION

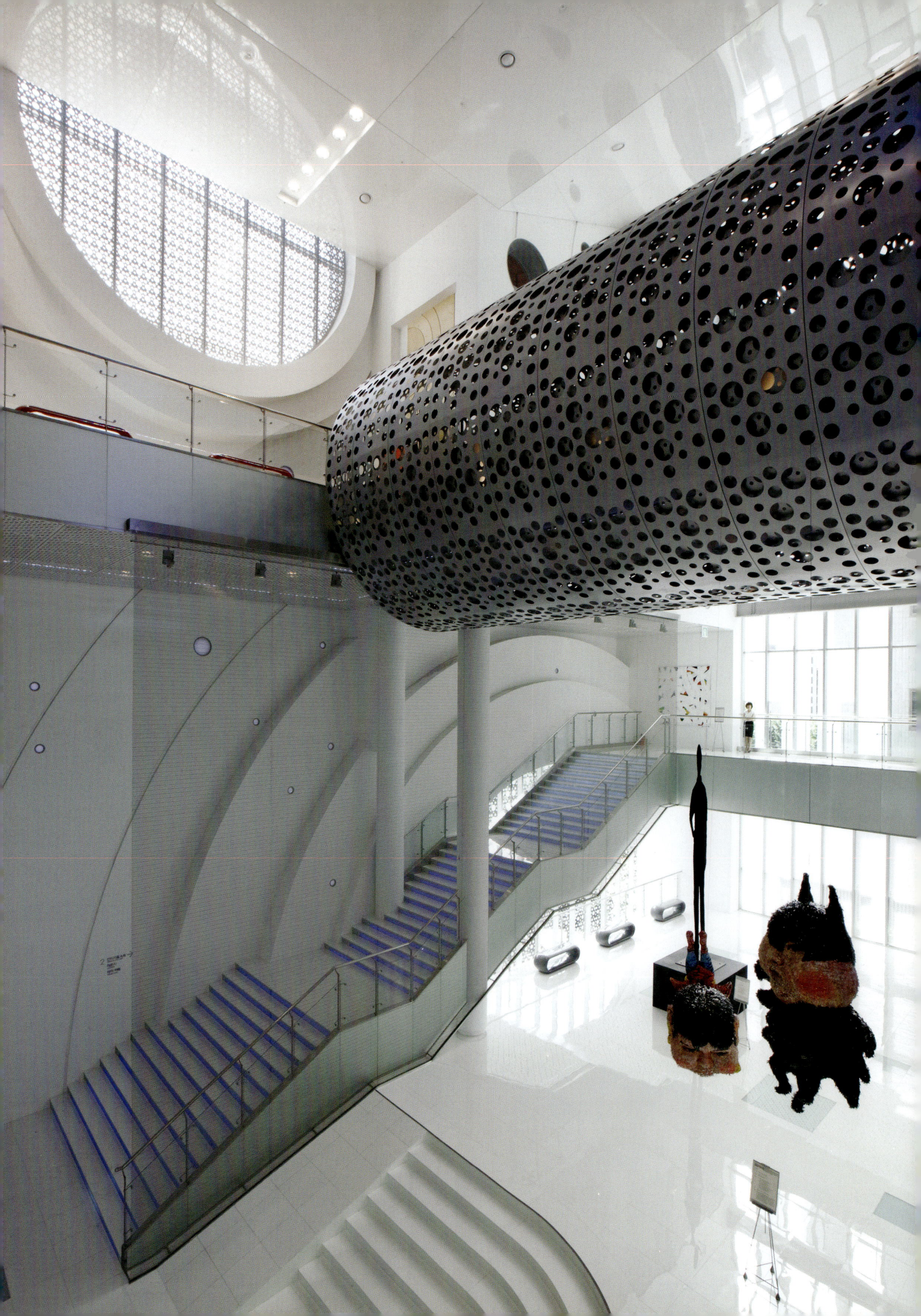

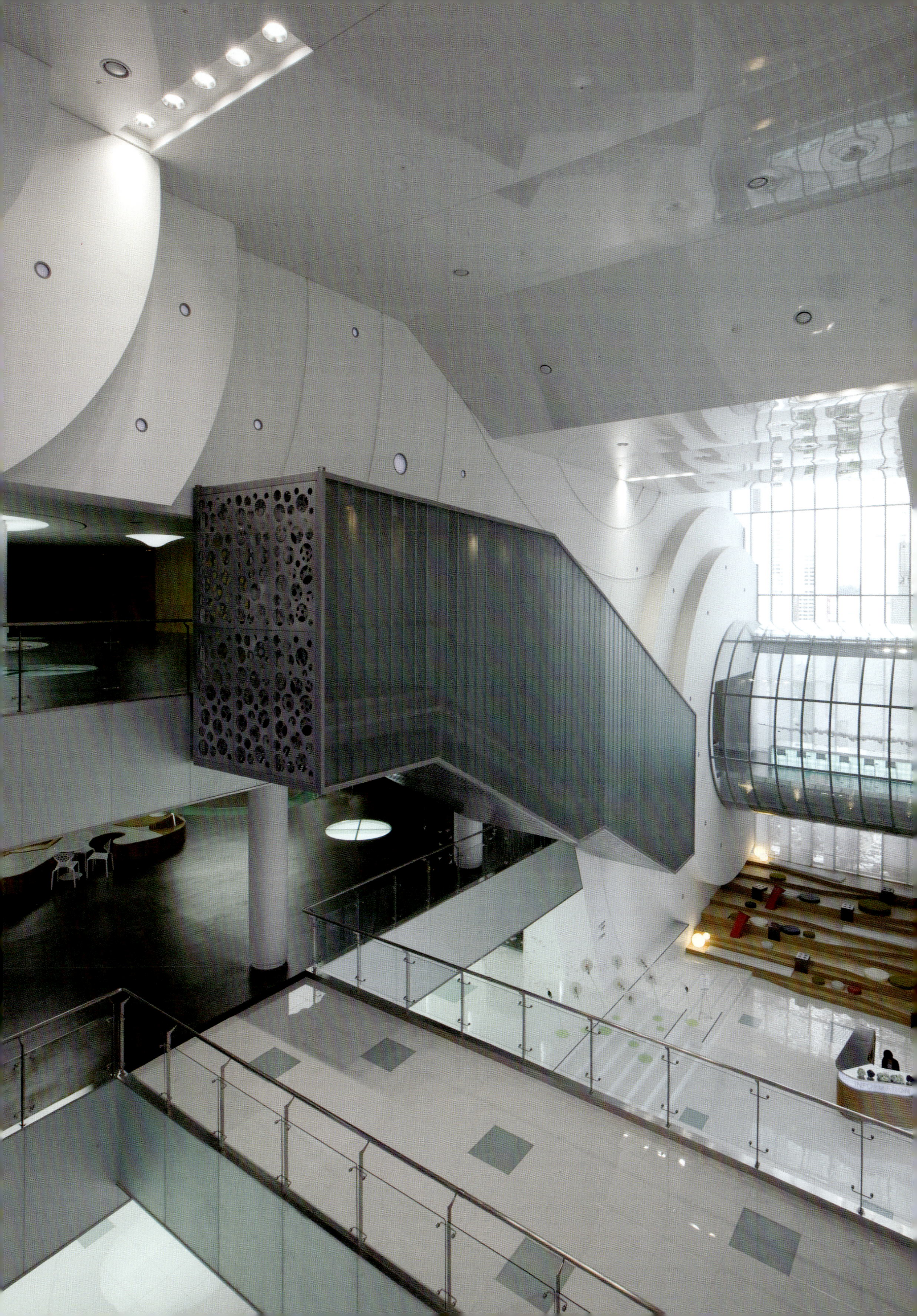

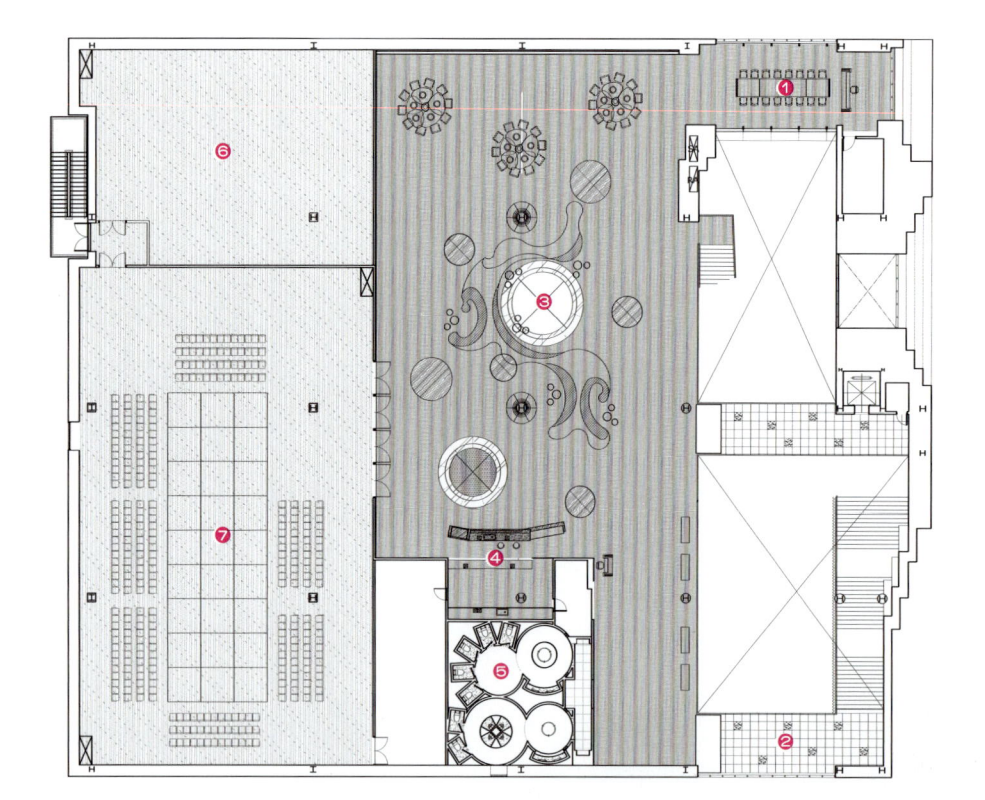

2ND FLOOR PLAN

1. Meeting Room
2. Bridge
3. Public Lounge
4. Cafe
5. Toilets
6. Life Style Room
7. Vintage Hall

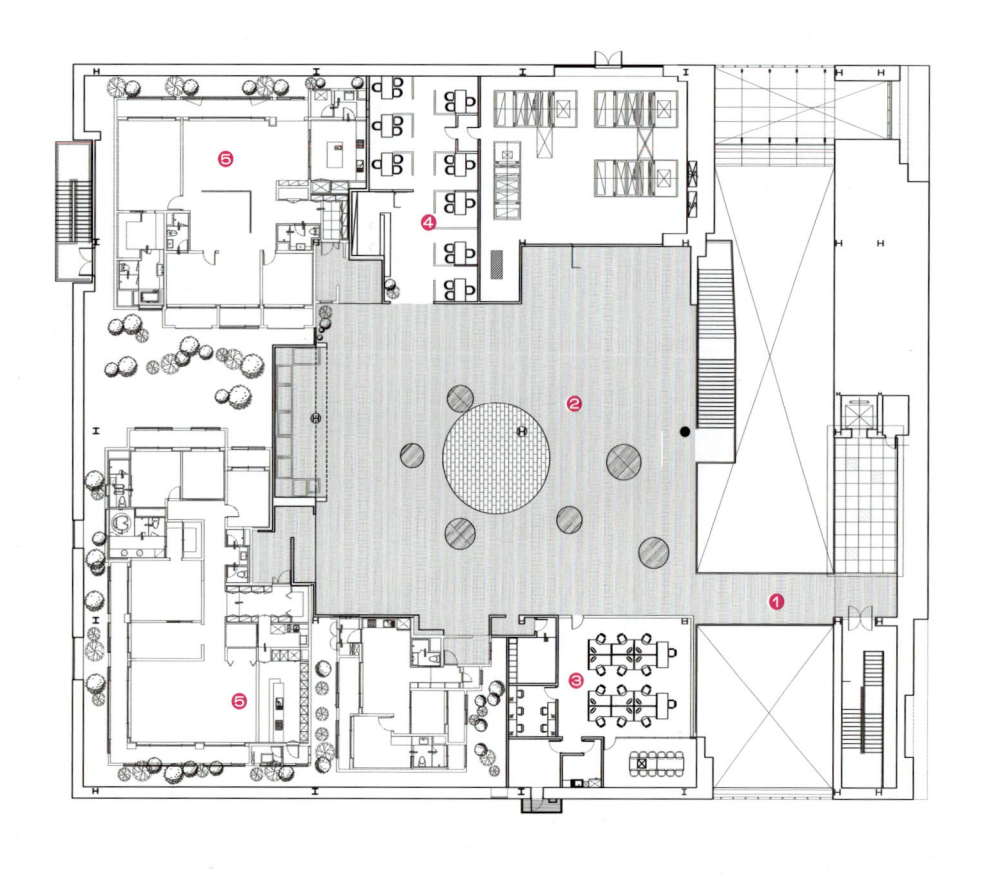

3RD FLOOR PLAN

1. Bridge
2. Exhibition Hall
3. Offices
4. Consultation Area
5. Model Apartment

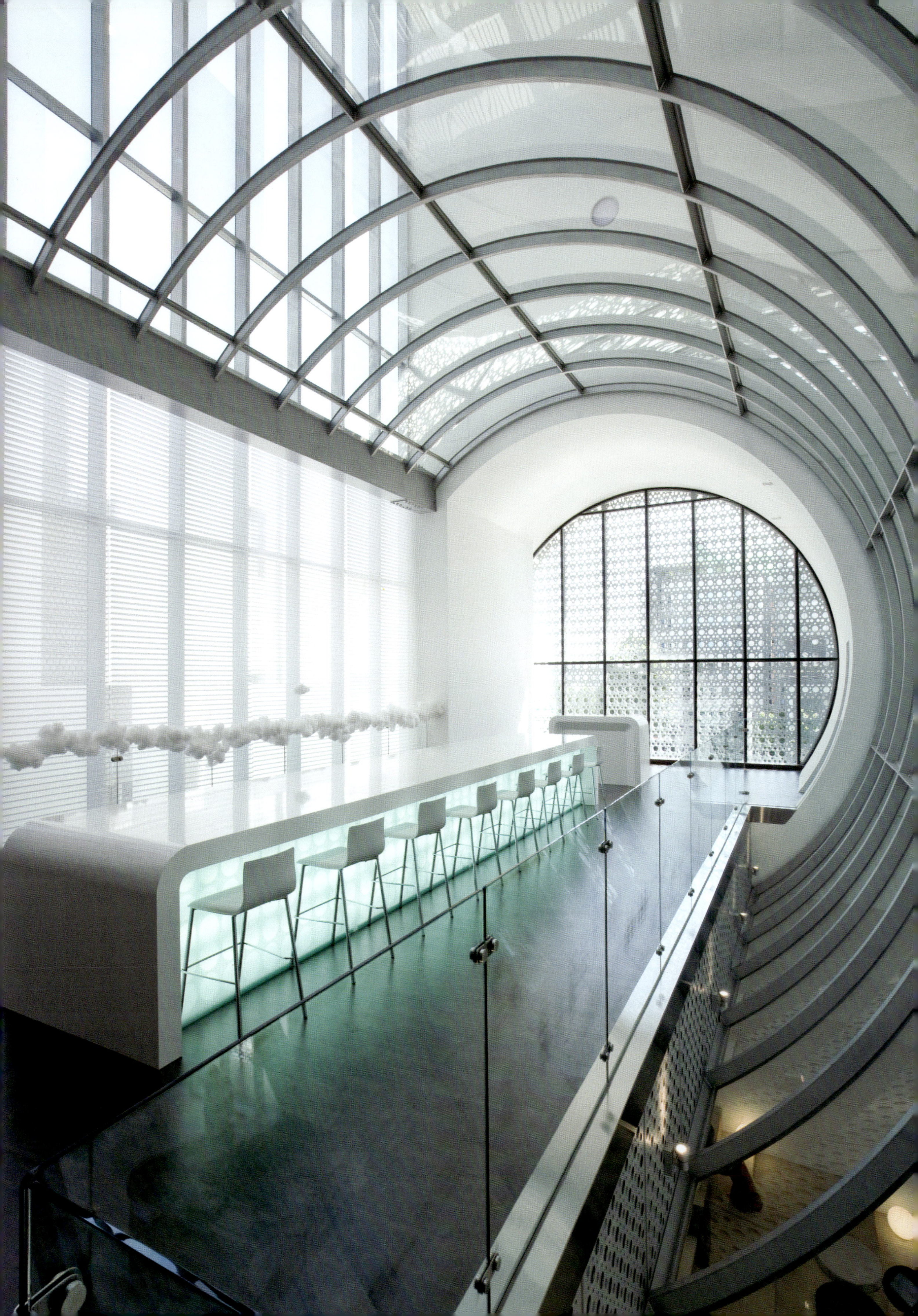

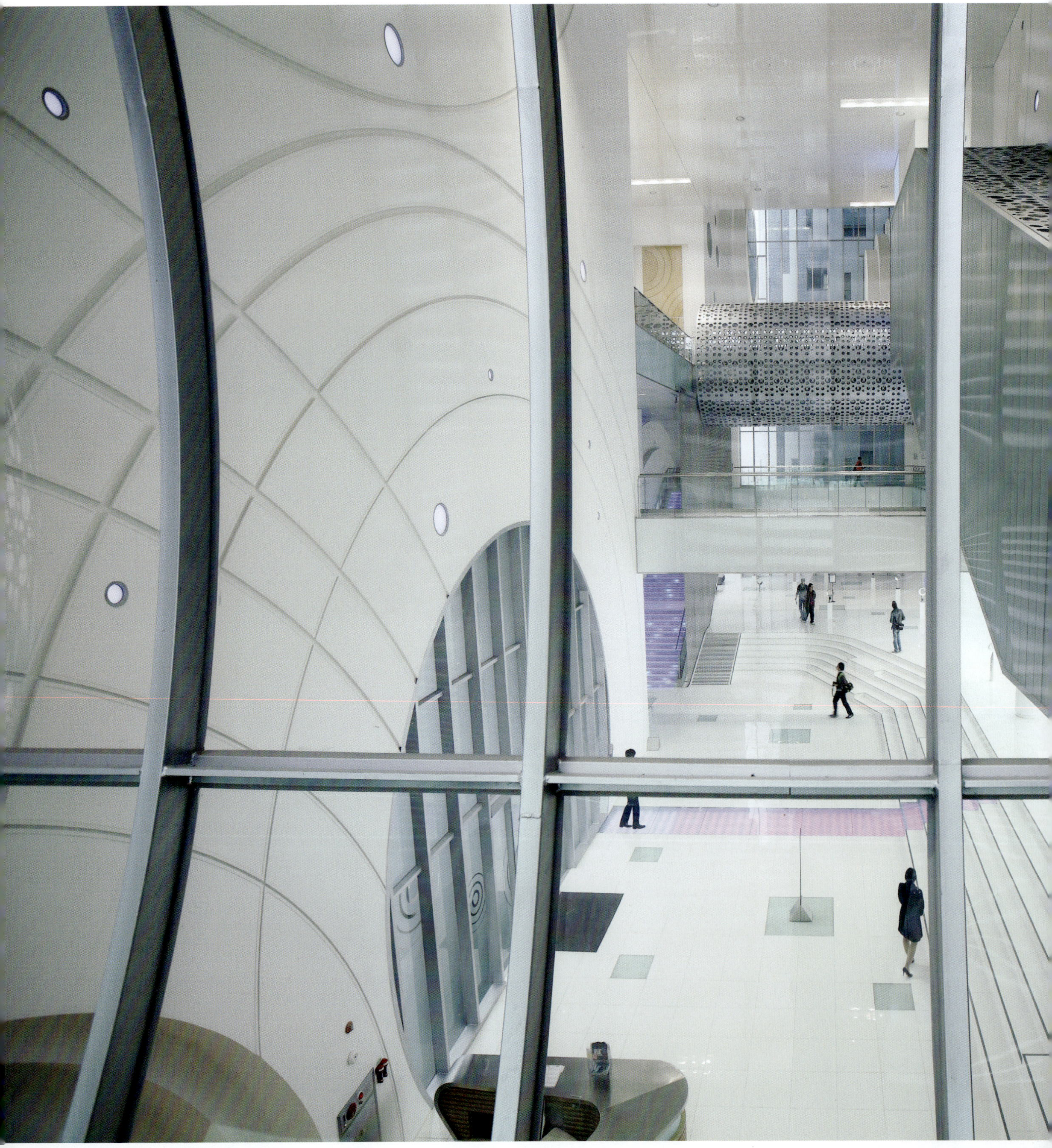

COMPOUND BODY 75

Model World
text Benjamin Budde, Interior Design Magazine

When visiting a model apart- ment with a mind to buying your own pied-a-terre, is enough simply to examine your future home's layout, fixtures, and furnishings?
Unsangdong Architects, led by principal Yoon Gyoo Jang and Chang Hoon SHin, are betting that apartment buyers want to know much more than that. So when their firm was hired by the giant South Korean real estate developer and builder Kumho Engineering & Construction to design a building is Seoul to exhibition model apart- ments for the corporation's luxury condominium brand. Uwoolim, the architects were determined that the structure be highly conceptual, a concrete reflection of the sensibility, lifestyle, and identity that the client markets.
Uwoolim is a Korean word that can be translated as "community in harmony." and the company cultivates a brand image centered on the idea of living in concord with neighbors, nature, and shared values. Unsangdong took this notion of the fully integrated life-aworld in which the individual, society, culture, commercem technology, and the natural environment interact fluidly and fruitfully-and explored it architecturally. So, rather than simply being a collection of model apartments, their building shows how life in an Uwoolim condomini- um interacts with the surrounding community.
In fact, there are only three model apartments in the entire 75,000 square-foot, three-story building. The rest of the space functions as a cultural complex for a variety of curated events and exhibition, includ- ing dance performances, art installations, and design competitions. The liberal allocation of square footage to nonresidential purposes reflects Jang and Shin's belief that lifestyle are shifting and that archi- tecture must respond to changing modes of living. "Today's lifestyle demands an unpredictable architecture." sats Jang. "As wats of life are transformed. architecture also shifts away from a single restricted form."
This philosophy finds dramatic expression in the building's stainless- steel facade, which is covered in a series of enormous circular aper- tures. Each takes the form of a series of layered, concentric rings-like a cross between the ripples on a pond and a whirlpool-that funnel though the thick facade into the building's interior. While the largest of these cutouts surrounds a panel of LEDs that use flash program- ming to create an animated image of an archetypal cityscape, the others are mostly big windows, some of which front steel-and-glass tubes that crisscross the airy spaces inside.
These round openings not only give the building its name-Kring, which is Dutch for "ring"-but also reverberate with multiple mean- ings and associations. Along with rippling water, their allusions to the natural world run the gamut from the tiny orbitals of subatomic particles to the vast circling of planets around the sun. There are also echoes of man-made forms-Greek amphitheaters, Gothic rose windows, the spiraling ramp of New 어l's Solomon R, Guggenheim Museum-as well as social structures and hierarchies. As such, Kring's facade is the most public embodiment of the architects' stated inten- tion: "to create scenarios that harmonize nature, life, and the city's various elements."

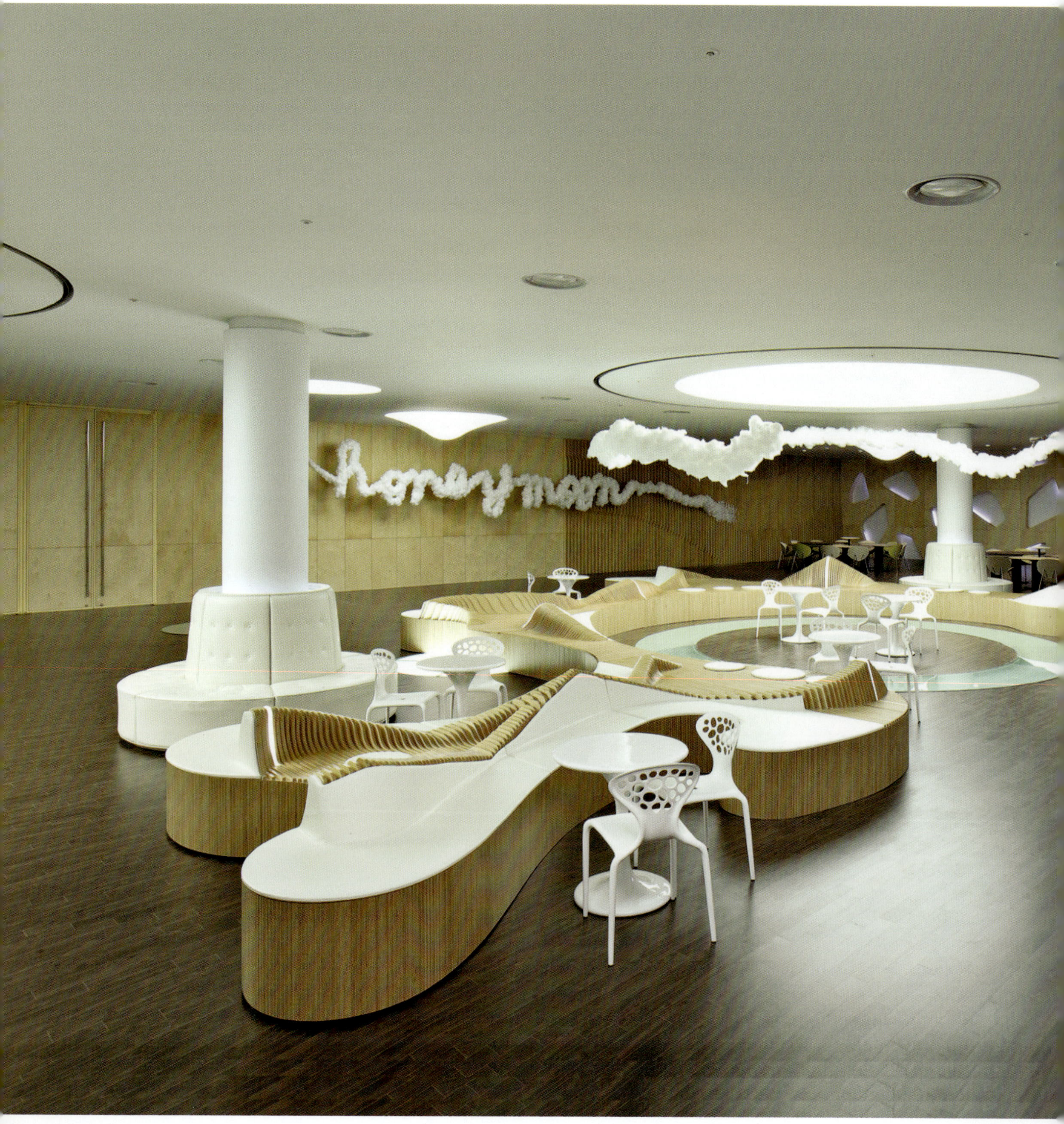
honeymoon

Kring's interior is no less allusive or radical. The main entry, though one of the giant rings, leads into a huge, shiny white atrium that soars the building's full three-story height. Shin calls this large, echoing volume "the big sounds hole," and links its white emptiness to the concept of dreaming-a blank screen on which to project reveries and visions. The cavernous space is spanned at various heights by walkways and a couple of tubular bridges, one enclosed in glass, the other sheathed in perforated steel. As connecting elements, these airborne structures are natural metaphors for the realms of social interaction and creative imagination. As the architects put it: "The cylinders penetrating the space are images expressing dreams, passions, and communication."

Kring will continue functioning as a cultural center after Uwoolim dismantles its model apartments. (In South Korea, residential exhibition buildings like this one are usually demolished once their promotional purpose has bees served.) Unsangdong cheerfully acknowledges that its aim is to "realize progressive architecture," and it's difficult to imagine an American real estate developer letting a design firm experiment so dramatically on a structure that's primarily intended to sell product. But Kumho evidently feels its luxury brand has been very well served by Kring. Plus it's a distinctive piece of urban sculpture that incorporates a rich array of influences-it even evokes a giant Swiss cheese from some angles-and certainly enlivens Seoul's mostly uninspiring cityscape. "Social identity is related more directly to consumption than production." explains Jang. "Through the process of consumption, 'manufactured space' can stimulate the consumer's desires," Sold!

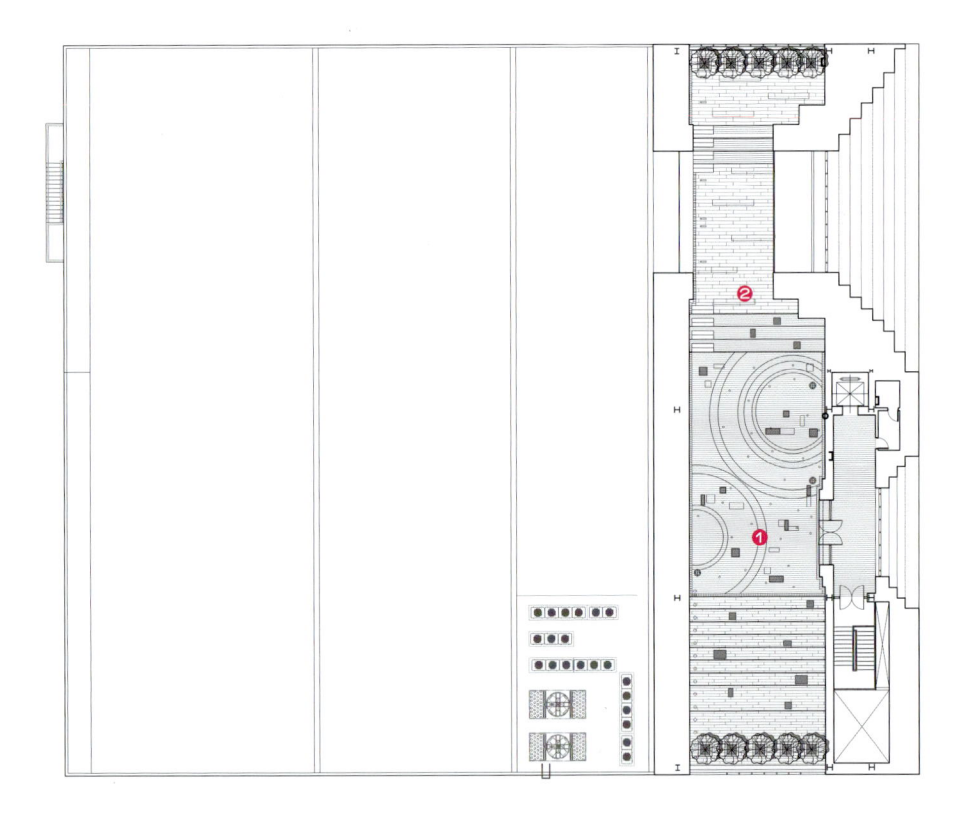

ROOF PLAN
1. Dream Park
2. Dream Deck

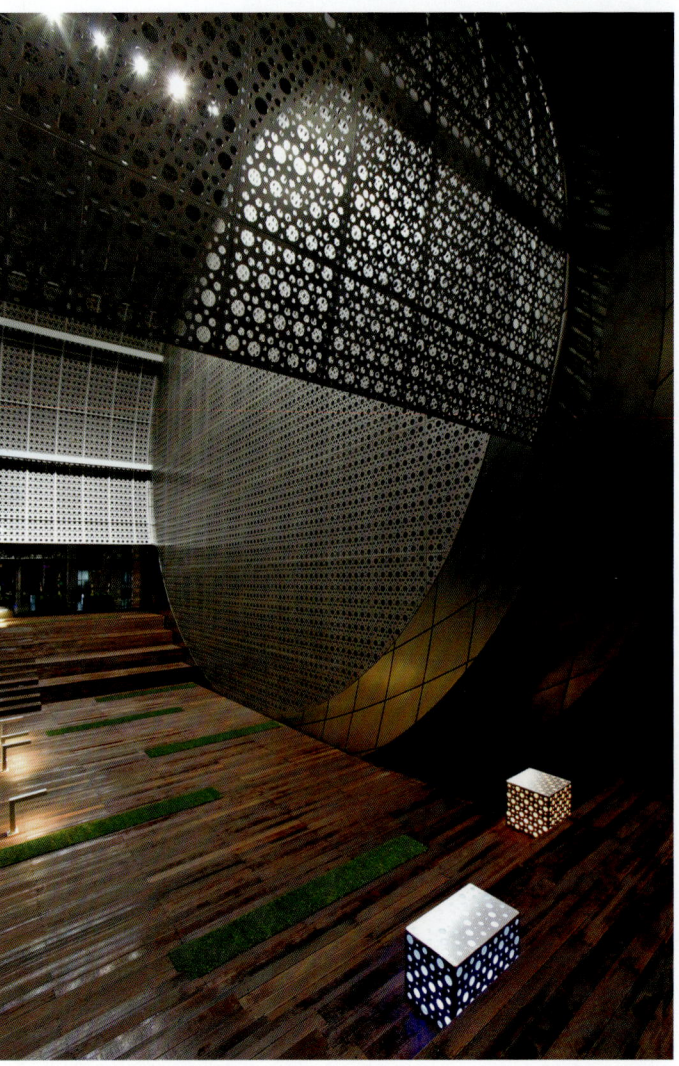

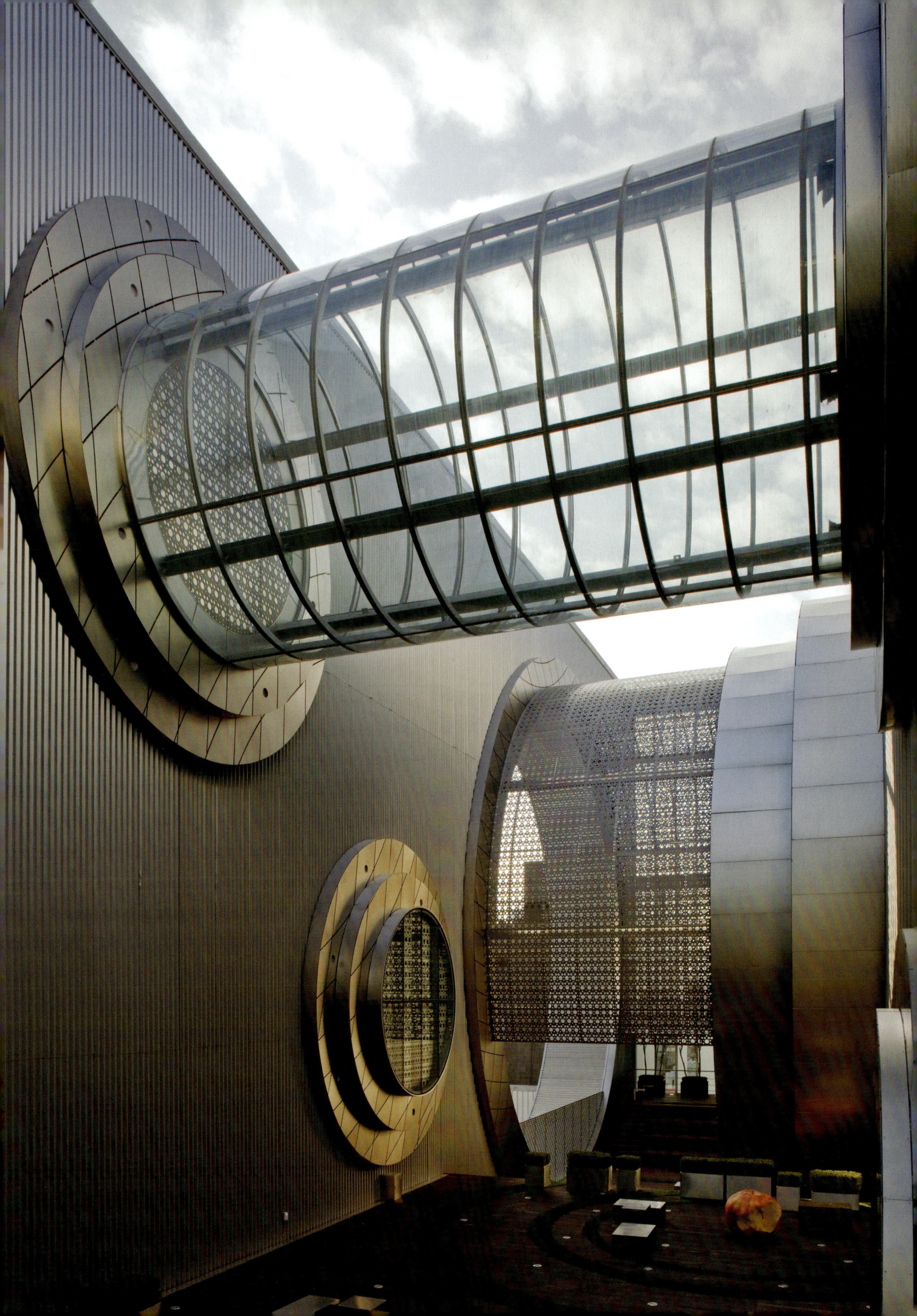

LIGHTING ART

Marking use of lighting art, each of these seven ulimtong is illuminated with graphics that convey massages to the public aboust life, ecology, the city, living, housing and the company's brand. The rings of sound waves on the interactive media wall symbolize an exhalation of images towards the city and an inhalation of energy from the city. The imagery of ulimtong is also adopted throughout the interior space: on the walls, in the flooring and in the horizontal cylindrical volumes. These pierced hollow tubes serve both as passageways and simply as huge ornaments. According to the architects, they have a 'dreamlike' symbolic meaning, which is their translation of the client's motto to create premier living space that is in harmony with humanity, nature and state-of-the-art construction technology.

text from **MARK**

Program Lighting   Star Lighting   Material Lighting

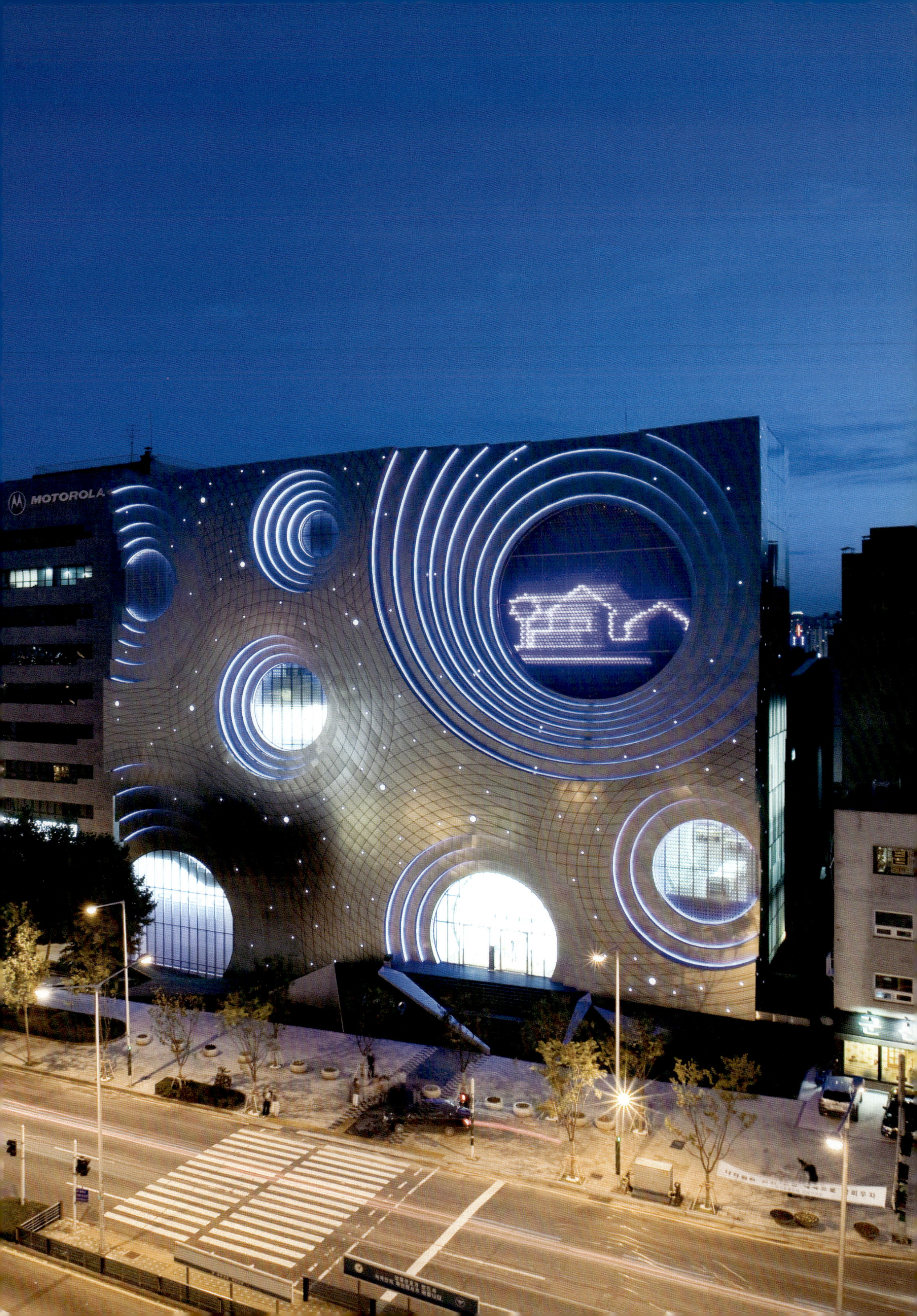
MOTOROLA

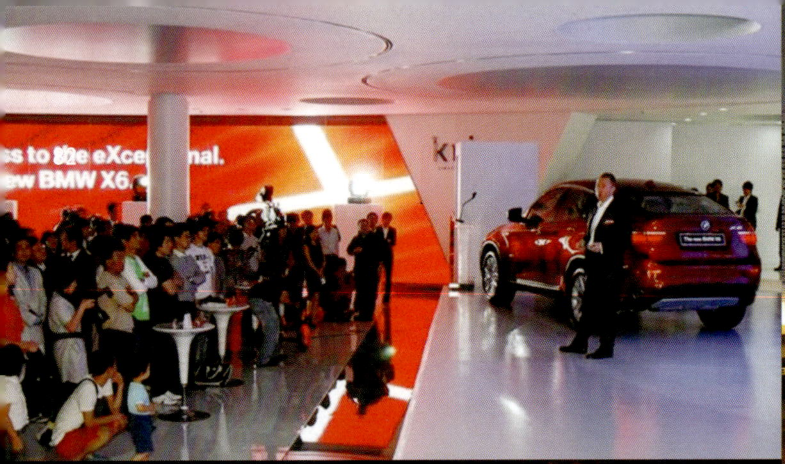

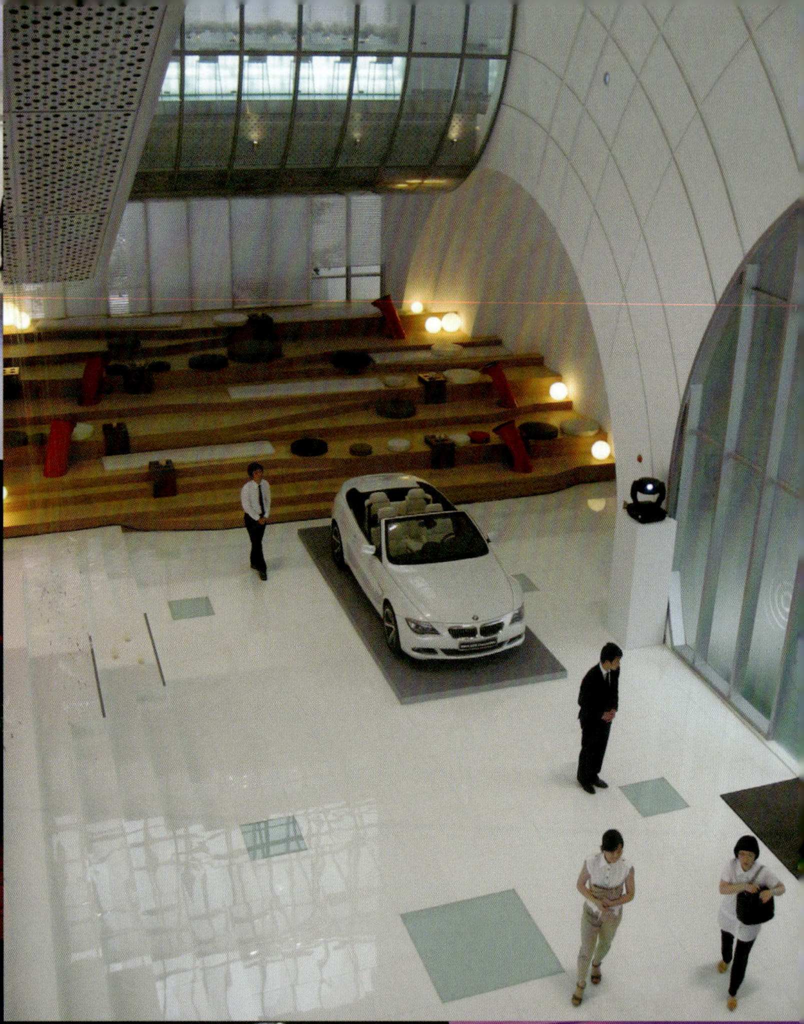

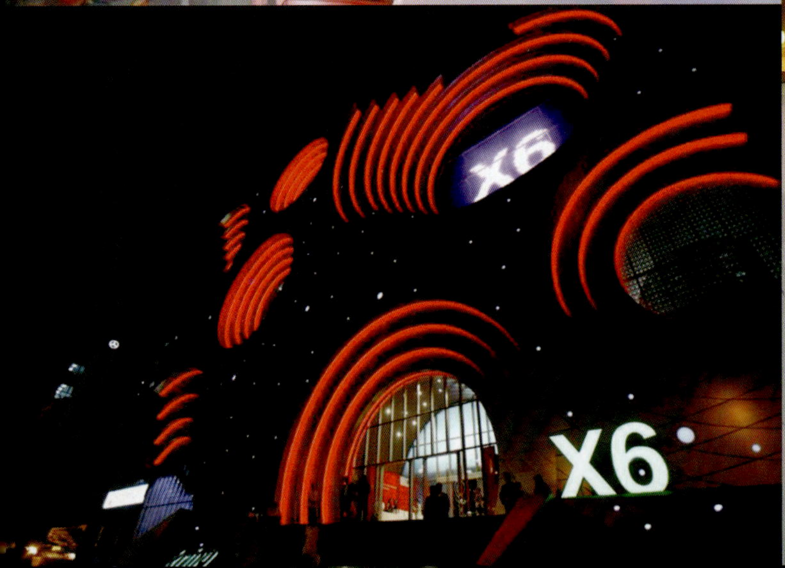
X6
X6

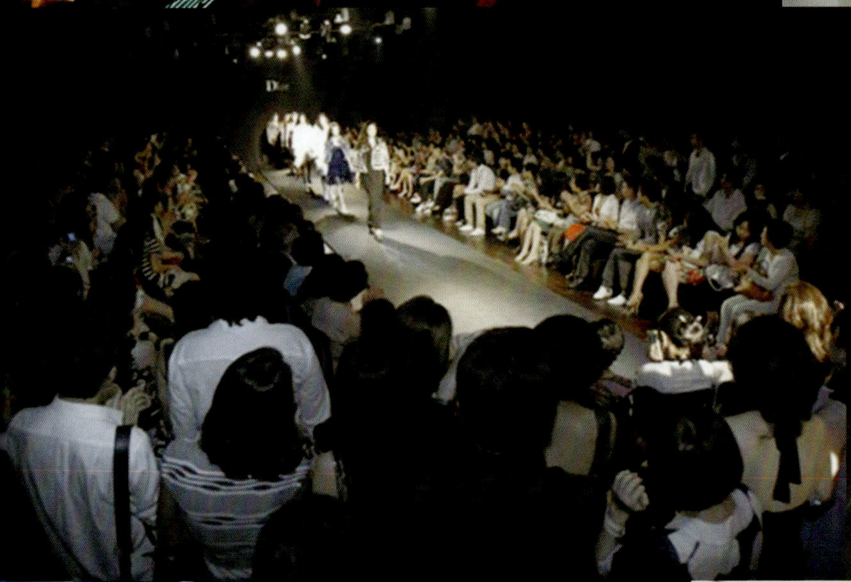

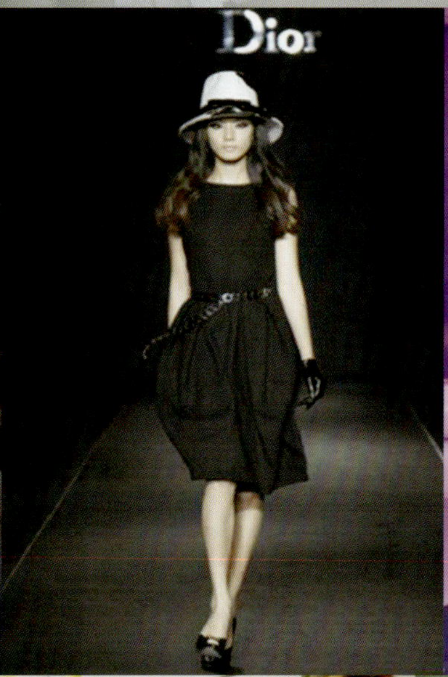
Dior

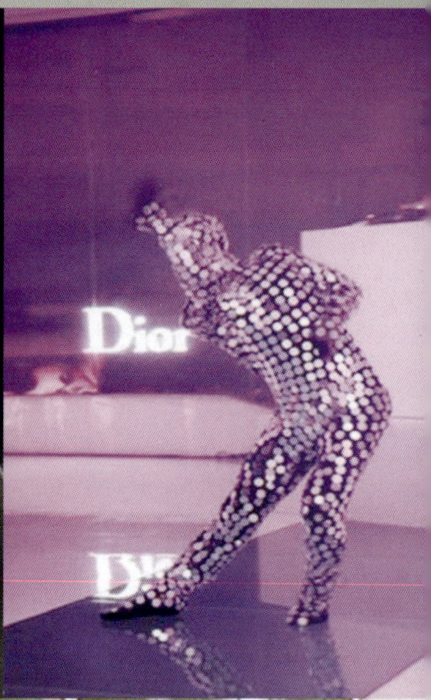
Dior

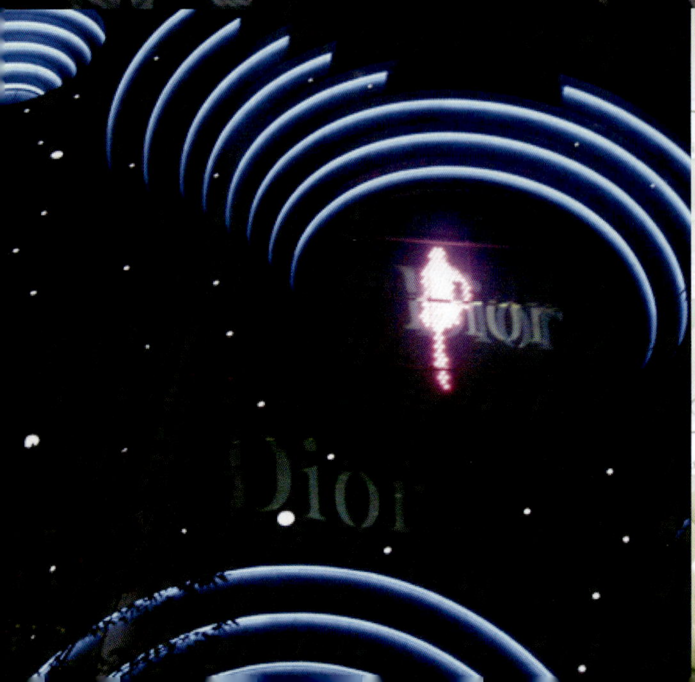
Dior
Dior

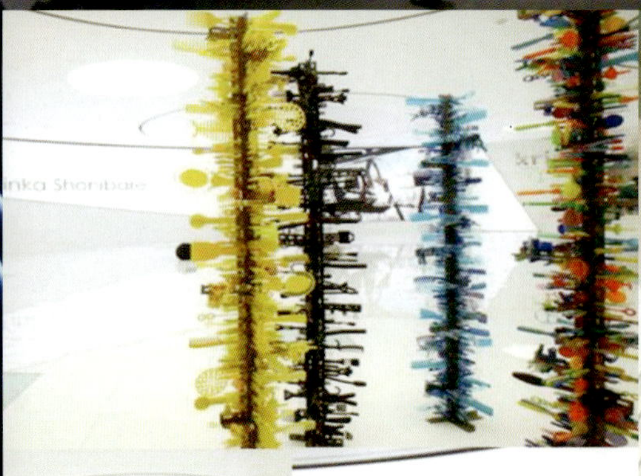

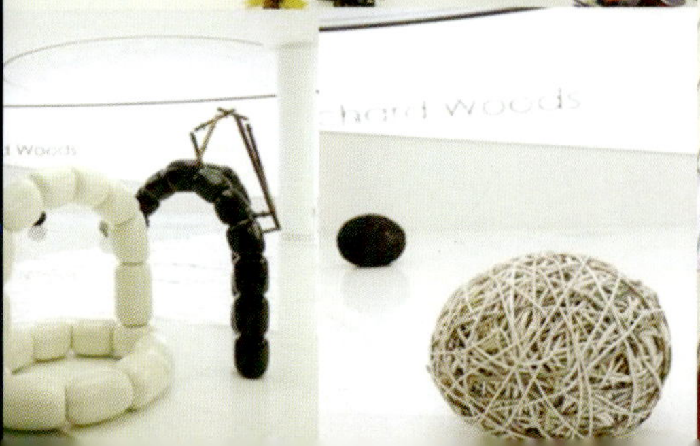

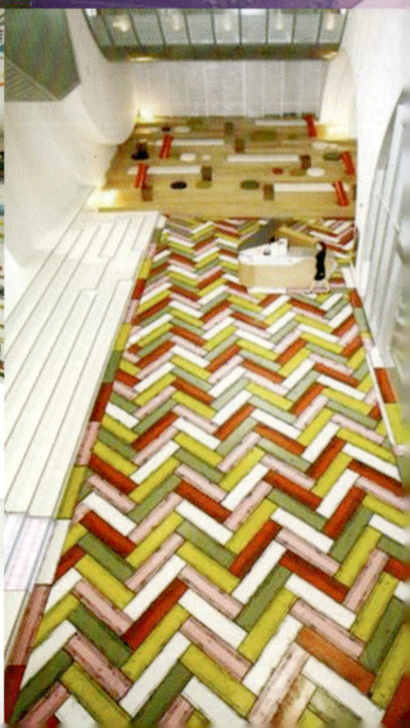

DROPS OF GLASS ON THE CITY

In South Korea, at Seoul, Kring, the multi-target and multi-functional macro-object, covers an ambitious real estate investment with the poetry of art. Exhibition space on the ground and first floors, a conference room on the second, space for the sale of real estate on the third, and a sky garden on the fourth and last level, a futuristic destination for a sensorial itinerary, narrating a work of architecture that is both a marketing tool and an urban container. The dance of two drops of water never misses a beat. One after the other, the movement seems to be held in place by the way it repeatedly hits the same target. It digs into the pores of a steel box, like stone, hollowing and then inserting the sea, a sea of new ideas. An imposing presence, for the perplexed faces of a charmless metropolis. Seoul has the talent of a middle zone, and perhaps we will see what it will become. Because the ratrace, plunging and soaring, forces another sort of sustainability, that of the architectural object that generates profit in its own right. Darwin is still here in our midst, facing a glass cylinder, a meeting room suspended over the big entrance lobby. From a distance, he watches the architects Yoon Gyoo Jang and Chang Hoon Shin as they discuss things with the management of Kumho E&C, a leader in the real estate sector. Seven times the thickness unveils its layers, revealing its time and that of the next generation. Kring will leave a mark even when we have forgotten its forms, because its program has invented a new way of doing architecture. The first five years of the new millennium were for the new patrons, who thanks to the fever of consumption filled cubes and towers with neon and high fashion. Architecture, the most intelligent promotional message, marketing tool, three-dimensional in look, two-dimensional in perception, mono-dimensional in content, was filled with new demagogic symbols. But not Kring. It keeps the course, but finds another port of call, that of evolution. So a real estate company commissions a multi-target work, and fills it with functional itineraries, apparently distinct from the original aim. The functional program penetrates the facade volume with white reliefs that frame glassy irises, seven like the epicenters of the streetfront. Circular, vertical and horizontal, radiated and reflected, the absolute principle of this project clad in steel passages pointed toward the city. Beyond the threshold, sculpture floats in shiny white, the offices are set back, beyond the cinema toward the internal facade, while the gaze loses its bearings on the three open ramps that climb, excessive, to the first slab and the cafe zone, the expanded foyer of the multi-purpose conference room. It pulsates, reduces, dilates; the parallelepiped is a frozen lake. Outside, its openings retreat amidst luminous rings that form a vertical amphitheater for the contours of the city. The circular incisions are the reverberations of a drop, another, another still. Inside, from the glazed vertebrate cylinder, on 'dives' into the void, in the glare of many suns, satellites of the visitor who, curious, grasps at the 'porous, suspended tunnel' of the third level. The secret of Kring is finally, discreetly, revealed. Wrapped by wooden suspended ceilings and walls, in 6 glass rooms, in 12 round, swiveling chars, those who wandered through flying sculptures, took part in a conference, listened to music, perhaps with a cup of coffee, can finally, if they so wish, buy a house. They can also think it over, going up to the last level, a lunar landscape, on a long, undulated deck, under drops of steel from a clear blue sky. Seats scattered like perforated ice cubes, a bitten apple in the background, and beyond another oversized eye gazes at the occidental silhouettes of the city, the worksite of changes, and a drop of glass, like a tear, joins to steel skins.

text **Sergio Pirrone**

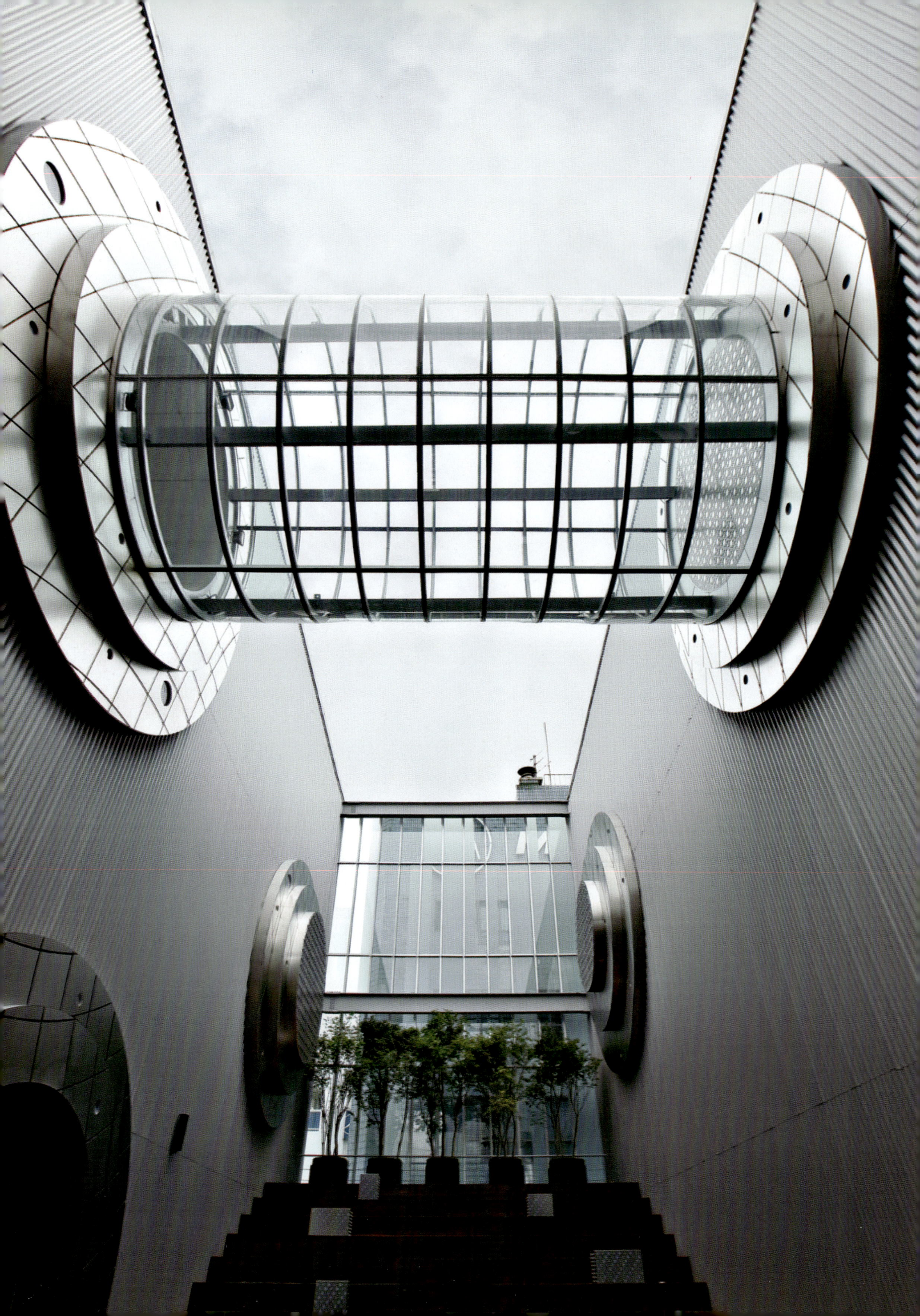

Architects
Jang Yoon Gyoo, Shin Chang Hoon, Kim Kyeung Tae
Project Team
Kim Sung Min, Moon Sang Ho, Kim Se Jln, Kang Seung Hyeun,
Kim Bong Kyun, Seo Hye Lim, Goh Young Dong, Yi Na Ra
Location
968-3, Daechi-dong, Gangnam, Seoul, Korea
Use Temporary building (Model house)
Site Area 4,110.9m²
Building Area 3,153.58m²
Gross Floor Area 7,144.53m²
Building Coverage 76.71%
Floor Space Index 173.06%
Building Scope 3F
Structure Steel
Design Period 2007. 5 ~ 2008. 7
Exterior Finishing
Stainless steel, ETFE, Paired glass, LED
Interior Finishing
Painting on birch plywood & gypsum board, Barrisol, LED

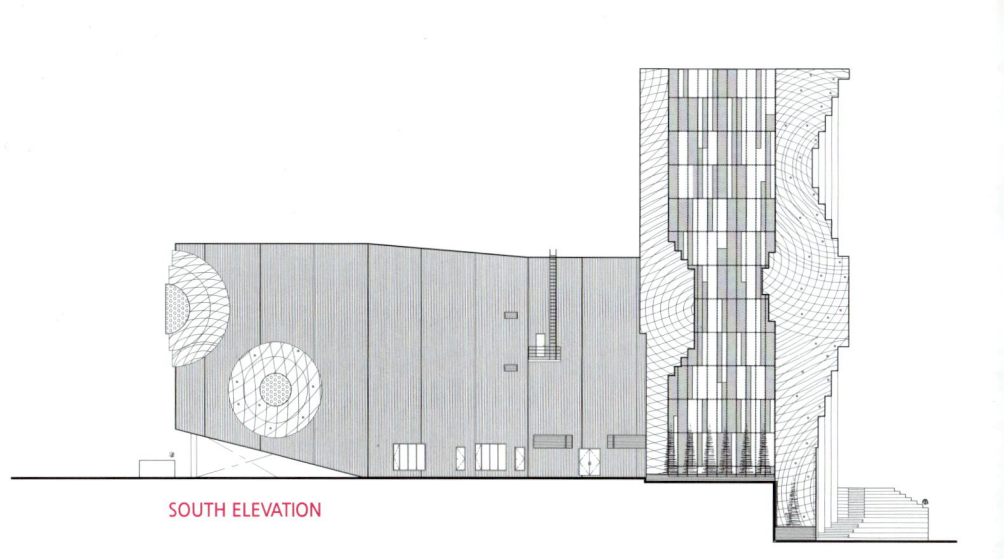

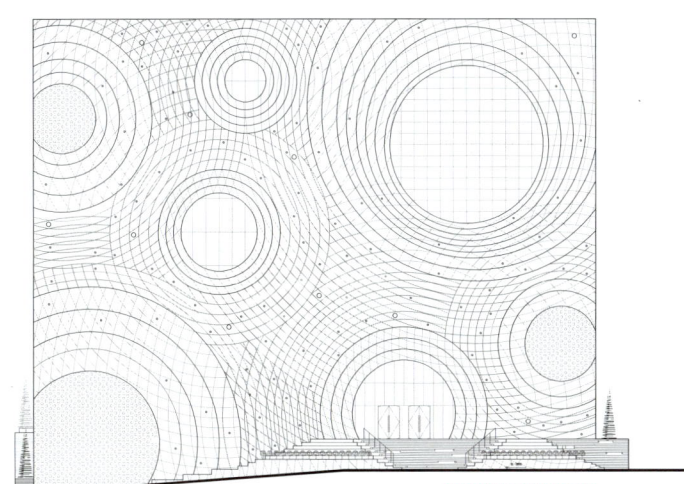

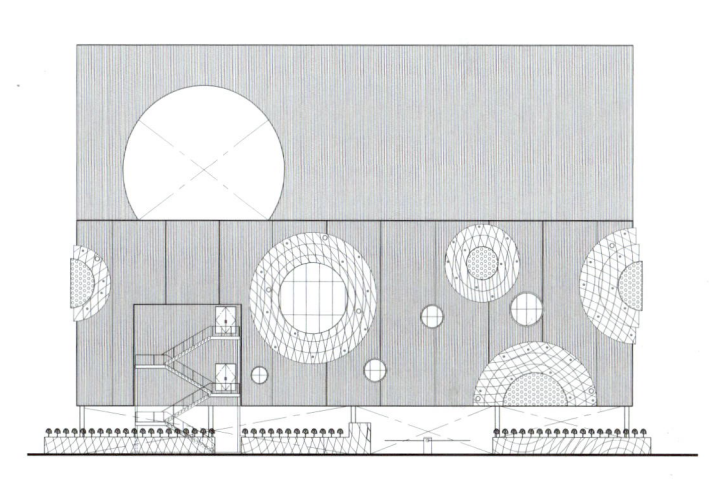

SOUTH ELEVATION

FRONT ELEVATION

REAR ELEVATION

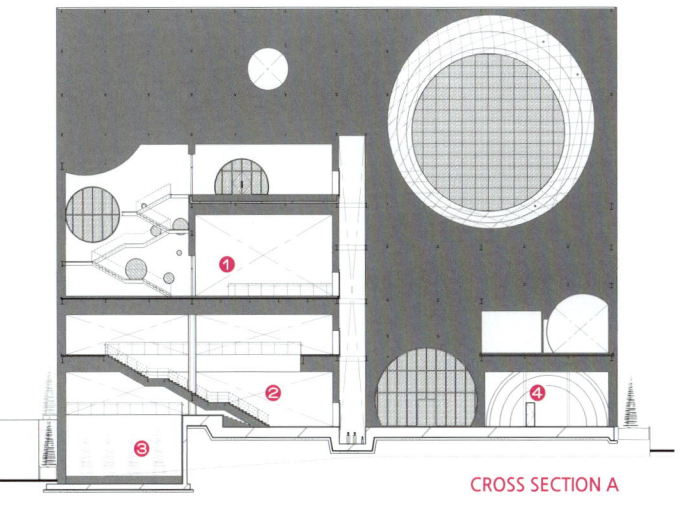

CROSS SECTION A
1. Bridge
2. Atrium
3. Artificial Planting
4. Storage

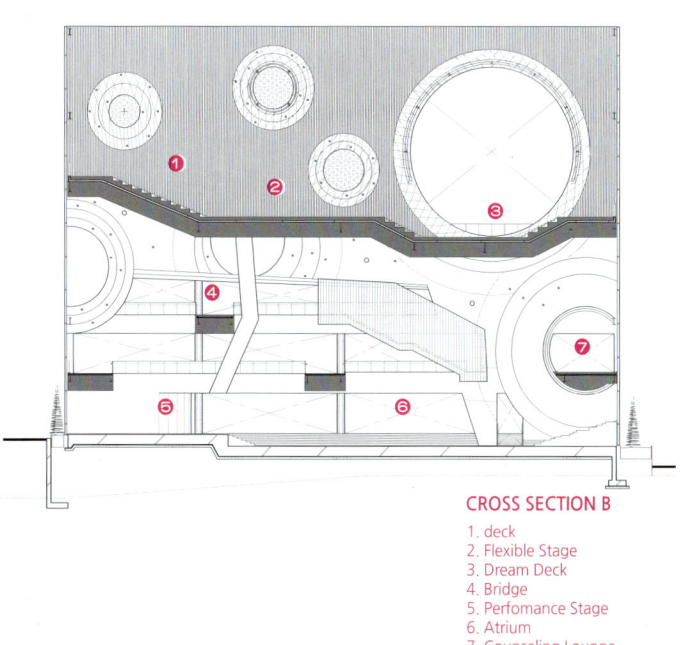

CROSS SECTION B
1. deck
2. Flexible Stage
3. Dream Deck
4. Bridge
5. Perfomance Stage
6. Atrium
7. Counseling Lounge

STRUCTURE STUDY

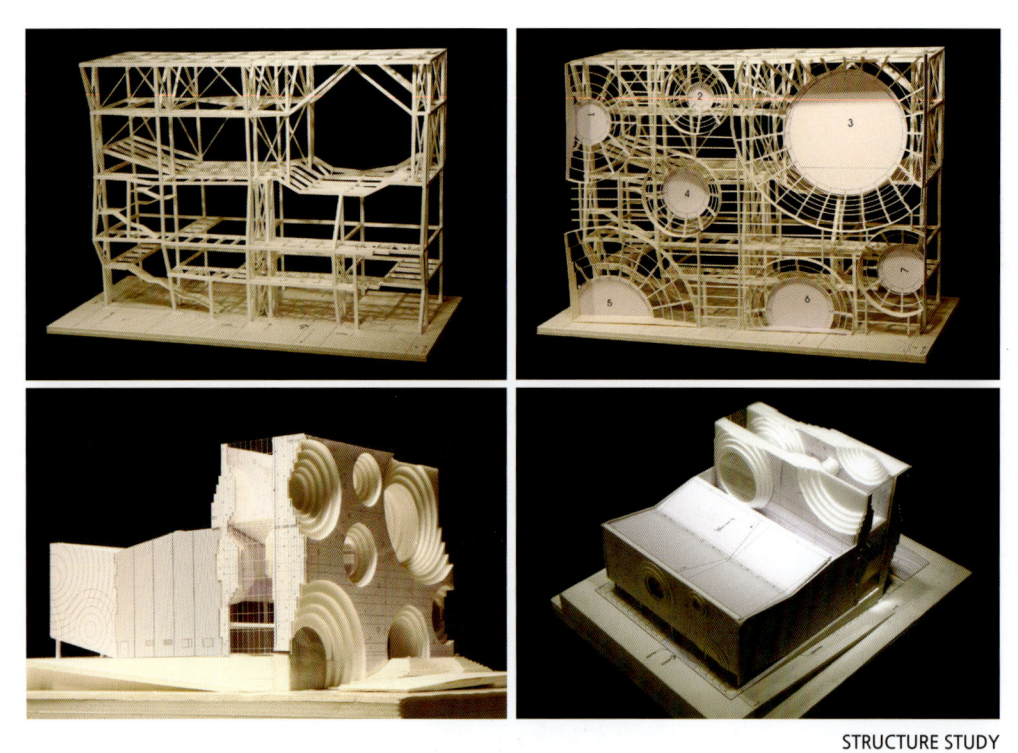

CONSTRUCTION PROCESS

CONSTRUCTION FRAME

'The biggest constraint was to keep the steel frame. We added a big atrium to the front part of the structure and preserved the rest. The initial design had to work around this,' the architects explain, Another technical challenge was the construction of the stainless steel curtain wall. When this was first presented to the client, the reactions were mixed. Some adored it for its 'out-of-the-box' sculpture-like configuration, while others thought it was too complicated and difficult to construct. Undeniably, the method of constructing the facade, which is drilled with seven differently sized three-dimensional spiral contours resembling ulimtong or reverberating sound waves, was the first in South Korea and it faced strict inspection.

text from **MARK**

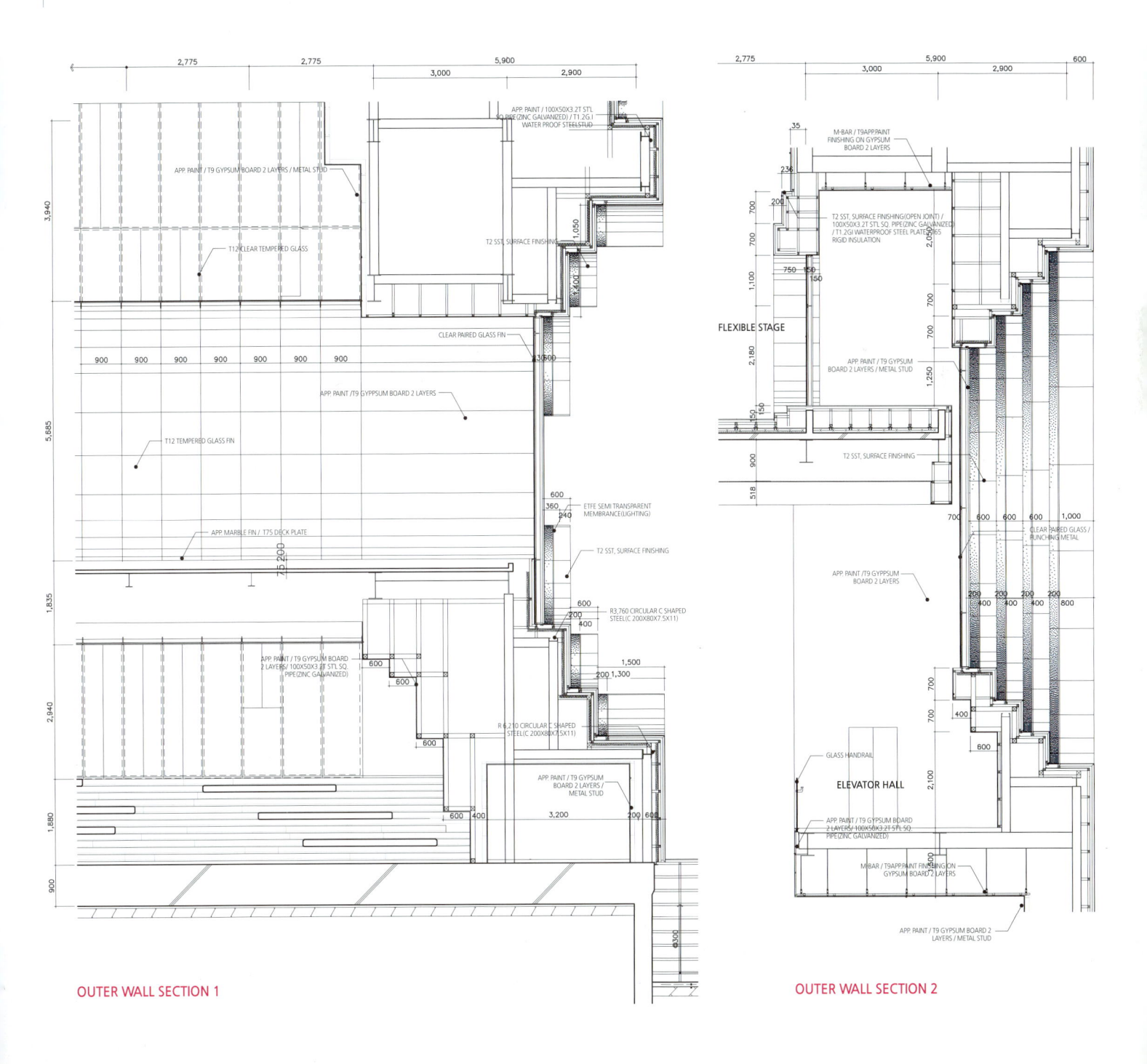

OUTER WALL SECTION 1

OUTER WALL SECTION 2

PARTIAL ELEVATION

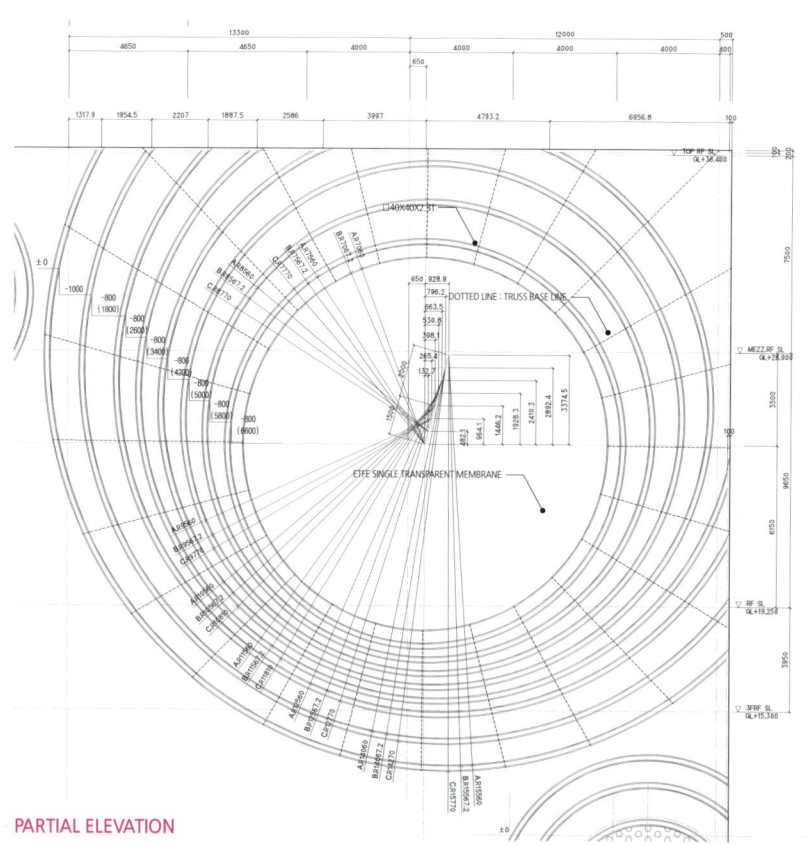

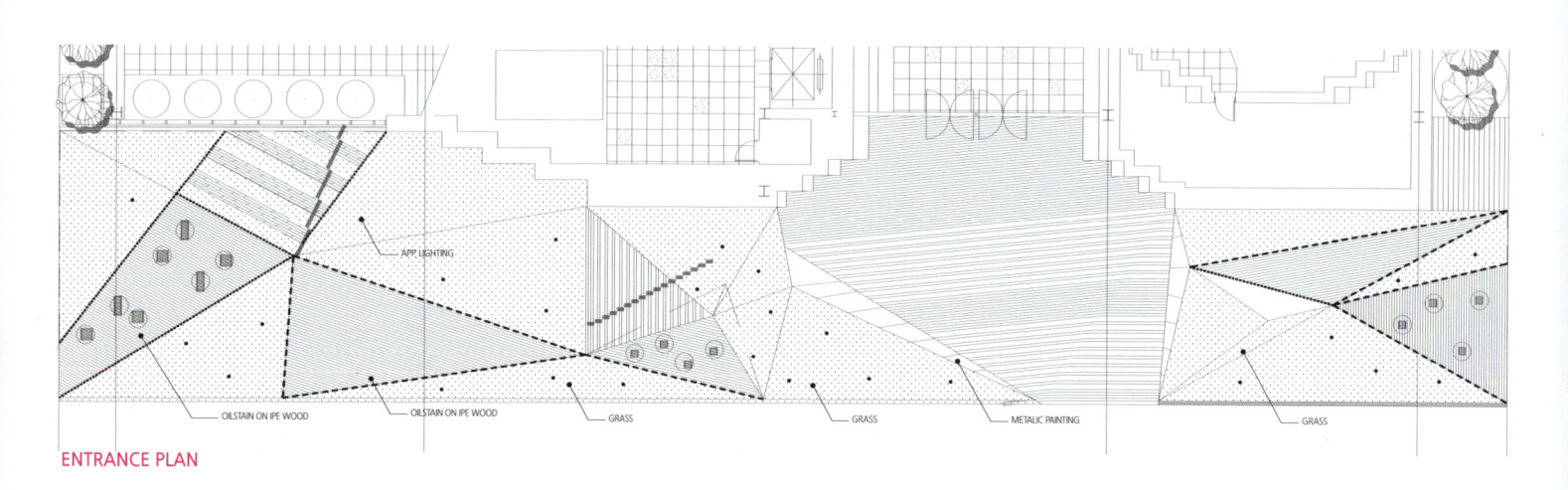

ENTRANCE PLAN

COMPOUND BODY 89

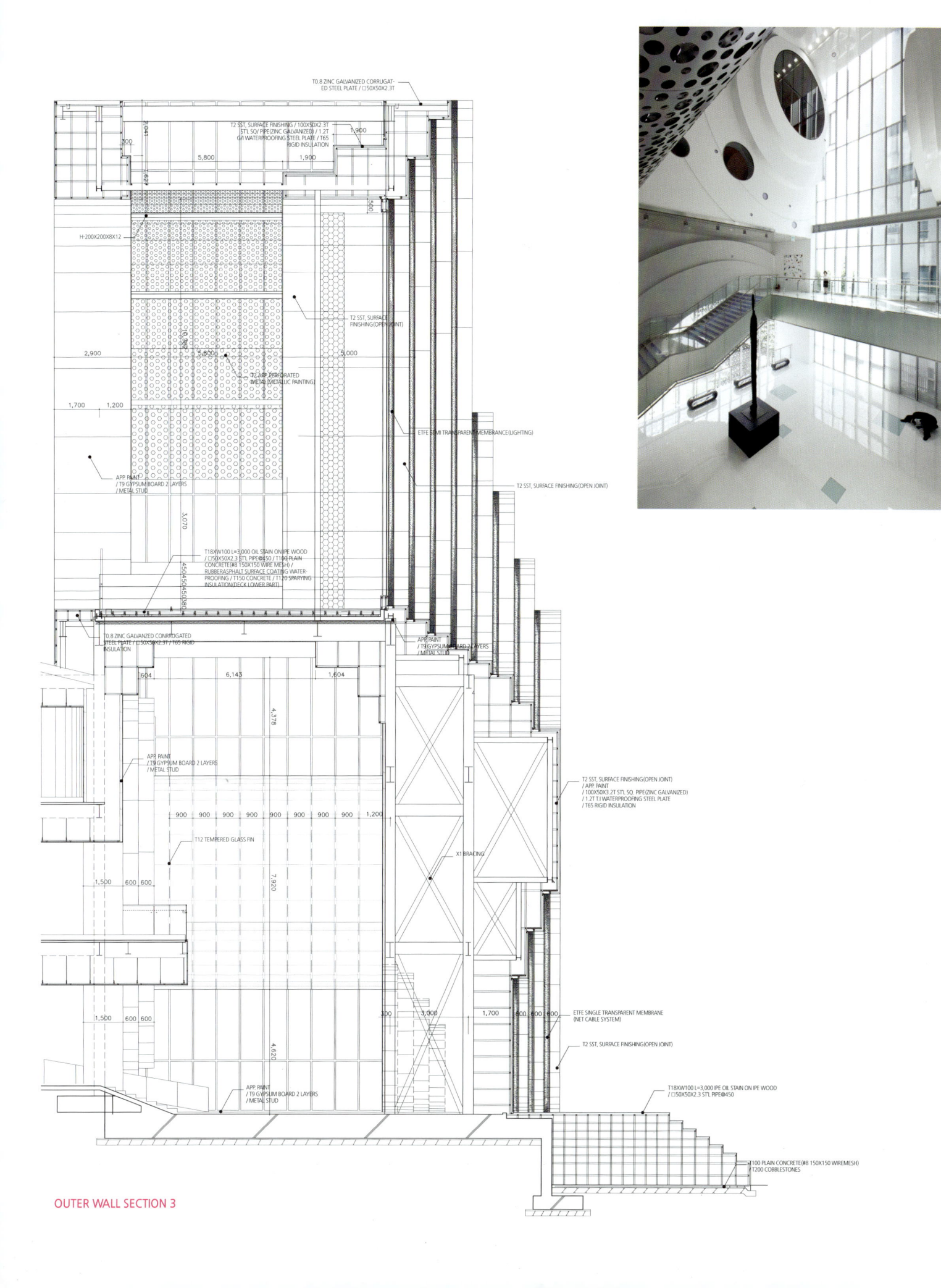

OUTER WALL SECTION 3

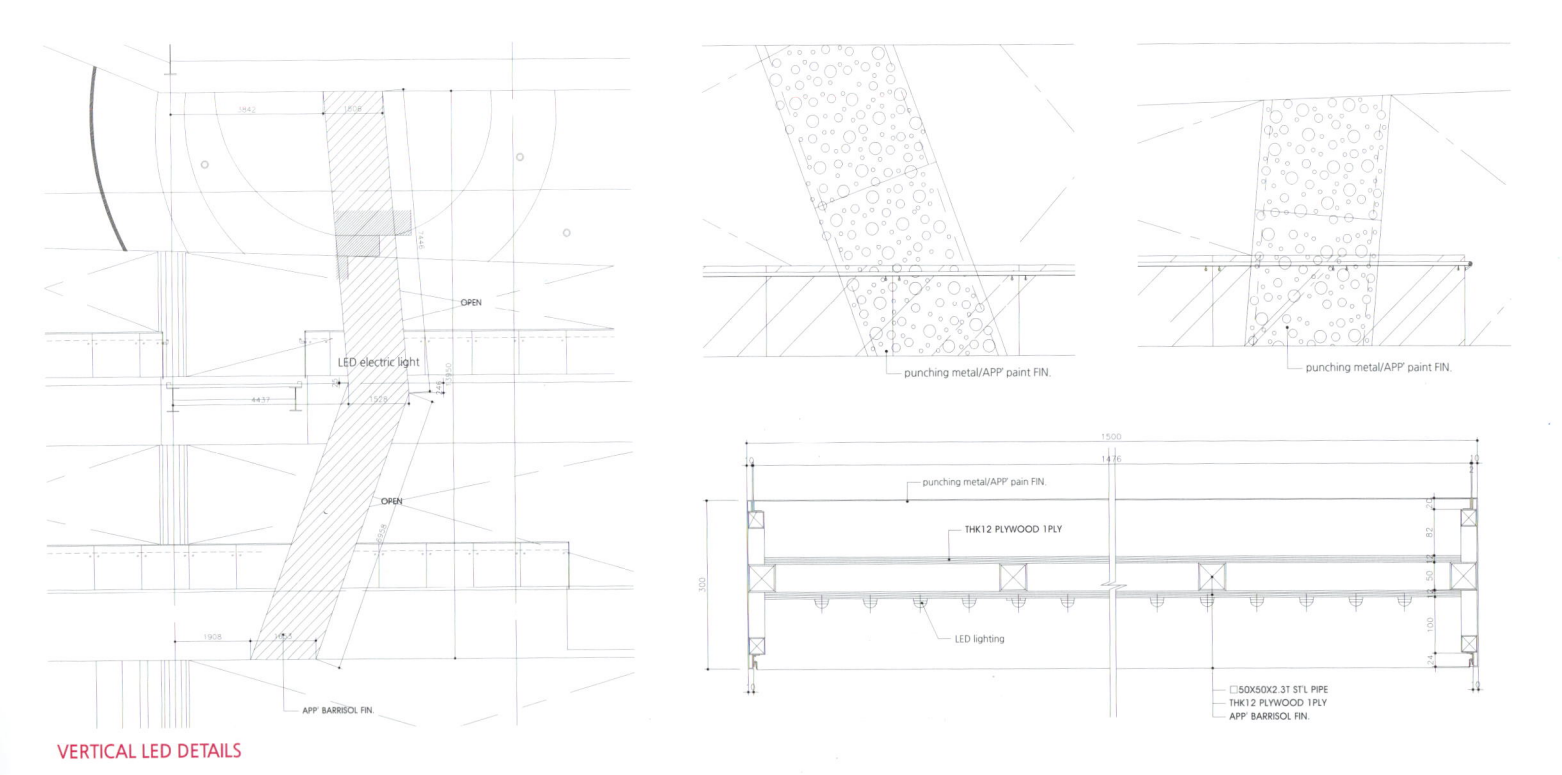

VERTICAL LED DETAILS

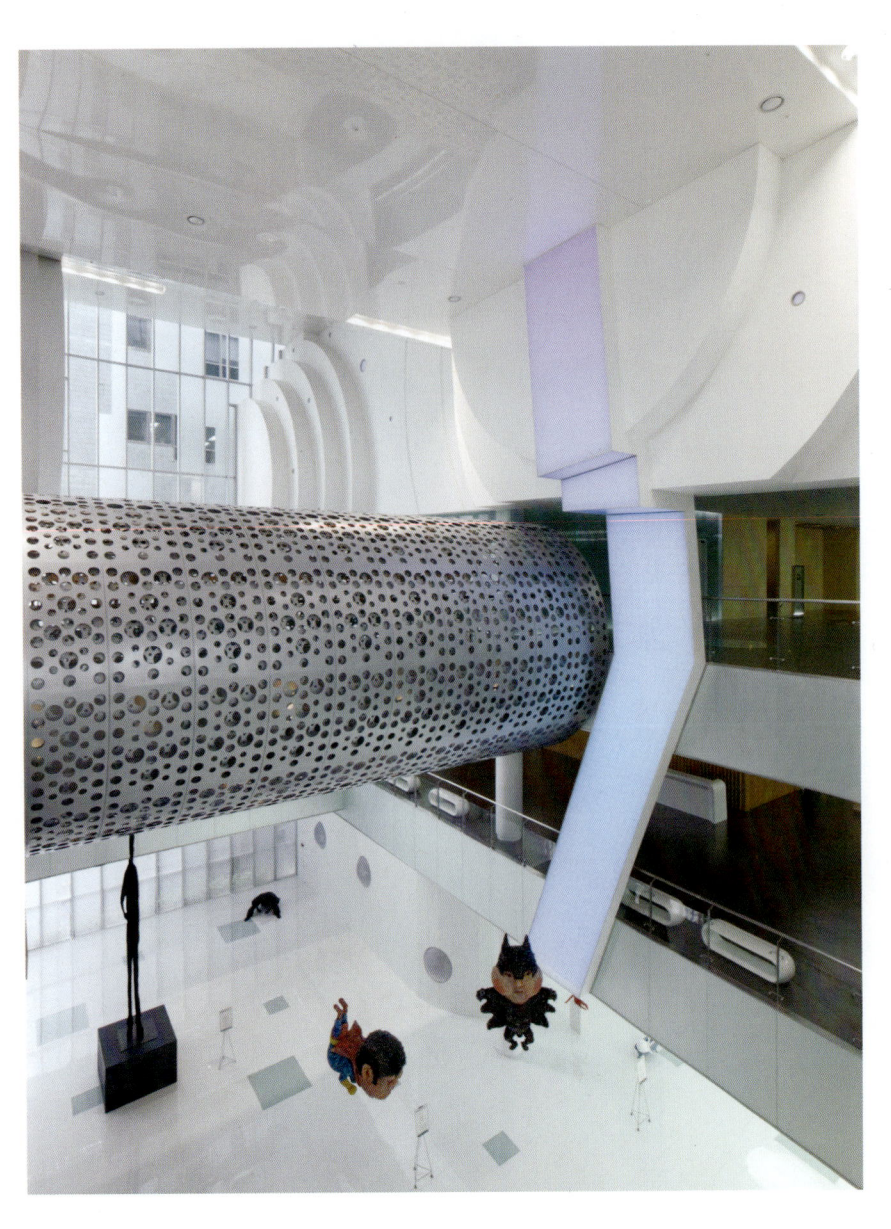

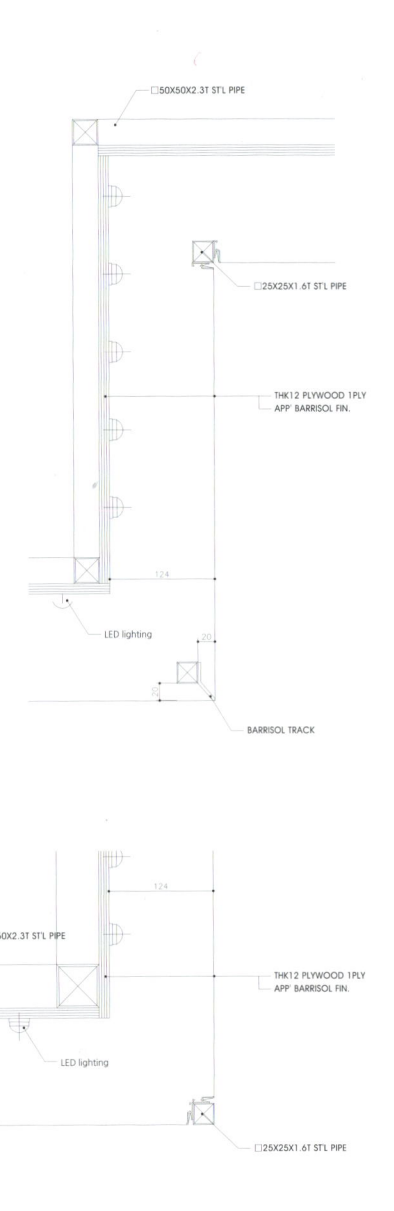

punching metal/APP' paint FIN.
punching metal/APP' paint FIN.
punching metal/APP' pain FIN.
THK12 PLYWOOD 1PLY
LED lighting
□50X50X2.3T ST'L PIPE
THK12 PLYWOOD 1PLY
APP' BARRISOL FIN.

LED electric light
OPEN
OPEN
APP' BARRISOL FIN.

□50X50X2.3T ST'L PIPE
□25X25X1.6T ST'L PIPE
THK12 PLYWOOD 1PLY
APP' BARRISOL FIN.
LED lighting
BARRISOL TRACK

□50X50X2.3T ST'L PIPE
THK12 PLYWOOD 1PLY
APP' BARRISOL FIN.
LED lighting
□25X25X1.6T ST'L PIPE

COMPOUND BODY 91

INTERIOR WALL DETAILS

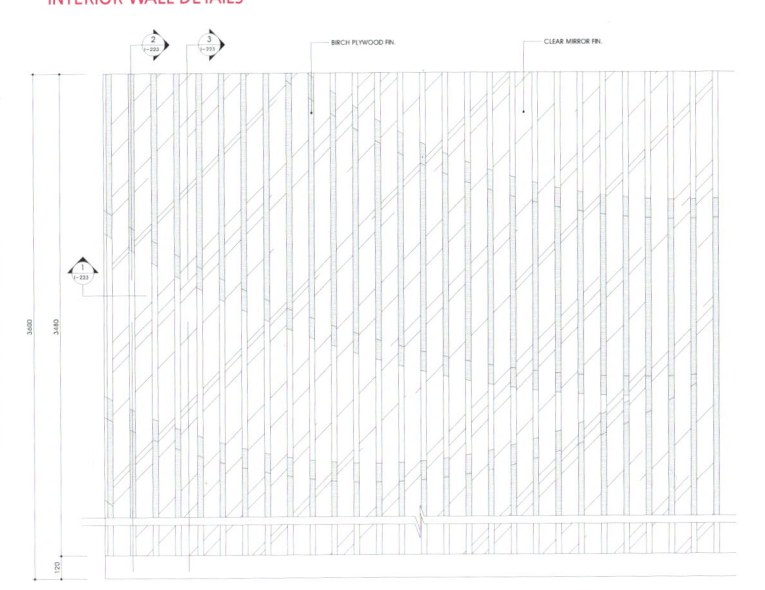

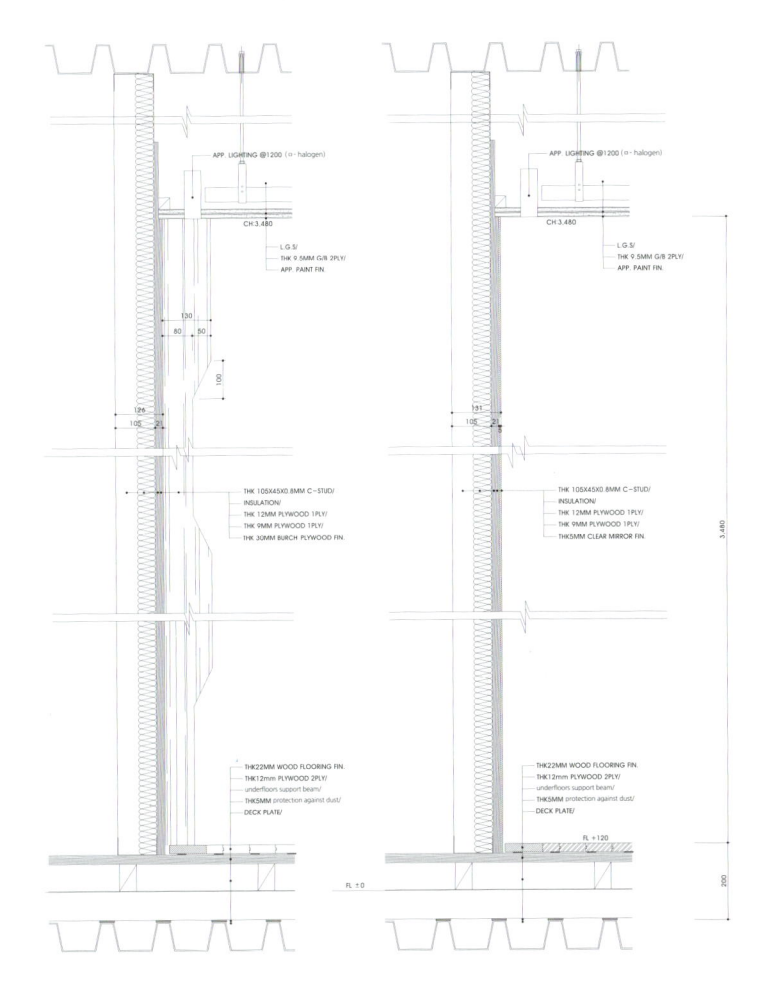

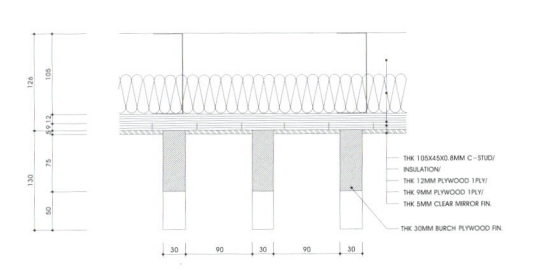

Gallery YEH

Making
urban campus

Architectural Review commended award
Architecture Record Vangauard Award
Award of Korean Architects Institute
Architecture Award of Seoul Metropolitan City
Award of Korean Architecture & Culture

Architects Jang Yoon Gyoo, Shin Chang Hoon, Kim Youn Soo
Client Gallery YEH
Photographer Kim Yong Kwan

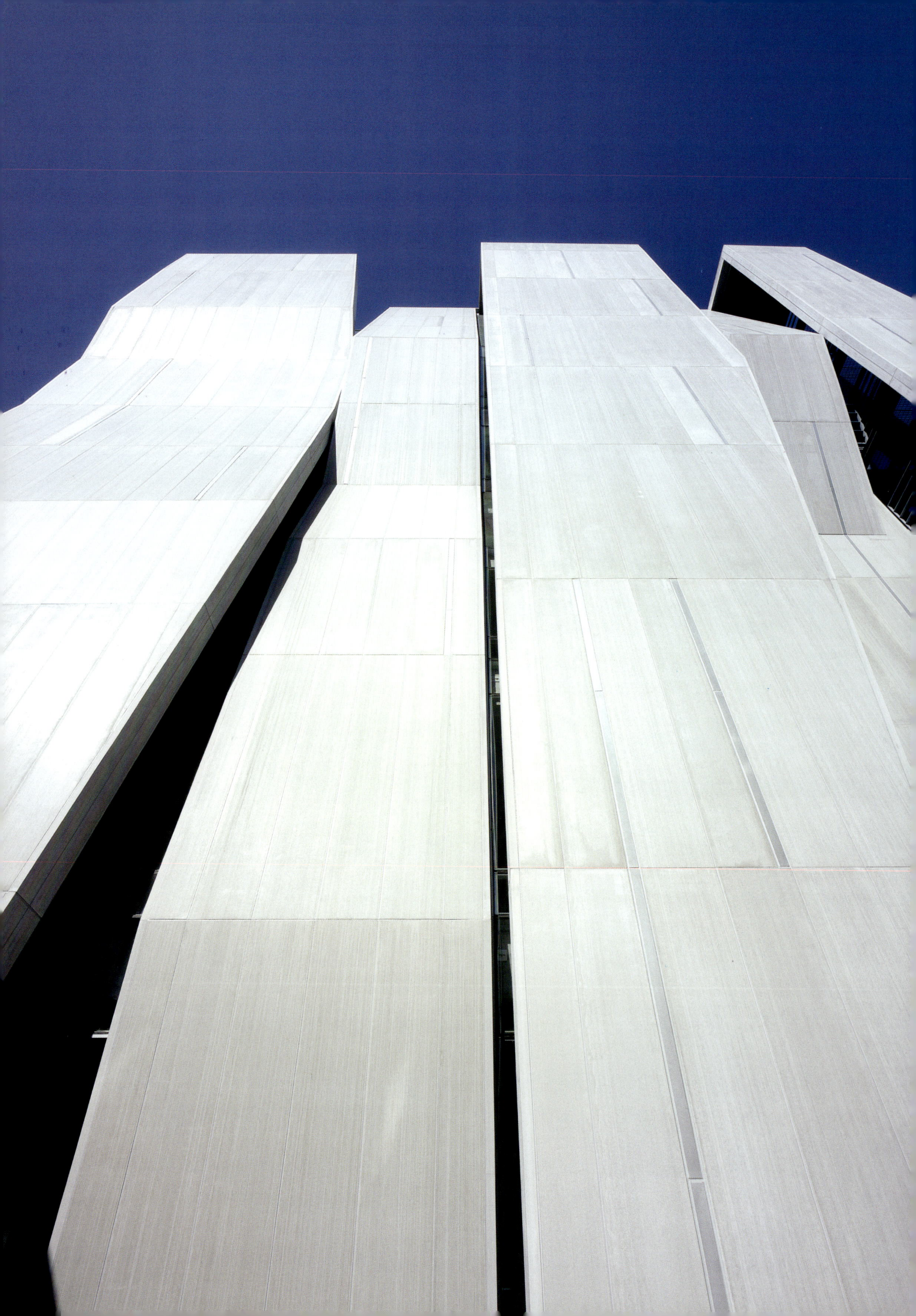

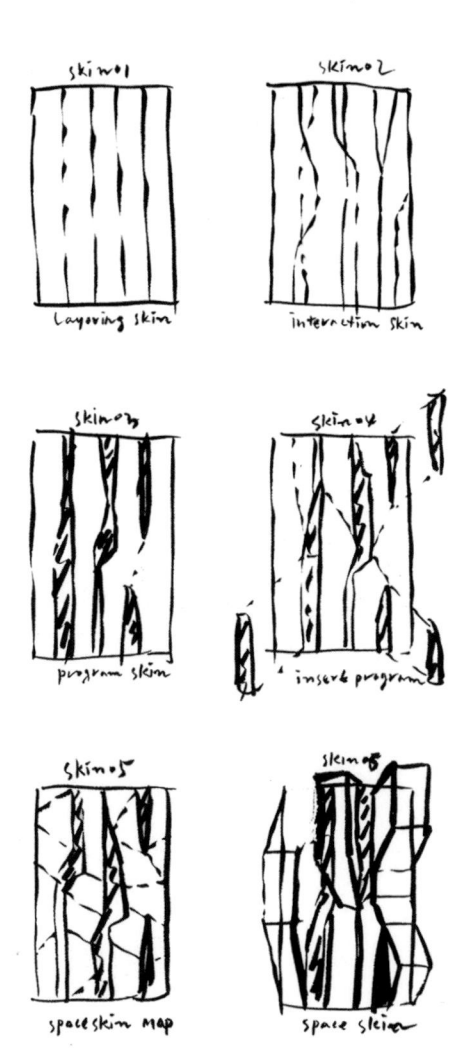

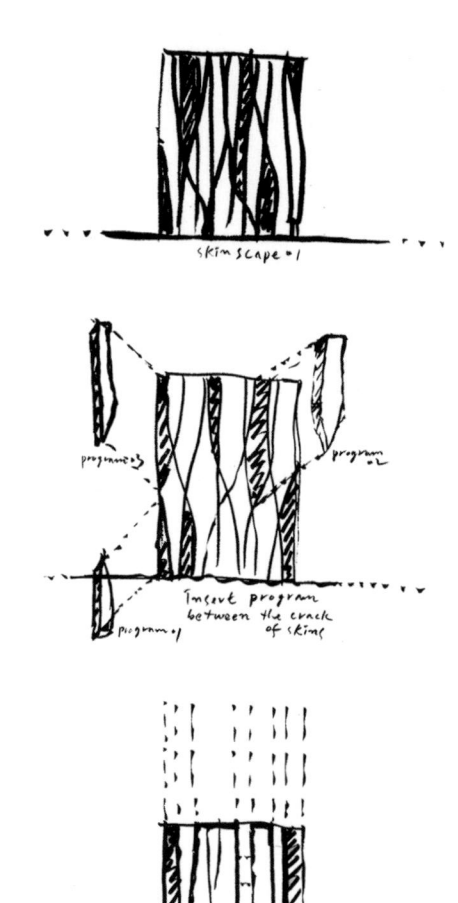

MAKING URBAN CANVAS

Enormous urban ⟨canvas⟩ has been attempted through the project ⟨Gallery Yeh⟩. ⟨Canvas⟩ is the wall of the building as well as a piece of experimental artwork that indicates a sign of the upcoming change of the new gallery. If typical canvas can be thought as two-dimensional medium, the canvas we have developed for the gallery is the spatial skin developed out of the new code found between the floor plan and the three-dimensional medium. Two-dimensional aspects of the wall have now become the opportunity to deform into space. Such work is similar to searching for the new generation of space out of structure between the folded and smooth, continuous skin. ⟨Spatial skin of the fold⟩ indicates the process of generating multiple layers hidden behind the single layer of the architectural skin. Skinscape can be initiated by simply acknowledging urban fabric as rather the envelope structure. Looking at the city as an enormous folded surface, continuous and sequential.

⟨Skinscape⟩ can be said an experimental text attempted by combining the architectural skin and the loose meaning of the term ⟨scape⟩. It is organized through the formula of skin plus other elements and layers as variable? skin plus structure, skin plus space, skin plus program… and etc. Then we can imagine its physical deformation. Process of finding the new spatial model is closely linked with ⟨Skinscape⟩, with its variables possible to be maximized by removing the excessive spatial elements or adding up more spatial 'fat'.

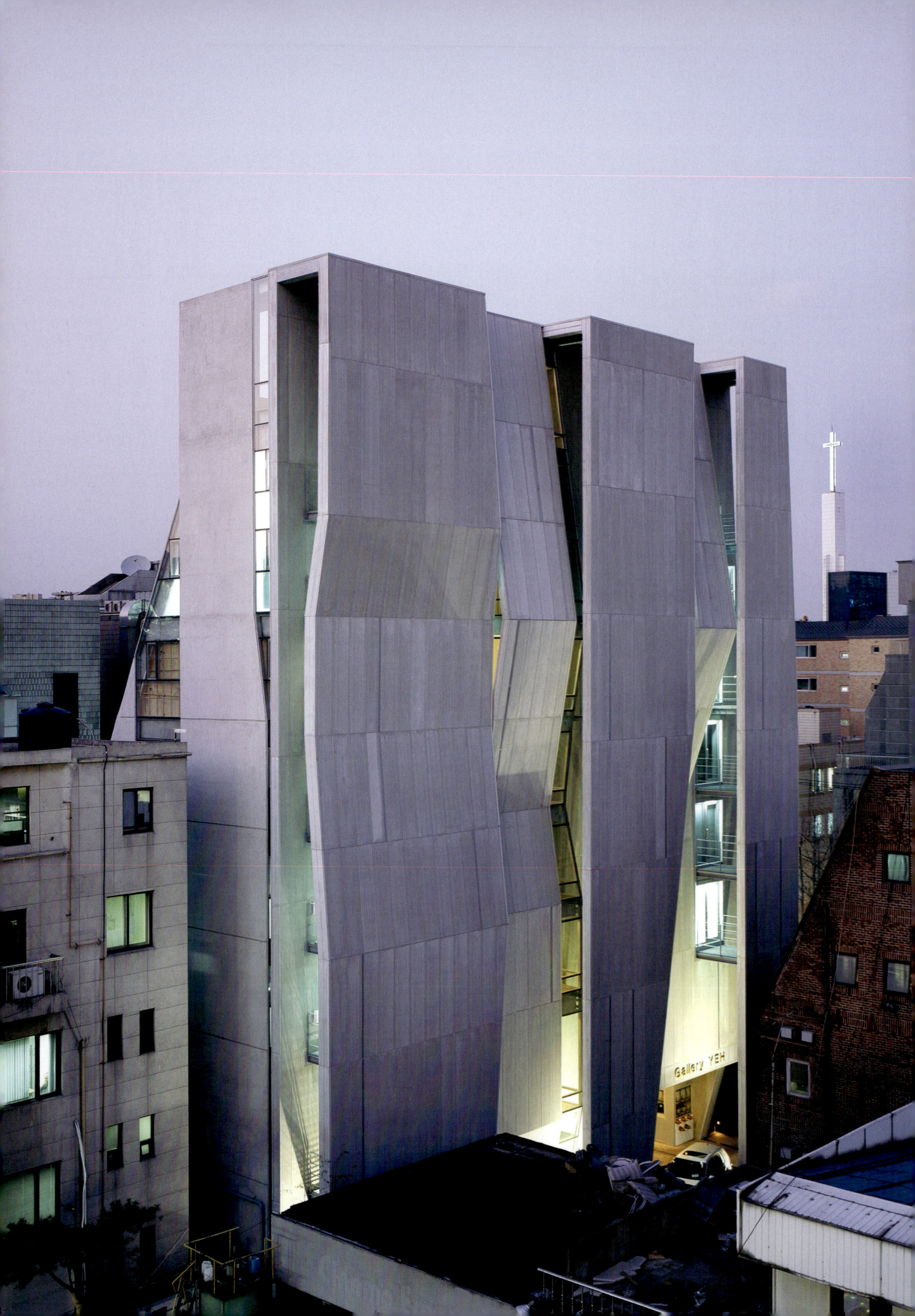
Gallery YEH

Architects
Jang Yoon Gyoo, Shin Chang Hoon, Kim Youn Soo
Location
SinsaDong, GangNam, Seoul
Use Mixed - use facility
Site Area 567.5m²
Gross Floor Area 1,995.14m²
Building Coverage Ratio 58.62%
Bldg. Scale
Two stories bellow ground / Seven stories above ground
Structure R.C
Exterior Finishing
T50 base panel, Exposed concrete, T24 transparent pair grass
Interior Finishing
Epoxy coating, Base panel. Exposed concrete
Client Gallery YEH (www.galleryyeh.com)
Construction
GuJin Industrial Development Co.Ltd

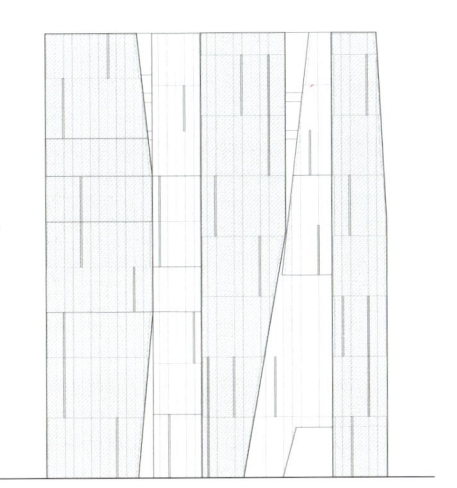

SOUTH ELEVATION

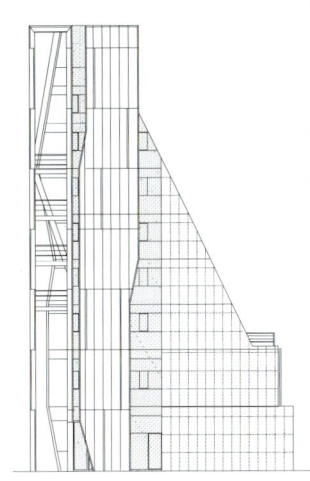

EAST ELEVATION

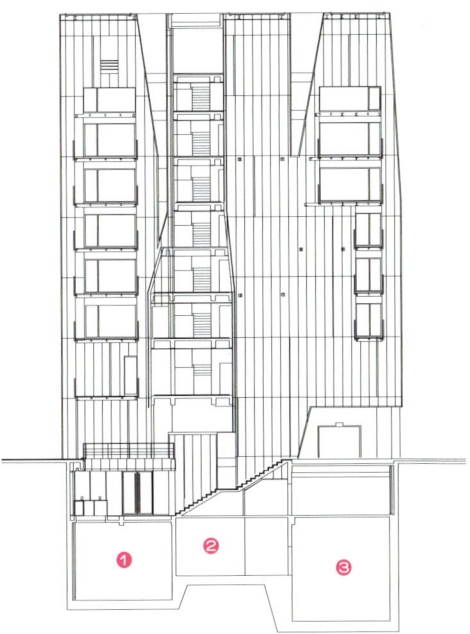

SECTION A
1. Electrical
2. Storage
3. Parking

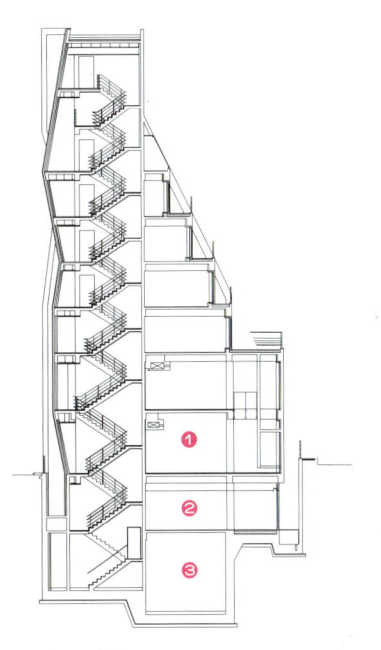

SECTION B
1. Exhibition
2. Cafeteria

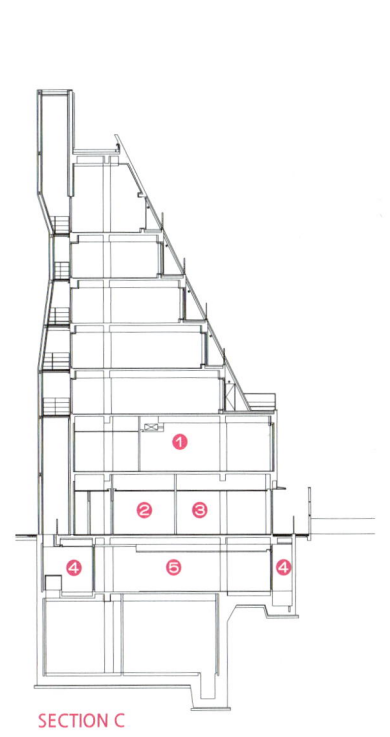

SECTION C
1. Exhibition
2. Information
3. Principal's Office
4. Sunken
5. Cafeteria

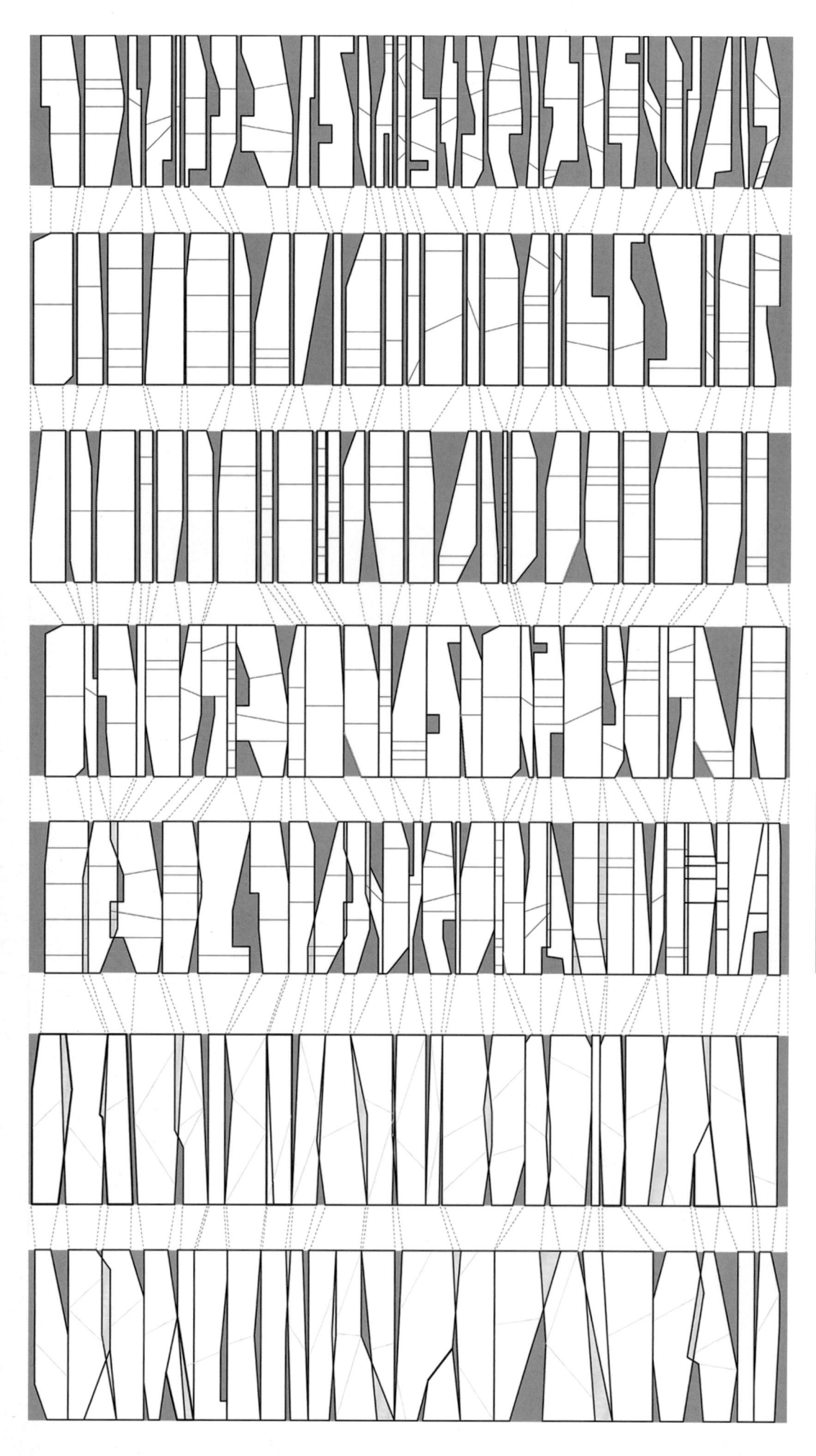

The concept applied in <Gallery Yeh> can be categorized as <Spatialization of Skin> and/or <Mediazation of Skin> - screen for the skinscape can be the medium to provide exhibit information as well as the huge canvas attracting outside events. Space for the skinscape offers unique spatial experience of puncturing through multiple layers of skin, in which each of its layers come as different spatial quality. <Spatial Surfing>, <Skin Surfing>, <Pictorial Surfing>, <Organizational Surfing>, ··· are some of the codes appearing along such experience, while each surfing twists and intertwines to create spatial complexity as a whole.
Like <Crack of Armor>, skin is not the surface that envelopes the space, but is bound by air that is light material and metaphorical interpretation and irony behind the new possibilities of space. The framework of heaviness is gained through the lightness, the quality of the skin is linked with the possibilities of creating gaps, so thus the space become enriching experience of discovering the hidden layers of logic and irony.

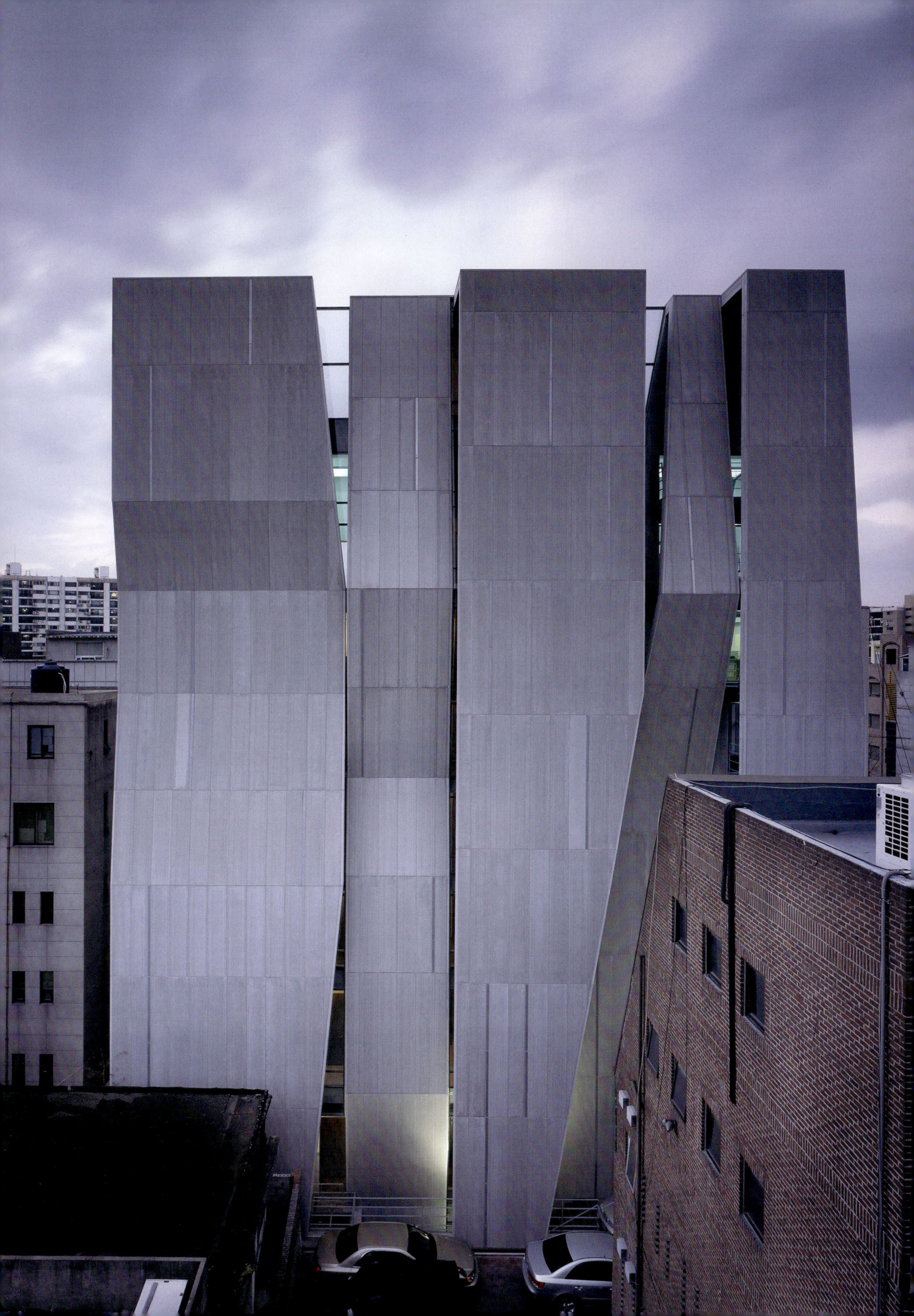

100

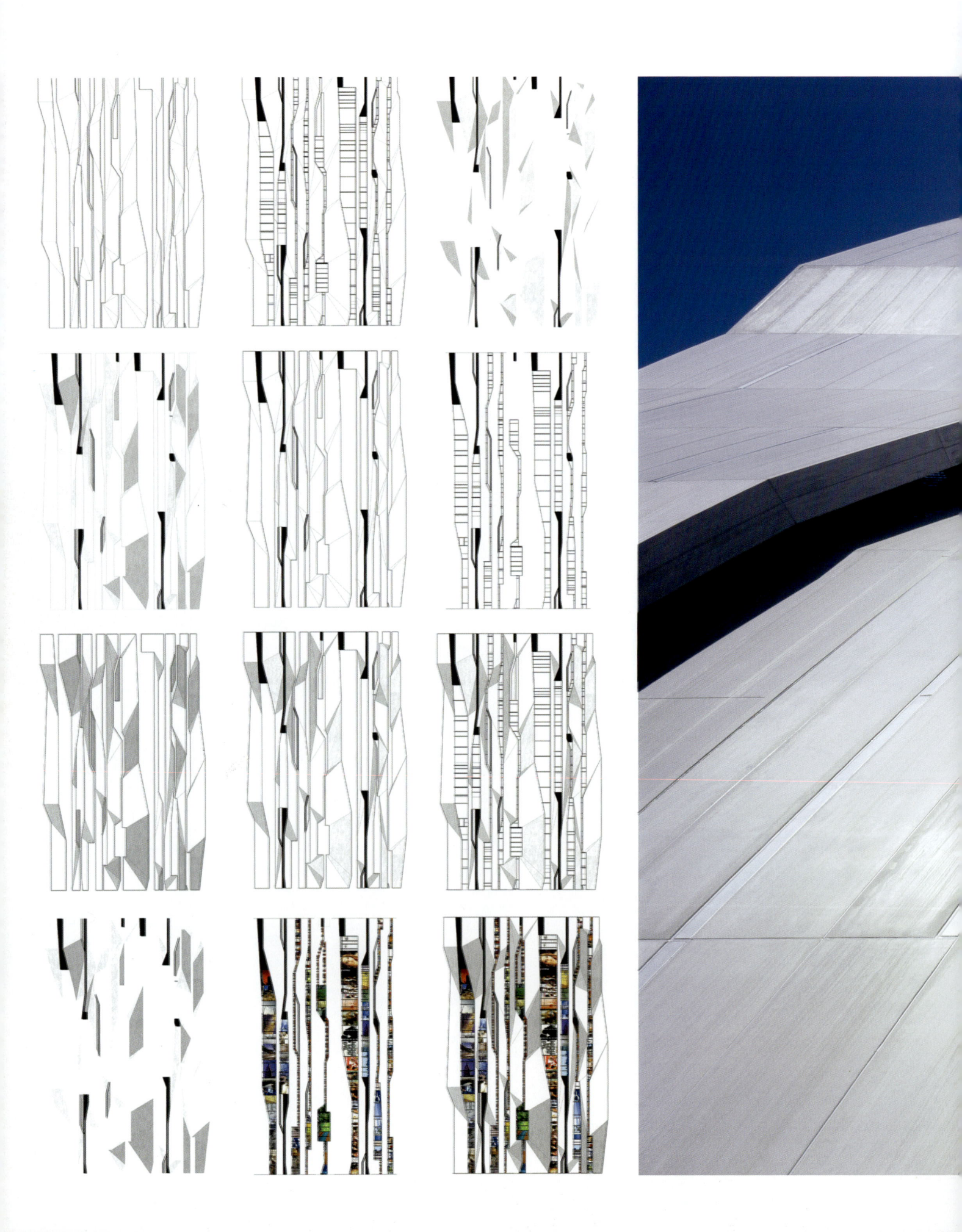

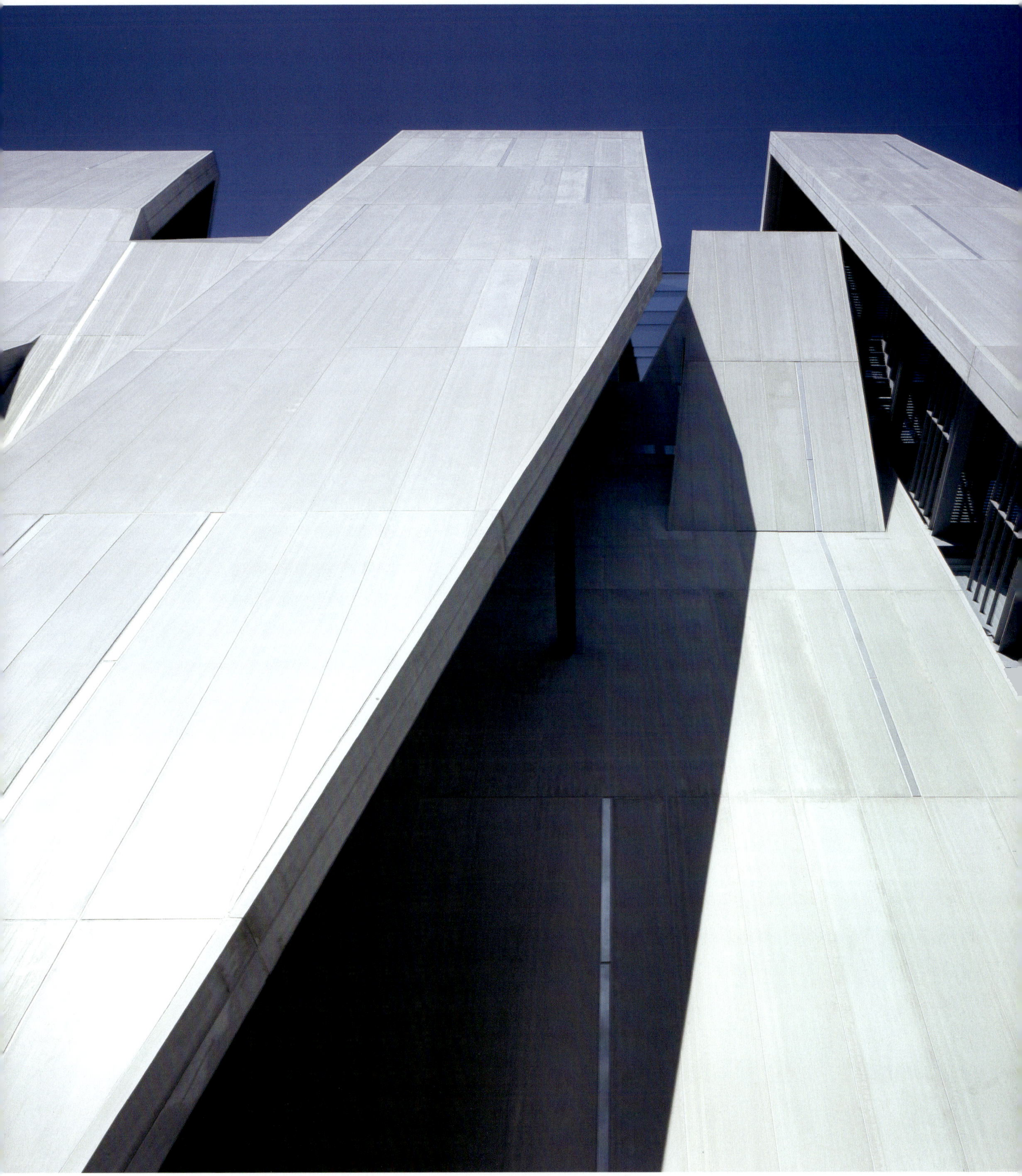

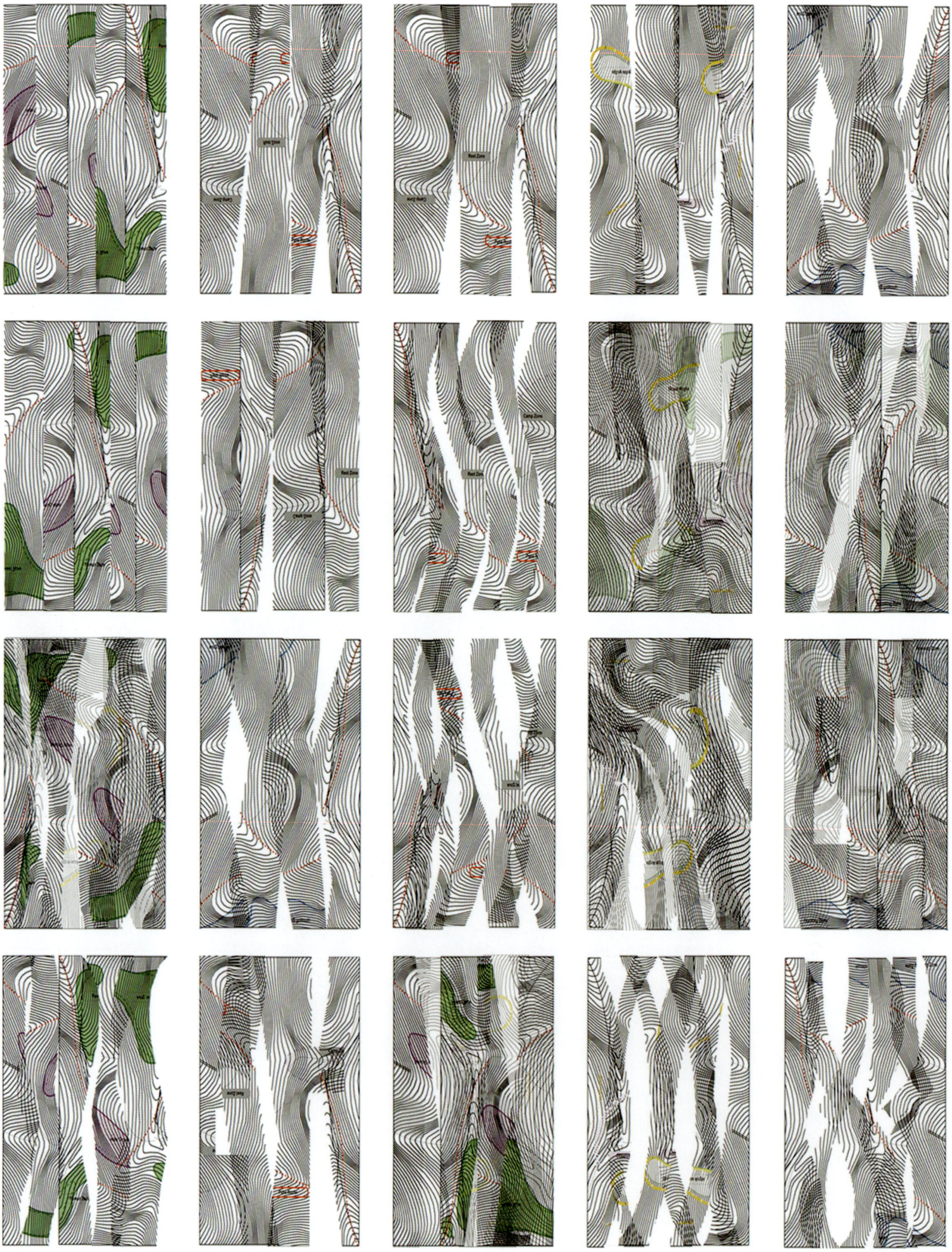

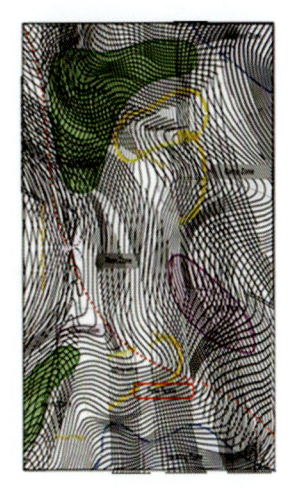

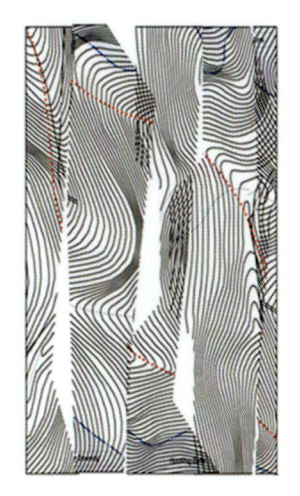

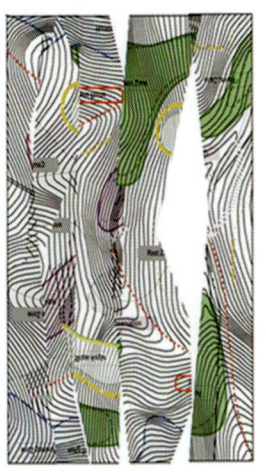

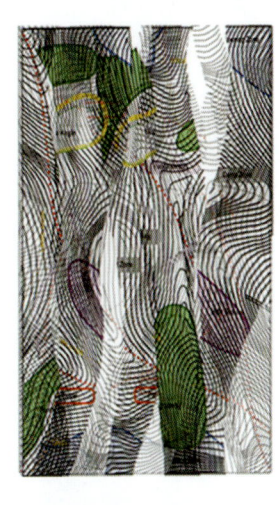

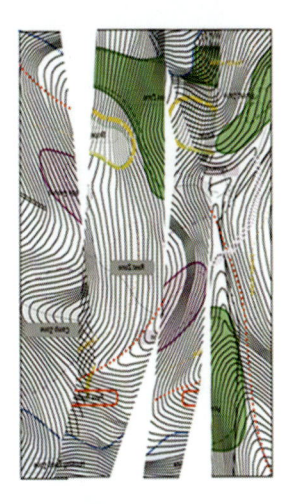

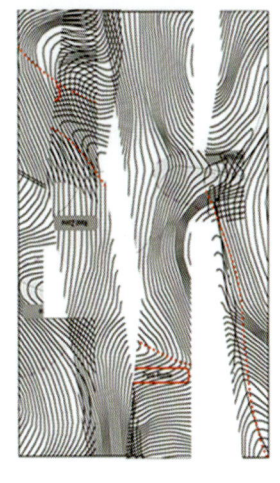

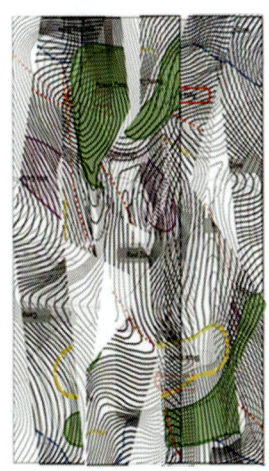

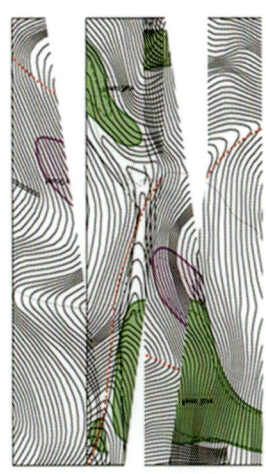

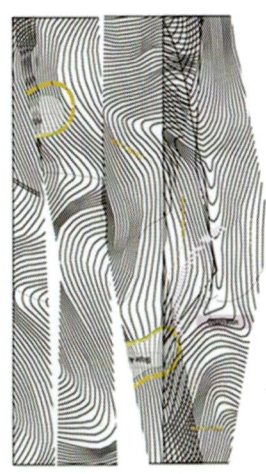

FASSADENRAUM
text Mathias Remmele

Unsangdong Architects is established in 2001 by architects, YoonGyu Jang and ChangHoon Shin. They are the only architects who haven't left Korea for any purpose, job or study. Nevertheless, they claim their concept as a part of avant-garde which is international architectural trends. They are distinguished not only their buildings but also displaying design, architectural thesis and gallerist.

On the southern part of Seoul divided by Hanriver, GangNam-gu which is the most important commercial center today is situated. Along the wide road, high-raised business building, huge hotel and shopping mall are embraced on one side. On the other hand, narrow and heterogeneous pathways have chic boutique, furniture store, gallery, restaurant, coffee shop and karaoke bar. Moreover, because of the centricity, it is also loved as residential place- and also expensive with same reason. On the one narrow pathway in GangNam, 7 stories building which is vividly distinguished with surrounding buildings stands attracting by bizarre elegant appearance like impressive sculpture. Main facade is consisted of 5 vertical concrete structures irregularly composed. These are separated by linear crack. The facade structures which fall down vertically waving front and back give unique dynamics even though they seem to be heavy and massive. Something is veiled behind of these linearly cracked and dynamic concrete bars. Approach starts from narrow side, and then Facade structure goes to the front of main building. And a type of long fireplace is revealed between them. Big signboard written >>Yeh Gallery<< lets know that the main usage of this building is art gallery. It is the first step explaining unfamiliar spatial sense.

// Skinscape can be initiated by simply acknowledging urban fabric as rather the envelope structure. Looking at the city as an enormous folded surface, continuous and sequential.

Gallery YEH

Spatialization of skin

Unsangdong Architects finished business building in 2006 asked by Yeh gallery and 2 stories are used as gallery. The design of building starts from point which is related and close to culture and art. And architects themselves do artists' work and it contributes to find out contacting point with contemporary art. They have run gallery JungMiSo which is specialized in experimental and conceptual art since 2003.

They want the facade of Yeh gallery to be comprehended as one of art, urban canvas, sensational screen and experimental art piece. This intension becomes a base of concept and Unsangdong Architects name it Spatialization of Skin. According as they regard designing building as consumable process, it is also called as Skin plus Structure, Skin plus Room and Skin plus Program..

Most important figurative motive is fold. Their aim which they want to achieve with fold is creating new generation of space and more.

···And its realization

How are spatial and functional load of skin accomplished successfully. Accurate view of the space behind facade structure is realized it. Inner space is embraced in that empty space. Because of the structure crossing through the empty space.

By this way, linear crack of facade structure provides a view of empty inner spcae and surround it. This spatial permission makes small projected balcony possible above 3rd floor. However, there is a different view for the quality of facade room. Visitors get less intensive and imaginative impression an it is only small space for short smoking break.

Overall prospect from building is unique and spectacle. But inside of facade zone is dark and nar-

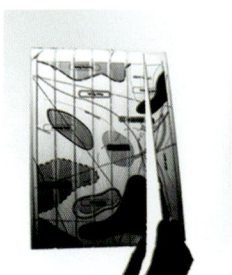

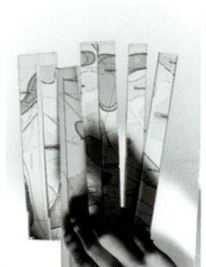

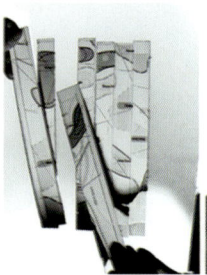

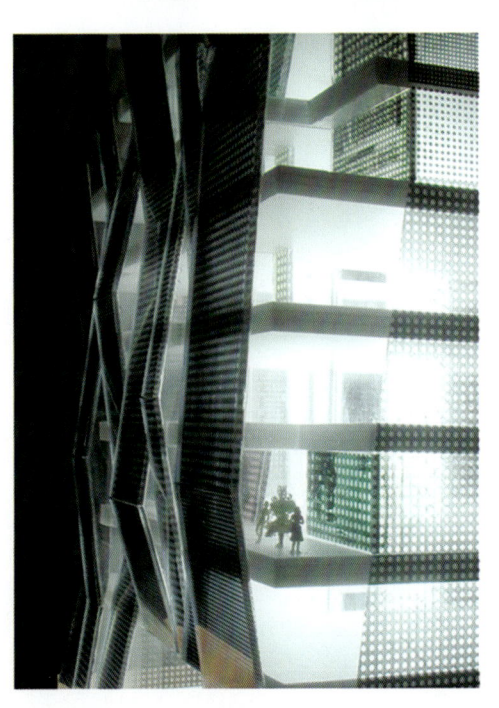

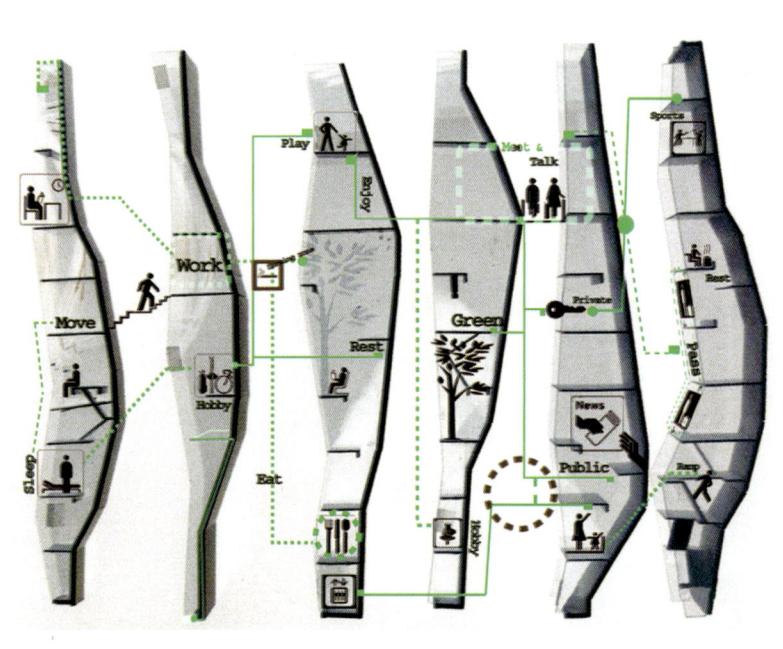

// skinscape can be the medium to provide exhibit information as well as the huge canvas attracting outside events.

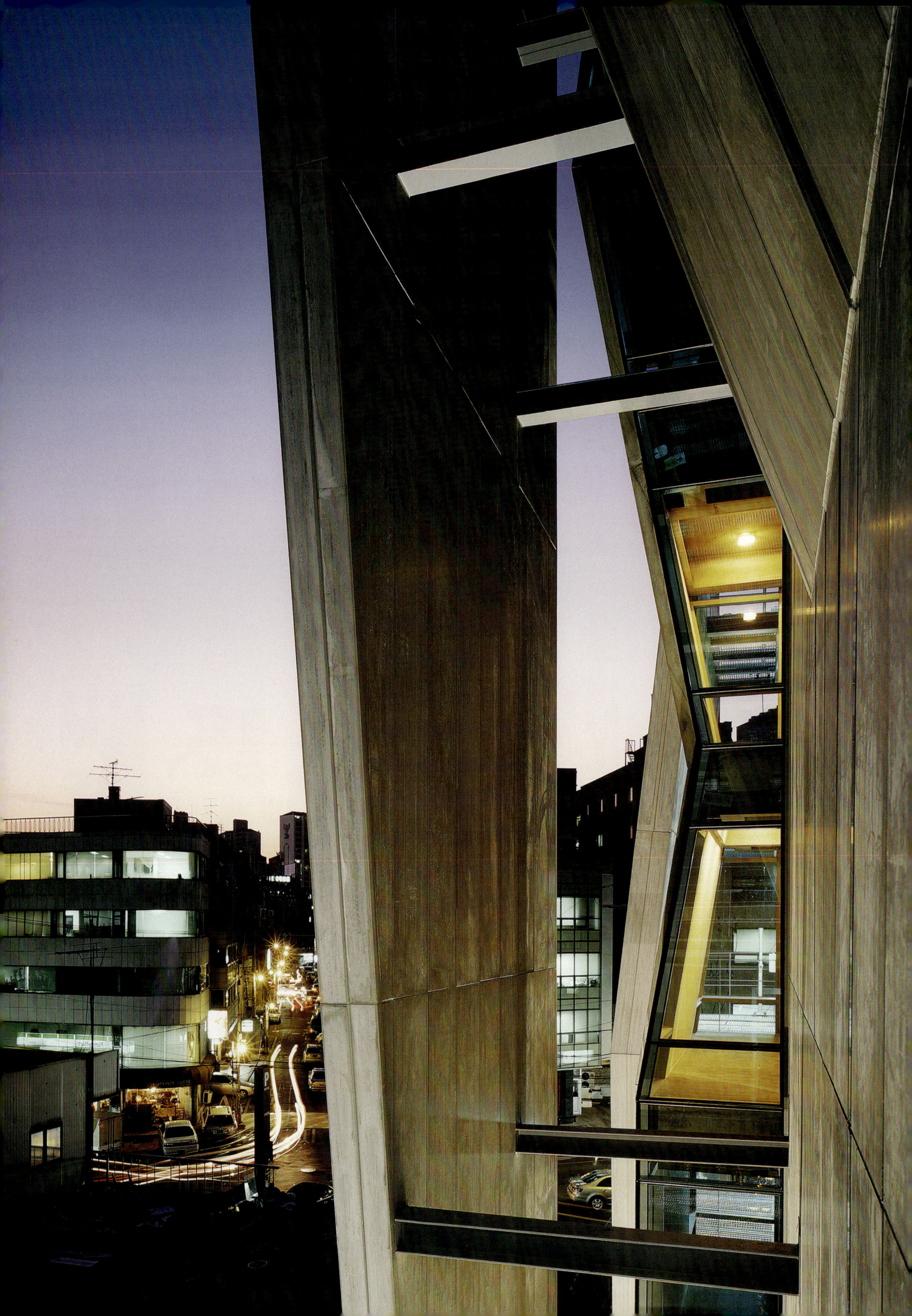

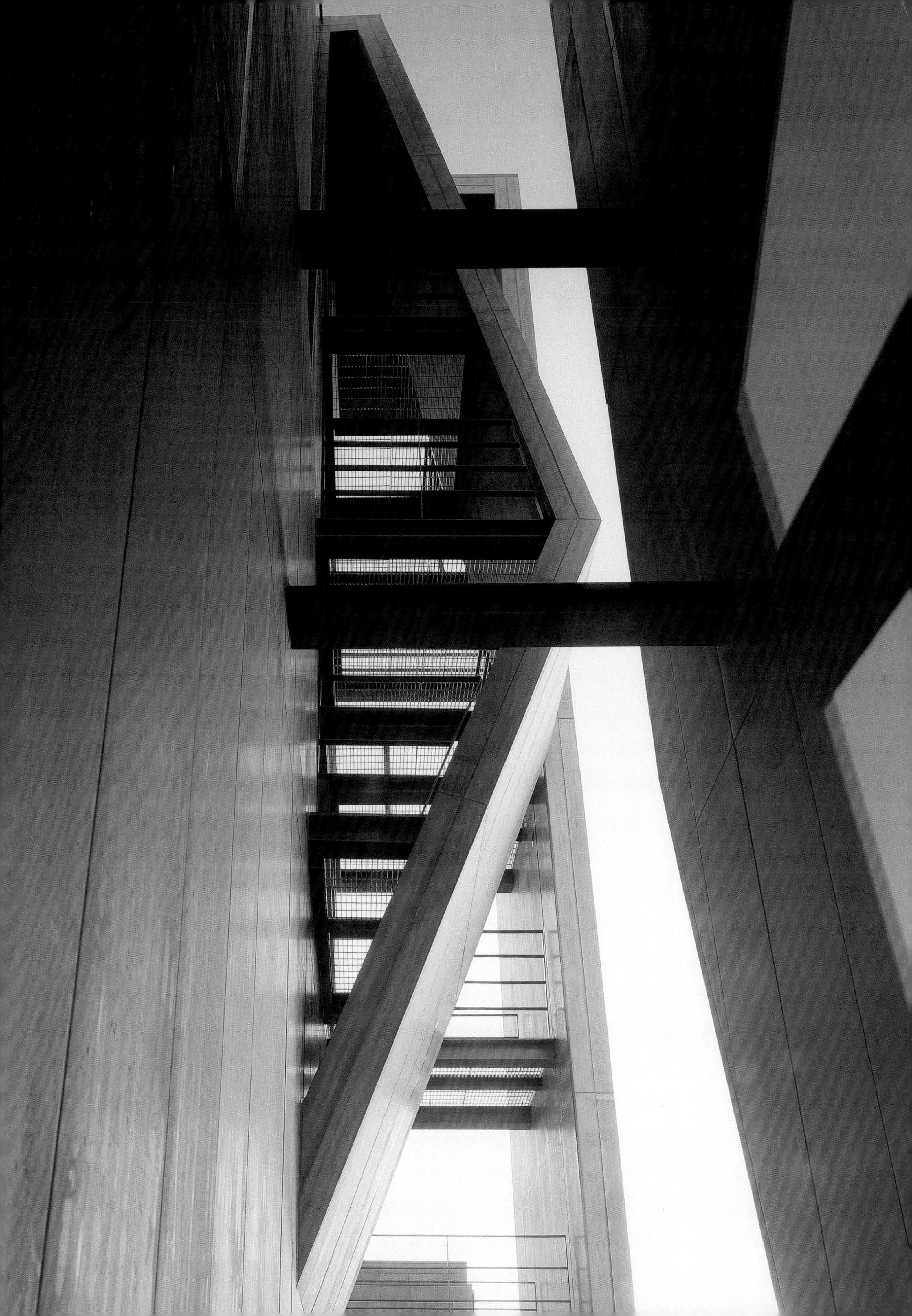

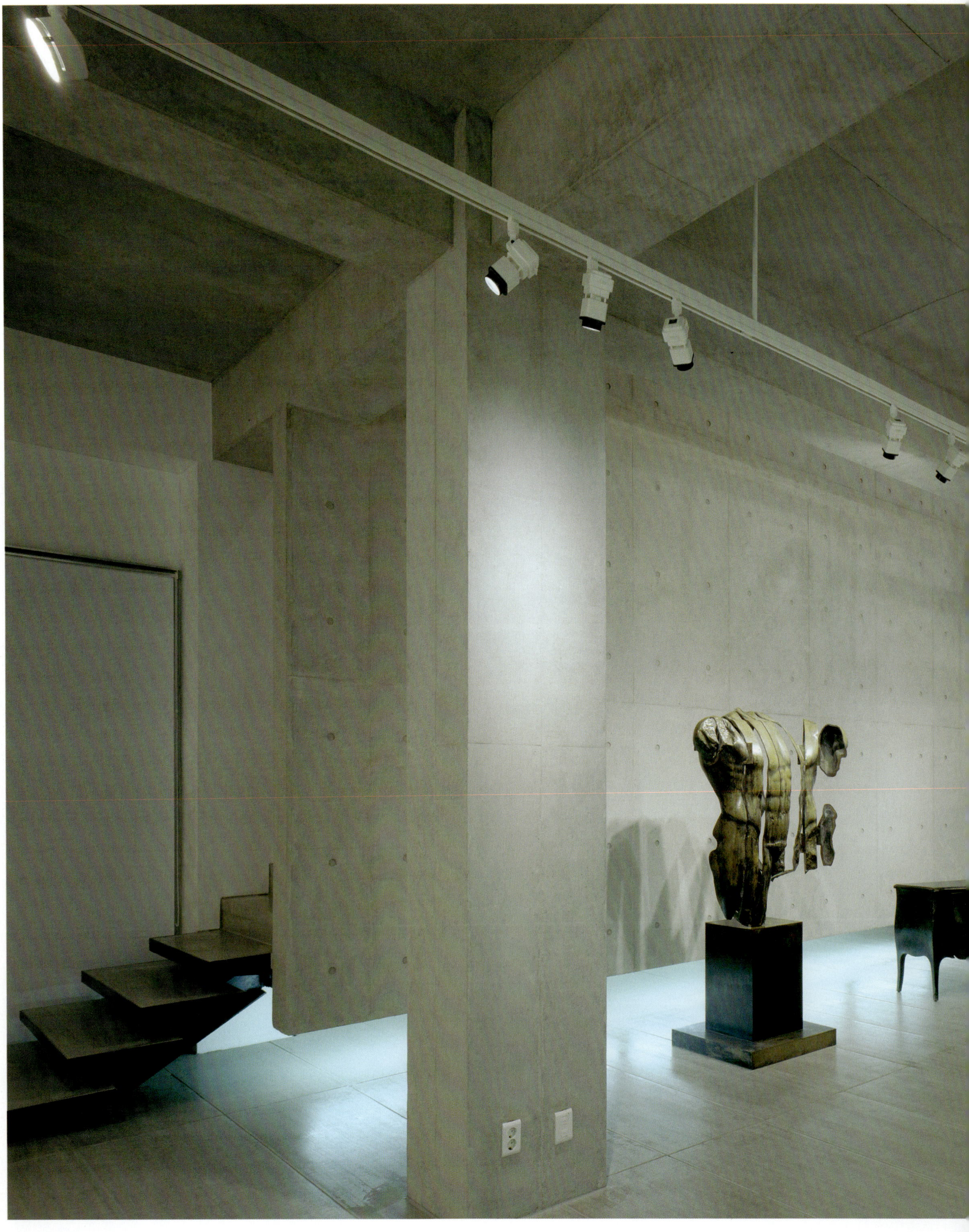

COMPOUND BODY 109

row, so it is harder to feel stability as time goes by. It is not improved in even their aesthetic effect. When visitors pass by middle zone arousing their curiosity entering the building, their sight goes up to upper space like smoke sucked into chimney from fireplace. There is a question for our imagination about what facade is and something challenging existing spatial experience.

Inner space of building is less bizarre than facade area. 1st floor and 2nd floor are used as the landlord's cultural gallery. The height of exhibition area is higher than the other floor and is connected through inner stair case. Inner structure is simple. Concrete floor, white plaster wall and crossbeam-style ceiling made by fresh-concrete connecting beneath of air conditioning facility are composed. Floating fresh-concrete wall is eye catching factor hiding a stair which goes upstairs exhibition room.

3rd to 6th floor space is used as commerce and office. The area of sable space is getting smaller according as floor gets higher. And it goes with sharp shape towards upside. This impressive spatial use provides tall height of roof floor and wide sight for urban view.

A chronic problem of architecture which is based on polish concept is that constructed reality is hardly ever synchronized with theoretical and schematic ideal. However the benefit of architecture which is progressed on the concept is huge potentiality for numerous innovations on the plan. Yeh Gallery by Unsangdong Architects is an example belonging to both. A doubt about creating new generation of space is still remained. But as a space which shows huge aesthetic attraction, the fact that becomes origin of new and interesting facade with depth effect is worth of attention.

text **Mathias Remmele**

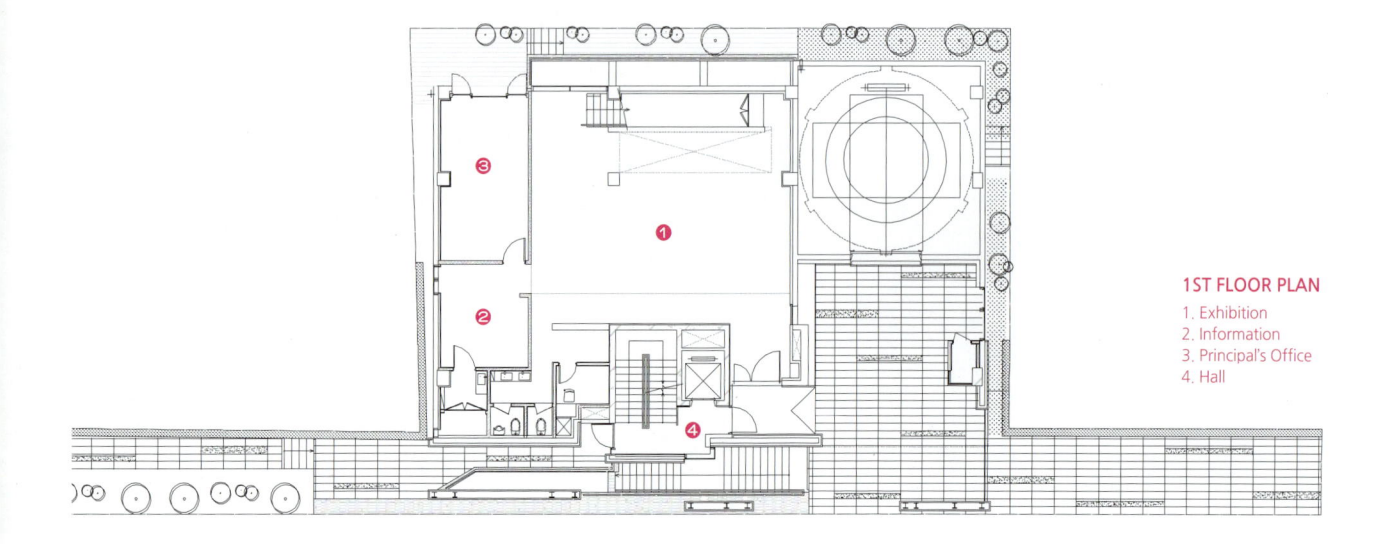

1ST FLOOR PLAN
1. Exhibition
2. Information
3. Principal's Office
4. Hall

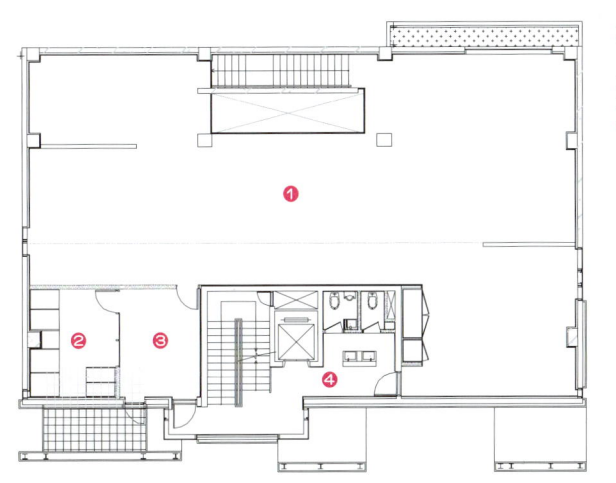

2ND FLOOR PLAN
1. Exhibition
2. Data Room
3. Office
4. Hall

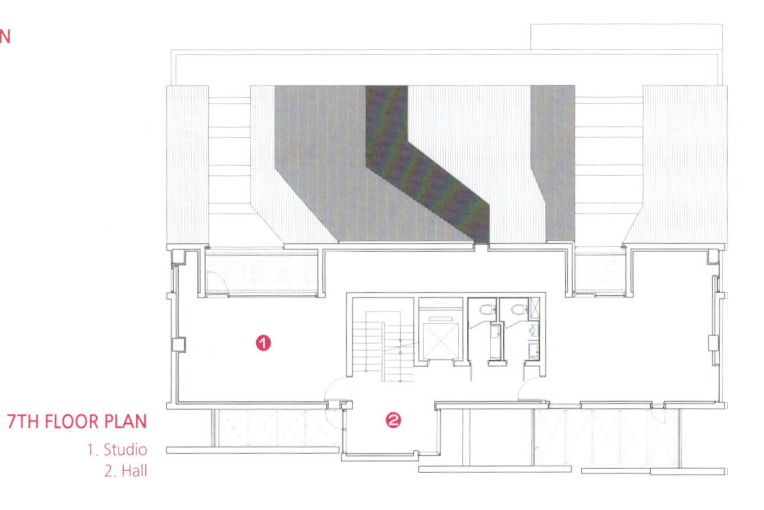

7TH FLOOR PLAN
1. Studio
2. Hall

SECTION DETAIL

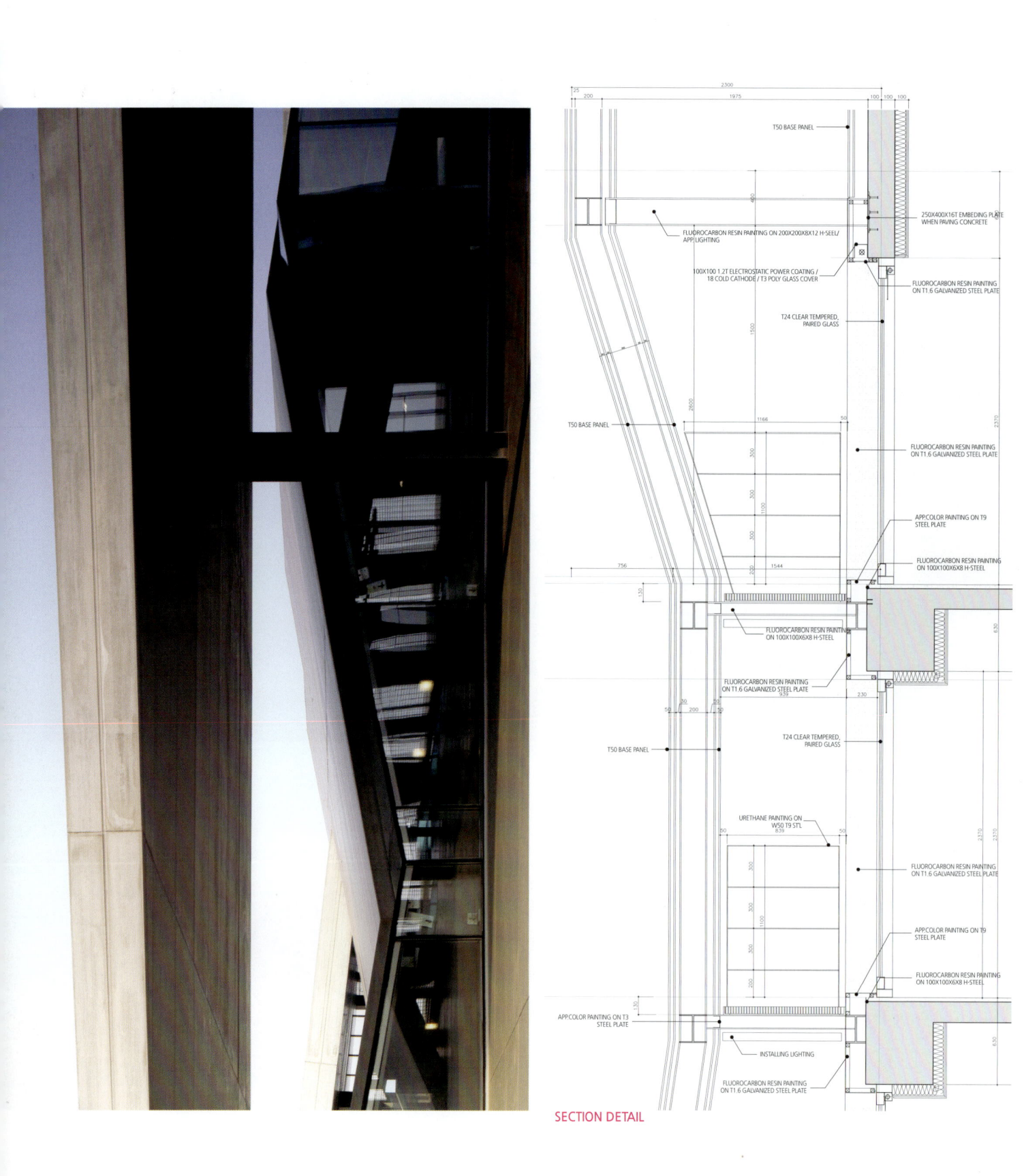

COMPOUND BODY 113

Yeosu Expo Thematic Pavillon

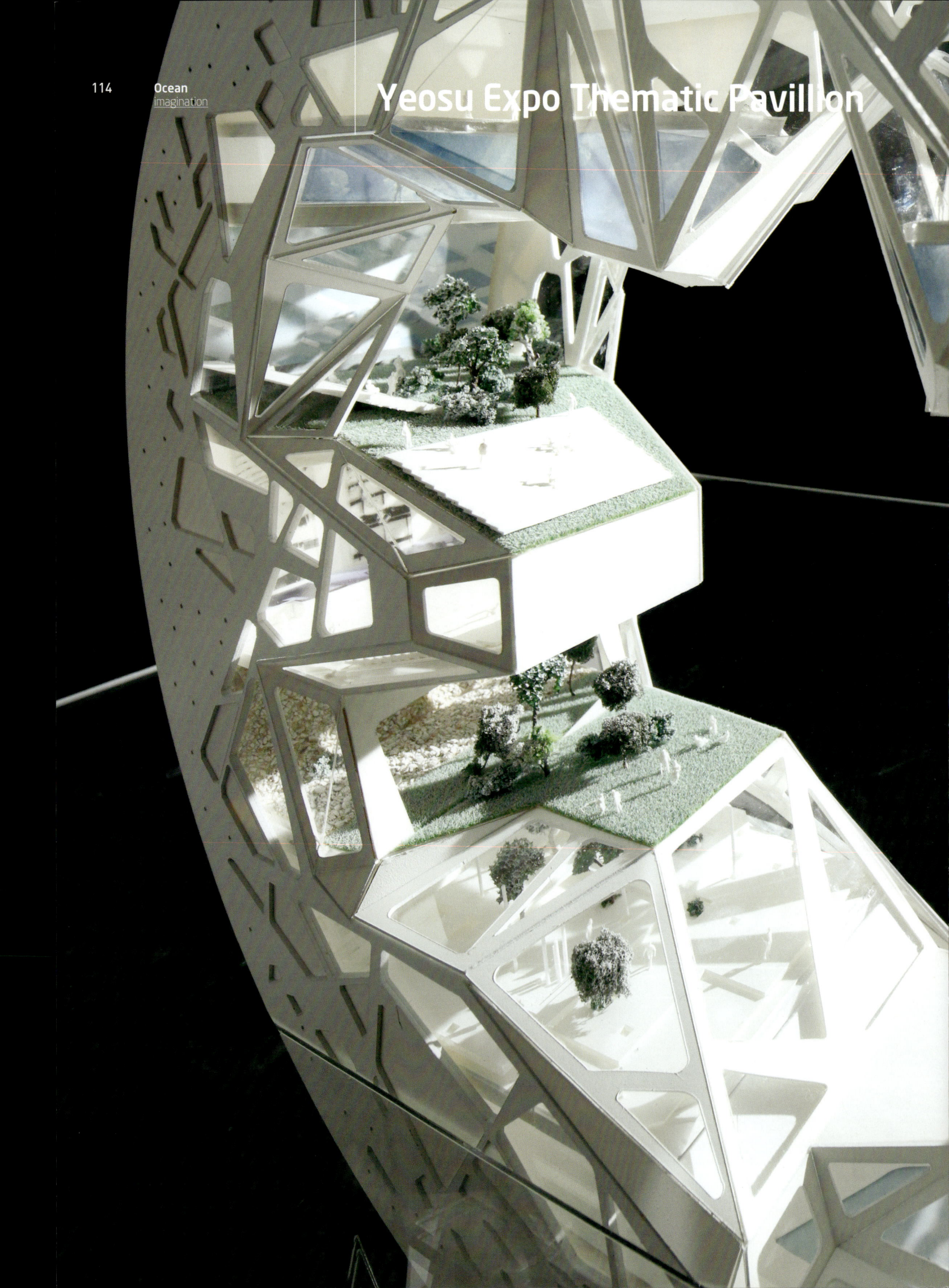

International Competition Honorable Prize

Architects Jang Yoon Gyoo, Shin Chang Hoon,
Kim Woo Young, Kim Bong Kyun, Kang Seong Hyun
Photographer Kim Jae Kyung

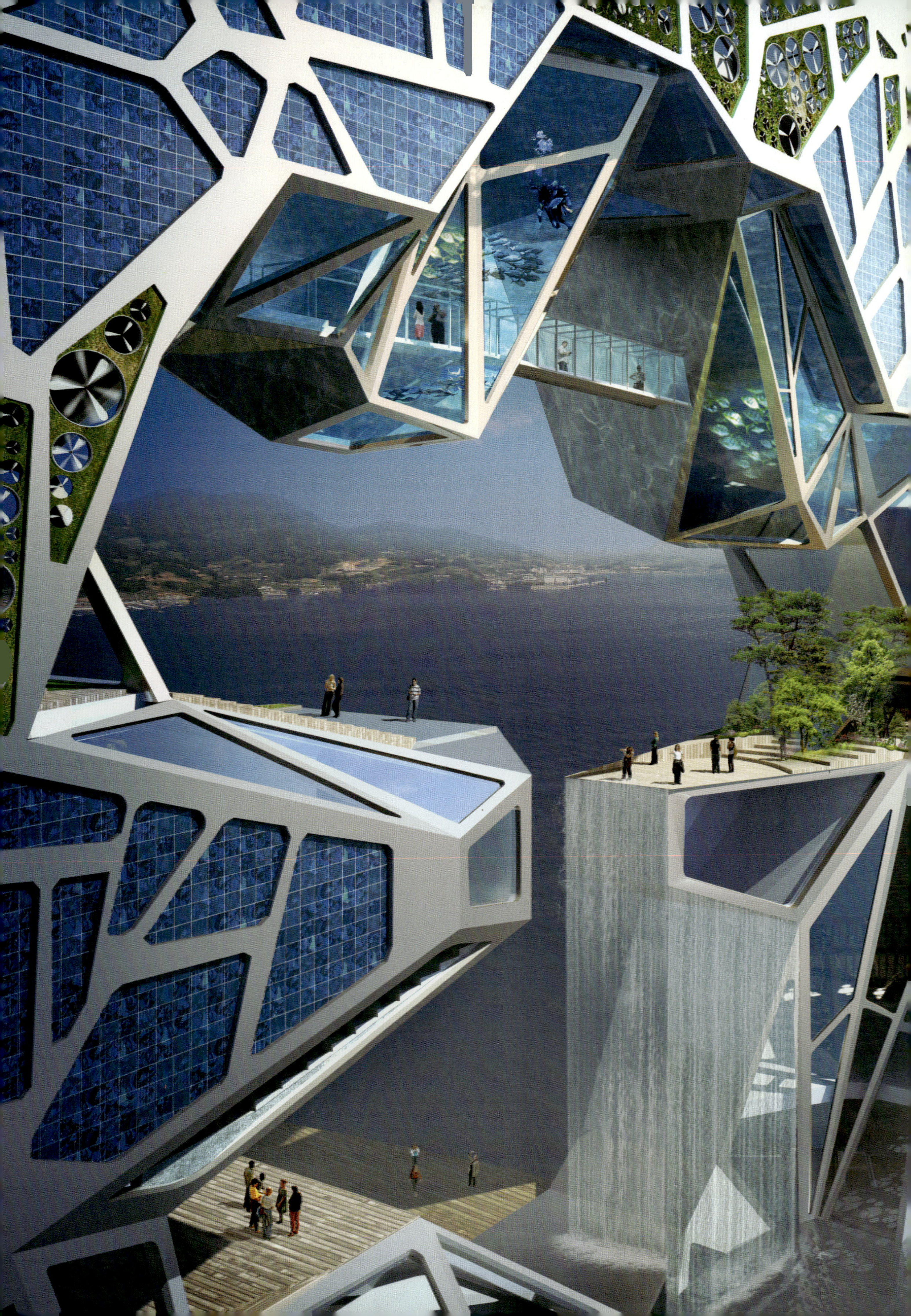

OCEAN IMAGINATION

Ocean and Imagination Compounds
Our emphasis is that by combining Ocean Nature and Imagination, we would make the best use of infinite possibility of nature. Having decided to show the exhibition space in a subtle way, we took rather unique way. We link the place, architecture and exhibition. We consider 'Ocean Eco Compounds' to realise the main theme of this exposition which consists of marine technology, architecture engineering, civil engineering, information technology and so on. We allow visitors experience ecosystem of the ocean and every kind of experience or exhibit which is related with the man-made nature in the Main exhibition area. 'Landscape-Architecture' i.e. architecture which is linked closely with landscape or Ecological-Architecture' are of far more importance. It is straight forward that we need to channel more support to sustainable structure when it comes to building up a new synthesis of architecture and nature.

SITE PLAN

OCEAN IMAGINATION

// Core Attraction _ Blue Eco-Polis
We set a place for festival of human being, ocean and technology.
We set up a path for pedestrian which is extension of breakwater.
It will take a role as a sort of a gallery which shows ocean exhibits in the Ocean exposition (Big O). Nonetheless, water was originally used as a horizontal component, Ocean Gate is cutting edge architecture which is vertical transformation of water. &Big O*, as core attractions for visitors, is connected with other exhibition facilities. There will be &Eco-void space* on the extension of main hallway of exhibition area. In accordance with the changes and event of the eco-void space, visitors would be able to understand the main theme of this exposition.

COMPOUND BODY 119

// Aqua area which was formed by access path becomes an 'Aqua Park' by displaying restored ocean. Aqua park looks different by tides. Visitors will enjoy the changing space, landscape element and Eco-sculptures as time passes.

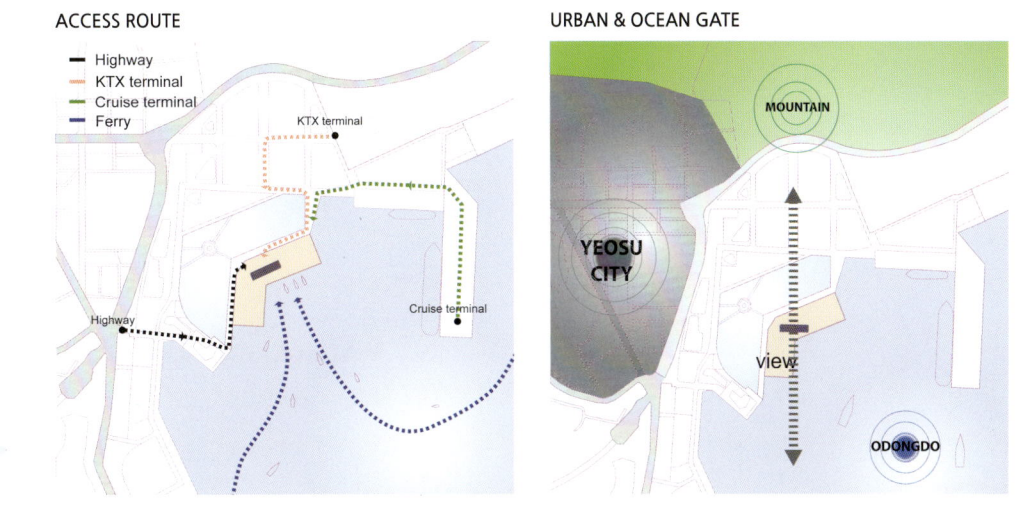

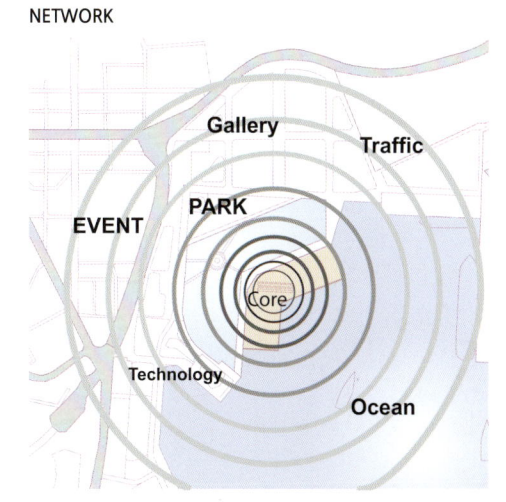

ACCESS ROUTE
- Highway
- KTX terminal
- Cruise terminal
- Ferry

URBAN & OCEAN GATE

NETWORK

Original Program

Inserting Eco Program

Theme Exhibition
BPA Exhibiion

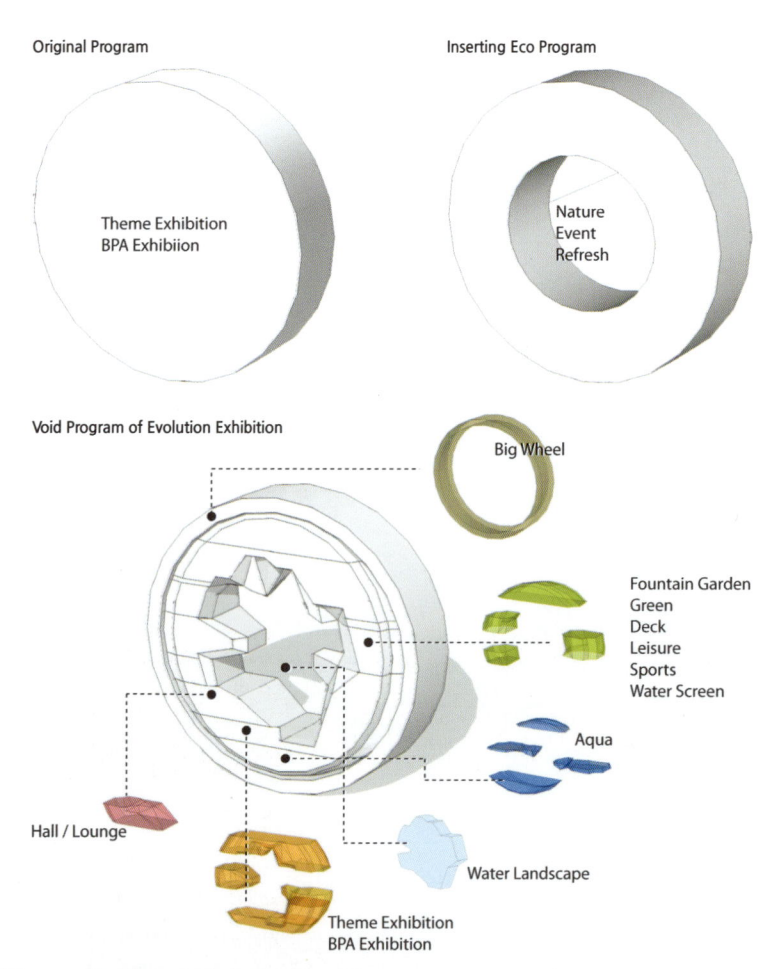

Nature
Event
Refresh

Void Program of Evolution Exhibition

- Big Wheel
- Fountain Garden / Green / Deck / Leisure / Sports / Water Screen
- Aqua
- Water Landscape
- Theme Exhibition / BPA Exhibition
- Hall / Lounge

// Expected Experience in Ferris wheel is as follows,
1. Submarine Experience
2. Experiencing Land and Deep Sea
3. Experiencing Forest and Sea
4. Experiencing Wind and Island
5. Experiencing Sky, Ocean and Exposition
   It will be a monumental landmark as it is allowing visitors to experience all these superb activity.

Creative Exhibition for Ocean Experiences
Circular-shaped Green Imagination symbolises the chief exhibition area and induces people to experience various things as a breathing architecture. Along the side of the building, visitors would be able to enjoy the beautiful scenery in a Ferris wheel. We call it 'a Moving Imaginative Compounds'.

A scenery carved out by mountain and water
We imagine an artificial bowl which has nature in it. It is combined with a symbolic figure of Korean landscape. In the view of Oriental philosophy toward nature, nature is translated into a &Mechanism of Time∗. Nature has a lot of signs of the past and present. We consider a chief exhibition area as an artificially created nature. This symbiotic structure is defined by a point of contact for dynamism and contemporary aesthetics. We carve out the traditional korean mind of loving nature. Artificial bowl is a ground for blending the way of illustrating and reinterpreting the nature. We conceive diverse way of structuring through applicances of Korean topography. Abstraction and illustration of Korean land enables us to have a profound spaces. Korean nature such as ocean water, island, wetland, mountain, valley and so forth are carved in the space.

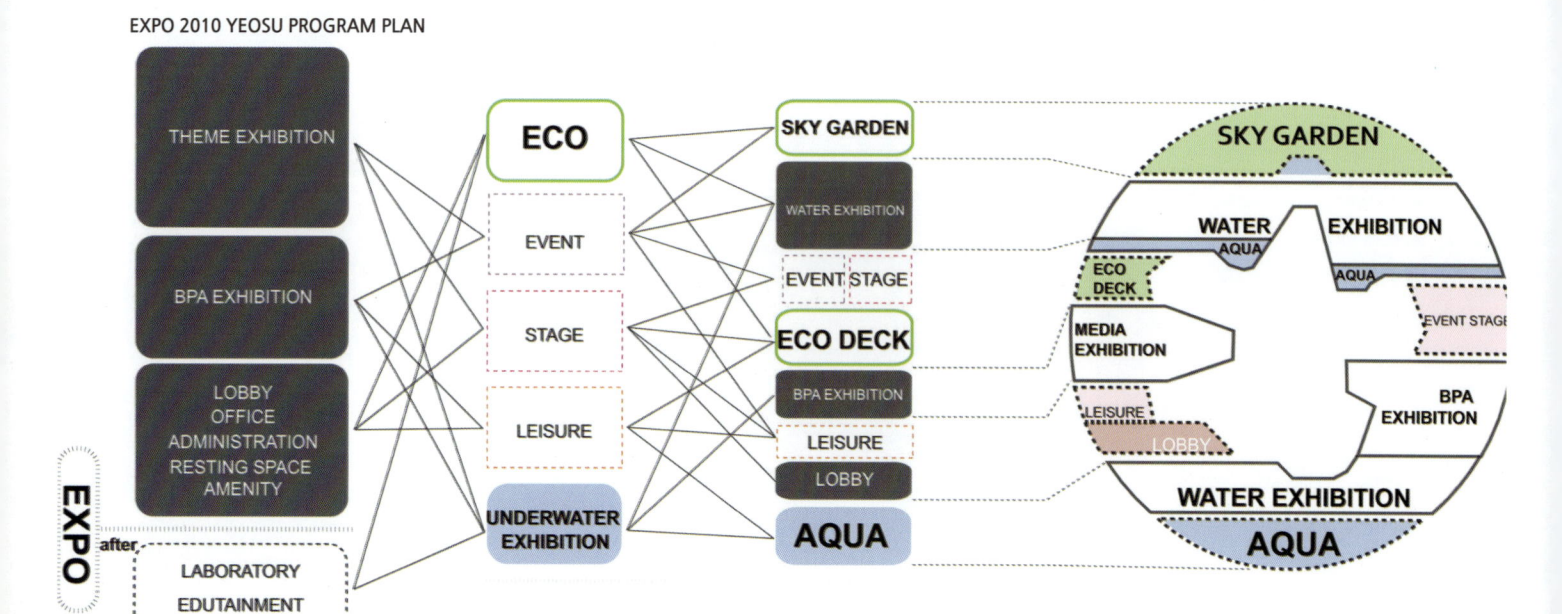

EXPO 2010 YEOSU PROGRAM PLAN

COMPOUND BODY 121

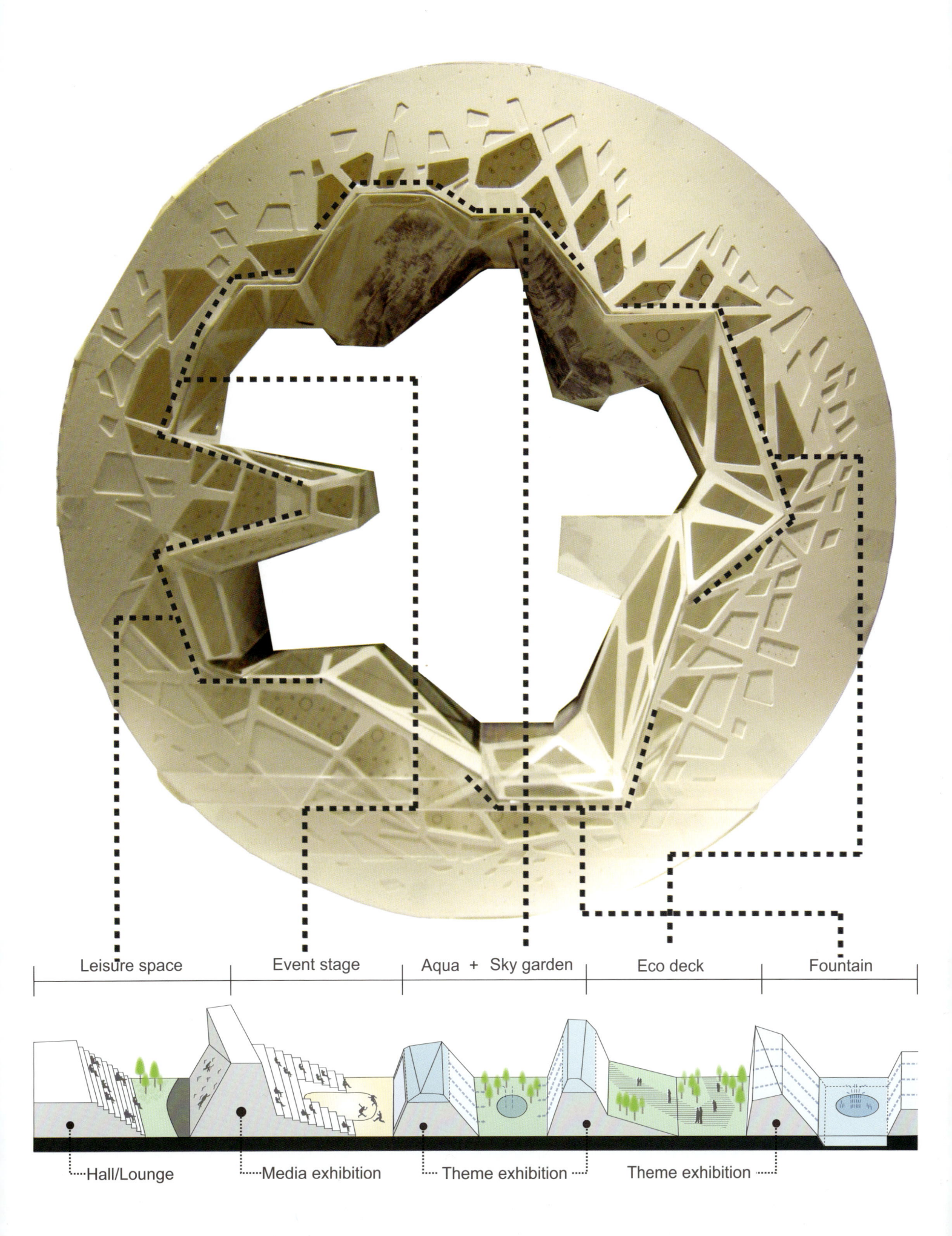

Leisure space | Event stage | Aqua + Sky garden | Eco deck | Fountain

Hall/Lounge · Media exhibition · Theme exhibition · Theme exhibition

**Dynamically Stacked Programme
_ Vertically Composed Programme**
Stacked programme is quite similar with natural phenomenon; and even, it is like a living thing which reacts to time passing. It represents history of nature but also civilisation of human being. We consider it as a ingenious way of liking past, present and future. It is our intention to allow people to experience the space and exhibition simultaneously as opposed to just arrange exhibition area with relevant technology. Visitors would experience ocean exhibits through vertically stacked programme and intersected ourdoor and indoor space. Stacked programme is linked with nature element. In the centre of the building there is 'Eco void space'.
This space is tied up to other spaces like:
1_Main Hall > 2_1st Event Nature > 3_Media Exhibition > 4_2nd Event Nature > 5_1st Main Theme Exhibition > 6_Scenery Observing Deck > 7_2nd Main Theme Exhibition > 8_3rd Event Nature > 9_3rd Main Theme Exhibition> 10_Aquarium > 11_Deep Sea Lounge

Eternally Shining Lighthouse in Yeo-Su
Ocean Imagination is a sustainable building which produces energy through renewable resources like the wind, the sun and the water. We intend a circular-shaped lighthouse which is shining brilliantly in the night sky by using renewable energy. It will keep twinkling for everlasting as well as during the exposition period. We imagine that it could be a glamorous scenery. Pedestrians might be able to enjoy dramatic scenery. At first glance, circular-shaped light is floating above the sea. And then, it would be reflected on the surface of the sea like a sunshine in the daytime. The light of the lighthouse stands for a 'Light Gate' which leads visitors to the Exposition Yeo-su. Furthermore, it will represent vision of Yeo-su which expands toward the ocean to an unlimited extent.

'A Light Symphony' will be performed by time and sort of programme.

PROGRAMME OF ALIVE LIGHT IN THE SHINING LIGHTHOUSE

Light for Metropolis

Media Art Show

Laser Show

Advertising & Promoting Exposition

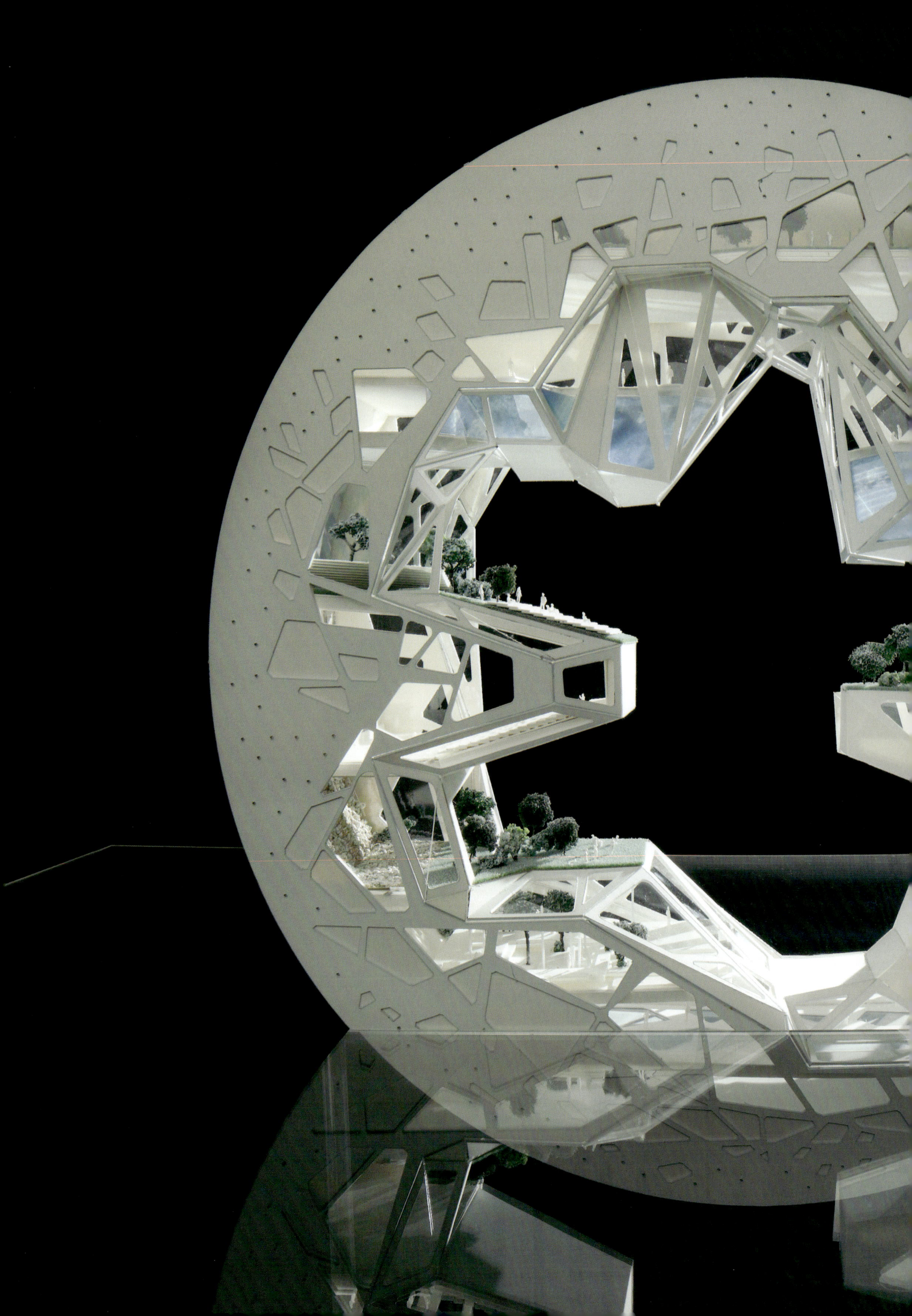

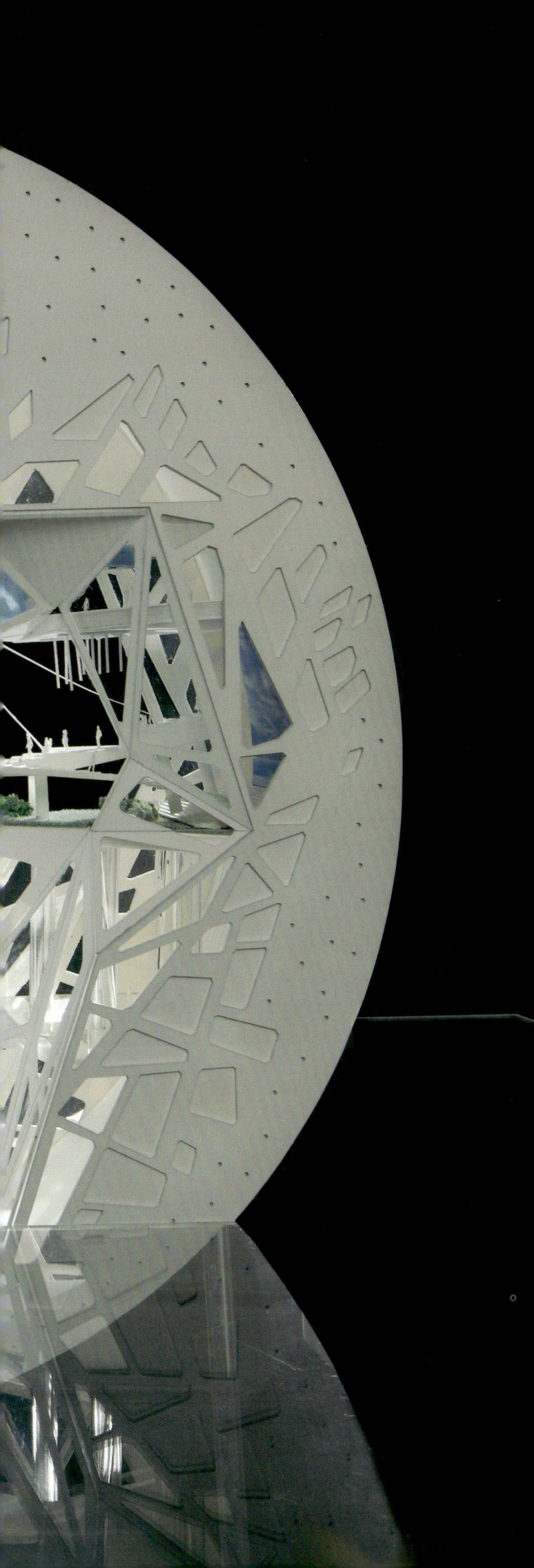

Blue Economy
It goes without saying that the environment is in crisis as new technologies change our society. Cost-driven society which is the crux of capitalism causes serious ramifications namely global warming, exhaustion of natural resources. What's more, it would be a daunting prospect if we overlook the expansion of big cities because it consumes lots of dwelling spaces, infrastructures and food. In the end, it threatens ecosystem. It is called for to picture of our future life through speculating about environment. 'Landscape-Architecture' i.e. architecture which is linked closely with landscape or 'Ecological-Architecture' are of far more importance. It is straight forward that we need to channel more support to sustainable structure when it comes to building up a new synthesis of architecture and nature.

Ocean Gate_Vertical Landmark
To build up of the theme of this project : the Living Ocean and Coast, we propose a 'Big Ocean Gate' which appears to play a key role as an information hub in the area. 'Ocean Gate', the notion shows lives and cultures on the sea shore vertically. It becomes a vertical gate which combines ocean ecosystem and architecture in accordance with the main theme of this project, 'Ocean & Life'. Visitors would enjoy a host of ocean related experience through 'Eco-void' in this vertical landmark. Our strategy is to give a message and vision of this exposition to the public constantly.

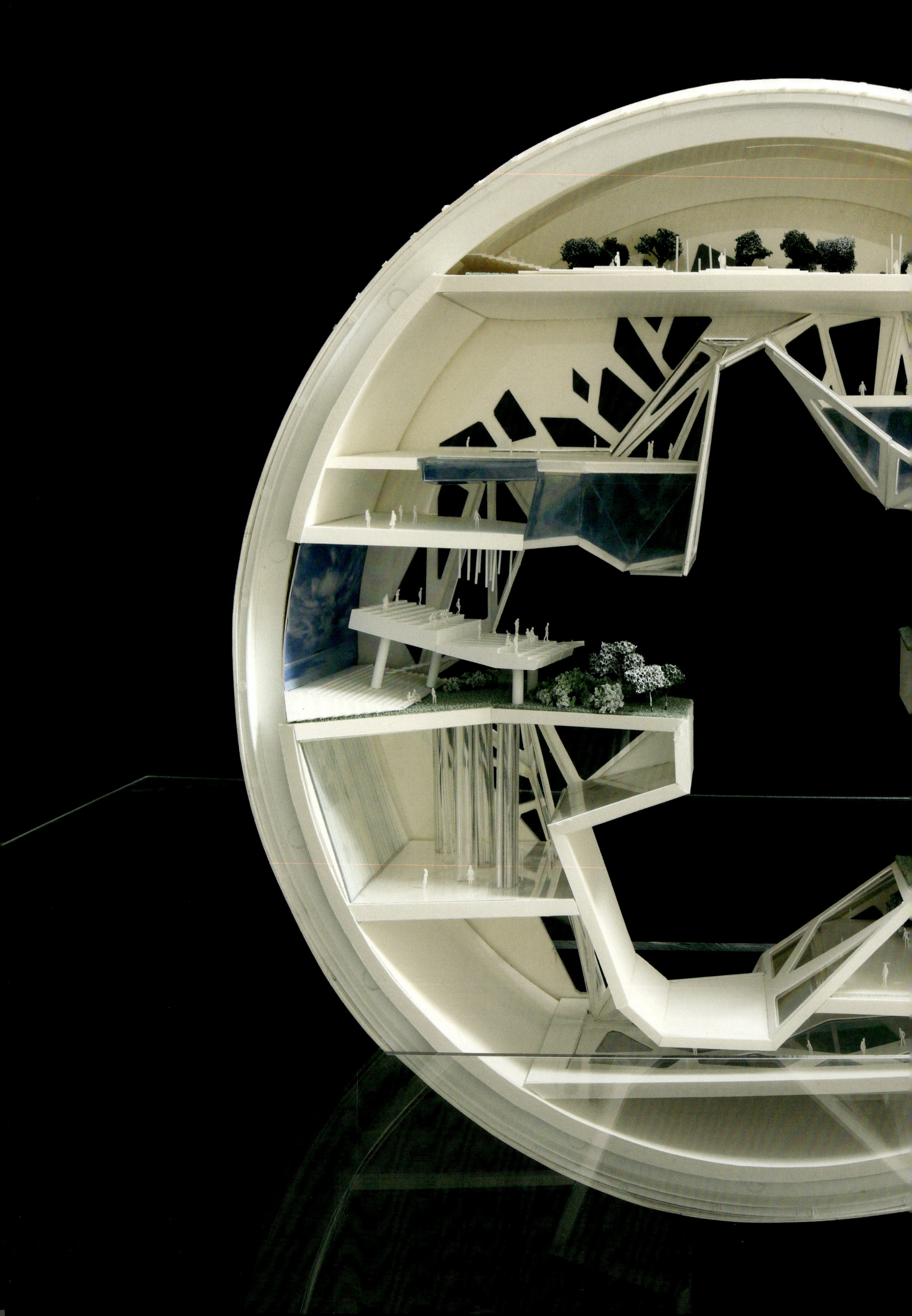

Ocean Void Space_ Organism of Scenery
'Sustainable Ocean void space' is formed from combination of flowing water and ecological environment. We assume that there might be a limit if we persist to put the rooms for exhibition only inside the building. To curb this problem, we decided to use outer space as a part of exhibition space. Those carries out different kinds of event such as Water-Valley, Media-Valley, Play-Valley, Green-Valley and so on. In the main exhibition space, we categorized it by four seasons of Korea. The scenery is surprisingly diverse in Korean landscape according to the seasons. We define it as an 'Organism of Scenery'. In spring, flowers bloom everywhere. In summer, the scenery contains dramatic waterfalls and thick forests. In fall, the leaves on the trees turn yellow. In winter, a blanket of snow lay on the ground like a black and white drawing of traditional korean painting. Combination of panoramic vistas creates an original architecture like Korean paintings. It would accommodate a host of programme as they mirror the characteristic of nature and lead us forward into a new era. Form of the organism becomes an organic system which changes flexibly as time passes by.

EL+90000

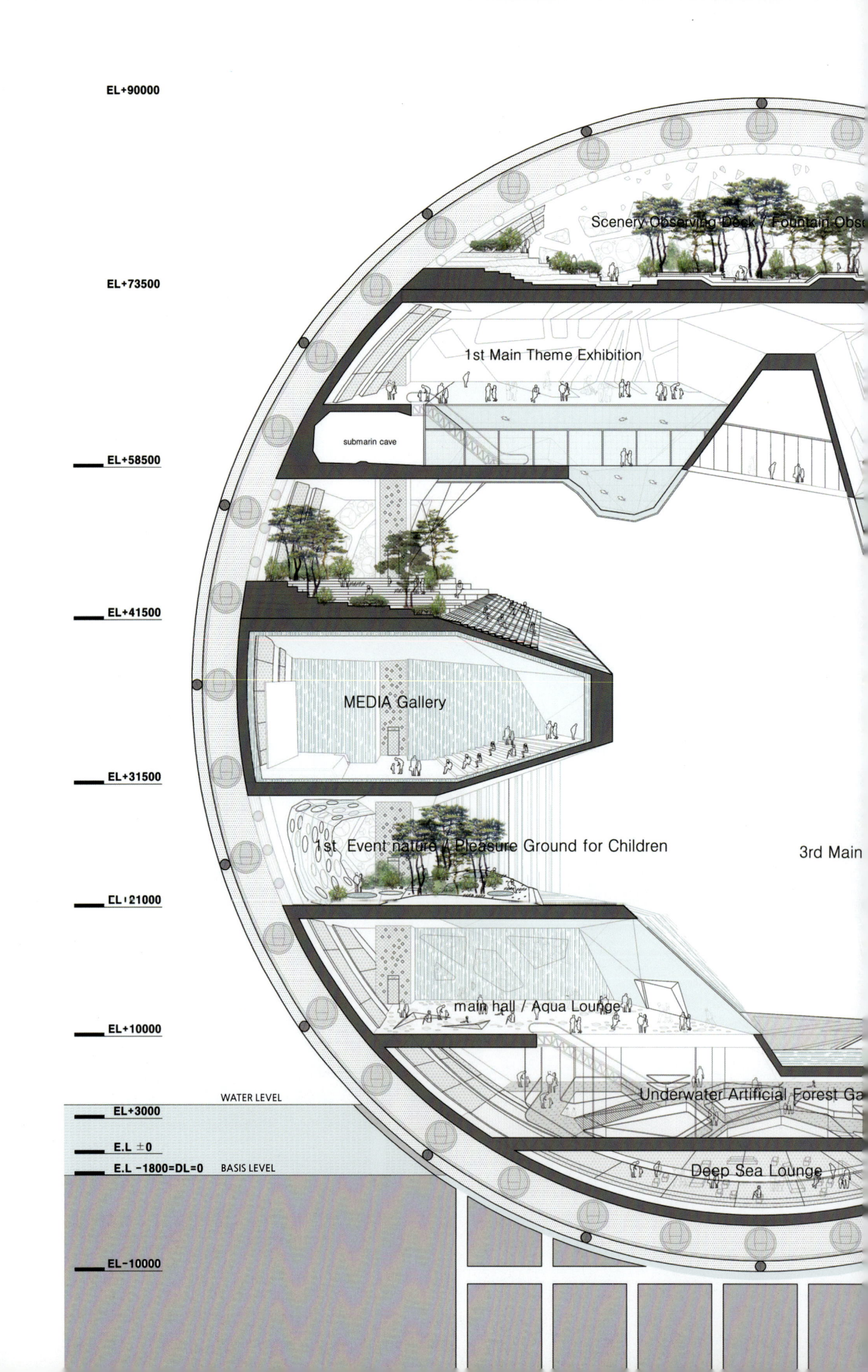

EL+73500 — Scenery Observing Deck / Fountain Obs...

1st Main Theme Exhibition

EL+58500 — submarin cave

EL+41500

MEDIA Gallery

EL+31500

1st Event nature / Pleasure Ground for Children   3rd Main

EL+21000

main hall / Aqua Lounge

EL+10000

WATER LEVEL
EL+3000
E.L ±0
E.L −1800=DL=0   BASIS LEVEL

Underwater Artificial Forest Ga...

Deep Sea Lounge

EL−10000

COMPOUND BODY 129

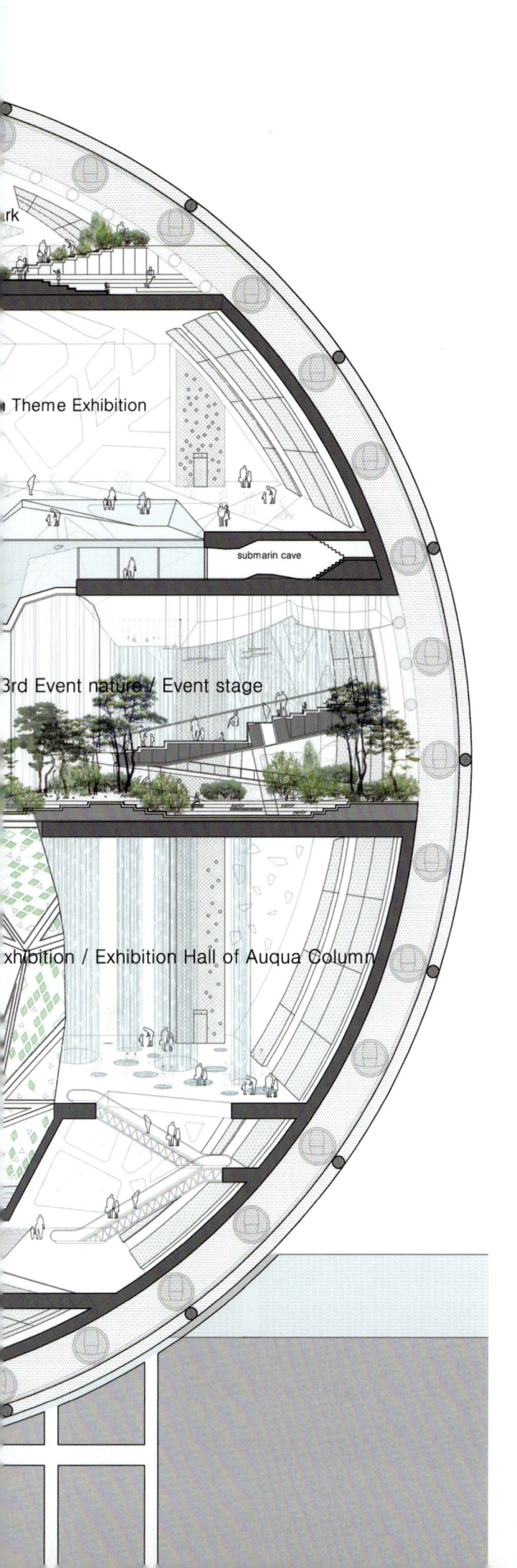

1. Aqua Lounge
Visitors walk along the huge aqua wall in the entry.

2. Pleasure Ground for Children
Children will have various activity by playing with water.

3. Media Exhibition
Every wall in this area is aquarium.
People would watch a short film about ocean eco system through a screen which is surrounding the visitors in every direction with circular shape. The screen is just a glass wall, however, it changes to a translucent screen by an electric equipment.

4. Water-Stairway Garden
A Park which is made with Dynamic Landscape Stairway and water space.It provides a peaceful rest place for people.

5. 1st Thematic Exhibition
Various kinds of exhibition will held on the water as the floor of the gallery will be made with an aquarium.

6. Fountain Observation Park
People will observe the sea and all over the area of this thematic pavilion at this area. There will be pine tree forest and fountain. It is an event space which contains several elements of Korean traditional garden.

7. 2nd Thematic Exhibition
Various kinds of exhibition will held on the water as the floor of the gallery will be made with an aquarium.

8. Event Stage
This area compromises various event and performances with using water.

9. Exhibition Hall of Aqua Column
Different size of water column will be placed as elements of exhibition.

10. Underwater Artificial Forest Gallery
People will enjoy exhibit real ocean by travelling on a transparent tube.

11. Deep Sea Lounge
Visitors take a rest in a space which is situated in deep sea.

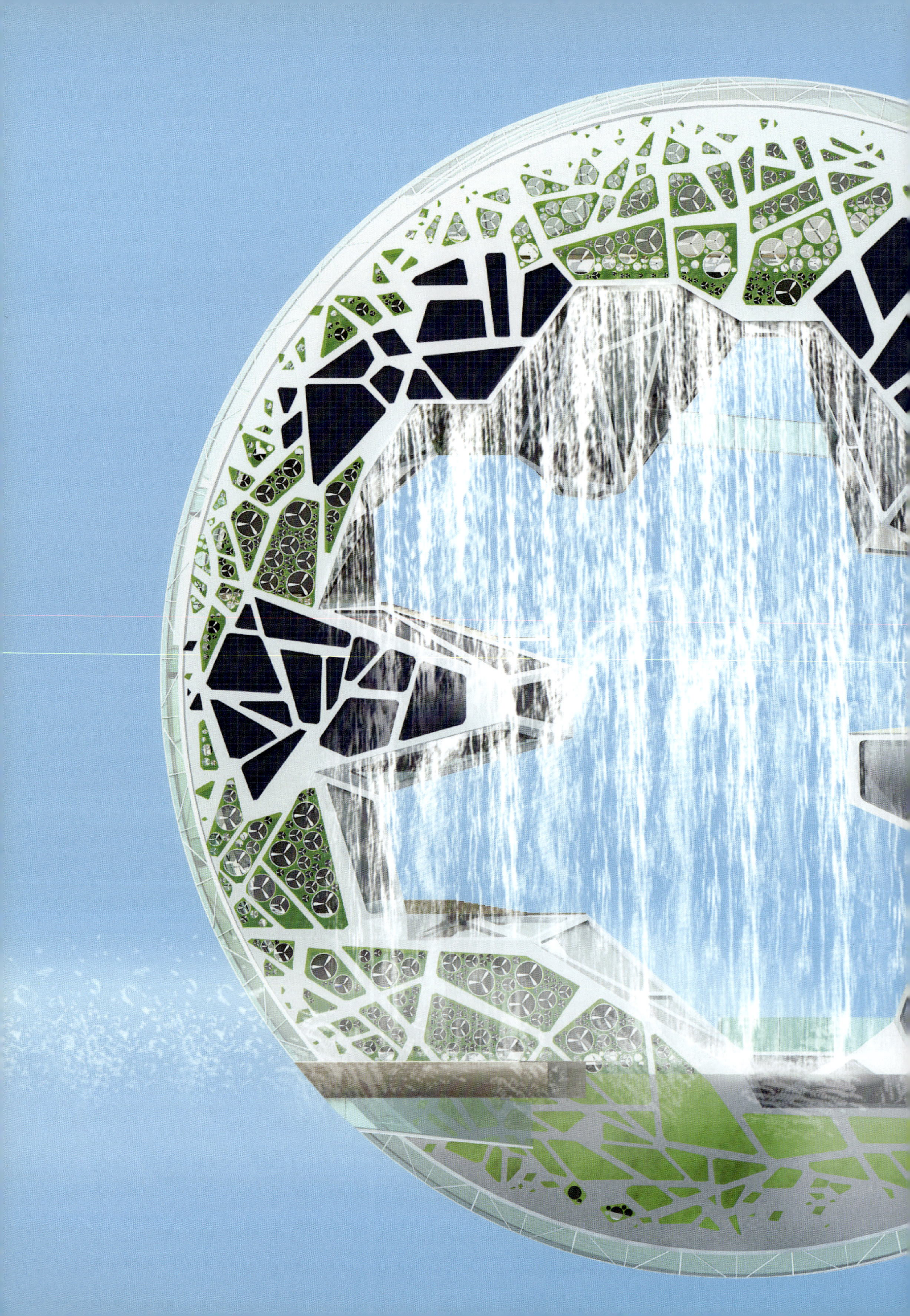

// **Water Stream_ Media Waterfall**
Water is used to set up the media wall. It acts as a nature experiencing programme. Water is a dynamic element in Korean traditional architecture like inishing touch in painting. Eco-void space accommodates different phase of water streaming. Water skin is changing as time goes on. It shows different signal in accordance with the subject of exhibition. There are a host of water space namely, waterfall, fountain, fog and so on. It could be a media screen of huge information about the exposition. Otherwise, it can be a light screen controlled by specific programme. It will freshen up the city-scape by producing various kinds of images and lights. Visitors would find that it reacts to their action in the void space. This urban skin provides vast information to the visitors to advertise and promote the exposition.

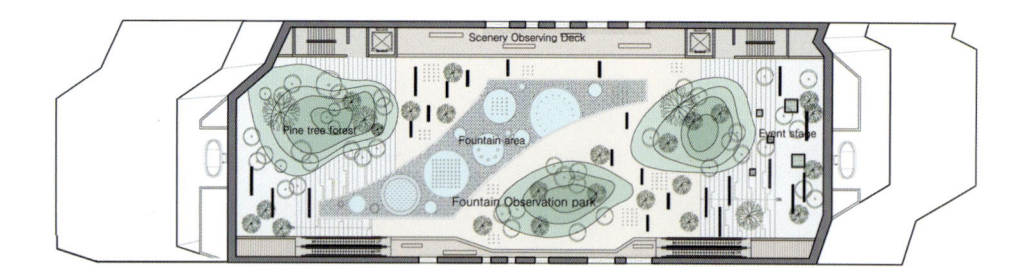

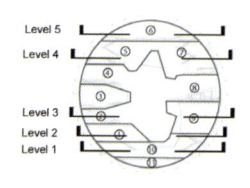

LEVEL 5
Fountain Observation Park

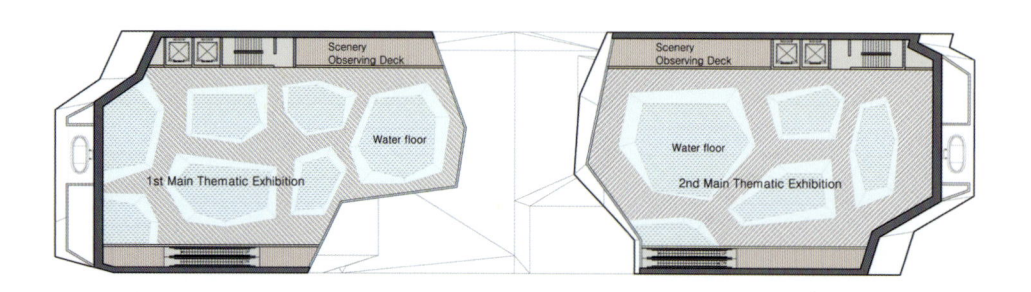

LEVEL 4
Thematic Exhibition

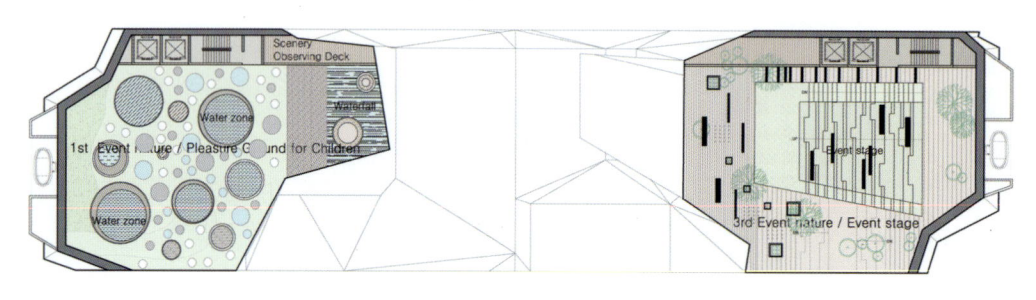

LEVEL 3
Pleasure Ground for Children

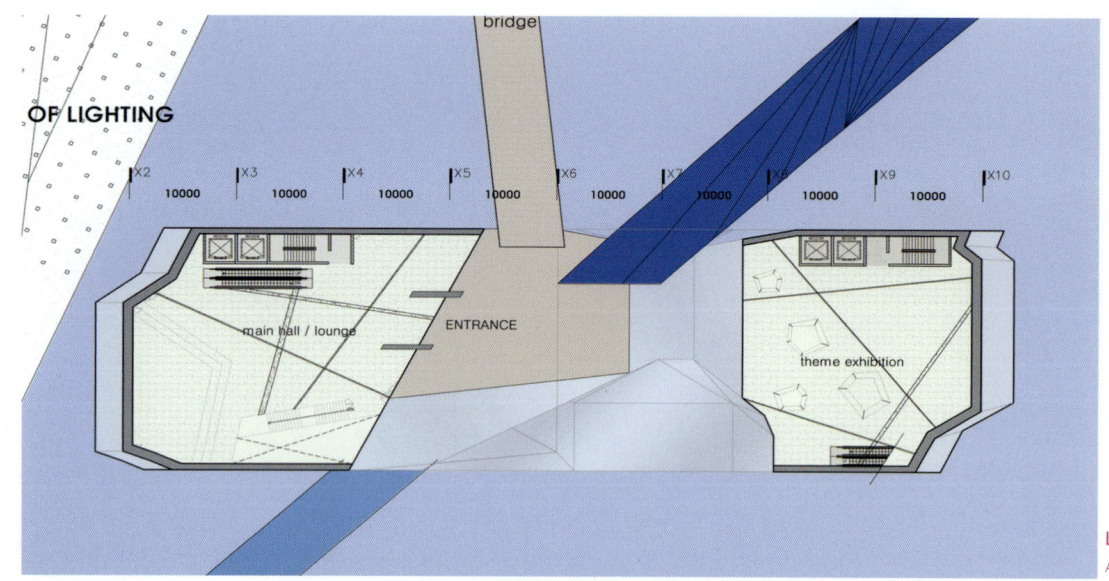

LEVEL 2
Aqua Lounge

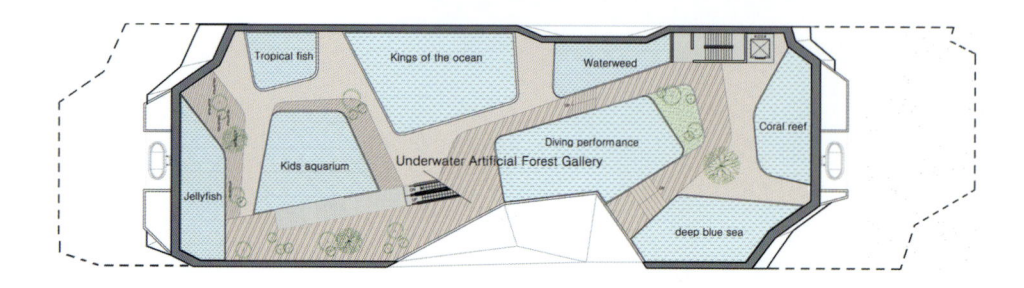

LEVEL 1
Underwater Artificial Forest Gallery

COMPOUND BODY 133

// **Movement**
We set a clear movement by separating path for vehicle and pedestrian. Elevator and excalator will be intersected for visitors to move more readily when they want to move to different floor. What * s more, people will experience exhibits on the move.

A. PEDESTRIAN MOVEMENT
1_Main Hall > 2_1st Event Nature > 3_Media Exhibition > 4_2nd Event Nature > 5_1st Main Theme Exhibition > 6_Scenery Observing Deck > 7_2nd Main Theme Exhibition > 8_3rd Event Nature > 9_3rd Main Theme Exhibition> 10_Aquarium > 11_Deep Sea Lounge

B. OBSERVATION
A transparent spinning elevator for observation will be placed on the edge of the thematic pavillion. It carries people from underwater to sky garden. People will be able to watch diverse scenery.

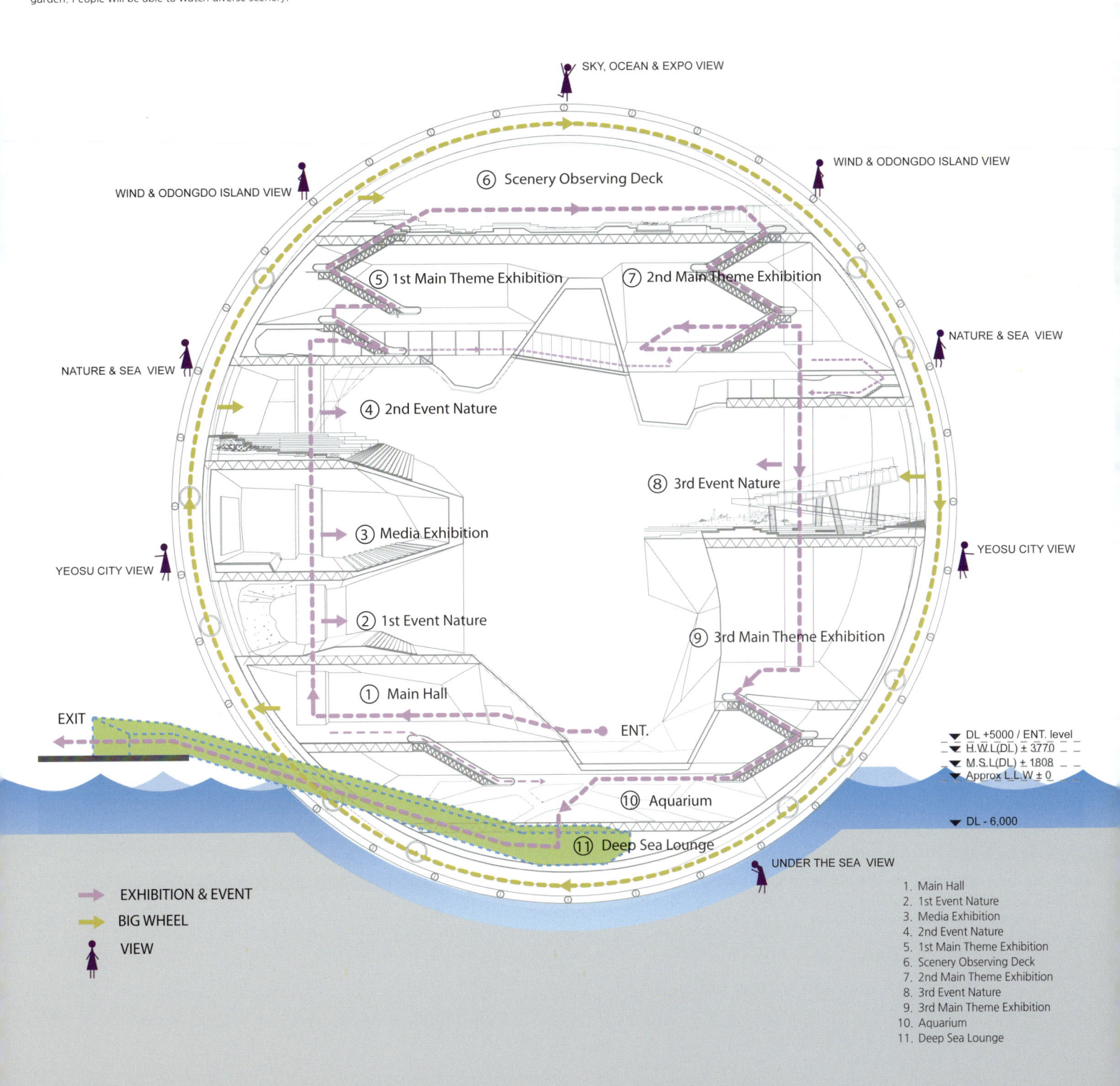

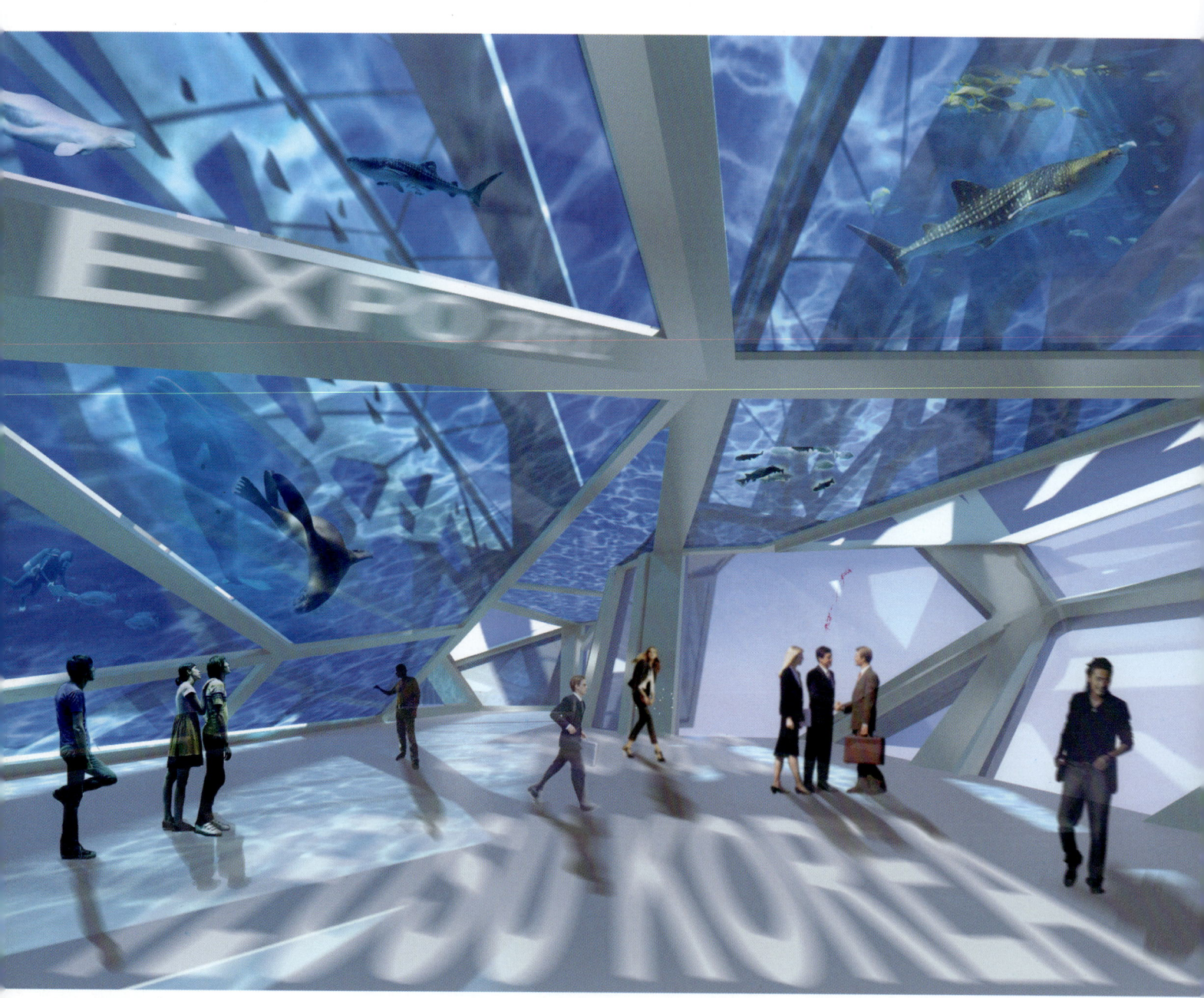

// **Deep Sea Lounge**
Visitors take a rest in a space which is situated in deep sea.

// **Thematic Exhibition**
Various kinds of exhibition will held on the water as the floor of the gallery will be made with an aquarium.

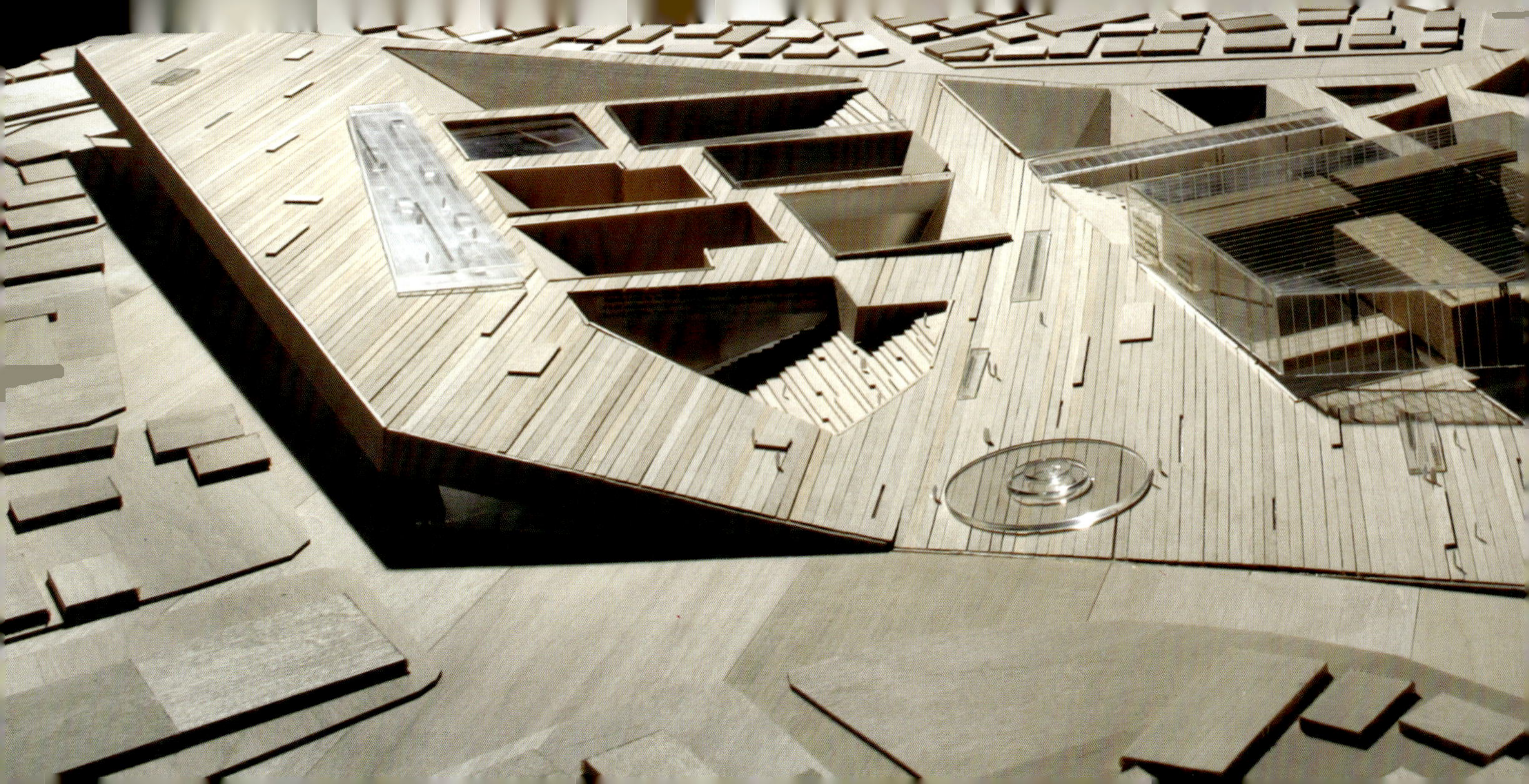

International Competition, 3rd Prize

Architects Jang Yoon Gyoo, Shin Chang Hoon, Kim Woo Il, Kim Woo Young
Photographer Kim Jae Kyung

COMPOUND BODY 137

○ INTERACTIVE CULTURE STAGE

INTERACTIVE CULTURE STAGE

We propose to constitute a stage that acts as a new container for the culture and everyday events. If new stage for the city is creating an empty open space out of penetrations pathways and plazas, making the new 'city stage' is as same as to conduct an enormous mapping operation with penetrating programs and landscape. We propose the Asian Culture Complex as the earth in between creation and disappearance. The earth that is transformed into fragmented pieces and become urban landscape filled with memories of the site and historical evolution of various spectrums of relationships.

Culture Canvas on Urban Plaza

We provide culture canvas that can be filled-in by the citizens of Gwangju. Setting up the open space as the platform to hose. "audience-driven" acts. Not just empty and void, the open space acts as a sheet of canvas to host constant change in time and media. This canvas is filled and generated by the audience's participation. Each audience becomes a protagonist in this "Plaza of Participation". Through changing boundaries and shifting programs, the plaza is a set of infrastructure that provides diverse range of experiences to the citizens. It opens up to host various events at regular intervals including indoor/outdoor exhibits and performances, while flexible enough to accomodate the needs for the special occasions.

Circle of the Earth
Between Creation and Disappearance of the Earth

We propose the Asian Culture Complex as the earth in between creation and disappearance. The earth that is transformed into fragmented pieces and become urban landscape filled with memories of the site and historical evolution of various spectrums of relationships. Creation and Disappearance includes a series of relationships of which the beginning/end, yin/yang, straight/curve, existant/extinct, and chaos/order are generated in every life cycles of the earth. Nevertheless they are the few examples of dichotomy taking place in all the universal relationships, creation and disappearance harbors the evolution of intricate process of infinite amount of associations.

The Asian Culture Complex stands in the middle of these complex nature of evolutions. Creating "inbetween" space at the leveled ground of the earth. "inbetween" includes the countless facts of certain environmental conditions. Fluctuating within the dichotomy of creation and disappearance, the term symbolizes infinite potential and dynamics, as well as the main driving force that can harmonize the nature - according to the eastern thought. Asian Culture Complex Gwangju is like conducting an operation to make new earth, generating new open space that accomodates changing programs and events in time, and lasts as a place to record all of the layers in history and memories of creation and disappearance.

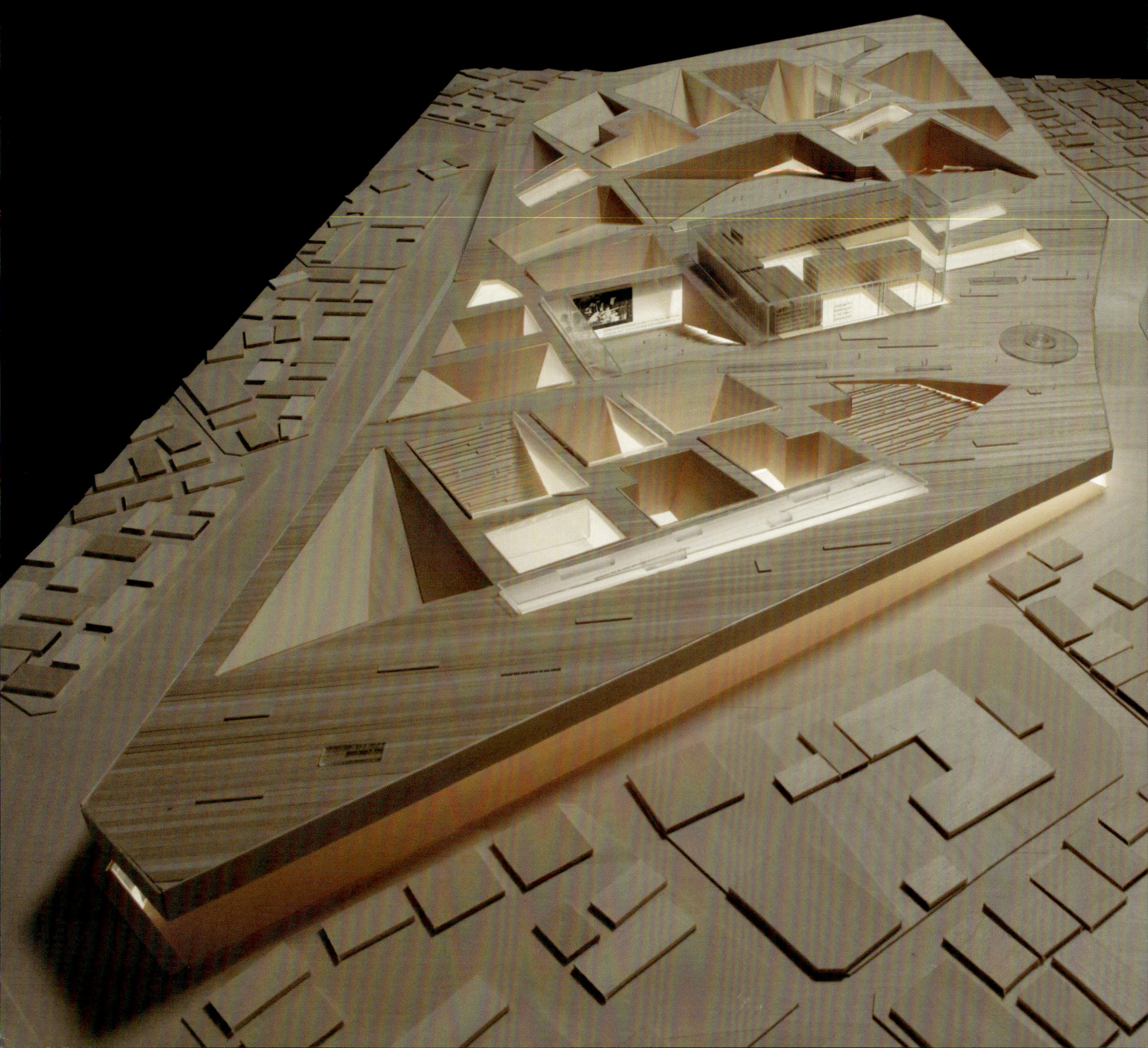

Interactive Sections - Interactive Skins

We propose the skin of the earth to act as the framework for the Asian Culture Complex Gwangju. Two-dimensional skin if the plaza is extruded to become spatial skin. Not only stopping at changing the urban topography through spatial morphing, the plaza is rearranged by matching with diverse codes required cultural code, artistic code, urban code,···.matched with spatial code. The plaza is not a two-dimensional urban surface, but rather the multi-dimensional space with layers and folds of spaces that is matched by several codes. It becomes the framework of earthly generation that accommodate multiple channels of arts.

SKIN 01 Culture Stage

City Stage for historical memories and cultural activities Making a city - scale urban plaza of Culturescape Street Mat City - We propose the process of extruding out the existing city structures and fabrics as a way of recording the history of Gwangju existing bands of streets are extruded to become the volume in order to frame the new city condition. This means that the city's existing fabric with historical value is also the spaces and streets with historical memories and events. Through the reversal of old streets and masses, city-scale urban mat is defined, followed by morphing it into the earthly monument. Urban mat framed out by the streets then forms the landscape slicing through the surrounding urban panorama, hosting various events and programs, while providing needed circulations.

Three-dimensional event plaza embedded in the urban mat during the culture stage (stage 01), is inserted in between streets to become the multi-dimensional skin containing cultural programs and activities. In cohesive with outside landscape elements, it acts as a stage to host diverse events. Outdoor spaces framed out by the streets constitute various themes of programs parks, commercial facilities, cultural and media centers and others.

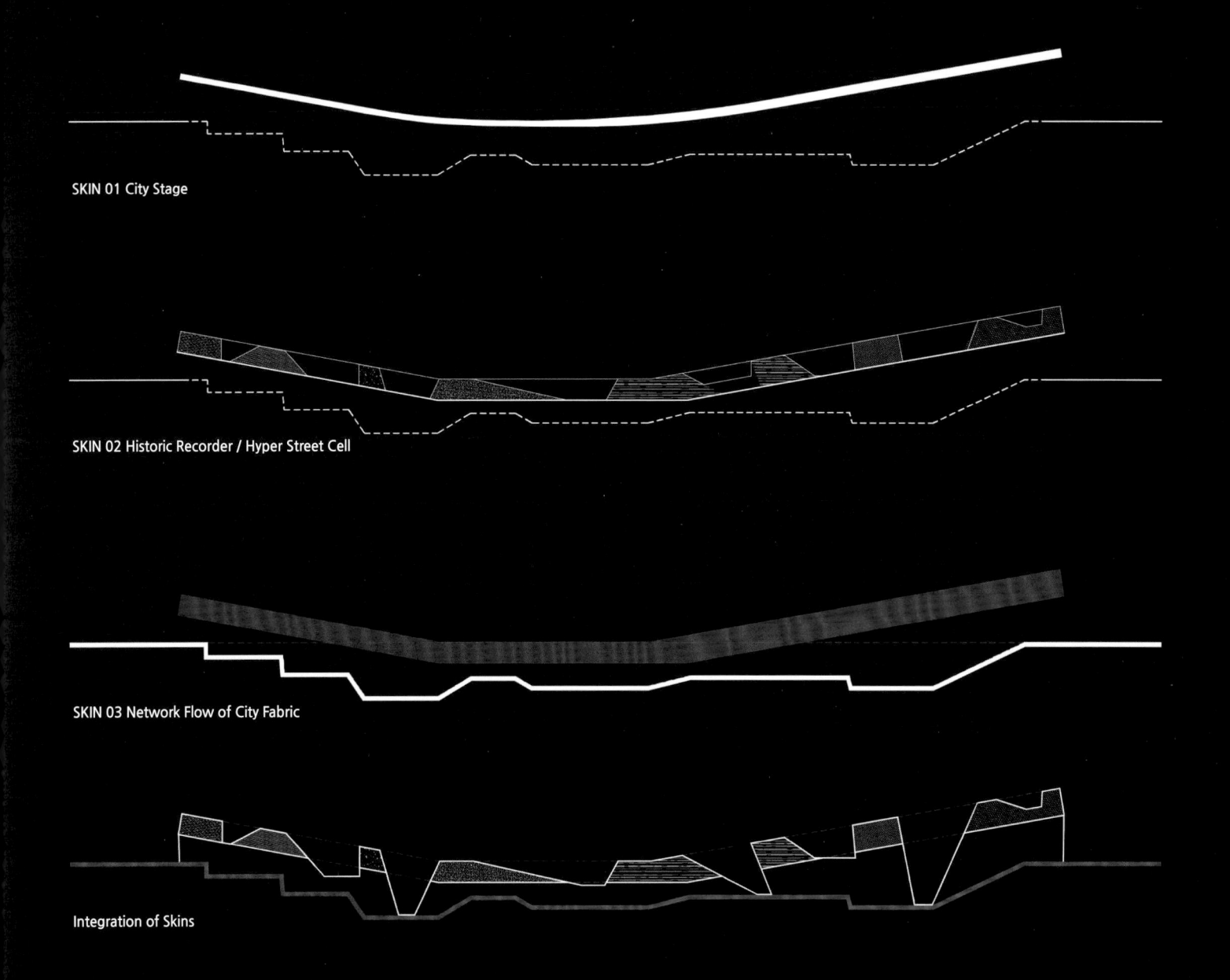

SKIN 01 City Stage

SKIN 02 Historic Recorder / Hyper Street Cell

SKIN 03 Network Flow of City Fabric

Integration of Skins

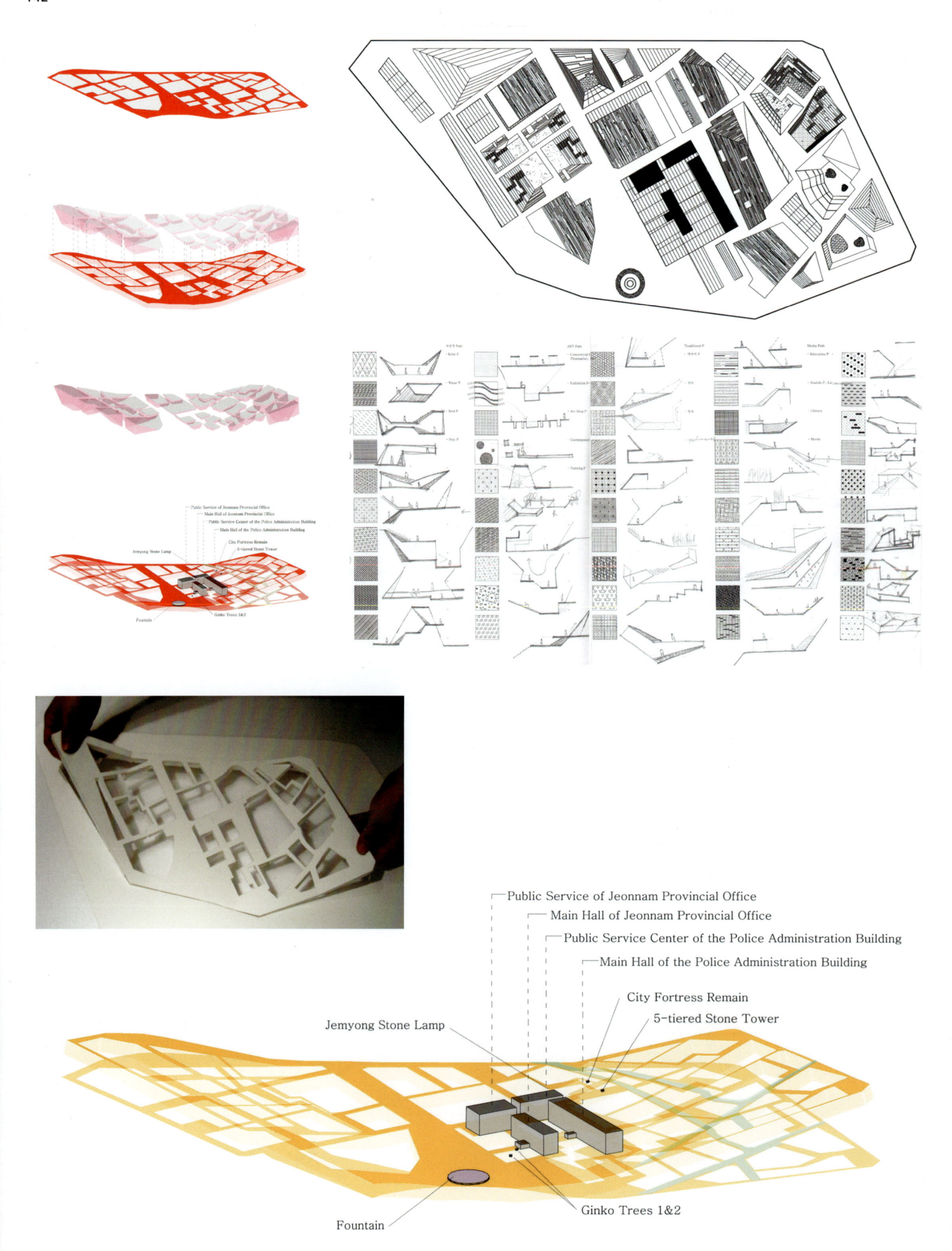

Public Service of Jeonnam Provincial Office
Main Hall of Jeonnam Provincial Office
Public Service Center of the Police Administration Building
Main Hall of the Police Administration Building
City Fortress Remain
5-tiered Stone Tower
Jemyong Stone Lamp
Fountain
Ginko Trees 1&2

SKIN 02   Street Cell - Historic Recorder

Through a process of spatial reversal, the three-dimensional volume of the streets become 'objet' to which its combinations are formed as a historical matrix. Streets are no longer the left-out voids of the city, but to become an active framework containing diverse range of programs.Through each street being accentuated by the city's important historical events over time, programs and boundaries are defined for the Historic Recorder.Reaching beyond the limits of the concept that a gallery describes only the historical events, historical matrix are generated as a symbolic space for the memories and commemoration.
New cultural network is organized at the heart of the cross-road connecting the city of Gwangju and Asia. Cultural network acts as one of apparatus linking functional mechanisms of the surrounding area with the topological context of the site. Through the rearrangement of lines and orientations embedded in the network, the compound body is created out of the existing pathways of the history and the future cultural pathways still to come.

Street cells segmented by the historical events are generated by the cultural hyper-link map and the event stage in the form of a landscape. Upper level of city stage ⟨skin 01⟩, lower level of landscape plaza ⟨skin 03⟩ combined with the existing city fabric, and the hyper street cell ⟨skin 02⟩ integrated as a network, are altogether organized into the following spatial elements and their combinations:

SKIN 03 Network Flow

Hyper-street map, acting as the city plaza and landscape, is organized by the series of network cells. The site is not an isolated property, but rather becomes an open stage. The lower level of the city stage is a network of space freely interacted by the people, while the event stage at the upper level is penetrated by the series of programs to possess ideal urban dynamics.

INTERACTIVE PROGRAM MAP

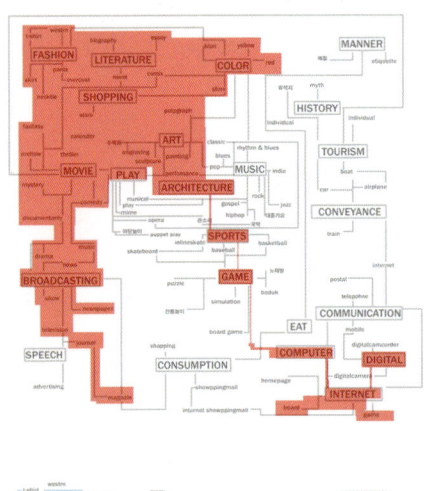

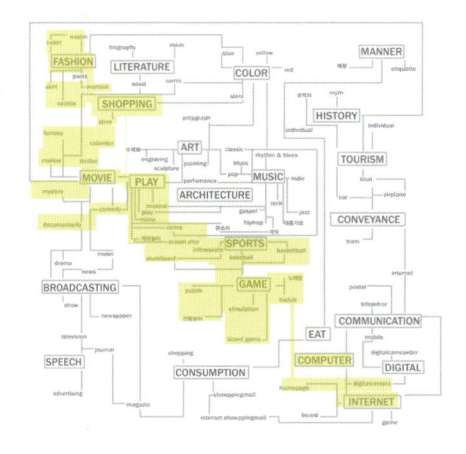

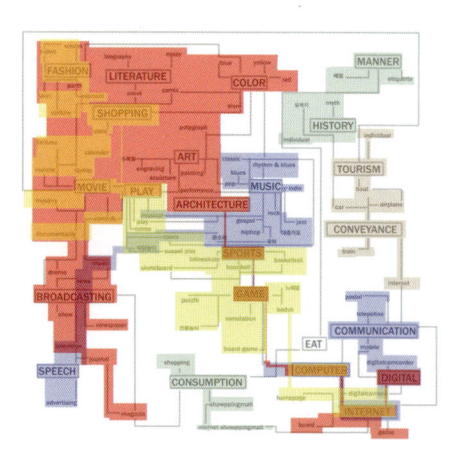

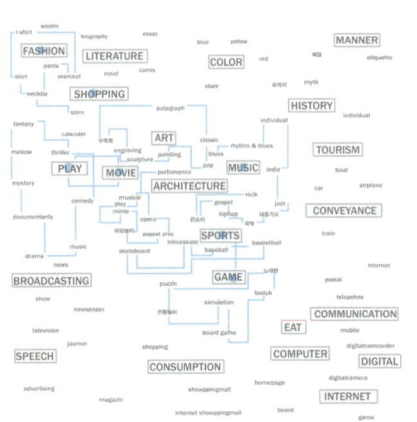

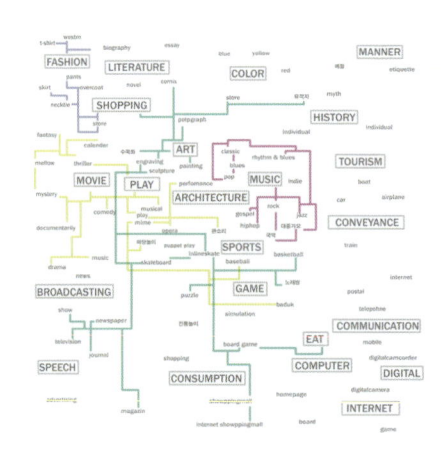

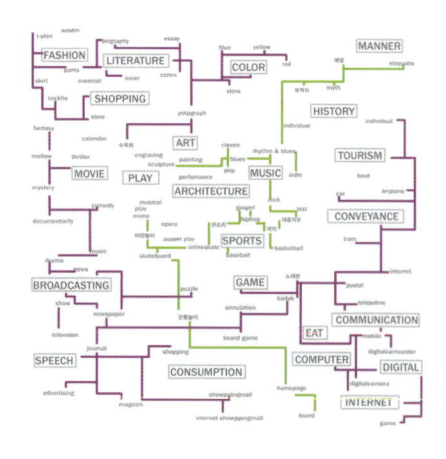

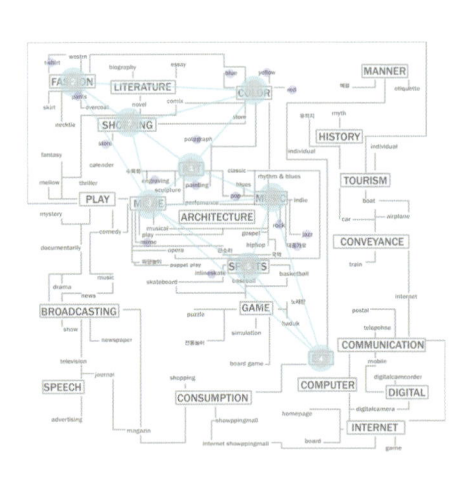

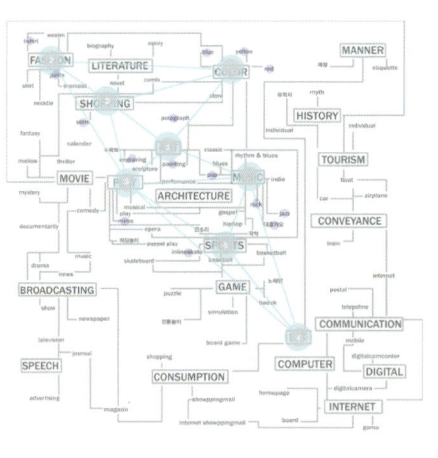

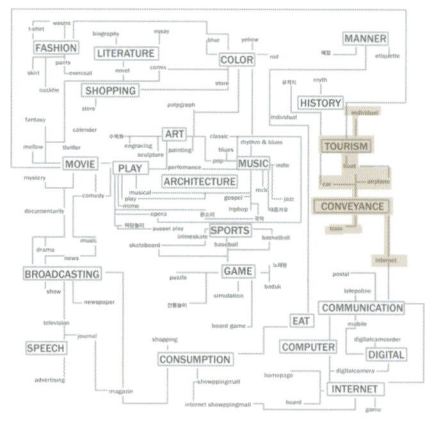

COMPOUND BODY   145

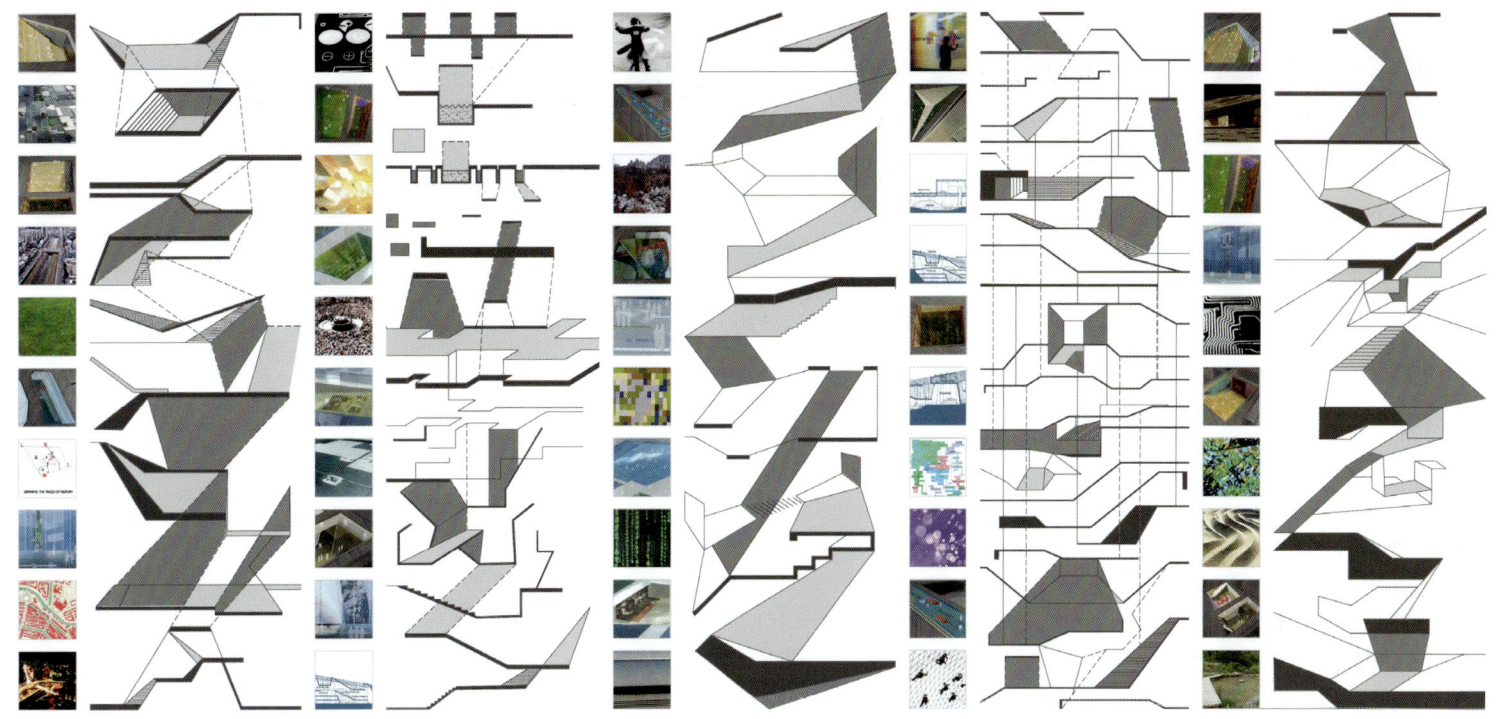

URBAN VOID PROGRAM: VERTICAL INTERACTION

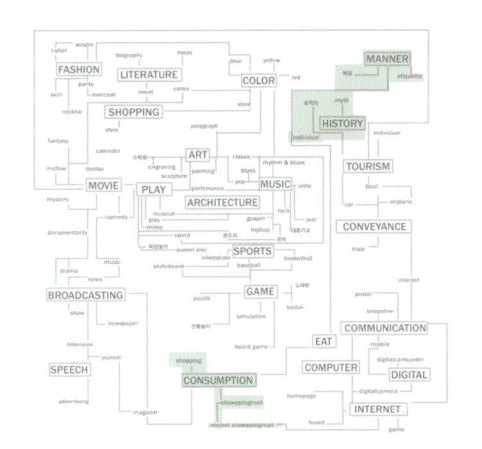

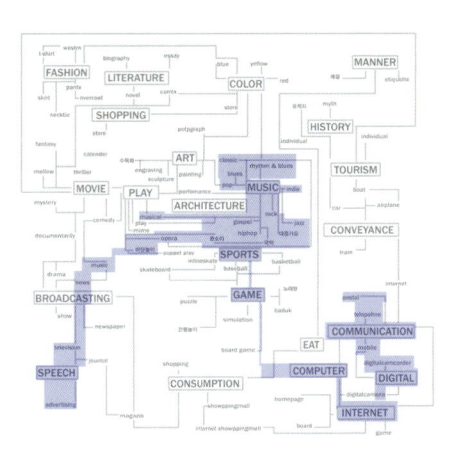

TRANSITION PROCESSING

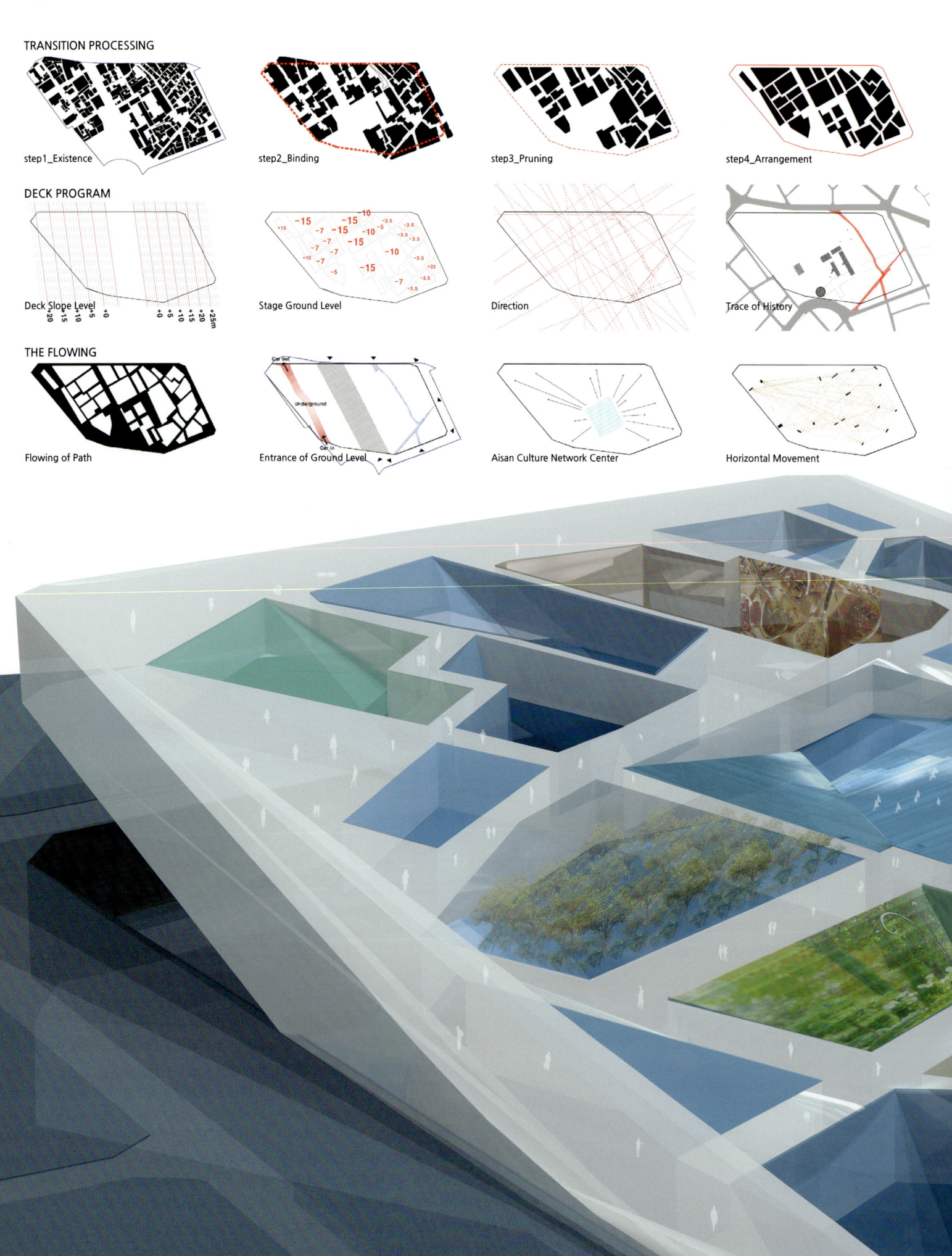

step1_Existence | step2_Binding | step3_Pruning | step4_Arrangement

DECK PROGRAM

Deck Slope Level | Stage Ground Level | Direction | Trace of History

THE FLOWING

Flowing of Path | Entrance of Ground Level | Aisan Culture Network Center | Horizontal Movement

COMPOUND BODY 147

SKIN1 _ CITY STAGE

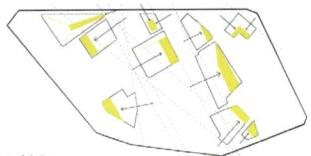

Multi Stage 　　　　　Landscape Stage 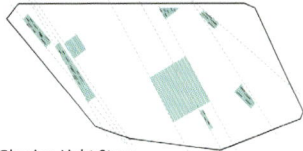　　　　　Glassing-Light Stage 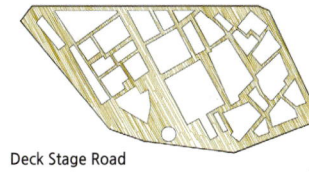　　　　　Deck Stage Road

SKIN2 _ STREET CELL / HISTORIC RECORDER

Combine with Stage 　　　　　Natural Contour of Step 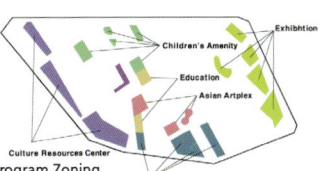　　　　　Program Zoning 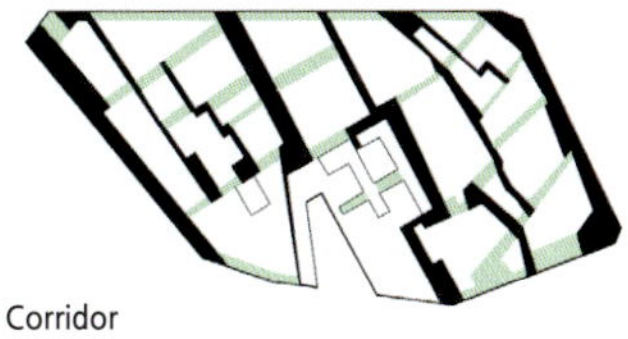　　　　　Corridor

SKIN3 _ NETWORK FLOW / HYPER-STREET MAP

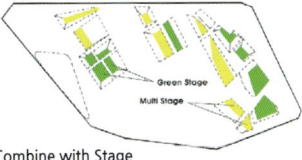

Combine with Stage 　　　　　Natural Program Contour 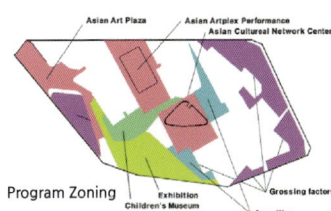　　　　　Program Zoning　　　　　Plug in Gardens

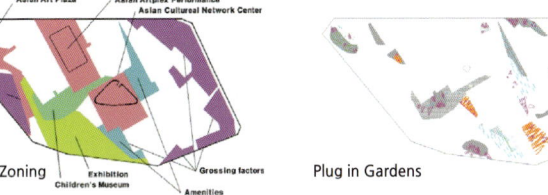

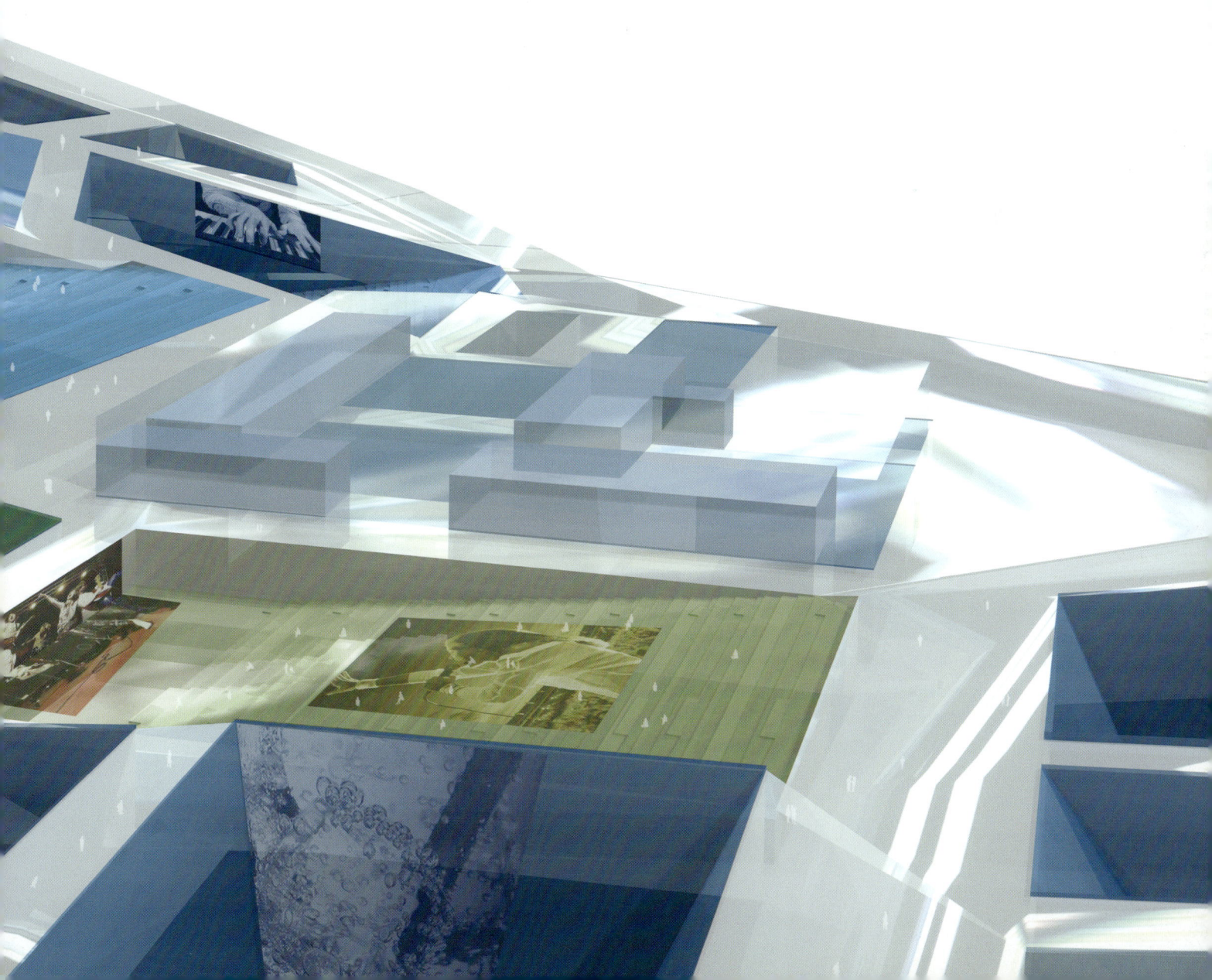

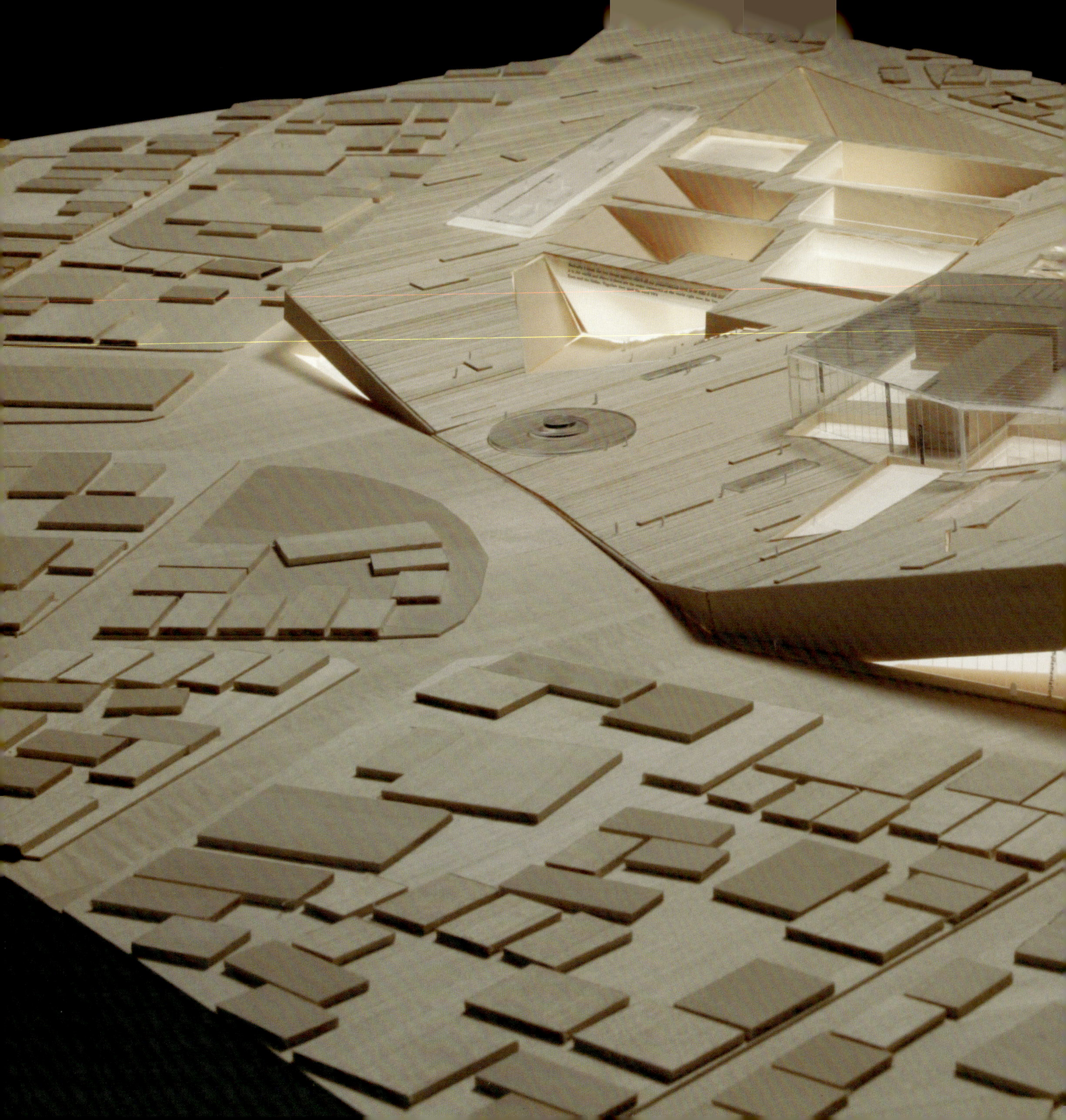

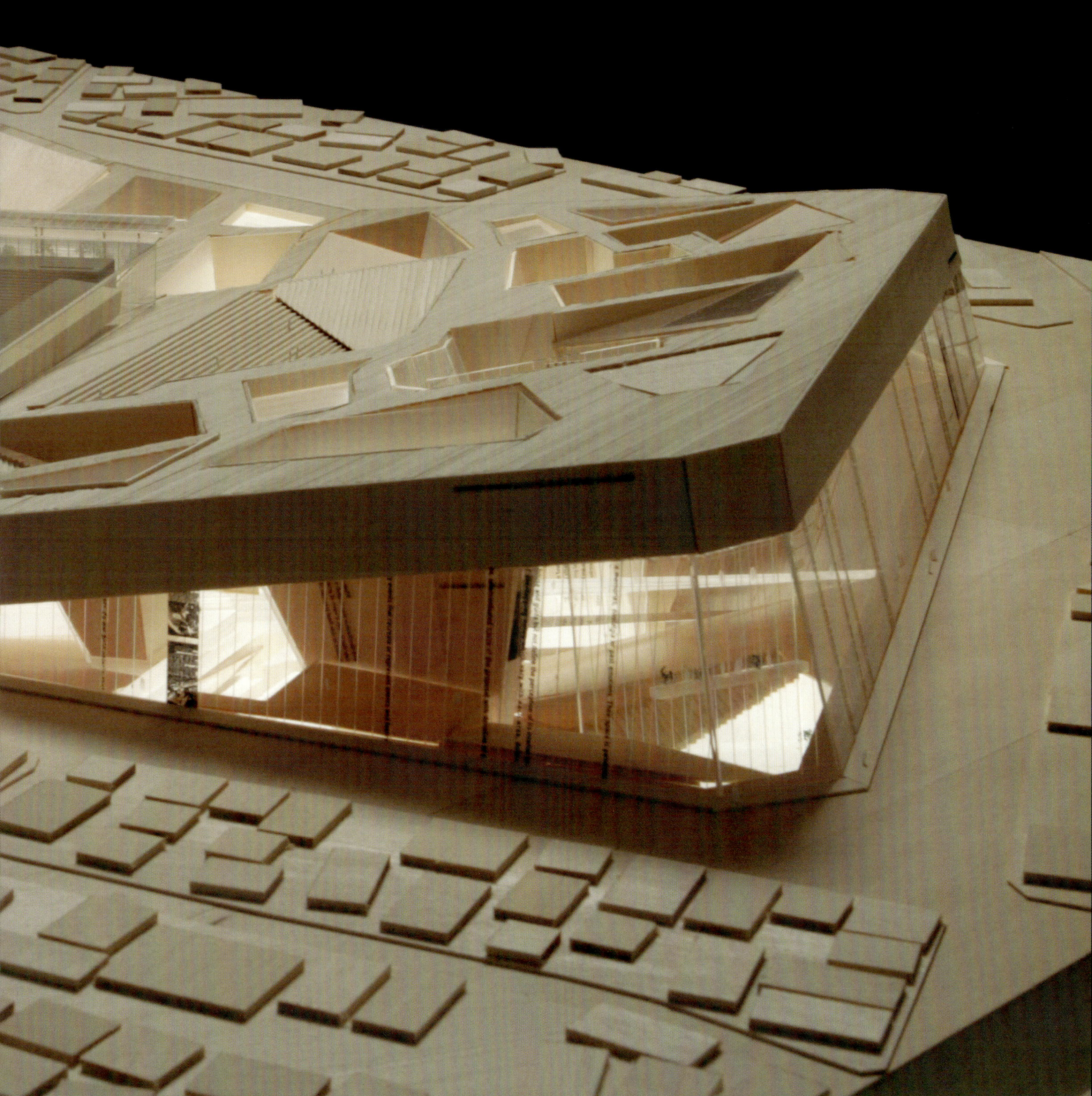

Jangdong Rotary

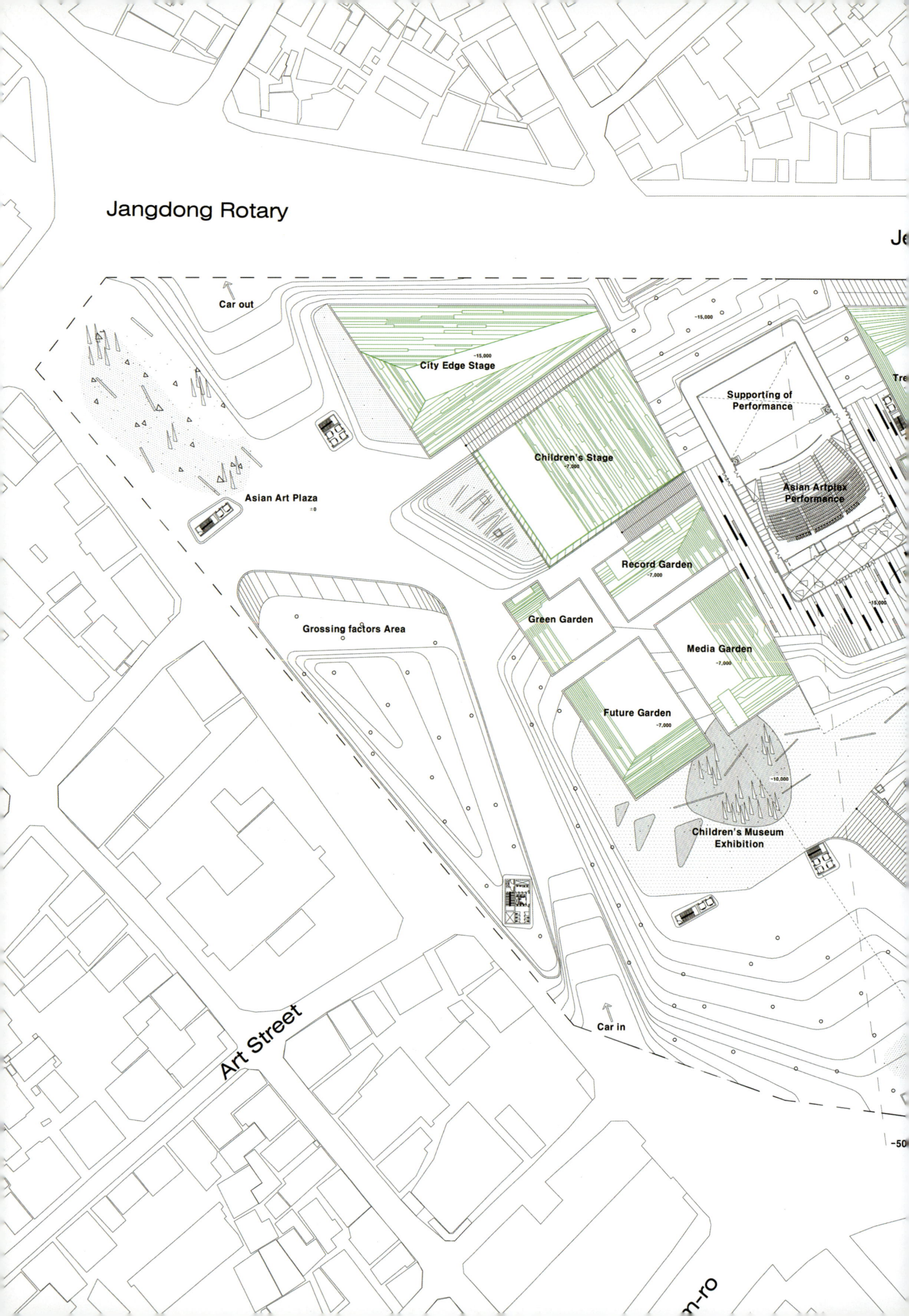

Car out

City Edge Stage
−15,000

Supporting of Performance

Asian Art Plaza
±0

Children's Stage
−7,000

Asian Artplex Performance

Record Garden
−7,000

Green Garden

Grossing factors Area

Media Garden
−7,000

Future Garden
−7,000

Children's Museum Exhibition
−10,000

Art Street

Car in

ro

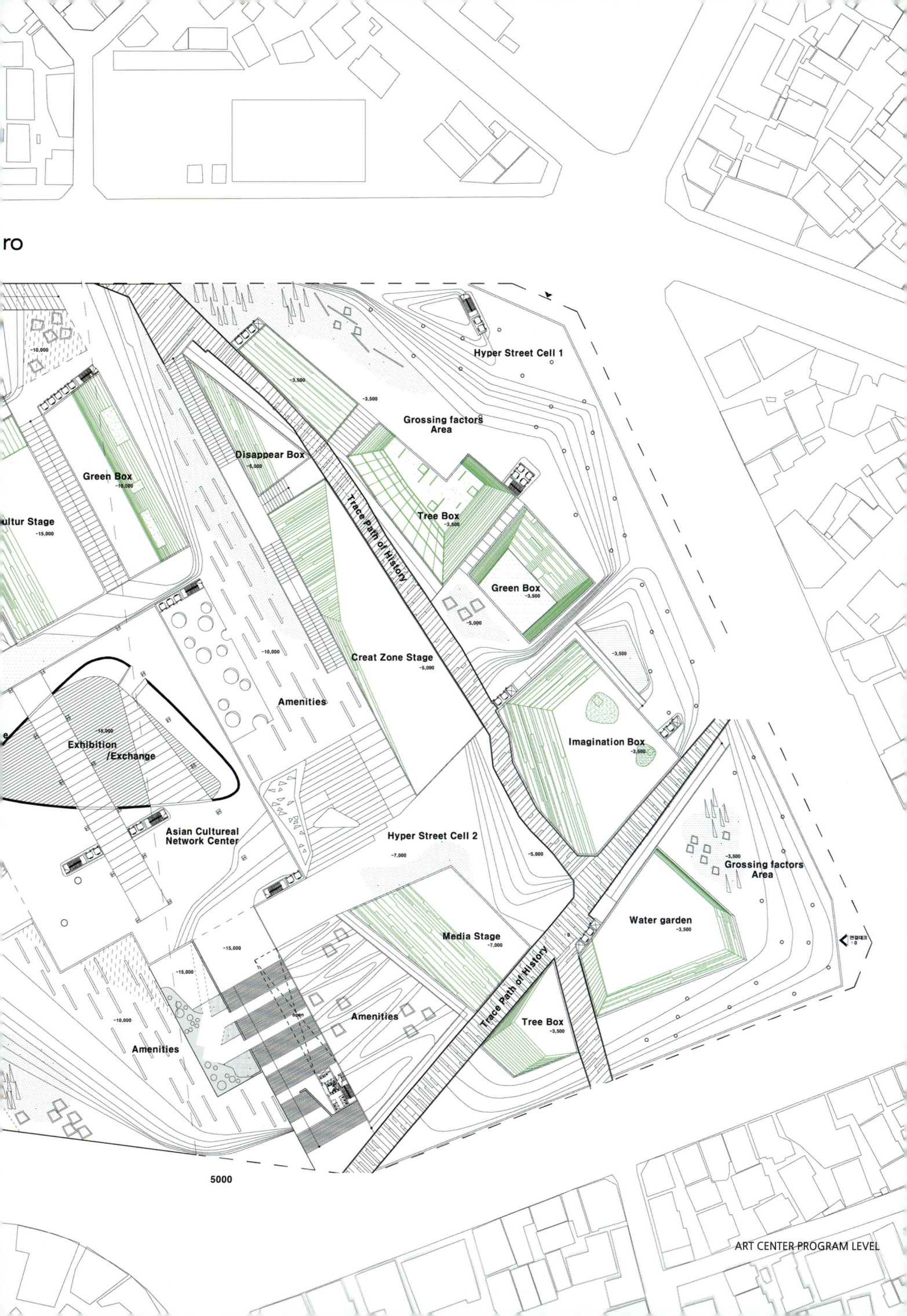

-10,000

Hyper Street Cell 1

Grossing factors Area

Disappear Box
-5,000

Green Box
-10,000

Trace Path of History

Tree Box
-3,500

ultur Stage
-15,000

Green Box
-3,500

-10,000

Creat Zone Stage
-5,000

-3,500

Amenities

Exhibition /Exchange
15,000

Imagination Box
-3,500

Asian Cultureal Network Center

Hyper Street Cell 2
-7,000

-5,000

Grossing factors Area

-15,000

Water garden
-3,500

Media Stage
-7,000

-10,000

Amenities

Trace Path of History

Amenities

Tree Box
-3,500

5000

ART CENTER PROGRAM LEVEL

Jangdong Rotary Jebong-ro

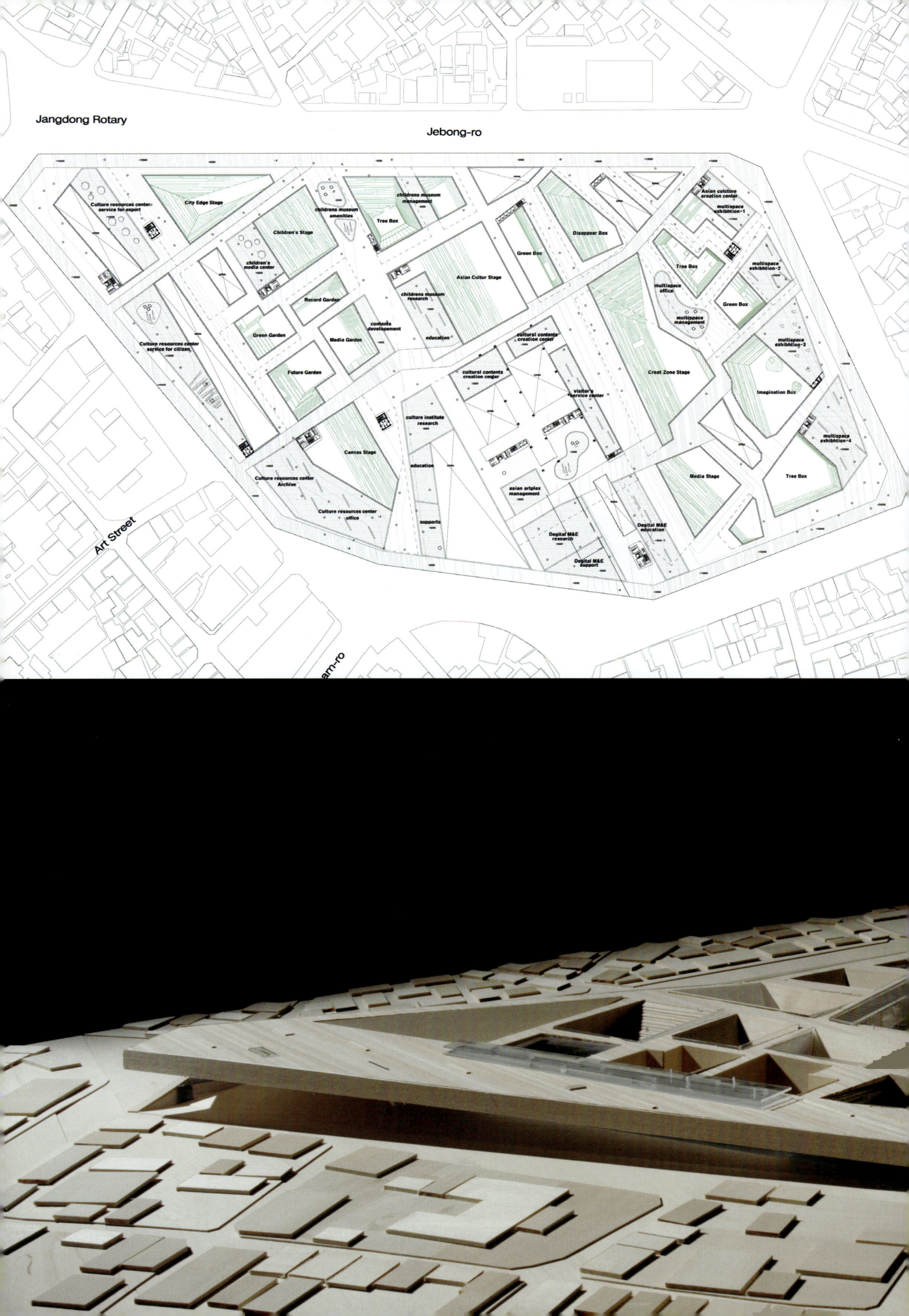

Art Street

Jangdong Rotary
Jebong-ro

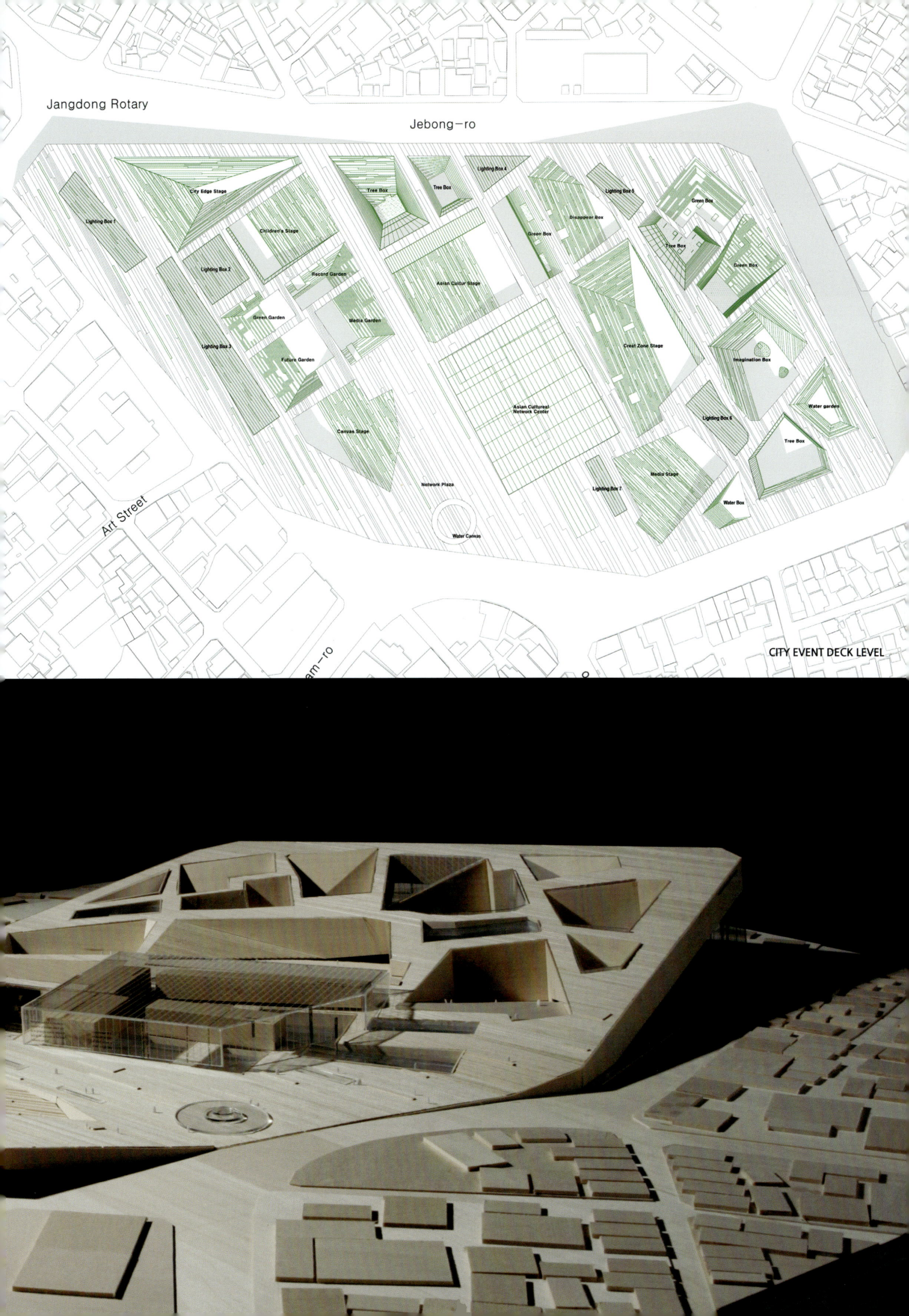

Lighting Box 1
City Edge Stage
Tree Box
Tree Box
Lighting Box 4
Lighting Box 5
Green Box
Children's Stage
Disappear Box
Green Box
Lighting Box 2
Record Garden
Tree Box
Green Garden
Asian Cultur Stage
Green Box
Media Garden
Lighting Box 3
Future Garden
Creat Zone Stage
Imagination Box
Canvas Stage
Asian Cultureal Network Center
Water garden
Lighting Box 6
Tree Box
Network Plaza
Lighting Box 7
Media Stage
Water Box

Art Street

Water Canvas

am-ro

CITY EVENT DECK LEVEL

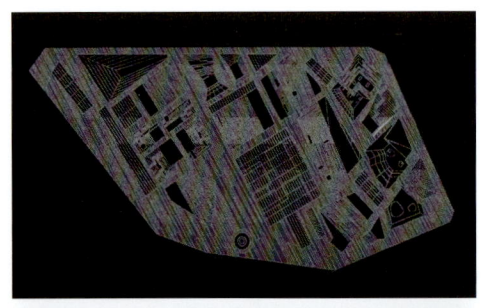

Defining the Trace of History

History Mapping

Street Cell

Cultural Link

Event Stage Mapping

Event Stage Link

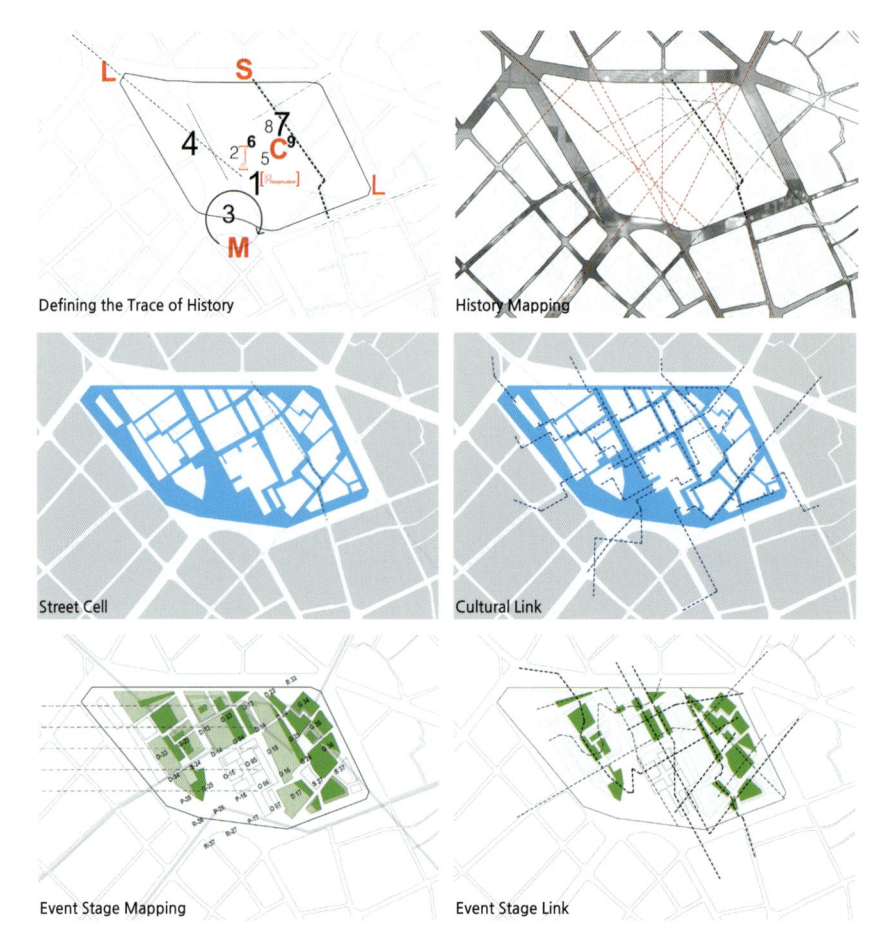

Trace of History

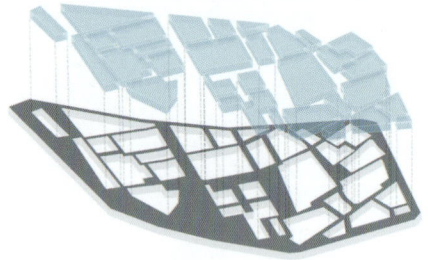

Urban Landscape of Historical Memories

Event Stage for Activities

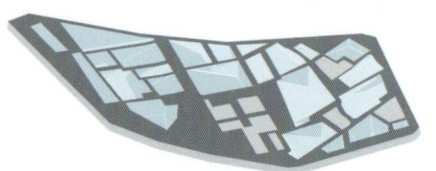

Integration of Stage

Extruded Plaza as Compound Body
We propose to make the new plaza as the compound body a system that randomly assembles urban fabric, landscape, paths, open space, built structure, and programs through which the new cultural courage can be generated. Two-dimensional skin of the plaza is extruded to become spatial skin. Not only stopping at changing the urban topography through spatial morphing, the plaza is rearranged by matching with diverse codes required cultural code, artistic code, urban code, ... matched with spatial code. The plaza is not a two-dimensional urban surface, but rather the multi-dimensional space with layers and folds of spaces that is matched by several codes. It becomes the framework of earthly generation that accommodate multiple channels of arts.

Recording of Gwangju
- History and Urban Fabric
We propose to establish the Complex through morphing the earth. The Complex becomes the strata of contours tracing the history of Gwangju and its memories of various events, while preserving the existing urban fabric.
1) Trace of History
2) Urban Landscape of Historical Memories
3) Event Stage for Activities
4) Integration of Stages

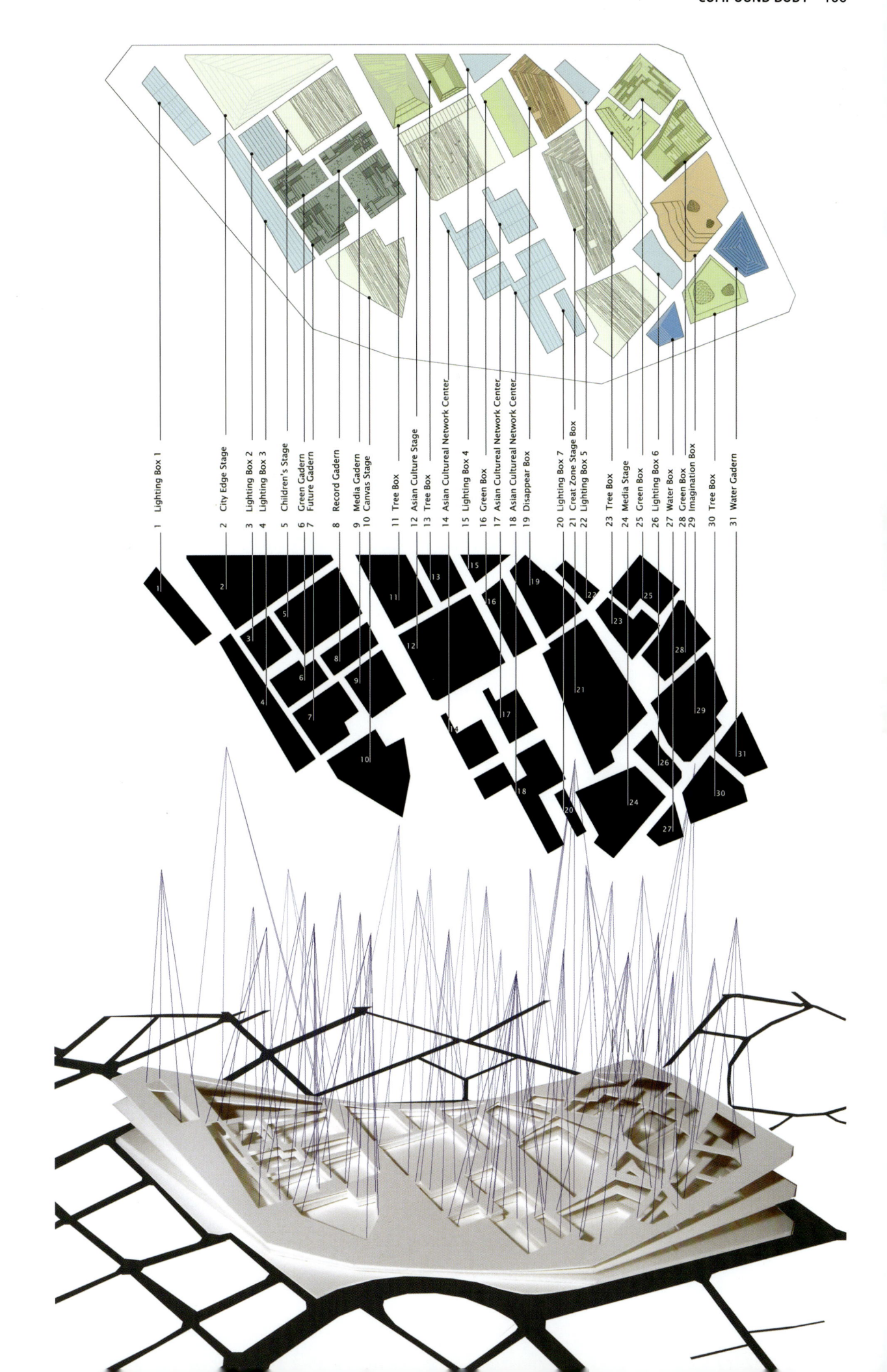

COMPOUND BODY 155

1 Lighting Box 1
2 City Edge Stage
3 Lighting Box 2
4 Lighting Box 3
5 Children's Stage
6 Green Gadern
7 Future Gadern
8 Record Gadern
9 Media Gadern
10 Canvas Stage
11 Tree Box
12 Asian Culture Stage
13 Tree Box
14 Asian Cultureal Network Center
15 Lighting Box 4
16 Green Box
17 Asian Cultureal Network Center
18 Asian Cultureal Network Center
19 Disappear Box
20 Lighting Box 7
21 Creat Zone Stage Box
22 Lighting Box 5
23 Tree Box
24 Media Stage
25 Green Box
26 Lighting Box 6
27 Water Box
28 Green Box
29 Imagination Box
30 Tree Box
31 Water Gadern

Defining the Trace of History

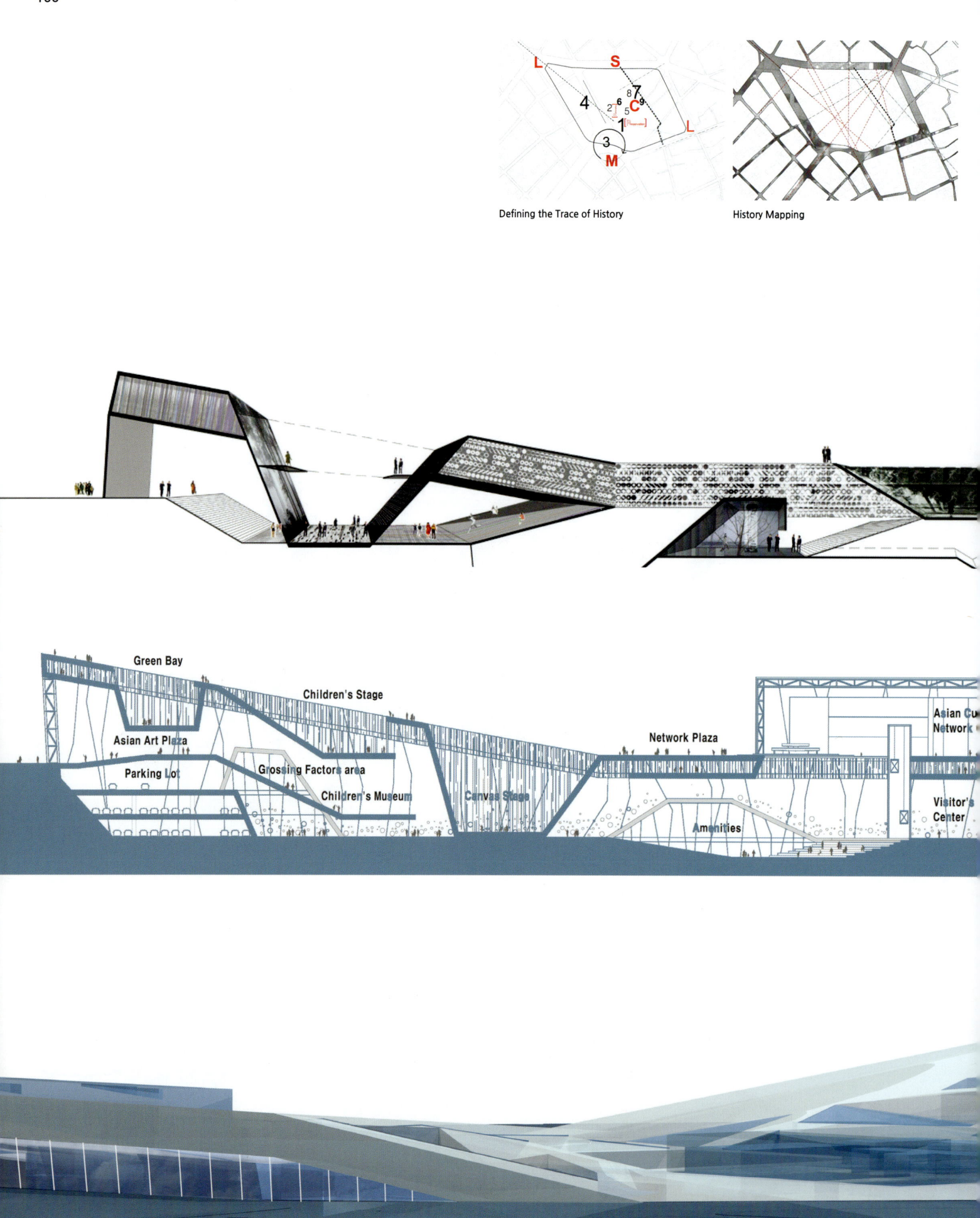

History Mapping

Green Bay
Children's Stage
Asian Art Plaza
Network Plaza
Parking Lot
Crossing Factors area
Children's Museum
Canvas Stage
Amenities
Asian Cu Network
Visitor's Center

COMPOUND BODY 157

Street Cell

Cultural Link

Event Stage Mapping

Event Stage Link

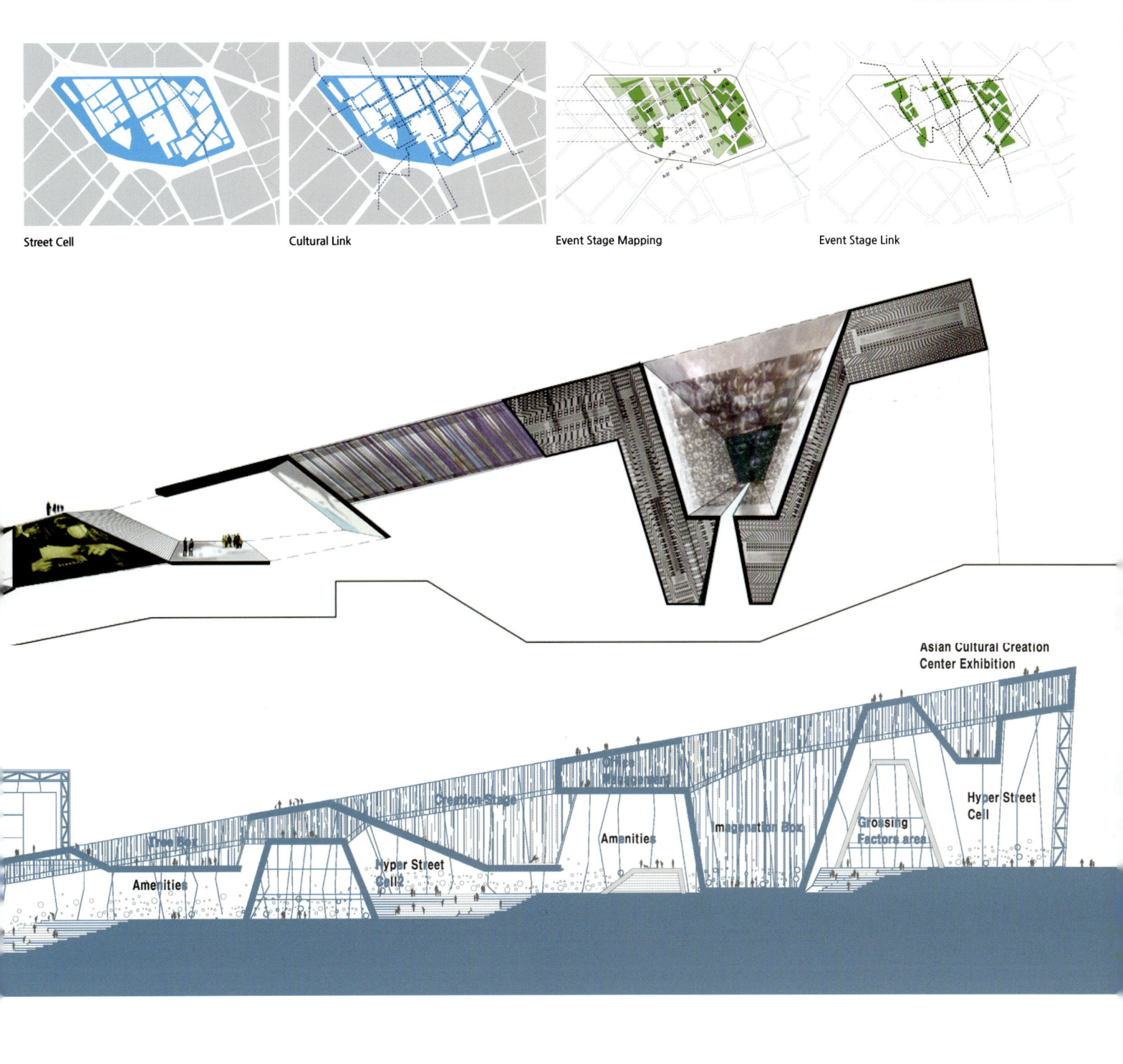

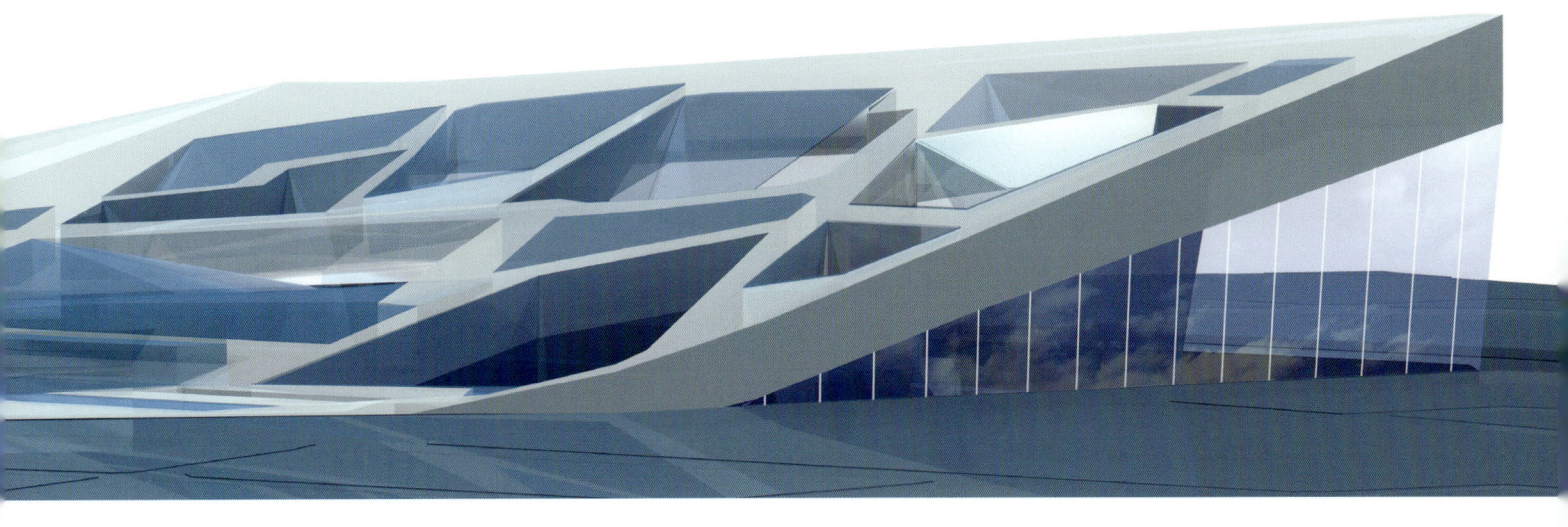

Asian Cultural Creation Center Exhibition

Extruded Plasz

COMPOUND BODY 159

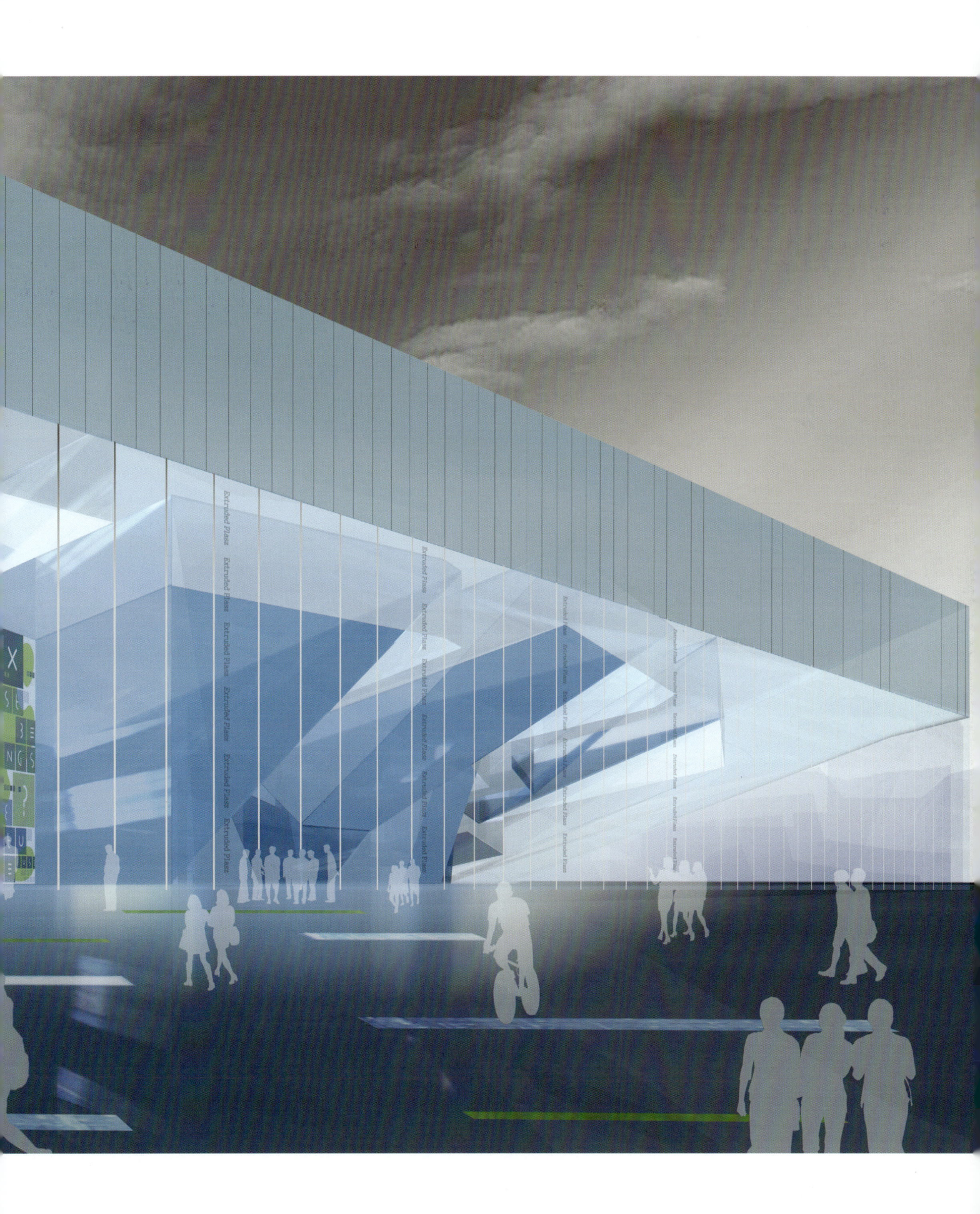

160 Interactive
music stage with evnet bubble

Music Pad
Outdoor Amphitheater for Youth in Nodeul Island

| International Competition Winner | **Architects** Jang Yoon Gyoo, Shin Chang Hoon
Photographer Kim Bong Kyun | **COMPOUND BODY** 181 |

NODEL ISLAND

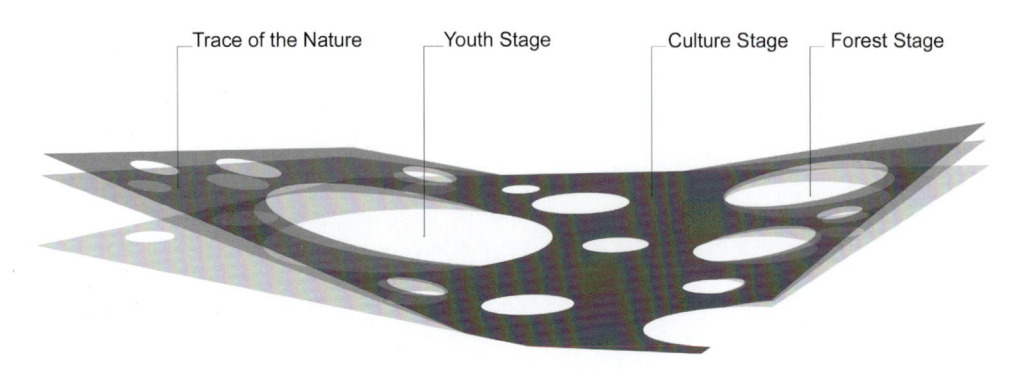

Trace of the Nature — Youth Stage — Culture Stage — Forest Stage

INTERACTIVE MUSIC STAGE

INTERACTIVE MUSIC STAGE with EVENT BUBBLE

Music Stage

We suggest "Outdoor Youth Amphitheatre at Nodeul Island" as a music stage accommodating both various musical events and Landscape. The new topographic frame we suggest is a combination of landscape and stage.

The new topography resembling a mat consists of various cultural stages which are a combination of bubble map and landscape map. On the cracks of the Lifted topography, the main function; a concert hall for the youth makes musical performances possible on the site. The relationship between the important factors filling the site that include metaphorical expressions of music, water waves, open sky and various programs are being re-interpreted. And The Music Pad, The Water Pad, The Sky Pad are suggested through the building method of nature.

Folding & Flowing

Wave Length

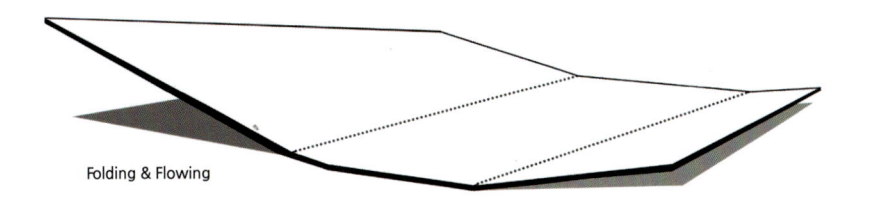

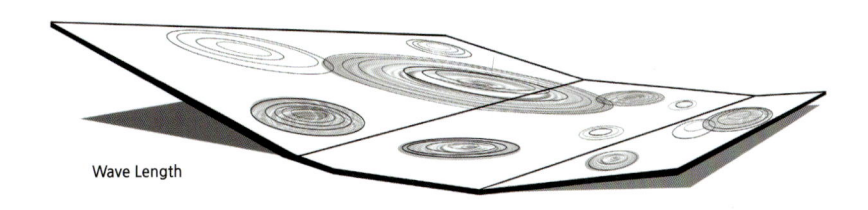

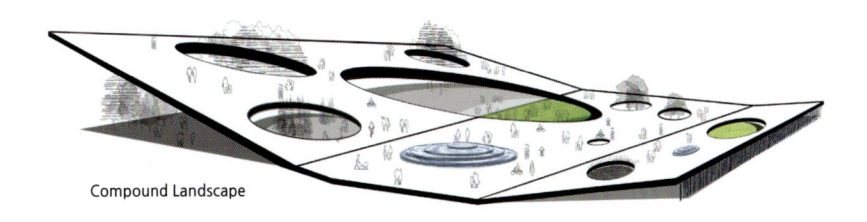

Compound Landscape

FOLDING AND WAVELENGTH LANDSCAPE

Landscape Compound
Outdoor concert stages, nature, light and water have no boundaries and these factors which exceed a single purpose, constitute organic form and programs.
Artificial Deck connects nature with humans and programs, interactively changed by the time and the purpose as networking equipment. Nature Hub filled with many activities is opened to both art and the audience.

3-dimensional Plaza
The space of Nodeul Island isn't just nature with separated skins, but a connection of manipulated topographic levels according to programs that provide urban and cultural public space. To make compound green space, we suggest Folding and Wavelength Landscape which will make continuous flow on the site. Different landscaping programs are laid within a transformed 3-dimensional site. Half outdoor landscape will be a cultural container filled with architecture, culture and youth providing a new experience

Culture Plaza

Our aim is to set up a stage like a bowl filling with culture and music of Seoul. It makes a topographic skin as it forms an outdoor concert hall. The skin transformation to the spatial plaza and the musical combination of various codes such as landscape, event, performance and concerts will make up the cultural plaza. The role of Nodeul Island, beyond Natural Island, will represent a cultural code of Seoul, producing musical depths and youth culture.

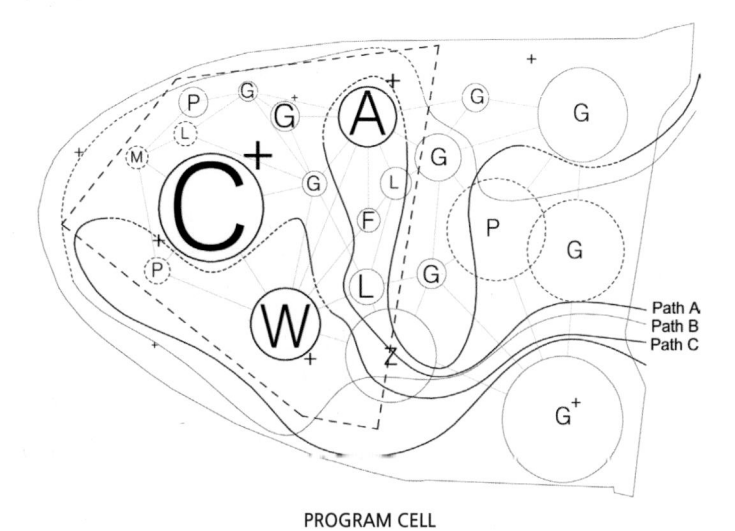

PROGRAM CELL

NETWORK FLOW IN LANDSCAPE

Musical Wave Mat

Our suggestion is starting with a young stage of leading voluntary youth culture. The young generation's breath is pounding like waves of lively heartbeats from Music Pad. It will fill the whole of Nodeul Island with youth and hopeful sounds.

Music Pad

Sound field of the landscape.
Each music pads are filled with these factors below.
Music Pad-01 : Youth outdoor concert hall
Music Pad-02 : The concert hall of water
Music Pad-03 : The sound of water
Music Pad-04 : The sound of wind and tree
Music Pad-05 : The sound of light
The waves of different music pads will be harmonized and overlapped, and the site will sing along with them.
The sounds, which are the essence of music, have sensory factors such as steady pitch, volume and tone and the difference is distinguished by them. Eventually the material of music is the sound which is caused by the physical phenomenon, wave. It will become an art of time that expresses philosophy and emotions by regular forms and rules such as tempo, melody, harmony, tone and so on.

Water Pad

Inside consists of the factors below.
Water Pad-01 : Water Garden
Water Pad-02 : Dropping water and rainbow
Water Pad-03 : the site and flowing water
Water Pad-04 : Tree and dancing water
Han River and Nodeul Island are connected visually through water space, so Water Pad will produce abundant experiences.

Sky Pad

Artificial site combined with youth concert halls will produce a seat for new music concerts below the roof of nature. Sky Pad is opened to nature and the structure works as an aperture towards sky. This is scenery equipment.

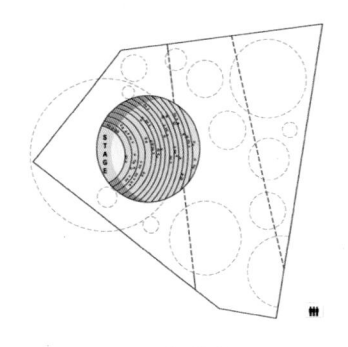

COMPOUND BODY 165

STAGE 01 BASIC CONCERT HALL	STAGE 02 EXTENSION STAGE	STAGE 03 LANDSCAPE STAGE
CULTURE STAGE	HARMONY, MUSIC PAD	LIGHTING SCAPE & WATER POINT
STRUCTURE	MOVING LANDSCAPE	TOPOGROPHY OF THE LANDSCAPE
NATURE HUB	MUSIC PAD	WATER PAD

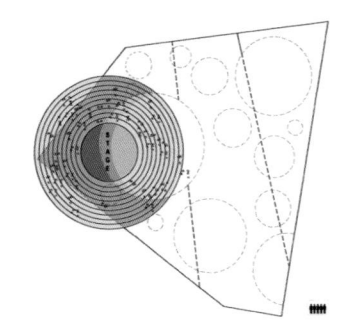

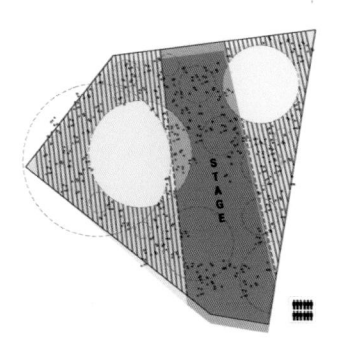

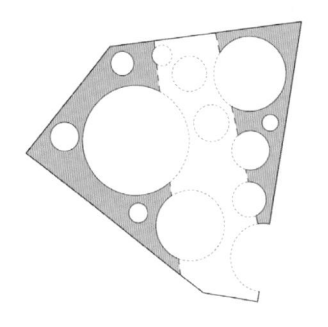

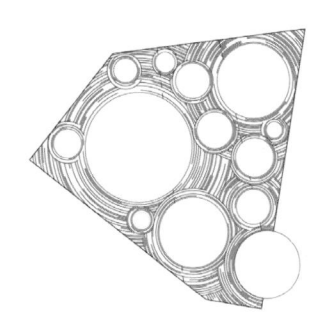

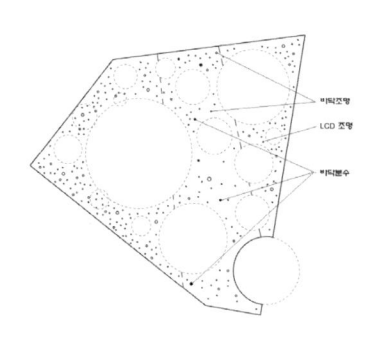

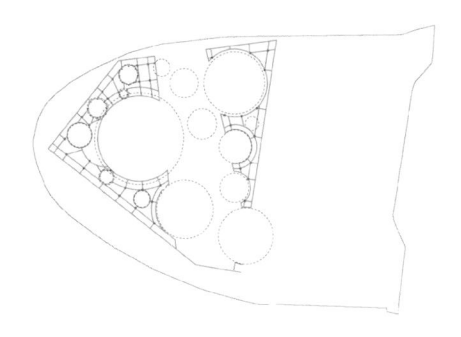

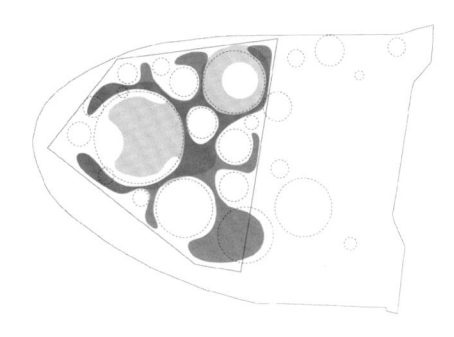

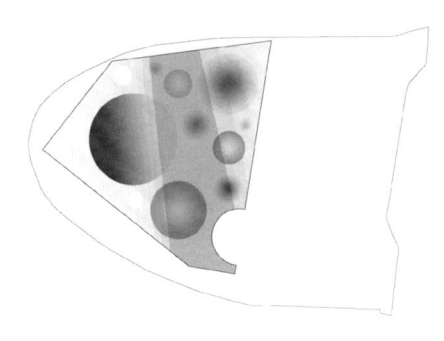

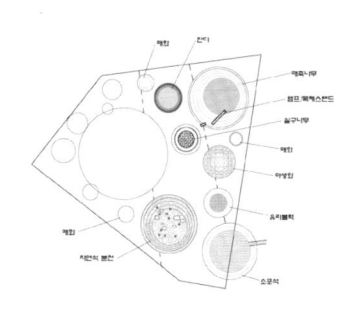

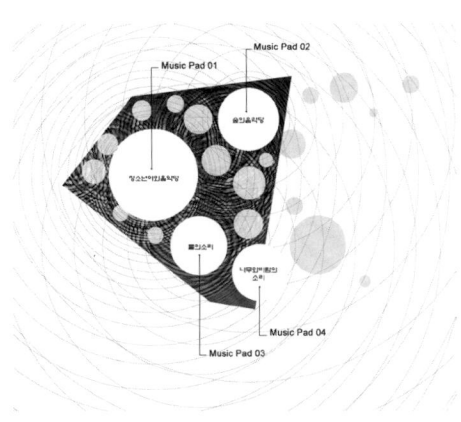

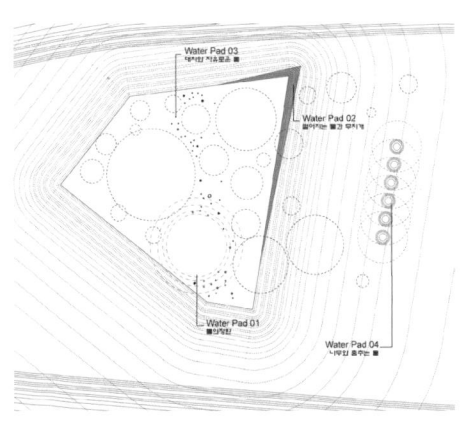

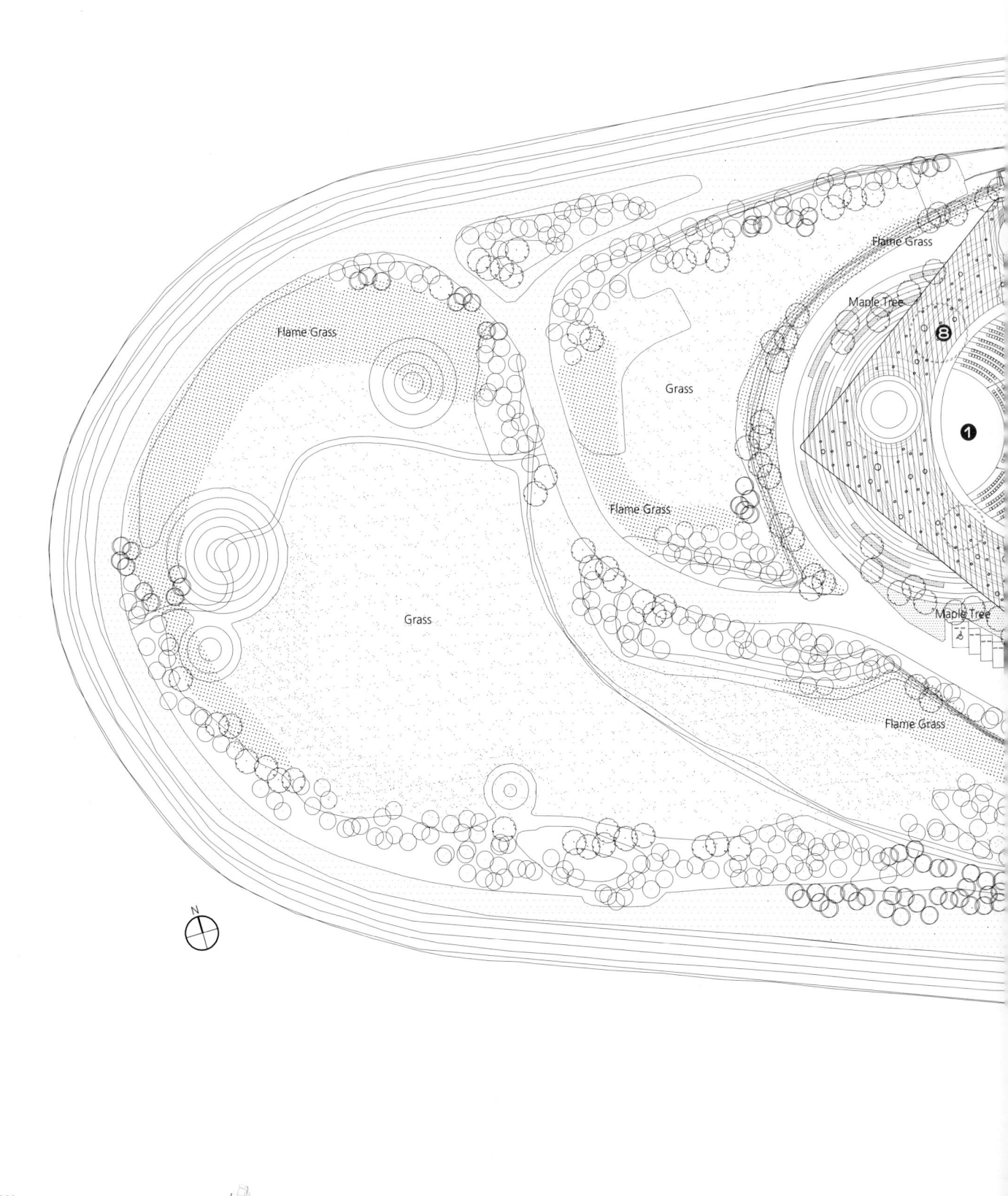

Flame Grass
Maple Tree
Flame Grass
Grass
Flame Grass
Grass
Maple Tree
Flame Grass

LEVEL +14,000
LEVEL −1,000
LEVEL −5,000

Green
Stage
Event Stage

Willow Tree
ese Apricot Tree
Snowbell Tree
Lamp / Wood Stand
Japanese Apricot Tree
Apricot Tree
Zelkova Tree
Flame Grass
Poplar Tree
Flame Grass

MASTER PLAN
1. Youth Concert Stage
2. Water Garden
3. Meeting Plaza
4. Grass Garden
5. Amphitheater of Forest
6. Soil Garden
7. Flower Garden
8. Parking

Green   Land Object Stage   Lighting

LEVEL +4,000

LEVEL ± 0

The Garden of Water Streaming

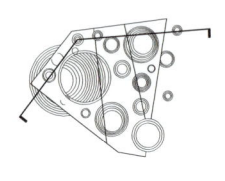

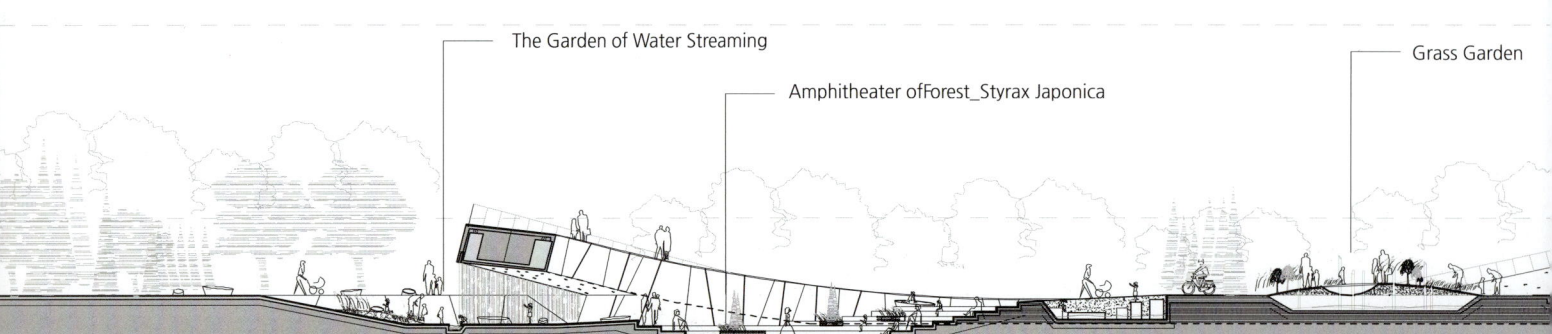

Amphitheater of Forest_Styrax Japonica

Grass Garden

COMPOUND BODY 169

Location
302-146 Ichon-dong Yongsang-gu Seoul, Korea
Use
Outdoor Youth Amphitheatre
Site Area 22,613m²
Building Area 557m²
Gross Floor Area 716.45m²
Building Coverage 2.55%
Floor Space Index 3.17%
Building Scope 2F
Structure
Steel, Reinforced Concrete
Design Period 2006. 11

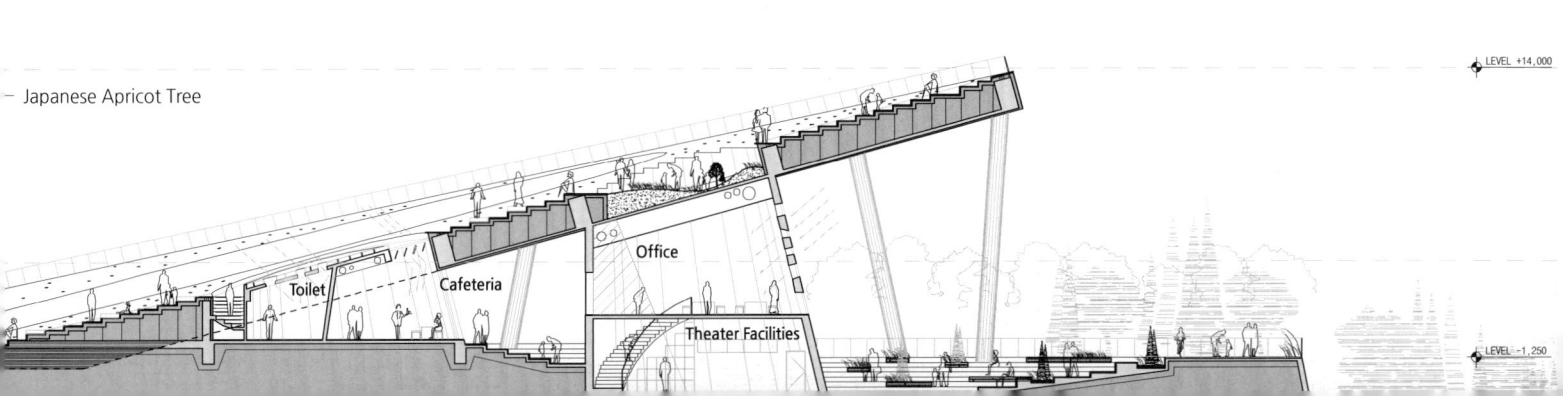

Japanese Apricot Tree

KTNG Complex Center

FLYING
CITY

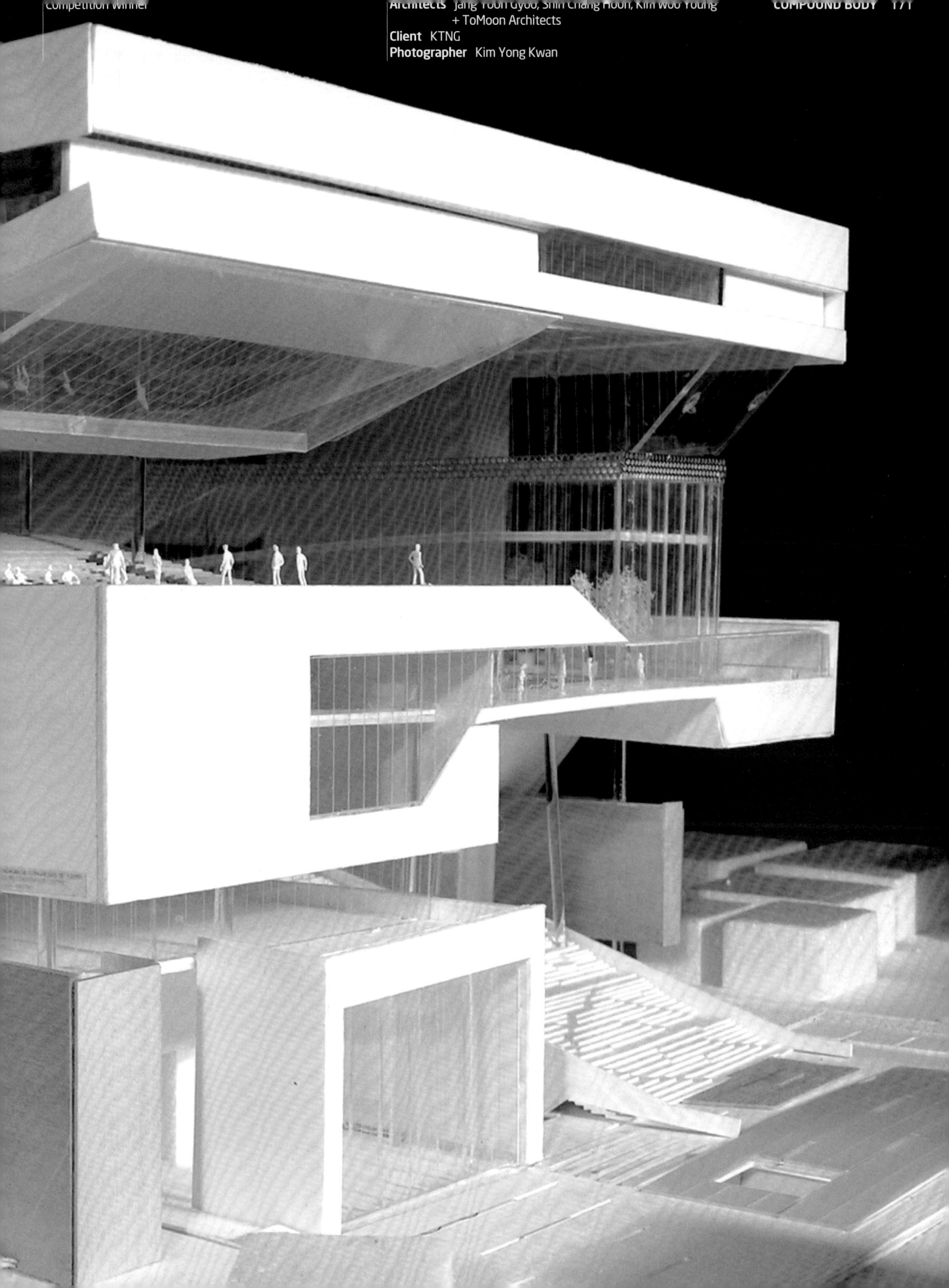

Architects Jang Yoon Gyoo, Shin Chang Hoon, Kim Woo Young
+ ToMoon Architects
Client KTNG
Photographer Kim Yong Kwan

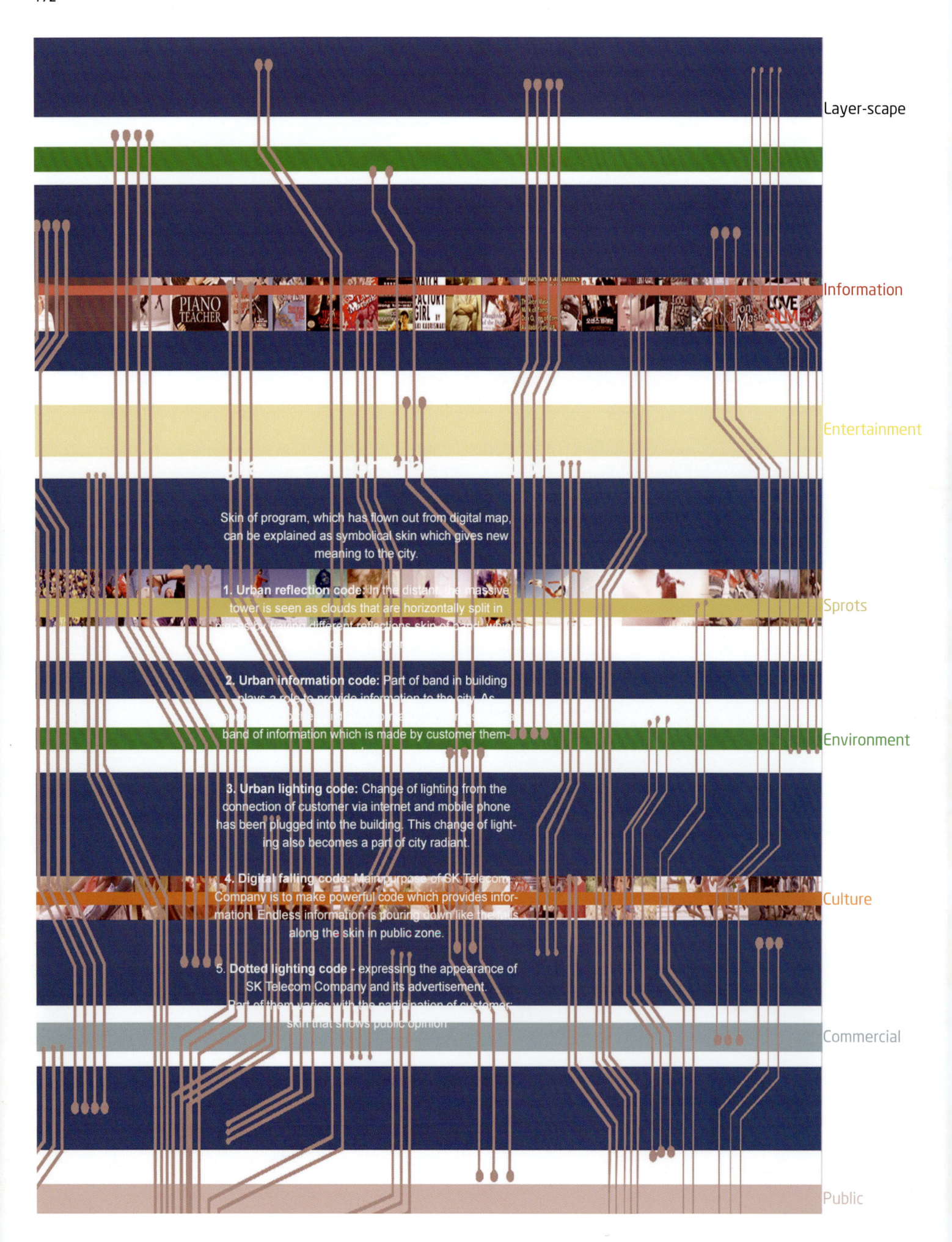

Skin of program, which has flown out from digital map, can be explained as symbolical skin which gives new meaning to the city.

1. Urban reflection code: In the distance, the massive tower is seen as clouds that are horizontally split in spaces by having different reflections skin of band. March of seasons…

2. Urban information code: Part of band in building plays a role to provide information to the city. As such… Plug-in… zone…. It is a band of information which is made by customer themselves.

3. Urban lighting code: Change of lighting from the connection of customer via internet and mobile phone has been plugged into the building. This change of lighting also becomes a part of city radiant.

4. Digital falling code: Main purpose of SK Telecom Company is to make powerful code which provides information. Endless information is pouring down like the falls along the skin in public zone.

5. Dotted lighting code - expressing the appearance of SK Telecom Company and its advertisement. Part of them varies with the participation of customer: skin that shows public opinion.

Layer-scape
Information
Entertainment
Sprots
Environment
Culture
Commercial
Public

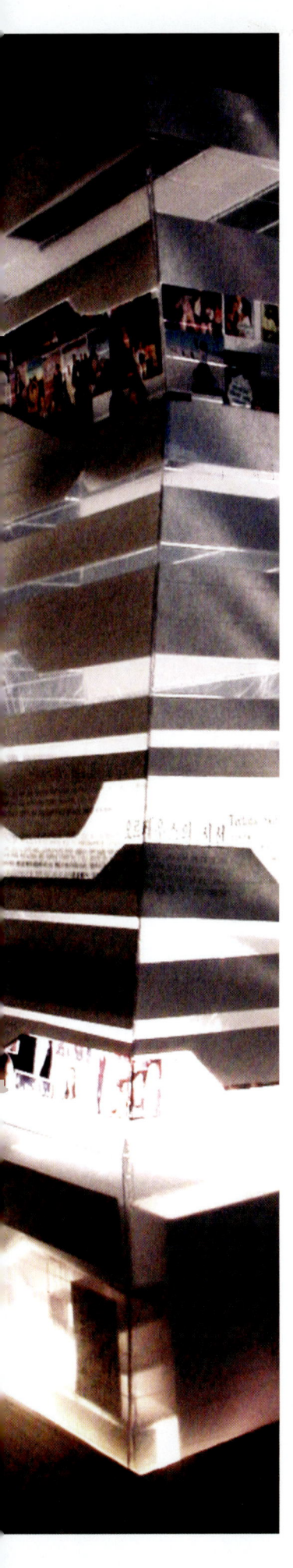

FLYING CITY

Imagine a flying city free from the ground. This floating city is an urban hovering in the air saturated with freshness, The youth mesmerized with this imaginative spirit nurture new fantasies, Numerous cityscapes are clustered together layer after layer and from the flying city of vast commercial and cultural space. This gravity-free zone rearranges streets, plazas, forest, shops, amusement park, and park. It is a city of imagination that is free from the earth.

Theatrical Space as a multicultural space, the flying city will actively help young people to perform leading roles in expanding stage volumn. The theatrical spaces, the trademark of the flying city, serves as a cultural center that can provide various imaginative resources by building events such as shopping, game, entertainment, multimedia, education, clinic, and community activities. Moving street The maximum employment of the commercial belt on the horizontal streets allows the building to host three dimensional spaces where various programs can be easily applied, The contents of this spaces are to be composed of experimental works with young spirit. Therefore, the space will function as a festive venue for youngsters. Imaginative Atrium The imaginative atrium provides infinite resources of information.

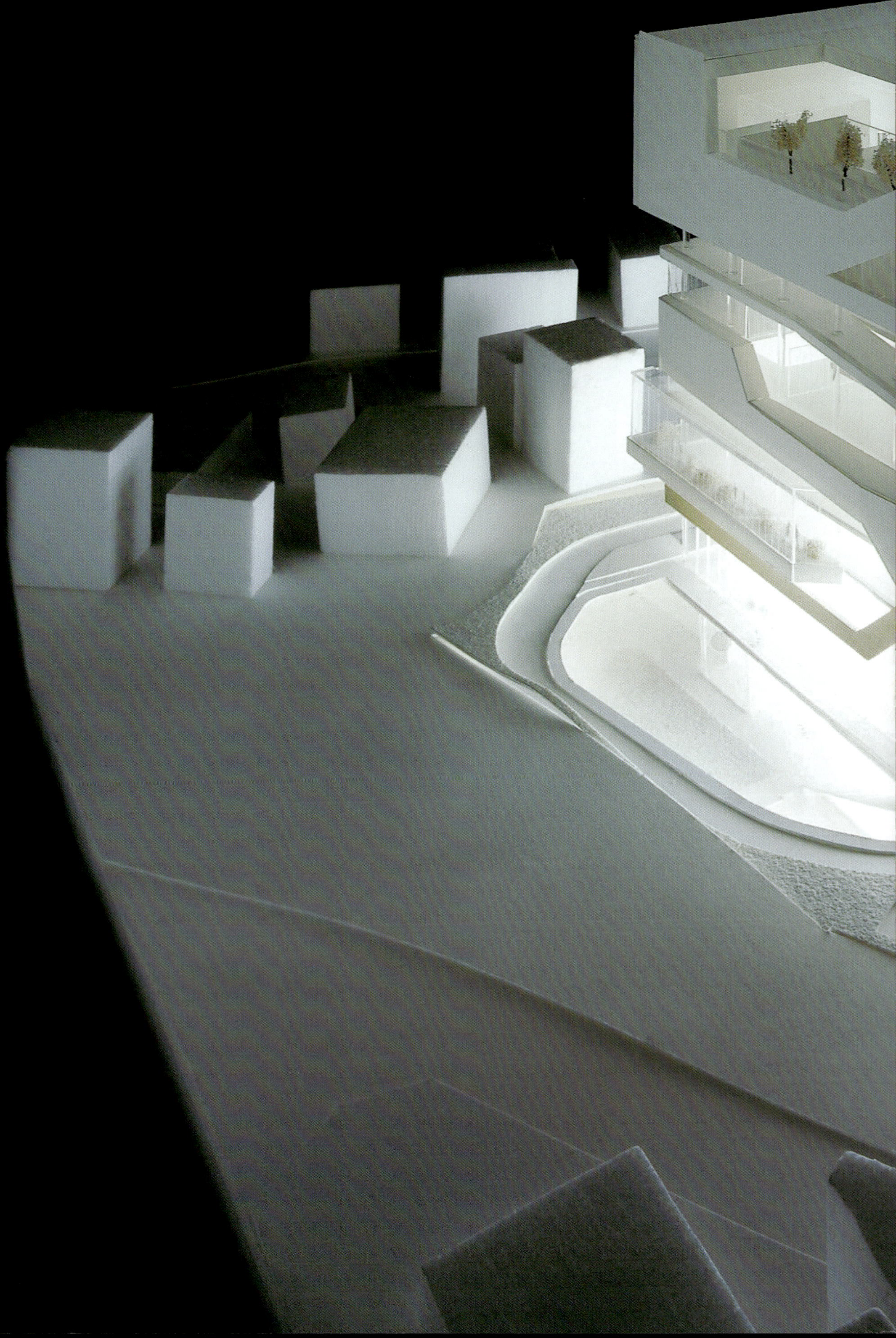

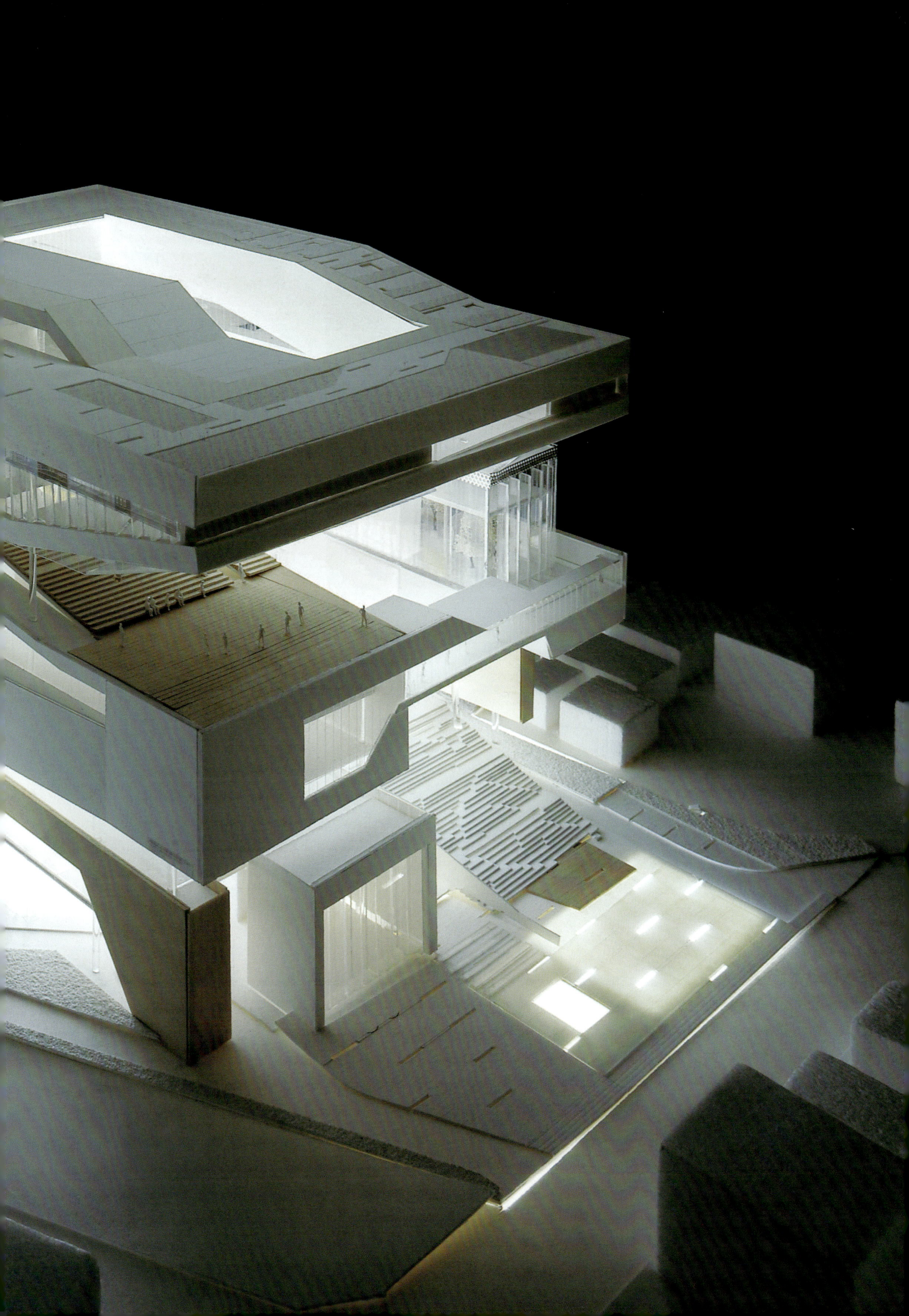

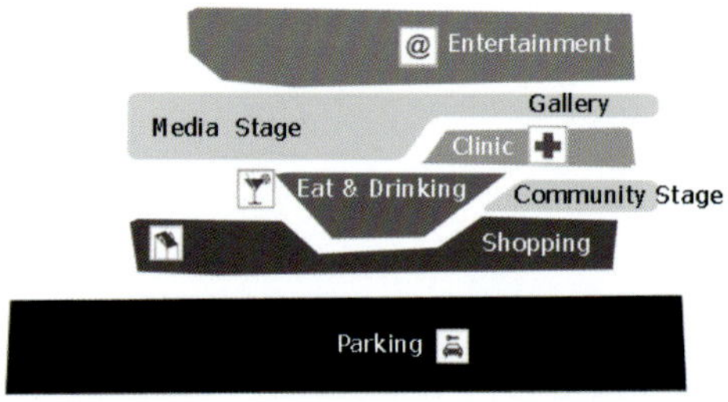
Entertainment
Media Stage
Gallery
Clinic
Eat & Drinking
Community Stage
Shopping
Parking

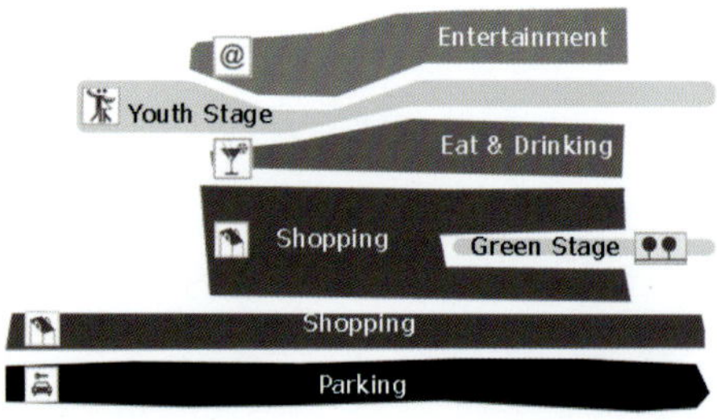
Entertainment
Youth Stage
Eat & Drinking
Shopping
Green Stage
Shopping
Parking

GREEN
MEDIA
Youth stage
imagination stage
COMMUNITY STAGE
GREEN STAGE

Sports
Education
Clinic
Entertainment
Eat & Drinking
Shopping
Parking

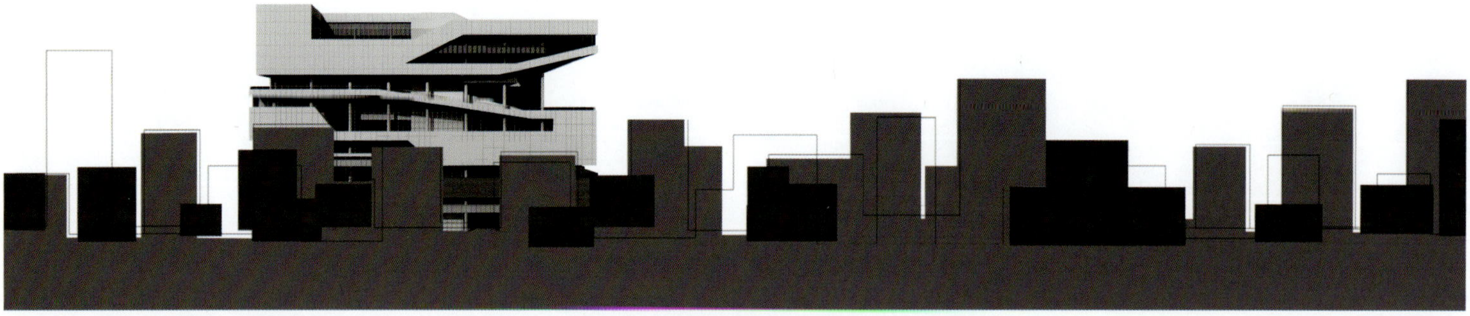

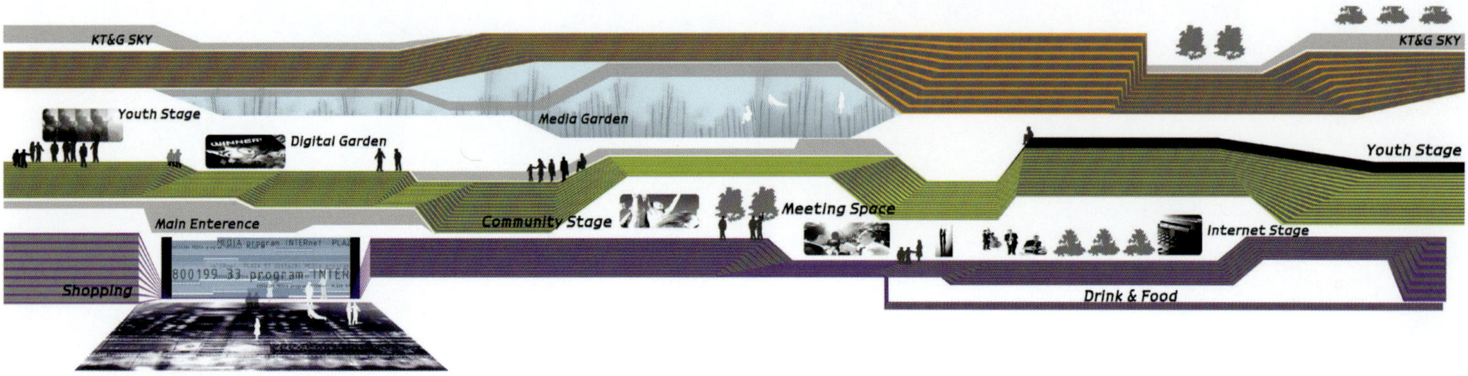
KT&G SKY
KT&G SKY
Youth Stage
Media Garden
Digital Garden
Youth Stage
Main Enterence
Community Stage
Meeting Space
Internet Stage
Shopping
Drink & Food

COMPOUND BODY 177

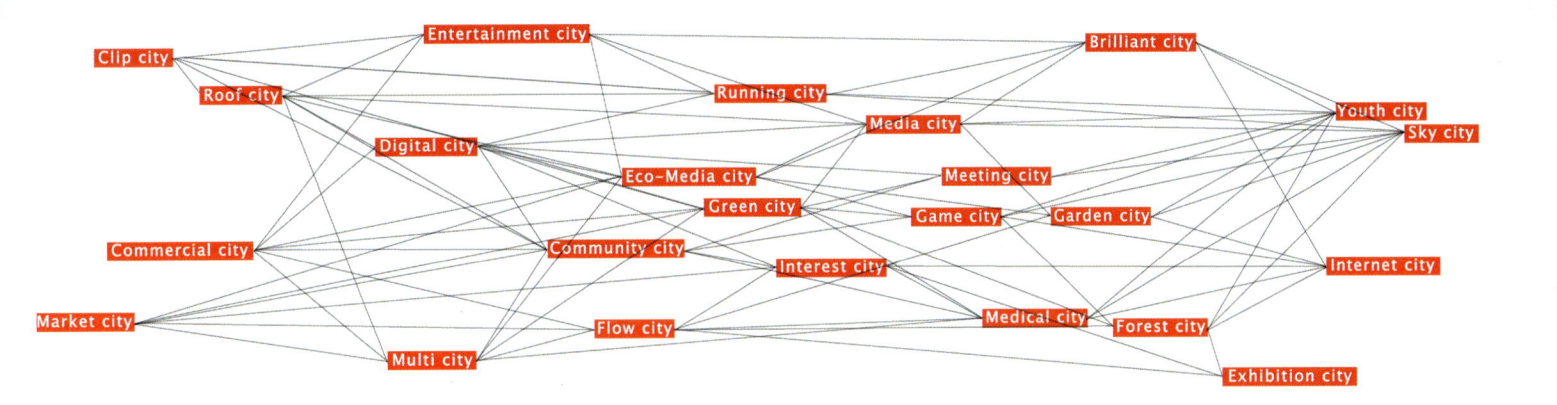

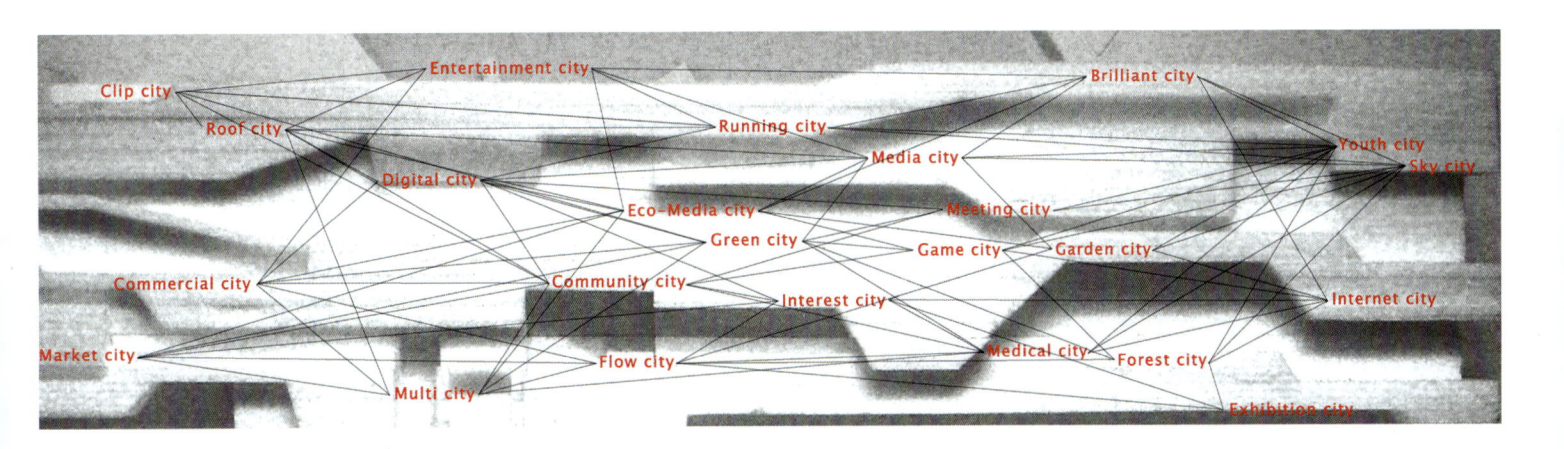

8,9F Entertainment

6,7F Youth Stage/Eat & Drinking

5F Shopping

4F Shopping

3F Shopping

2F Shopping

1F Shopping

COMPOUND BODY 179

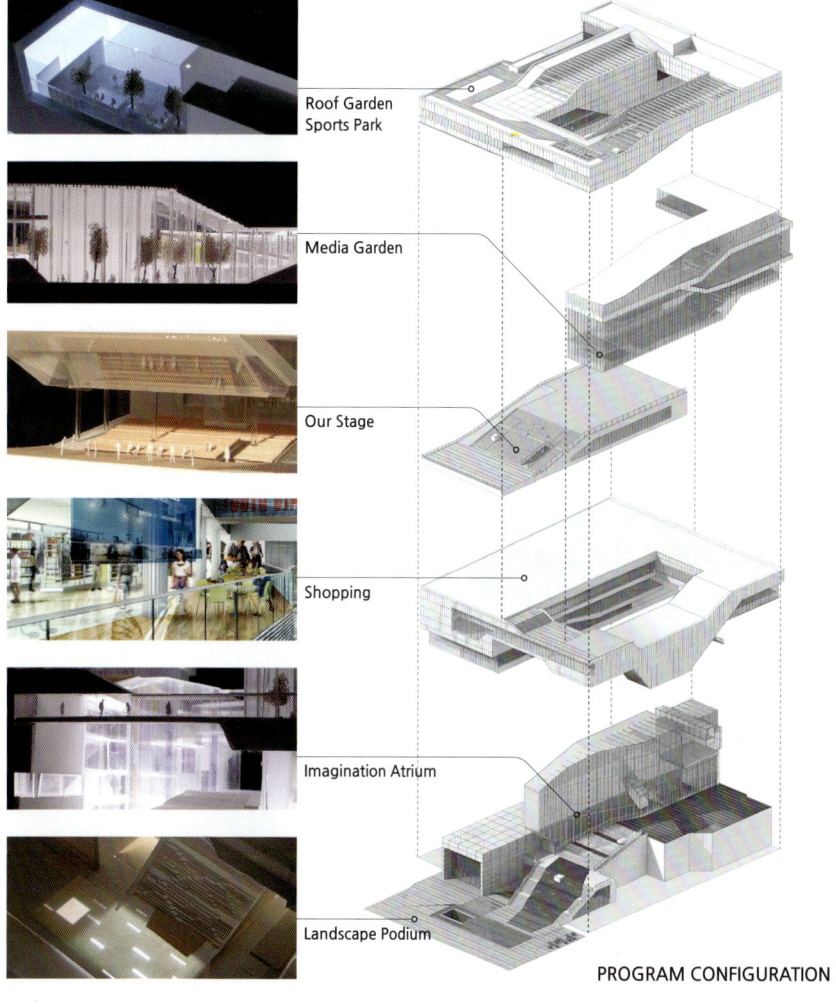

Roof Garden Sports Park

Media Garden

Our Stage

Shopping

Imagination Atrium

Landscape Podium

PROGRAM CONFIGURATION

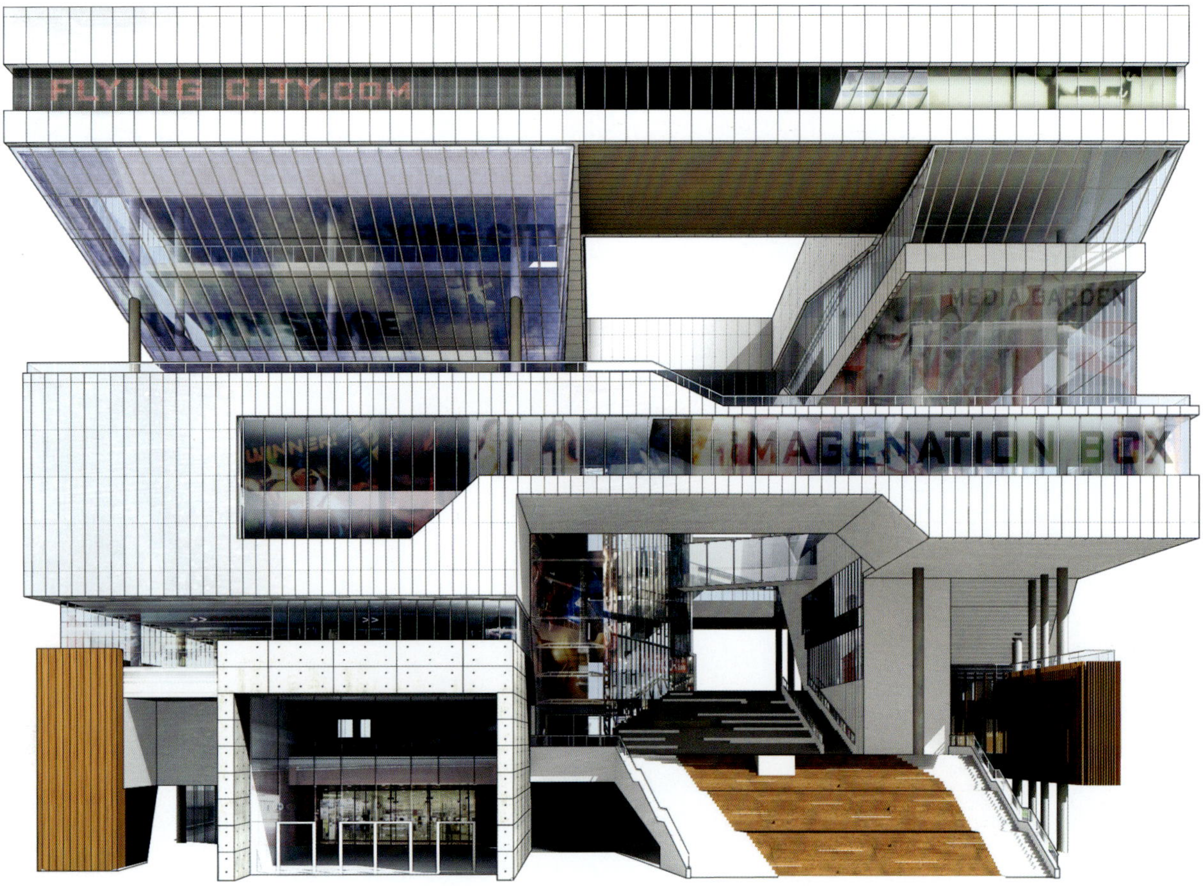
FLYING CITY.COM
MEDIA GARDEN
IMAGENATION BOX

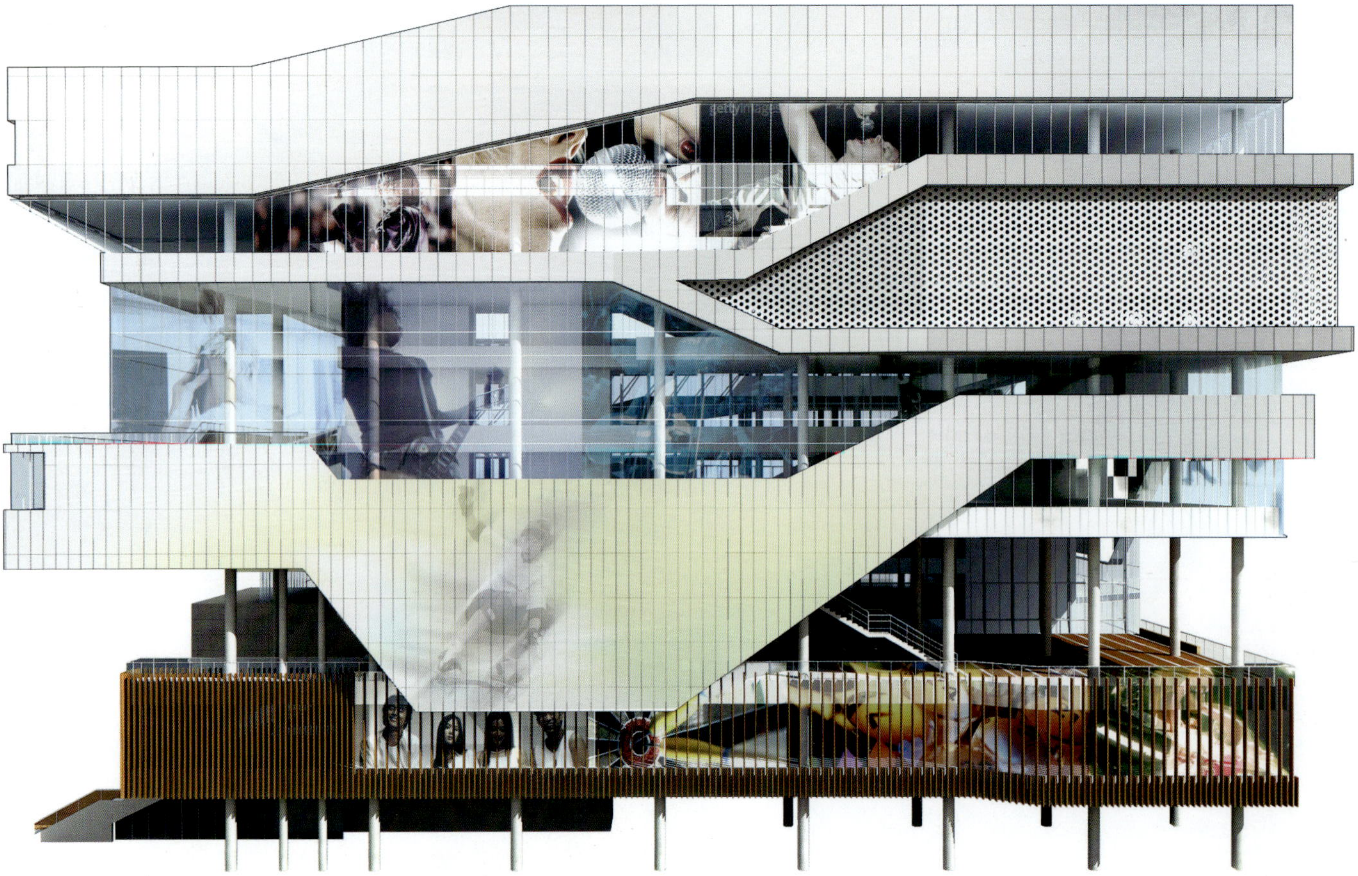

The imaginary wall installed within the atrium serves as a canvas for better communication with the youth. Information about shops and events are to be posted. Program interactive The flying city was not designed to serve one purpose, An interacting program like the one+one strategy generates shopping space+park, and shopping space+stage plaza formula. The crossover between artistic completeness and commercial programs spawns a strong synergy effect. while going through the imaginative atrium and the inner garden, various commercial programs earn authenticity from the synergy effect. A space the deserves a visit is the direction of the multicultural space. So, being interactive is a key to the success. Cubistic Landscape this space is a hybrid of architecture and landscape design.
In other words, the cubistic landscape means various experimental architectural programs that meet elements of landscape design such as green lands, information, lights, and events. The plaza at the facade leads its way to a deck in the building and composes a podium on the cubistic ground which links the space form 1st to 3rd floor. On this cubistic landscape there will be community stage and outdoor screen. The floating landscape that penetrates a part of the whole building provides an exotic rooftop garden where you can enjoy sports and rest. Landmark-Light Sculpture the basic structure of the imaginative box is a mixture of various young imaginative elements. It not only symbolizes liberal spirits of the youth, but also serves as a landmark for young community that can deliver information through the programmed lights. Flying City, Immagination Box

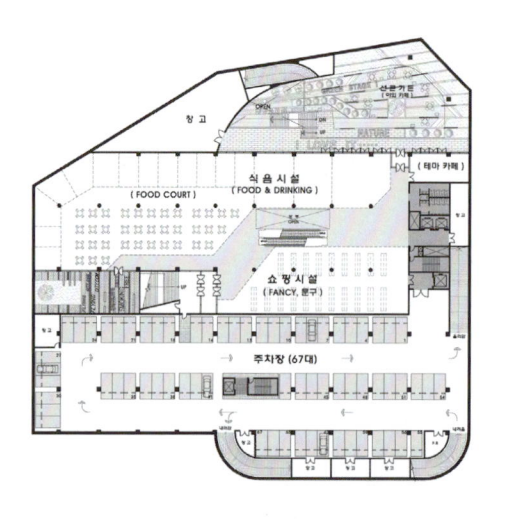

BACEMENT FLOOR PLAN

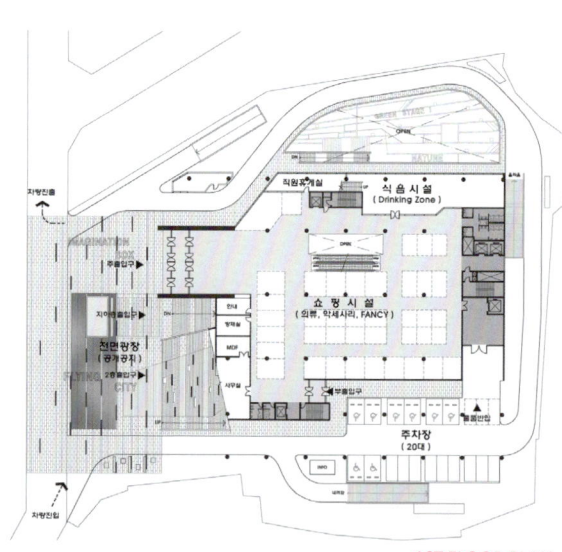

1ST FLOOR PLAN

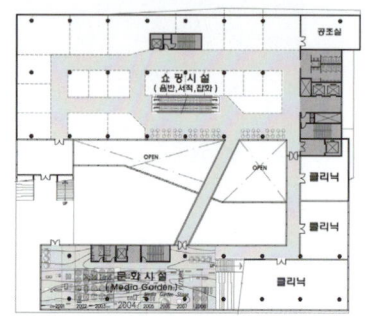

5TH FLOOR PLAN

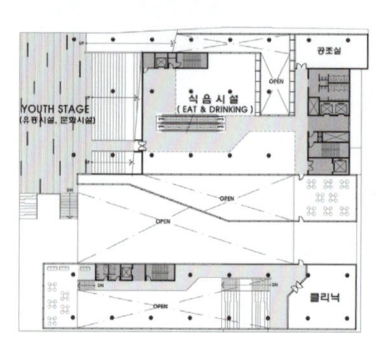

6TH FLOOR PLAN

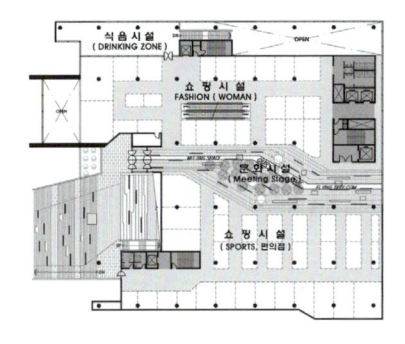

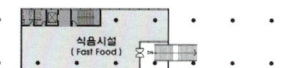

2ND FLOOR PLAN 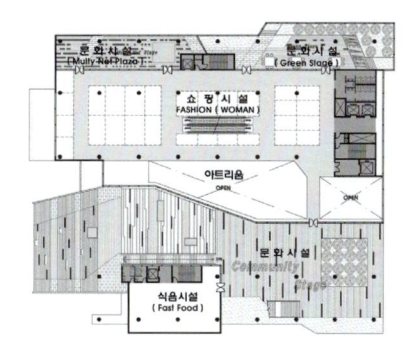   3RD FLOOR PLAN 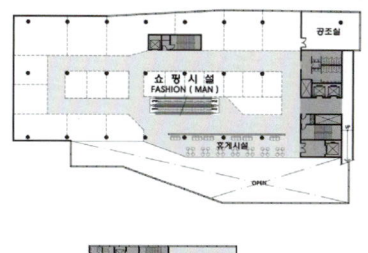   4TH FLOOR PLAN

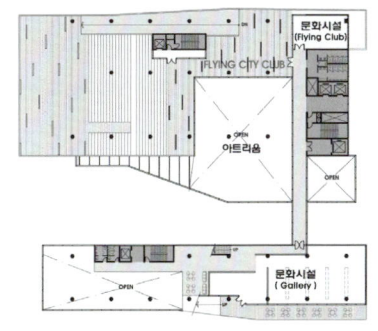

7TH FLOOR PLAN 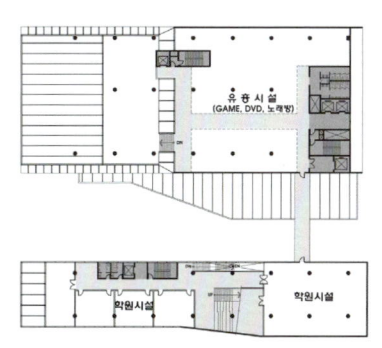   8TH FLOOR PLAN    9TH FLOOR PLAN

Interactive
program

Design Center in Gwangju

Competition Winner

Architects Jang Yoon Gyoo, Kim Woo Il + ToMoon Architects
Photographer Lee Ki Hwan

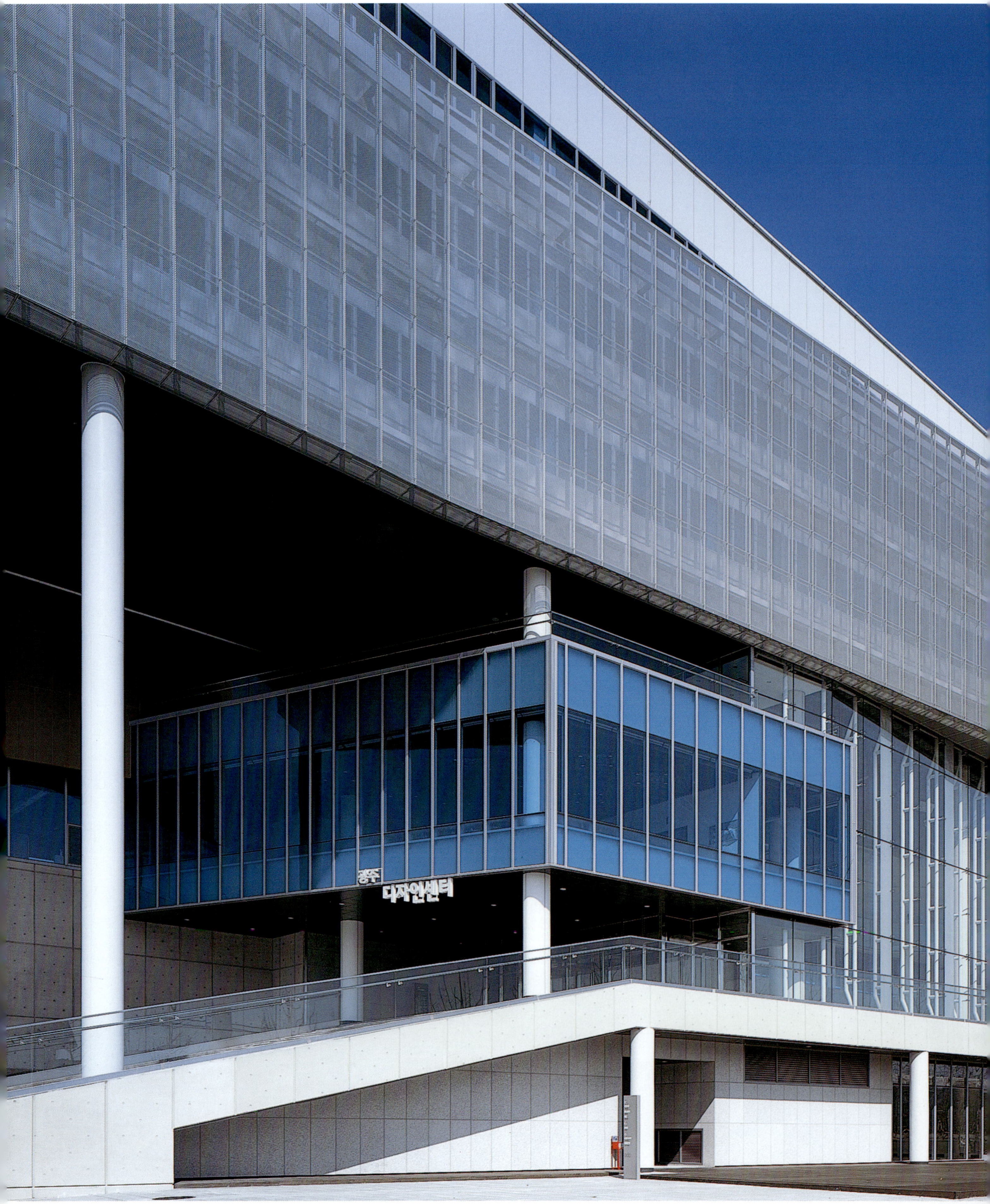
광주
디자인센터

COMPOUND BODY 187

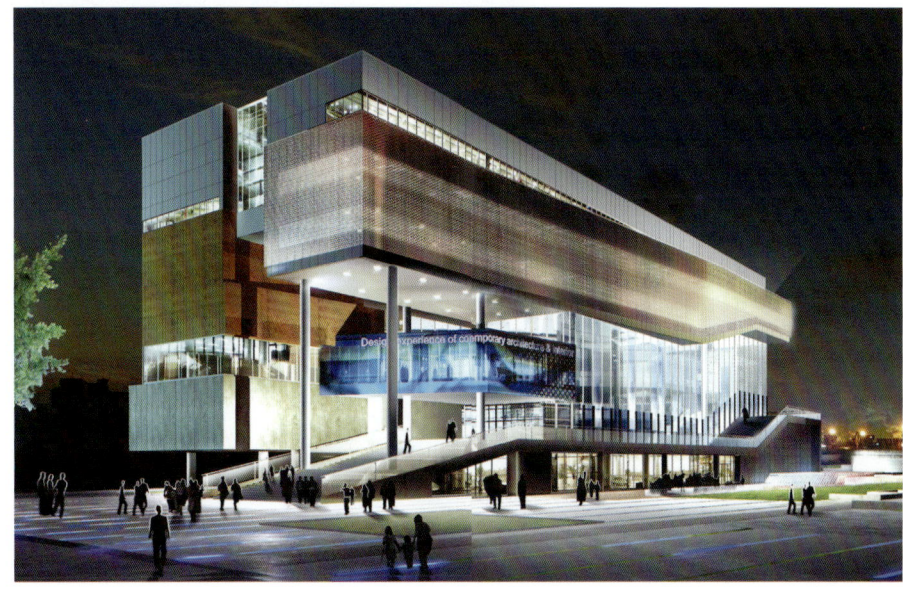

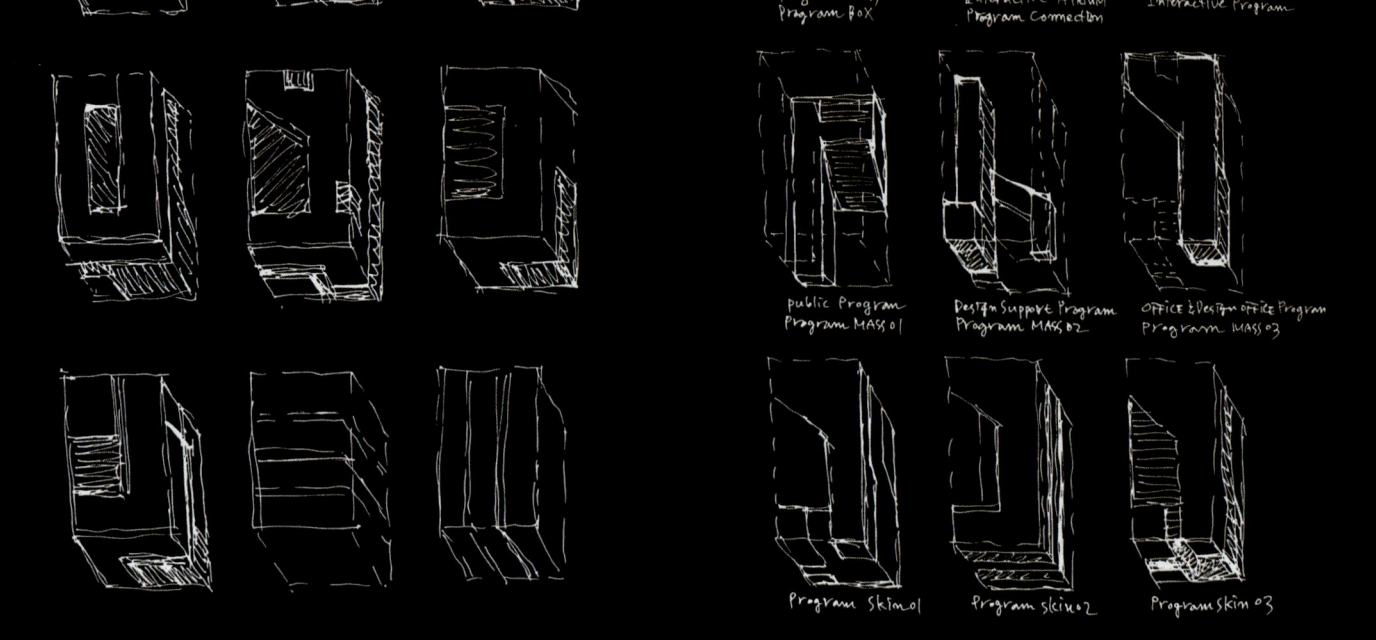

LIGHTING LANDSCAPE

PROGRAM MASS

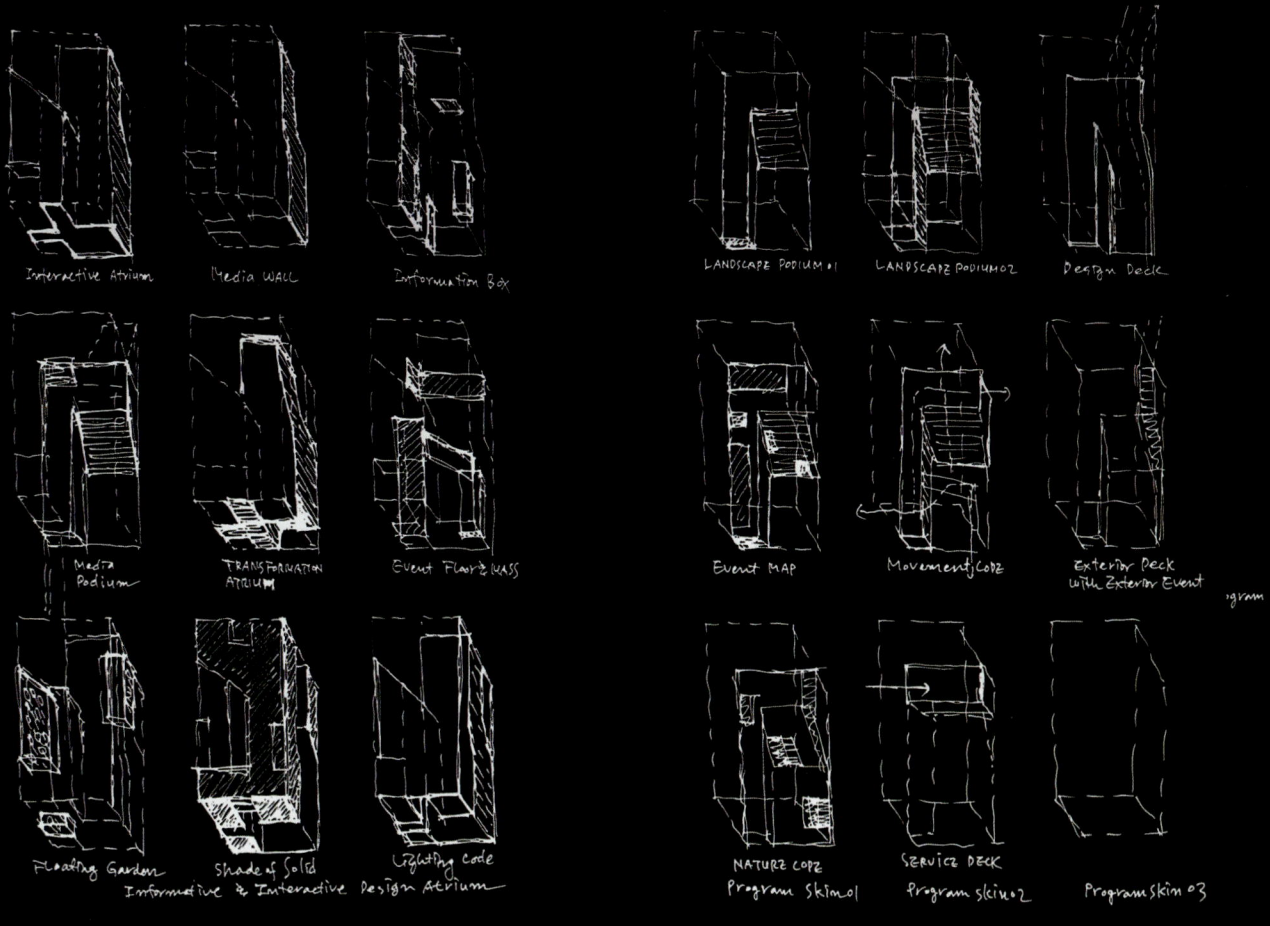

Interactive Atrium	Media Wall	Information Box	Landscape Podium 01	Landscape Podium 02	Design Deck
Media Podium	Transformation Atrium	Event Floor & Glass	Event Map	Movement Code	Exterior Deck with Exterior Event
Floating Garden Informative & Interactive	Shade of Solid Design Atrium	Lighting Code	Nature Code Program Skin 01	Service Deck Program Skin 02	Program Skin 03

DESIGN ARTRIUM   **LANDSCAPE FODIUM**

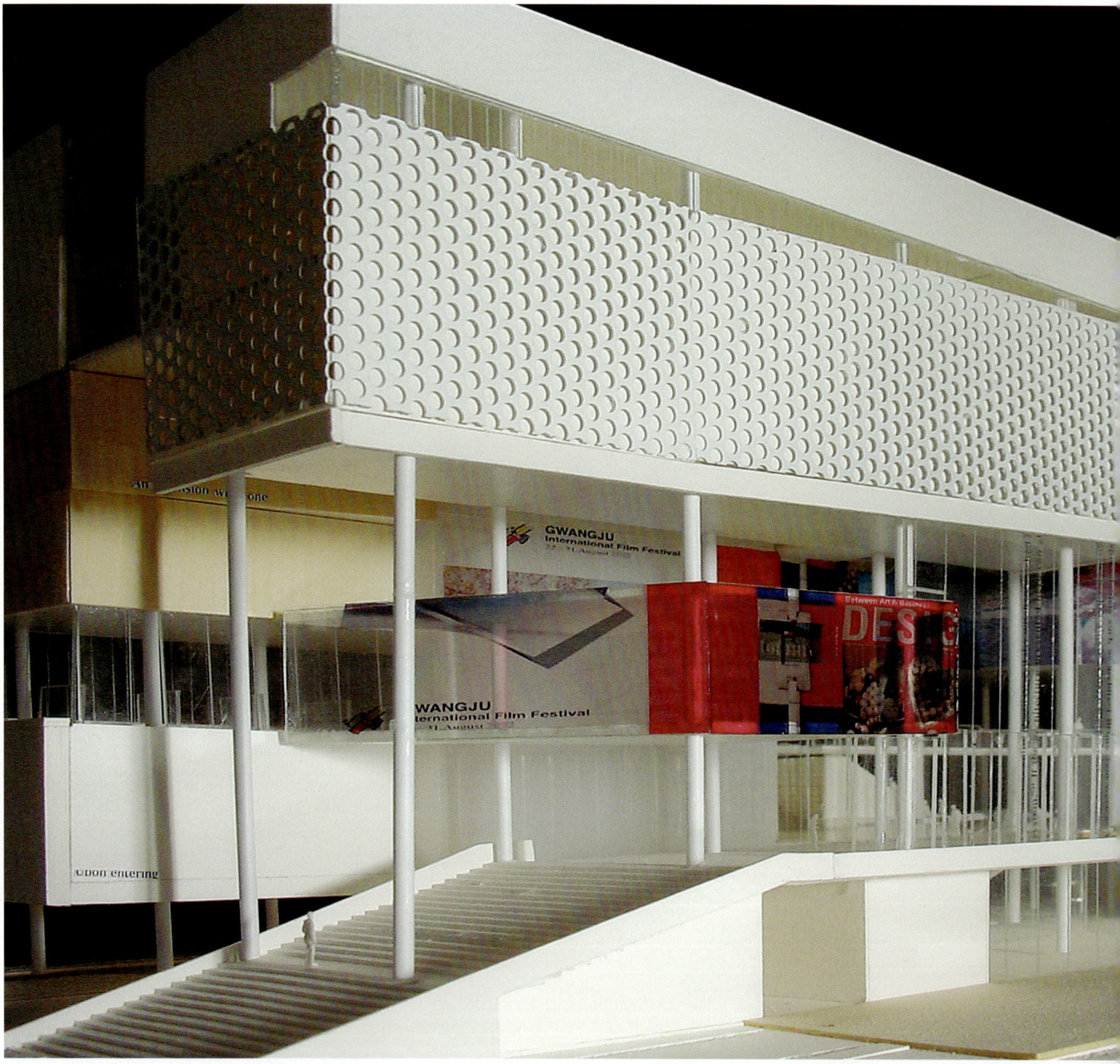
GWANGJU
International Film Festival

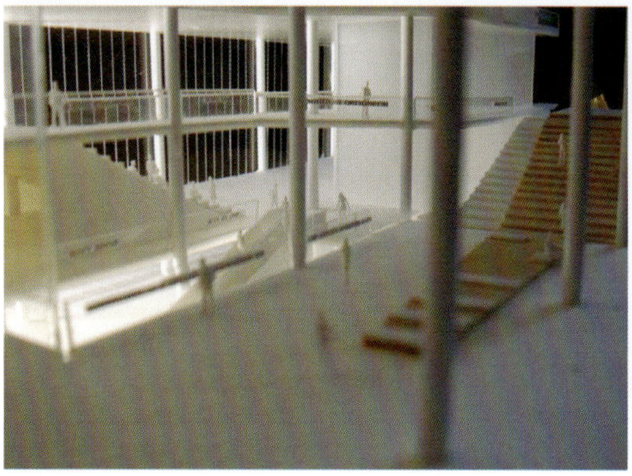

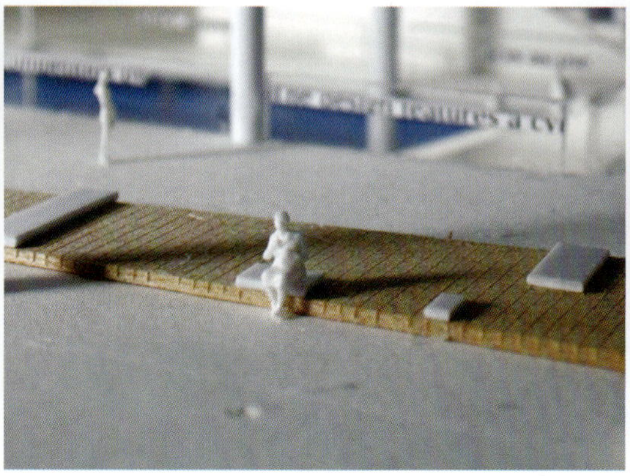

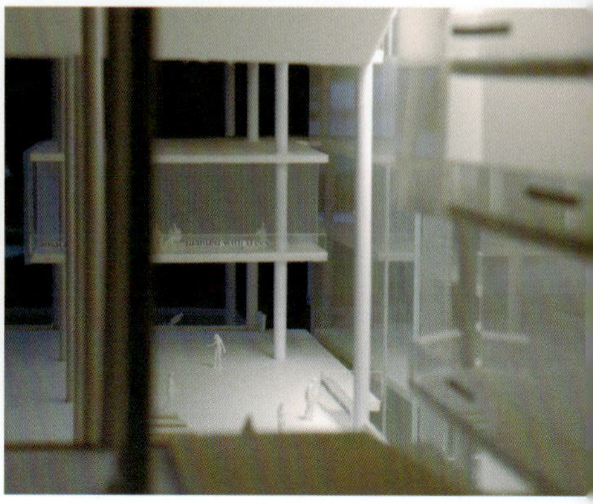

COMPOUND BODY 191

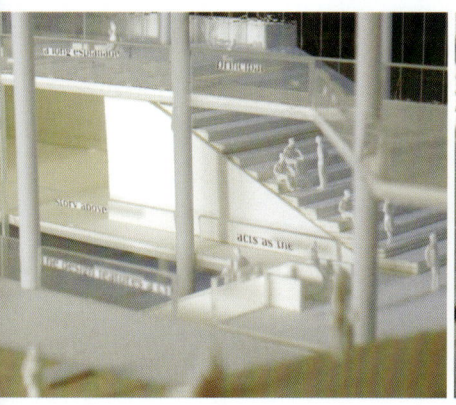

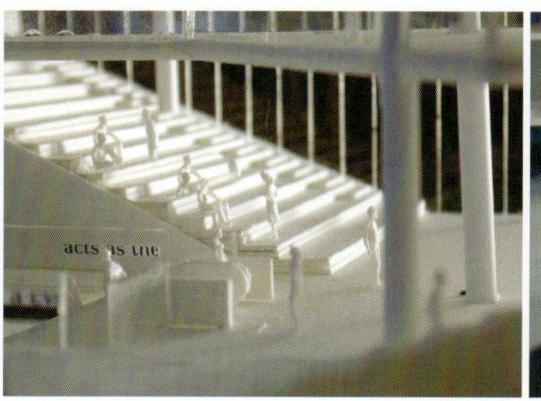

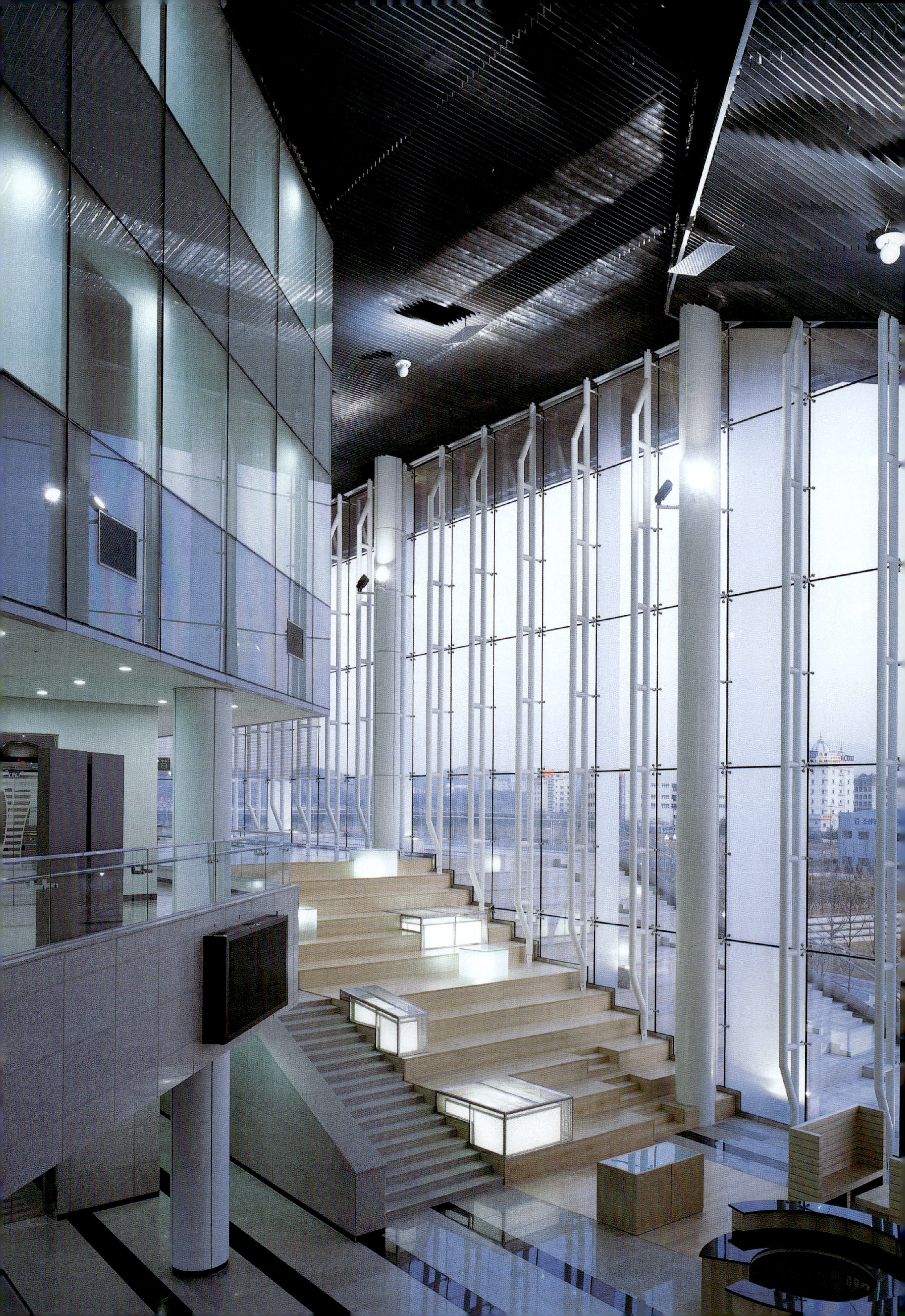

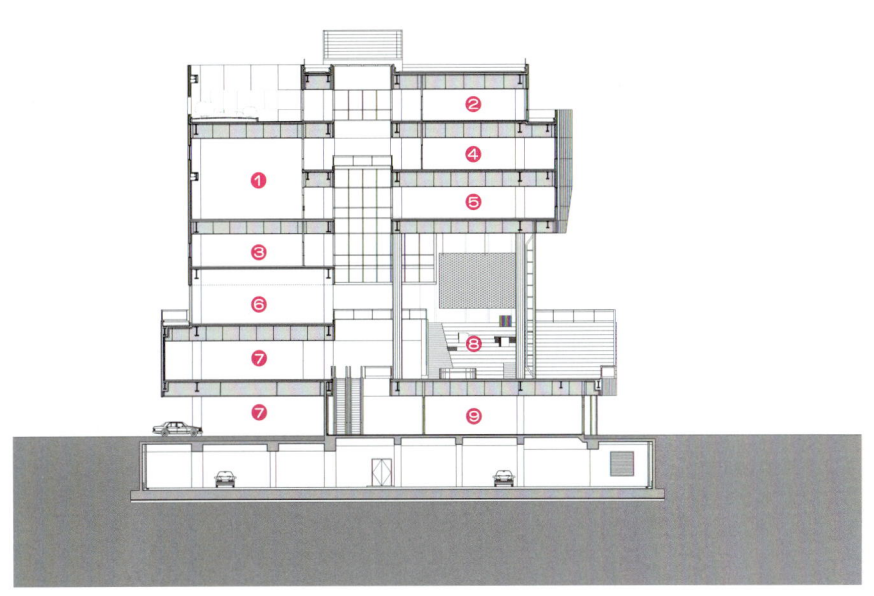

INTERACTIVE PROGRAM

The large complex facilities is demanded the thing other than sensuous design generally. It must treat total system with the solution of structural things and technical part. Design center of GwanJu is the A to Z of design infrastructure combined design education, support faculty, related facilities, exhibition, and public relation office. On this account there needs goes in gear system with each program doesn't conflict. when seeing from outside, the form which stack up or insert with boxes of different shape and materials to apply various program. The space is abundanted and escape from monotony through division, constructing and design of space. At this time, important thing is what is the mechanism in the space and form with uniting elements.

Intractive box

We propose to make space using interactive map. Program of the design center which is presented basically in laminate fan shape and composes the system which connects this with each other. Design center is put on the center of the design network which recomposes a program. culture, nature, information, design, etc., It could be connected with the city. This place accompishes a role with the place of the flow which makes the culture network and the natural network. We propose the landscape podium is connected inside and outside with artificial site creating on the flat three-dimensional site. The landscape podium which is a three-dimensional continuation of the site recomposes of a program and the level which

CROSS SECTION A
1. Roof Garden
2. Office
3. Library
4. Business Incubator
5. Recess Hall
6. Seminar
7. Design Exhibition
8. Lobby & Design Public Relations Hall
9. Cafeteria

CROSS SECTION B
1. Principal's Room
2. Meeting Room
3. Office
4. Business Incubator
5. Recess Hall
6. Experience Hall
7. Cafeteria
8. Lobby
9. Event Hall

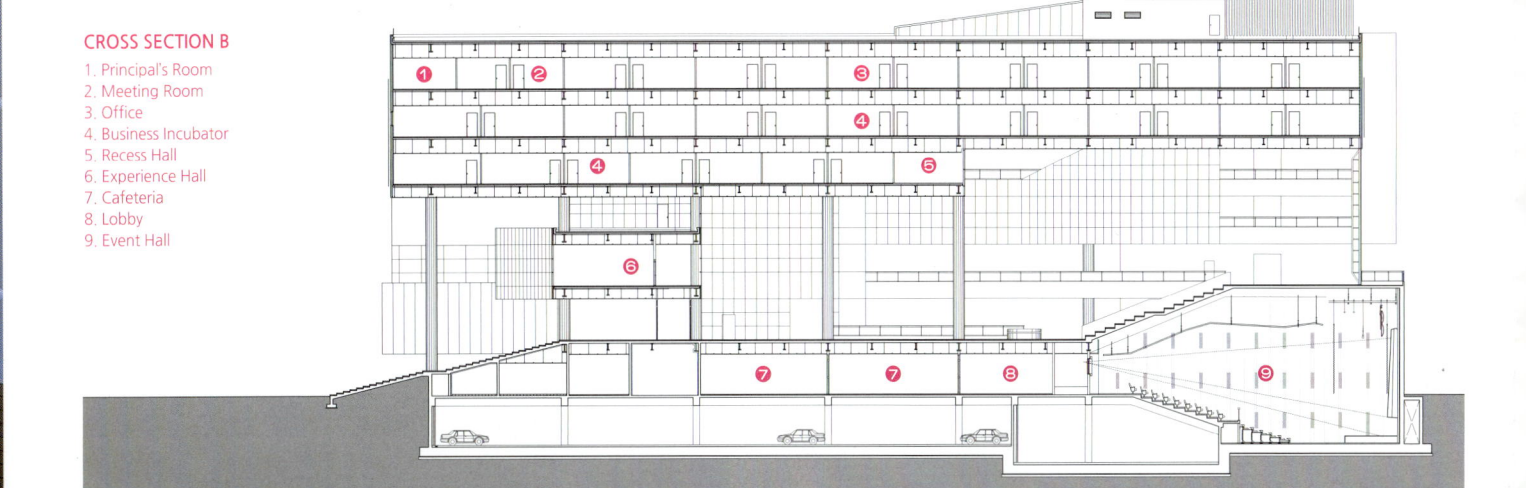

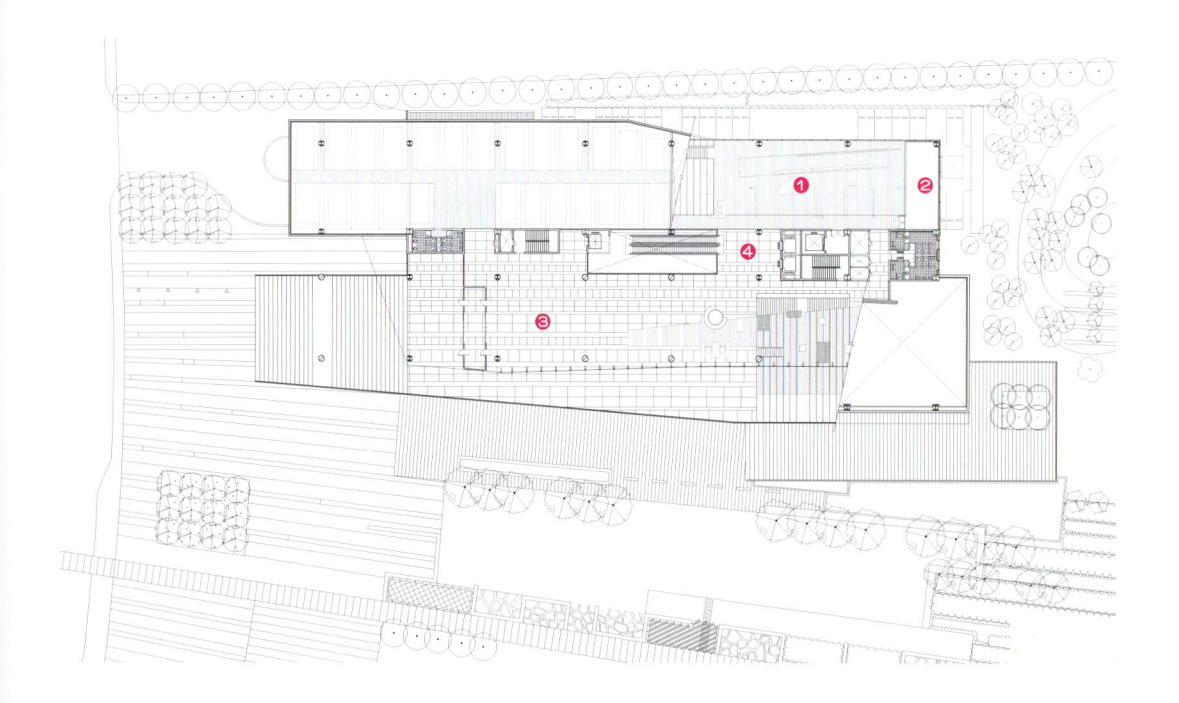

2ND FLOOR PLAN
1. Design Exhibition
2. Storage
3. Lobby & Design Public Relations Hall
4. Hall

1ST FLOOR PLAN
1. Cafeteria
2. Lobby
3. Event Hall
4. Outdoor Deck
5. Parking

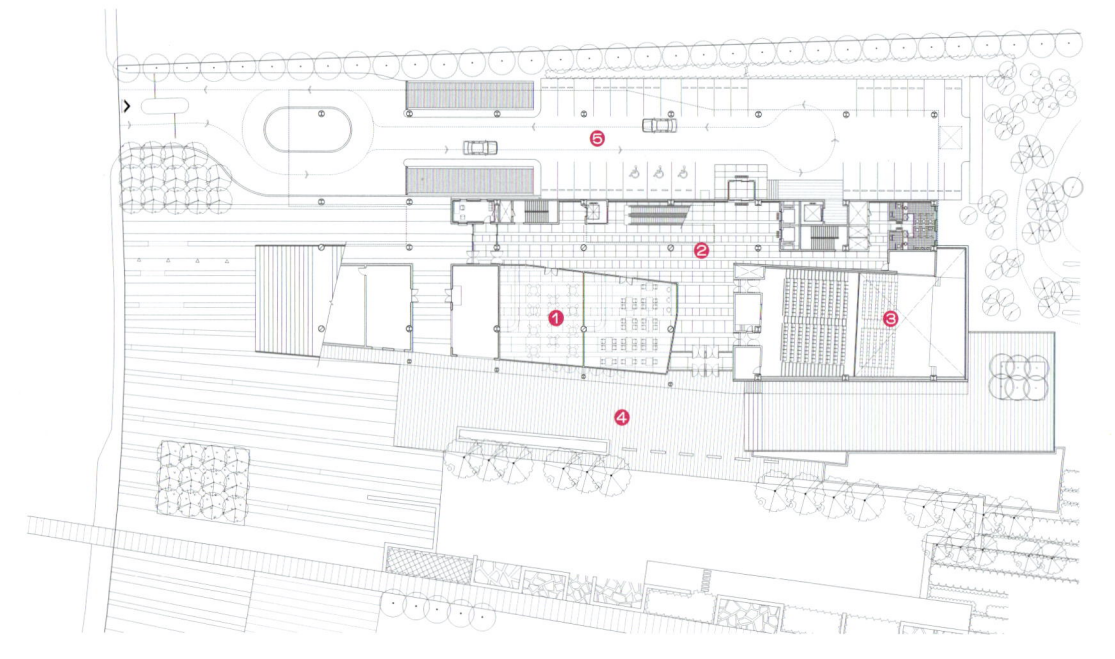

SPACE PROGRAM

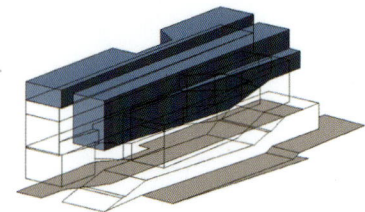

Design Office

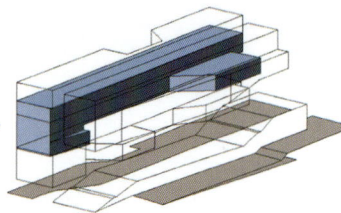

Design Support

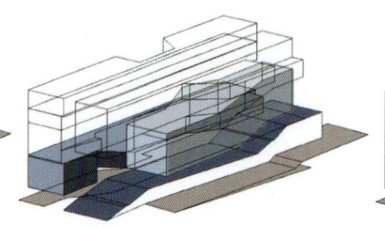

Design Atrium

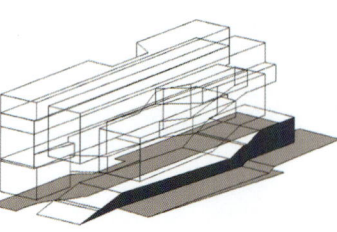

Design Public

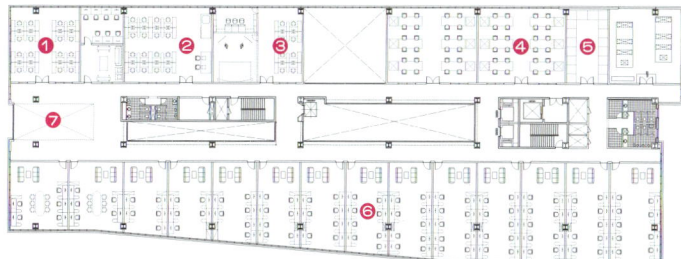

COMPOUND BODY 195

6TH FLOOR PLAN
1. Graphic Design Room
2. 3D Modeling Room
3. Web Design Room
4. Workshop
5. Storage
6. Business Incubator
7. Recess Hall

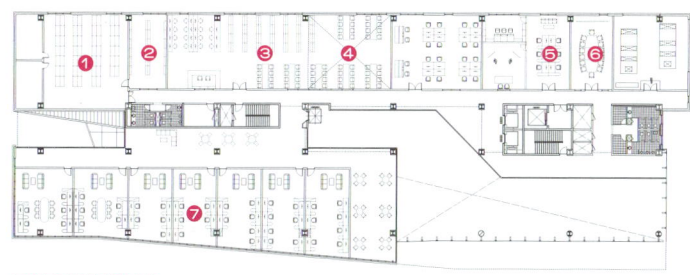

5TH FLOOR PLAN
1. Computer Room
2. Data Room
3. Library
4. Reading Room
5. Studio
6. Presentation Room
7. Business Incubator

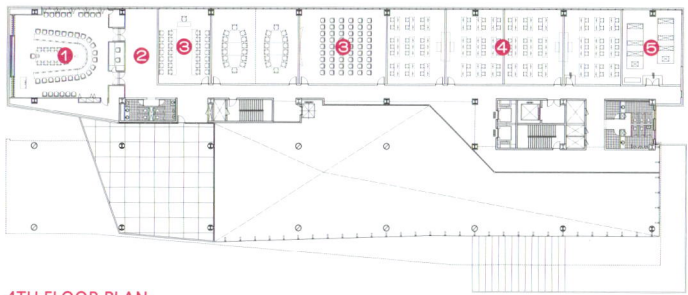

4TH FLOOR PLAN
1. Conference Room
2. Hall
3. Seminar
4. Design Education Center
5. HVAC

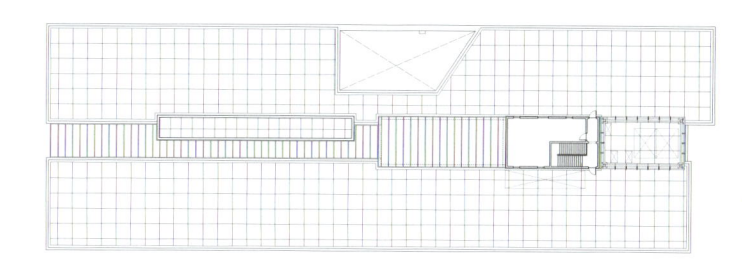

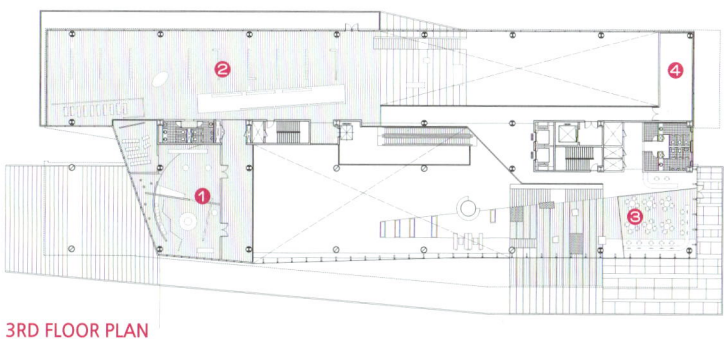

3RD FLOOR PLAN
1. Experience Hall
2. Design Exhibition
3. Cafeteria
4. Storage

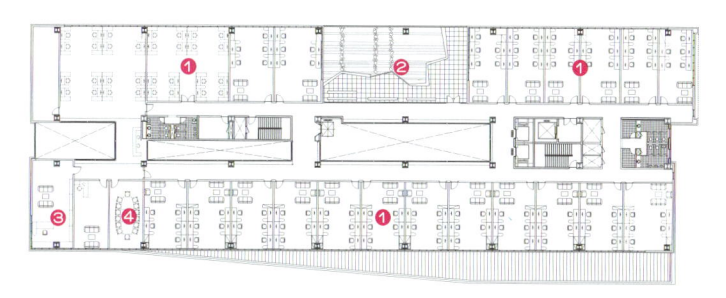

ROOF PLAN

7TH FLOOR PLAN
1. Office
2. Roof Garden
3. Principal's Room
4. Meeting Room

exhibit space and a lobby space of the design center becomes new site. There is meaning to commpose the view of the flat three-dimensional site as the land system. The space of the public character which includes outside sqare and exhibition space is not separated as well as composed landscape podium for continous or three-dimensional deck place. We proposes program skin with the concept which the program inside does make facade immediately. Outside skin replects inside programs. It applies the concept with separates materials by order of space function. It composes with following program and each other different material and physical properties even in landscape design. Also it applies the concept of the program field which provides a different program in landscape design in fan shape.

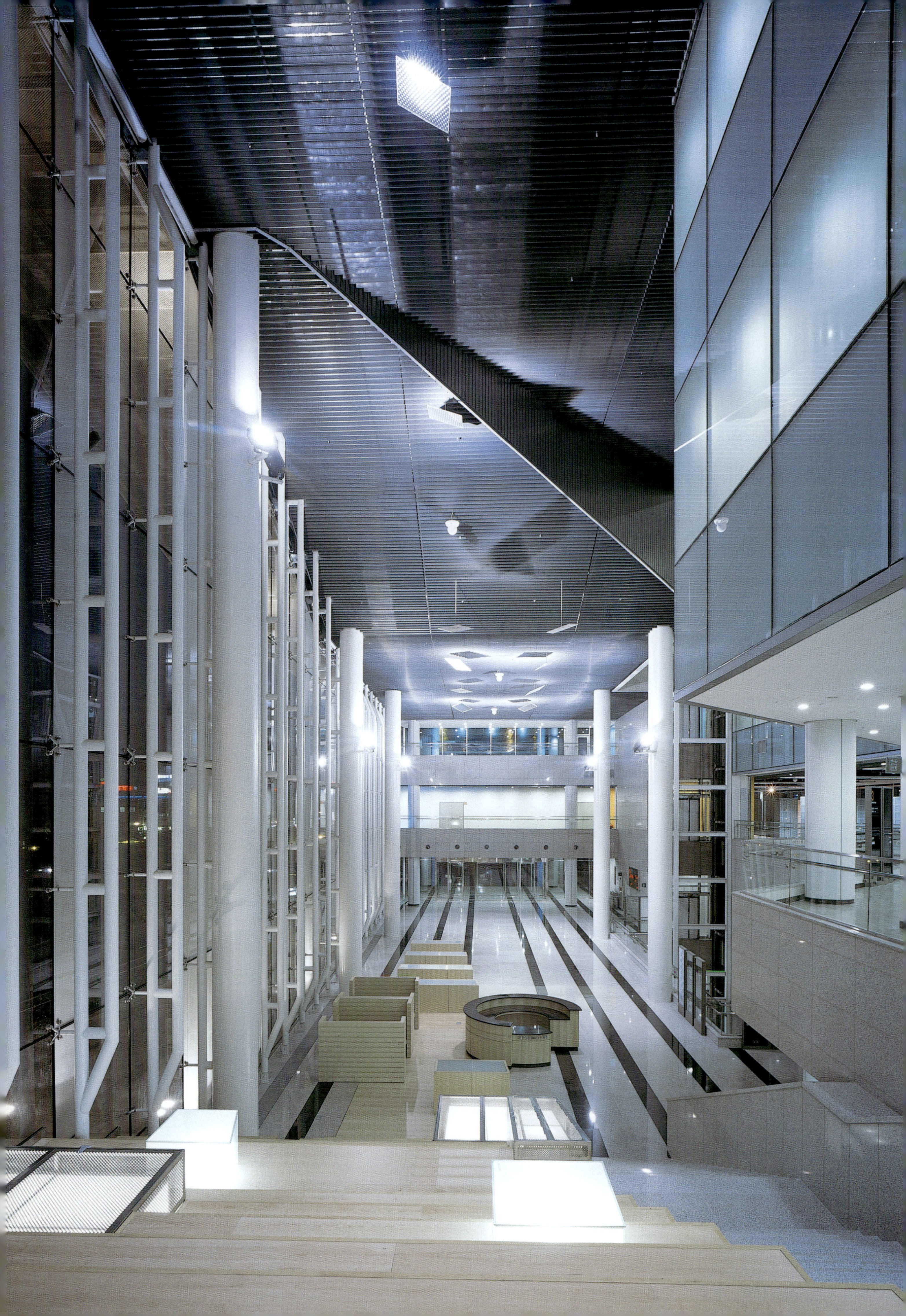

Location
OrYongDong, Bukgu, GwangJu
Site Area 33,056.9m²
Building Area 3,216.77m²
Gross Floor Area 17,247.22m²
Building Coverage Ratio 9.73%
Gross Floor Ratio 40.7%
Building Scale
One story below ground, Seven stories above ground
Structure
R.C. + Steel frame
Exterior Finishing
T24 Pair grass, CRC panel, Stone, Aluminium Panel, Punching metal
Interior Finishing
T30 Granite, Carpet tile, Wood panel

Flagship Tower

Interactive
flagship void

Architects Jang Yoon Gyoo, Shin Chang Hoon, Kim Youn Soo
Photographer Kim Jae Kyung, Kim Bong Kyun

COMPOUND BODY 199

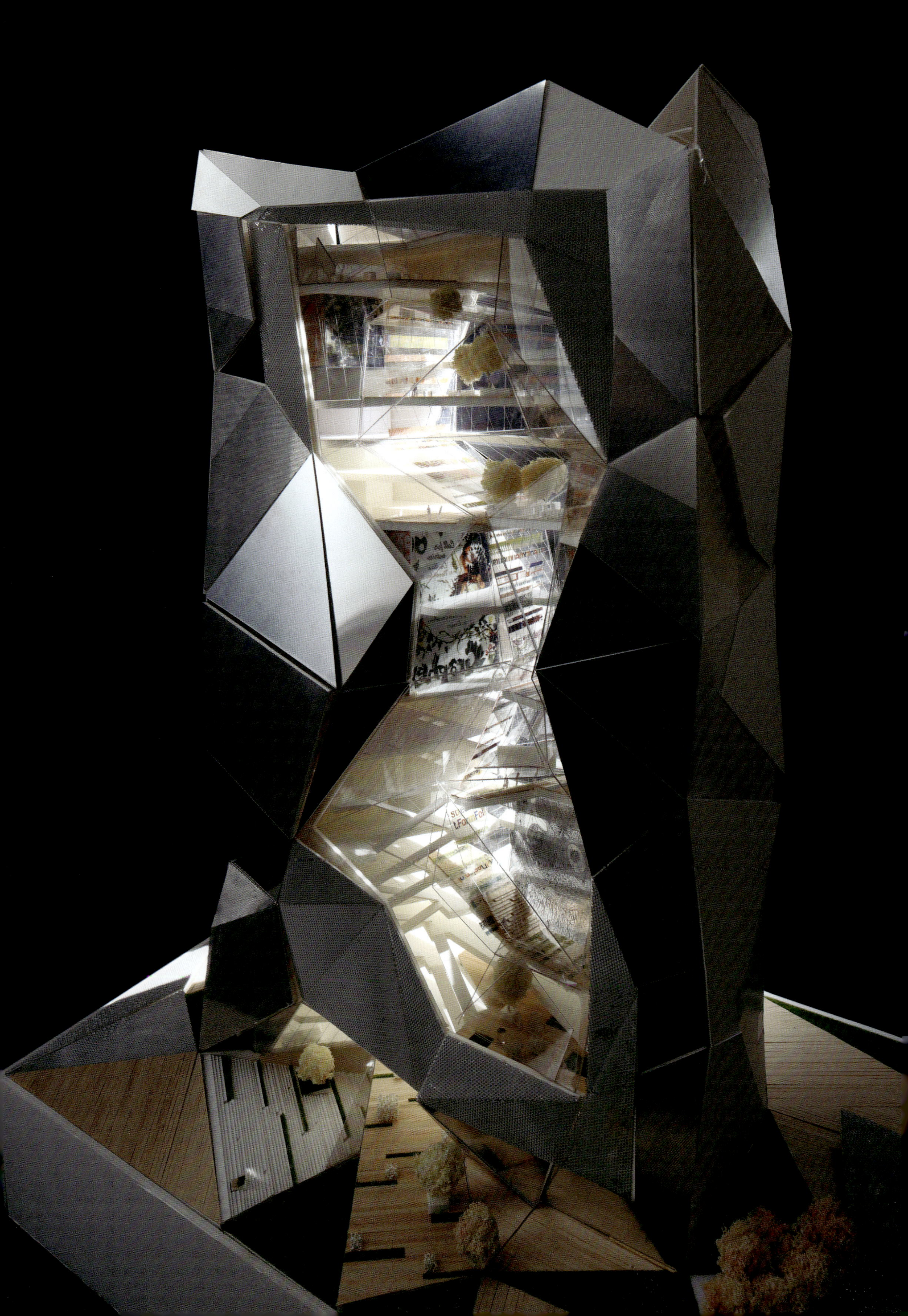

INTERACTIVE FLAGSHIP VOID

A membership space with various services in one place is composed. This advanced emotional space connecting customers to products and enterprise recognizes the brand image through experience. Close contact and understanding with the customers is actualized off-line. The 1st strategy for gathering customers is the urban sculpture-like architecture. A new lifestyle combines with commercial space and to provide diverse images of enterprise.

Flagship Core

We suggest Flagship Core, penetrating the whole architecture. It is a resting space and a floating art garden for urban people who are exhausted by daily routine. It is a new type of urban garden combining art and culture. Environmental friendly resting space such as Floating Forest, Green Square and Refresh Terrace produces diverse cultures. Flagship Core is a network system connecting accumulated programs on each floor. The demand for events happening in the meditating space between programs is accommodated with an urban stage. It is a cultural charging station for early adopters who are always chasing after something new. It is a cultural heart creating new urban emotions and the experience of new items such as the Media Forest, Entertainment Lobby, Performance Stage, and Ubiquitous Garden. An interactive Media Skin is inserted to the Flagship Core adopting the ubiquitous environment. Diverse information according to user's demands and emotions is provided through the Media Skin. The Media Skin is a sculpture itself expanding art wall 3-dimensionally.

Flagship Core plays a role as an urban void. It is not only an icon for promotion and sale, but it releases the image of enterprise towards the city.

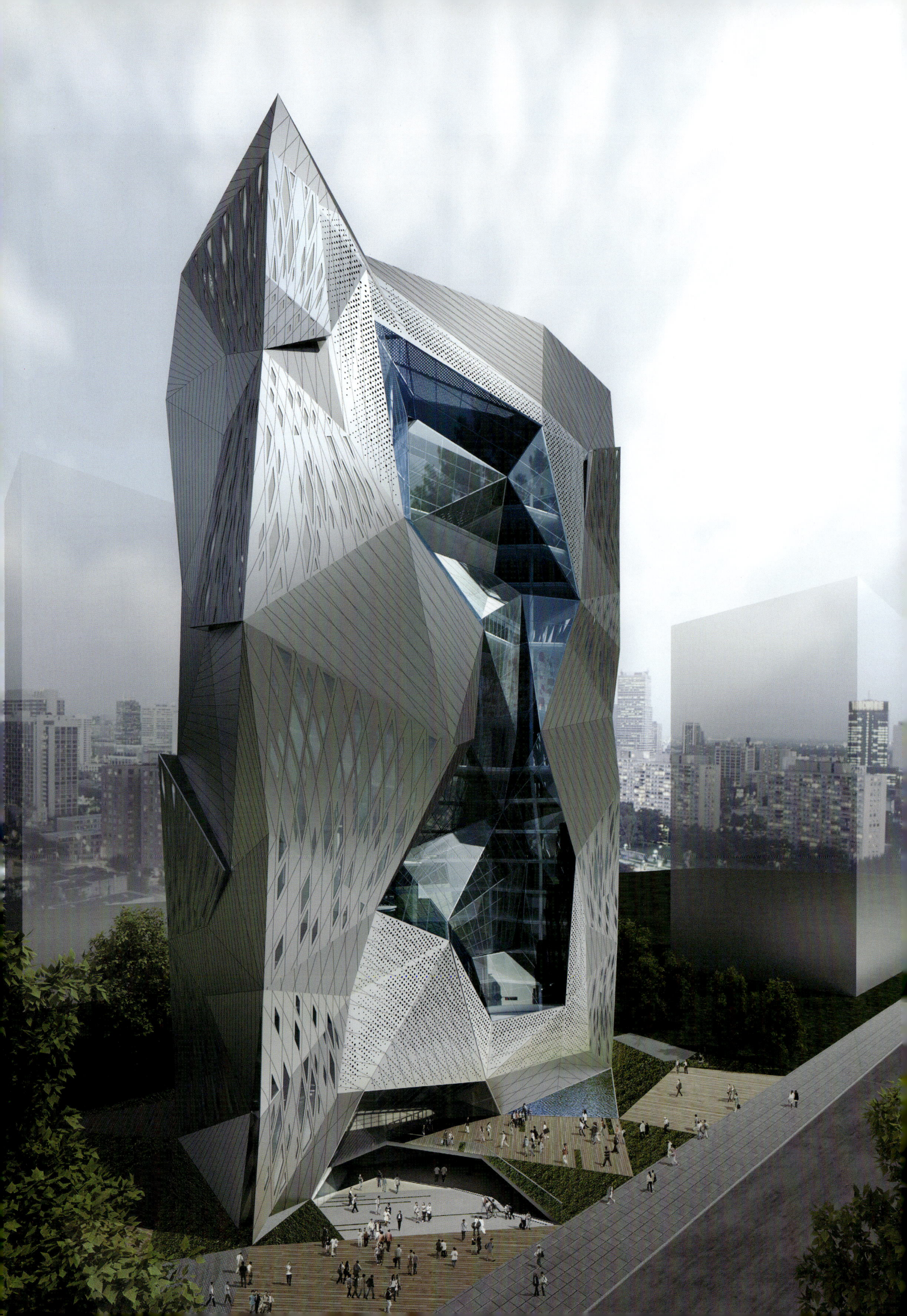

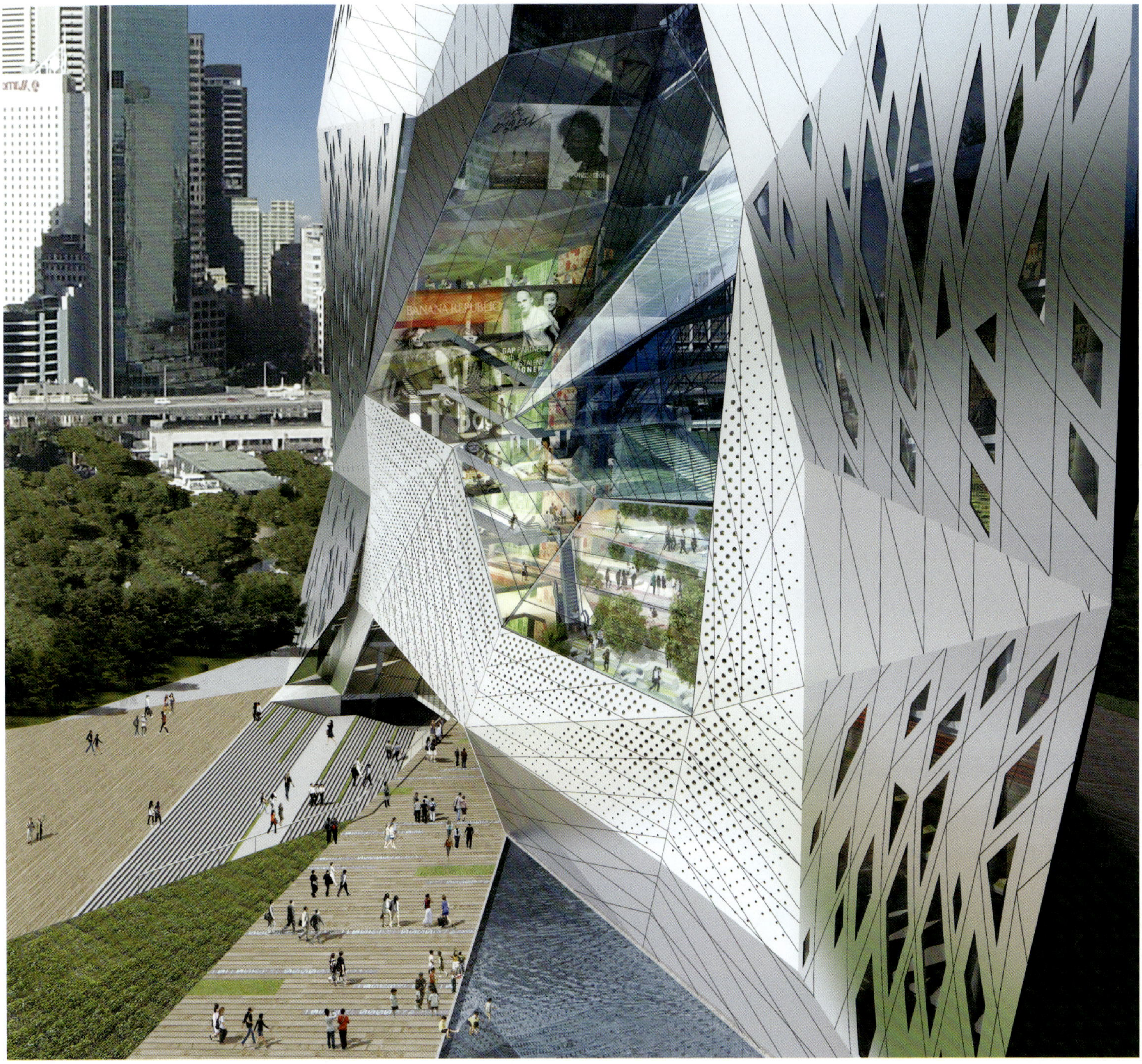
BANANA REPUBLIC

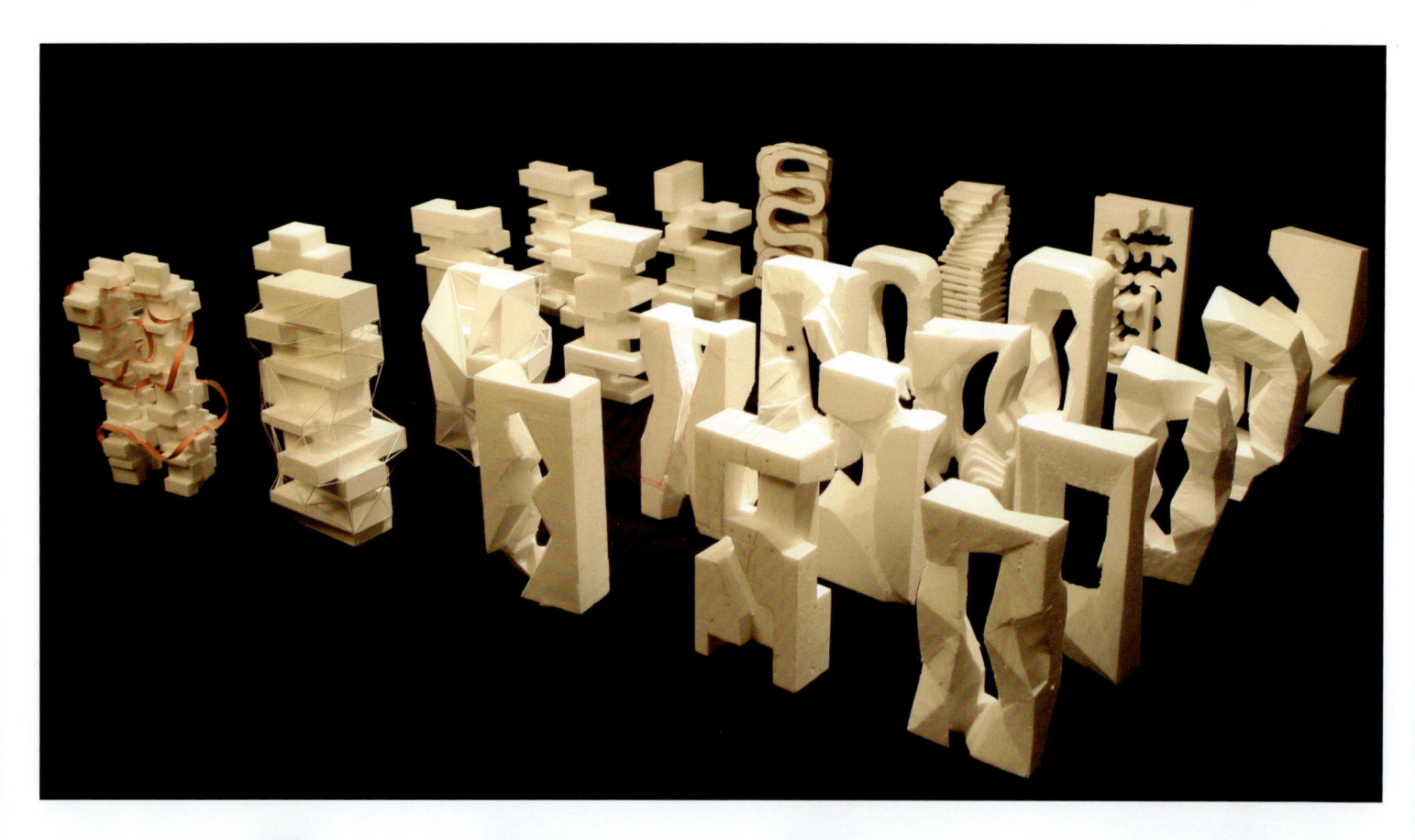

Various Activity on the Earth Skin	Ordinary Building System	Isolated Program by Slabs	Various Programs on the urban network
Earth Interconnects to Main Program	Big Scale Community Space : Penetration	Program Interaction	Urban Activities Interconnect to Main Program
Attaching Earth Program on the Skin	Interactive Penetration core Vertical Network Matrix	Interaction Program by Void Tube	Wrapping Skin by Urban Activities

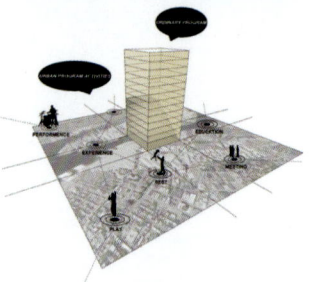

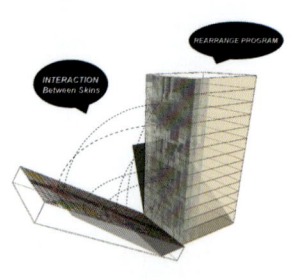

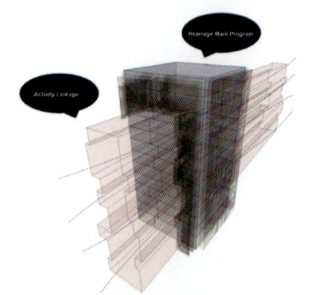

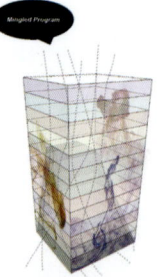

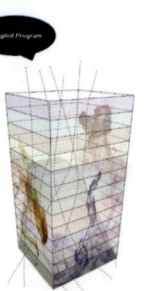

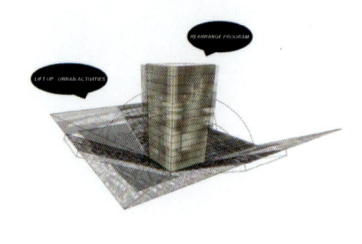

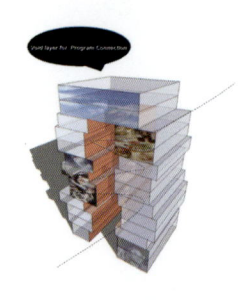

COMPOUND BODY 205

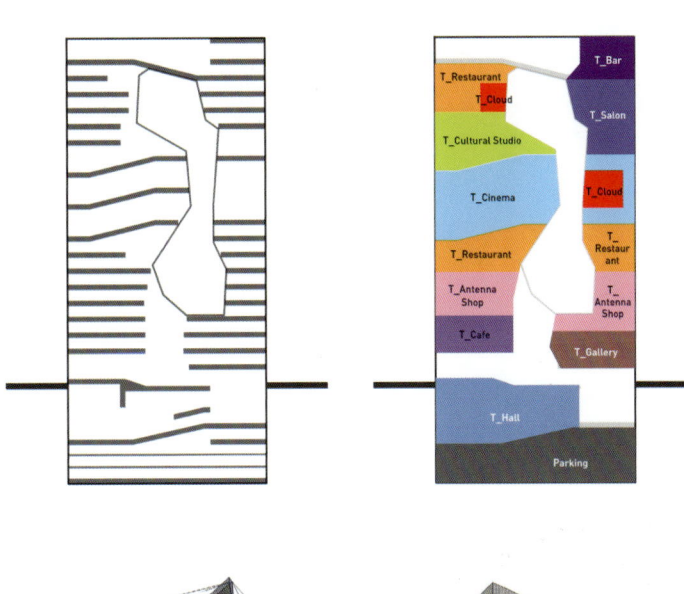

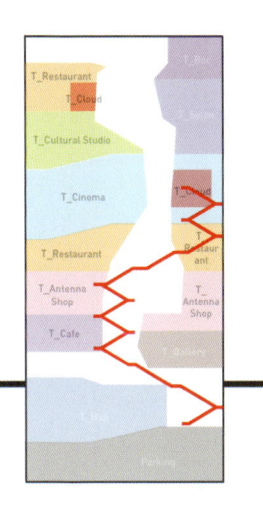

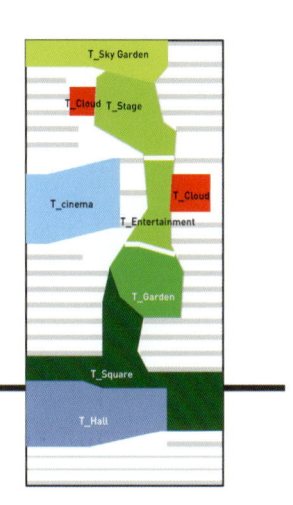

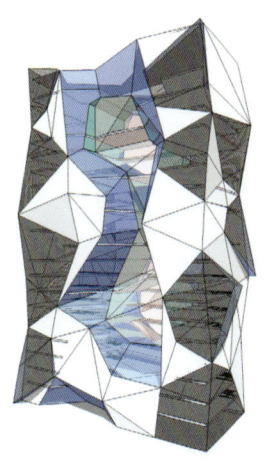

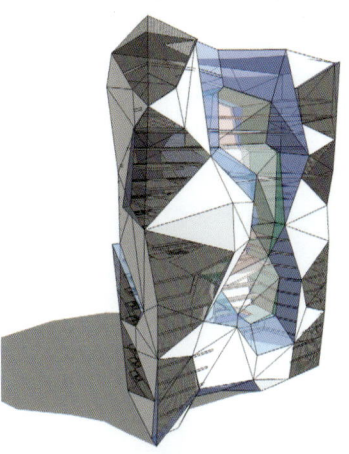

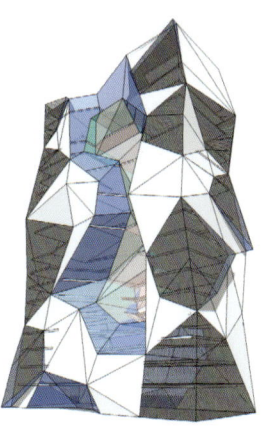

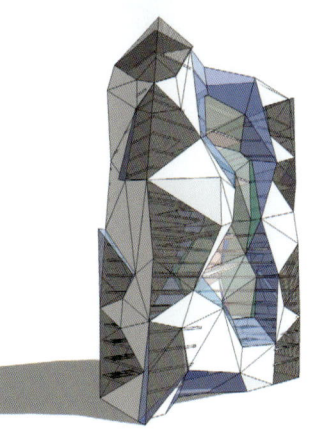

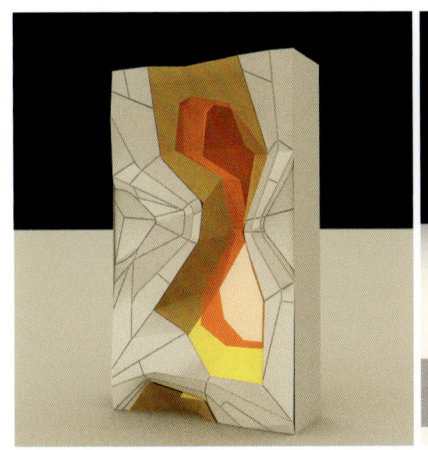

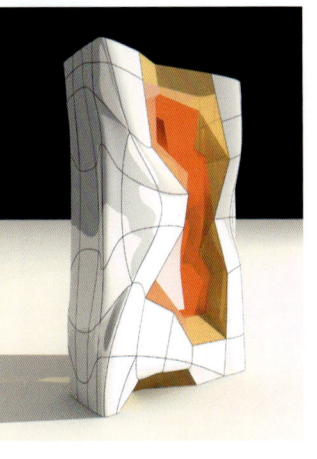

CRYSTAL N - UBIQUITOUS CULTUREWORK FLAGSHIP

Crystal

Emotional Space

Wing

LIGHTING SYMPHONY

// **Dream City Icon** Brand Icon which is continuously changing and symbolized. Symbol of dream made from urban background.

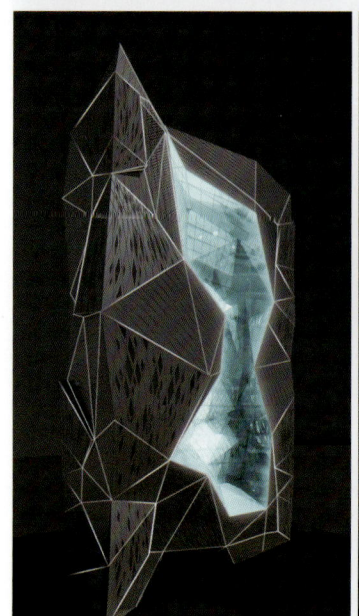

// **Lighting Crystal**
Lighting performance towards the city
Lighting Icon which lights up the city is suggested by program; Crystal Line symbolizing network, Star Light symbolizing shining dream, Wing Light symbolizing item which comes close to customer.

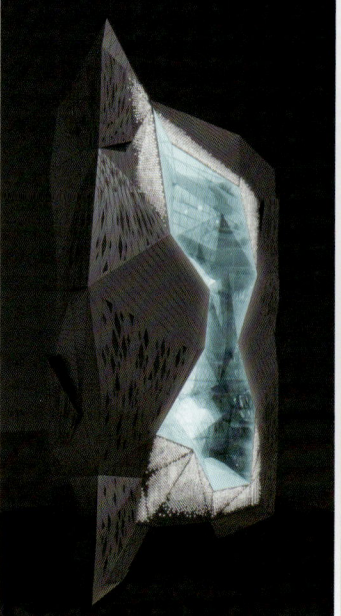

Crystal Line

Star Light

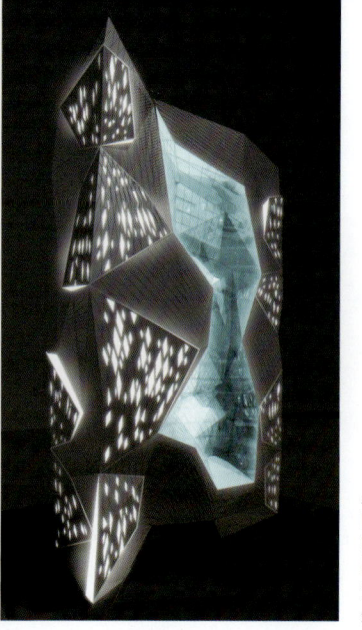

Wing Light

COMPOUND BODY 207

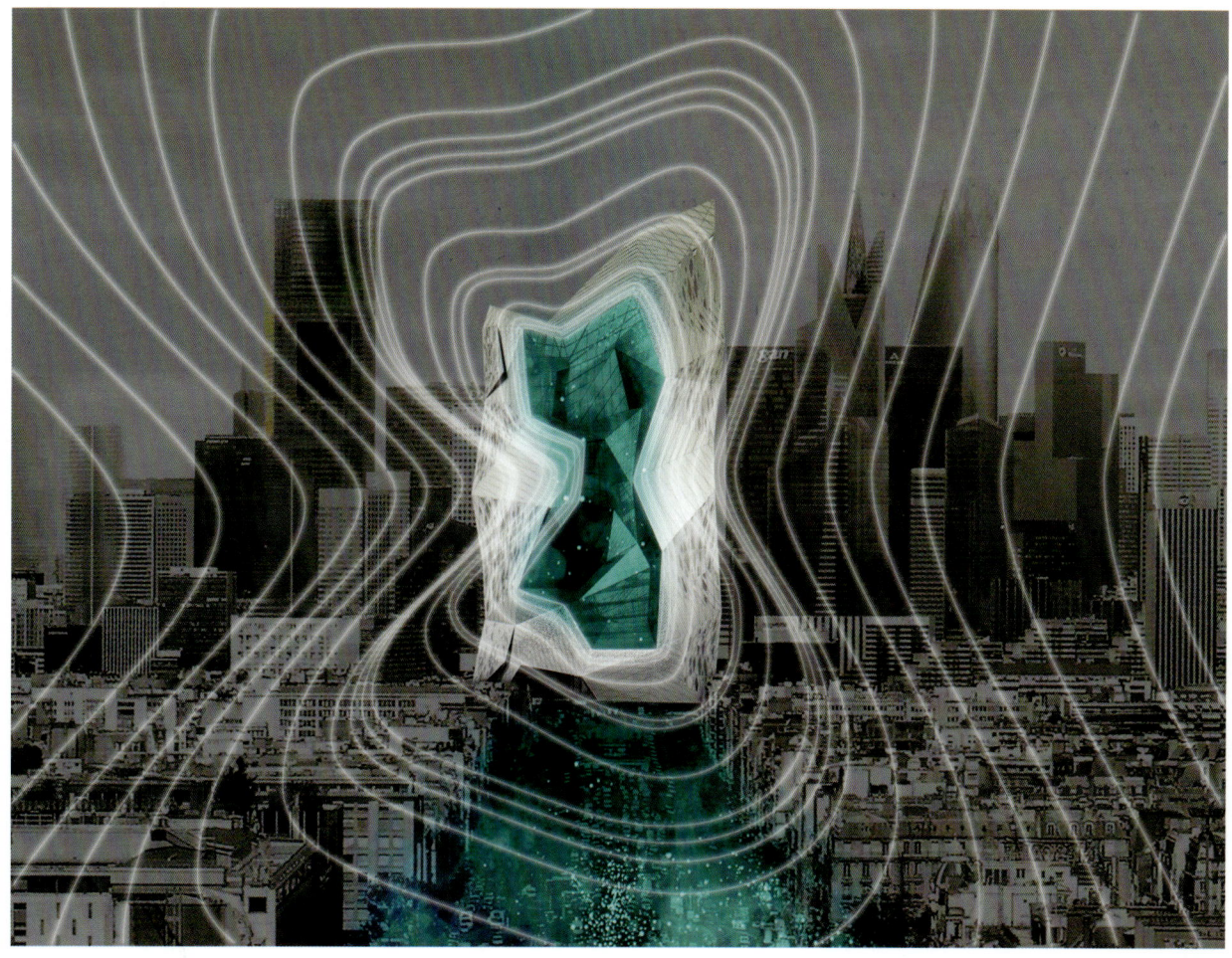

BUTTERFLY EFFECT

// **Interactive Media Skin**
Ubiquitous space made by new technology
Interactive Media Skin adopts ubiquitous environment.
Diverse information according to user's demand and emotion is provided through media skin, and that performance itself becomes cultural performance formatting art wall.

Culture Skin   Emotion Skin

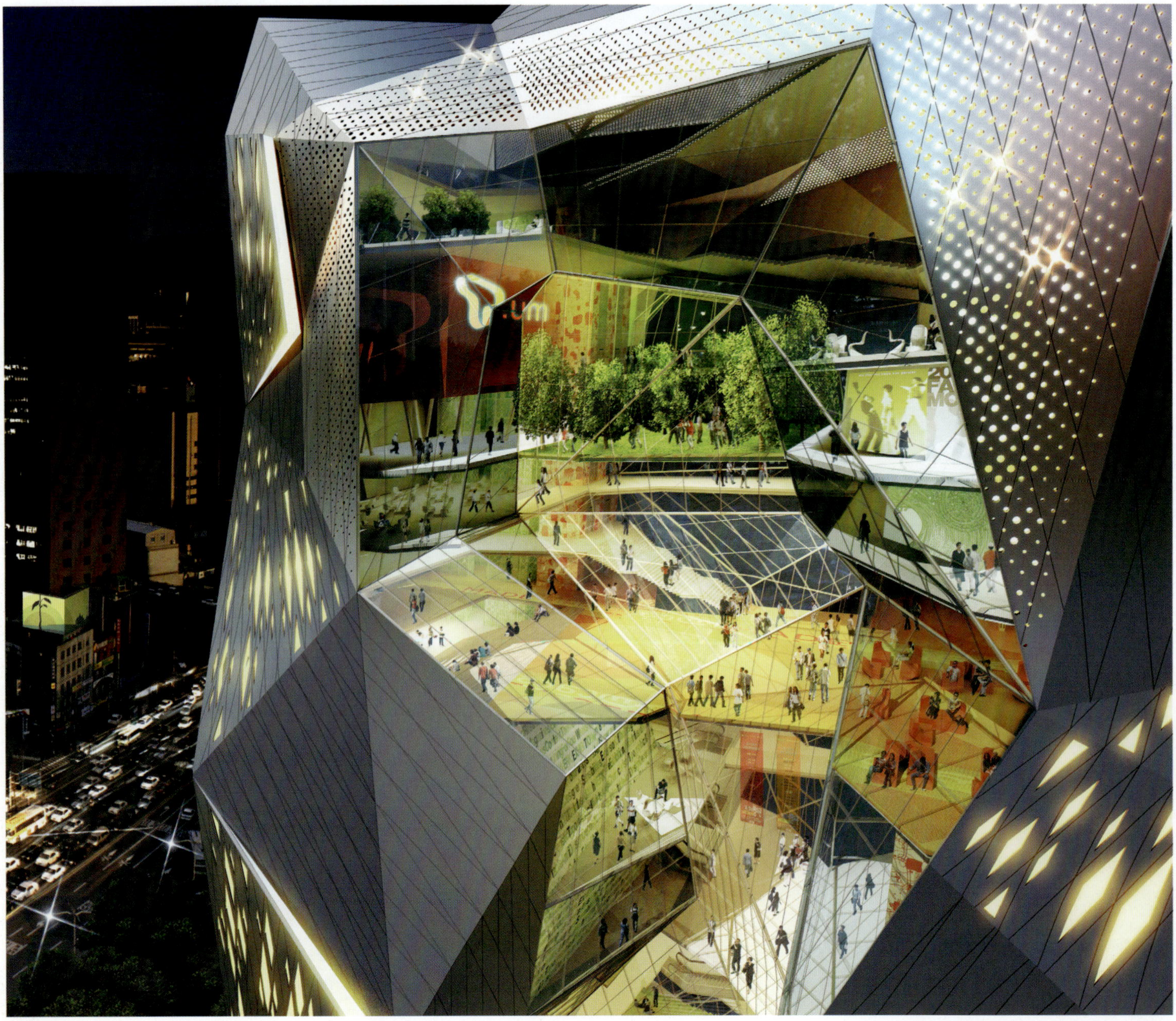

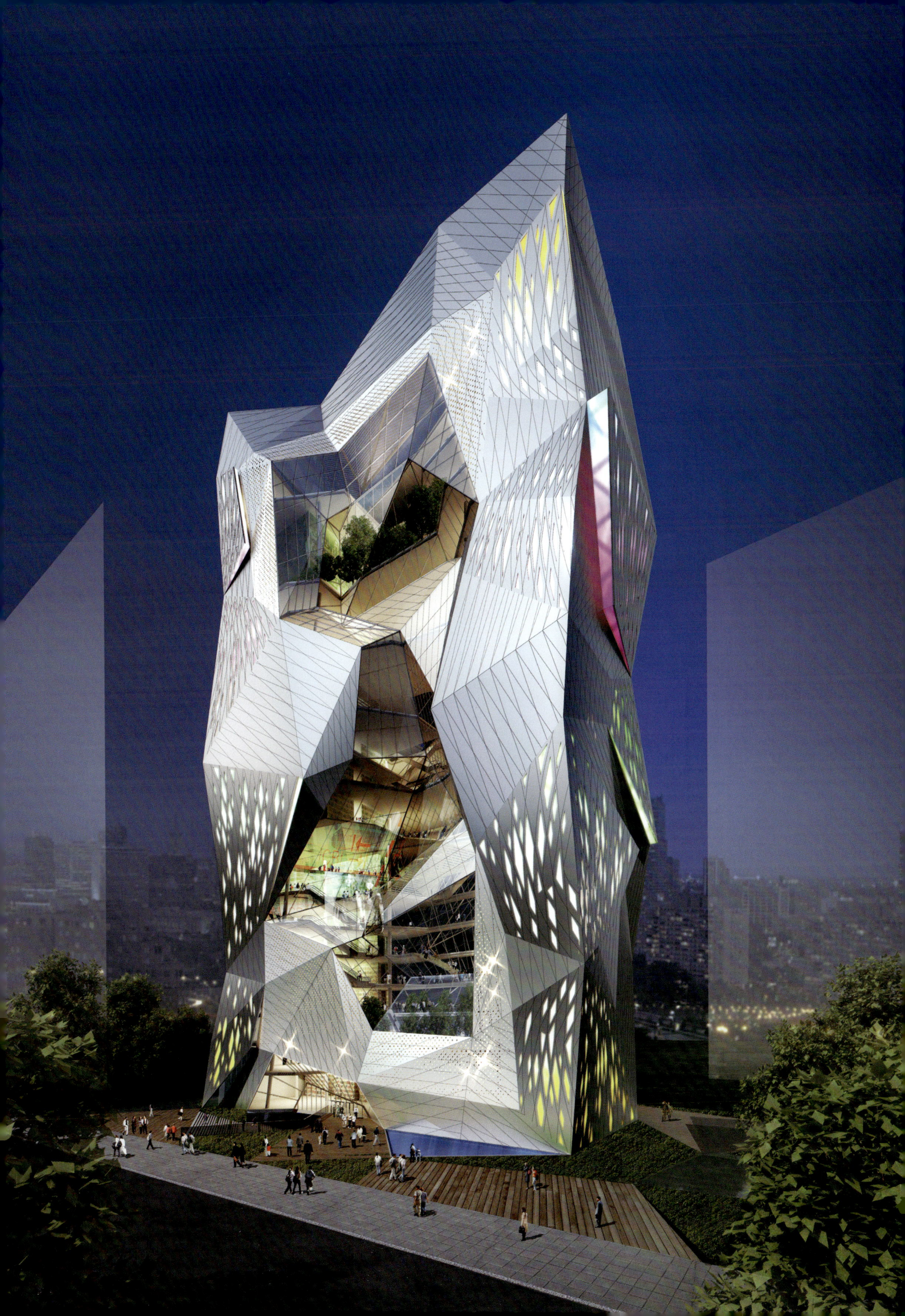

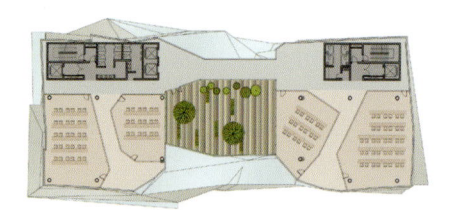

210

13F Culture Studio

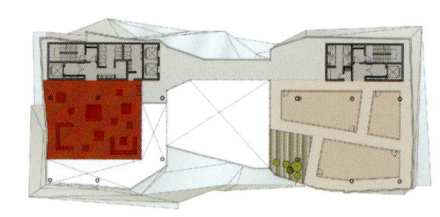

14F Culture Studio / Lounge

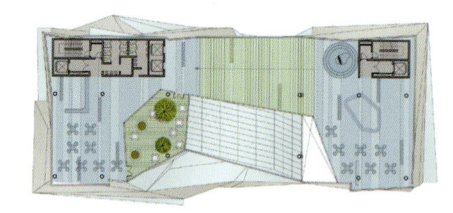

15F Bar

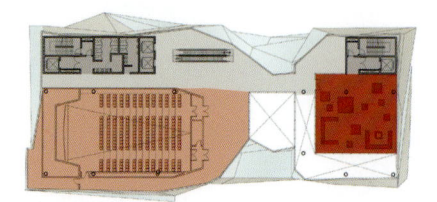

10F Cinema / Lounge

11F Drama

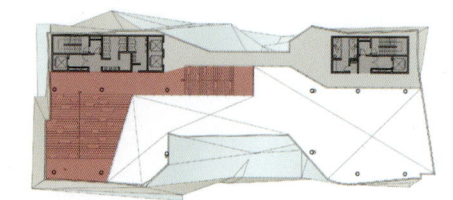

12F Drama

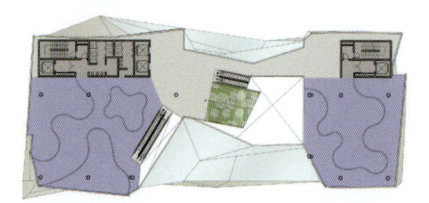

7F Antenna Shop

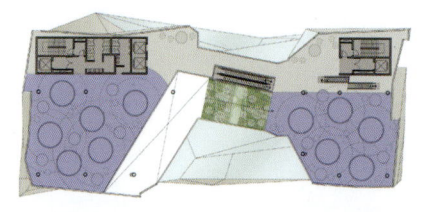

8F Antenna Shop

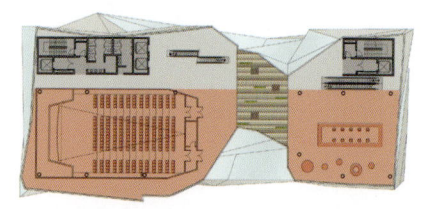

9F Cinema

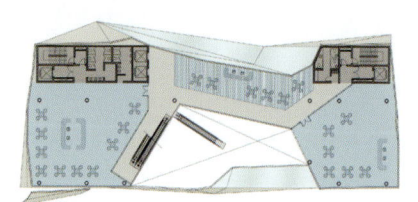

4F Restaurant / Antenna Shop

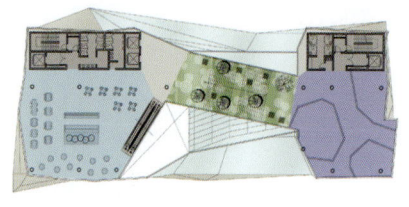

5F Restaurant / Antenna Shop

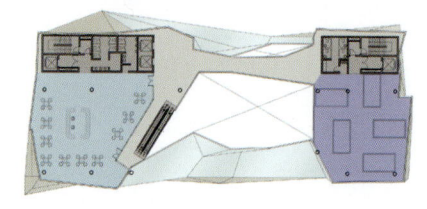

6F Restaurant / Antenna Shop

1F World

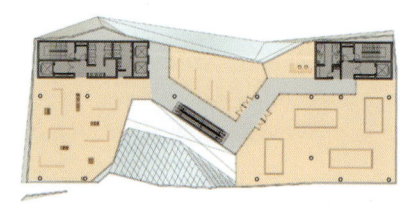

2F Gallery

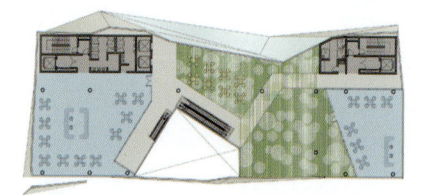

3F Restaurant

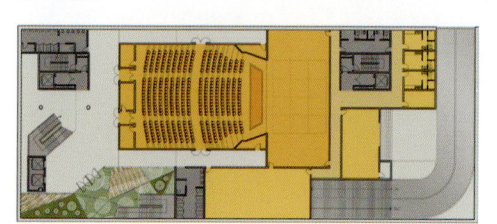

B1F Hall

COMPOUND BODY   211

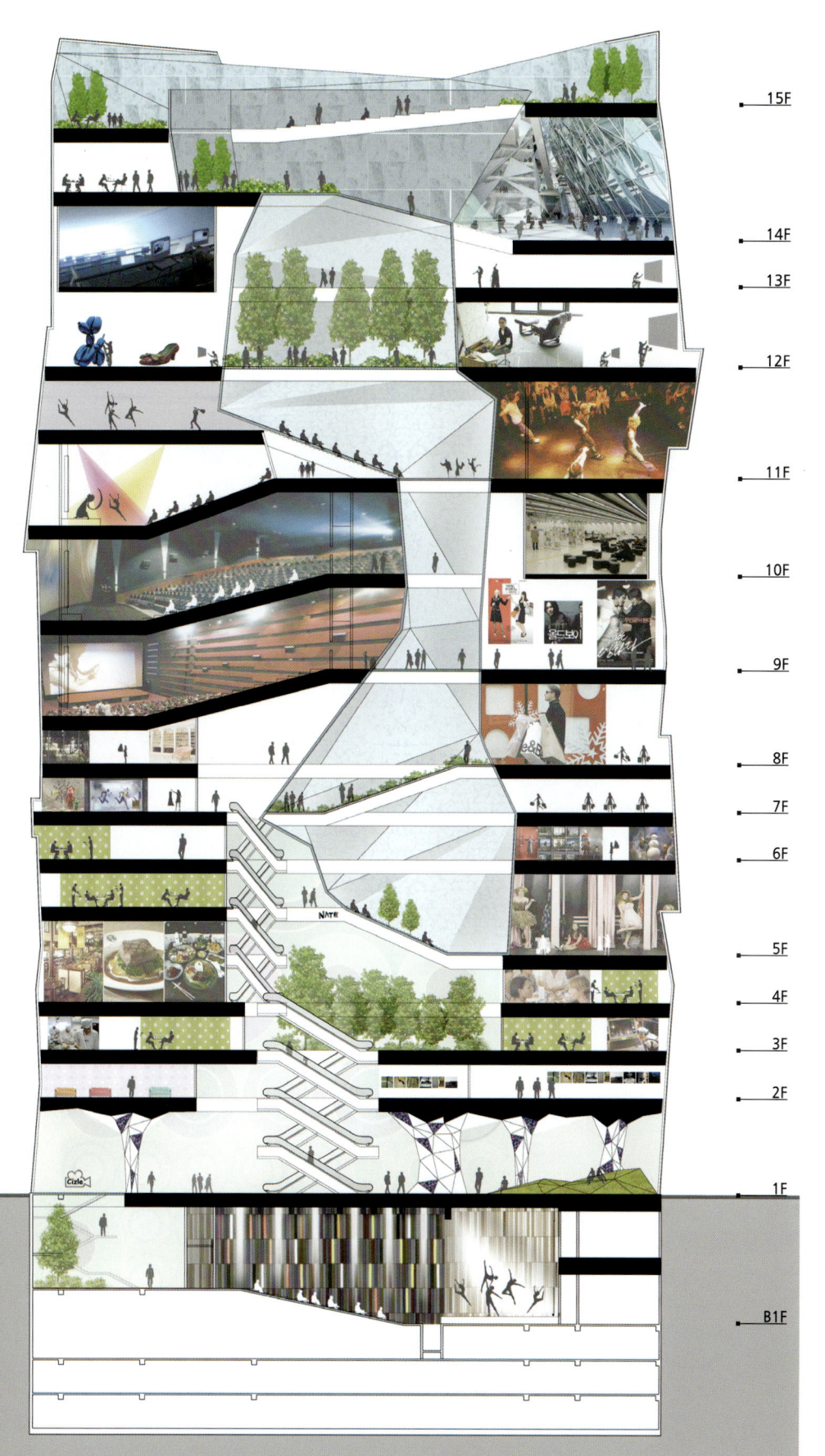

Culture Network Program
The idea 'like-a-communication' is providing a window for diverse contents and culture whenever and wherever for you to enjoy. Interactive programs which actualize that idea are accumulated. We suggest the compound program of art and culture which makes you experience and interact with resting and amusement. Stacked programs combined to Flagship Core form a more unique experience.

Bar Symbolic space representing the stylish life of young trend setters.

Lounge As a membership space, luxury and convenient service is provided like a lounge in hotel.

Culture Studio Space for cultural class for membership customers.

Cinema/Drama Theater for movie and plays, distinguished complex cultural contents provided.

Antenna Shop Experiencing space for high-technological products which are on sale exclusively.

Restaurant Zone Food zone combined with special events, menus and services.

Zone Resting place suggesting a new life style.

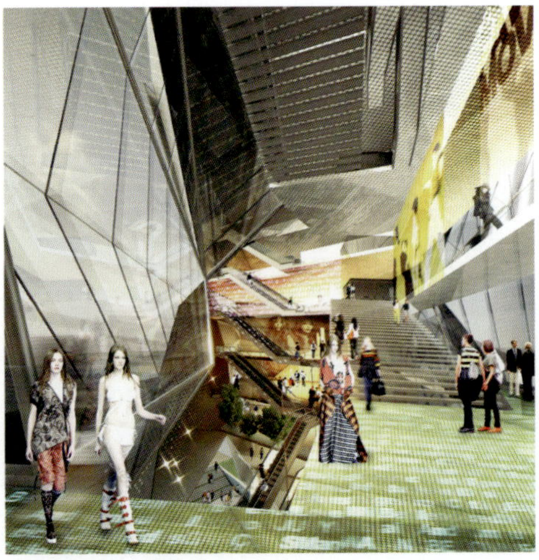

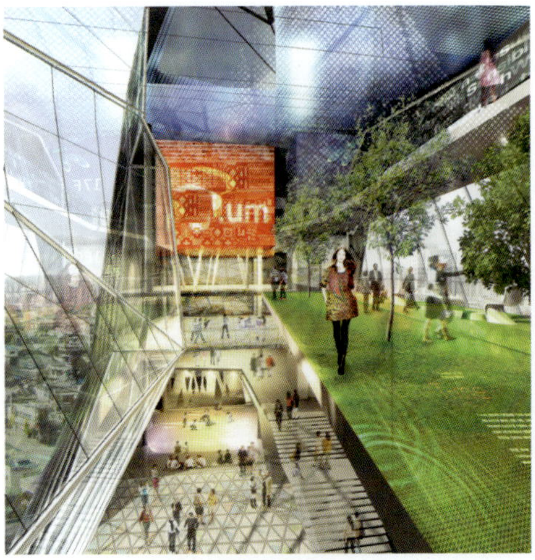

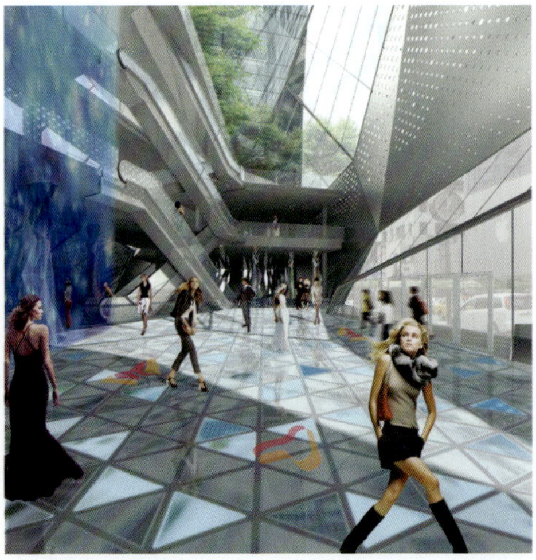

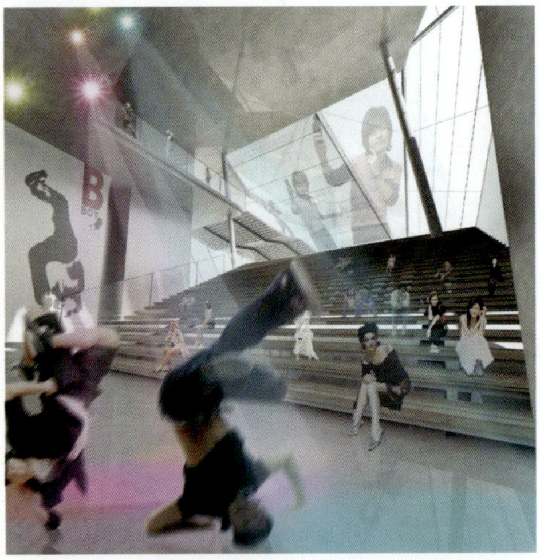

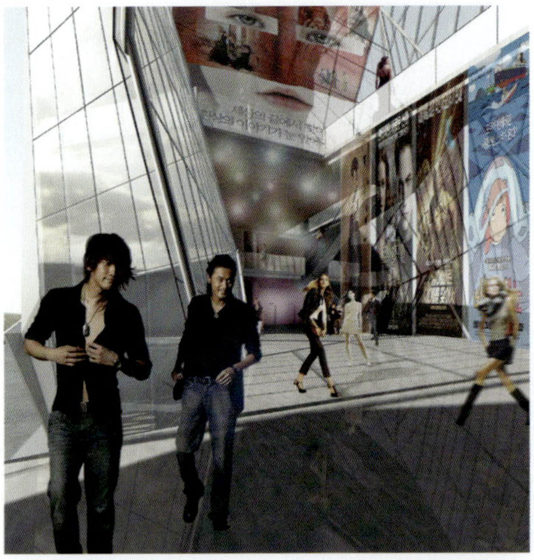

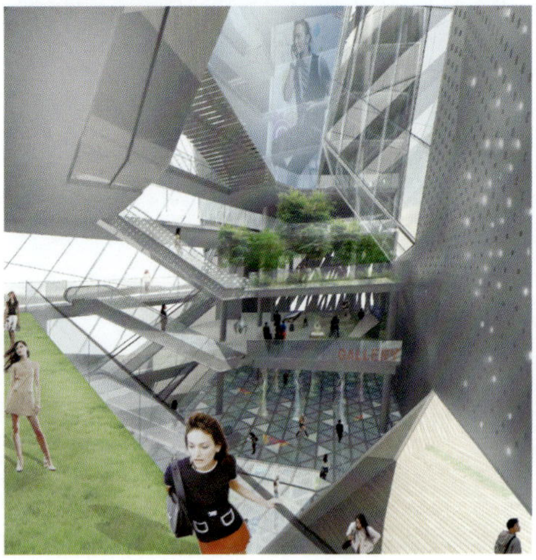

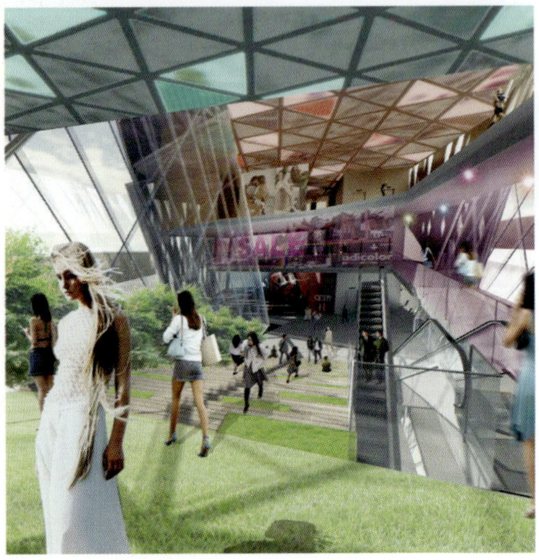

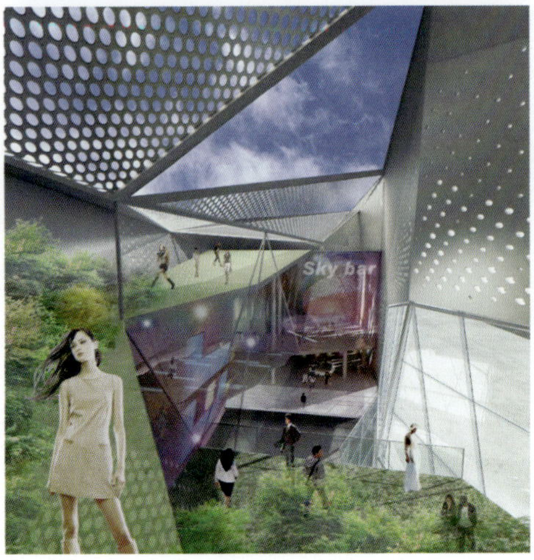
Sky bar

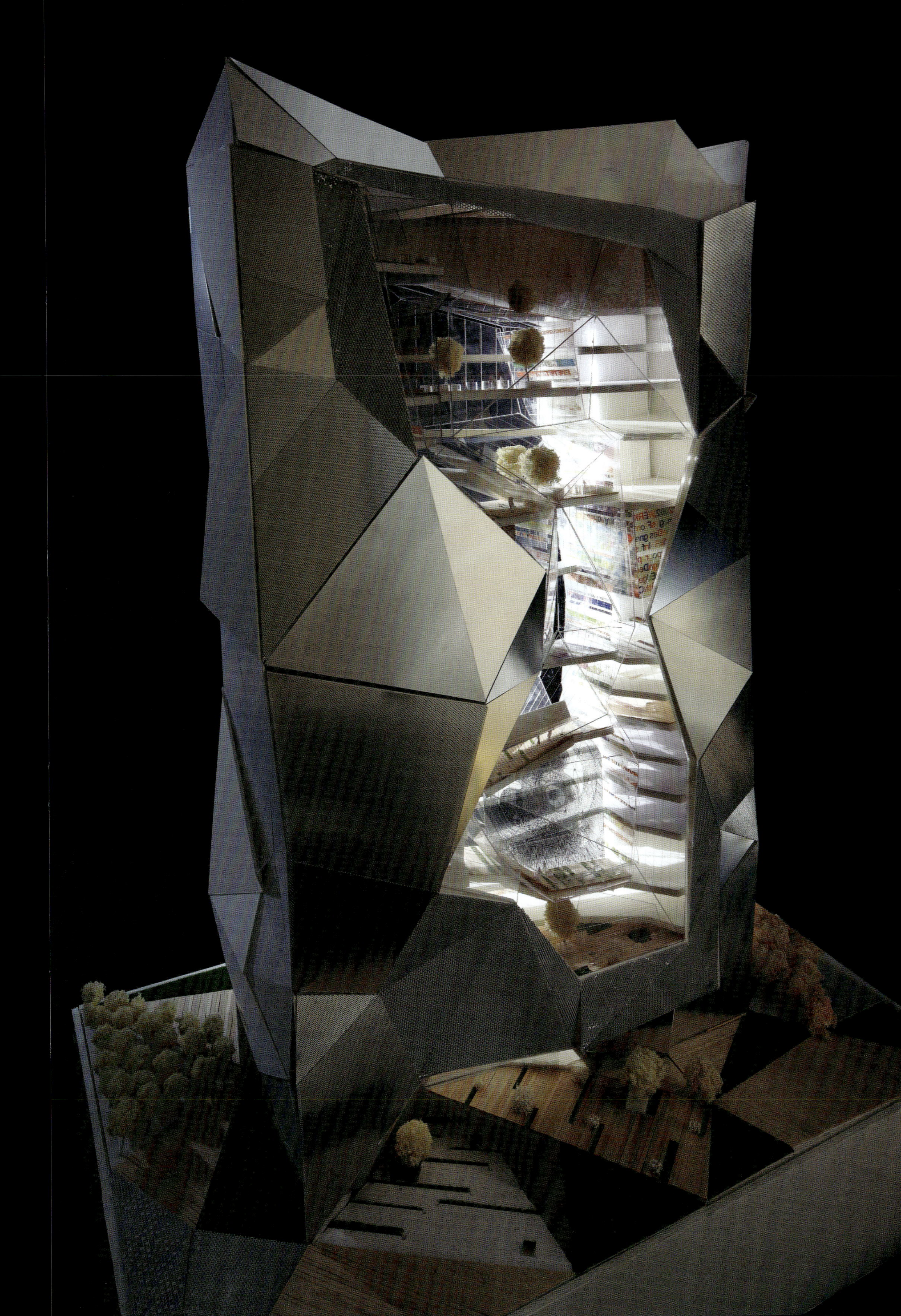

Life & Power Press in PaJu Book City

Cultural topography
stacking contour

Architecture Award of KyungKi Province

Architects Jang Yoon Gyoo, Shin Chang Hoon, Kim Youn Soo
Client Life & Power Press, Kim Seung Ki
Photographer Namgoong Sun

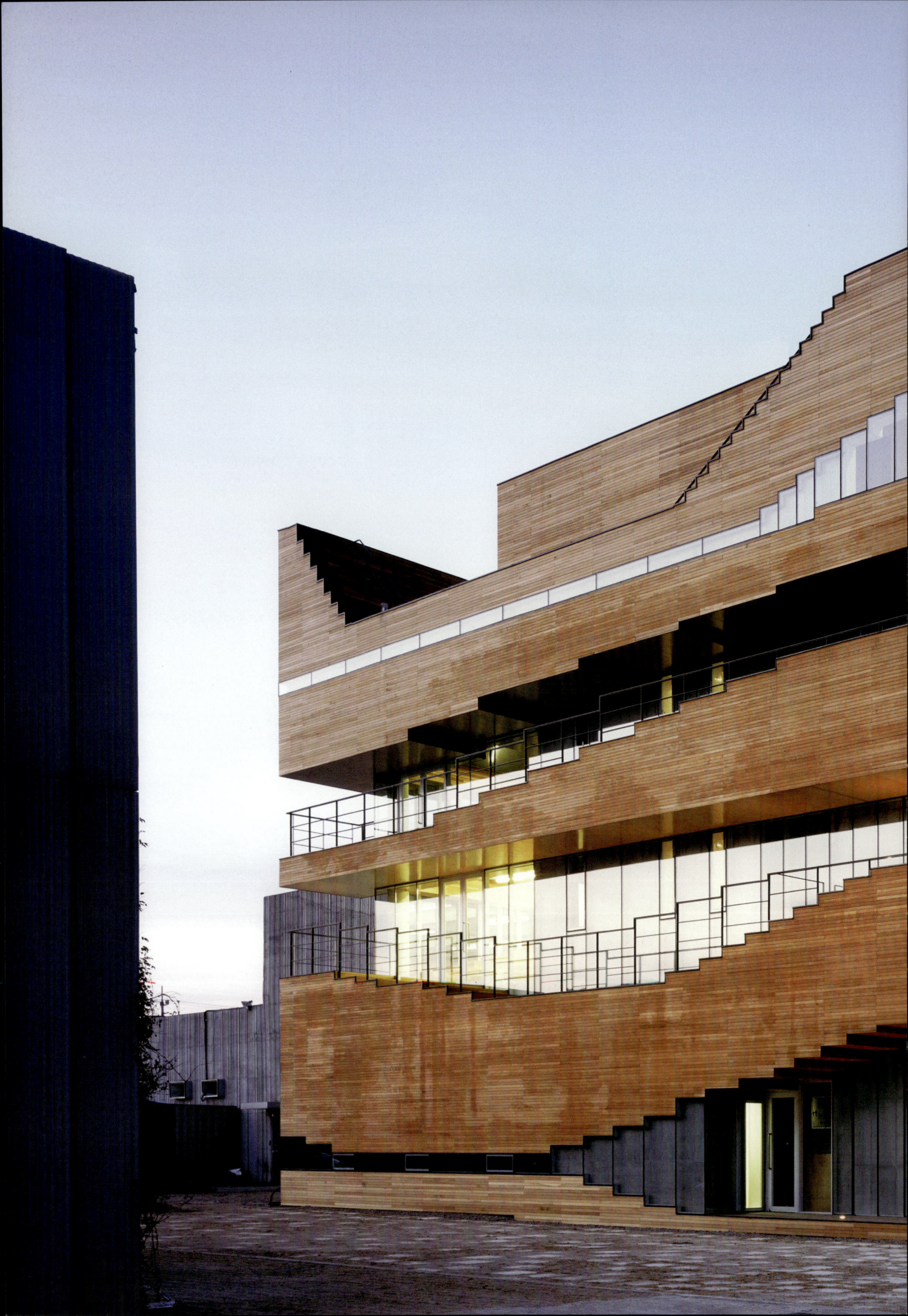

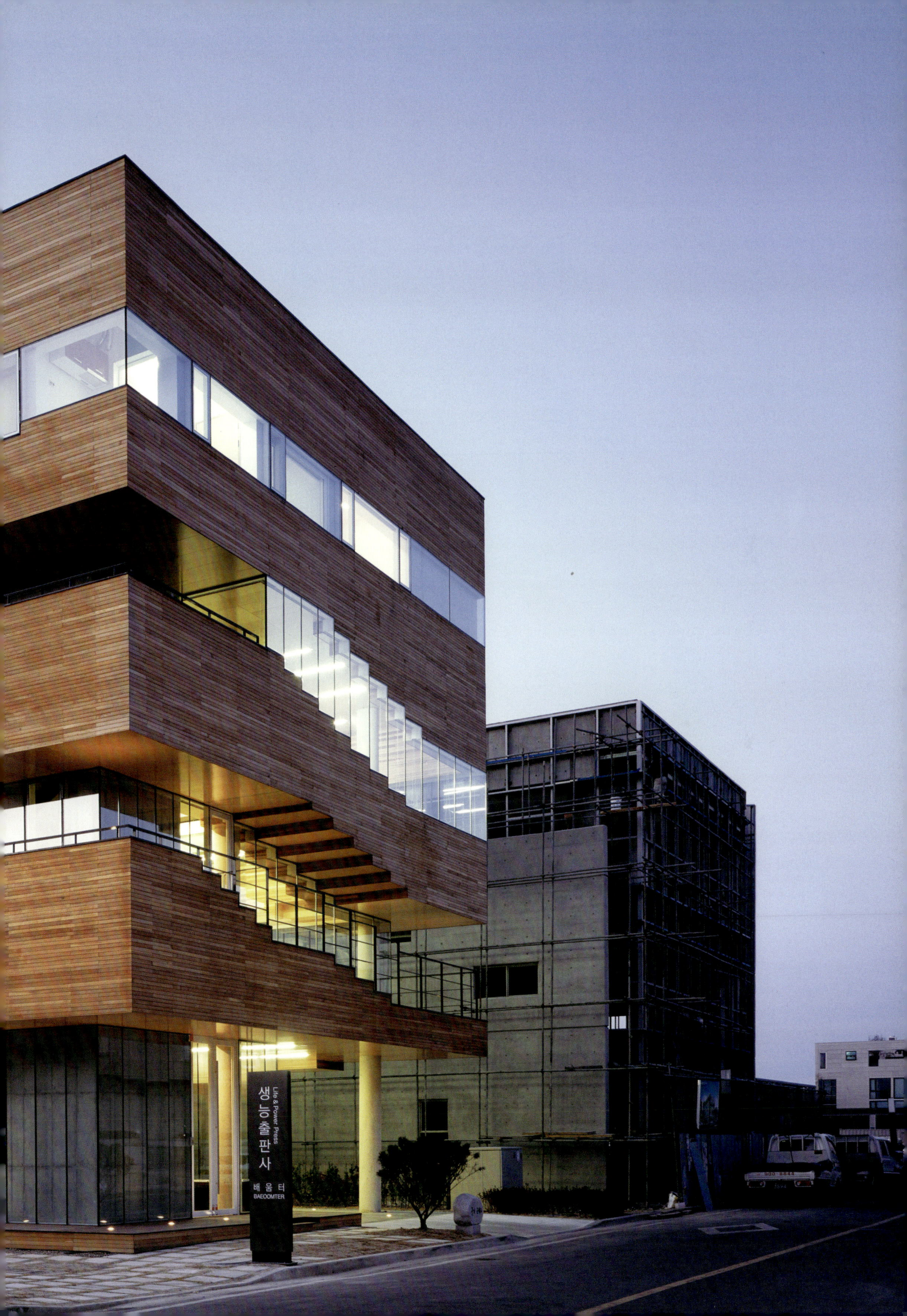
생능출판사
Life & Power Press
배 움 터
BAEOOMTER

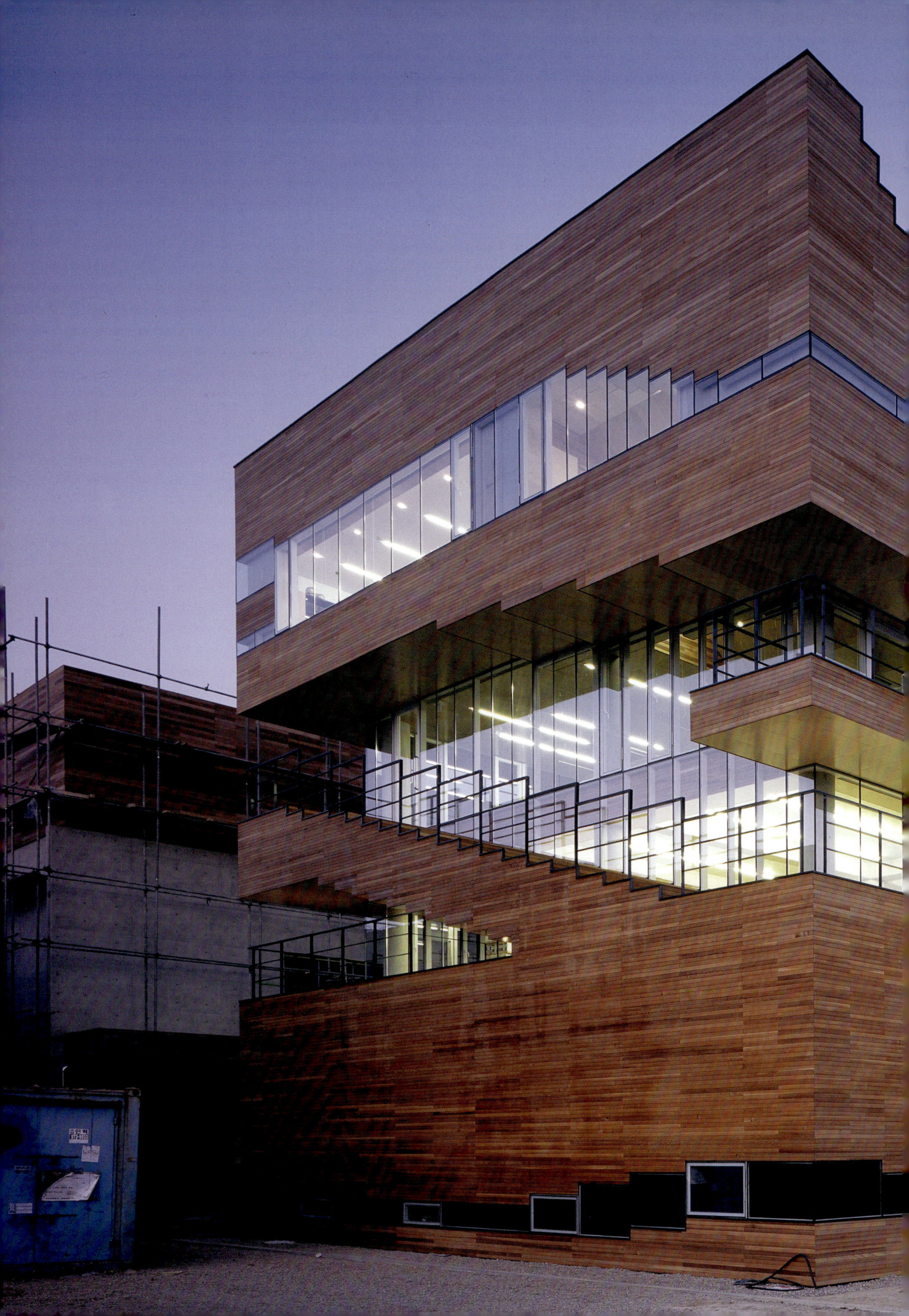

Architects
Jang Yoon Gyoo, Shin Chang Hoon, Kim Youn Soo
Location
507-12 Munbal-li, Kyoha-eup, Paju City
Use Office
Site Area 727.20m²
Gross Floor Area 995.77m²
Building Coverage Ratio 48.47%
Gross Floor Ratio 135.24%
Bldg. Scale
One story below ground/ Seven stories above ground
Structure R.C
Interior Finishing
Preserved wood + T24 transparent pair glass
Client Life & Power Press, Kim seung Ki

CULTURAL TOPOGRAPHY
- STACKING CONTOUR

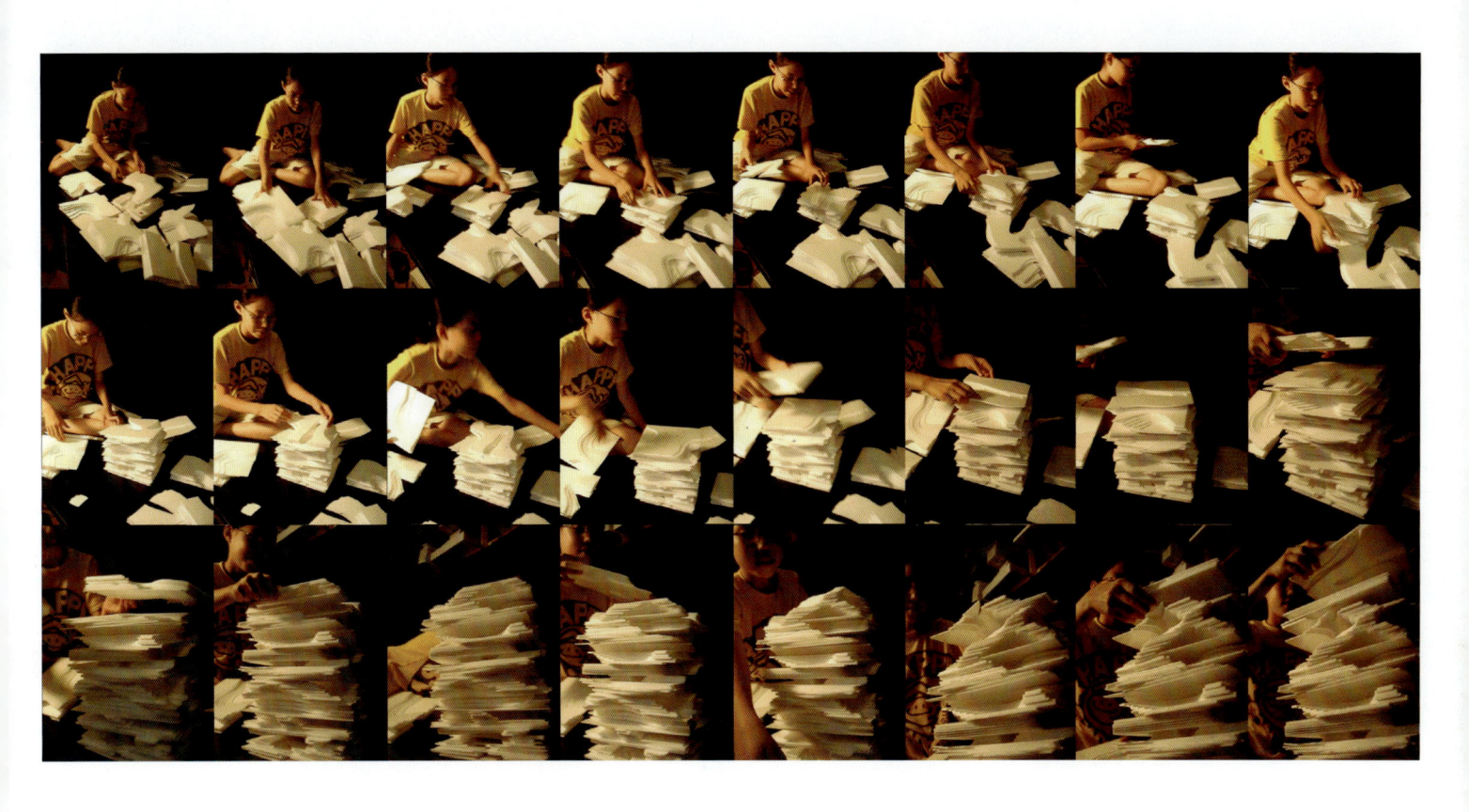

CULTURAL TOPOGRAPHY
- STACKING CONTOUR

In the huge gray planned Paju Book-city, there is a building releasing warm energy giving life to its environment. On too arranged site without no characteristic topography and curve, the only recue is coiled up wooden stairs with topographic energy. It takes a couple of glances to find the entrance and the number of floors inside.

Stack a Topographic map of contour

Finding certain building without guide map is not an easy thing to do in Paju Book-city. It's like an architectural competition of trend and concepts. Topography, which Architect Jang Yoon-Gyoo, suggests incompatible in-between space, causing conflicts and collision. In other words, containers of new topography, so to speak, can't avoid conflicts with the other architects. So the structure of interaction should contain of co-operation and understanding, and an interactive map system should be constituted. Meanwhile, conflicting topography is studied, enjoying talking and debating with each other.

He adopted this idea to the Life & Power Press Project. New container of topography inserts wrinkled lands into existing exhibition space. And the space by this operation makes up a different experience. Transformed topography contains not only physical form, but sharing ideal parts of cultural contents.

Jang Yoon-Gyoo suggests "Map of Stacking Contour" which transforms the topography abstractly.

The Programmatic limit, office, changes to new potentiality by extension of skin space. In particular, the stair-shape balcony, which produces silence rest, predicts different programmatic variations such as performance, gallery and seminar.

All the buildings on that street have similar volume with vertical rising. Therefore he focused on horizontal stacking. He believes that inside of a building bears its own topography. To find topographical structure in it, "stacking" is the

Contour

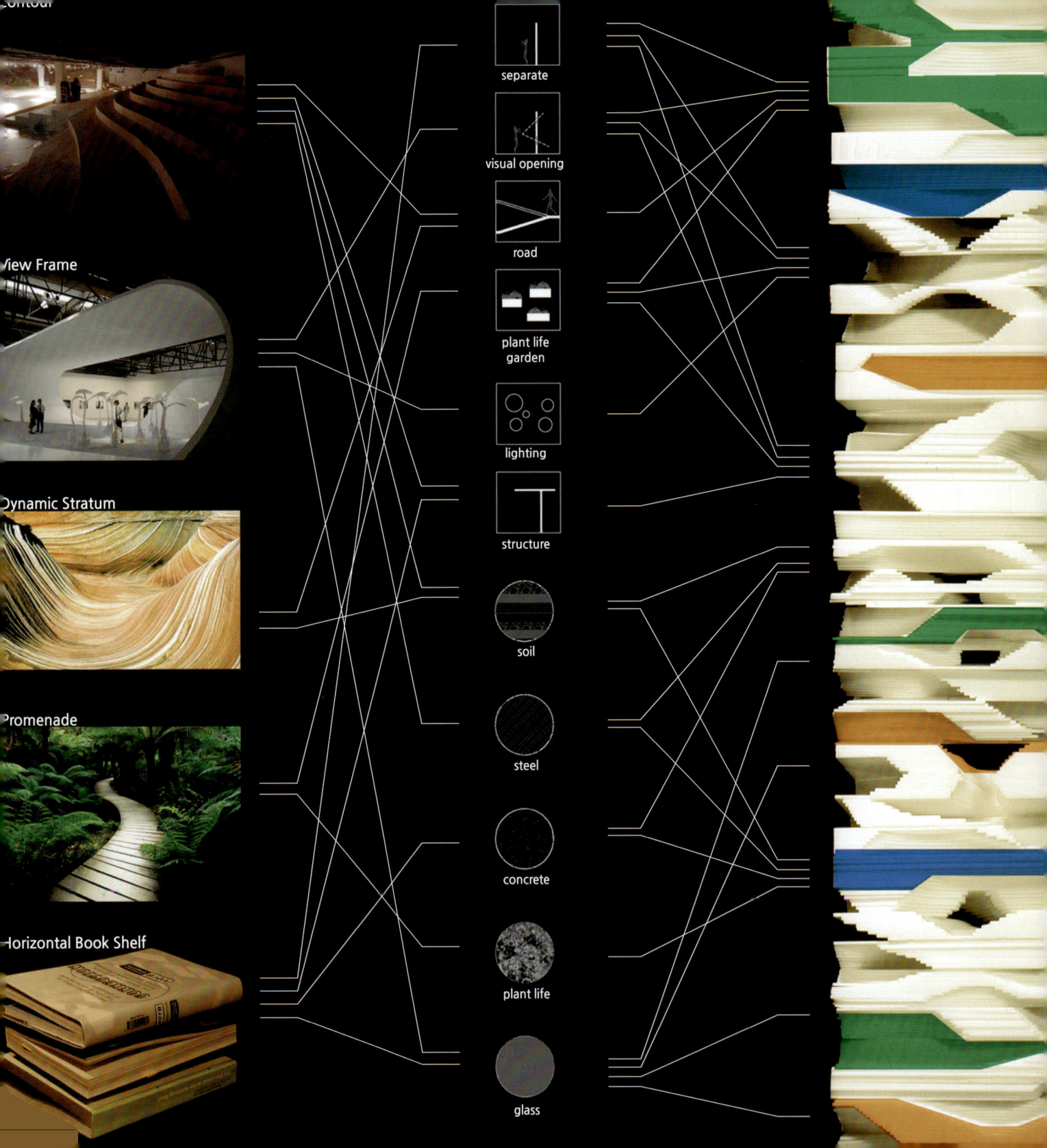

View Frame

Dynamic Stratum

Promenade

Horizontal Book Shelf

separate

visual opening

road

plant life
garden

lighting

structure

soil

steel

concrete

plant life

glass

COMPOUND BODY 223

Dynamic Stratum

View Frame

CULTURAL TOPOGRAPHY

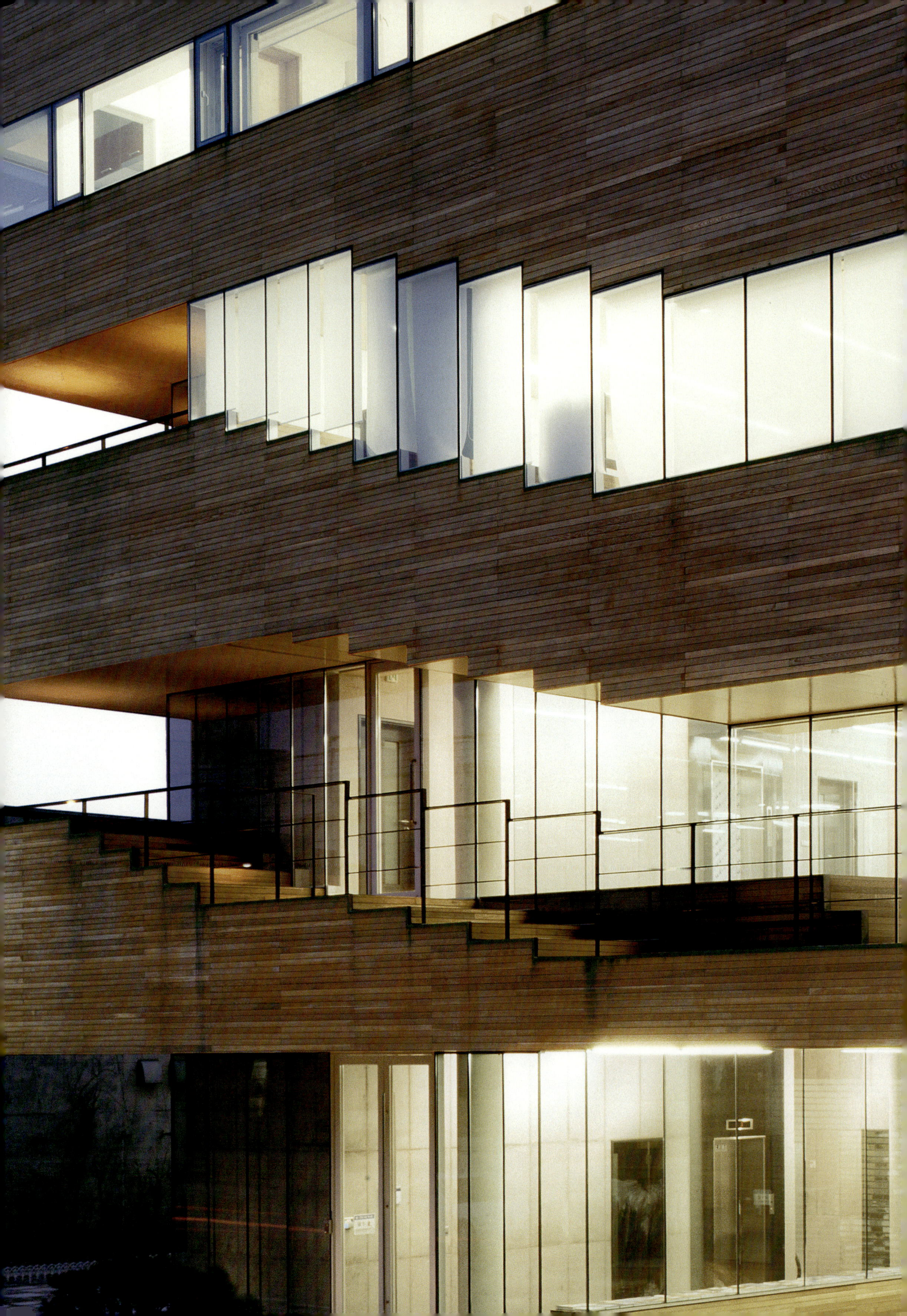

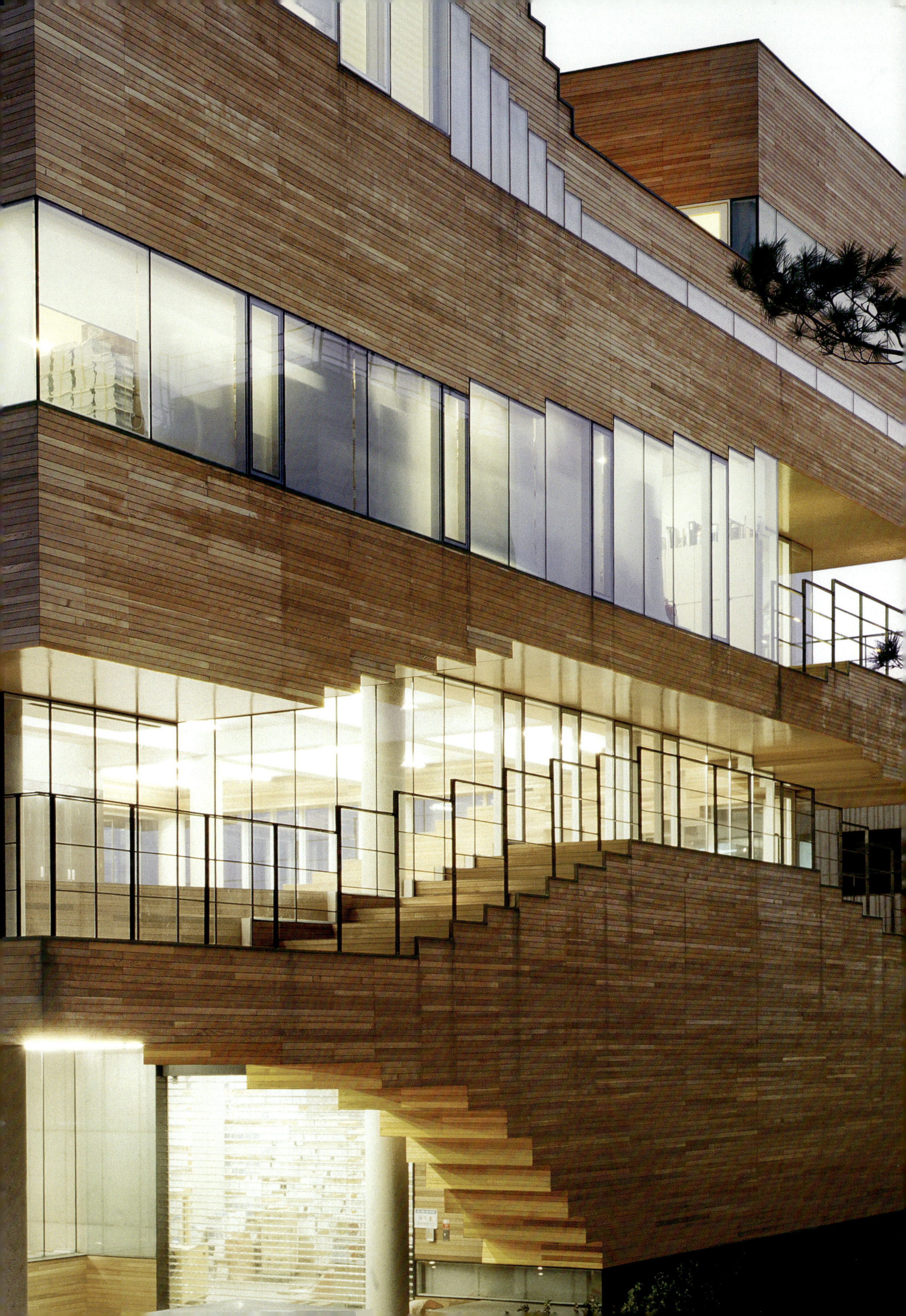

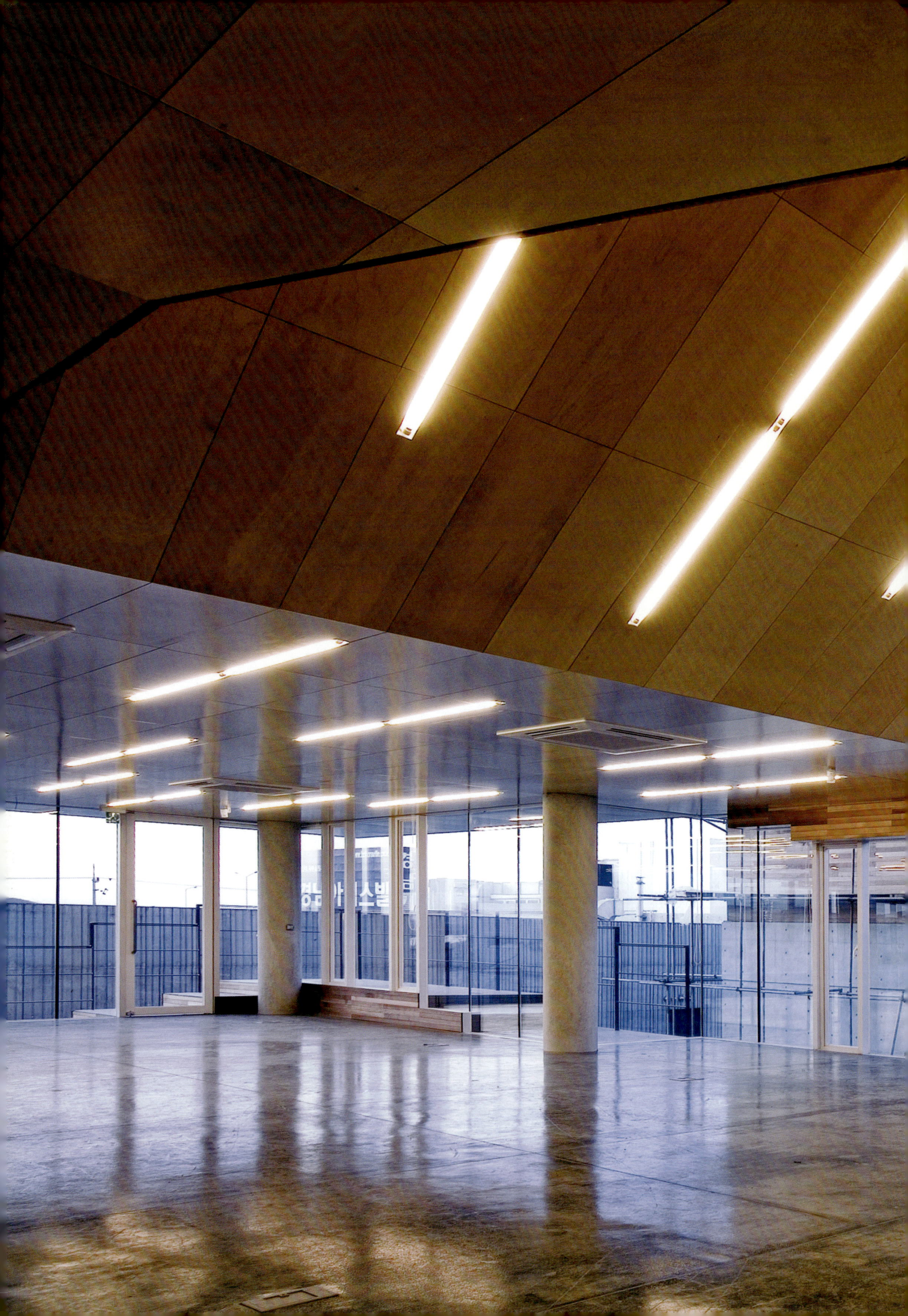

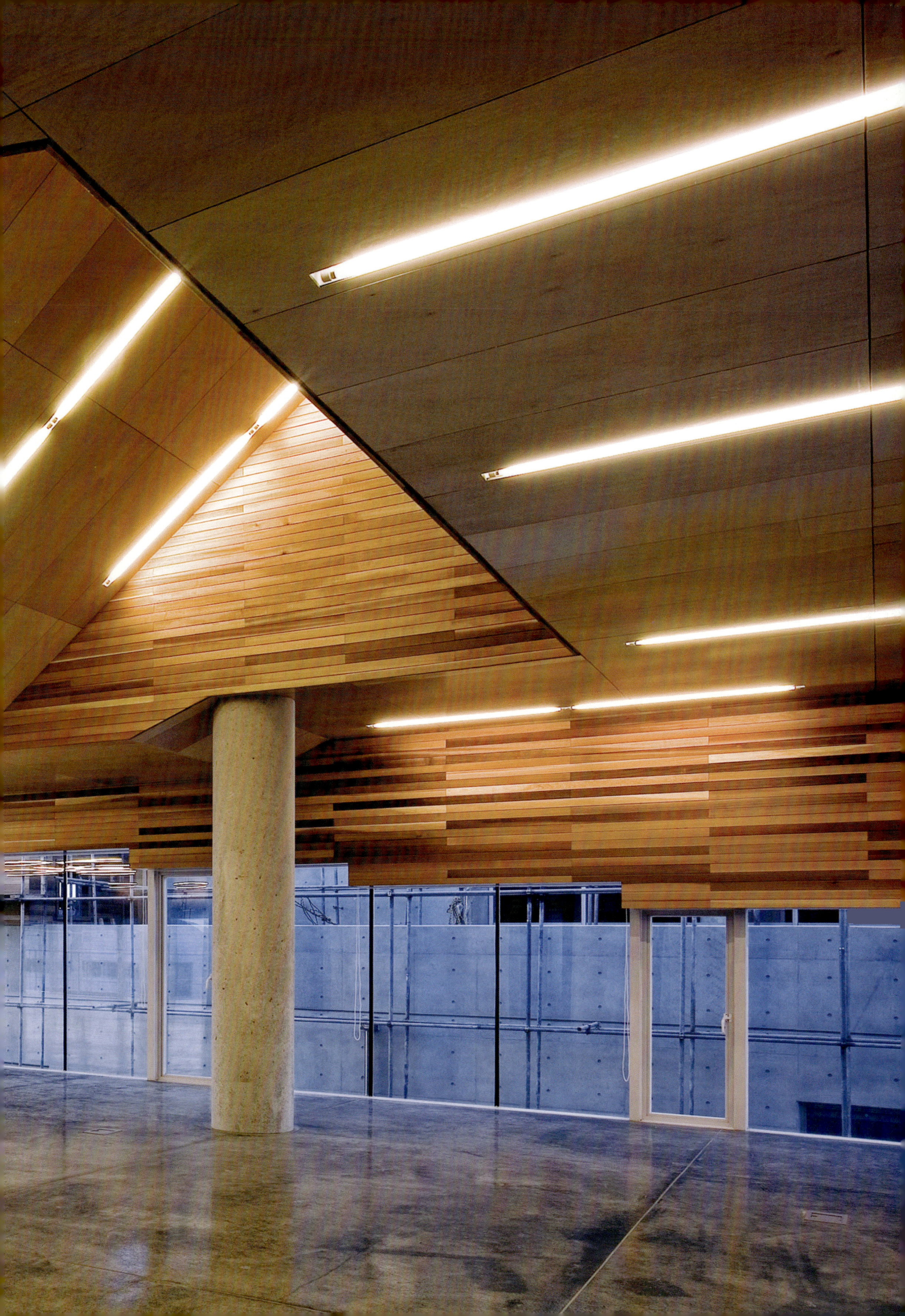

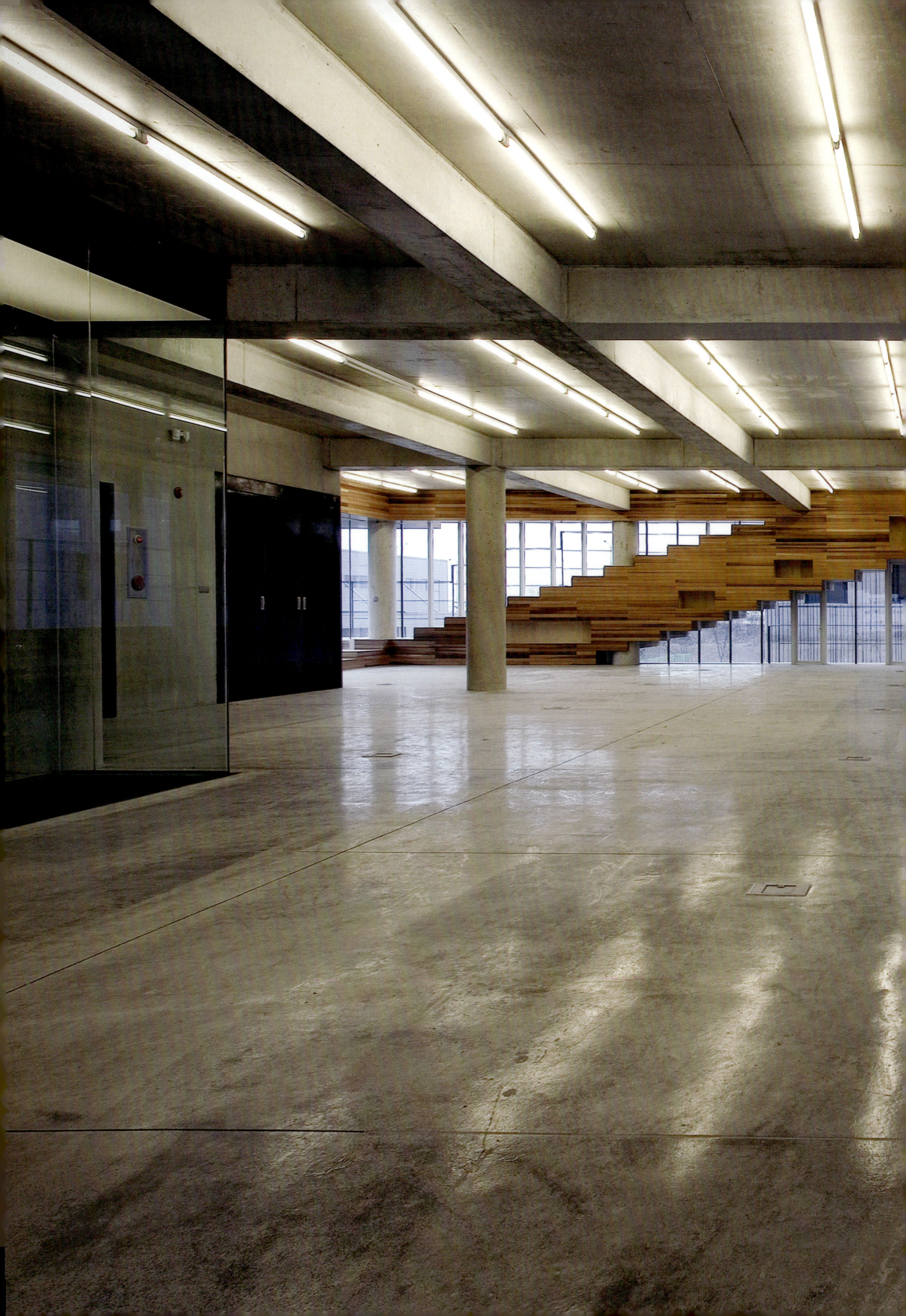

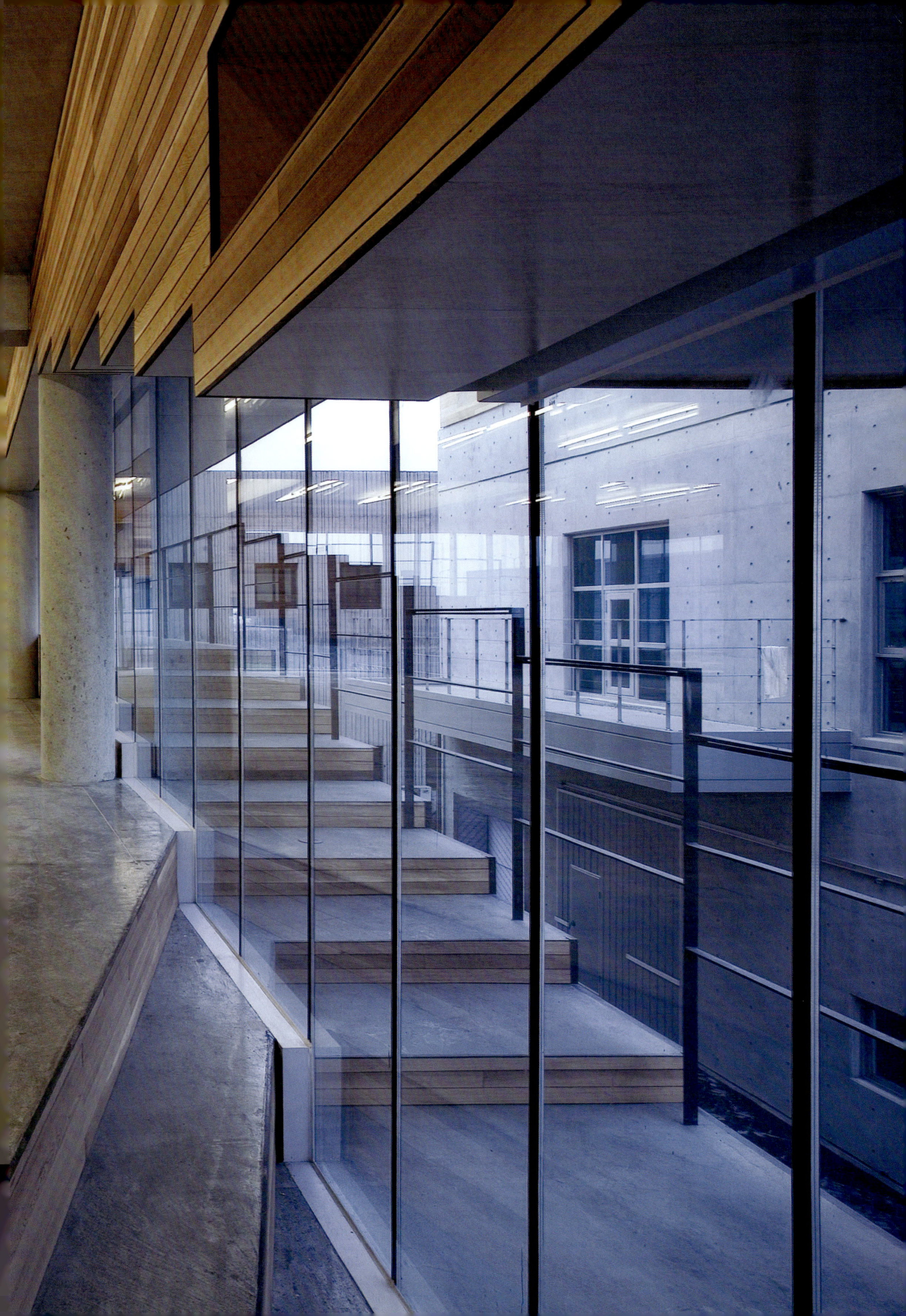

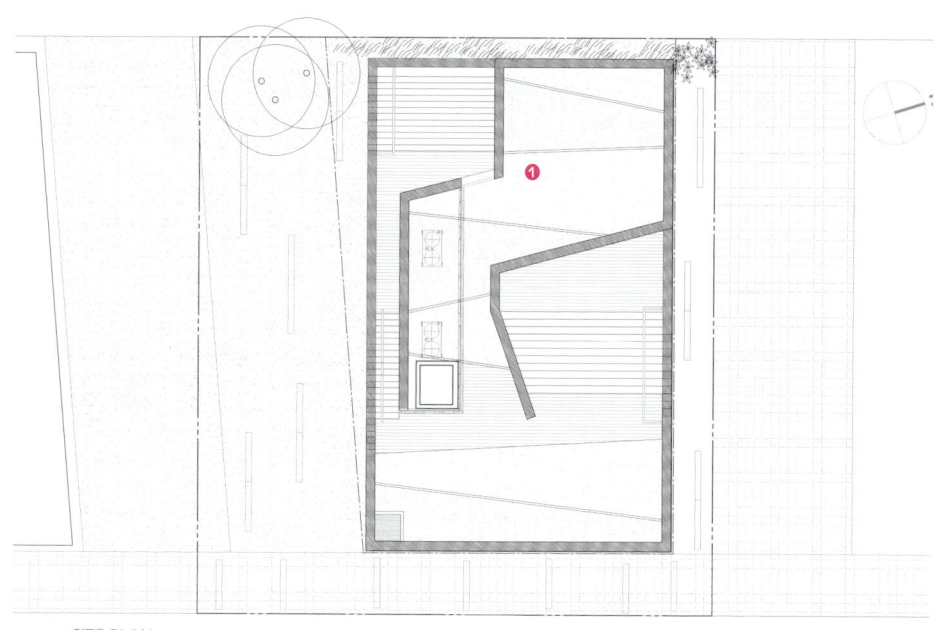

SITE PLAN
1. Roof Garden

way to construct a new building. Here comes another key word, "Compound body" which is the overlapping two objects but both still moderately existing, not completely melted like a single object. For this idea, outside ceiling is finished with warm timber; the lower part of the building is enclosed with transparent glass. Until the last decision of mass, Unsangdong Architects had made 10 different models while working on this project. The number 10 is not just the total number of models, but the modeling groups that show the accurate concept.

The program of this building is unpredictably simple. The 1st floor is a warehouse and gallery and the rest is office space. The upper space belongs to the owner. He collapses these spatial divisions with a composition of scenery like something that can be watched through the windows. Because his theory is that light emerging through spatial cracks determines the matter of volume.

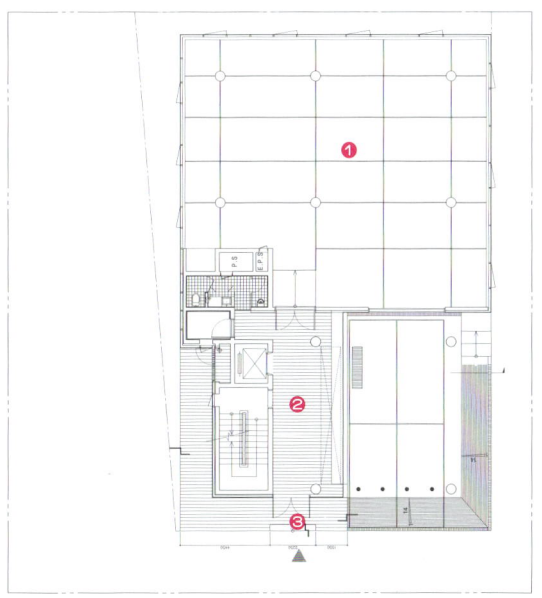

1ST FLOOR PLAN

1. Exhibit Hall
2. Hall
3. Entrance

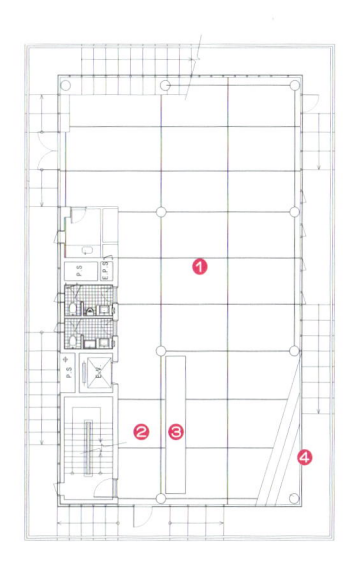

2ND FLOOR PLAN

1. Storage
2. Hall
3. Open
4. Balcony

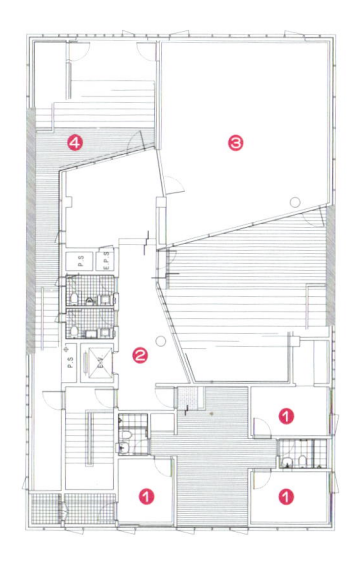

4TH FLOOR PLAN

1. Studio
2. Hall
3. Conference Room
4. Roof Garden

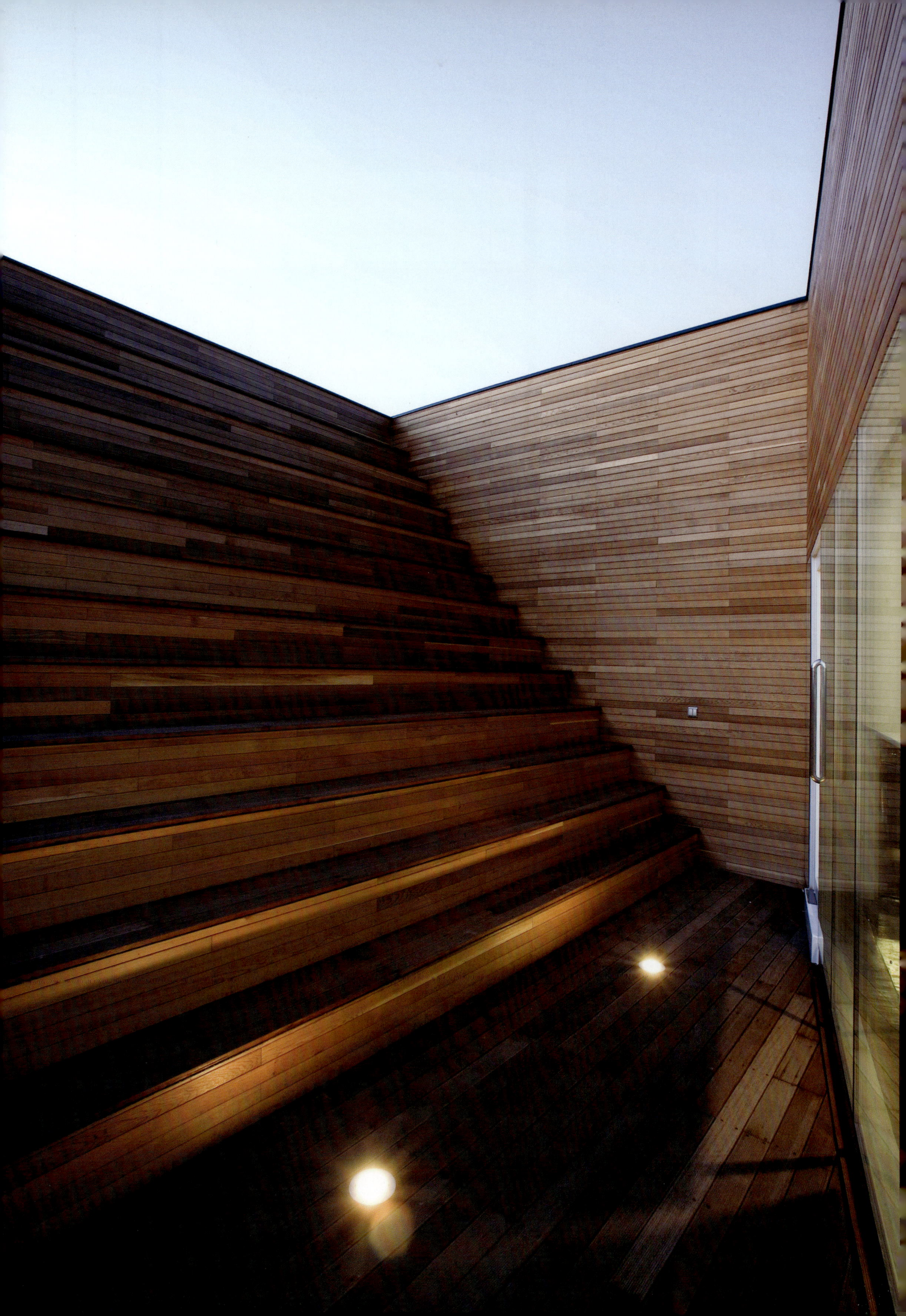

Admire architecture as culture
Requests of a press office building in Paju Book-city are made by coordinators, architects and architects recommended by them. At the same time, he is evaluated as an artist who can shed light on the gray city concept. He regards architecture as the combination of unlike means, not just space or form. Life & Power Press is also on the way of that study. Wooden plates are not simply stacked. They are formed to mass by cutting and emptying, producing an image like four books stacked together.
In the beginning of his studies on architecture, he was more interested in poetry. But he chose architecture finally because it is a more integrated field with literature, aesthetics and making physical matter. However, architecture needs to be built then formed plus spatial matter conflicts with his ideas.

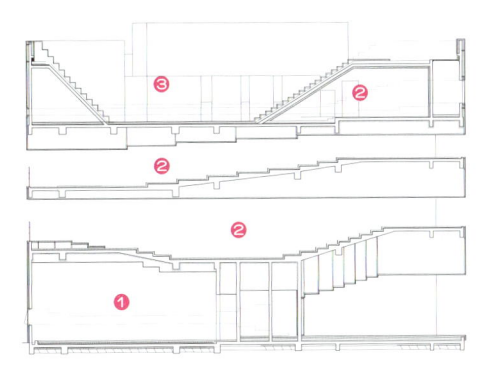

CROSS SECTION A
1. Exhibit Hall
2. Balcony
3. Roof Garden

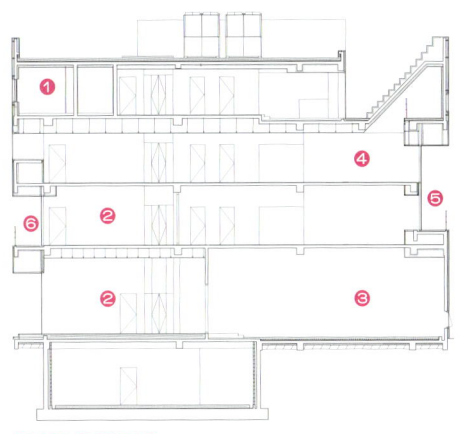

CROSS SECTION B
1. Studio
2. Hall
3. Exhibit Hall
4. Office
5. Stair
6. Balcony

EAST ELEVATION

NORTH ELEVATION

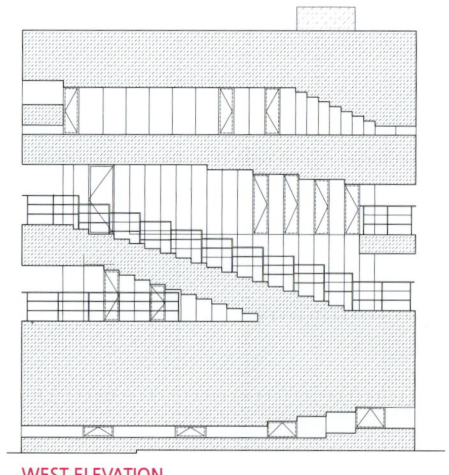

WEST ELEVATION

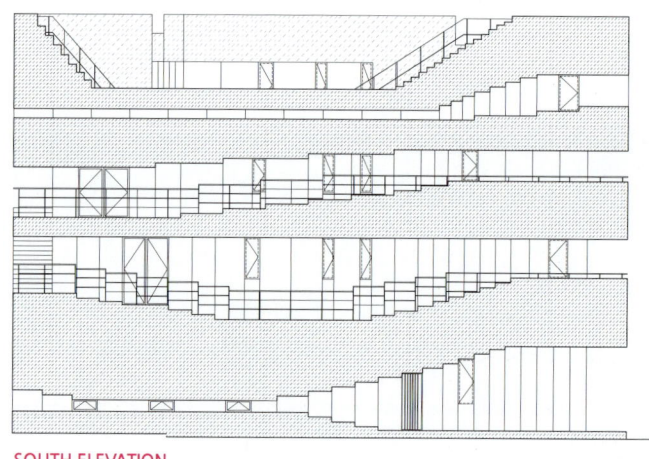

SOUTH ELEVATION

"Compound body." It is what he does every time when he starts a design. He researches the city to form a relation between combination and compound, and with the results he finds the way to constitute new architecture. Thus his preposterous combinations are born. And also architecture is not only an object standing alone but it requires context, programs which are combined newly physically. In other words, walls can be space or form and it is actually working on. Perhaps his architecture comes from watching architectural culture on a philosophic background.
Architecture should become a code like culture. So he asks himself how to realize this. He is also concerned about the way to bond various kinds of artists to work on something all together. It is why he interacts with young artists.
He admires architecture more as a social role than just the building a house. Through his role in society, he believes society can change and architecture can become a culture itself. Good architecture makes a good city, and a good city makes good culture. He will try to make good architecture as long as he can and he will keep suggesting new trends and directions. In the end, when it meets the other artists, he dreams that his efforts are recognized talked about.

text from **V-Magazine**

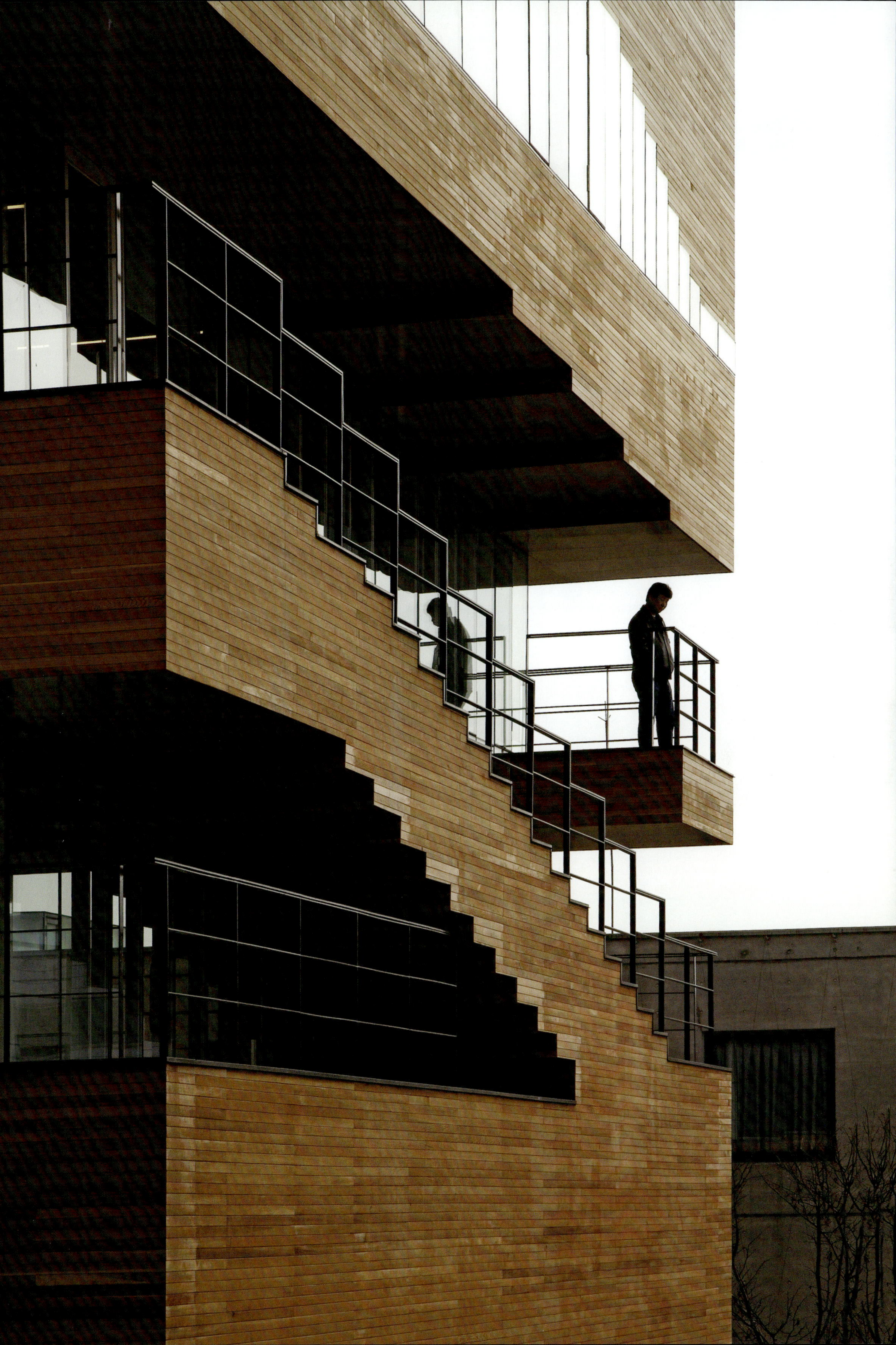

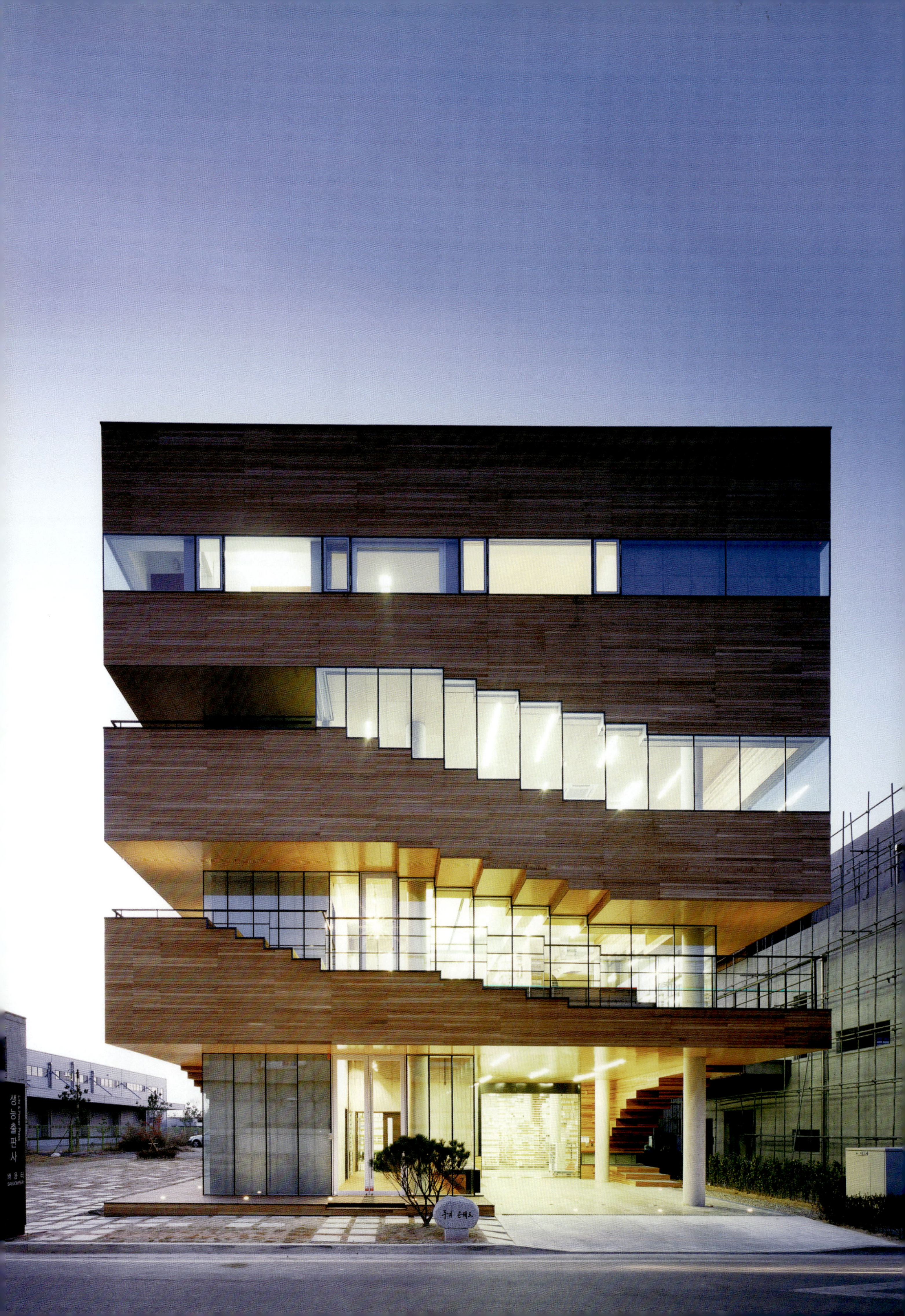

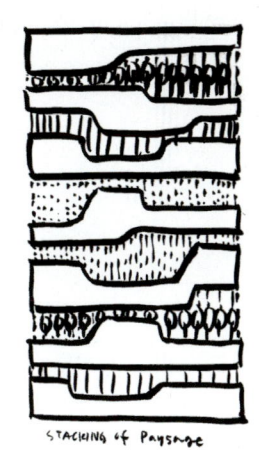

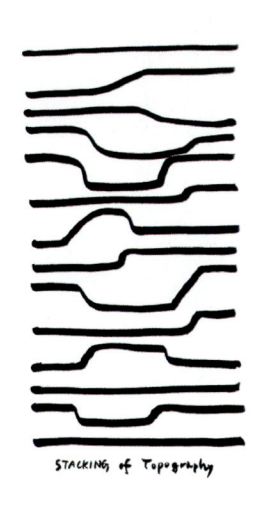

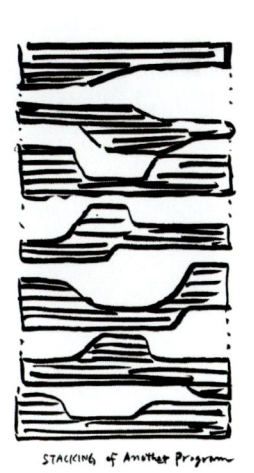

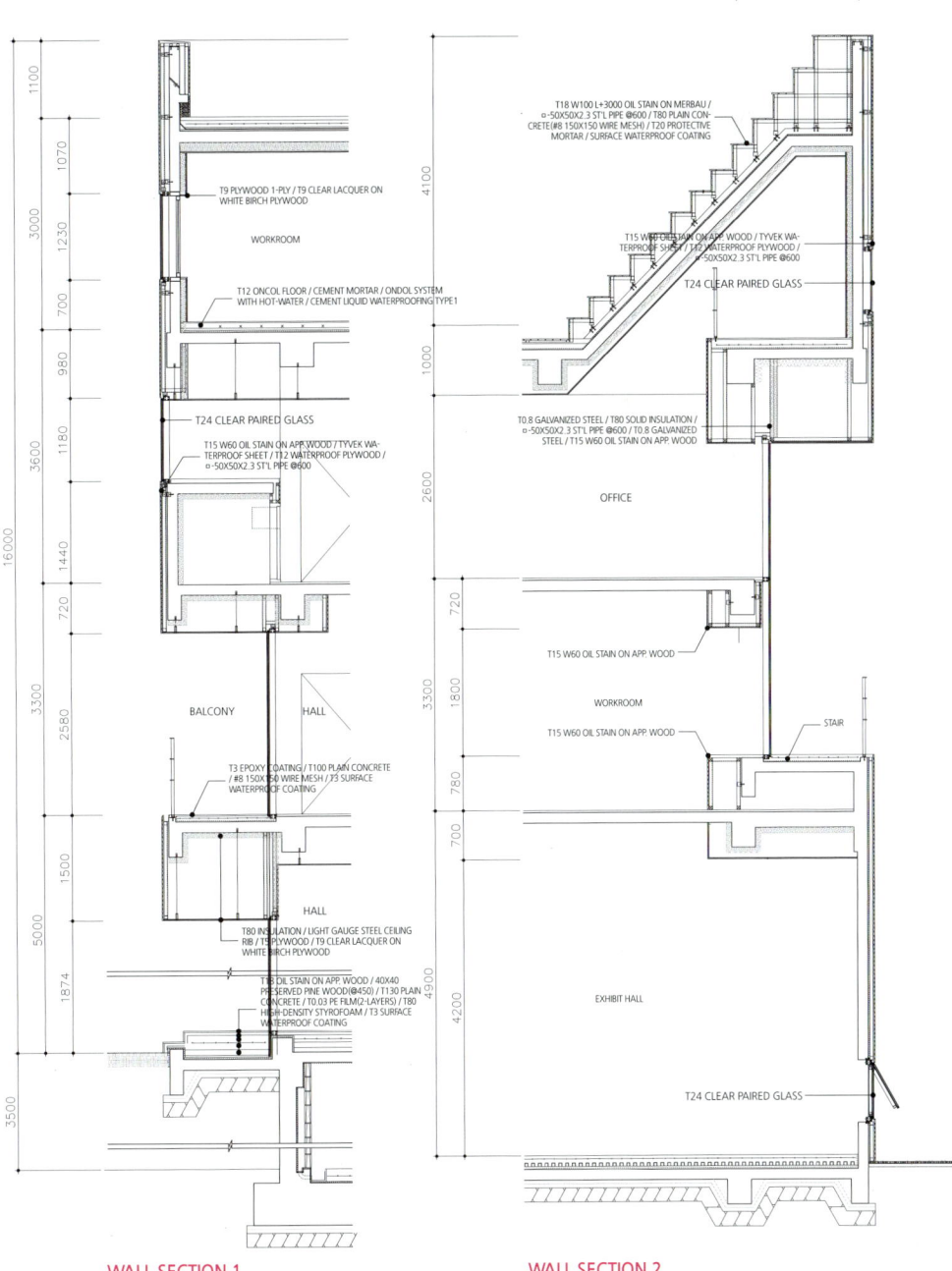

STACKING of Paysage   STACKING of Topography   STACKING of Another Program

PARTIAL ELEVATION   WALL SECTION 1   WALL SECTION 2

Theater Contour

Architects Jang Yoon Gyoo, Shin Chang Hoon
Photographer Kim Jae Kyung

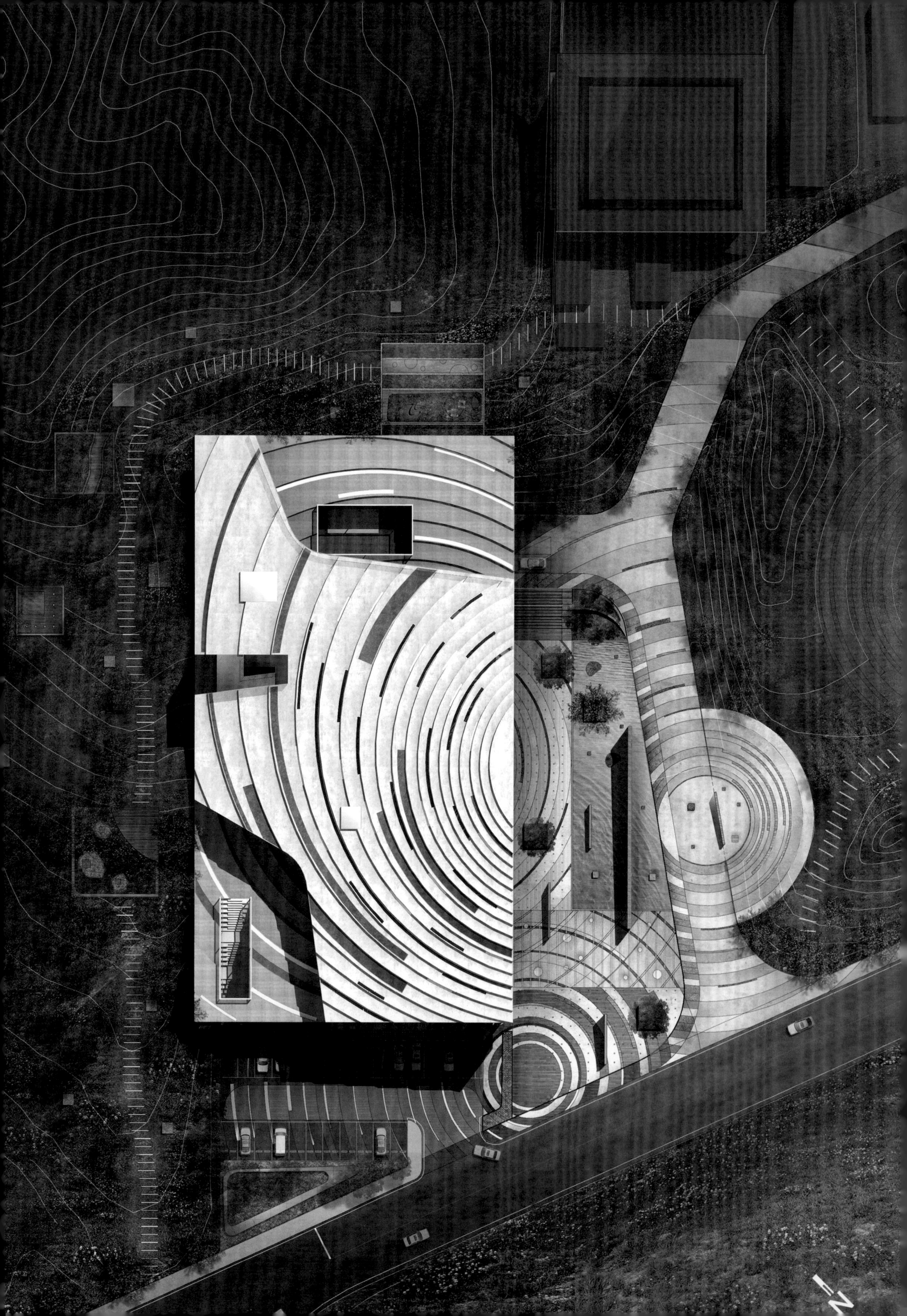
N

TOPOGRAPHY STAGE OF CONTOUR _ SOUND FIELD OF THE LANDSCAPE

Our aim is creating a stage like container for our cultural performance. As a basic frame of consisting theater, topographic skin is interpreted to continuation of topography from the site. Skin of plaza; 2-dimensinal skin is substituted to spatial skin. Required diverse codes are combined and change the cultural plaza. The culture plaza is substituted according to set-up of cultural codes, artistic code, natural code and urban code. NamSaDang Theater becomes diverse dimensional space with spatial layers and represents cultural code of AnSeong above local theater. It is the plaza for young culture accommodating artistic diverse channel actively. It provides playing space in the true sense of the term which contains Korean recreation culture. To Korean, aesthetic thing is natural thing rather than the natural thing is the aesthetic thing. Beauty of Korean old architecture is from making nature more standing out than itself. Architecture is objet of nature as well as background. Korean topography symbolizes mountain, ground and beautiful line. Korean beauty is discovered while the process of finding symbiotic code in harmony of nature and human.

Topography Stage
Between the mountain and valley, there is what by wide yard opened and river running through them. And houses are built and village is founded in there. Roof of the houses resembles the mountain at the back of their houses. Contemporary society gets lost communication with surrounding nature treating the mountain as developing target. We suggest NamSaDang Theater is natural stage resembling the figure of our local nature. The line combines human physical sense rather than visual. It is easy about modification and changes all the time. Korean line aims for movable physical beauty and unique aesthetic form organizing relationship of human and nature.

Panorama Nature
The Stage consisted of Korean topographic figure adopts Panorama Nature to inside from outside. Background of the stage is not fixed architecture but living nature. Korean four-season becomes the background giving experiences our nature through scenery frames.

Stage of Sound
All sound has sensual factors such as certain pitch, loudness and tone. The sound which is the result of wave is material. And tempo, melody, harmony and tone are synthesized by certain rule and convention and our emotion and thought are expressed by it. Play is developed according to flow of the time and reflects the time and circumstance as an active genre. Architecture and nature doesn't guard each other. Each factor is ecologic and inclusive in entire site above single purpose and constructs the organic form and program. Environment of the site becomes compound nature.

COMPOUND GREEN GLASS

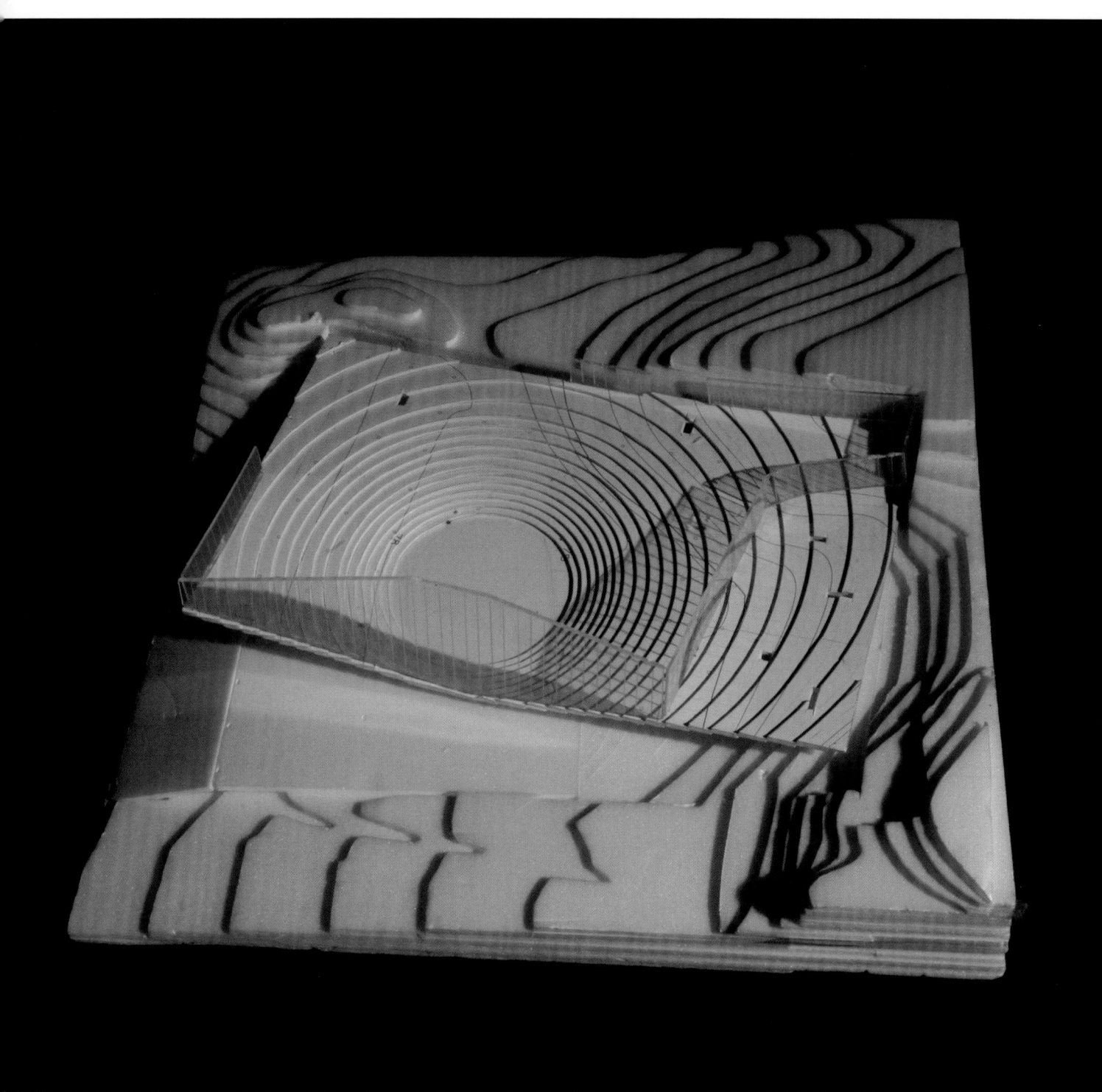

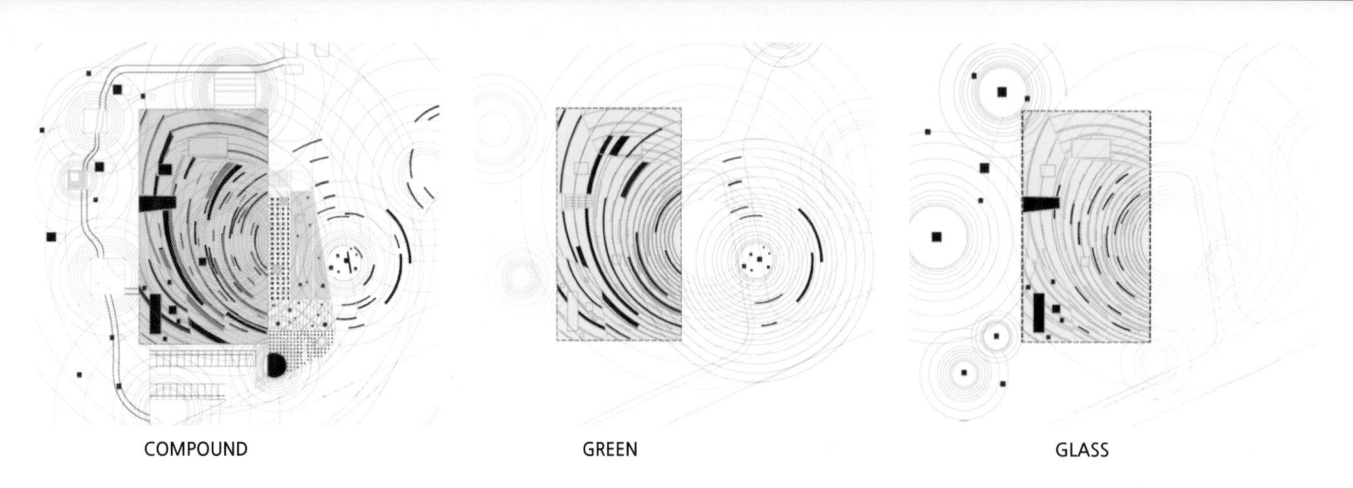

COMPOUND BODY 243

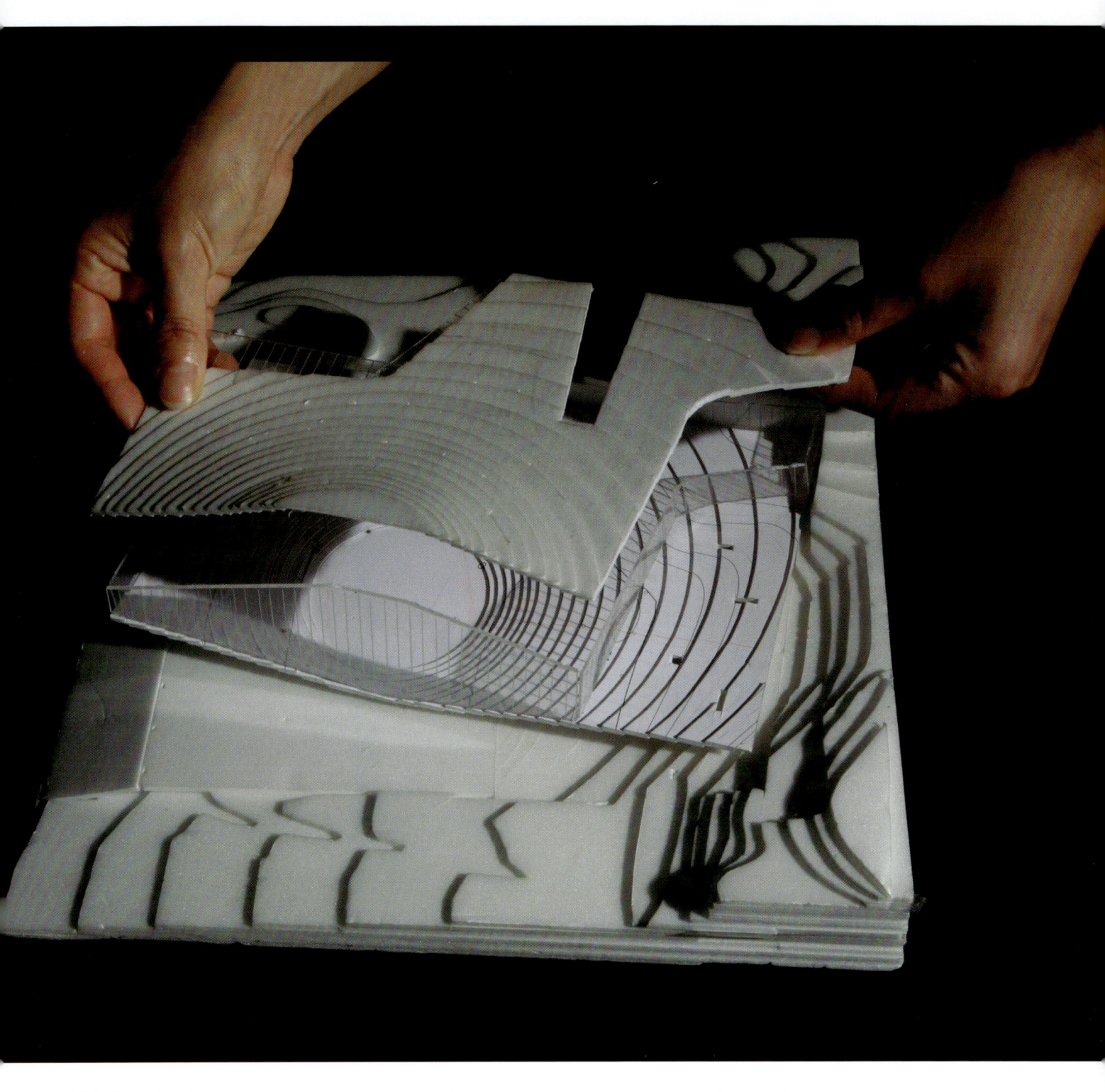

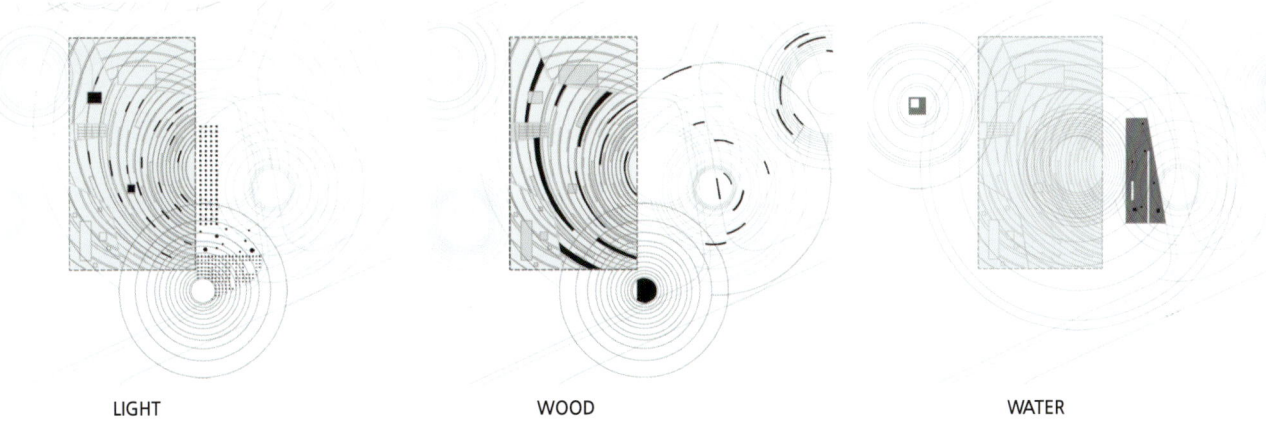

LIGHT	WOOD	WATER

ELEVATION

KEY MAP

KEY MAP

COMPOUND BODY 245

Location MT 31, Bokpyungri, Bogemyun, Ansung, Kyunggido, South Korea
Use Korean cultural performance
Site Area 8264.5㎡
Building Area 2411㎡
Total Floor Area 3147.19㎡
Building Coverage Ratio 31.56%
Floor Area Ratio 36.51 %
Building Scale Two Stories
Structure Steel Structure + R.C. Structure

THEATER FLOOR

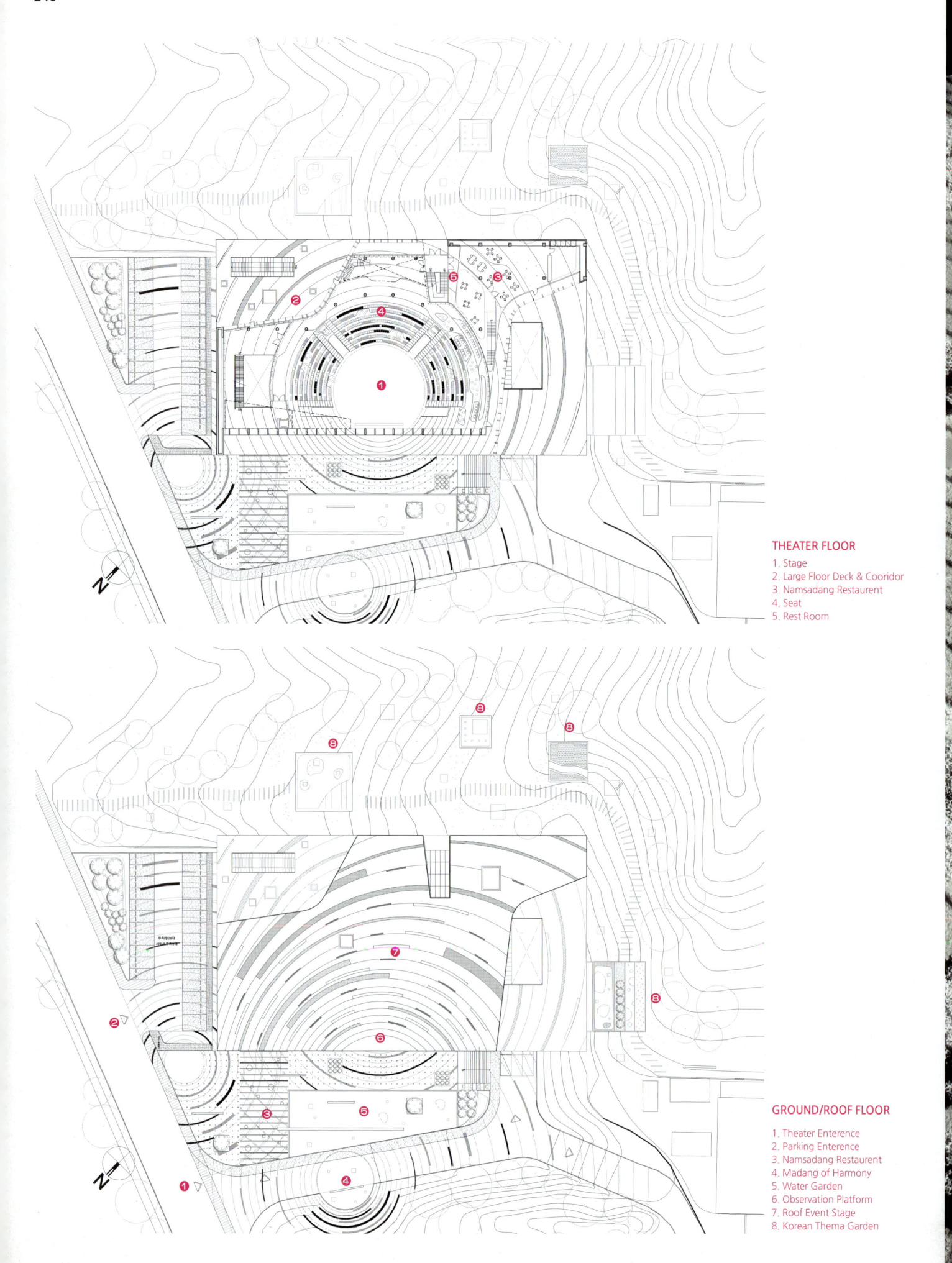

1. Stage
2. Large Floor Deck & Cooridor
3. Namsadang Restaurent
4. Madang of Harmony
5. Rest Room

GROUND/ROOF FLOOR

1. Theater Enterence
2. Parking Enterence
3. Namsadang Restaurent
4. Madang of Harmony
5. Water Garden
6. Observation Platform
7. Roof Event Stage
8. Korean Thema Garden

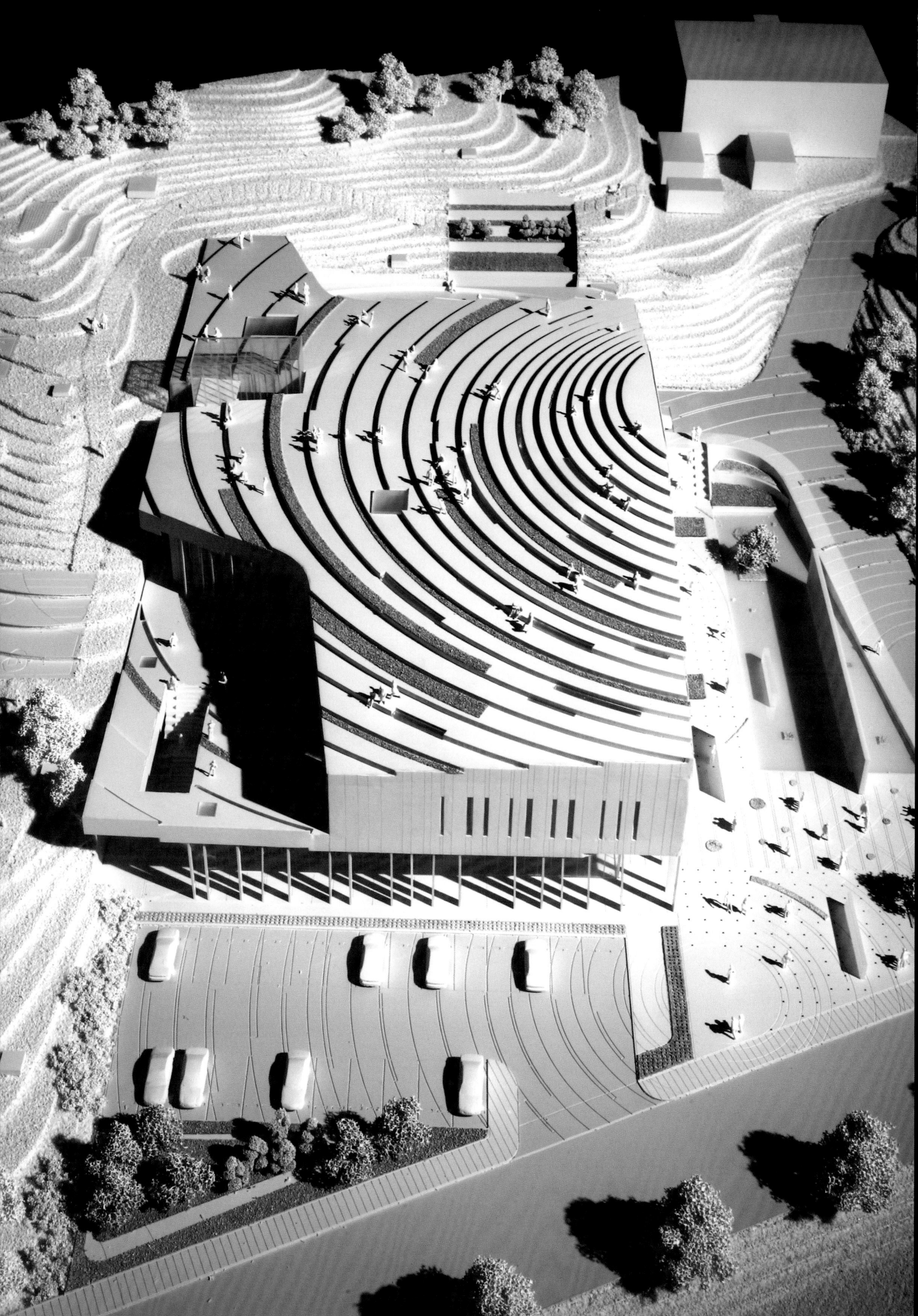

Prehistoric Museum

Interactive topography

Architects Jang Yoon Gyoo, Shin Chang Hoon, Kim Woo Young
Photographer Kim Jae Kyung

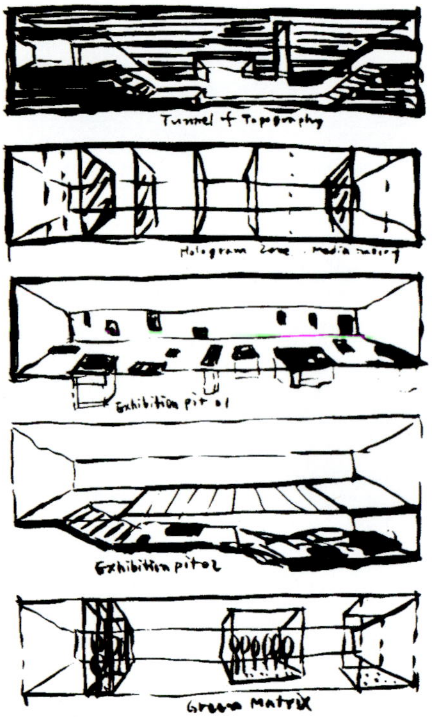
Tunnel of Topography
Hologram Zone
Exhibition pit 01
Exhibition pit 02
Green Matrix

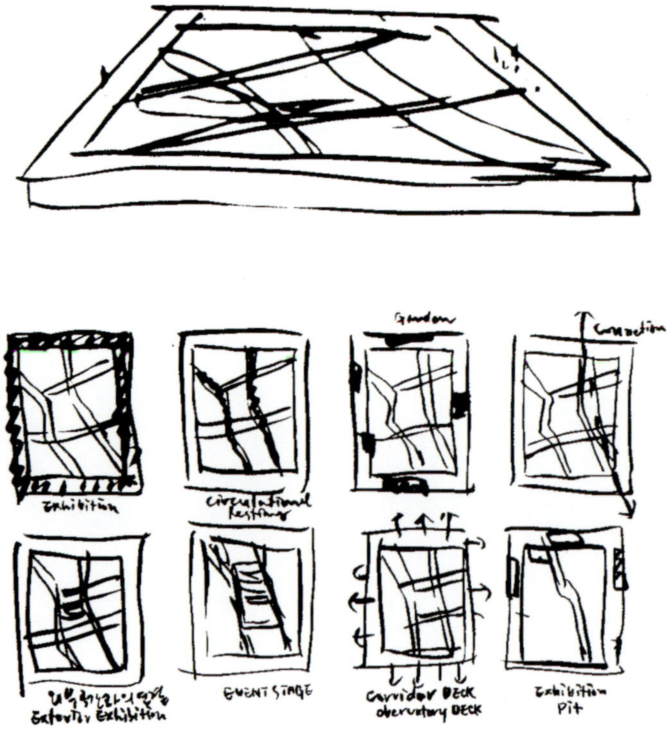
Garden
Connection
Exhibition
Circulation and Resting
EVENT STAGE
Corridor DECK
observatory DECK
Exhibition
Pit
Exterior Exhibition

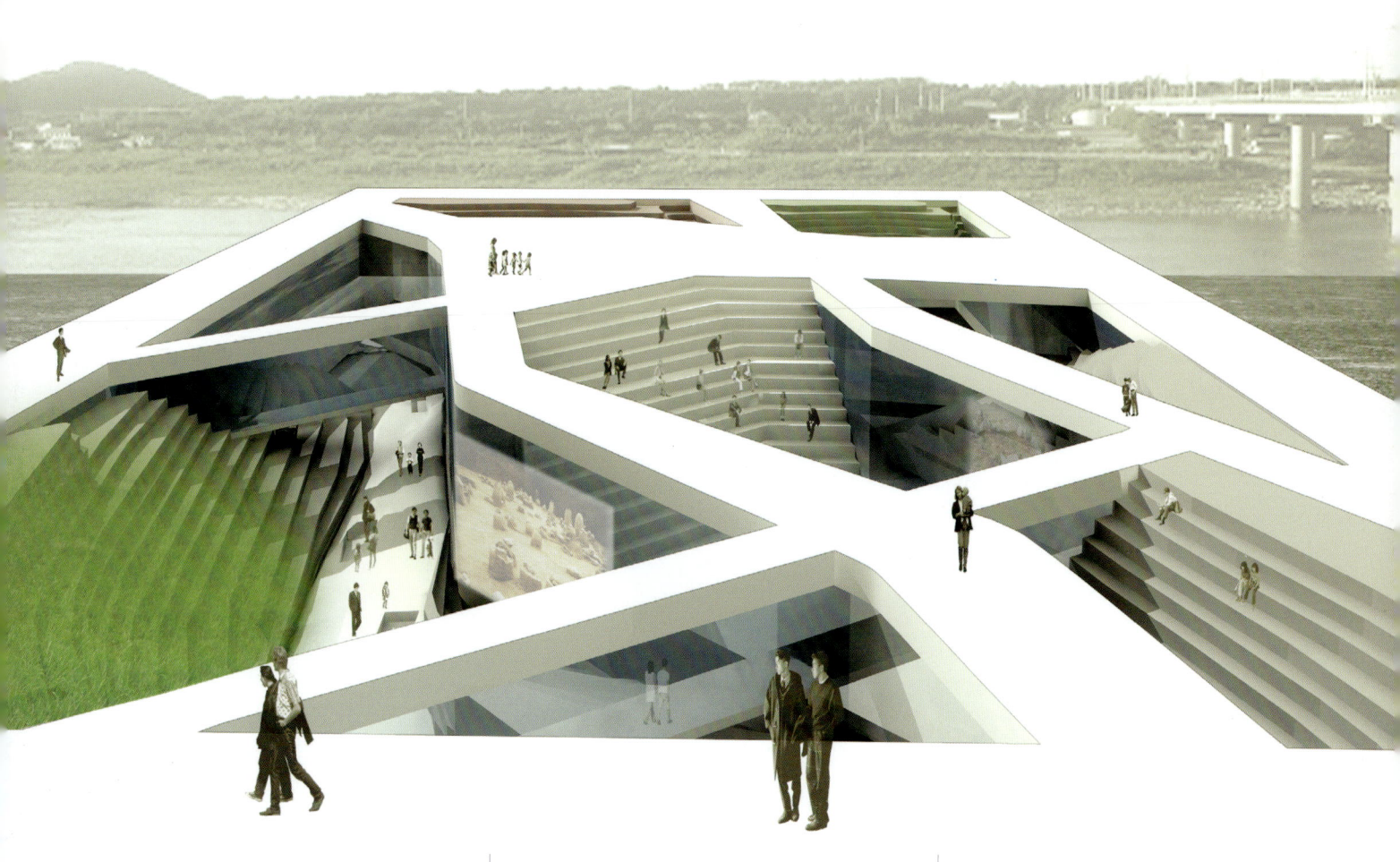

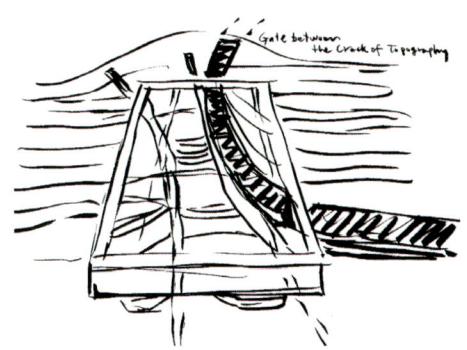

INTERACTIVE TOPOGRAPHY

The Transformation of Topography

We propose creating a museum program and space by trans-morphing the earth. The outcome would represent the evolution of nature while the body acts as the change of time. The natural topography of Jeongok-ri is a major element of the site as well as its formal motif and programmatic constituency. Through topography, programs can be defined and prescribed for our past, present, and future in conjunction with mankind's fluid and ever evolving cultural landscape. The topography will evolved into the outdoor exhibit by establishing an area for a prehistoric experience, open space, event hall, a basalt precipice exhibition, Observatory over the Hantan river, etc. Through the Time Corridor, the evolution of each space will form a network and become a framework for the entire museum. Reaching beyond the idea of the museum, which focuses on prehistory, we hope to enervate the museum, creating a living, dynamic body that reacts and breathes with the thriving diversity of mankind and changing demands.and become urban landscape filled with memories of the site and historical evolution of various spectrums of relationships.

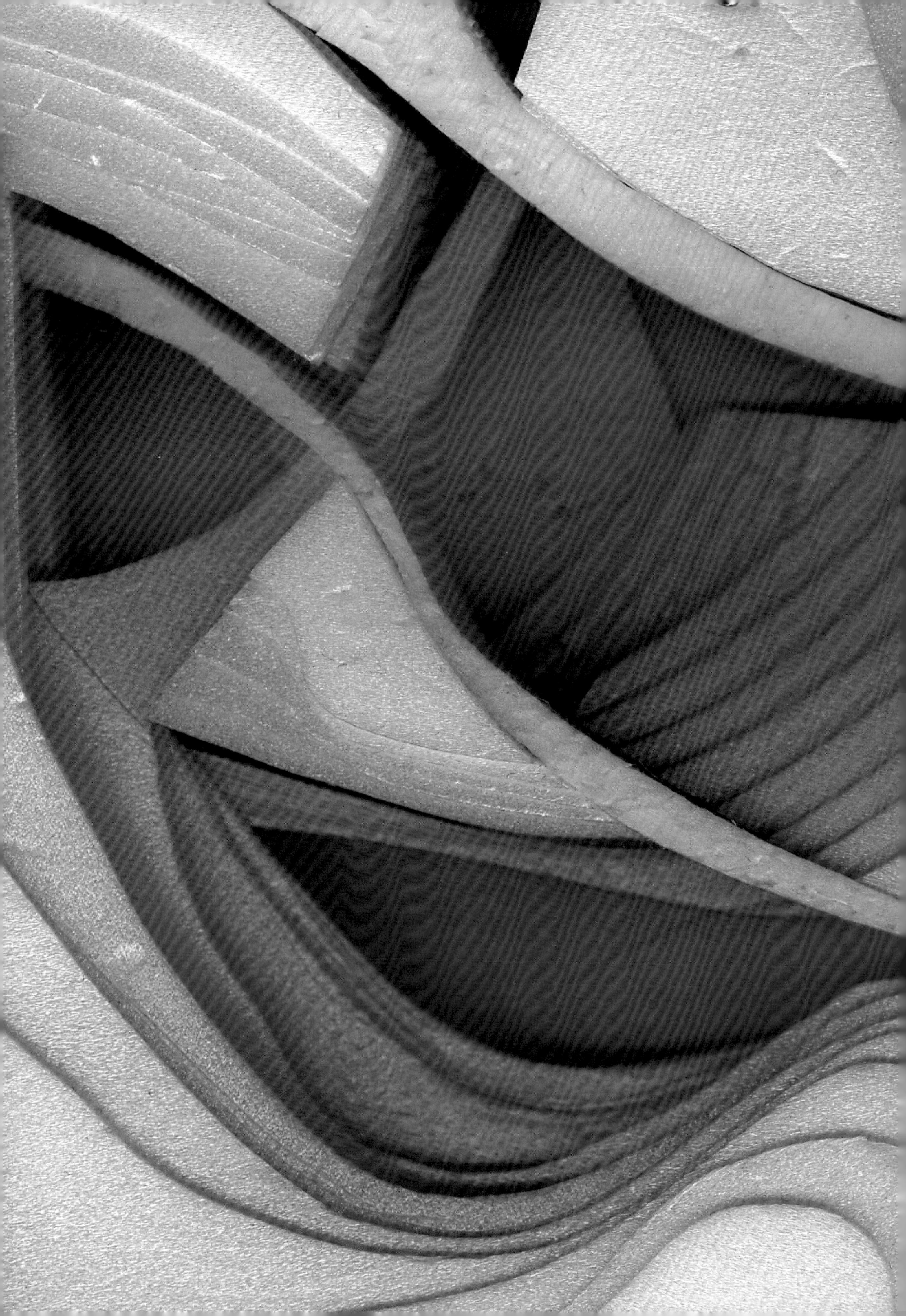

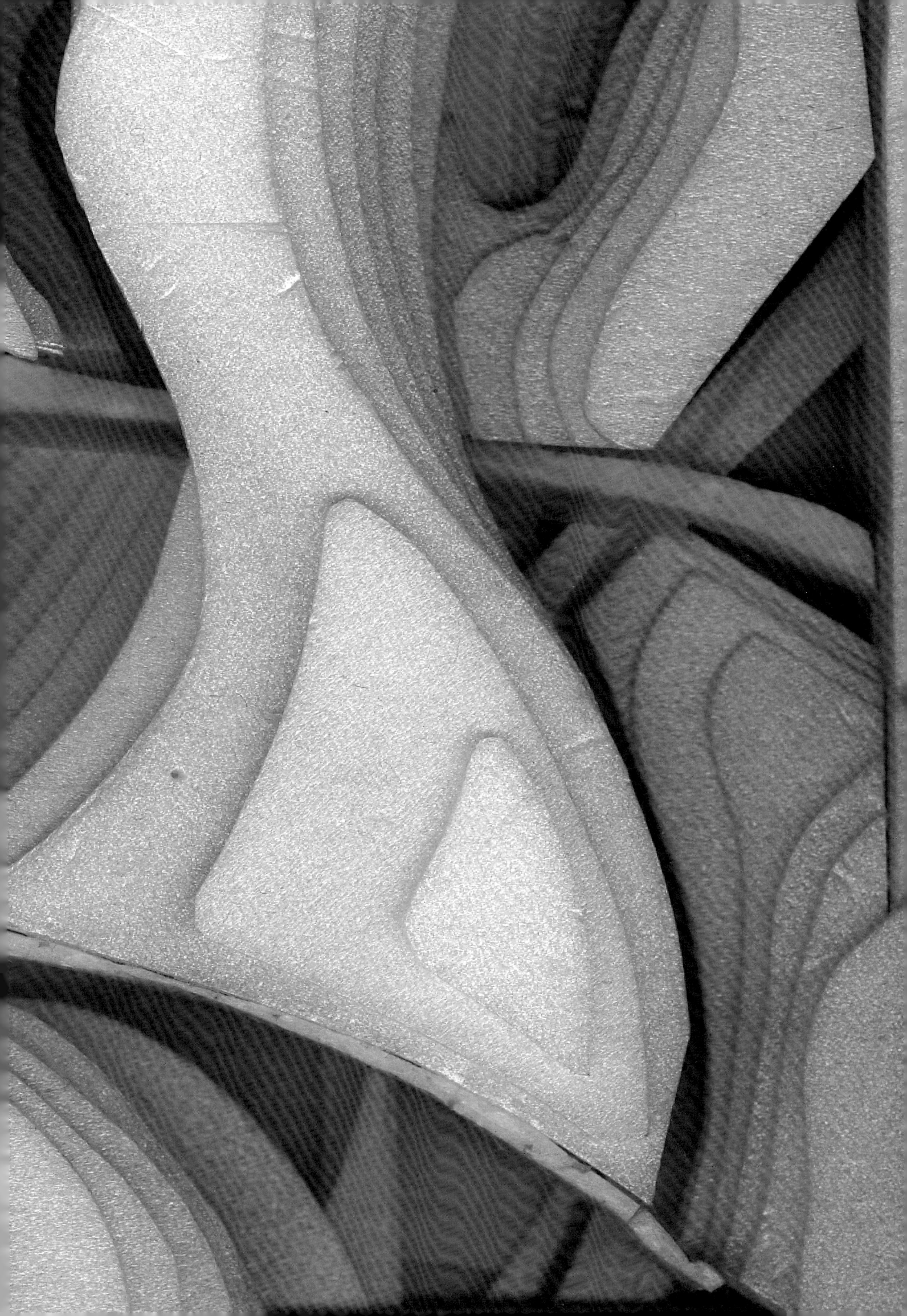

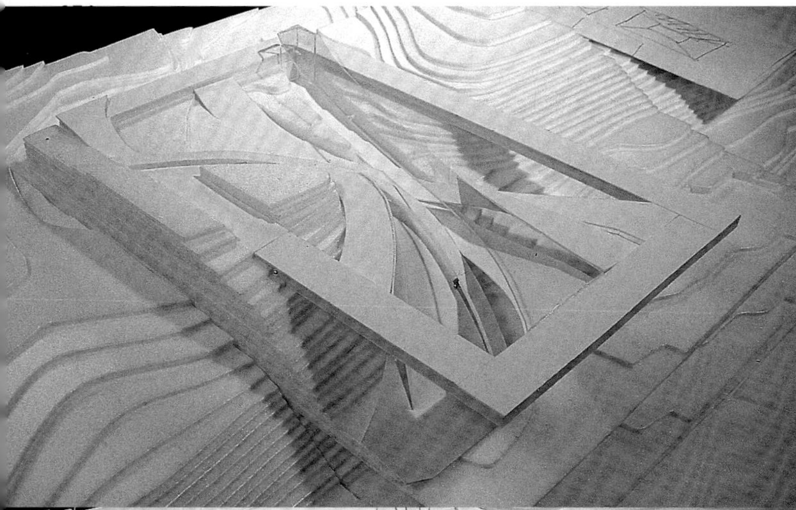
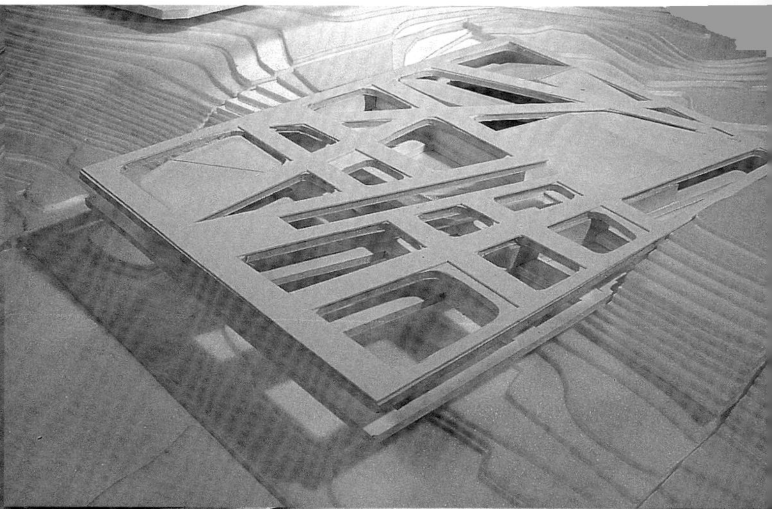
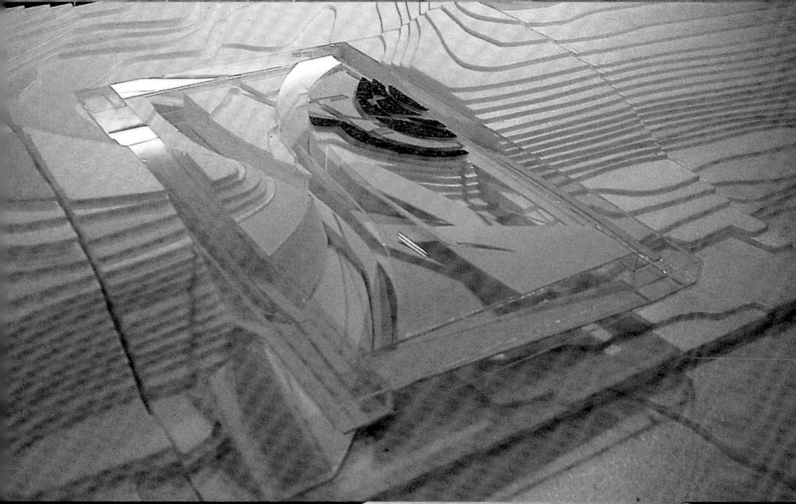
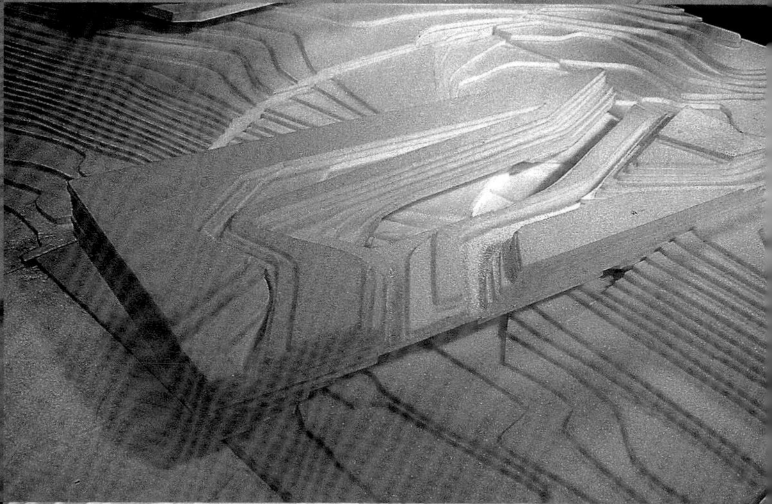
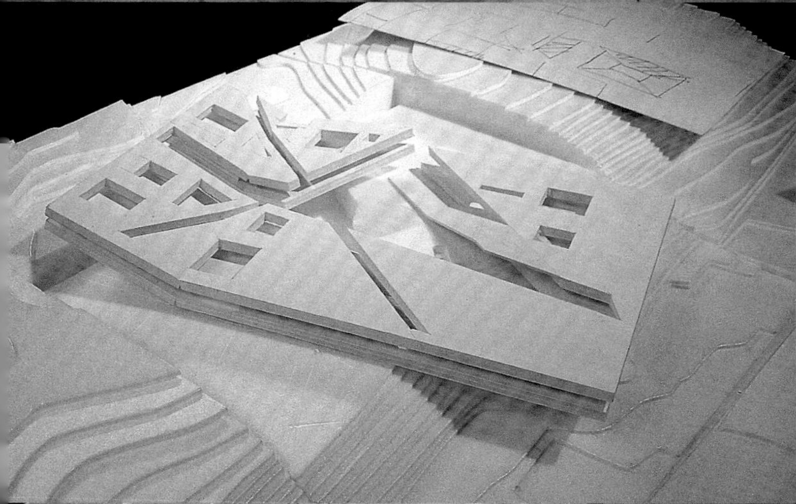
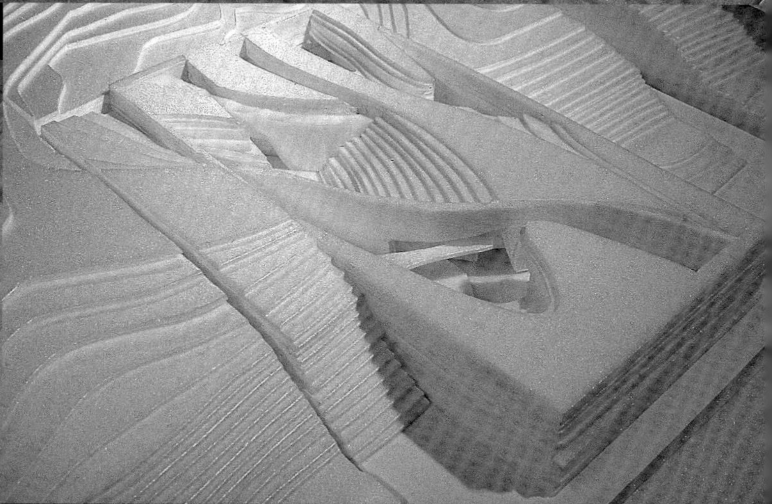
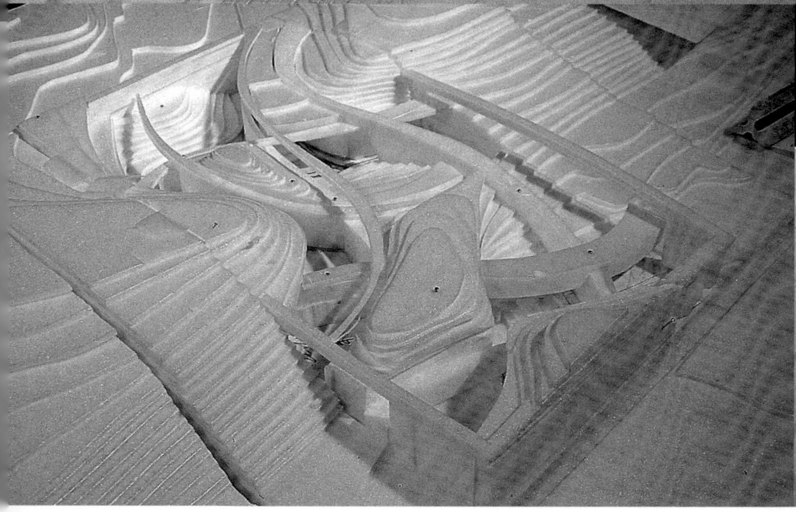
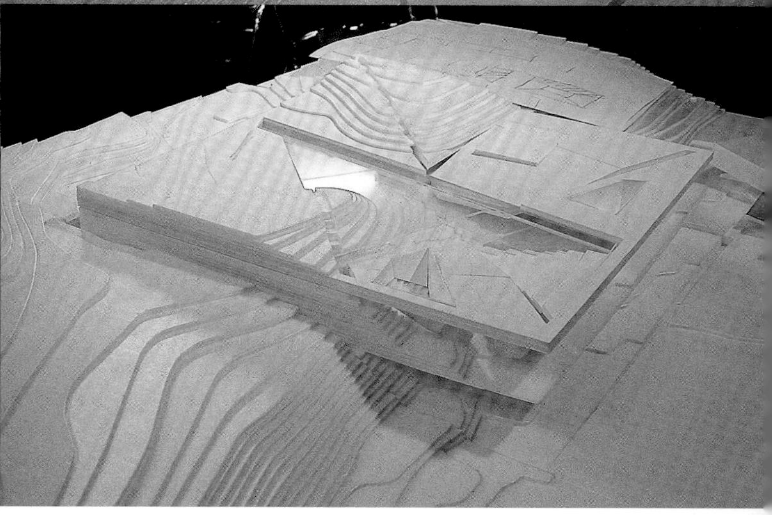

COMPOUND BODY 255

THE LAYOUT OF TIMES

INSERT

PULL OUT

CRACK

CONNECTION

TRANSFORMATION

IDENTITY

CONNECTION

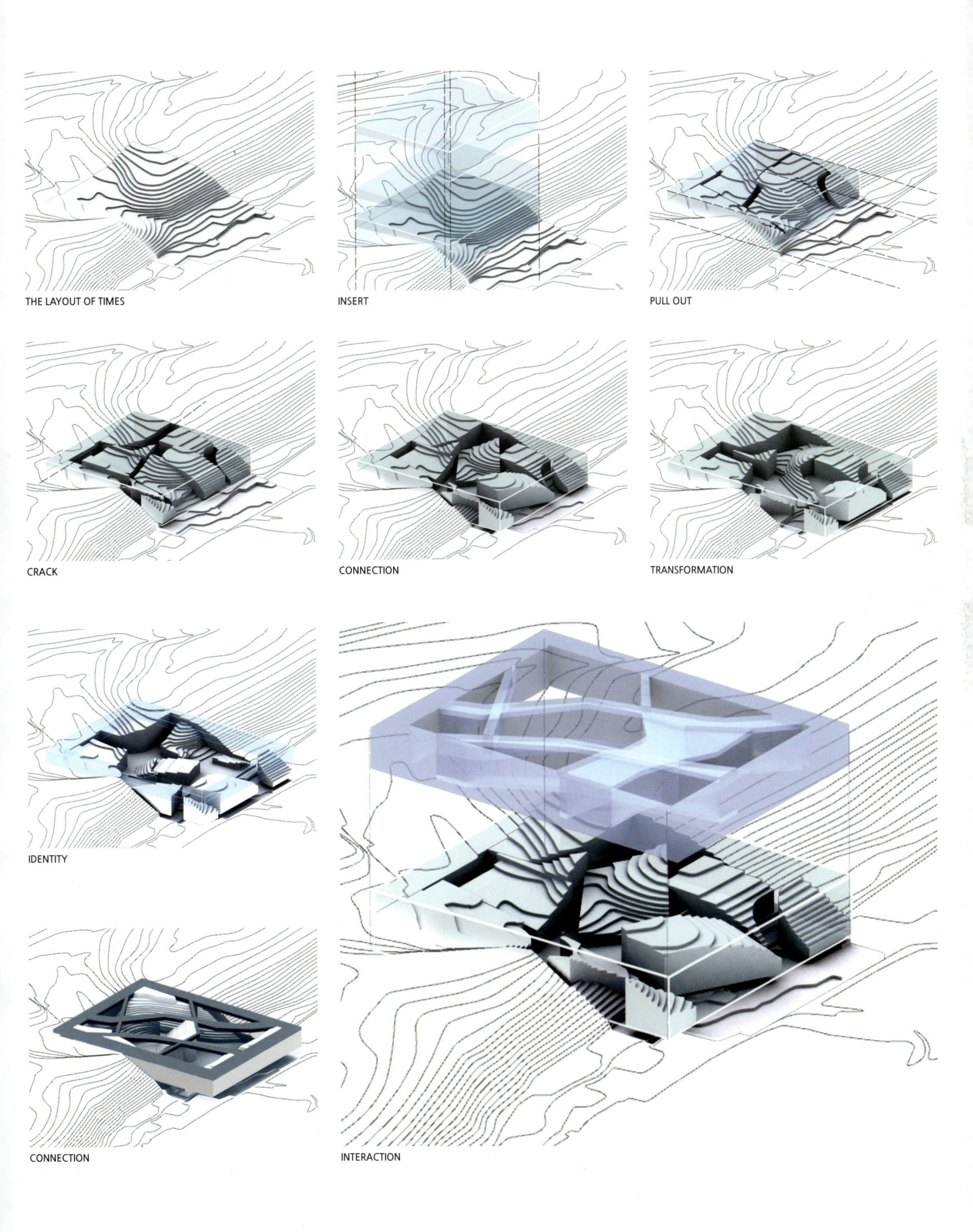

INTERACTION

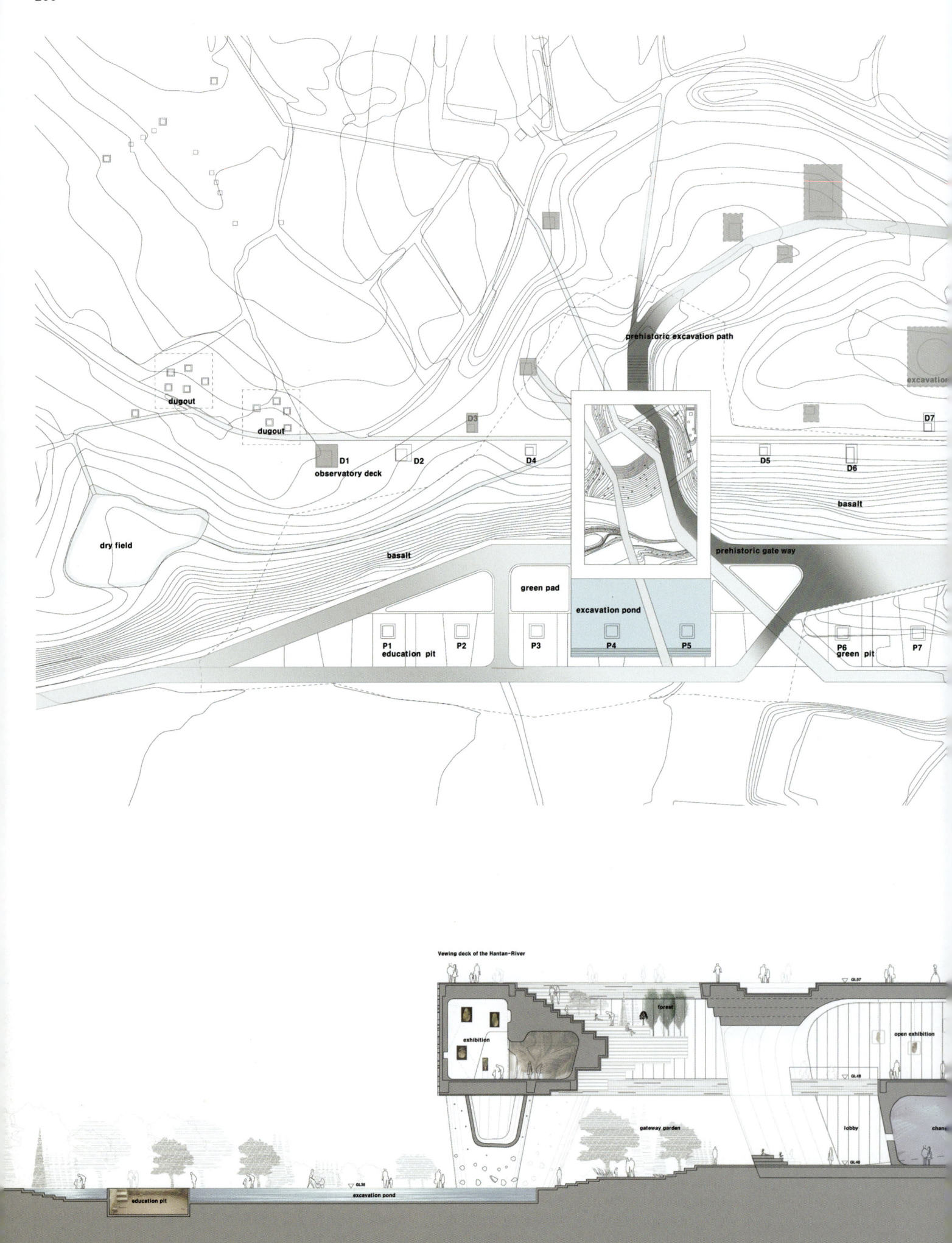

dugout
dugout
D1 observatory deck
D2
D3
D4
D5
D6
D7
dry field
basalt
basalt
prehistoric excavation path
prehistoric gate way
green pad
excavation pond
P1 education pit
P2
P3
P4
P5
P6 green pit
P7
excavation

Vewing deck of the Hantan-River
exhibition
forest
open exhibition
gateway garden
lobby
chan
education pit
excavation pond

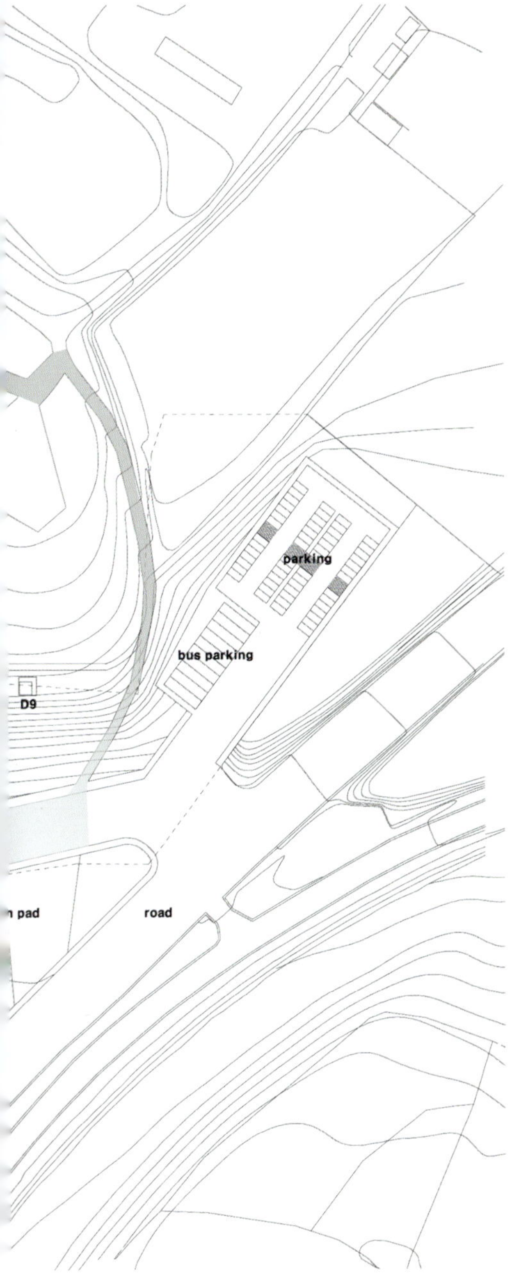

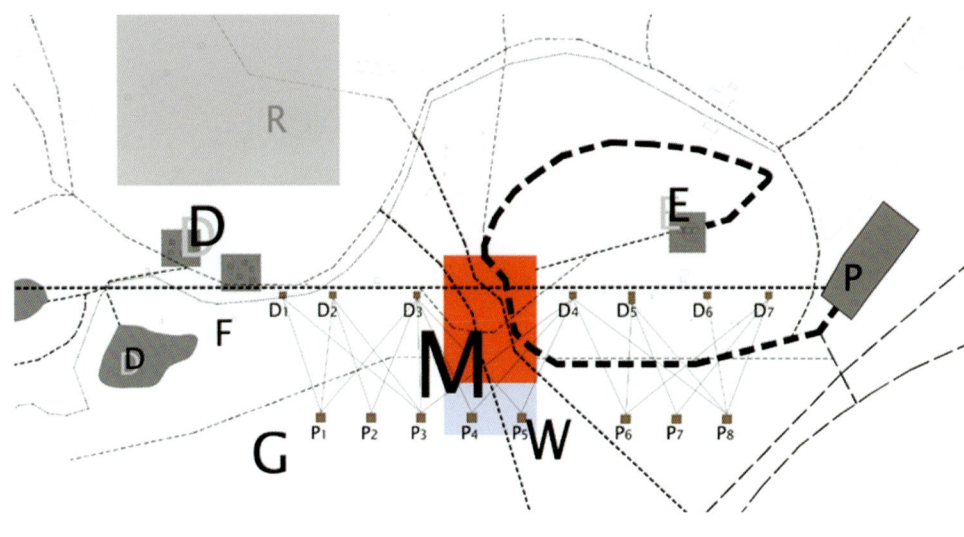

Time Gate between the Crack of Topography
The site for the proposed gate is a gateway entering into the prehistoric excavation site. We propose a system in which visitors will walk through the cracks of the earth, thus providing a gateway for them to travel between the past and present. The gate symbolizes the experience and journey through time that leads to "The nature and man coming across, and for the encounter among prehistory, present, and future." At the Time-gate, the approach to the excavation site is located in a crack within basalt layers, thereby acting as physical connection, as well as providing opportunities for the exhibit against its walls, conserving the existing topography while providing a symbolic gateway for the complexity of prehistoric experiences.

Interactive Program - Interactive Topography: Extruded Topography as a Compound Body
We propose creating an interactive topography and program in the compound's body - a system that randomly assembles urban fabrics, landscapes, paths, open spaces, built structure, and programs through which new cultural courage can be generated.

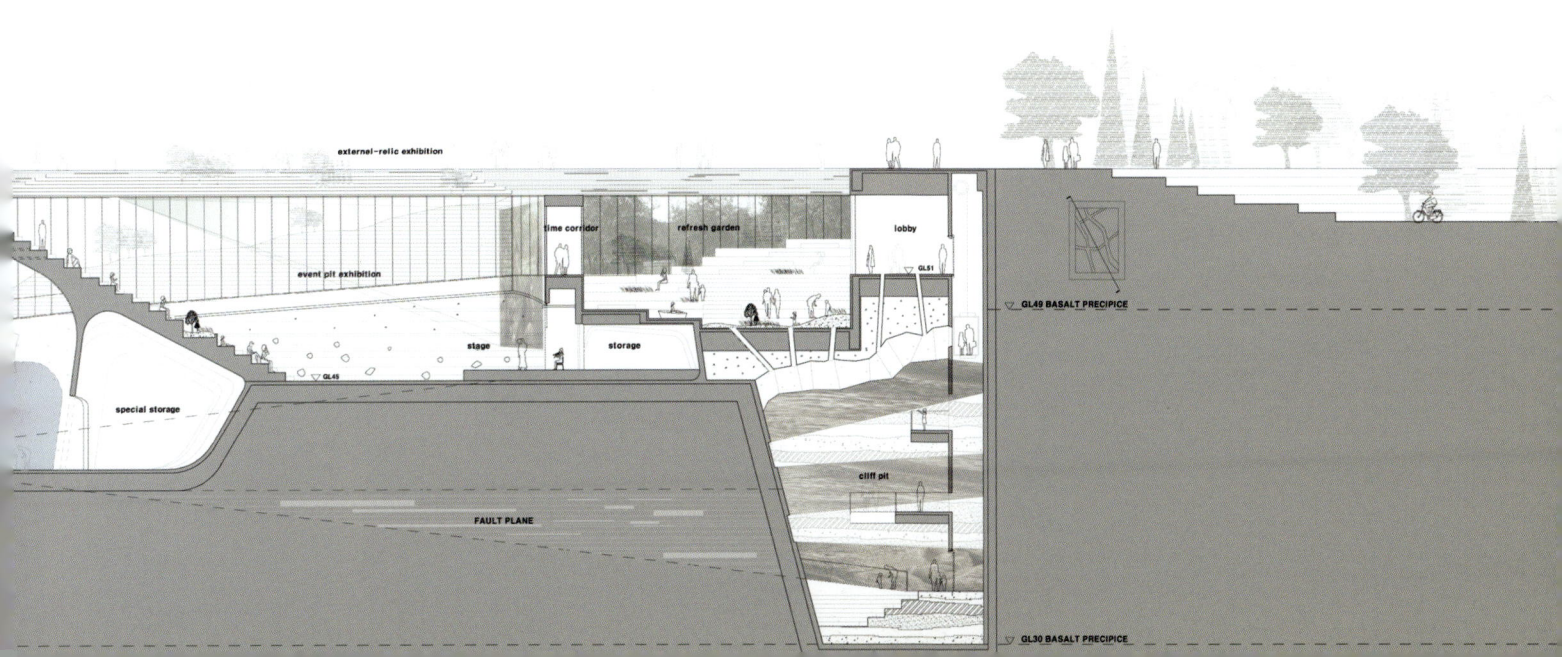

EVENT STAGE FOR CULTURAL ACTIVITIES

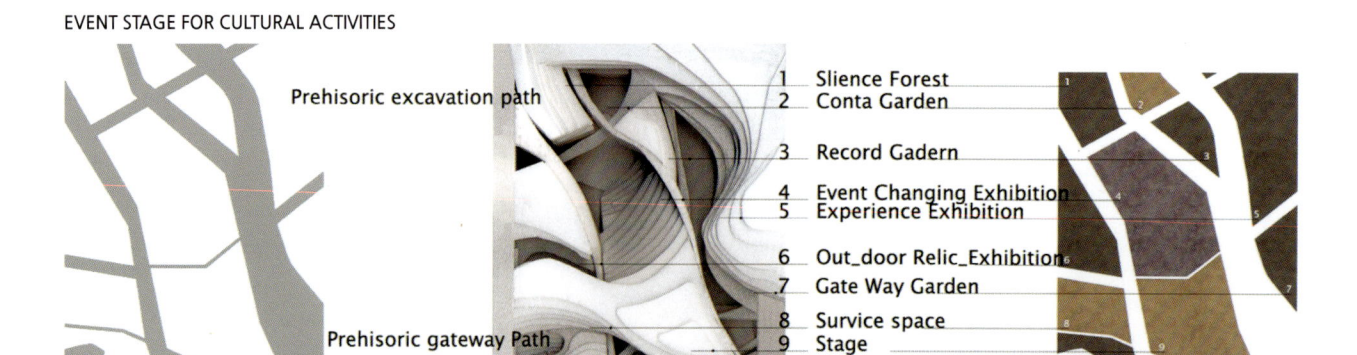

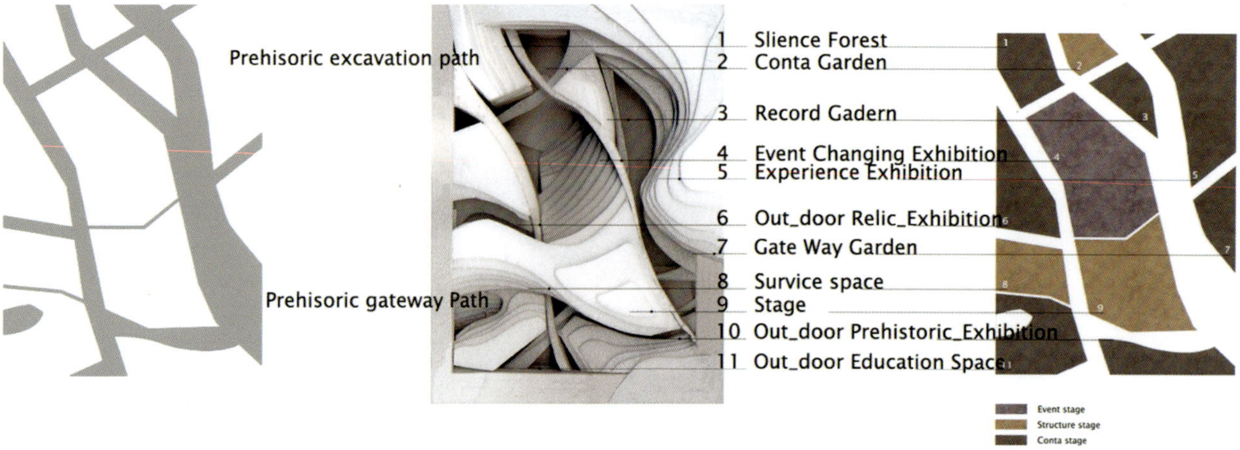

Prehisoric excavation path

Prehisoric gateway Path

1. Slience Forest
2. Conta Garden
3. Record Gadern
4. Event Changing Exhibition
5. Experience Exhibition
6. Out_door Relic_Exhibition
7. Gate Way Garden
8. Survice space
9. Stage
10. Out_door Prehistoric_Exhibition
11. Out_door Education Space

- Event stage
- Structure stage
- Conta stage

INTERACTIVE PROGRAM - INTERACTIVE TOPOGRAPHY EXTRUDED

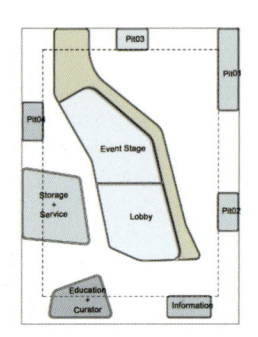

Ground Level 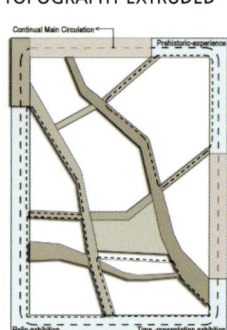 | The Main Exhibition Level 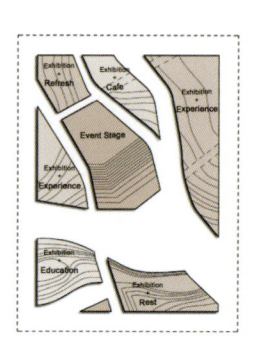 | The Topography Level 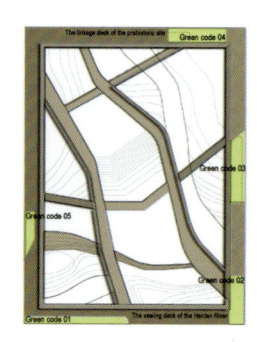 | The Roof Deck Level

TIME CORRIDOR - PREHISTORIC RECORDER

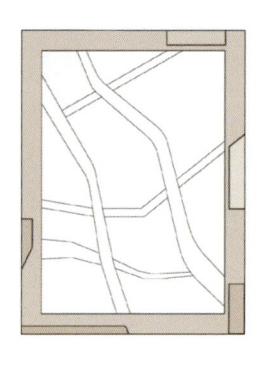

Exhibition 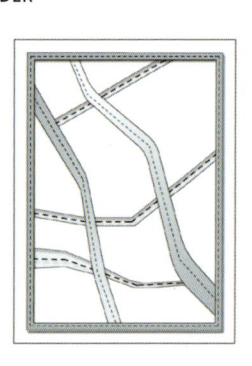 | Circulation 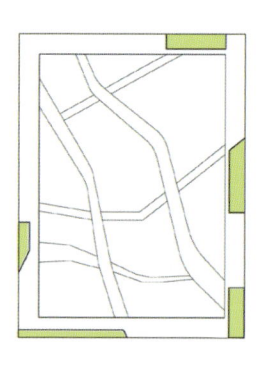 | Exhibition Inter Garden 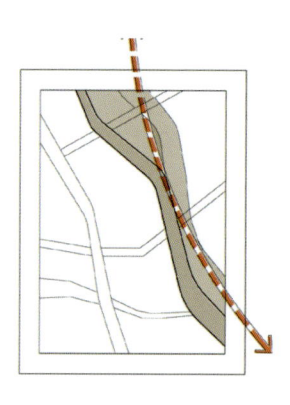 | Landscape Connection

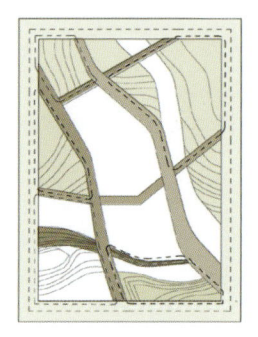

Exterial Exhibition 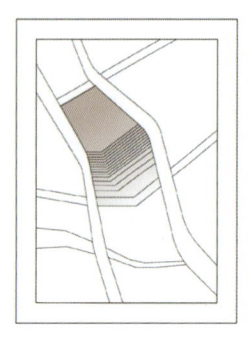 | Event Stage 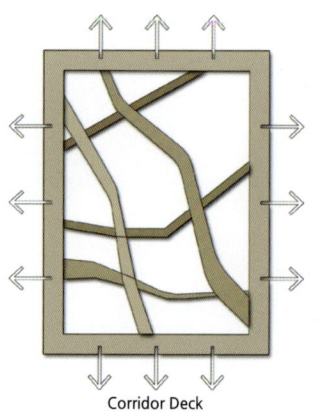 | Corridor Deck 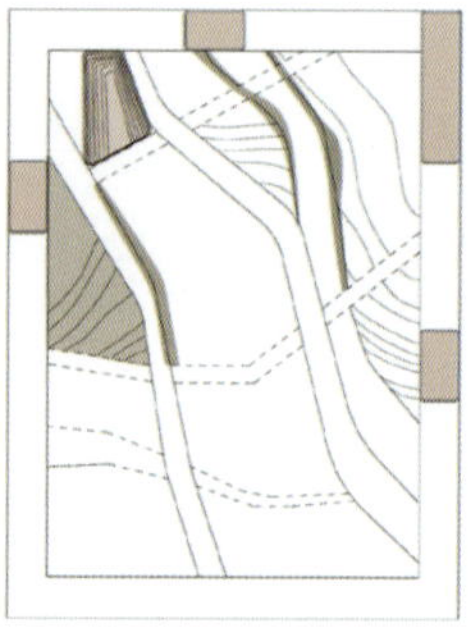 | Basalt Precipice

Time Corridor

The prehistoric Recorder Time Corridor, which is the essential element for the 'earth between its creation and distinction', will be the fundamental medium. At the juncture leading to the prehistoric excavation site of the Jeongok-ri, the new cultural network will be established to represent the new opportunities for mankind, culture and nature. Its pathways wil be considered
apparatuses connecting the existing functions and the site's context. The insertion of linear paths throughout the network will establish the linkage between the existing land and the new topographical code, thereby becoming the medium for the journey through time.

Stage Mapping Event Landscape for Exterior Exhibition

We propose for the museum reach beyond the typical exhibition experience by establishing trans-programmatic elements between the exhibition spaces such as outdoor event halls and stages. Not only will this deform the topography in the physical dimension, but the museum will also become a cultural stage through the cohesion with a diverse array of required codes. These codes the archaeological code, historical code, cultural code, artistic code, etc., conjoin with the spatial code in order to generate a new series of multi-dimensional spaces.

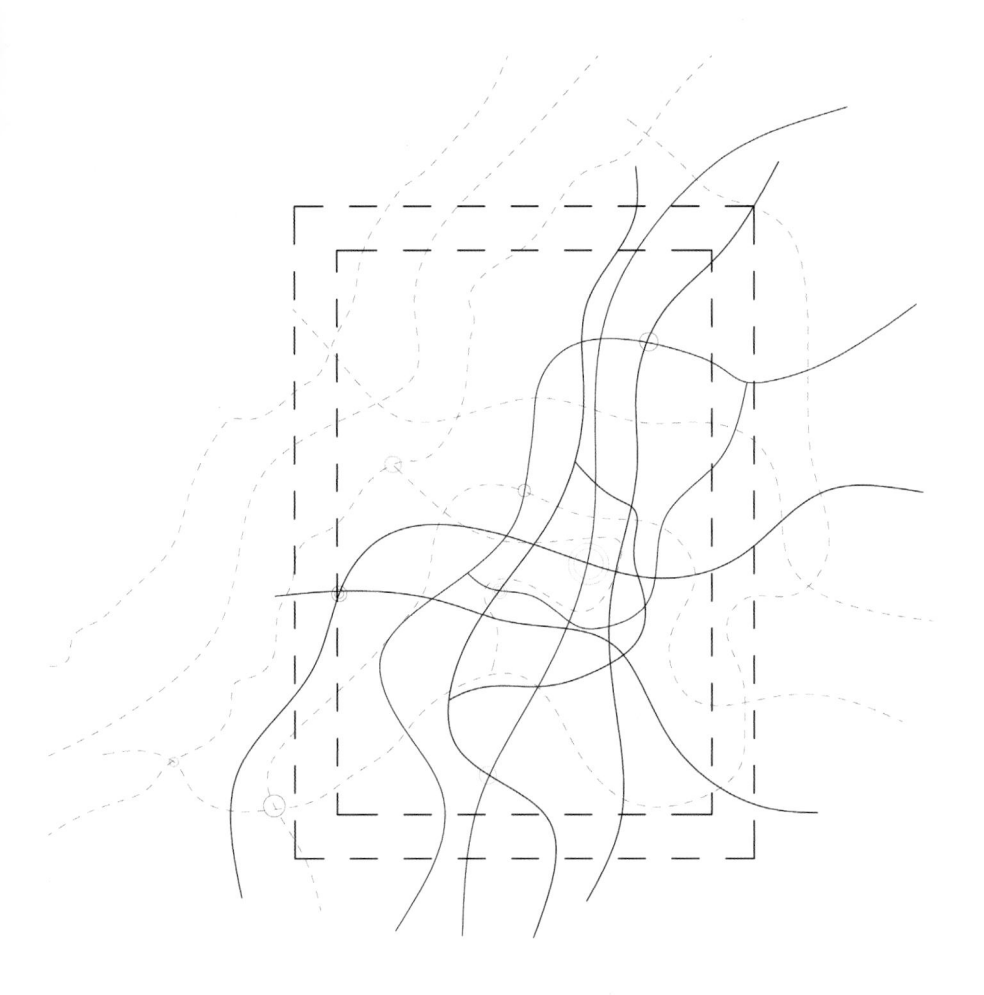

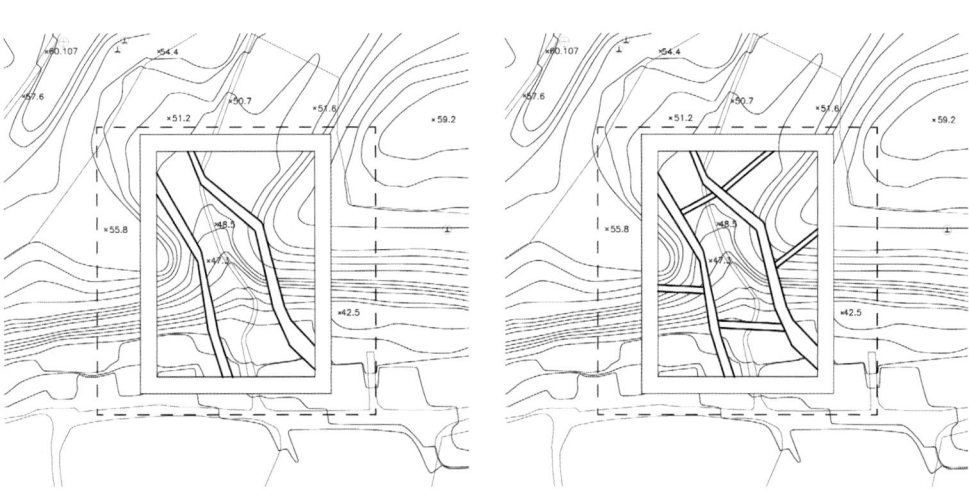

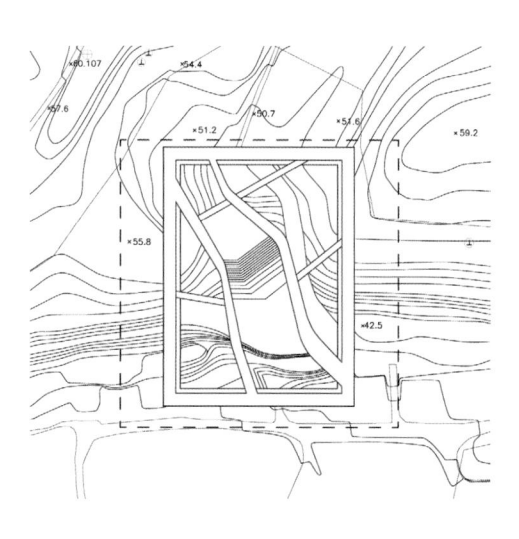

EVOLVING TOPOGRAPHY

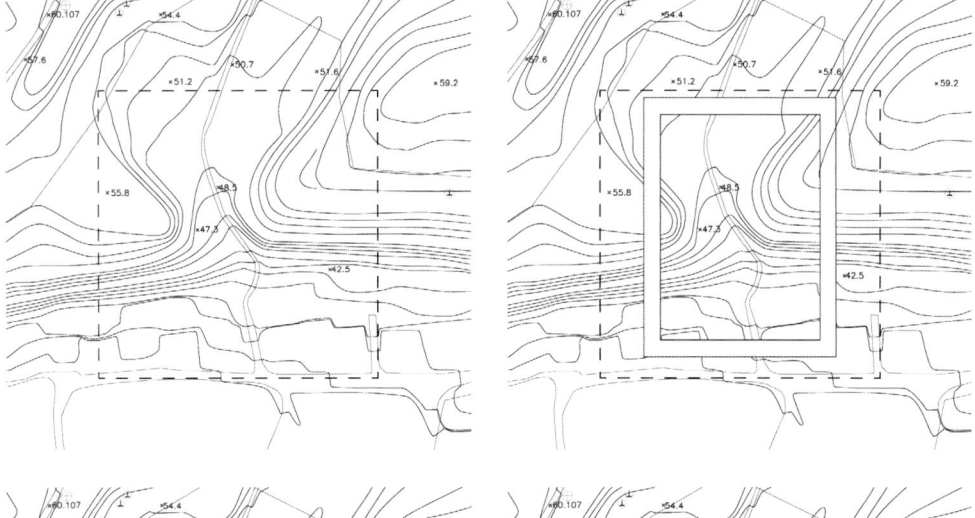

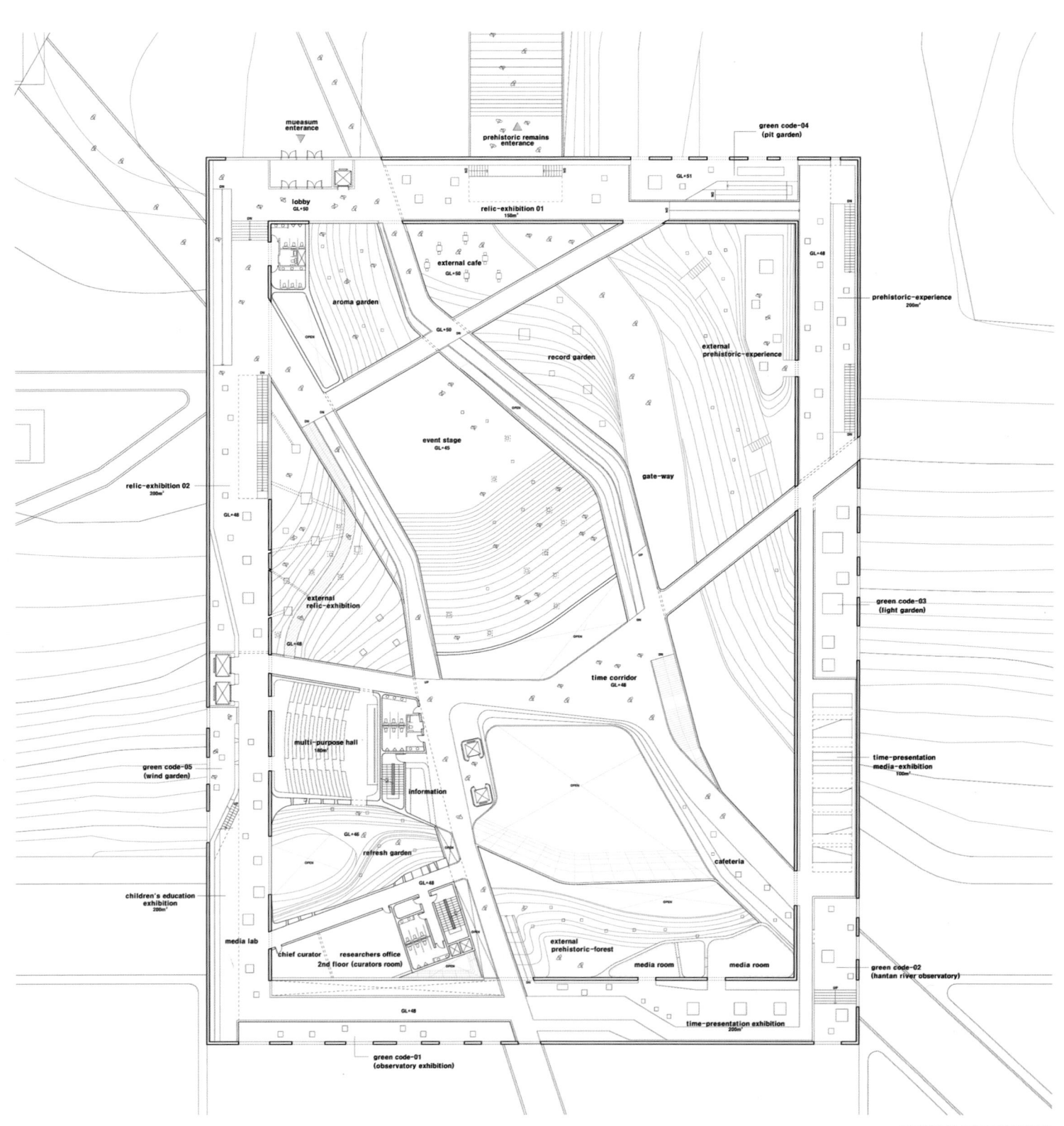

MUSEUM GALLERY LEVEL

COMPOUND BODY 261

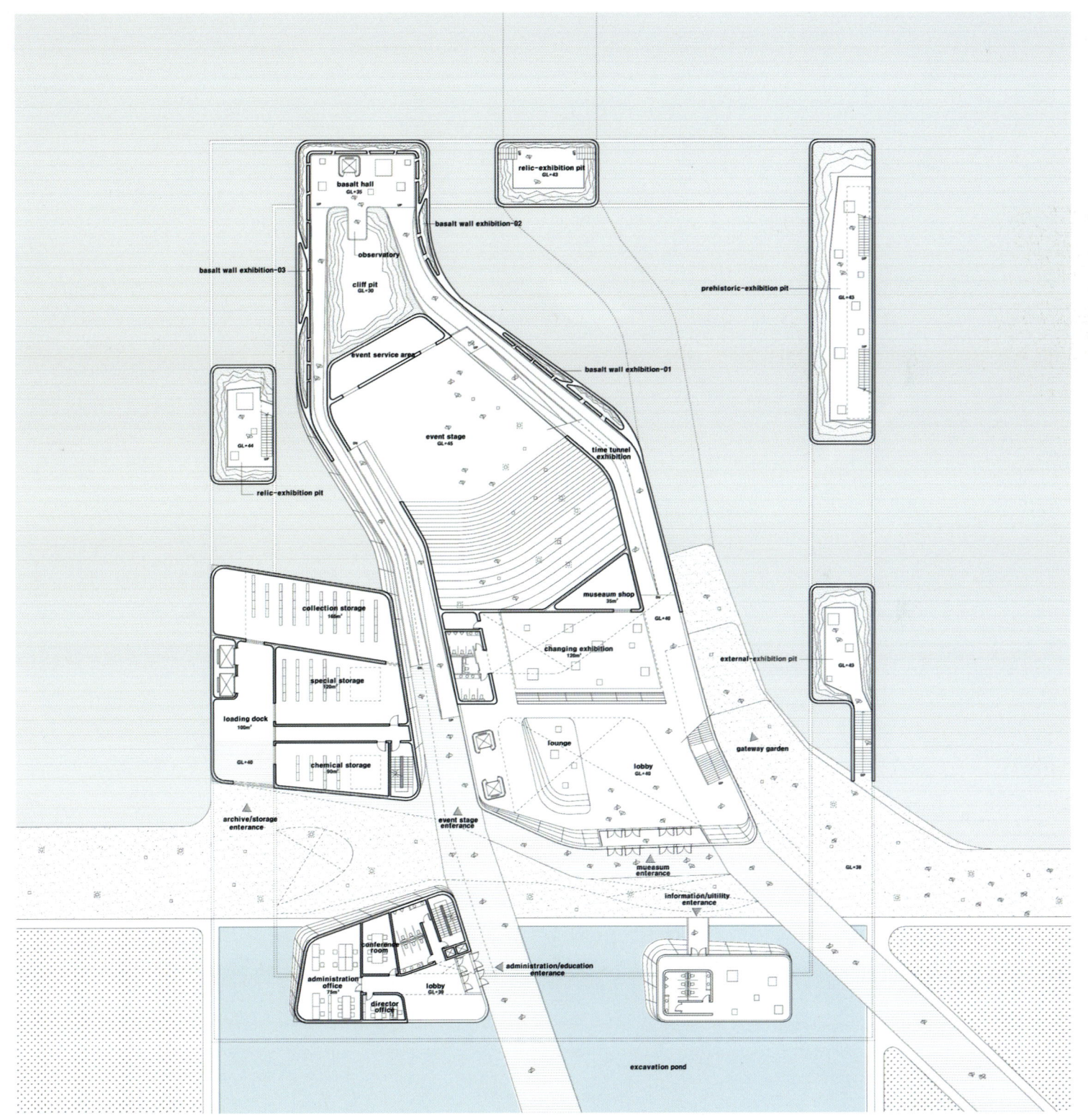

MUSEUM APPROACH LEVEL

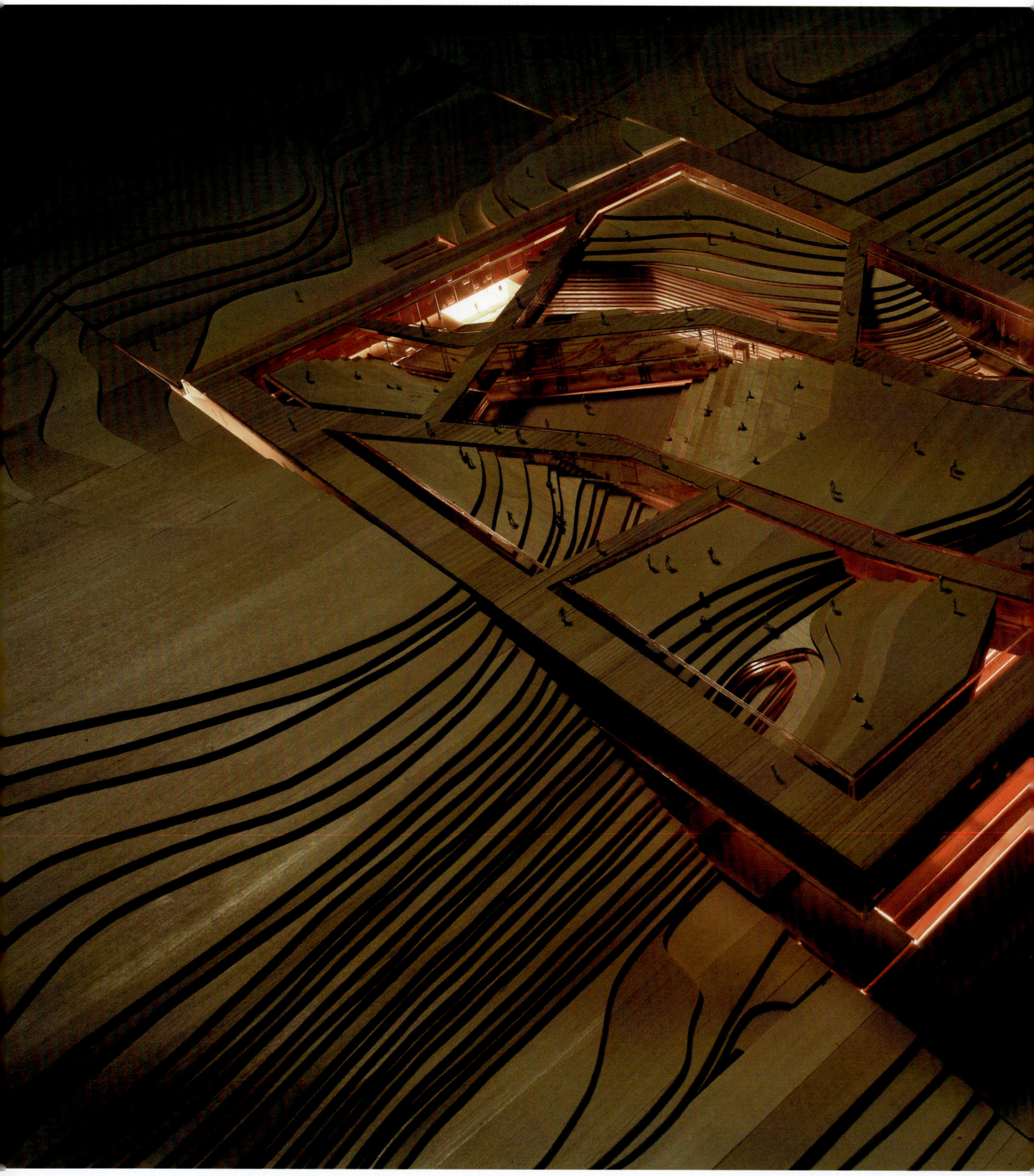

COMPOUND BODY 263

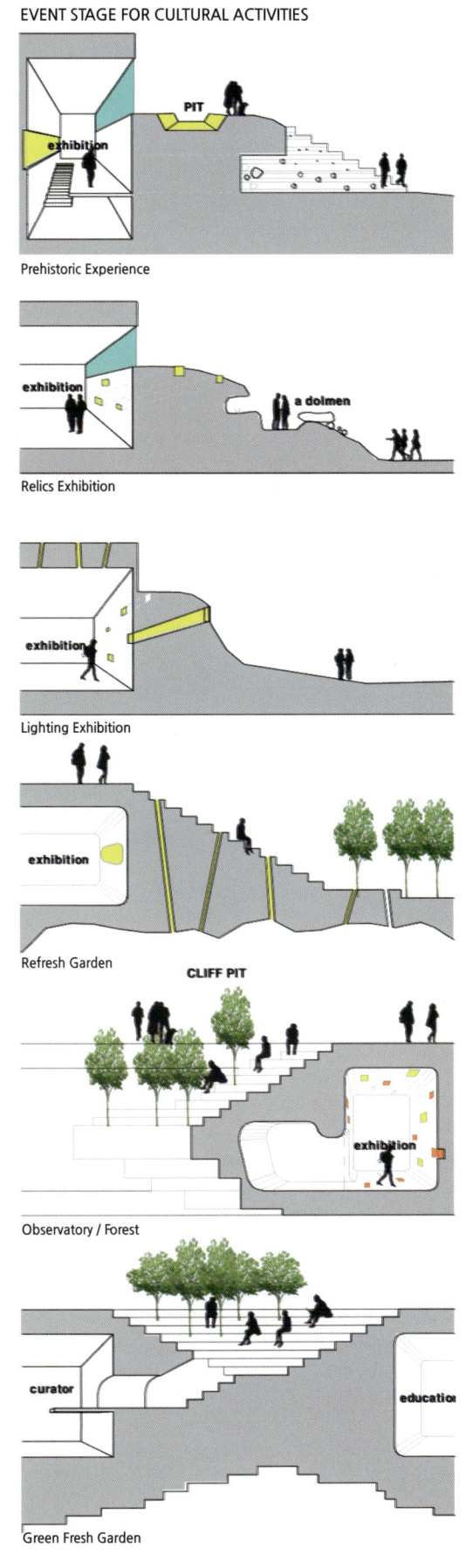

EVENT STAGE FOR CULTURAL ACTIVITIES

Prehistoric Experience

Relics Exhibition

Lighting Exhibition

Refresh Garden

Observatory / Forest

Green Fresh Garden

264

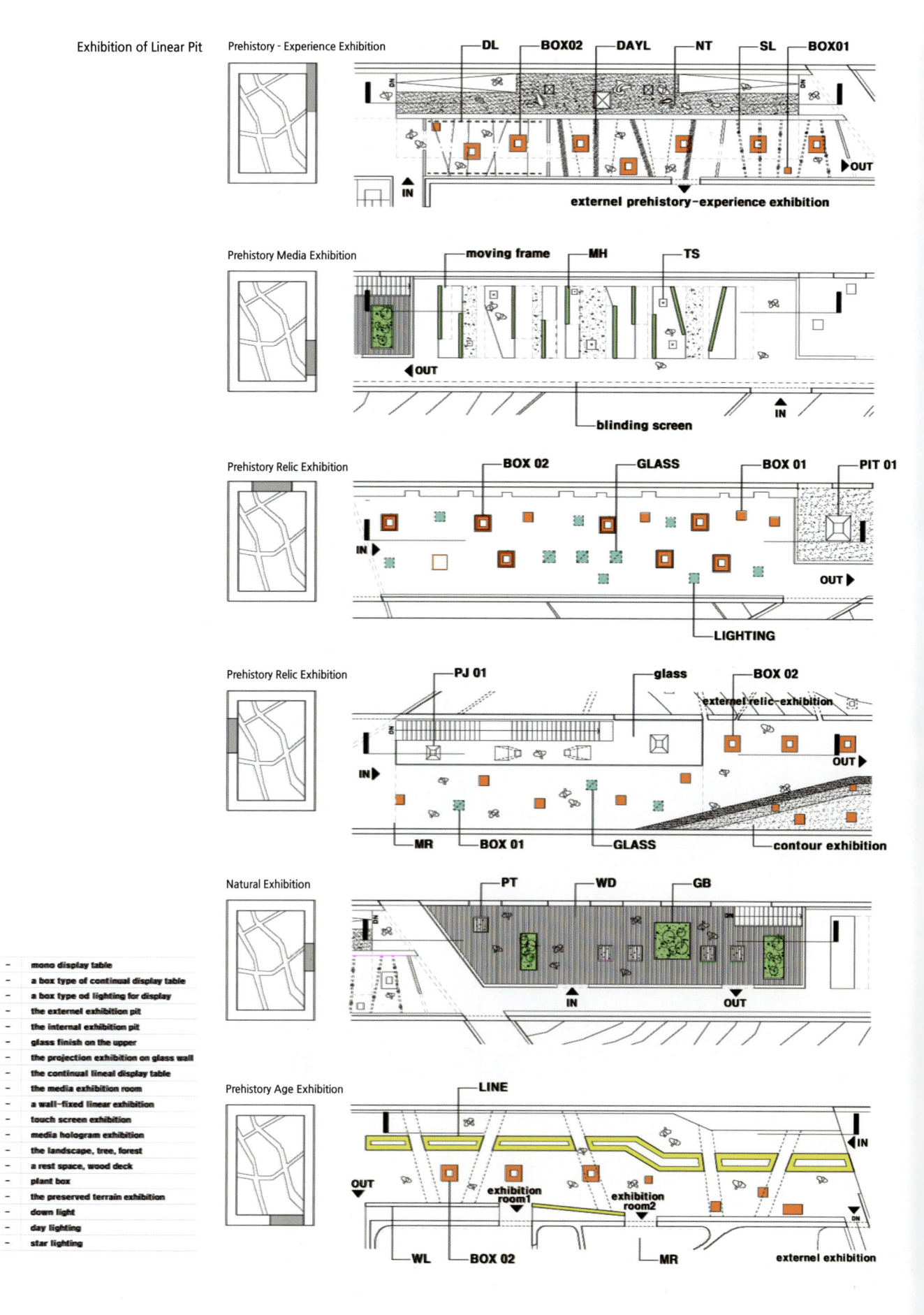

Exhibition of Linear Pit

Prehistory - Experience Exhibition

DL — BOX02 — DAYL — NT — SL — BOX01

externel prehistory-experience exhibition

Prehistory Media Exhibition

moving frame — MH — TS

blinding screen

Prehistory Relic Exhibition

BOX 02 — GLASS — BOX 01 — PIT 01

LIGHTING

Prehistory Relic Exhibition

PJ 01 — glass — BOX 02 — external relic-exhibition

MR — BOX 01 — GLASS — contour exhibition

Natural Exhibition

PT — WD — GB

Prehistory Age Exhibition

LINE

exhibition room1 — exhibition room2

WL — BOX 02 — MR — externel exhibition

	BOX 01	-	mono display table
	BOX 02	-	a box type of continual display table
	LIGHT 01	-	a box type od lighting for display
	PIT 01	-	the externel exhibition pit
	PIT 02	-	the internal exhibition pit
	GLASS	-	glass finish on the upper
	PJ 01	-	the projection exhibition on glass wall
	LINE	-	the continual lineal display table
	MR	-	the media exhibition room
	WL	-	a wall-fixed linear exhibition
	TS	-	touch screen exhibition
	MH	-	media hologram exhibition
	GB	-	the landscape, tree, forest
	WD	-	a rest space, wood deck
	PT	-	plant box
	NT	-	the preserved terrain exhibition
	DL	-	down light
	DAY L	-	day lighting
	SL	-	star lighting

COMPOUND BODY 265

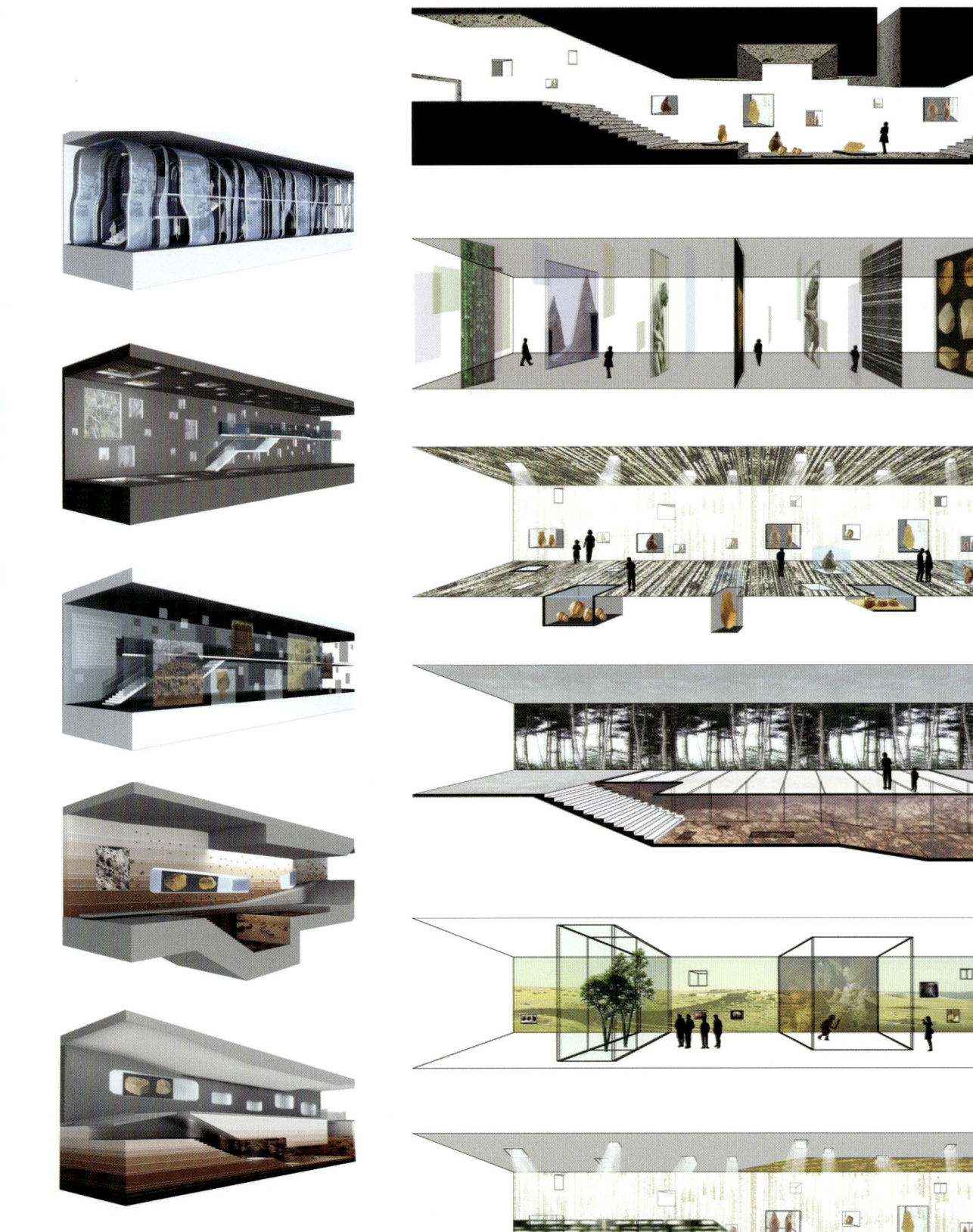

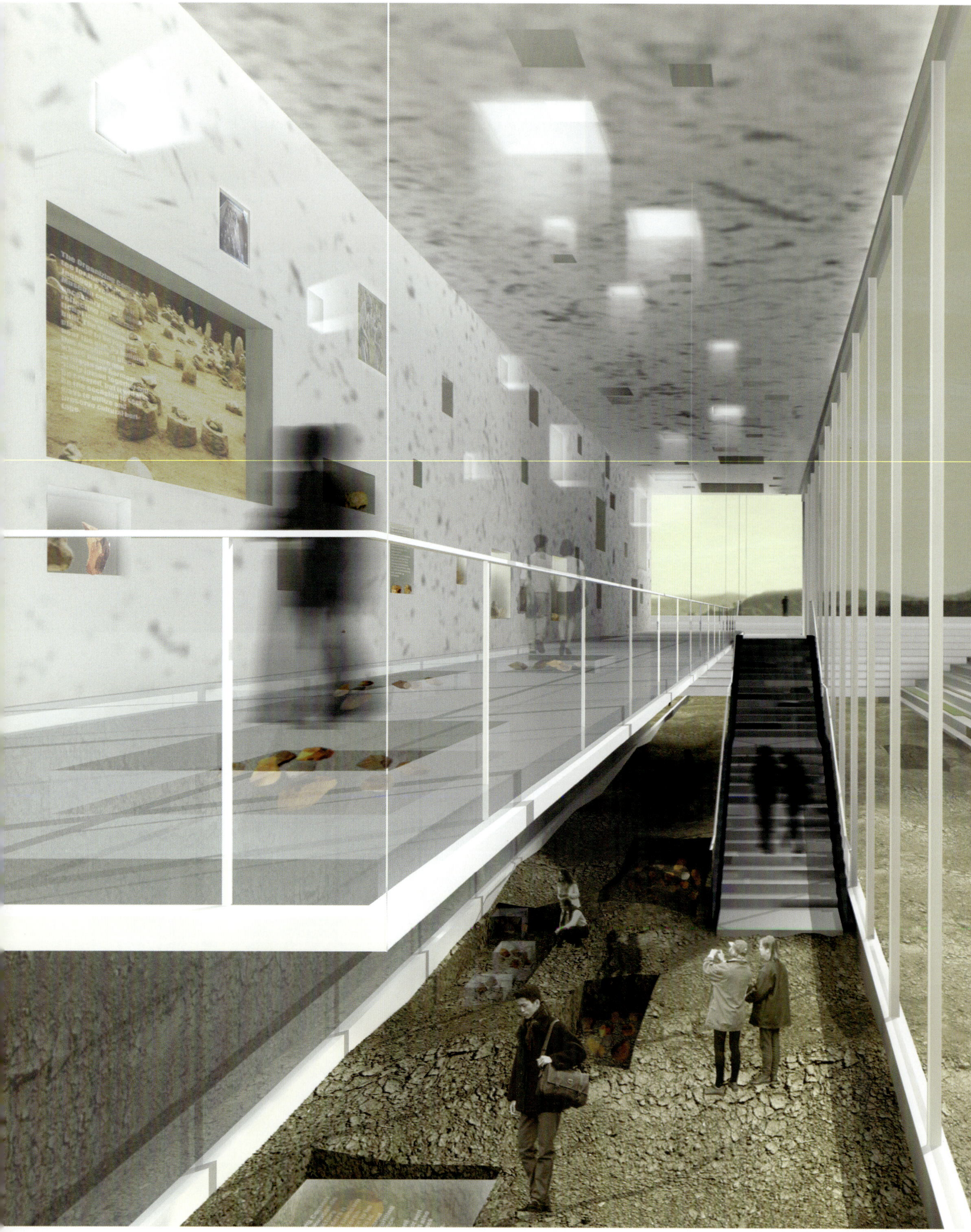

COMPOUND BODY 267

Architects Jang Yoon Gyoo, Shin Chang Hoon
Project Team Kim Woo Young, Kim Youn Soo, Kim Sung Min, Choi Hyae Jin,
　　　　　　　Kwon Woo Suk , Jung Bok Joo
Location 528-1 Jeongok, Yeonchun, Gyeoggi-doa

山水彫刻
Shanghai EXPO Industrial Pavilion

Architects Jang Yoon Gyoo, Shin Chang Hoon
Photographer Kim Jae Kyung

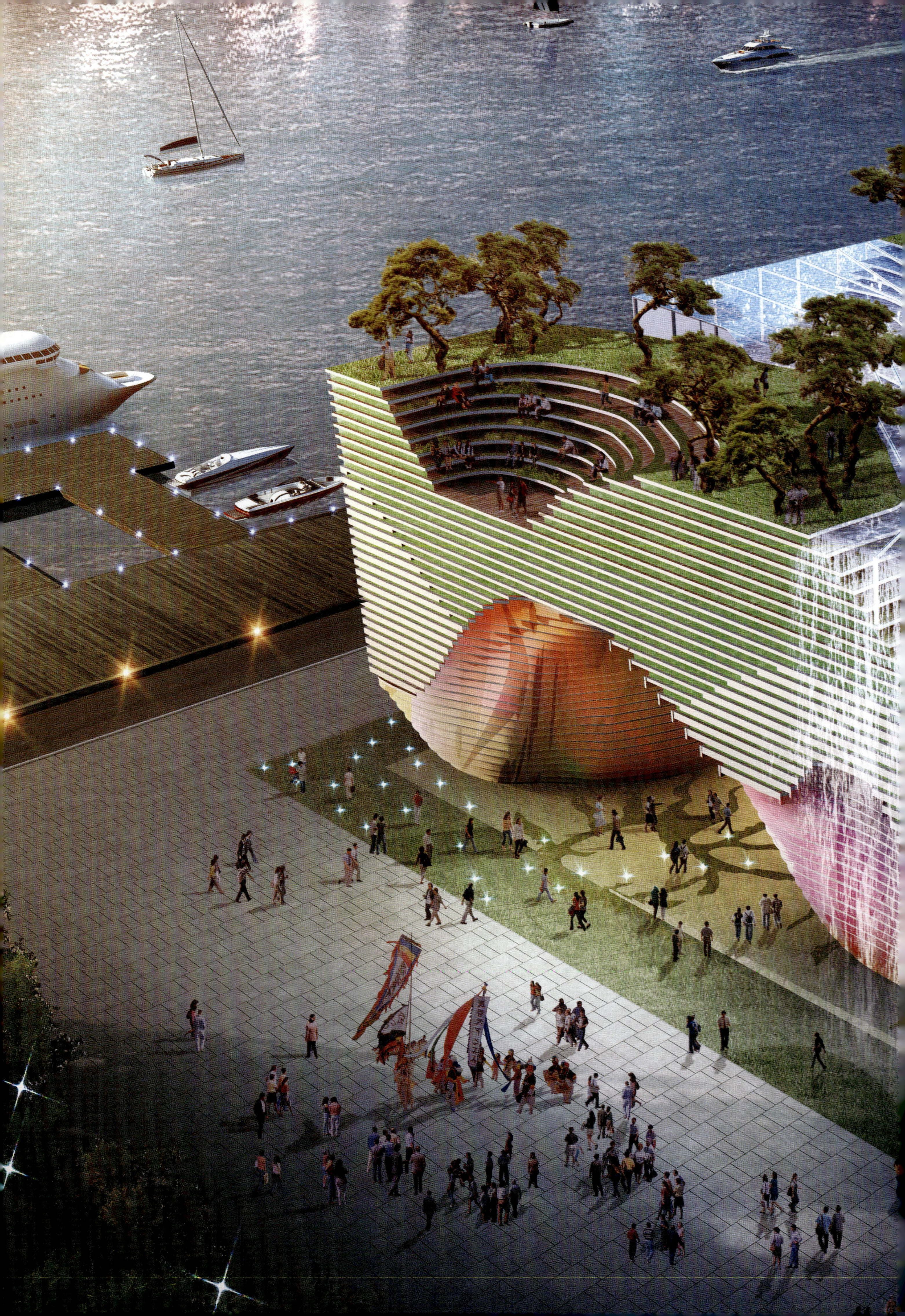

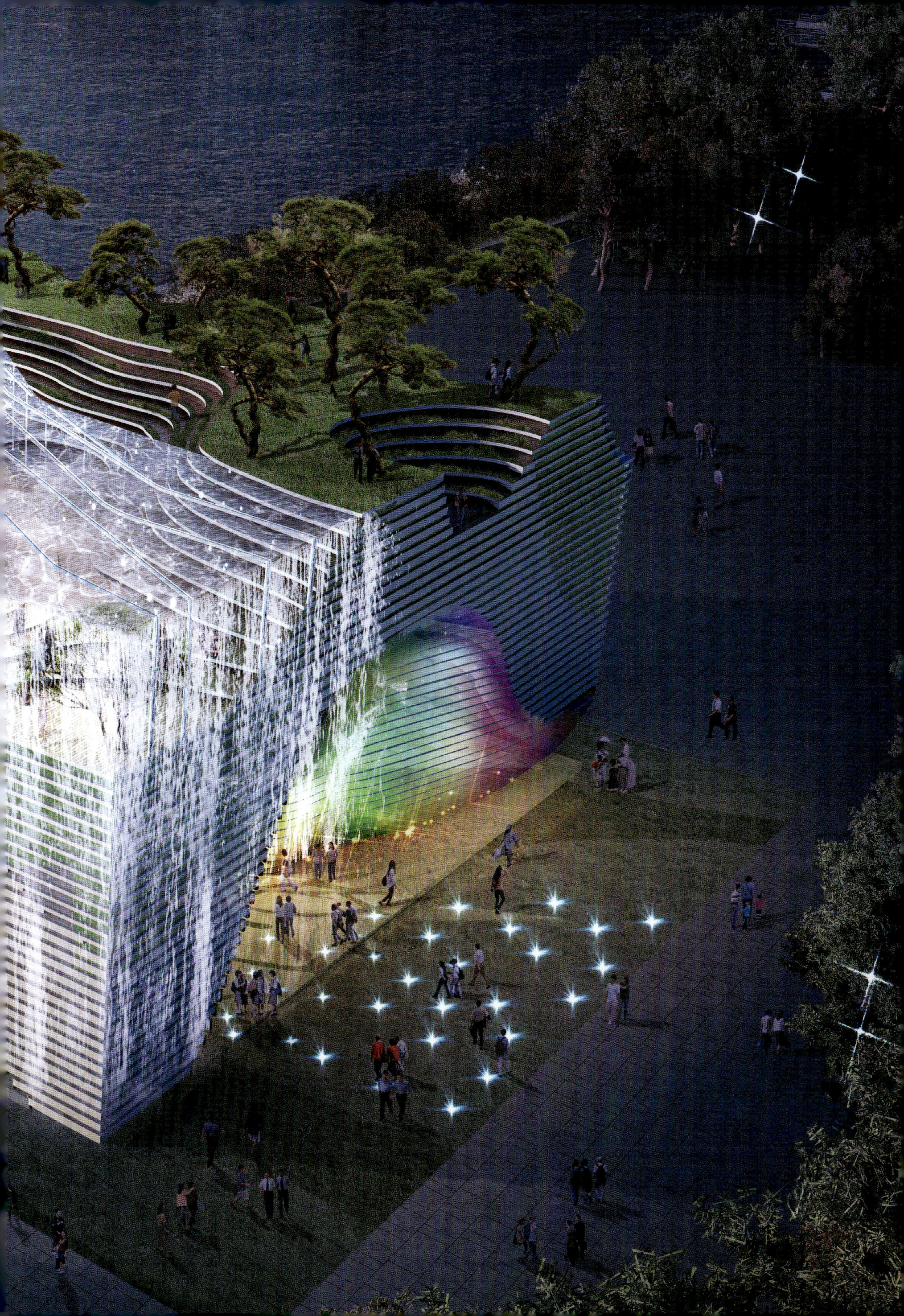

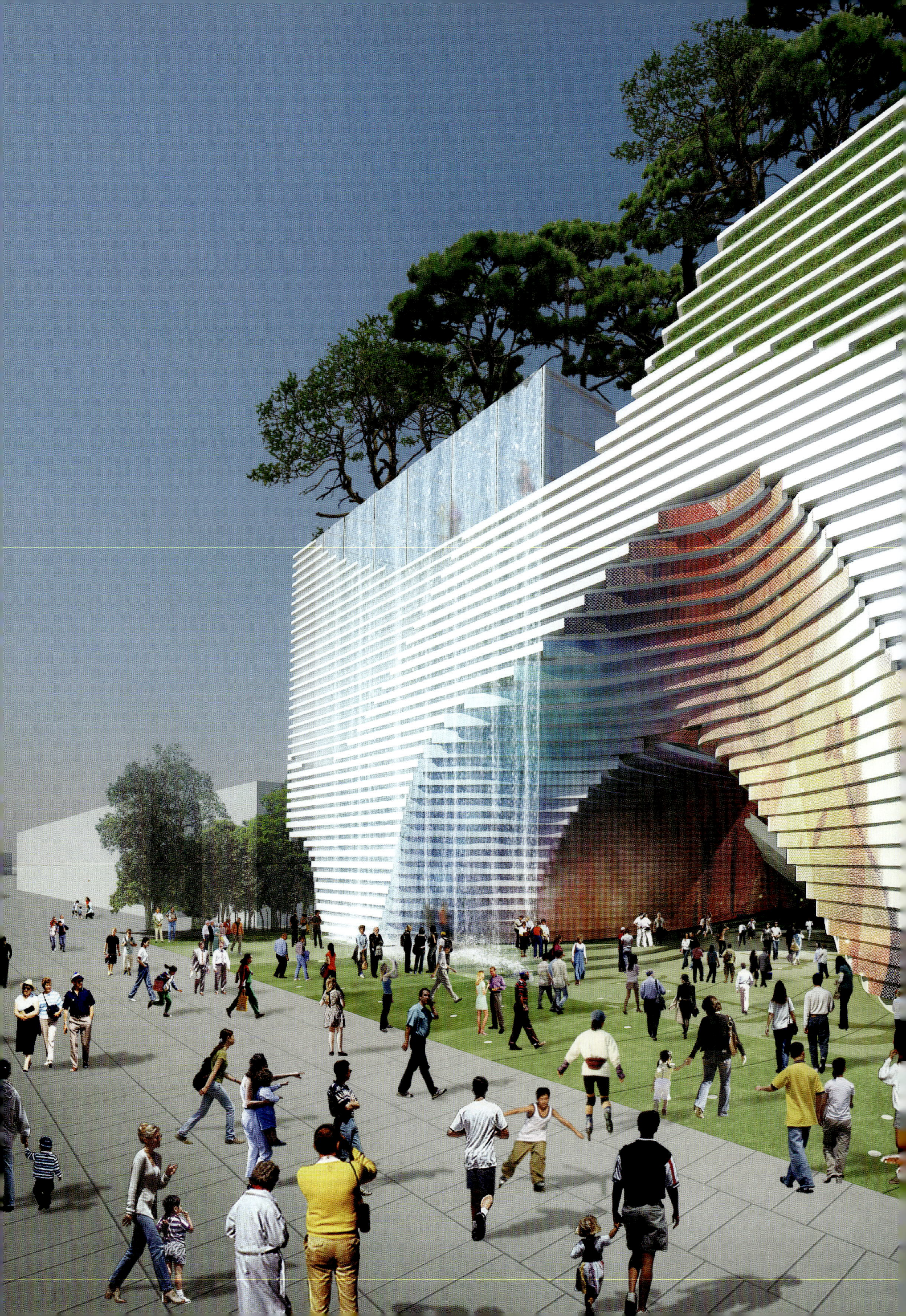

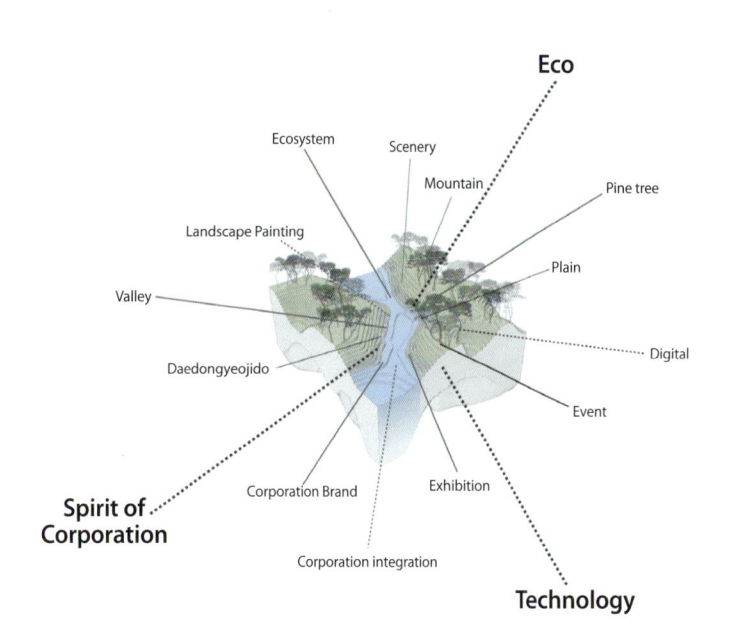

COMPOUND BODY 273

Eco

Ecosystem Scenery
          Mountain   Pine tree
Landscape Painting
                              Plain
Valley
                              Digital
      Daedongyeojido
                              Event
Spirit of   Corporation Brand   Exhibition
Corporation
             Corporation integration
                              Technology

GREEN IMAGINATION

We imagine Korean Corporate Pavilion coinciding with the subjects; Green city and Green life. It is named Communi-Imagination and it holds introspection of environment together with innovation of technology. Korea got over the unfortunate situation of the Korean War which didn't seem to be possible and has achieved unimaginable development and innovation. This space represents technology and spirit of Korean enterprises which is the main agent of these accomplishments. The spirit and the technology of 12 Korean enterprises which are developing towards higher-tech such as information technology, distribution, aviation, electronic, vehicle, chemistry and shipbuilding are represented in the architecture by diverse exhibitions and videos. This recordable scale of expo is held in China which is the biggest market in the world. We hope to promote advanced Korean technology and brand, and re-establish a new relationship for economy and cultural exchange between Korea and China. We hope to promote new competiveness of Korean enterprises with new awareness of nature and Korean high-technology. In conclusion, Environmental Communi-Imagination connects Asia to the world and suggests a new vision.

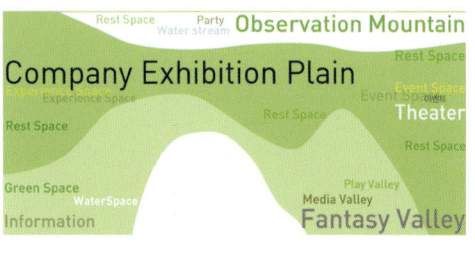

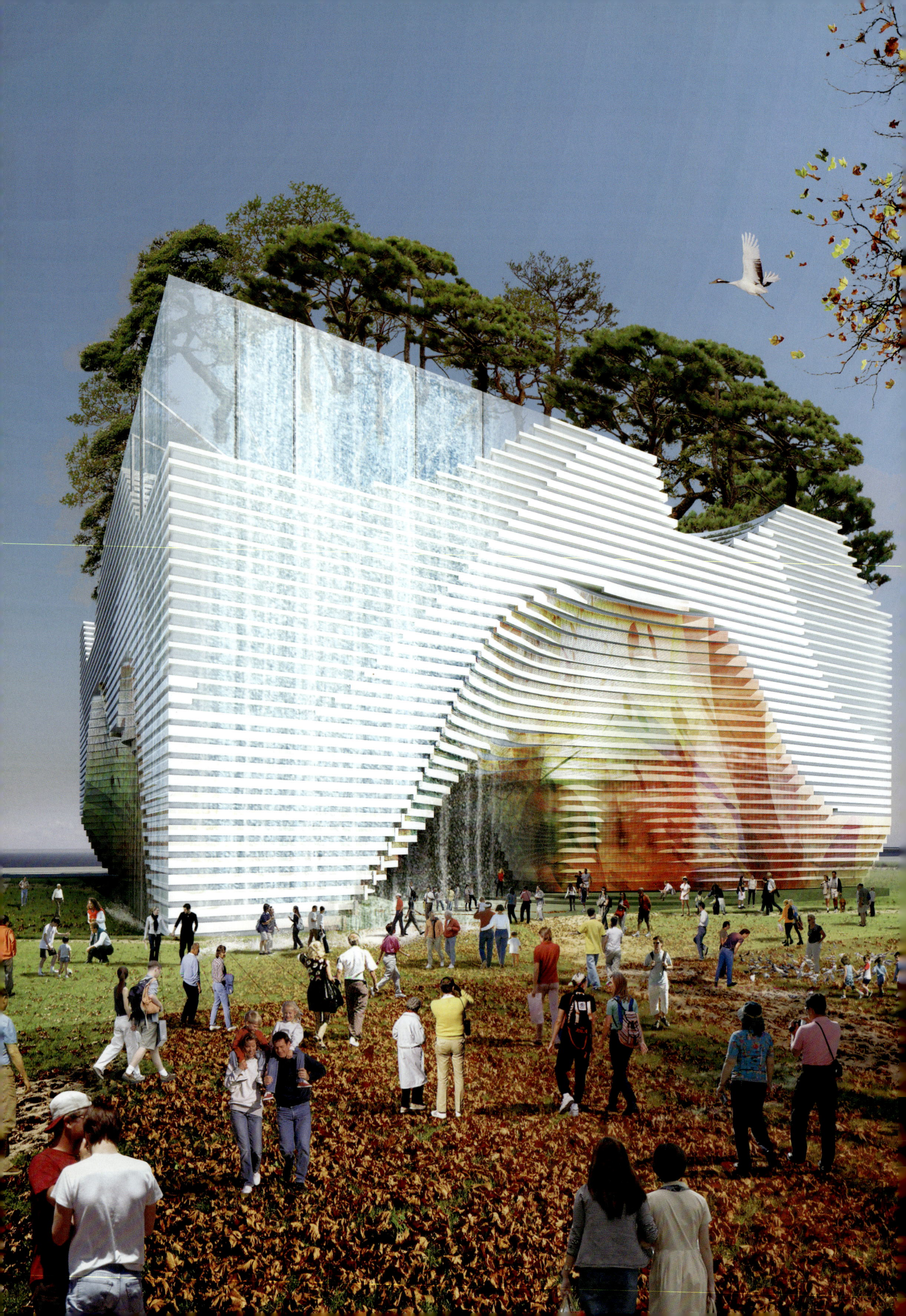

GREEN-IMAGINATION

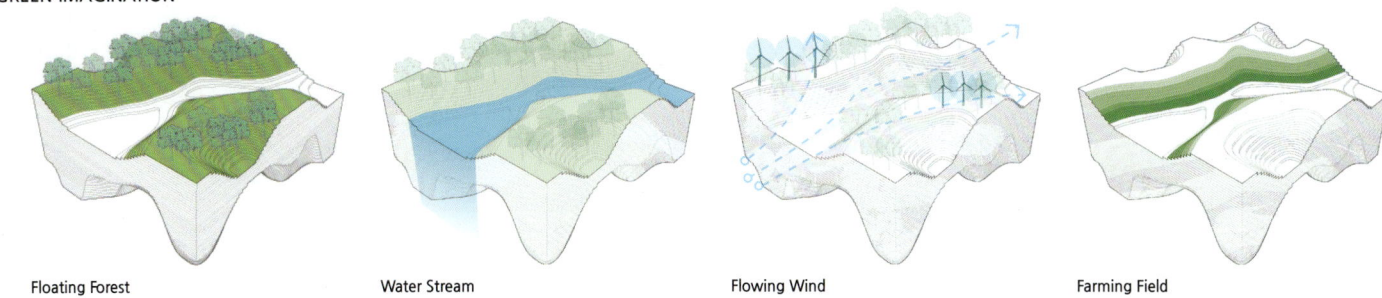

Floating Forest   Water Stream   Flowing Wind   Farming Field

// Green Imagination 01: Combination of Green and Imagination
We suggest Korean Corporate Pavilion containing exhibition and experience of natural nature and artificial nature. The shape of the pavilion is taken from nature. It brings parts of it to the architecture as an artificial container. Green-Imagination means the combination of Green and Imagination which re-produces an unlimited potentiality of nature and the power of making imagination true in order to express the spirit and the technology of Korean enterprise.
As society is getting civilized, the condition of nature goes to ruin. Global warming and depletion of natural sources which the consumption-driven society in capitalism causes are important issues now, and we can't avoid the environmental subjects. Especially the unlimited expansion of population, architecture and infrastructure in big cities predict overall natural exhaustion threatening the ecosystem. Korean enterprises also need to suggest new values for the future through introspection of nature. Therefore, a new system gained from the combination and symbiosis of nature and human is suggested such as landscape architecture and ecological architecture. This system is the active integration of architecture and nature from deep introspection of sustainability.

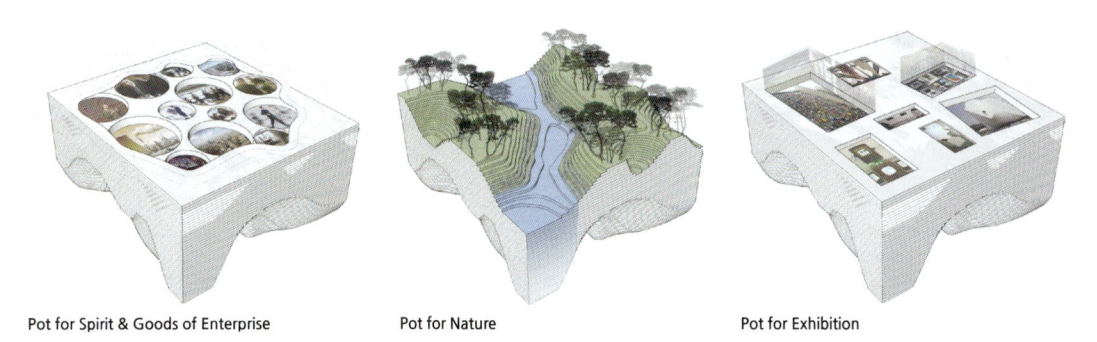

Pot for Spirit & Goods of Enterprise   Pot for Nature   Pot for Exhibition

// Green Imagination 02: Compound of nature component_ a container holding nature
Korean Corporate Pavilion is a pot-like architecture. The pot is an artificial container in which nature is put in. The pot is a technological container maintaining and creating diverse figures of nature. In this technologic container, 12 Korean enterprises are combined. The exhibit hall provides potentiality of futuristic high-technology through cooperation and communication among each other. This pot-like architecture is composed with a 3-dimensional digital space at ground level, exhibition space on the 2nd floor and space for enterprise prospecting on the 3rd floor. Eventually it is a huge pot of a pine grove penetrating the whole system.
The artificial pot putting nature in embodies and combines nature by diverse methods. This diverse composition is generated by a 3-dimensional combination of natural topography. Various Korean topographies are abstracted and its components such as mountain, field, valley and river are combined with architecture.

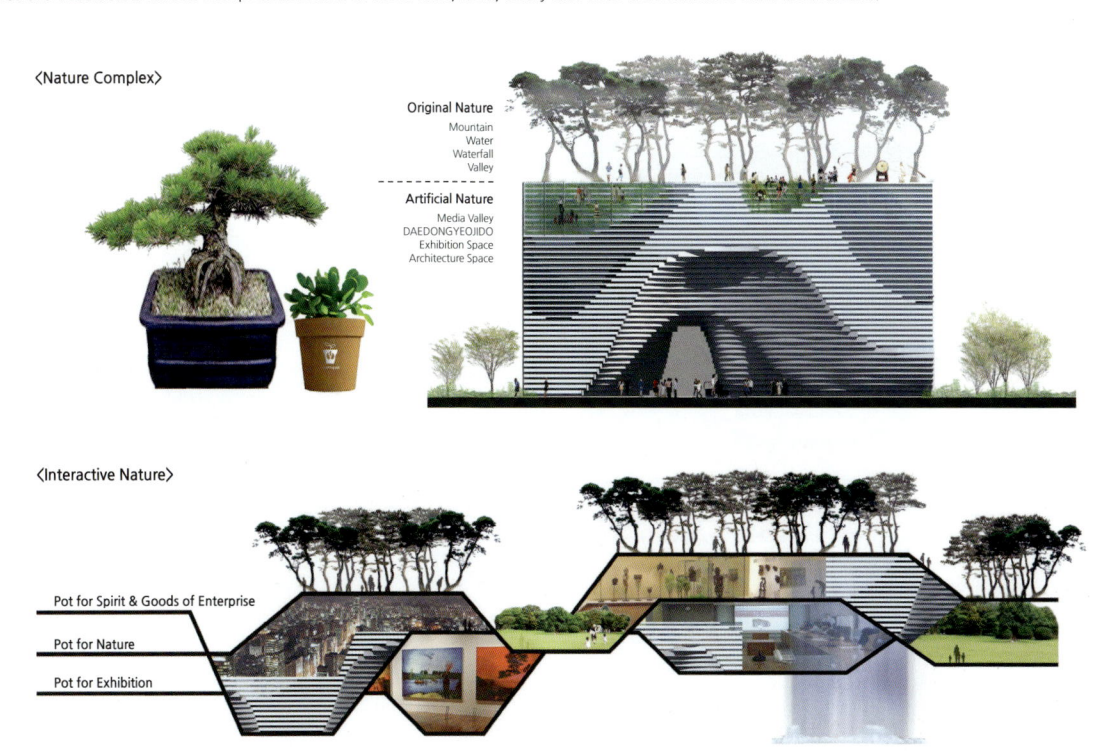

⟨Nature Complex⟩

Original Nature
Mountain
Water
Waterfall
Valley

Artificial Nature
Media Valley
DAEDONGYEOJIDO
Exhibition Space
Architecture Space

⟨Interactive Nature⟩

Pot for Spirit & Goods of Enterprise
Pot for Nature
Pot for Exhibition

SILHOUETTE OF NATURE 山水彫刻

SCULPT KOREAN SCENERY

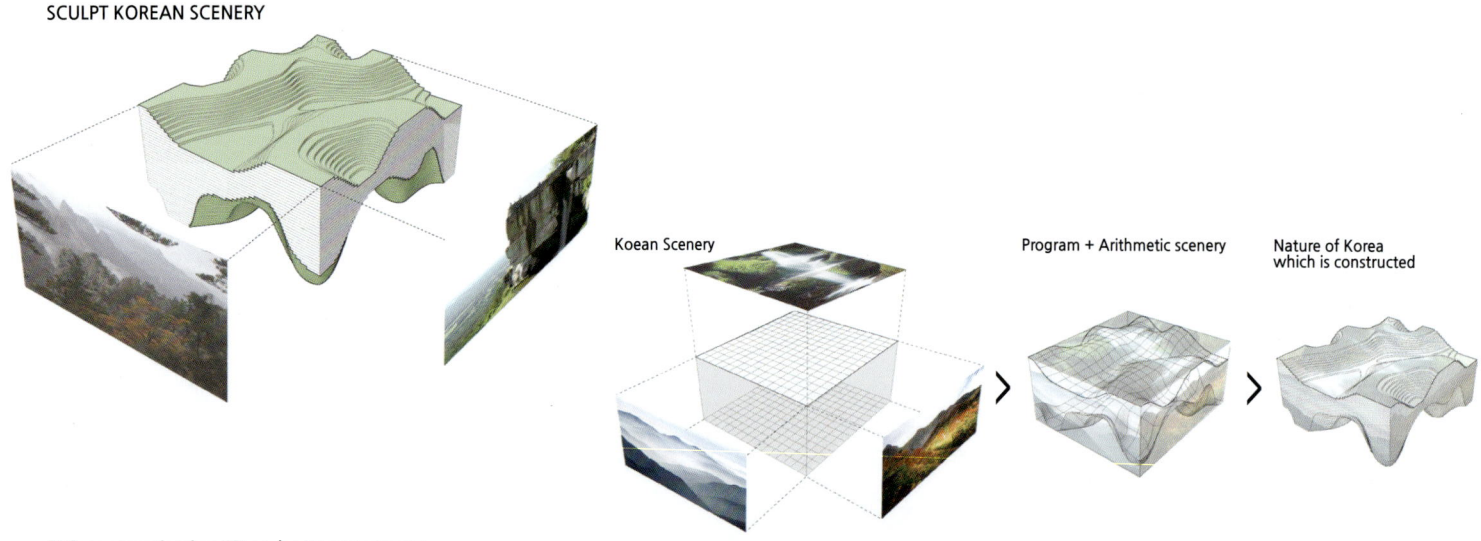

// Green-Imagination 03: sculpt Korean scenery
The artificial pot putting in nature contains eternity and change of Korean landscape; mountain and water. In the oriental view of nature, scenery is interpreted as a temporal medium which contains traces and the involving the past and the future. Korean Corporate Pavilion as artificial nature is an organic body breathing with mysterious nature which keeps changing unlimitedly. Korean Corporate Pavilion is a symbiotic structure at the contact point of lively dynamics and contemporary esthetics.
To sculpt Korean scenery_ Korean corporate pavilion intents a Korean environmental-friendly spirit. Korean nature like landscape painting is engraved.

// Green Imagination 04: topography of communication
Korean identity is introduced to the world, furthermore, a communicating topography is provided at the center of Asian emotion. The communicating topography consists of the pot in order to provide diverse experiences for visitors and the exhibition of Korean enterprise. Especially at the ground level, communicating structure which digital nature-plaza composes is dynamically opened except for necessary programs in order to overcome the conditions of small site. It is a waiting area before appreciating the exhibition. They get in touch naturally with promotional images of Korean enterprises while staying in the waiting area. At the 2nd level, universal space engages diverse exhibitions. It not only advertises individual enterprise but also advertises Korea overall as a brand. The 3rd floor, which is a nature observing space integrating all the Korean enterprises provides surrealistic communication combining real and technological nature. Lastly the pine glove is a space like paradise harmonizing nature and human.

CIRCULATIVE ECOSYSTEM

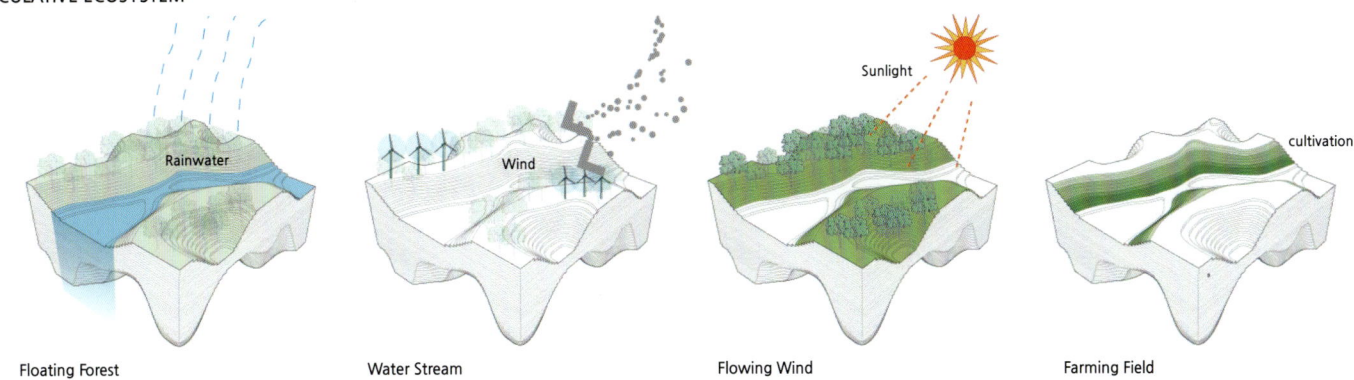

Floating Forest | **Water Stream** | **Flowing Wind** | **Farming Field**

// Green Imagination 05: circulative ecosystem
We suggest the forest to be like enormous tree pot moved. At the top, there is an ecosystem with the pine grove, water space, roof garden and windmill. As visitors move, they experience nature such as water, energy, pine grove and grass. The composition is that Korean nature is placed in the huge pot.
We suggest not only a small ecosystem but a self-sufficient environmental system. Rainwater penetrating the whole architecture is filtered to drinking water, and the windmill produces energy using wind from the roof floor. The lake on the top floor runs through the gauze like a curtain and it reaches the root of trees in order to help their growing. It is a vertical landscape realizing the saving water, light, energy and time.

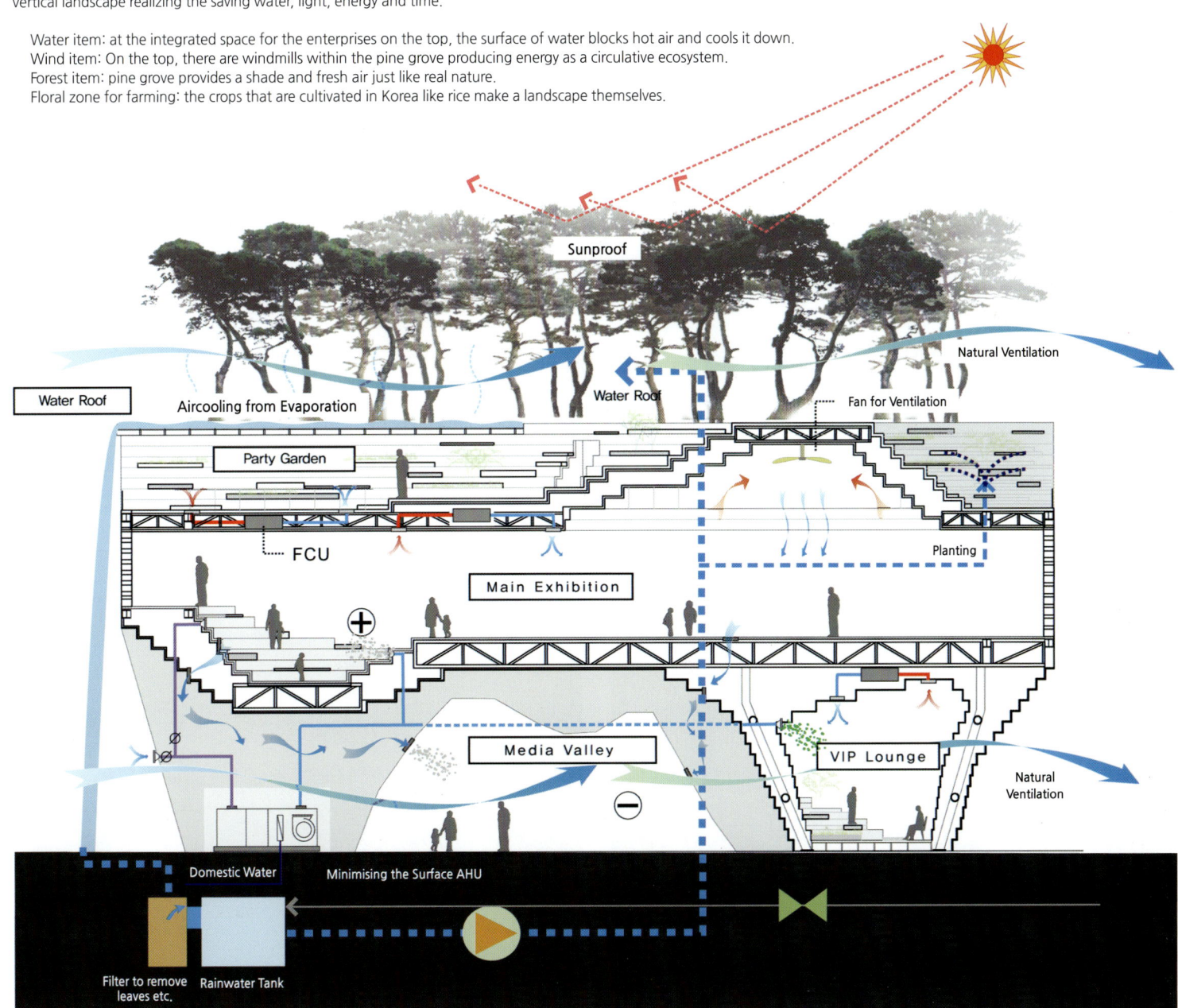

Water item: at the integrated space for the enterprises on the top, the surface of water blocks hot air and cools it down.
Wind item: On the top, there are windmills within the pine grove producing energy as a circulative ecosystem.
Forest item: pine grove provides a shade and fresh air just like real nature.
Floral zone for farming: the crops that are cultivated in Korea like rice make a landscape themselves.

ACCUMULATED EVENT NATURE

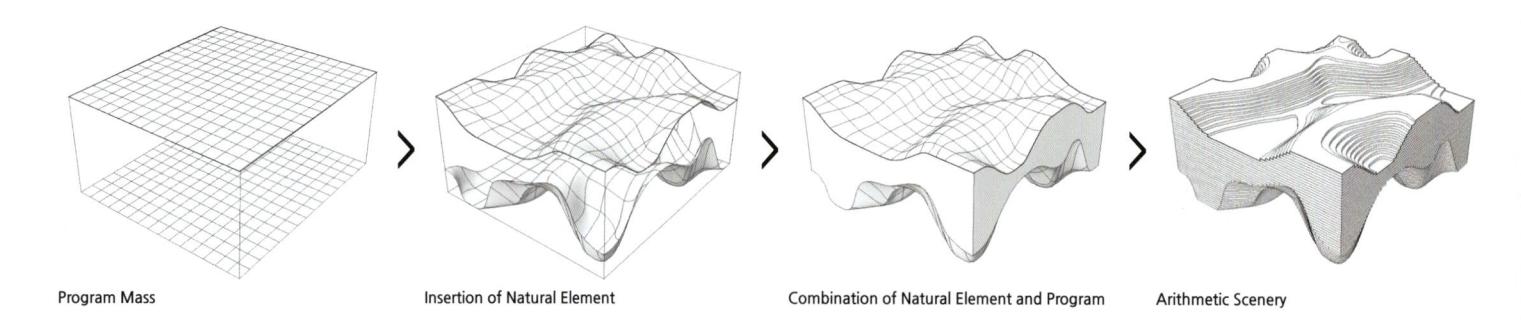

| Program Mass | Insertion of Natural Element | Combination of Natural Element and Program | Arithmetic Scenery |

// **Vertical composition of program_ accumulated event nature**

We suggest Korean Corporate Pavilion providing an experience of nature. It doesn't show the spirit and the technology of Korean enterprises by a simple exhibition. Spatial experience becomes an exhibition itself through nature displayed on different levels such as media valley, universal topography, nature-observatory and pine grove.
The pot putting in nature is composed by the accumulation of topographic language. The language of accumulated topography is abstracted and constructs the shape of nature. Accumulated topography is a result representing the natural phenomenon and responding to the time flow like an organism. Diverse technology and spirit which connect past, present and future are contained in the topography. Topography is not only an accumulated phenomena of time but a historical phenomenon holding human civilization and historical records. Topographic accumulation is not only a matter of shape but program. Moreover the combination of them and events produce diverse accumulations.

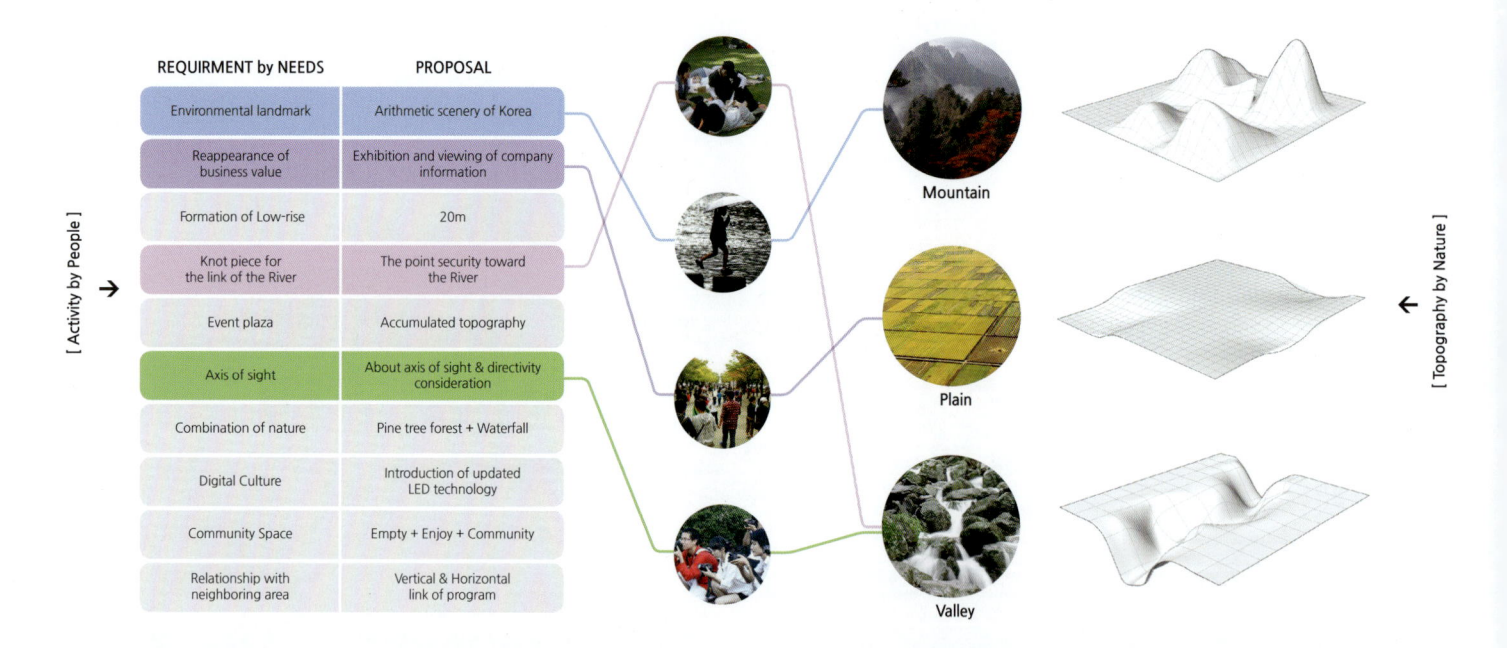

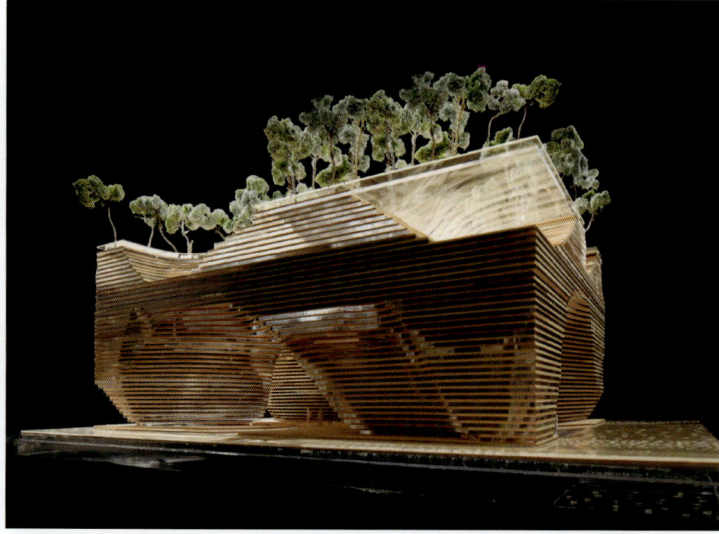

REQUIRMENT by NEEDS	PROPOSAL
Environmental landmark	Arithmetic scenery of Korea
Reappearance of business value	Exhibition and viewing of company information
Formation of Low-rise	20m
Knot piece for the link of the River	The point security toward the River
Event plaza	Accumulated topography
Axis of sight	About axis of sight & directivity consideration
Combination of nature	Pine tree forest + Waterfall
Digital Culture	Introduction of updated LED technology
Community Space	Empty + Enjoy + Community
Relationship with neighboring area	Vertical & Horizontal link of program

[Activity by People]

Mountain

Plain

Valley

[Topography by Nature]

COMPOUND BODY 279

MAKING PLACE

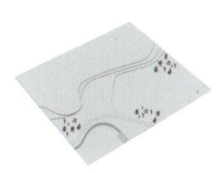

LV +0	LV +3000	LV +6000	LV +12000	LV +16000	LV +20000
Partition of the site	Partition of the site	Connection of Vertical Circulation	Formation of exhibit space	Party/Event area differentiation	Insertion of landscape space

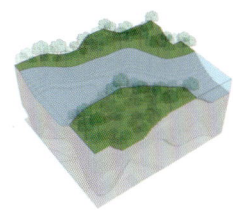

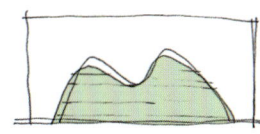

Mountain	Waterfall	Cliff	Sand Dune	Columnar Joint

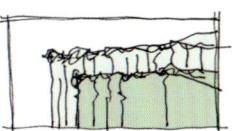

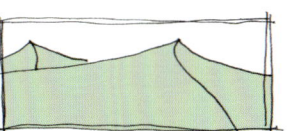

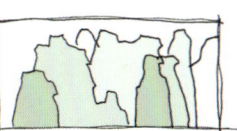

——— ICONIC NATURE ELEVATION ———

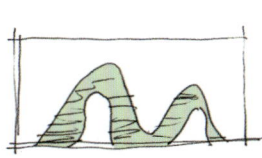

Valley	Forest	Contour Linces	Cascaded Arable Land	Water Flow	Plain

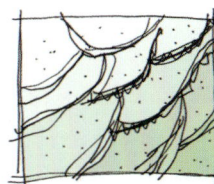

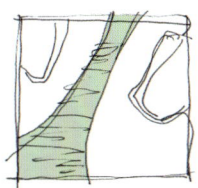

——— ICONIC NATURE PLAN ———

SOUTH ELEVATION A
山水彫刻 which sees from the River

+20.2 RF
+16.2 3F
+10.2 2F
+0.2 1F

4500
6000
9500

COMPOUND BODY 281

EAST ELEVATION B
山水彫刻 which sees at the plaza

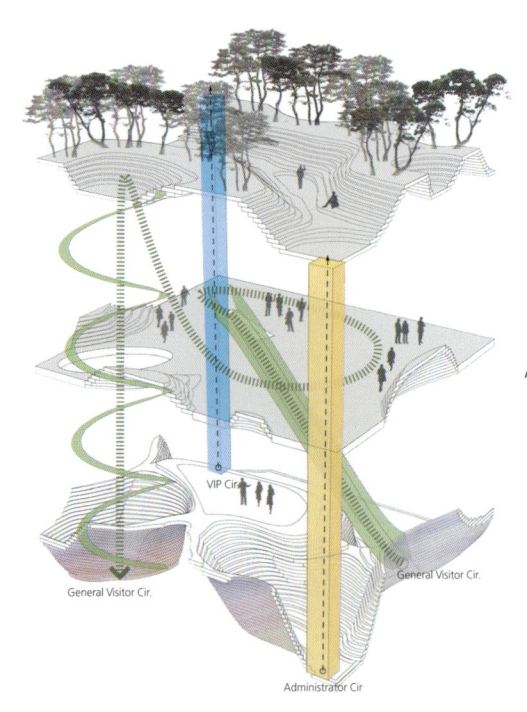

// **Circulation**

General visitor circulation_ 1st floor has waiting and approaching area in the plaza. They enter and wait through the media valley which is an open exhibition space for images. A vertically moving escalator from plaza level goes through the digital valley and moves up to different levels.
VIP and the disabled circulation_ a different entrance and an elevator going to the observatory and enterprise event space are suggested. Media valley is appreciated in a separated VIP lounge as well.

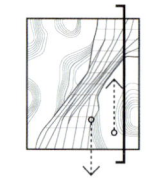

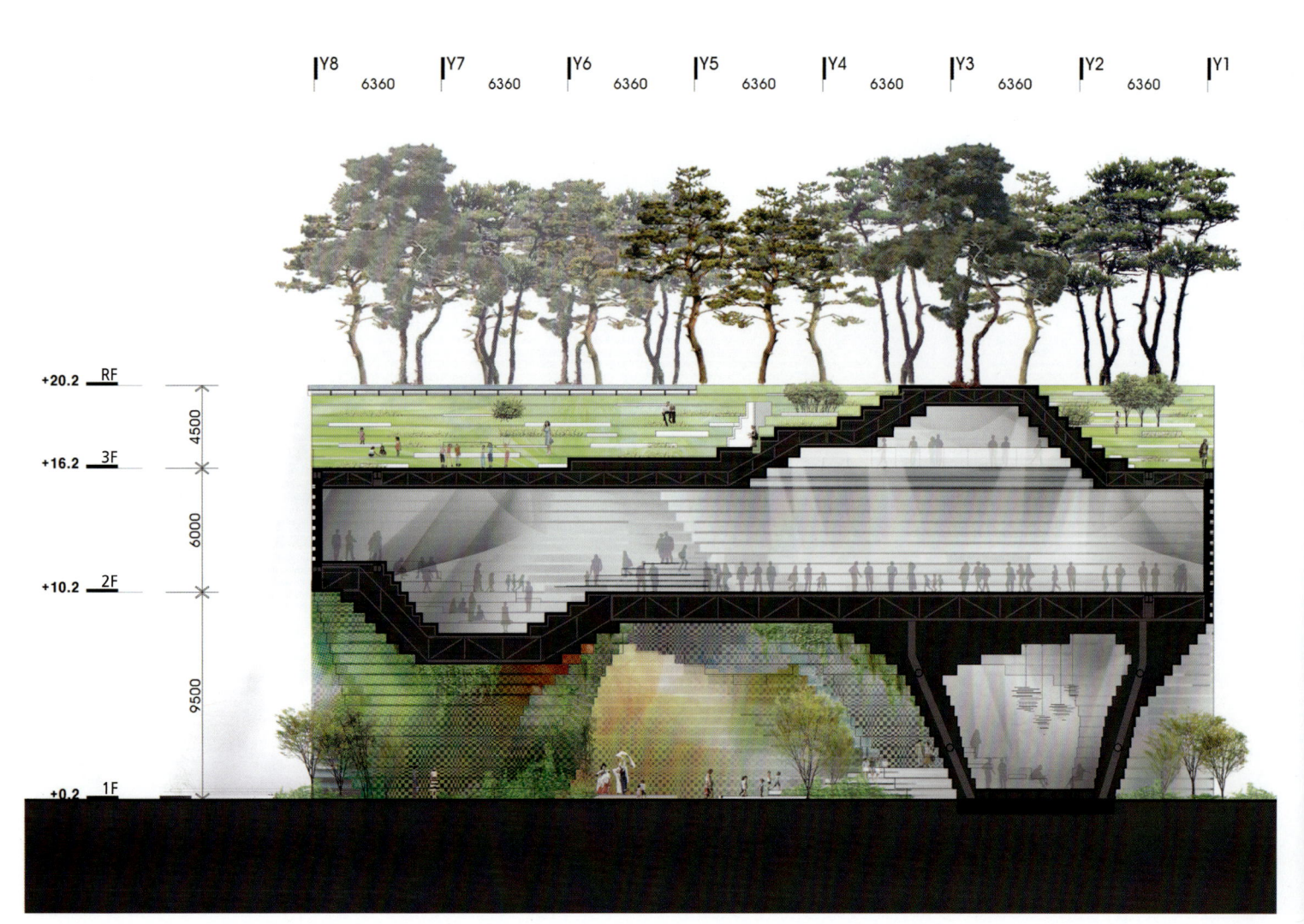

INTERACTIVE SECTIONAL COMPOSITION

Observation Mountain

Company Exhibition Mountain

Fantasy Valley

Stacked Program

Interactive Program by Topography

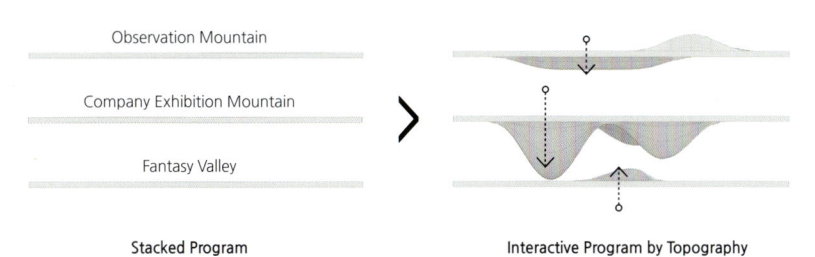

Interactive Sectional Composition and Circulation
3-dimensional topographic section is composed. Diverse scenery frames are experienced and a circulation inducing lively movements of waiting, image, exhibition, promotion, event, outdoor exhibition, resting and commemoration is set. Circulation for general visitors, VIP and services is separated in different spaces.

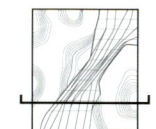

1ST FLOOR PLAN / media valley, digital natural space
1. Public open space - media valley, circulation by escalator, information center, souvenir shop + exit for media cylinder, visitor's toilet
2. VIP space - VIP lounge, VIP entrance, service and management room, conference room
3. Service space - control room, media cylinder, mechanic room

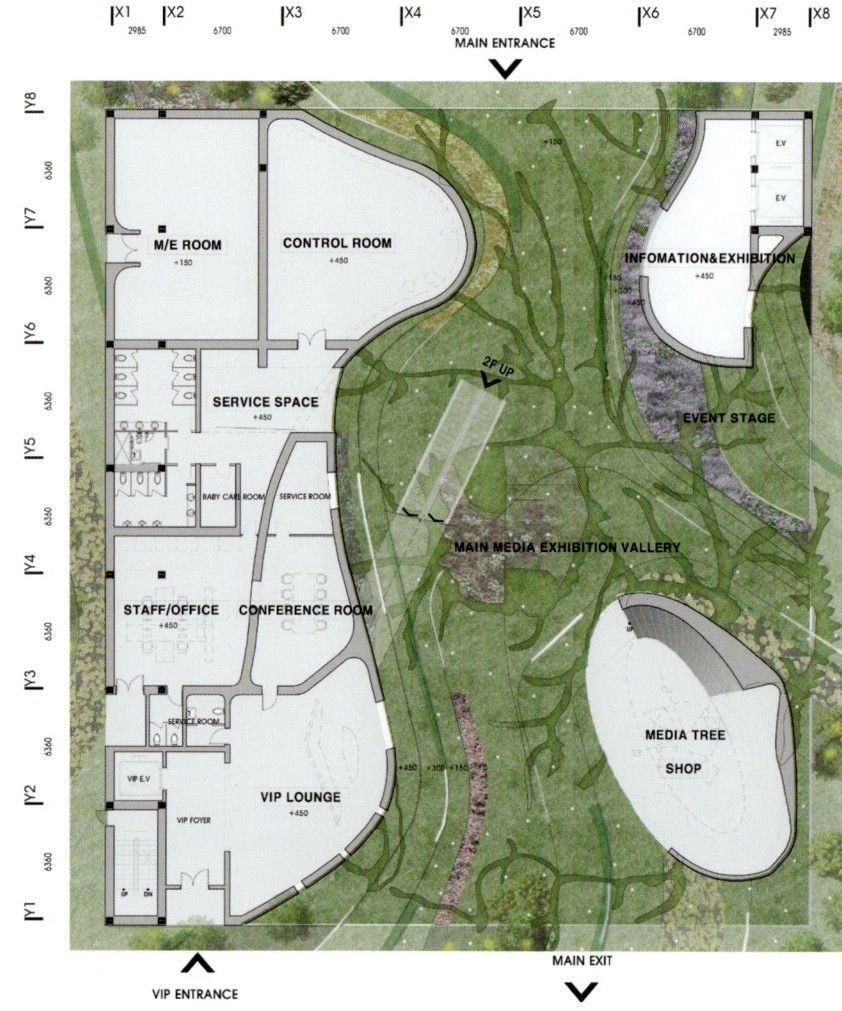

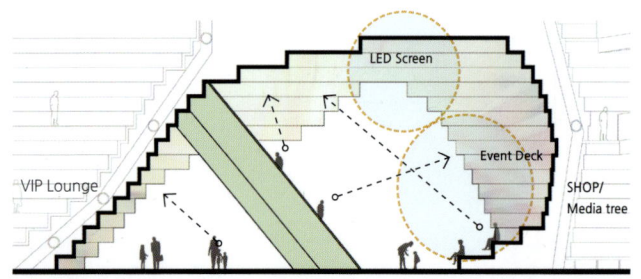

// Media valley 01- digital valley: 1st floor
Expo Korean enterprise hall is an open space with images, exhibition, resting and events for visitors. As a waiting and moving space for visitors, it accommodates many people. This public plaza is composed with the concept of an image-hall and an event-plaza as semi-outdoor space. The event plaza which is open to 4 directions is artificial digital nature confronting natural landscape. By spatial display using information and media, natural topographic form and digital technology is grafted. It is a new technical Digital Nature.

2ND FLOOR PLAN / natural space for enterprise exhibition
Exhibition space for enterprise, resting space, media cylinder, visitor toilet, circulation by escalator, service core

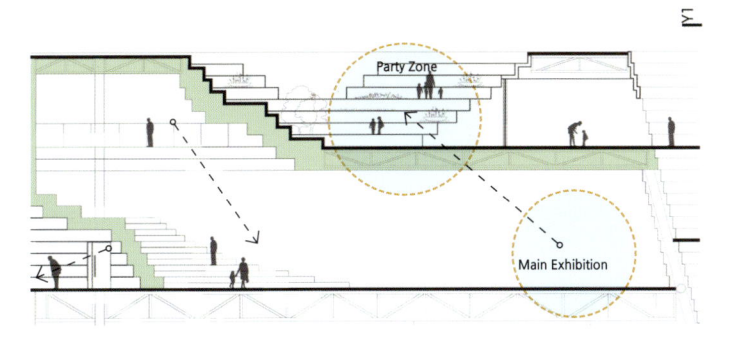

// **Universal exhibition space_ enterprise exhibition space: 2nd floor**
The Universal space concept accommodates contents and methods of diverse exhibitions. Brand, spirit, and value of enterprise are accommodated in open planned space. The common theme among the 12 enterprises and brand identity is provided and given an exhibition. To supplement and verify the planar open plan, topographic carved down space provides an image exhibition. 3-Dimensional exhibitions according to the change of the ceiling level produce diverse sectional compositions. The entrance to media valley is composed by an escalator penetrating the media valley. After appreciating the exhibition, a final exhibition is finished through the media cylinder.

3RD FLOOR PLAN / nature-observatory space for all enterprise
Nature-observatory, service and management space, media cylinder

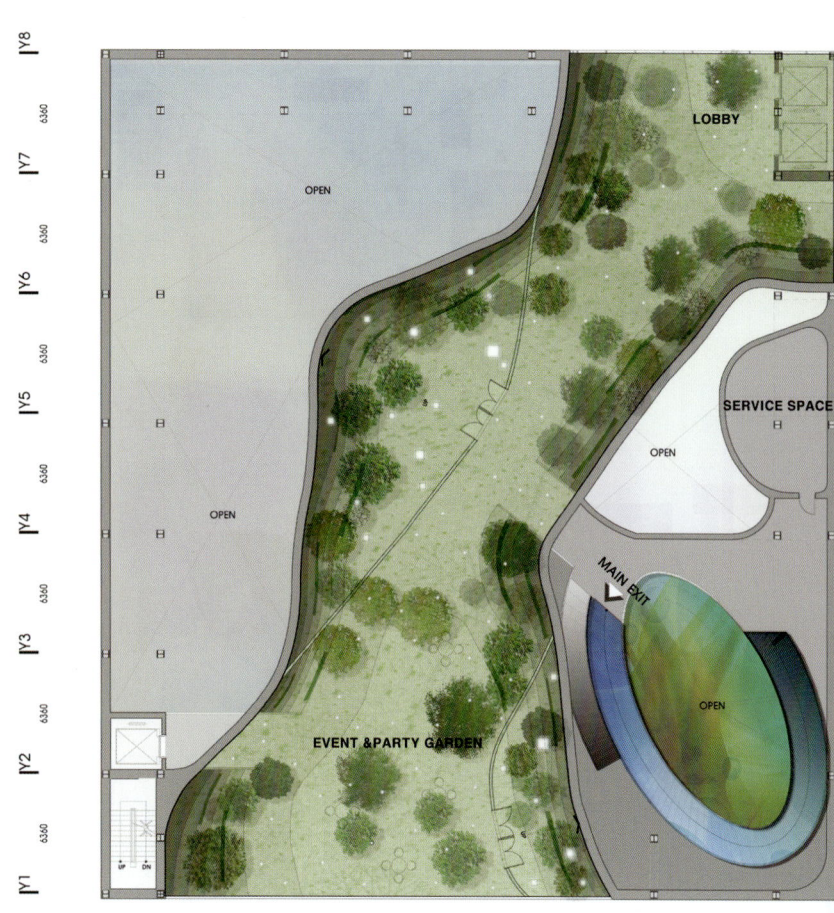

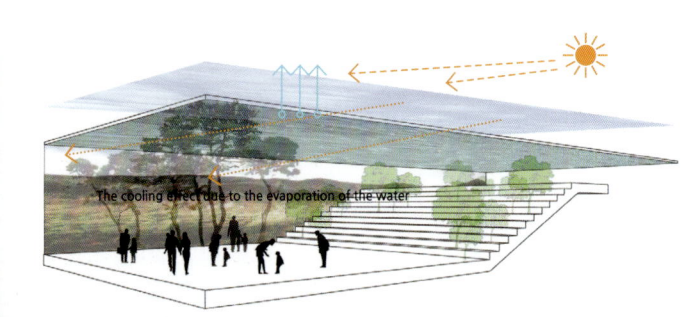

// **Nature observatory_ enterprise integrating space; 3rd floor**
It is an expansion of universal space accommodating diverse contents and methods of exhibition. Stair-shape natural topographic space holds interesting events such as inner theme exhibition, promotion, small concerts and parties. During each period of the 12 enterprises, diverse spatial demands are accommodated in this changeable displaying space. It is party place in nature with water in the sky and exhibition on the floor. The ceiling is finished with a glass skin so pine grove and the sky are brought to the inside. The glass skin displays water space. The wall provides images of a waterfall and the ceiling reflects an image of water so that it gives an experience of being in the water.

ROOF FLOOR PLAN
Outdoor exhibition space in the pine grove

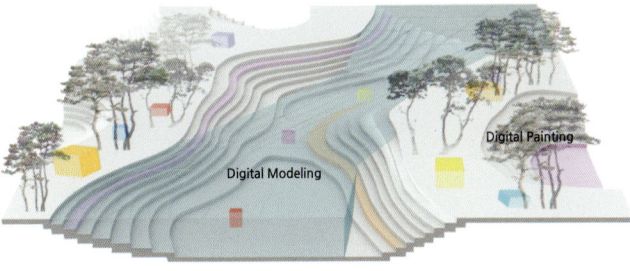

// Pine grove_ nature paradise roof floor plan
The last space level for the enterprise exhibition is a multi-purpose space accommodating outer exhibitions. Nature-observatory is connected and enforced to the experience of a forest and exhibition. Its purifier is the landscape itself and it also purifies the spirit and a new understanding of nature. Korean emotion and spirit produced in this identical space is combined with the components of Korean garden as the climax space. Sharing the characters of the sky garden, it is an ultimate nature experience helping us develop our physics and spirit.

TRANSITION OF EVENT VALLEY

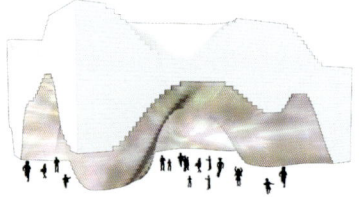

Media Valley    Play Valley    Water Valley    Green Valley

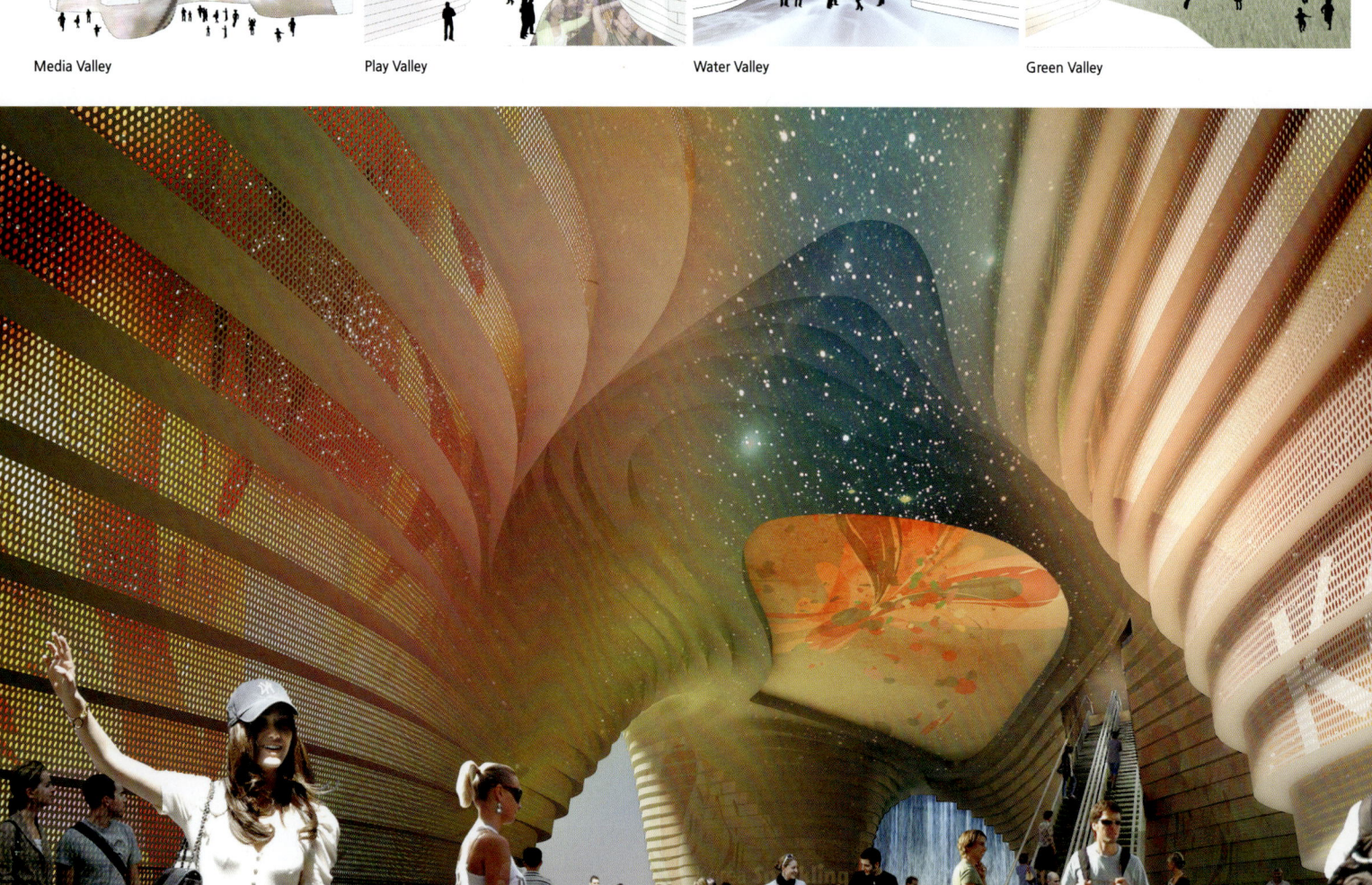

COMPOUND BODY 289

TRANSITION OF EVENT VALLEY

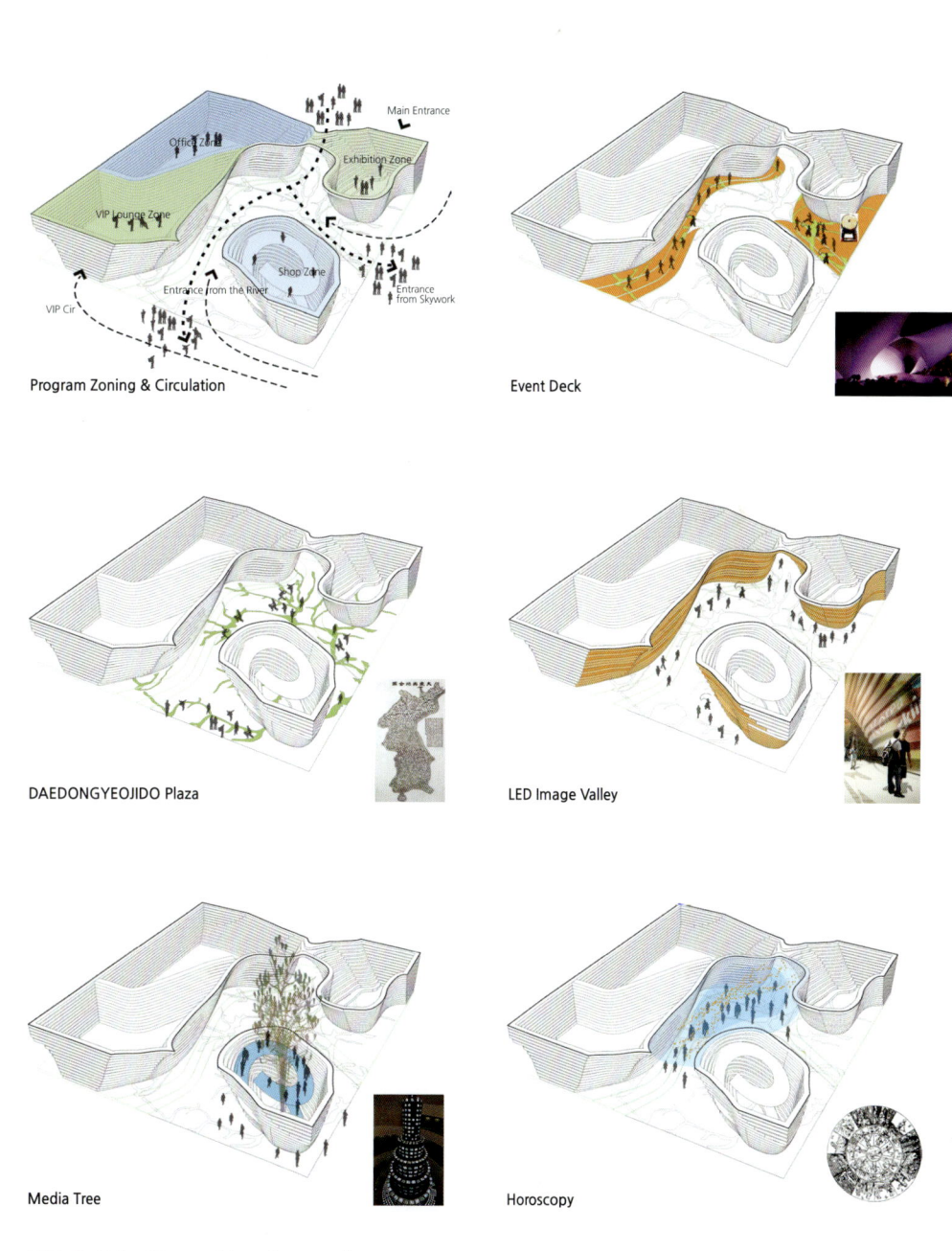

Program Zoning & Circulation

Event Deck

DAEDONGYEOJIDO Plaza

LED Image Valley

Media Tree

Horoscopy

// Media Valley 02_ transition of event valley
The combination of the spirit of enterprise and technology provide accommodation of a combination among public space, expo network and cultural events. It becomes a changing plaza responding to diverse events such as media valley, play valley and water valley.

Digital Skin 1   Digital Skin 2   Digital Skin 3

// **Digital scenery**
The Korean landscape engraved digital skin changes urban expressions using diverse LED images and light. It is an urban skin providing advertisement of enterprises and necessary information for visitors.

// **Organic of scenery_ landscape and lighting concept**
The four seasons of Korean nature are displayed. Korean landscape has different beauties according to its season. Organism of scenery is like ink-and-wash painting presenting spring- bright flower scene, summer- cool water fall and green forest scene, autumn- beautiful autumn colors of leaf scene and winter- modest cold mountain scene.
The panorama harmonizing inner space and outer space composes architecture like a new landscape.
The spatial structure and the program included reflect properties of nature and accommodate diverse naturalized programs relating new circumstances of the new age.
Constructed shape consists of an organism system which keeps changing with the relationship between people and time beyond separated category weather it is scene or not. It is new oriental painting harmonizing digital and nature.

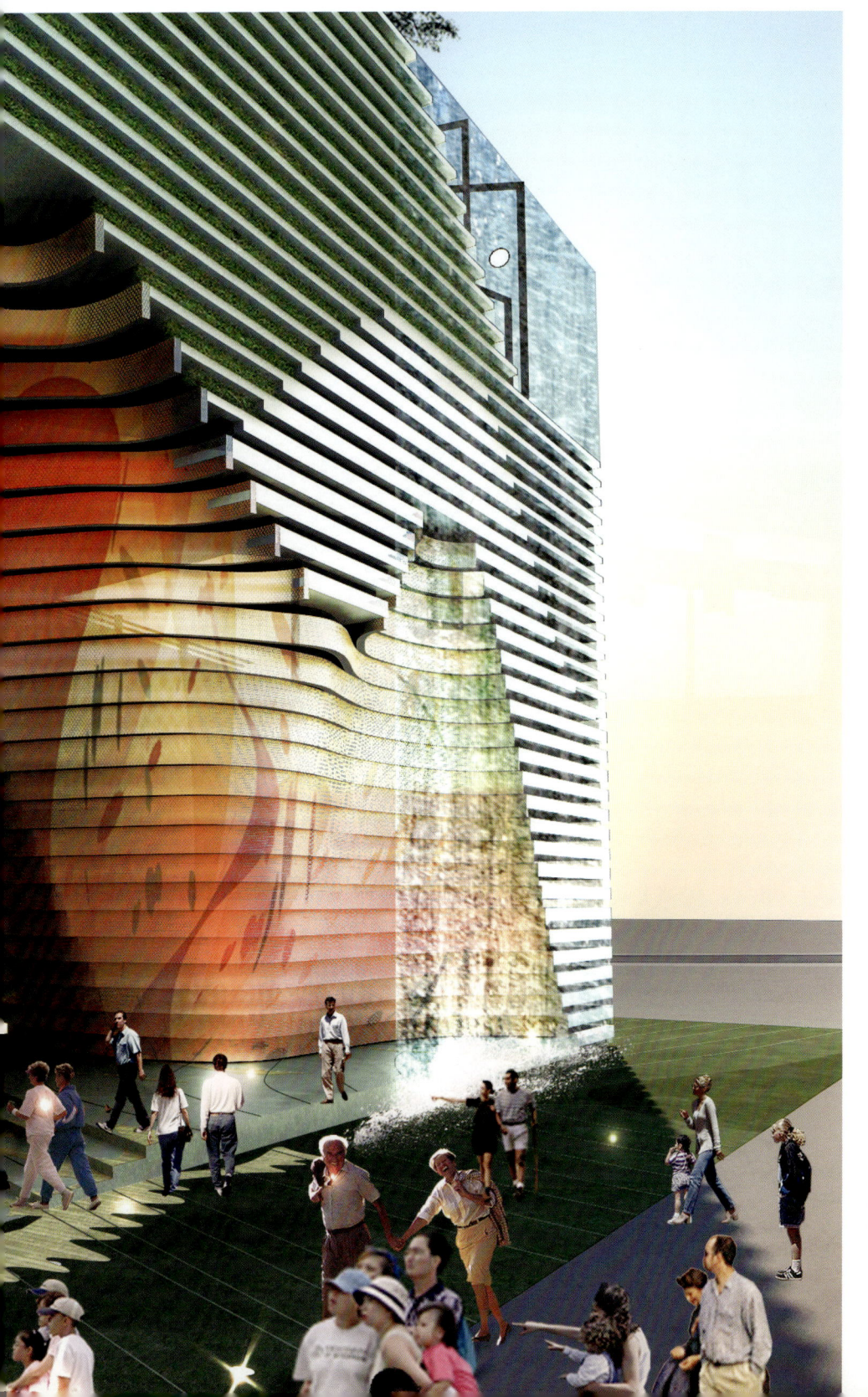

// **Water Stream**
As part of experiencing nature on elevation, water skin starting from the nature-observing space changes as time period goes by. It floods to the enterprise hall like a waterfall. It is a dynamic fact working as a finishing stroke in Korean scenery. The waterfall is located in the entrance and the river side, and the visitors' spectacular experience is amplified according to their movement.

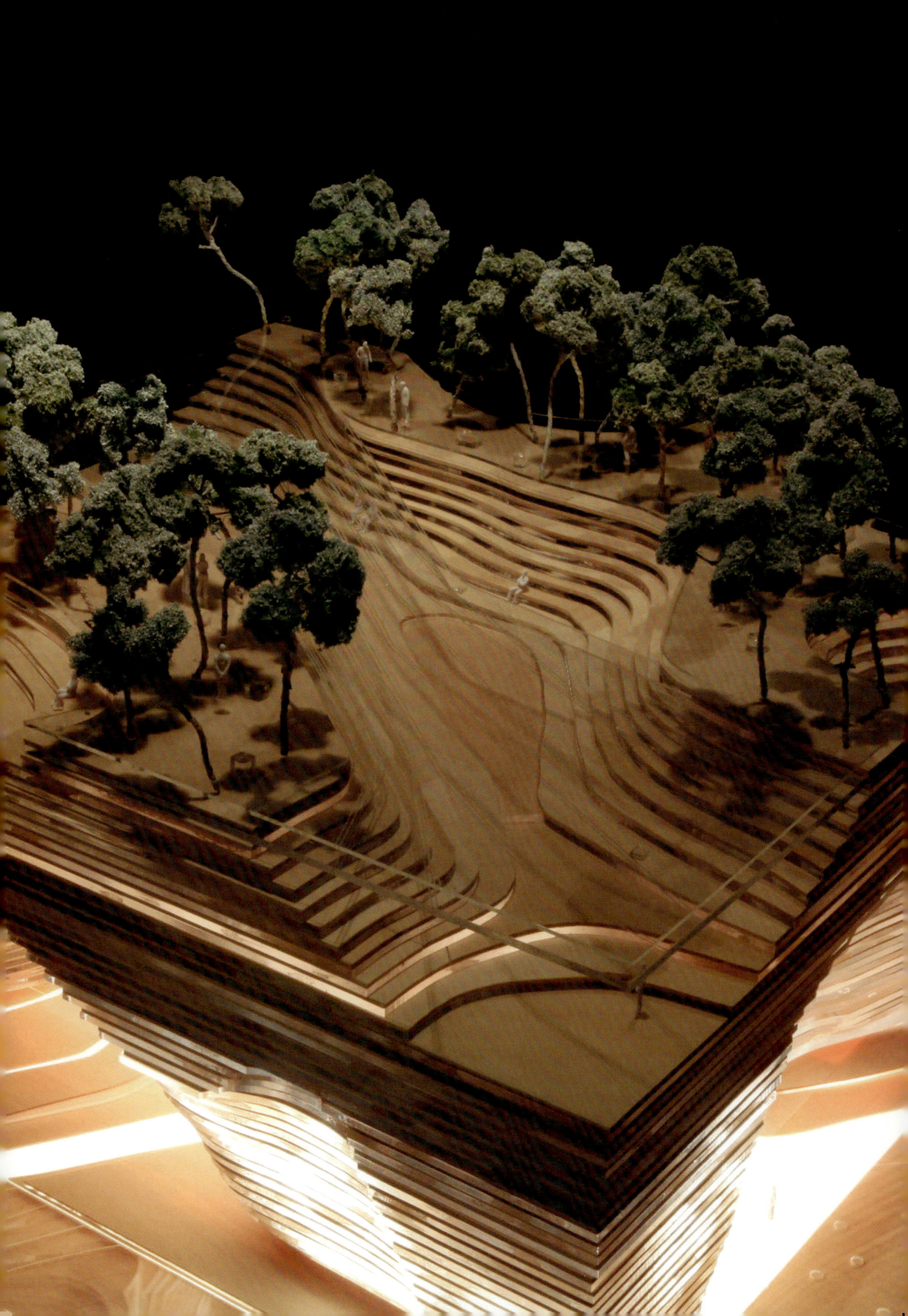

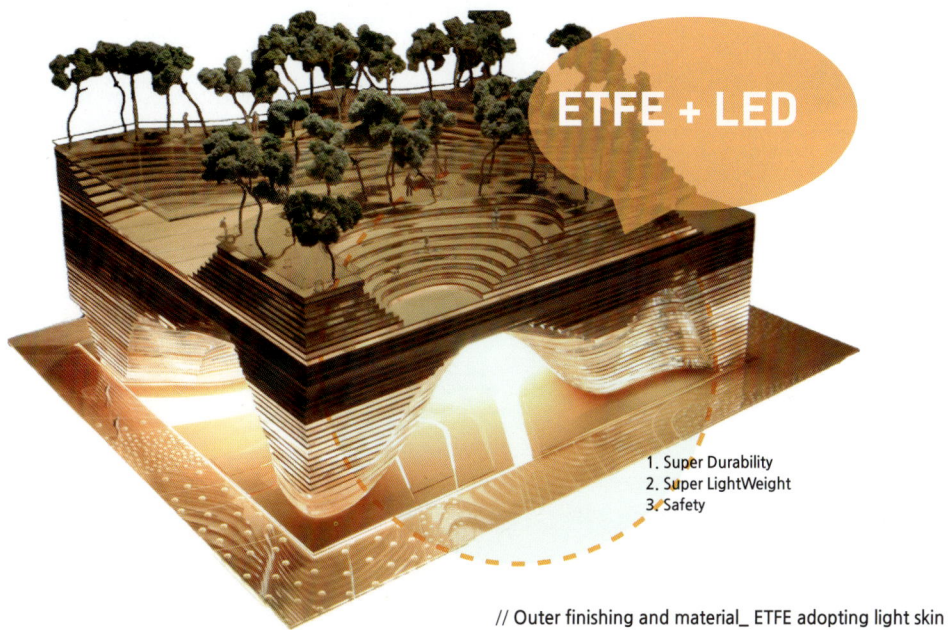

ETFE + LED

1. Super Durability
2. Super LightWeight
3. Safety

// Outer finishing and material_ ETFE adopting light skin

For the shortening of constructing time and easier deconstruction, a semi-transparent ETFE film and steel louver is used. ETFE film is possible of making a free curved frame. Its advantage is that it is lighter than any other material. Low-friction, adhesion, water-proof and oil proof which is the surface-feature of fluoroplastic helps maintenance. The printing on the surface, the LED light, and the projection of images provide diverse night views.

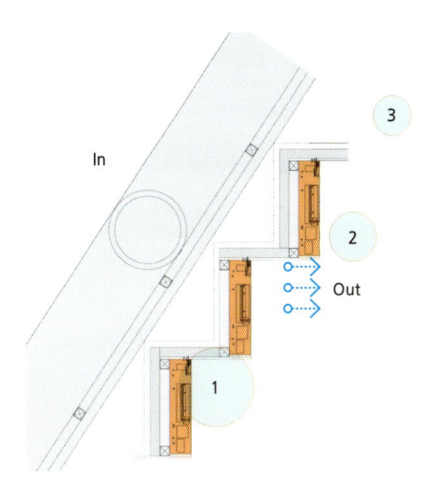

A Type: LED

1. 10mm LED
2. THK 10 STL PLATE / APP. PAINT
3. ▫-50x50 STL PIPE

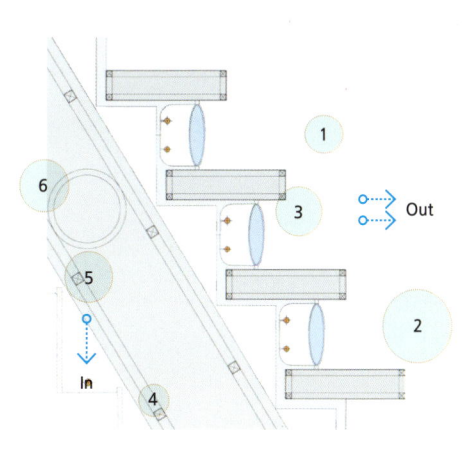

B Type: ETFE + LED

1. THK 1.6T STL PLATE
2. ETFE PAIRED MEMBRANE FILM
3. LED 2EA
4. ETFE FILM
5. LED
6. 2 LAYERD PLY WOOD / APP. PAINT

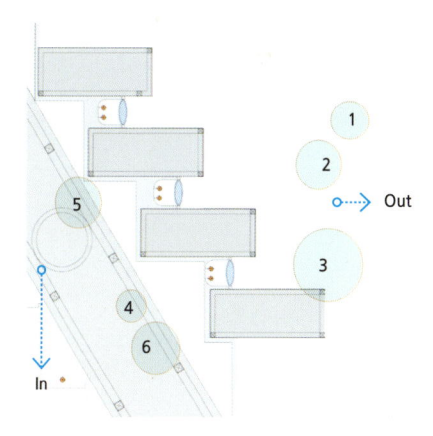

C Type: ETFE + LED

1. THK 1.6T STL PLATE
2. ETFE PAIRED MEMBRANE FILM
3. LED 2EA
4. ETFE FILM
5. LED
6. 2 LAYERD PLY WOOD / APP. PAINT

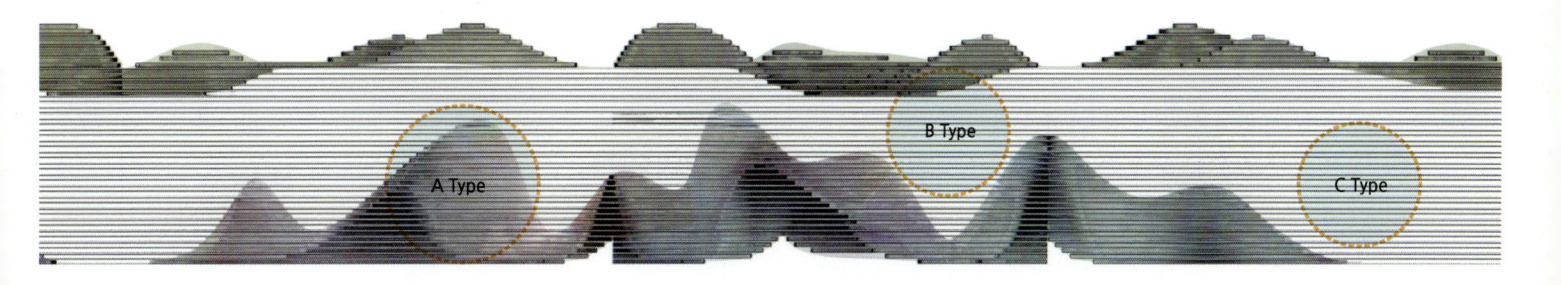

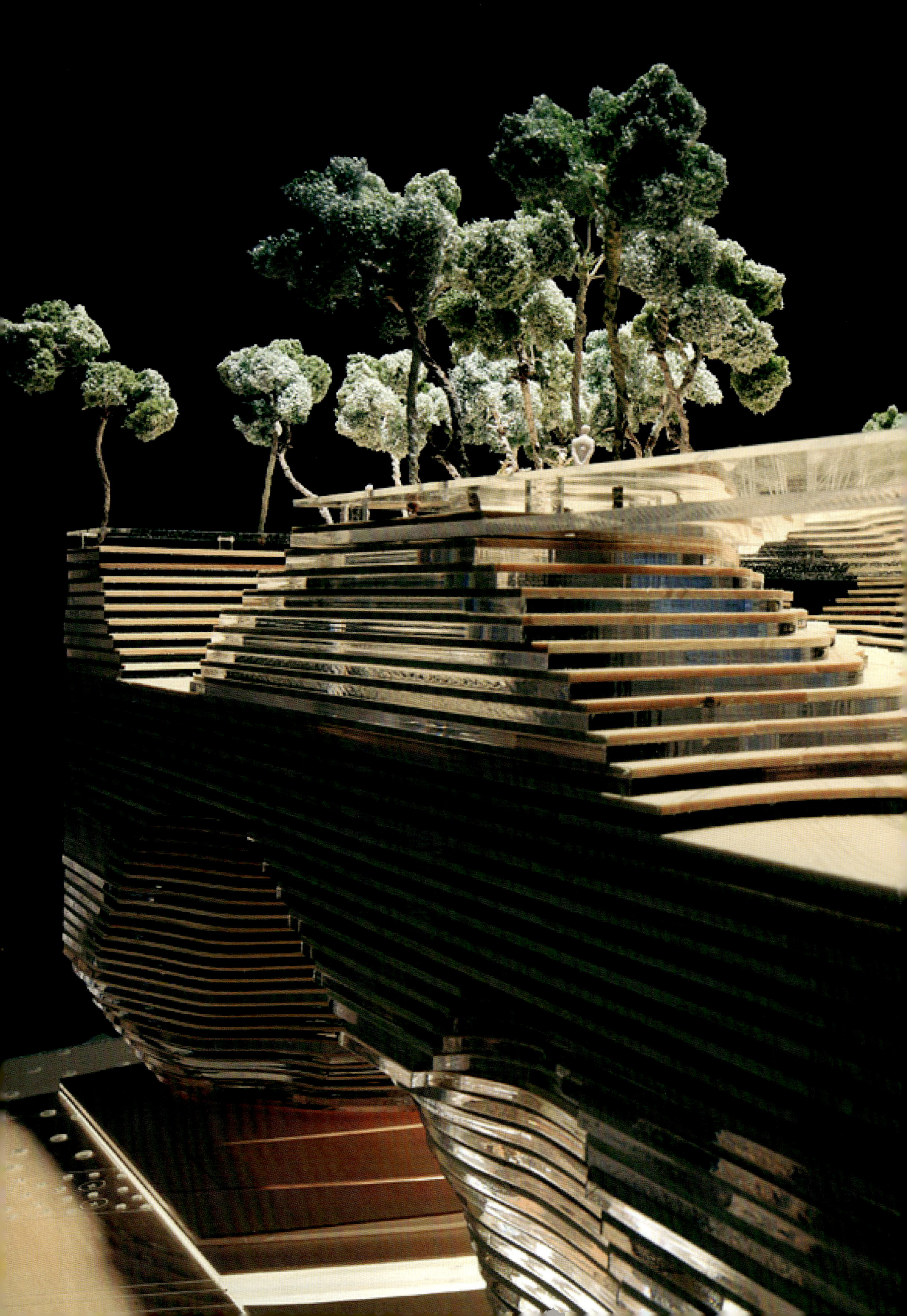

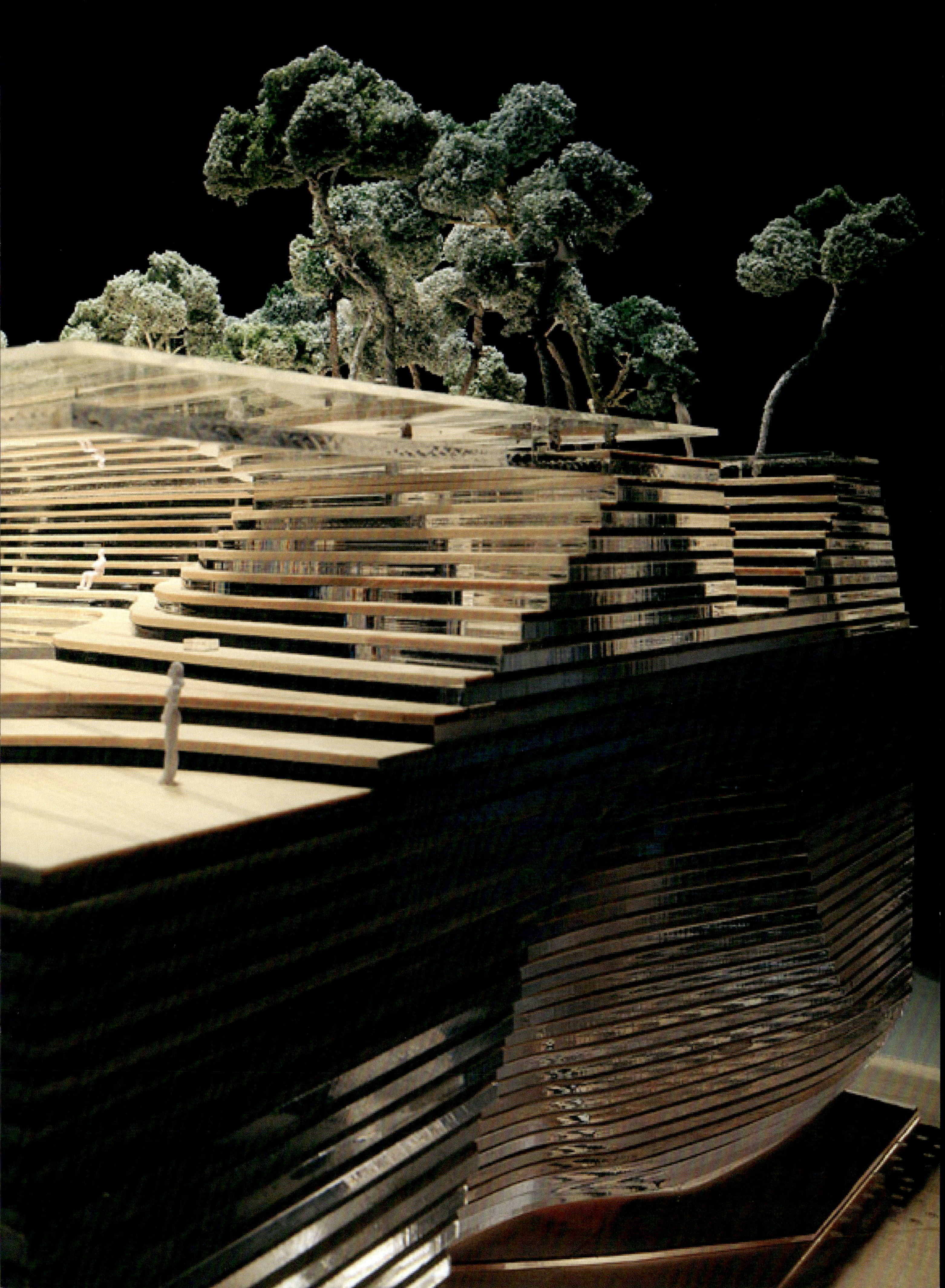

Crystal
sculpture

Gallery 303

Honorable Prize of Korean Good Design Award | **Architects** Jang Yoon Gyoo, Shin Chang Hoon, Kim Sung Min
Client AMJ Development, Lim Kwang Taek
Photographer Namgoong Sun

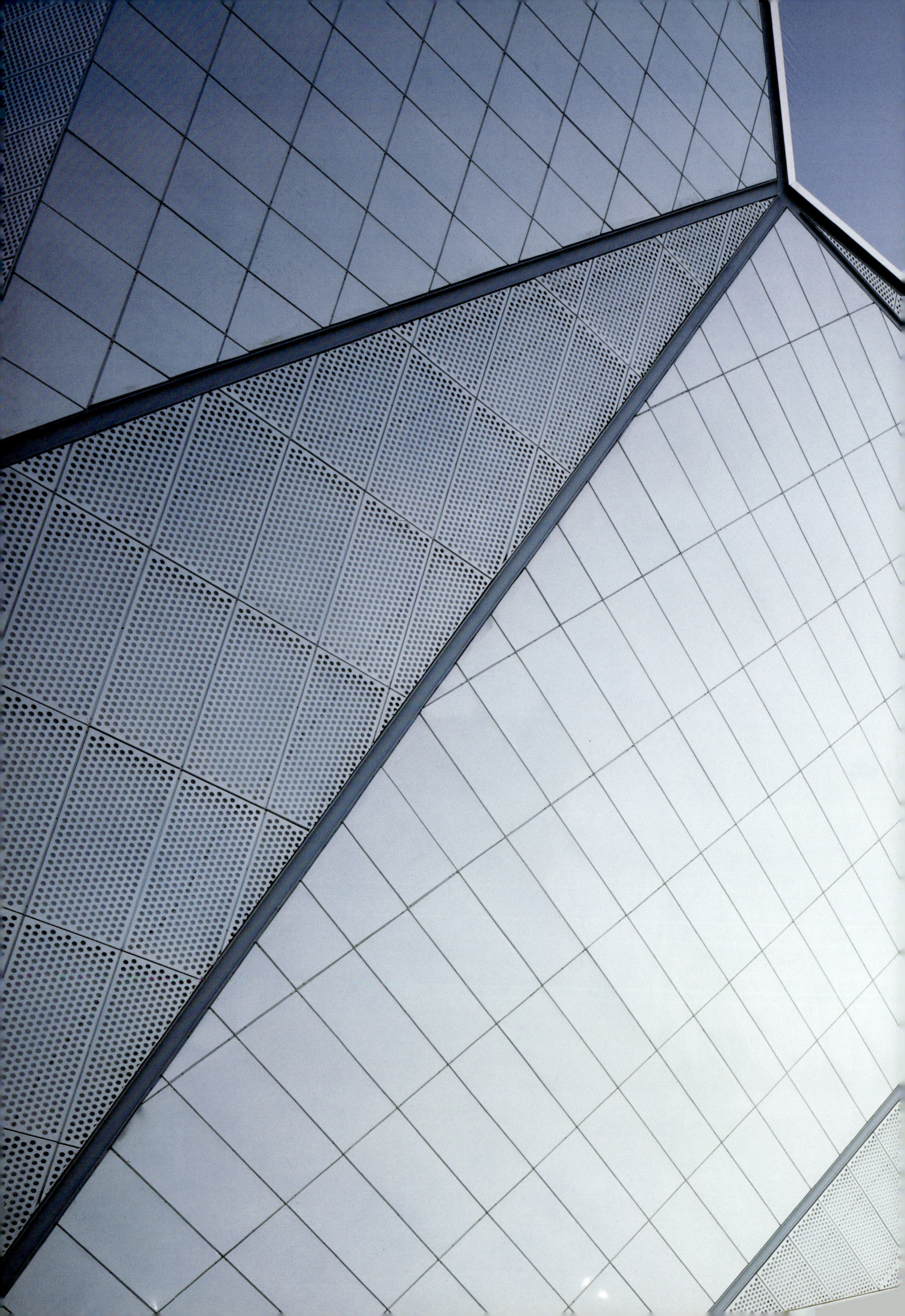

GALLERY 305
contemporary

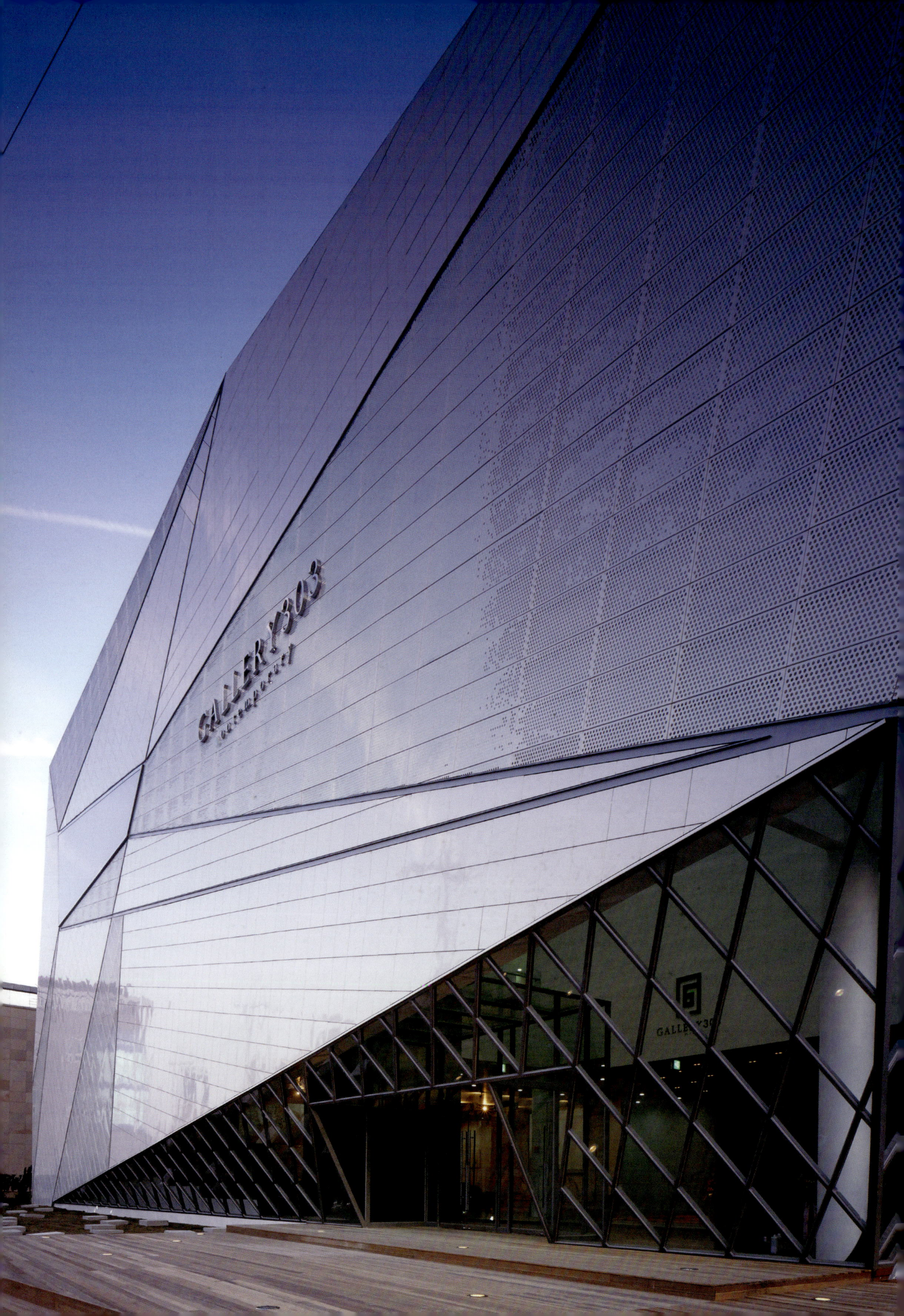
GALLERY303
GALLERY303

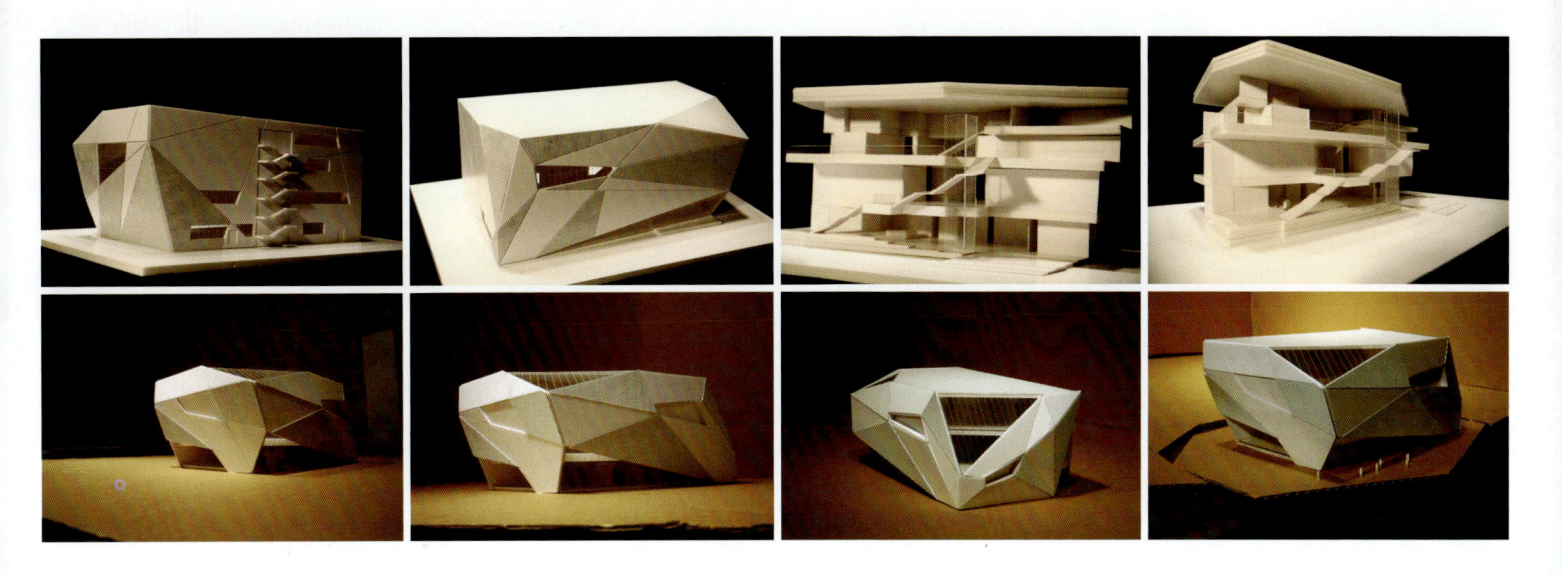

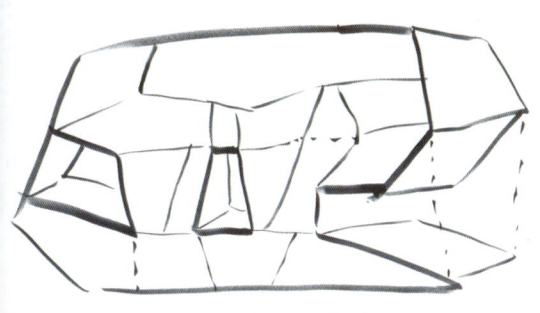

CRYSTAL SCULPTURE

Gallery 303 is the only apartment complex reflecting a global life style incorporating business, cuture, and art located in Gwang-Ju.
We designed the model house like a gallery to catch people's fancy using a of a simple white material. The gallery atmosphere is also evident in the interior materials of the base panel and stainless steel.
Compared to existing model houses, Gallery 303 proposes a new shape as a urban sculpture something like a city's jewel.
The Gwang-ju model house provides information about the new type of model house that breaks from preconceived notions of temporary buildings that perfectly align the interior and exterior.
Based on the plan of the exhibition space, performance space, and restaurant, this complex offers a real Community space for the residents.
The Interiors form long and tall unit spaces using natural three dimensions. The stairs connect different spaces to forme of a gallery. Using light iris, the lighting display provides a meaningful experience for the visitor.
Changing the image of the sculpture to different points of view make it seem alive. We want the white crystal to impact the city. The general idea of a crystal sculpture is to make it differentiate itself from others by cutting the mass. On the pure white, the matching red is reminiscent of Kumho's corporate identification in a natural way. The use of natural wood and a gray base panel in the interior provide special features for the minimal gallery space.
To secure efficient space, simple materials and methods of construction were specially chosen. This also lowered the per unit price for construction. The plans call for selecting materials that promote easy construction and tear down as well as recycled materials.

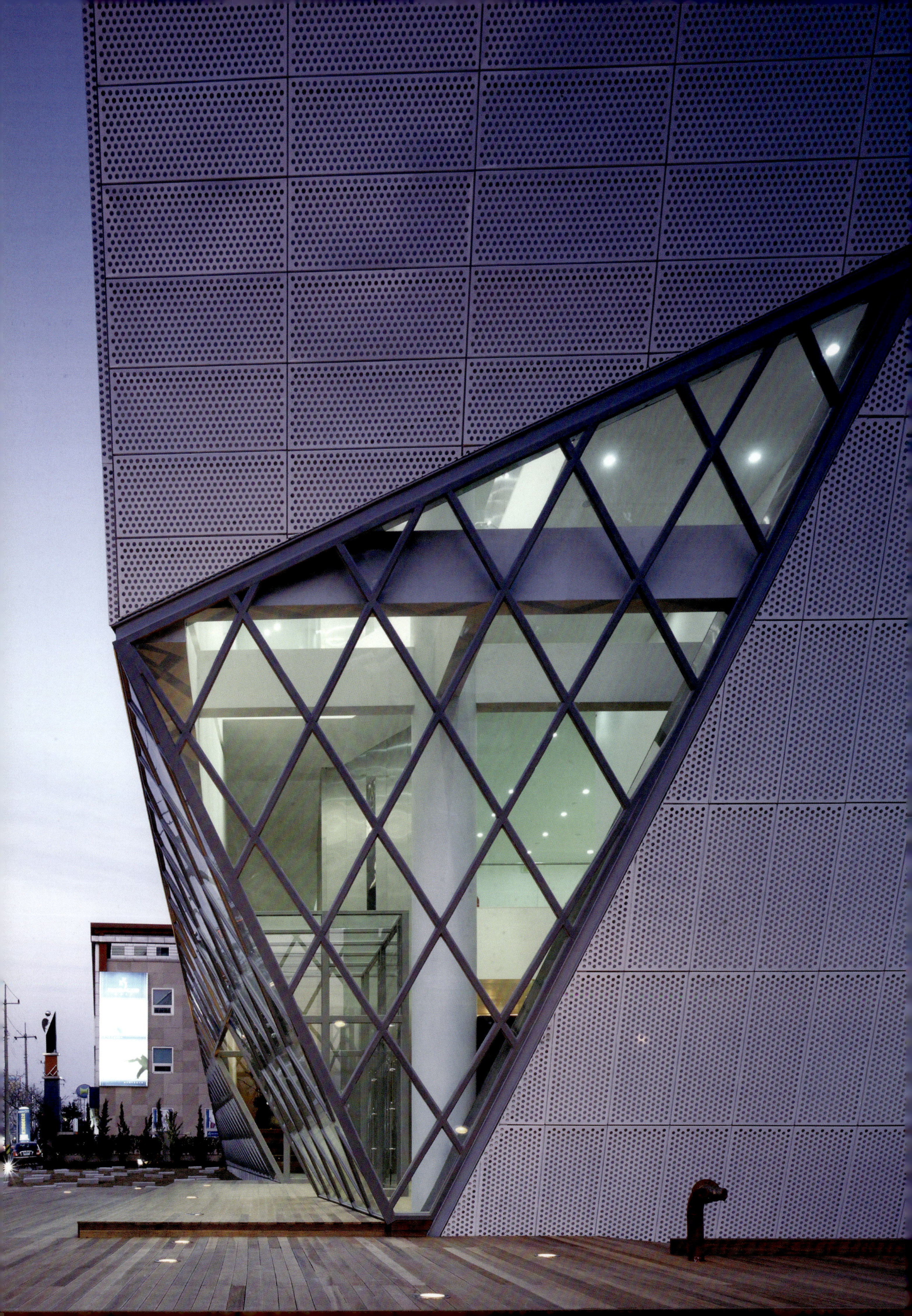

COMPOUND BODY 303

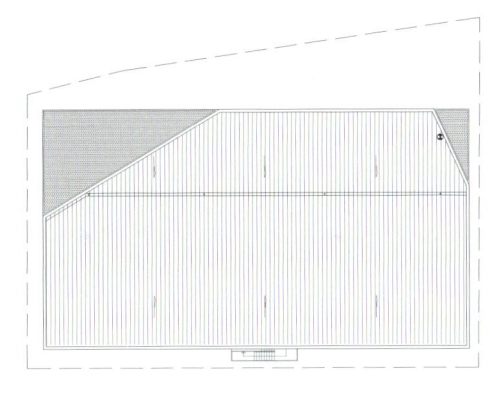

ROOF PLAN

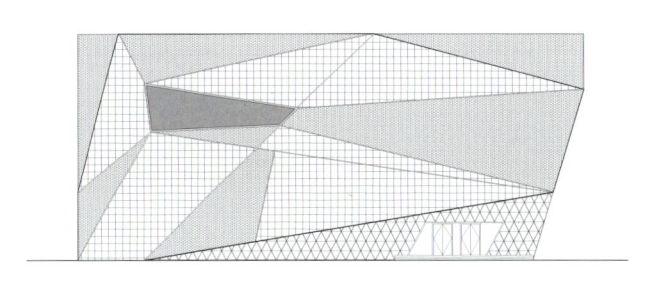

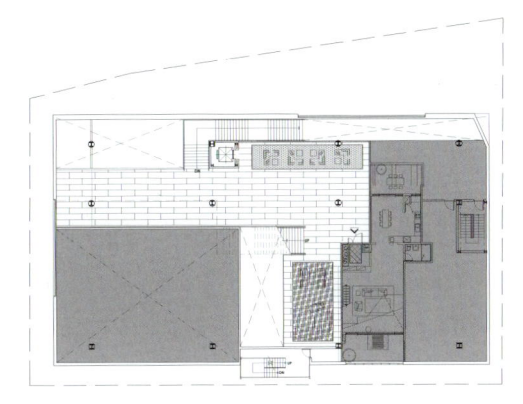

3RD FLOOR PLAN

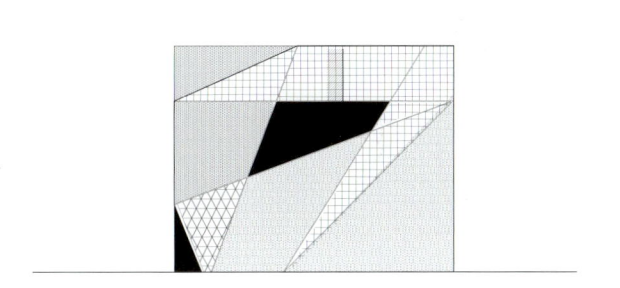

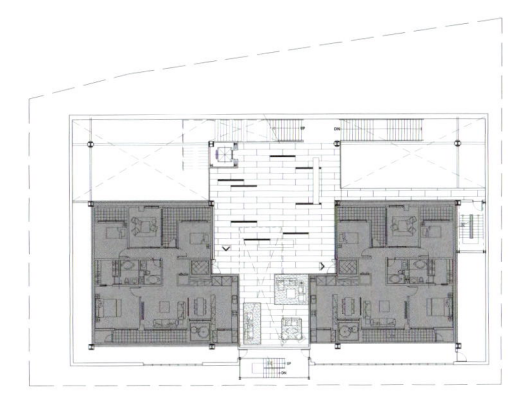

2ND FLOOR PLAN

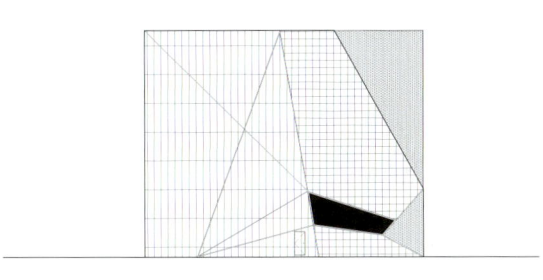

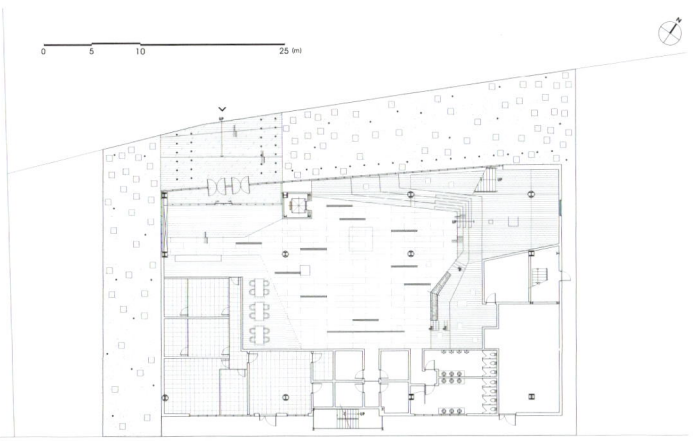

GROUND FLOOR PLAN

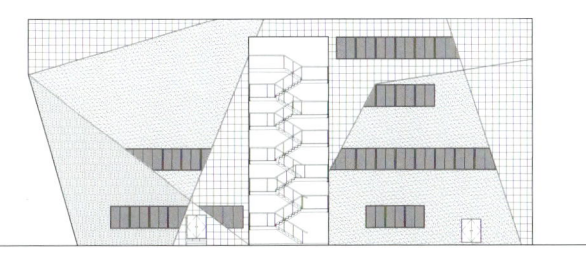

ELEVATION

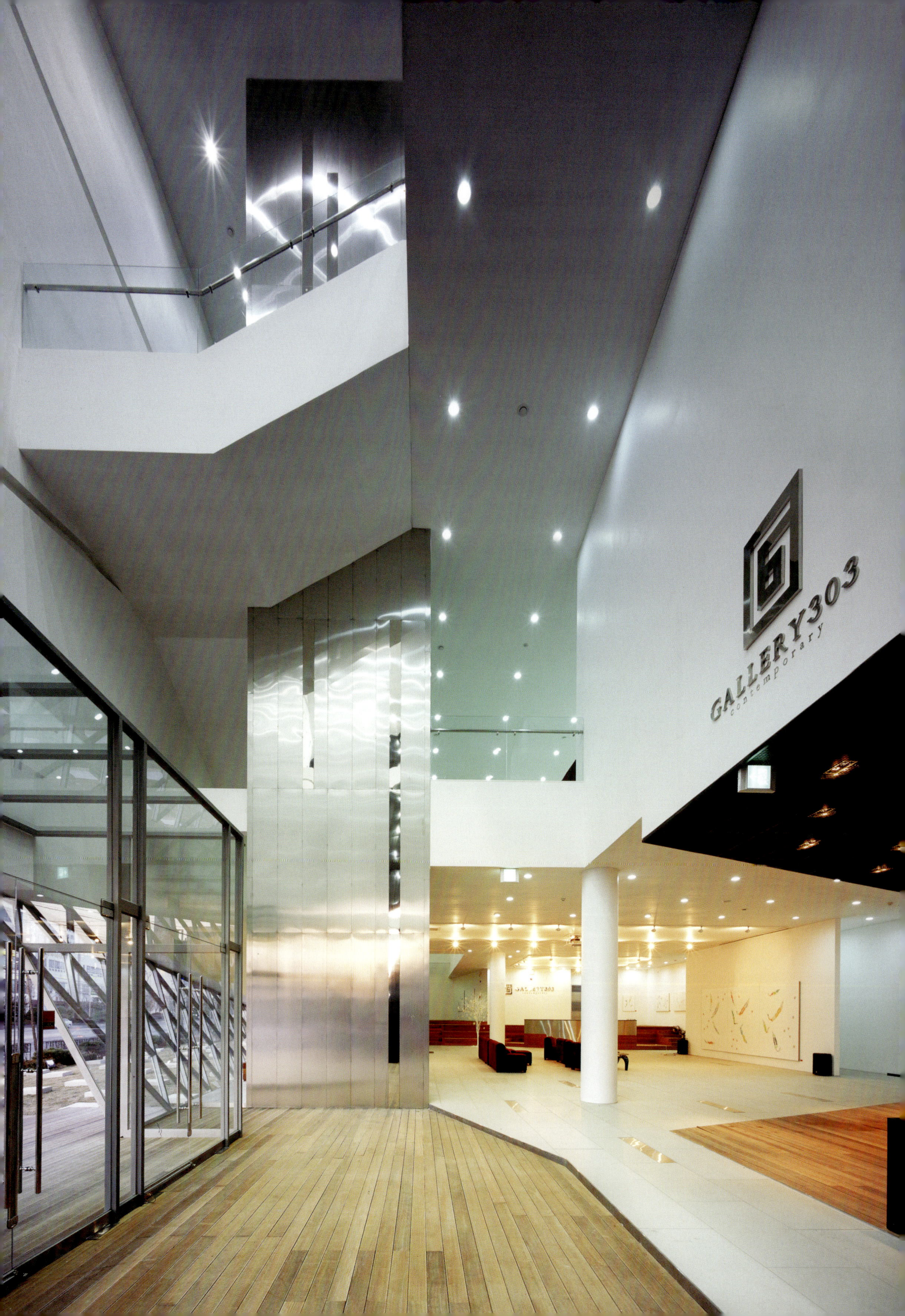
GALLERY303
contemporary

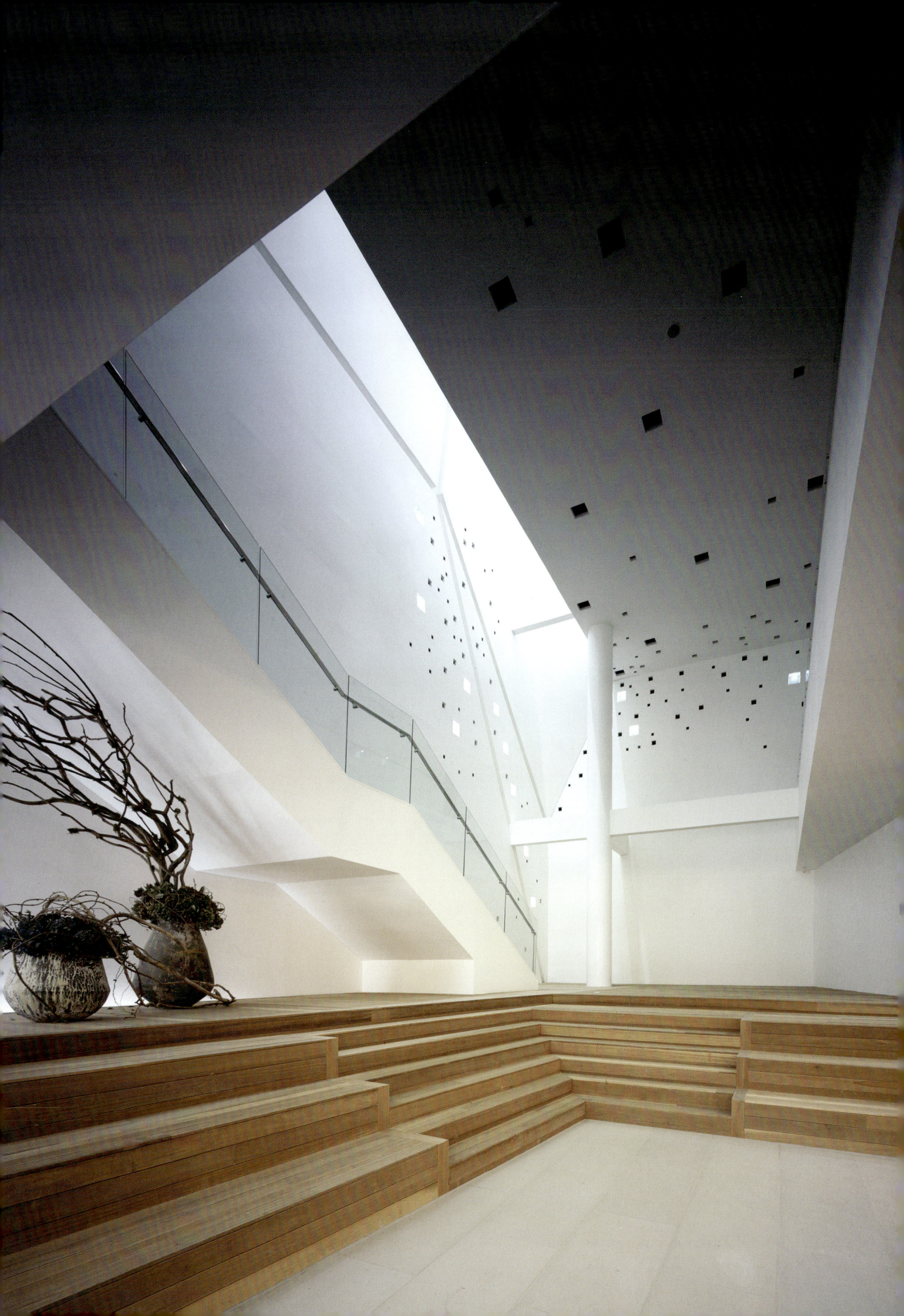

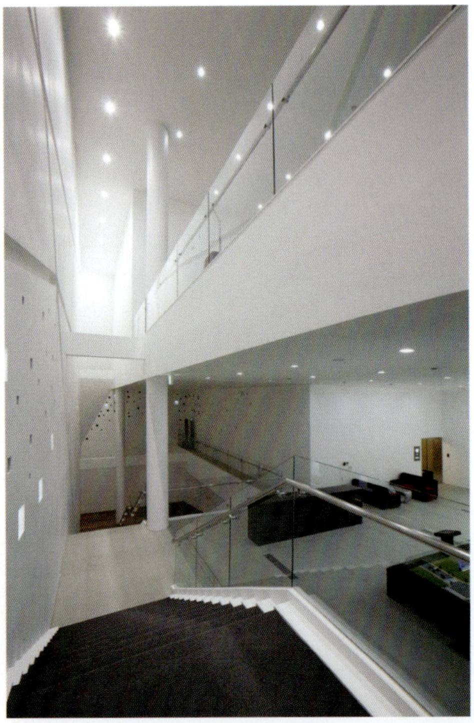

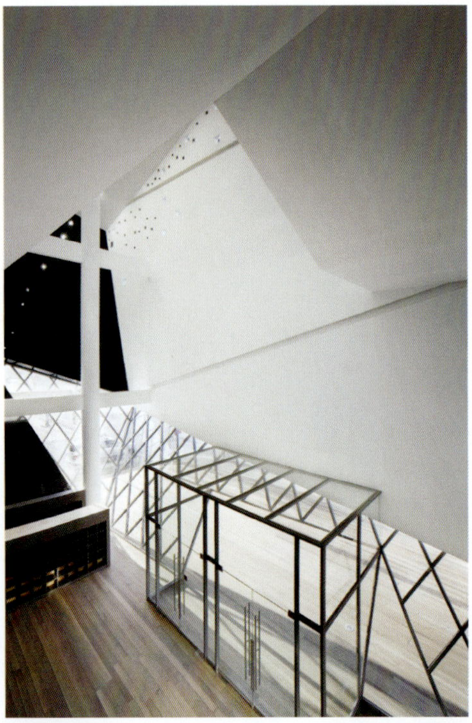

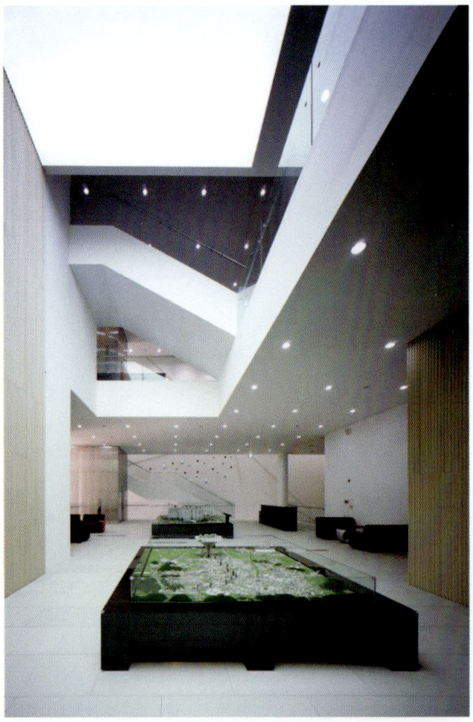

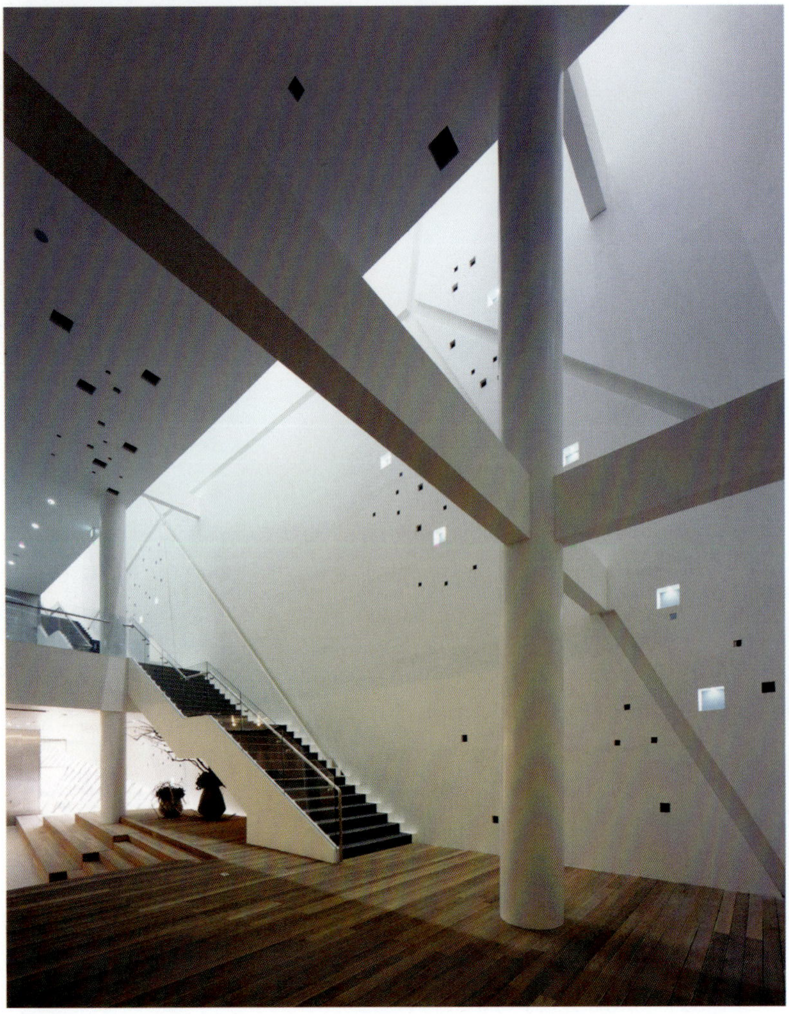

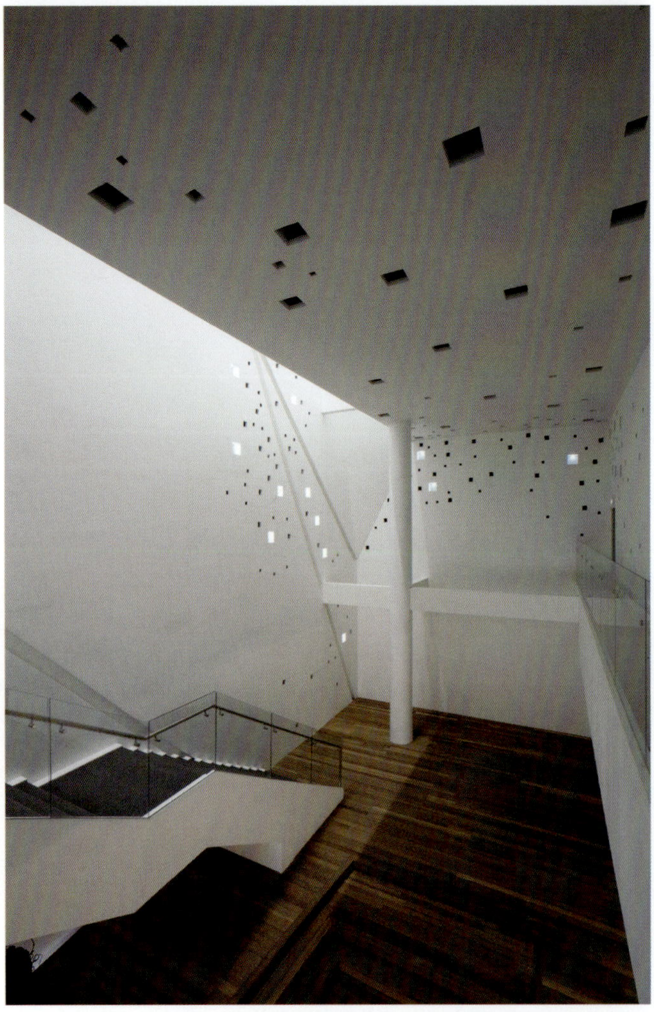

Project Name
Gallery 303 (Gumho Culture of Housing Gallery)
Architects
Jang Yoon Gyoo, Shin Chang Hoon, Kim Sung Min
Project Team
Kim Se Jin, Kim Min Tae, Kang Seung Hyun
Client
AMJ Developmnet, Lim Kwang Taek
Location
167-8, 167-69, 167-73, 167-72, Su-gu, Mareuk-dong, GwangJu
Use
Temporary Building
Site Area 1,493.00m²
Building Area 1,152.09m²
Gross Floor Area 2,777.86m²
Building Coverage 32.98%
Gross Floor Ratio 79.52%
Building Scope 3F
Structure Steel Structure
Parking 75cars
Exterior Finishing
Punching metal + THK24 Duble Glazing +THK30 Stone (whIte color)

Gallery The Hill

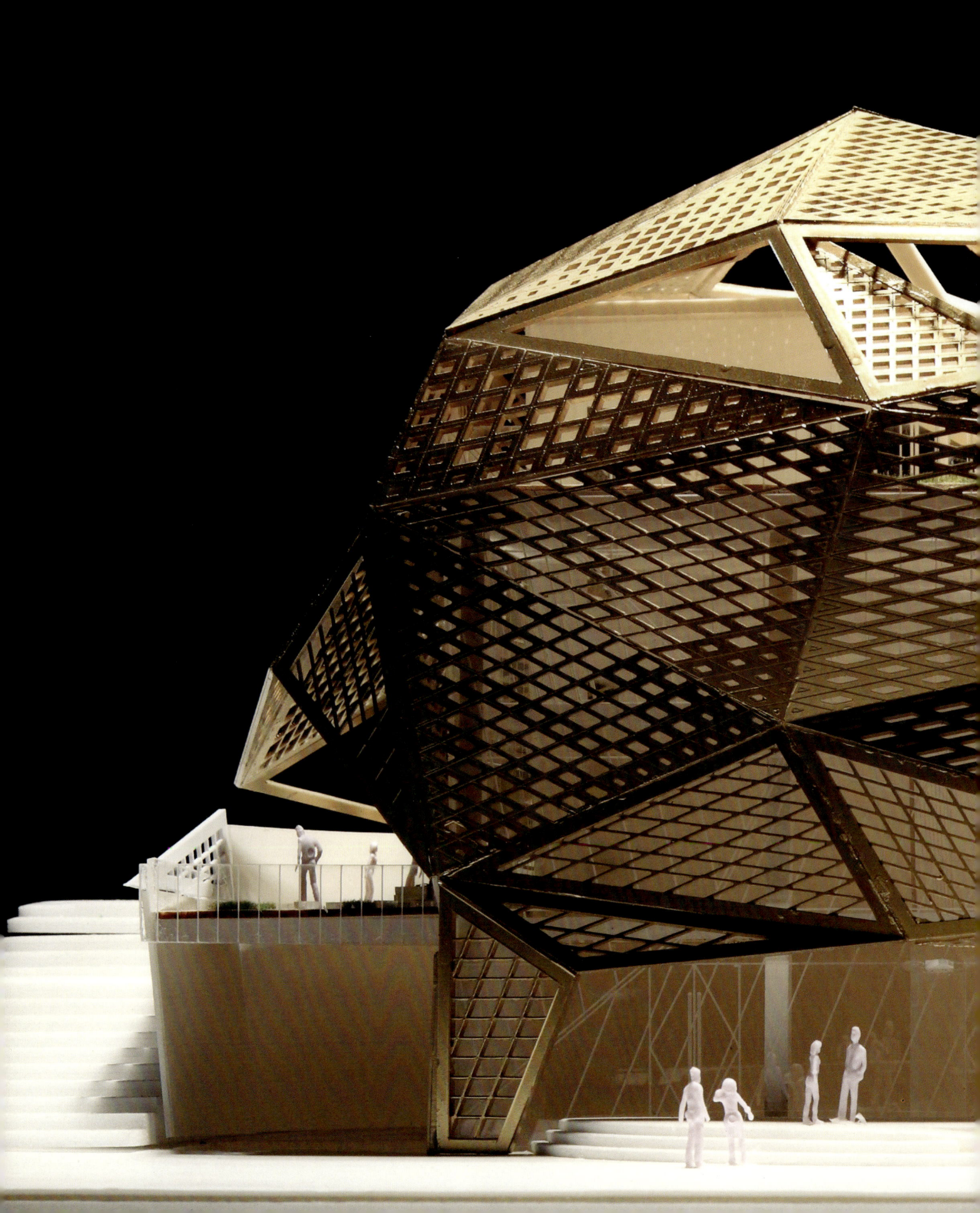

Crystal
mountain

Architects Jang Yoon Gyoo, Shin Chang Hoon, Kim Kyung Tae
Client Han's Jaram AMC Co. Ltd
Photographer Kim Jae Kyung

COMPOUND BODY 309

SKIN DETAIL PLAN

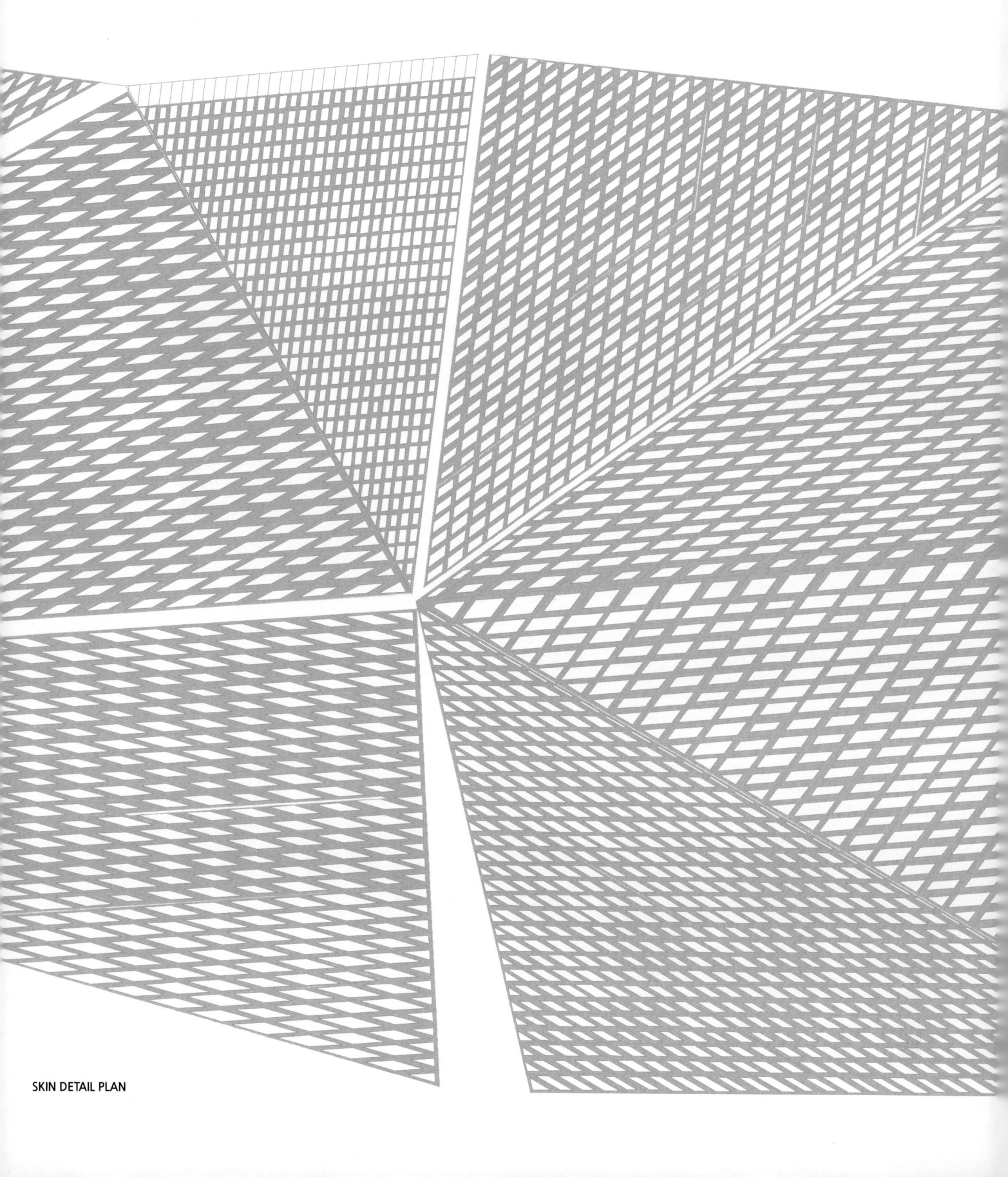

CRYSTAL MOUNTAIN

We suggest The Hill Gallery, a community facility in the housing district at Hannam-dong, by replacing the neighborhood facility to the topography. The neighborhood facility is considered a subordinate architecture which doesn't care much about its design. Our aim is to restore the role of this subordinate building as the local community program.

In the process of composing a large scale housing block, severance of nature which happened as a result of topographic destruction is reverted using a new topographic map. It acts like an artificial mountain connecting nature and the urban. The shape of the site is converted to an abstract skin consisted of a triangular pattern. It becomes the landscape and a land mark as a light mountain.
The frame of the site rising along the slope accommodates festivals and events.

A half transparent skin is suggested which changes according to the change of the inner programs and the functions. Leaning skin and the outdoor frame consist of the dynamic lighting mountain. The landscape, locating partial void including an eco deck, is a green space in the artificial mountain. It also plays a role of a gate and a link between the city and housing. As an urban connection approaching the city, it provides cultural space for example, a cultural vision deck, recording the memory of Hannam housing and being the observatory for the community.

The artificial skin system holding various architectural programs holds an environmental system which acts differently with various architectural functions and program change. The artificial mountain adopts many eco friendly systems. The light condition is managed by the double skinned roof, and the void on the roof for the natural wind path helps air conditioning. The alternative energy is collected by solar louver, and rain drops are saved for the water space. The landscape system uses the outdoor deck and the retail gallery accommodates various events. The eco roof provides resting and events and the void space with the stage, the forest and the garden provide an eco friendly environment to the residences.

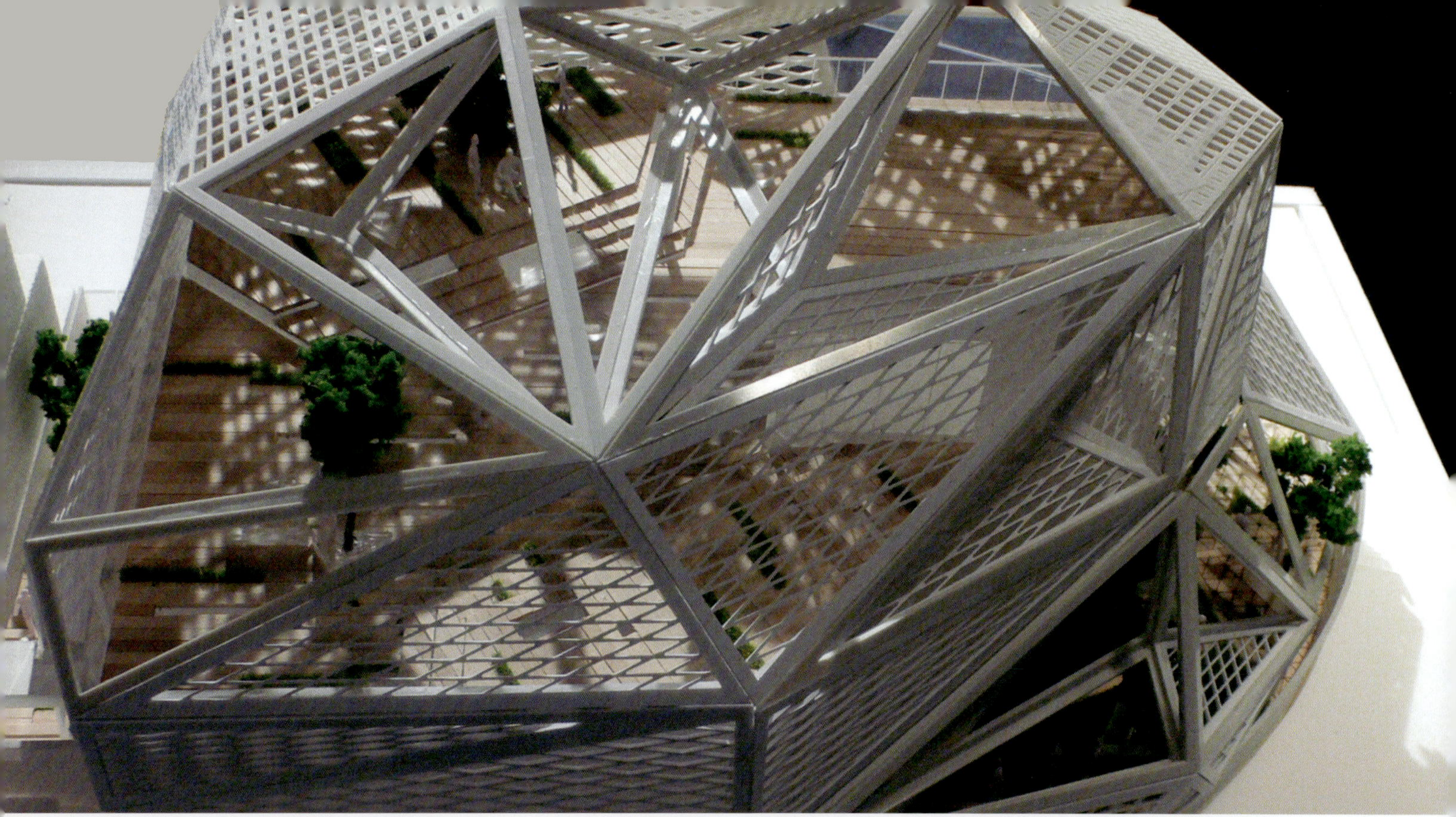
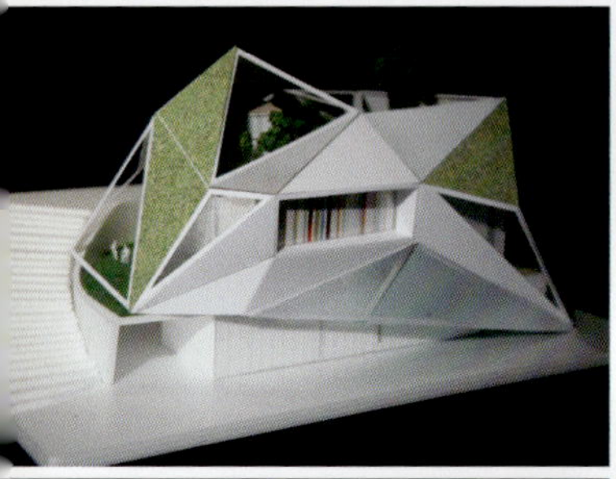
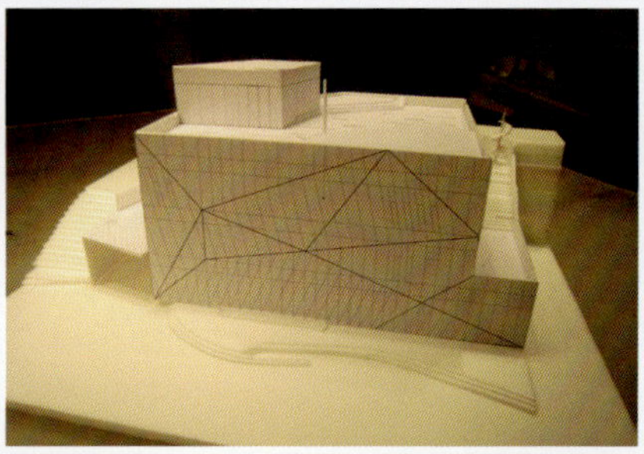
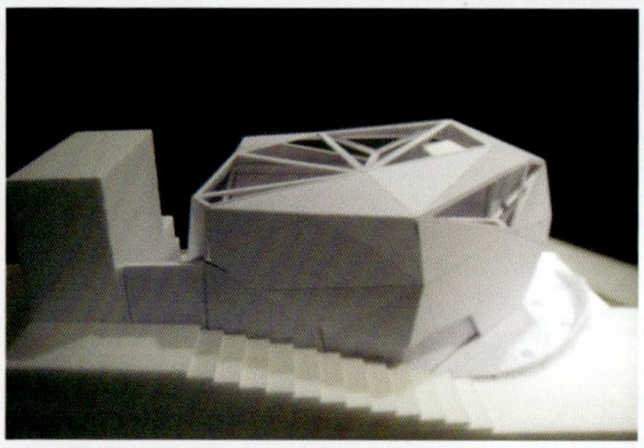
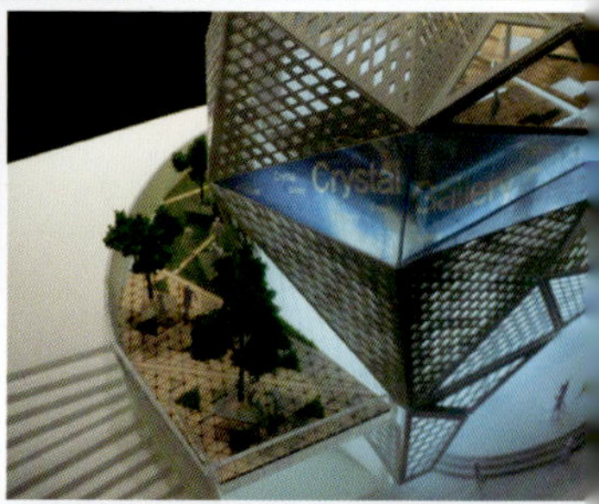
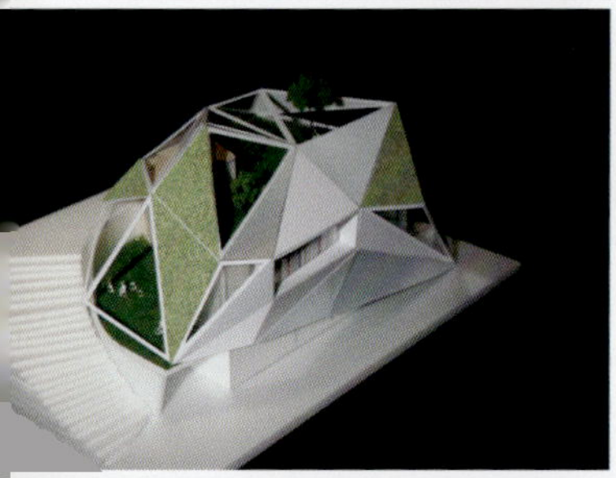
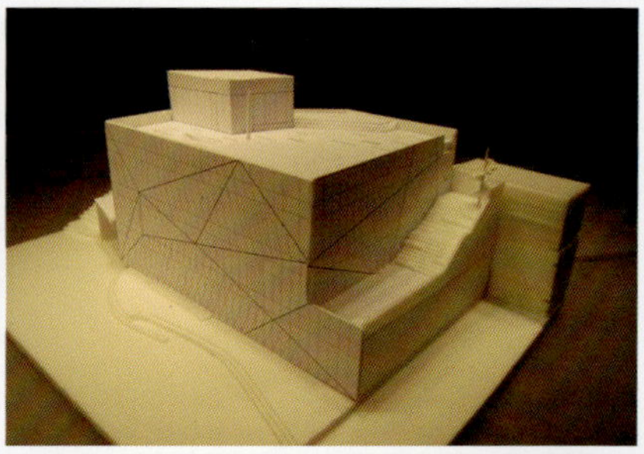
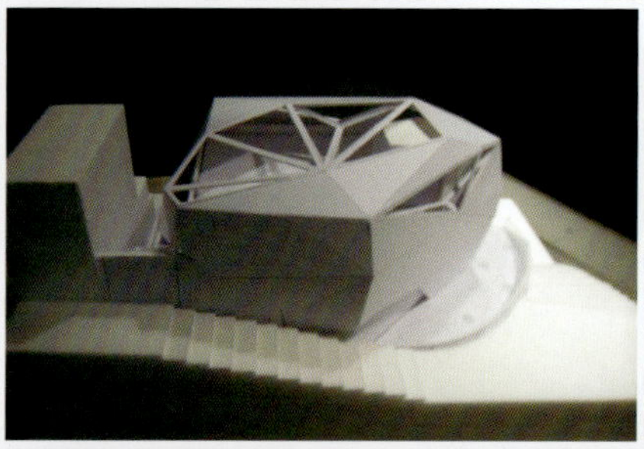
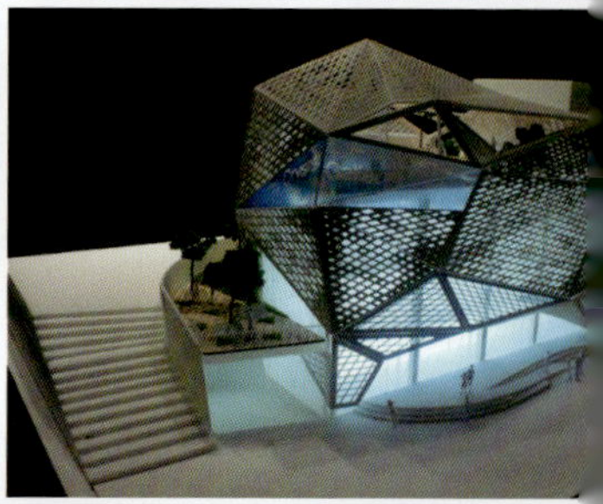
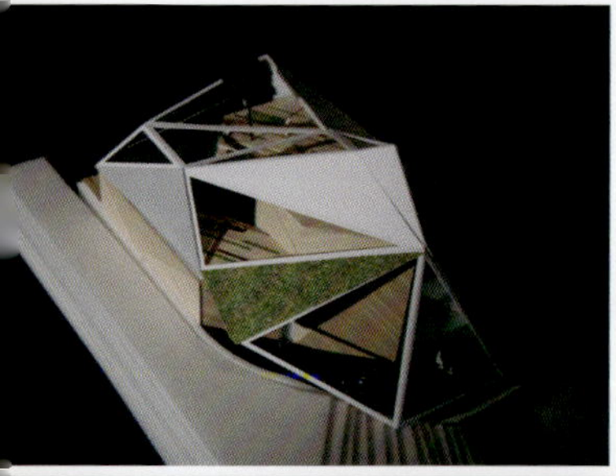
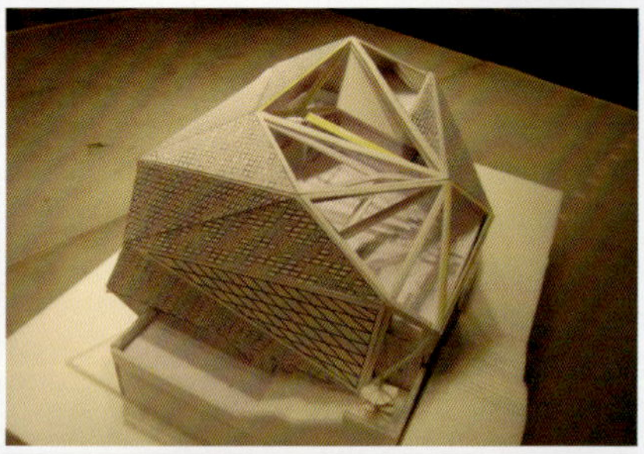
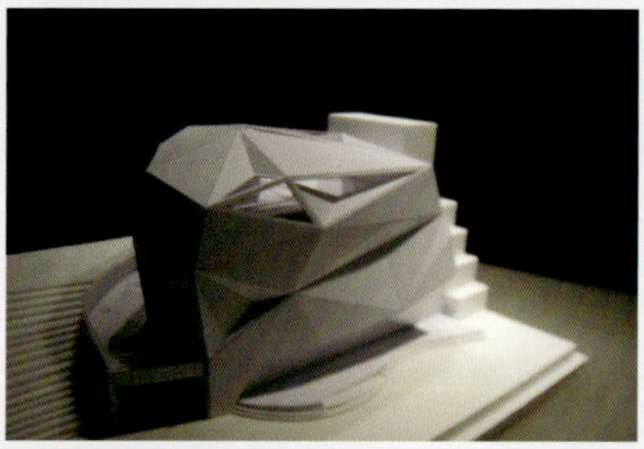
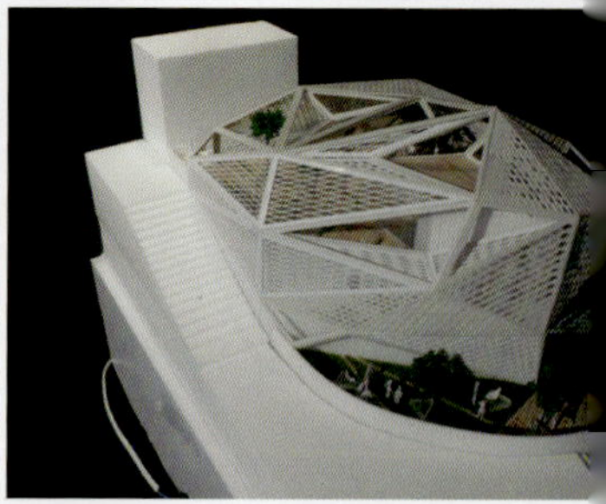
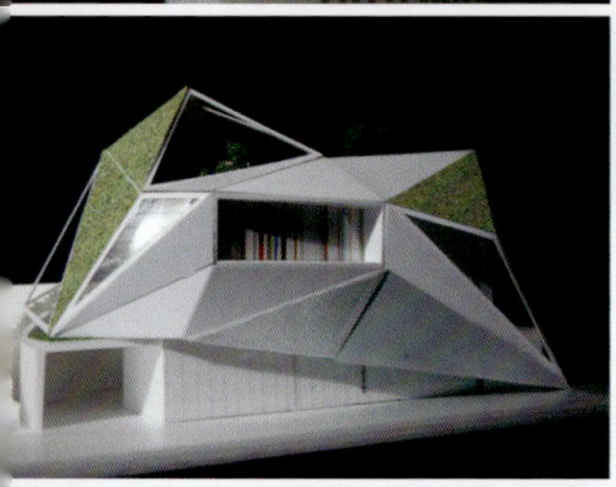
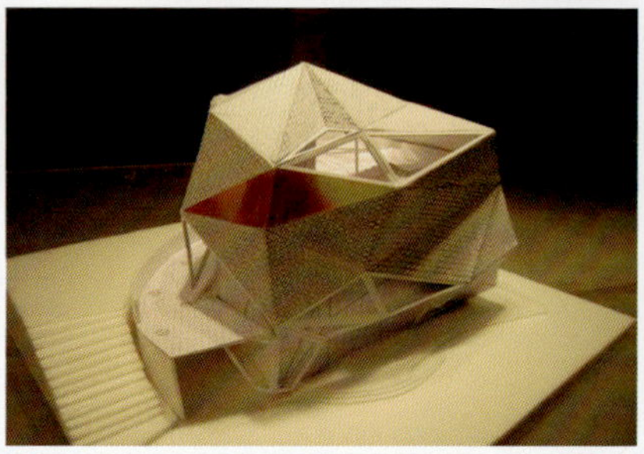
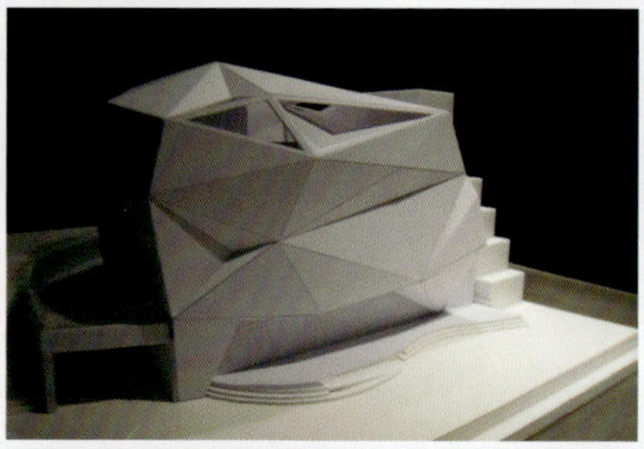
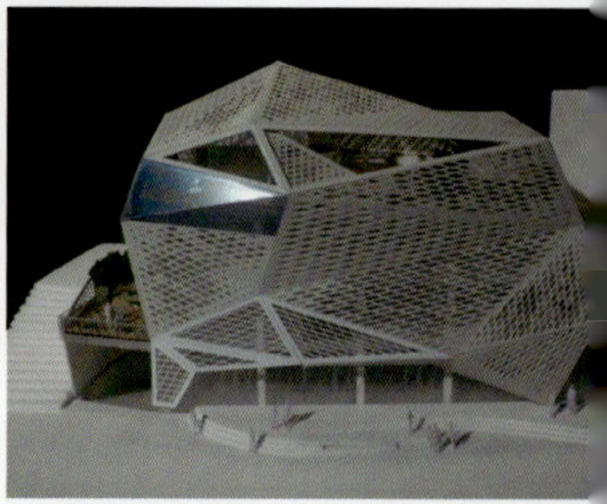
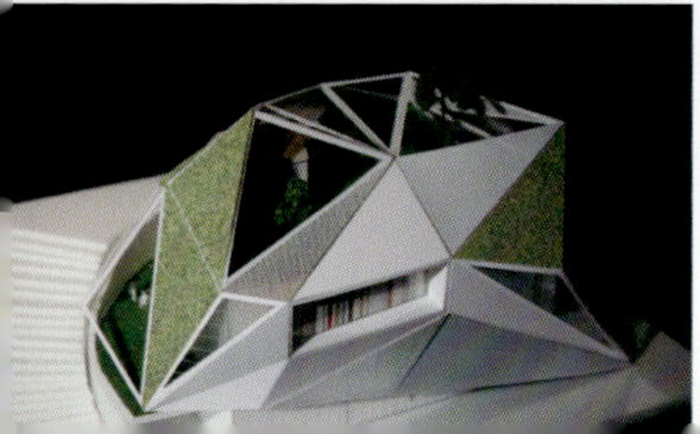
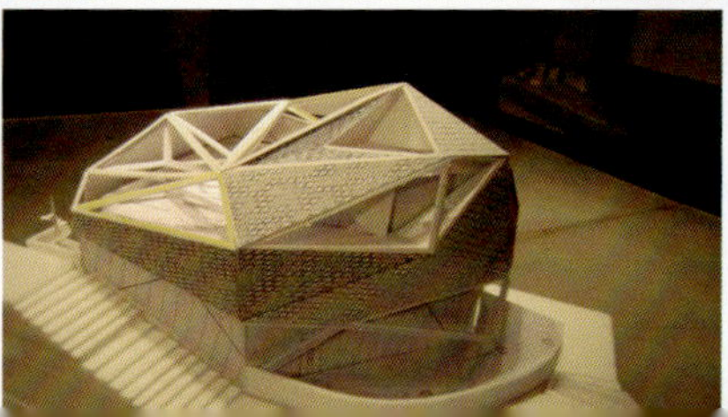
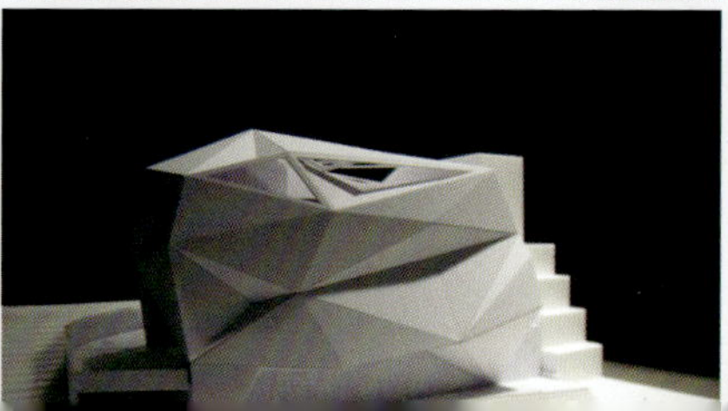
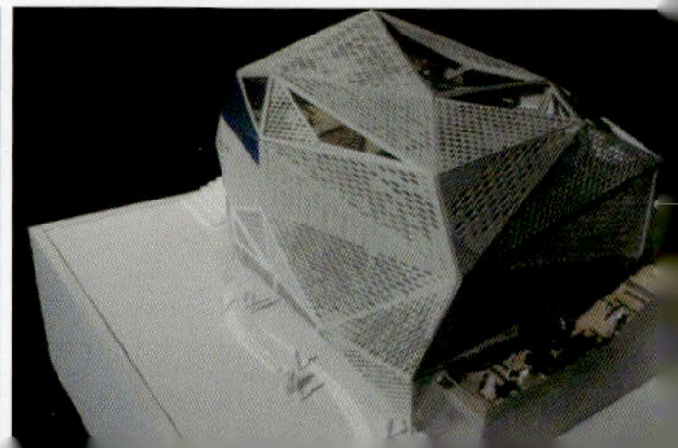

SKIN DETAIL

- Punch Panel
- ATP' Panel
- A
- B
- Stainless Mesh

지정판넬타공
T-FRAME STL
HEAVY COATING

ST'S T13X30

STL 자물쇠 D:25 고정

T-FRAME STL
HEAVY COATING

T-FRAME STL

PUNCH PANEL DETAIL

MODULE DIM.   MODULE DIM.

Panel
chemical adhisive
Fill glue seal

84 59
    25

84X65 STL T-FRAME/HEAVY COATING

ST'S MESH DETAIL

ST'S T13X30
STL 자물쇠 D:25 고정
판1관 판2는 용접
판2와 AL바는 볼트조임

DOUBLE SKIN DETAIL

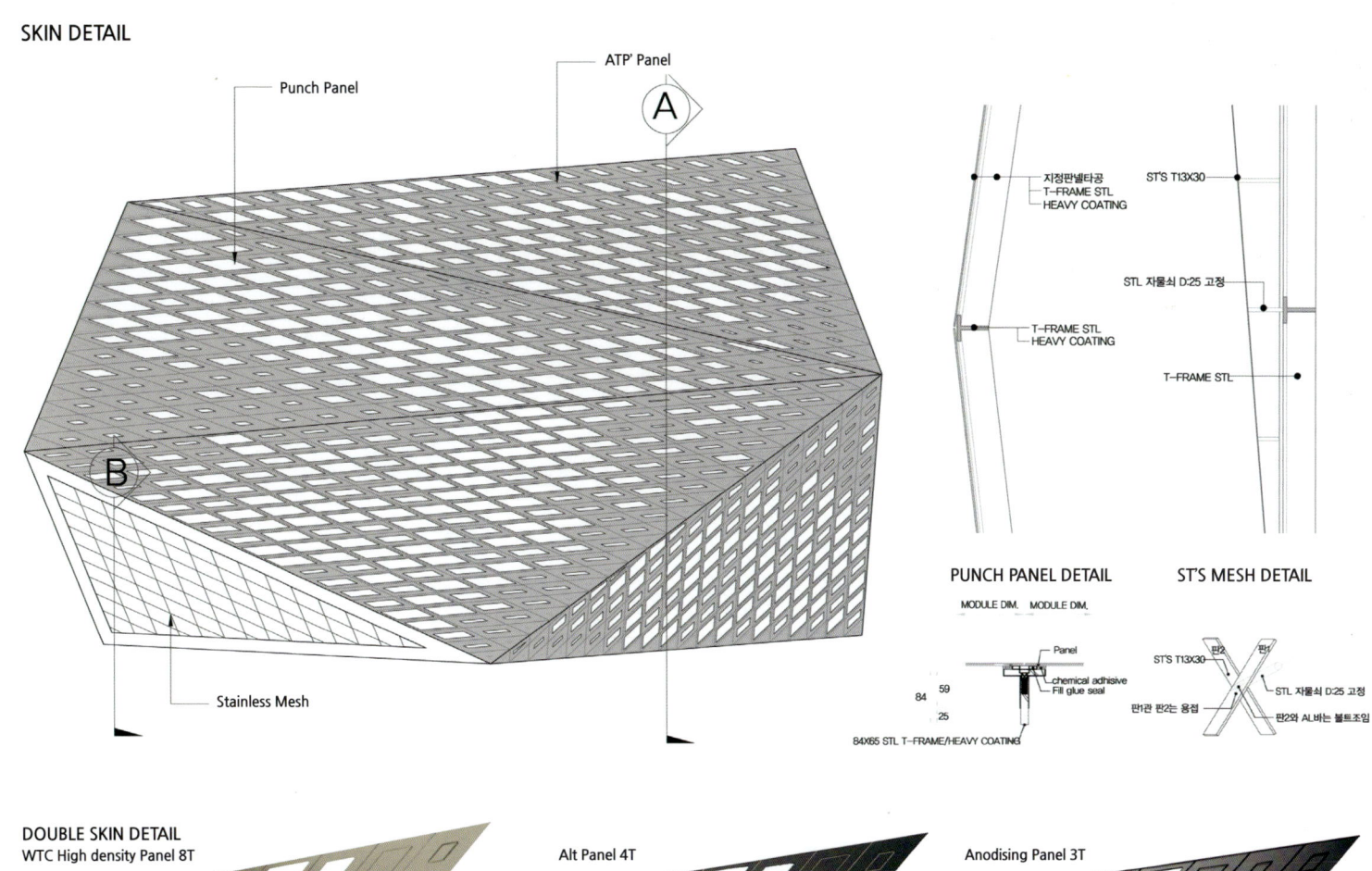

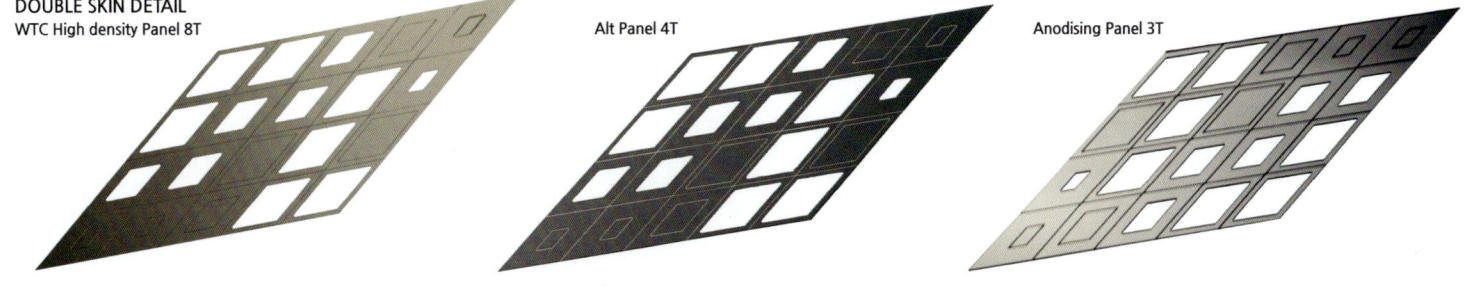

WTC High density Panel 8T | Alt Panel 4T | Anodising Panel 3T

// The shape of the site is converted to an abstract skin consisted of a triangular pattern. It becomes the landscape and a land mark as a light mountain.

COMMUNITY PROGRAM

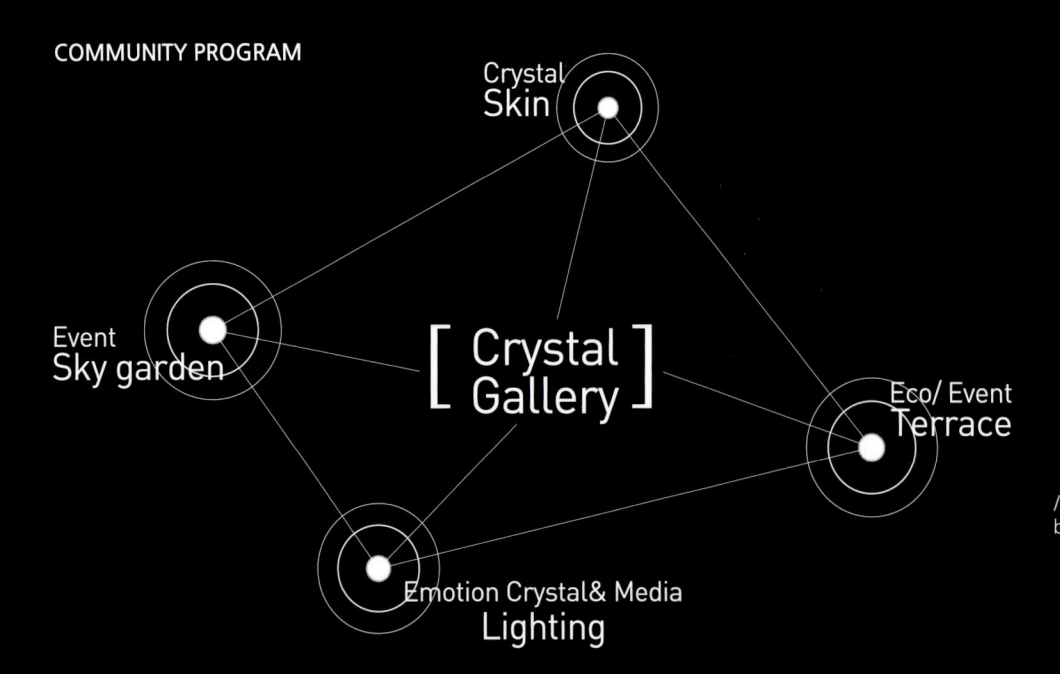

Crystal **Skin**

Event **Sky garden**

[Crystal **Gallery**]

Eco/ Event **Terrace**

Emotion Crystal & Media **Lighting**

// Our aim is to restore the role of this subordinate building as the local community program.

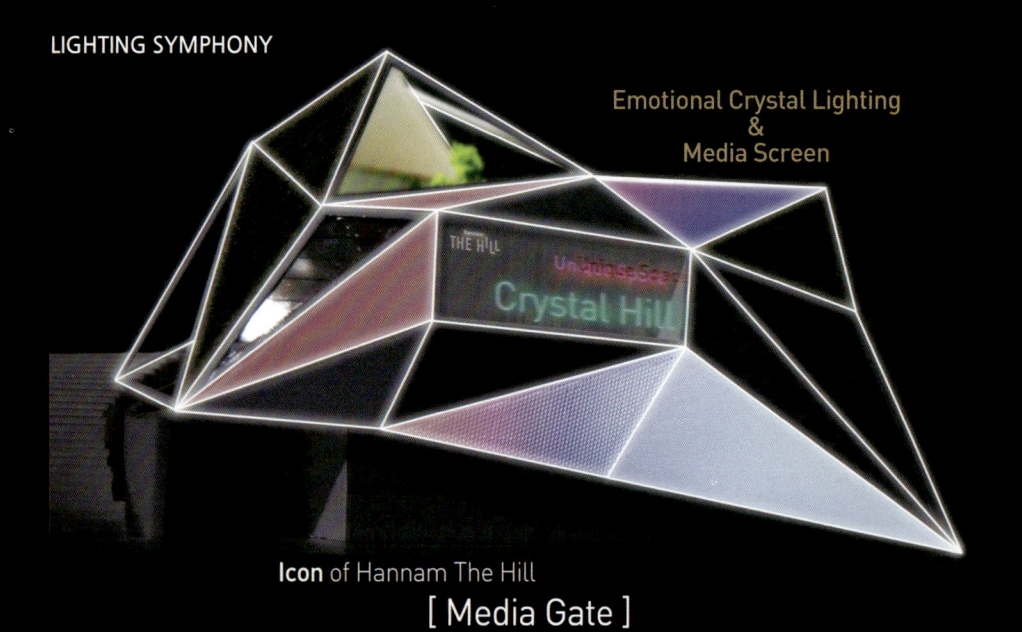

LIGHTING SYMPHONY

Emotional Crystal Lighting & Media Screen

// A half transparent skin is suggested which changes according to the change of the inner programs and the functions. Leaning skin and the outdoor frame consist of the dynamic lighting mountain

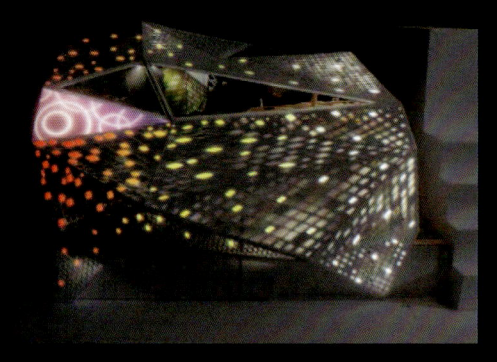

Icon of Hannam The Hill
[Media Gate]

Media Lighting

Crystal Lighting

Star Lighting

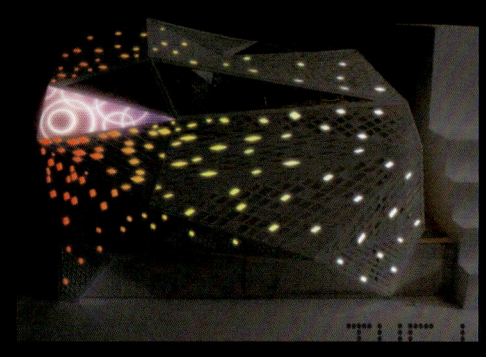

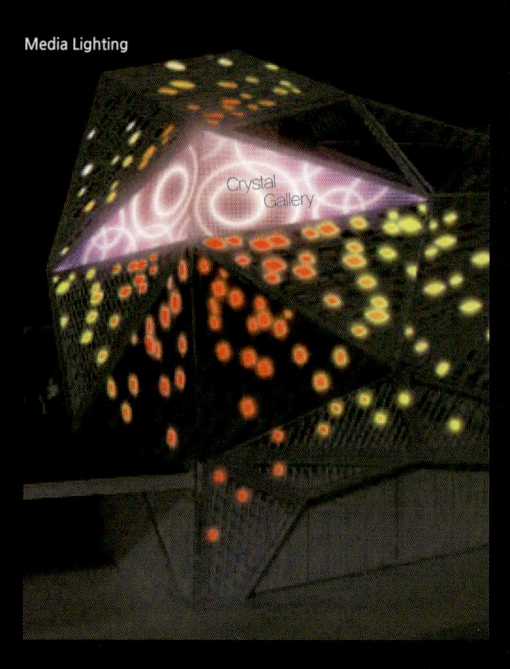

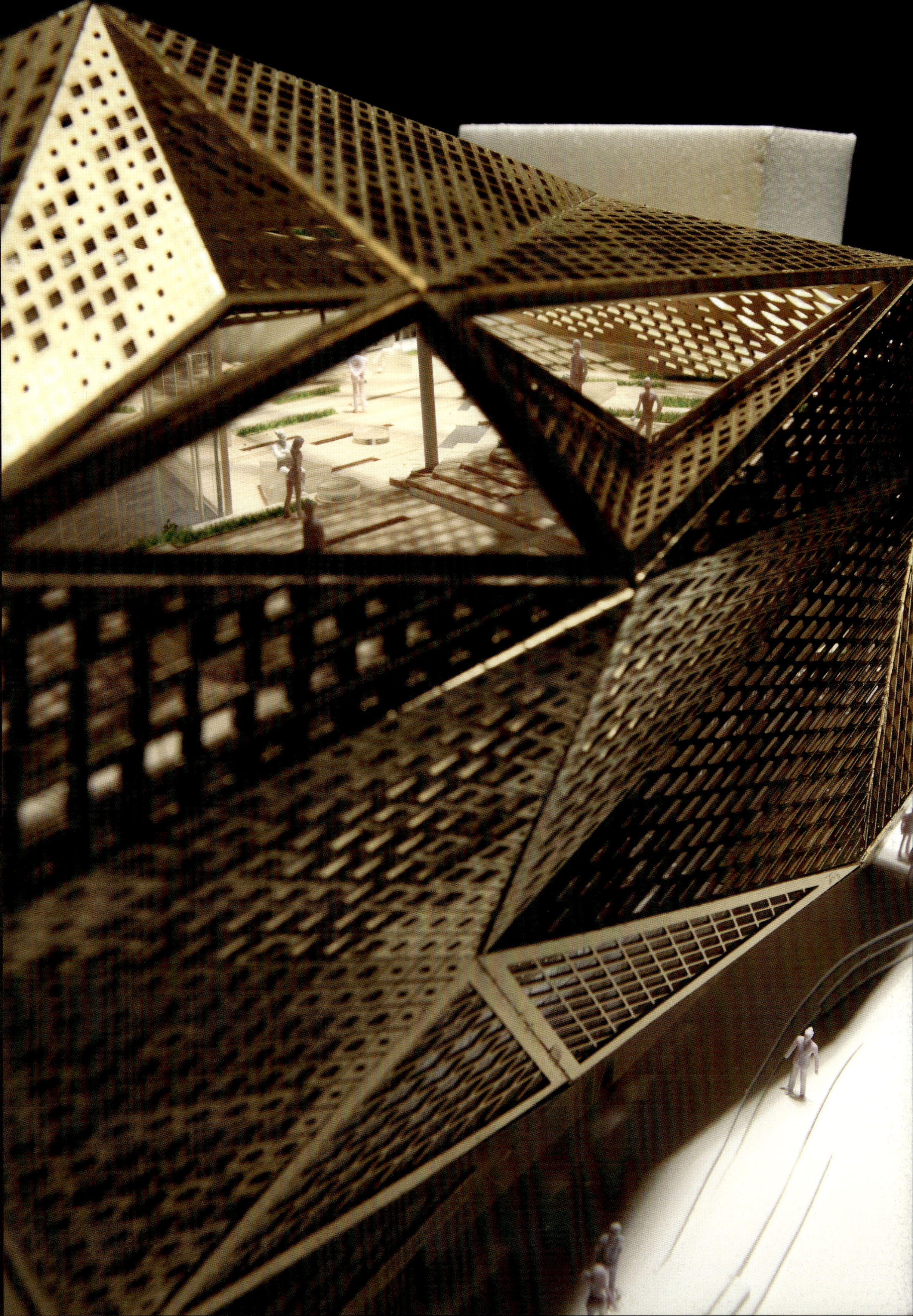

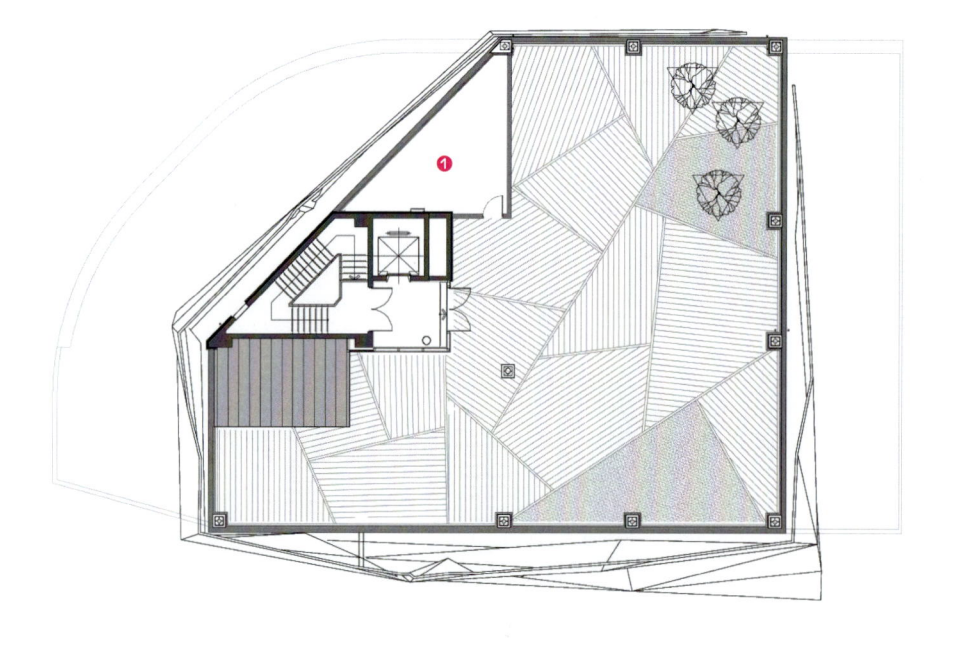

ROOF FLOOR PLAN
1. Office

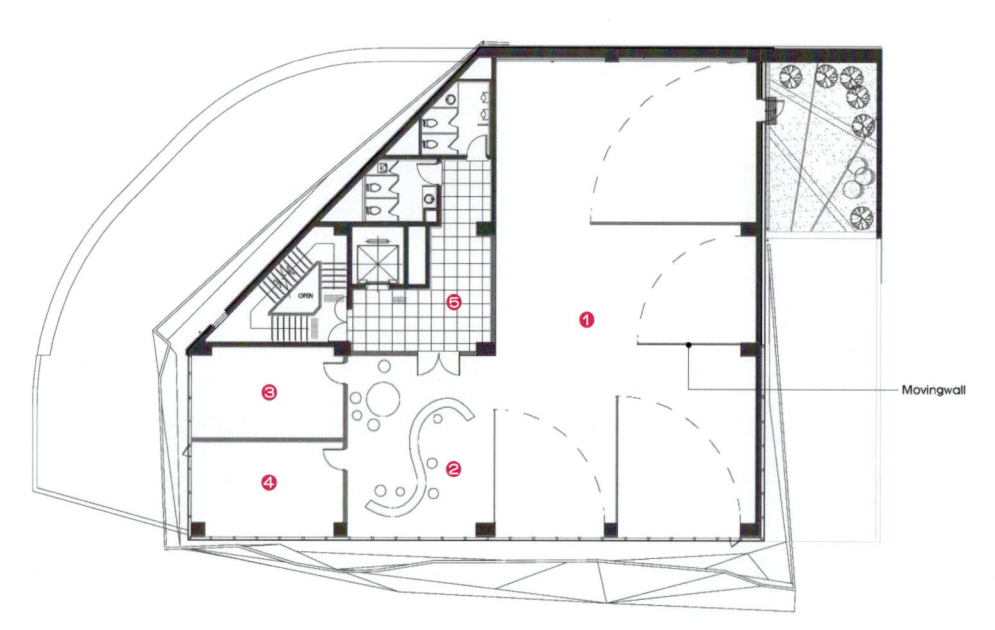

2ND FLOOR PLAN
1. Gallery
2. Gallery Lounge
3. Meeting Room
4. Office
5. Hall

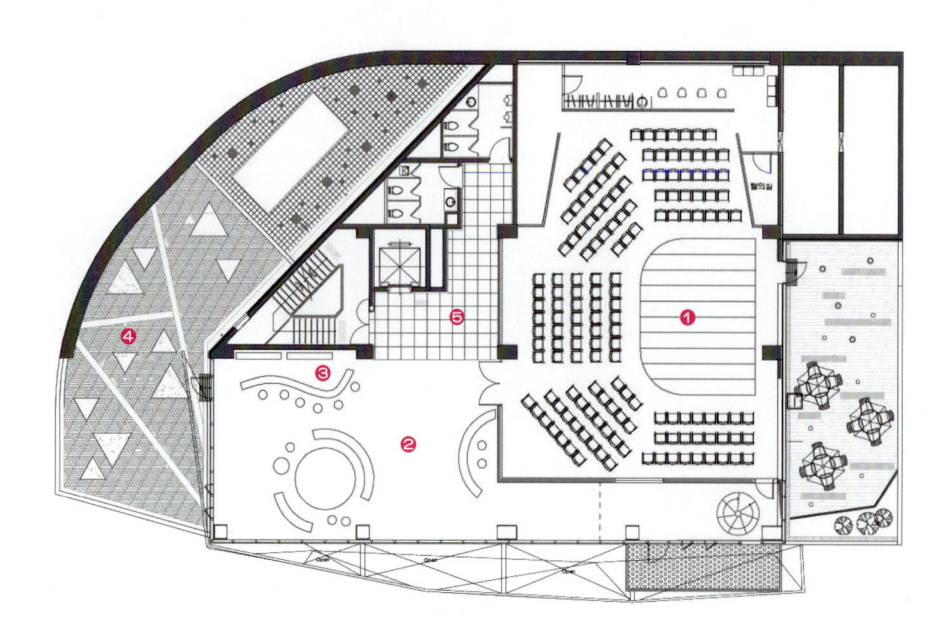

1ST FLOOR PLAN
1. Theater
2. Lounge
3. Cafeteria
4. Eco-Terrace
5. Hall

Roof Deck

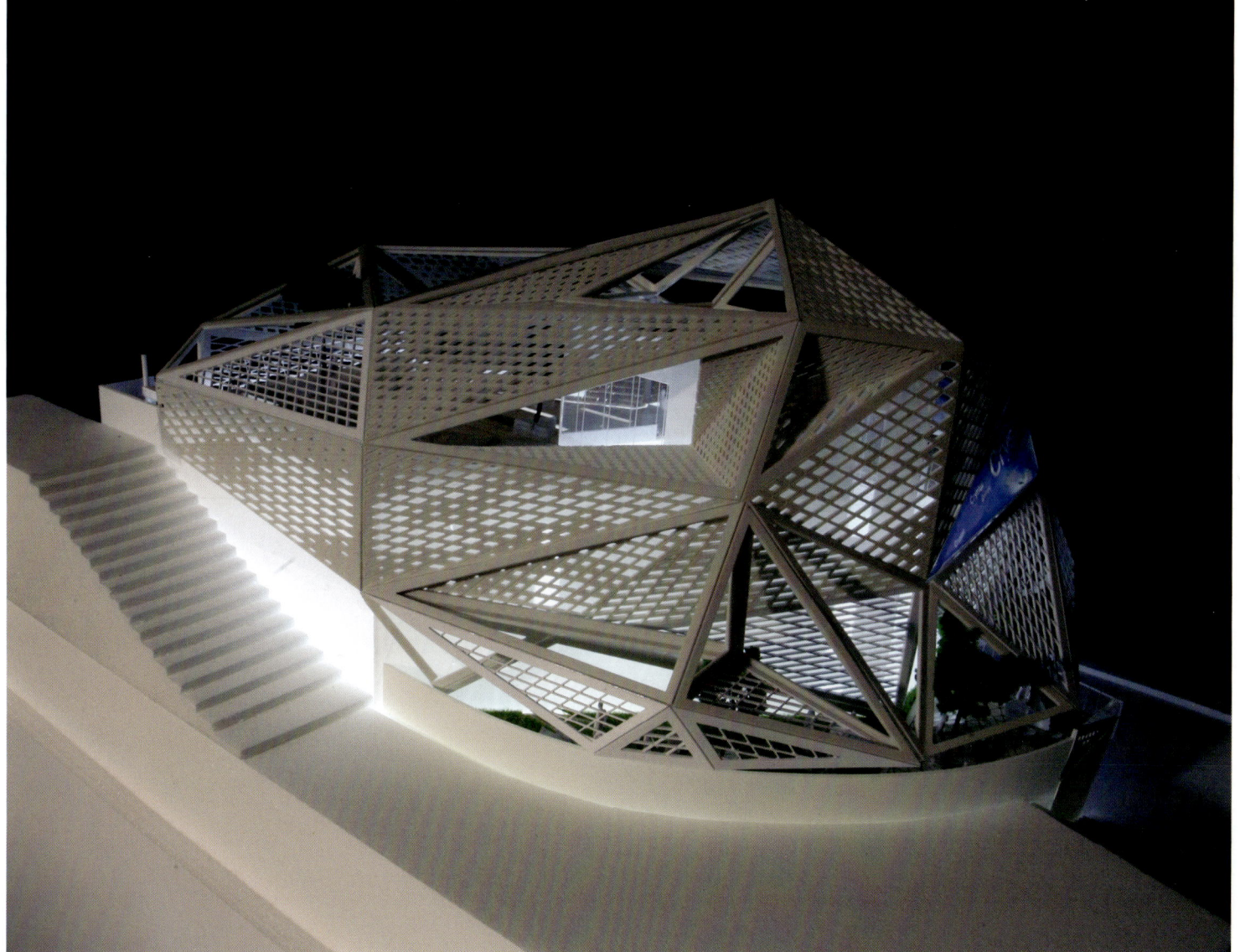

Main Hall

Gallery

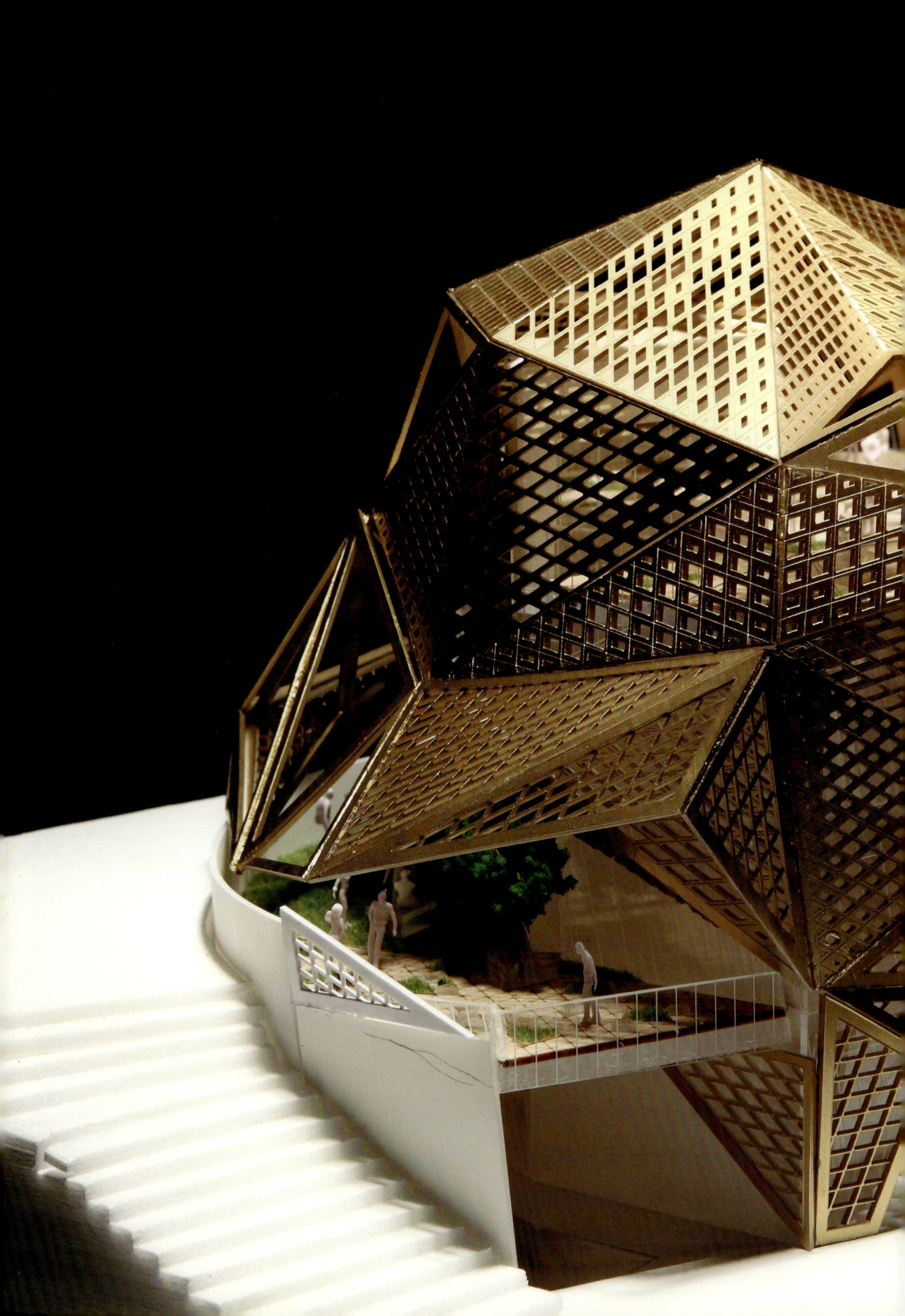

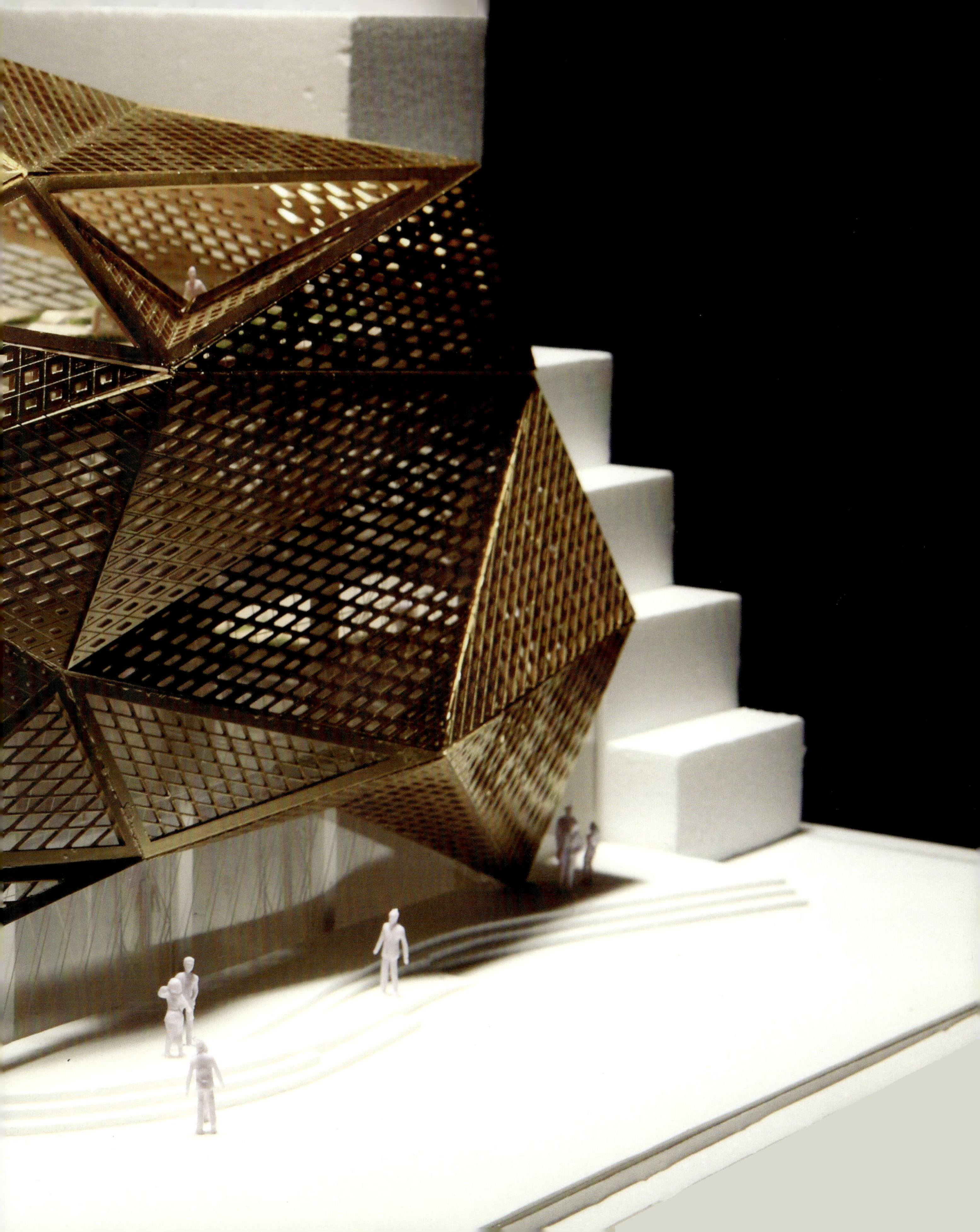

Sculpture
floating stone

Stacking Gallery in ChungJu

Architects Jang Yoon Gyoo, Shin Chang Hoon, Kim Sung Min
Client IDEA Development & Construction
Photographer Namgoong Sun

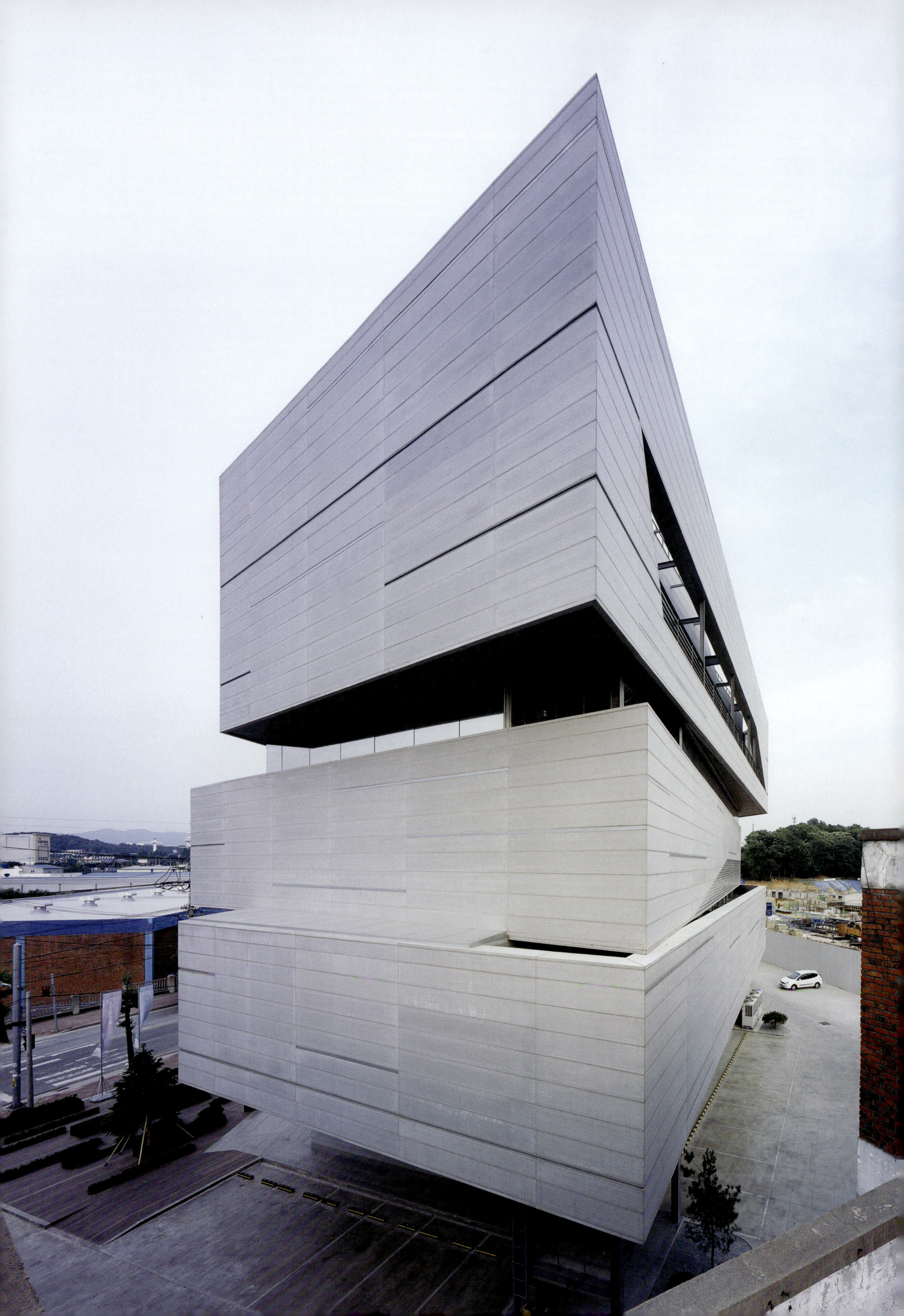

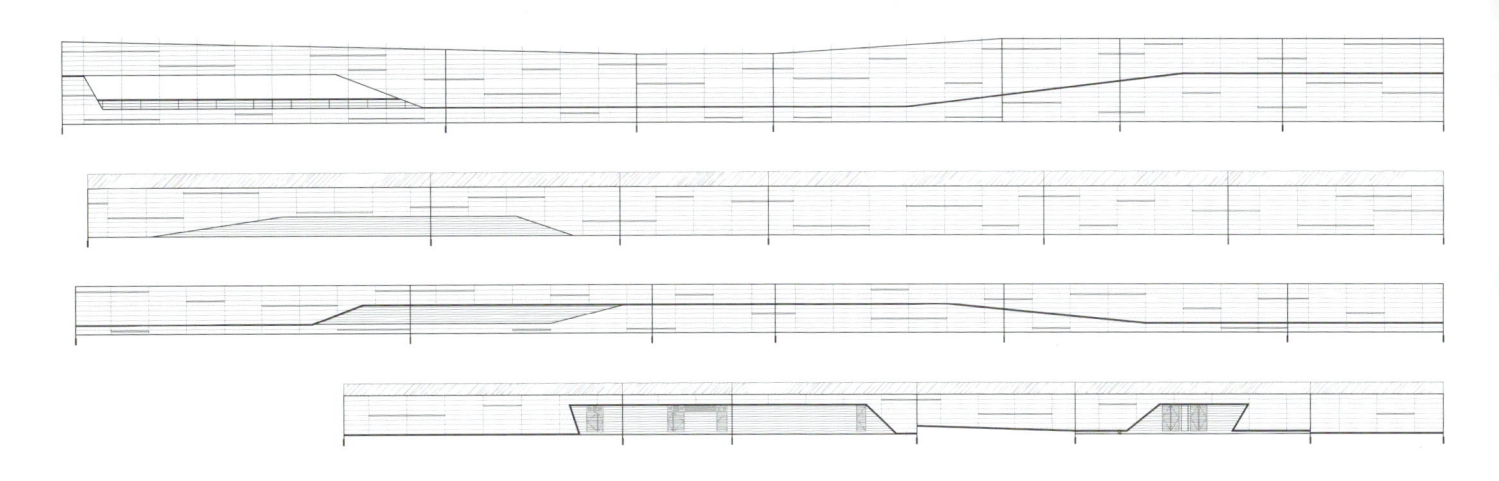

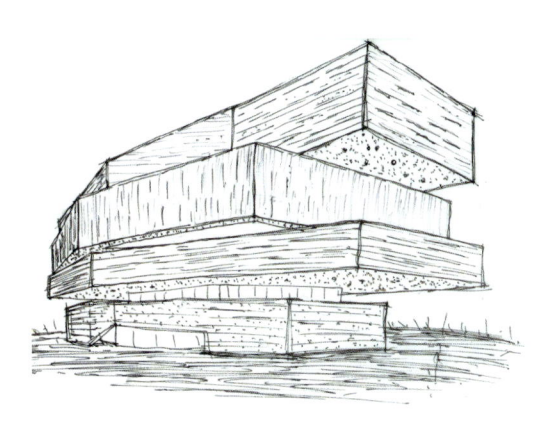

FLOATING STONE

The "Kumho [e]ulim Modelhouse" in Cheongju goes beyond the function of a simple display of a house and suggests a role of a "cultural building" that houses various lives of residents. Each floor has planned community spaces along with the modelhouse display spaces, where people can take a break and enjoy the cultural and natural spaces, which suggest being a living cultural place where humans can connect to the culture of living, rather than a model home as a commercial place.

Four huge masses that cross each other become a gigantic urban environmental sculpture. The four masses have various images and expressions, such as an urban sign, a landmark, a work of art, media and a brand. The existing wall that used to be full of flashy and dizzy signs has converted into an empty wall that makes it feel like entering an art gallery. The three dimensional wall plays a role of an urban canvas that changes with various promotions and lights. The place is planned to function as a community house after the pre-sale.

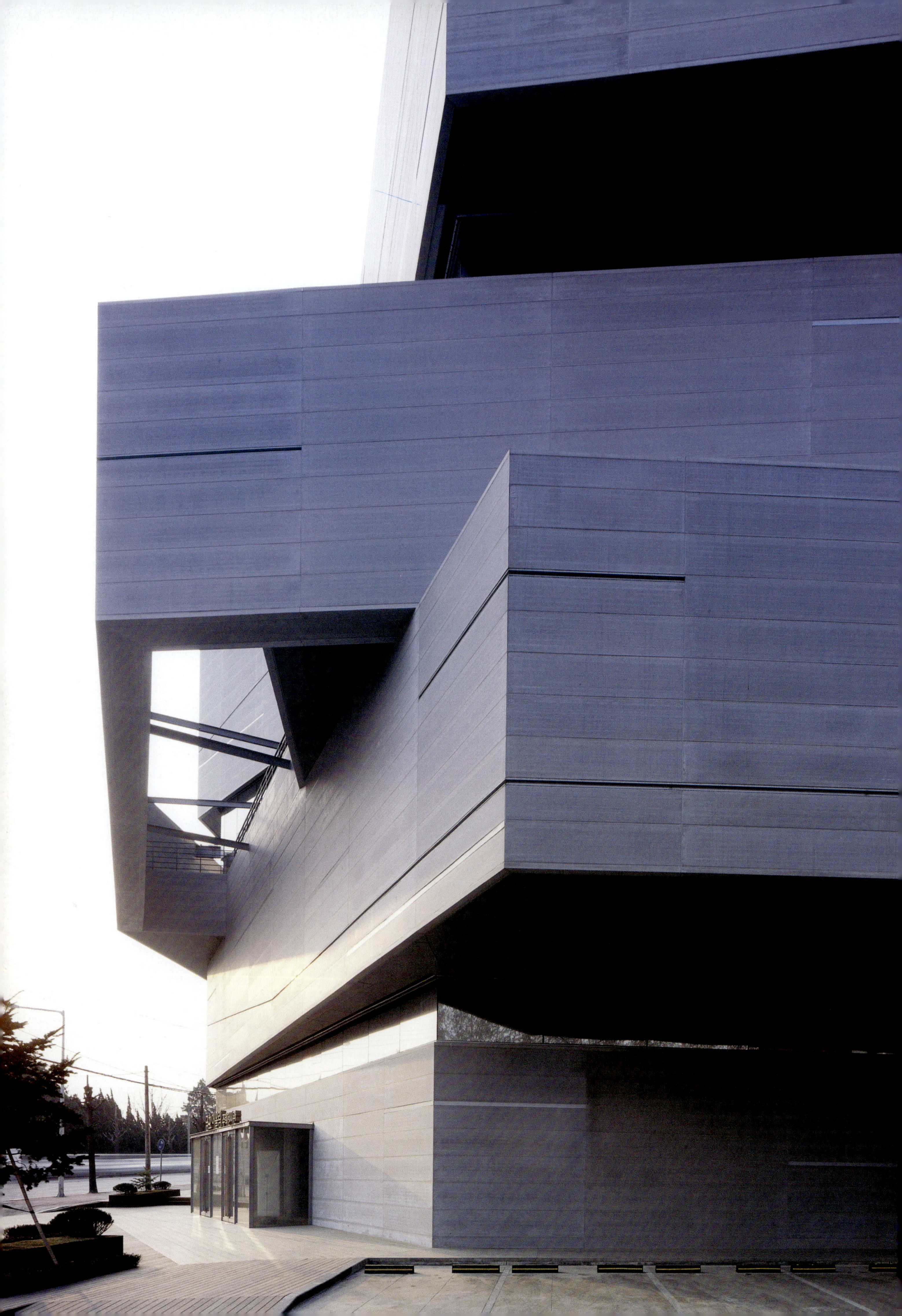

Design Team
Lee Sunpyo, Kim Sung Min
Location
292-3,7 Songjung-Dong, Hongduk-Gu, Chungju, South Korea
Use
Temporary Building
Site Area 2,486m²
Building Area 1,292.85m²
Total Floor Area 3,664.52m²
Building Coverage Ratio 52.01%
Floor Area Ratio 147.41%
Building Scale Four Stories
Structure Steel Structure

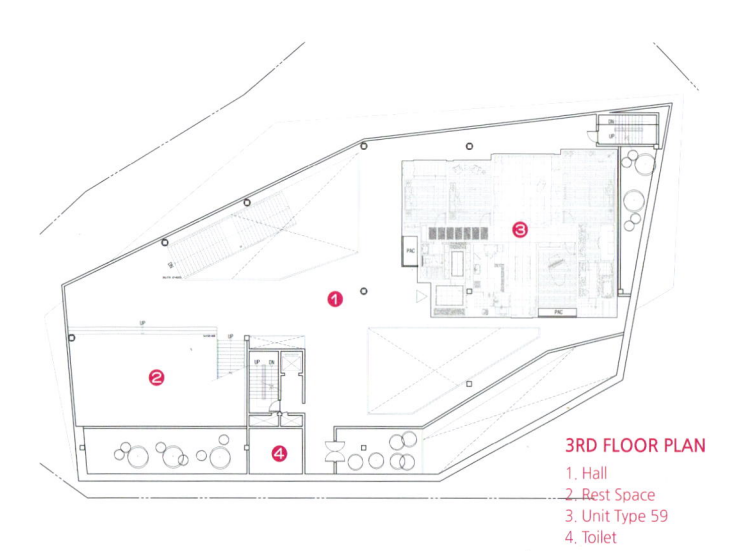

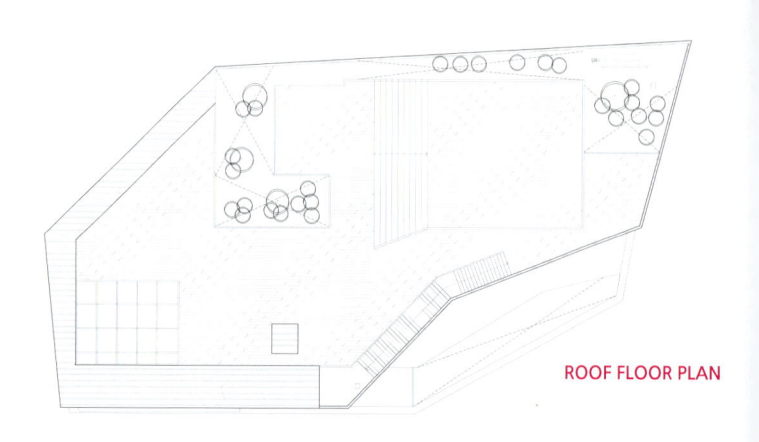

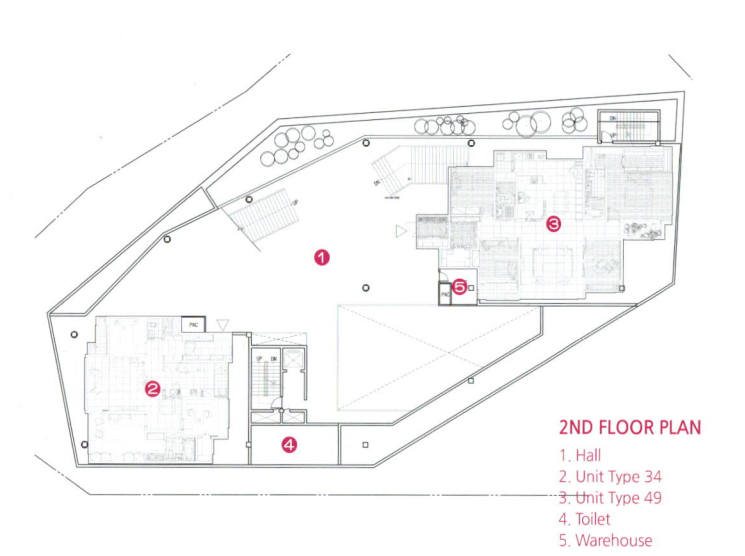

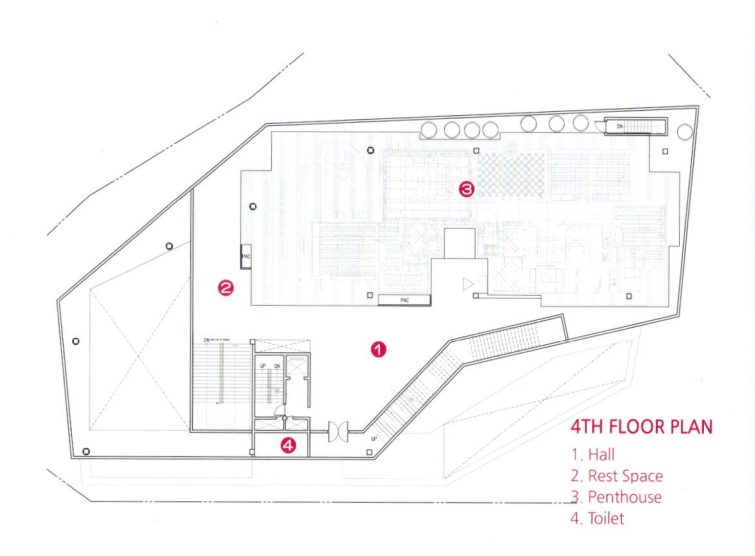

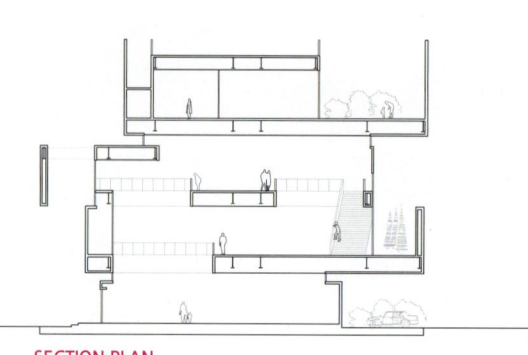

3RD FLOOR PLAN
1. Hall
2. Rest Space
3. Unit Type 59
4. Toilet

ROOF FLOOR PLAN

2ND FLOOR PLAN
1. Hall
2. Unit Type 34
3. Unit Type 49
4. Toilet
5. Warehouse

4TH FLOOR PLAN
1. Hall
2. Rest Space
3. Penthouse
4. Toilet

GROUND FLOOR PLAN
1. Garden
2. Hall
3. Information
4. Restaurant / Meeting Room
5. VIP Room
6. Office
7. Warehouse

SECTION PLAN

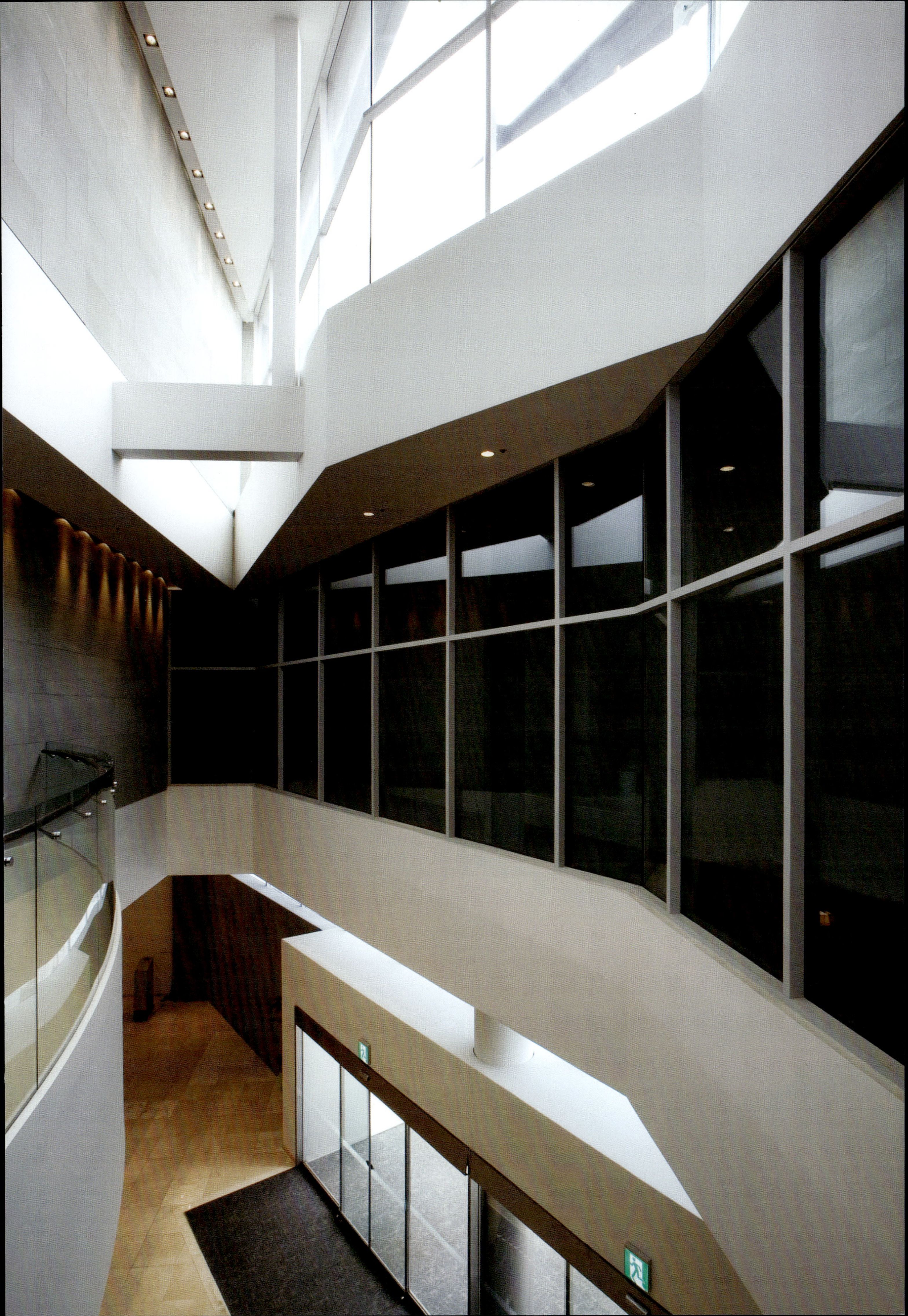

Dream Art Hall in Sung Dong

| Competition Winner | **Architects** Jang Yoon Gyoo, Shin Chang Hoon
Client SeongDong-Gu
Photographer Kim Jae Kyung

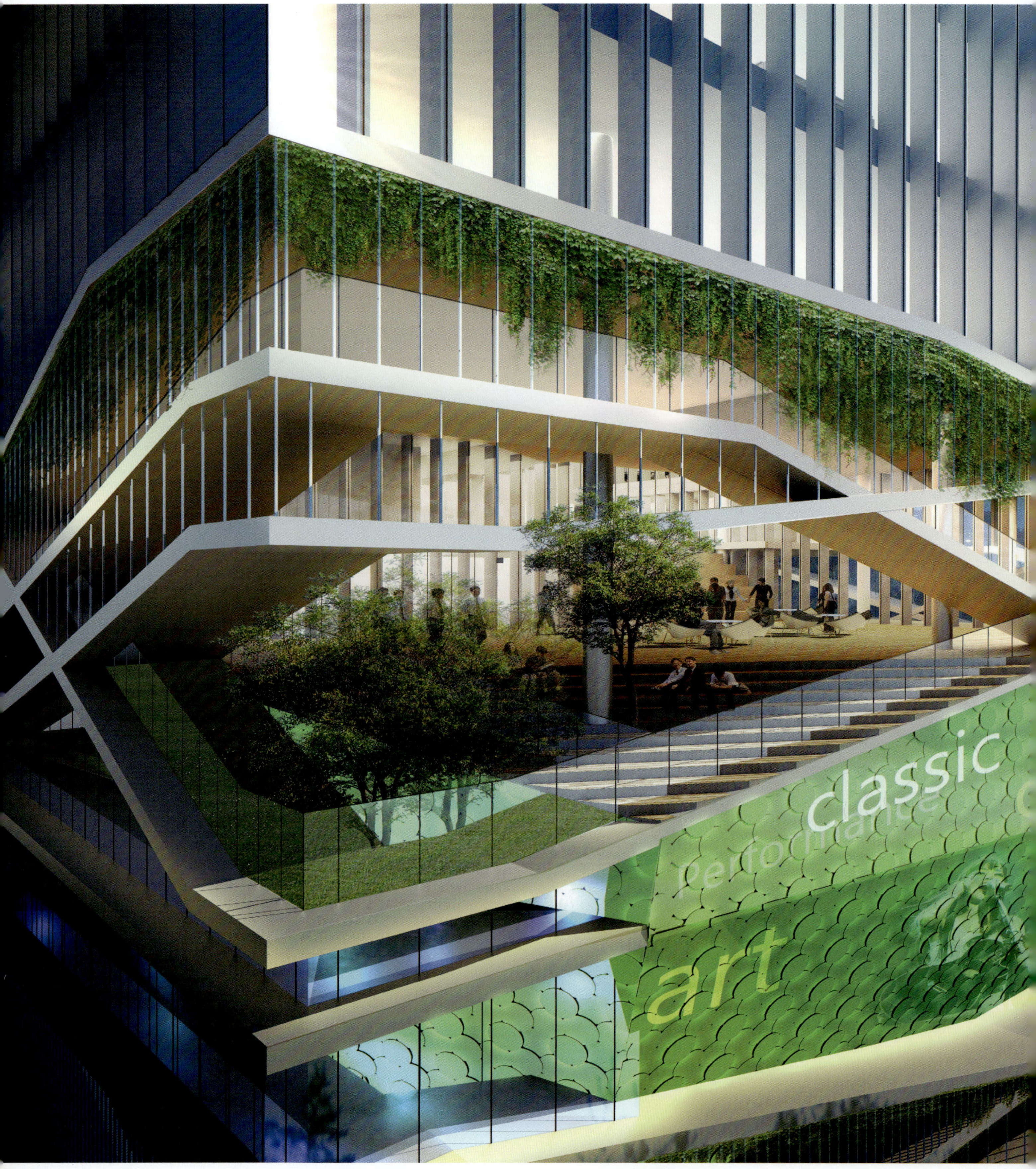
classic
performance
art

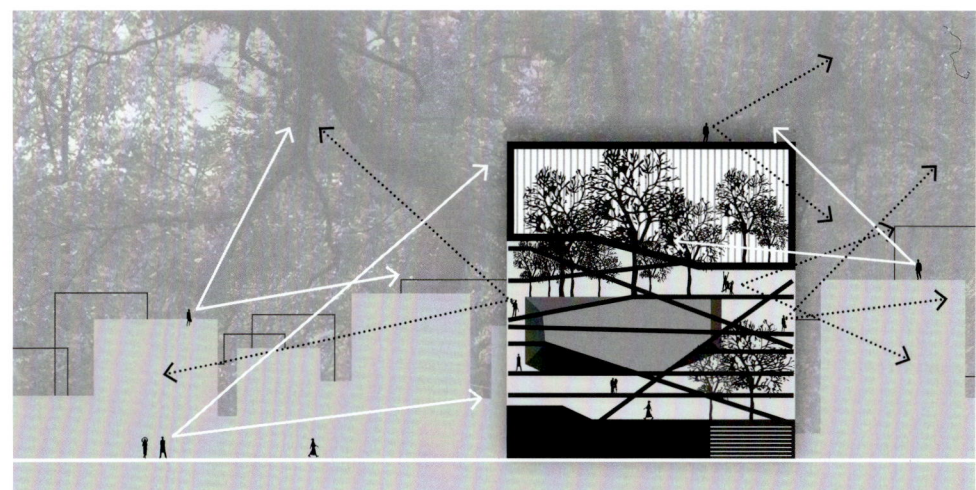

城東風景
Scenery of Seongdong

CULTURE FOREST

Forest lets us experience nature, heals our soul and mind, and makes us dream of a new future. In a forest, natural substances such as air, trees, water, soil and wind do not exist separately. The natural substances in a forest are linked together. Since forests provide a beautiful voice and stunning experiences, many people are amused with the harmony of forests and moon over the space of forests. The scenery looking at Seongdong will be as opened as possible, providing a landscape of intensive and storytelling experience. By planning eco-friendly architecture, the new cultural space will become a dreaming space. Each program consists of an eco friendly and creative cultural space by floating rest, events and green area. The space skin of culture will unify architecture and nature through green walls and generates energy by solar powered panel skin.

The flying theater has a unique and creative form. By geometrical patterns and forms of nature, the skin inside is a logical space for the sound. The entire space of the theater will be filled with dark wine color.

By using the crack of the inside skin, the lighting will become atypical and organic, suggestion an attractive theater space connecting reality, ideal and dream.

The walkway around the building naturally connects each program and becomes an intensive cultural street, converting from inside to outside and outside to inside.

In order to become a sustainable culture space, the space should get over the basic rules. A multi culture complex is suggested to actively realize the needs of residents. Becoming a multi cultural facility that provides eco-friendly and healthy cultural living. Culture Forest will create various library programs for residents such as concerts, women's culture and children playing area and become a landmark with beautiful culture, future-oriented dreams and passion of SeongDong.

// The walkway around the building naturally connects each program and becomes an intensive cultural street, converting from inside to outside and outside to inside.

ELEVATION PROGRAM

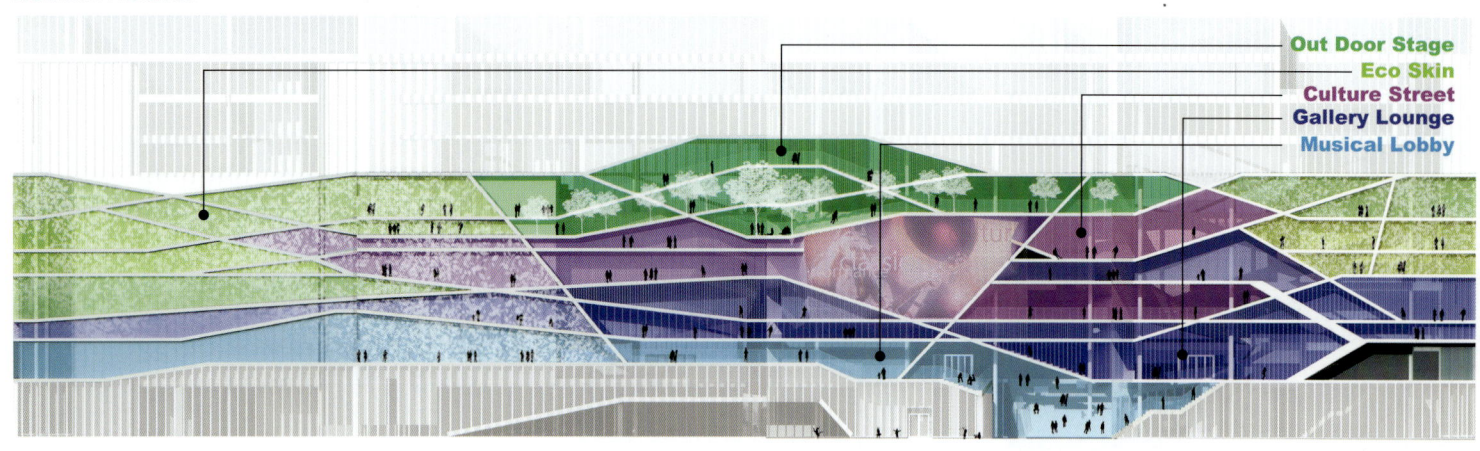

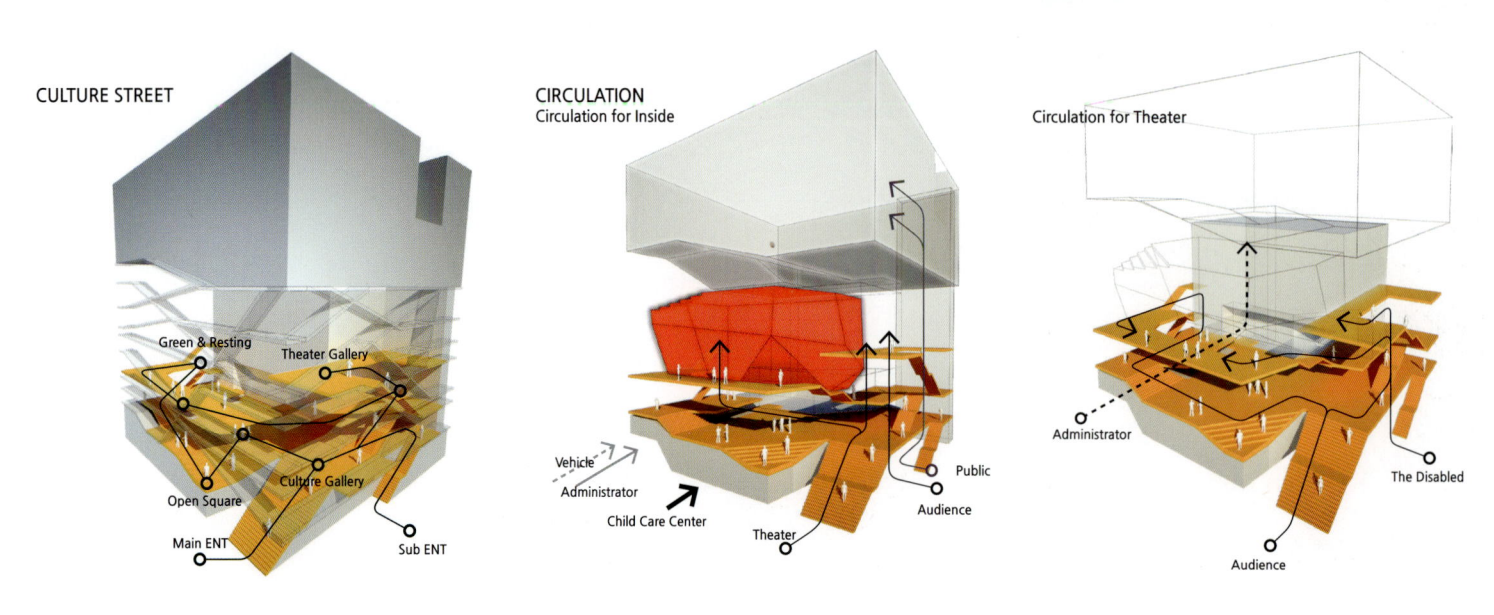

- Out Door Stage
- Eco Skin
- Culture Street
- Gallery Lounge
- Musical Lobby

CULTURE STREET

- Green & Resting
- Theater Gallery
- Open Square
- Culture Gallery
- Main ENT
- Sub ENT

CIRCULATION
Circulation for Inside

- Vehicle
- Administrator
- Child Care Center
- Theater
- Public
- Audience

Circulation for Theater

- Administrator
- Audience
- The Disabled

COMPOUND BODY 333

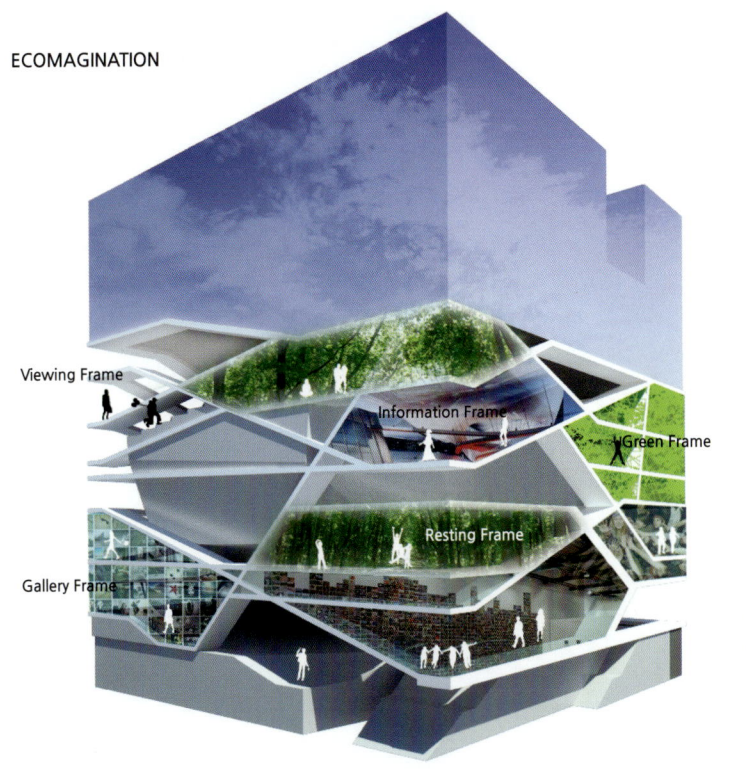

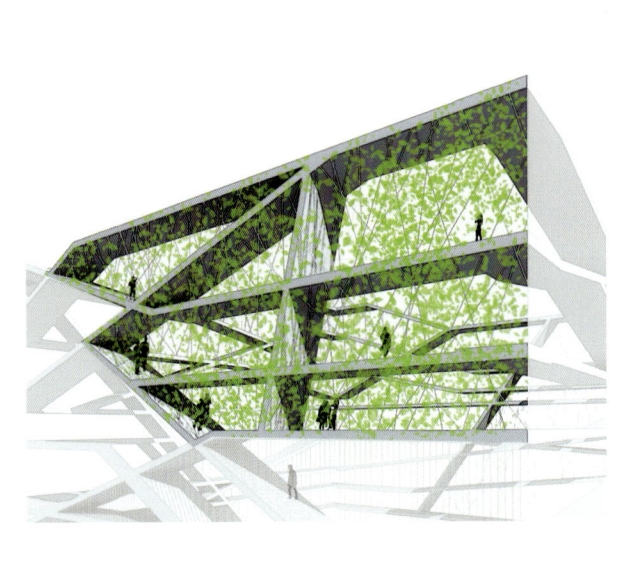

ECOMAGINATION

Viewing Frame
Information Frame
Green Frame
Resting Frame
Gallery Frame

// Each program consists of an eco friendly and creative cultural space by floating rest, events and green area. The space skin of culture will unify architecture and nature through green walls and generates energy by solar powered panel skin.

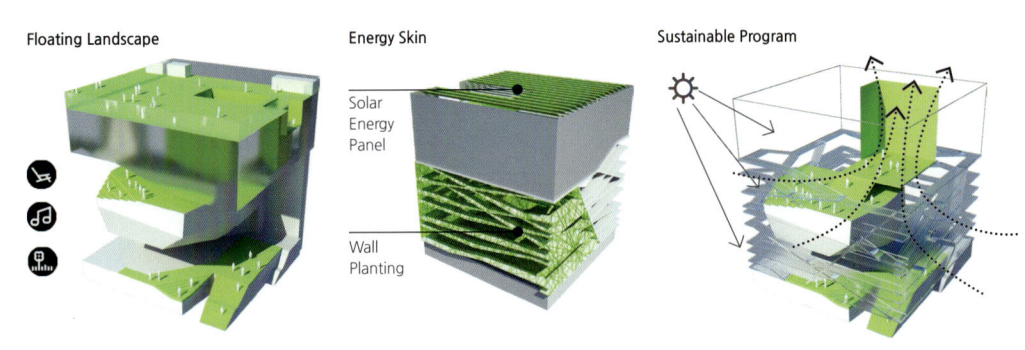

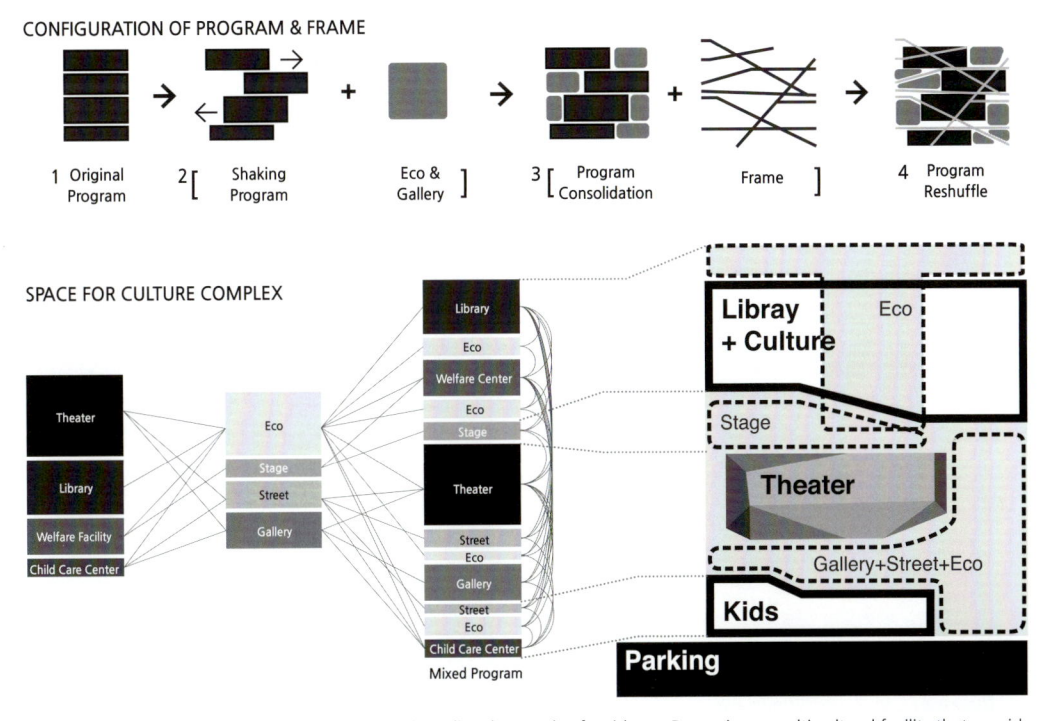

Floating Landscape

Energy Skin
- Solar Energy Panel
- Wall Planting

Sustainable Program

CONFIGURATION OF PROGRAM & FRAME

1 Original Program → 2 [Shaking Program + Eco & Gallery] → 3 [Program Consolidation + Frame] → 4 Program Reshuffle

SPACE FOR CULTURE COMPLEX

Theater, Library, Welfare Facility, Child Care Center → Eco, Stage, Street, Gallery → Library, Eco, Welfare Center, Eco, Stage, Theater, Street, Eco, Gallery, Street, Eco, Child Care Center (Mixed Program)

- Libray + Culture / Eco
- Stage
- Theater
- Gallery+Street+Eco
- Kids
- Parking

// A multi culture complex is suggested to actively realize the needs of residents. Becoming a multi cultural facility that provides eco-friendly and healthy cultural living.

OUR STAGE

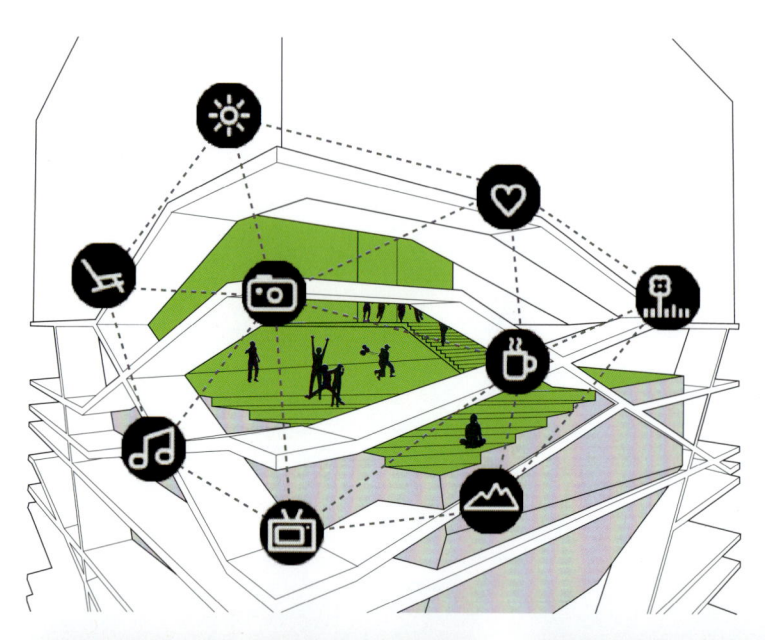

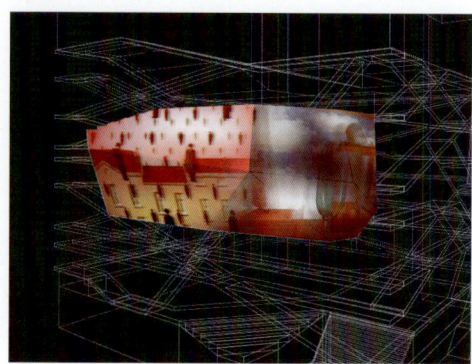

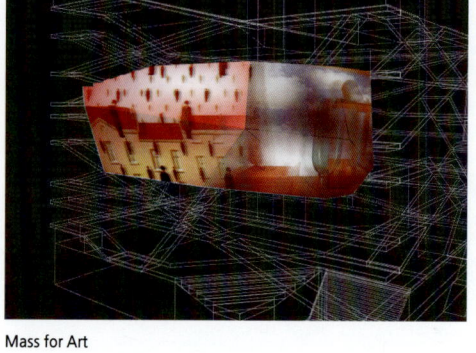

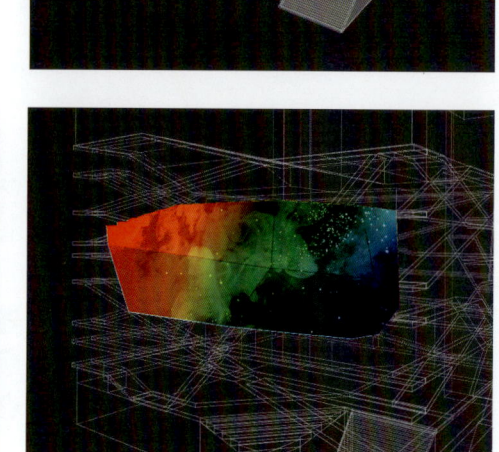

EMOTIONAL THEATER

Library & Welfare Facility

Flying Mass

Child Care Center

Mass for Media

Mass for Art

Colorful Mass

SYMPHONY OF LIGHT

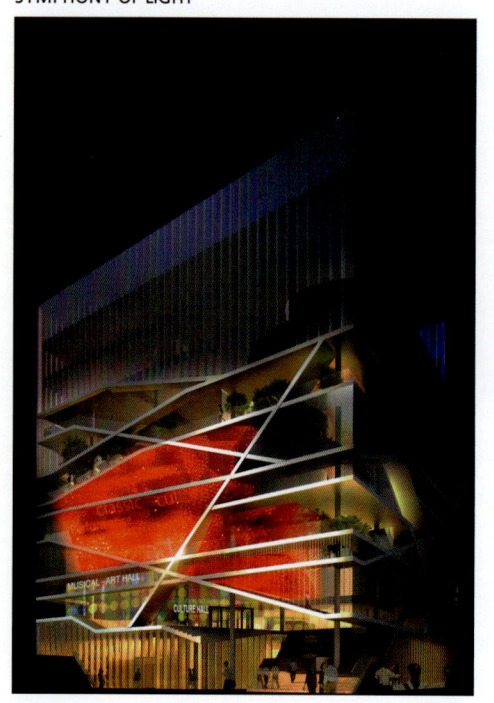

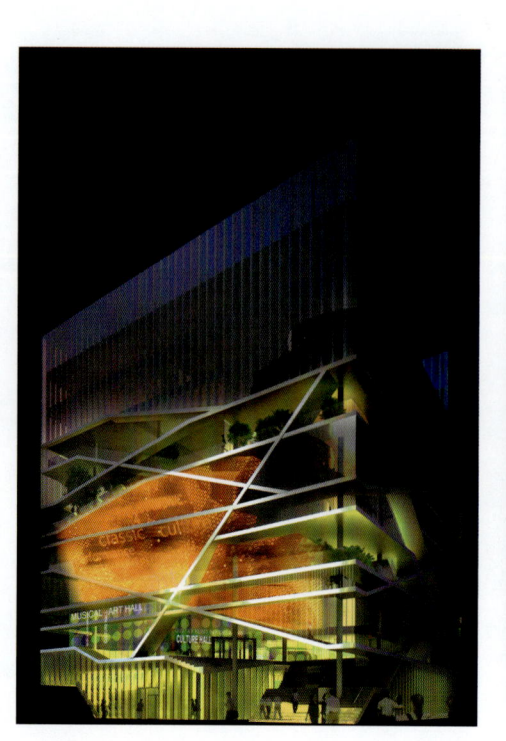

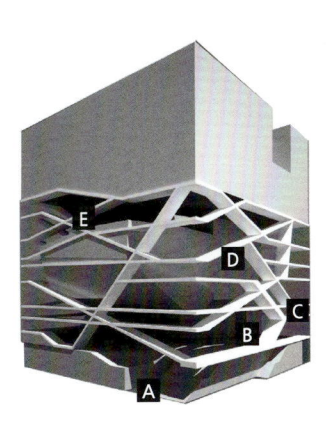

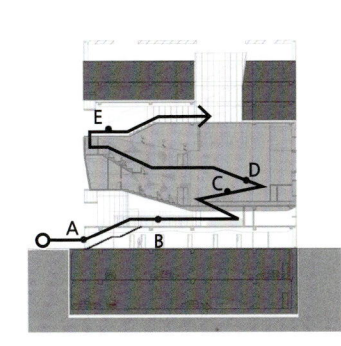

THEATER SECTION

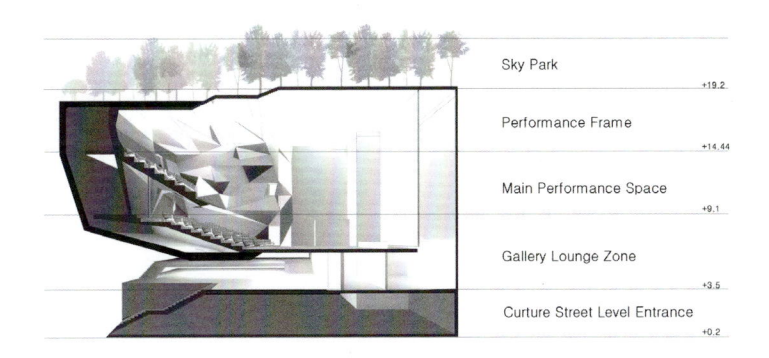

Sky Park	+19.2
Performance Frame	+14.44
Main Performance Space	+9.1
Gallery Lounge Zone	+3.5
Curture Street Level Entrance	+0.2

THEATER PLANNING

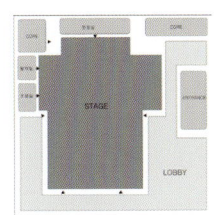

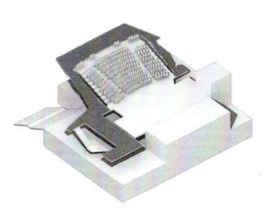

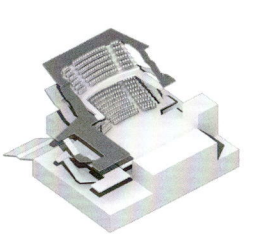

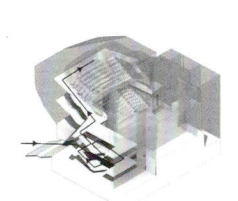

POSITION	Gallery Lounge	Main Performance Space	Performance Frame	Sky Park
LEVEL	+3.5	+9.1	+14.44	+19.2
PEOPLE	360	221	126	360

Architects
Jang Yoon Gyoo, Shin Chang Hoon, Kim Sung Min
Project Team
Kim Min Tae, Seo Hye Lim, Kim Won Il, Ahn Bo Young, Cho Eun Chong
Location
656-323, SeongSu-dong, SeongDong-gu, Seoul, South Korea
Use
welfare, education and research, culture, nursery school
Site Area 1,694m²
Building Area 1,001.77m²
Gross Floor Area 9,597.37m²
Building Coverage 59.13%
Gross Floor Ratio 398.98%
Building Scale
three stories below ground and seven stories above ground
Structure
Steel framed reinforcement concrete
Client
Municipality of SeongDong-gu
Status
1st prize winning project, will be completed in next year.

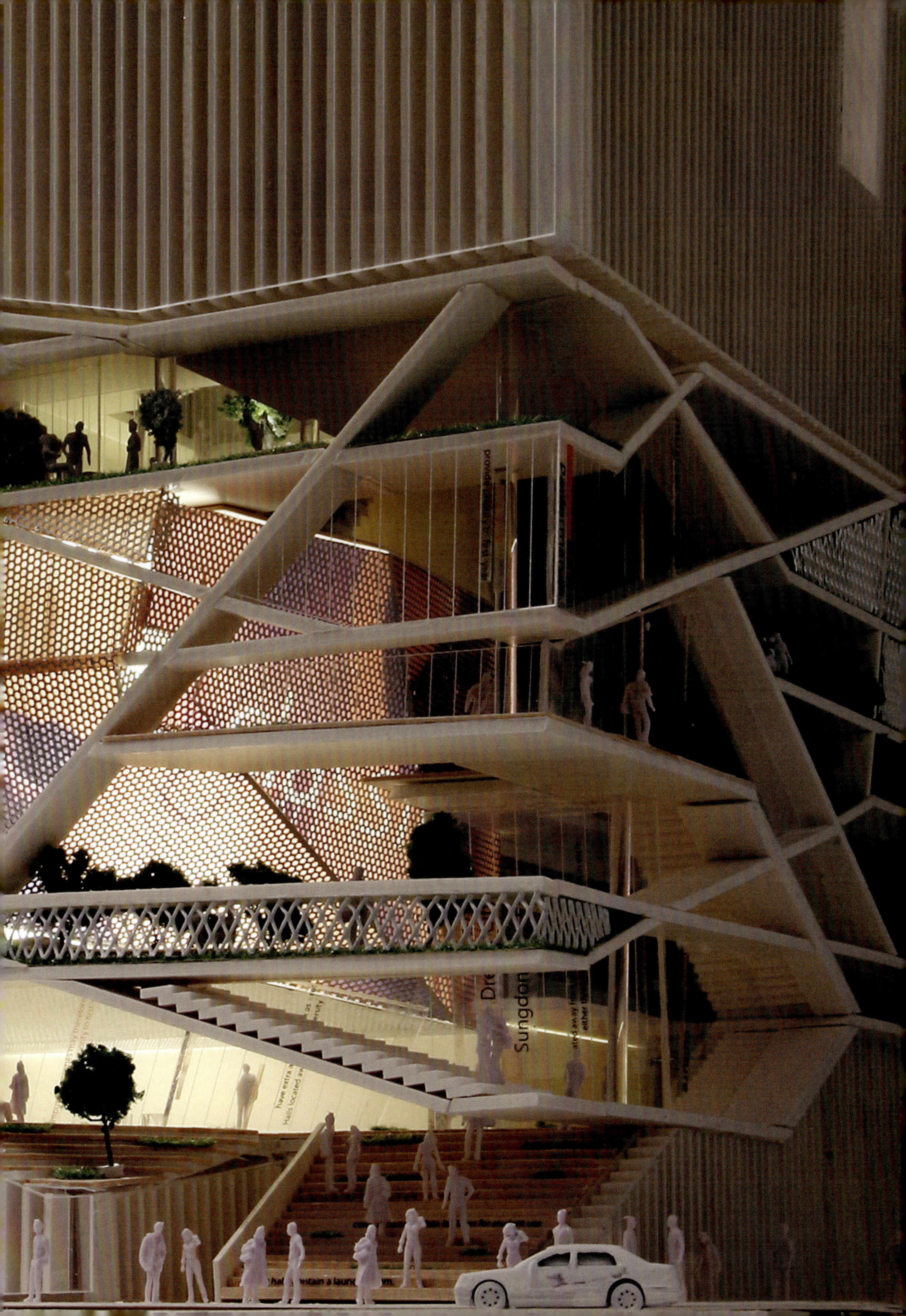

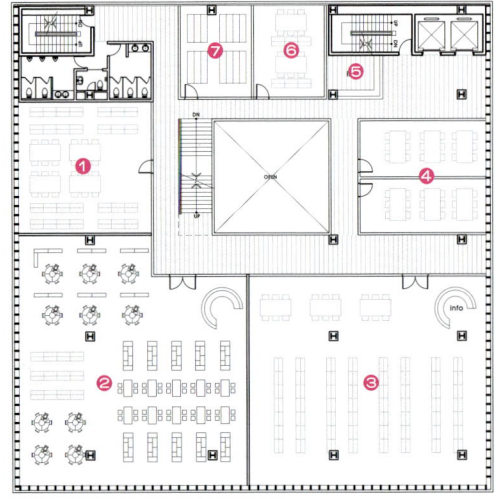

6TH FLOOR PLAN
1. Reading Room
2. Kids Reading Room
3. Literature Intelligence Center
4. Cultural Course Room
5. Information
6. Family Reading Room
7. Arrangement Stands Room

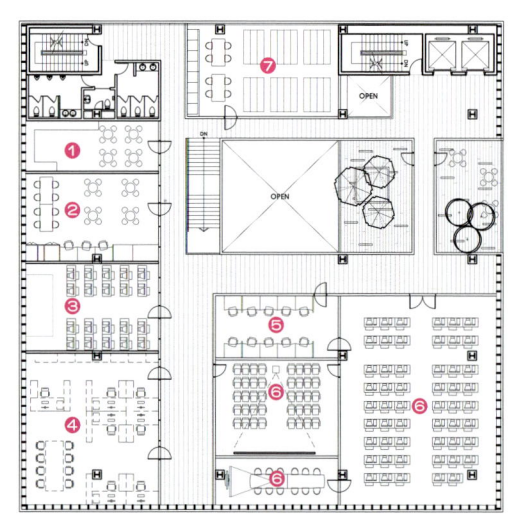

7TH FLOOR PLAN
1. Entrance
2. Reading Discussion
3. Computer Education Room
4. Office
5. Design Information Room
6. Audiovisual Room
7. Preservation Stands

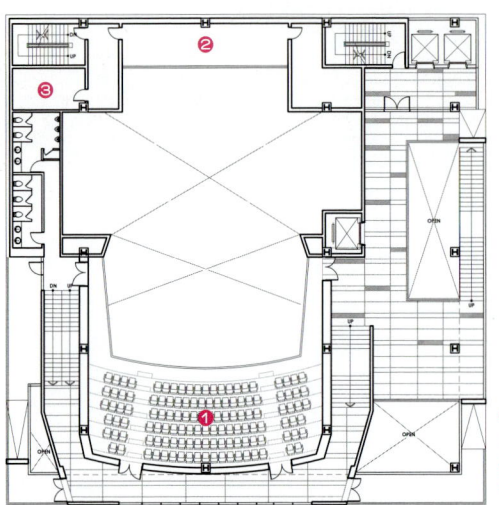

4TH FLOOR PLAN
1. 2F Seat Hall
2. Fly Gallery
3. Warehouse Room

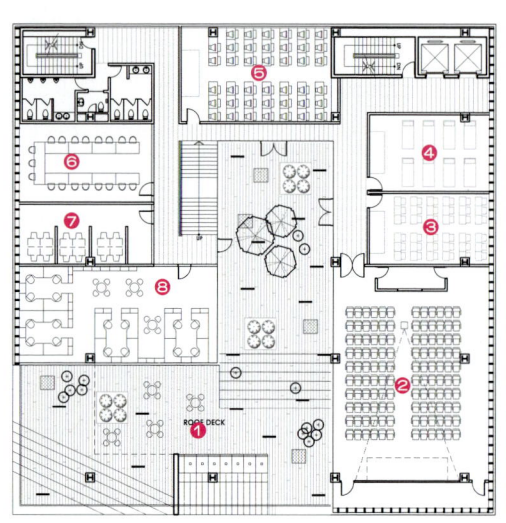

5TH FLOOR PLAN
1. Roof Deck
2. Auditorium
3. Establishment Lecture Room
4. Cooking Room
5. Computer Lecture Room
6. Group Consultation Room
7. Individual Consultation Room
8. Integrated Management Office

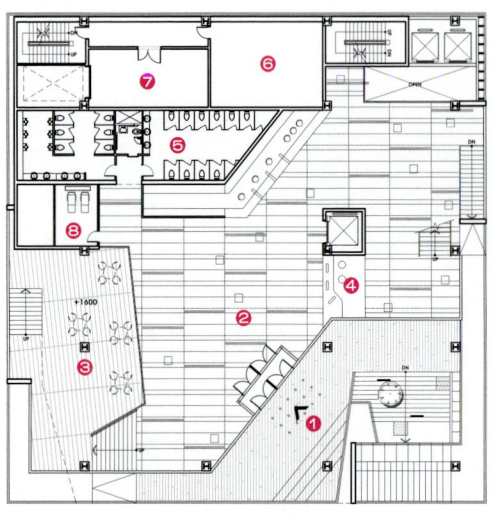

2ND FLOOR PLAN
1. Theater Enterence
2. Gallery Lounge
3. Gallery Cafe
4. Information Desk
5. Toilet
6. Practice Room
7. Warehouse Room
8. Breastfeeding Room

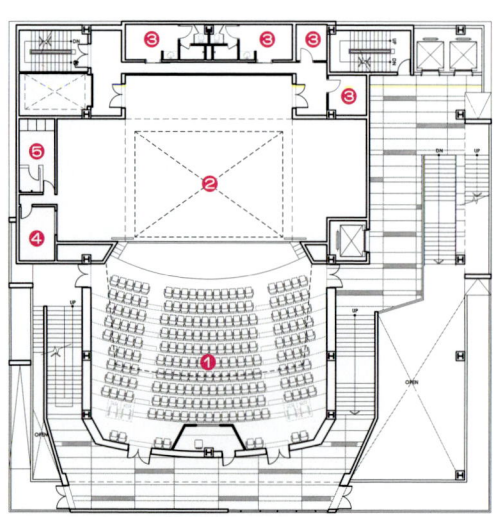

3RD FLOOR PLAN
1. 1F Seat Hall
2. Main Stage
3. Make-up Room
4. Exhibition Hall
5. Control Room
6. Fitting & Shower Room

GROUND FLOOR PLAN
1. Public Lobby Enterence
2. 1F Theater Lobby Enterence
3. Kids House Enterence
4. Bus Parking Enterence
5. Theater Parking Enterence
6. Public Culture Gallery & Lobby
7. Indoor Kids Playground
8. Kids Chief Office
9. Kids Gallery

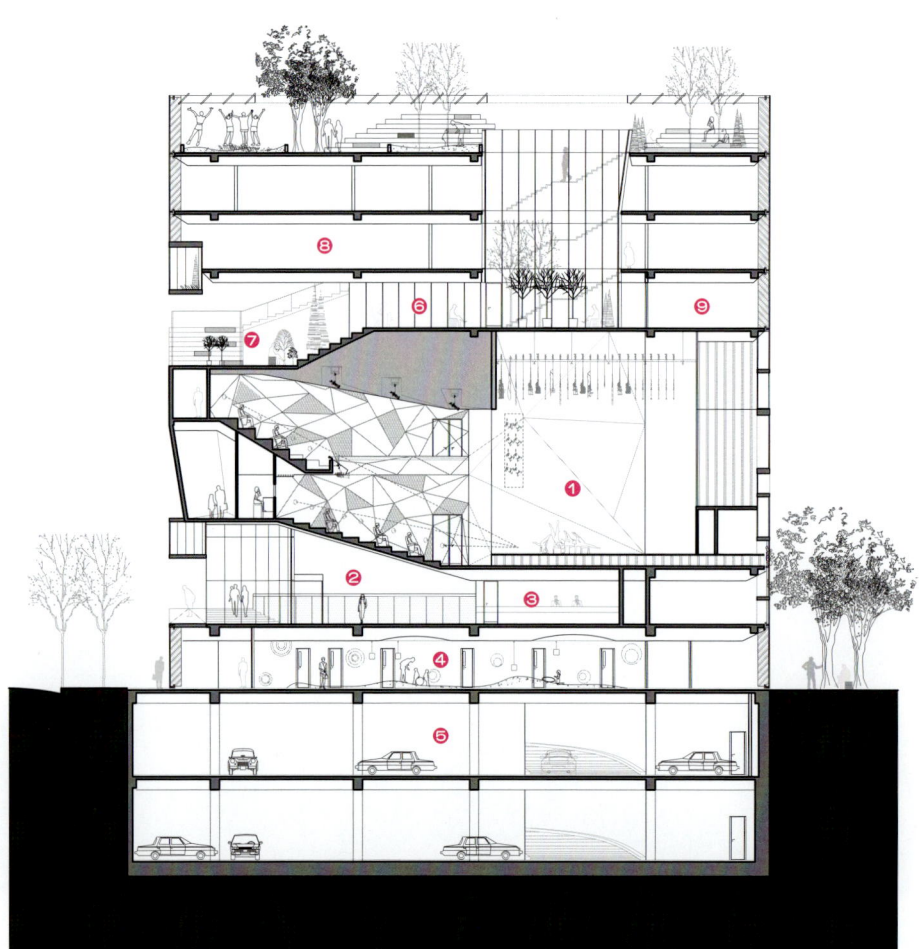

SECTION
1. Theater
2. 1F Theater Lobby
3. Ticket Booth
4. Indoor Kids Playground
5. Parking
6. Roof Deck
7. Gallery Frame
8. Literature Intelligence Center
9. Computer Lecture Room

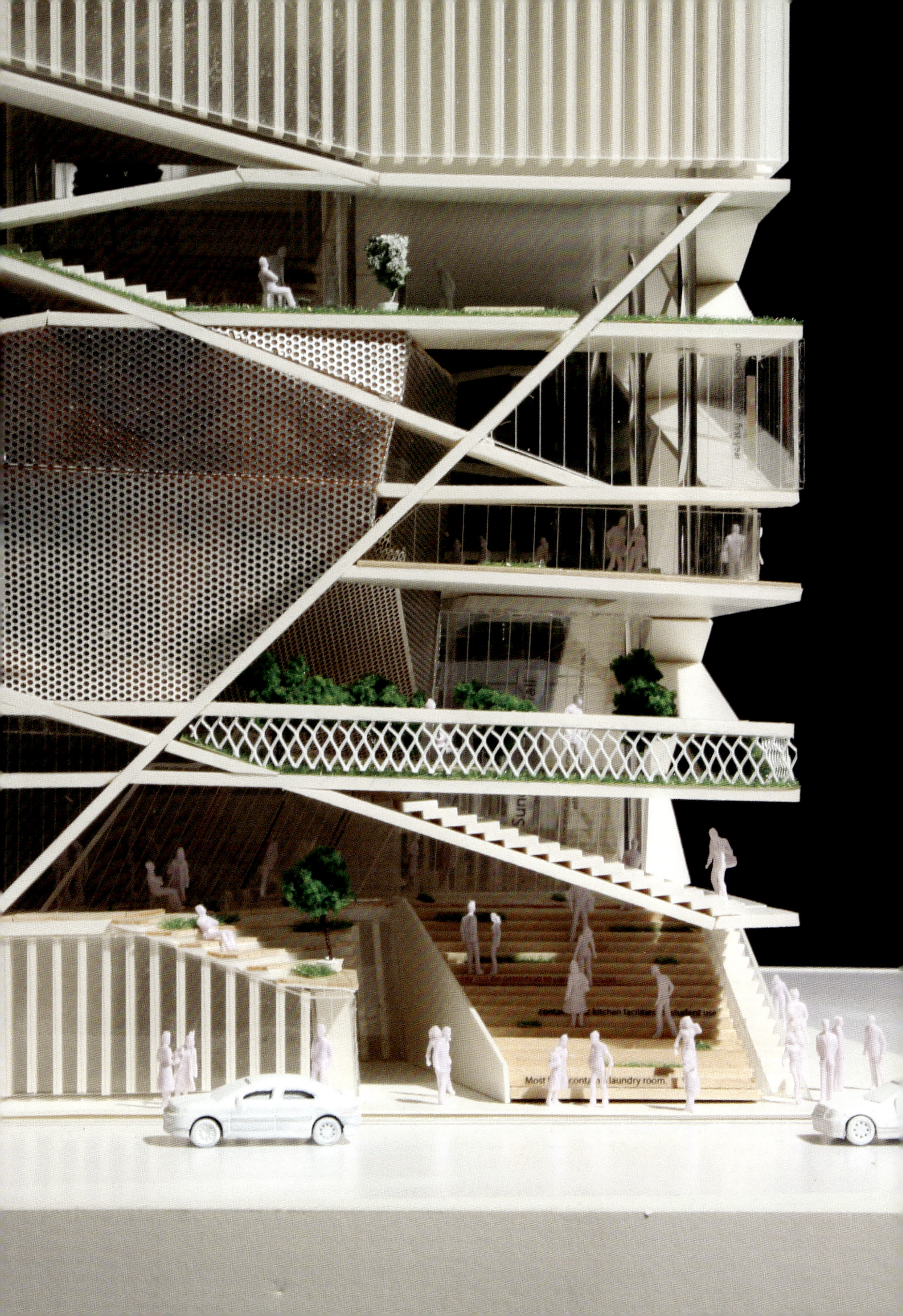

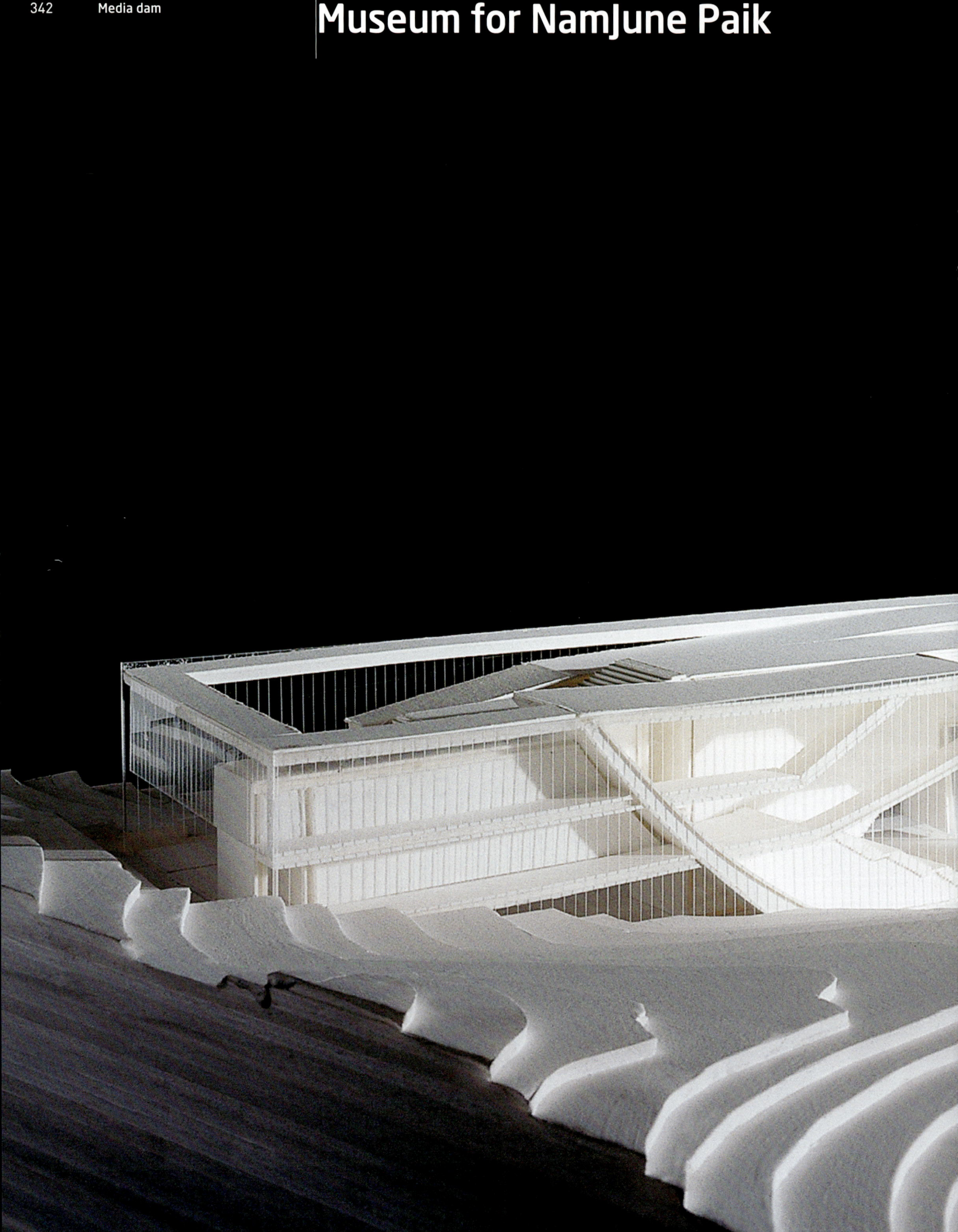

… Media dam … Museum for NamJune Paik

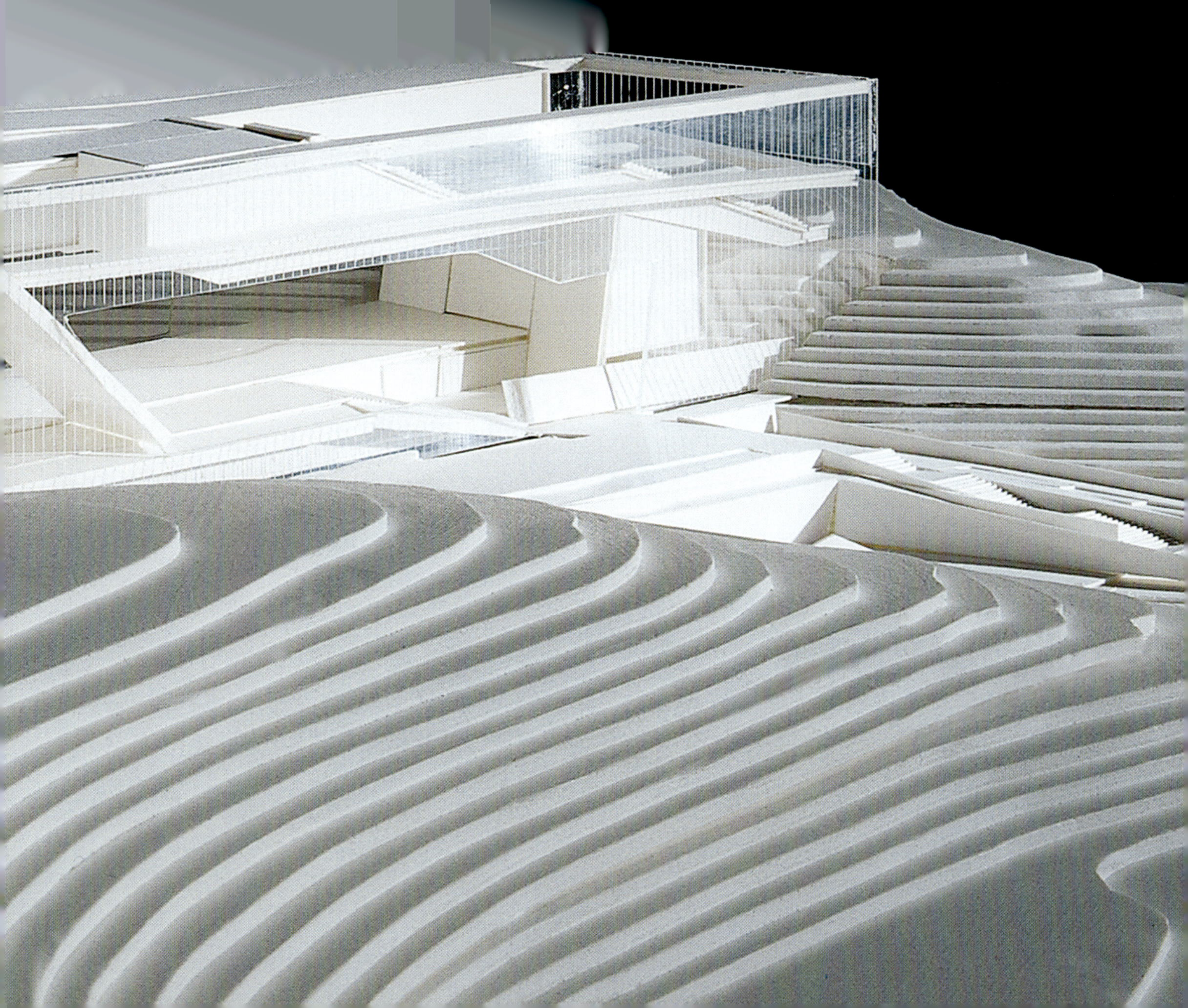

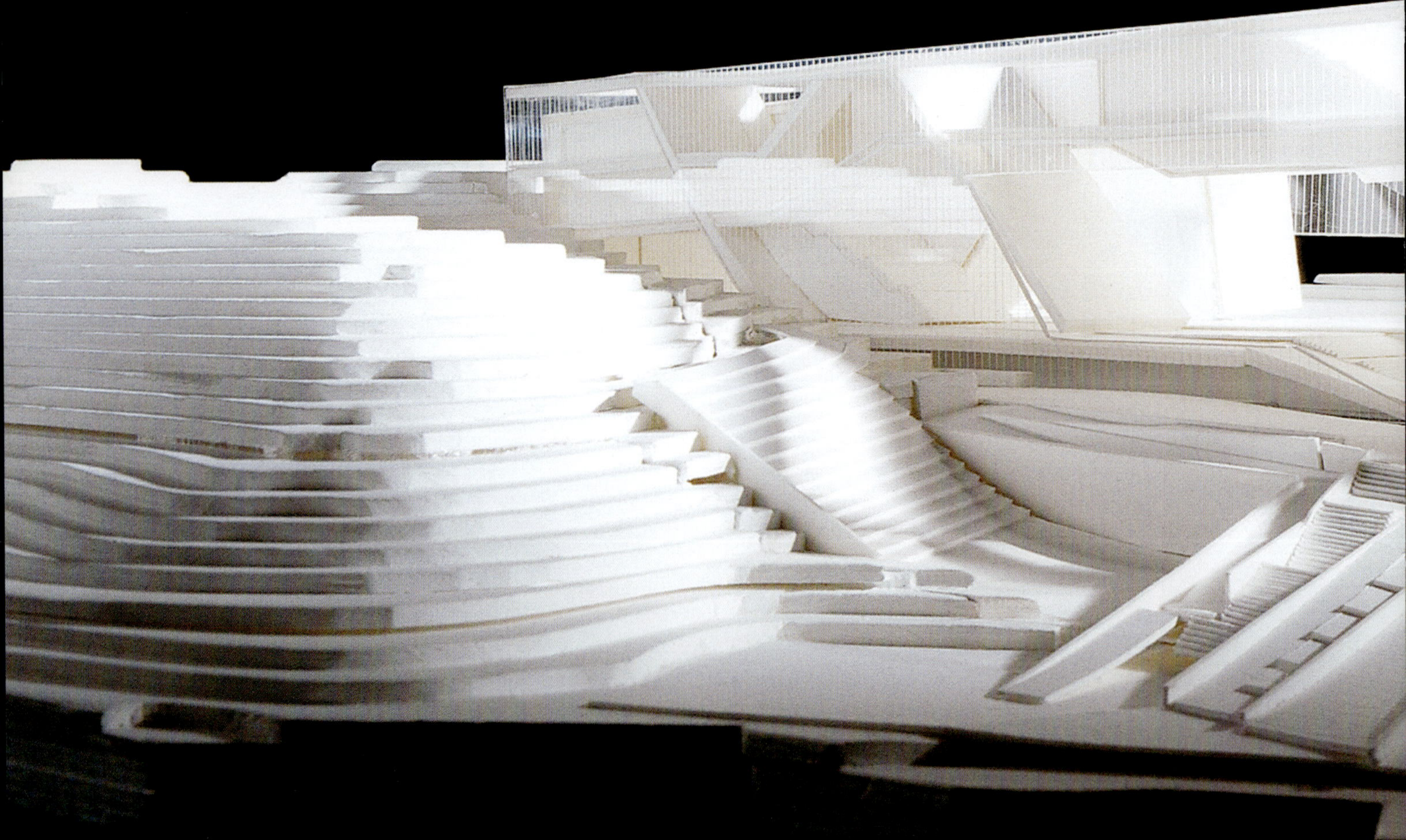

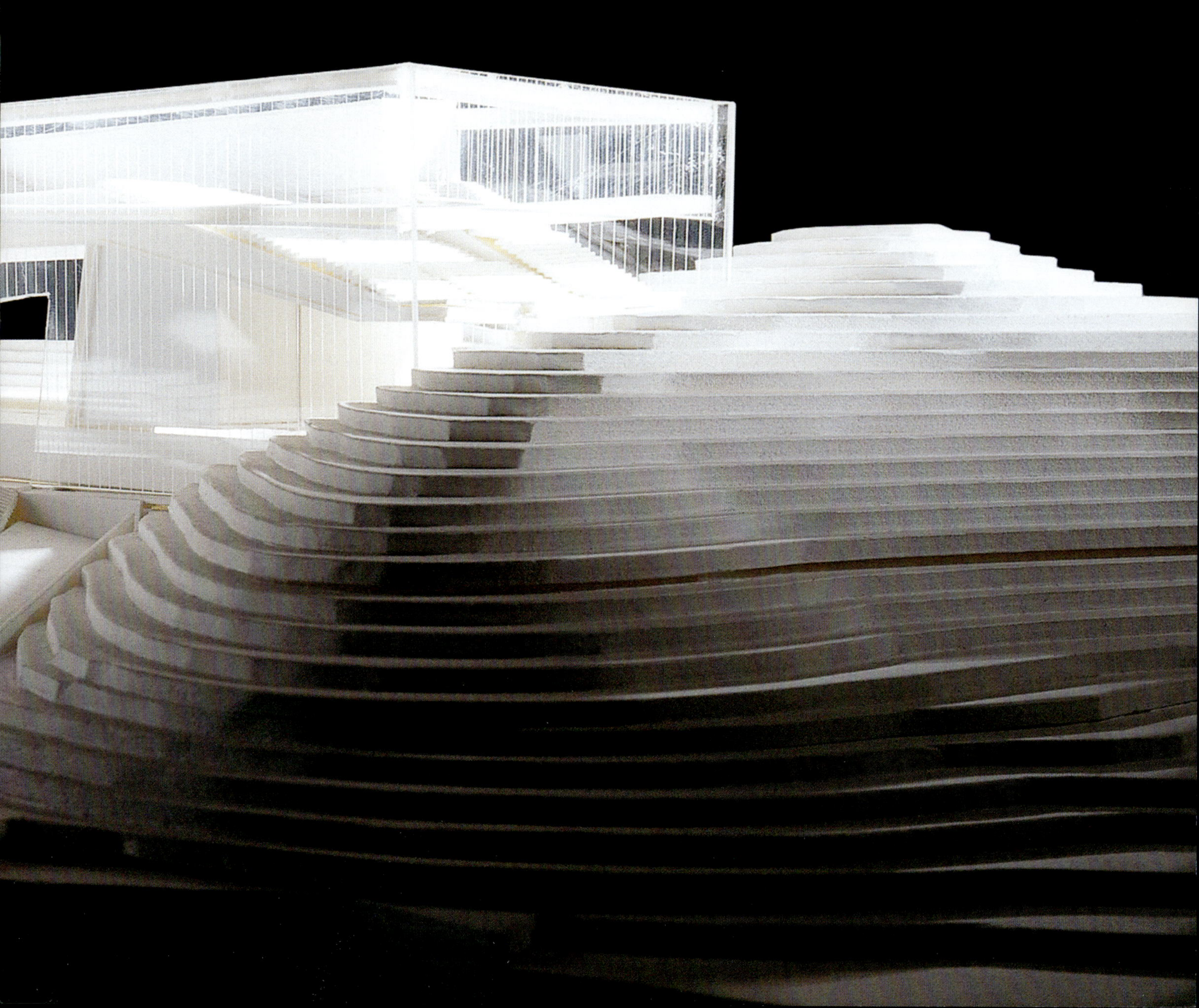

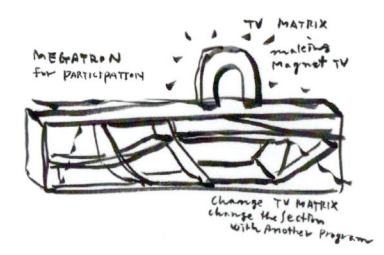

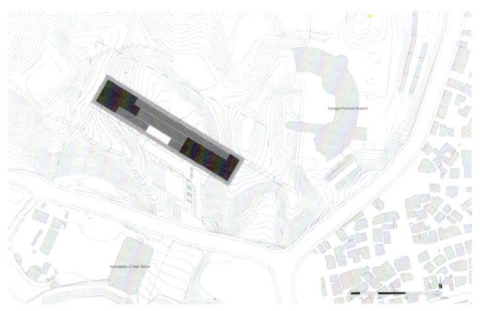

SITE PLAN

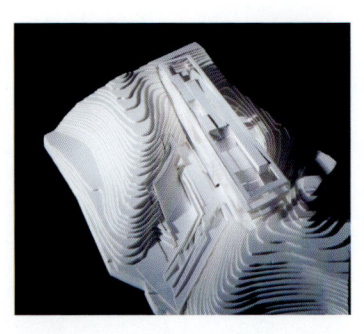

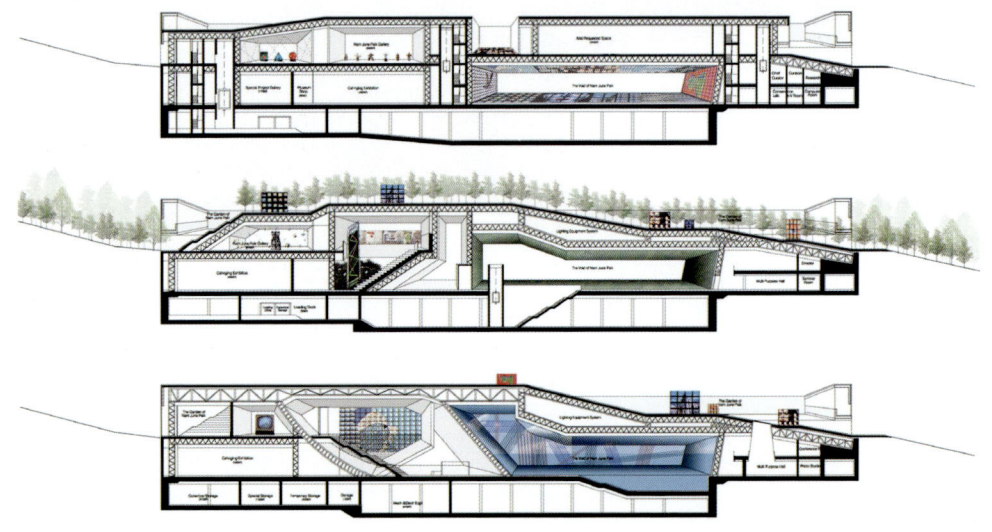

INTERACTIVE PLATES WITH PROGRAM SECTION

MEDIA DAM

Containing Channels of Nam June Paik

The main idea of this Nam June Paik Memorial is to achieve a specific architectural structure in this building as a mediator for containing various media. The proposal running across the valley in our site is called Media Dam, which can be working as a huge container to operate and control the diverse art media including Nam June Paik's works. The programs in the gallery of media are a kind of materials for playing and creating spatial and sectional varieties. This Media Dam is a void canvas to be occupied by his new spirits and works and a bridge to connect cultural points around the site. In this Media Dam are there four spatial channels supposed to the space of Nam June Paik.

Media Falling
Imaginary Landscape
Structure for Radiating media

Media Dam has the character of adopting structure but, on the other hand, Media Falling can constitute the character of radiating structure for the reproduction toward our society and cities. It means we are focusing on reacting mechanism to adopt and radiate his spirit and art toward our society beyond the simple action of exhibiting his work. The vertical layer from Media Gallery is for getting spatial heterogeneity ideally to penetrate into the whole building and also Media Falling is working as a digital falling having the spatial depth beyond surface device such as digital wall.

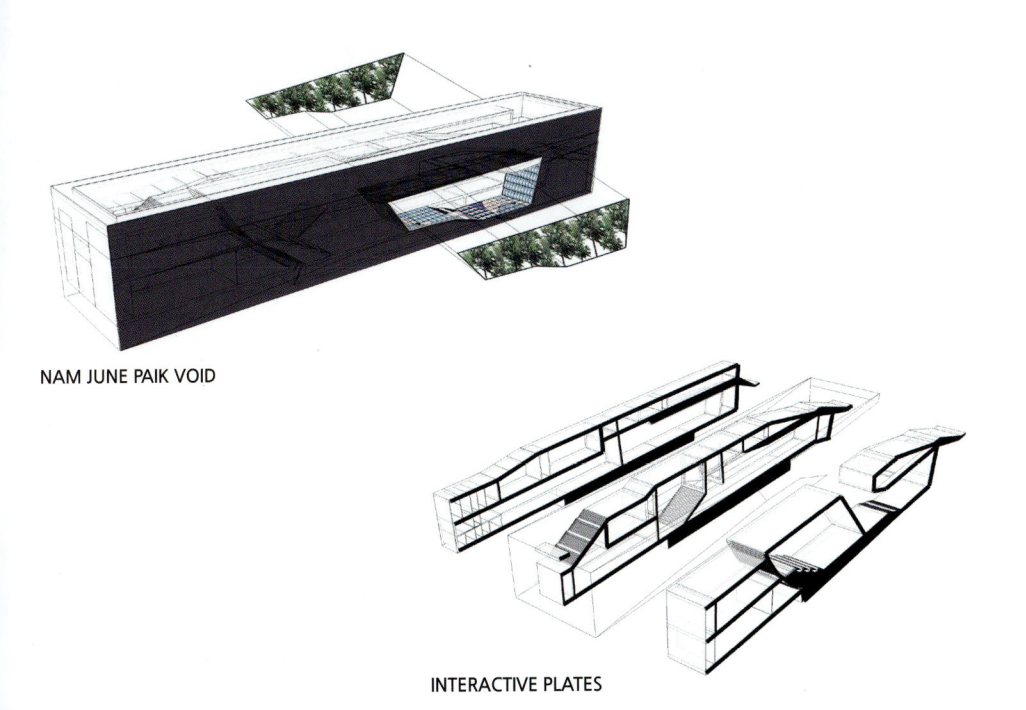

NAM JUNE PAIK VOID

INTERACTIVE PLATES

Media Falling
Imaginary Landscape
Structure for Radiating media

Media Dam has the character of adopting structure but, on the other hand, Media Falling can constitute the character of radiating structure for the reproduction toward our society and cities. It means we are focusing on reacting mechanism to adopt and radiate his spirit and art toward our society beyond the simple action of exhibiting his work. The vertical layer from Media Gallery is for getting spatial heterogeneity ideally to penetrate into the whole building and also Media Falling is working as a digital falling having the spatial depth beyond surface device such as digital wall.

Channel 01_Void
Modulation in Sync ⟨Unoccupied Monitor⟩
We are proposing a huge void for his completed works and it has another possibility and flexibility for future. This unoccupied space having special character such as ⟨participation TV⟩ is a huge monitor for Nam June Paik, which can react with his feelings and visions as an artist. In there, the devices for many artistic needs and changes are concealed ingeniously and various artistic performances can be played, communicated, and participated. This new participation device, Nam June Paik Void is working as a threshold to connect to internet and broadcasting system.

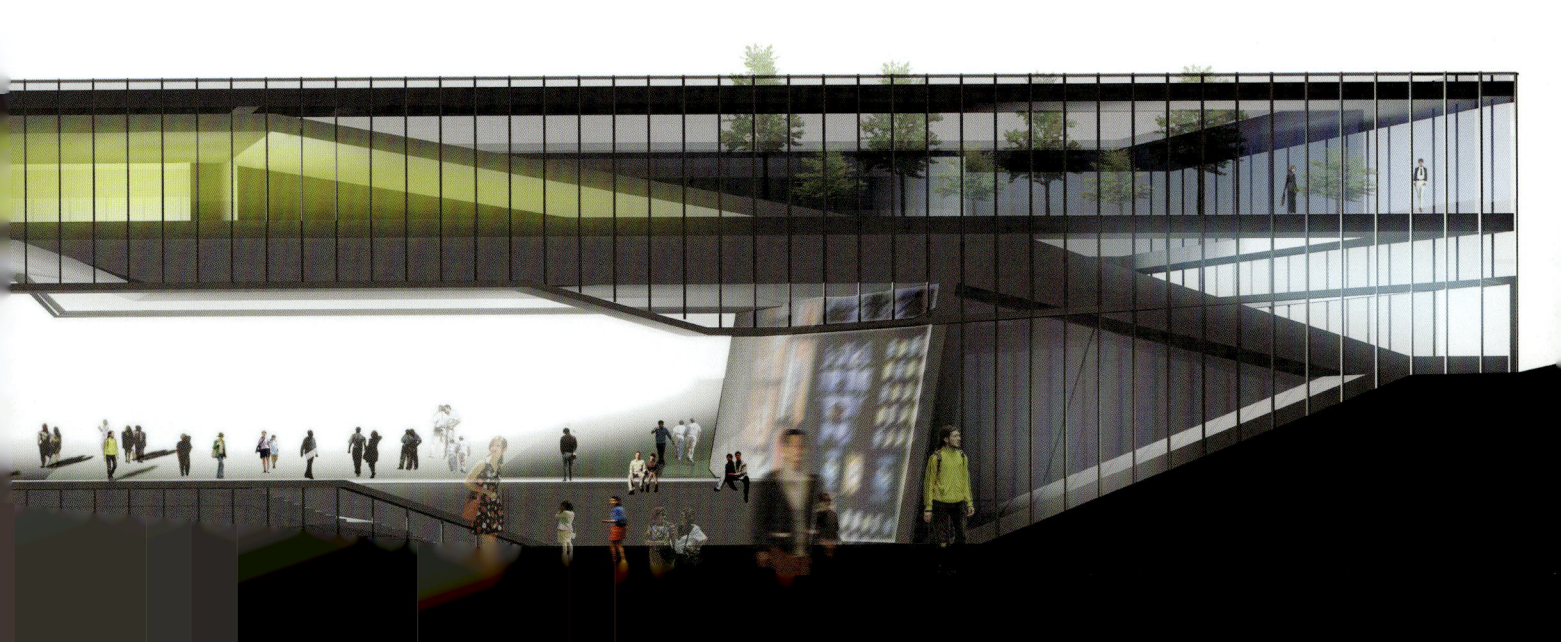

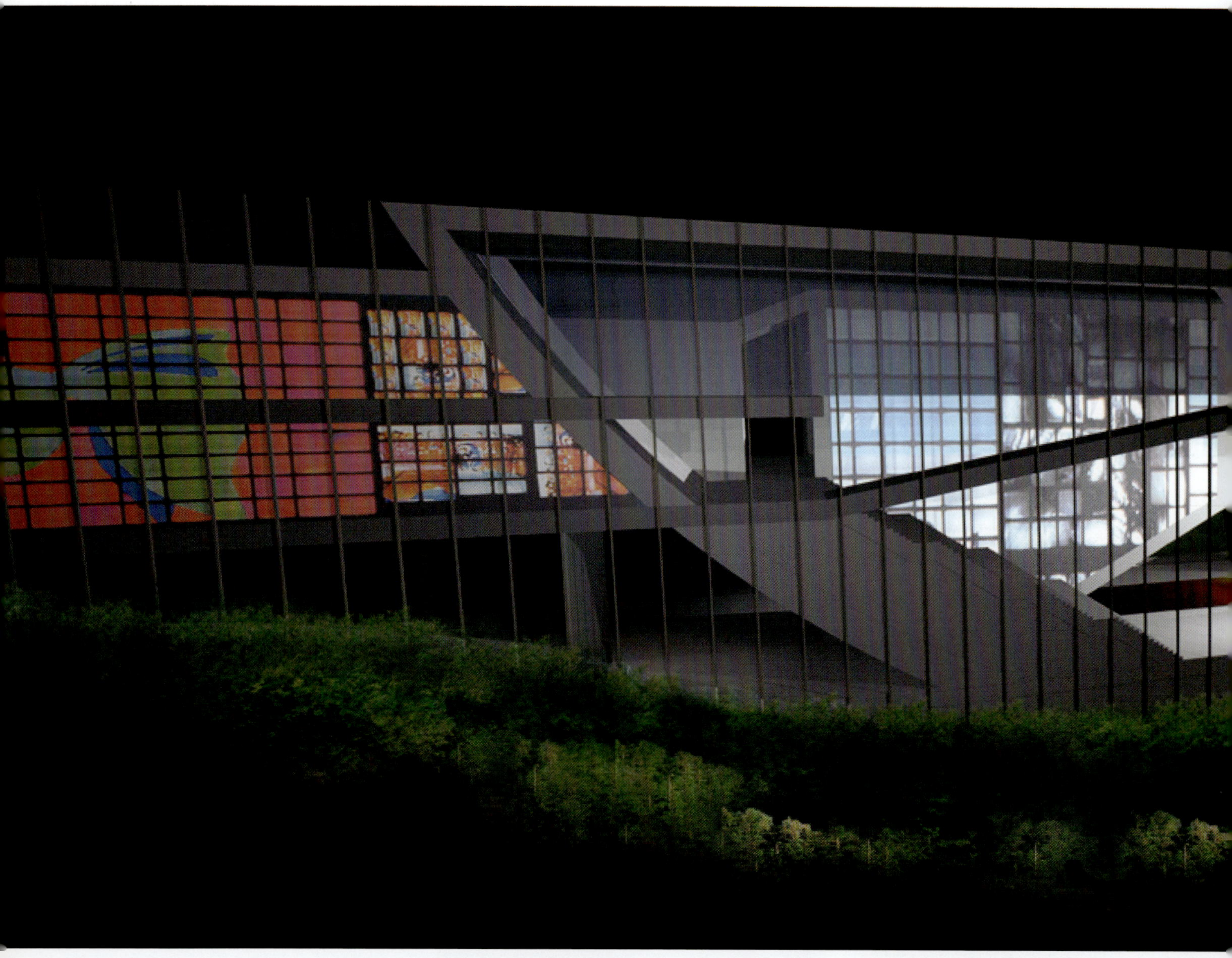

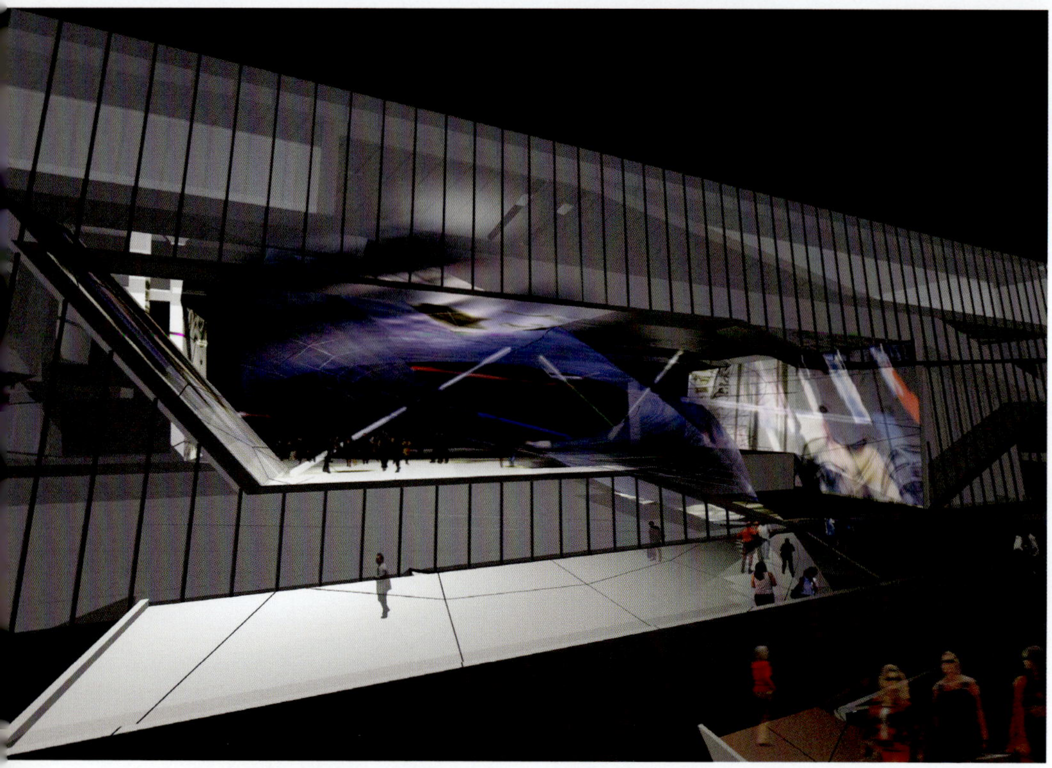

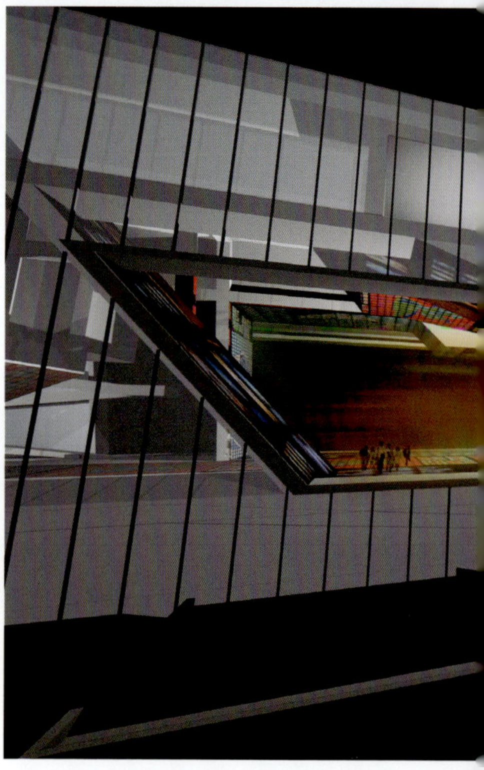

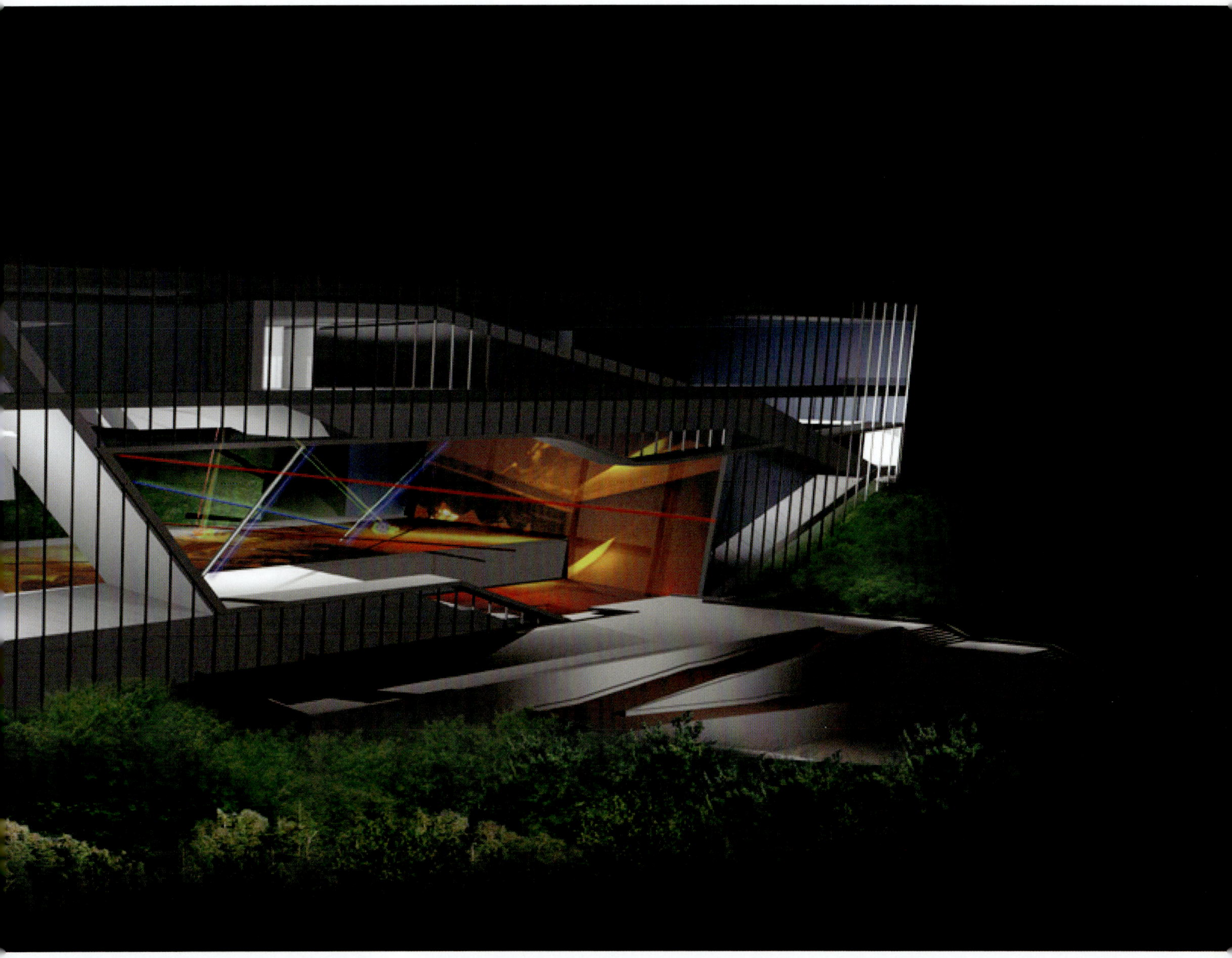

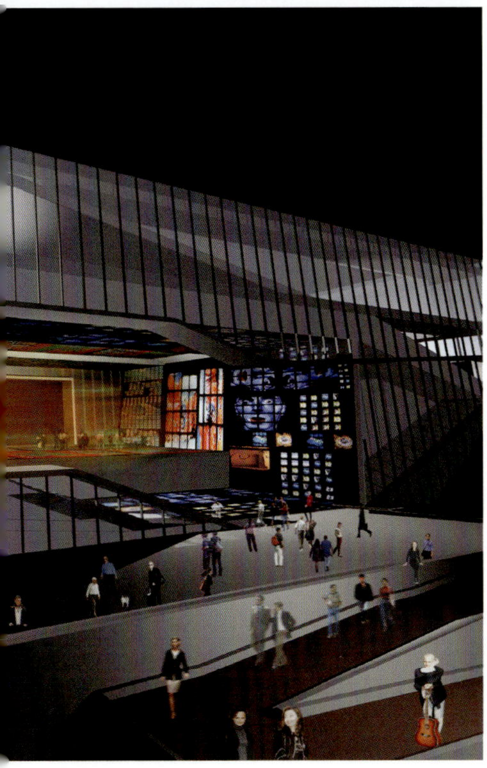

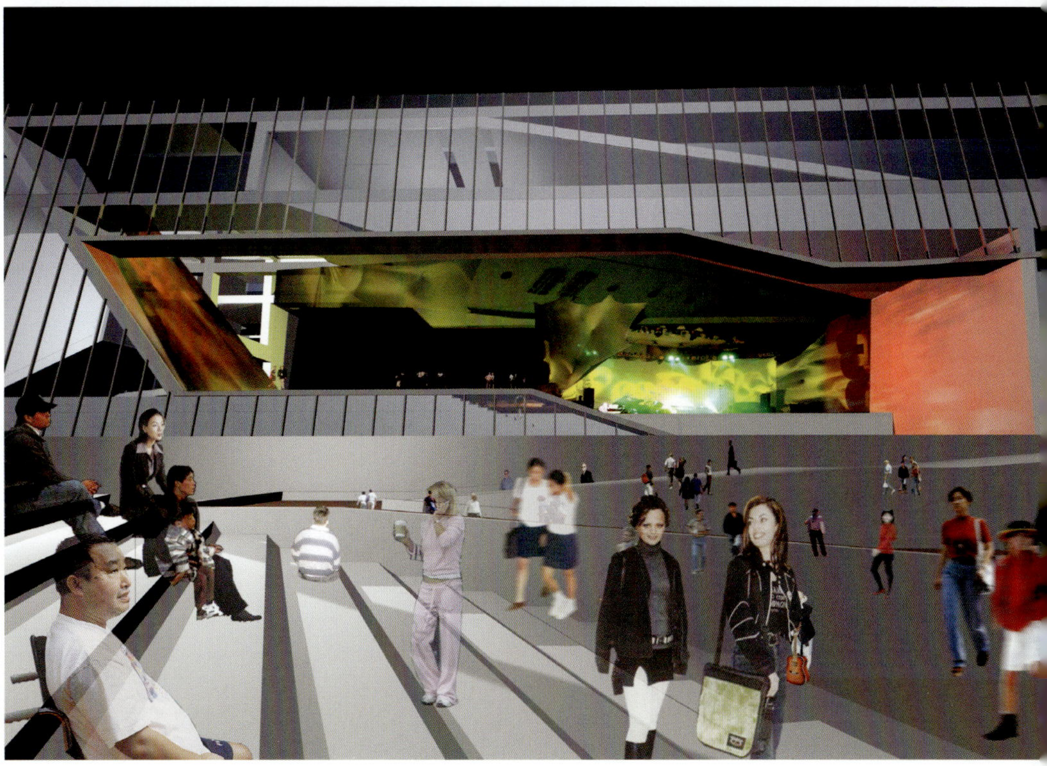

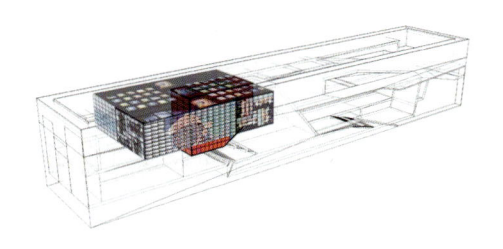

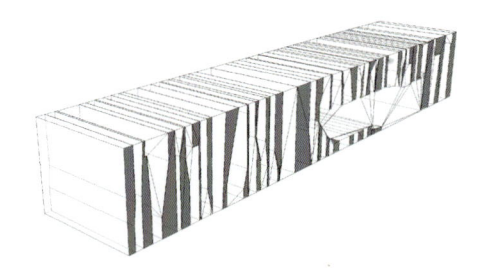

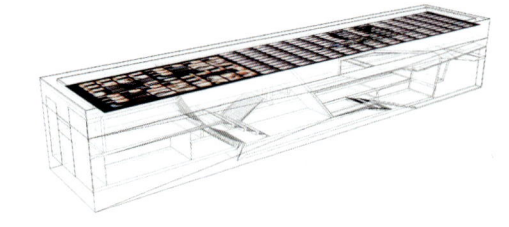

NAM JUNE PAIK GARDEN

MEDIA COLONNADE

NAM JUNE PAIK MUSEUM

CHANNEL 02 MEDIA SCULPTURE

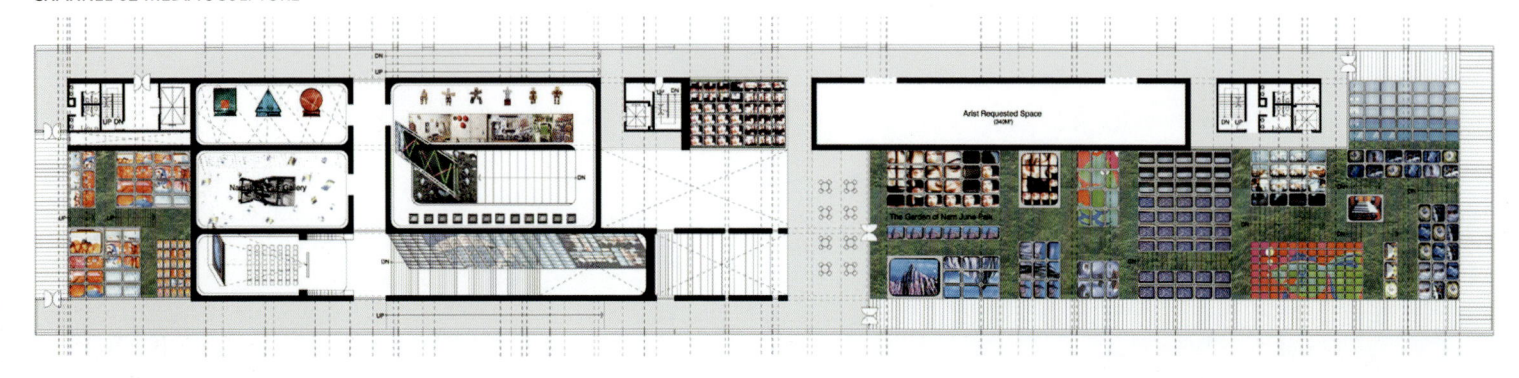

CHANNEL 03 MEDIA GARDEN

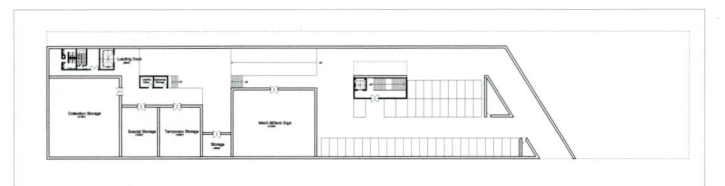

Basement Floor Plan

Ground Floor Plan

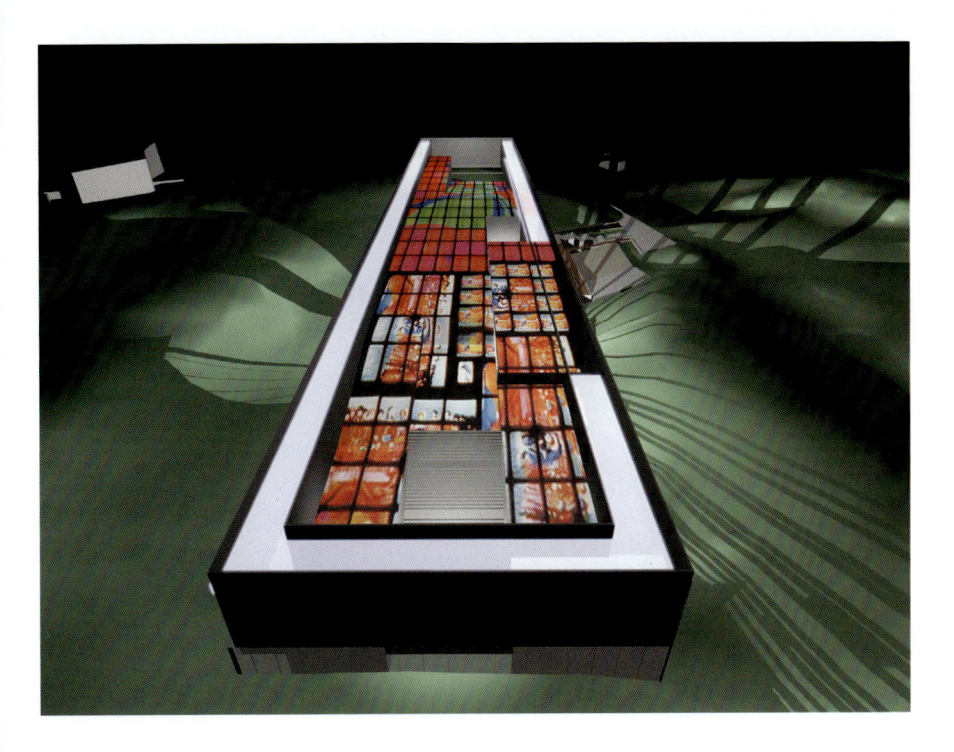

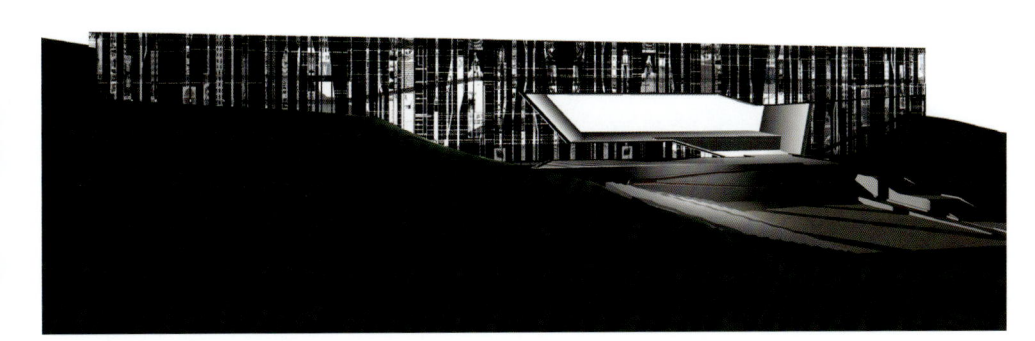

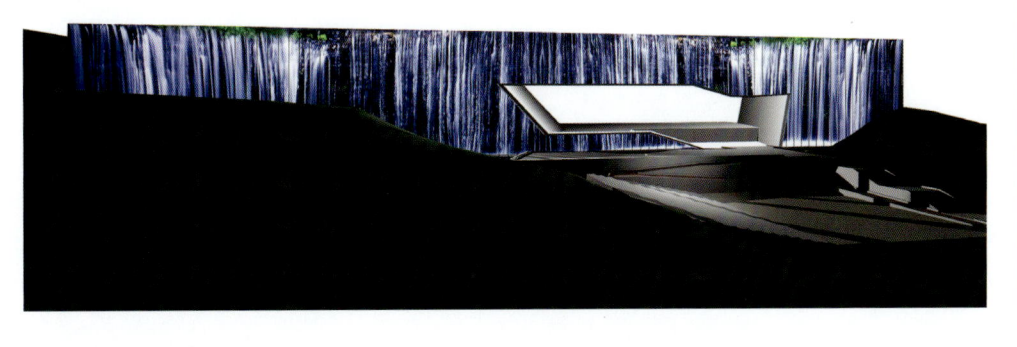

Channel 02_
Nam June Paik Museum Media Sculpture
Nam June Paik Museum is another channel space, which is called ⟨Media Sculpture⟩ in whole gallery space. This one has different section and spatial depth through main theme of each exhibition. This sectional space is proposed to have various exhibition ways and routes and creates multi-layered dramatic space in each different section. Nam June Paik Museum is a Media Sculpture and a reaction device for symphony of 20 spaces in a huge glass box

Channel 03_
Nam June Paik Garden -Media Garden
Visitors can meet a special garden at the roof gallery of this building. It is a sort of mediating space to connect in between interior and exterior exhibition spaces, which is unfixed and changeable for his needs on new exhibition. The whole exterior space of it is constituted by landscape map like ⟨Matrix⟩ and this exhibition area is flexible on the size, height, capacity, and lighting. This Nam June Paik Garden is a framed-structure of digital environment for horizontal events and exhibitions on the roof garden.

Channel 04_
Media Colonnade
Media Colonnade is another channel of Nam June Paik to make the digital surface of media, which is reacting an information layer in between double surfaces and gallery space. The glass box provided by electrical device is a digital skin, a frame to make various media space, and a transparent-translucent device to make a huge Media Falling by various information and media skin.

Pusan Tower

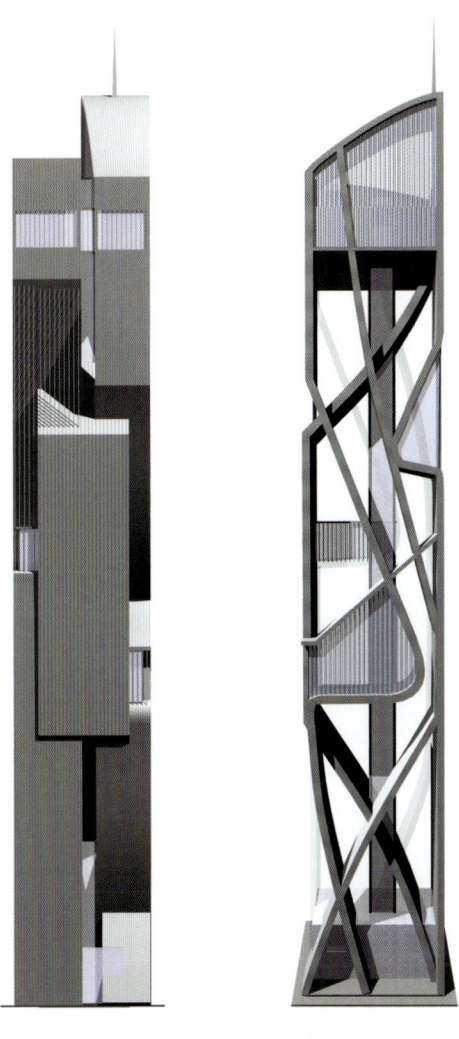

Architects Jang Yoon Gyoo, Shin Chang Hoon, Park Byung Kyu, Lee Mee Young

COMPOUND BODY 353

VARIOUS OBSERVATORY LEVEL PERSPECTIVE

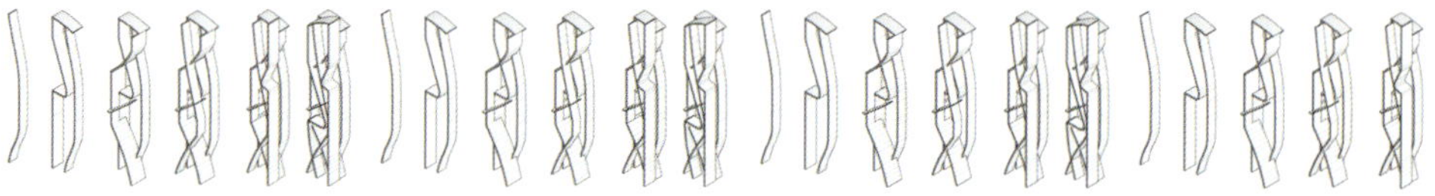

INTERACTIVE PASSAGE

Interactive Scape Map - Section of Wave
As city and its society cannot be described as singular organization and code, observatory building programs requires varieties. The frame work for variety is created by architectural system that has multi-layered structure, as interactive structure. A strategy is to formed New Busan Tower by inserting interactive map into observatory. The experience is not made partly or immediately, but with vertical and horizontal continuity by applying the concept of interactive plates. In here, interactive structure has meaning of <Trans-Programming> <Trans-Space> ..... and <Trans-Structure> by Symbolic Wave Cross Map. Map of interactive-scape, which is drafted from the compounding skin, is also the map that represents symbolical appearance the Sea Wave, DNA, ...,and Dragon movement. It is also a representation that describes the connection of the city, human, media, information,.... and digital future.

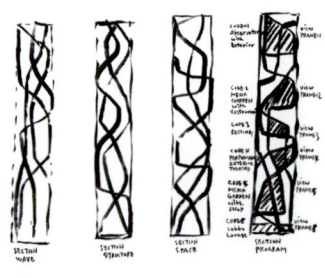

Interactive Plates Landscape for Yongdu Hill Park
In master plan concept, interactive plates concept will apply and make interactive landscape plates with exhibition hall, monuments, dragon tower, wefare hall, and parking,..etc.
Interactive Landscape Plate bands is about displaying the program that generates from functional and urban contextual reaction, within Yongdu hill park. Band of interactive plate was formed by applying the concept of, firstly, layer that are programmed with natural and environmental thoughts derived from site, and secondly, memorial information layers that provides urban park needs such as resting, memory, visibility, approach, identification and information.

Compound Body between Space and Structure
These continuous interactive skins of multi-waves, are operated folding and flowing space, have ambiguity of space between exterior and interior. These is transformed into the hyper-dimensional skin.
These continuous waved plates create structure of Compound Body between Space and Structure, between Skin and Structure ..... and between Wall and Floor. There is no distribution of general architectural element.
This compound body, which is rigid structure, make Spacial Structure and Structural Space with Hyper-Folding & Flowing.
Interactive Plates with Program Section. These Continuous Skins of multi-section is operated to the Plate with Observatory Function. The Transformation of program on waved plates is started from the continuous exchange of these elements : Program skin, Media skin, Information skin, Landscape skin, Cultural skin, ... etc. The horizontal plates exchange into the program which is related to observatory function. It is program, ground level-main lobby, second level-media garden, third level-restaurant, fourth level-media garden, fifth level-exterior performance, sixth level-resting, seventh level-panoramic observatory, eighth level-exterior observatory and media garden.

Various Picture Frame
Structure of compound body becomes another observatory with different view frames for various kinds of view interface. Under the concept of interactive map, Busan Tower will be designed not for unique view frame, but for the visitors to experience various senses by the section of continuous folding, flowing and crossing plates. Various Section of view frame make different experience of urban panoramic view-scape.

Informative Map - Media Falling and Light Falling
City and society of future will not be organization that is intermittently constituted by singular code. Busan Tower stands at heart that provides and link various information city. We can draw the needs of information and digital of future in the interactive map.
Urban lighting code : Change of lighting from the connection of the cityscape becomes apart of urban luminary.
Medial Falling code : Busan tower is to make powerful code which provides information. Media information is pouring down like is falls along the folded plates.
The Media Flow inner folding plates not only provides basic information for visitor but also events by employing various installations such as media projection, sound, smell and light, 3-dimensional loop will form, starting from public main lobby to different observatories on different levels and functions.

INTERACTIVE PLATES LANDSCAPE FOR YONGDU HILL PARK

COMPOUND BODY

INFORMATIVE- MEDIA FALLING AND LIGHT FALLING

Landscpae
stacking

City Tower in ChungLa

Architects Jang Yoon Gyoo, Shin Chang Hoon, Kang Seung Hyun

ELEVATION

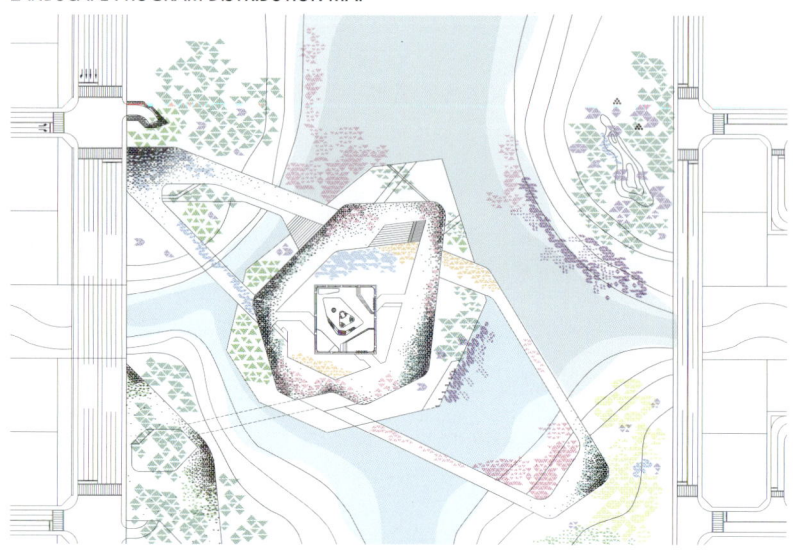

LANDSCAPE PROGRAM DISTRIBUTION MAP

SCENERY OF LANDSCAPE

MYTHOLOGICAL STUPA

Bulguksa Seokgatap | Bulguksa Dabotap | Citytower | Hwangnyongsa 9 Floors Wood Stupa

LANDSCAPE STACKING WITH PASSAGE

Scenery of Landscape
We suggest the city tower be the scenery of Landscape. It represents the variation and perpetuity of nature. In the oriental view of nature the scenery of Landscape is perceived as a scene of changing nature through time. The tower interacts with the ever-changing spectacle of nature that shifts through time yet exists like a living organism. Various new experiences and functions for observation can be combined together, creating a compound tower. The tower will provide wider publicity to Korea, and become a visionary milestone in the city of Inchun.

Mythological Stupa
The new city tower should be a symbolic gesture of the progressing urban culture while representing the desire for new social ideals. We can create a city tower as a mythological existence similar to Korea's historic stupa which implies various cultural, social, and political hopes. It will constantly change and reflect contemporary issues, becoming the center of interactive communication.

Stacking City Program with Nature

We suggests City Tower be a vertical stacking of various urban fabrics and programs. The strategy is to re-organize and pile up diverse programs clipped from horizontal urban structures. The common organization of conventional tower, with an observation platform on top and a commercial program in the lower part, can be dissolved as the programs are distributed vertically throughout the whole tower. The tower could be a compound of programs such as parks, cultural space, sports and leisure, and shopping mall. The form of stacking varies according to the qualities of various programs and their volumes. This morphologic, volumetric variation creates the stacked tower of urban programs. The various programs on various levels remain independent, but they also interact with each other deriving diverse experiences. By stacking the natural and artificial elements vertically, the tower becomes a condensed entity of city and nature.

Scenic Organism

The observation platform exhibits fascinating sceneries from four seasons of Korea's landscape. Each of the morphing-sections can be composed of semi-exterior space for a complex experience of both internal programs and external scenery.

1. Inserting Korea's Natural landscape
The tower as a scenic organism will provide various visages : fields of flowers in spring, flourishing greens and refreshing waterfalls in summer, colorful leaves in fall, and sublime snow-scapes in winter.

2. Structural skin as a frame for scenic views
Between the interior space and the outside environment, the structural skin becomes a medium that captures the dramatic scenery of Korean landscape.

3. City reactor as an artificial landscape
Standing in the center of the Cheongna district in Inchun, the tower is a city reactor that interacts with changing seasons, events, and time like an organic body. It transforms and reacts to the natural environment and the condition of the city with diverse devices, such as the digital cascade, mirage-like smog, continuously changing eco skin and the interactive city lightings.

COMPOUND BODY 361

STACKING PERFORMANCE

City   Forest   Program   History

INSERTING PROGRAM

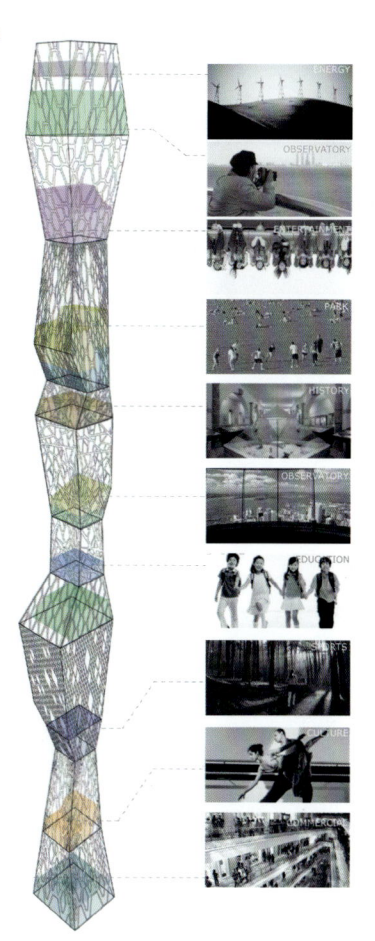

STACKING CITY PROGRAM

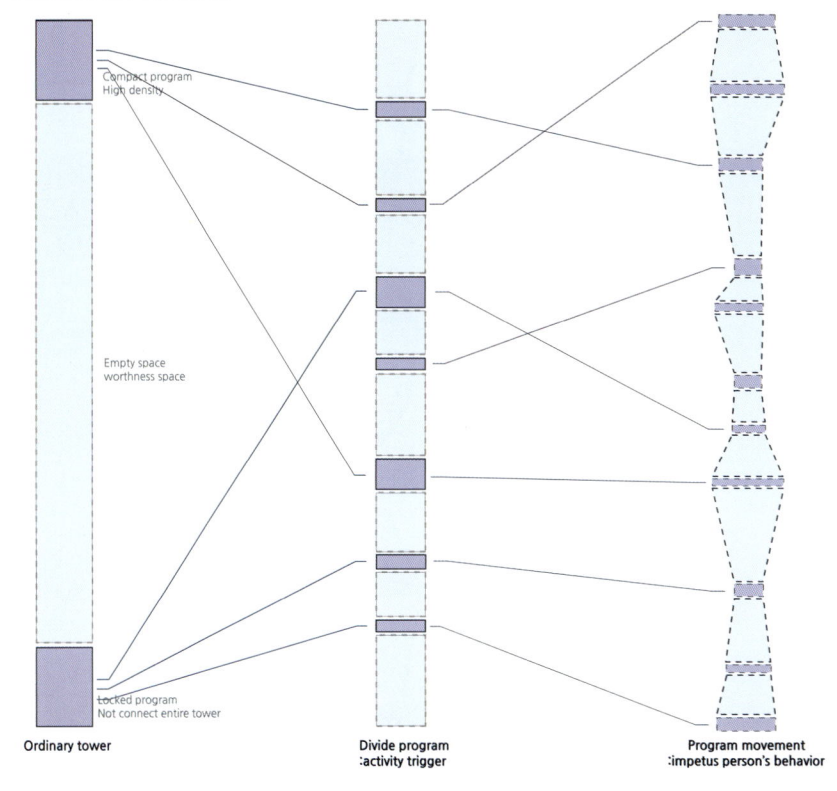

Compact program
High density

Empty space
worthness space

Locked program
Not connect entire tower

Ordinary tower   Divide program
:activity trigger   Program movement
:impetus person's behavior

SCENIC ORGANISM

Spring   Summer   Fog

ROLE OF PROGRAM

REQUIRMENT BY SCENARIO	PROPOSAL	PROGRAM	SQUARE	WELFARE	SHOPPING	MOVEMENT	STOP	HISTORY	SUSTAINABLE
Empty of Facade	Common Ownership	Square Join							
History preservation	History Office	History Museum							
Reappearance of Past Trace	Apply to Past Element	Floor Pattern							
Axis Usage (Road and View)	Axis arrangement	Right side Extand							
High rise buinding	450m	Sunken and Double Layer							
Platform to Dynamic	Standard of Plot Plan	Construct by View Axis							
Platform to Sea	Vista toward sea	Mass design for Vista							
Community Space	Empty + Enjoy + Community	Agora							
Control Box / Speculation Box	Flexible Space / Silent Space	Mass and Ground form							
Plus Nature	Water +Green	Front Water Founding							
Connection Path	Vertical and Horizantal Pass	Reinforce of Connection							
Shelter of Weak	Social Restoration	Nursery / Shelter							
View Axis	Vista toward	Mass design for Vista							
Passage from front to rear	Sublation Filling of Building	Thin and Division Mass							
New Digital Culture	Intention of Intelligent Digital	Mediatheque							
Less Builing, More Complex Square	Double Using of Total Space	Various out, Ind							

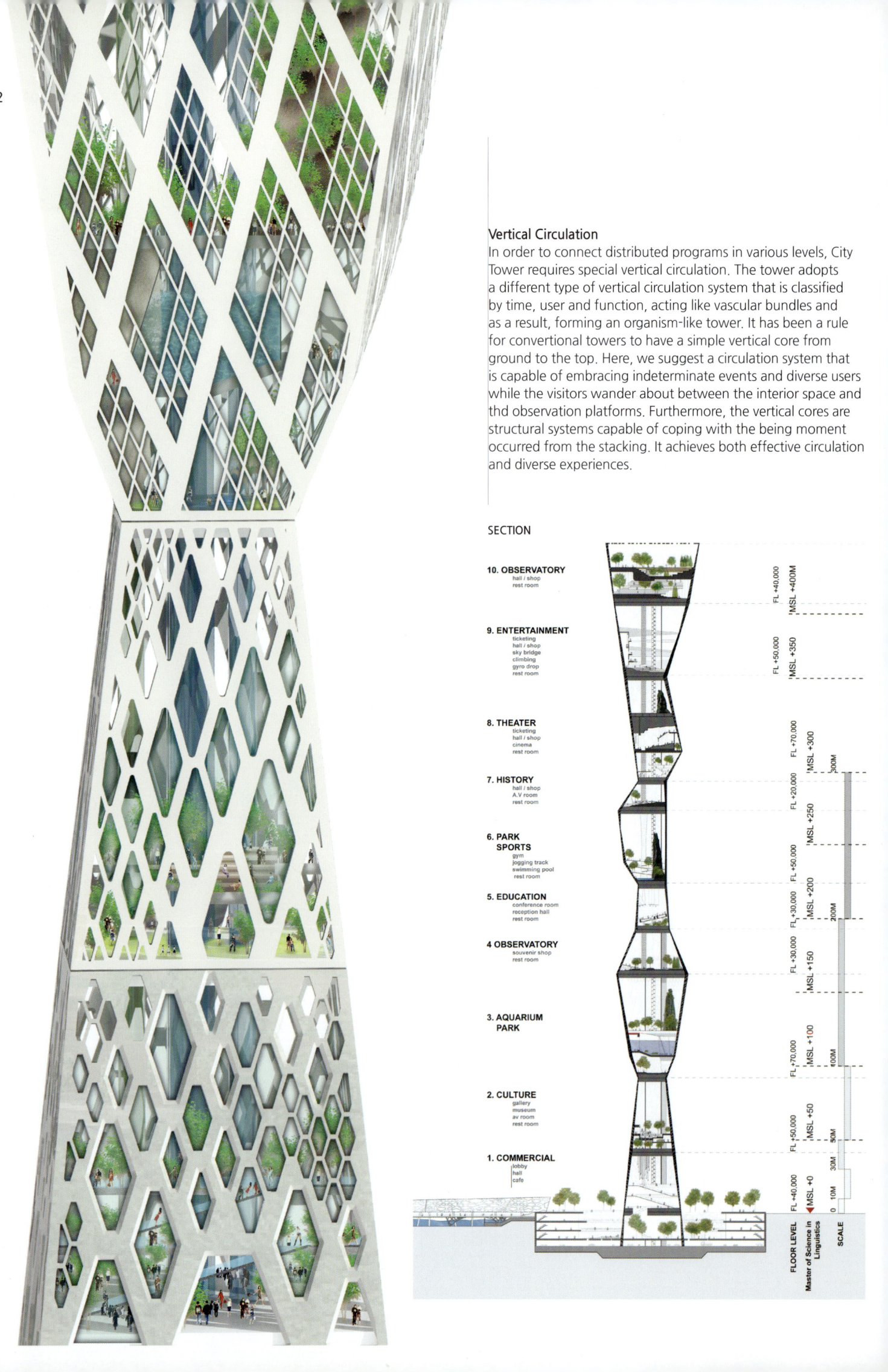

Vertical Circulation

In order to connect distributed programs in various levels, City Tower requires special vertical circulation. The tower adopts a different type of vertical circulation system that is classified by time, user and function, acting like vascular bundles and as a result, forming an organism-like tower. It has been a rule for convertional towers to have a simple vertical core from ground to the top. Here, we suggest a circulation system that is capable of embracing indeterminate events and diverse users while the visitors wander about between the interior space and thd observation platforms. Furthermore, the vertical cores are structural systems capable of coping with the being moment occurred from the stacking. It achieves both effective circulation and diverse experiences.

SECTION

10. OBSERVATORY
    hall / shop
    rest room

9. ENTERTAINMENT
    ticketing
    hall / shop
    sky bridge
    climbing
    gyro drop
    rest room

8. THEATER
    ticketing
    hall / shop
    cinema
    rest room

7. HISTORY
    hall / shop
    A.V room
    rest room

6. PARK
   SPORTS
    gym
    jogging track
    swimming pool
    rest room

5. EDUCATION
    conference room
    reception hall
    rest room

4. OBSERVATORY
    souvenir shop
    rest room

3. AQUARIUM
   PARK

2. CULTURE
    gallery
    museum
    av room
    rest room

1. COMMERCIAL
    lobby
    hall
    cafe

STACKING COMPOSITION

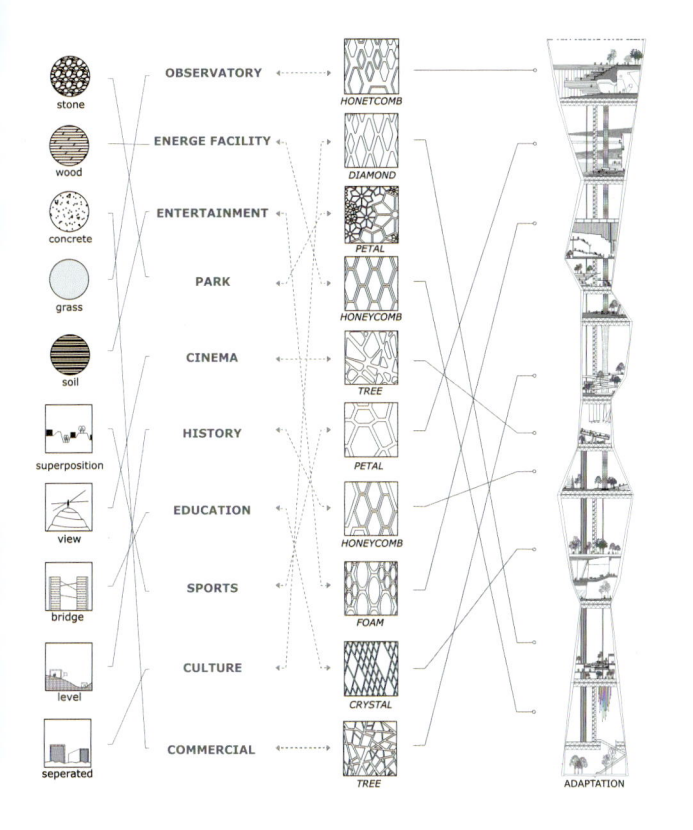

stone	OBSERVATORY — HONEYCOMB
wood	ENERGE FACILITY — DIAMOND
concrete	ENTERTAINMENT — PETAL
grass	PARK — HONEYCOMB
soil	CINEMA — TREE
superposition	HISTORY — PETAL
view	EDUCATION — HONEYCOMB
bridge	SPORTS — FOAM
level	CULTURE — CRYSTAL
seperated	COMMERCIAL — TREE

ADAPTATION

SKIN STRUCTURE

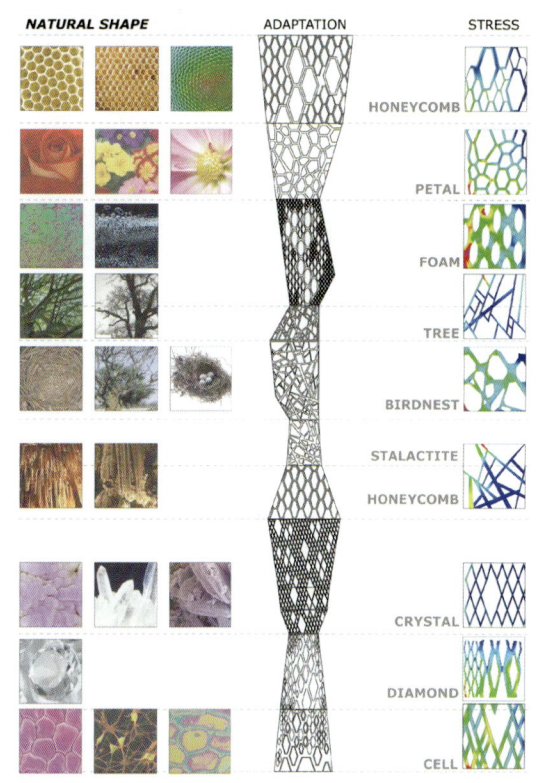

NATURAL SHAPE — ADAPTATION — STRESS

- HONEYCOMB
- PETAL
- FOAM
- TREE
- BIRDNEST
- STALACTITE
- HONEYCOMB
- CRYSTAL
- DIAMOND
- CELL

1. Compound Structure - The dynamic structure of the tower itself is integrated to the skin of the building, forming a synthetic and vigorous enentity. The integration occurs in a side rage of elements: structure and skin, structure and view frame, structure and inner program, skin and programs, skin and view frame.
2. Stacked Structure - the strategy for the structures of the tower is the stacking and joining of each independently stable structure, like the way that programs are stacked and connected. When each structure integrates with different programs they are transformed into various forms of skin structures and applied.
3. Nature Motive - Motive of the skin and structure is derived from the materials and organizations of the nature. Forms such as honeycomb, bark, bubble and diamond provides ideas for highly stable and organic structures. Each stacked part of the skin independently stands on its own.

VERTICAL CIRCULATION

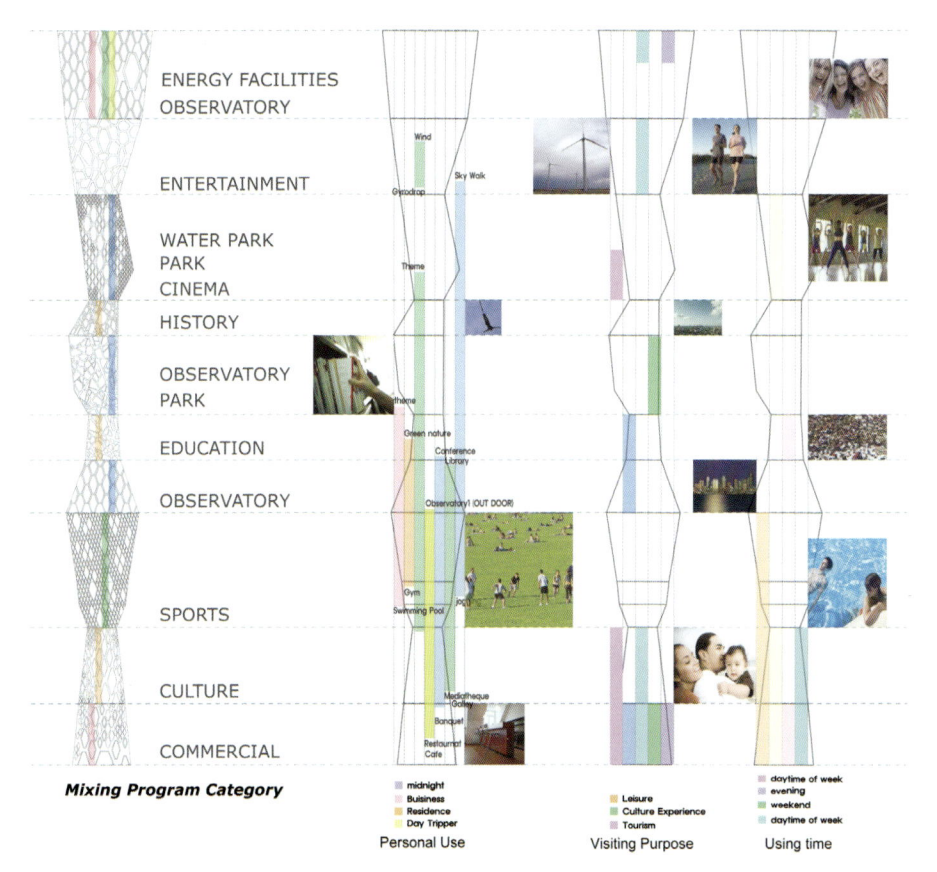

- ENERGY FACILITIES / OBSERVATORY
- ENTERTAINMENT
- WATER PARK / PARK / CINEMA
- HISTORY
- OBSERVATORY / PARK
- EDUCATION
- OBSERVATORY
- SPORTS
- CULTURE
- COMMERCIAL

Mixing Program Category

Personal Use: midnight, Buisiness, Residence, Day Tripper
Visiting Purpose: Leisure, Culture Experience, Tourism
Using time: daytime of week, evening, weekend, daytime of week

1. Efficency core - The efficiency core is a direct connection on between the ground floor and observation platform on the top floor. It vertically passes throung the whole tower providing a sequential view of various stacked programs on each floor.
2. Experience core - We suggest several branches of divided circulation core that intimately connect vertically stacked programs while providing an interesting experience. Penetrating the natural, artificial, programmed space, the circulation cores offer diverse experiences.

INTERACTIVE EXPERIENCE FIELD

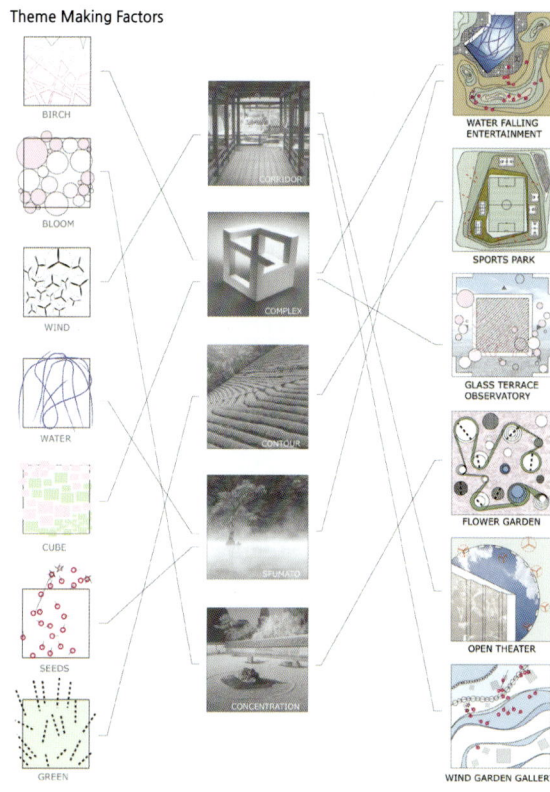

Theme Making Factors

- BIRCH — CORRIDOR — WATER FALLING ENTERTAINMENT
- BLOOM — COMPLEX — SPORTS PARK
- WIND — CONTOUR — GLASS TERRACE OBSERVATORY
- WATER — FLOWER GARDEN
- CUBE — OPEN THEATER
- SEEDS — CONCENTRATION — WIND GARDEN GALLERY
- GREEN

// Instead of plane, flat floor plan arrangement, we organized the programs such as nature, culture, sports, education and leisure three-dimensionally. The spaces for various events and observation activities are arranged and combined adequately. For example, the artificial mountian lifted up 300m from the ground will offer a whole new experience of superb nature, and the two separate glass observatory terrace will provide a spectacular view of east-northern asia. Also, the wind flowing valley, rest space with cascade falling, an extreme park, the children education programs, entertainment facilities and information center will be included in the tower, offering diverse experiences for a wide range of people.

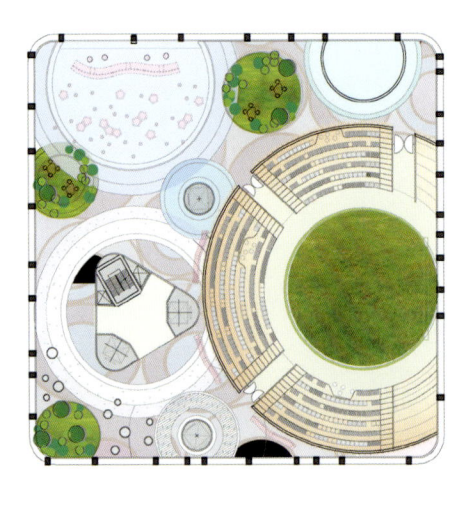

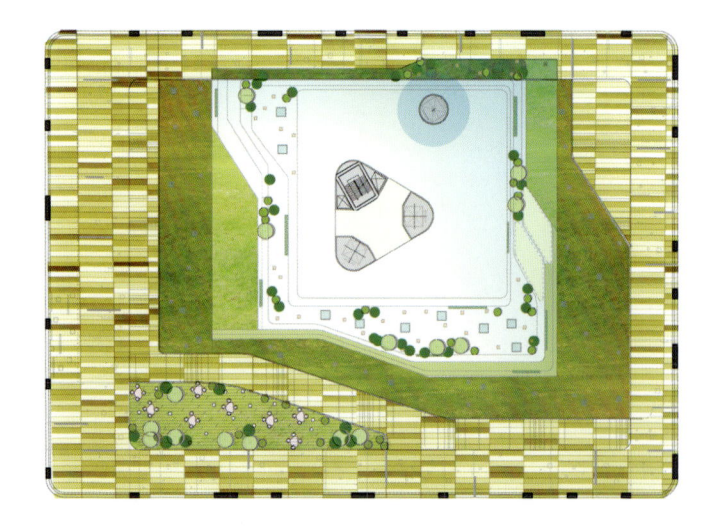

▶ **Theater park**

It is one of the gardens of four seasons, and it is an exotic space with Korean landscape garden and cinema combined together.

3D Media theater

It is a multi-functional space showing dynamic images and performances

▶ **Event roof_
outdoor observation platform on the top floor**

Terraced space that can hold various events like city stage.

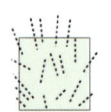

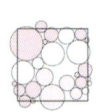

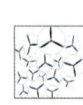

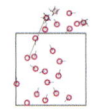

COMPOUND BODY 365

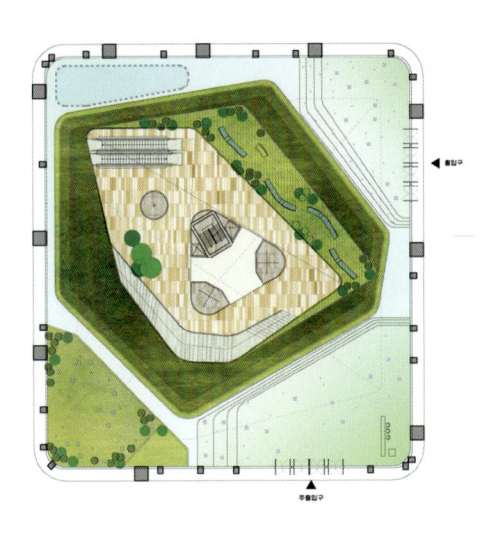

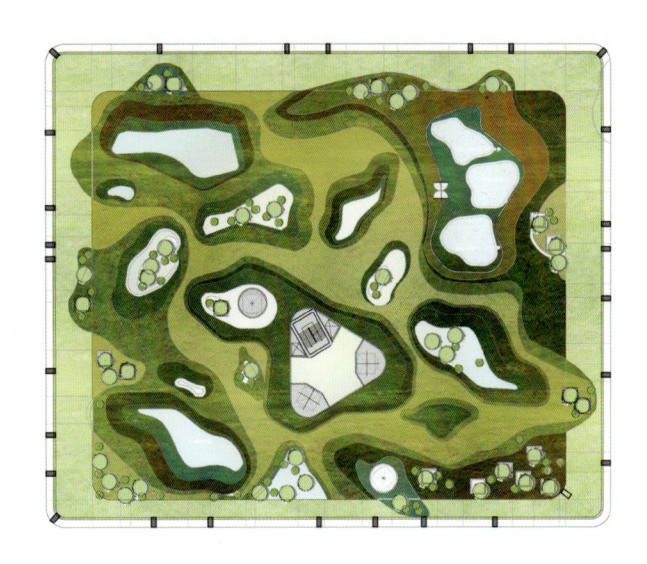

▶ **Commercial park**

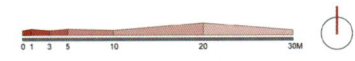

Small shops along the ramp and the promenade form a park-like commercial space. It is connected to the main lobby space which is accessible from both ground and underground level.

▶ **Sub-observatory**

It is an indoor observatory offering close view of the city and providing space for temporary events

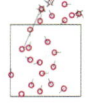

SUSTAINABLE PROGRAM

RECYCLING WATER | WIND FORCE | ACTIVE SOLAR | PIEZOELECTRONIC

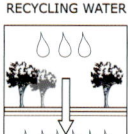

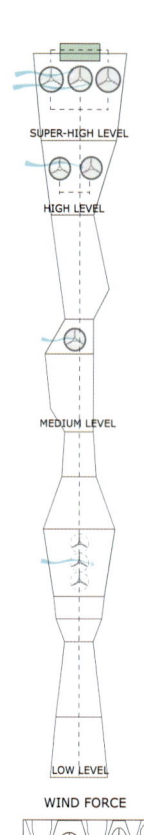

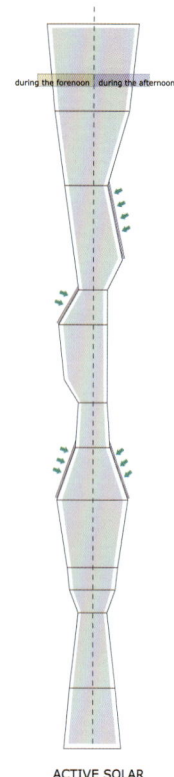

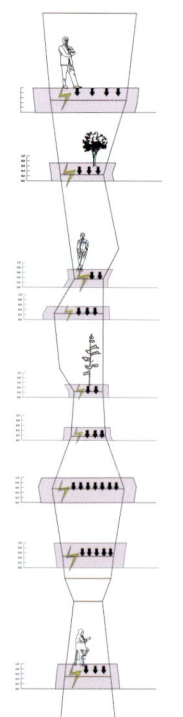

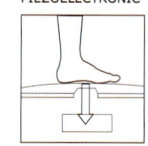

Sustainable Program

The tower is open to various new experiences being created through the association of different programs beyond their categories. The 450m tower consists of a sequence of diverse spaces. The currently emptied space or outdoor spaces can be transformed to hold the new associated programs that continuously being generated. The empty spaces inside the tower operate as a resonating container for vibrant urban events.

1. Flexible skin structure - inside the frame of the skin and the structure, the city tower enables various programs to interact and conjugate with each other. The void spaces are capable of transforming into a space for holding programs of the demands of the times. It reflects both the continuity and transformation of the city through time.

2. Skin-eco
Various forms and types of skin are applied according to the requirements and conditions of the each program inside: 1) plant-like skin 2) solar panels integrated to skin 3) glass skin in lens form 4) wind power plant skin.

3. Water circulation
Water from sea and rain is collected and circulated from bottom to top, utilizing it for various functions of the tower. The after-use water is purified by the circulating process and recycled without letting contaminated water outside the tower. By this system, the tower is self-sufficient and eco-friendly

STRUCTURE CONCEPT EXPOSITION_SKIN
SKIN STRUCTURE PLAN
Wind load decrease proposal

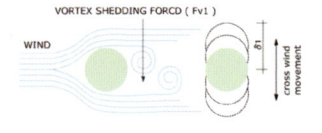

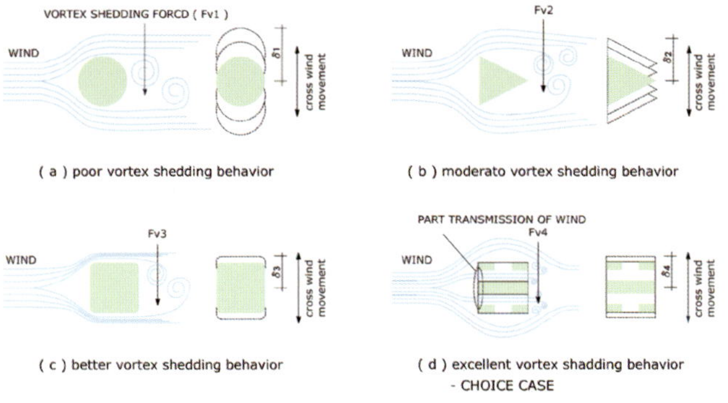

(a) poor vortex shedding behavior
(b) moderato vortex shedding behavior
(c) better vortex shedding behavior
(d) excellent vortex shadding behavior — CHOICE CASE

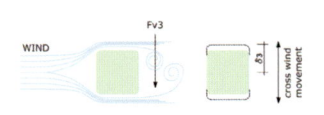

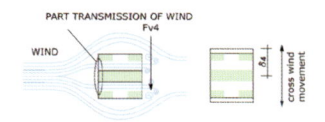

$Fv1 > Fv2 > Fv3 > Fv4 \rightarrow \delta1 > \delta2 > \delta3 > \delta4$

Stress & Deformation of each skin type

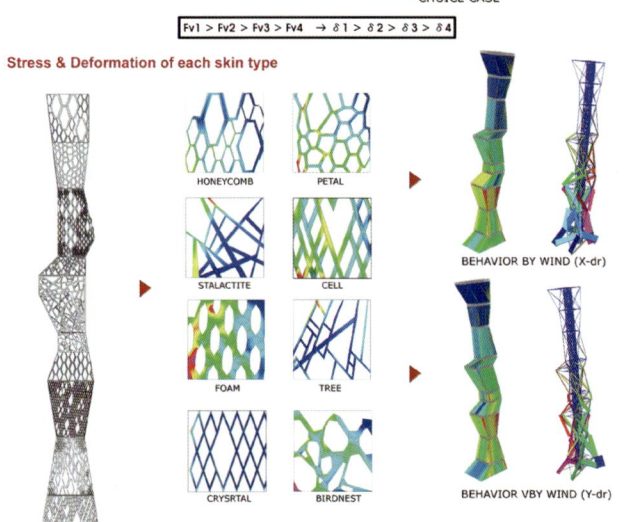

HONEYCOMB / PETAL / STALACTITE / CELL / FOAM / TREE / CRYSRTAL / BIRDNEST

BEHAVIOR BY WIND (X-dr)
BEHAVIOR VBY WIND (Y-dr)

STRUCTURE CONCEPT EXPOSITION_STACK
SLENDER TOWER

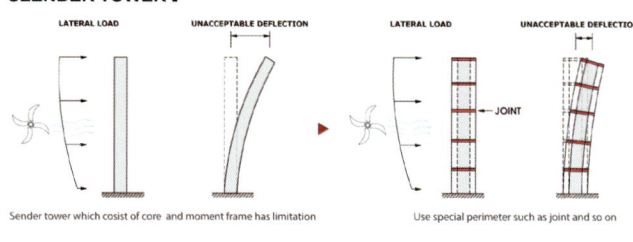

LATERAL LOAD — UNACCEPTABLE DEFLECTION — LATERAL LOAD — UNACCEPTABLE DEFLECTION — JOINT

Sender tower which cosist of core and moment frame has limitation
Use special perimeter such as joint and so on

JOINT STRUCTURE | Strong link between MASS to MASS ▶ Joint Structure

MASS + MASS = MASS LINK MASS + MASS = MASS LINK MASS LINK MASS

| Slenderness Ratio : Average 7~8 | Very Slender type | Need a special LATERAL - LOAD residence system | Apply BAMBOO to structure | a BAMBOO with Joint Structure / Higher Slenderness ratio (over 10) |

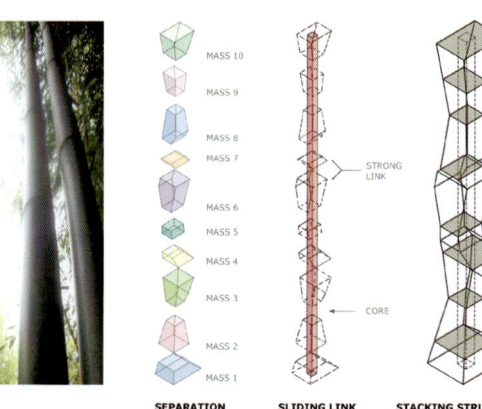

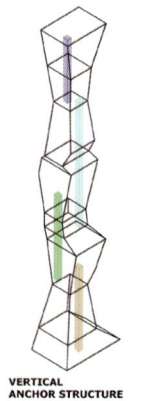

MASS 10 / MASS 9 / MASS 8 / MASS 7 / MASS 6 / MASS 5 / MASS 4 / MASS 3 / MASS 2 / MASS 1

STRONG LINK — CORE

SEPARATION — SLIDING LINK — STACKING STRUCTURE — VERTICAL ANCHOR STRUCTURE

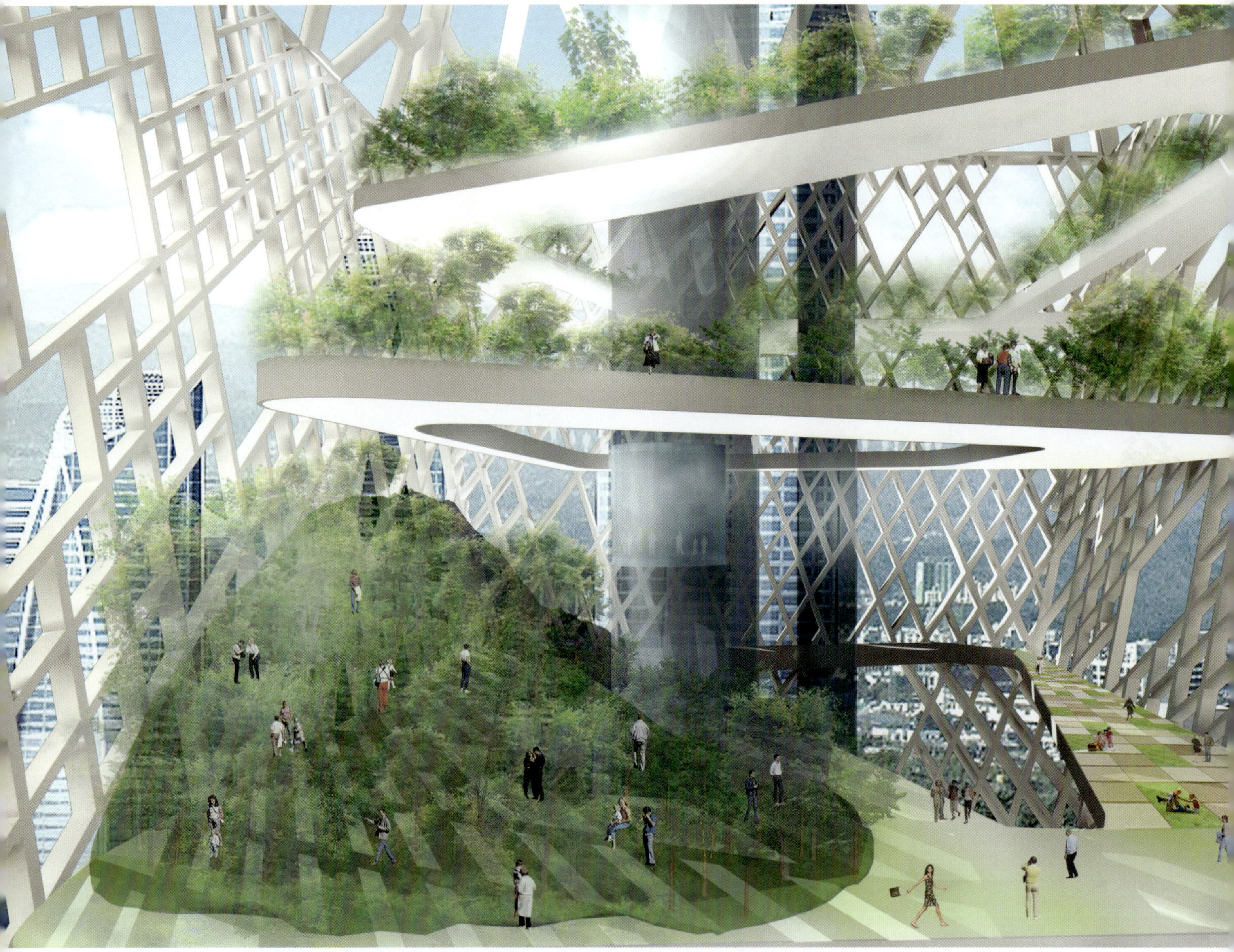

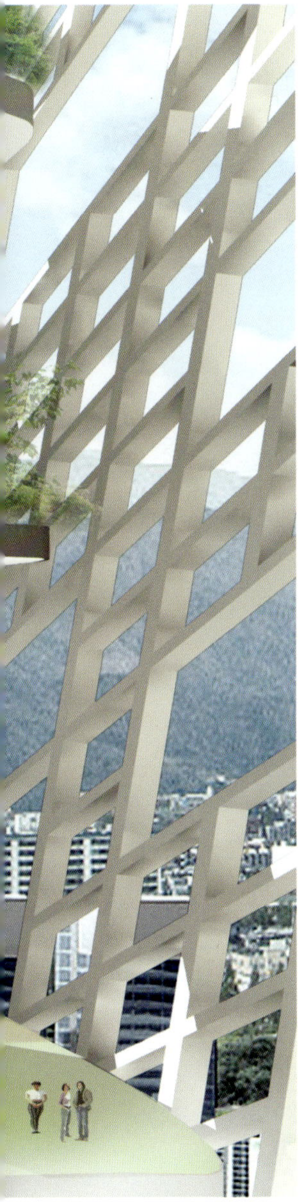
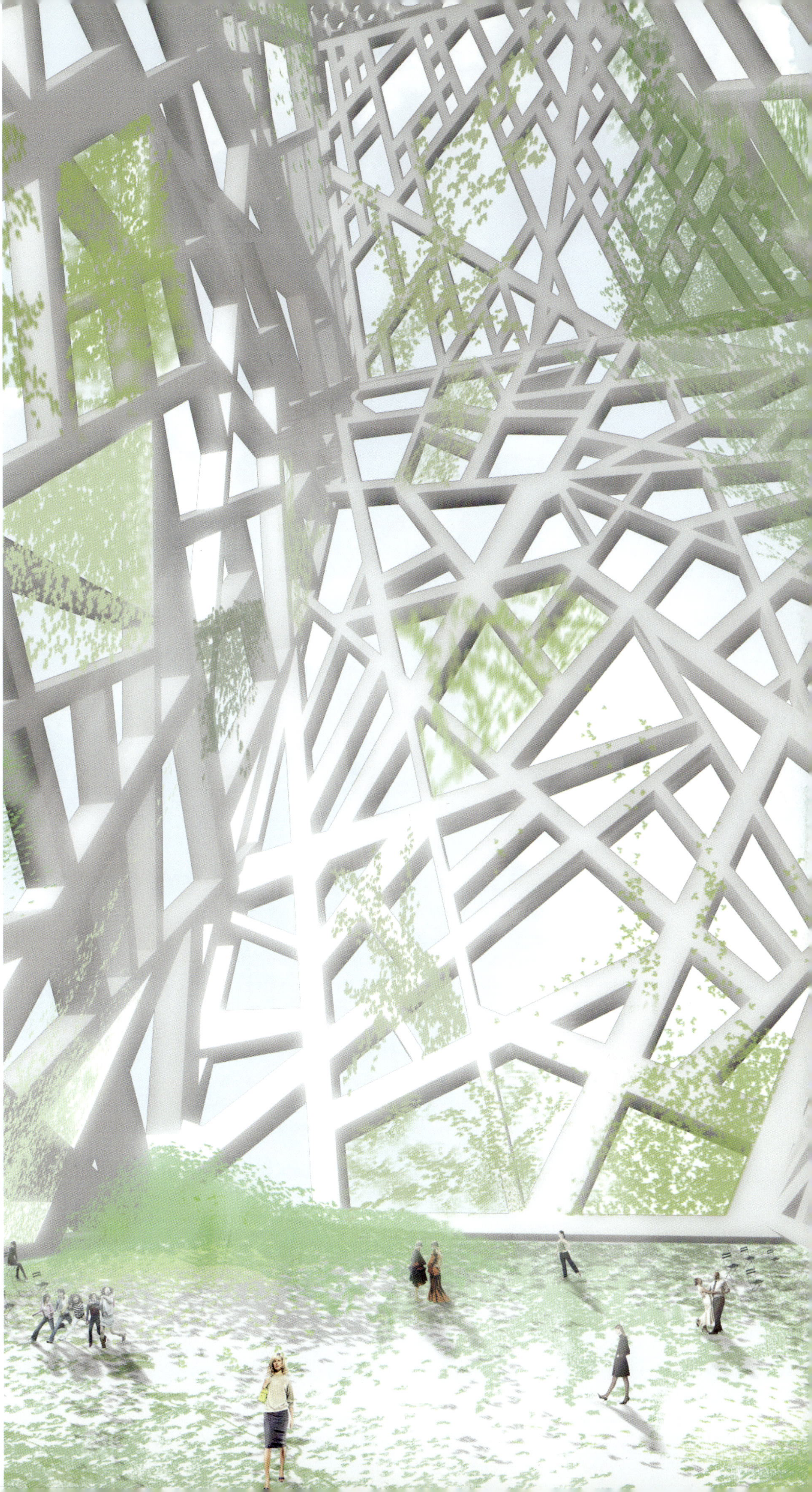

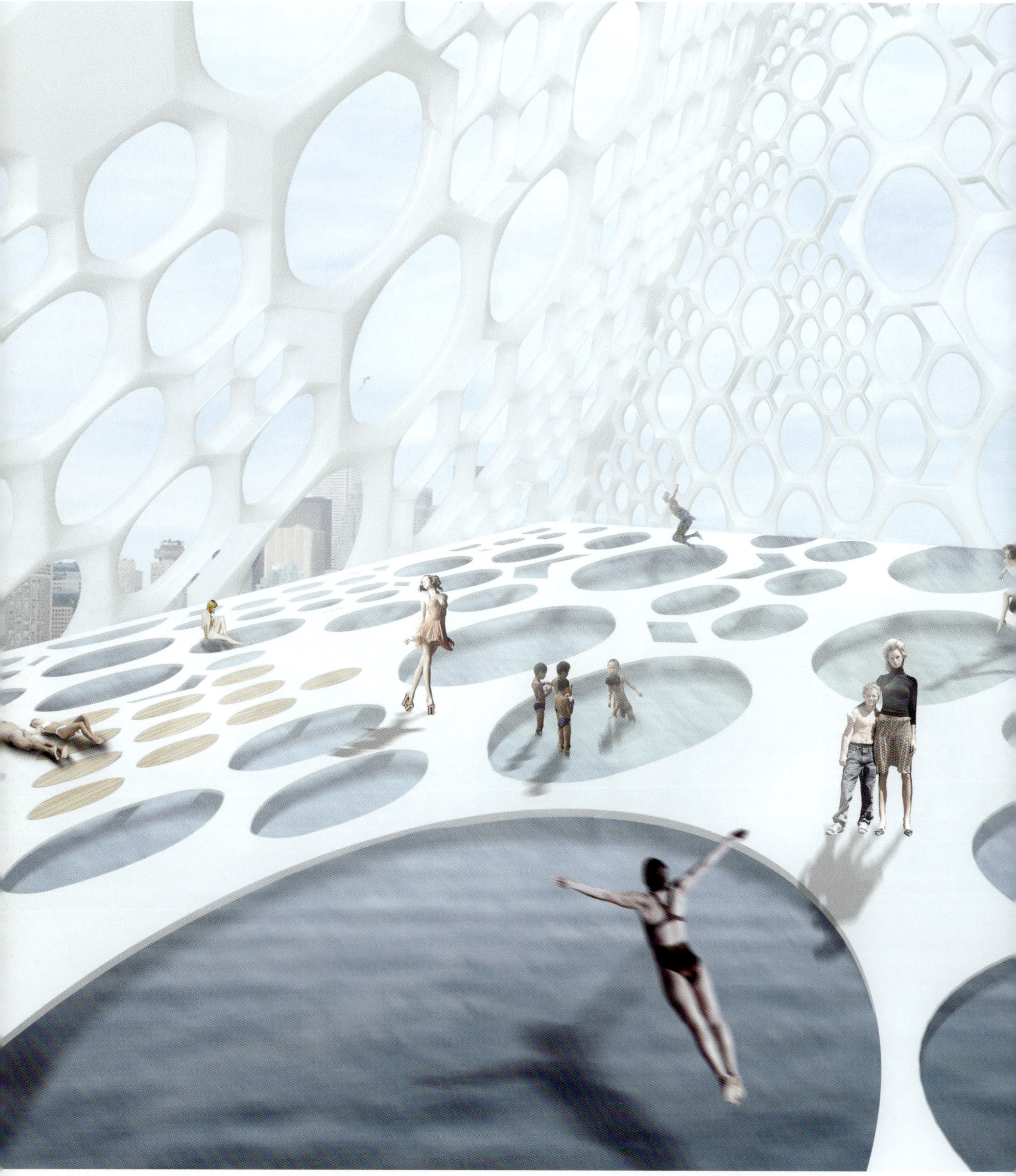

COMPOUND BODY 371

Architects Jang Yoon Gyoo, Shin Chang Hoon
Project Team Kim Sung Min, Seo Hye Lim, Kim Se Jin, Kim Min Tae, Kang Seung Hyun, Goh Young Dong, Yi Tae Hyun, Choi Ji Won, Oh Yeun Keung
Location CheongLa Incheon, South Korea
Use Tower
Site Area 110,425.0m²

ChiChi Memorial

Architects Jang Yoon Gyoo, Shin Chang Hoon

COMPOUND BODY 373

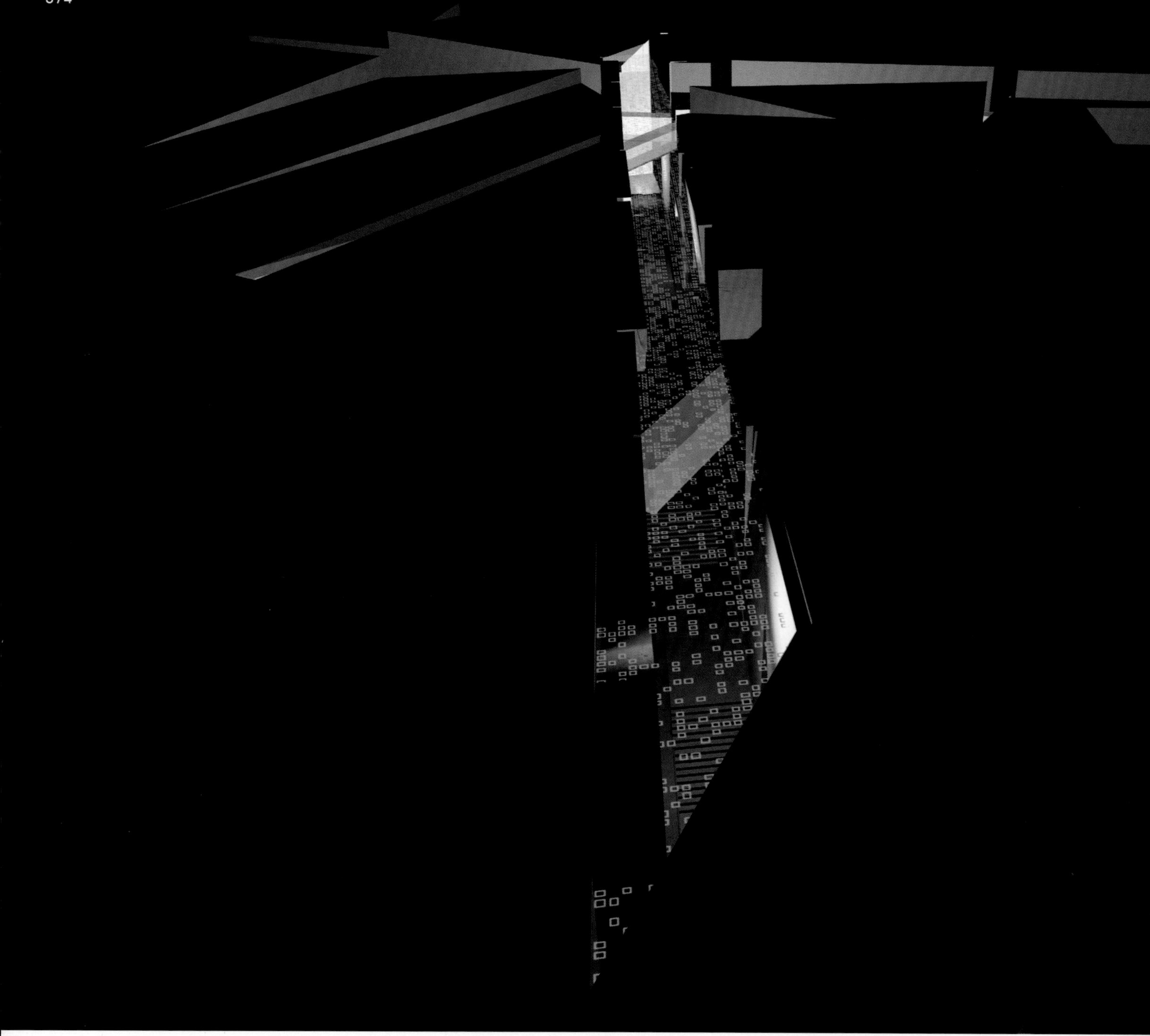

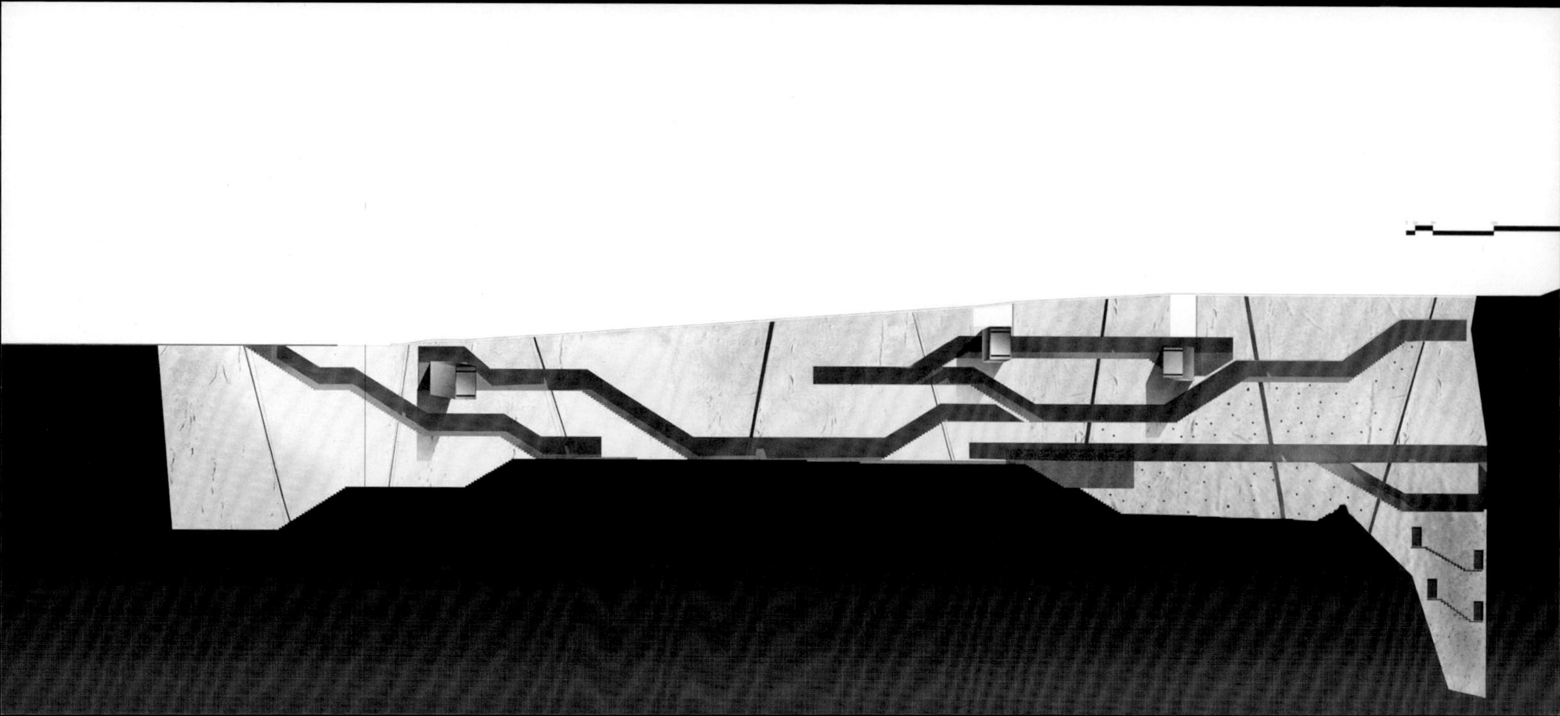

Our first attempt to define the concept of the CHICHI MEMORIAL is to see the whole site as one piece of monument. Instead of positioning the object at a certain spot, we try to find a way to disclose the dormant monumentality in the site.
This way, every piece of the site becomes the subject of monumentality including the underground part of it. What makes us to see the site as a monument itself, is the fact that memories of exclamation is melted inside the ground. This project starts from the notion of monumentality and the understanding of the historical and sociological background of the project. Based on a critical approach to the monumentality, this project also includes open-ended narratives and implicit suggestion.

First, it deals with the three notions of monumentality to establish the conceptual premise.
1. monumentality is defined by what is remained at present, what remind the trace of the past, and especially what has to be achieved in the future.
2. monumentality is based on the memory shared by person and group of people. This research is focused on the shift from the personal memory to the memory of group.
3. monumentality is accompanied by the demand of continuous transformation to be remembered in time.

Secondly, while the existing monumental space emphasizes significance of the message, it is focused on the response of the messages from the monumental space itself.

Thirdly, the context of CHICHI 921 vaguely written in the site is transformed into the design elements and spatial concepts. It is also implied in design senario, circulation system plan, land use plan, and master plan.

// **FINDING the QUAKE**   An earthquake is a sudden, rapid shaking of the Earth caused by the breaking and shifting of rock beneath the Earth's surface. For hundreds of millions of years, the forces of plate tectonics have shaped the Earth as the huge plates that form the Earth's surface move slowly over, under, and past each other. Sometimes the movement is gradual. At other times, the plates are locked together, unable to release the accumulating energy. When the accumulated energy grows strong enough, the plates break free causing the ground to shake. Most earthquakes occur at the boundaries where the plates meet; however, some earthquakes occur in the middle of plates.
Trying to disclose the dormant monumentality in the site, we find several meaningful lines in the site including the trace of collapsed buildings and forces from the origin of earthquake.
We regard these lines not just as lines on the surface, but as outlines of the ground plates beneath the Earth's surface. We intend to imply the monumentality both on the surface and inside of these plates.

// **QUAKE-SCAPE : CRACKING the land_SCAPE**
generated quake / transformed landscape
Cracking the landscape is the way to expose the plates beneath the Earth's surface.
Through the generated quake of CHICHI 921, the whole site is transformed into one piece of quake-scape. This quake produces vertical and horizontal movement of plates.
We choose this process to disclose the dormant monumentality in the site.

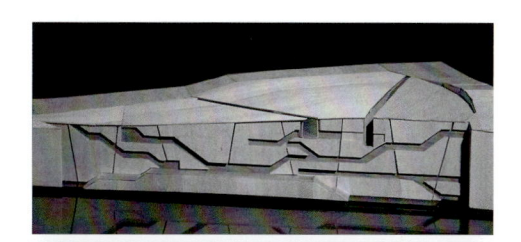

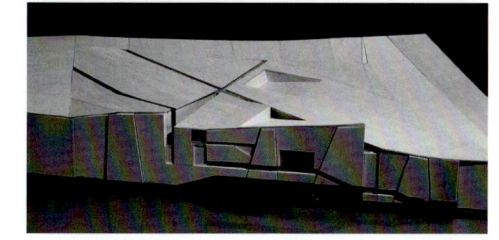

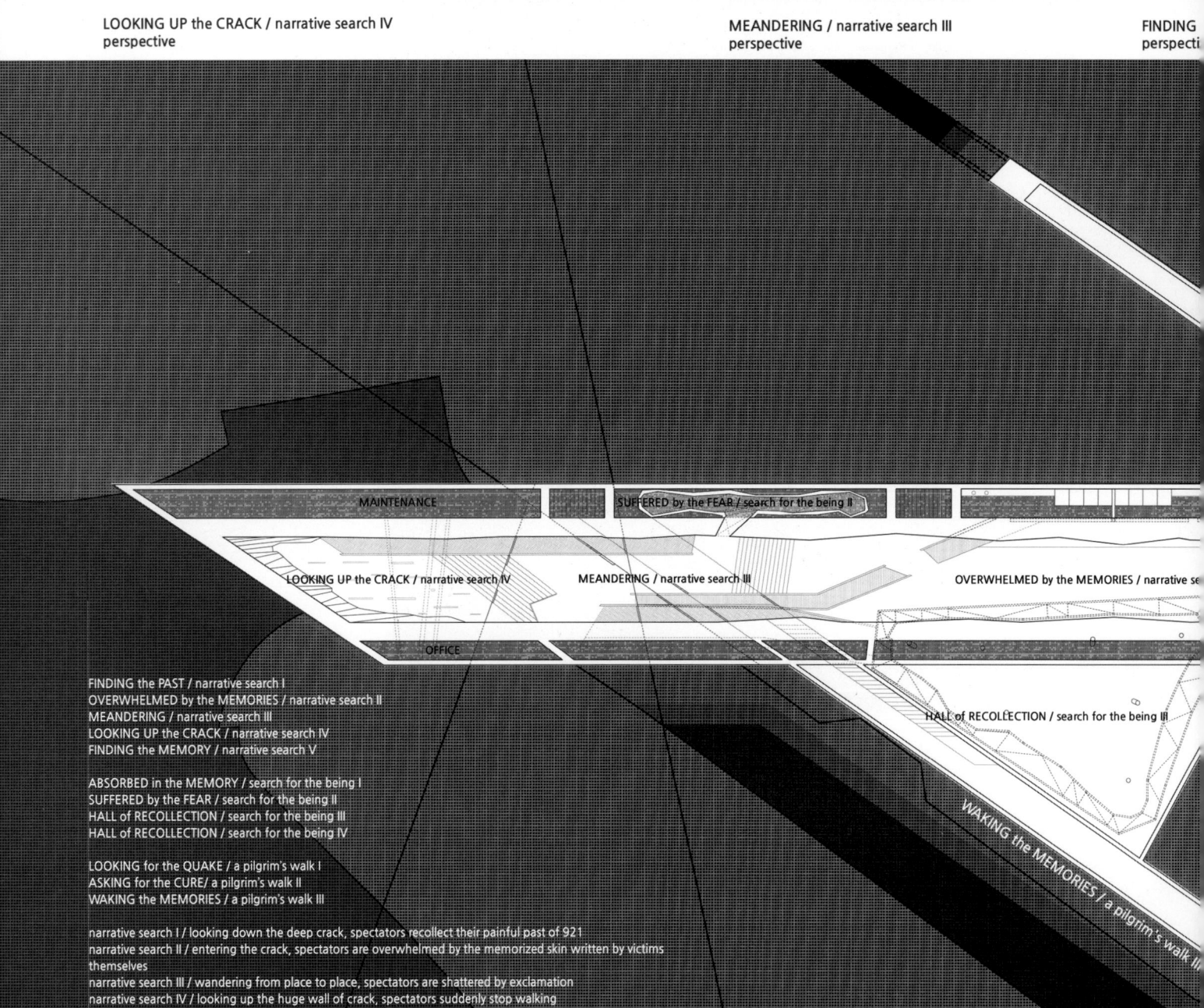

LOOKING UP the CRACK / narrative search IV
perspective

MEANDERING / narrative search III
perspective

FINDING
perspecti

MAINTENANCE
SUFFERED by the FEAR / search for the being II
LOOKING UP the CRACK / narrative search IV
MEANDERING / narrative search III
OVERWHELMED by the MEMORIES / narrative se
OFFICE
HALL of RECOLLECTION / search for the being III
WAKING the MEMORIES / a pilgrim's walk III

FINDING the PAST / narrative search I
OVERWHELMED by the MEMORIES / narrative search II
MEANDERING / narrative search III
LOOKING UP the CRACK / narrative search IV
FINDING the MEMORY / narrative search V

ABSORBED in the MEMORY / search for the being I
SUFFERED by the FEAR / search for the being II
HALL of RECOLLECTION / search for the being III
HALL of RECOLLECTION / search for the being IV

LOOKING for the QUAKE / a pilgrim's walk I
ASKING for the CURE / a pilgrim's walk II
WAKING the MEMORIES / a pilgrim's walk III

narrative search I / looking down the deep crack, spectators recollect their painful past of 921
narrative search II / entering the crack, spectators are overwhelmed by the memorized skin written by victims themselves
narrative search III / wandering from place to place, spectators are shattered by exclamation
narrative search IV / looking up the huge wall of crack, spectators suddenly stop walking
narrative search V / along the pathway, spectators find individual memories of 921

search for the being I / exhibition chamber / ABSORBED in the MEMORY
search for the being II / exhibition chamber / SUFFERED by the FEAR
search for the being III / multipurpose hall / temporary exhibition
search for the being IV / multipurpose hall / temporary exhibition

a pilgrim's walk I / walking along the trace of quake, spectators settle themselves
a pilgrim's walk II / walking across the present and the past, spectators pursuing the cure
a pilgrim's walk III / walking around the remnant of the past, spectators wake memories of the serenity

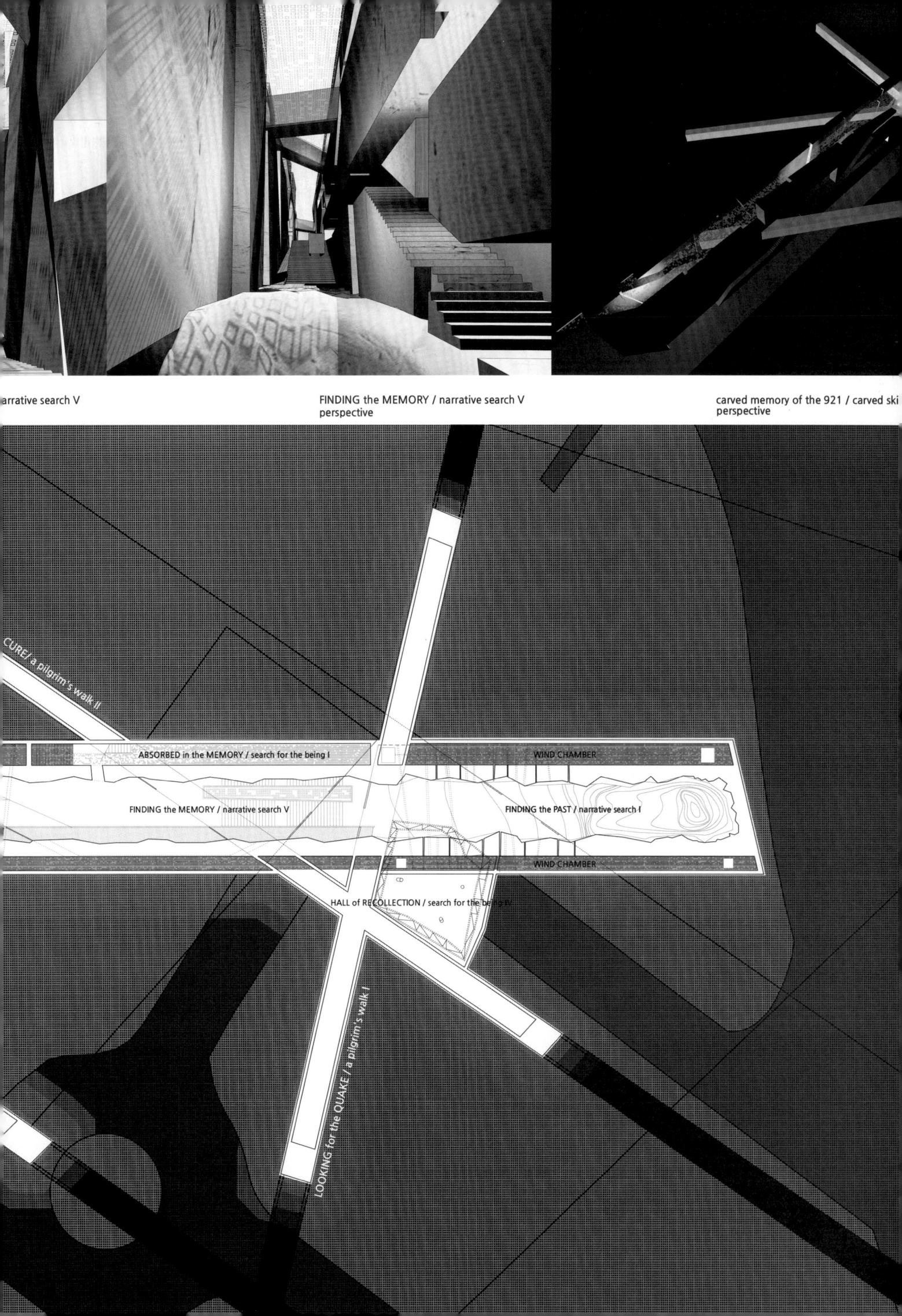

narrative search V · FINDING the MEMORY / narrative search V
perspective

carved memory of the 921 / carved ski
perspective

CURE / a pilgrim's walk II

ABSORBED in the MEMORY / search for the being I

WIND CHAMBER

FINDING the MEMORY / narrative search V

FINDING the PAST / narrative search I

WIND CHAMBER

HALL of RECOLLECTION / search for the being IV

LOOKING for the QUAKE / a pilgrim's walk I

378 | Urban connecting
sculpture

Thousand Palace
Palace of May _ Hi Seoul Festival Stage Sculpture

Hi Seoul Festival 2009

Architects Jang Yoon Gyoo, Shin Chang Hoon + Mak Max Korea
Co-Artist Ahn Eun Mi
Client Seoul Foundation Arts and Culture
Photographer Sergio Pirrone

COMPOUND BODY 379

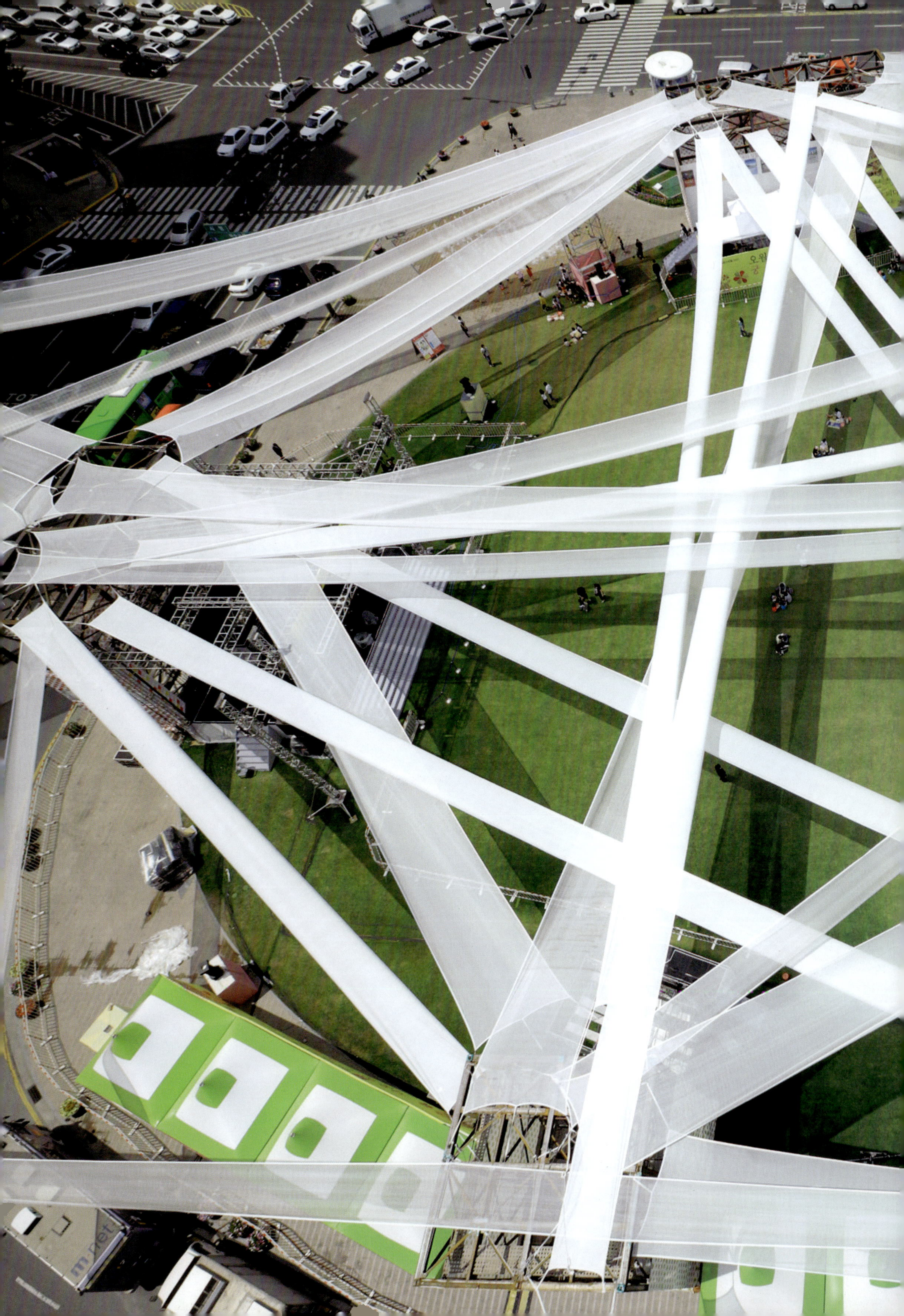

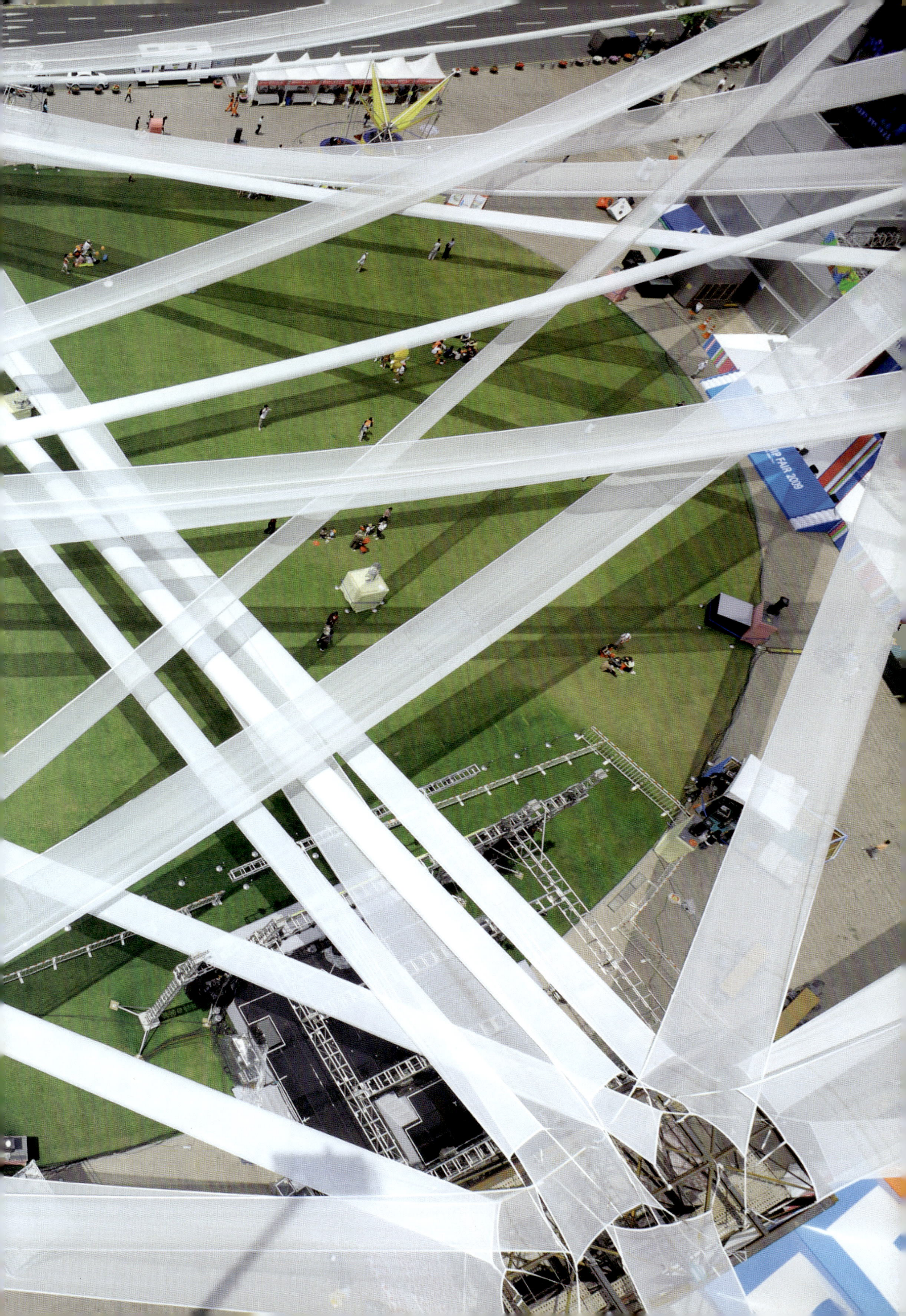

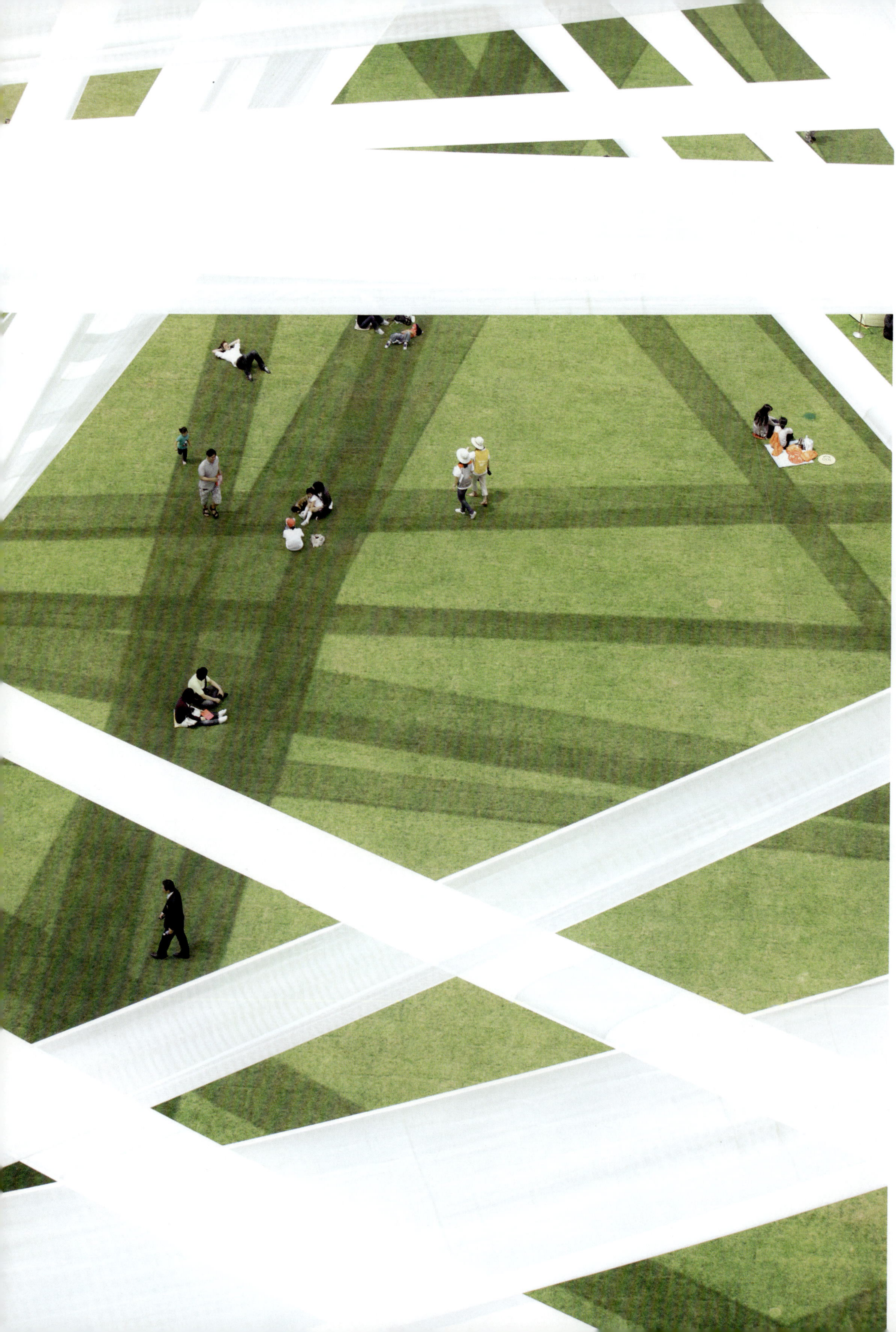

URBAN CONNECTING SCULPTURE

'Palace of May' comes into being a symbolic sculpture of 'Hi Seoul Festival 2009' in the heart of Seoul, Seoul Plaza. There will be not merely the opening ceremony but also various kinds of event namely Palsekmudohe(the eight coloured banquet i.e. A Korean traditional ball). Last year, the theme of the festival was 'Digital Palace' which represents the state of the art IT technology of Seoul. This year, its theme is sustainable and futuristic Seoul by dealing with interchanging between environment, human being and technology. World-class Artist, Ahn Eun Mi is the Director. Jang Yoon Gyoo who is one of the leading architects in Korea was designated as the Design Director.

'Palace of May _Cheon Goong' is not only a gigantic environmental and urban sculpture but also a landmark of this festival. It consists of 60 pieces of fabric. The maximum length of it is about 200-metre-long. They connects City hall, buildings around the plaza.

The scheme is motivated by the concept of Korean traditional sunshade of the Palace, 'Yong Bong Cha Il'. It means that all the citizens have to be treated like the King and the Queen. This type of sunshade was quite special in bygone days. Even a loyal subject was not allowed to use this and was sentenced to jail due to asking for using it.

The aims of the 'Palace of May' for the festival are connecting and communicating between buildings, square and streets. It enables the festival would extends all over the city as well as in the Seoul Plaza. This structure is soaring towards sky. Simultaneously it creates a convergent point of the city and of the world. 'Palace of May' mix well tradition and high technology. It made the best use of natural sources. Wind, which rises alongside buildings, that contributes to the fluidity. Light, which enters from the white translucent fabric, is the natural element that provides a spectacular space to visitors.

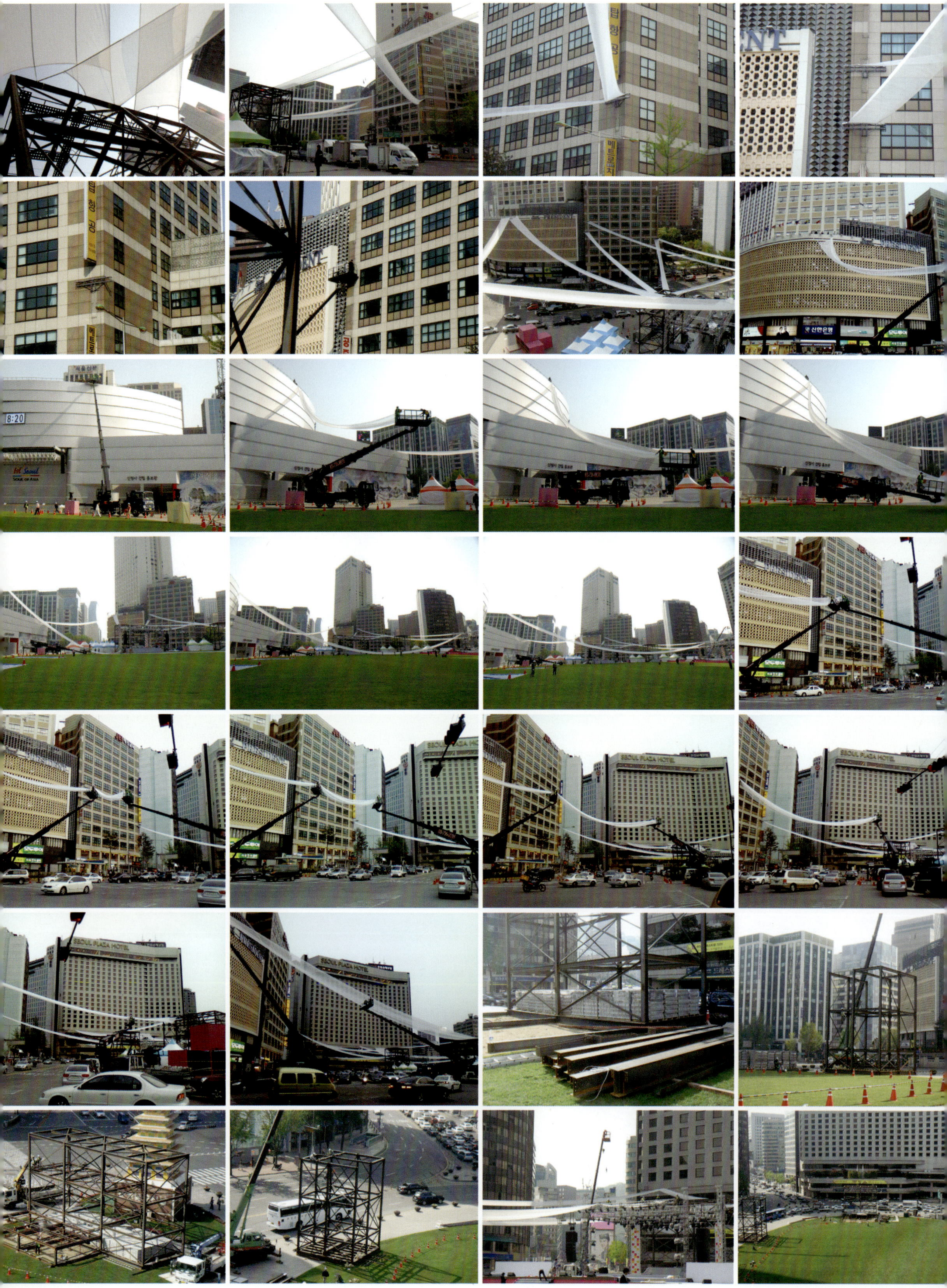
8:20
SEOUL PLAZA HOTEL

COMPOUND BODY 385

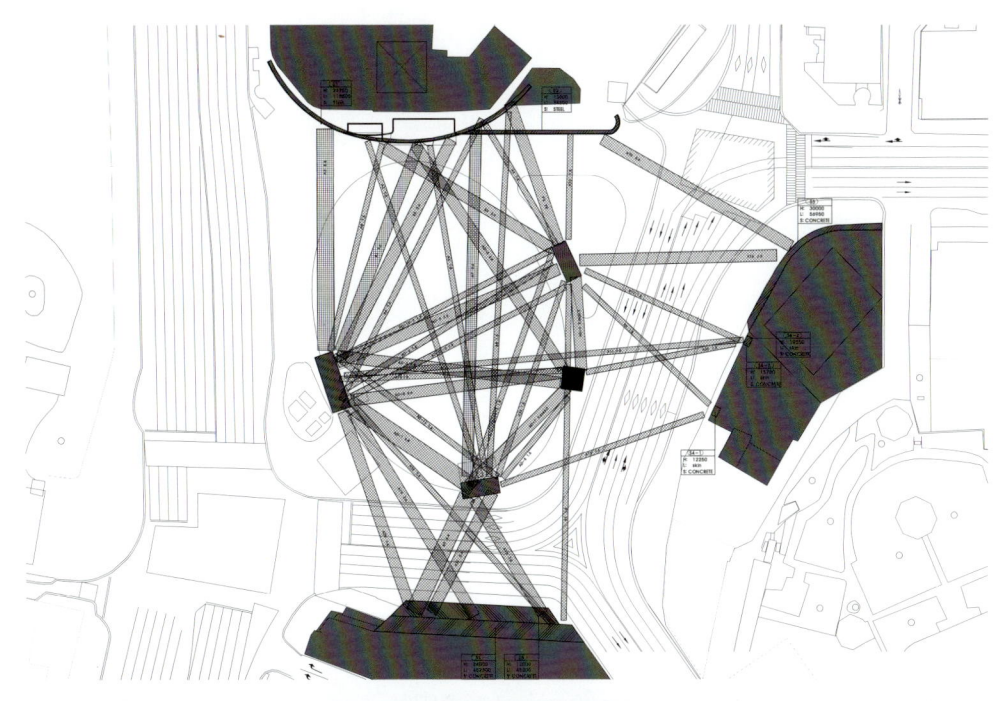

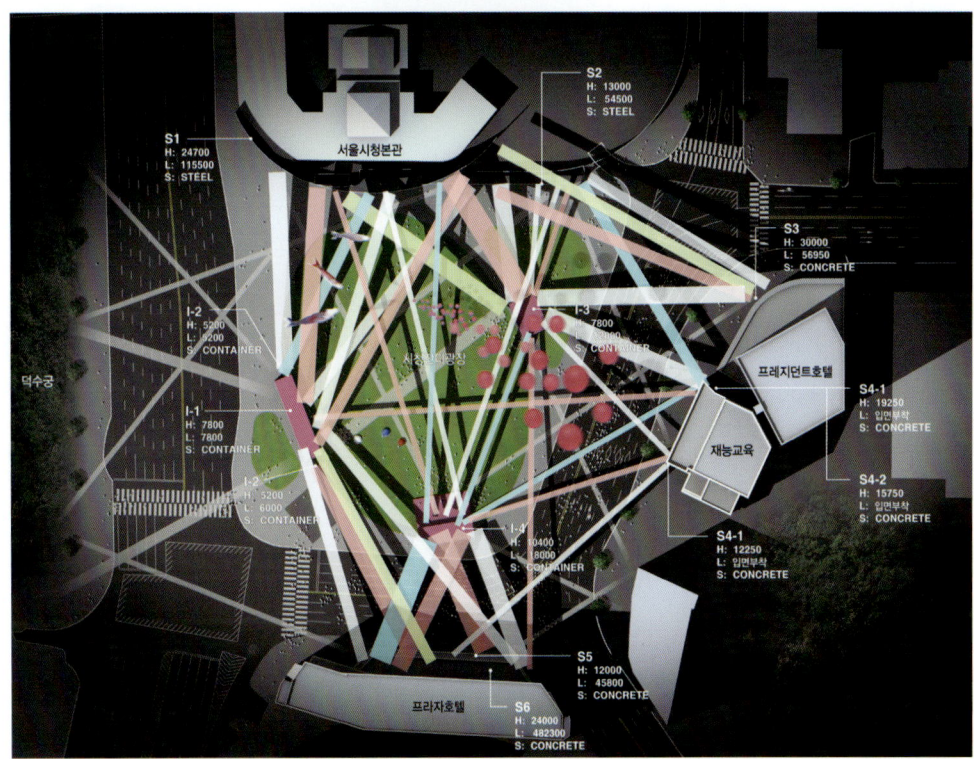

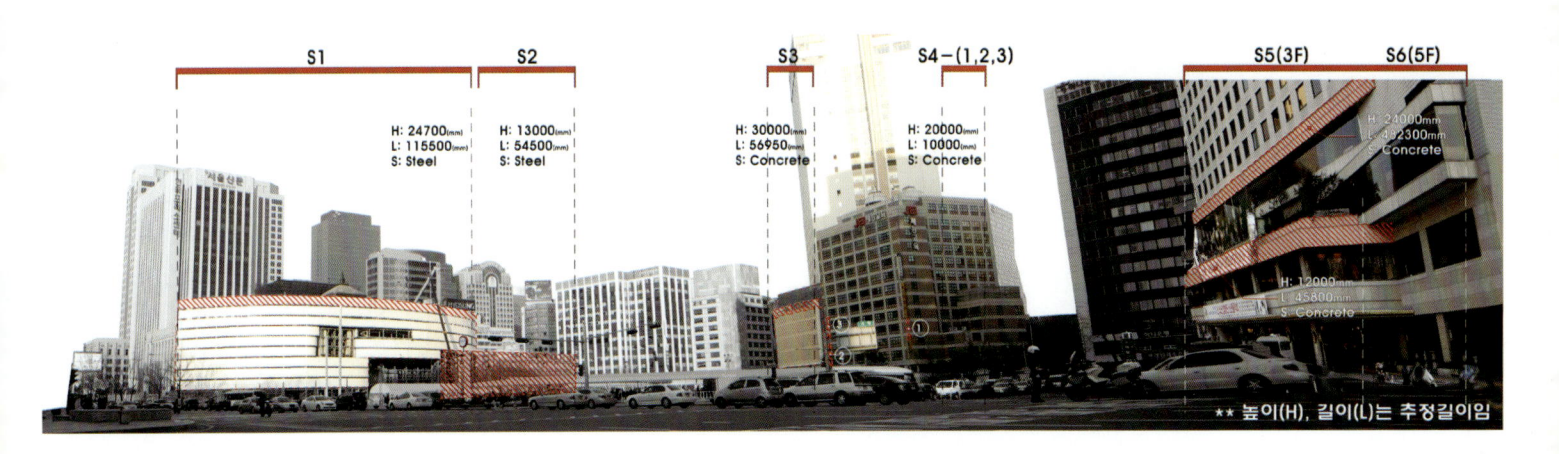

** 높이(H), 길이(L)는 추정길이임

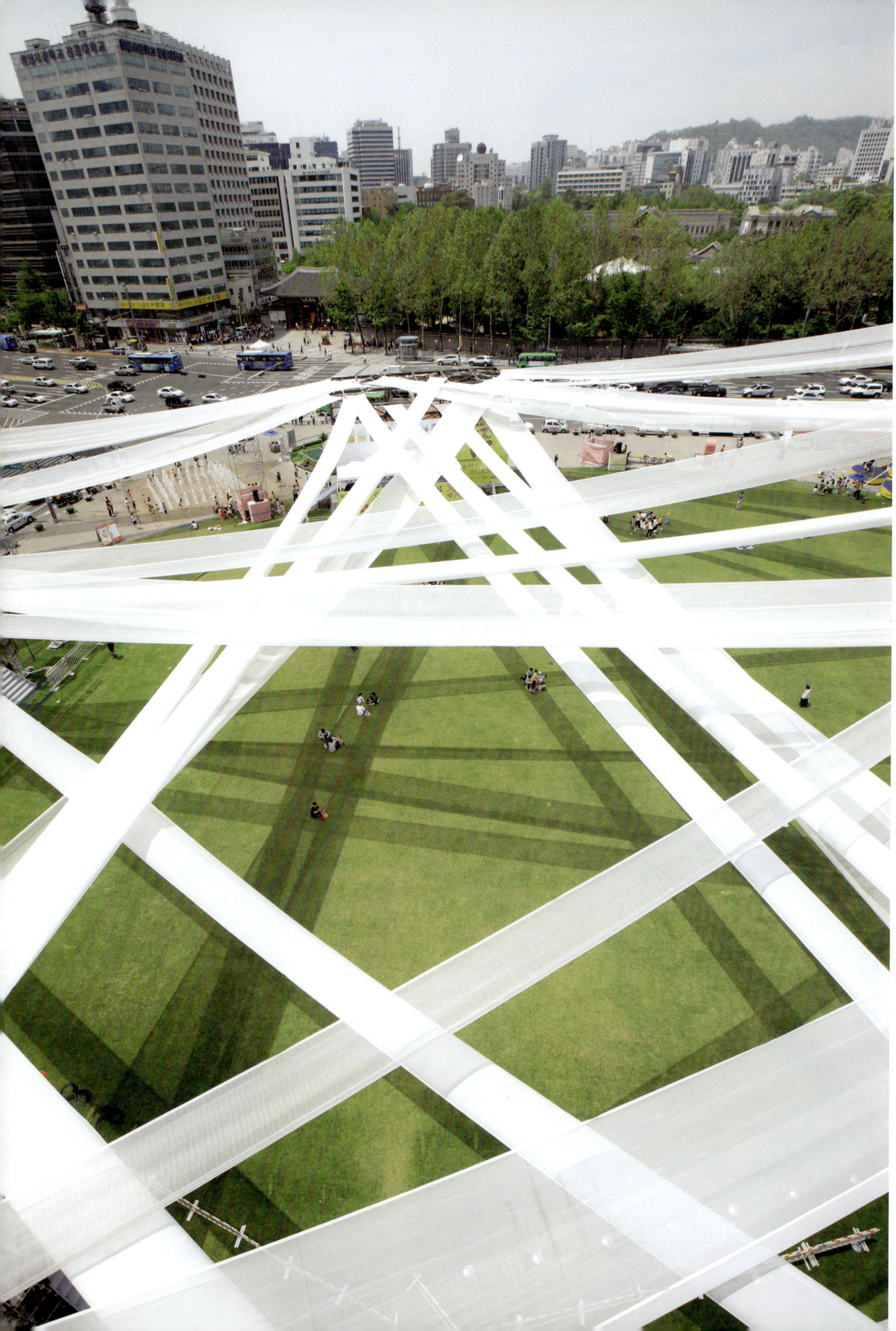

'Palace of May', which was just a monotonous plaza as a part of urban space, acts as a conspicuous and brilliant stage. An experimental architect, Jang Yoon Gyoo, is in charge of this project design.
He's been trying to demonstrate that Architecture is the heart of culture. Through this project, Palace of May, he realised a place where people can recharge and relish this festival as best as it can be.
In the words of the architect 'Palace of May _ Cheon Goong(This word from Chinese character. It is a homonym. Its pronunciation and spelling are all same in Korean. Having said that though, it bears various senses. Cheon means Sky, Stream and Thousand) is made of clouds in the sky. It is a virtual stream which flows in the space. It has thousands of phases which is changing by sunlight, wind and lighting.' 'Hopefully it will be a modern palace of the festival for all the citizens.' He added.

天宮 : Sky Palace
川宮 : Stream Palace
千宮 : Thousand Palace

Cheon Goong is not only a place for festival but also a linking object which enables citizens to realize their dream and imagination. It is a moving and reacting object for people who attend the festival in many ways.

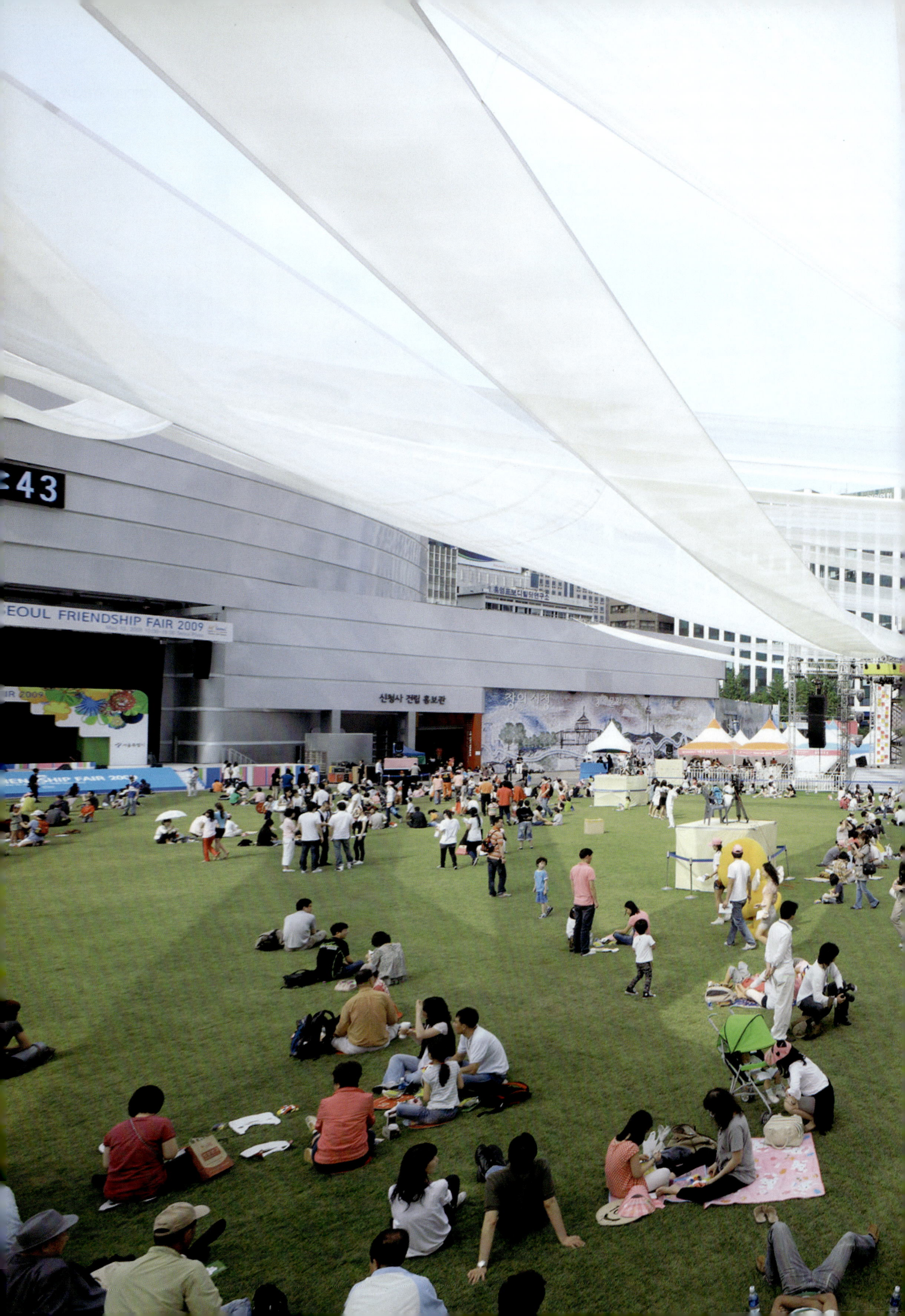
43
EOUL FRIENDSHIP FAIR 2009
신청사 건립 홍보관

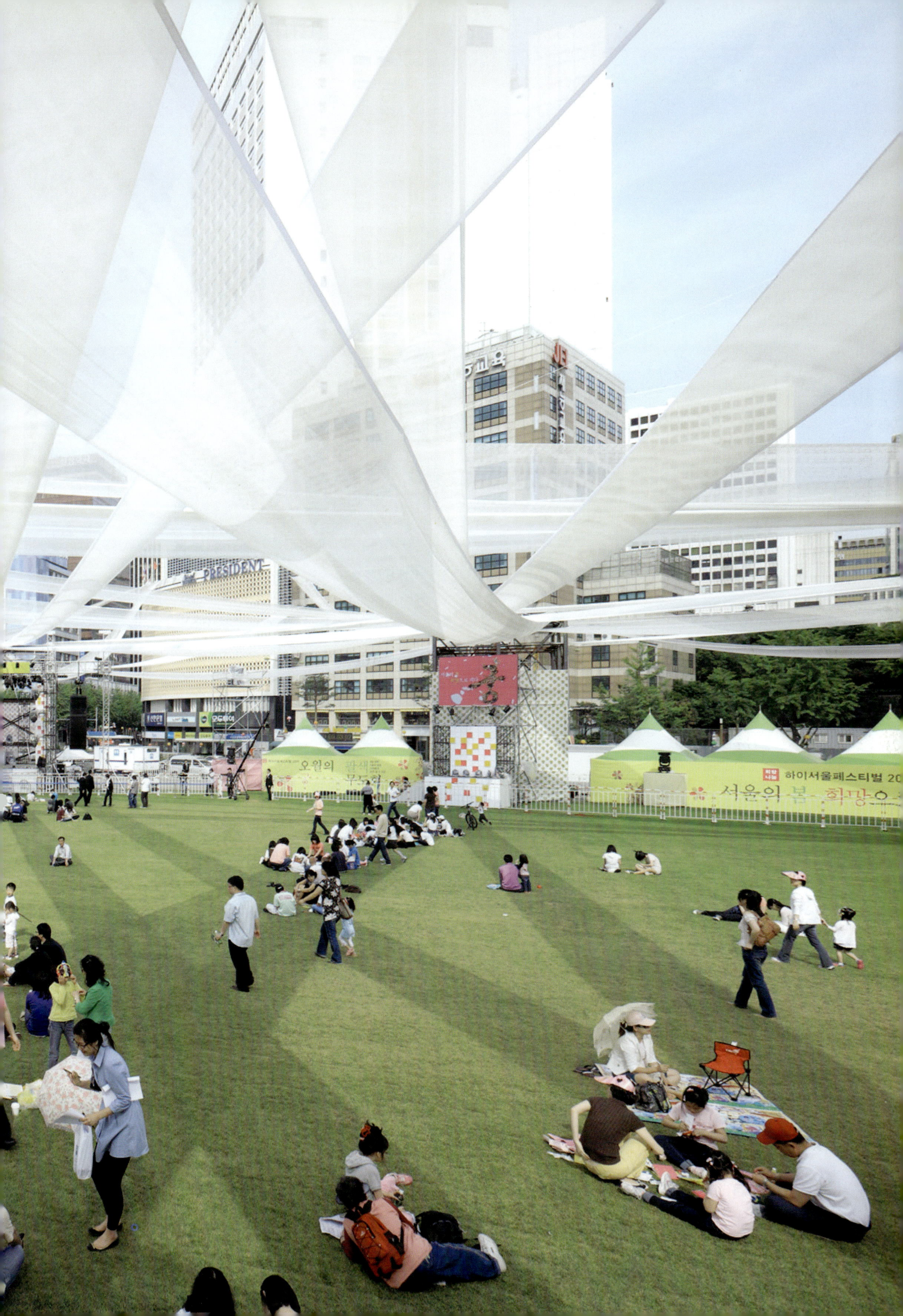
PRESIDENT
하이서울페스티벌

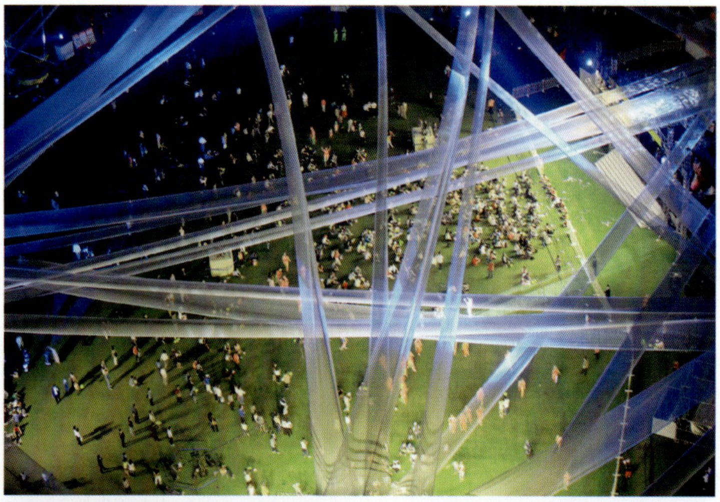
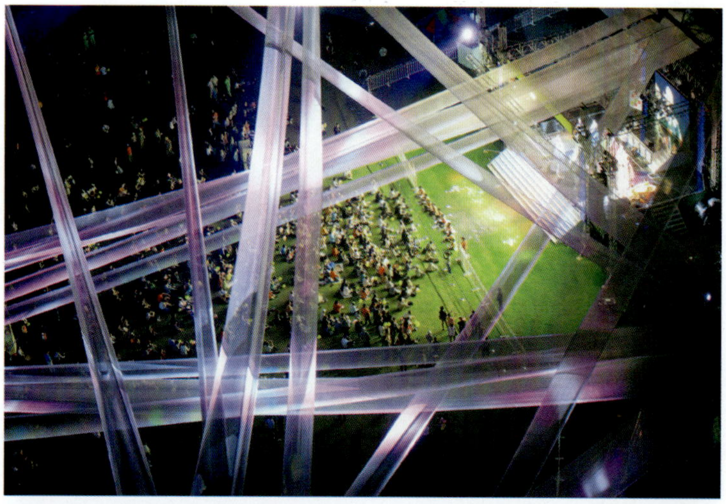
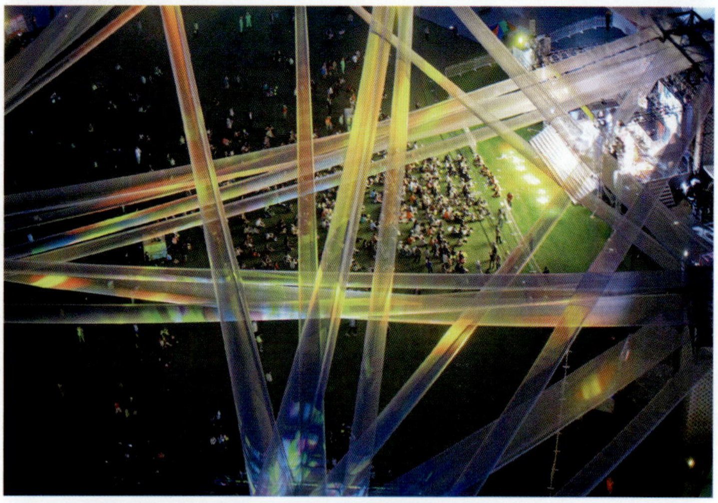
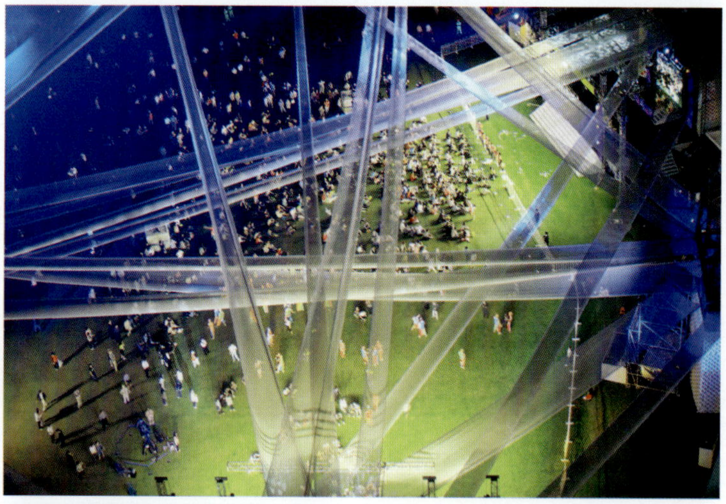
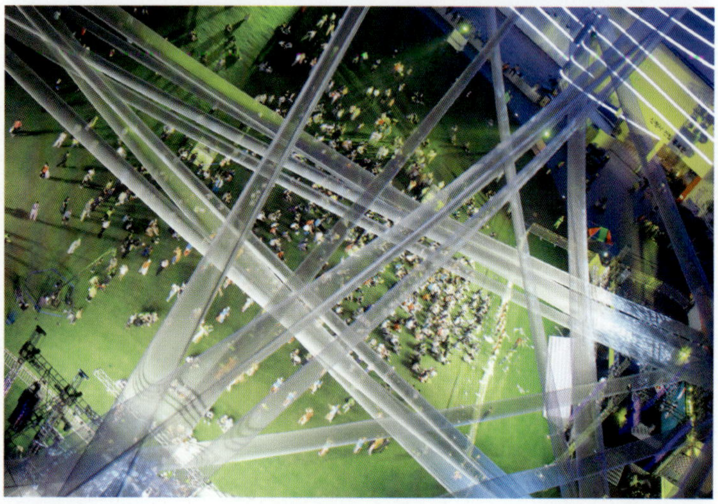
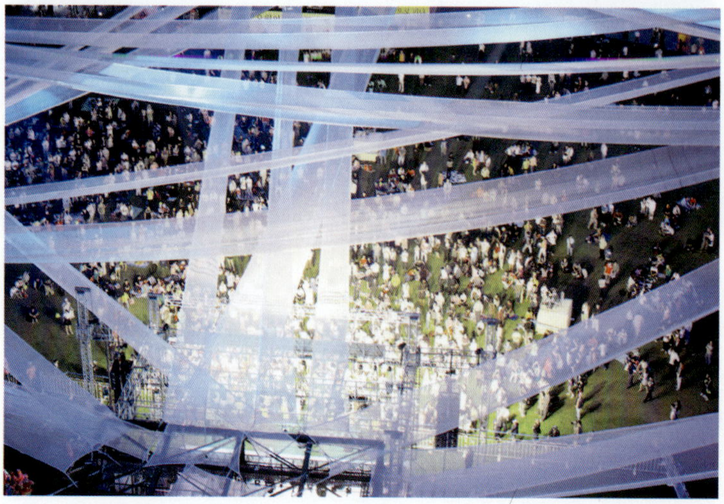

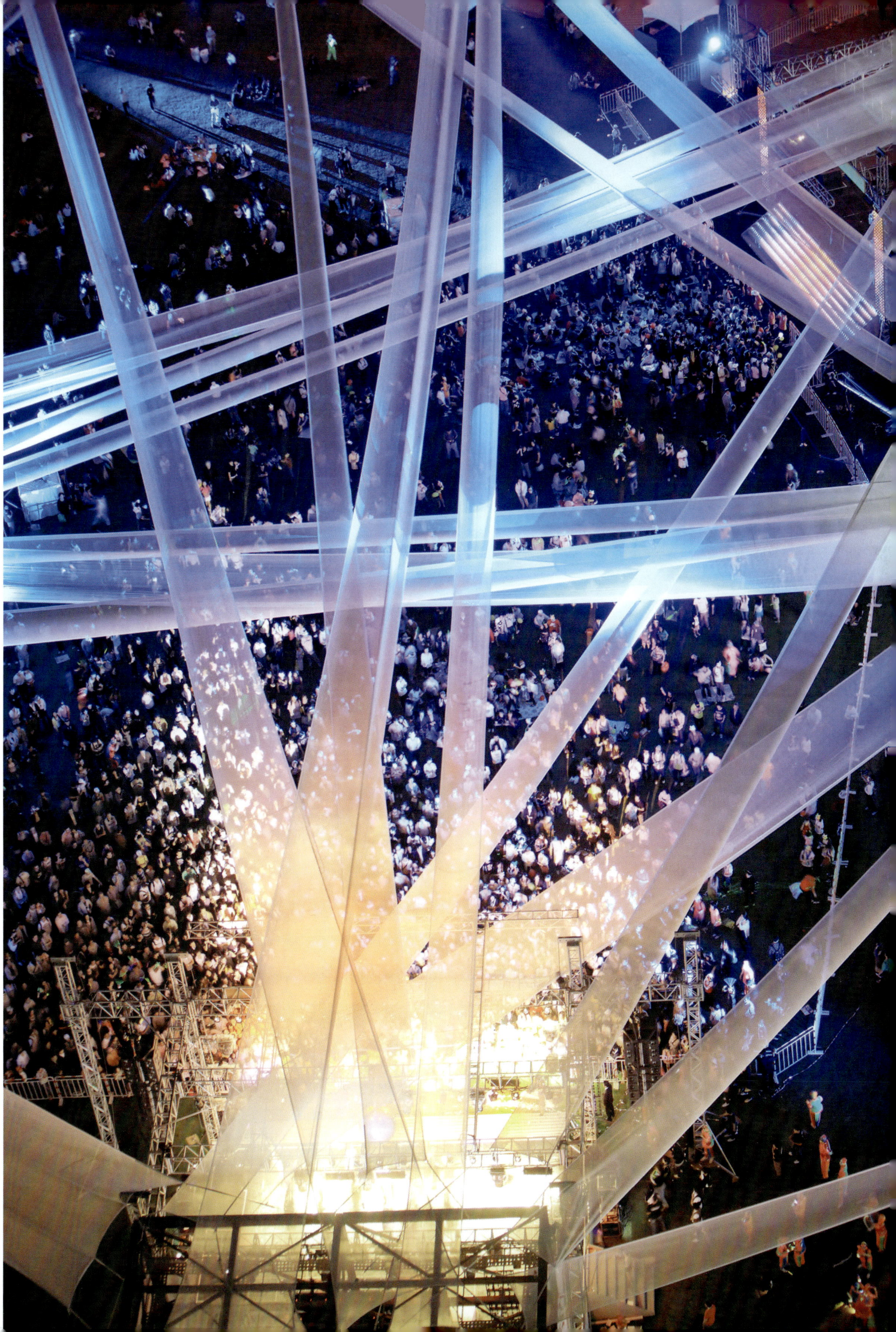

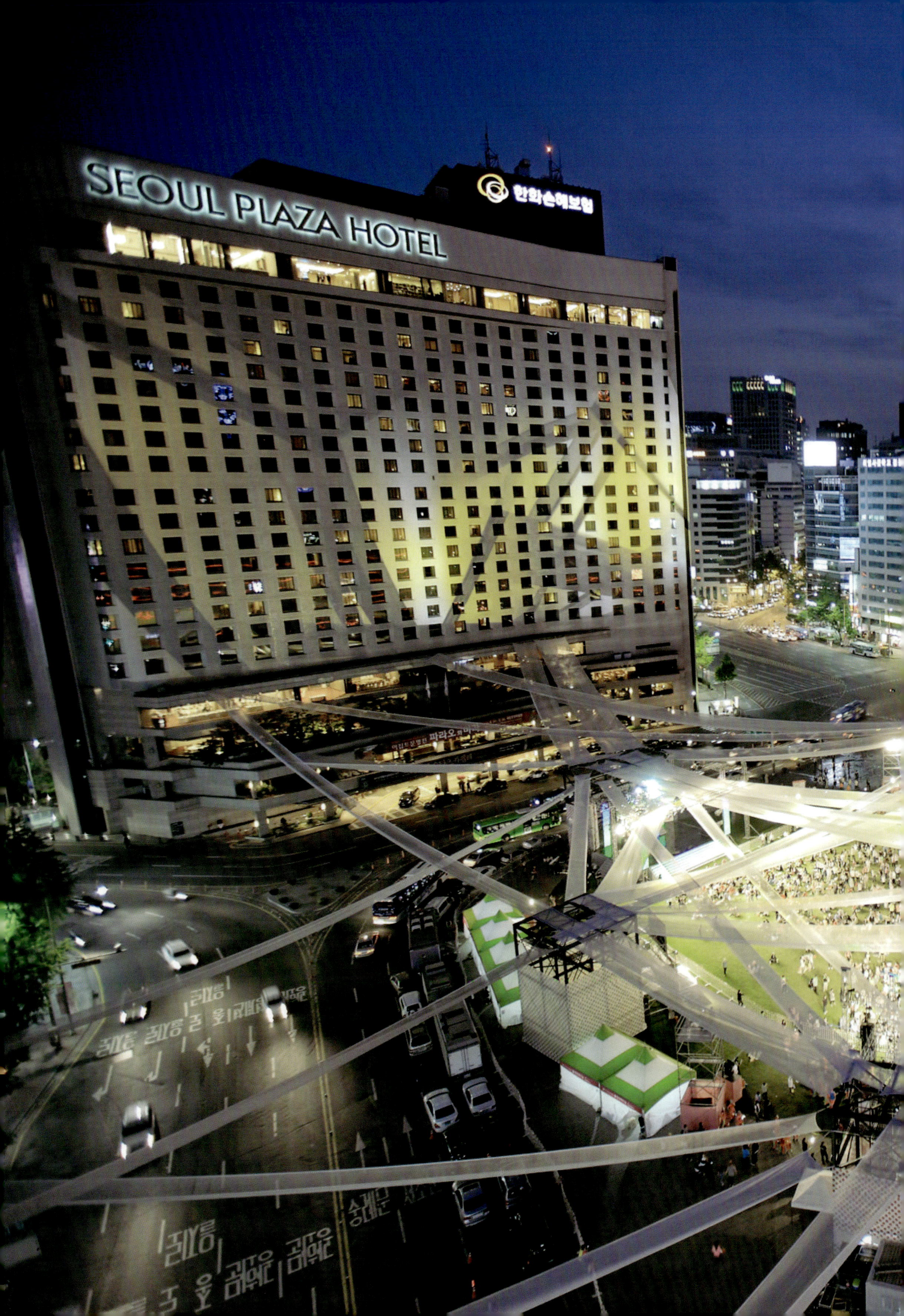
SEOUL PLAZA HOTEL
한화손해보험

Client
Seoul Metropolitan Government
Architects
UnSangDong Architects Cooperation
Principals
Jang Yoon Gyoo, Shin Chang Hoon
Structural Engineer
MakMax Korea
Site
Seoul Plaza, Seoul, South Korea
Allied Building around the site
Seoul City Hall, Seoul Plaza Hotel, JEI,
Materials
3D MAK MESH(2 layered fabric made of translucent vinyl fiber)

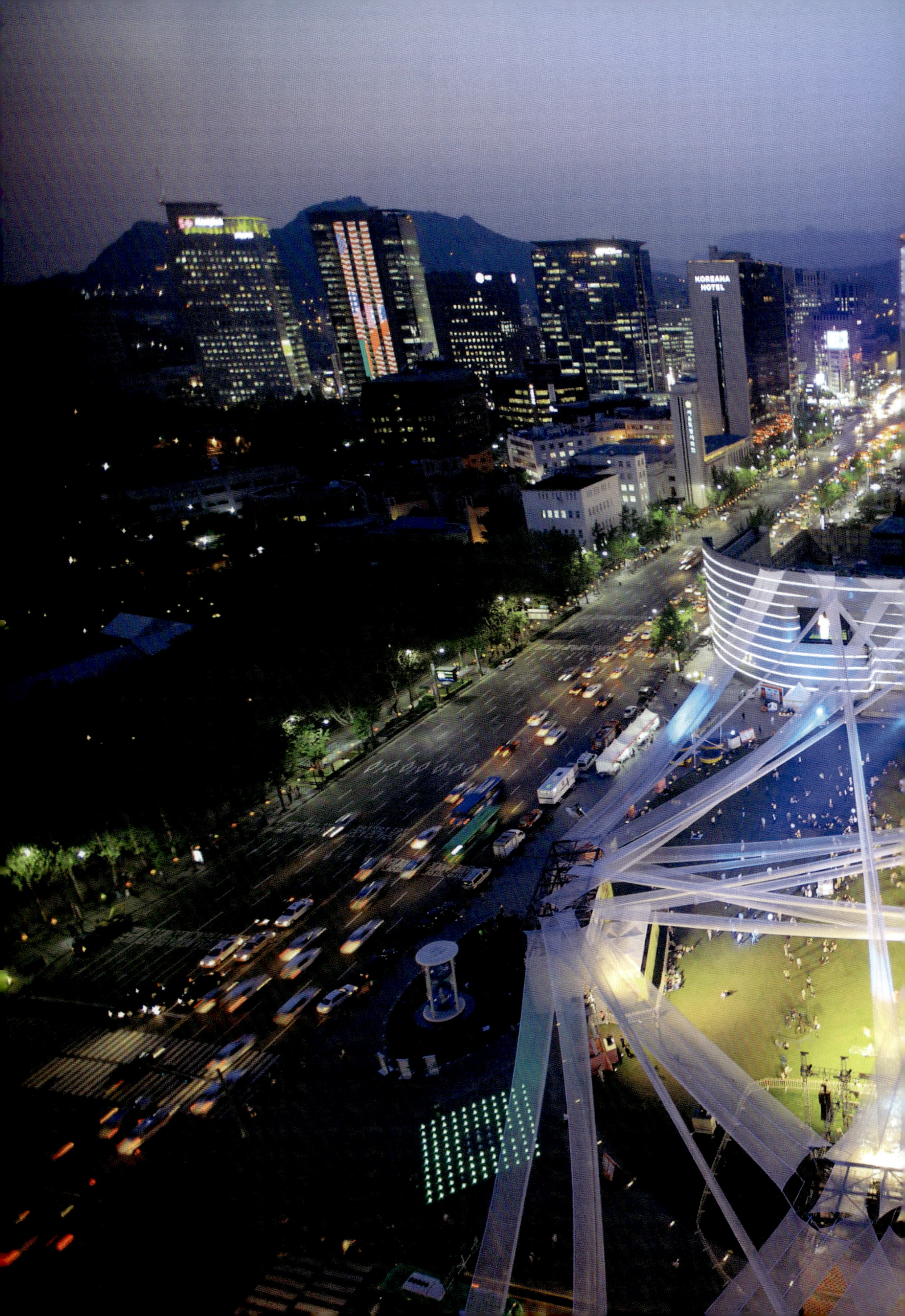
KOREANA
HOTEL

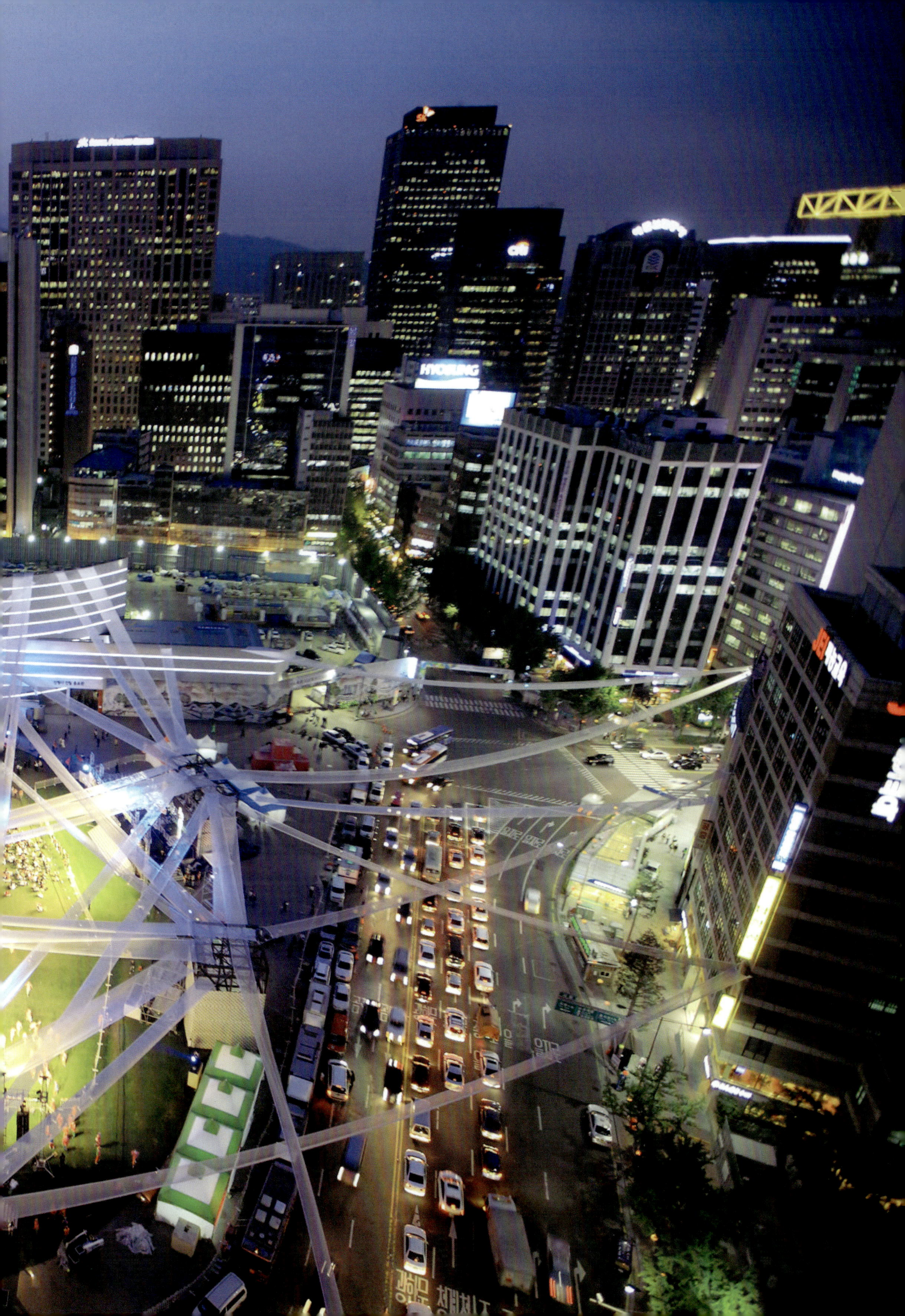
HYOSUNG

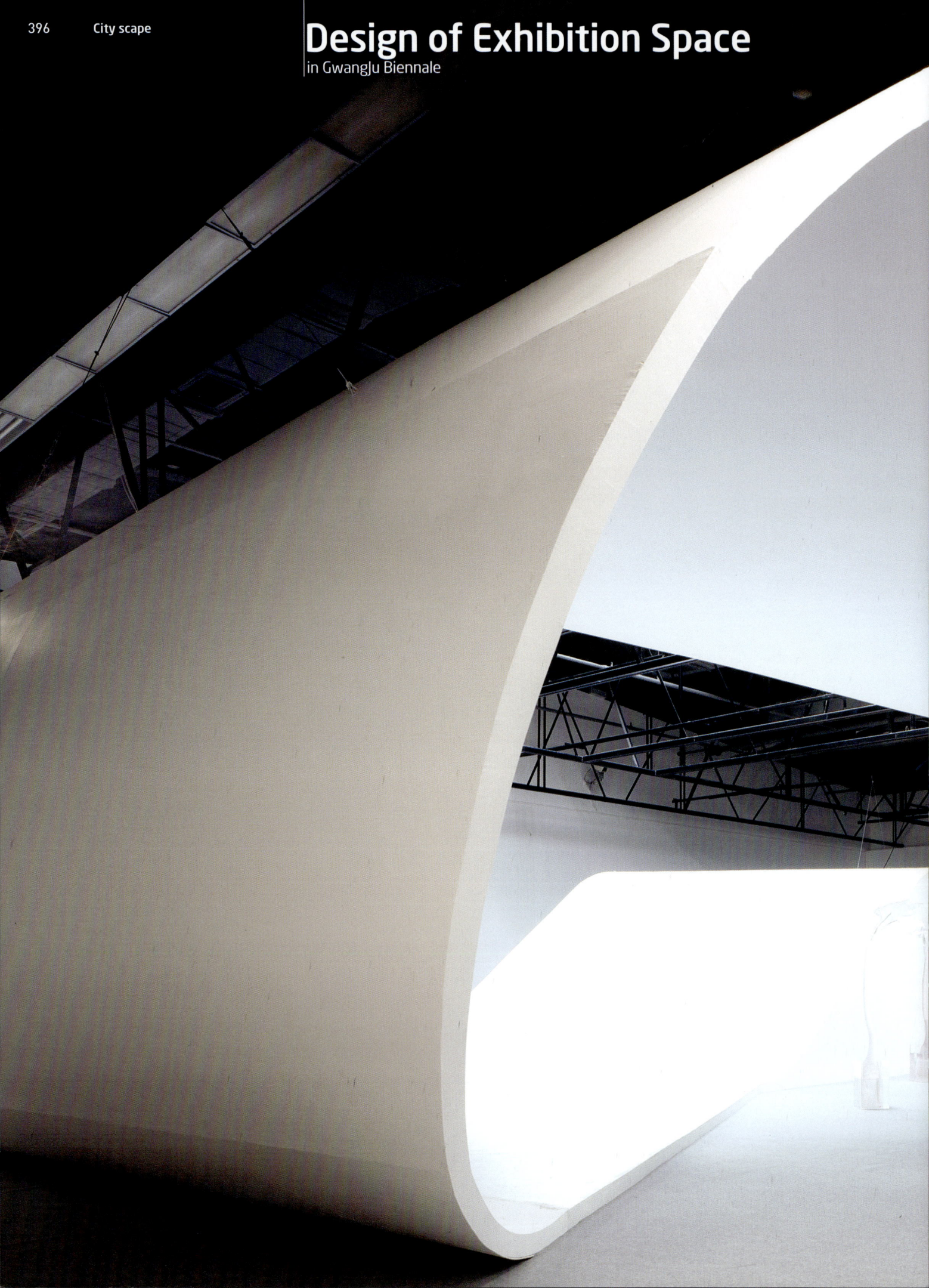

Design of Exhibition Space
in GwangJu Biennale

Architects Jang Yoon Gyoo, Shin Chang Hoon
Photographer Jin Hyu Sook

COMPOUND BODY 397

398

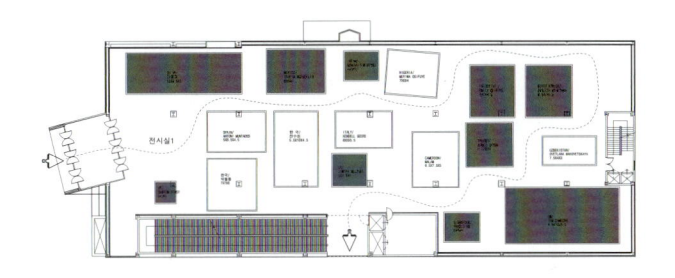

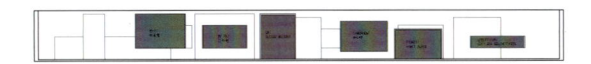

CITY SCAPE

Theme01
GRAIN of DUST_ MAP of CELL

The "Dust" exhibition seeks the stories related to the big questions about human civilization. 'Cell', which is the essential element for the 'earth between its creation and distinction', will be the fundamental medium. I propose a space where we can construct whole topography with cells. The arrangement of cells and the void space made by the movements in between are the principles for the creation of topography. Dust is always with us in the forms (and substances) of everyday life: dreams, frustrations, outcry, relief, and so on; it reacts to time by changing and sometimes disappearing.

The cell of dust becomes a living creature thanks to humans, time, and water. And it is an artistic expression of living subjects that fills and empties the 'earth between its creation and extinction.' Based on the concept of cell units. I will organize the small units of exhibition booths all over the space. A cell consists of the whole and the whole volume of media that stands for the scale and form of a city and nature. The whole space needed by the artists will be composed of cell units; and each unit will be arranged according to the spatial flow, which is formed by the interrelation between the units.

The viewer will have the illusion that he/she is walking through a city. The structures and the organized space where the viewer walks reflect the deserted urban environment created in the name of "city". Cells will be established as a box space, the simplest and smallest element, and be arranged as a map of a city by the movements of viewers and the relationships between the artists. We will adopt the spatial chaos and ambiguity as the fundamental mode of arrangement. Entering viewers will experience the order of chaos, which is actually aimed at expressing the chaos of an urban map.

A box attached to the earth, a box flooting above the earth, a box of material change... we experience the movement of space that can be attained on the side. The void made out of the boxes consists a visible and reachable moving space and a visible but unreachable space. The void also makes the chaos of movement. The viewer will experience the exhibition realized in the booth by the changing location following the viewpoints of the moving viewer.

Theme 02
A DROP of WATER_ MAP of FLOW
By making a connector like "water', we can give a life to the deserted structure of dust, inducing mutual power. This exhibition consists of a three-dimensional representation of the landscape that shows the flow of water. Dispersed like pixels on a monitor, the sources of water produce streams of water that flow over the wavy surface and become one to form a body of water in the exhibition booths. People can walk through the booths that span all over the exhibition space like a map of the water flows. By transforming the floor, walls, and ceilings of the booths, the exhibition lets the viewer experience the changing wavy space. We put a strong element that form the "wave", a heterogeneous leeway, into the homogeneous space, which occupies the space in a whole new way.

The map of ' skinscape" changes the flat structural surface into the space of continuous waves, The continuous curtains erase the division of spatial elements, avoid the basic definition of the elements, and reproduce a new spatial structure". Crossing the space, the three-dimensional "skin" changes the map of dust into the map of continuous flows. the skin makes space while it is a part of exhibition and changes into variety of layers, also turning the continuously changing life force of water into a skin of landscape. The skin covering the whole gallery space is an interactive device that connects two different works or spaces. The life force of water expands itself form the status of simple water to that of connector. If the theme of the exhibition, "Dust", gives the space a chaotic order, the space is the place that is synthesized by moving skins, and that produces the unity of spatial flow.

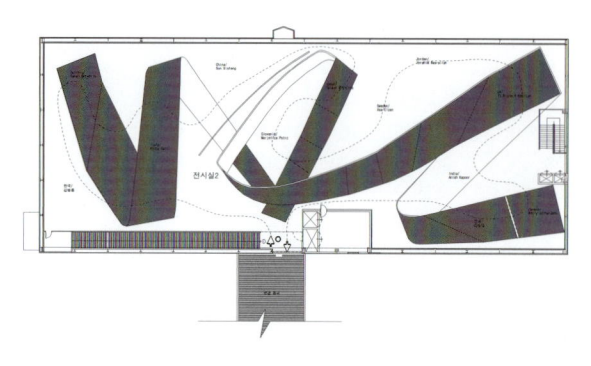

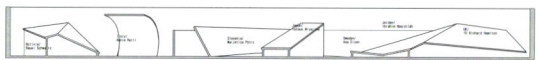

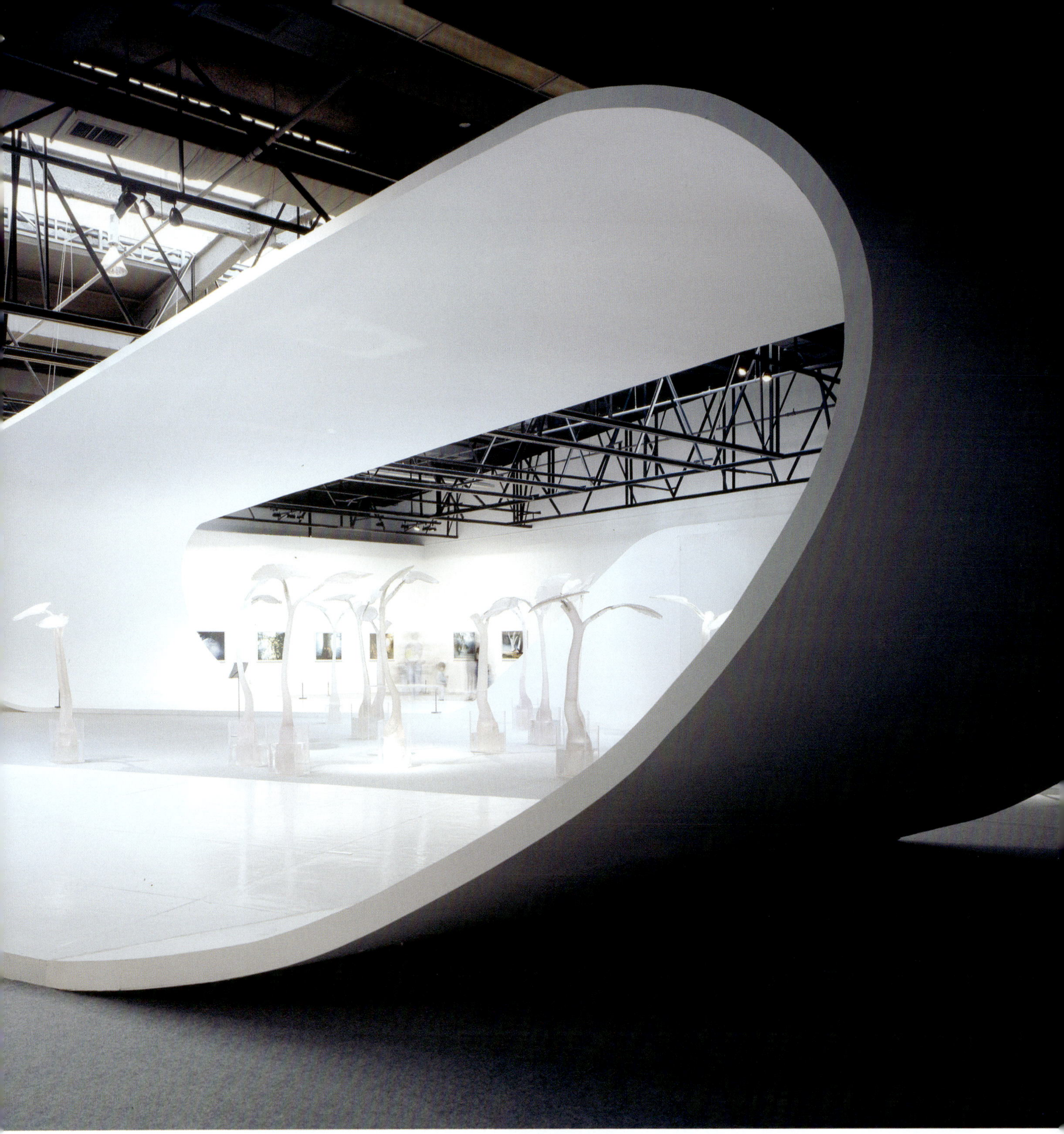

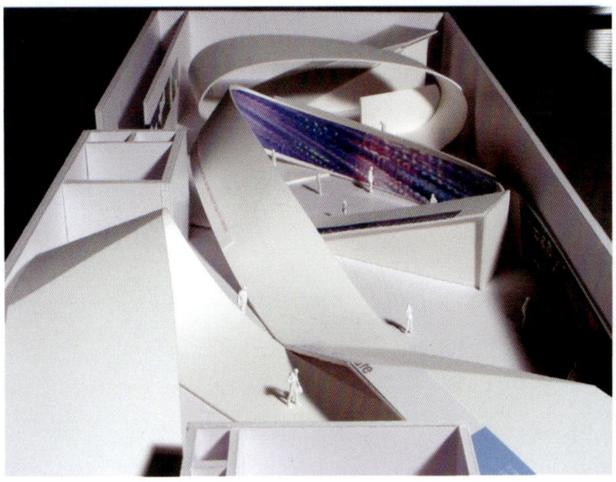

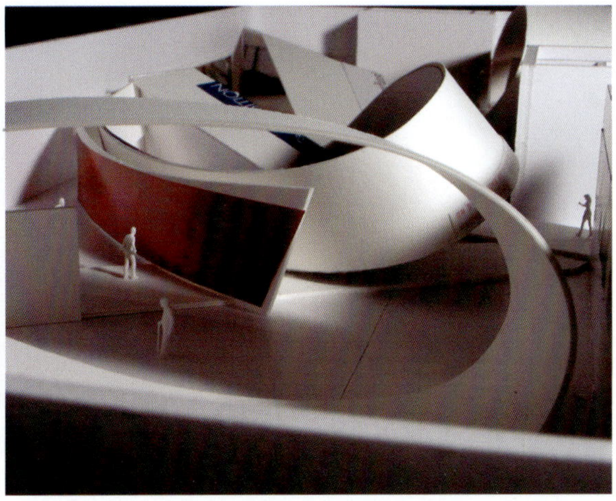

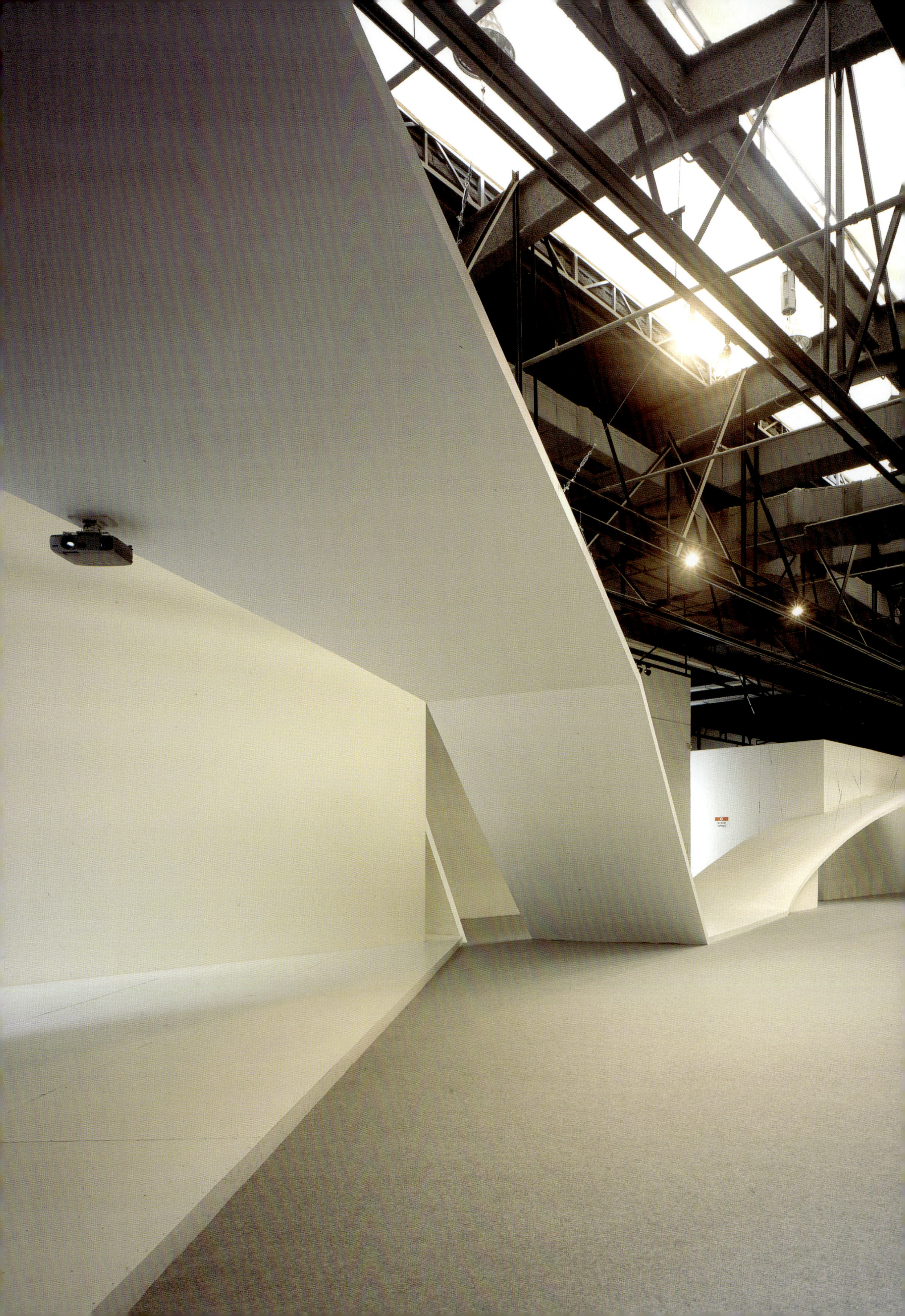

COMPOUND BODY 403

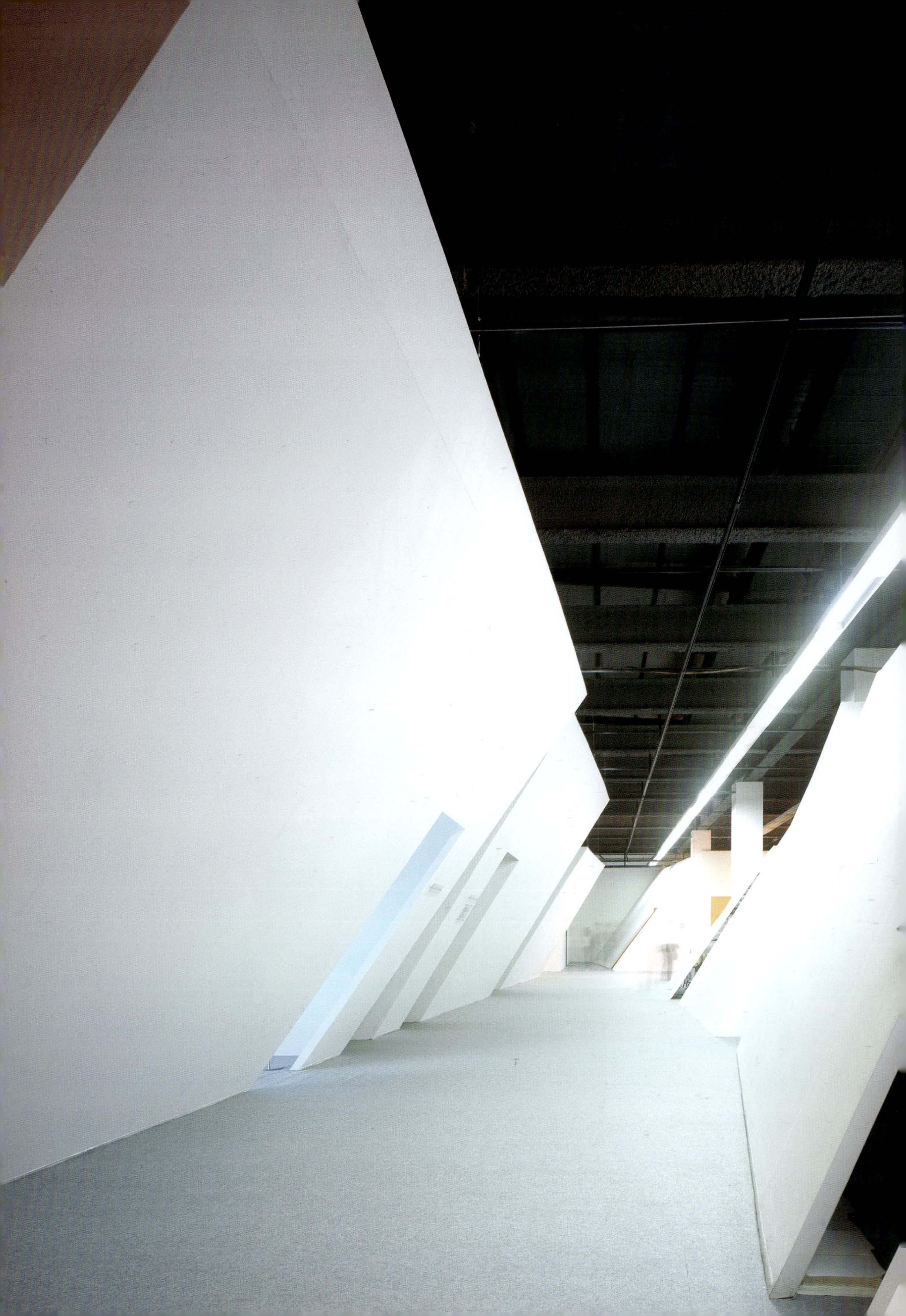

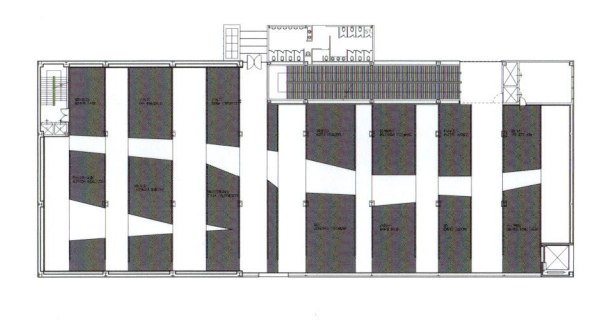

Theme 03
DUST+WATER SYNTHESIS MAP of CREATION/DISAPPEARANCE_ MAP of TRACK

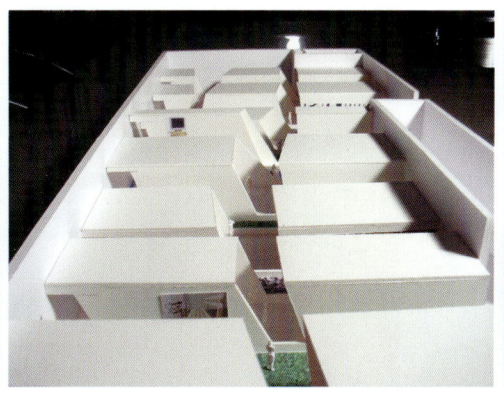

The "Dust" exhibition seeks the stories related to the big questions about human civilization. 'Cell', which is the essential element for the 'earth between its creation and distinction', will be the fundamental medium. I propose a space where we can construct whole topography with cells. The arrangement of cells and the void space made by the movements in between are the principles for the creation of topography. Dust is always with us in the forms (and substances) of everyday life: dreams, frustrations, outcry, relief, and so on; it reacts to time by changing and sometimes disappearing. The cell of dust becomes a living creature thanks to humans, time, and water. And it is an artistic expression of living subjects that fills and empties the 'earth between its creation and extinction.' Based on the concept of cell units. I will organize the small units of exhibition booths all over the space. A cell consists of the whole and the whole volume of media that stands for the scale and form of a city and nature. The whole space needed by the artists will be composed of cell units; and each unit will be arranged according to the spatial flow, which is formed by the interrelation between the units. The viewer will have the illusion that he/she is walking through a city. The structures and the organized space where the viewer walks reflect the deserted urban environment created in the name of "city". Cells will be established as a box space, the simplest and smallest element, and be arranged as a map of a city by the movements of viewers and the relationships between the artists. We will adopt the spatial chaos and ambiguity as the fundamental mode of arrangement. Entering viewers will experience the order of chaos, which is actually aimed at expressing the chaos of an urban map.

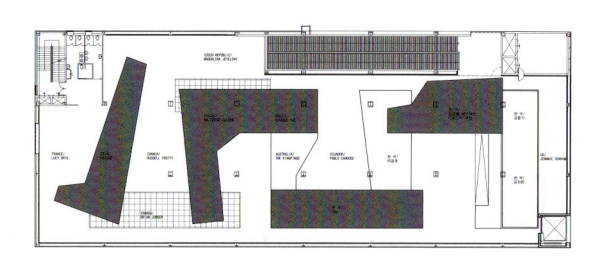

A box attached to the earth, a box flooting above the earth, a box of material change... we experience the movement of space that can be attained on the side. The void made out of the boxes consists a visible and reachable moving space and a visible but unreachable space. The void also makes the chaos of movement. The viewer will experience the exhibition realized in the booth by the changing location following the viewpoints of the moving viewer.

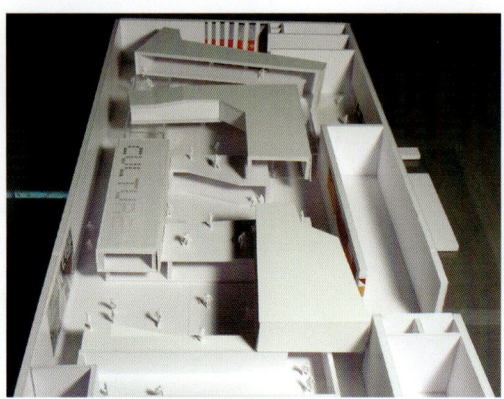

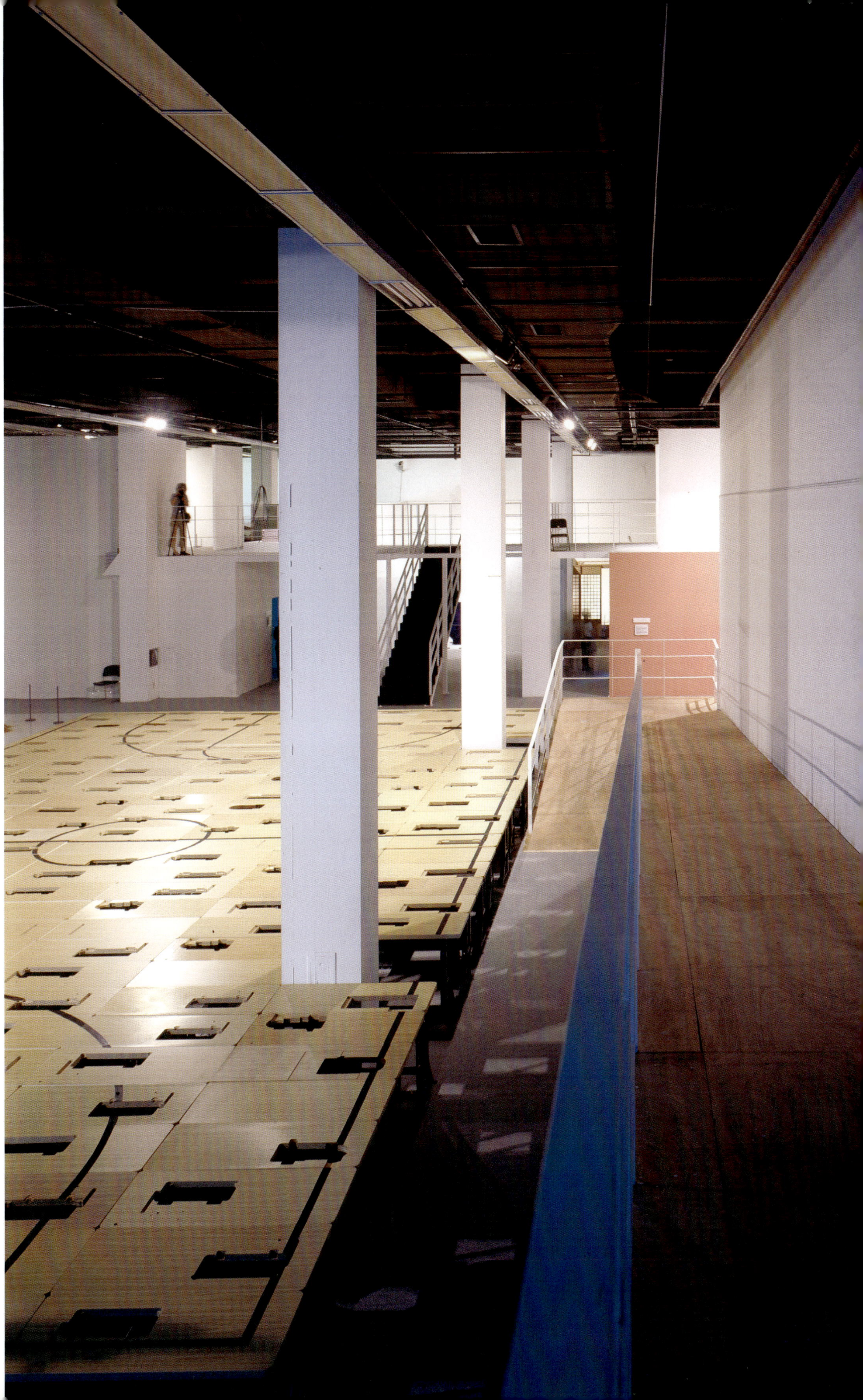

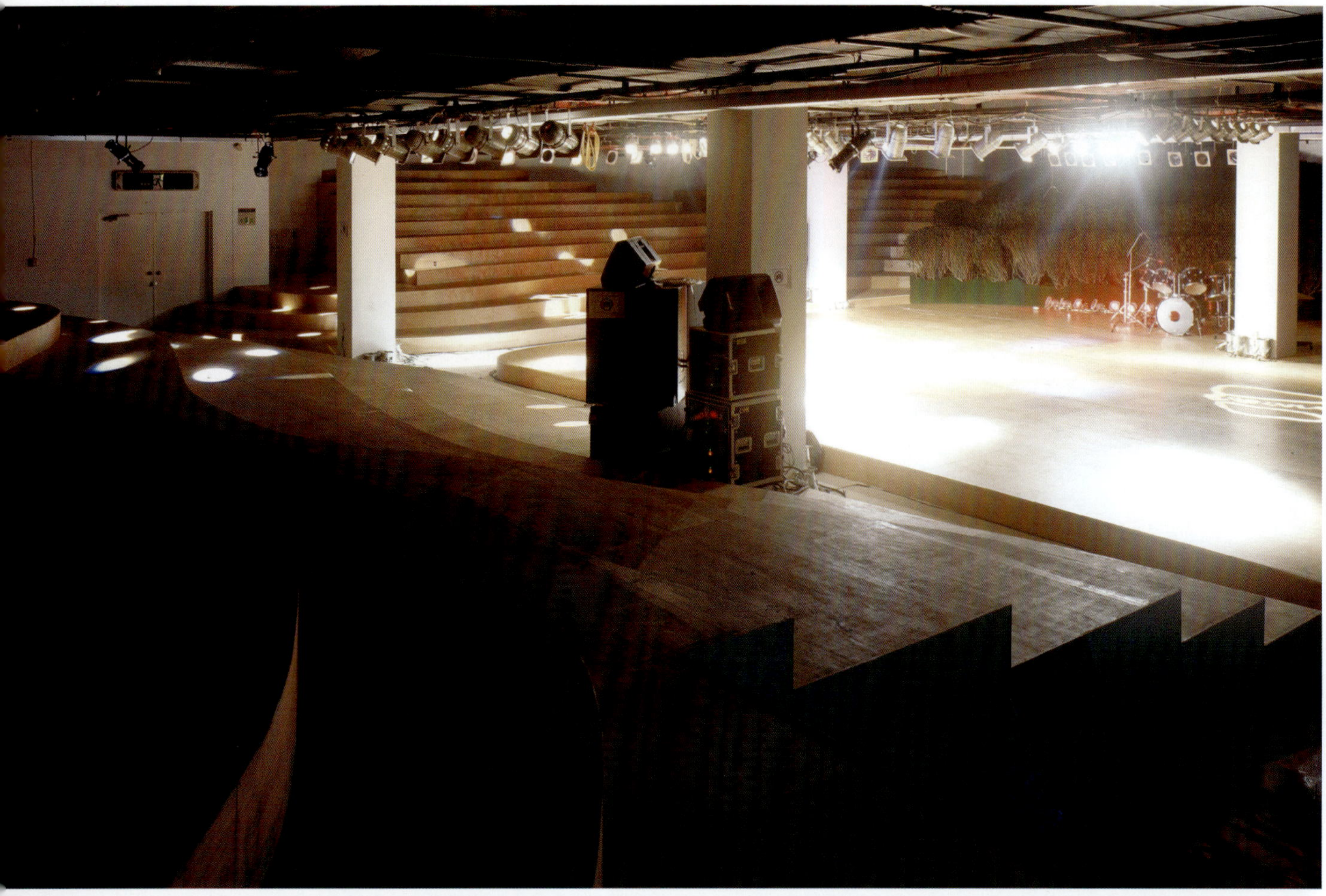

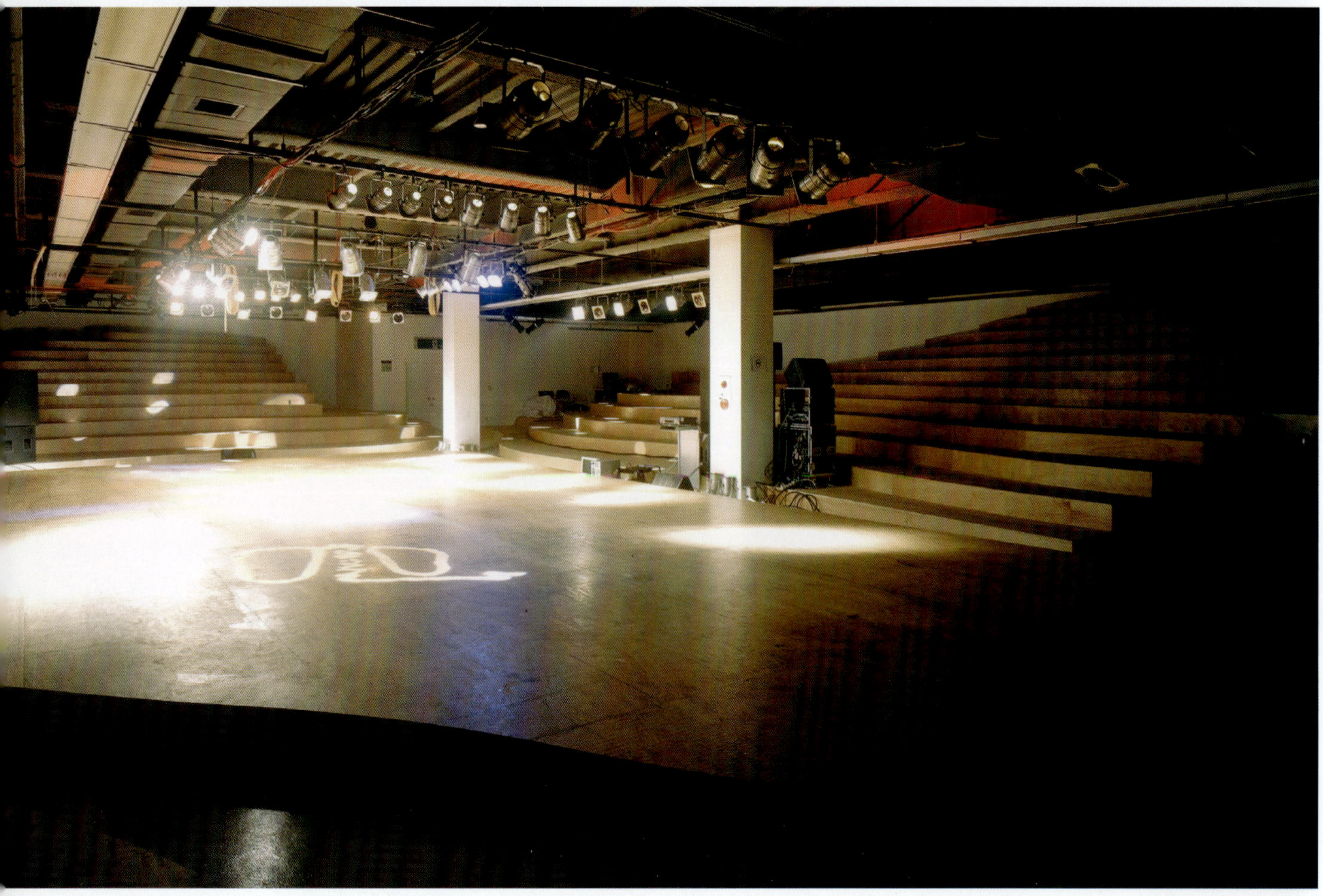

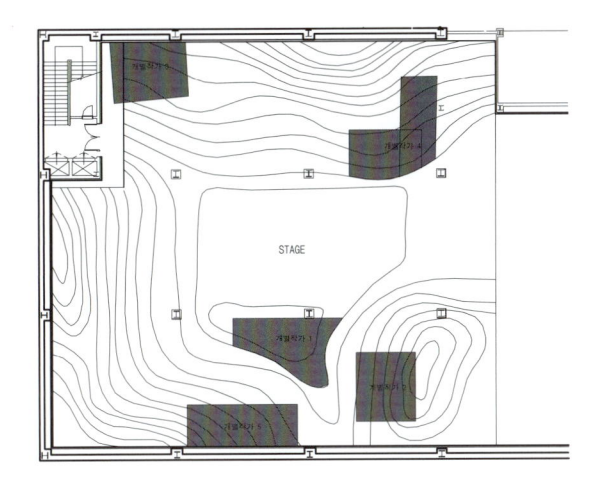

Theme 04
CLUB CONTOUR_ THEATRICAL TOPOGRAPHY

We will make-the "Theatrical Topography" a space for the' active viewer. 'The club space will reflect the real topography by applying the abstract image of it to the floor. The topography that reconstructed in the club is "Theatrical Topography" that has no clear boundaries between the works of art and the real topography. The Theatrical "Topography" works as canvas for the artists, but changes through various new media. And this "canvas" is an open space where the viewer can particpate an a center of the work, which means that he/she can join the dialogues as a curator in the "theatrical Topography". making the whole work a celebration of art. This will be a new artistic experience. The exhibition space and the works are part of an effort to find a certain structural whole, and at the same time, of fun and delight for the audience. The space (or the multi-purpose topography) is a protean map of club, show, seminar, lecture, performance, etc. The interactive works are a sort of toy that the viewers can touch. step on, and play with in very common activities in everyday life, but uncommon in a gallery space. In this new artist environment, the viewer does not just "view" the work of art anymore, but acts as a part of it.

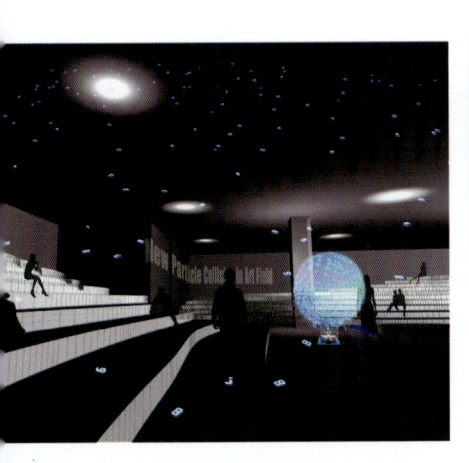

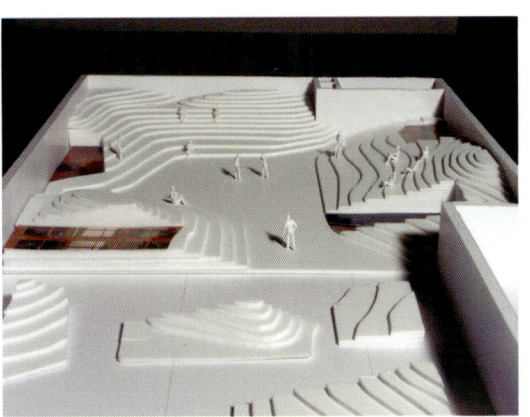

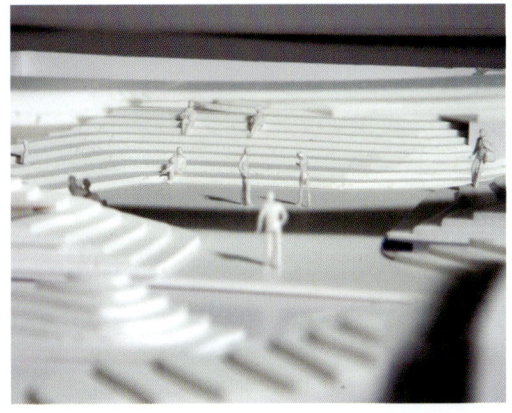

Paris Olympic Memorial

Architects Jang Yoon Gyoo, Shin Chang Hoon, Suh Soo Kyung

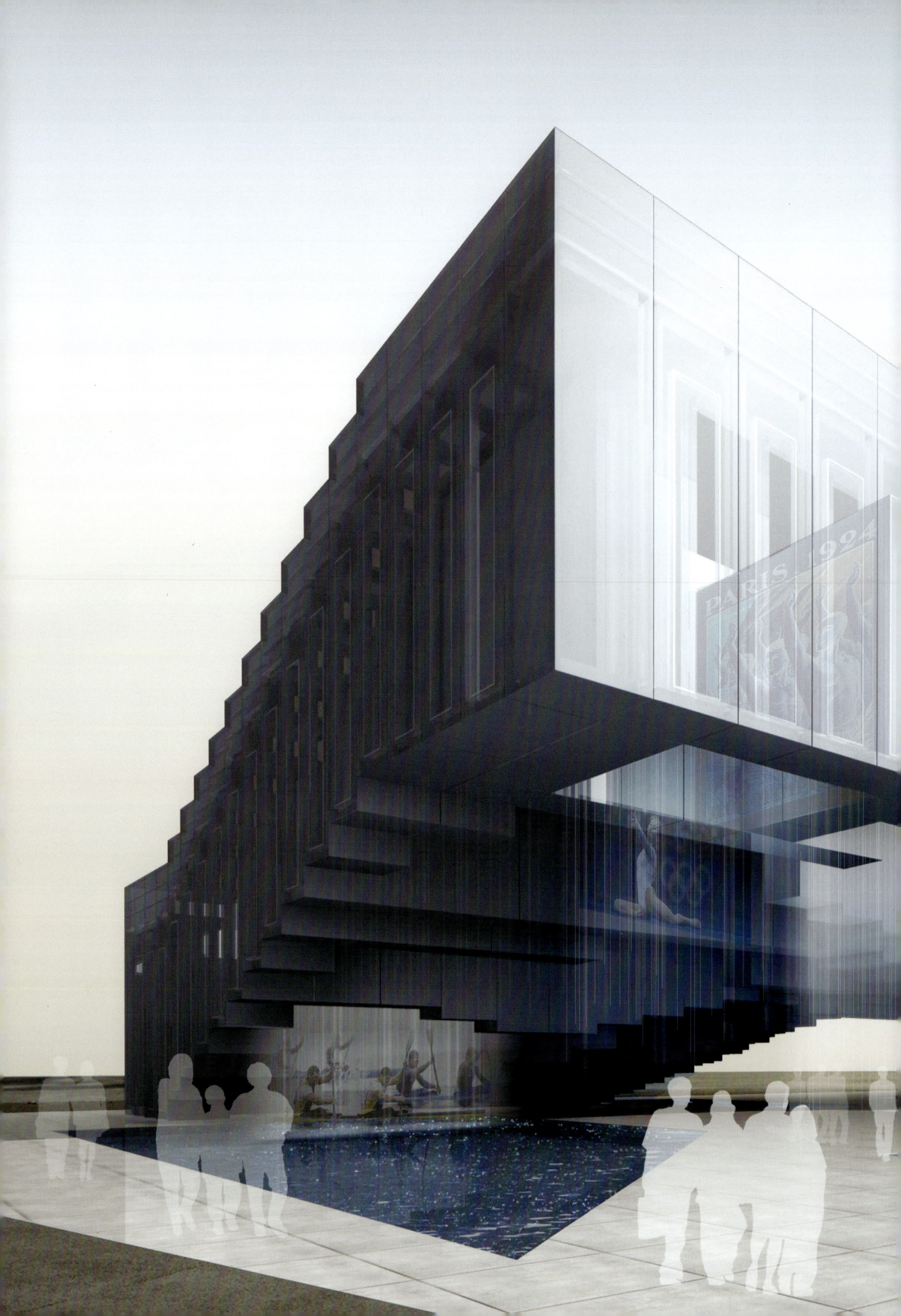
PARIS 1924

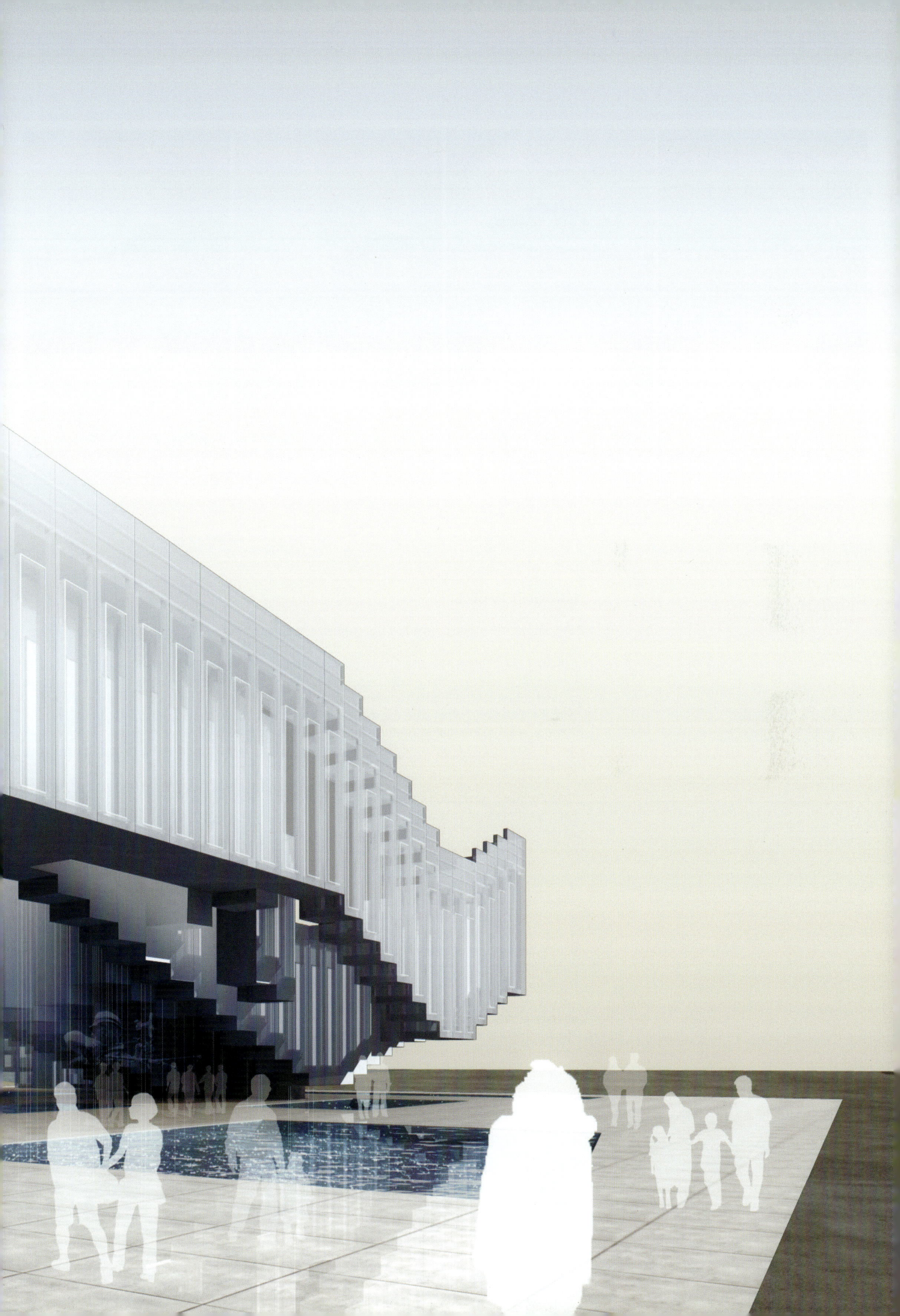

NAVIGATION CELL

We propose an olympic landmark using an abstract map of the earth. Every race and region in the world is represented by a map of abstract cells. The whole landmark map is composed of vertically extruded cells. 3-dimensional and zero gravity matrix is constructed by mechanical puzzle joints which tightly connect vertical sides of each cell. The map of newly positioned cells from the existing ground composes the 3-dimensional matt-like space and provides connection link to communicate with the ground, to experience the space, and to navigate inside and outside the landmark. Through a re-organizational assembly of anti-gravity cells, it becomes a live landmark, which can be transformed into pixels of scenery, pixels of landscape, pixels of light, pixels of color, pixcels of glass, and etc.

Time Capsule - Navigation Capsule
Each cell is made of time capsules in memory of the Olympic. Each cell is transformable to contain diverse memories inside, which can be collected by media, program, nature, material, and so on. The whole map, which exists and intersects each other on different levels and positions, proposes leveled and abstract re-construction of the earth including human, nature, culture, sports, material, and spirit. Emptied capsules are reserved for the record of the future Olympic.

Interactive Walking into Navigation Cell
This landmark is not just an object to see, but a matrix of cells in the shape of frame, providing the inside experience of the landmark itself. Walking above or below the cell matrix and moving around inside the cell structure, one can experience new perspectives over the Olympic Park and Paris. At the same time the spaces inside the consecutive cells produce spectacular scenery. Walking on the abstract topography of the earth over the cells, one can enjoy the surrounding scenery.

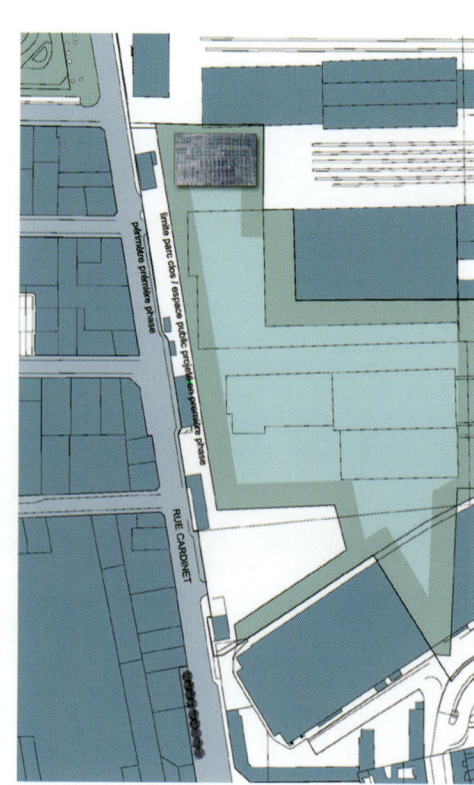

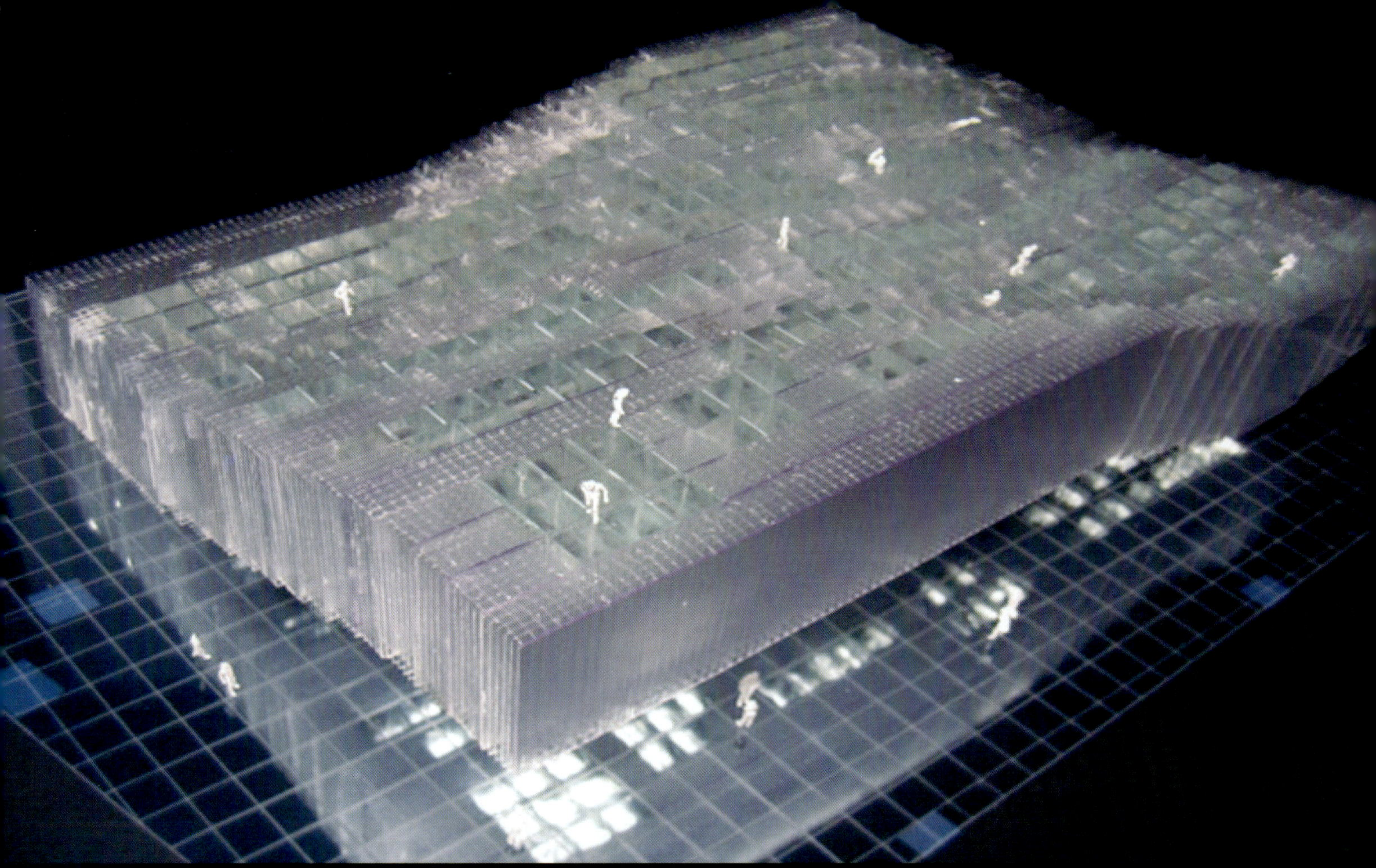

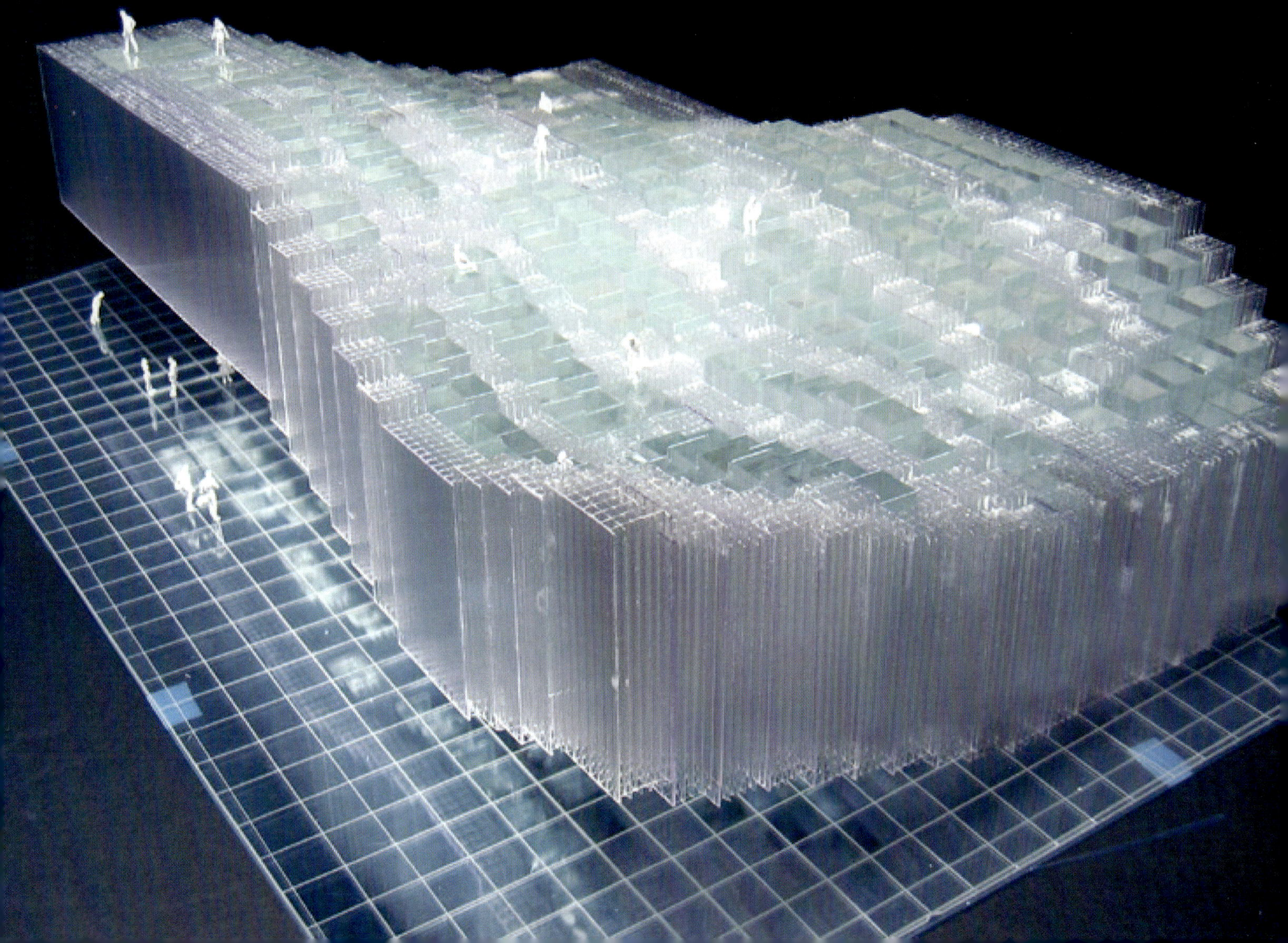

TRANSFORMATION PROCESS

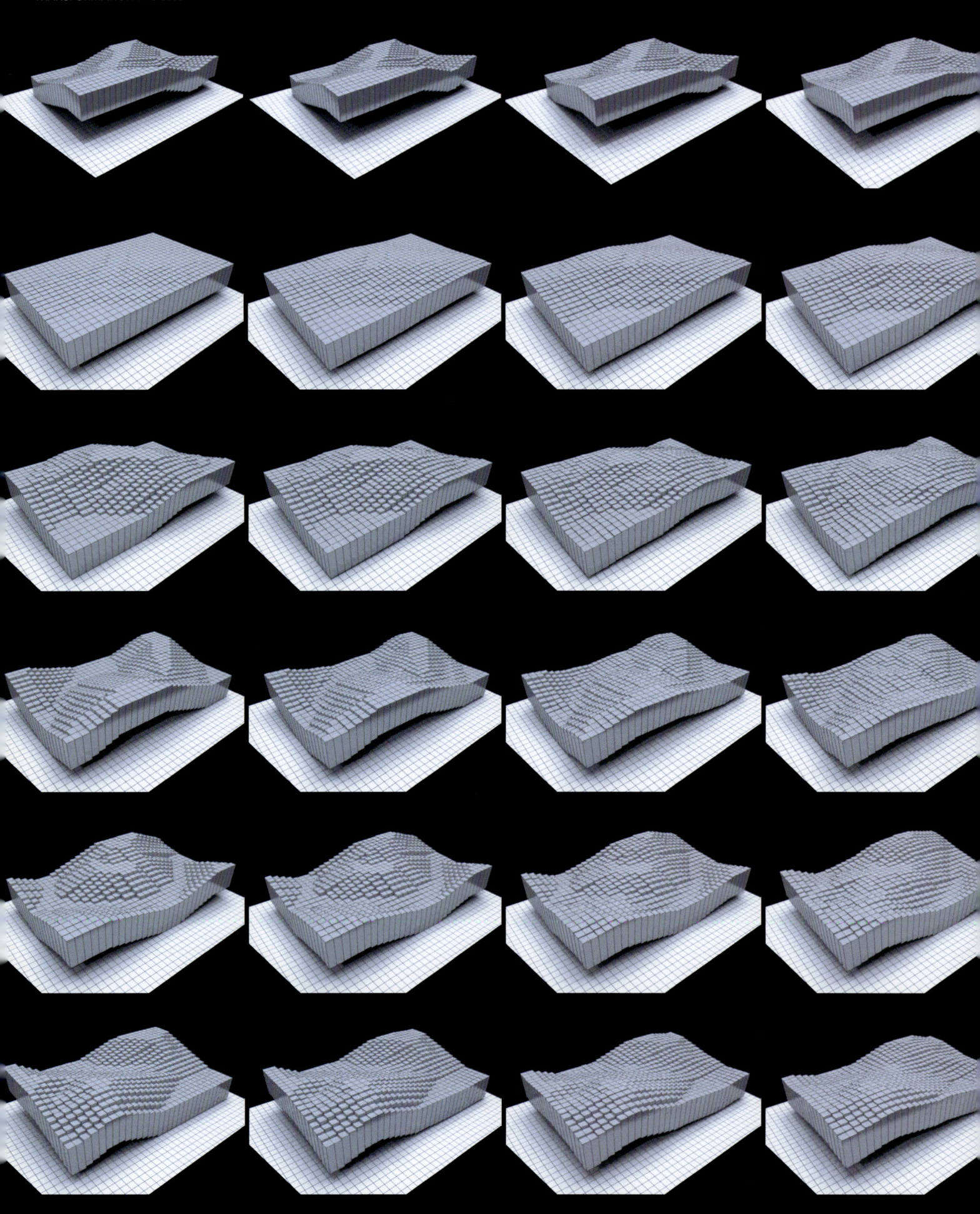

COMPOUND BODY 417

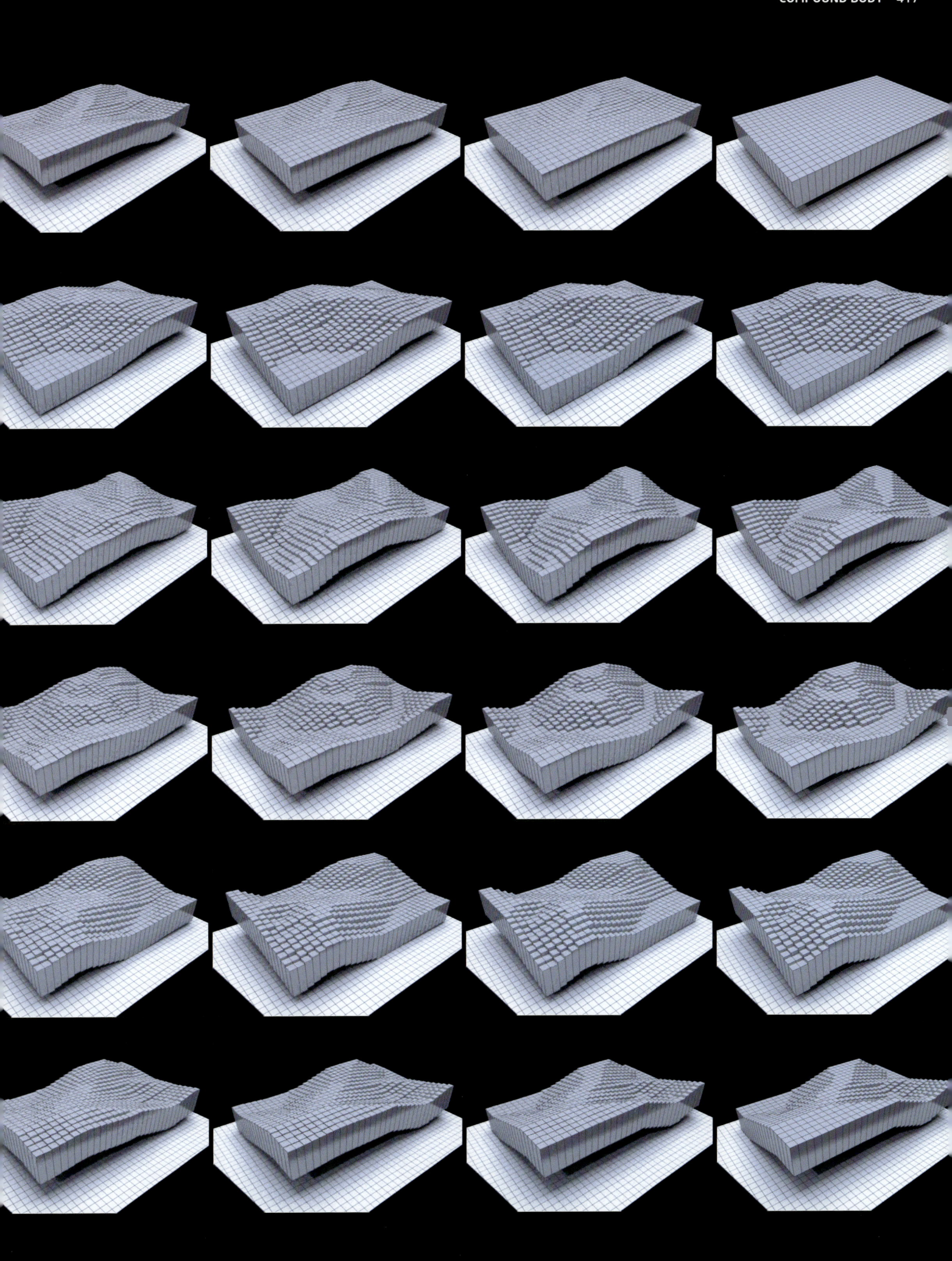

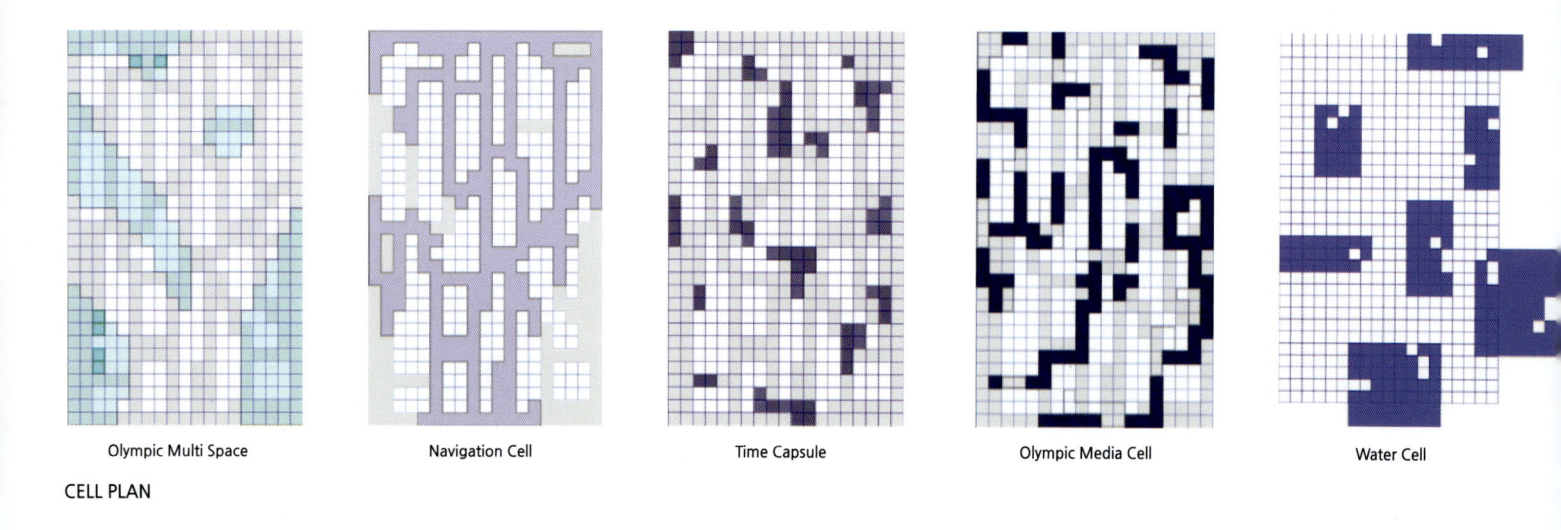

418

Olympic Multi Space   Navigation Cell   Time Capsule   Olympic Media Cell   Water Cell

CELL PLAN

C Olympic multi space
T Toilet
C Time capsule
O/M Olympic multi space / Media cell

E Elevator
M Media map
O/C Olympic / Time capsule

PLAN

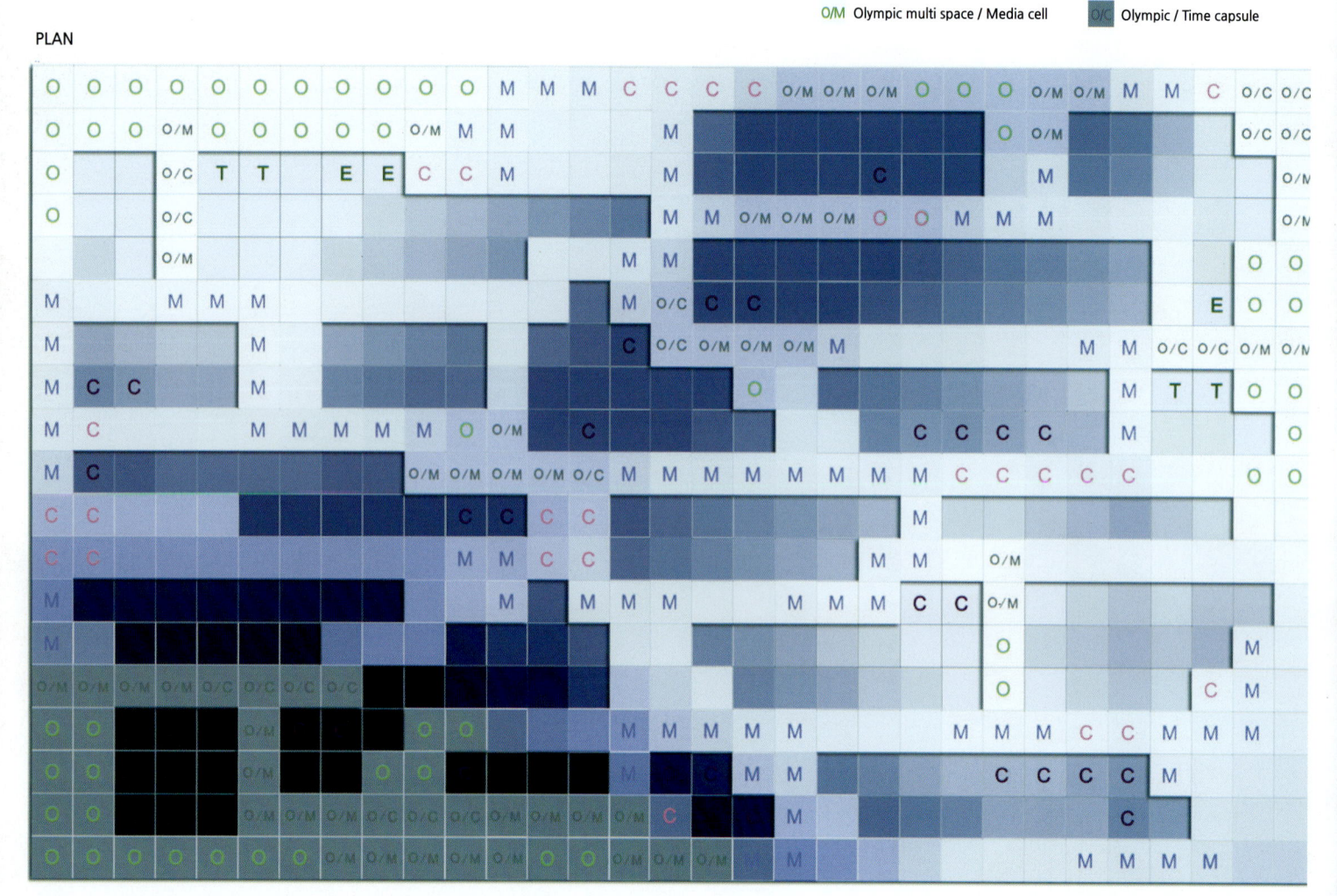

Container Structure
The combination of vertical cells produces horizontal and anti-gravitational structure. Using 3-dimentional position shift of the consecutively combined cells, 3-dimentional void connected to the ground has been created. The whole structure has been made by the union of the cantilevered cells, which is growing from the four anchoring spots on the ground. Like vertical LEGO block without permanent glue, each unit cell is combined together using gravitational friction and suspension structure.

Programmed Void
Emptied void space becomes a frame which contains events of the city temporary and hypothetically. From time to time, each void space is transformed into gallery or event space on the ground level. The whole concaved 3-dimensional void becomes stage-like space for the crucial event in the city.

Alternative Re-use
Because this Olympic landmark is using simple mechanic joint, which is disjointable, the combination of cells can be transformed into the various forms of matrix reflecting the condition, need, and scenery of the different site. Horizontal and vertical combination of the cells, the location and size of the void, and the shape of wave(concave) can be presented in a quite different way.

NORTH ELEVATION

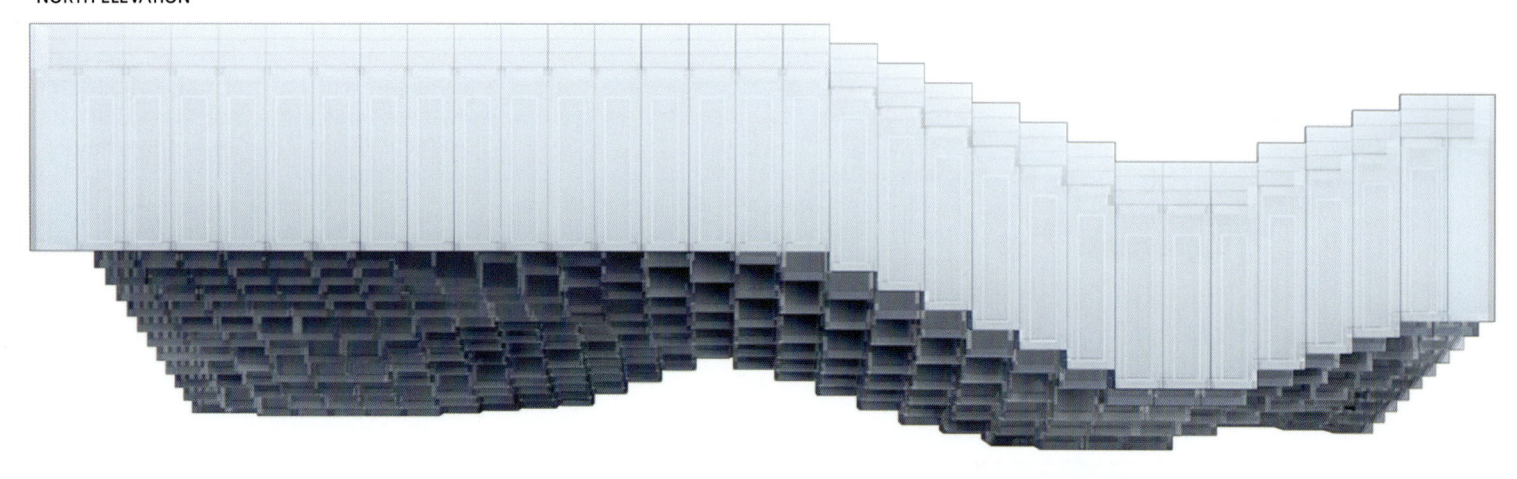

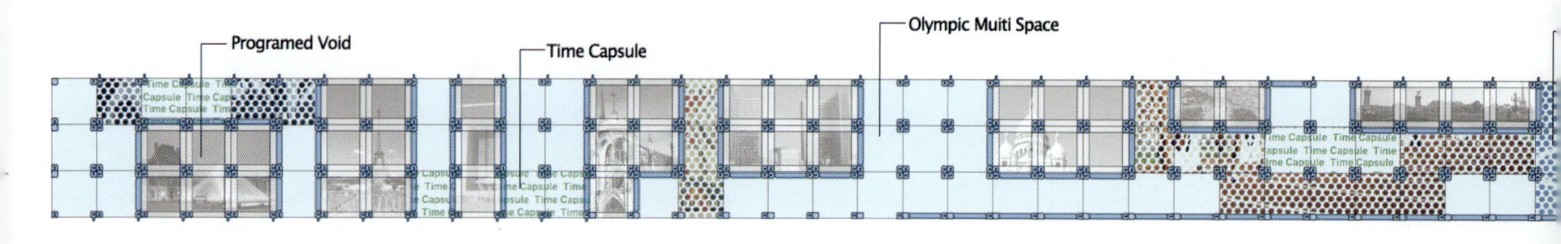

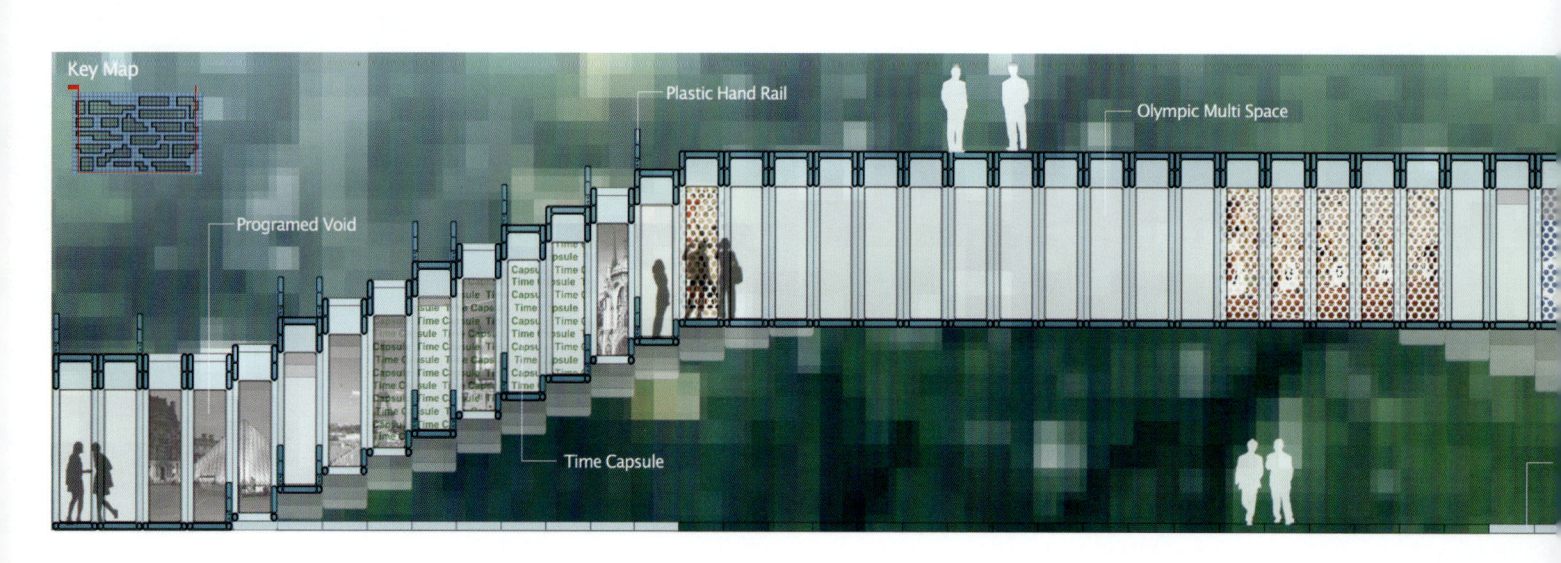

- Programed Void
- Time Capsule
- Olympic Multi Space

Key Map

- Programed Void
- Time Capsule
- Plastic Hand Rail
- Olympic Multi Space

COMPOUND BODY 421

SOUTH ELEVATION

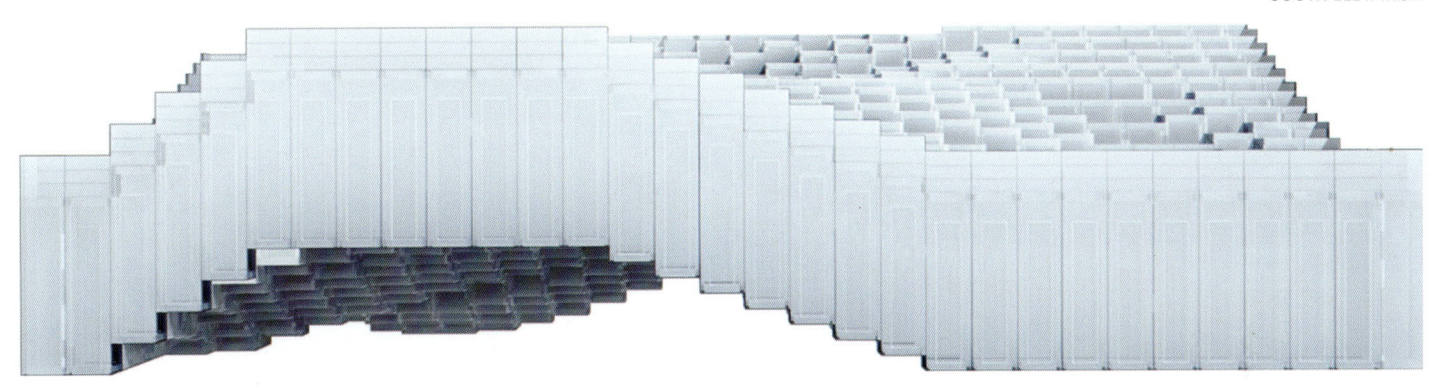

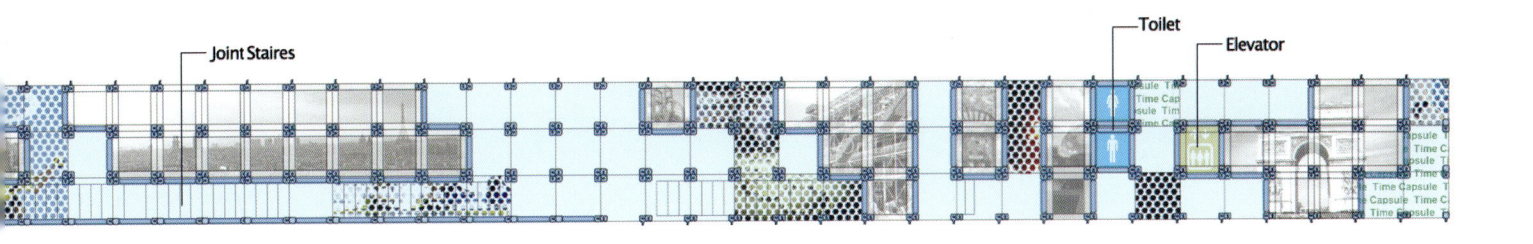

Joint Staires — Toilet — Elevator

SECTION

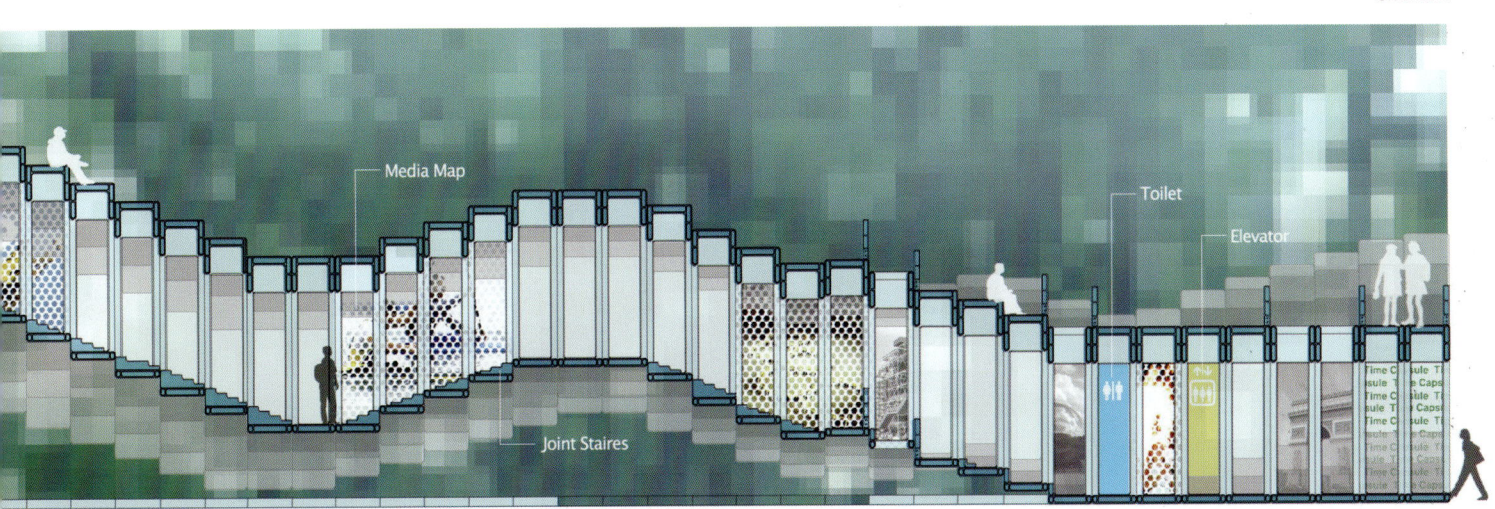

Media Map — Toilet — Elevator

Joint Staires

STRUCTURE ANALYSIS

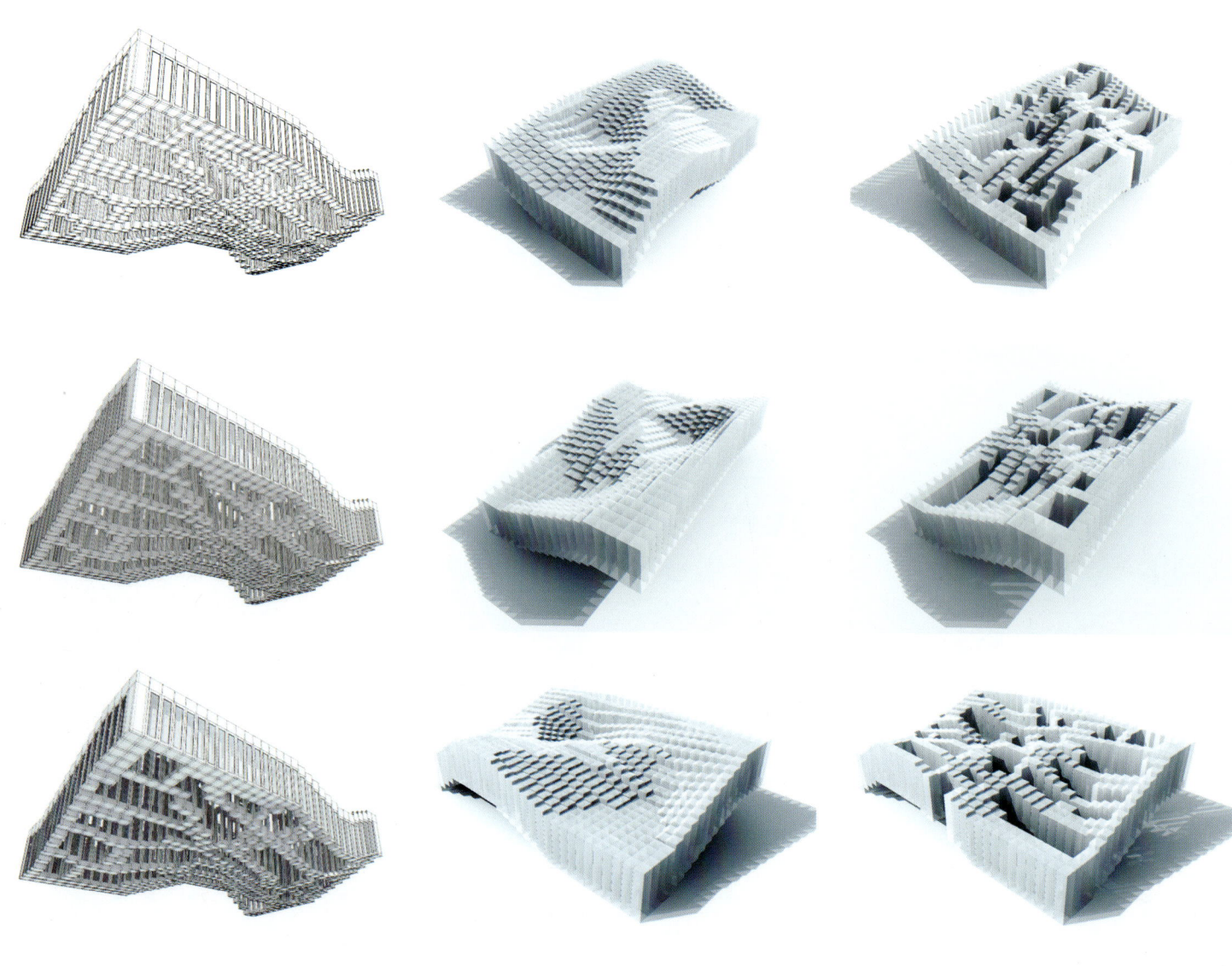

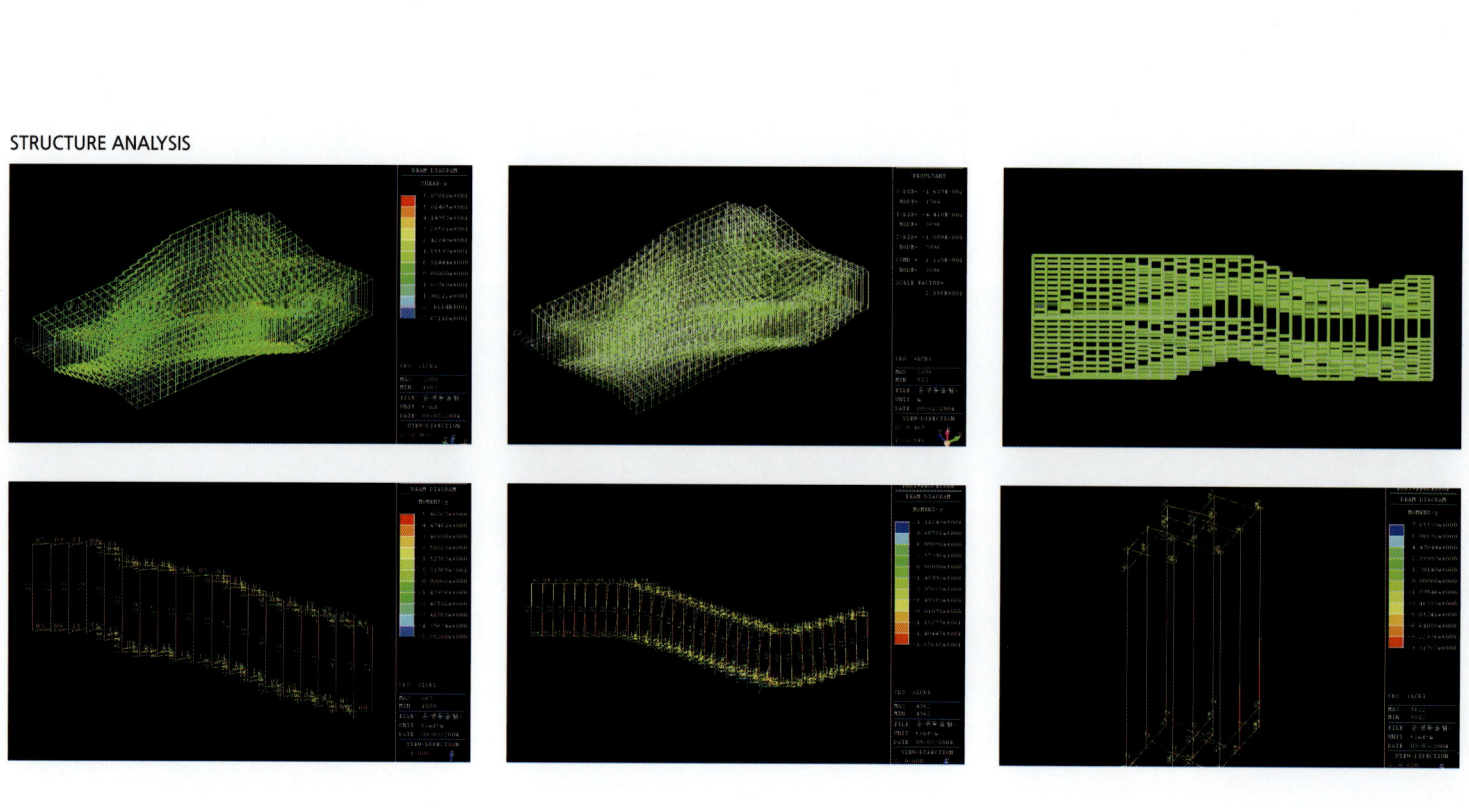

UNIT DETAIL

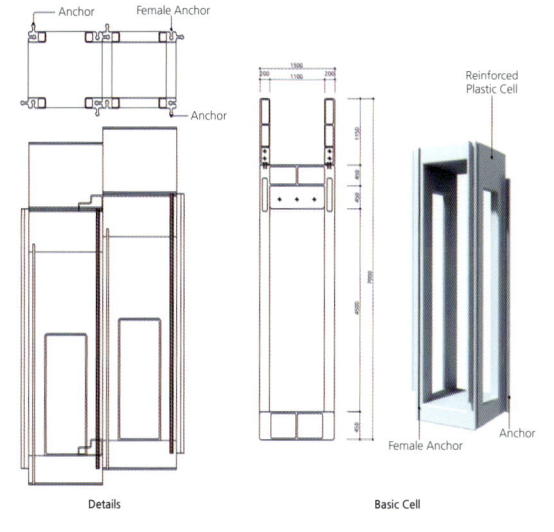

Details — Basic Cell

Unit Cell — Union Cell

Reinforced Plastic Cell

The whole landmark is made of reinforced plastic cells which can be assembled consecutively. The whole assembly system can be made by a simple and basic mold unit. It's reinforced plastic unit made of inter-connectable joints, circulation corridor, and floor covering top side and bottom side of it. It has changable connection joints using the friction of gravitational force. Additional circulation stairs, lighting boxes, observation windows, railings, and etc. can be combined with these basic unit cells depending on the site and program condition.

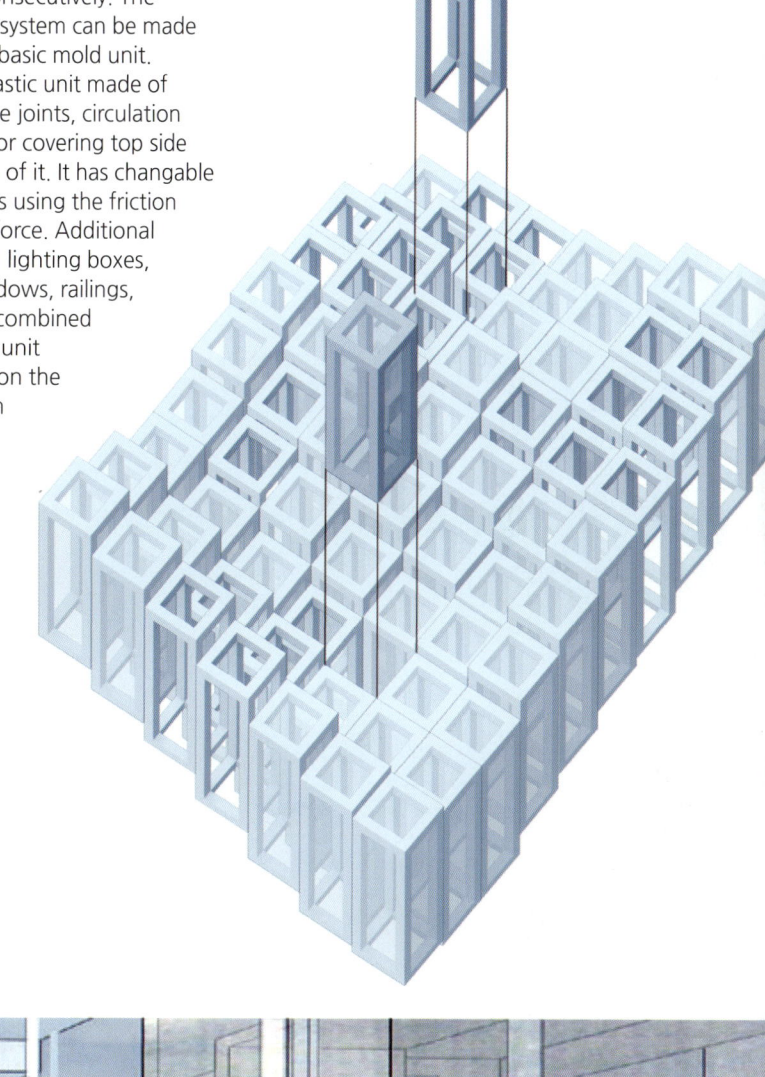

Gallery JUNGMISO

Architects Jang Yoon Gyoo, Shin Chang Hoon
Client Yoon Suk Hwa
Photographer Song Jae Young

COMPOUND BODY 425

LOOKING THROUGH THE GLASS

A devastated place has changed to 'Gallery JUNGMISO'. Head office of a monthly music magazine, GAEKSUK(AUDITORIUM) has transformed into a 'symbolic aspect of culture(finding)'. It, however, has long been a medium for reading. 'Alice' is looking at a mirror as if she could get something that she had been craving for ages. We put a huge glass instead of the existing floor. We visualise that what it would be like if we look through the glass. It is neither a ceiling nor a floor. It might look like a pit in 'Alice in Wonderland'. It is becoming a kind of linkage which conveys a host of artworks to the society and to the general public like a curtain in a theatre. Since the curtain is situated between the floor(stage) and the ceiling. Gallery JUNGMISO was constructed as a space which is filled with people's hopes and dreams. We could get a haven for young artists by adding few tales to the gallery rather

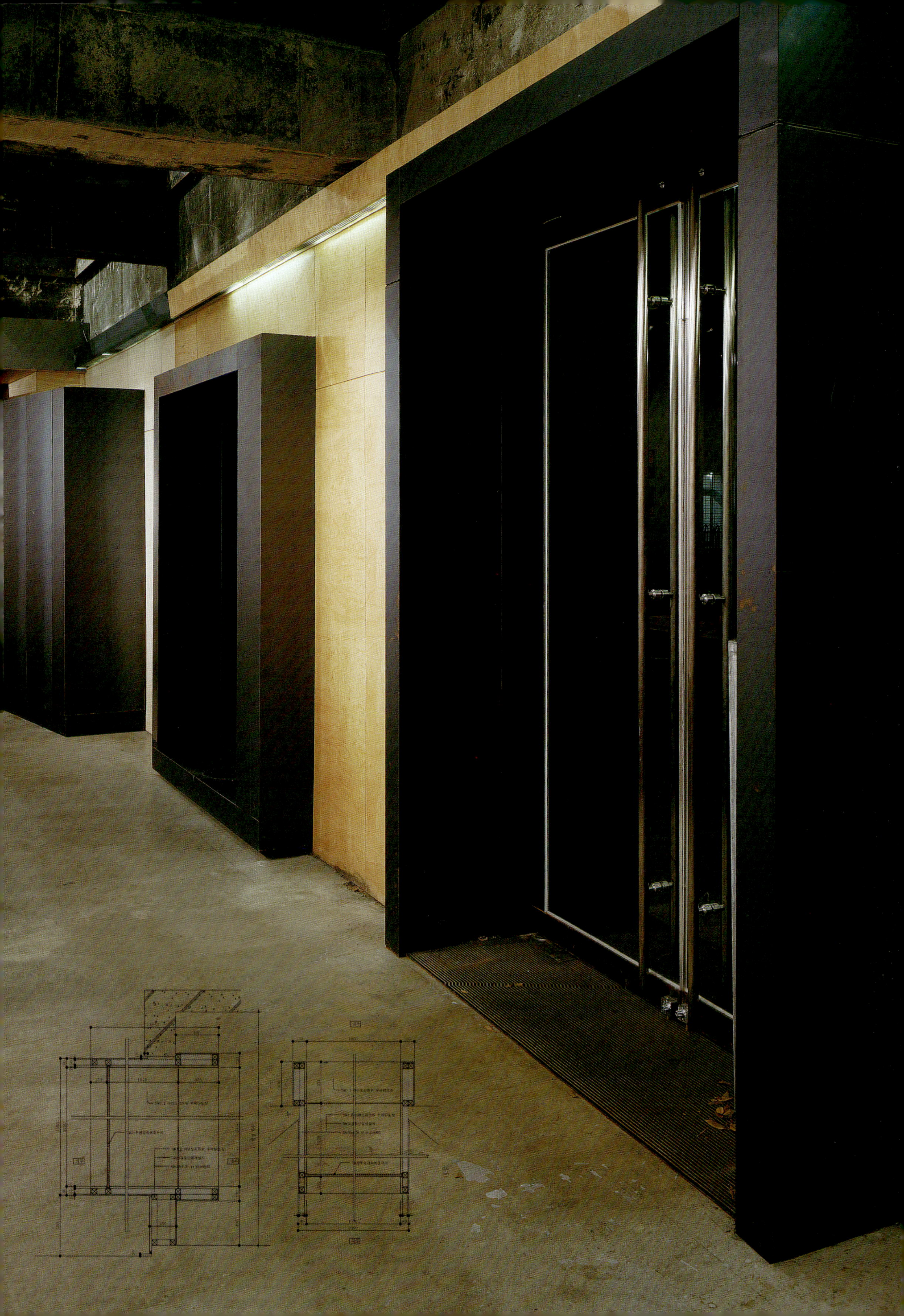

than eliminating every element to renovate it. Artist could build a network through the gallery as its space infuses with poetic aspects. The glass floor of the gallery is also the ceiling of the theatre's lobby. It represent a seed which is a network of hope. "We bring a glass floor like the mirror of Alice." It connects architecture and artwork. The Glass Floor is not only a surface but light, a screen which carrying images and media like a canvas.

PLAN

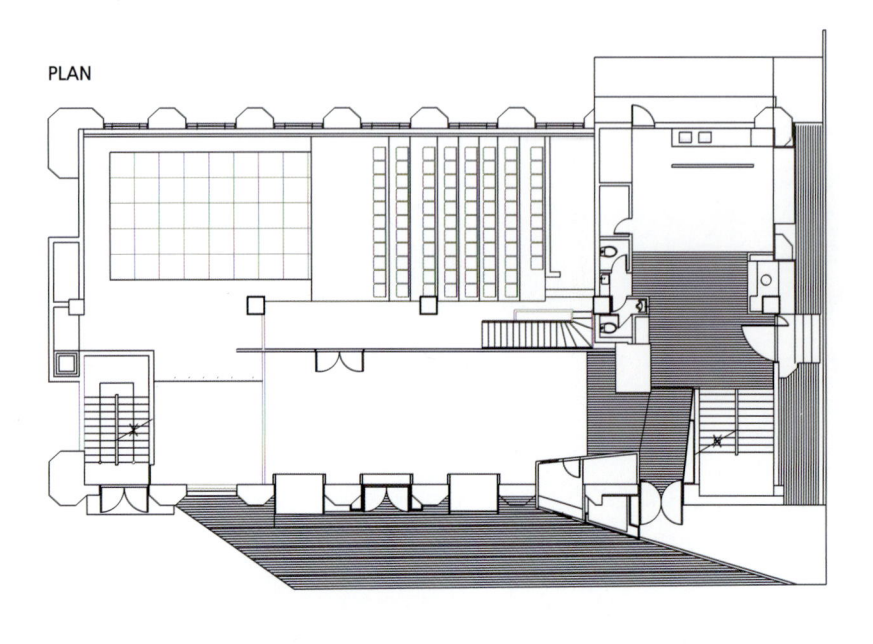

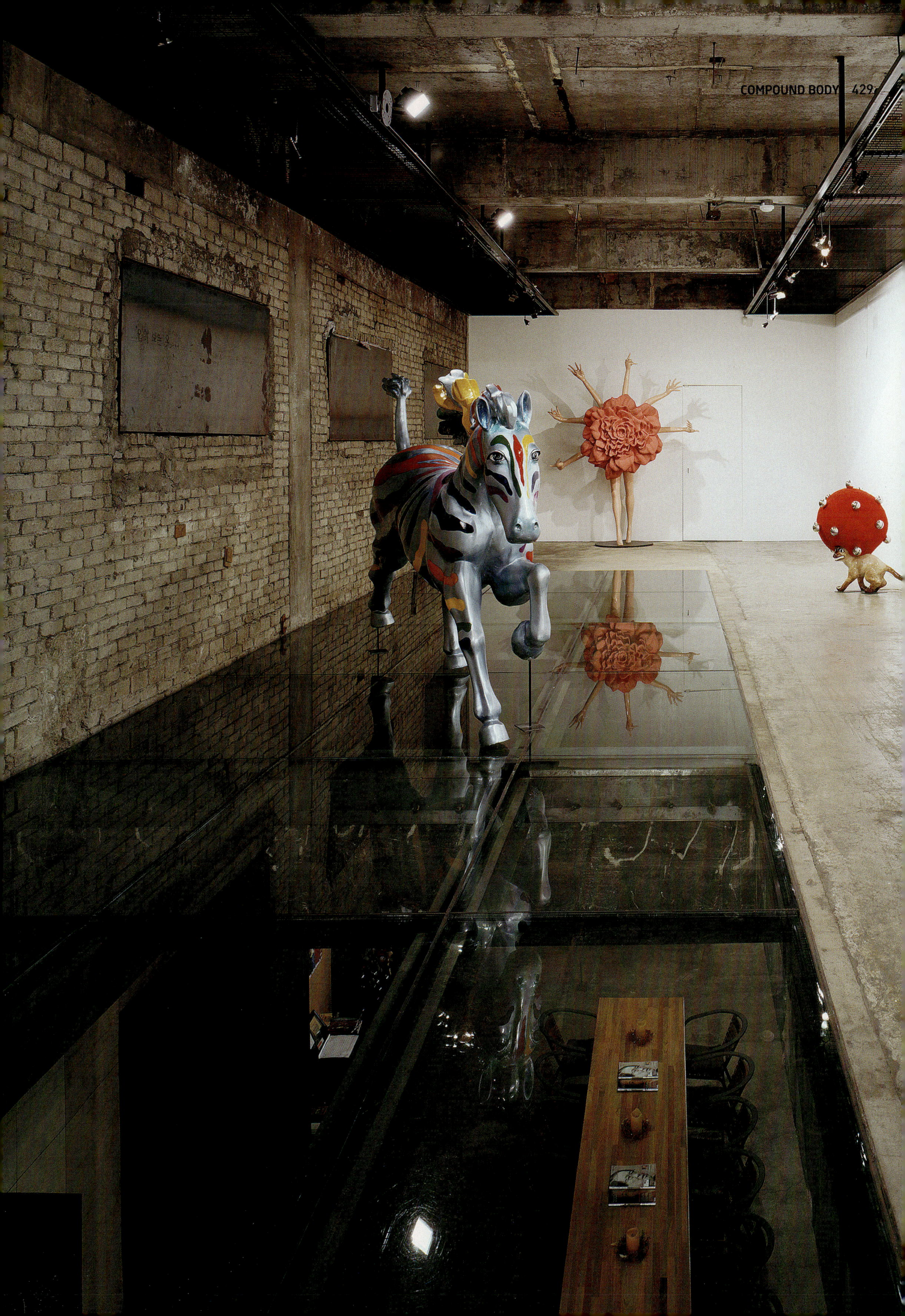

Cloud
skin

Actress ⟨YOONSUKHWA⟩ Space
for Performance

Architects Jang Yoon dyoo
Co-Artist Jang Yoon Sung
Client Yoon Suk Hwa
Photographer Moon Jung Sik

COMPOUND BODY 431

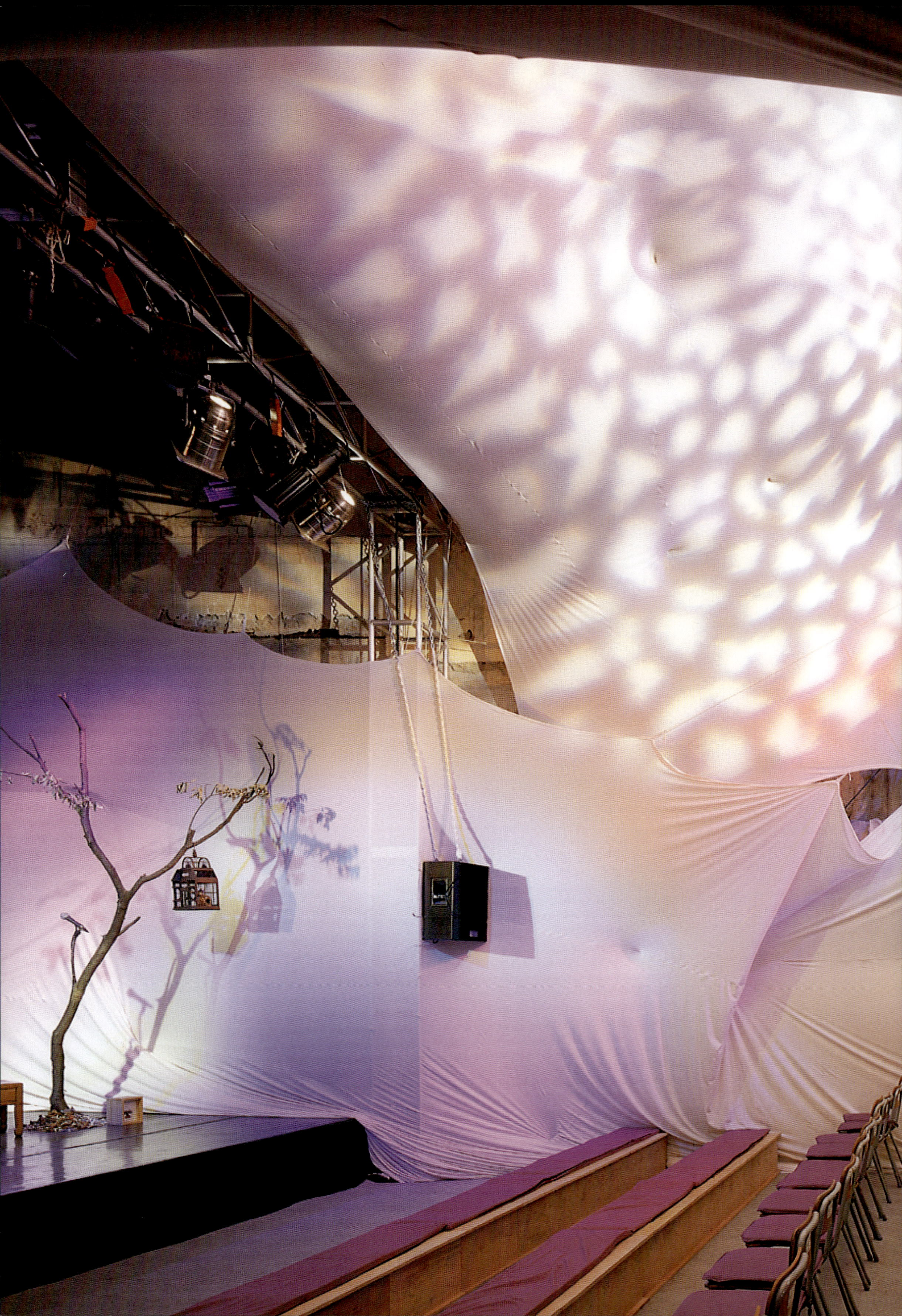

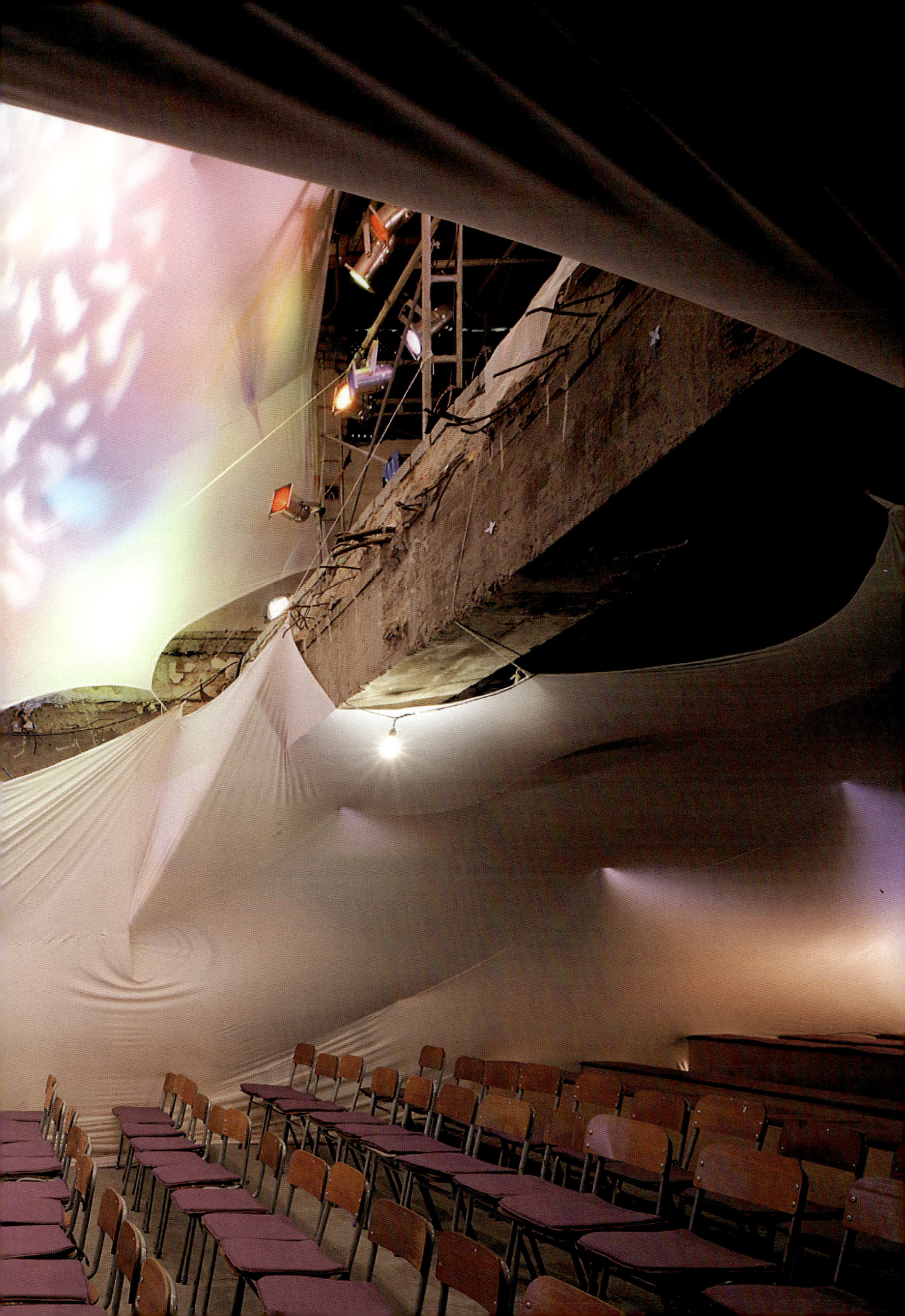

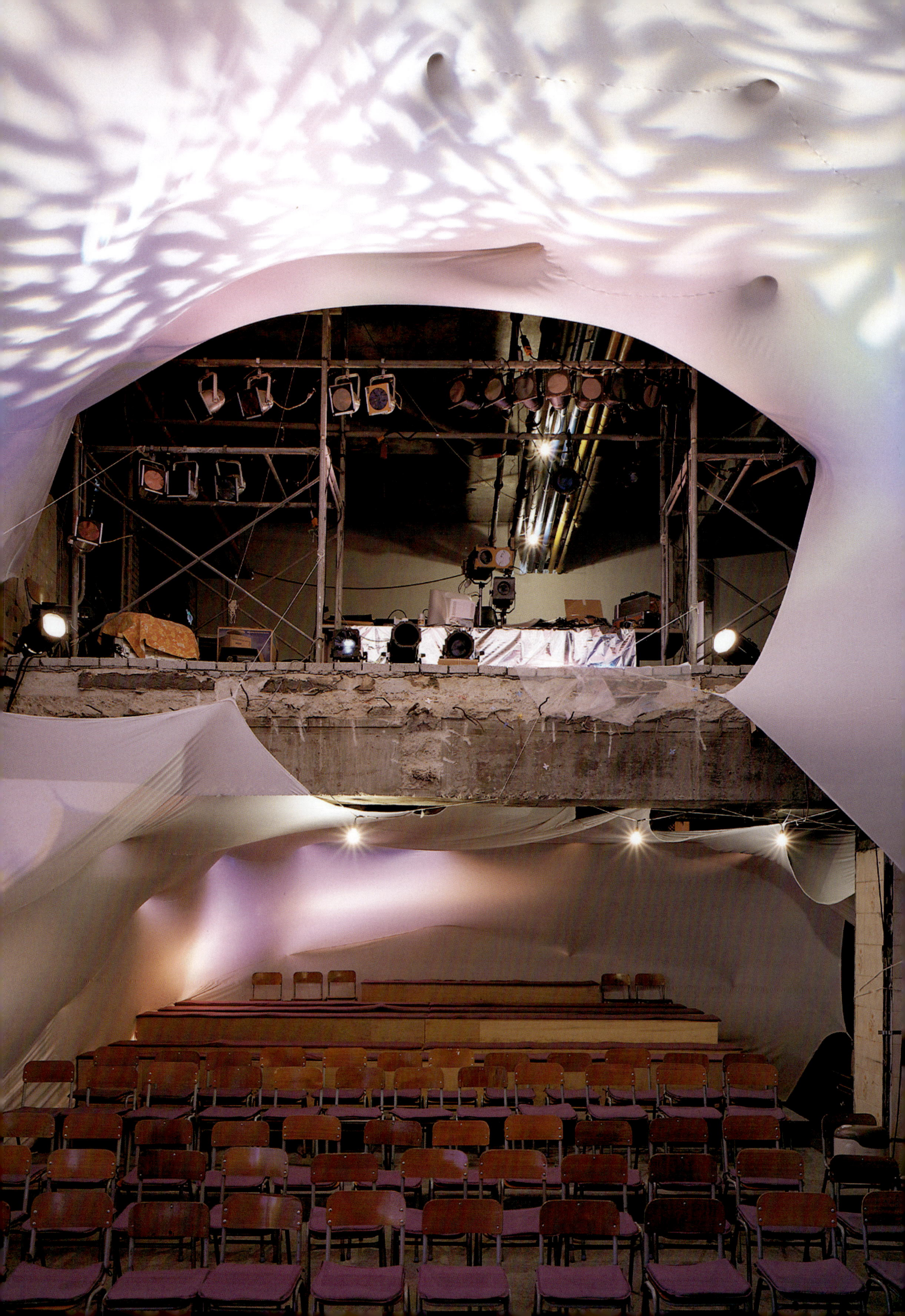

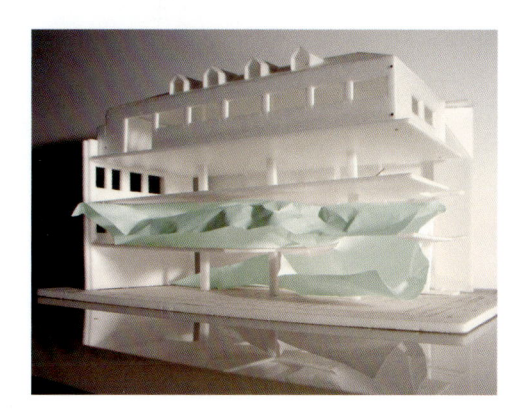

ACTRESS YOON SUK-HWA'S SPACE, THEATER JUNGMISO STORY

There is a small theater, Jungmiso, occupying the 1st and 2nd floor of Gaek-Suk Building. Demolished concrete skin, iron bars sticking out, holes on the ceiling and pipes… Indescribable ruins even get tears dry.
I found this ruined space so beautiful. I want to change the unpleasant air to abundance like a flower garden. I want it to bear the depth of poetic space. I ask myself what it means to eliminate a deserted thing and replace it with something new. The reason why the Acropolis in Grease, Athens is impressive is because it is a ruined place with trace of time. A ruined space combined with the Mediterranean light and air is what catches our eyes. The theater scene on the outdoor stage of the Acropolis gives us a thrill that transcends time. The emotion of a flower blooming in the ruins will fill up the space at Jungmiso. Instead of clean and neat interior or architecture, the ruins will be a little bit organized and a huge curtain will be inserted like a theater stage or installation art. This installed curtain will be a 3-dimensional flower bed, emitting light and scent. This space will not stay ruined. It will change and grow with constant plays and events. Growing Space is not only for one person. It will be made by all the participants with their affection and concern. In other words, it will start as an empty space with the least spatial manipulation, different from a wholly completed space.

Consecutive artists' stages will fulfill the space of Jungmiso. The themes of the space will change according to each artist's set up. It can be a scene full of sand, flowers and light bulbs hanging under the whole ceiling like stars. Poetry and picturesque theater space will be created from artists' imagination.
Theater generally consists of seats which make up the audiences' space and a stage which is the space within the space. At the end of many talks with Yoon Suk-hwa, we agreed to go with a new and experimental theater. It will not only used as a theater. It will be a multilayered space that includes cafe, gallery and events. I hope it to be a changeable space according to the concept of the stage and the cultural code of the play. A container for new space will be created so that programs irrelevant to the stage can be inserted.
Most of the plays are performed in the evening. So we thought the space for the seats could be filled with different events. The audiences who come here to watch the plays will come to appreciate art experiencing new events and the audiences who come to the gallery will watch the plays. The theater will form another space within the space. This abundant space will become an open plaza to everybody, embracing all factors such as cyber curtain, lights, play, resting place and people.

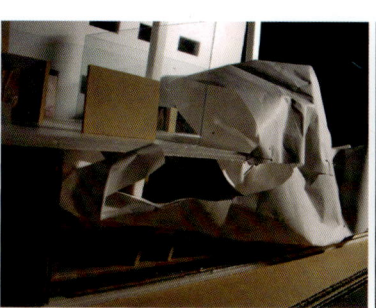

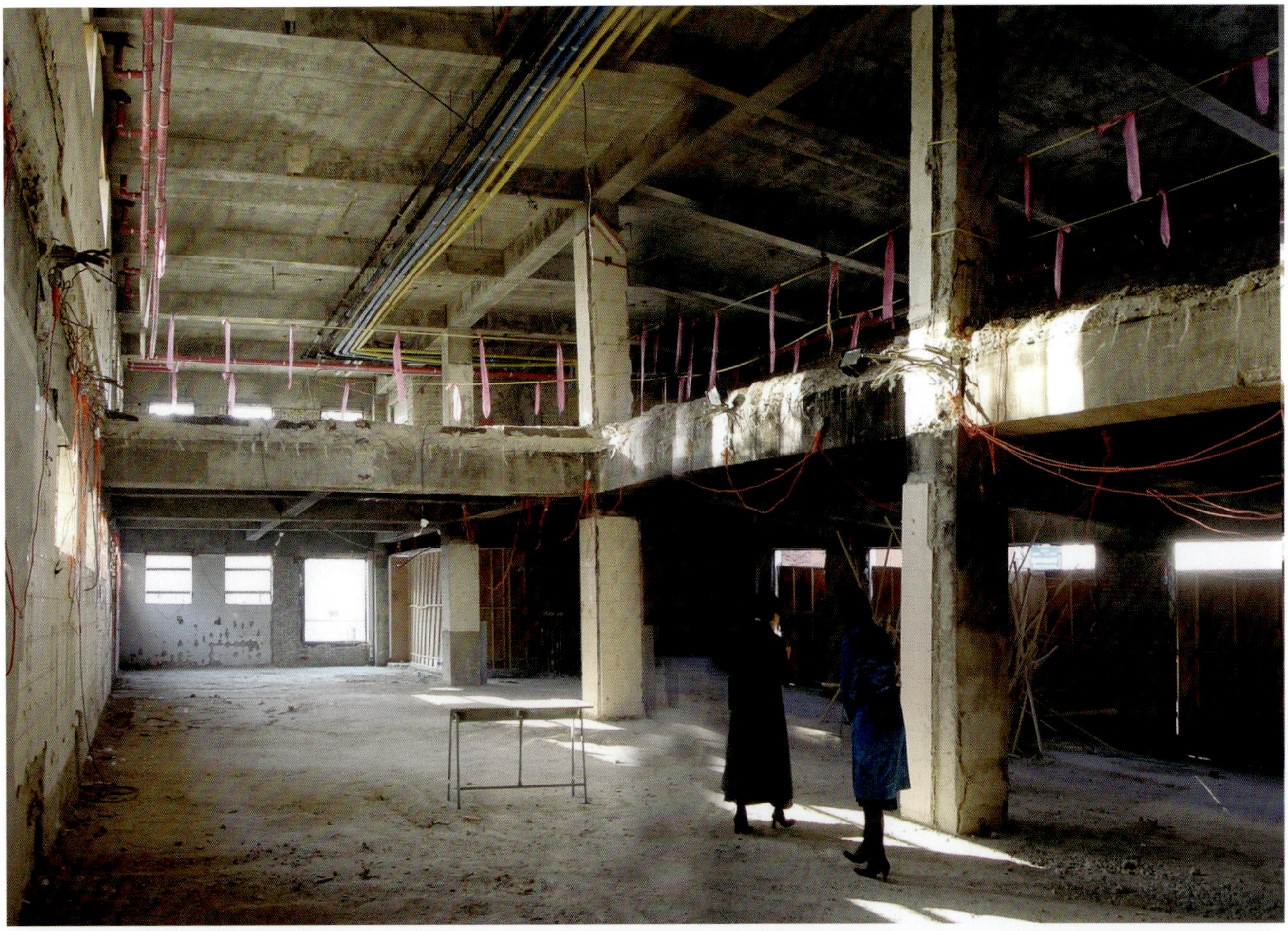

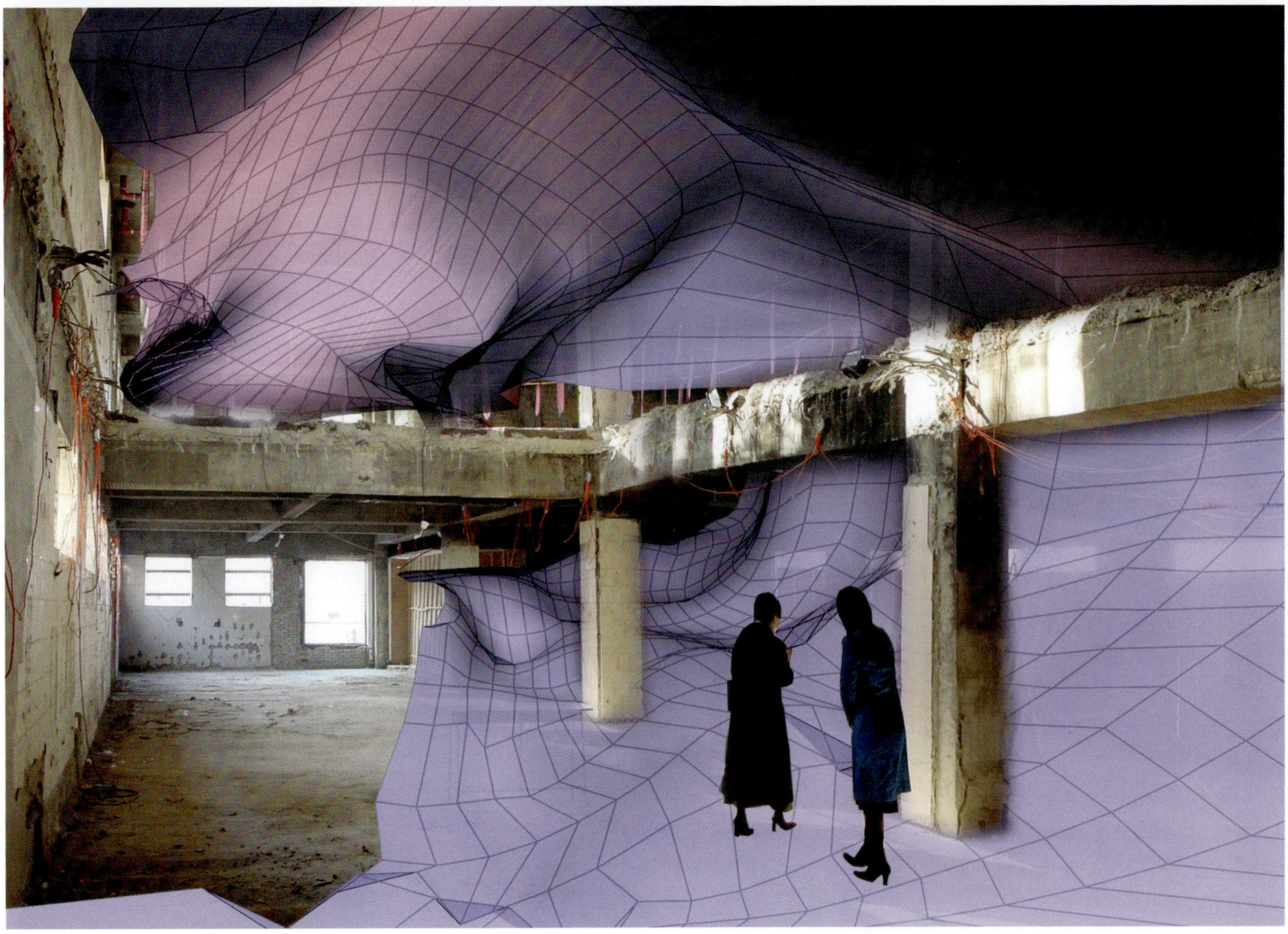

Yoon Suk-Hwa and I, imagine the huge curtain at the same time. Space for the play ⟨On the Flower garden⟩ will have the canvas curtain like installation art to insert program codes. The audiences will experience the huge curtain crossing over the whole theater. While they are watching the curtain, they will be curious and have an expectation of the play that will be performed, reminding actress Yoon Suk-Hwa. The stage-wise imagination will be hidden behind the curtain. We hope it to not stop just as a stage. The seats enclosed with the curtain will be another stage.

Theater and gallery, stage and audience, artistic code and spatial code, traditional space and alternative space… There is a question that defines these relationships newly in this space. I wish that it brings the audience and the performers close and eventually make them one. A white curtain is powerful equipment that replaces the whole theater. The curtain is not only developed on the wall but on to the floor and the ceiling enclosing inner space of the theater. The curved curtain can make strange spatial illusion.

There is a topic asking the relationship between a piece of art and audience. Walking on the curtain means enjoying art put under their feet. And furthermore it is the process of dragging the art down to their daily life. Not only stepping on it, but also touching it provides tactual reactions. Nobody will say "Don't touch." Tangible art wrapped over whole theater. The slippery property of the curtain changes to the epidermis of folds, meaning infinite baroque potentiality which Deleuze mentioned. The inner space of Jungmiso is transformed to spatial epidermis of the folds.

The space will become a living creature given life by the light. The huge curtain will not stay as physical skin but will become the light, the images and the media. It is a huge blank canvas. We will draw a picture of the light related the play. The canvas will be a media skin that reflects the theme of the play changing to screen, light, silhouette, image, and flowers. The audience will have become the leading role of the play touching this canvas inserted in the ruins.

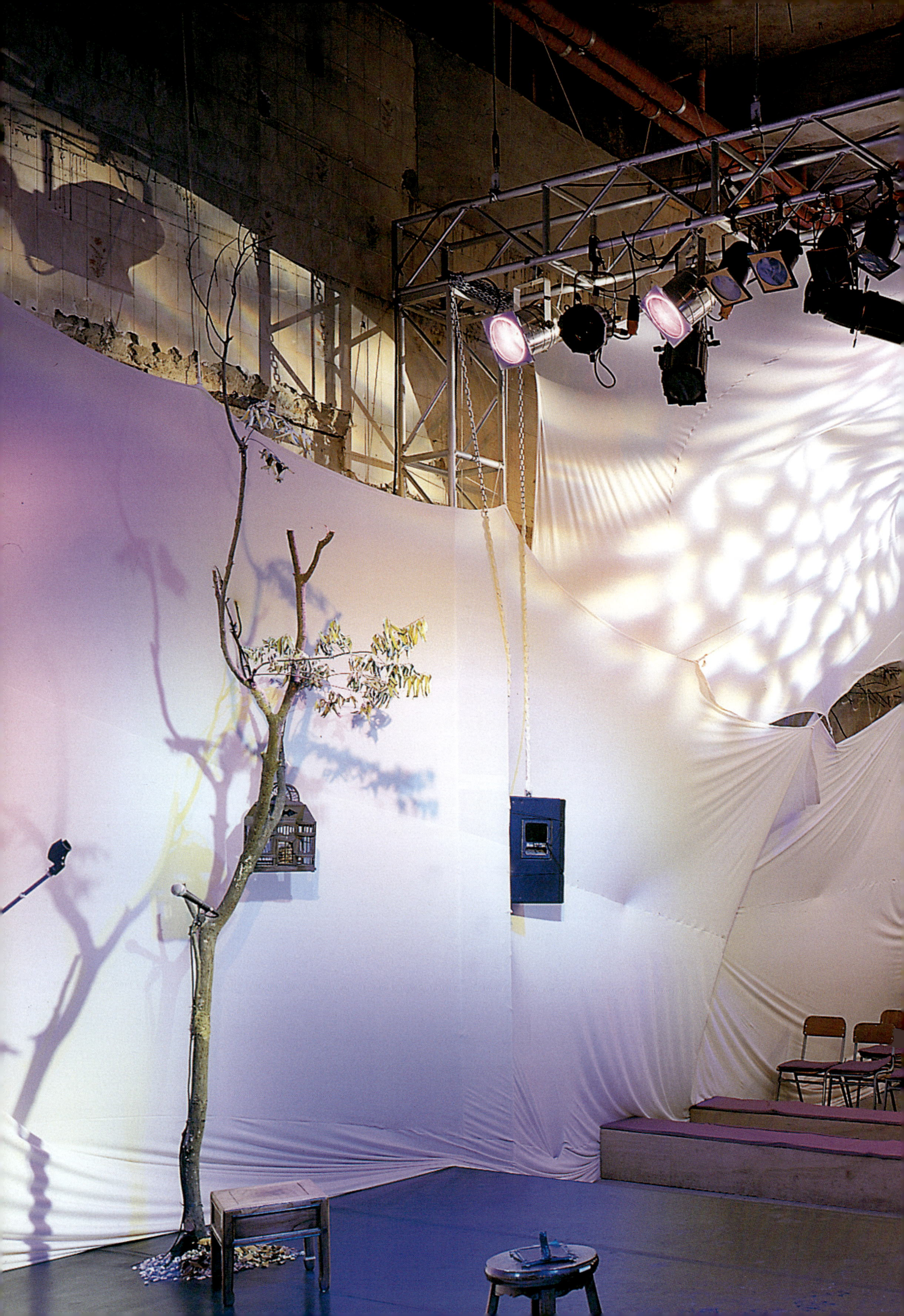

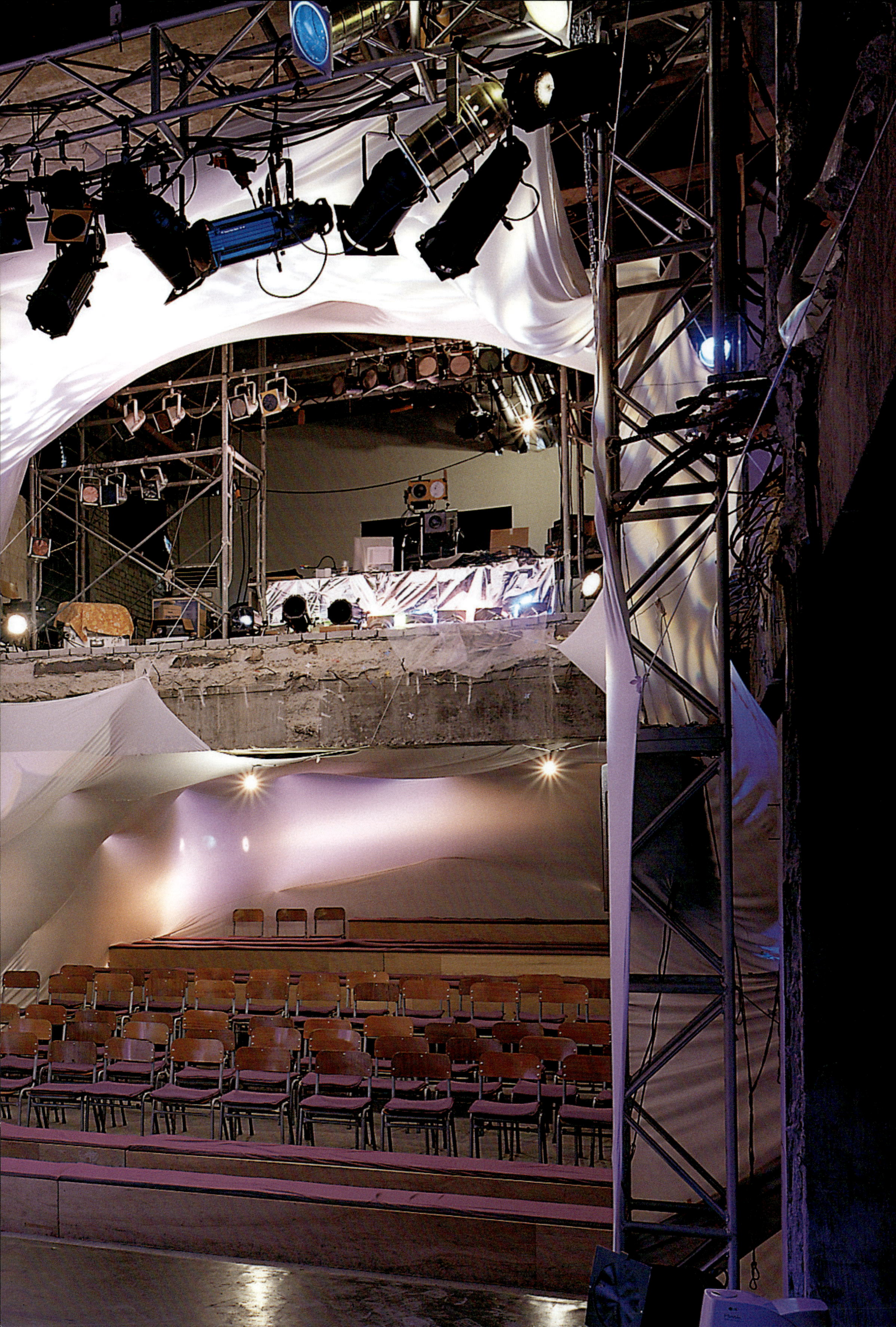

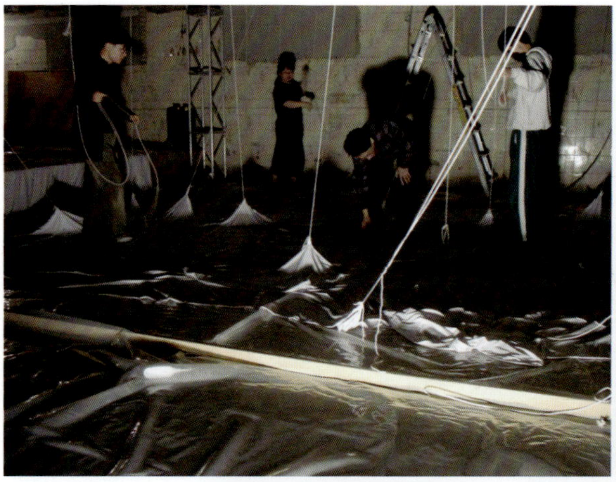

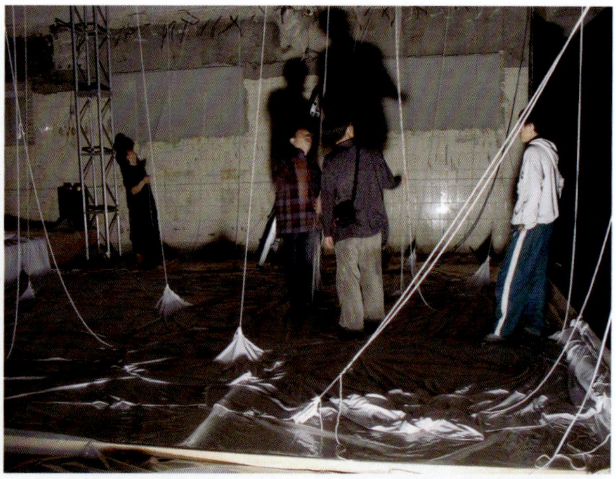

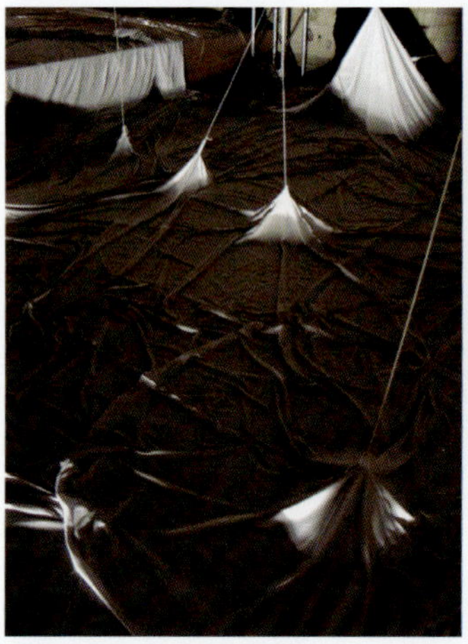

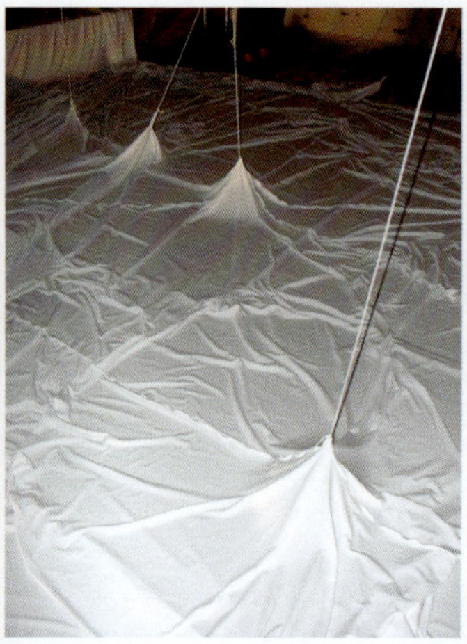

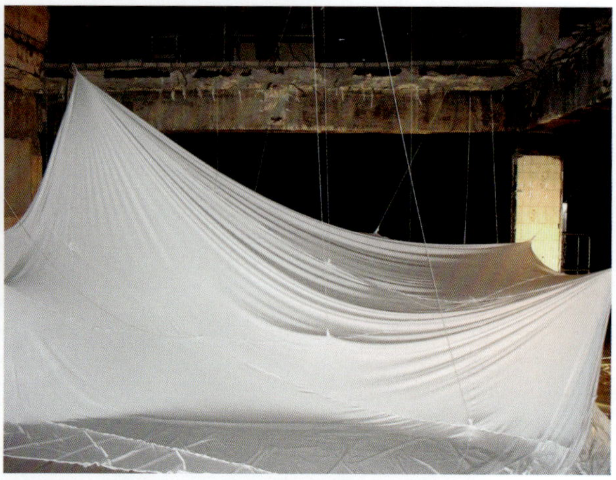

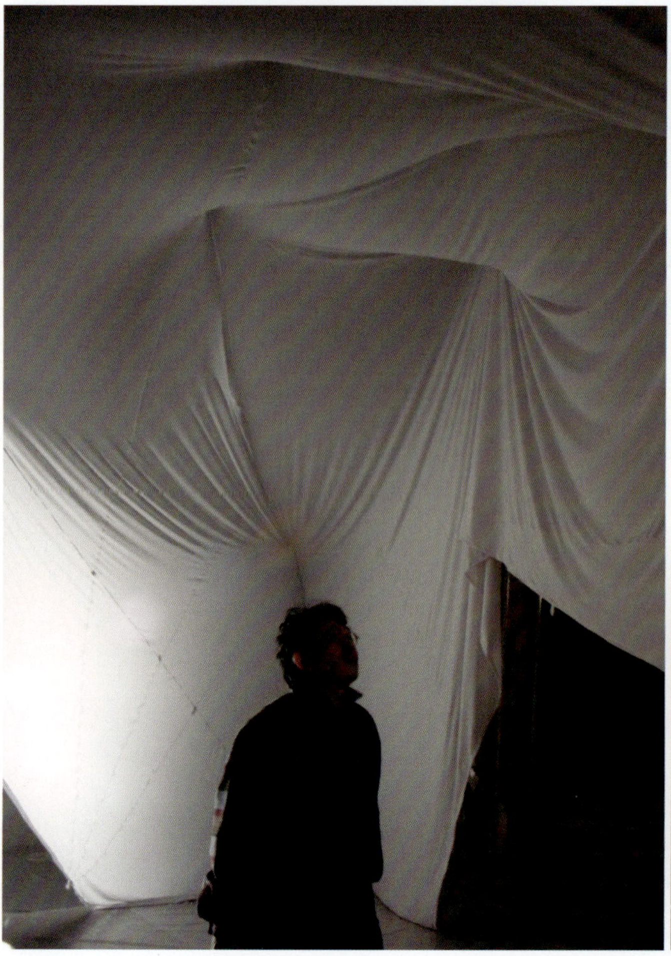

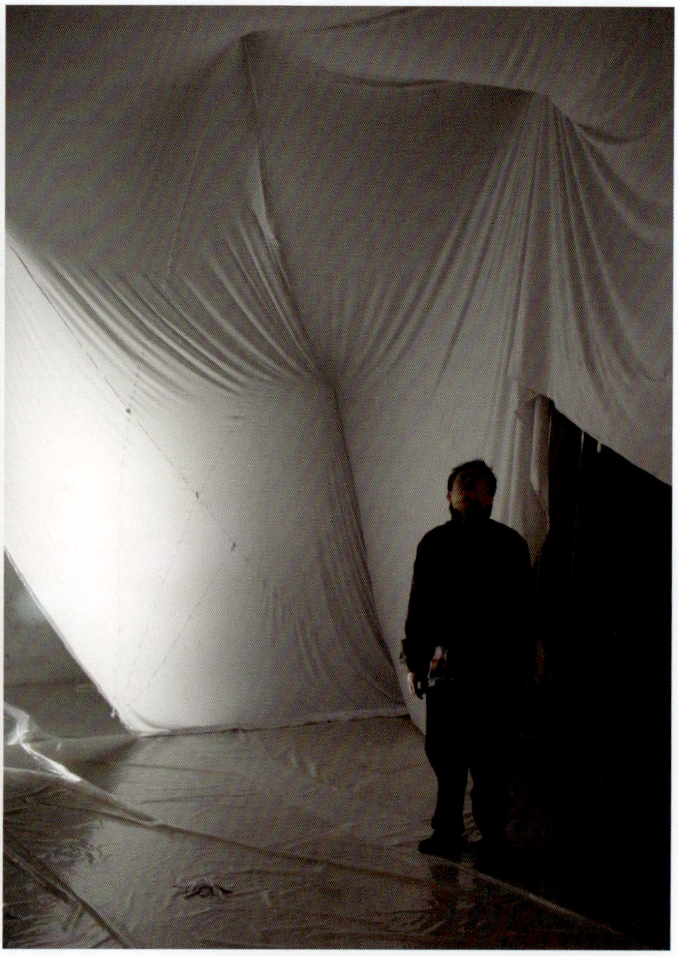

COMPOUND BODY 441

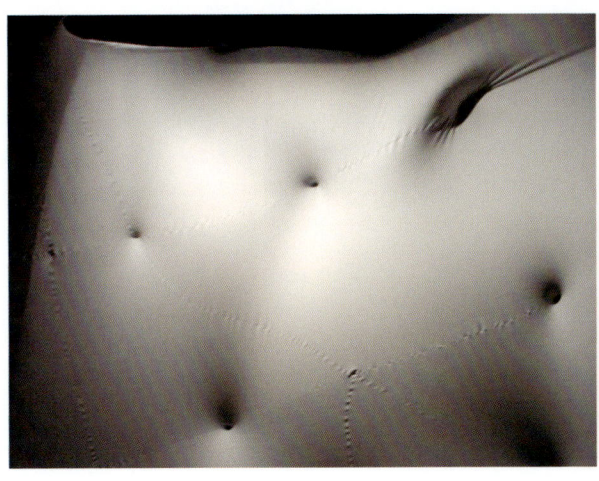

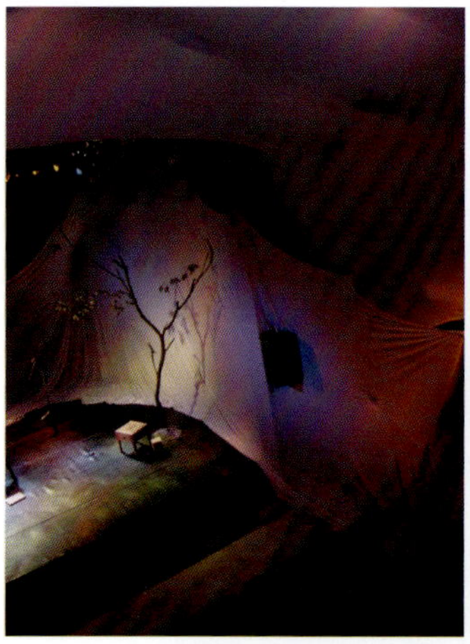
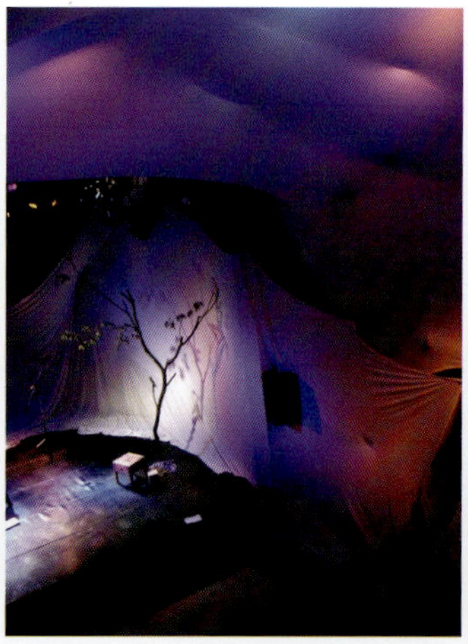
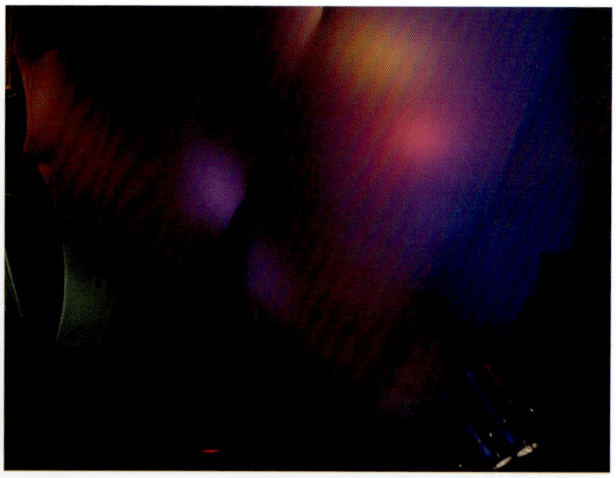
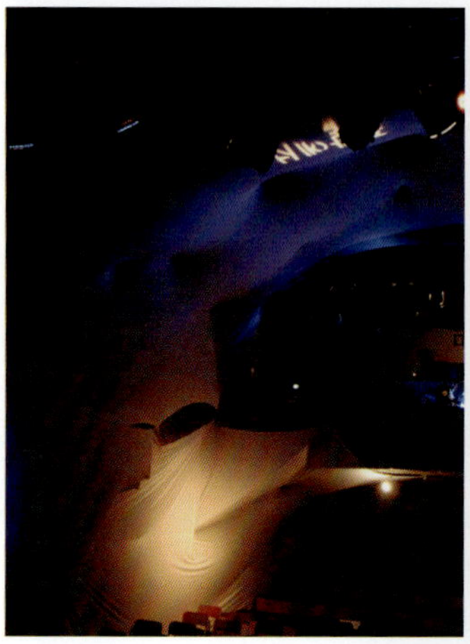
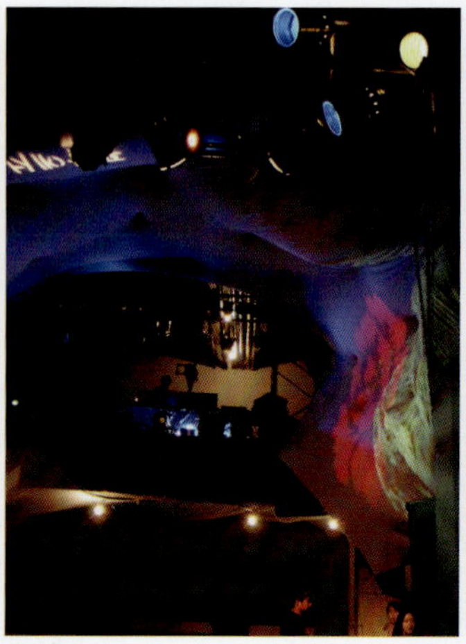
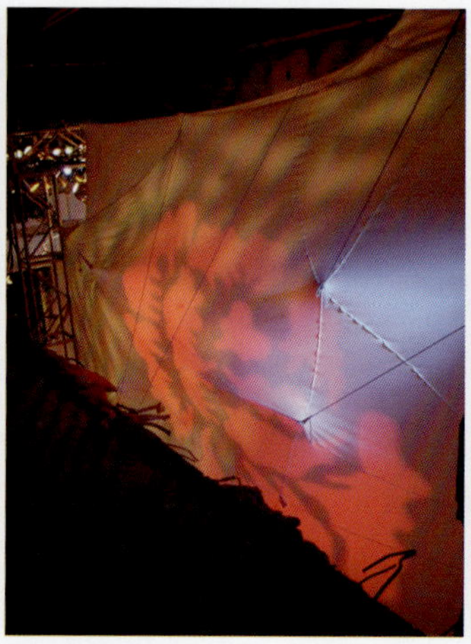
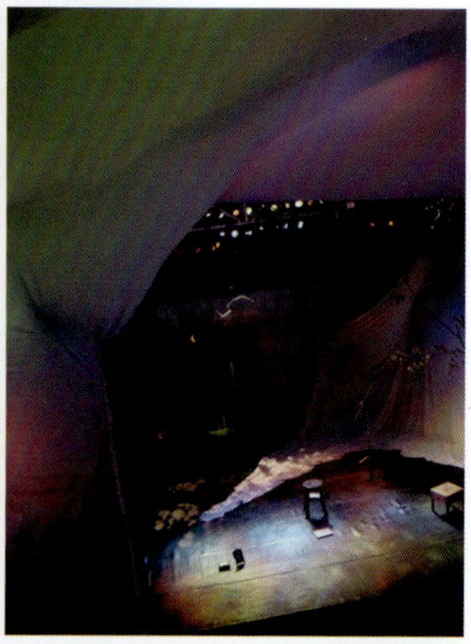
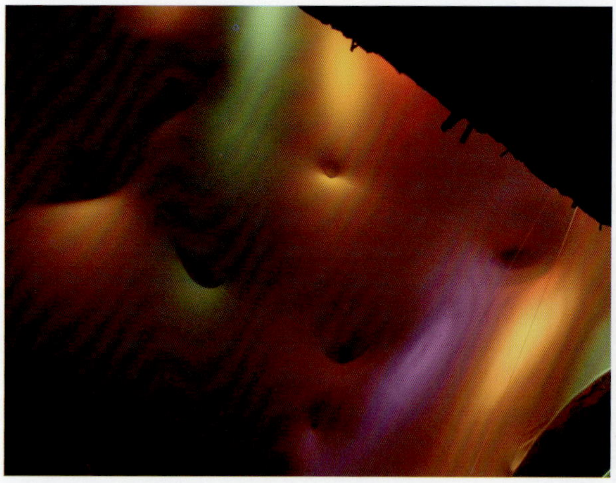
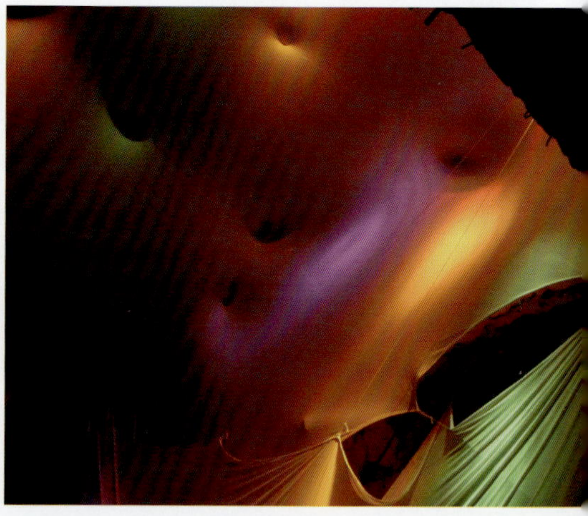
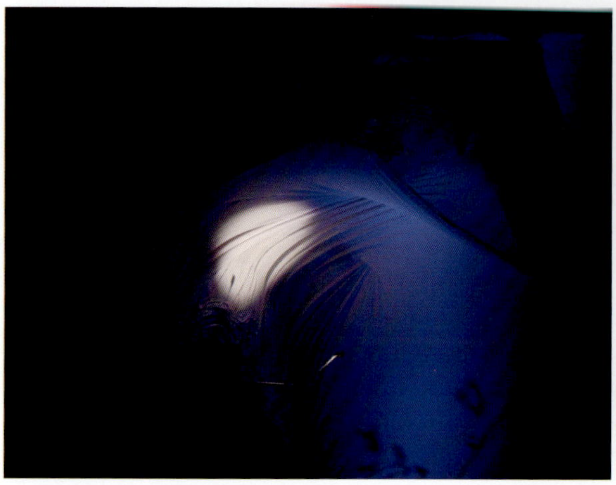
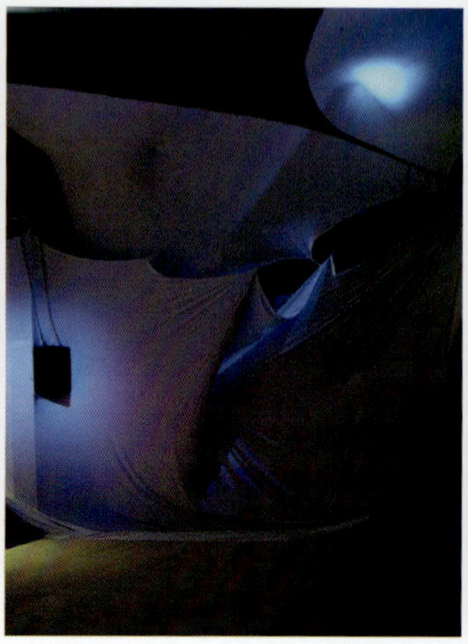

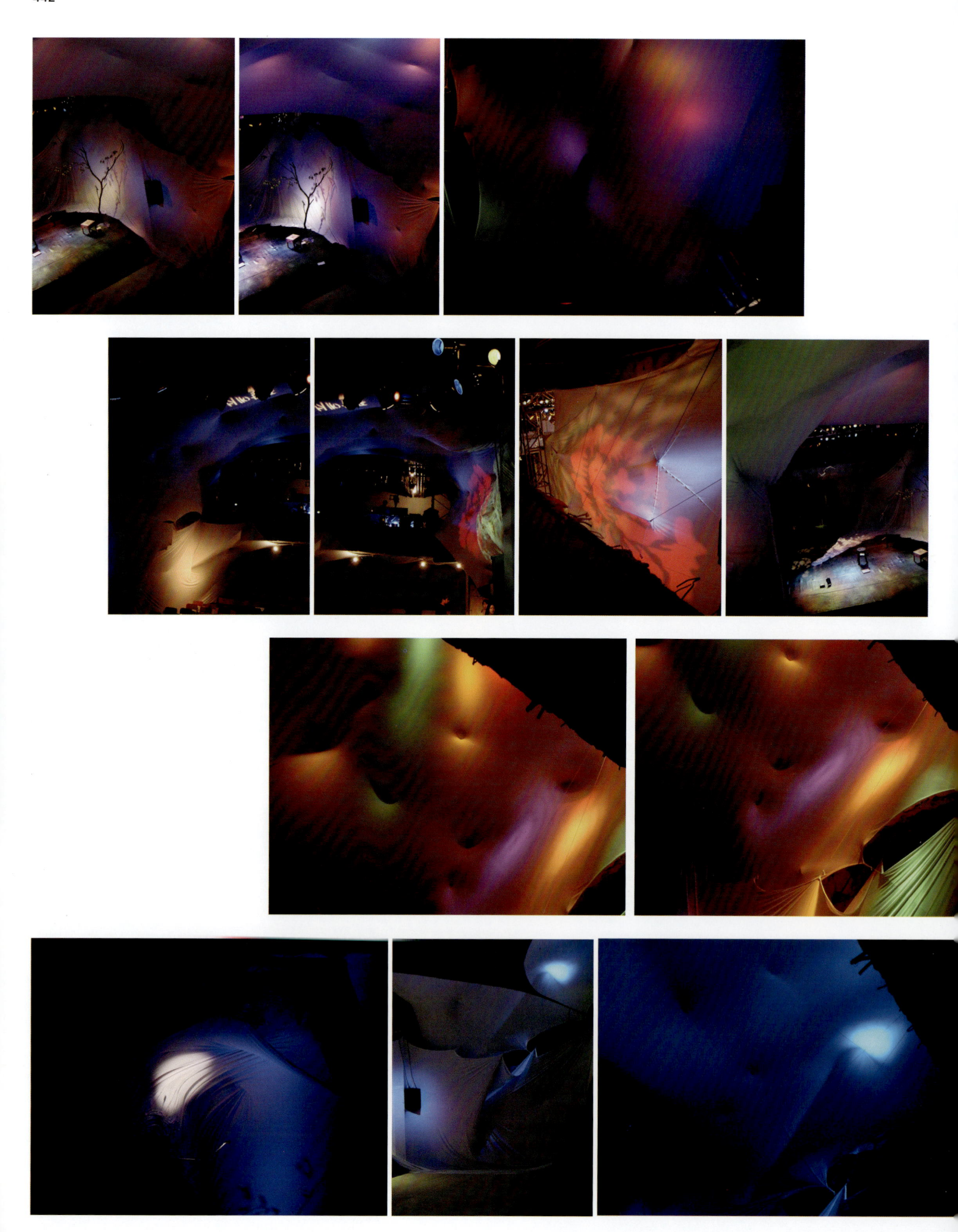

COMPOUND BODY 443

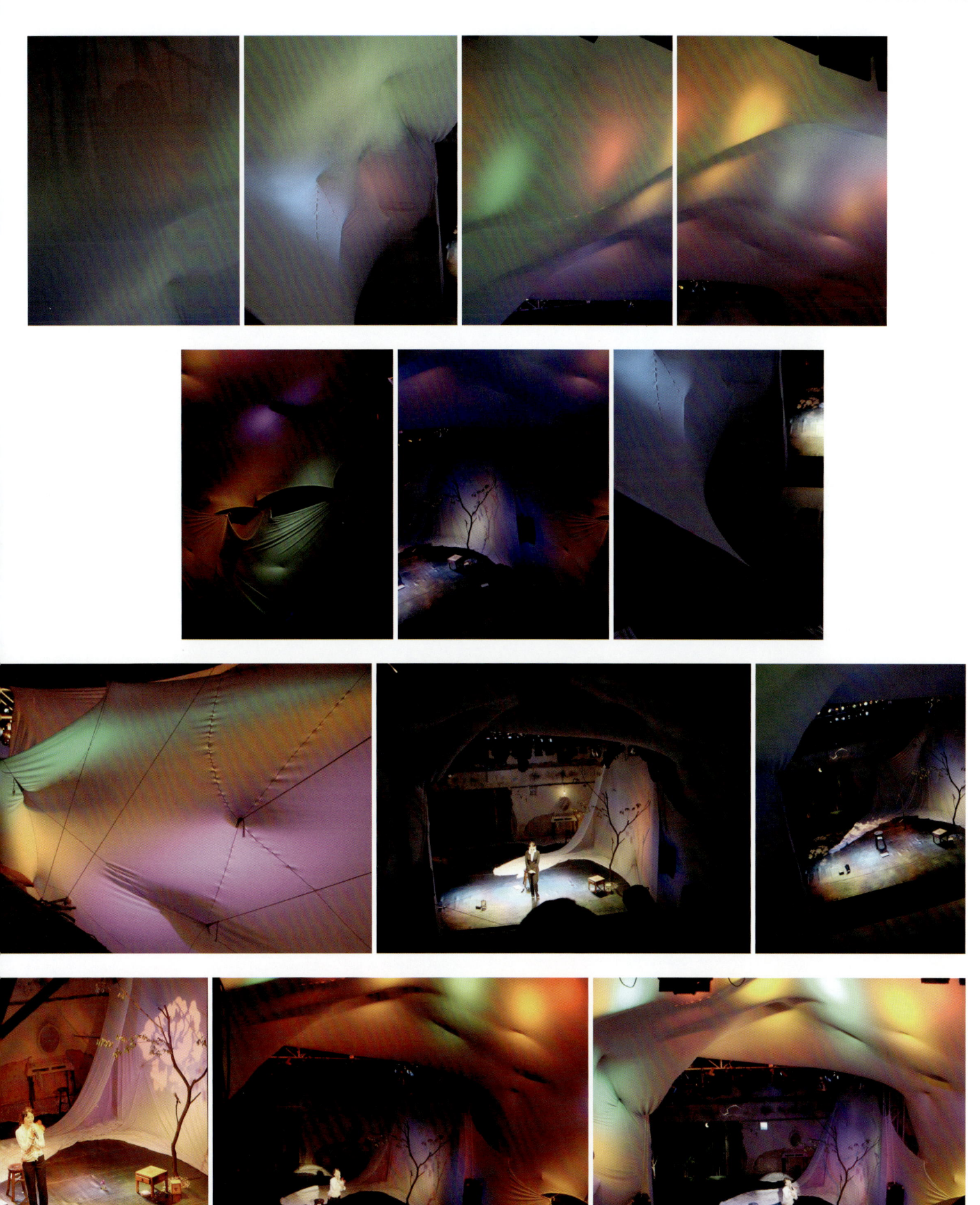

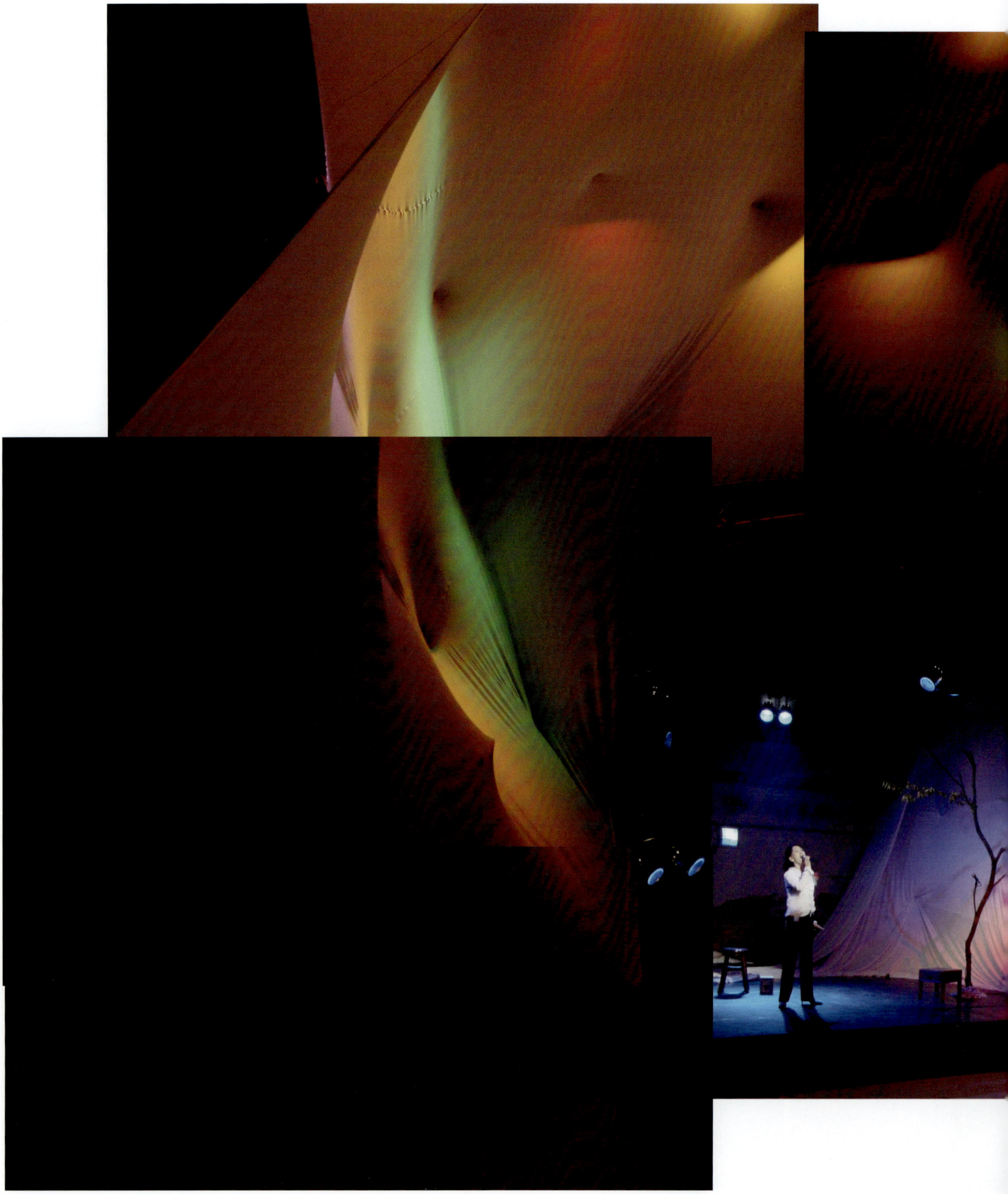

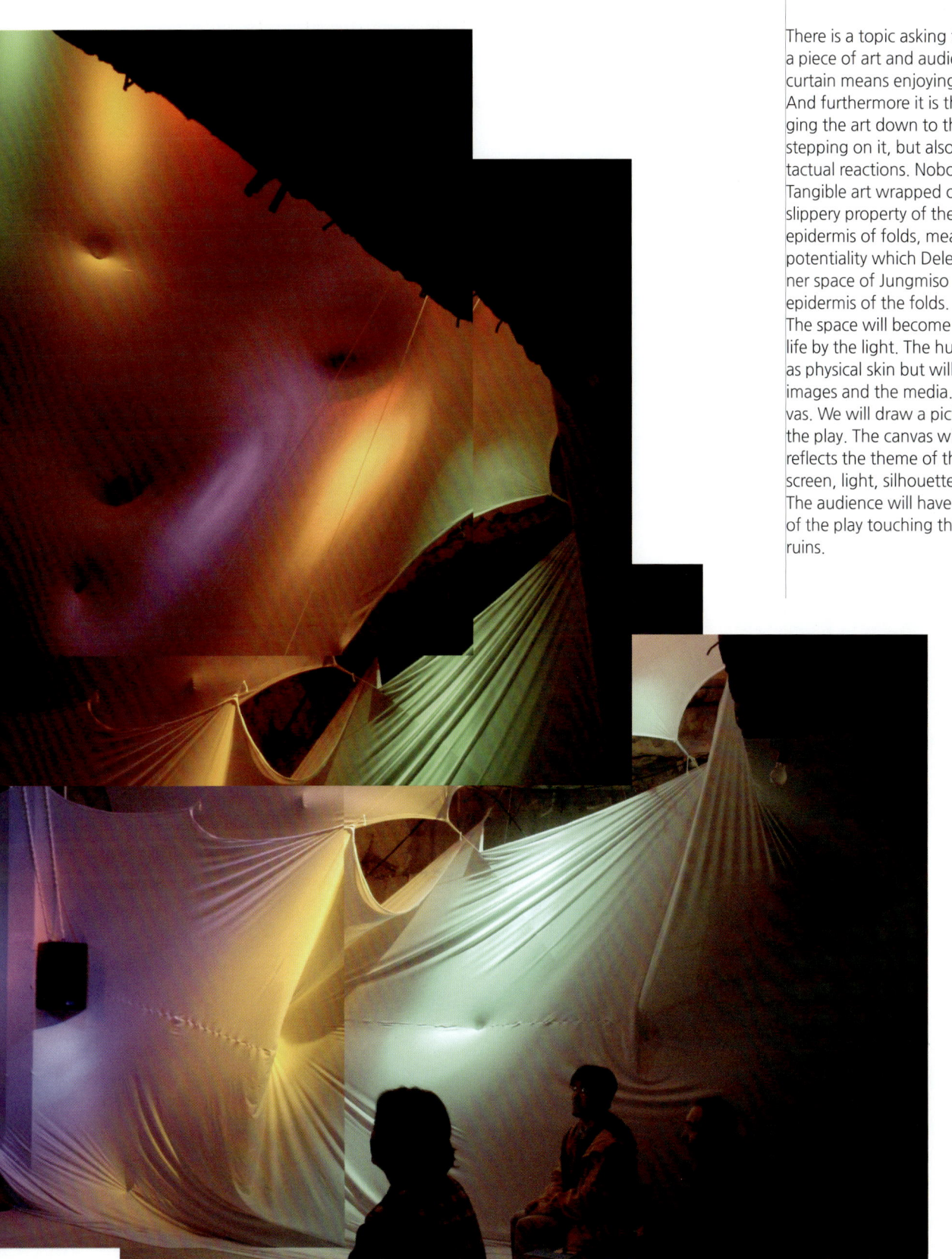

COMPOUND BODY 445

There is a topic asking the relationship between a piece of art and audience. Walking on the curtain means enjoying art put under their feet. And furthermore it is the process of dragging the art down to their daily life. Not only stepping on it, but also touching it provides tactual reactions. Nobody will say "Don't touch." Tangible art wrapped over whole theater. The slippery property of the curtain changes to the epidermis of folds, meaning infinite baroque potentiality which Deleuze mentioned. The inner space of Jungmiso is transformed to spatial epidermis of the folds.

The space will become a living creature given life by the light. The huge curtain will not stay as physical skin but will become the light, the images and the media. It is a huge blank canvas. We will draw a picture of the light related the play. The canvas will be a media skin that reflects the theme of the play changing to screen, light, silhouette, image, and flowers. The audience will have become the leading role of the play touching this canvas inserted in the ruins.

Gallery JUNSOOCHUN

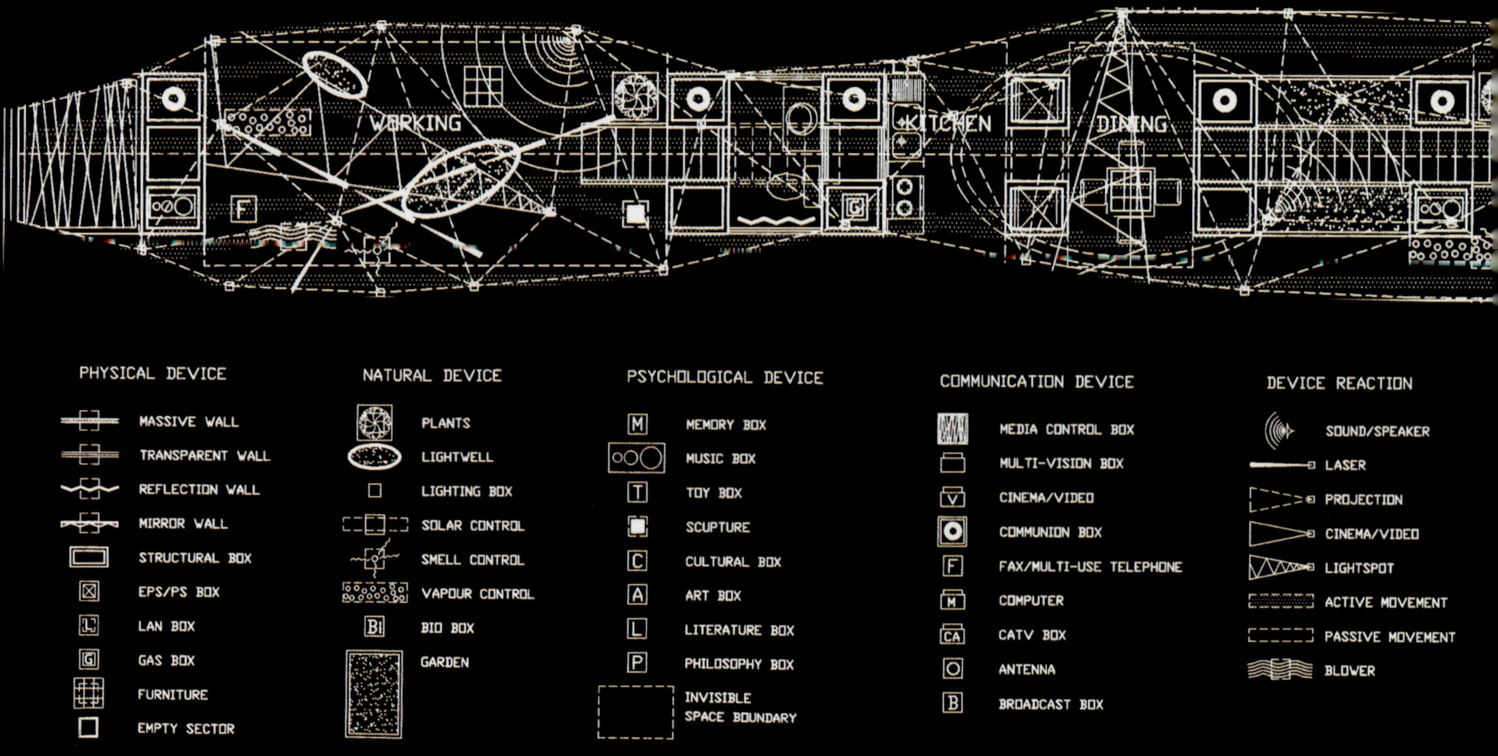

PHYSICAL DEVICE	NATURAL DEVICE	PSYCHOLOGICAL DEVICE	COMMUNICATION DEVICE	DEVICE REACTION
MASSIVE WALL	PLANTS	MEMORY BOX	MEDIA CONTROL BOX	SOUND/SPEAKER
TRANSPARENT WALL	LIGHTWELL	MUSIC BOX	MULTI-VISION BOX	LASER
REFLECTION WALL	LIGHTING BOX	TOY BOX	CINEMA/VIDEO	PROJECTION
MIRROR WALL	SOLAR CONTROL	SCUPTURE	COMMUNION BOX	CINEMA/VIDEO
STRUCTURAL BOX	SMELL CONTROL	CULTURAL BOX	FAX/MULTI-USE TELEPHONE	LIGHTSPOT
EPS/PS BOX	VAPOUR CONTROL	ART BOX	COMPUTER	ACTIVE MOVEMENT
LAN BOX	BIO BOX	LITERATURE BOX	CATV BOX	PASSIVE MOVEMENT
GAS BOX	GARDEN	PHILOSOPHY BOX	ANTENNA	BLOWER
FURNITURE		INVISIBLE SPACE BOUNDARY	BROADCAST BOX	
EMPTY SECTOR				

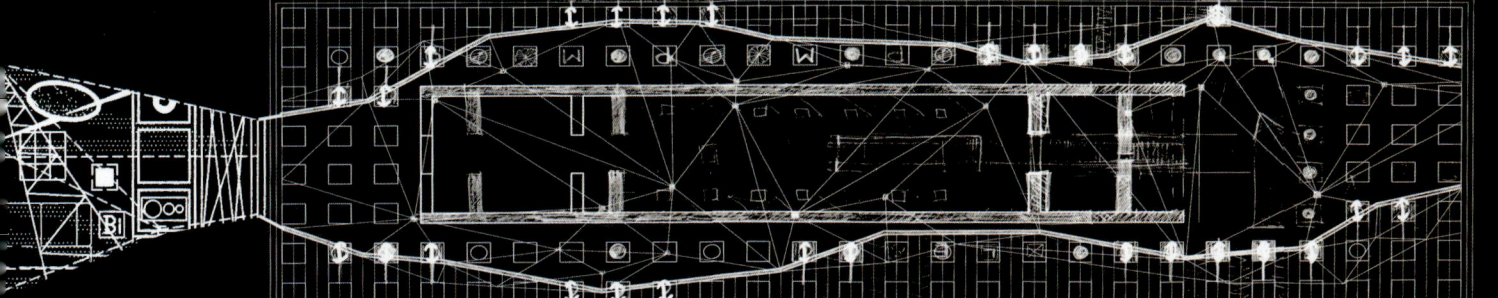

Architects Jang Yoon Gyoo, Kim Min Tae

COMPOUND BODY 447

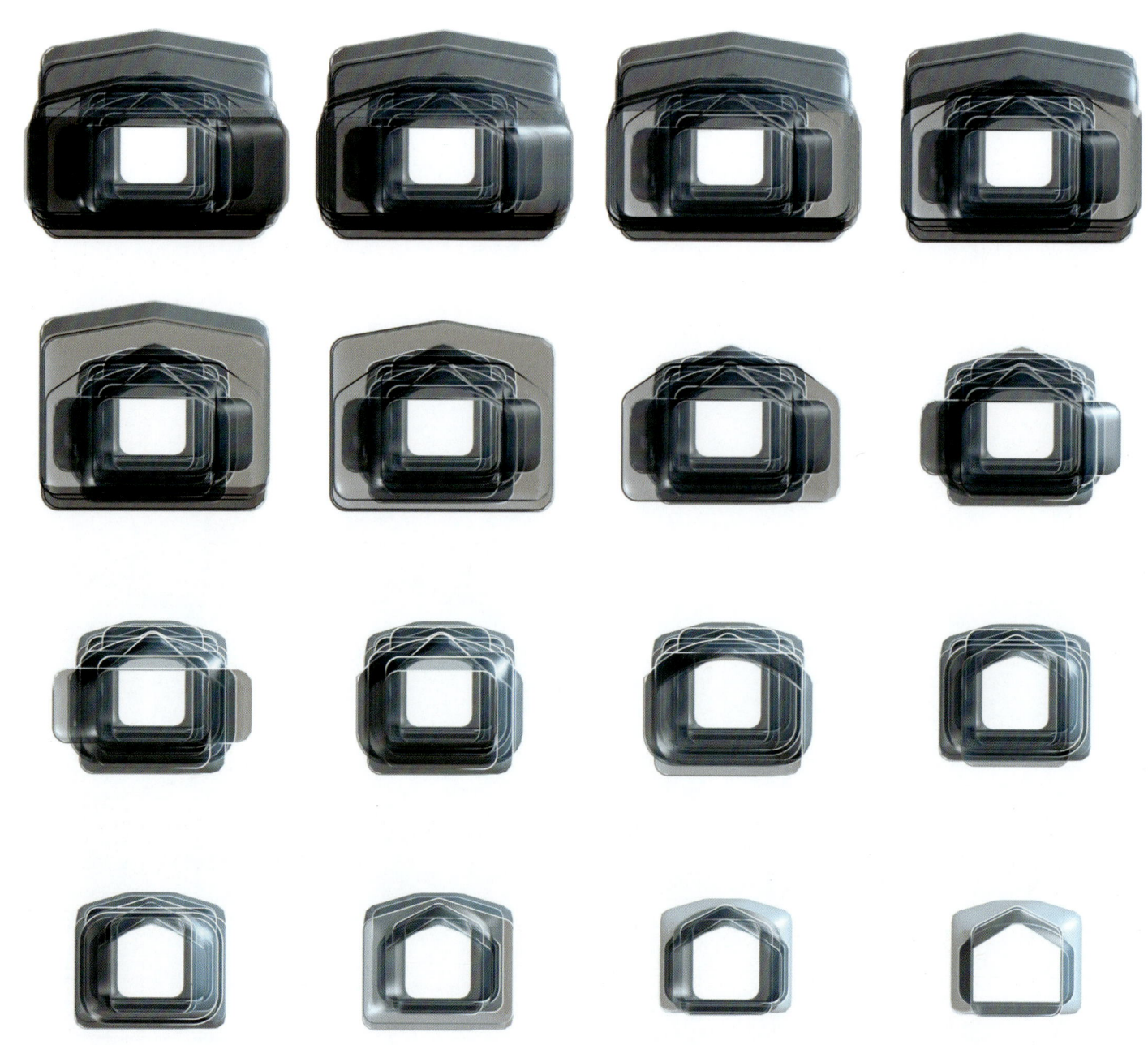

SECTION

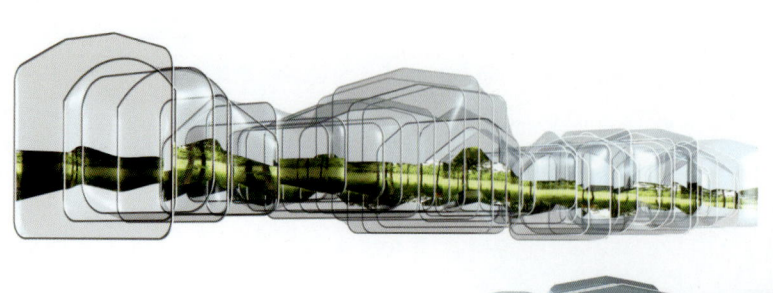

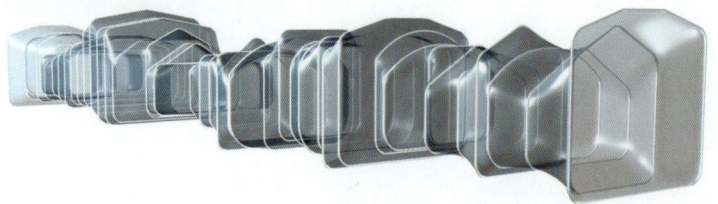

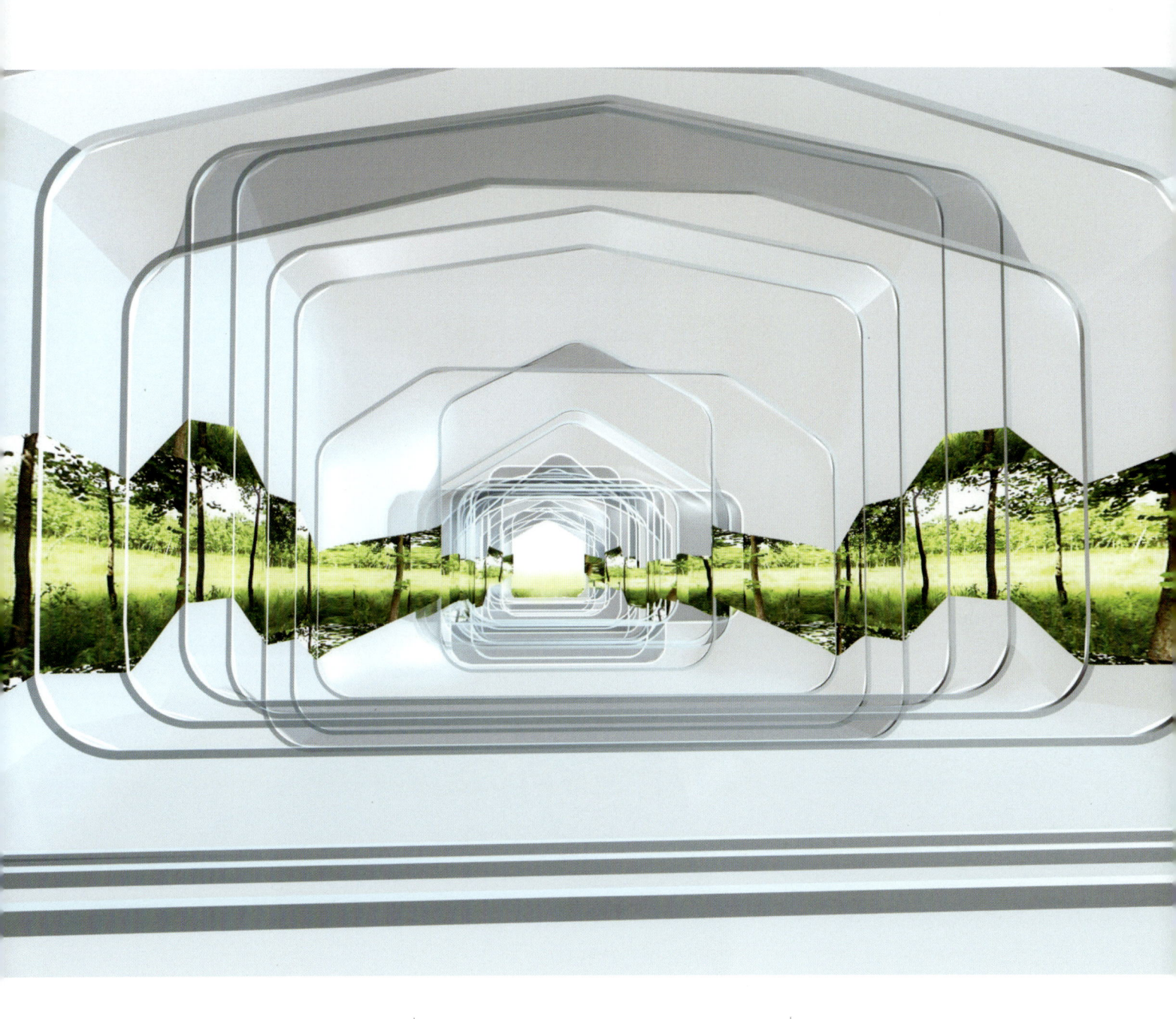

VINYL HOUSE

A vinyl house for indoor farming was suggested for JunSooChun Space. So far, vinyl has not been able to be used for architectural construction, but the material no longer refuse to be used for architecture. This transparent working environment closely associated with earth allows for a tight insertion of natural codes. The entire workspace has some farming codes. Like farming, artistic activities have a scheme of reproduction tightly structured. This space reminds us that art is a kind of production or reproduction. The goal of this space lies in creation of a surfing structure of transparency and translucency or a framework for Zen-like landscape and transparent vinyl. A space being accelerated lightly was conceived by substituting free structures for bolting structure of a vinyl house. The continuum of the sections displaced spatially was borrowed from a morphing form to reflect the diverse structures of Jun, Soo Chun's works. Zen-like structural framework hints that this workspace would be not simply workplace but an impressive exhibition space for the audience. This exhibition space not isolated from the nature looks as if it were an artwork displayed outdoor. Here, a hidden irony is the fact that the space formed with too cheap materials and structures is a shelter for valuable artworks.

Plaza of GwangJu Biennale

Architects Jang Yoon Gyoo, Shin Chang Hoon   COMPOUND BODY 451

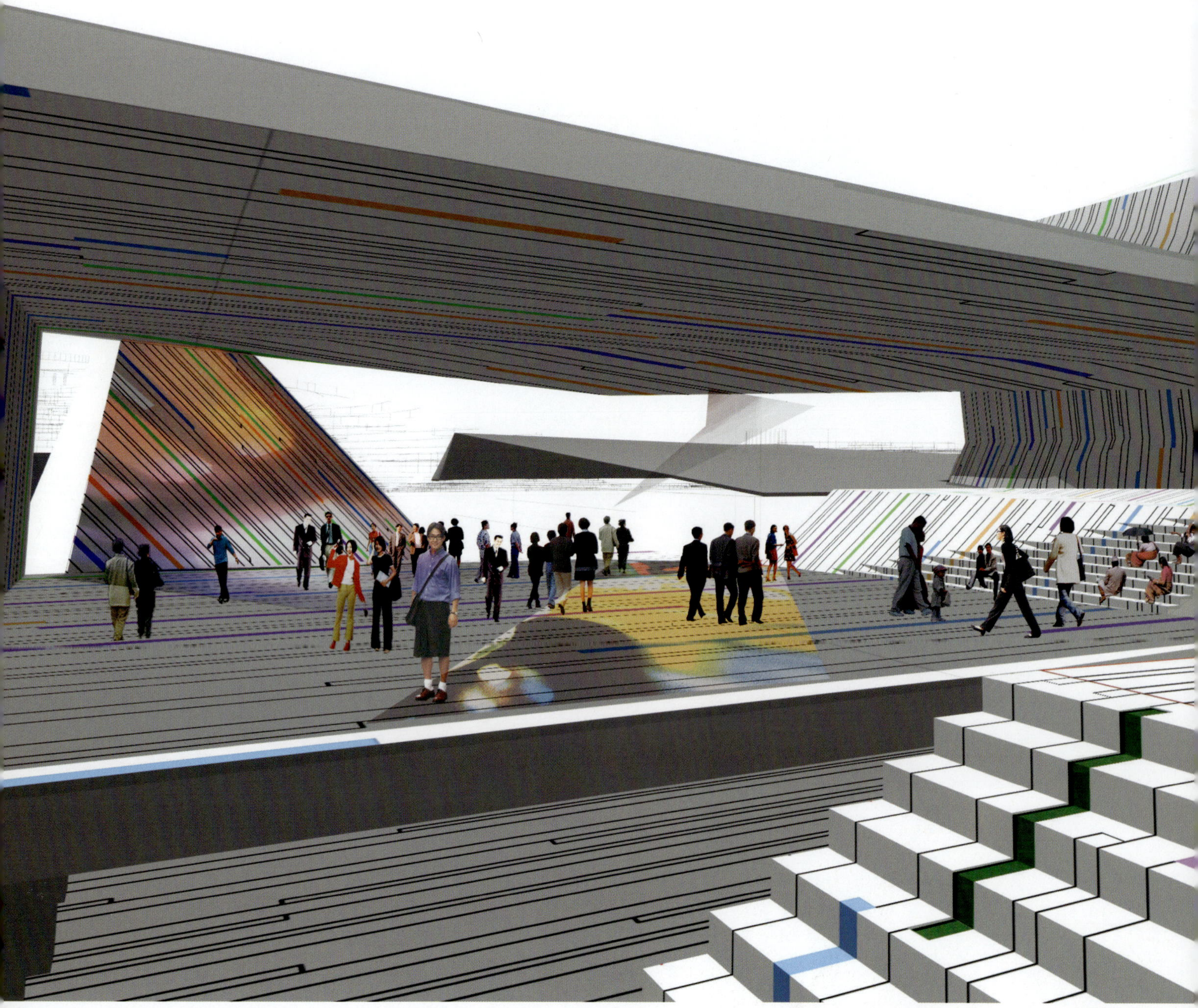

SCULPTURE OF THE EARTH

Signs a land between creation and extinction. A land is no longer a flat dump of earth with one fixed mark. It wakes up by the lands of artists who are full of creative spirit. Even a song hidden in the creative arouses. Circulation of light, water, and dust is revived on canvas. The land of GwangJu is a vessel where artists and viewers meet. The orbit of time is engraved on the land which circulates its own body.
The land is a media and sculpture by itself.

SITEPLAN

FOLDING & FLOWING LAND

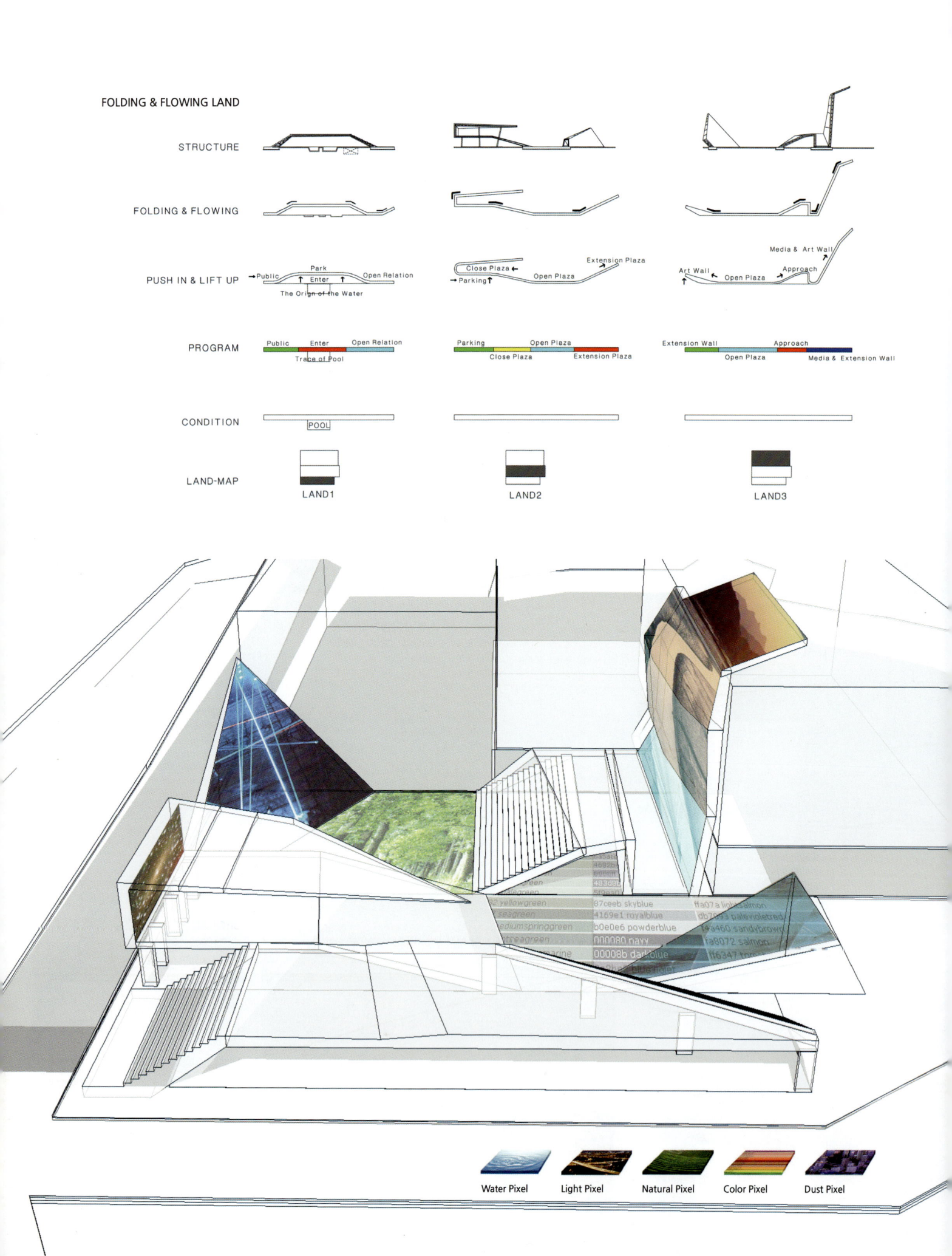

STRUCTURE

FOLDING & FLOWING

PUSH IN & LIFT UP
- Public → Park ← Open Relation / Enter / The Origin of the Water
- Close Plaza ← Extension Plaza / Parking ↑ Open Plaza
- Art Wall ← Open Plaza → Approach / Media & Art Wall

PROGRAM
- Public | Enter | Open Relation | Trace of Pool
- Parking | Close Plaza | Open Plaza | Extension Plaza
- Extension Wall | Open Plaza | Approach | Media & Extension Wall

CONDITION — POOL

LAND-MAP: LAND1 / LAND2 / LAND3

Water Pixel | Light Pixel | Natural Pixel | Color Pixel | Dust Pixel

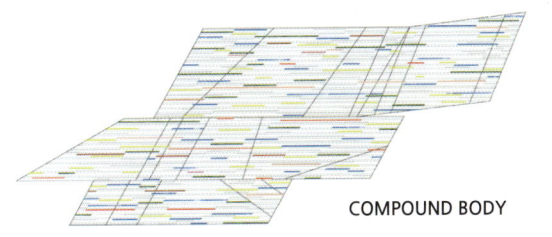

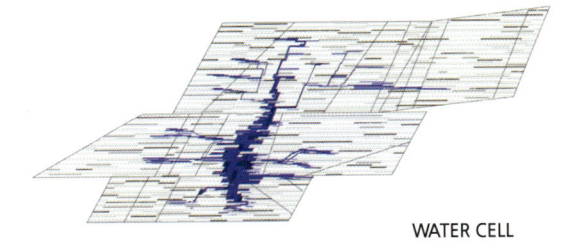

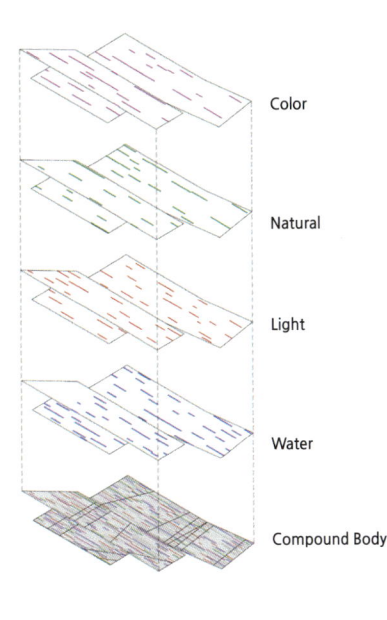

Circle of the Earth- between Creation and Disappearance of the Earth

A land and extinction is presented as the theme of the plaza. The relation of 'A dust, A water Drop' is transformed into a landscape-like terrain sculpture. Creation and Extinction makes the dichotomy between the beginning and the ending, yin and yang, curvy lines and strait lines, nonexistence and existence. 'Crack' created on the flat ground plays essential roles in clarifying the dichotomy. The program of the plaza and its agility to transform in accordance with time and people enable the place to remain as an archive of the history of creation and existence. Imagine the land as an origin of life.

Mediascape on Urban Plaza- Void Canvas on Urban Plaza

A plaza that makes viewers stood in the central position as 'subjective observers' is the concept of the design. The plaza at GwangJu Biennale is not simply an empty space but a canvas which interacts with various environments and media. Viewers become main actors and actresses in the 'Participating Plaza'. Be a curator yourself in this 'Participating Plaza' and feel another dimension of artistic experiences.

COMPOUND BODY

WATER CELL

Color

Natural

Light

Water

Compound Body

level +500 Plan   level +4500 Plan   level Roof Plan

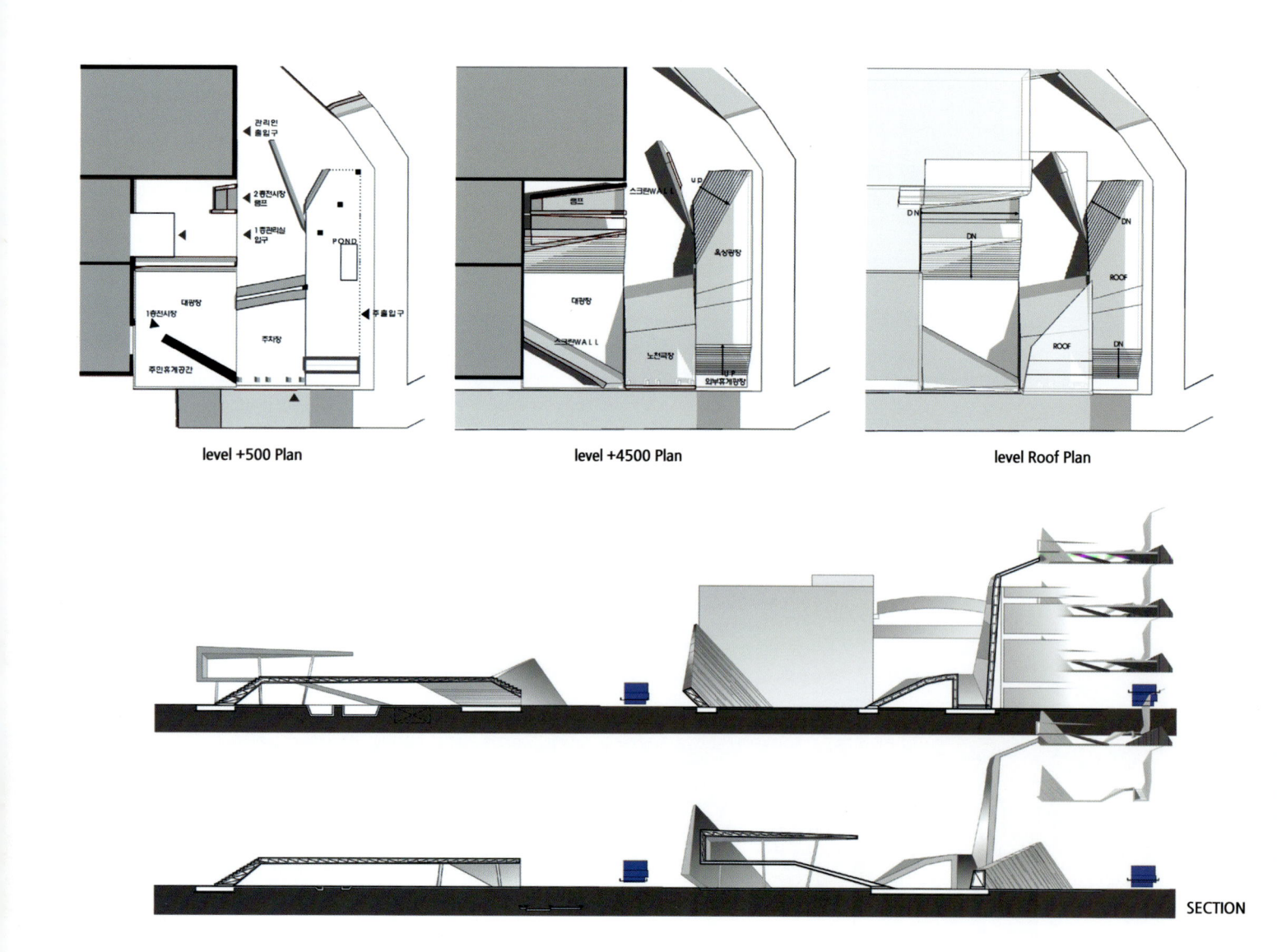

SECTION

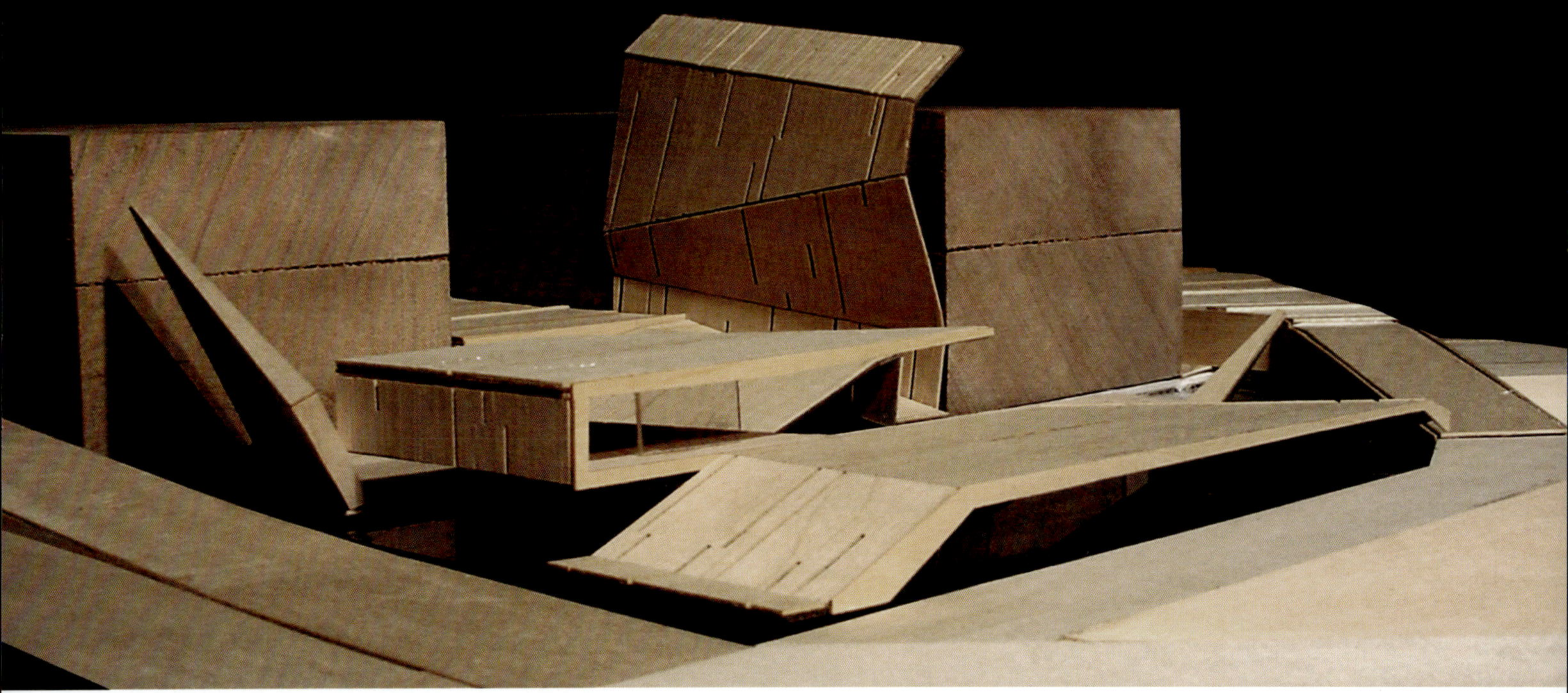
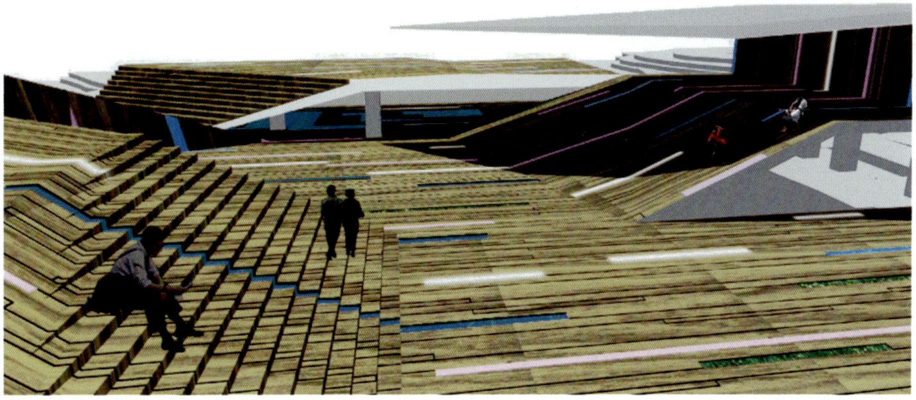
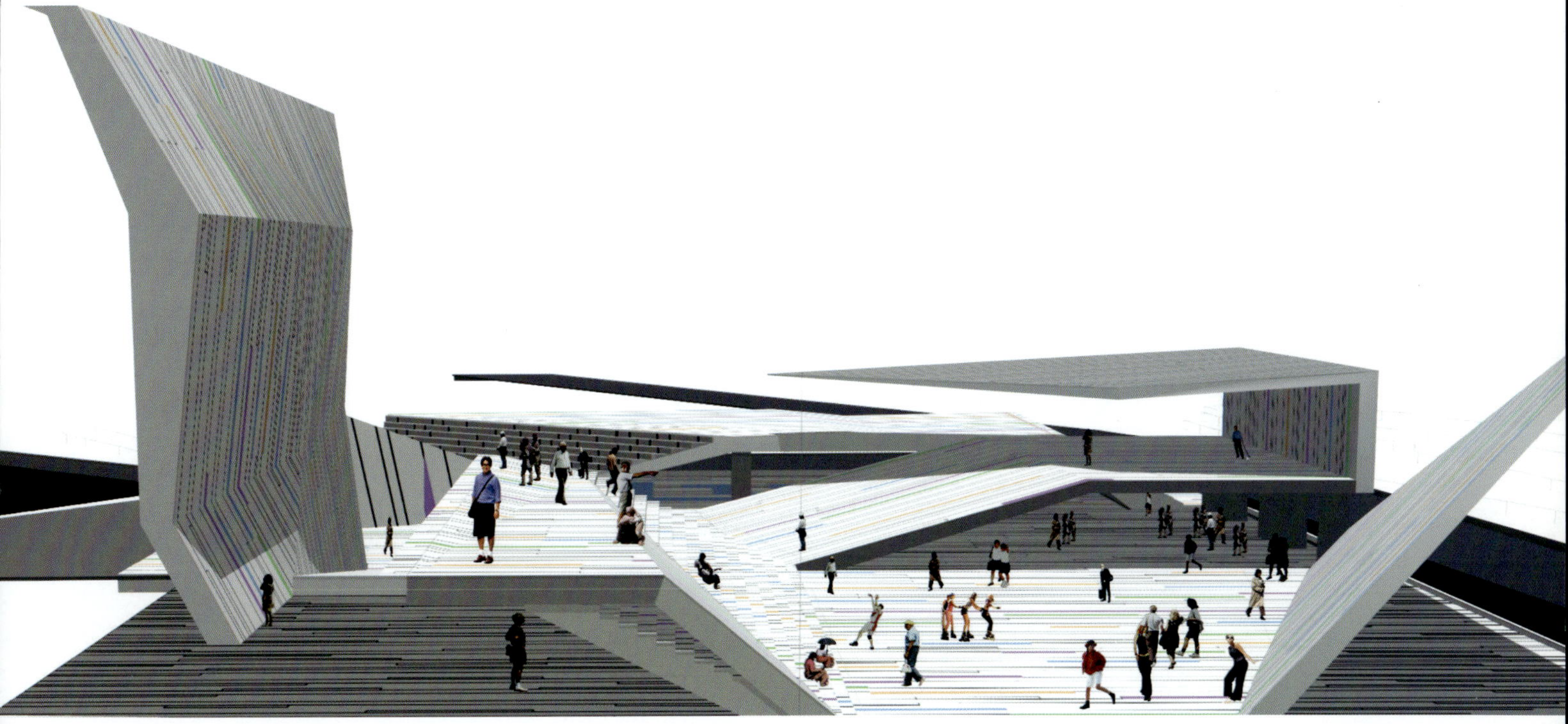

Ravin Peace Plaza Vertical Interaction

International Competition Finalist | **Architects** Jang Yoon Gyoo, Lee Mee Young | **COMPOUND BODY** 459

460

VOIDSCAPE FOR PEACE FORUM

VOIDSCAPE 01
Inspiration of Urban Void
One of many stratagems on this proposal is the thing that inspires eventfulness, activity, and attaches in exterior and interior spaces around urban block. What is important is to make a complex accelerating many urban elements and fragments not only filling up functions in space. Urban Plaza mean to not only filling with program and mass but also voiding of urban space for public needs.

VOIDSCAPE 02
Floating Skin with Void
A new layer of horizontal plate rises from the earth to form another floating and flowing skin. This layer is a symbol of Peace. The new layer transform into different skins of movement code. These new 'skins of folding and flowing' are filled with different demands of different elements and charges them with new activity of new life. The new infilled layer is not only a fragment of a physical city structure but as a materialistic realization of the spiritual foundation of Peace and Culture. This 'Floating Skin' acts as a new space of exchange and peace intercourse.

VOIDSCAPE 03
Spiritual Landscape, the Skin of the BIBLE
Peace Forum should be take a place for intermingle of different cultures, the stage for understanding of fellow people around the world. The BIBLE with differential languages of the world is placed on the skin of forum, proposed site, as a symbol of international exchange. The Forum of the Bible is reborn as medium of understanding and exchanging different cultures of Peace.

VOIDSCAPE 04
Transprogramming of Plaza
Urban blocks are not physical objects but spiritual voids waiting for paroxysm. This idea is gaining "Oscillation of Free City" toward future. Therefore, void must accommodate many elements and fragments like politics, economics, society, culture, art, sports, and etc. Creating floated skin with Void is another experiment getting anti-reaction in existing urban fabric. This skin is filled-up many elements derived from city. They are not simple fragments of physical urban structure but physical transformation based on spirituality.

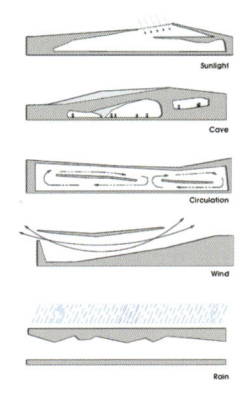

VOIDSCAPE 05
Continuous Skin with Hyper-Folding & Flowing
The essential requirement of urban plaza is reaction with the variety of urban program. therefore, the 2-dimensional skin of urban plaza is transformed into the hyper-dimensional skin. These Continuous skins of multi-levels, are operated folding and flowing space, have ambiguity of space between exterior and interior.
Urban skin can get free only through folding and flowing. This skin is opened all direction. It becomes a complex for accelerating all of urban life, and it combines with various layers as to urban necessity.
The Continuous Skin of Urban Plaza is operated to the Plate with Multi-Urban Function. The Transformation of program on Urban Plaza is started from the continuous exchange of these elements : Media skin, Information skin, Landscape skin, Historical skin, Cultural skin, ... etc.

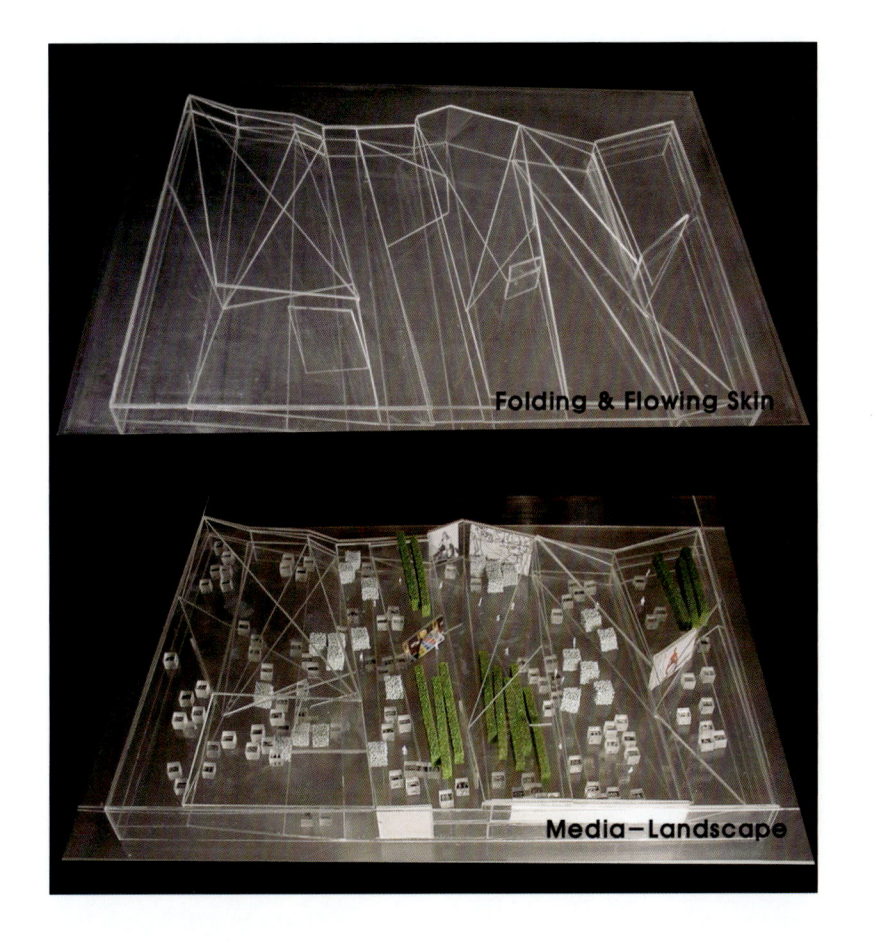

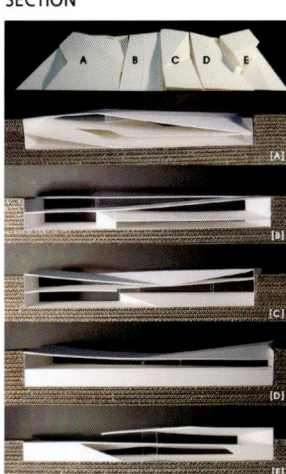

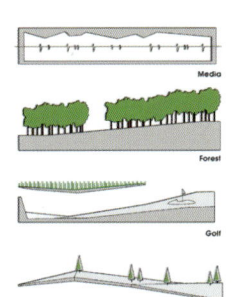

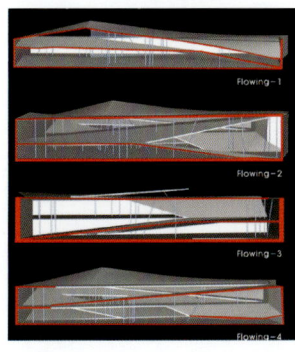

Dancing Apartment

Dong-a Ilbo Serial Architects Jang Yoon Gyoo, Seo Hye Lim COMPOUND BODY 463

Elevation

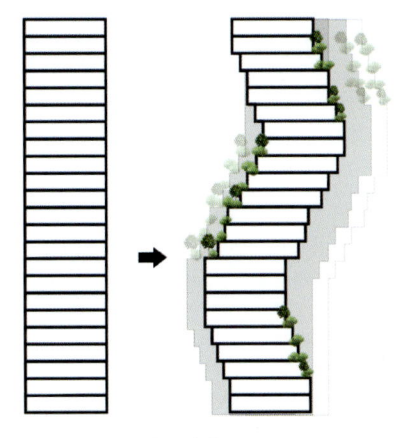

DEFORMING

Dancing apartment becomes terrace of nature. I inadvertently thought that I could make a three-dimensional apartment when I saw the movie Transformers, In which robots transform into cars and vice versa. A three-dimensional apartment would add variety to life. If existing apartments are built oblique lines in which each unit would be made of a natural terrace. As such, the apartment would seem to be dancing, providing an enjoyable view and breath of fresh air by making three-dimensional terraces of various sizes in each unit.

It would be created as if like a vertical skin of land made by vertical mountains. The intention is to lifestyle of the inhabitants, the terraces can be decorated like a greenhouse, a spa, a flower garden, of an exercise space.

If the apartment is yet a form building in which unrelieved furniture space is housed, we can now suggest a space inside be coupled with a variety of three-dimensional indoor spaces. In uniform apartment in a uniform building, the differences stem from the indoor spaces- which also meet the necessities required of a residence. Some units can raise a living room's ceiling height while others can create two stories inside. Thus, the three-dimensional approach will overcome limitations in residence programs. For example, if one family likes playing in water, they can make small pool on the terrace; if other family likes nature, they can create a garden on terrace. For families who like movies, it can be a theater; for families who like art, it can be a gallery. The terrace will be based on one's lifestyle and necessities - perhaps a music studio, children's playroom, or game room. Moreover, we can dream of creating complementary spaces for the elderly, single parents, and individuals can live in harmony.

Existing apartments are like individual buildings and communities of mutual exchanges that are made separately. However, the Dancing apartment system can create life associations by mixing units, putting differences between units. Each community can use small three-dimensional park, leisure facilities, culture space, event space, media space, library, performance space, etc. -which might create a new community network that adheres closely to life.

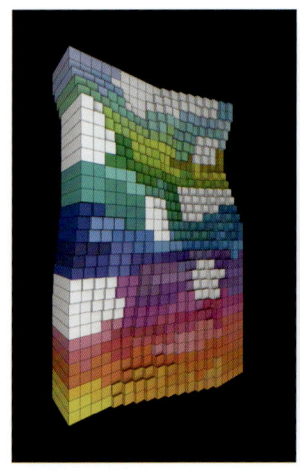

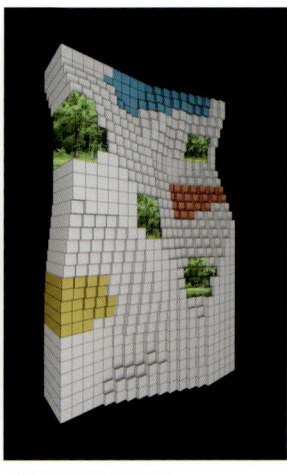

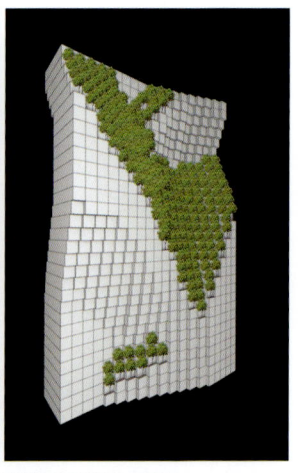

VARIOUS UNIT   COMMUNITY SPACE   TERRACE OF NATURE

ELEVATION

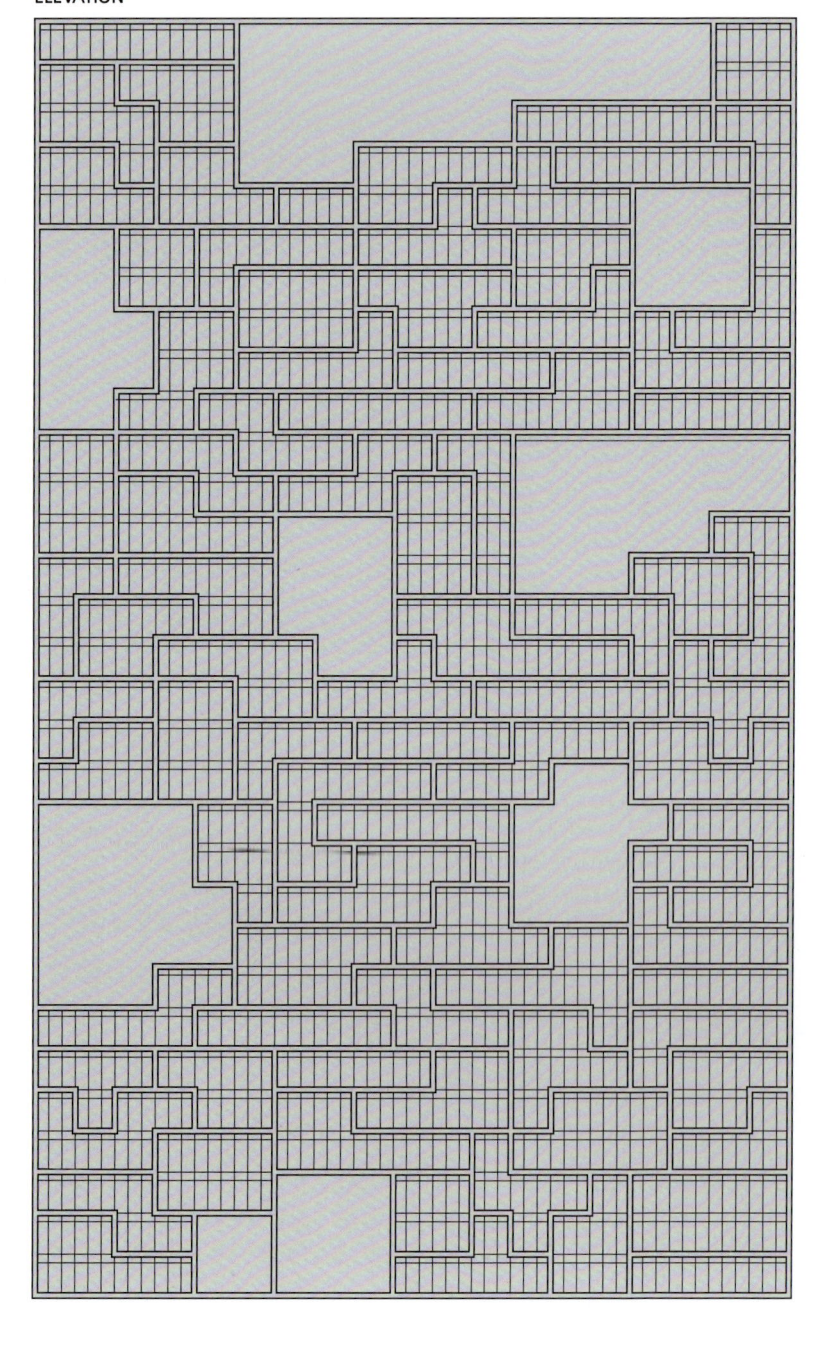

Dancing aptment-let get terrace of nature
Accidentally I thought that can I make the three-dimensional apartment when I saw that movie's name is transformer about between car and robot trans.
It is three-dimensional apartment to put into variety life.
The three-dimensional apartment starts in very simplicity conception.
The change is big that even if some small modifications, a building method of vertical expansion. In other words we have tried to build going in and out incessantly like dancing each of units that is originally vertical plate of shape.
If existing apartment is built systematically, three-dimensional apartment becomes that is layed up zigzag or an obique line, each units be made naturally terrace.
That will become a form of apartment which like a dancing. It can enjoy a view and breathe of air from being made three-dimensional various size of terraces in each units.

Elevation like a woods-each terrace plant trees
If the plant trees on the terrace which is built three-dimensional, the apartment elevation will be changed like forest being inside.
As if it is made like a vertical skin of land, that made vertical mountains.
It intend mountains come into a apartment. Nevertheless all terrace don't need planting wood. As it may chance about lifestyle who living in, it can decorate like a greenhouse, a spa, a flpwer garden, a exercises space.

COMPOUND BODY 467

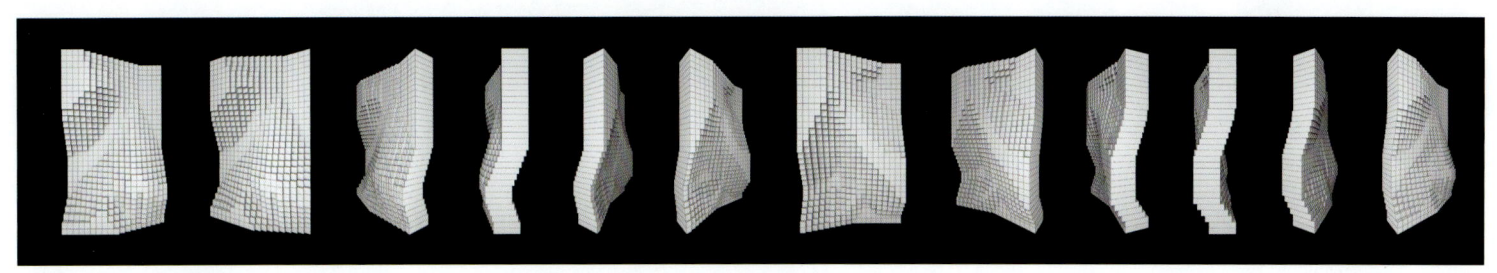

VARIOUS VIEW OF DANCING APARTMENT

THREE DIMENSIONAL RESIDING SPACE

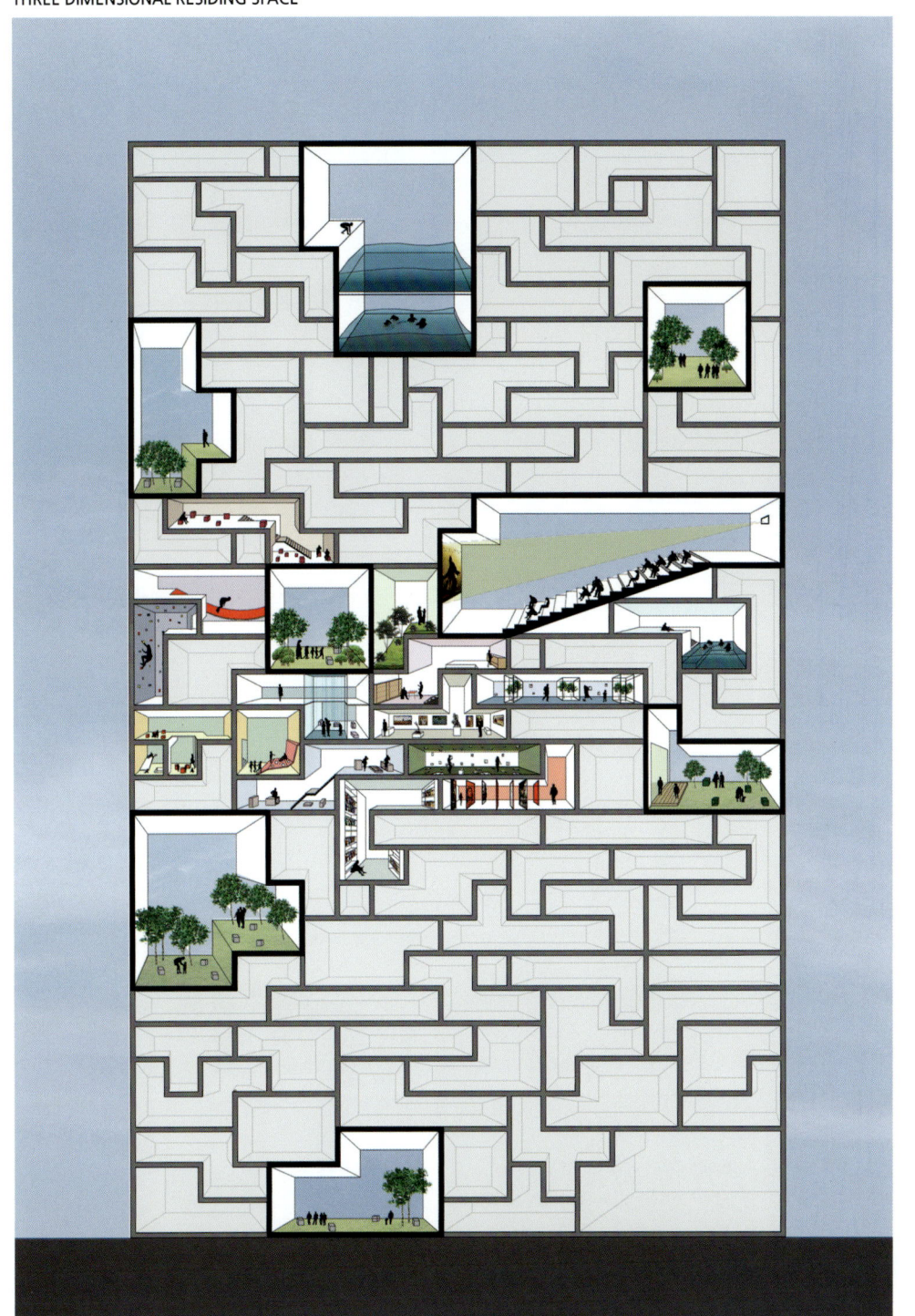

Three-dimensional residing space - choice lifestyle

If as yet apartment is a form building unrelieved furniture space, now we suggest space of inside of coupled with variety and three-dimensional indoor space.

If any same apartment, same building is being, it is made each difference indoor space to necessity or order of living residence.

Inside spaces are different between lower residence, upper residence and next-doors.

Some of units can raise a living room's ceiling height and other unit can make 2 stories inside. If will overcome standardization , residence program will change three-dimensional.

Simply living room, kitchen, and dinning room will change in a variety.

If some family like playing in water, they can make small pool in terrace and if other family like nature, they can make garden in terrace.

To some family like movie can be made like a theater, to any family like art can be made like gallery in terrace that can make one self style choicely from necessity like a music studio, children play room and game room.

Moreover we can dream making complementary space which the aged family, single mammy and a single person can live joinning together. Existing apartment exist as individual buildings and community of mutuality exchanging made separately. But Dancing apartment suggest system to making association life of mixed from putting units between units.

Each community can use small three-dimensional park, leisure facilities, and culture space, event space, media space, a library, a performance space etc,.

In that event, that might make a new community network to adhere closely with life

Kolon Theme Housing

Architecs Jang Yoon Gyo, Shin Chang Hoon
Client Kolon ENC
Photographer Kim Bong Kyun

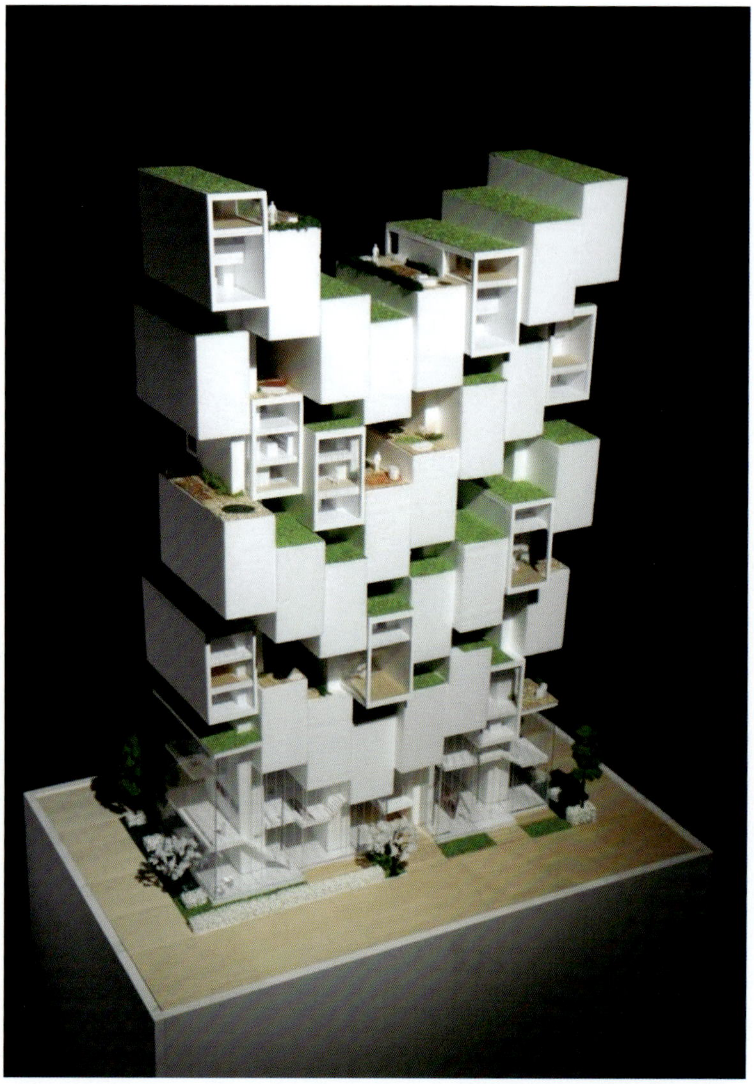

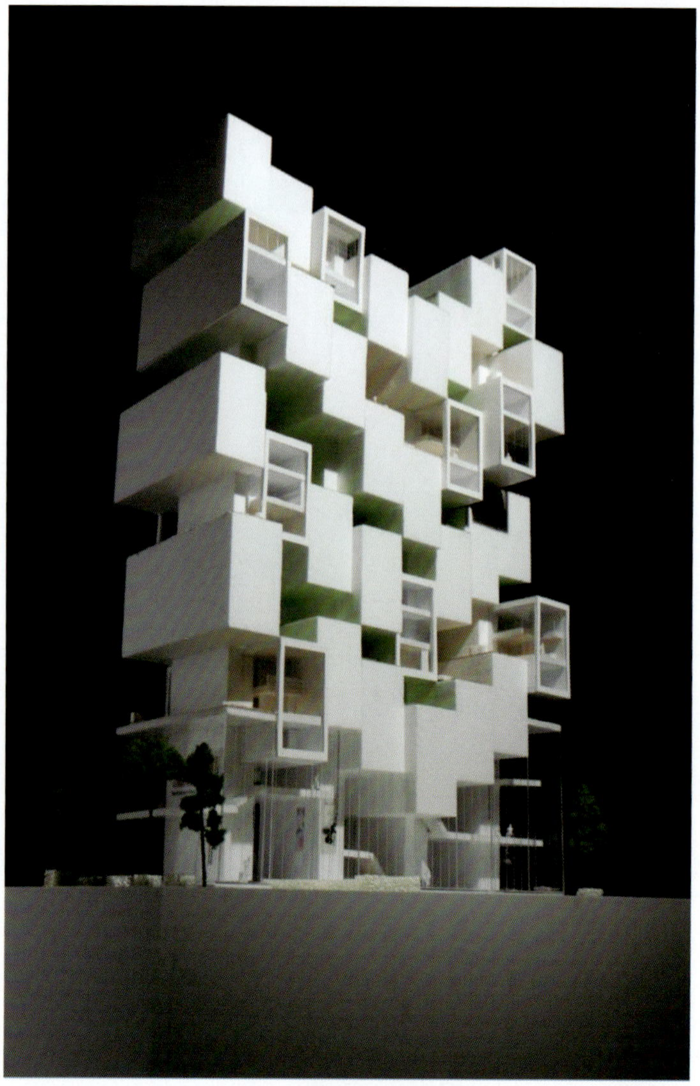

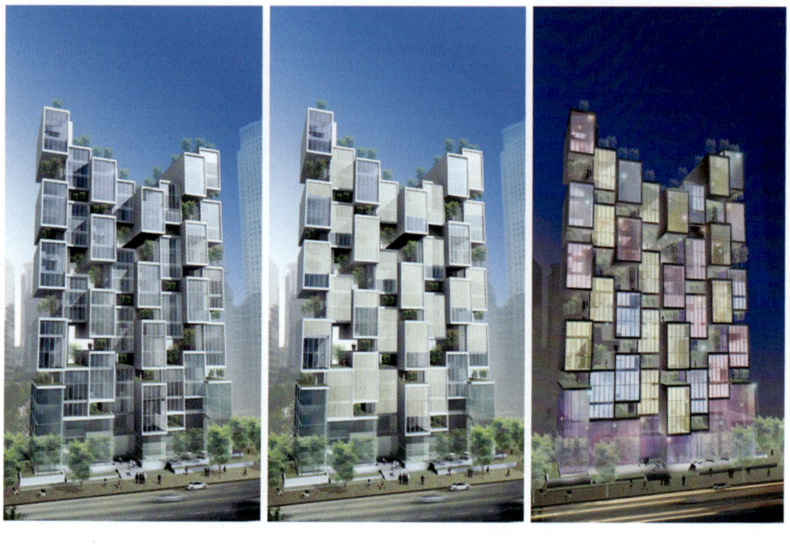

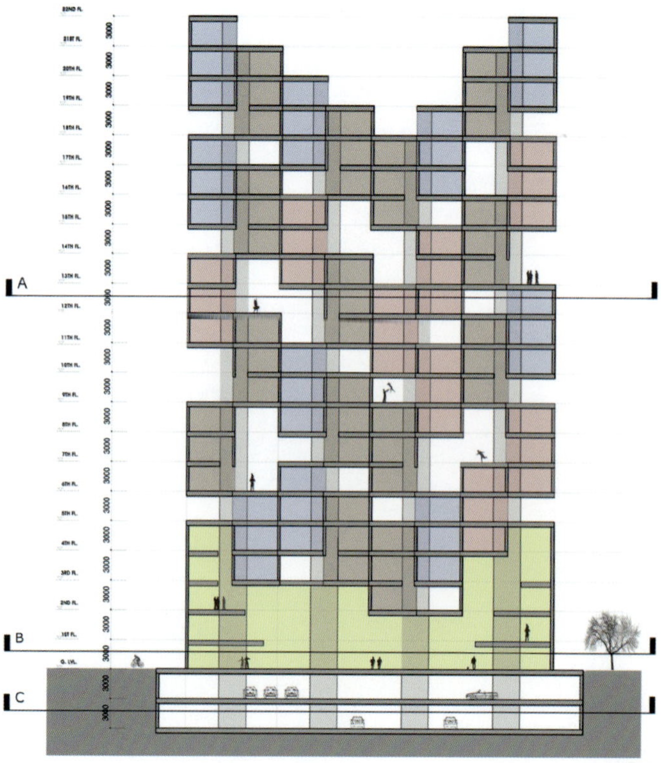
A
B
C

COMPOUND BODY 471

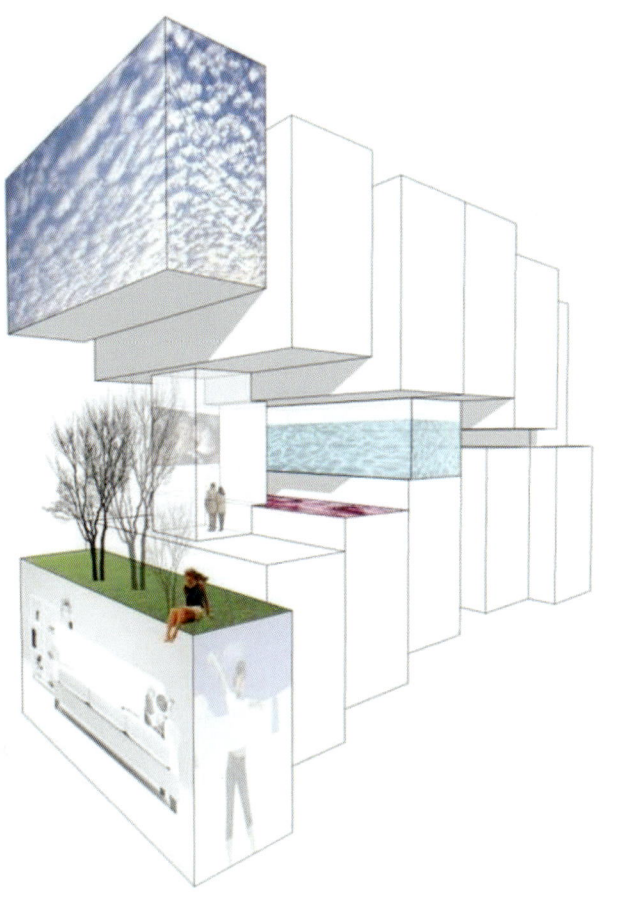

Solutions to design problems:
1. Each unit uses the roof top of adjacent unit as private outdoor terrace, creating a series of 'floating terraces'. The location of the outdoor terrace (1st, 2nd, 3rd floor) determines the program characteristic of each unit.
2. The main program of each unit (see below) type extends into adjacent outdoor terrace, providing flexible use of indoor and outdoor space.
3. These units can be stacked vertically for a dense urban environment, or can be organized horizontally for a low-density suburban environment.
4. Units cantilever from the service core, allowing all units to have direct access to the service core.
5. Flexible combination system allows the building to expand from a basic one-core form to multi-core (2, 3, 4, 5+) form.
6. This combination system creates interesting facade as the units shift both horizontally and vertically.

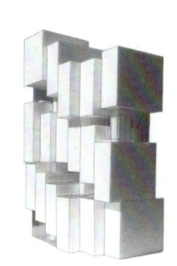

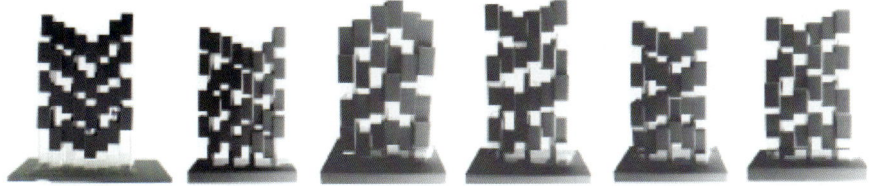

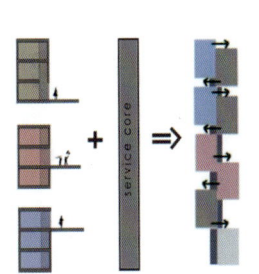

// Unit Formation Diagram
- Three unit types to accommodate various lifestyle needs
- Each unit uses the rooftop of adjacent unit as terrace
- Units cantilever from service core
- Flexible combination

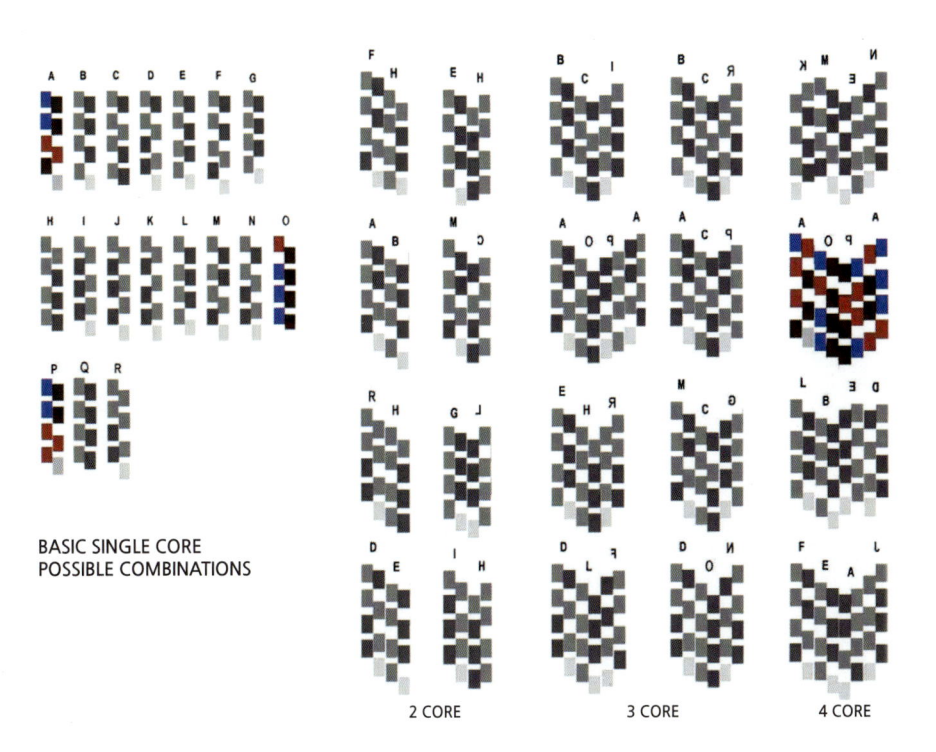

BASIC SINGLE CORE
POSSIBLE COMBINATIONS

2 CORE   3 CORE   4 CORE

THREE UNIT TYPES PER LIFESTYLE NEEDS
Main program of each unit expands into adjacent terrace space

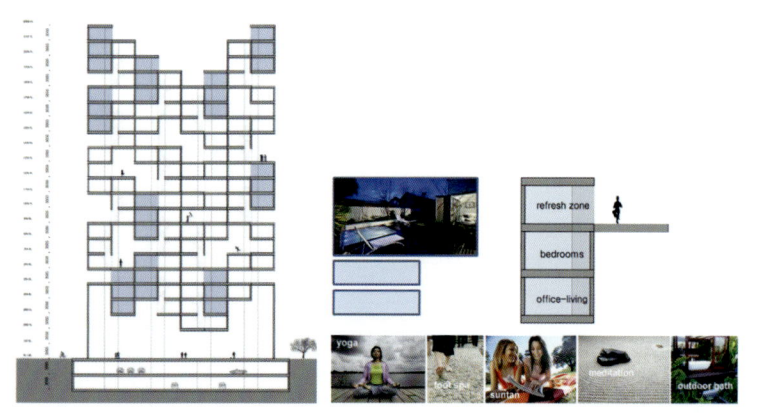

// **Dream Terrace**
OFFICE & RELAXATION ZONE + HOUSING
outdoor extends from 3rd floor relaxation zone for spa/recreative purpose

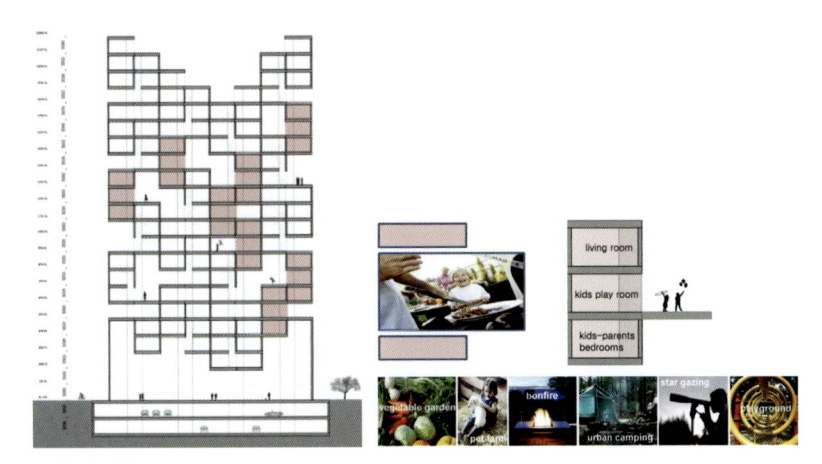

// **Happy Terrace**
KIDS & FAMILY + HOUSING
outdoor extends from 2rd floor kids play room for additional picnic and play space

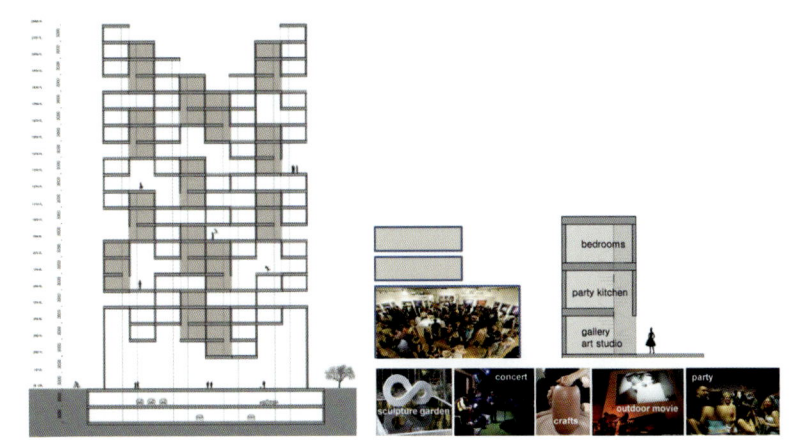

// **Creative Terrace**
CREATIVE STUDIO + HOUSING
outdoor extends from 1st floor art studio for exhibition and social activities

Prugio Labotega Officetel

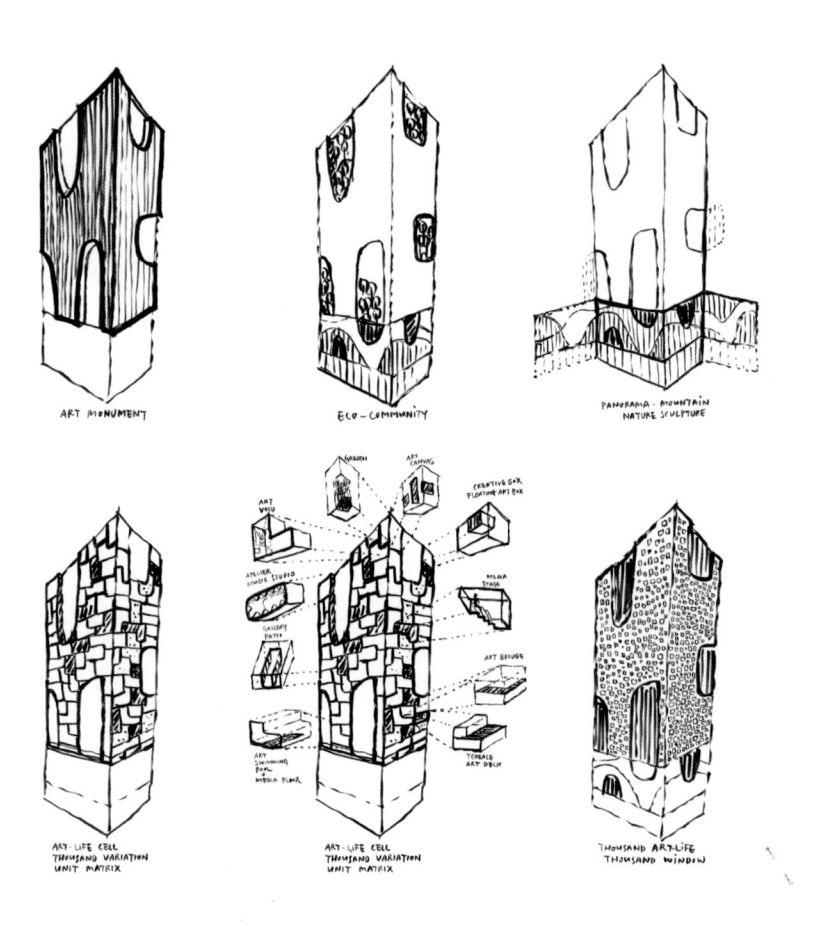

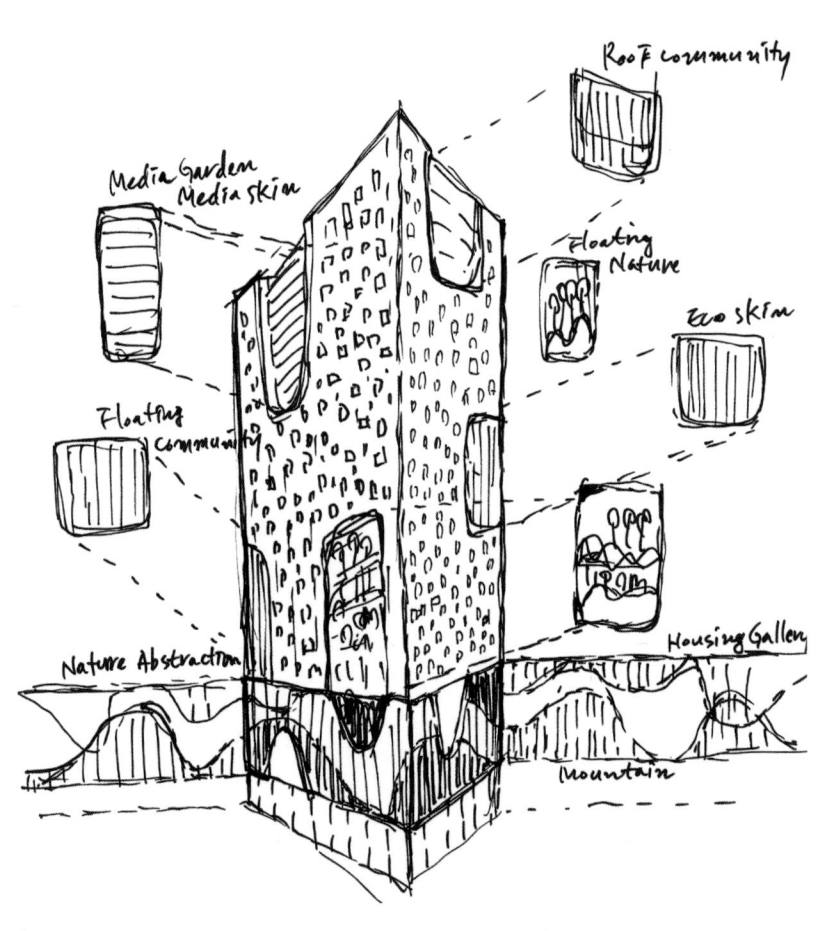

THOUSAND LIFE

The architecture is like a container of our life and changes it. Our life is on the age demanding the highest speed of alteration. Examination and reflection ourselves of public housing as the society develops is the foundation of creating new type of housing. The architecture for the contemporary society needs to change interactive. People want to bring the forest in their house because of pursuit of well-being life. And the life with new community defining the relationship with other people who live together is a important issue at this moment.

The aim of Dogok Purgio Art-Polis, we suggest, is bringing aspect of life to housing in order to achieve spiritual abundant enjoying art. Our suggestion for residential concept is related to the art. "Officetell" which is unique type of residence in Korea can be defines the middle of residence and business. Purgio Art-Polis re-interprets its meaning and combines with art. Eventually it creates high-end life.

The high-end life in the past tends to be for luxurious life showing their social state. So the masterpiece housing is evaluated by its physical condition such as size of residence and expensive material. New masterpiece-life should bear art and culture issues such as emotion, philosophy, value and identity. So-ho in New York and Chelsea are used be slum. But after the artists occupied, they became an art village with luxury dwelling. It is a good example of how much important factor the combination of art and culture is in masterpiece-life. The residence people longing for is not something like hotel-service holding Louis Vuitton or Hermes bag, but the container of their own unique life style with the art and the culture. The hotel residence like Trump So-ho is situated in the artists' street, so-ho. And Kobe art village and Heyri art village are also other examples of urban developing project with art. The artists and the residents have been cooperating in order to restore the value of whole village. Roppongi Hill in Tokyo is a sum of the artistic code like mori museum, the large commercial mall and the dwellings which enjoy them.

PRUGIO

COMPOUND BODY 477

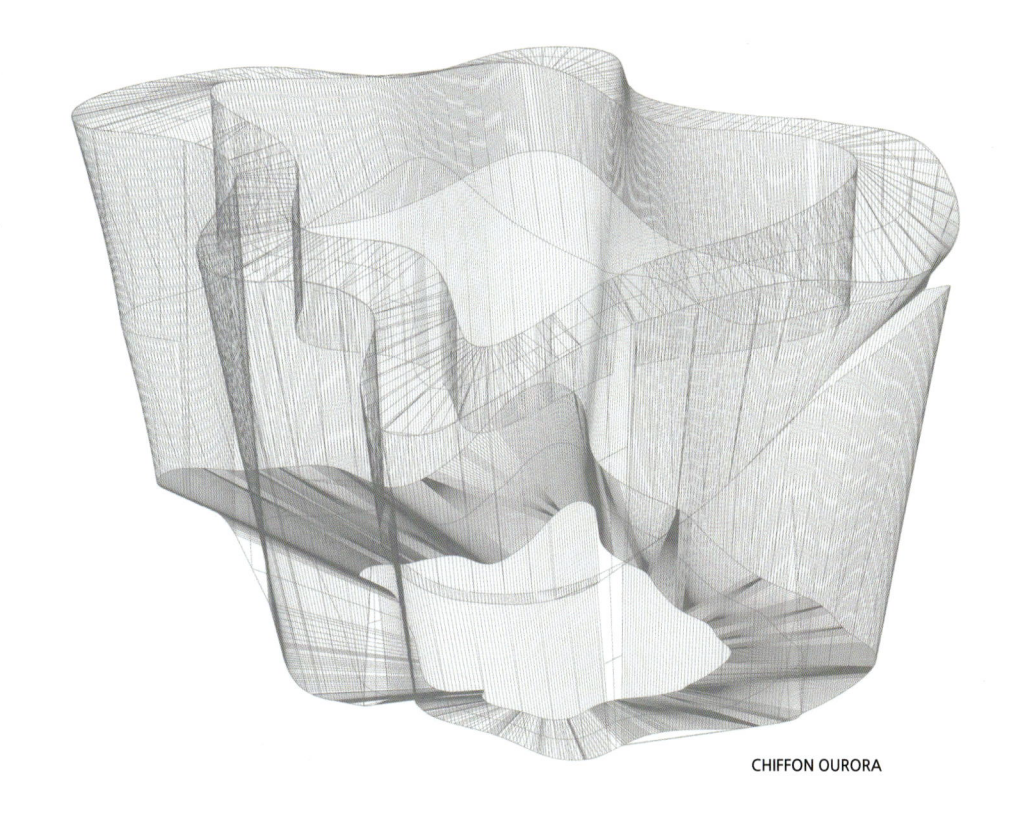

CHIFFON OURORA

The aim of Purgio Artpolis is that the desire for value of culture and art compound to the life directly. Whole composition is divided 3 parts, the culture and art community center show the life pattern and model house on lower part, personal officetell space is on middle part and the event garden is on the top. The unique composition is intervention of the model house. The existing showroom for housing changes to the dwellers' art center by meditating time of. It is used as gallery, theater, art shop, community, cafe and lounge meditating the time of use.

The importance of this project is on the innovation of individual residential units above using the art center and the personal dwelling separately. Artistic item and story combines and get into the residential space in order to innovative high-end life. Diverse art activities such as enjoy, producing, educating and integrating merge into the residence. The basic type of housing is designed to Green Gallery, Factory Loft, Atelier Beaux-art and Fantasy Pavilion.

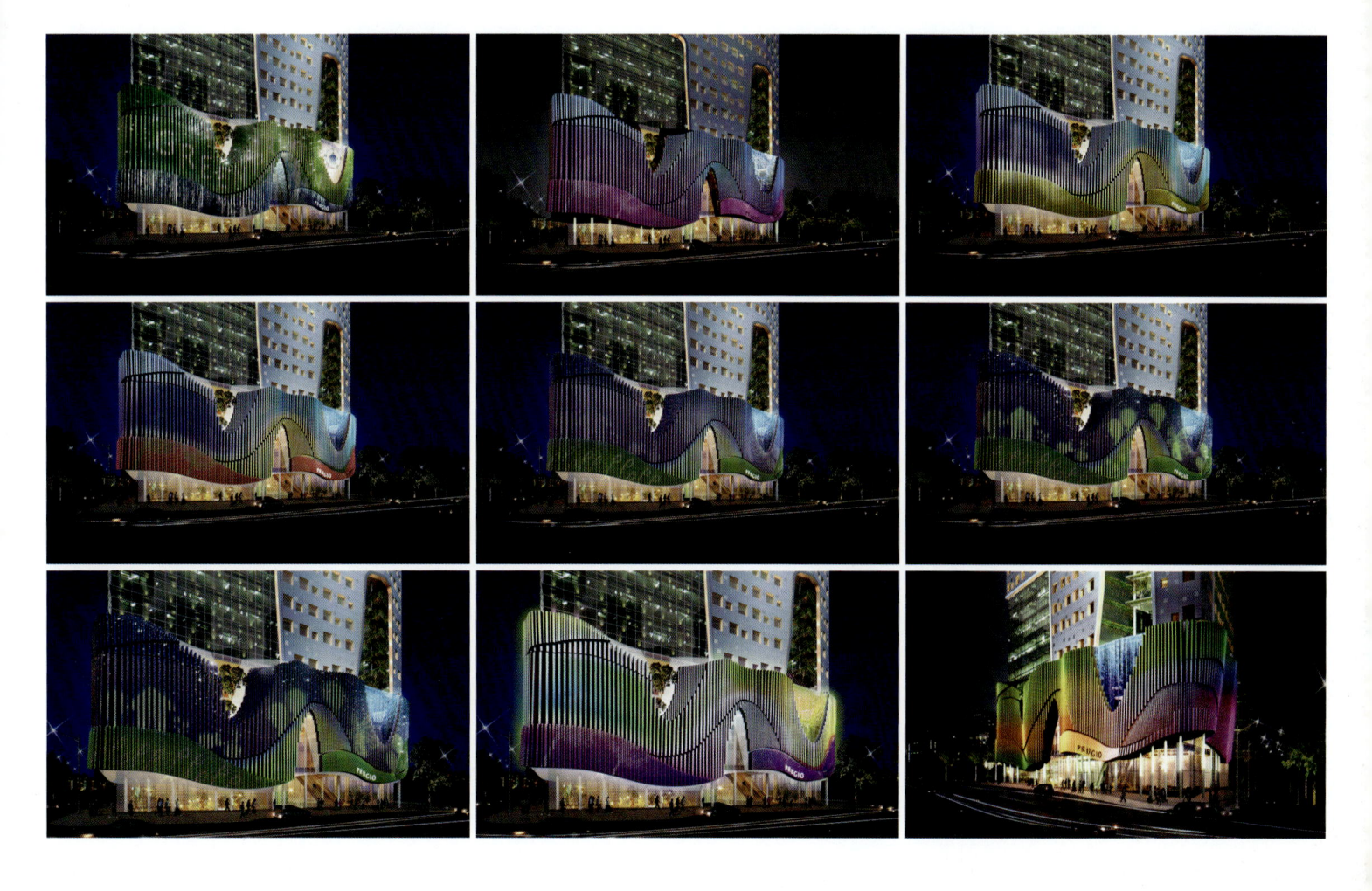

PANORAMA SKIN

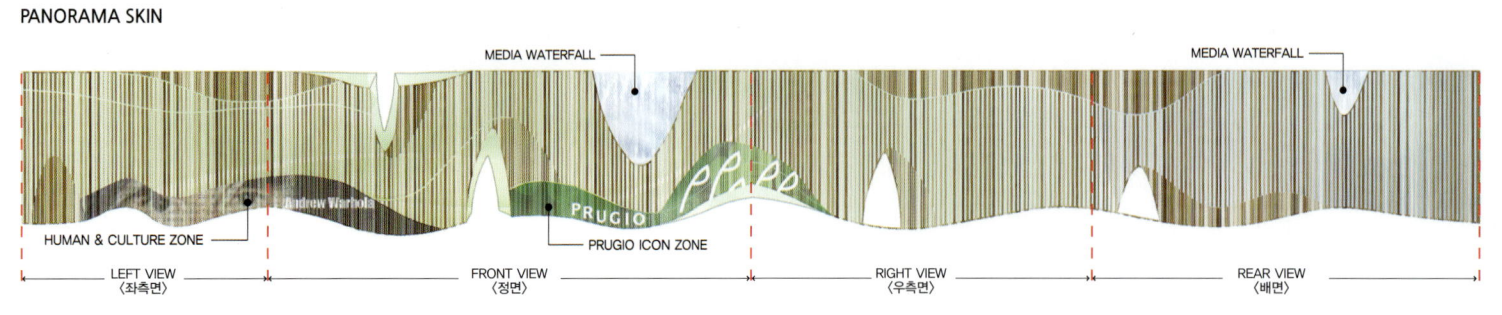

MEDIA WATERFALL

MEDIA WATERFALL

HUMAN & CULTURE ZONE

PRUGIO ICON ZONE

LEFT VIEW 〈좌측면〉 — FRONT VIEW 〈정면〉 — RIGHT VIEW 〈우측면〉 — REAR VIEW 〈배면〉

MATERIAL ZONE

SOLID + LOUVER   GLASS + LOUVER   GLASS

COMPOUND BODY 479

Nature Panorama 1

Nature Panorama 2

Nature Panorama 3

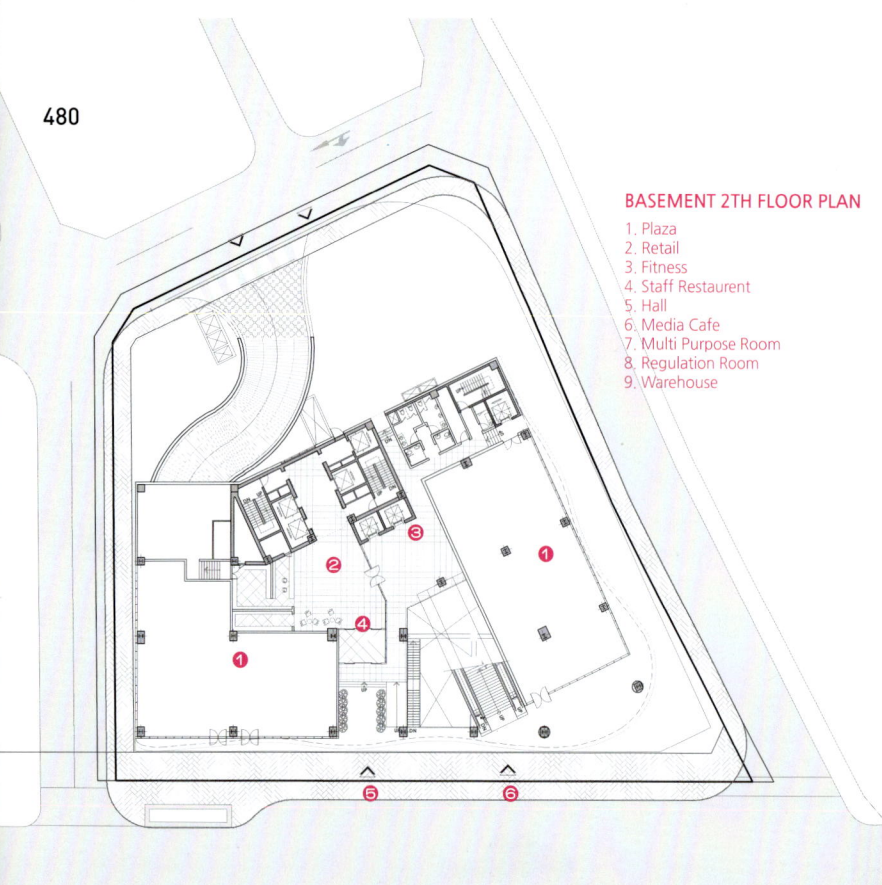

BASEMENT 2TH FLOOR PLAN
1. Plaza
2. Retail
3. Fitness
4. Staff Restaurent
5. Hall
6. Media Cafe
7. Multi Purpose Room
8. Regulation Room
9. Warehouse

For this art-based housing, the items which typical housing unit doesn't have combine to the units. For example, void, canvas wall, moving wall, garden, stage, studio, terrace, glass floor, bridge, pool, deck, patio, exhibition room, floating space, atelier and creative room are the items which are composed in the housing units distinctively.

The Fantasy Pavilion is a premium penthouse for artistic opinion leader. It is located on the top and has an advantage with sectional and spatial composition freely. On the middle of the unit, the void is inserted and the piece of art display and appreciate in it like a gallery. The void space penetrates 2 stories so it has expandable and flexible space for different size and

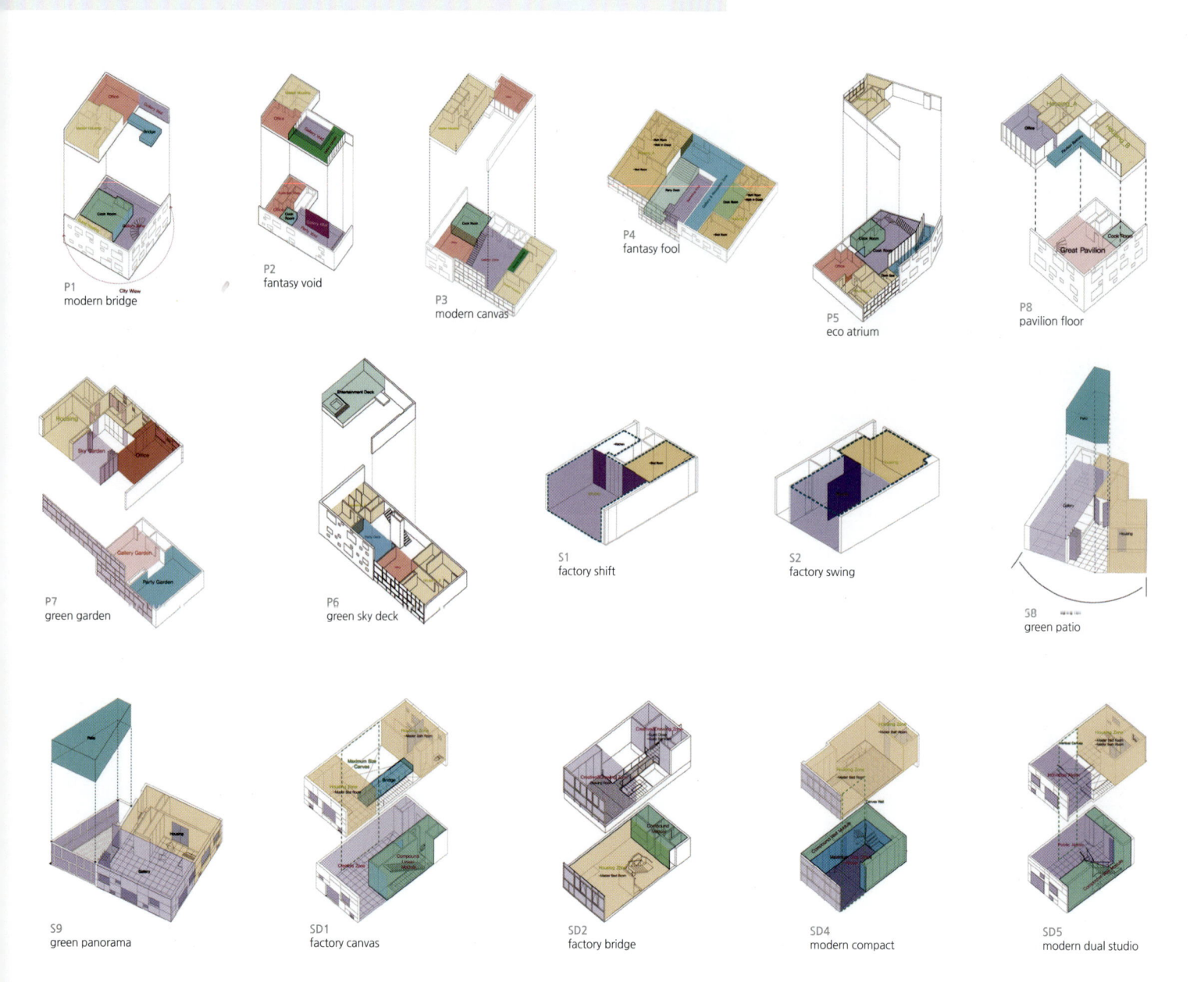

P1 modern bridge
P2 fantasy void
P3 modern canvas
P4 fantasy fool
P5 eco atrium
P8 pavilion floor
P7 green garden
P6 green sky deck
S1 factory shift
S2 factory swing
S8 green patio
S9 green panorama
SD1 factory canvas
SD2 factory bridge
SD4 modern compact
SD5 modern dual studio

COMPOUND BODY 481

scale of art works. The fantasy pavilion is based on Art Fantasy Void. The premium items, Art Modern Canvas, Art Modern Bridge, Art Fantasy Pool, Art Eco Atrium, Art Green Sky Deck, Art Green Garden and Art Great Pavilion give more unit variation transforming the basic type.

Factory Loft is both working space and living space for the artists like photo, paint, sculpture, media art and music and so on. The studio for working, exhibiting space and personal office are composed in single unit. By the diverse way to integrate or divide working space and living space, many aspects of the art will be accommodated. The Items for Factory Loft, which is in the middle of the studio and the dwelling are Art Factory Shift, Art Factory Swing, Art Factory Floating and Art Factory Vertical.

Green Gallery is housing for art enthusiast. It is in order to share their emotion and experience about art. The residents can exhibit their collection and have a meeting or party with the others. The gallery and outdoor terrace for small community are harmonized in living space. The way to insert nature, it is sorted Art Green Patio and Art Green Panorama.

Atelier Beaux-art is a duplex housing for artists of medium and their education and business. Creative work and educational activity are adopted in lower floor in Creative Atelier, Upper floor accommodates living program. There are 2 sorts of unit. Art Modern Compact Unit is that working-educating place completely separated. And Art Modern Flexibility Unit can be modified according to their demands of the each space.

P1 modern bridge

P2 fantasy void

P3 modern canvas

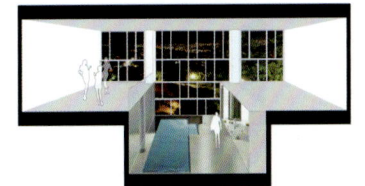

P4 fantasy fool

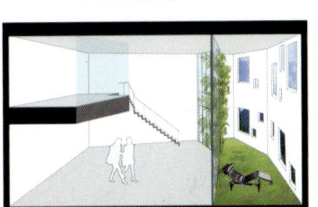

P5 eco atrium

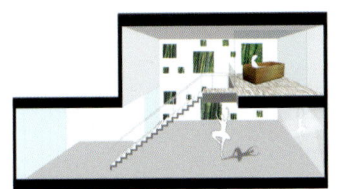

P6 green sky deck

P7 green garden

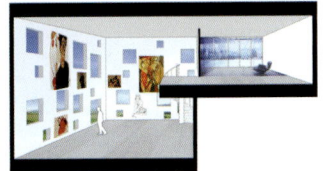

P8 pavilion floor

S1 factory shitf

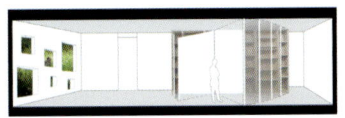

S2 factory swing

S8 green patio

S9 green panorama

SD1 factory canvas

SD2 factory bridge

SD4 modern compact

SD5 modern dual studio

PAVILION 1 FLOOR PLAN

PAVILION 2 FLOOR PLAN

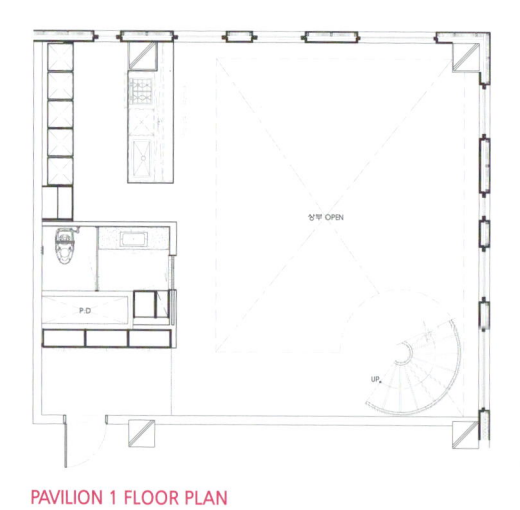

// **Art Pavilion Floor** 'Great Pavilion Floor' can be defined as a magnificent field of lives. It houses exhibition, banquet hall, lounge, office and drawing room. Our holistic approach is to separate upper part(residence) and lower part(public pavilion) of the building according to the programme.

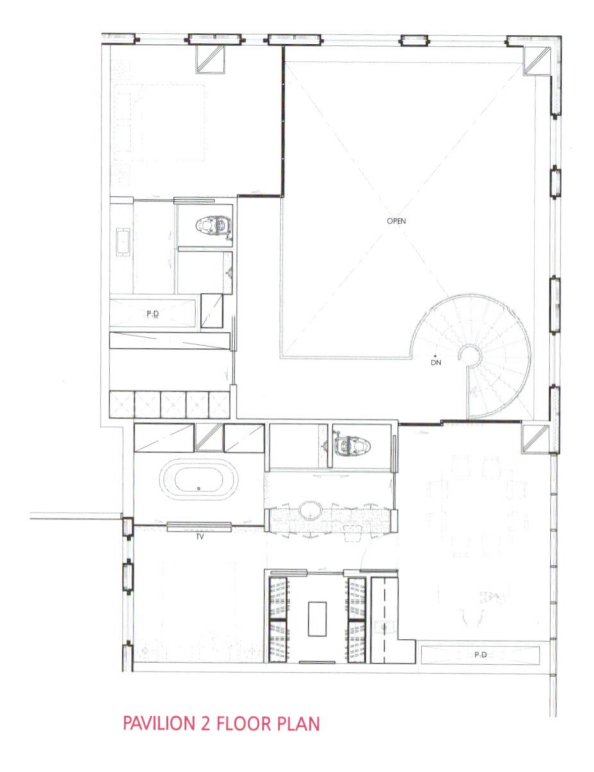

// **Art Eco Atrium** The building is a demonstration project incorporating lots of elements in nature within an exclusive architectural form and design strategy. Great openness provides us a light and airy space. Eco Atrium is a subtle way of adjusting garden in the sky.

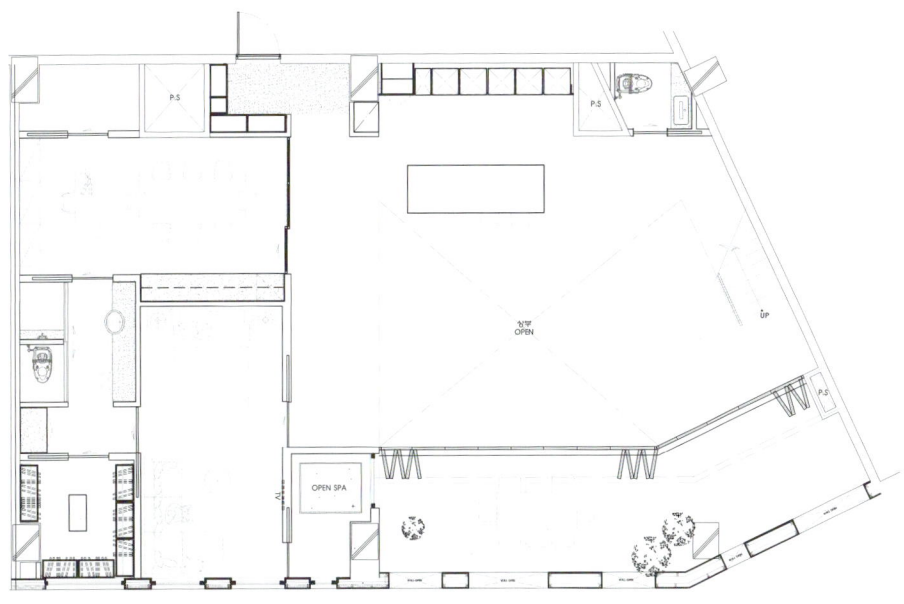

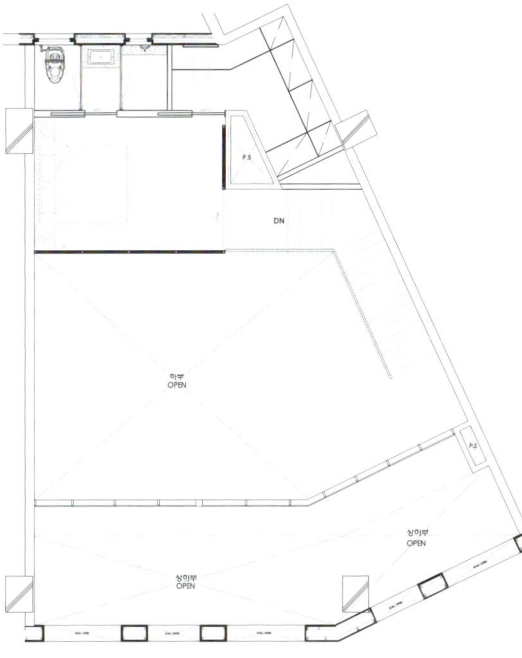

ECO ATRIUM 1 FLOOR PLAN

ECO ATRIUM 2 FLOOR PLAN

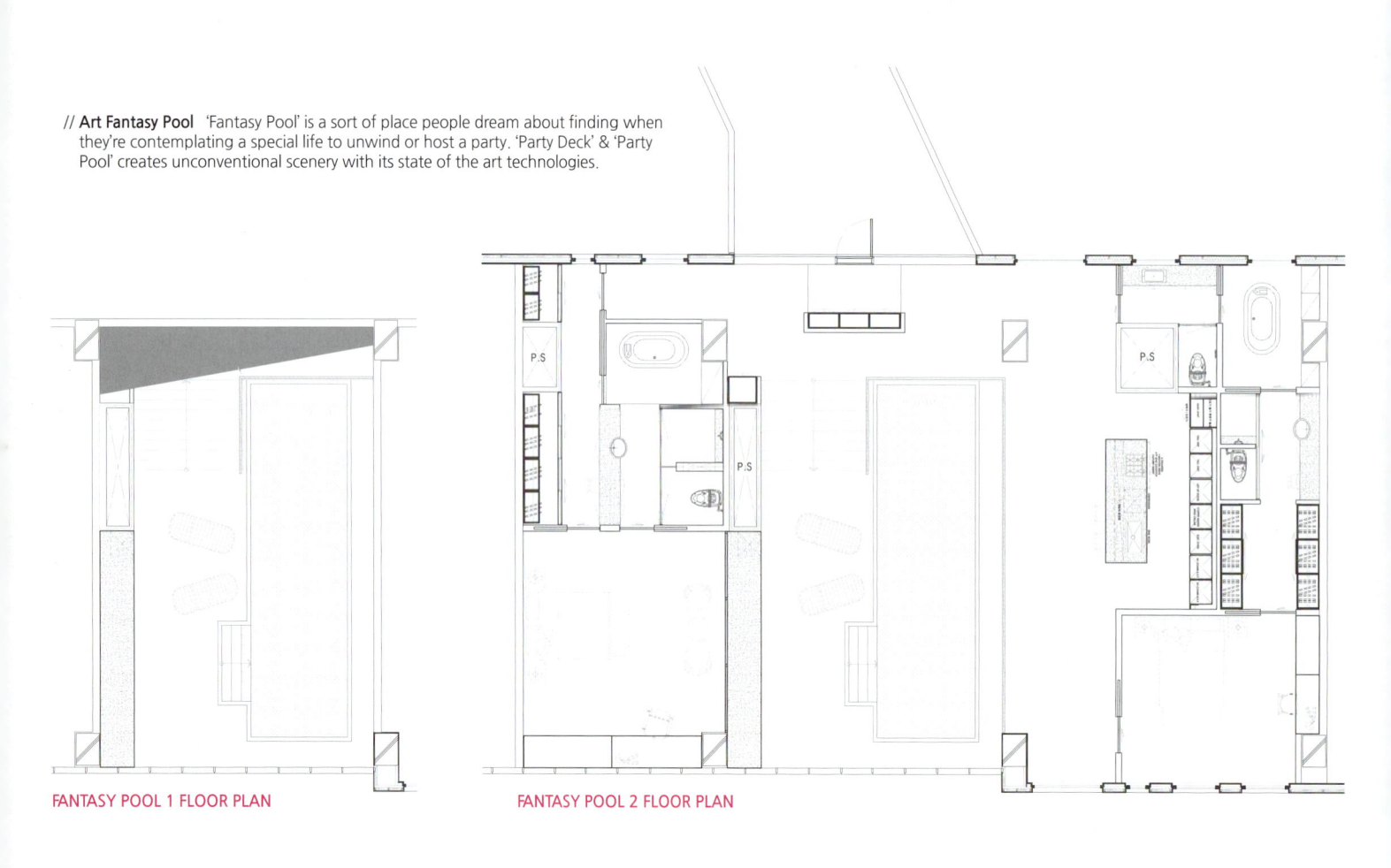

// **Art Fantasy Pool** 'Fantasy Pool' is a sort of place people dream about finding when they're contemplating a special life to unwind or host a party. 'Party Deck' & 'Party Pool' creates unconventional scenery with its state of the art technologies.

FANTASY POOL 1 FLOOR PLAN

FANTASY POOL 2 FLOOR PLAN

COMPOUND BODY 485

// Art Modern Bridge 'The bridge and spiral stairs' are also have a considerable overarching spatial quality. Since they're intended to allow people feel as if they're in an art gallery not an apartment. To put it another way, it can be said as an Art-Box Pavillion.

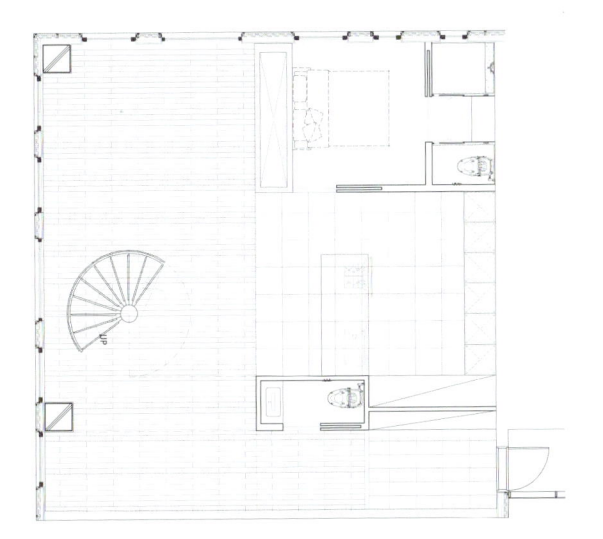

MODERN BRIDGE 1 FLOOR PLAN

MODERN BRIDGE 2 FLOOR PLAN

Headquater Office of SK Networks

Competition Winner

Architects Jang Yoon Gyoo, Shin Chang Hoon + JungLim Architects
Client SK networks
Photographer Kim Jae Kyung

COMPOUND BODY 487

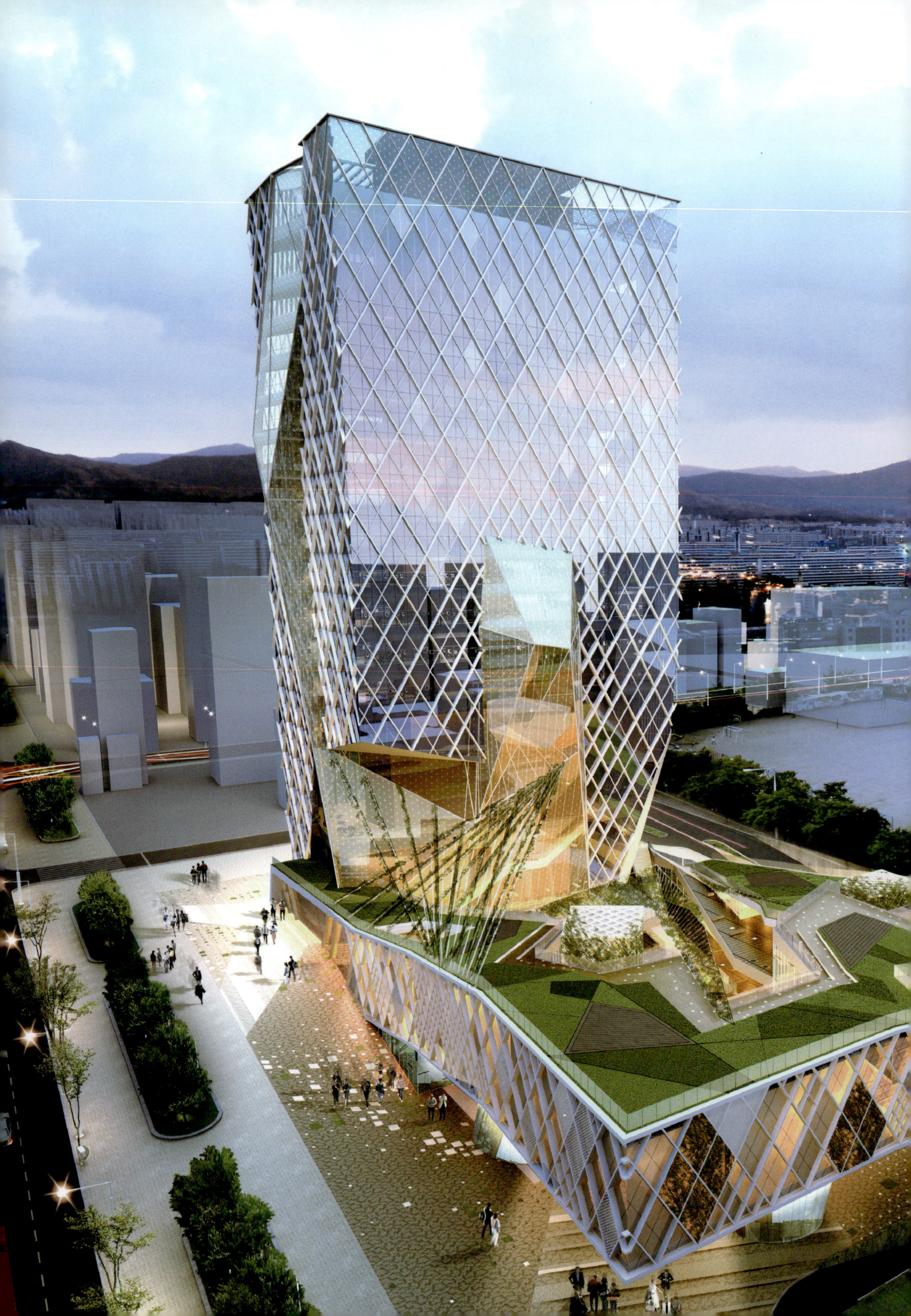

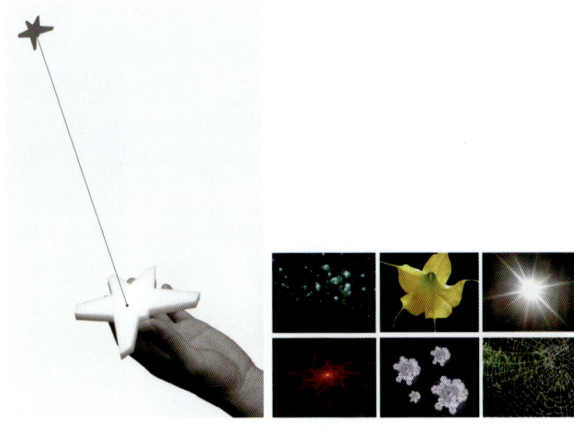

PLATFORM, CREATIVE OFFICE

This project starts from the question about the general model of an office space. Existing offices were based on efficiency and productivity so their aim was the simplest constitution of space and maximizing the potentiality of the functional space. Especially, office space is being required to change according to various demands in the contemporary society. This project in particular is for the new headquarter office of the SK Group so it has to work as a platform to realize various potentialities beyond just a typical office. It has to reflect new circumstances, provide different spaces and programmatic innovation to produce creative spaces. We adopt the concept of the creative office actively. To combine creative codes of the office job, we suggest concepts such as office landscape, creative zone, eco-friendly skin and growing office.

The purpose of the office landscape concept is divesting office space. According to area's usage on each floor and the user's demands, the layout of each floor is flexible with the interpretation of design factors such as scale, number of users, territory, and the relationship with the outdoors and so on. A program which performs a creative role in the office is inserted. To suggest creative groups for the individual and the group, the office combines information, rest and art. The media garden, personal meditation garden, terrace garden, and the forest garden are composed in there.

On the lower part, 3-dimensional cultural communication space is situated. There is a connecting zone for fluent communication between the visitors and the officers. This open community works as an urban connector, with the flowing surround infra.

Combining the creative zone and its symbolic property, we suggest The Wing of Happiness which resembles the symbol of SK Networks by the transformation of stacking masses.

The elevation changes with the eco equipment and the light. The Energy saving system and the wall planting make an eco friendly skin interacting with the environment.

It also has diversity according to the demands of the time. It is an evolving office. In 2010, the floor area ratio can be 250% and go up to 400% in 2020. Lastly in 2030, it expands till 800%.

The Evolving Program which will be developed with this volume expansion accommodates diverse programs including housing and cultural facilities.

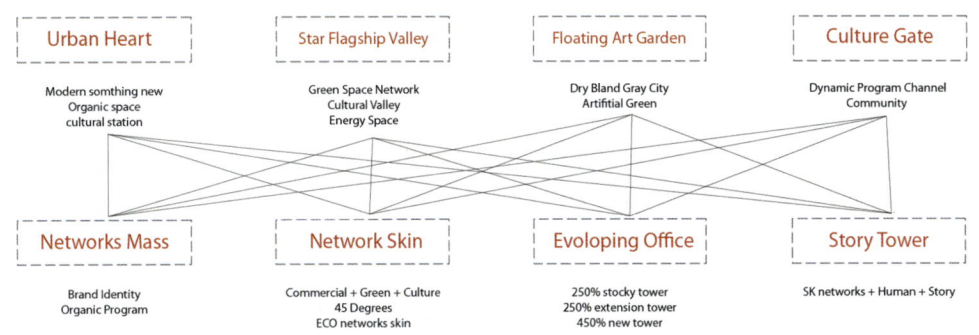

Urban Heart	Star Flagship Valley	Floating Art Garden	Culture Gate
Modern somthing new Organic space cultural station	Green Space Network Cultural Valley Energy Space	Dry Bland Gray City Artifitial Green	Dynamic Program Channel Community

Networks Mass	Network Skin	Evoloping Office	Story Tower
Brand Identity Organic Program	Commercial + Green + Culture 45 Degrees ECO networks skin	250% stocky tower 250% extension tower 450% new tower	SK networks + Human + Story

STAR FLAGSHIP VALL

NETWORK MASS

SPECIAL
REST
GALLERY
LOBBY

EVOLVING OFFICE

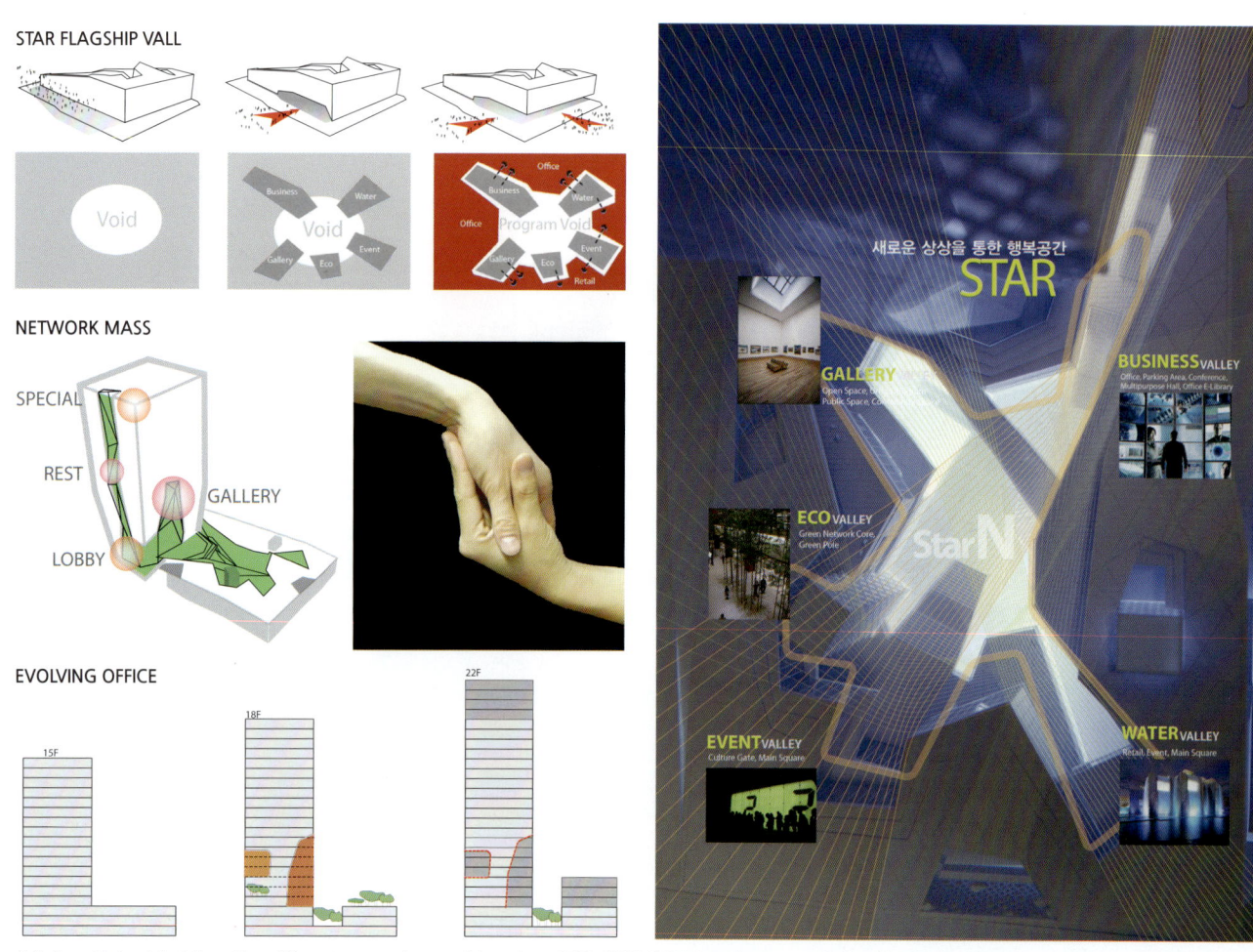

15F 18F 22F

새로운 상상을 통한 행복공간
STAR

GALLERY — Open Space, Public Space, Co...
BUSINESS VALLEY — Office, Parking Area, Conference, Multipurpose Hall, Office E-Library
ECO VALLEY — Green Network Core, Green Pole
EVENT VALLEY — Culture Gate, Main Square
WATER VALLEY — Retail, Event, Main Square

Star N

// **Culture Gate**   We take rather different approaches on this project, STAR-NETWORK. In a city, vast majority of buildings have platitude methodology by putting conventional programmes on the ground floor. You can explore what can be achieved within only a corporate headquarters; event plaza, nature, natural light, community and media.

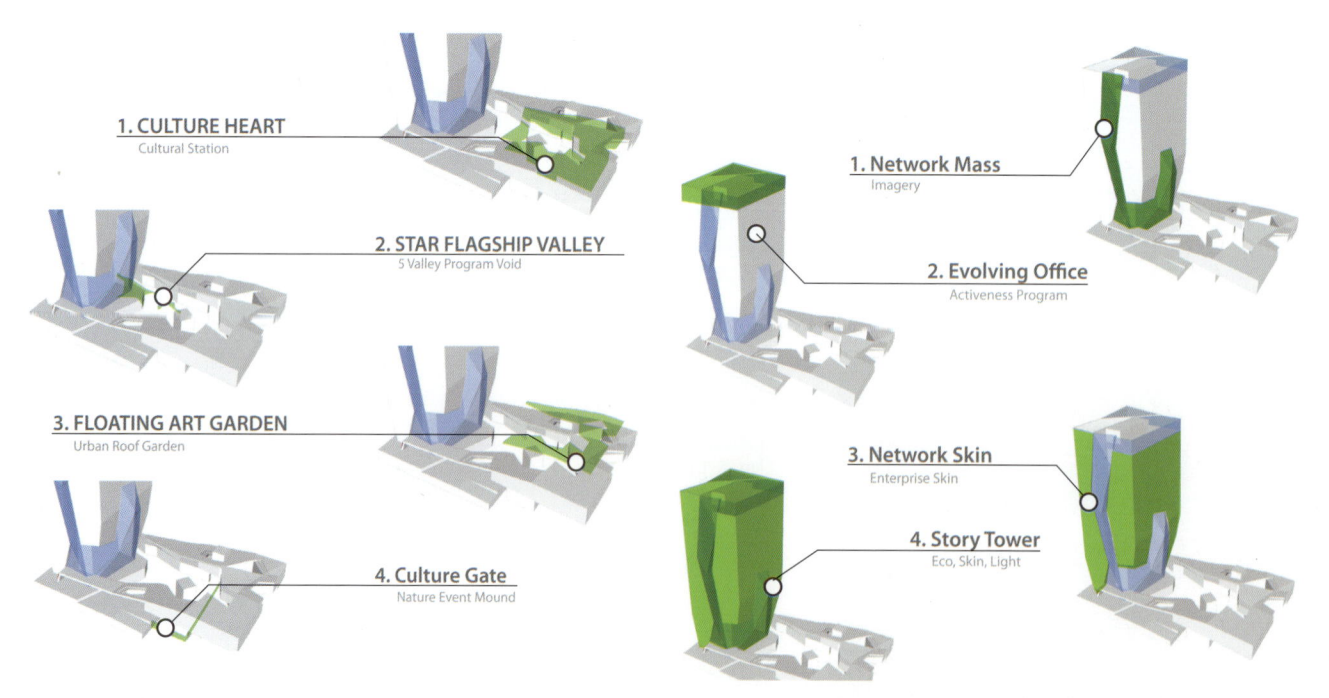

1. **CULTURE HEART** — Cultural Station
2. **STAR FLAGSHIP VALLEY** — 5 Valley Program Void
3. **FLOATING ART GARDEN** — Urban Roof Garden
4. **Culture Gate** — Nature Event Mound

1. **Network Mass** — Imagery
2. **Evolving Office** — Activeness Program
3. **Network Skin** — Enterprise Skin
4. **Story Tower** — Eco, Skin, Light

// **Star-network**, appears to play a key role in office programme. We make a difference on a global basis to achieve new vision of a brave new 'SK networks'. Through an office building, we boost corporate image as one of the most important companies in the world. 'Star Network' must be a big step towards being an innovative and go-ahead company.

| Office Zone | Art Garden Zone | Retail Zone | Public Zone |

Office / Office / Office / Office / Office
Health, Rest
Hall — Media Cafe
Business

Roof Garden
Restaurant
Sunken Space
Shopping, Food
Shopping, Delightful Playing
Culture Gate ◀ Public Space

// **Culture Heart** To meet the modern people's desire to pursue something new and creative, we suggest 'Culture Heart' which houses cultural facilities. Our holistic approach is not juxtaposing conventional programmes but creating organic and synthesis of spaces.
"A space could be a good source of energy for modern people."
Star Network will be lying at the heart of new culture.

3RD FLOOR PLAN
1. Office
2. Retail

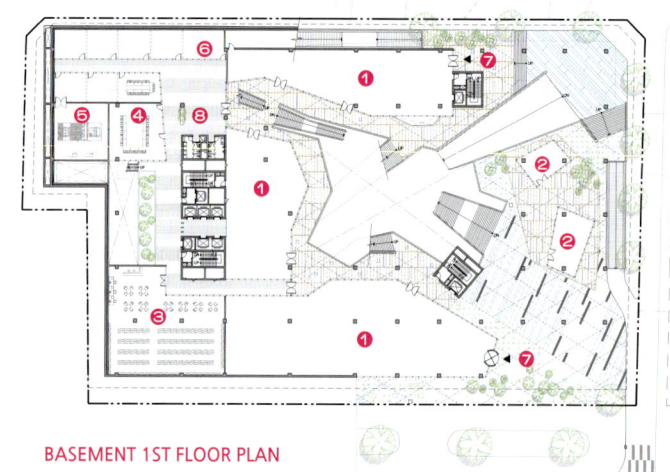

BASEMENT 1ST FLOOR PLAN
1. Office
2. Retail
3. Library & Support Facility
4. Meeting Room
5. Regulation Room
6. Reception Room
7. Office Entrance
8. Hall

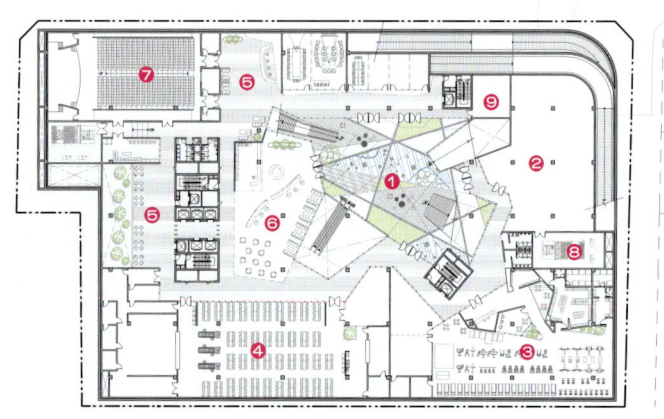

BASEMENT 2ND FLOOR PLAN
1. Plaza
2. Retail
3. Fitness
4. Staff Restaurant
5. Hall
6. Media Cafe
7. Multi Purpose Room
8. Regulation Room
9. Warehouse

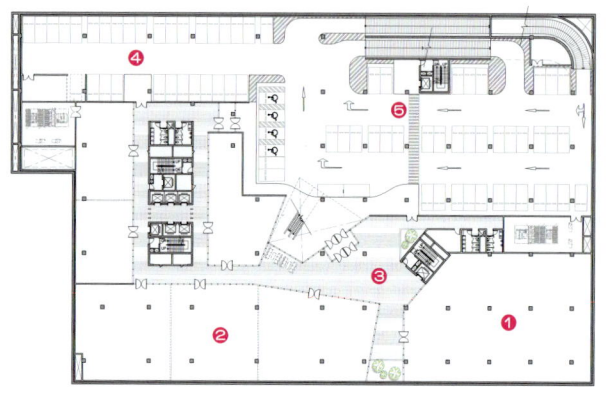

BASEMENT 3RD FLOOR PLAN
1. Mobile Experience Shop
2. Retail
3. Hall
4. VIP Parking
5. Parking

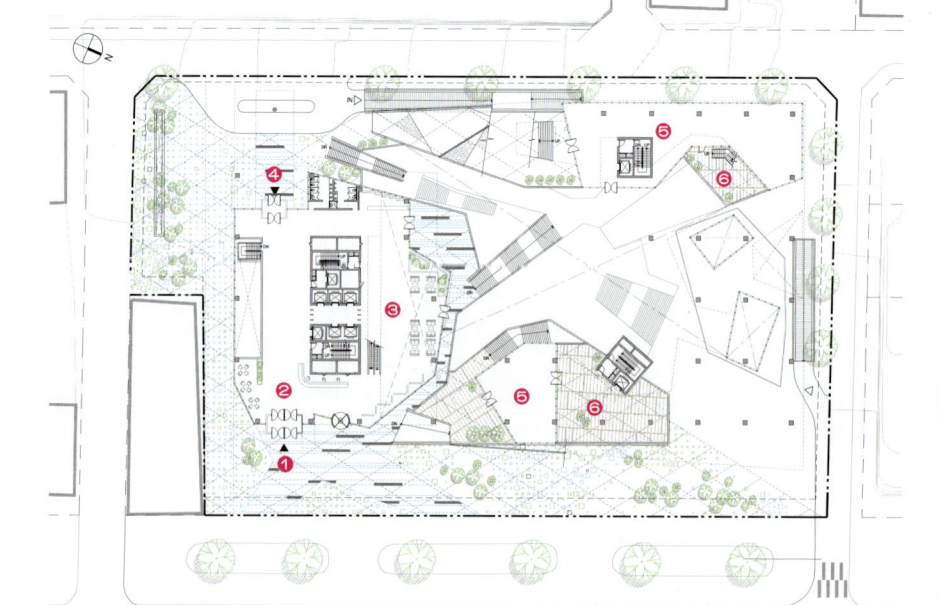

GROUND FLOOR PLAN
1. Office Main Entrance
2. Office Lobby
3. Office Lounge
4. VIP Entrance
5. Retail
6. Deck

// Floating Art Garden The goal of this project is to create an atmosphere that invites and promotes activity in an urban public space. 'Floating Art Garden' is a roof garden of the building. Its gentle slope mirrors the mountain shape to allow people feel as if they're on a mountain. 'Floating Art Garden' invites us to use the environmentally friendly programme such as green square, storytelling terrace and media water-fall.

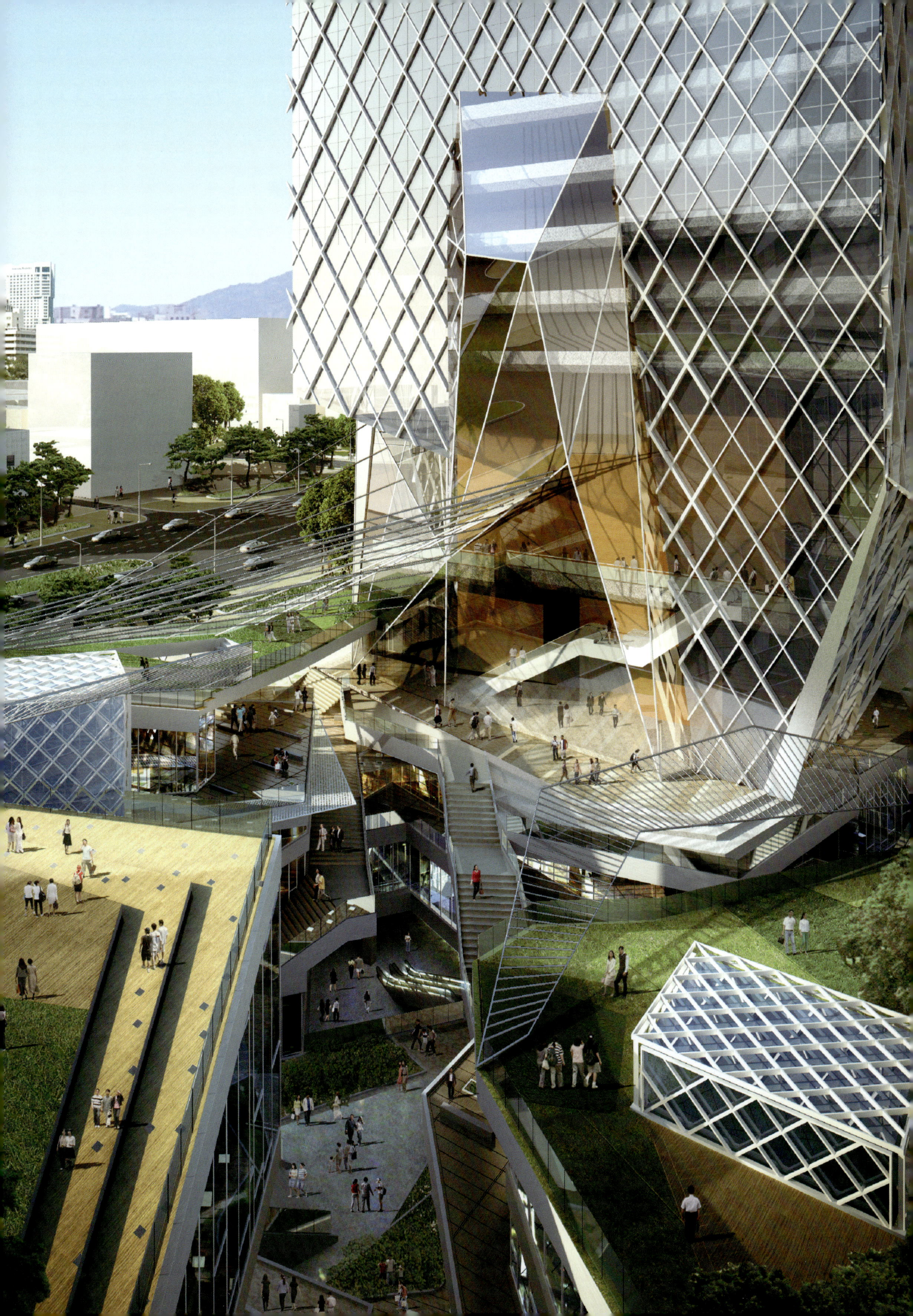

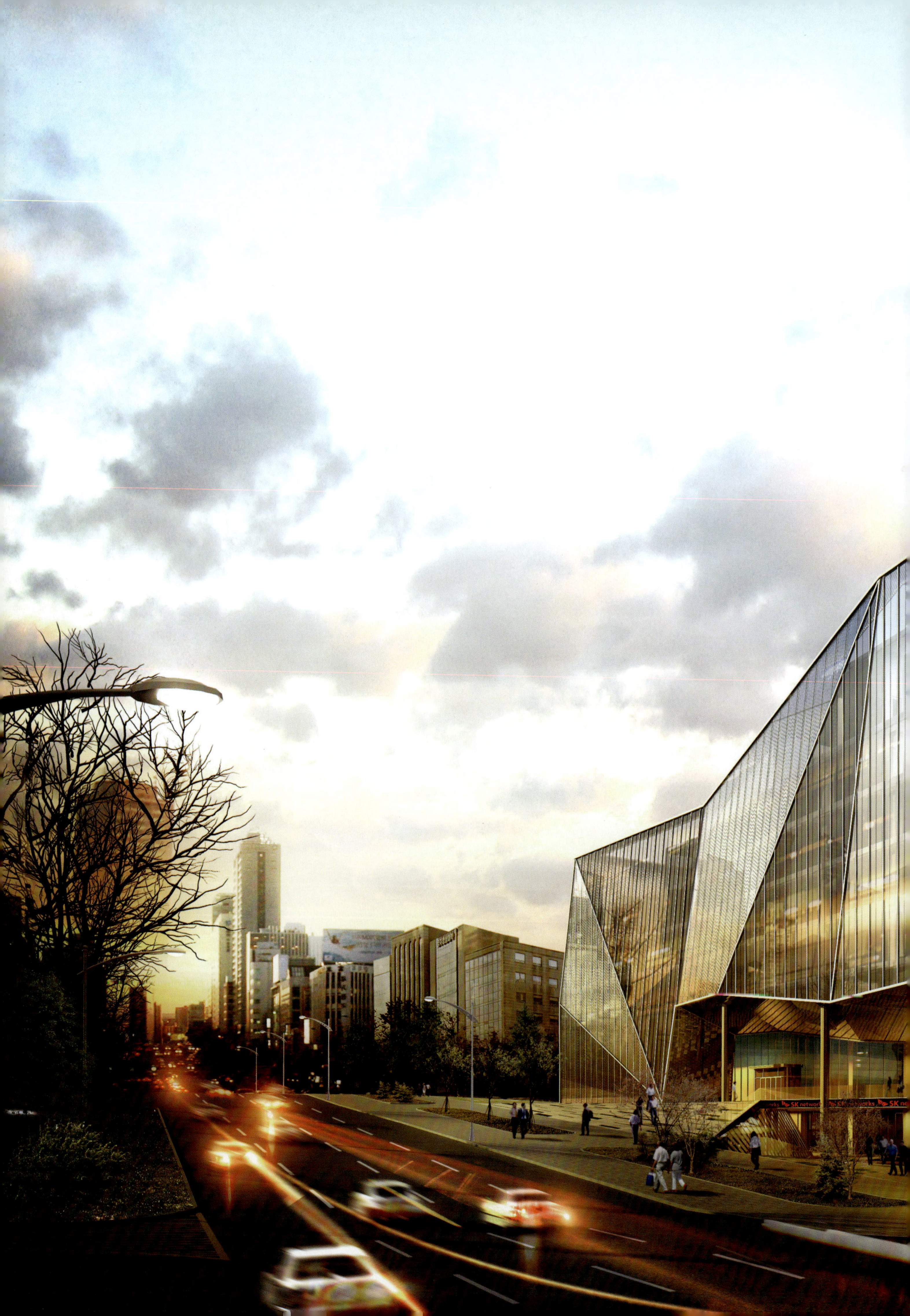
SK networks

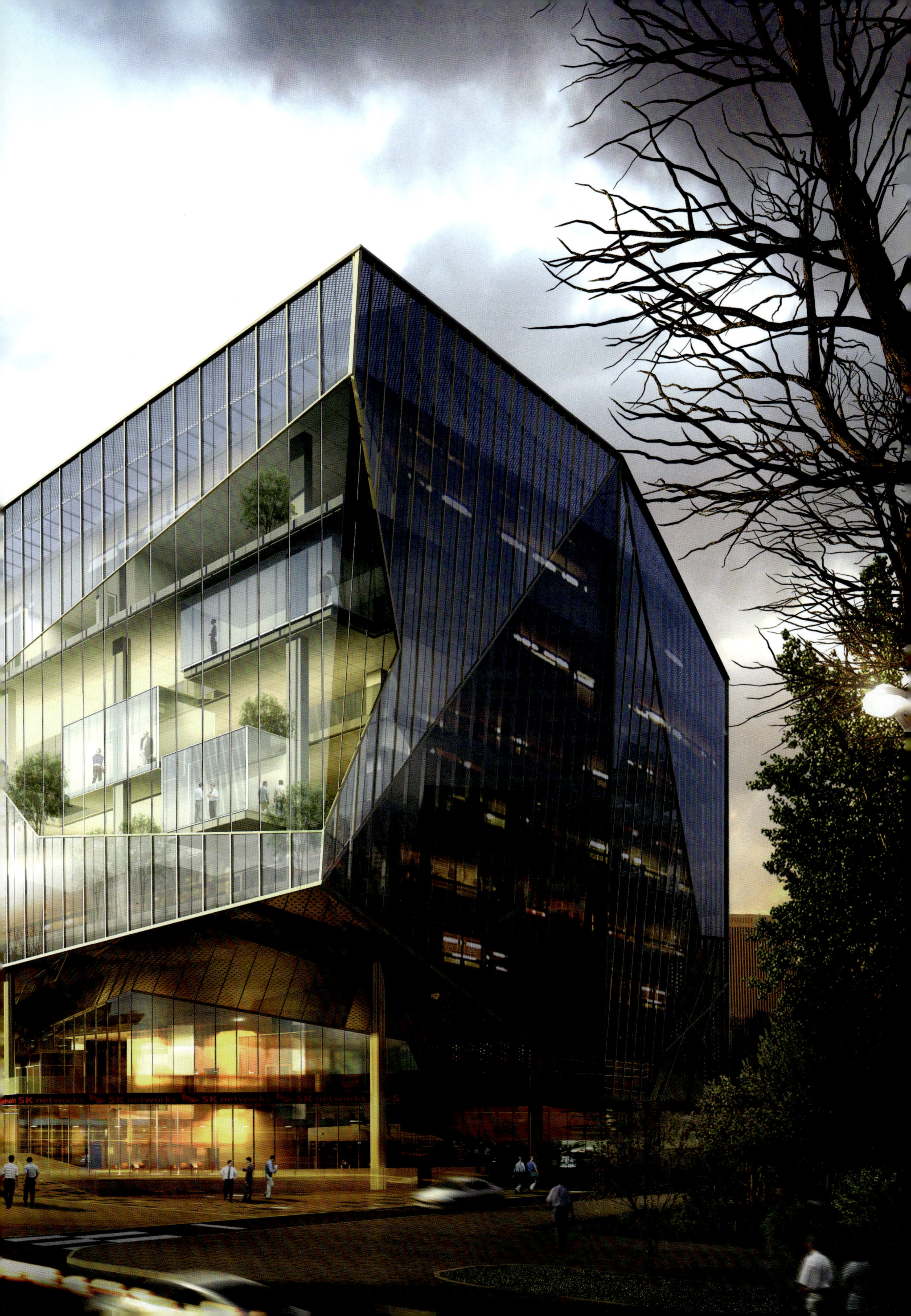
SK networks SK networks SK networks SK networks

Design
Jang Yoon Gyoo, Shin Chang Hoon + JungLim Architects
Design Team
Kim Bong Kyun, Sim Hyung Sun, Sim Jae Hyun, Kim Ho Jin, Choi Jin Gyu
Location
948-1 DaeChi-Dong, GangNam-Gu, Seoul
Use
Temporary Building
Site Area 8,267.10m²
Building Area 52,055.62m²
Total Floor Area 7144.53m²
Building Coverage Ratio 49.95%
Floor Area Ratio 249.66 %

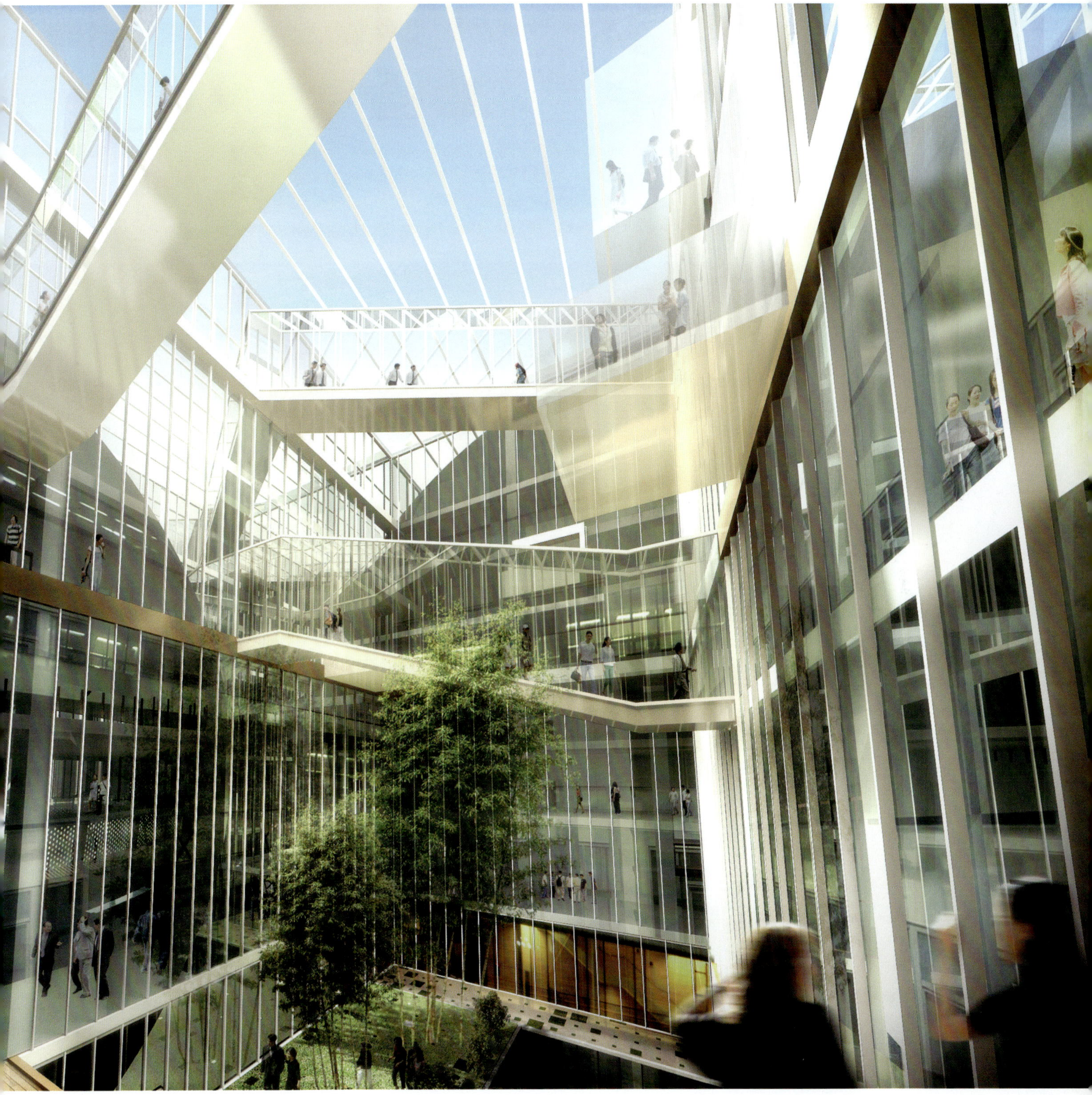

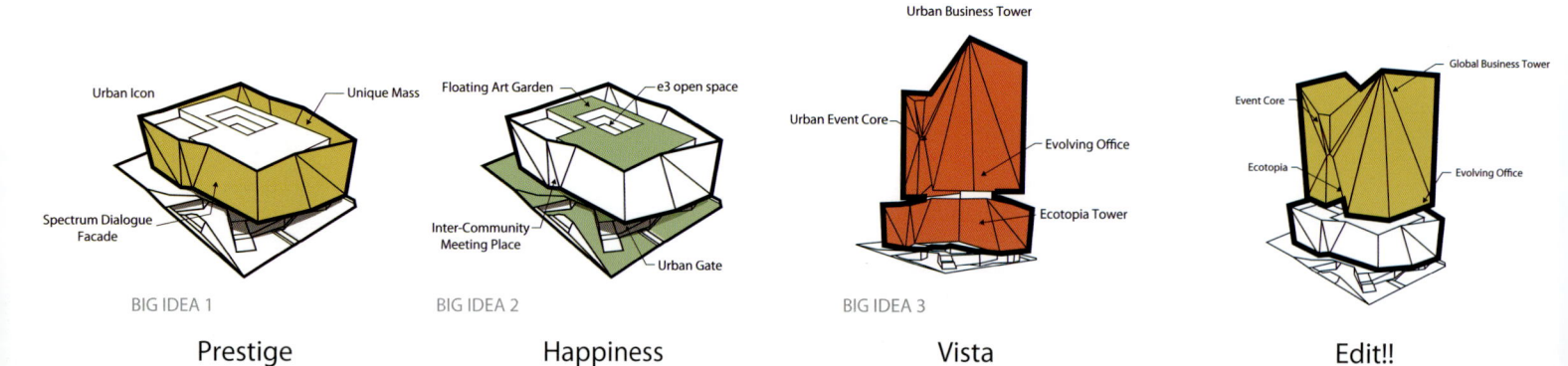

BIG IDEA 1 — Prestige
- Urban Icon
- Unique Mass
- Spectrum Dialogue Facade

BIG IDEA 2 — Happiness
- Floating Art Garden
- e3 open space
- Inter-Community Meeting Place
- Urban Gate

BIG IDEA 3 — Vista
- Urban Business Tower
- Urban Event Core
- Evolving Office
- Ecotopia Tower

Edit!!
- Global Business Tower
- Event Core
- Ecotopia
- Evolving Office

// **Platform office**   In order to create a unique headquarters, we set goals on happiness to everyone(to the company, customers and also to the general public).

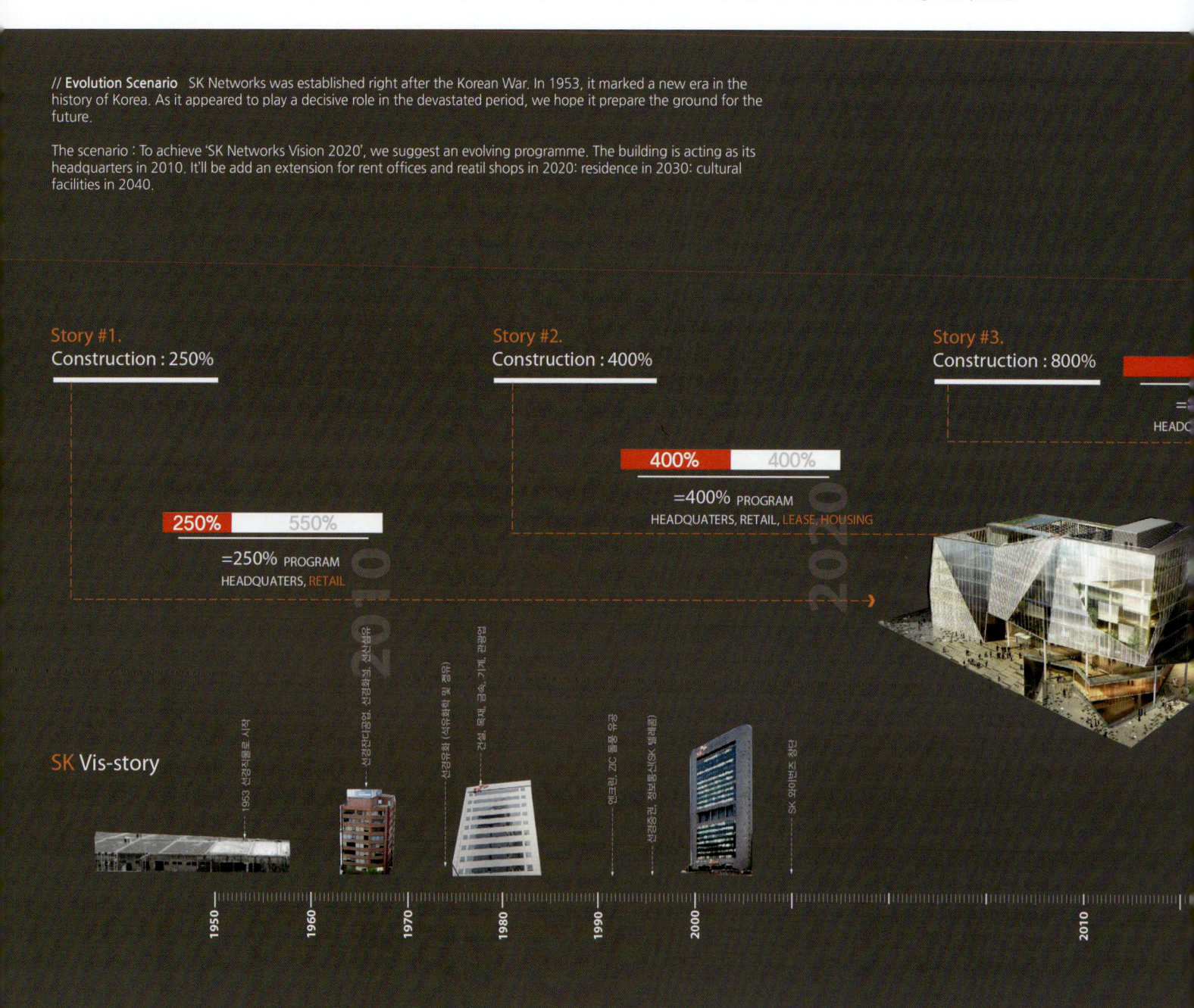

// **Evolution Scenario**   SK Networks was established right after the Korean War. In 1953, it marked a new era in the history of Korea. As it appeared to play a decisive role in the devastated period, we hope it prepare the ground for the future.

The scenario : To achieve 'SK Networks Vision 2020', we suggest an evolving programme. The building is acting as its headquarters in 2010. It'll be add an extension for rent offices and reatil shops in 2020: residence in 2030: cultural facilities in 2040.

Story #1.
Construction : 250%

250% | 550%
=250% PROGRAM
HEADQUATERS, RETAIL

Story #2.
Construction : 400%

400% | 400%
=400% PROGRAM
HEADQUATERS, RETAIL, LEASE, HOUSING

Story #3.
Construction : 800%

HEADQ

SK Vis-story

COMPOUND BODY 499

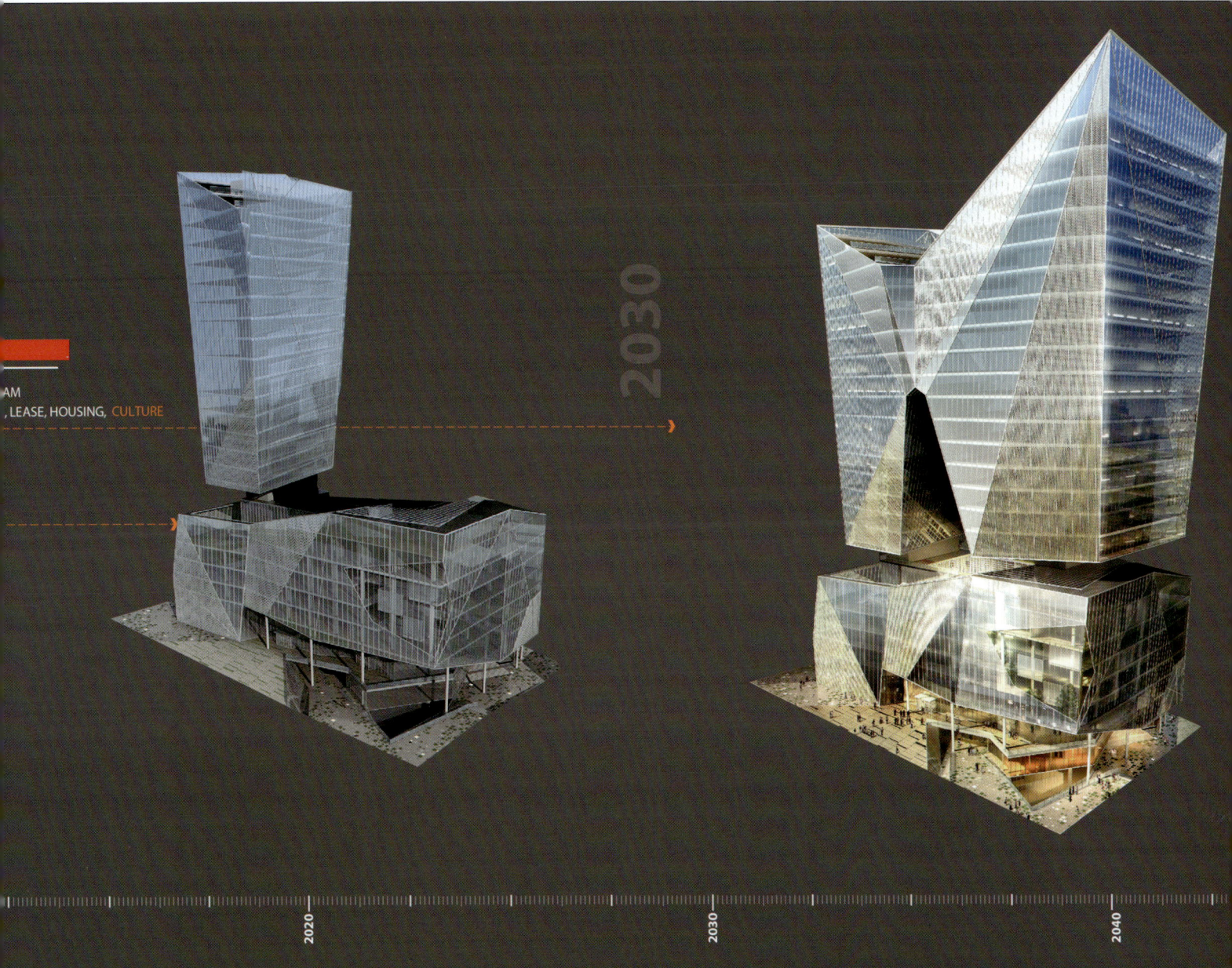

, LEASE, HOUSING, CULTURE

2030

2020　　2030　　2040

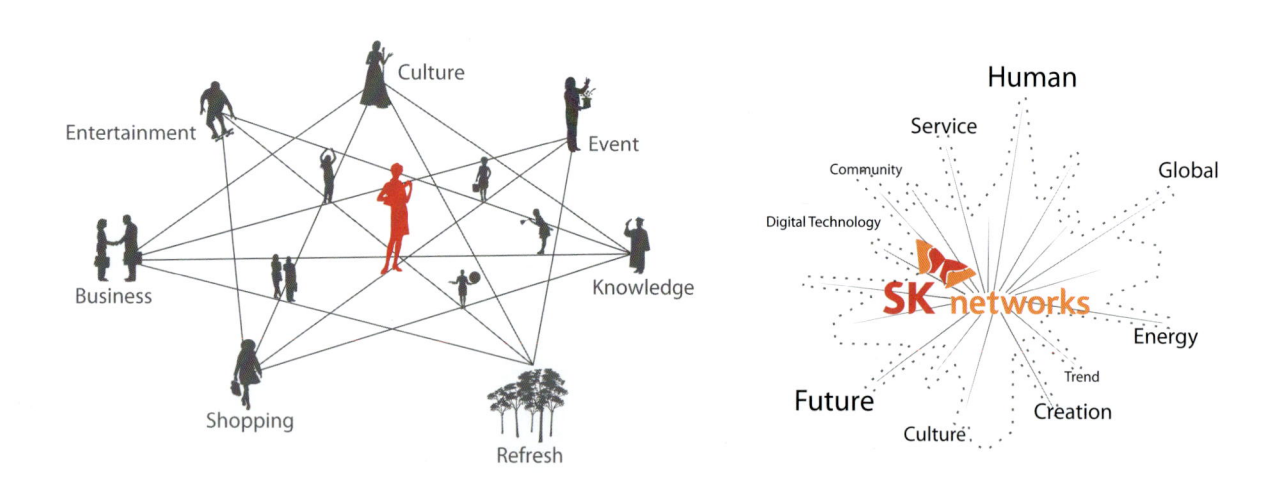

Culture
Entertainment
Event
Business
Knowledge
Shopping
Refresh

Human
Service
Community
Global
Digital Technology
SK networks
Energy
Trend
Future
Creation
Culture

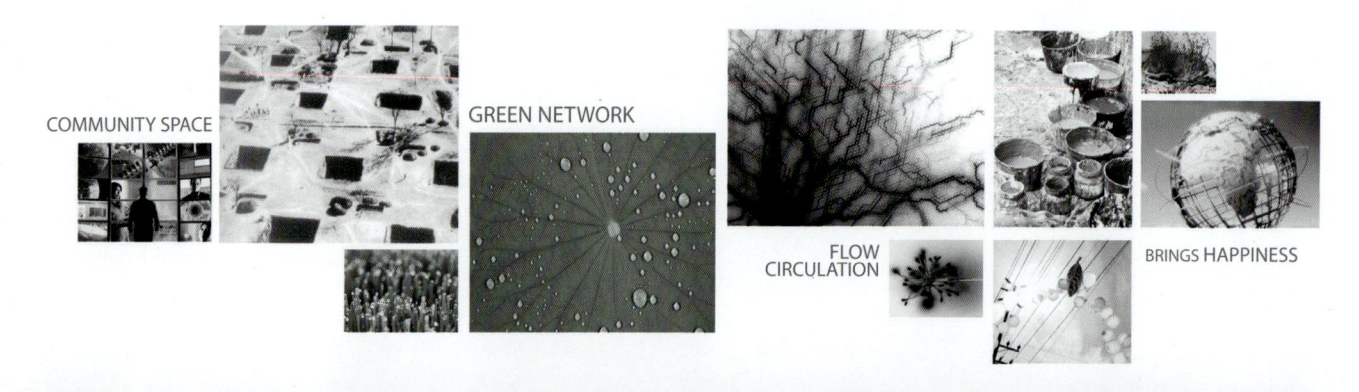

COMMUNITY SPACE

GREEN NETWORK

FLOW CIRCULATION

BRINGS HAPPINESS

// Continuous Flow_ Find the Potential Activities in City   'Crystal Platform' reflects its great potential growth with its distinctive form. It is a key part of the SK Networks. The goal of our strategy is being the first step toward the future. 'Crystal Platform', it would be a big step forward for the company.

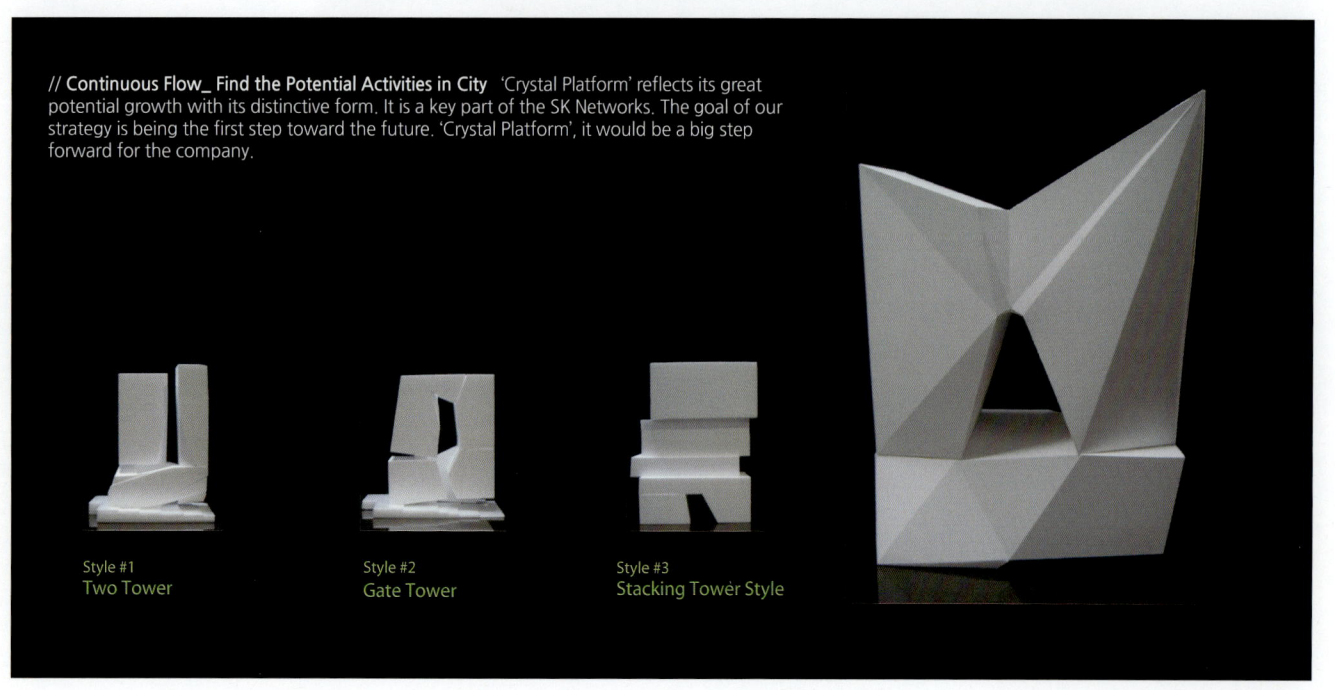

Style #1
Two Tower

Style #2
Gate Tower

Style #3
Stacking Tower Style

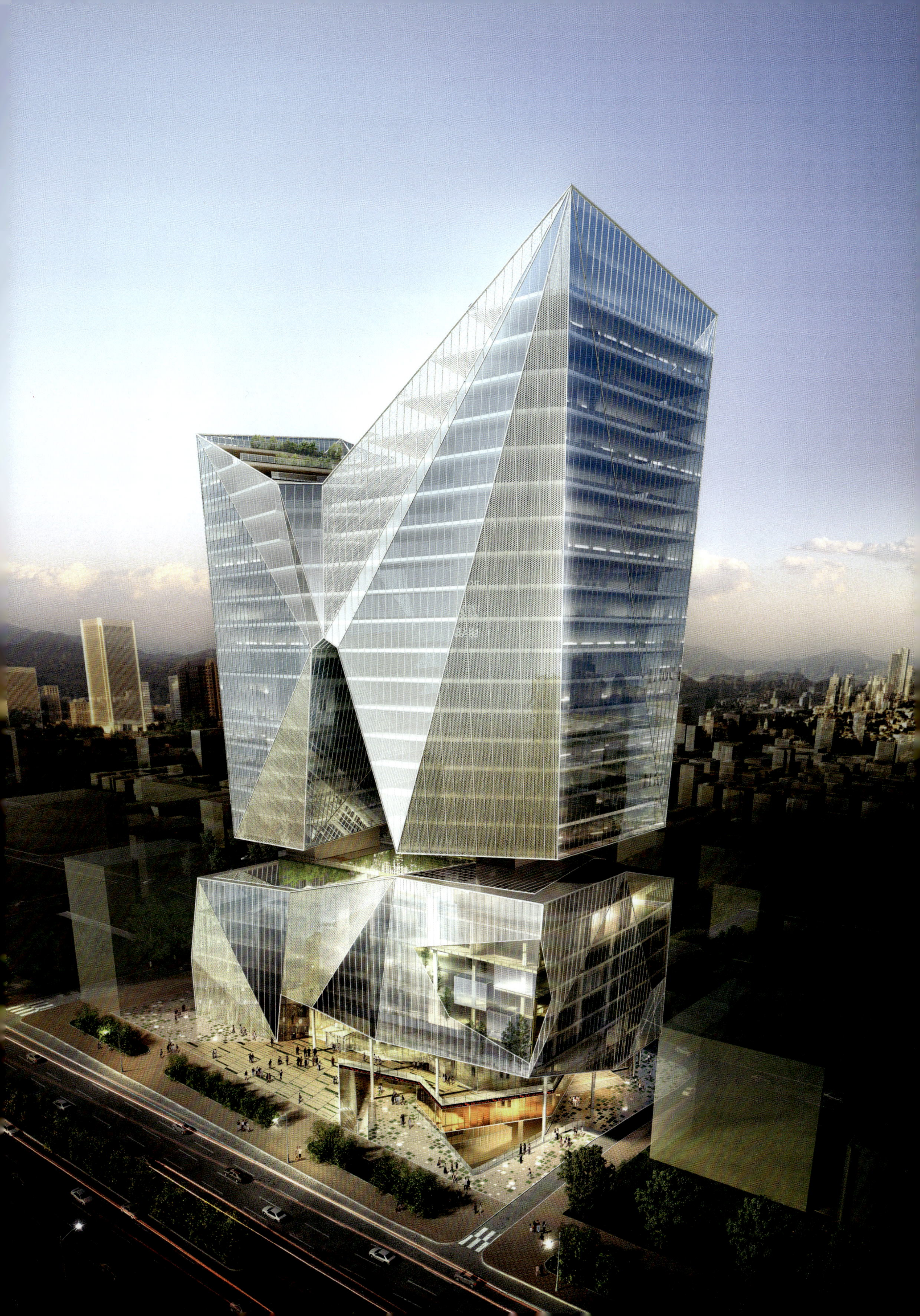

Brand space

Headquater Office of Evervill

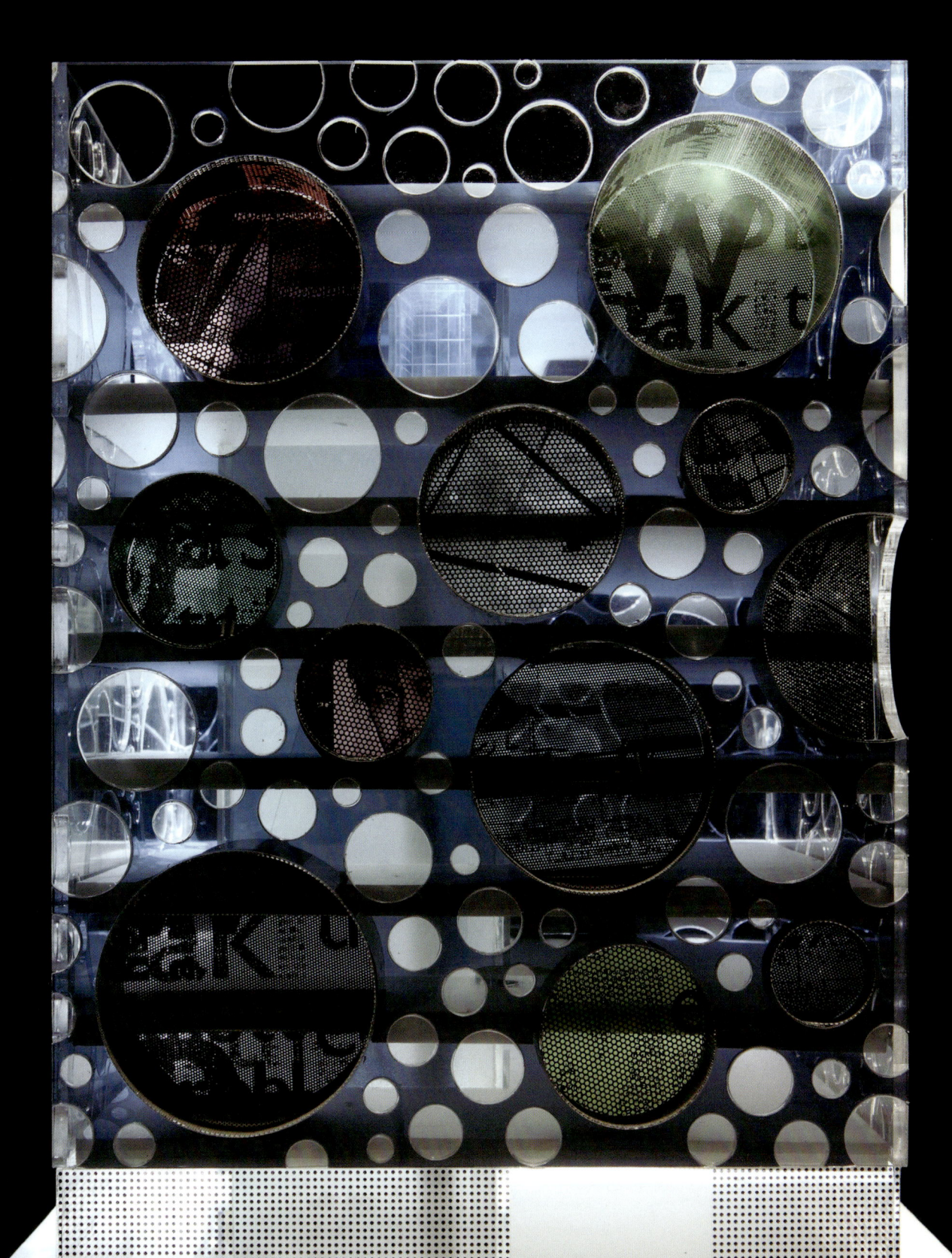

Architects Jang Yoon Gyoo, Shin Chang Hoon
Photographer Kim Jae Kyung

Location
968-3, Daechi-dong, Gangnam, Seoul, Korea
Use Temporary building(Model house)
Site area 4,110.9㎡
Building area 3,153.58㎡
Gross floor area 7,144.53㎡
Building coverage 76.71%
Floor space index 173.06%
Building scope 3F
Structure Steel
Design period 2007. 5 ~ 2008. 7
Exterior finishing
Stainless steel (PT), Pared glass, LED
Interior finishing
Paint, Laminates, Plywood & gypsum board, Barrisol, LED

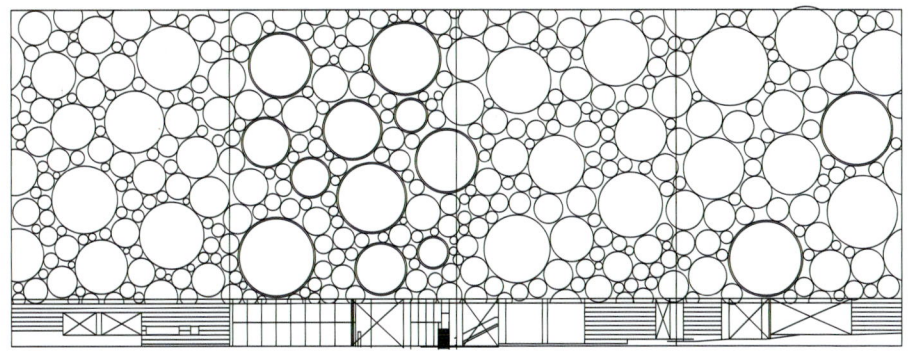

BRAND SPACE

Brand
The head office must accomplish enough for publicity of the enterprise and a role with office. Specially to be recognized the brand image of the enterprise which is evervill to the consuming public can decide directly role as future of the enterprise.
This head office building will be settled down with the brand icon which substitute for evervill from in the city.

Eco Office
There constructs office space of evervill for work, relaxation, and recharging at the boundary. In this way fabricated skin will provided the space of various program which is evaded from office facility. The program of echo office space came to be planned for conference room, consultation room, rest room, public information room, executive room, and private affair room centering around the office program by the selection of the different materials. It to be formed the icon of the program which is discriminated outside and inside.

Compound Frame
The element of outside skin constructed in simple one circular proto-type. Although these elements are created by the compound frame which is fundamental tool to make skin. Also outside skin related with the inside and it constructs inside space from compound frame inside. Compound frame of evervill will be taken another look with new city icon in the urban center.

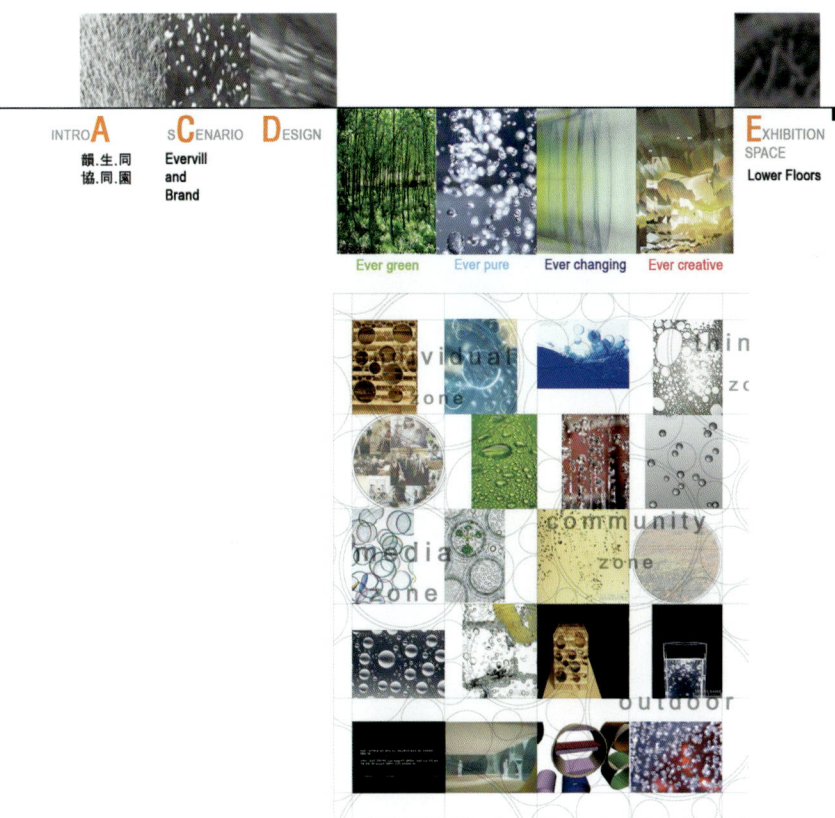

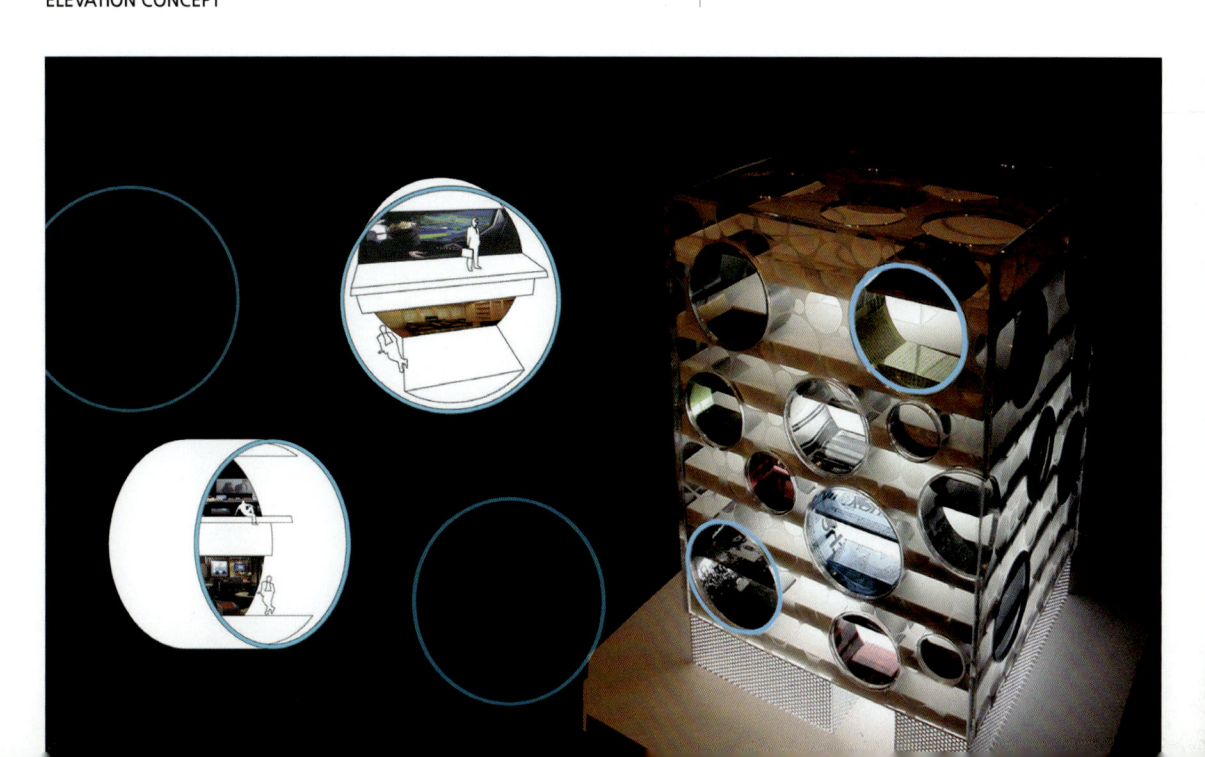

ELEVATION

ELEVATION CONCEPT

Campus Complex
in University of Seoul

Competition Winner
Architecture Award of Seoul Metropolitan City
Award of Korean Architecture & Culture

Architects Jang Yoon Gyoo, Shin Chang Hoon + Kim Woo Il
Client University of Seoul
Photographer Kim Jong Oh

COMPOUND BODY 507

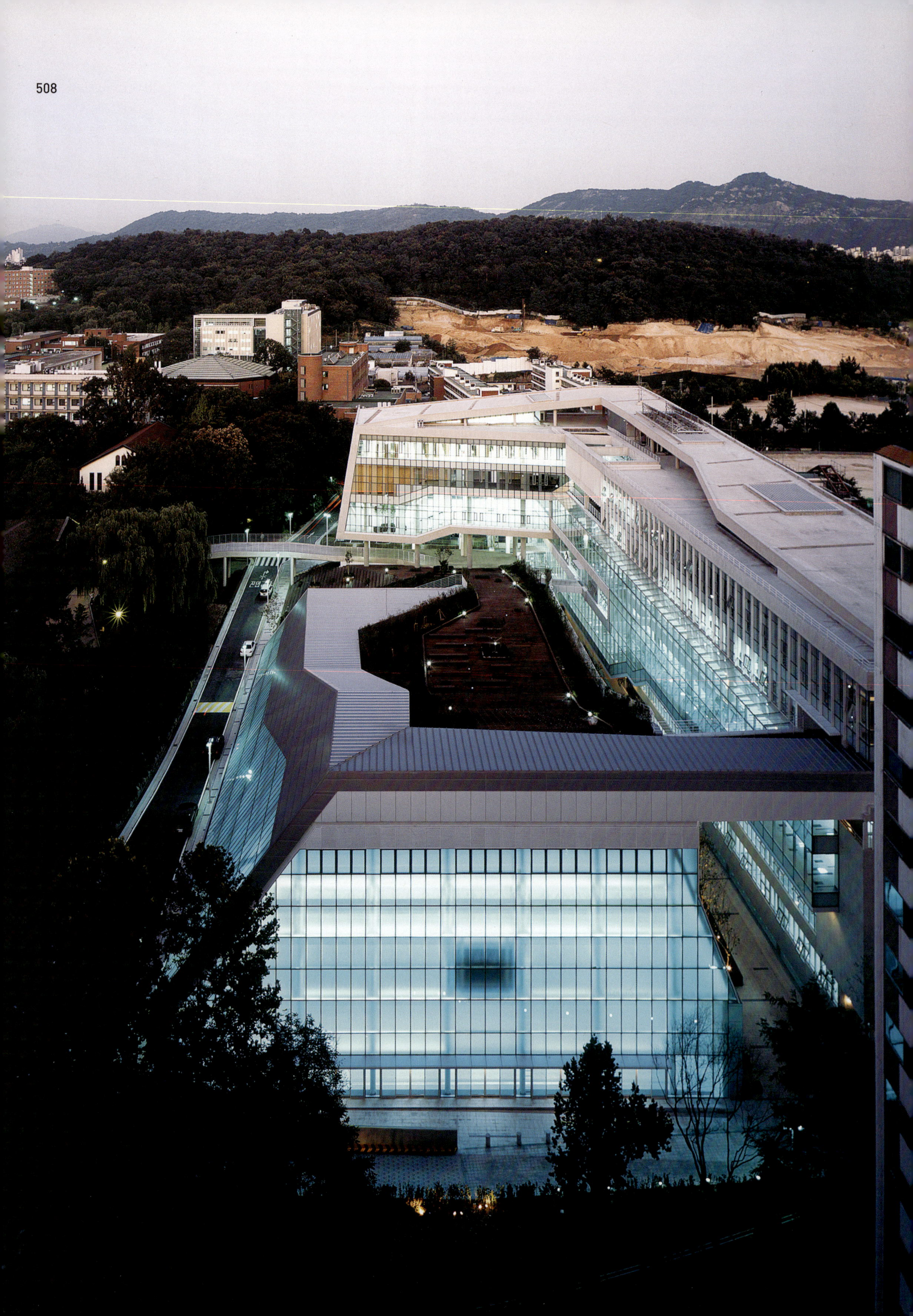

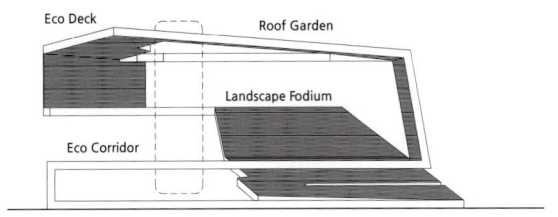

COMPOUND LANDSCAPE

The campus is composed of a great network of various programs, investigation, education, life, etc. The campus network (Landscape Plaza) is one frame that provides the space for a school facility and circumferential social event, as well as public space.

A given full site analyzes the Plaza as Public Space, with a plaza of multi-purpose skill toward the entrance-moving line and Youngnong-hall can be accepted as an idea of Universal Design for the activity of university students and the event of local residents. From the landscape plaze across the site, linear mass spare part of space to lecture and research. Then the lower part of the plaza provide space for gymnasium with eco landscape.
The Plaza as Public Space is actualized with ⟨Event Plaza⟩, ⟨Landscape Podium⟩, ⟨Eco Corridor⟩, ⟨Eco Valley⟩, and so on.

Event Stage -
Square as a event stage
The Plaza as Public Space through Campus mopology which is set accommodates the event which is various with the stage which comes to be opened proposed in same space. We suggest a three-dimensional plaza with unification of building elevation and floor, not a simple flat plaza. The wide deck open space would be located on gymnasium top and main lecture hall with the stage, which is wide glass facade wh located before that is set as the huge stage. The deck plaza is only an place of horizontal stage can be meet the people using other program each other and vertical stage can be see an act each other through the wide glass. A personal act is very private, but they are a hero or heroine as holding a vision each other in common.

Landscape Podium
we composed the plaza as a continuity of site. So we suggest a Landscape Podium connected with all direction. We composes campus plaza which is appropriate slope to connect vertical moving line and accommodate event.
The landscape podium becomes huge rest area which to offer nature, light, natural materials of flooring, water and so on. The upside podium which shape similar with site will disperse moving line and use for new main square of many students (over 1500 students) by acculturation of plaza and rest space. The podium and Atrium provide the scenery and sight through this we can get scenery frame which can make event from ordinary.

Eco Corridor
Eco vertical flow Connection system
We compose the eco-corridor which to offer at once efficient connection of whole moving line and eco rest area. The eco corridor is a system of vertical- moving line that be combined with landscape podium. Also it can be an environmental eco atrium of main lecture hall. Students can enjoy events and take a rest for studying within the environmental vertical-moving line system.

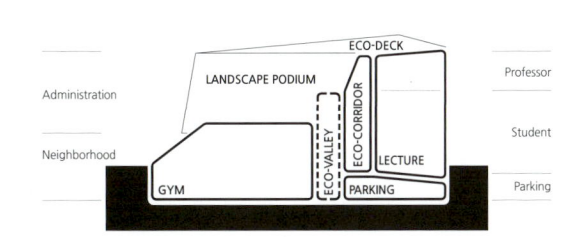

CAMPUS MARSTER PLAN

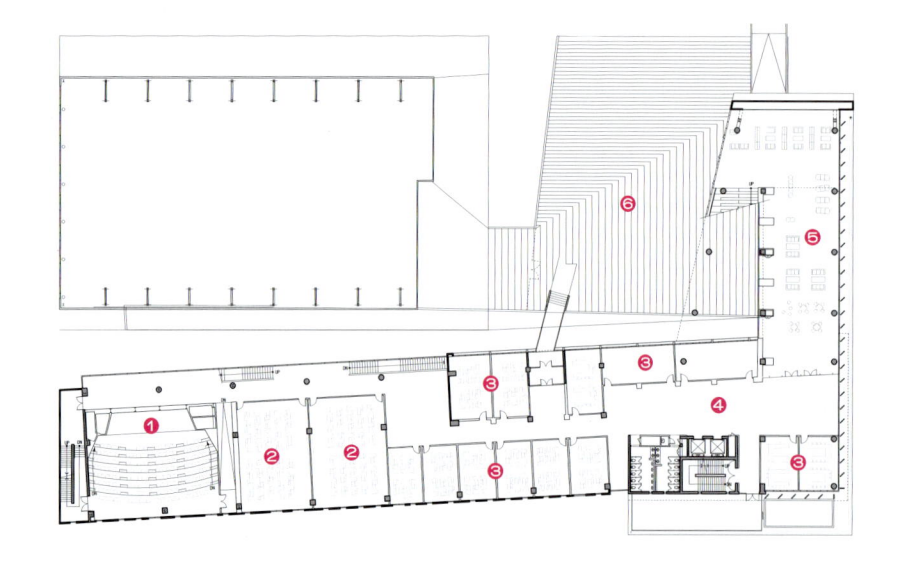

3RD FLOOR PLAN

1. Large-Lecture Room
2. Midium-Lecture Room
3. Small-Lecture Room
4. Hall
5. Students Lounge
6. Deck

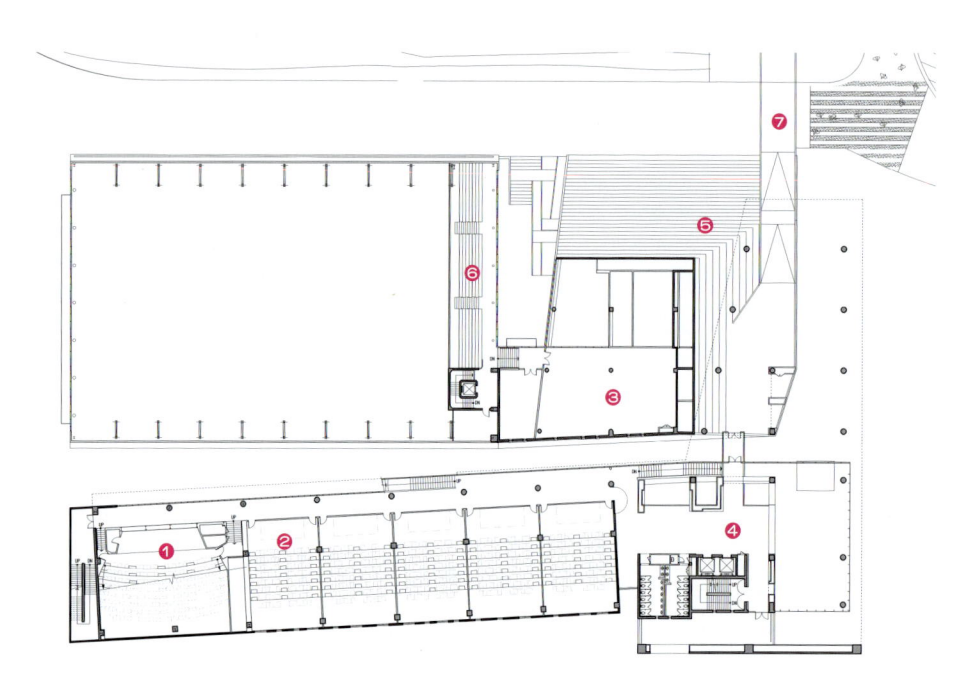

2ND FLOOR PLAN

1. Large-Lecture Room
2. Midium-Lecture Room
3. Multi Purpose Room
4. Hall
5. Deck
6. Seat
7. Bridge

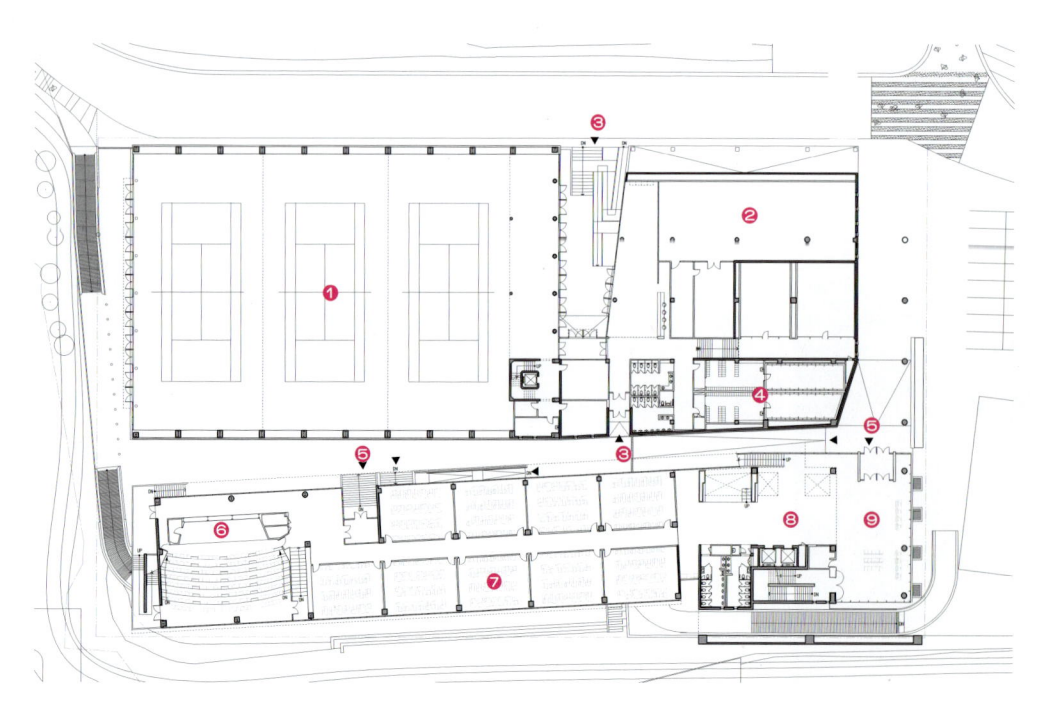

GROUND FLOOR PLAN

1. Indoor Tennis Court
2. Fitness Room
3. Gymnasium Entrance
4. Locker Room
5. Lecter Part Entrance
6. Large-Lecture Room
7. Small-Lecture Room
8. Hall
9. Lobby

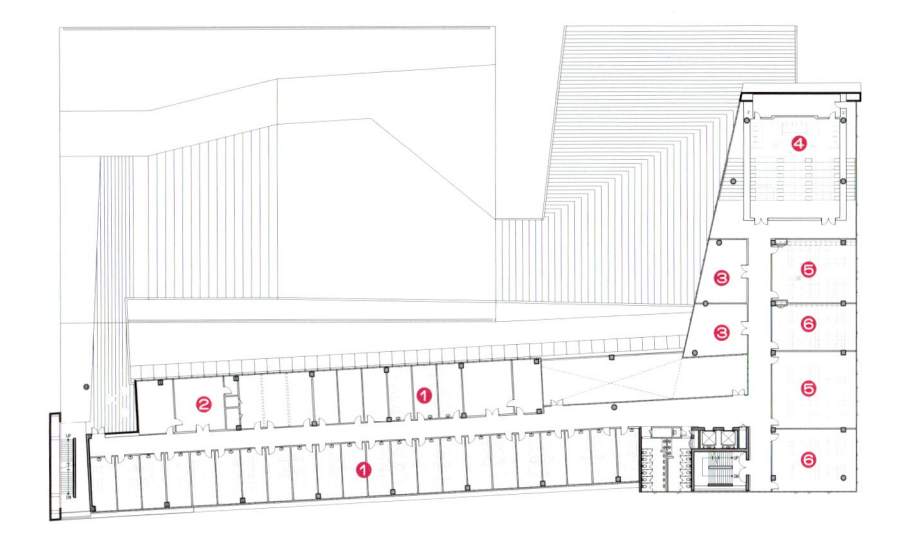

5TH FLOOR PLAN

1. Professor Room
2. Office
3. Seminar Room
4. Moot Court
5. Midium-Lecture Room
6. Small-Lecture Room

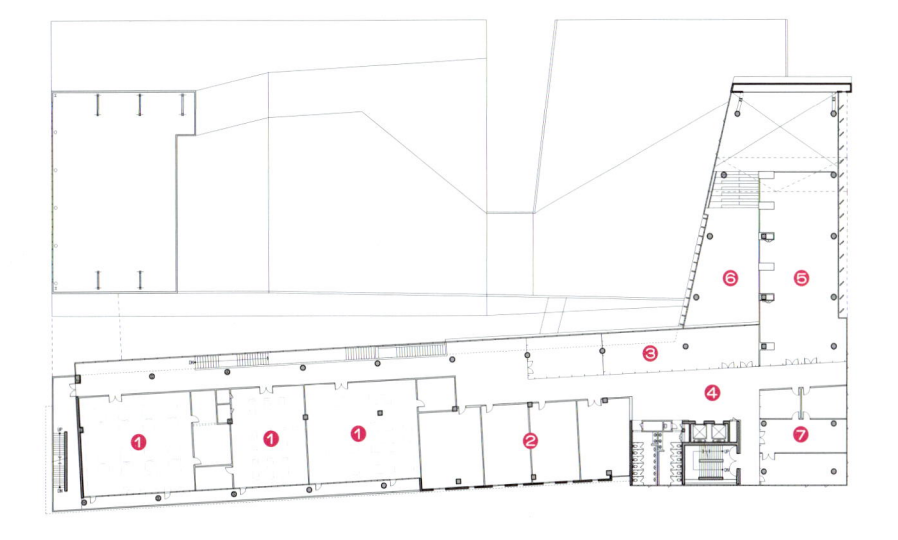

4TH FLOOR PLAN

1. Experiment Room
2. Research Room
3. Seminar Room
4. Hall
5. Law Lounge
6. Students Lounge
7. Chief Room

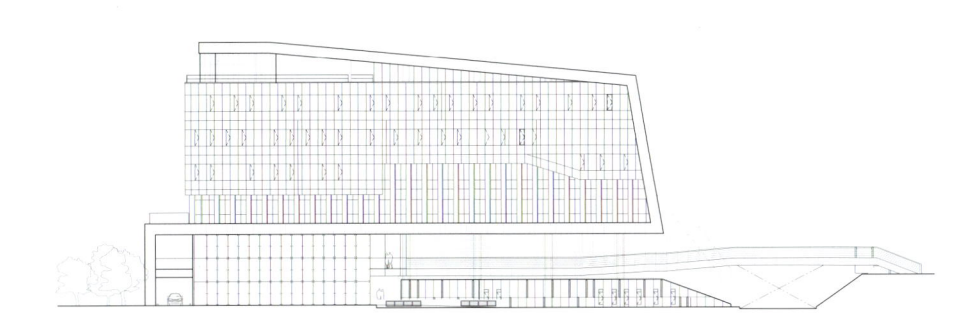

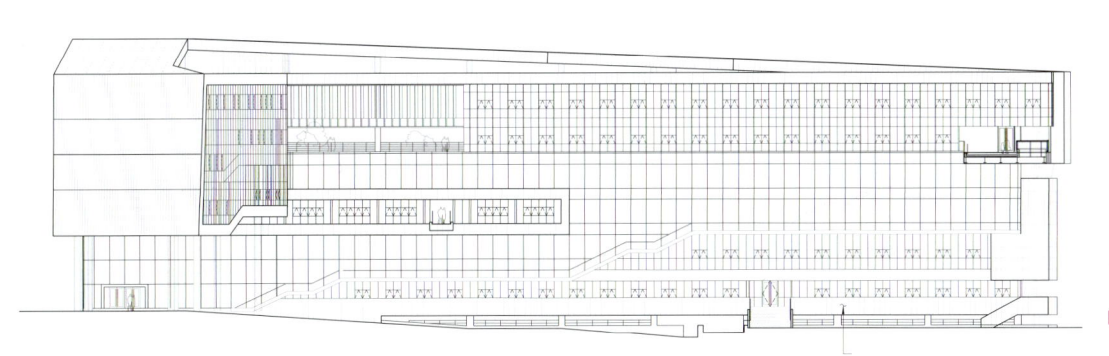

ELEVATION

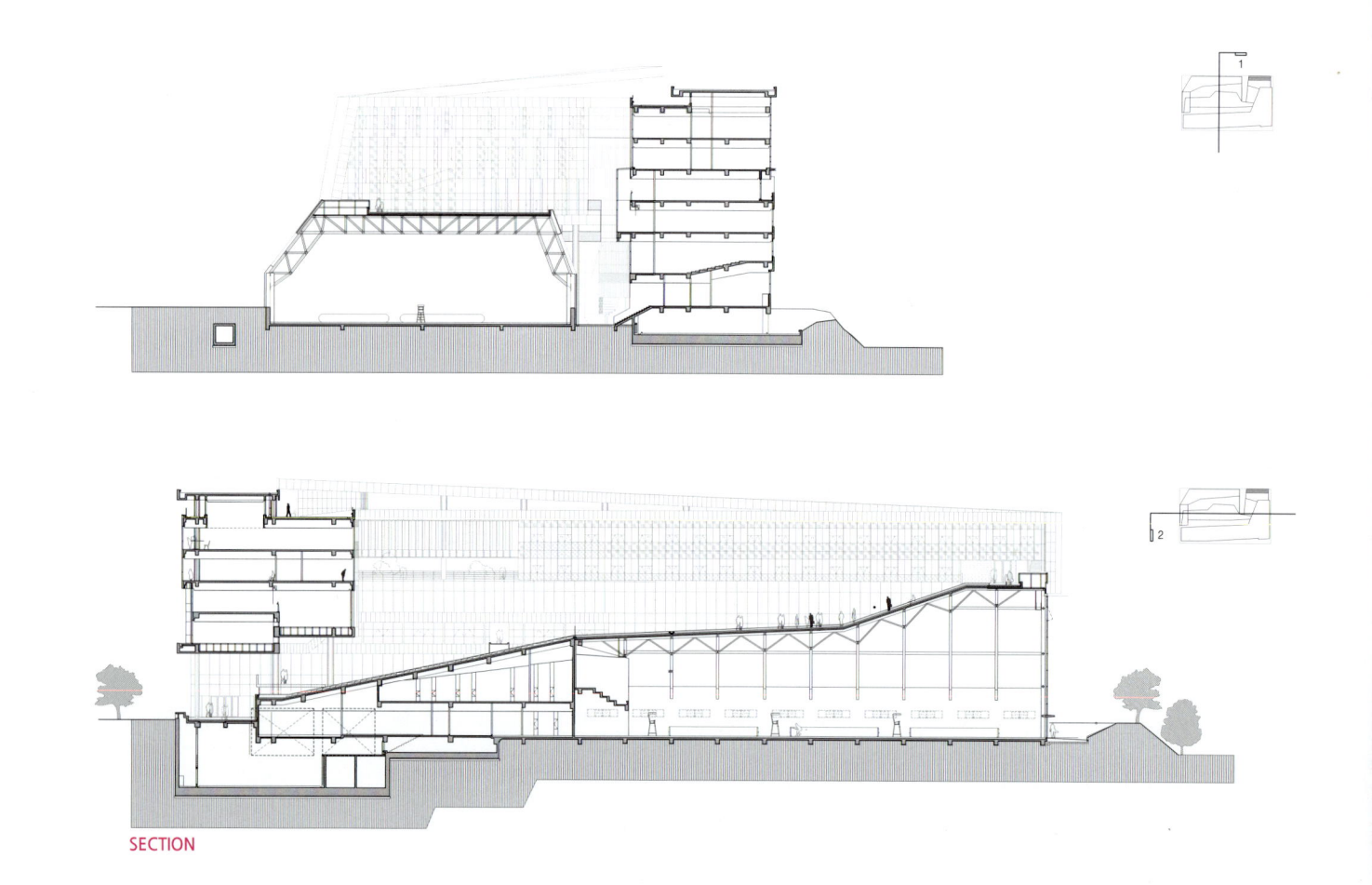

SECTION

SITE PLAN

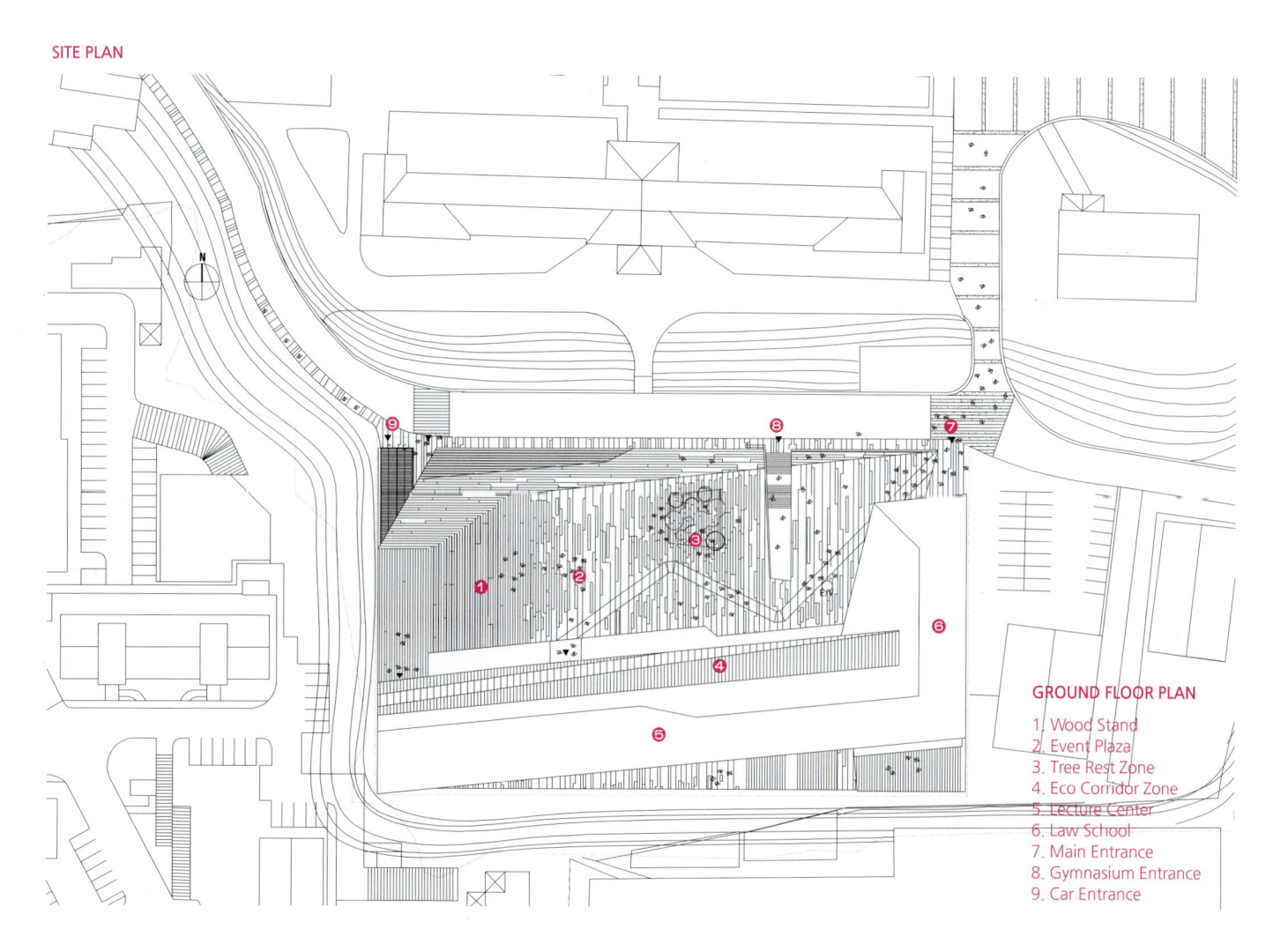

GROUND FLOOR PLAN

1. Wood Stand
2. Event Plaza
3. Tree Rest Zone
4. Eco Corridor Zone
5. Lecture Center
6. Law School
7. Main Entrance
8. Gymnasium Entrance
9. Car Entrance

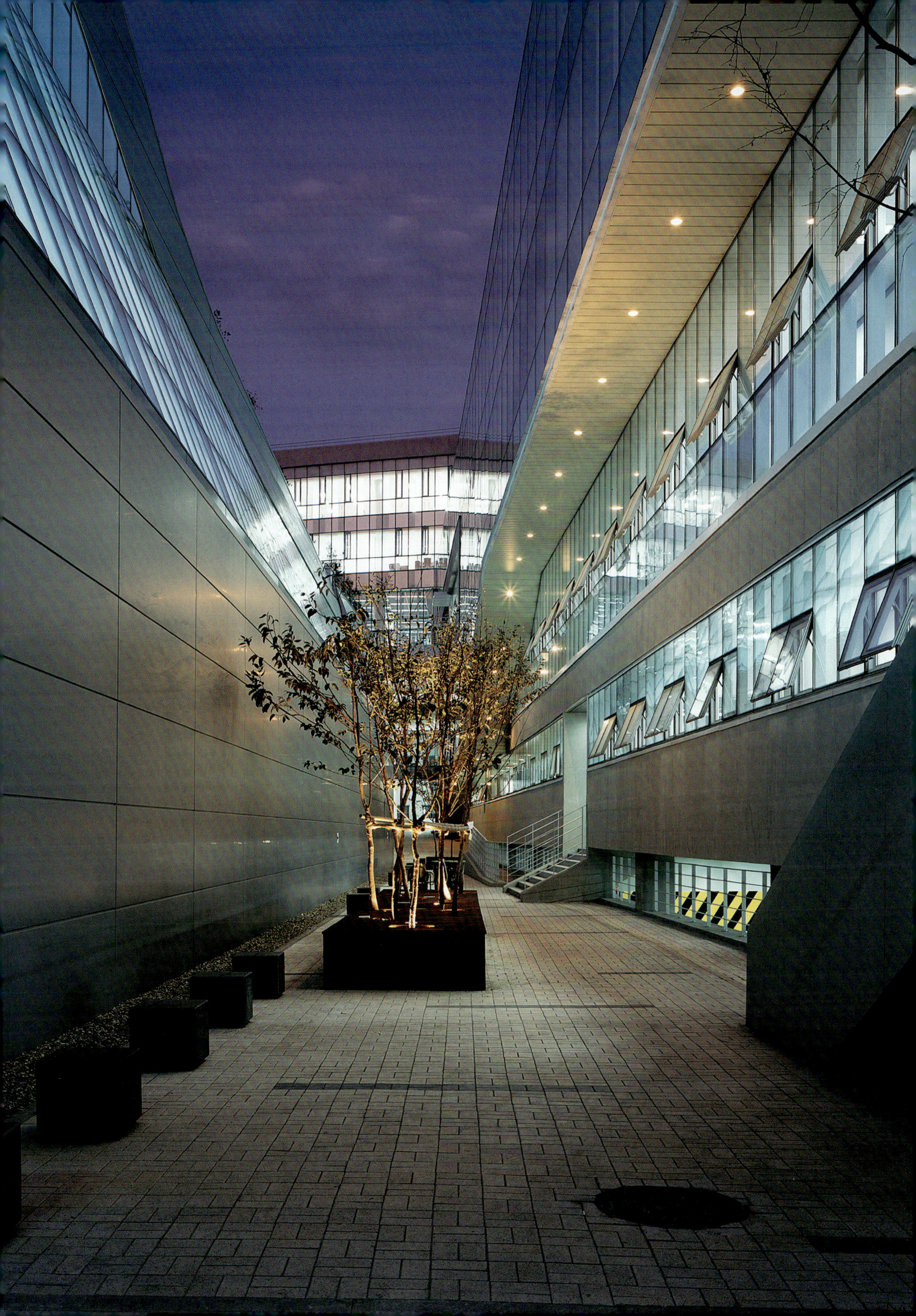

Project Name
Main lecture Hall at University of Seoul,
Scool of law building, Indoor tennis courts
Design
Jang Yoon Gyoo, Shin Chang Hoon + Kim Woo Il
Design Team
Jung Won Jin, Park Mi Jin, Kim Woo Young, Kim Youn Soo, Kim Sung Min, Kim Dong Chan, Yi Ho Sun
Location
90 Junnong-dong, University of Seoul, Seoul
District
1st General Residential Area, Natural Scenery District
Use
Education, Complx, Gymnasium
Site Area 270,600m² (7,603m²)
Building Area 6,071.49m²
Total Floor Area 18,763.97m²
Building Scope B2, 5F
Structure RC, Steel structure
Exterior Finishing
T24 Duble Glazing, Appointed wod panel Exposed Concrete
Interior Finishing
Exposed Concrete, Punching Metal, Sound absorbing wooden panel
Client University of Seoul

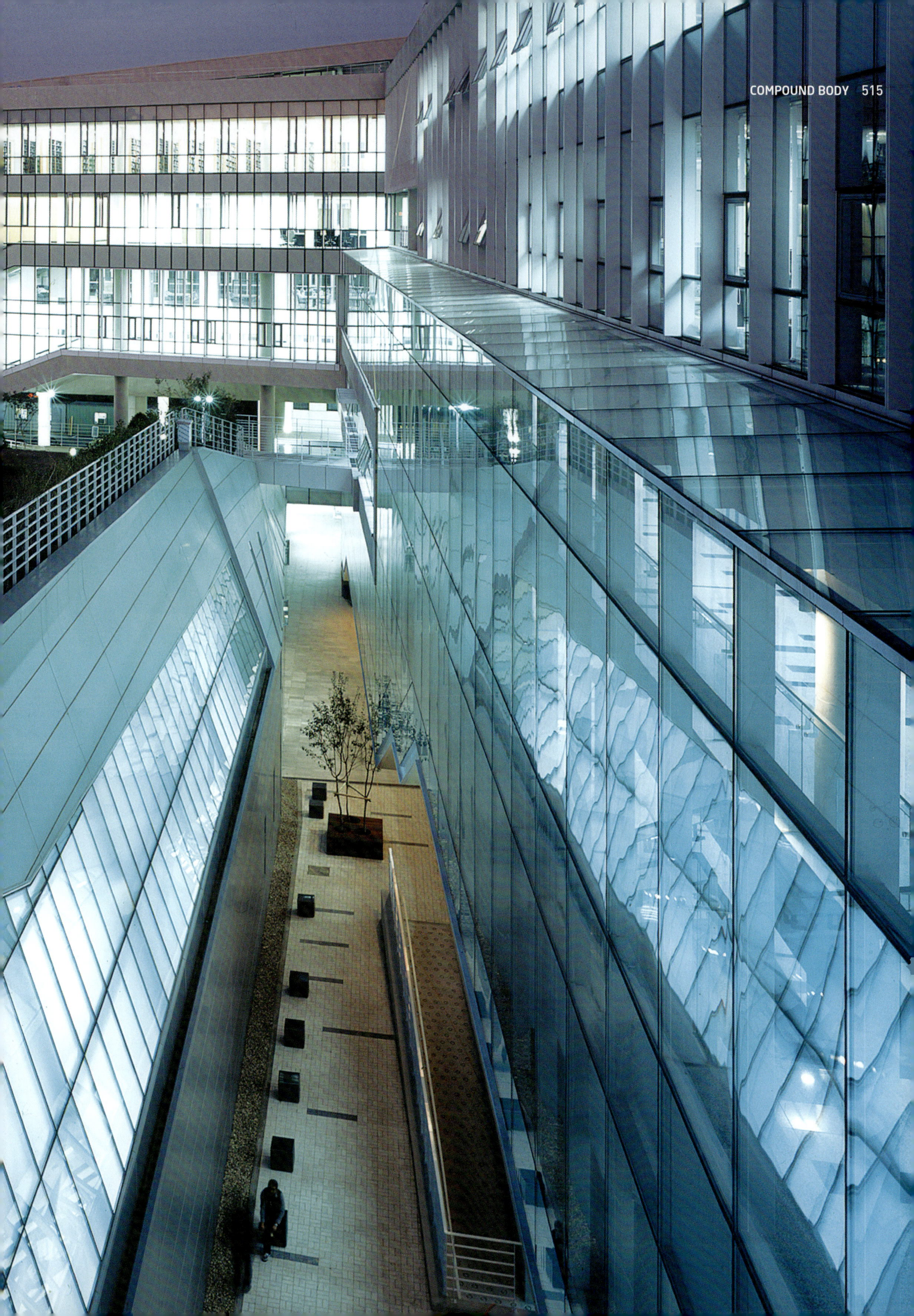

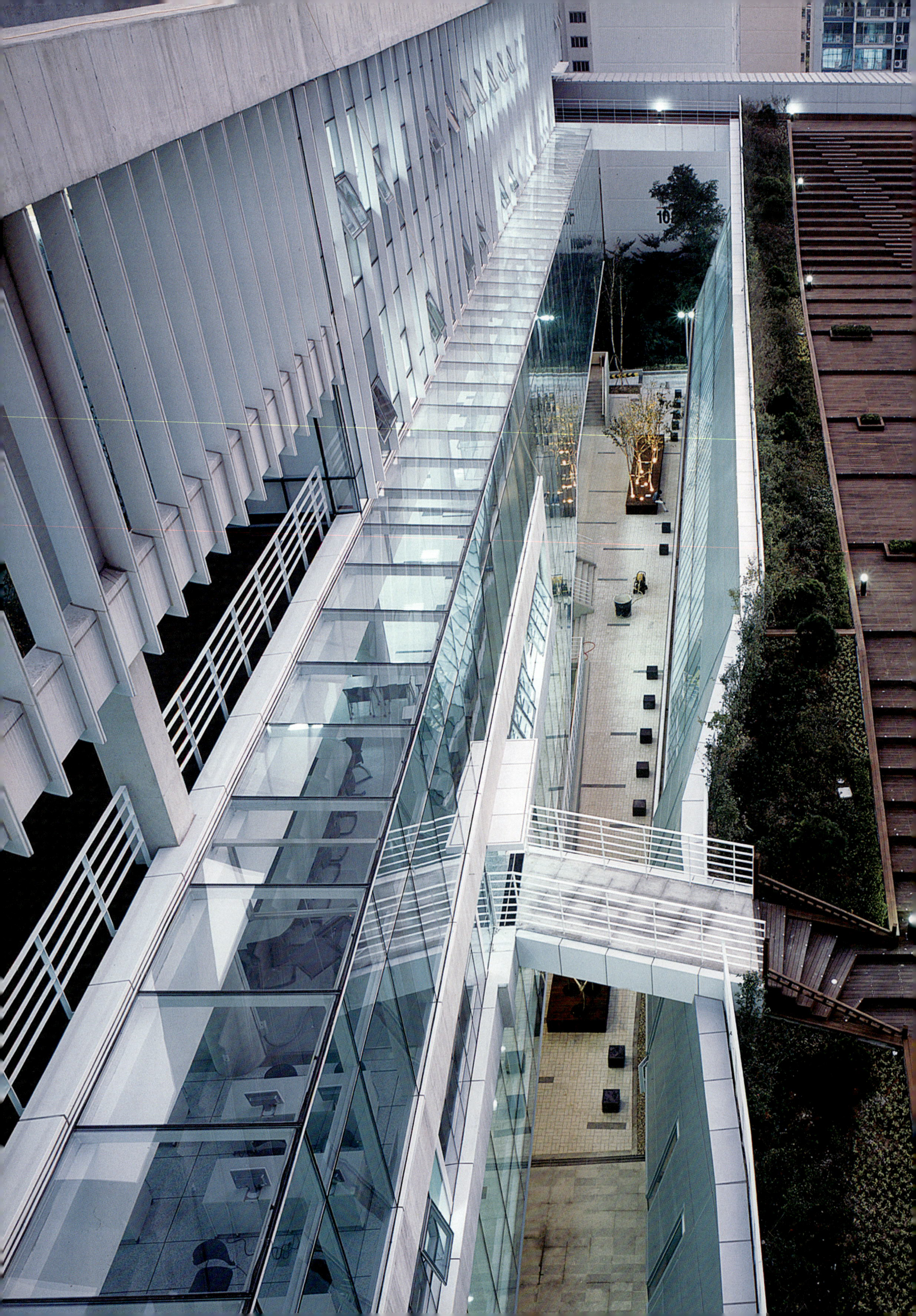

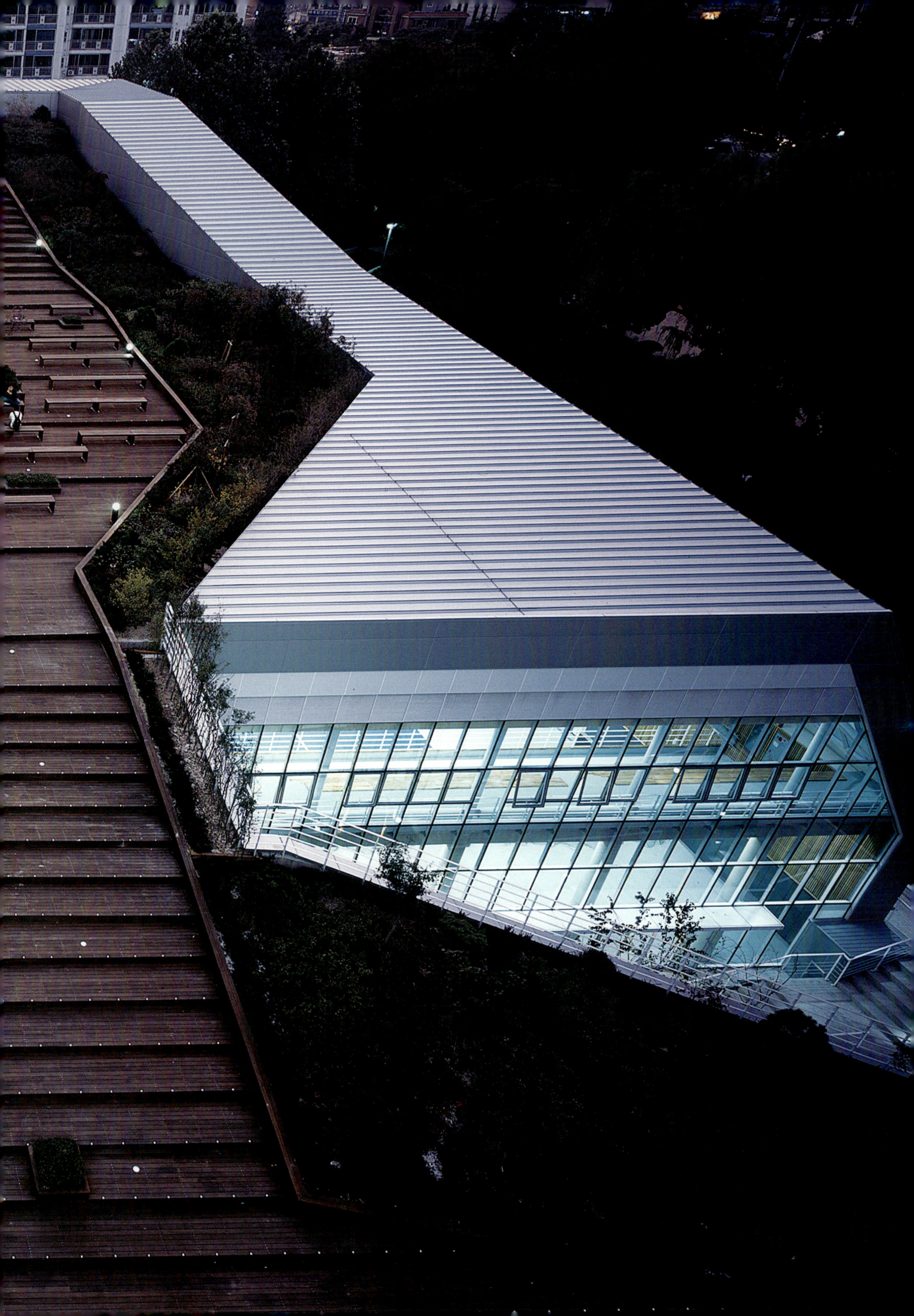

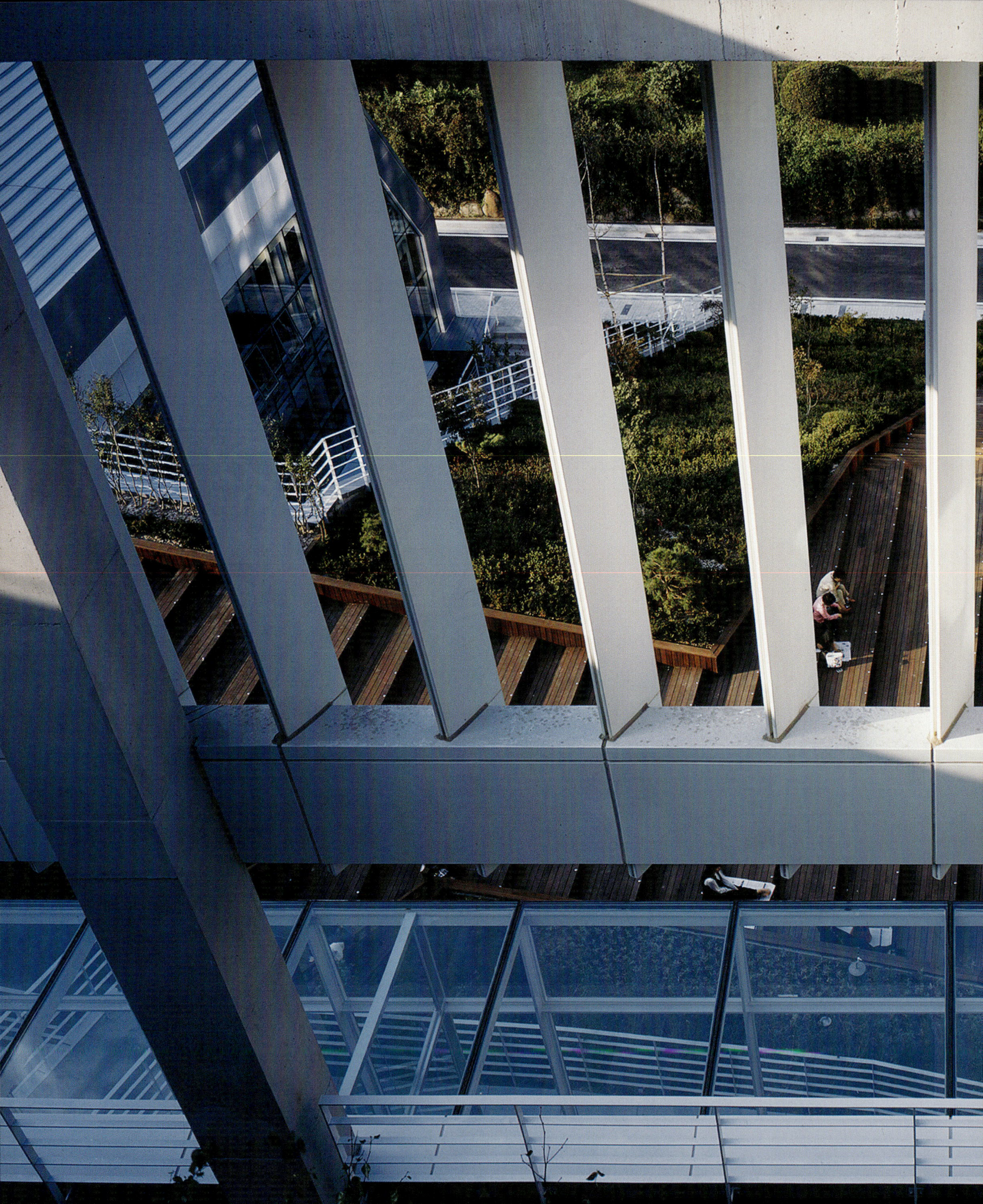

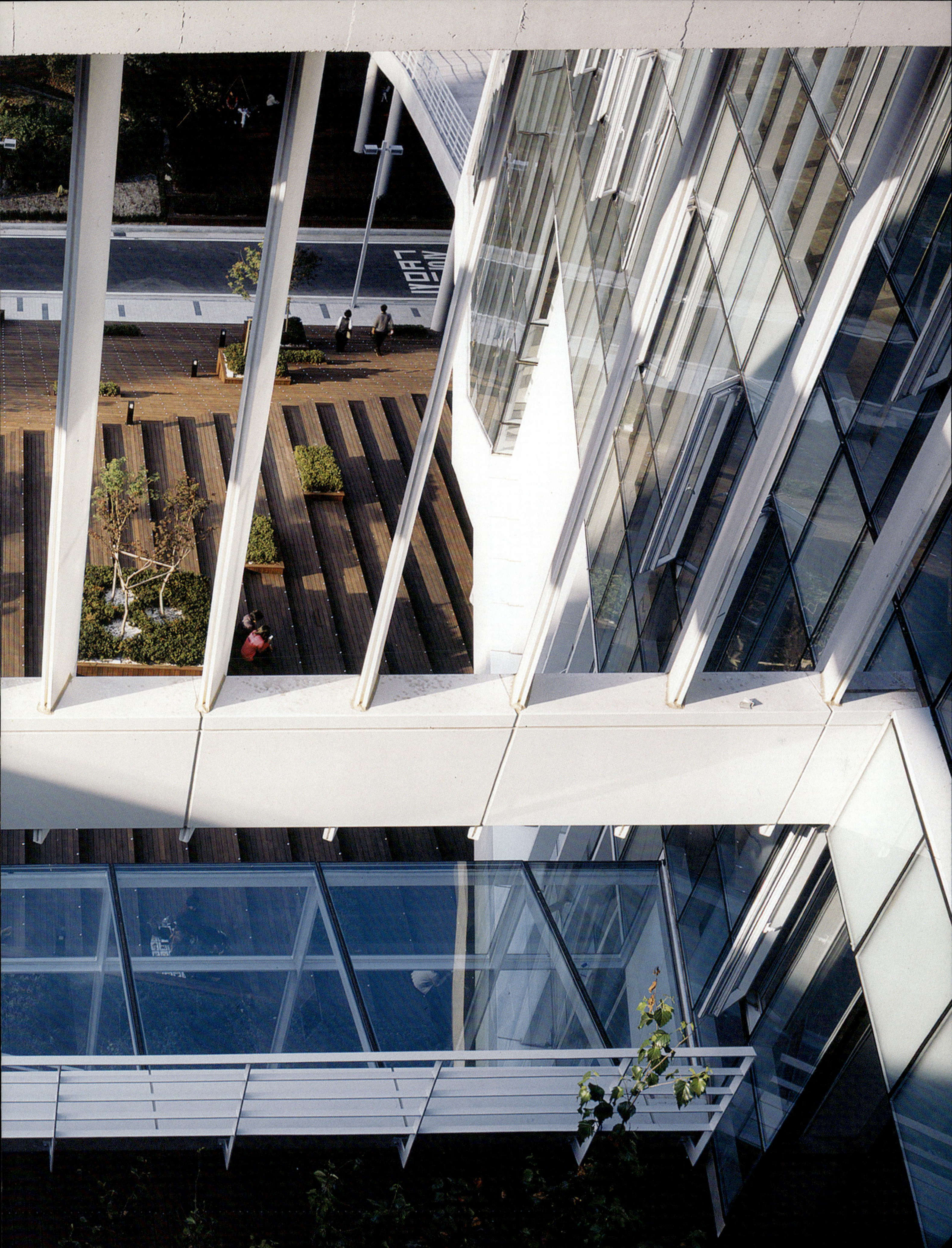

School of Architecture
in Seoul National University

Competition Winner
Architecture Award of Seoul Metropolitan City

Architects Jang Yoon Gyoo + JungLim Architects
Client Seoul National University
Photographer Kim Yong Kwan

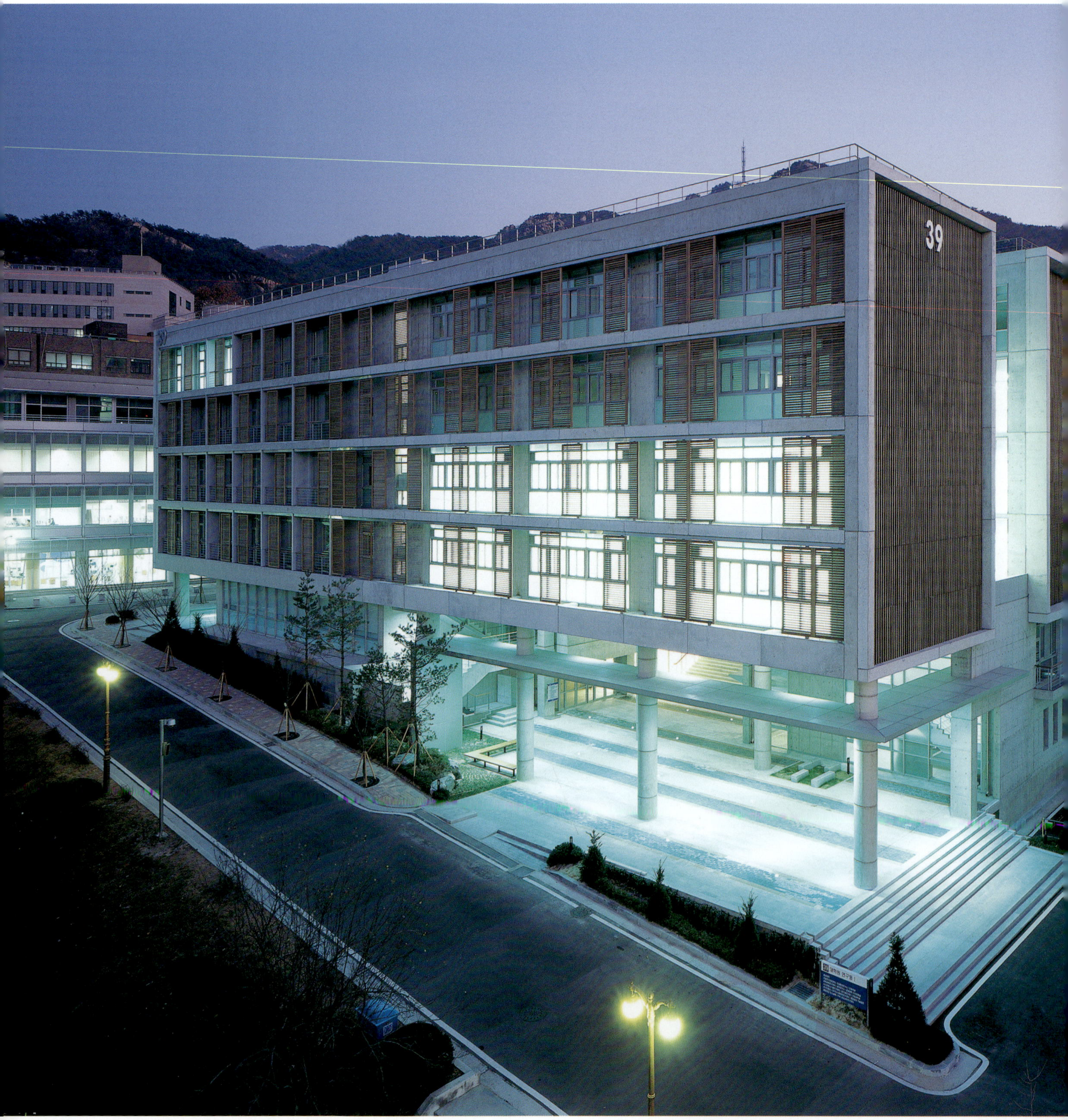
39

RESEARCH SCAPE

We adopt 'Landscape Podium' as a concept which procures whole property of architectural school at Seoul University. Nature connection is materialized accessing and connecting to the site from all direction. Existing experiment building was removed and nature which Gwanak originally has is revived. Also it is environmental code penetrating lower part for experiment and car park and upper linear mass for studying. This code consisting natural code links to required program from engineering school such as resting, cafeteria, lobby and physical fitness composes the open site. Landscape podium is not a single level structure. It composed stereo bate shape skin along the sloping site so that create 3 dimensional nature. Space for studying is base on rationality achieving environmental code. Above the landscape podium, 4 linear masses for studying are set. To achieve natural maximization, we suggest outdoor space combined with courtyard and linear exterior space. It comprises outdoor space with transformed linear studying mass. Maximum outdoor skin area and one-side-aisle system inside of the building fulfill general environmental code like natural light, ventilation and view. Linear mass makes systemic studying space based upon flexibility and changeability as premise.

This complex stands on an inclined site, linking the separate spaces through the landscape podium (the plaza) that lies along the length of the terrain. The masses of the four buildings as if floating over the pilotis are integrated actually by the underlying landscape podium. The event courtyards actively linked with the interior spaces are dispersed here and there for rest and chat, supporting and enriching the everyday activities of the students. New spaces with multiple purposes will be created by the students including the Media Garden for intellectual exchange, the Play Garden for maximizing the recess experiences in connection with the school store and the Gallery Garden for cultural experiences. In close connection with the spacious hallway which will host exhibitions and presentations by the students, these gardens propose a new type of public spaces. The design proposes a public place where diverse campus activities- exhibitions, performances, recesses, group other to encourage each other's growth.

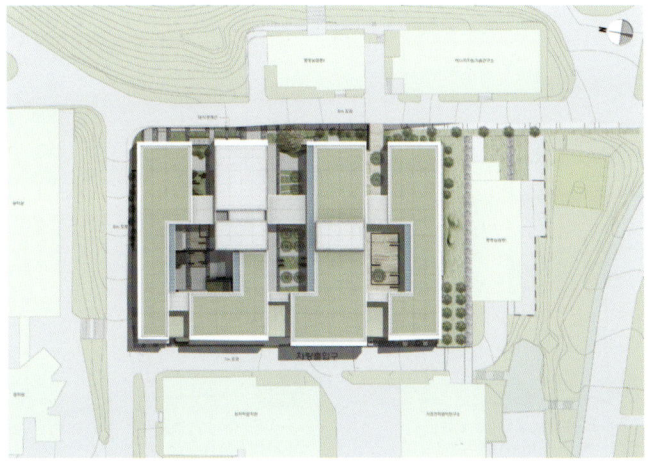

SITEPLAN

NATURE

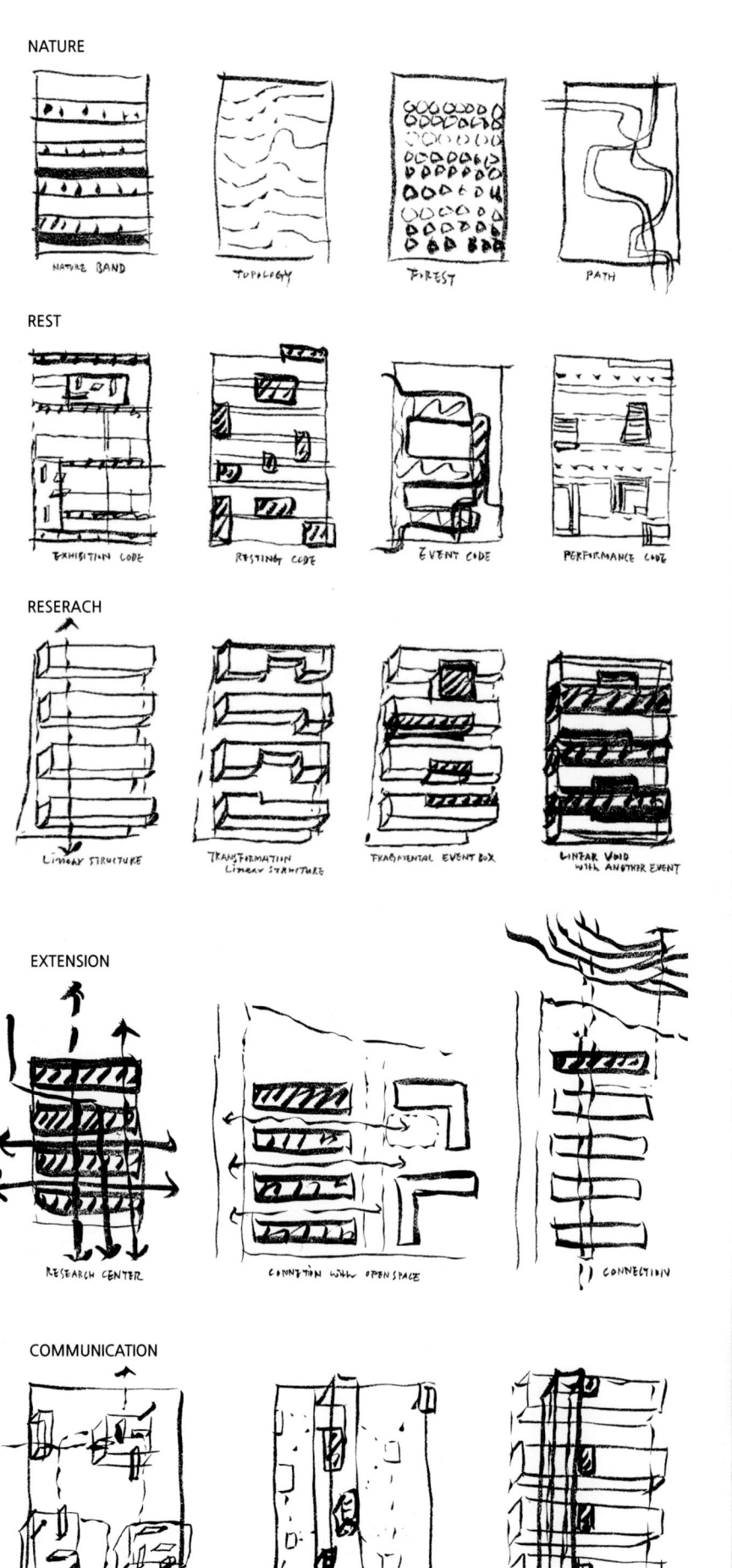

| NATURE BAND | TOPOLOGY | FOREST | PATH |

REST

| EXHIBITION CODE | RESTING CODE | EVENT CODE | PERFORMANCE CODE |

RESERACH

| LINEAR STRUCTURE | TRANSFORMATION LINEAR STRUCTURE | FRAGMENTAL EVENT BOX | LINEAR VOID WITH ANOTHER EVENT |

EXTENSION

| RESEARCH CENTER | CONNECTION WITH OPEN SPACE | CONNECTION |

COMMUNICATION

| EXTERIOR EXHIBITION | INTERIOR EVENT CODE with CIRCULATION | CIRCULATION SYSTEM EVENT CORRIDOR |

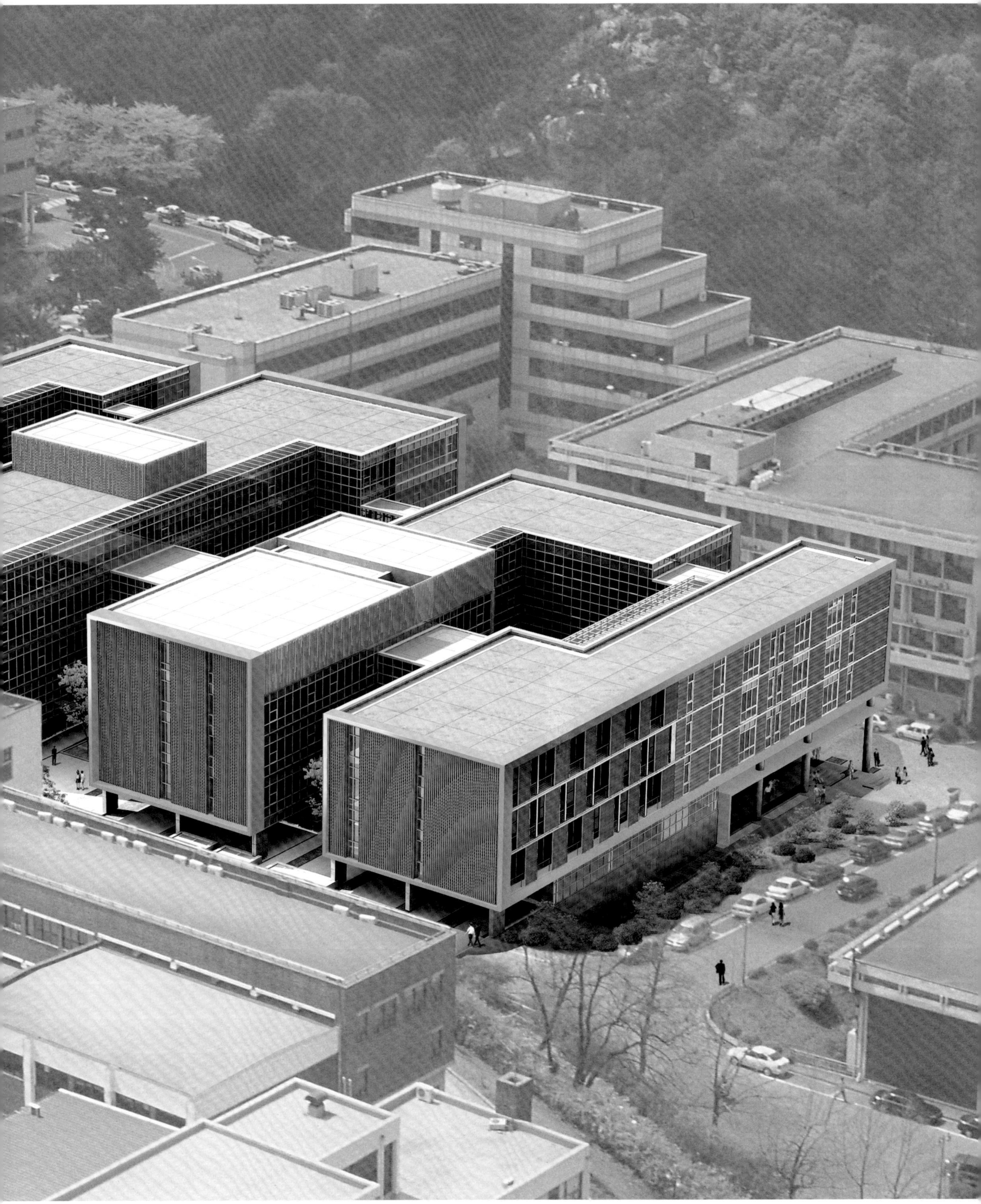

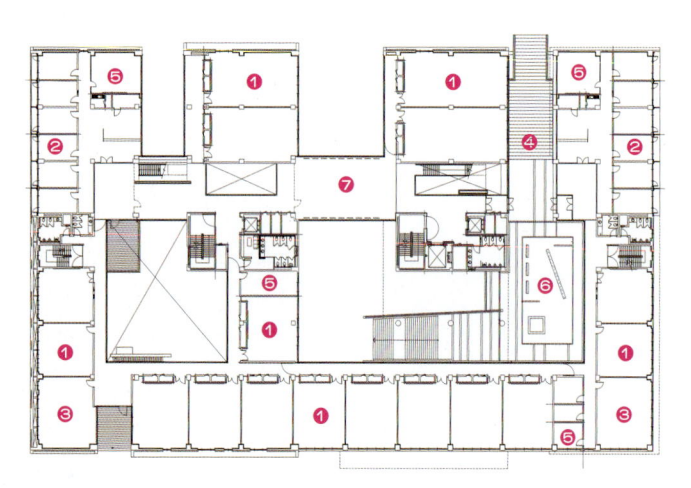

2ND FLOOR PLAN

1. Graduate Research Room
2. Professor Room
3. Seminar Room
4. Enterence
5. Rest Room
6. Gallery Garden
7. Multi Purpose Event Hall

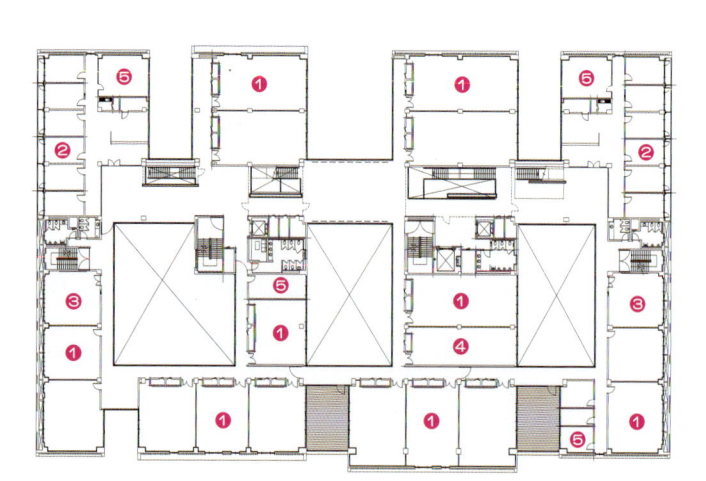

3RD FLOOR PLAN

1. Graduate Research Room
2. Professor Room
3. Seminar Room
4. Public Machinery and Tools
5. Rest Room

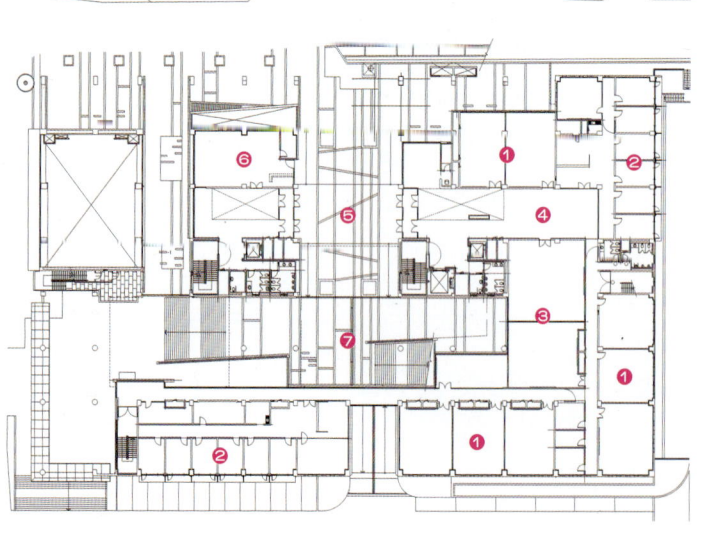

GROUND FLOOR PLAN

1. Graduate Research Room
2. Professor Room
3. Seminar Room
4. Lobby
5. Main Enterence
6. Store
7. Media Garden

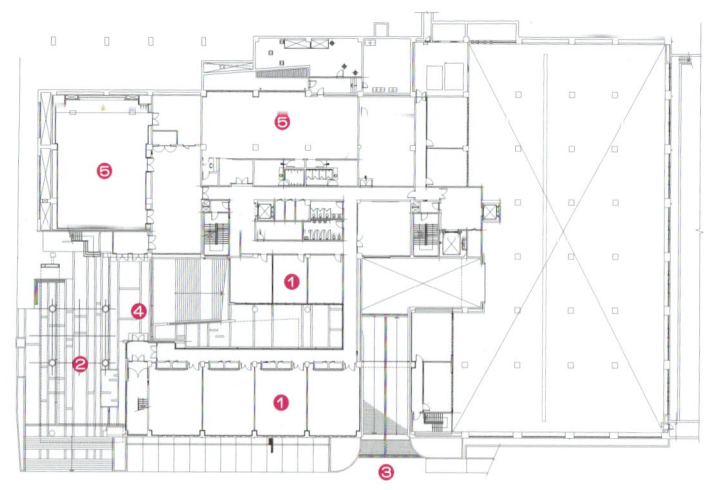

BASEMENT FLOOR PLAN

1. Graduate Research Room
2. Event Plaza
3. Car Enterence
4. Enterence
5. Seminar Hall

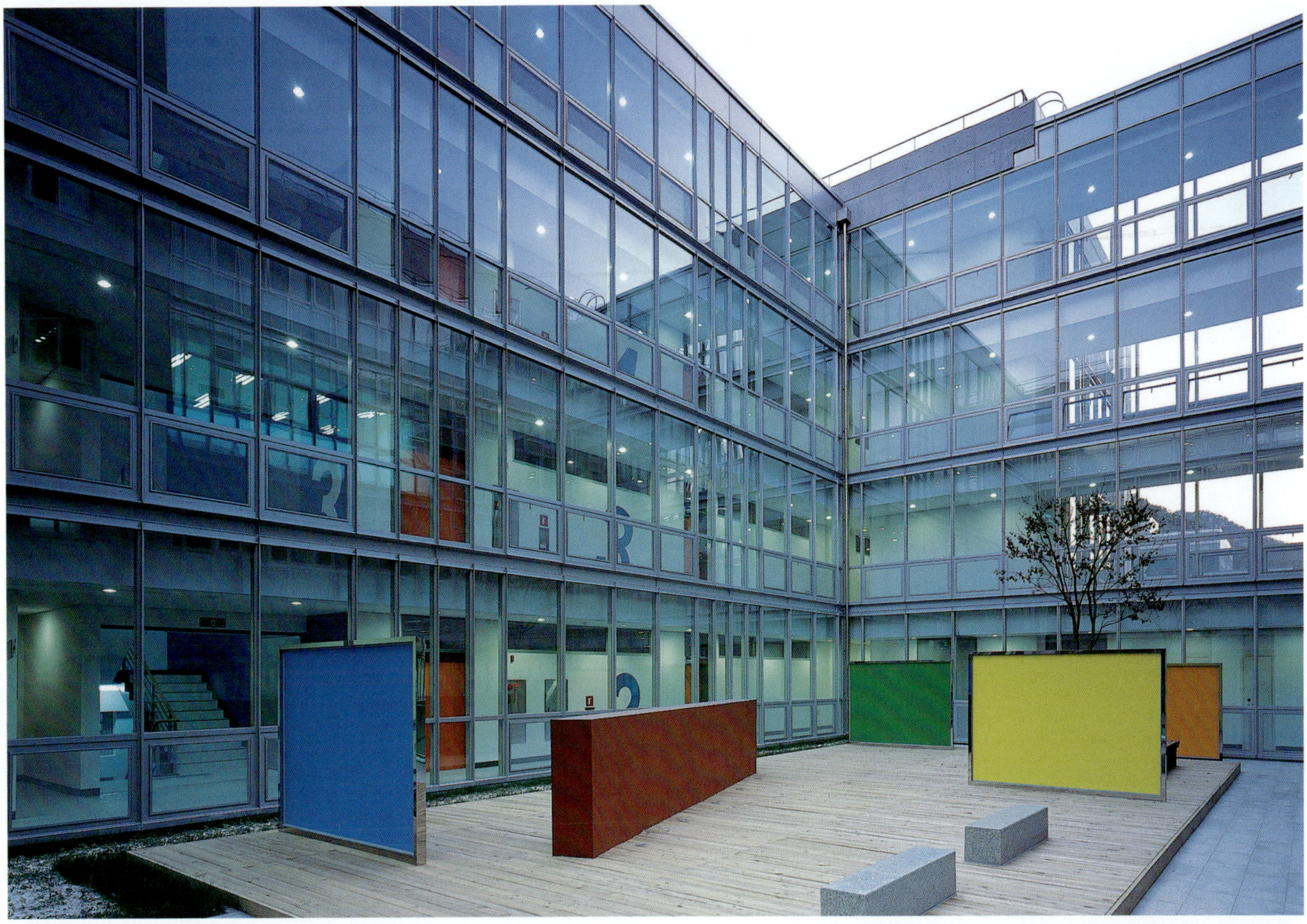

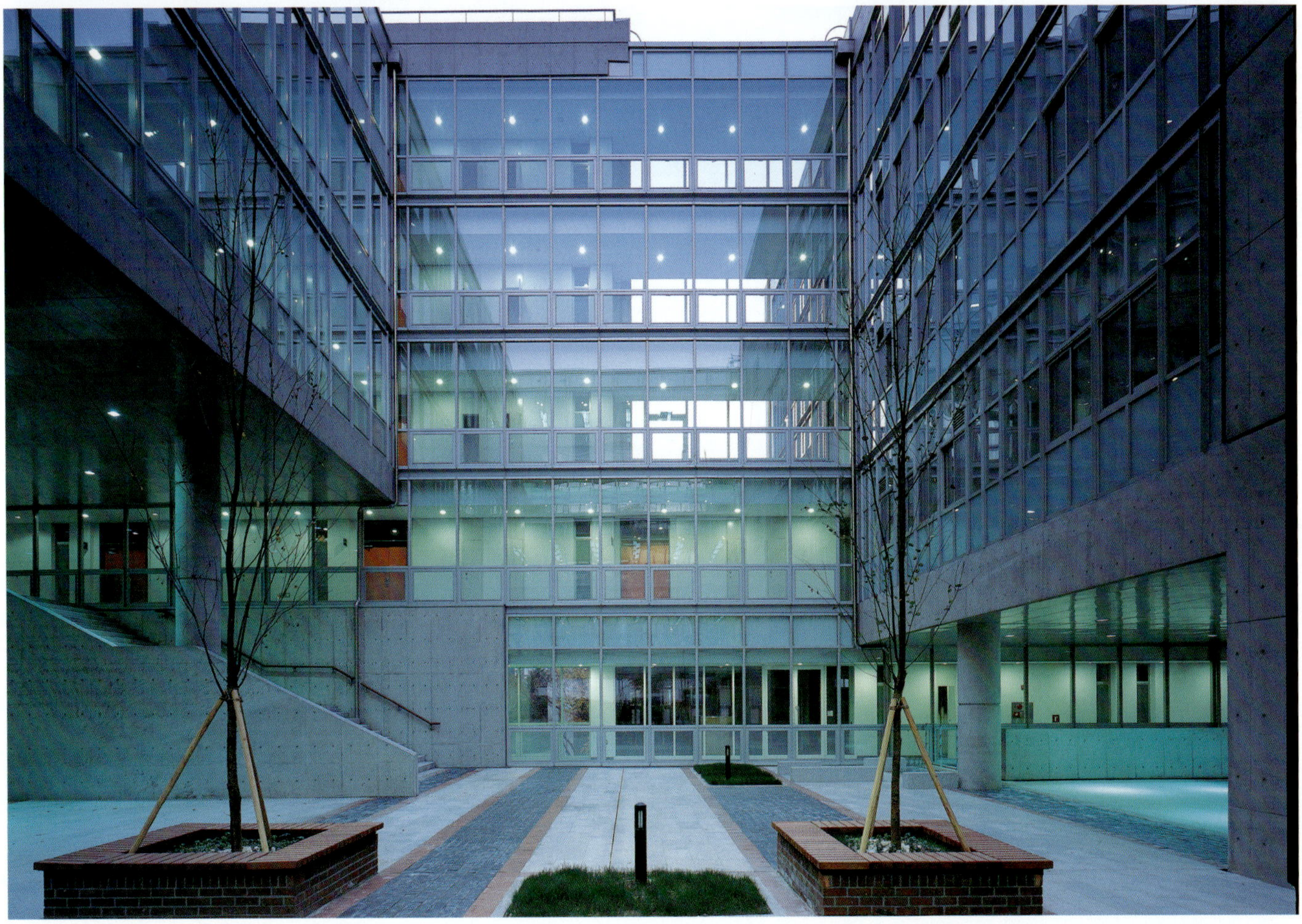

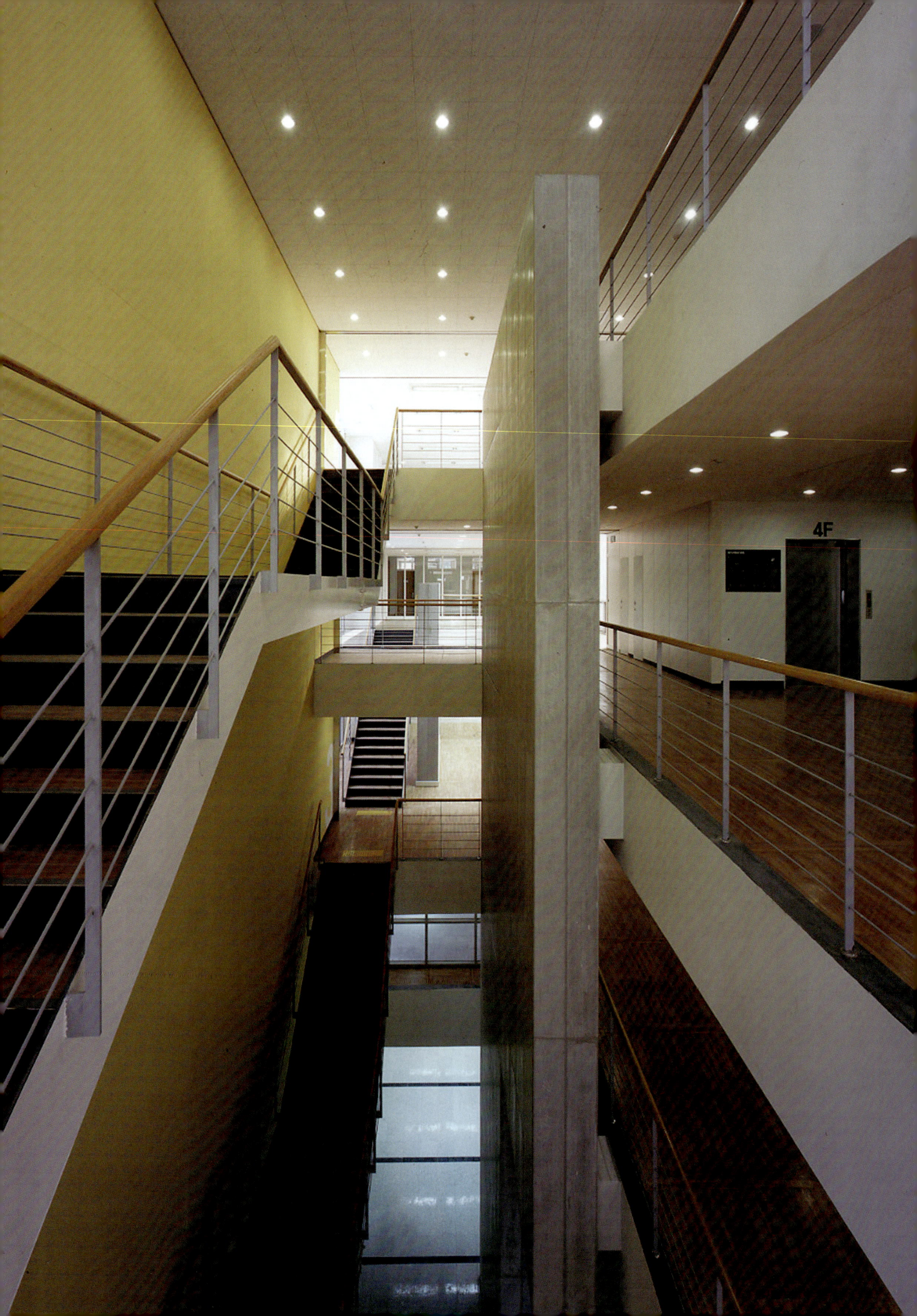
4F

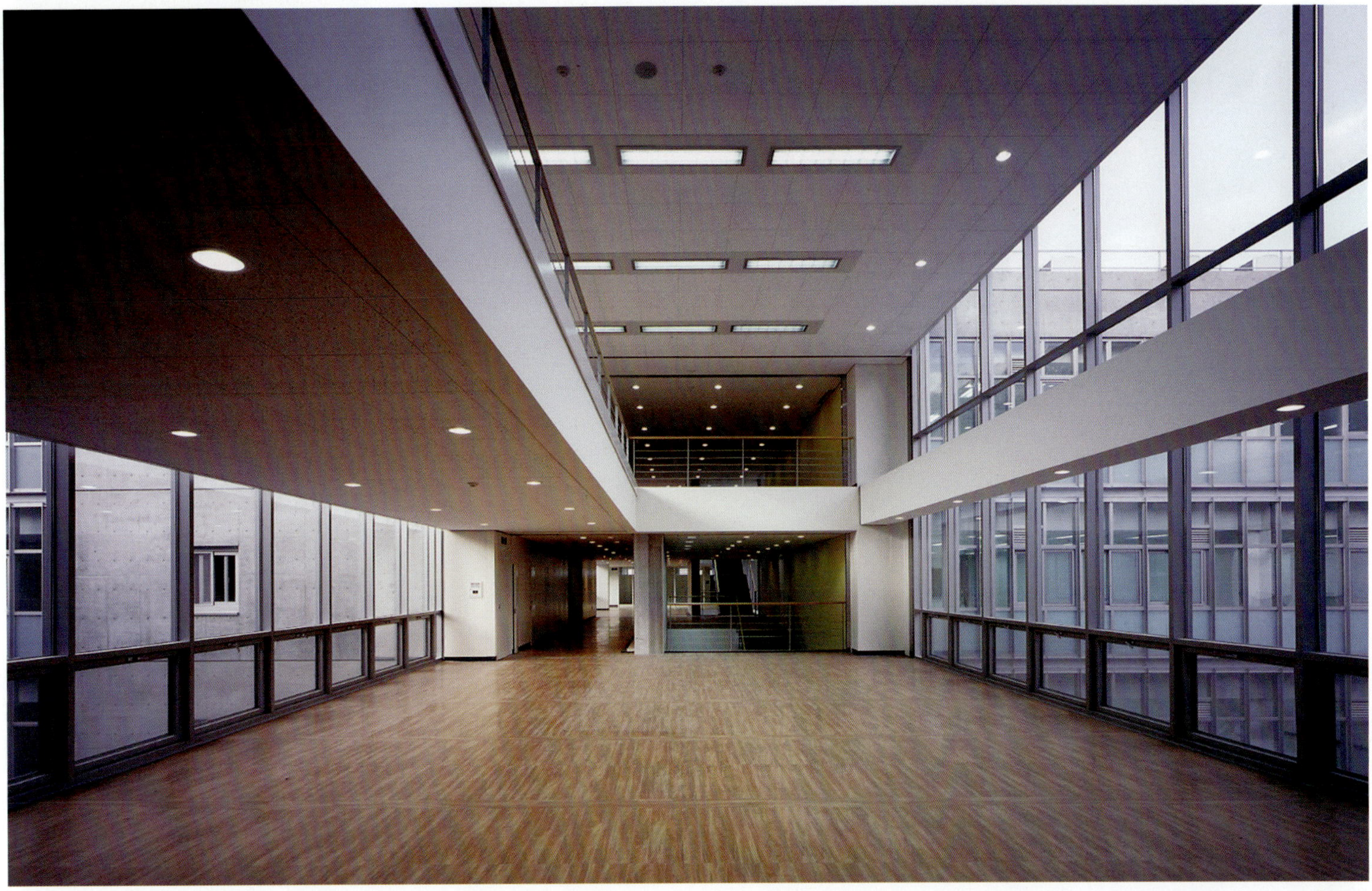

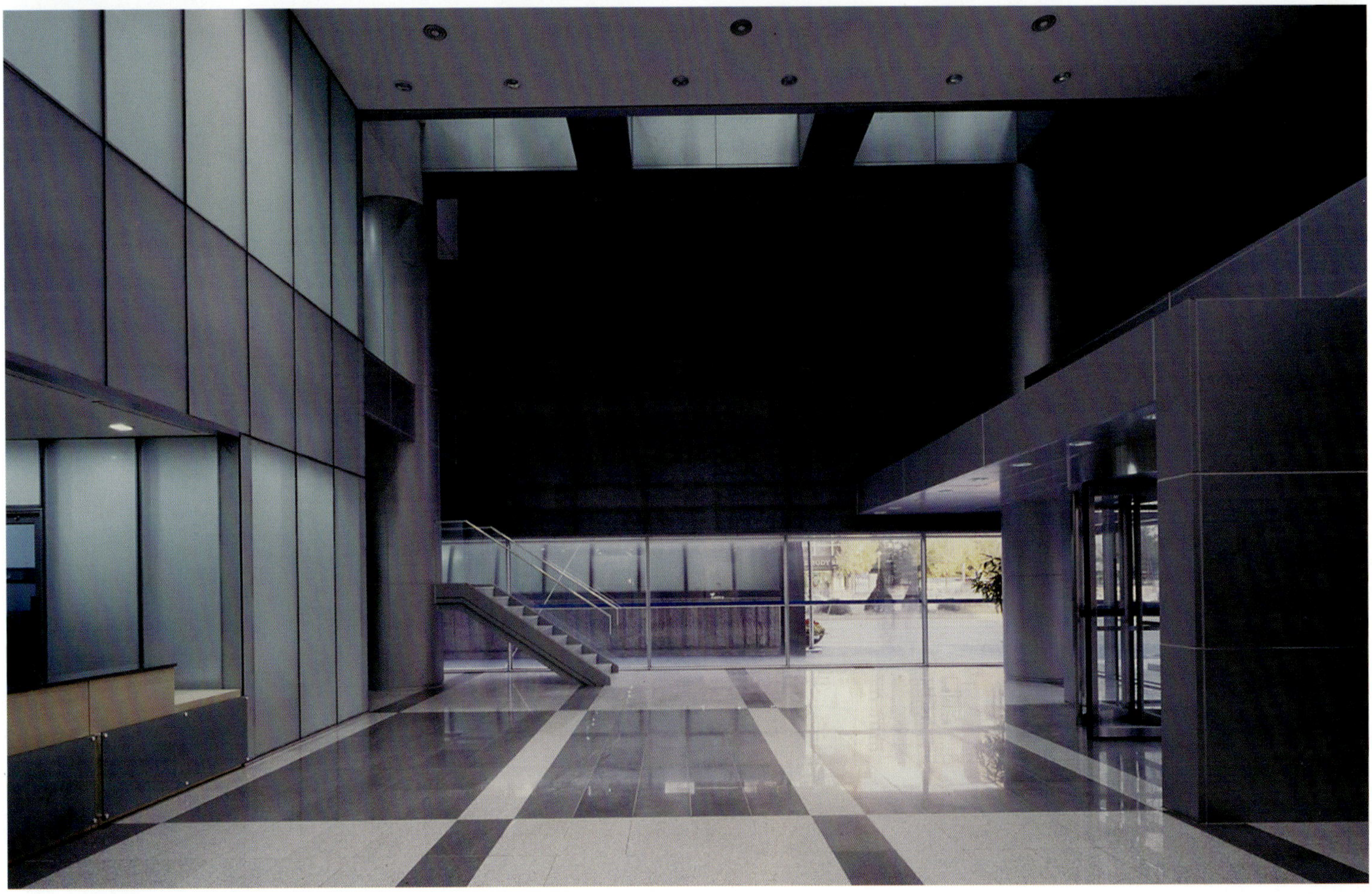

CheongShim Elementary School

Architects Jang Yoon Gyoo, Shim Chang Hoon, Kim Kyung Tae
Client Cheong Shim
Photographer Kim Bong Kyun

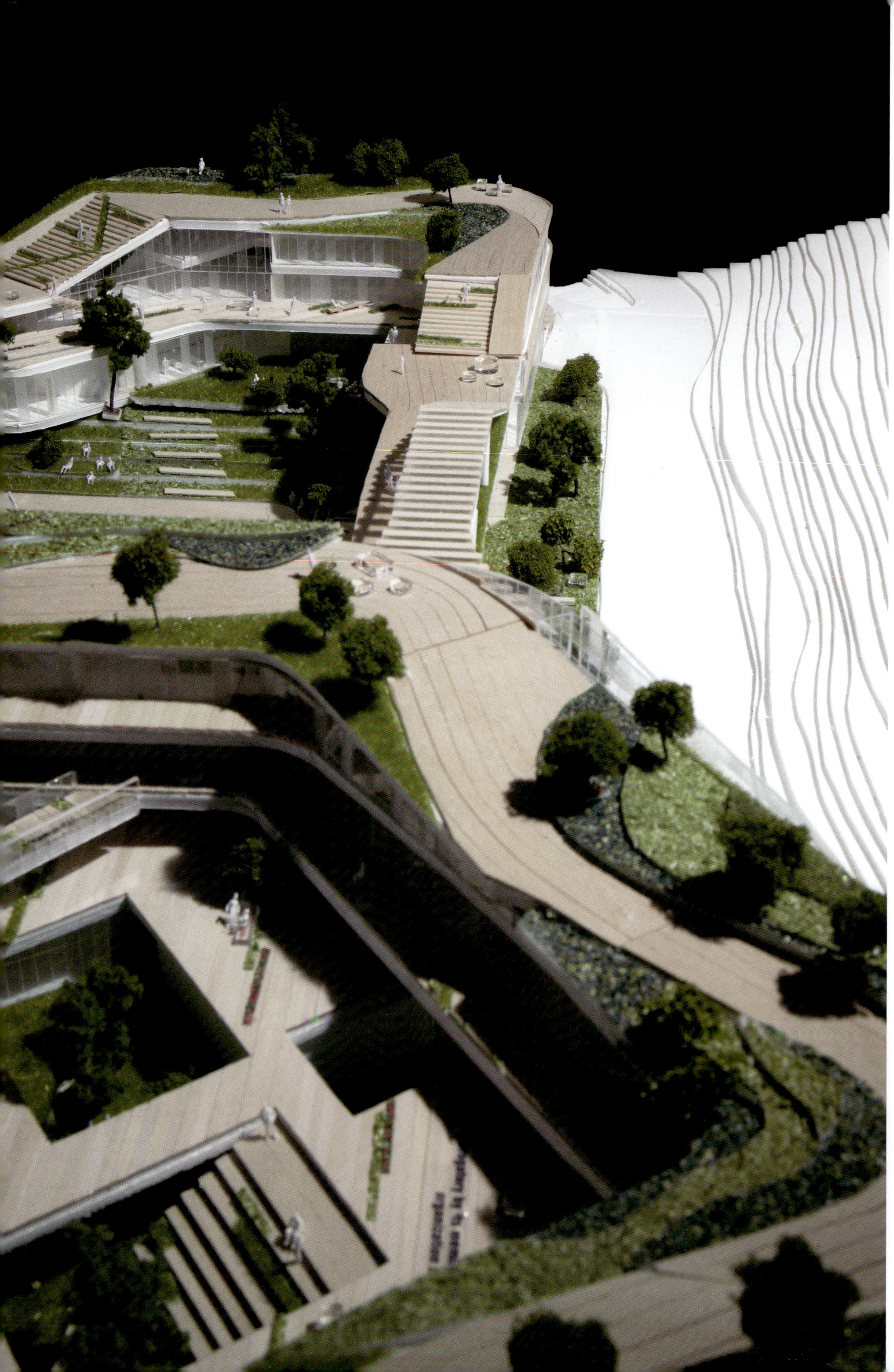

GREEN RING

Korean existing education tends to be a coercive structure for the entrance into a school of higher level. The educational aim of Cheongshim is cultivating global talented students. We suggest a spatial composition which can change the existing education system. Our aim is to make an eco-friendly educational space, the open educational space making creative thoughts, giving the power of execution and a 3-dimension educational space through diverse academic exchanges.

Cheongshim School, we suggest, will have an organic circulation system that adopts the topographic level and shape. It will have a close relationship with the Theological School and the International Middle and High school all working as teaching facilities. Systems for the Pre-school, the Playground and the Elementary School are all bonded closely to nature. The creative loop will be a sustainable tool, which will hold exchangeable educational programs.

The frame of Green Ring has an outdoor green agora, decks and a playground. It works as a dream ring connecting educational contents such as learning, exercising, art, nature and culture. The building and the landscape are not designed separately but integrated to make the environment closest to nature. The outdoor deck and the green deck are planned near to each classroom to take the advantages of ventilation and the skylight. In this building, the eco friendly plans are the most important theory that combines nature and imagination. It will develop to an education landscape, green skin and a sustainable program. They will be vocabulary consisting of pleasant educational space. Dream Trio Courtyard will bring the harmony of the outdoors, educational quality and the amenity of school life. In the whole loop, there is a small ring for the Pre-school and the building for the 1st and 2nd Grades, a medium ring for the building for the 3rd to 6th Grades and a centric playground. The 3 courtyards are not existing independently but more connected to each other and nature.

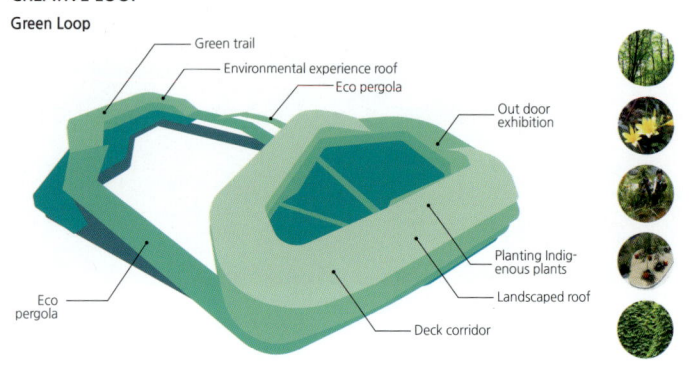

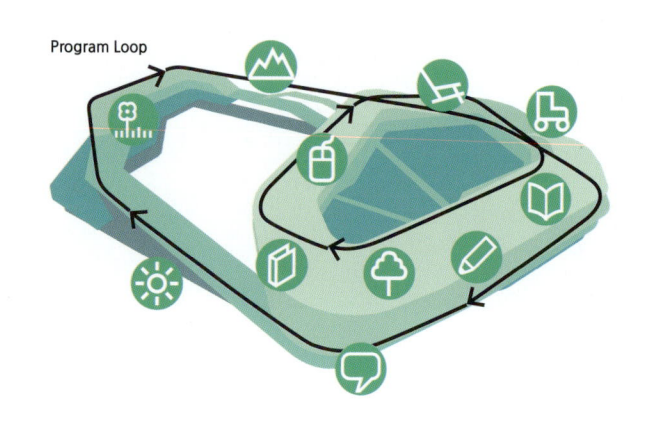

CREATIVE LOOP
Green Loop
- Green trail
- Environmental experience roof
- Eco pergola
- Out door exhibition
- Planting Indigenous plants
- Landscaped roof
- Deck corridor
- Eco pergola

Program Loop

ECO + IMAGINATION
Floating Landscape
- Roof garden Environmental Experience area
- Sports fields
- Entry Forecourt
- Landscaped roof

Kindergarten — Elementary

Green Skin
Covered in ivy | Louvre | Solar panel

Sustainable Program
- Natural light
- Increasing natural light
- Solar panel
- Courtyard/Basement floor: Natural ventilation

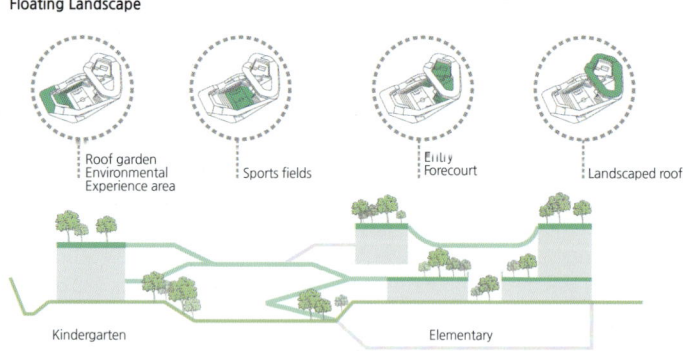

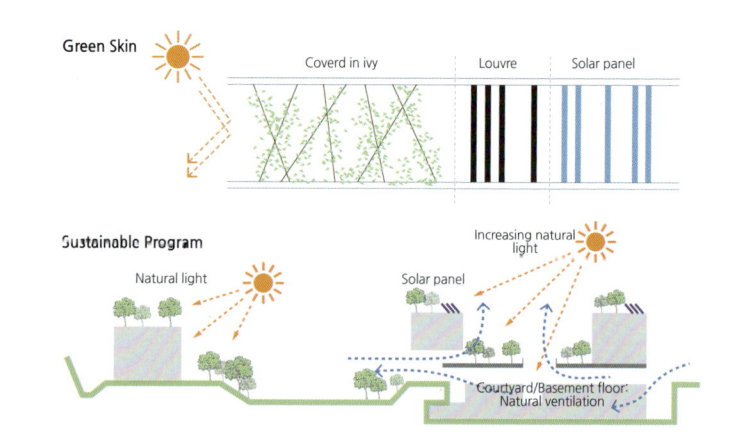

DREAM TRIO COURTYARD

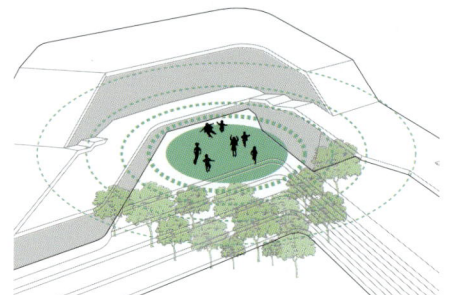

// **Kindergarten** Sheltered External Playground

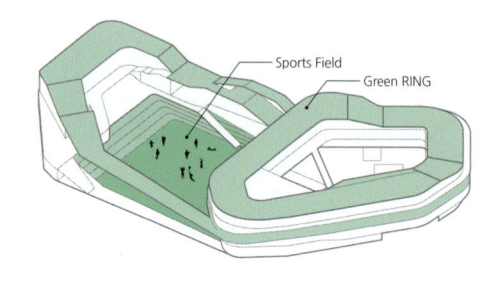

// **Sports Field** Green Ring surrounds a sheltered green sports field.
- Sports Field
- Green RING

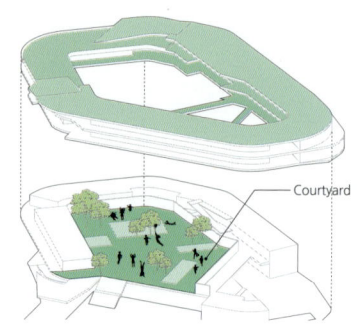

// **Elementary School** Maximising natural daylight, natural airflow into the courtyard
- Courtyard

// The courtyard of the Pre-School and the small ring building for the 1st and 2nd Grades is open playing space, consisting of water playing space, ecology learning space, grass mound space and an outdoor studying room.

Every ring has a courtyard. The courtyard of the Pre-School and the small ring building for the 1st and 2nd Grades is open playing space, consisting of water playing space, ecology learning space, grass mound space and an outdoor studying room. The courtyard of the medium ring for the 3rd to 6th Grades is filled with natural light and wind, and used as an outdoor classroom for extracurricular activities along with a wooden deck for resting, a bridge, an atrium, and event space. Lastly the courtyard for the playground ring is an active landscape connecting a shaded stand, a grass playground, a swimming pool and a roof garden.

We suggest a new space system for indoor studies in order to provide a creative educational system. The main building for the upper grades is an open plan classroom which is the main function of the ring on the 3rd floor to the 4th floor. Previously existing separated class rooms are integrated according to the grade and modified flexibly to curricular needs. Learning and playing, learning and art, learning and leisure… undivided spatial integration makes free thoughts and brings autonomy to the mind. The courtyard composed by the ring has the extracurricular space on the 2nd floor level. In the extracurricular space, a multi-room is centered and independent subjects like music, art, science and interactive curriculums are connected horizontally. Beyond it, there is a garden in the courtyard. The main space of the 1st floor level is a media center. The outdoor garden and each study room is floated and opened for the 1st level of the library. A teacher's room, promotion space and a reference room is closely composed. A half basement floor has a canteen connected to the playground, a theater and a multipurpose gym. In the lower part of the sub-building, the Pre-School is located and the middle part has the 1st and 2nd Grade students' classrooms. Study rooms are also opened according to their year. In the basement, a swimming pool and amenities are composed.

The skin of the building, we suggest, is planted and a solar panel is equipped to integrate with nature and produce an alternative energy. The eco friendly architecture gives the children a chance to experience environmental sustainability which also adds educational values.

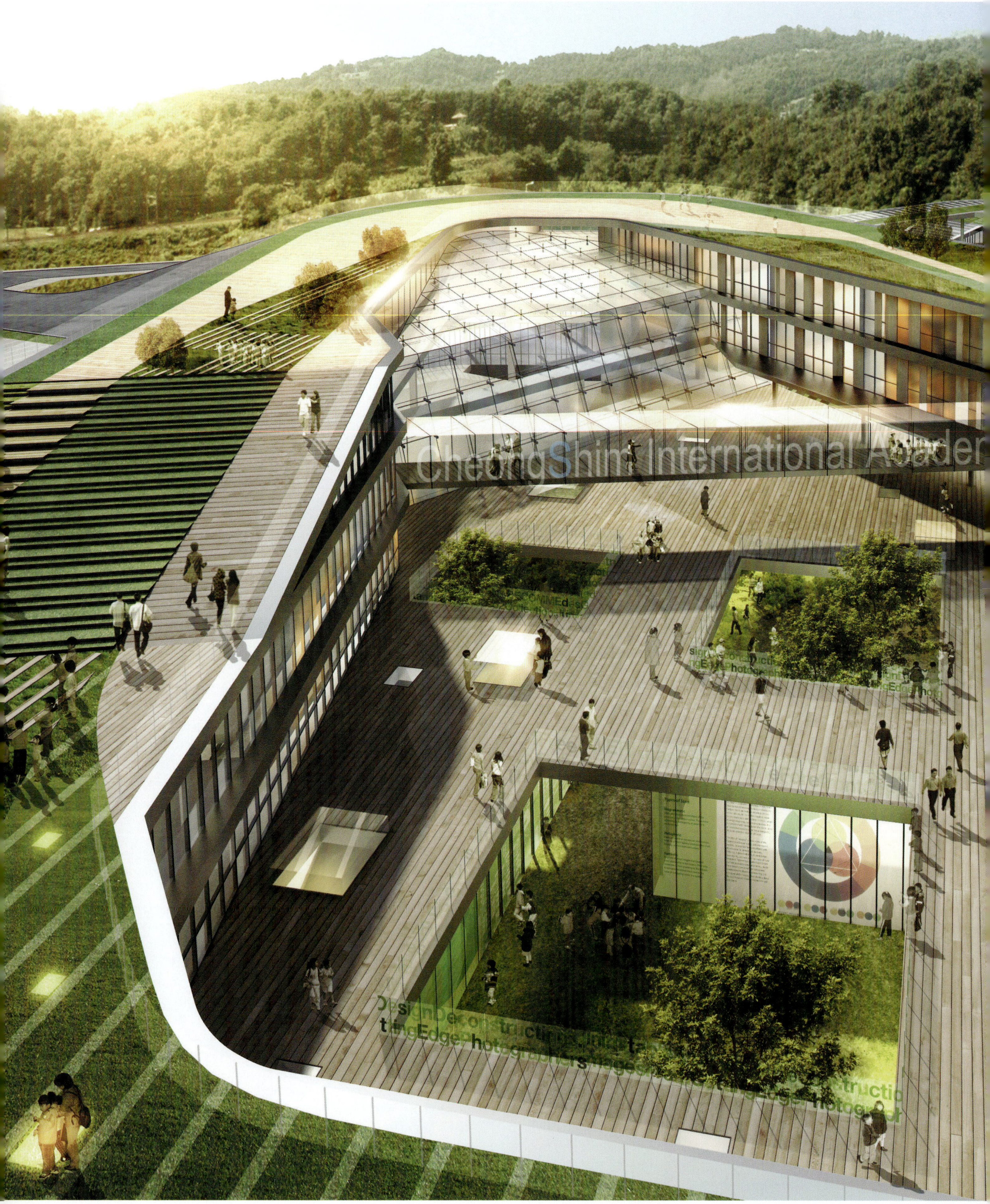
CheongShim International

COMPOUND BODY 537

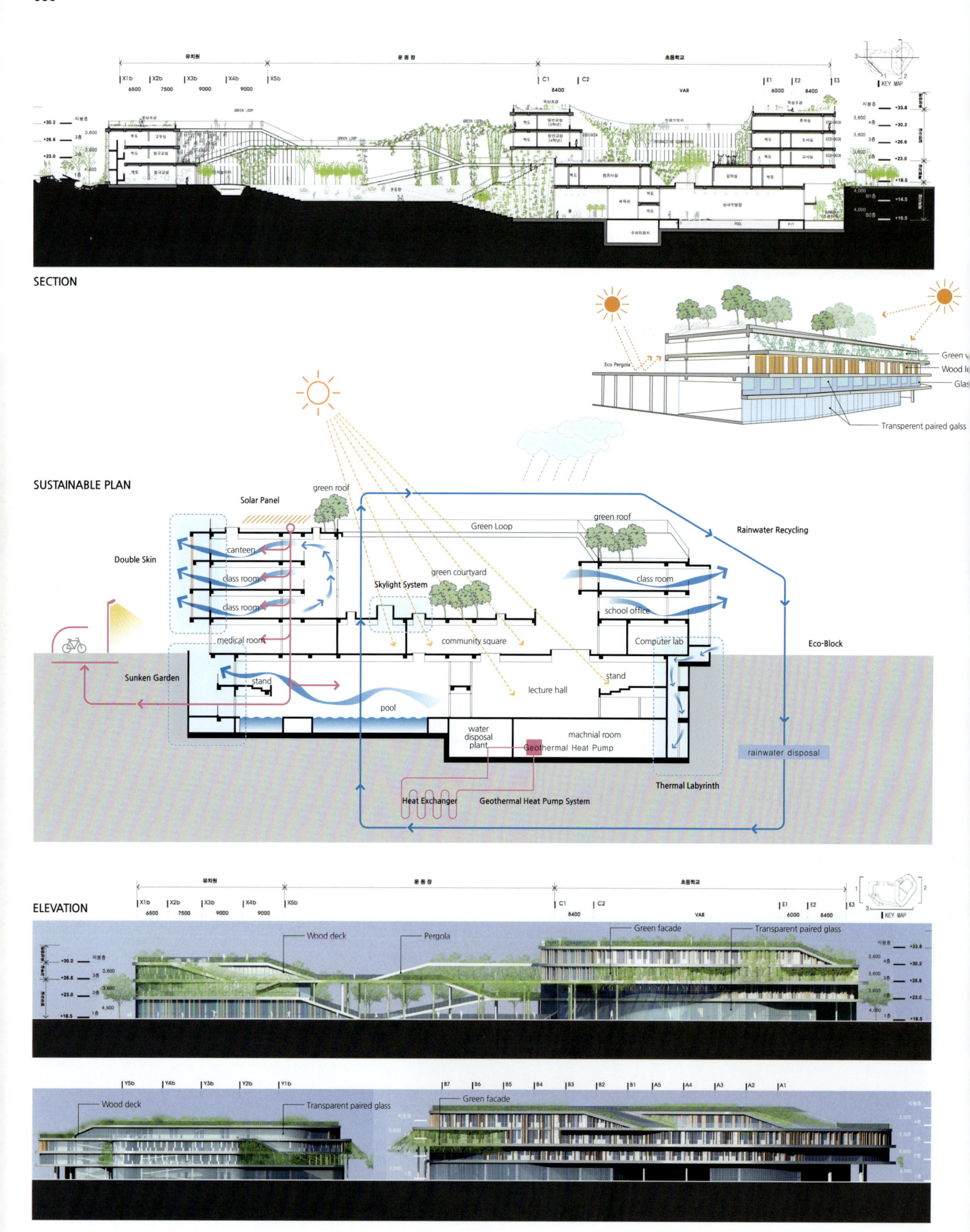

SECTION

SUSTAINABLE PLAN

ELEVATION

SUSTAINABLE EDUCATION SPACE

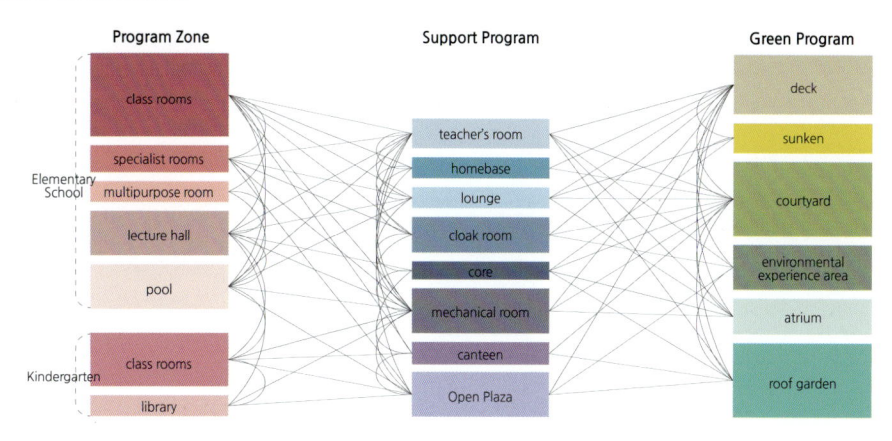

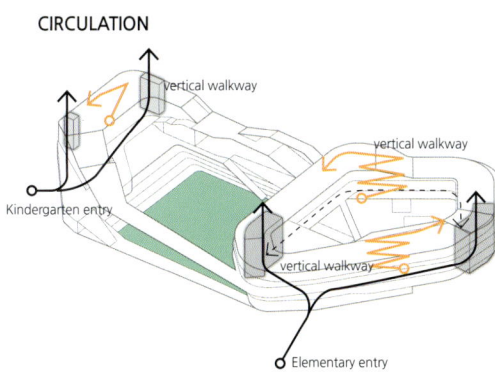

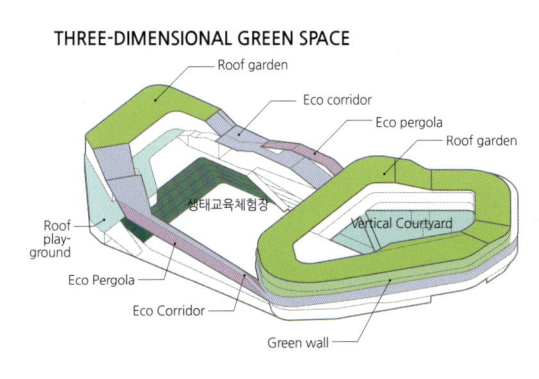

Program Zone	Support Program	Green Program
Elementary School: class rooms, specialist rooms, multipurpose room, lecture hall, pool	teacher's room, homebase, lounge, cloak room, core, mechanical room, canteen, Open Plaza	deck, sunken, courtyard, environmental experience area, atrium, roof garden
Kindergarten: class rooms, library		

CIRCULATION

- vertical walkway
- Kindergarten entry
- Elementary entry

THREE-DIMENSIONAL GREEN SPACE

- Roof garden
- Eco corridor
- Eco pergola
- Roof garden
- 생태교육체험장
- Vertical Courtyard
- Roof playground
- Eco Pergola
- Eco Corridor
- Green wall

540 Multi-
layered loop

Province Hall of ChungNam

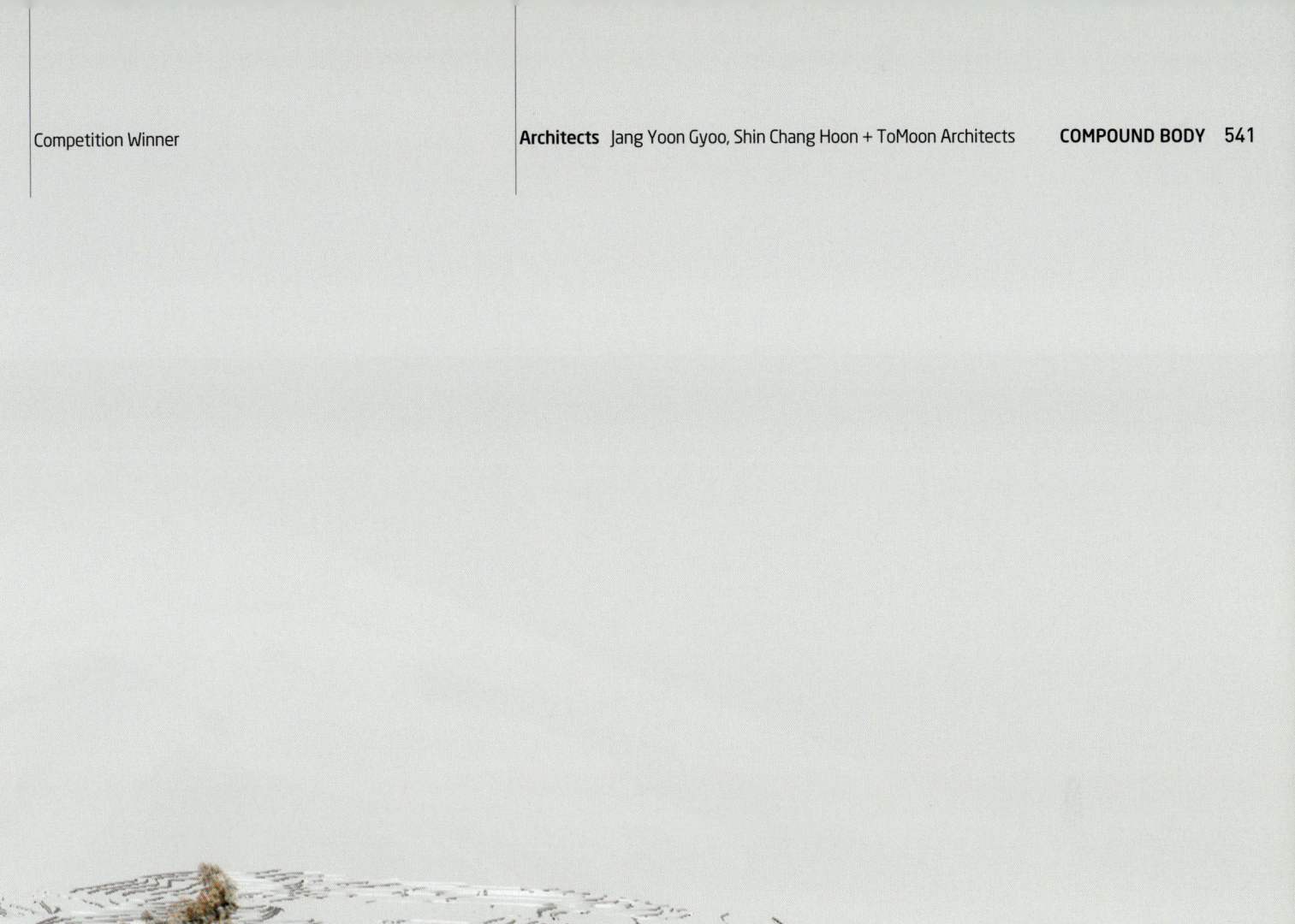

| Competition Winner | **Architects** Jang Yoon Gyoo, Shin Chang Hoon + ToMoon Architects | **COMPOUND BODY** 541

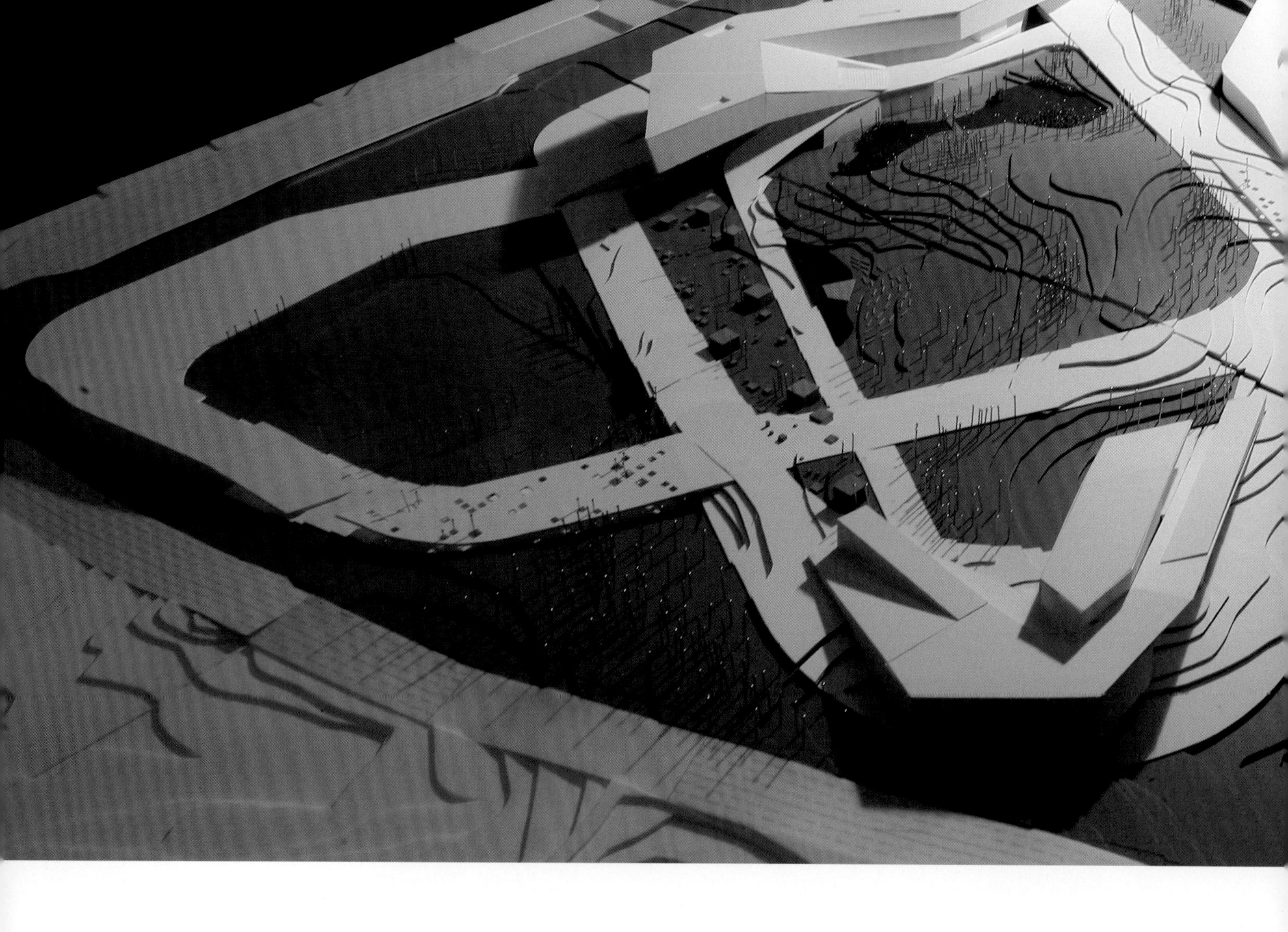

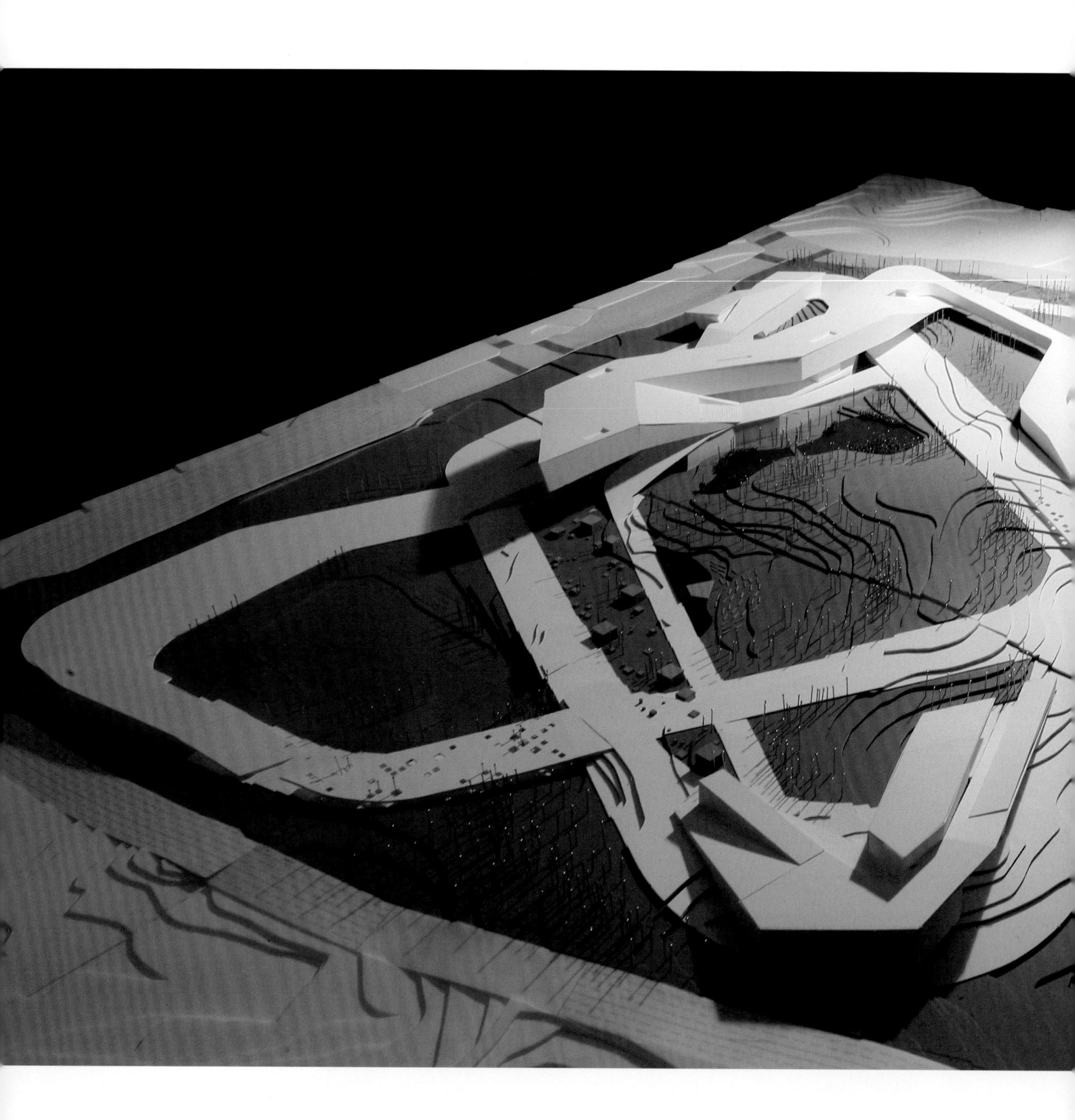

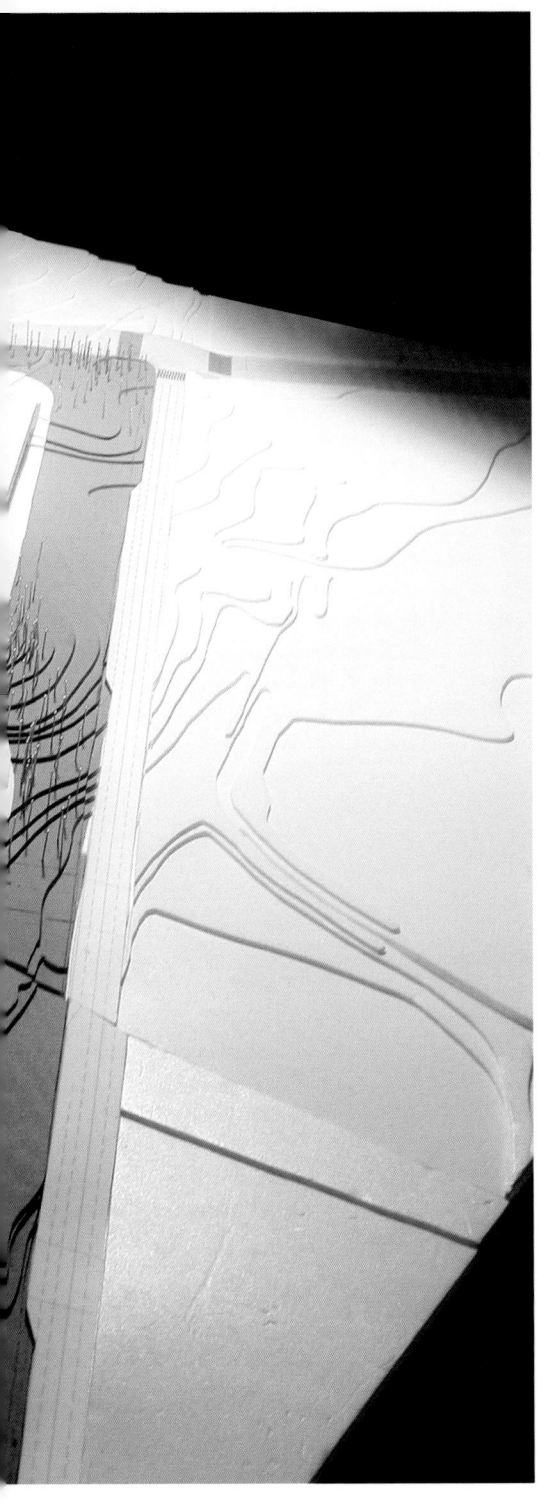

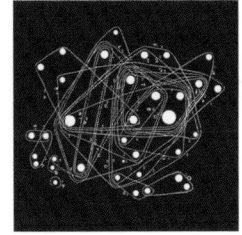

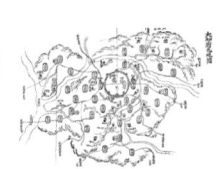

MULTI-LAYERED LOOP

In modern living, the role of the provinicial government office is not only a position of authority, but also a system that combine with democratic code in a horizontal relationship. People naturally meet in the space, which reproduces a variety of events and interests. Through the Chungcheongnam-do provincial government project, we tried to create a Multi-Layered Loop concept rather than a single roof. We composed the new geographically linked body in order to expand and go beyond the boundaries by changing the loof's position. Thus, every part of the multi-roof takes on a different role according to the landscape, event program, architectural function and correlation with the environs. The boundaries of the building between the interior and exterior disappear in the circulation and intersection of the continual multiple-layers.
The roof connects to a variety of cores, becoming a landscape with nature as well as a landmark in the city.

Muli-Core
We presented the new paradigm of a government office building that has its own functional multi-core (office, assembly, health, police,) and connections in the boundary of the Multi Layered Loop.

Eco-Landscape
We proposed the government office building be an environmentally friendly eco-garden that integrates nature into the site, thereby creating a green axis from YongBong-Mountain pass through the site, connecting the center of the city while sharing the characteristics and programs of each space.

Open-Landmark
We wish to realize open-landmark connected with the symbolic government office town that bring together nature and the city.
As an open space to civil society, it is possible to hold a variety events, becoming an open cultural space available for various uses connected with auditoriums, restaurants, and outdoor cafeterias. It is possible to move the loop dynamically as it is connected to the three-dimensional moving system.

Working in Nature
This project realized smooth office environment on the horizontal moving connection as the center of goverment offices to administer Chungchungnam-do.
It offers comfortable eco-office by providing a secure view, control of insolation, and the introduction of interior green spaces.

Flowing Loof   Being Platform   Making Place

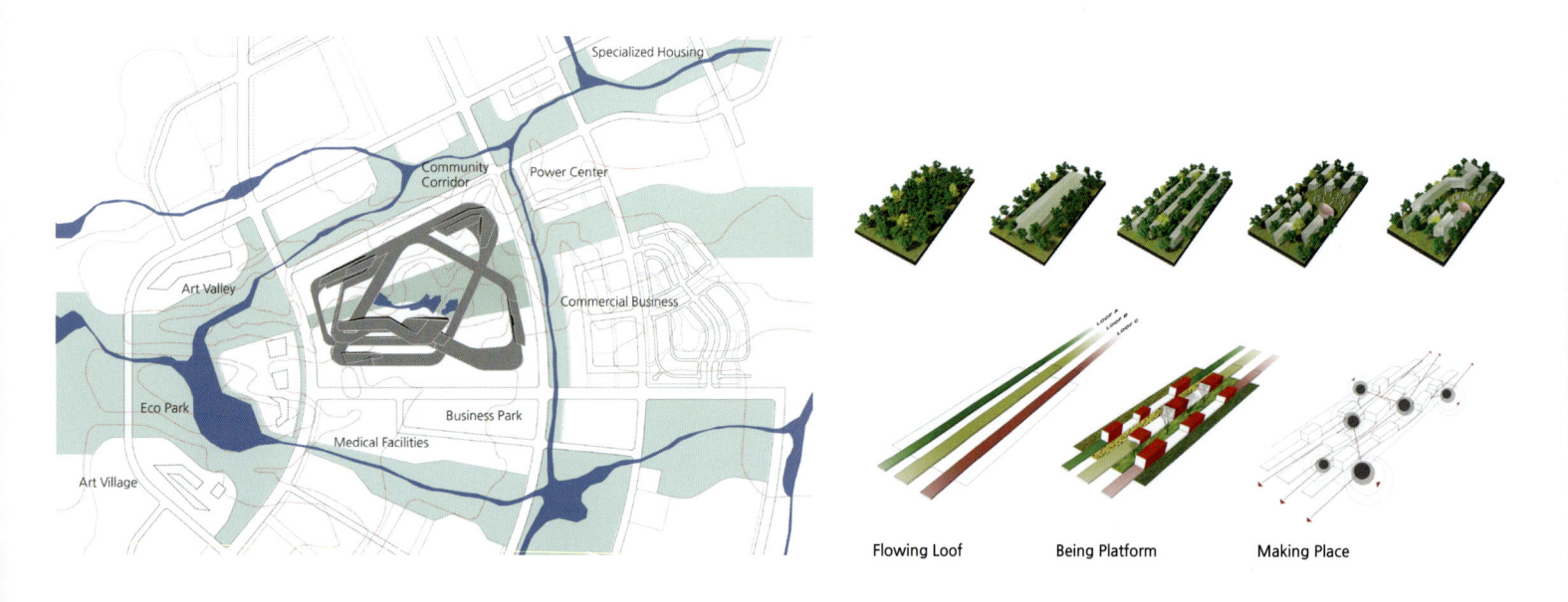

MASTER PLAN DIAGRAM

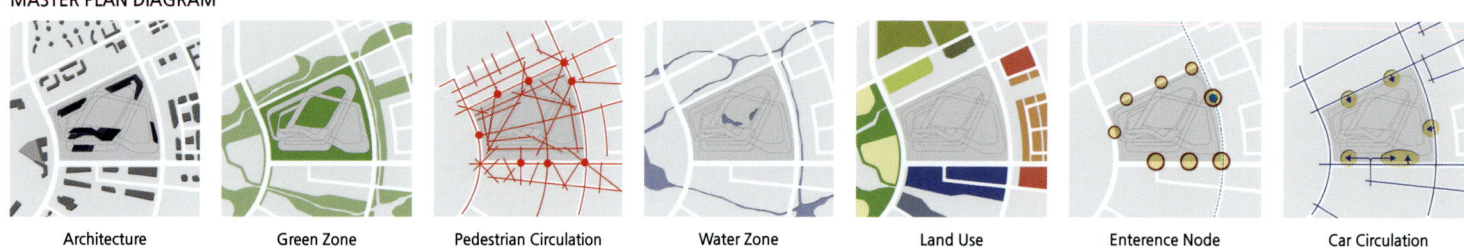

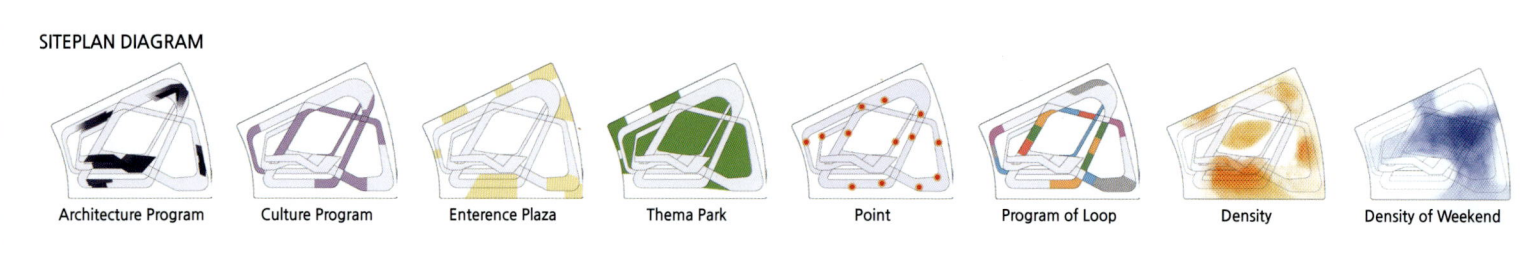

Architecture   Green Zone   Pedestrian Circulation   Water Zone   Land Use   Enterence Node   Car Circulation

SITEPLAN DIAGRAM

Architecture Program   Culture Program   Enterence Plaza   Thema Park   Point   Program of Loop   Density   Density of Weekend

SITEPLAN CONCEPT DIAGRAM

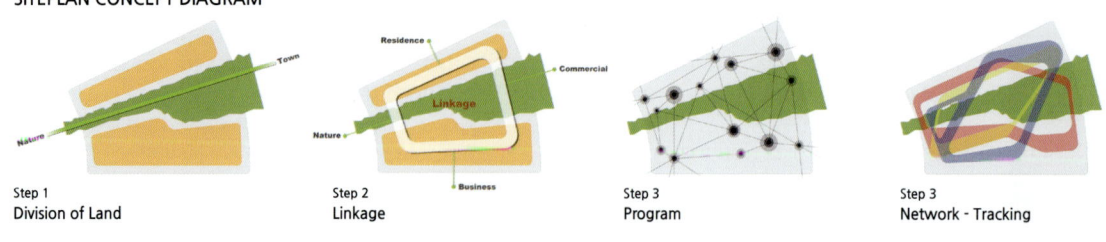

Step 1 — Division of Land
Step 2 — Linkage
Step 3 — Program
Step 3 — Network - Tracking

SITEPLAN CONCEPT VIEW

LEANER DISJOINTING

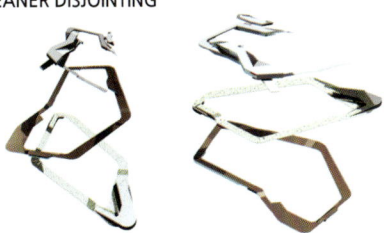

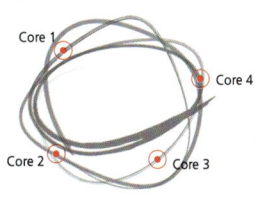

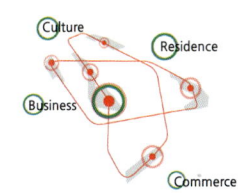

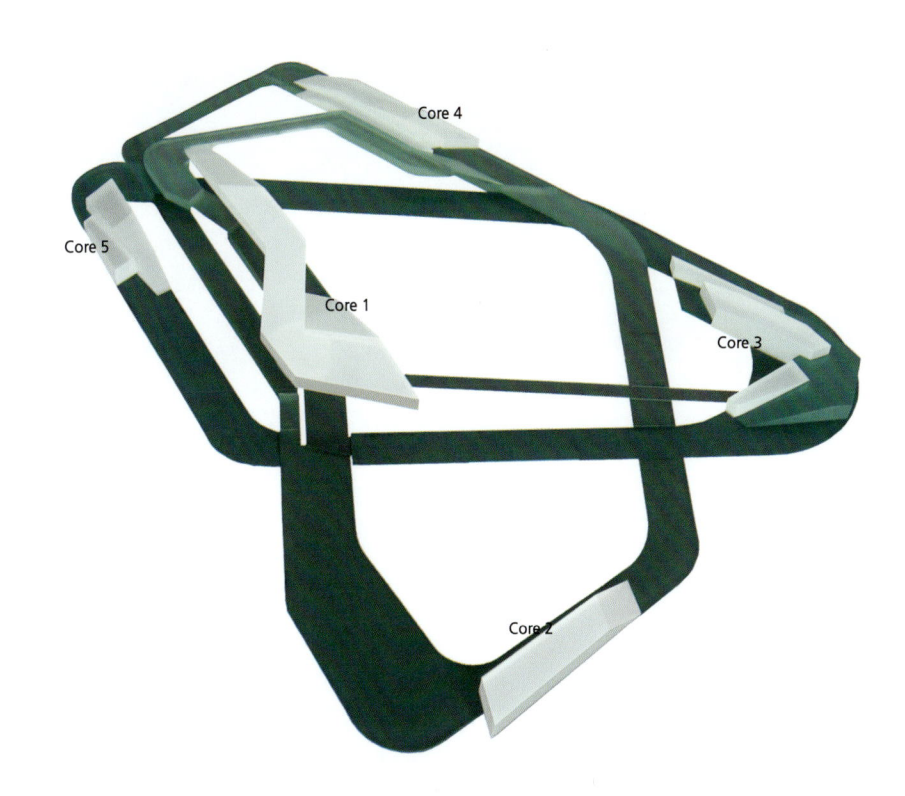

MULTI CORE

Core 1, Core 4, Core 2, Core 3

Culture, Residence, Business, Commerce

Core 4, Core 5, Core 1, Core 3, Core 2

LEANER PROCESS

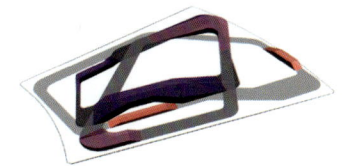

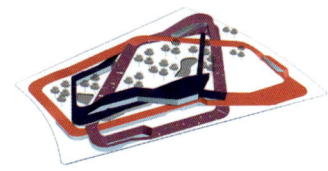

ROOF SECTION PANAROMA

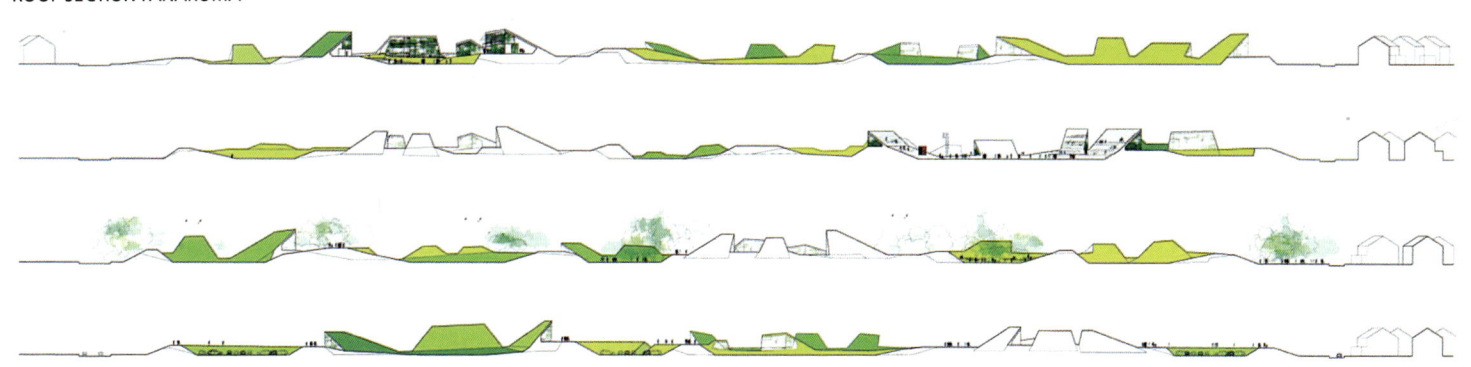

LANDSCAPE PROGRAM

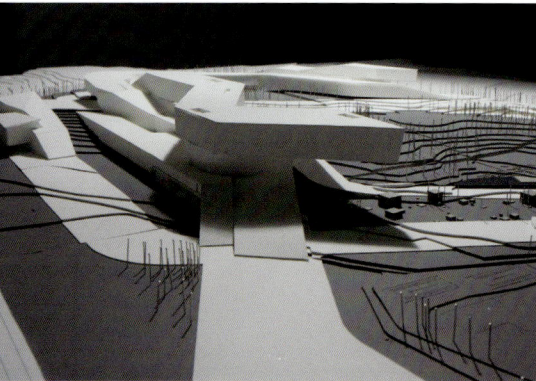

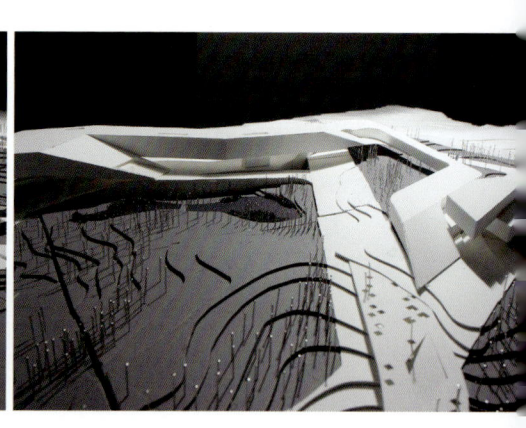

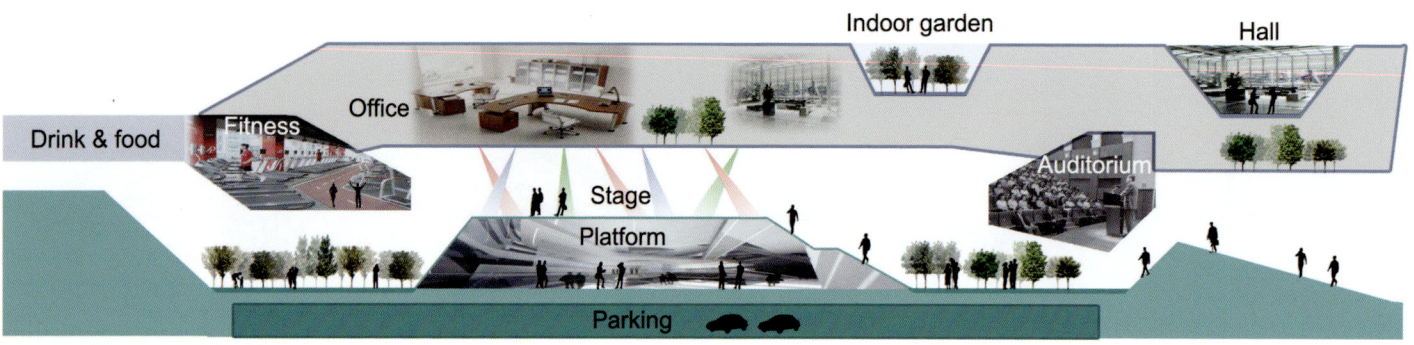

SECTION PROGRAM DIAGRAM

Drink & food | Fitness | Office | Indoor garden | Hall | Auditorium | Stage | Platform | Parking

SYSTEMIC DIAGRAM OF THE PLATFORM

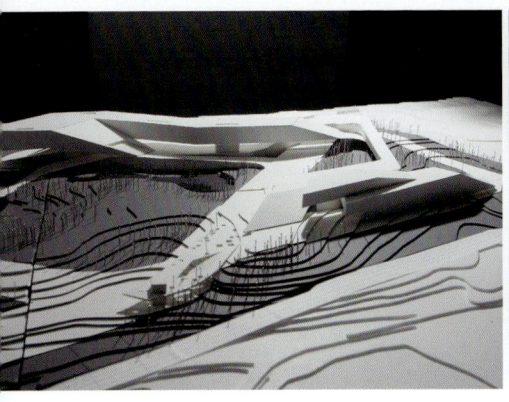

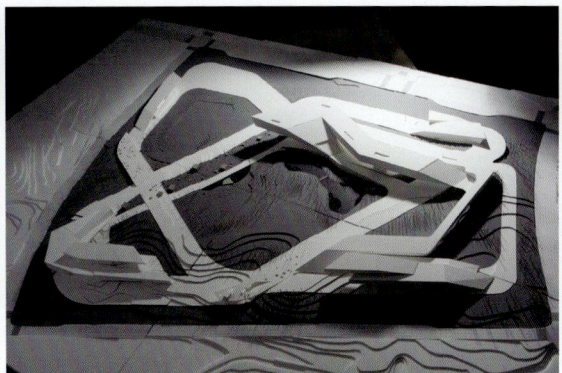

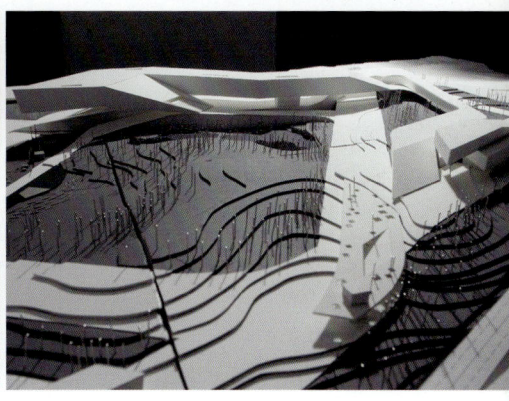

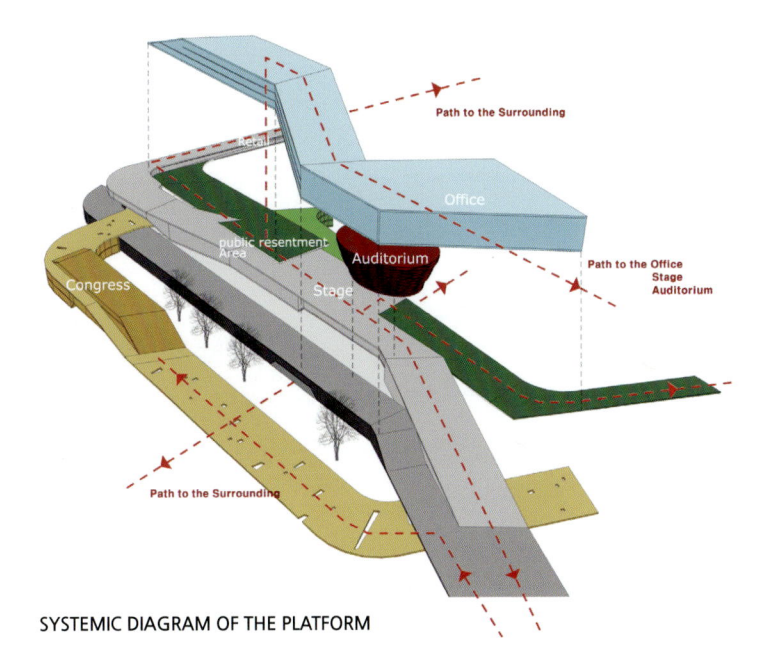

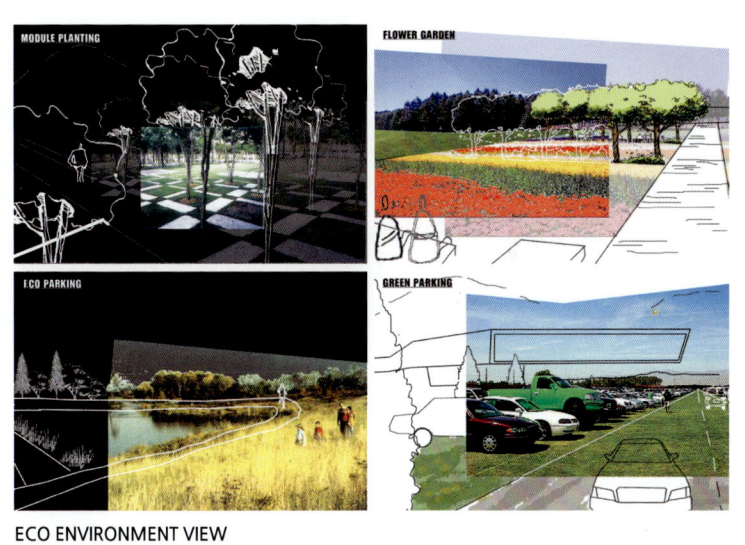

ECO ENVIRONMENT VIEW

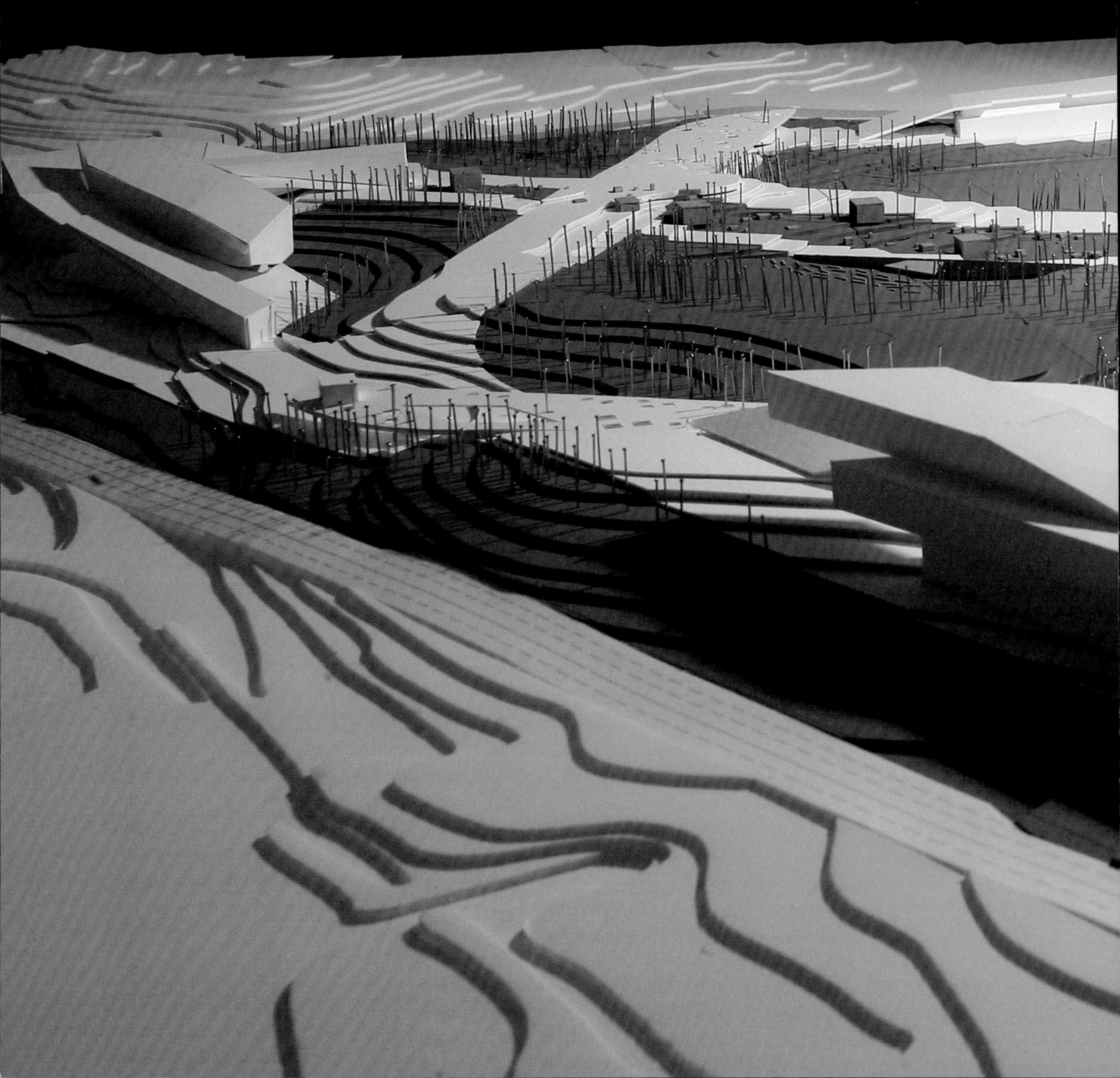

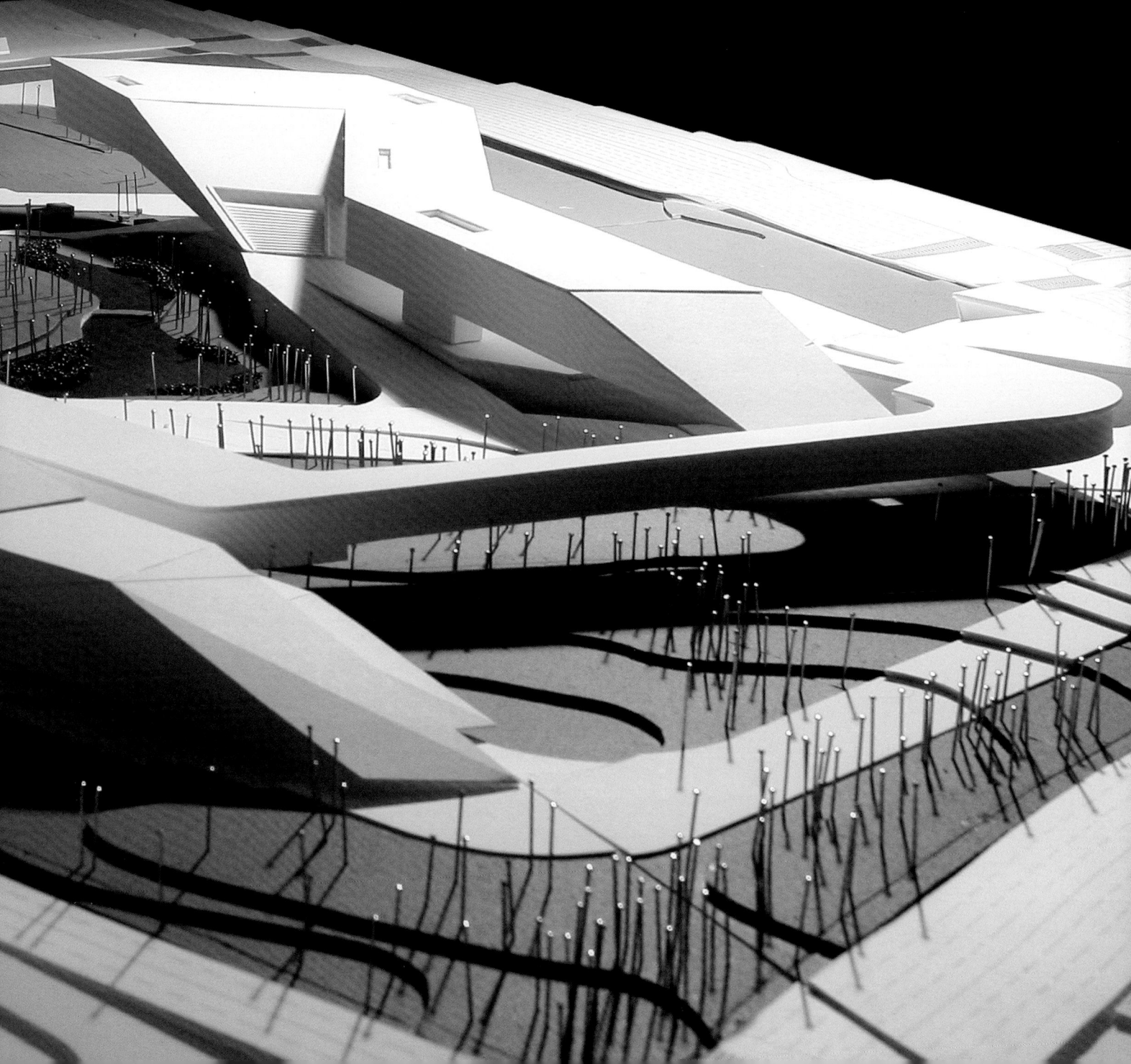

Project Name
Chungcheongnam-do provincial government office,
1st prize, Competition
Design
Jang Yoon Gyoo, Shin Chang Hoon, Kim Sung Min
+ Tomoon Engineering Architects
Design Team
Go Young Dong, Jin Jung Eun
Location
Chungcheongnam-do (at new administration town)
Use
Temporary Building
Site Area 231,406m²
Building Area 29,397m²
Total Floor Area 106,423m²
Building Coverage Ratio 12.70%
Floor Area Ratio 173.06%
Parking 1,562cars
Exterior Finishing
Metal panel, Color Duble Glazing
Structure
Steel Structure +Stainless Steel , Sandwich Panel

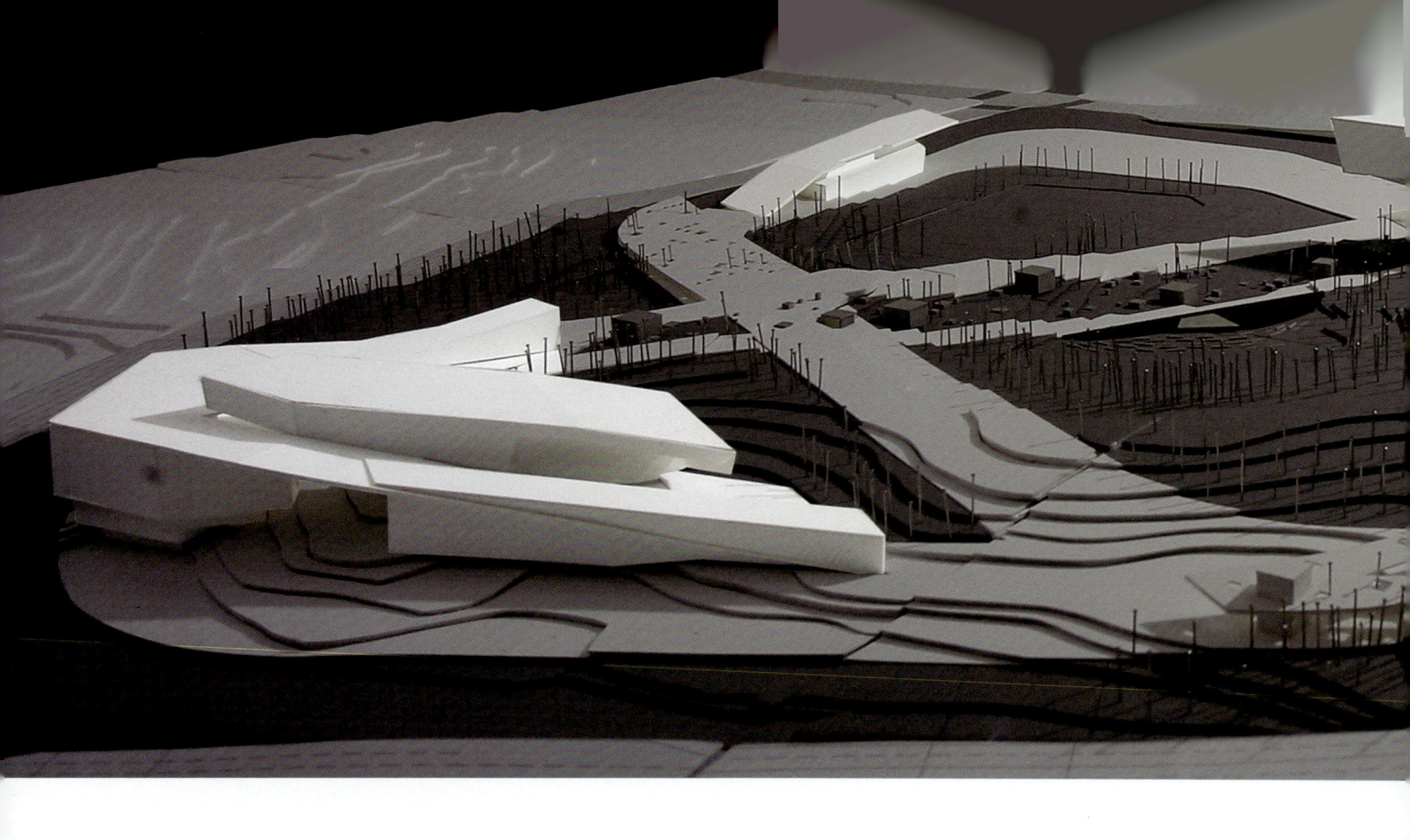

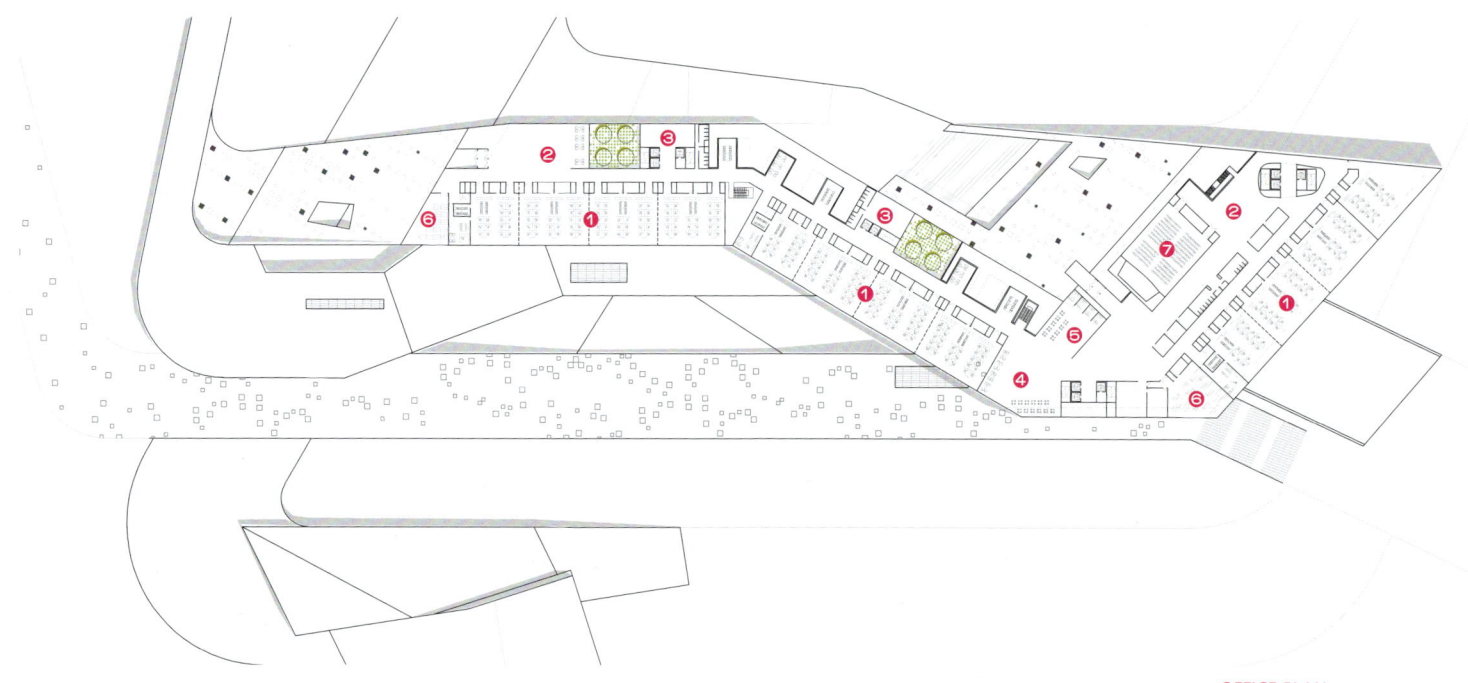

OFFICE PLAN
1. Office Facilitis
2. Hall
3. Rest Room
4. Lounge
5. Reception
6. Library
7. Main Metting Room

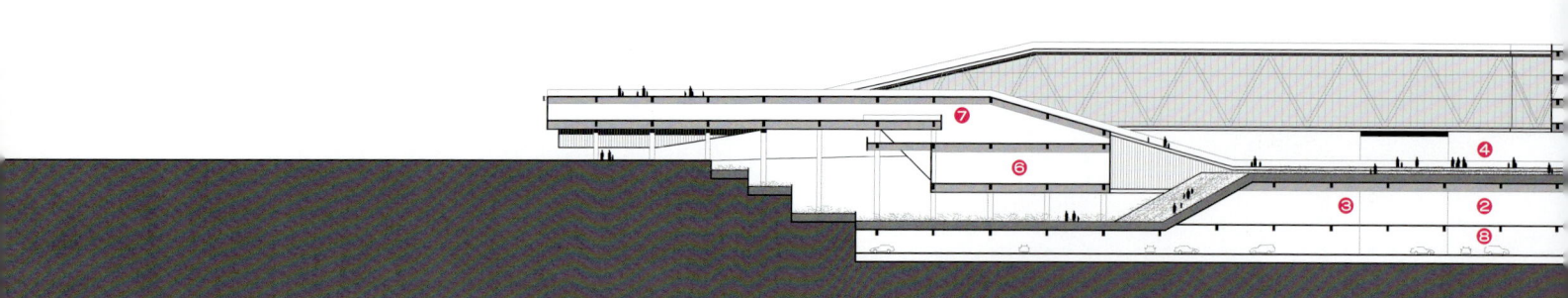

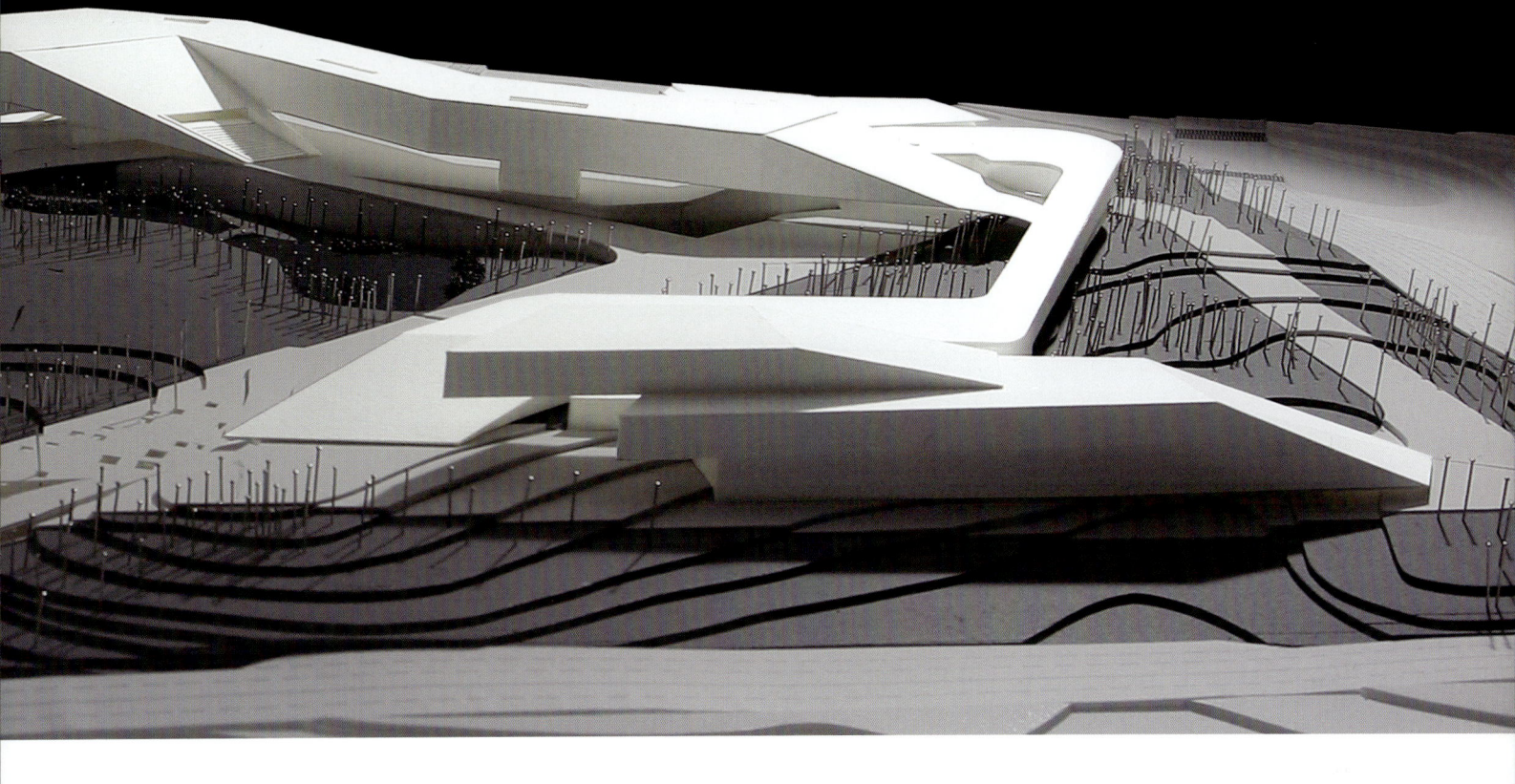

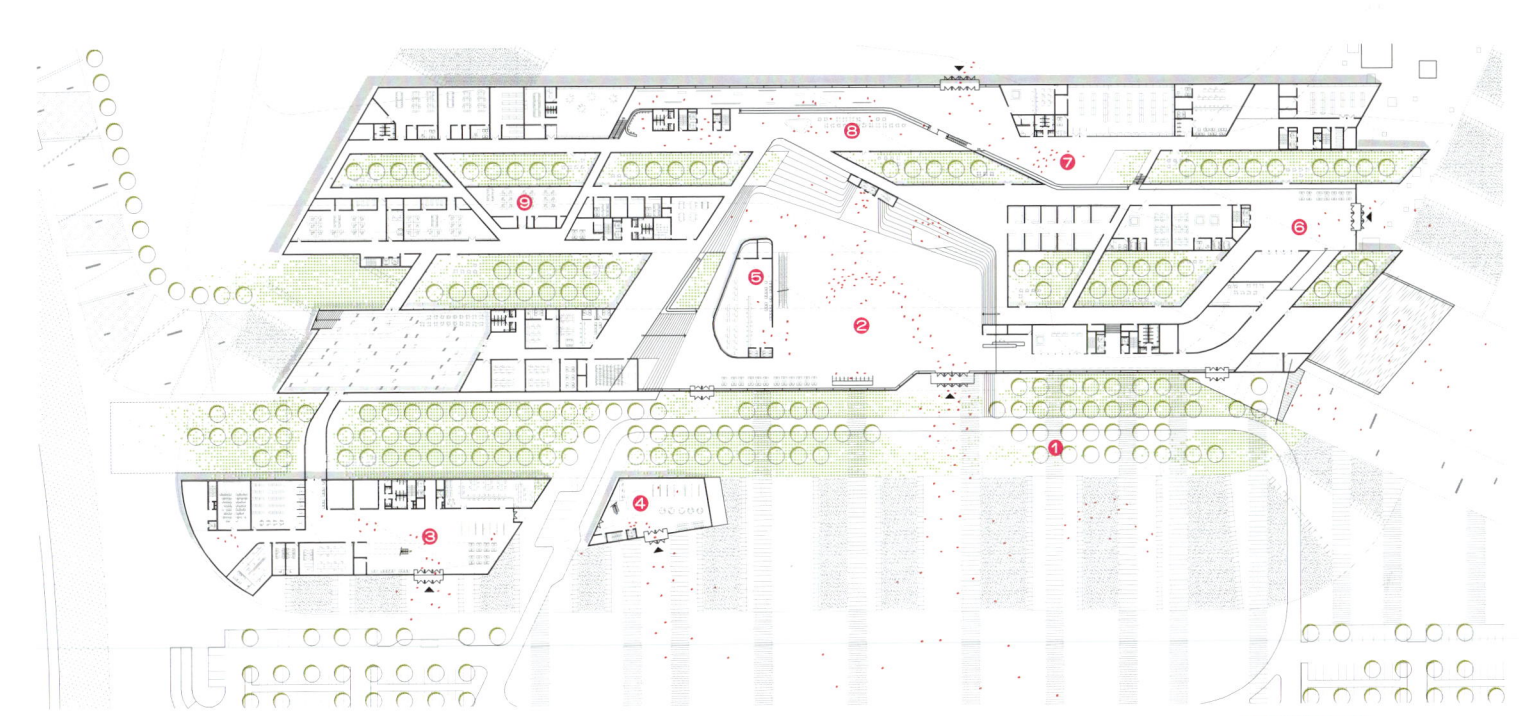

GROUND PLAN
1. Chungnam Honor Garden
2. Plaza
3. Committe Hall
4. Committe Research Gallery
5. Civil Appeal Service Center
6. Civil Appeal Hall
7. Event Garden
8. Cafeteria
9. Social Welfare Part

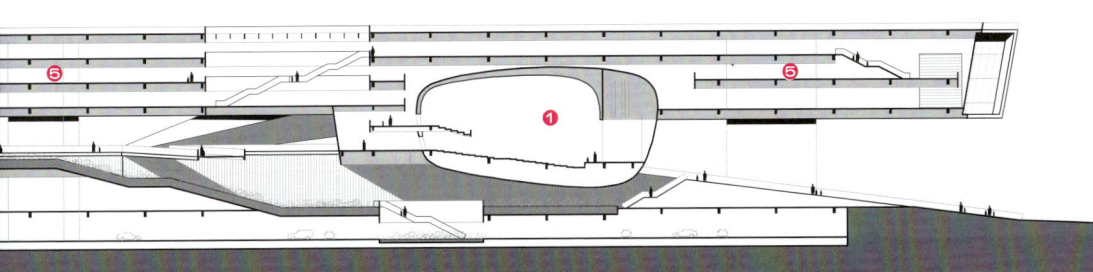

SECTION PLAN
1. Auditorium
2. Plaza
3. Civil Appeal Service Center
4. Open Deck
5. Office Facilitis
6. Video Conference Room
7. Fitness Center
8. Parking

ELEVATION

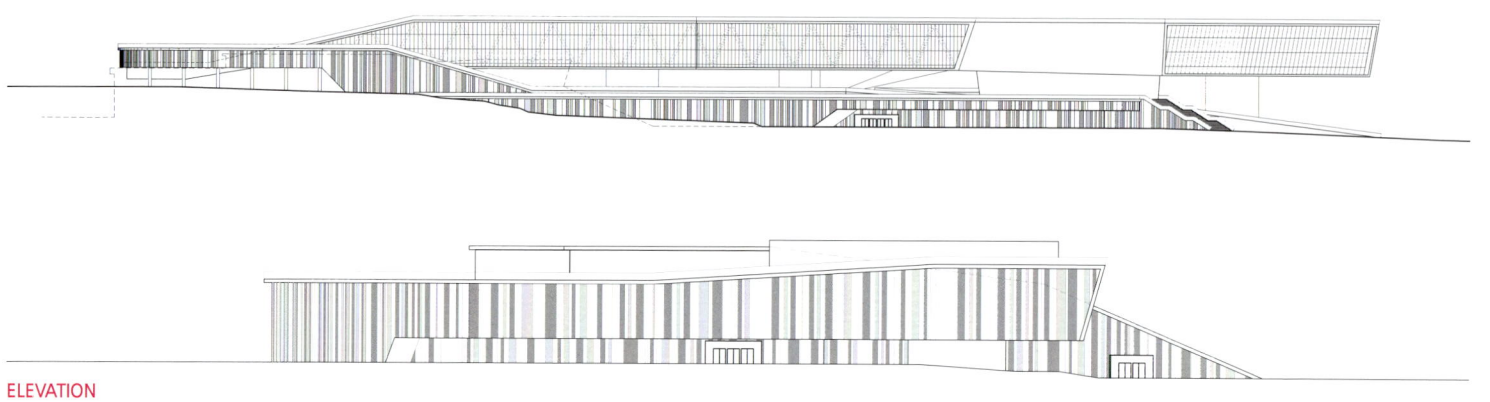

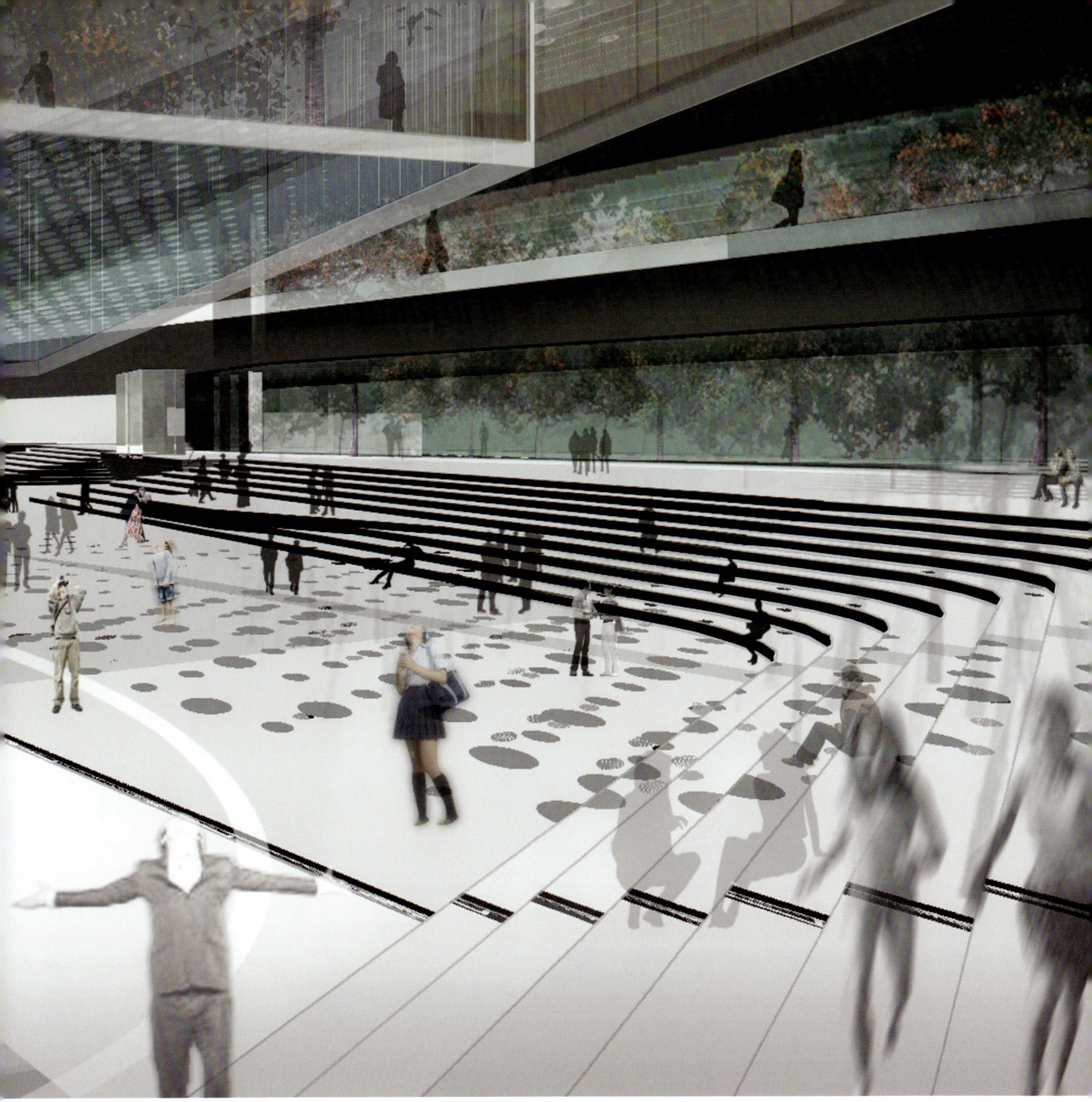

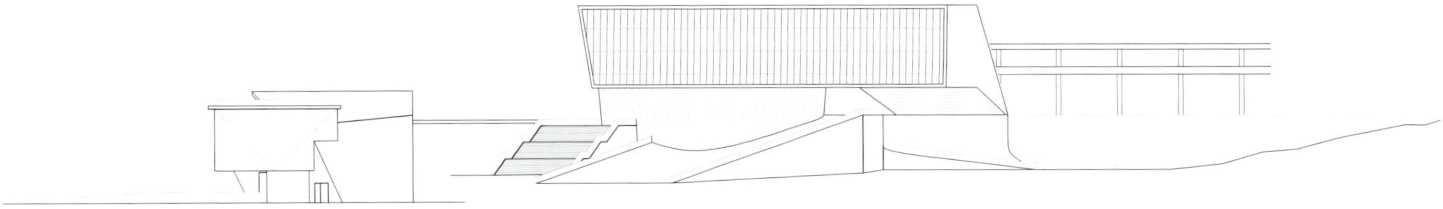

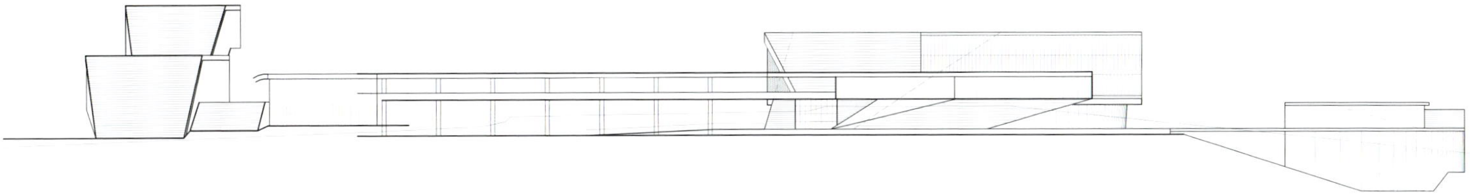

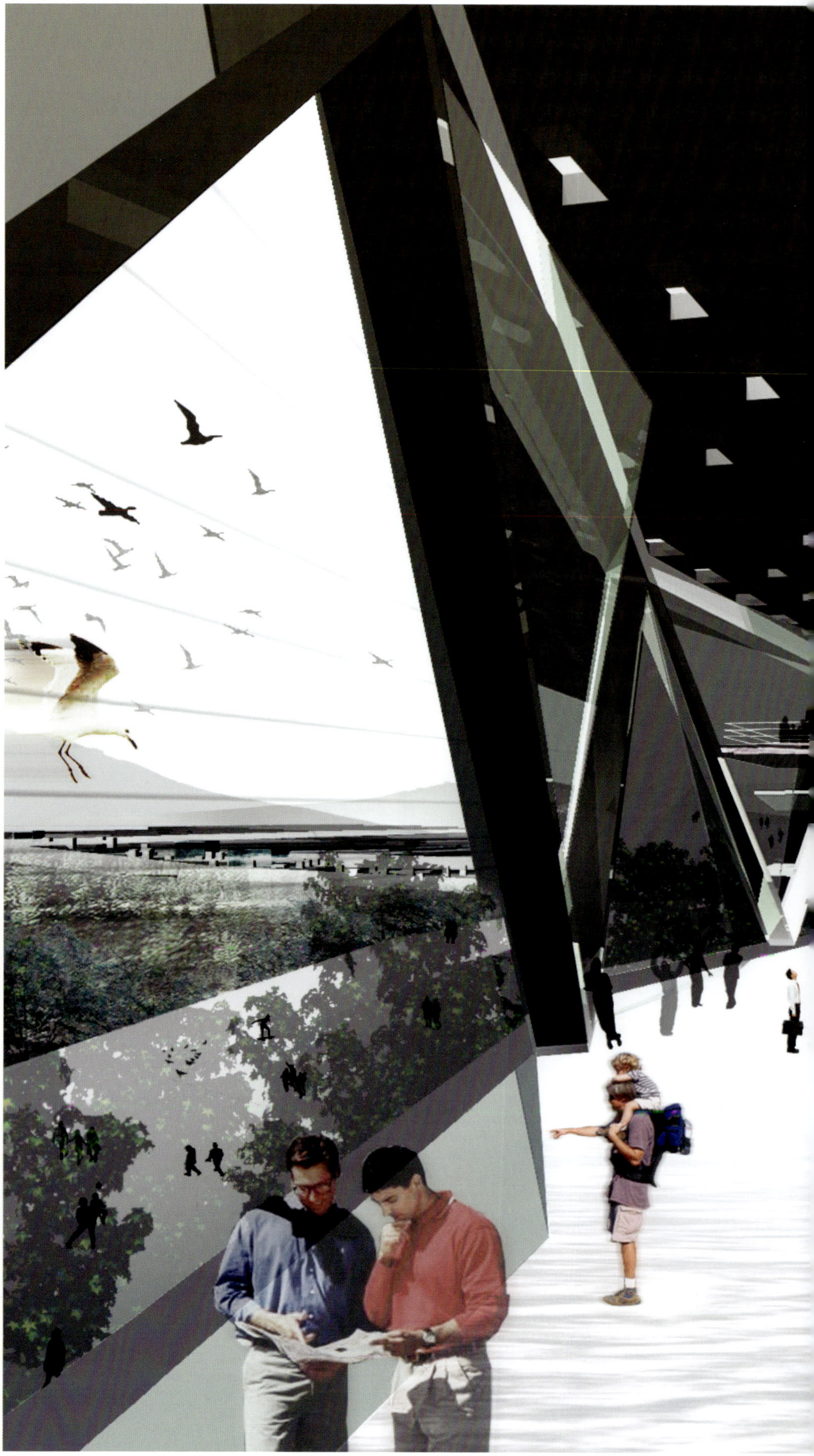

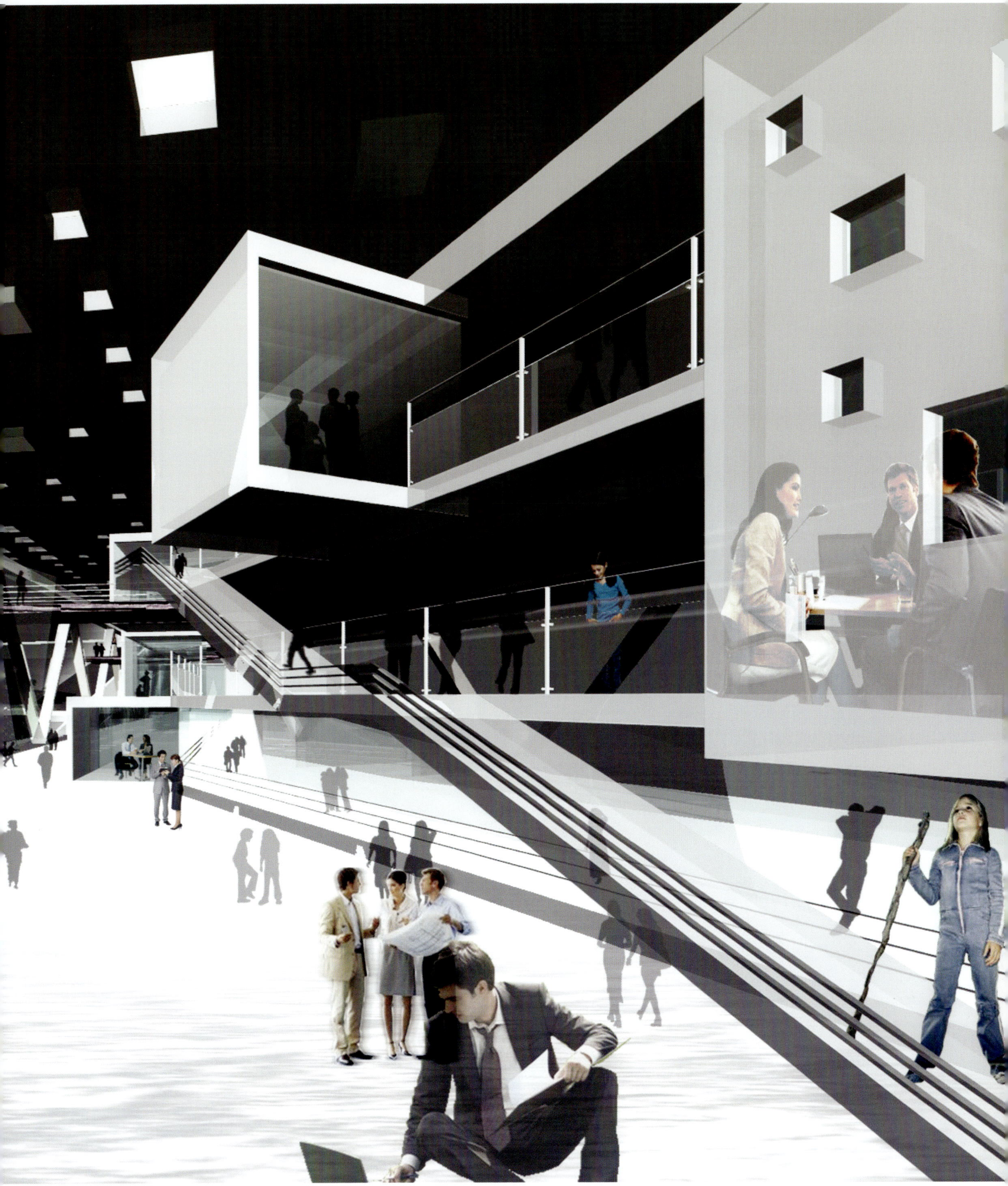

Kaleidoscope Gallery

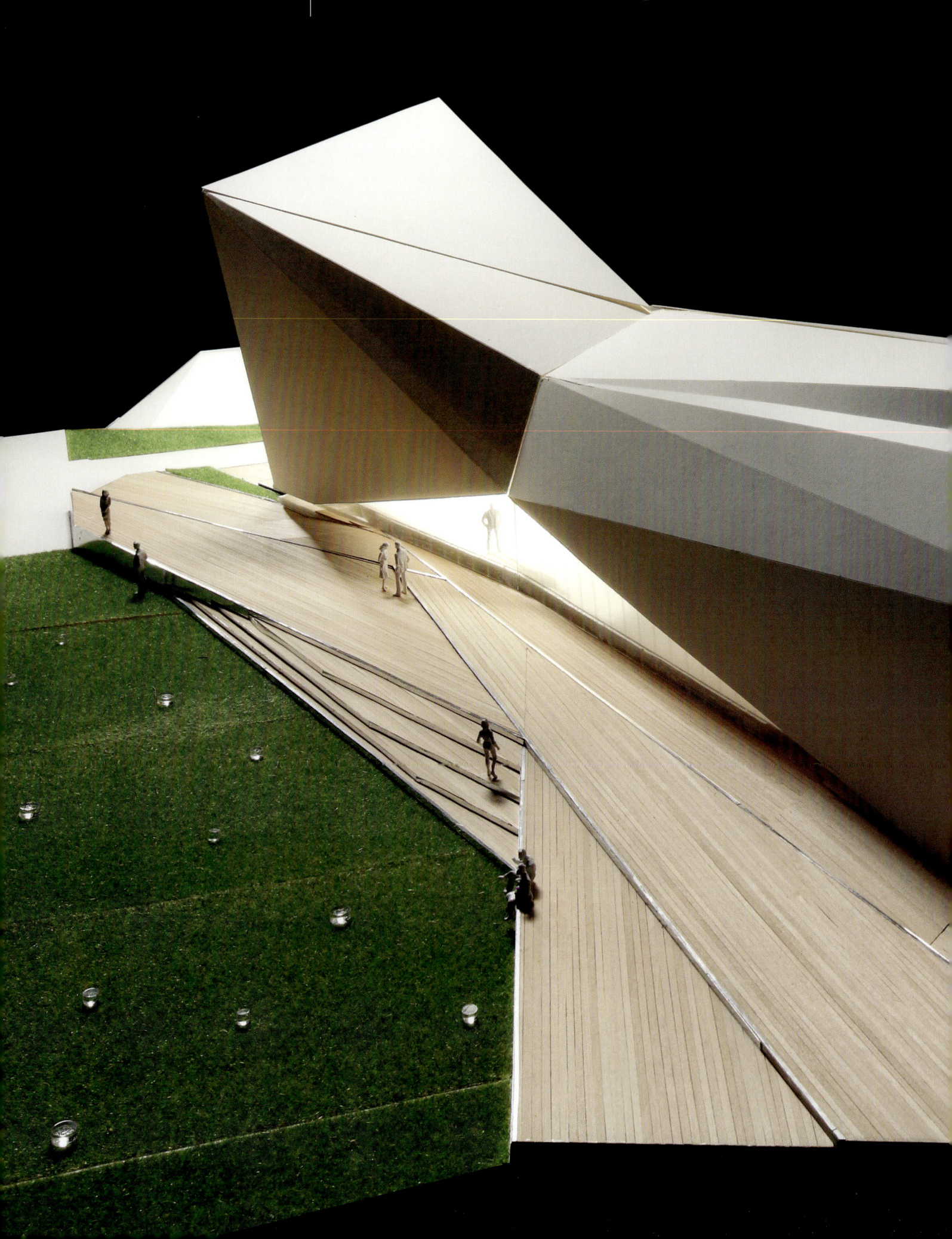

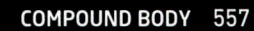

Architects Jang Yoon Gyoo, Shin Chang Hoon, Kim Sung Min, Kim Min Tae, Kang Seung Hyun
Client Jeong Geum Sook
Photographer Kim Jae Kyung

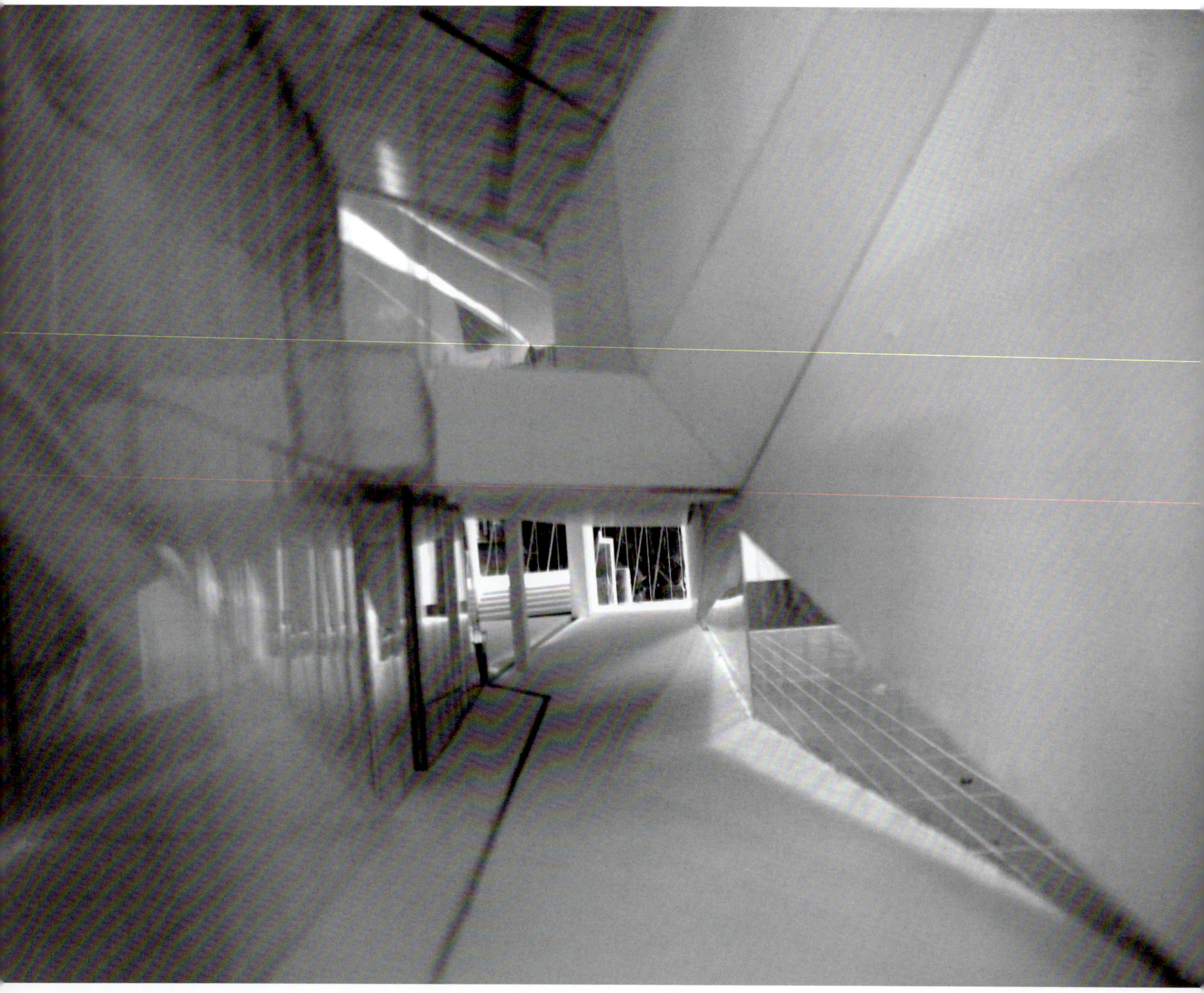

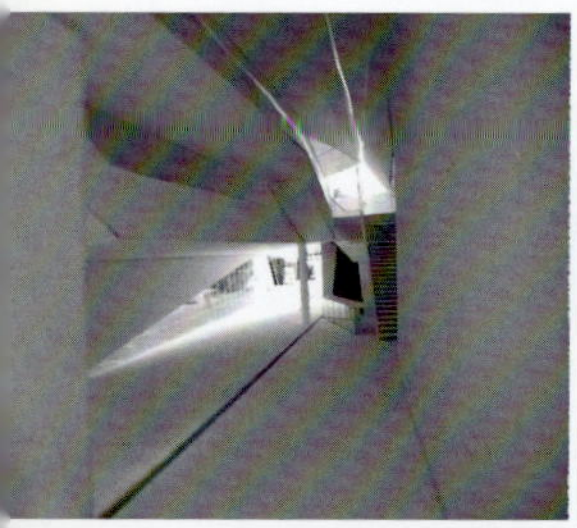
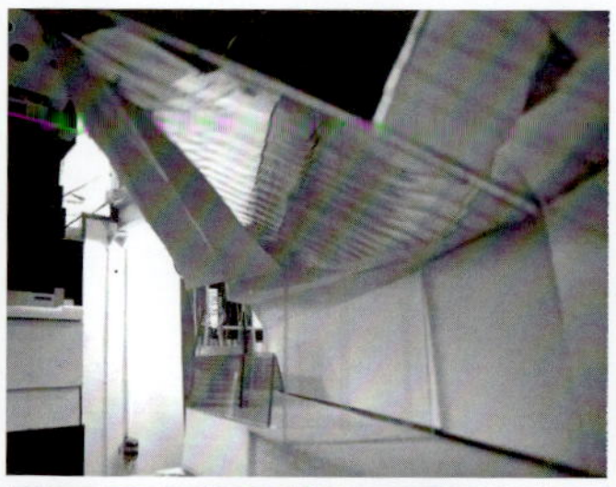
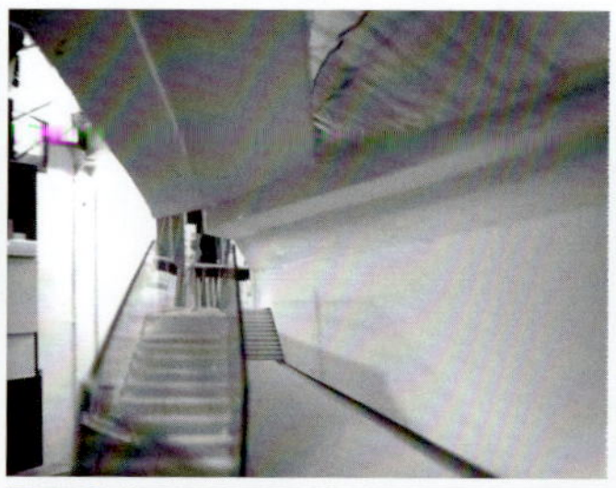
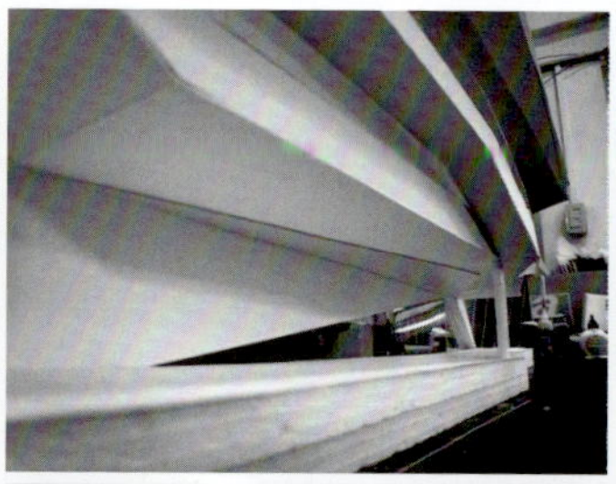
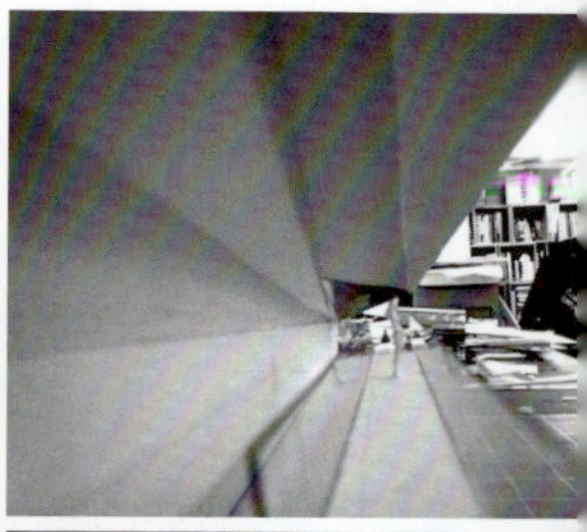

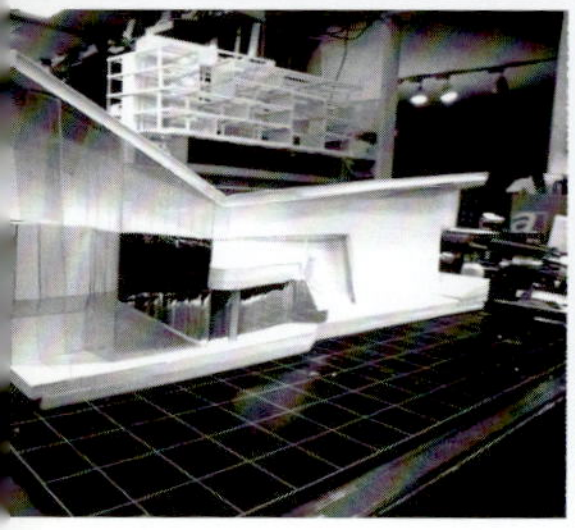
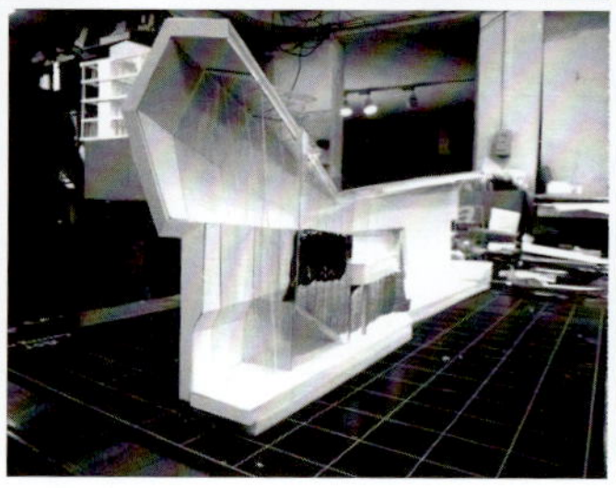
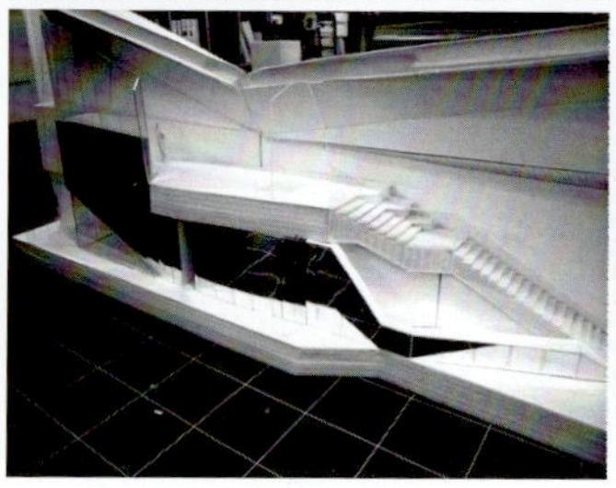
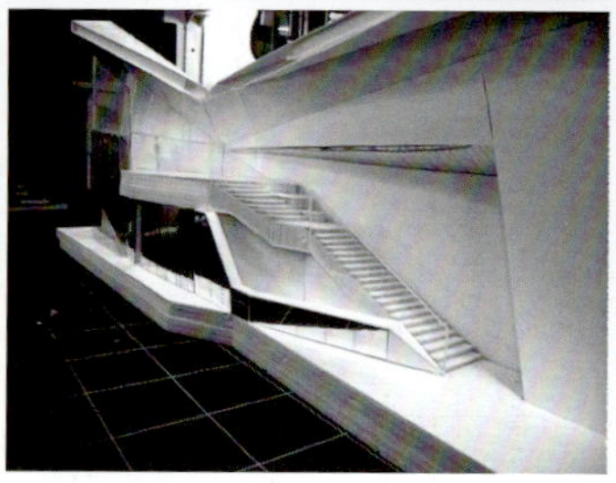
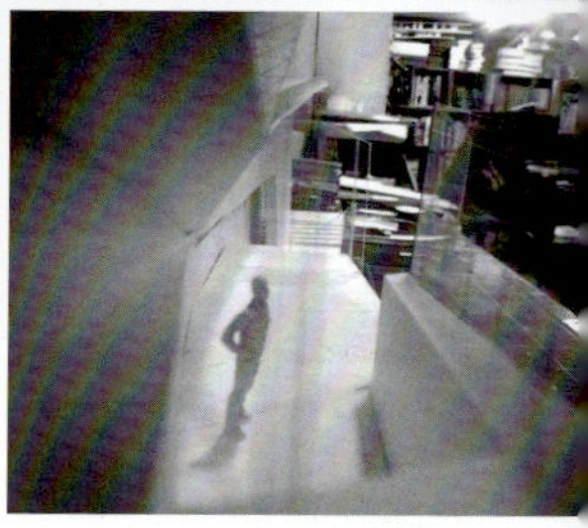

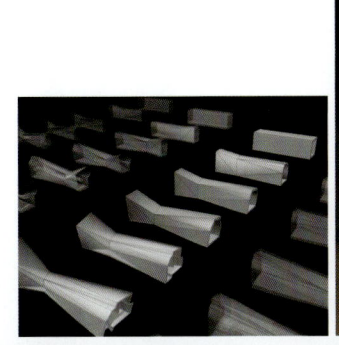

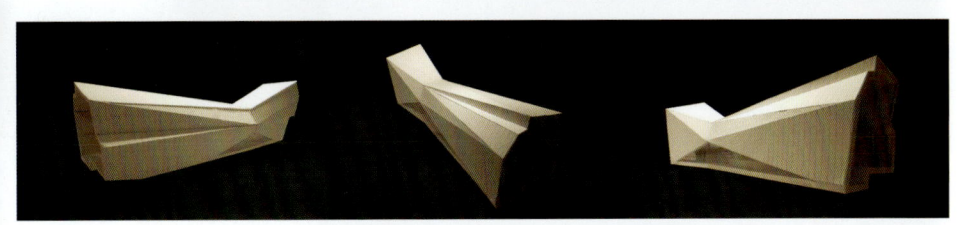

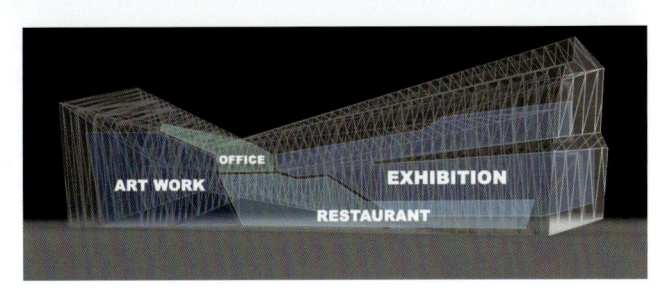

KALEIDOSCOPE GALLERY

On the express way to Won-ju, there are several long tunnels. While passing through them, I thought I wanted to make turn this interesting space of speed to an architectural work. Tunnels are an artificial and strong linking installation connecting severed two points. At the moment of penetrating a tunnel, I feel like I'm being moved to an unexpected place. Tunnels are a place like a kaleidoscope. This project, Kaleidoscope Gallery is one of the series of the transformed galleries. Yayoi Kusama's exhibition space shows limitless space like a kaleidoscope which reflects a limitless image. The Kaleidoscope space passes over the depth of fixed space and expands to a new range. The gallery, we suggest, has glass faces holding the scenery at both ends of it, and twisted linear masses are composed between them. The stress works at the medium point of the mass and it crumples the simple linear mass. Its end is white material contrasting the glass to provide surrealistic space. The images which are created in the gallery are not reflected totally. This delicate reflection makes resonance between the pieces of art. Clumped degree, depth of inner space, inserted duplex level and change of height verify spatial reflection and reaction.

SITE PLAN

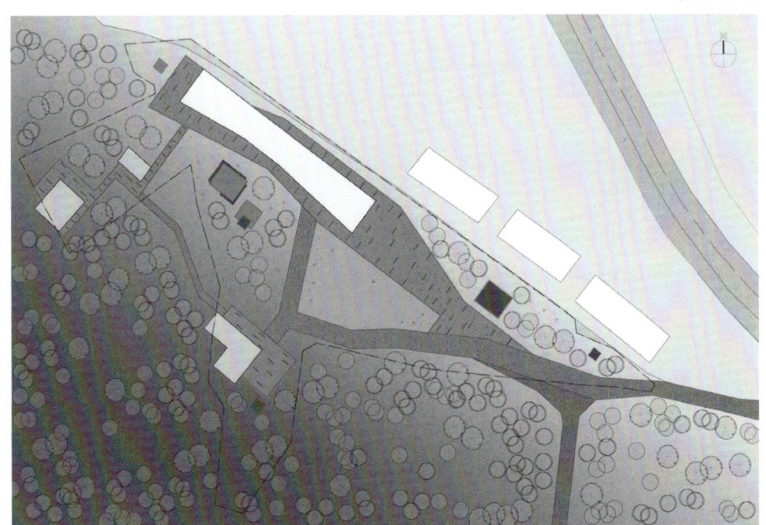

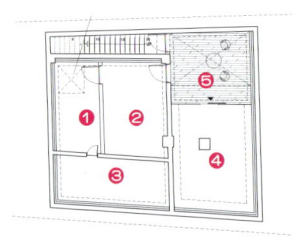

BASEMENT FLOOR PLAN
1. Machin Room
2. Electronic Room
3. Water Tank
4. Wine Seller Room
5. Sunken

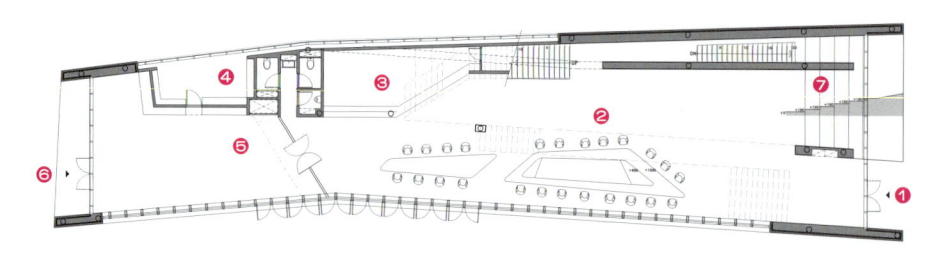

1ST FLOOR PLAN
1. Gallery Enterence
2. Gallery 1
3. Kitchen
4. Office
5. Studio
6. Atlier Enterence
7. Multi Event Deck

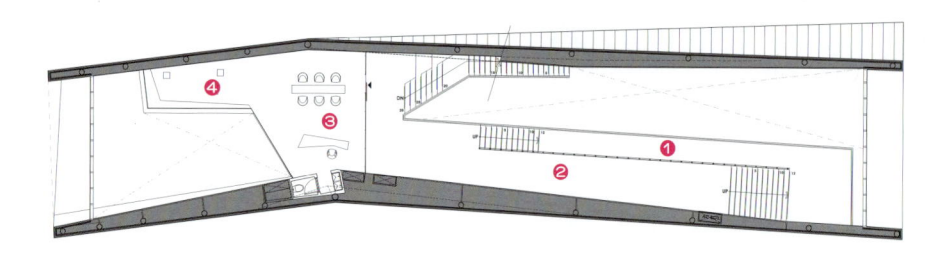

2ND FLOOR PLAN
1. Gallery 2
2. Mounting Shop
3. Principal's Office
4. Studio

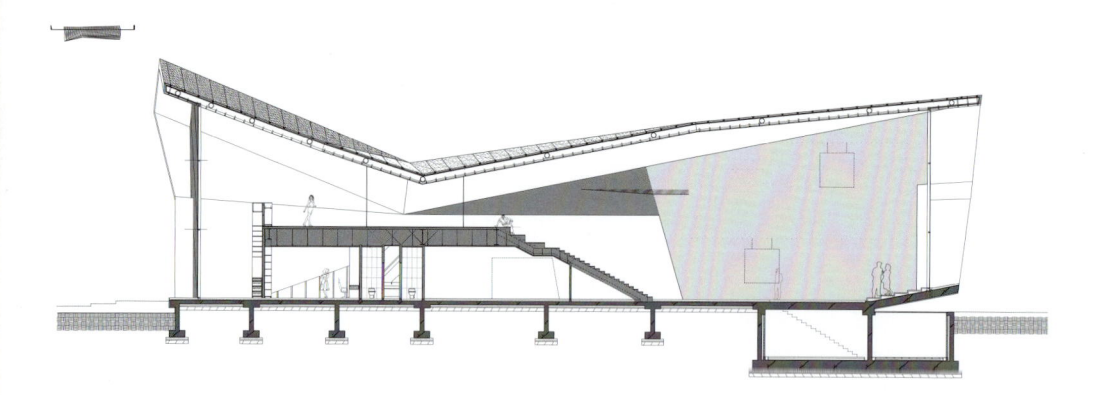

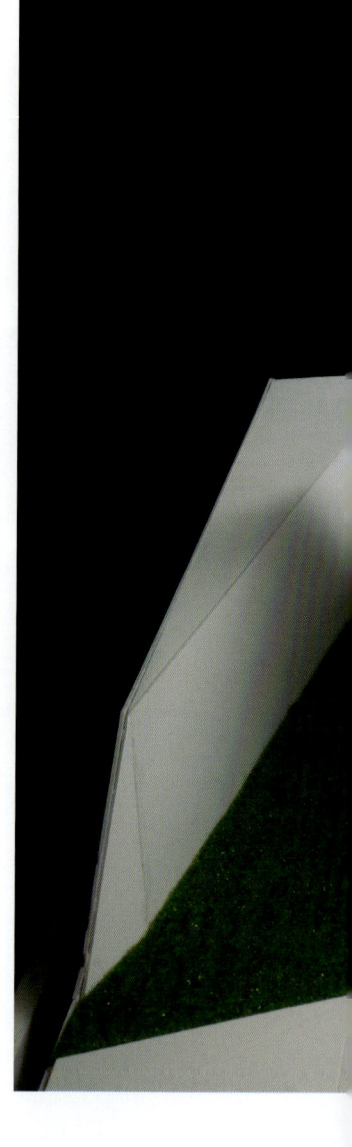

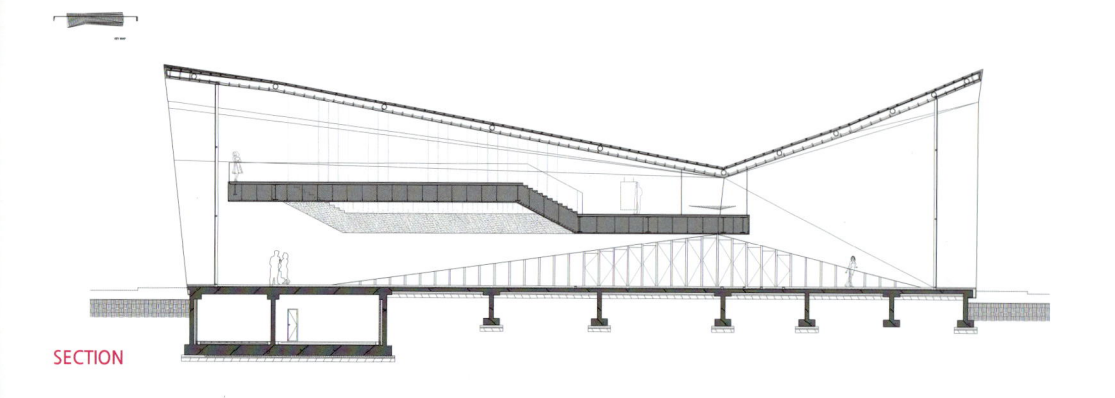

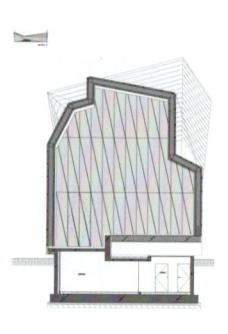

SECTION

COMPOUND BODY 561

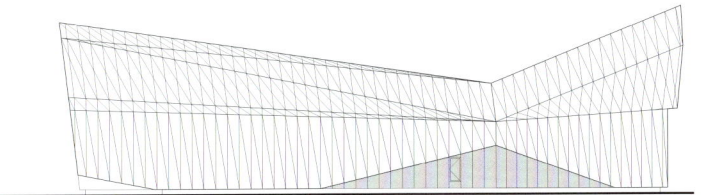

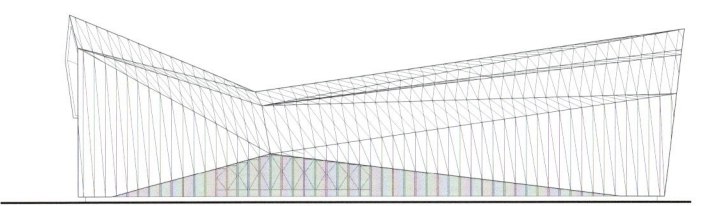

ELEVATION

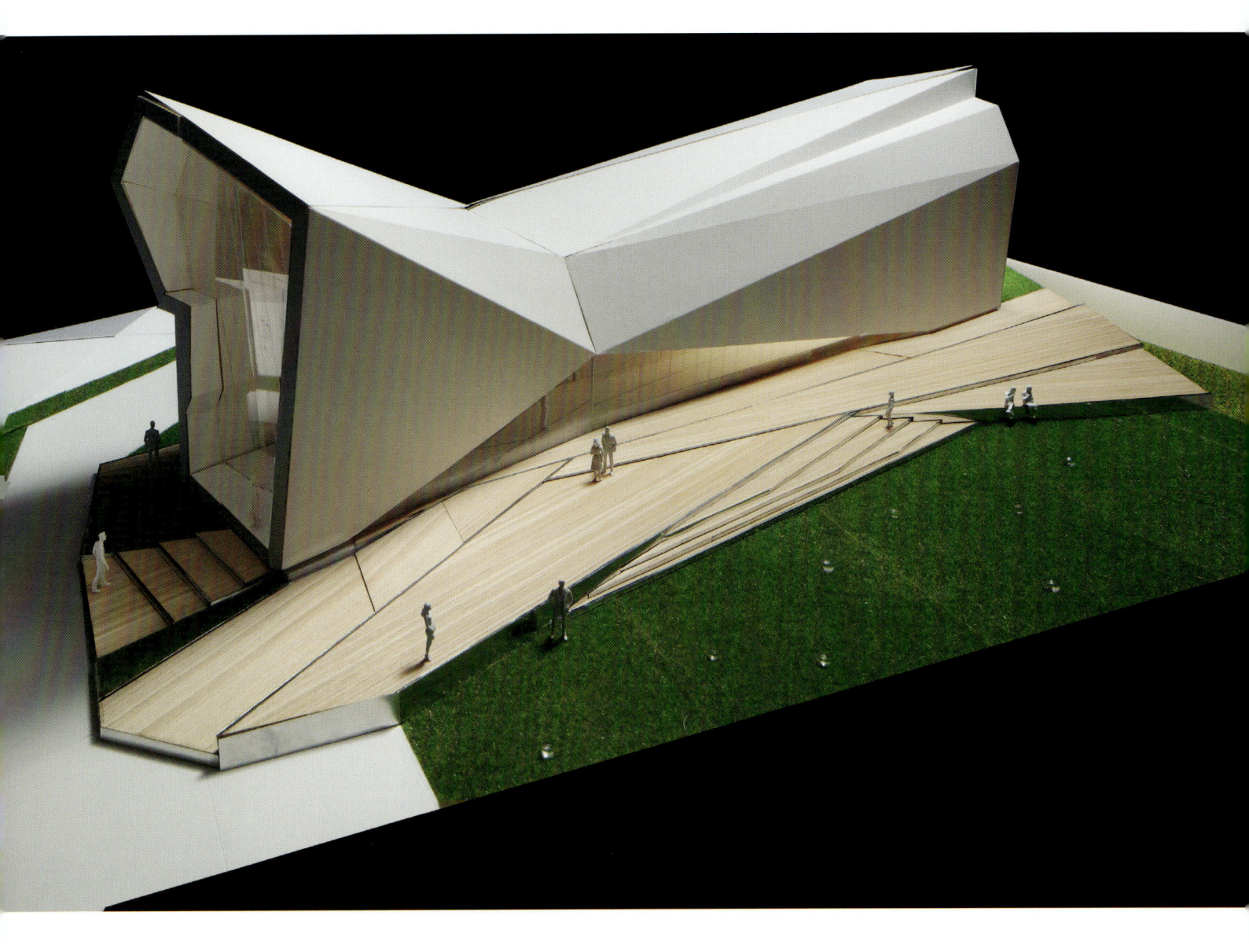

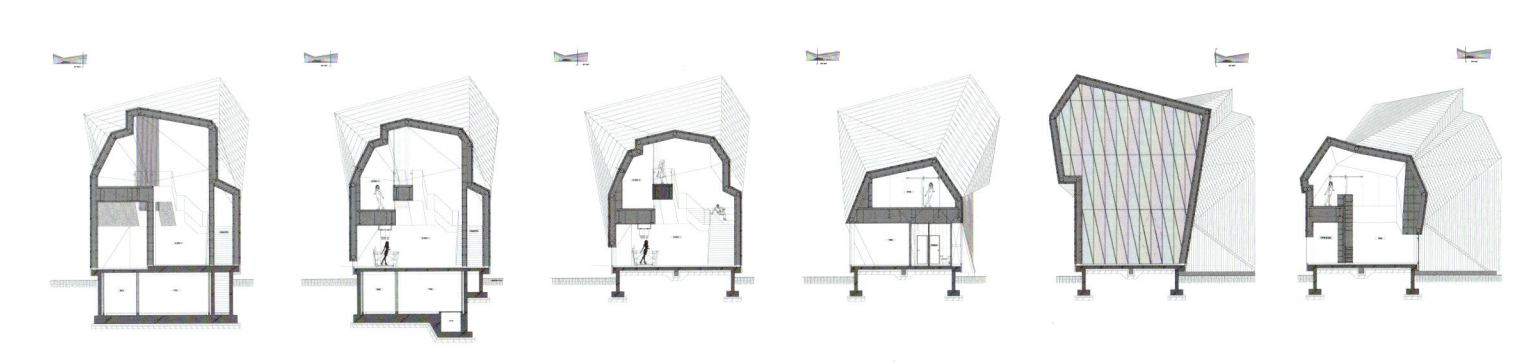

Passage
frame house

Atelier for Ceramic Artist

Architects Jang Yoon Gyoo, Shin Chang Hoon
Client Lee Jung Suk, Ko Hee Sook
Photographer Namgoong Sun

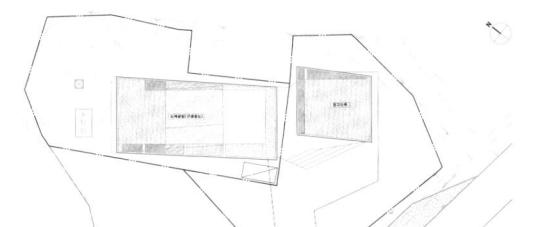

PASSAGE FRAME HOUSE

For a married couple who are potters, we propose this residential project as a frame house incorporate scenery. We create a simple concept with a minimum budget using passage frame, which collapses from a single plate.
After making a simple concrete plate structure in a box format, we can create economic forms between the plates to compose the inside space.
We then create the transformation body, which can change plates that are a combination of structure and skin, structure and view-frame, structure and program, ladscape and program, ladscape and view-frame, structure and moving, program and interactive map,etc., into the passage frame.

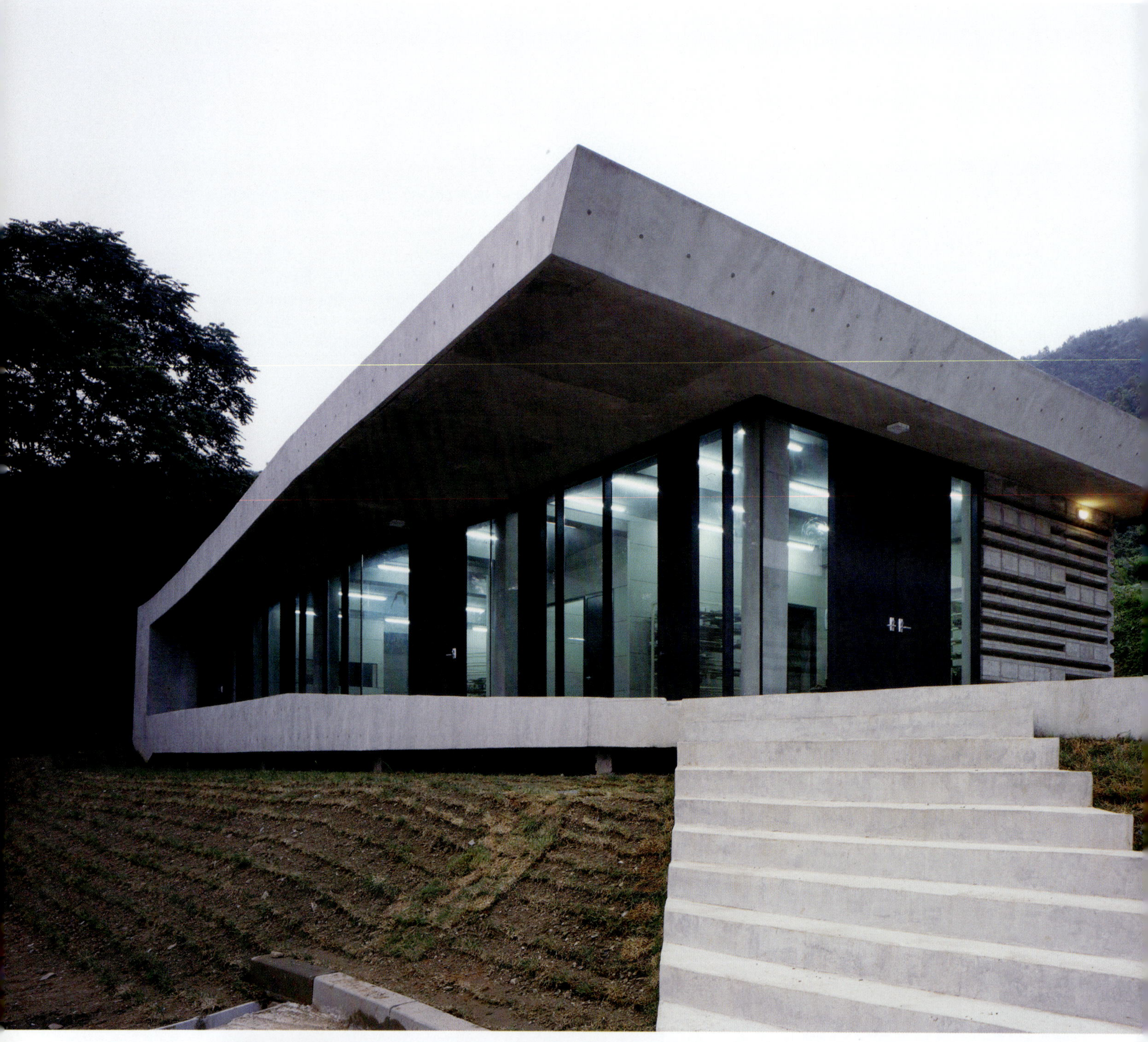

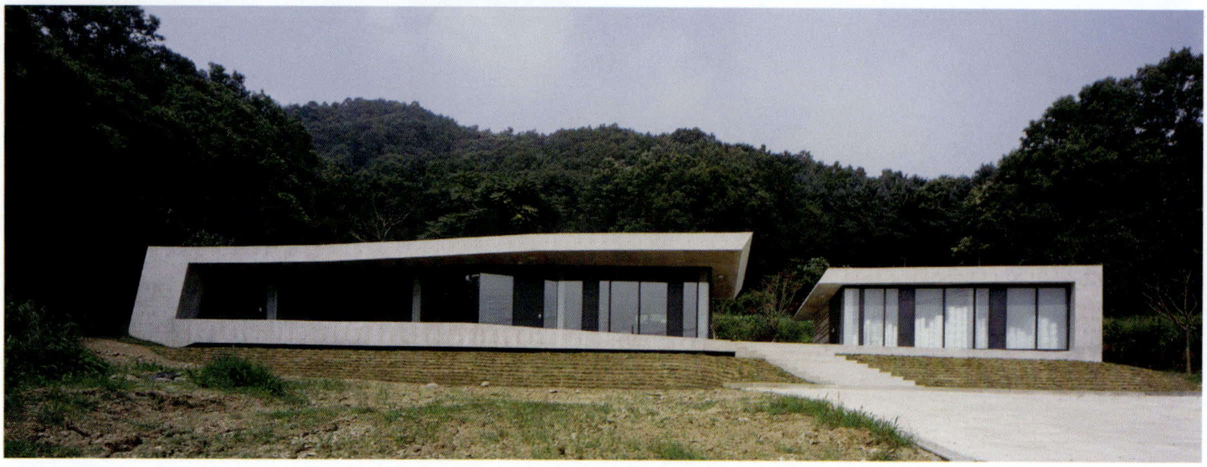

SOUTH-WEST ELEVATION

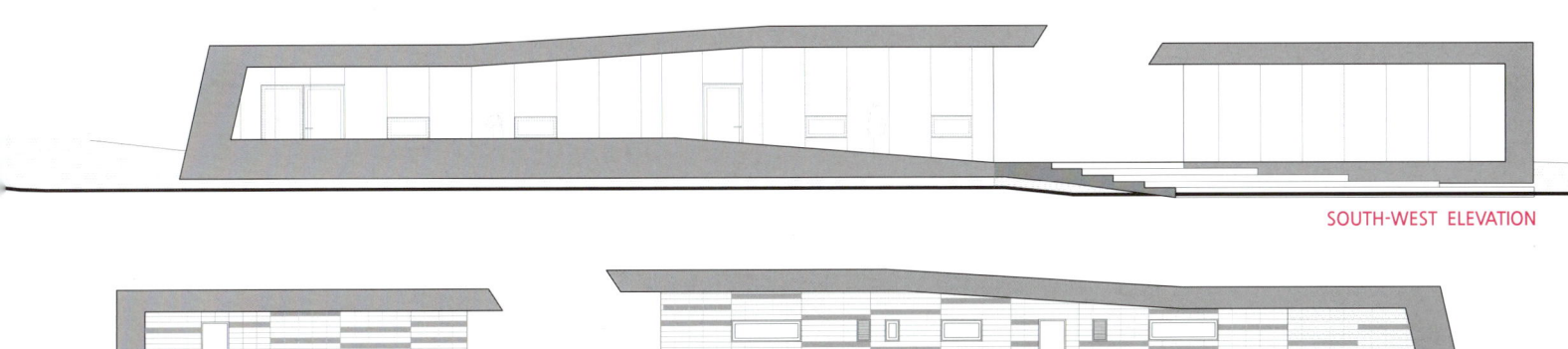

NORTH-EAST ELEVATION

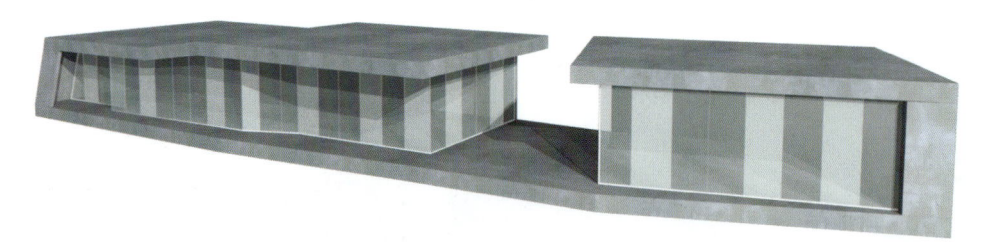

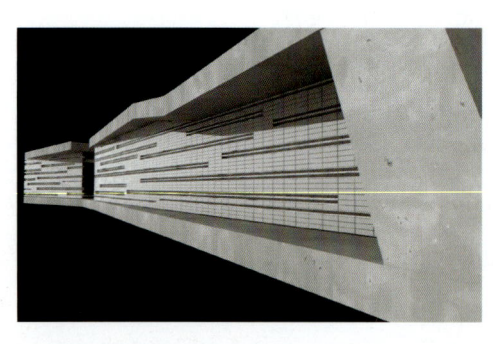

The suggested framework through the residential project becomes an Eco-friendly form that promotes enjoying and living with nature.
The pleasures of rural life offer a passage code from the natural landscape and environment. The passage frame is a similar vessel.
The transparent space filled in frame is a powerful device that accepts and admires nature without exaggerating it.
It is compose of the device frame which connects the residential function and natural landscape. It inserts spaces such as studios, outside decks, and indoor gardens into the frame space. The transparent space serves as a frame in which to incorporate the changes of nature. The space of the frame turns into a natural space when all the windows are open. It is similar to a vessel that can accommodate changes of nature and times.
The nature in the frame is also a nature frame that combines the changing and living.

FRAME

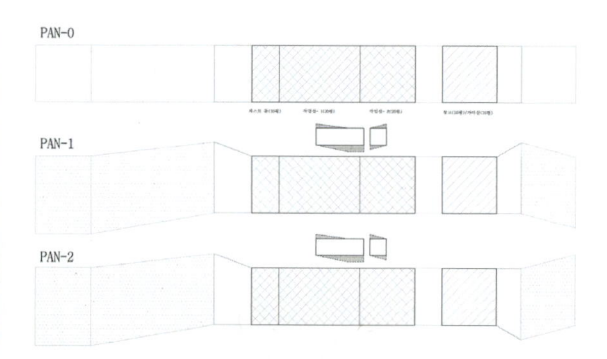

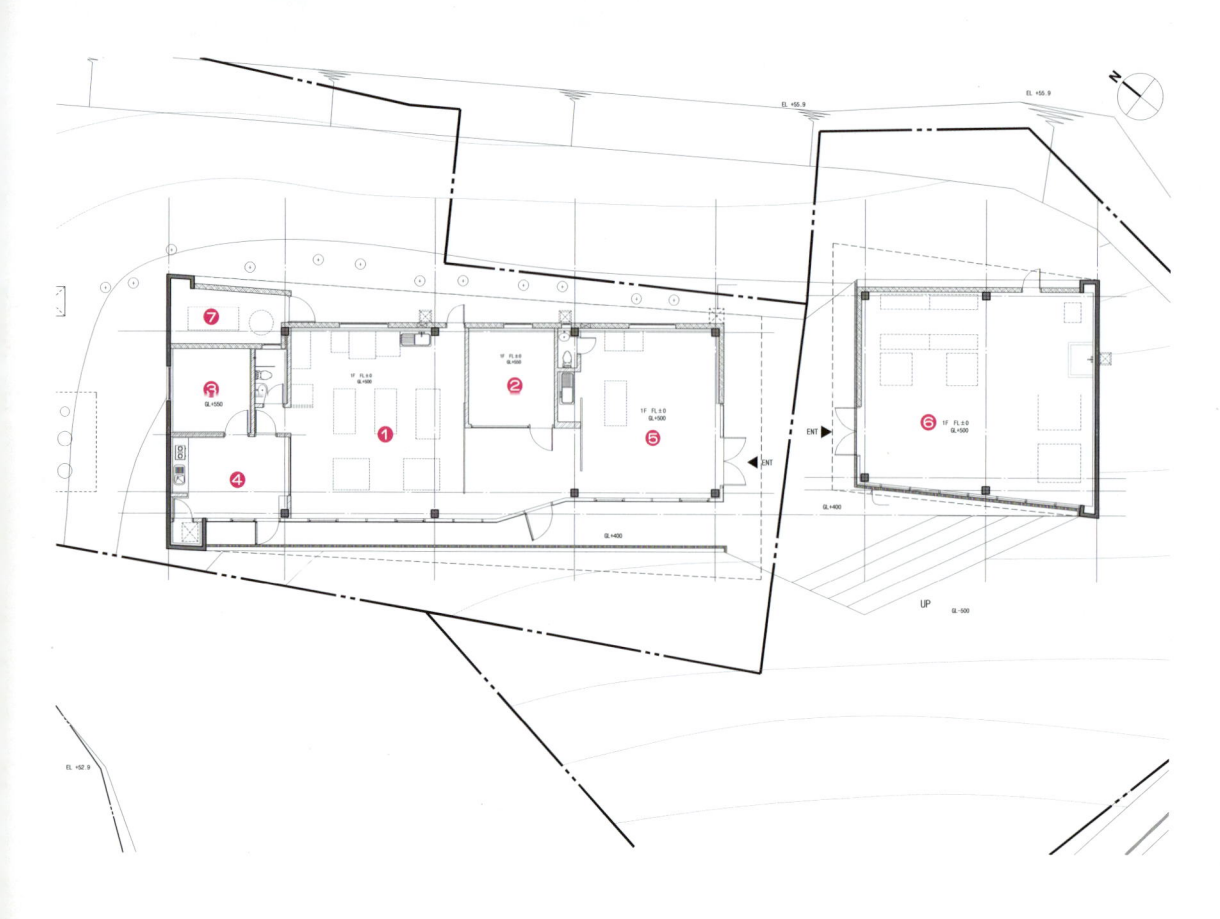

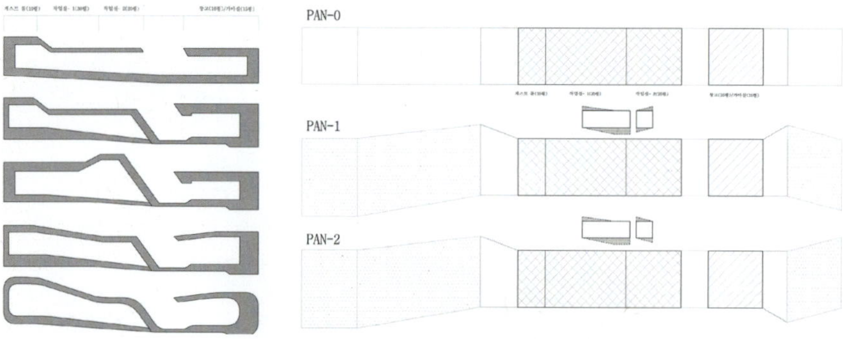

GROUND FLOOR PLAN
1. Studio
2. Achive Center
3. Bed Room
4. Living Room
5. Studay Room
6. Boiler room
7. Warehouse

Design Team
Lee Soon Pyo, Kim Min Tae
Location
258 Hu-ri, Sanbuk-myeon, Yeoju
Use Atelier and residence
Site Area 660㎡
Building Area 218.62㎡
Gross Floor Area 186.19㎡
Building Coverage 33.121%
Floor Space Index 28.21%
Building Scope 1F
Parking 1car

Eco Frame House

COMPOUND BODY 369

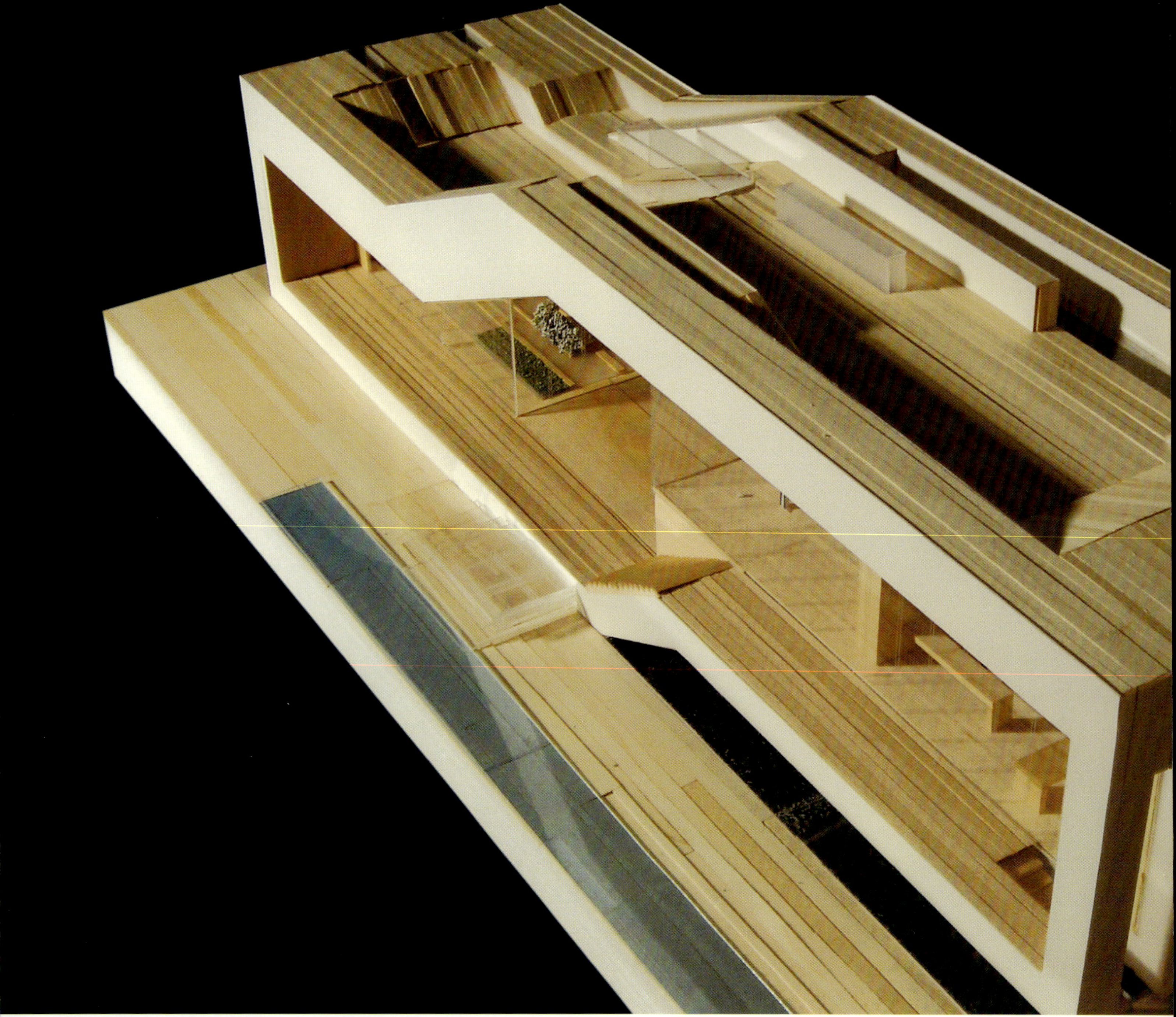

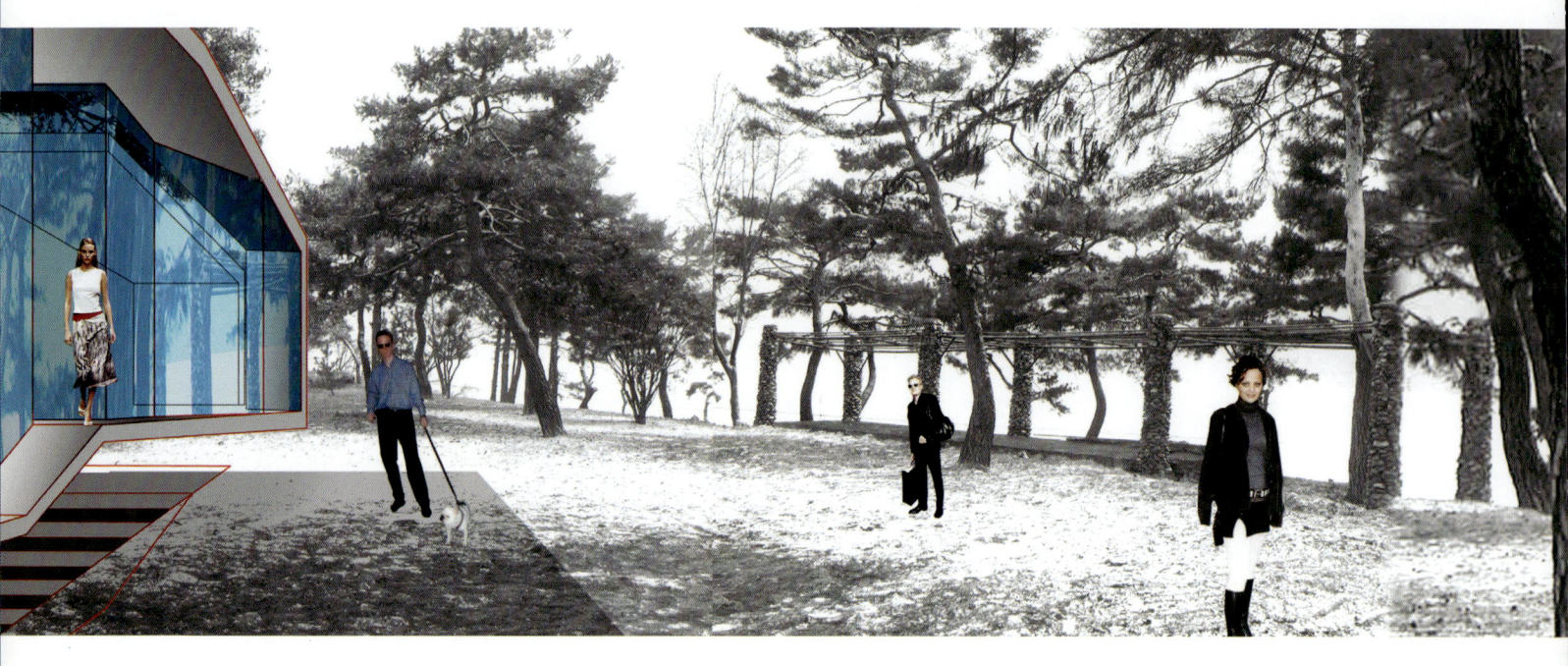

PASSAGE FRAME HOUSE

We suggest a housing which outdoor scenery is attracted in inner space. Interfering void which penetrates to each spaces through strong interactive map is suggested. Outdoor interactive map has synchronized code with inner scenery. Diverse layered frames piled on frames are arranged. Interfering void is scenery installation making sole scenery piled depth. The combination of structure and skin, structure and view frame, structure and inner programs, landscape and program, landscape and view frame, structure and movement, program and interactive map composes 'Landscape Compound'.

Passage between Nature-Artificial Codes
Scenery frame which is suggested by dwelling is environment-friendly amusing nature and living in it. Rural housing provides scenery code which is created in between circumstance and nature.

Interactive Frame
Scenery frame is sort of container putting in nature. Suggested frame has different section according to depth of space. Transparent space filled in the frame takes nature and dwellers amuse and experience as it is. It is installed frame connecting the function of housing and landscape from nature. Two-story-living room, outdoor deck space and indoor garden-changed function of warehouse-inserted in frame space.

Passage Frame
Transparent spatial frame holds change of nature. When all the doors open, the space in the frame changes whole nature space. It is like huge container accommodating change of nature by the time and season. Frame is a mold natural integrating natural changes and living in the housing

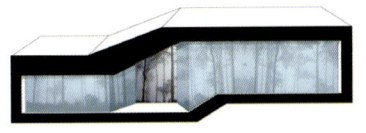

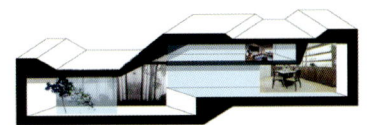

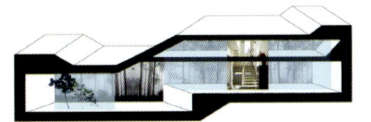

FRAME SECTION

FRAME TYPOLOGY FOR VIEW

ELEVATION

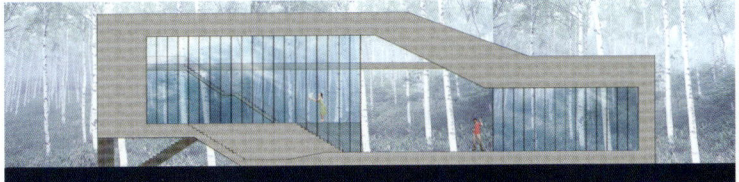

Kolon E+ Green Home

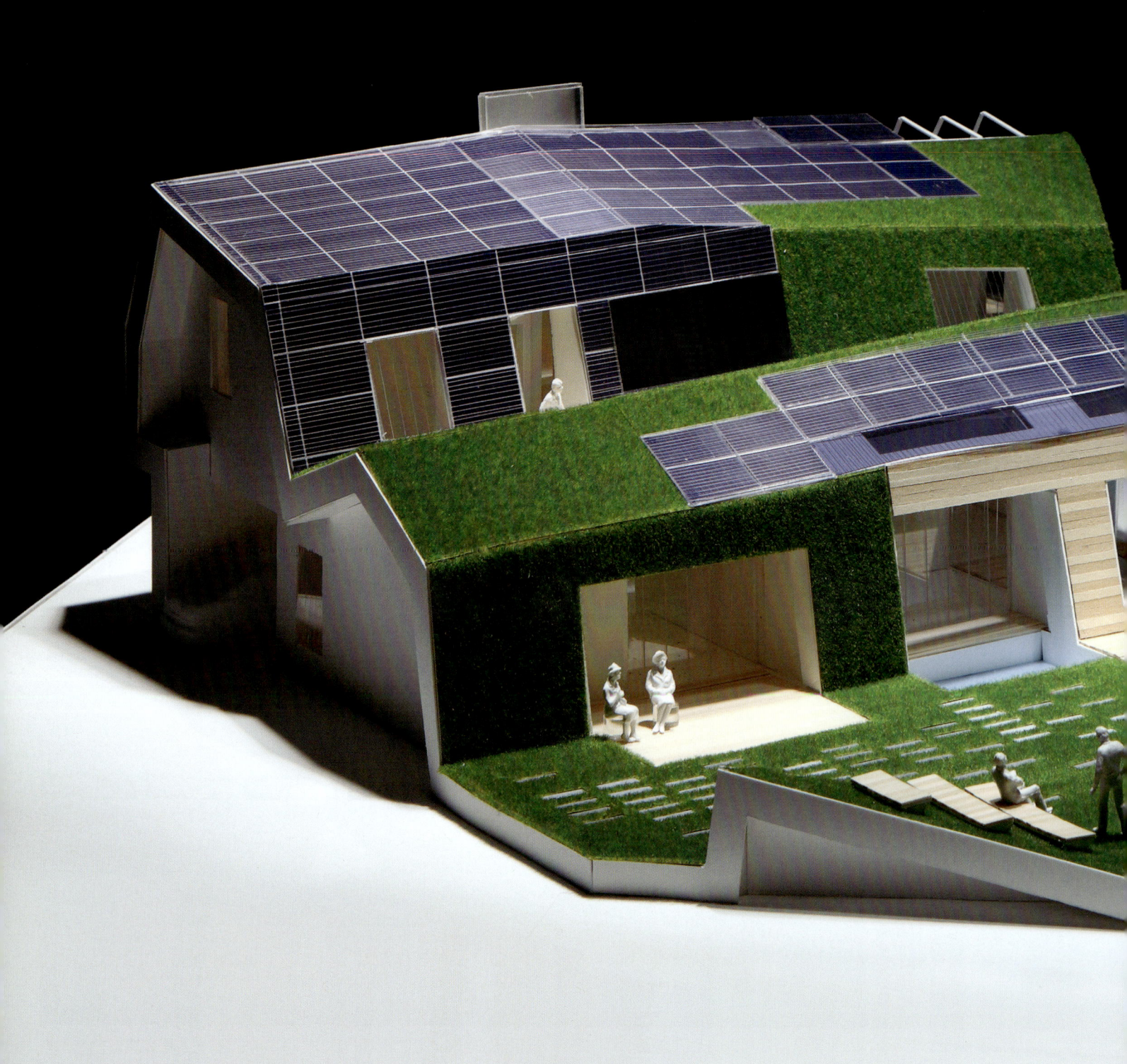

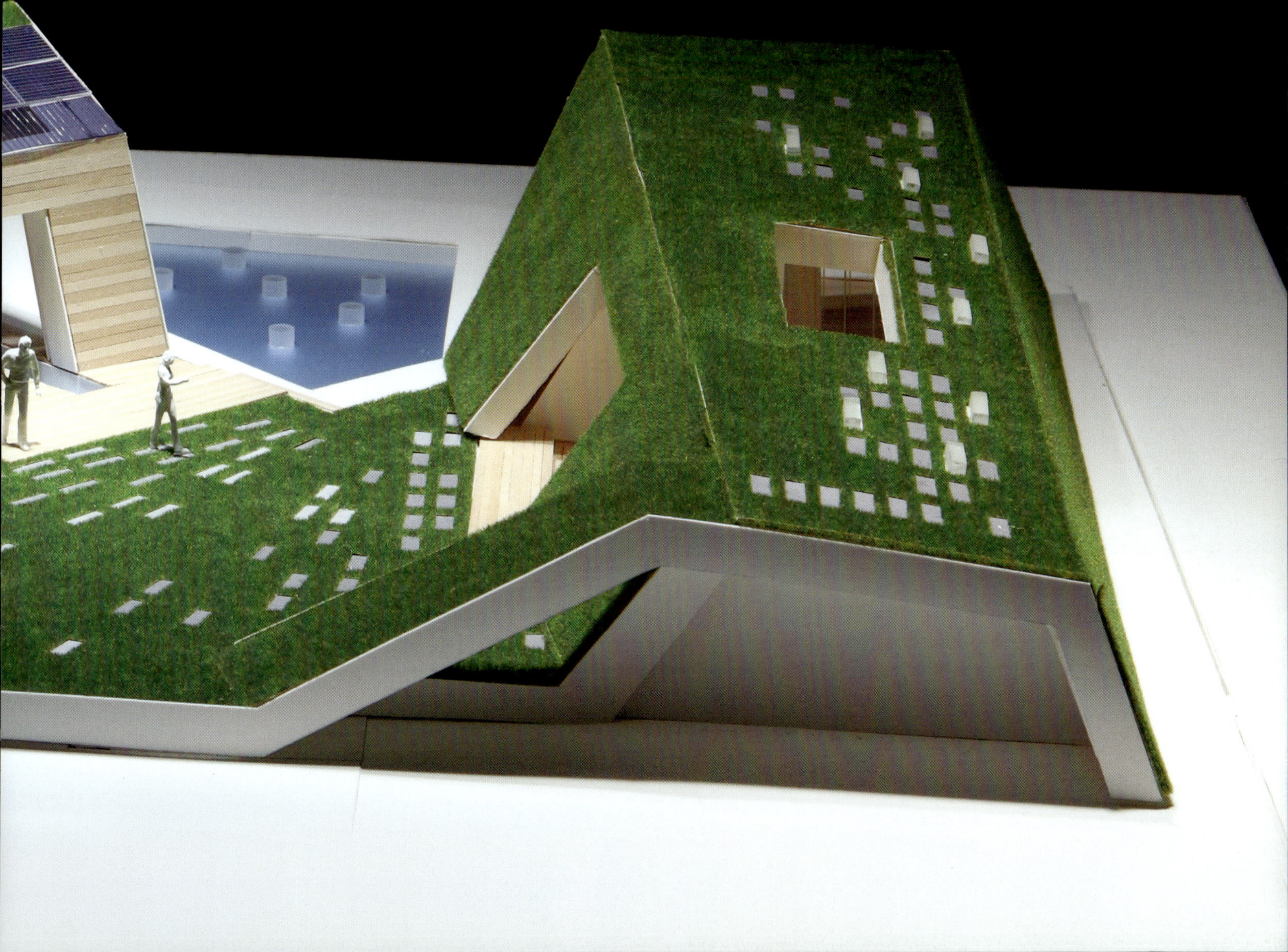

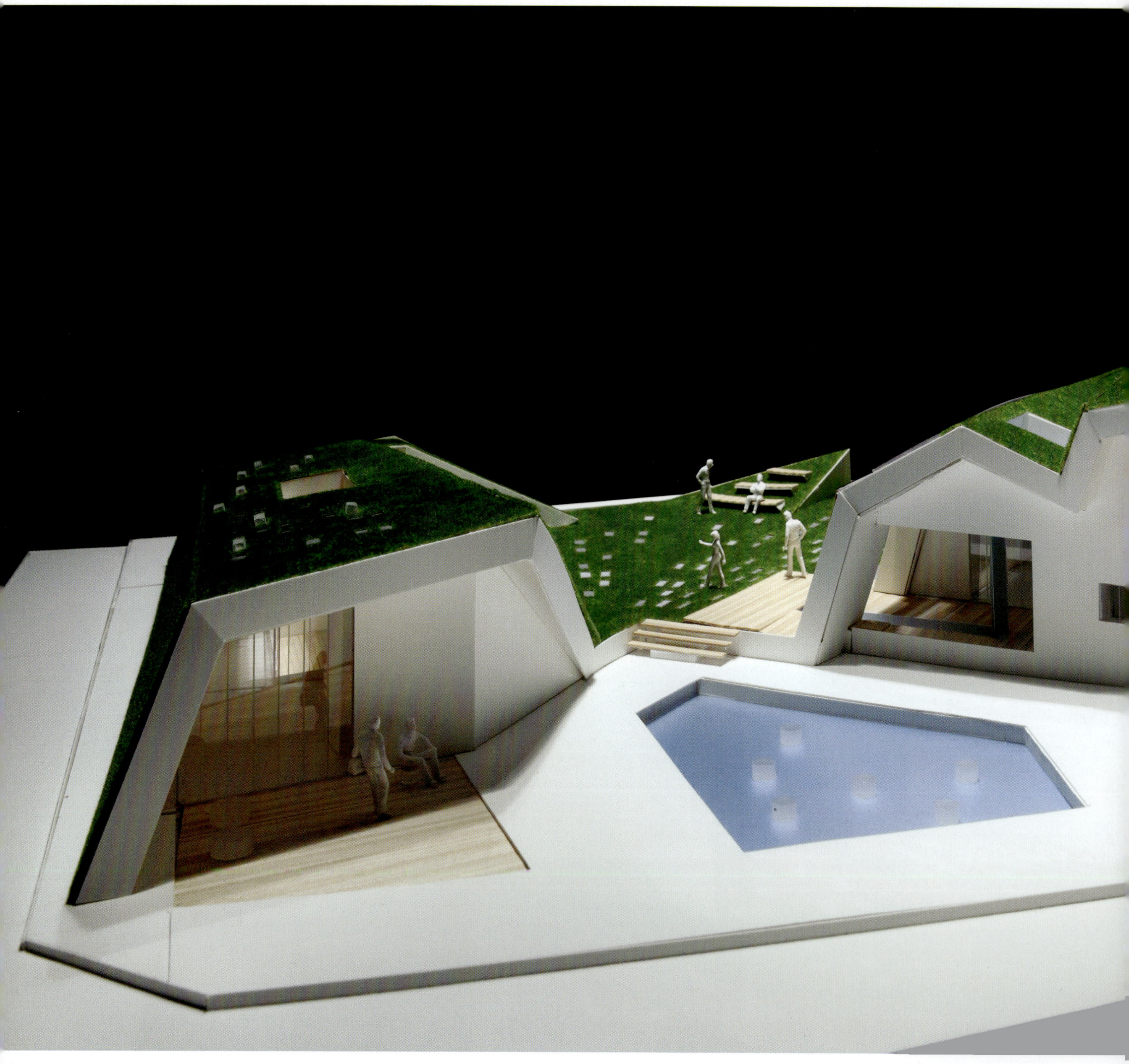

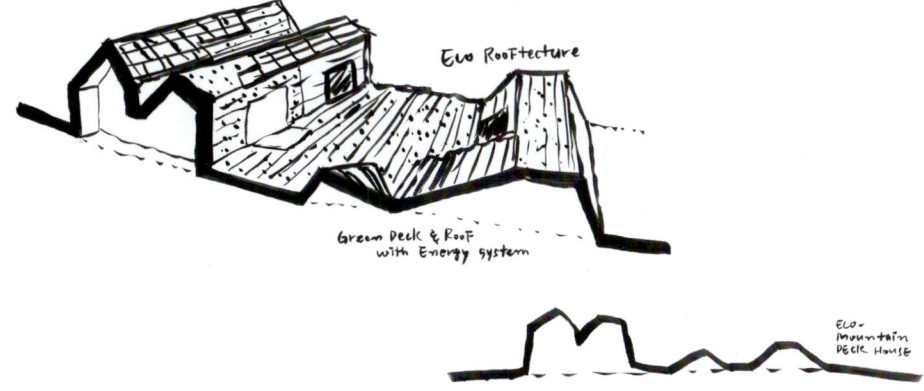

ECO-ROOFTECTURE

Our civilization, having been progressed on industrialization and information, confronts to absolute demand for coexistence with nature. All the traces of civilization from architectural activities could mean ruins from the nature's point of view. What we call civilization is producing dead architectural space and places by futuristic demands. As the society is civilizes the natural environment goes towards ruins. As capitalism is on progresses, the consumption-oriented society makes focus on environmental issues making global warming, exhaustion of natural resource and energy draining a subject that we can't avoid. Especially the population of big cities, architecture, infra… because of theses endless expansions and consumptions, a new type of urban residence is required. Based on Landscape Architecture and Ecological Architecture, the demands for eco friendly system achieved by the combination artificiality and nature and symbiosis is also in that issue.

As the theme of a new type of dwelling, we suggest Energy + Green Home above Energy Zero. It is a type of dwelling which is a combination of architectural products of natural properties and a production way of artificial technology. This green home includes diverse factors such as structural system, materials, spatial composition, landscape-enrichment and facilitated human life.

The roof concept integrating a landscape and energy system is accommodated. This work adopts shapes from nature such as chaos, fractal and folds to the space. Rooftecture is that the roof, which is the most important part of a shelter, brings natural shape and transforms to physical skin in a more abstract way. A technology skin including energy product system is combined with it. The system of Rooftecture with minimized energy loss, gain of maximum solar energy with the gradient of the roof, curved shape using water resource and outdoor terrace are teamed up and become a whole roof like a landscape with the appropriate crease, angle and bumpy face. The roof, like a consequent mountain shape efficiently uses natural resources such as the sun, water, earth and wind.

It is a sustainable housing producing energy with the optimum system adopted through eco friendly architectural technology. Architecture and nature are harmonized and residents meet nature factors in daily life. It is a rational and emotional housing taking shape and system from nature. New organic Architecture is extracted from nature inspired technology which studies the principle of all natural creatures.

PHASE 1

Type 1 Monolithic

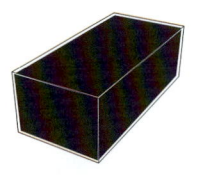

A simple mass that has no projecting part.

> Energy Efficiency
> Aesthetic
> Workability
> Economical

Type 2 Additional

Forming mass by stacking programmes, we can have a string of in-between spaces.

> Energy Efficiency
> Aesthetic
> Workability
> Economical

Type 3 Subtractive

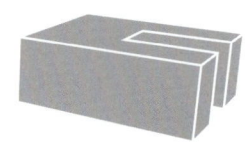

Getting fresh air and daylight in the central part of building through to the courtyard.

> Energy Efficiency
> Aesthetic
> Workability
> Economical

PHASE 3

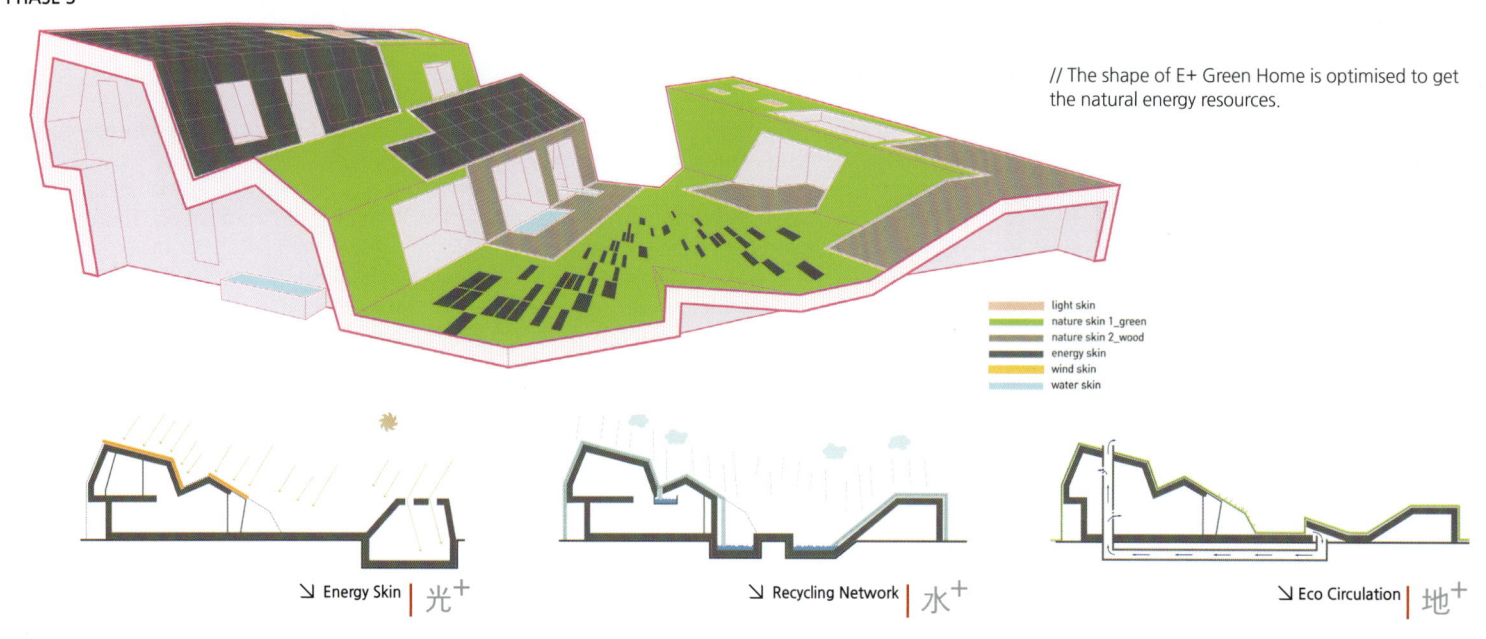

// The shape of E+ Green Home is optimised to get the natural energy resources.

light skin
nature skin 1_green
nature skin 2_wood
energy skin
wind skin
water skin

↘ Energy Skin | 光+

↘ Recycling Network | 水+

↘ Eco Circulation | 地+

GREEN PATIO

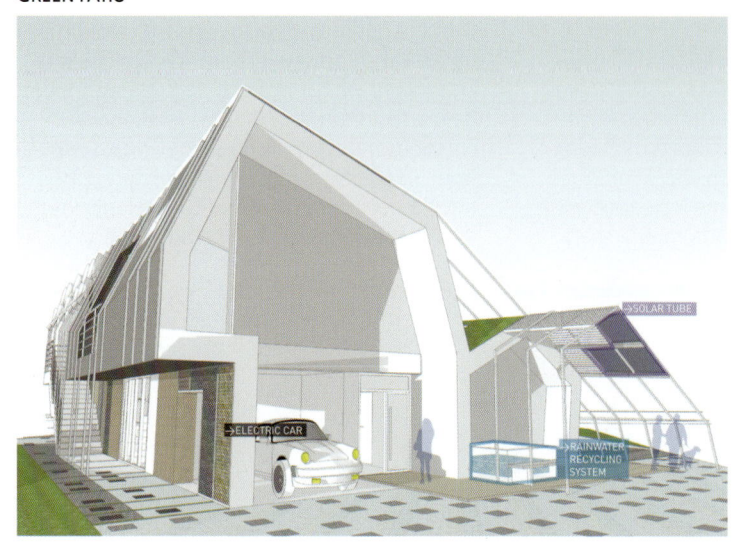

INFORMATION CENTRE

PHASE 2

1 **Program Mass** 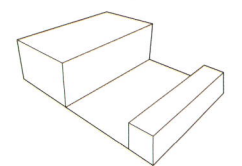
Minimising energy loss. No seperation or interpenetration.

2 **Solar System** 光+ light+
Tilting the roof to get the best use of solar energy.

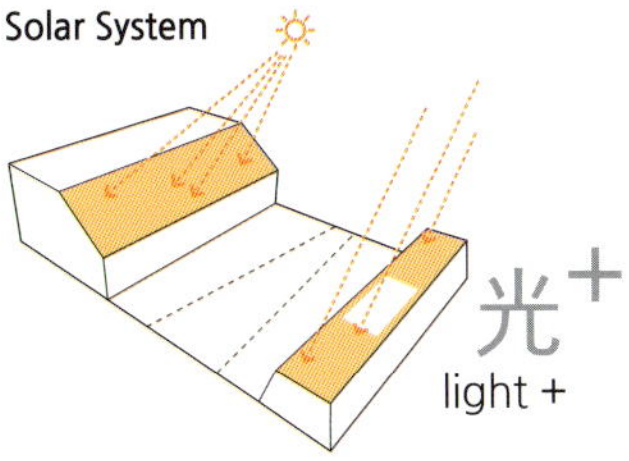

3 **Water Flowing** 水+ water+
Transforming and making up the shape to make better use of water energy.

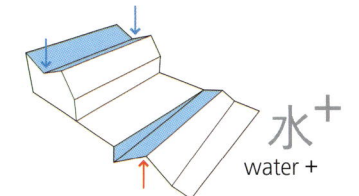

4 **Eco Landscape** 地+ land+
To maximise of using natural resources, all the facets are transformed.

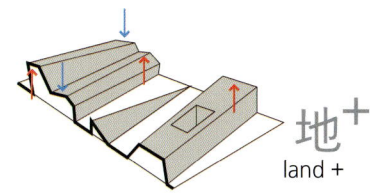

PHASE 4

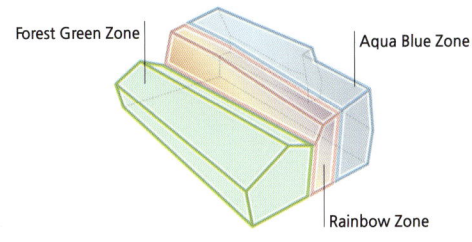

Forest Green Zone
Aqua Blue Zone
Rainbow Zone

↘ **Forest Green Zone** : Living Space facing South
↘ **Aqua Blue Zone** : Service area facing North
↘ **Rainbow Zone** : In-between space

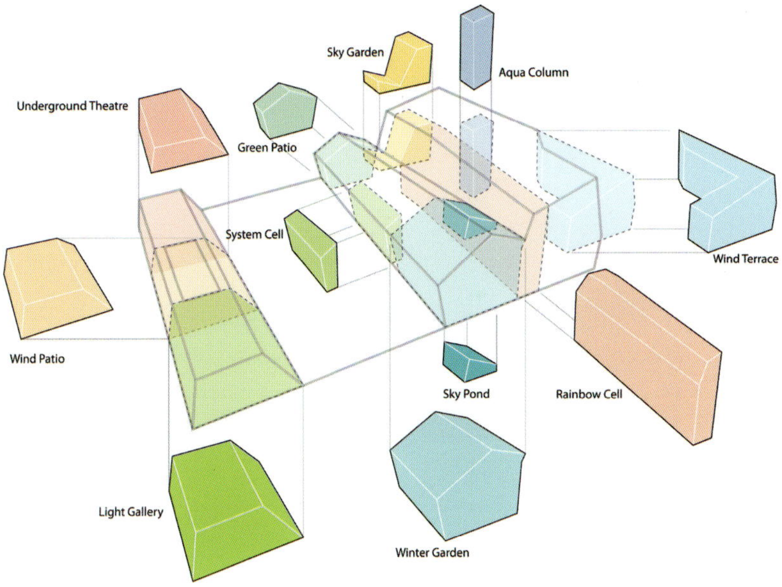

// There are different kinds of 'eco-spaces' in the building namely, rainbow cell, wind terrace, aqua column and so on. E+ Green Home would provide us a healthy living and qulity of life through these spaces.

Underground Theatre, Sky Garden, Aqua Column, Green Patio, System Cell, Wind Terrace, Wind Patio, Sky Pond, Rainbow Cell, Light Gallery, Winter Garden

FOREST GREEN ZONE

AQUA BLUE ZONE

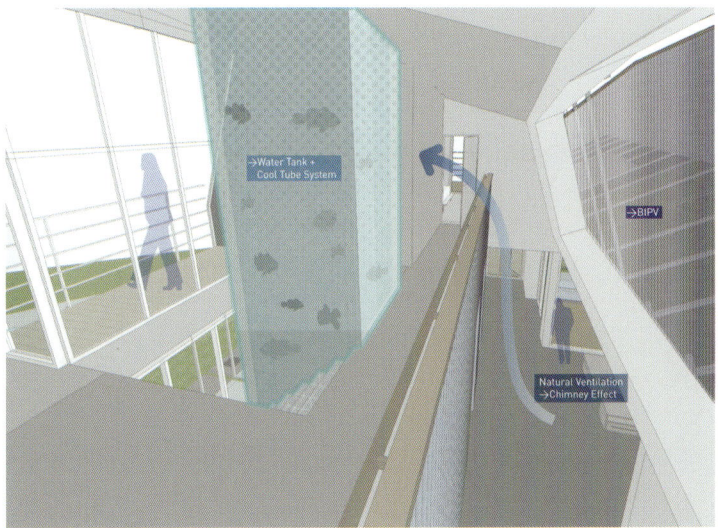

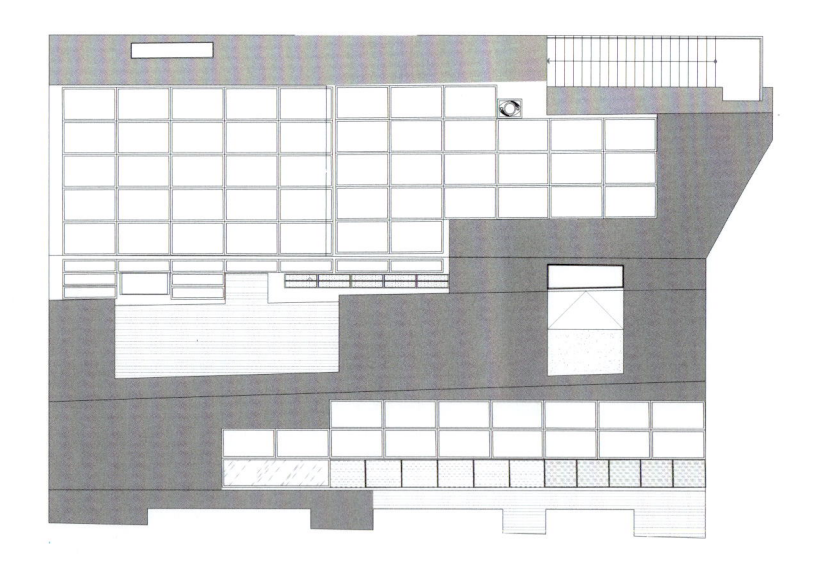

ROOF PLAN

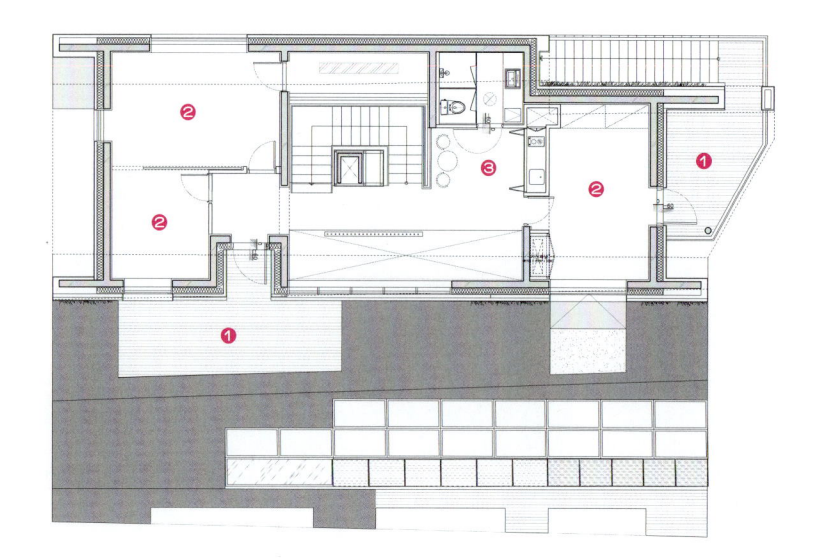

2ND FLOOR PLAN
1. Terrace
2. Bed Room
3. Kitchen

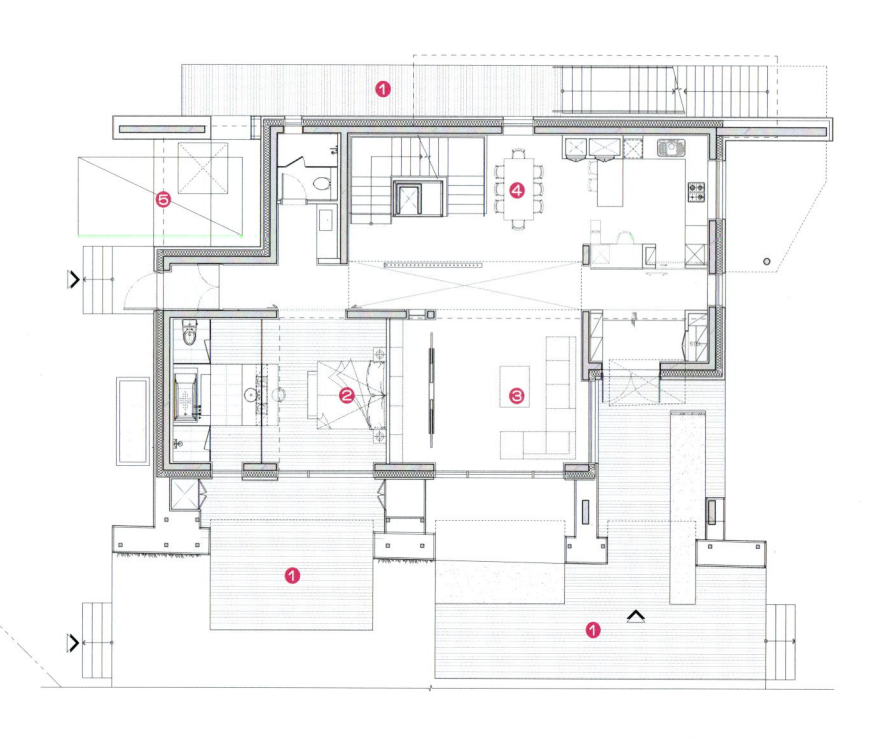

1ST FLOOR PLAN
1. Deck
2. Master Bed Room
3. Living Room
4. Dining Room
5. Parking

COMPOUND BODY

↘ Solar Energy　|光⁺

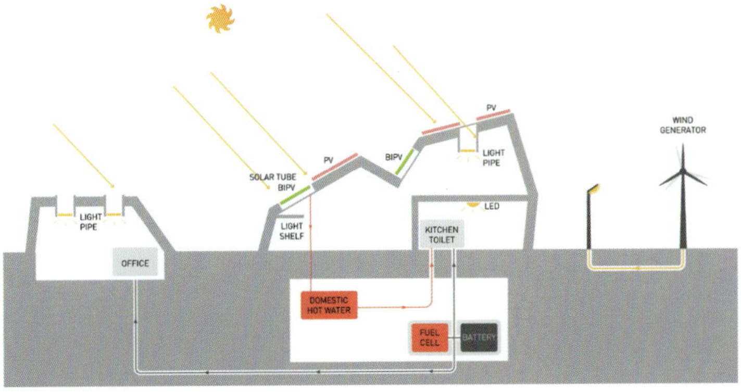

↘ Recycling Network　|水⁺

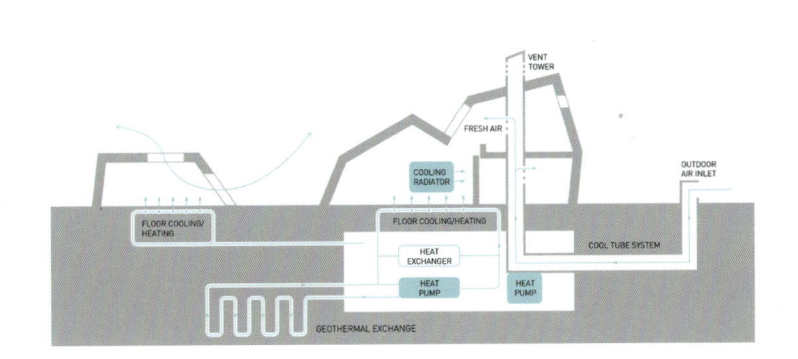

↘ Eco Circulation　|地⁺

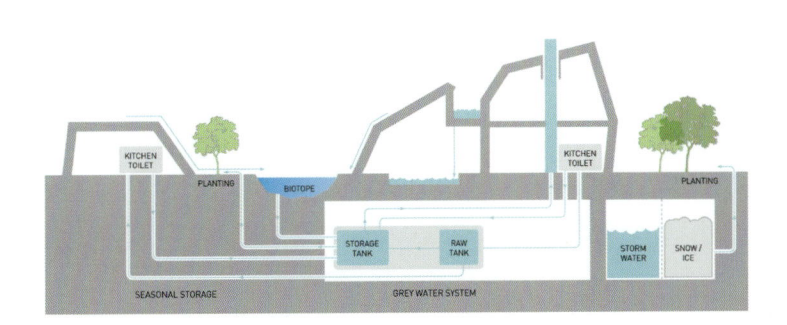

GEOTHERMAL ENERGY

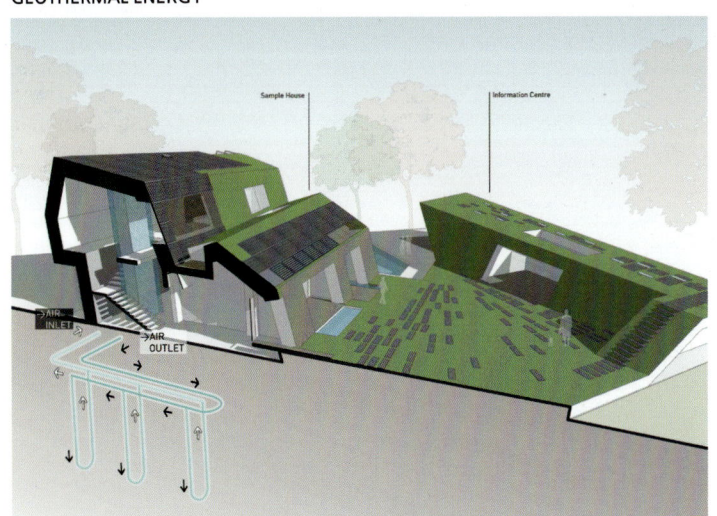

SOLAR ENERGY

- SOLAR PHOTOVOLTAIC ENERGY (PV's) **115m²**
- BIPV **14m²**
- SOLAR THERMAL ENERGY (HOT WATER) **13m²**

RAINWATER RECYCLING

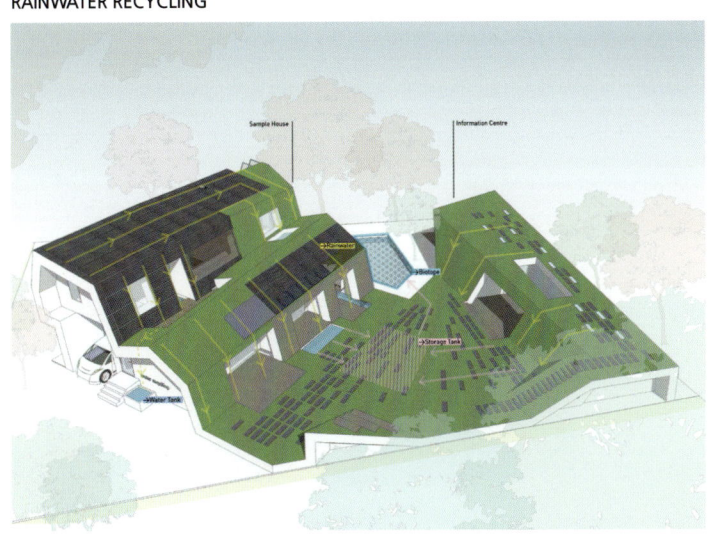

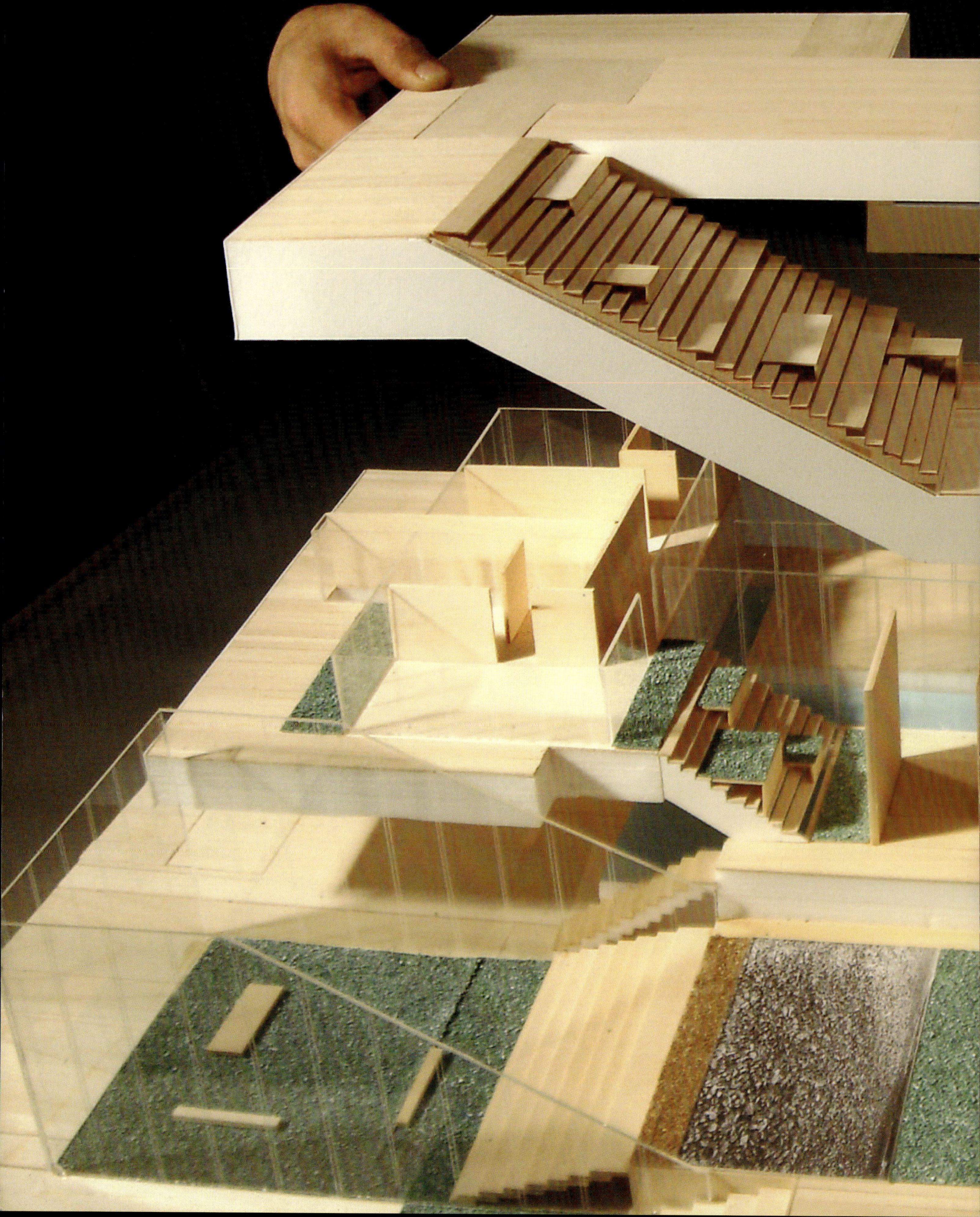

Competition Winner   **Architects** Jang Yoon Gyoo, Shin Chang Hoon, Lee Mee Young   **COMPOUND BODY** 581

VIEW FRAME

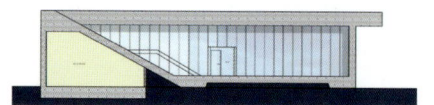

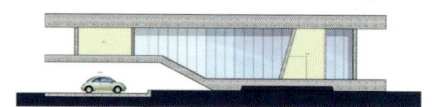

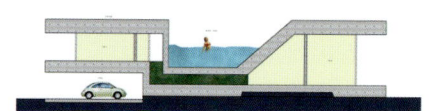

GROUND FLOOR PLAN

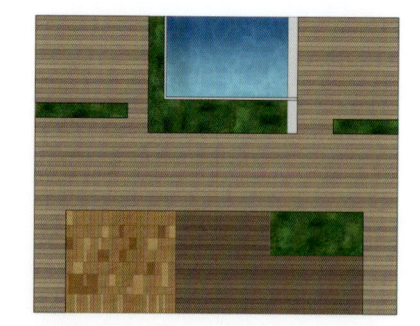

ROOF FLOOR PLAN

ELEVATION

INTERACTIVE PASSAGE

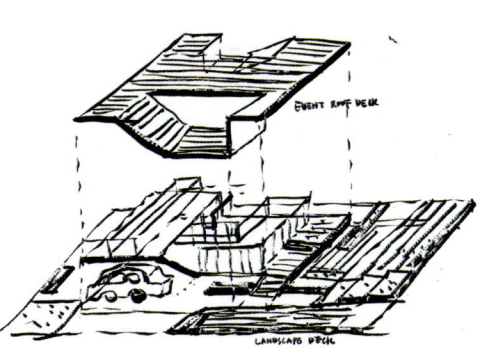

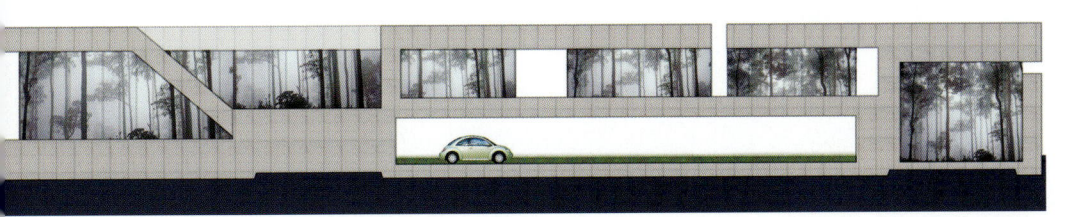

PASSAGE DECK HOUSE

Landscape Deck of topography is 3 dimensionally composed. Empty glass space existing in crack of two levels is a ring connecting outside and inside passage. The 3-dimensional deck erases boundary between living space and landscaping space. There are 2 decks on the ground floor which combines landscape and function and roof floor which has floating landscape.

Interactive Passage
Program which forms topographic scenery and grows it is inserted. The topographic scenery is not included in boring routine anymore. It creates the passage towards outdoor and control indoor passage. New boundary crossing passage and non-passage makes housing programs and materials relating each other and draws interactive map. Movement of passage is set up open relationship in order to control construct of site. Scenery and property of material composes interactive landscape through manipulation of architectural plate.

Landscape Deck 01_ Interactive Deck
We suggest composition which compound inner space relating living program and ground level deck extended landscape. A code inserting nature inside of housing program is composed. Housing function and natural landscape is sequential on the housing level. Materials such as green skin, artificial deck, terraced deck, inner deck, water space, gravel, grass and wooden deck and the variation of them make varied landscape.

Landscape Deck 02_ Event Roof deck
3-dimensional deck is composed on the roof level connected ground. This roof garden is extension of landscape. It plays role of adopting diverse events. Garden party, outdoor resting, walking, playing, watching stars, swimming… Landscape deck penetrates nature. Diverse dwellers lie down on the deck amusing nature. In conclusion, our aim is the architectural program of event roof deck which architecture is compounded with landscape and 3-dimensional landscape concept generally including the landscape factors such as green carpets, information, light, plaza and event.

Gallery CAMELLIA HILL

Architects Jang Yoon Gyoo, Shin Chang Hoon, Park Byung Kyu, Lee Mee Young
Client Yang Eon Bo, Camellia Hill

FRONT ELEVATION

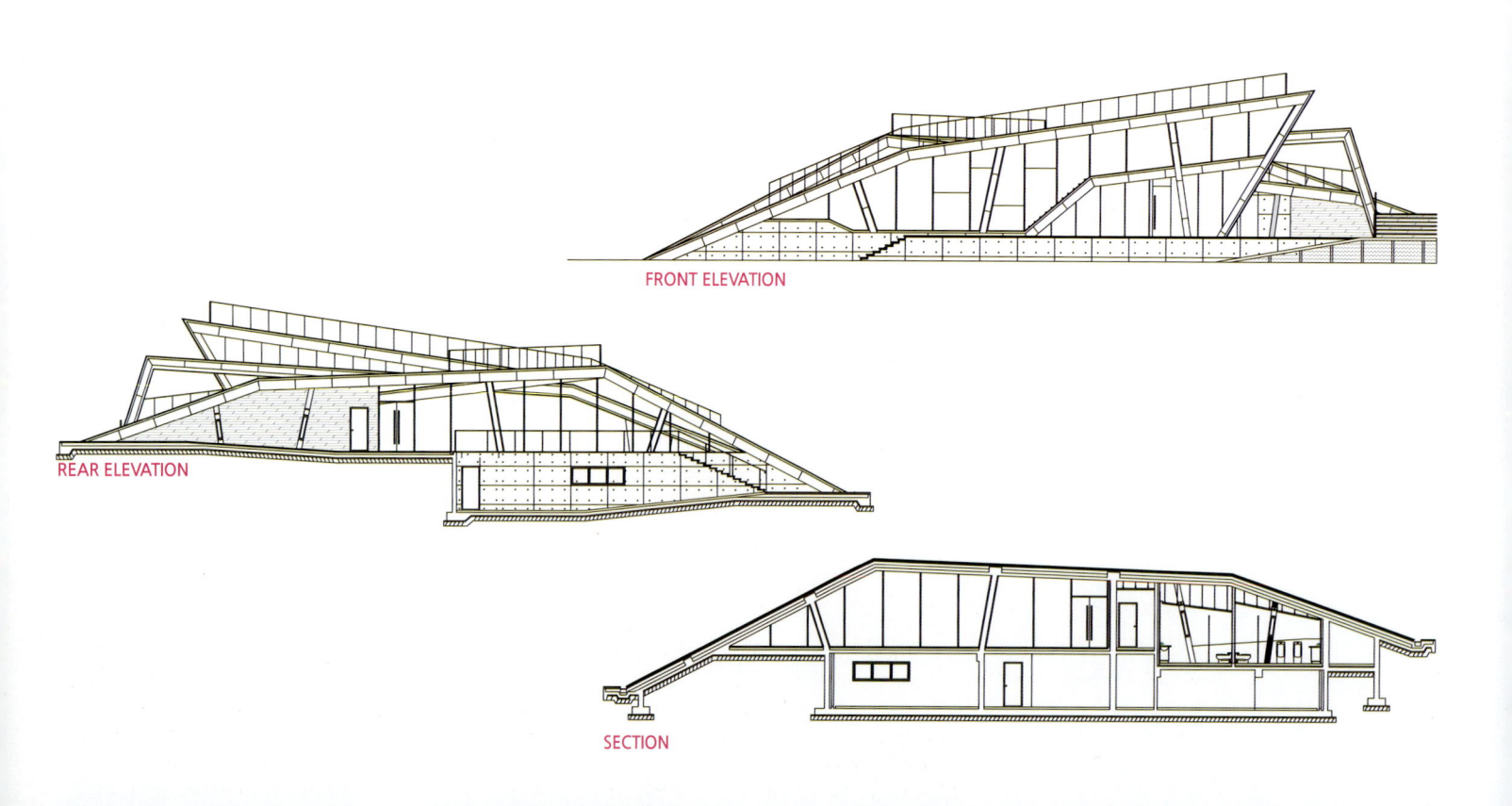

REAR ELEVATION

SECTION

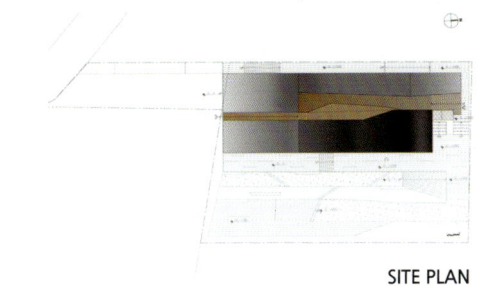

PASSAGE MOUND

We suggest a gallery with scene and mound. Scenery is fully appreciated, enjoyed and meditated at 'Passage Mound' gallery. Space of sequential scenery through inside and outside is combined by Interactive Passage Map. Exhibition program and nature program enriching life are crossed, so that interactive space is realized. Passage map is poetic code making cracks between function and program, space and mass. The program for exhibition is defined in relation of finding and making passage of site. The space with nature and scenery is suggested as a result of integrating skin and structure, skin and landscape.

Mound is a type of topography referring Small Mountain in JeJu Island. And it is the most figurative design factor among beautiful scenery in JeJu Island. The shape of this mound is transformed to spatial model. 4 layers with each different form construct the mound. It becomes a frame composing changes of outdoor space and indoor scenery differently.

It is not only exhibition hall composed by new understanding of the mound and transforming it, but integrated inside exhibition space to outside in compound body. Find out hidden space from the epidermal site and insert exhibition program into it. We suggest architecture as compound body which landscape, site and architecture are all integrated. The site is spatialized and transforming of different layers finds out crack in the topographic space. The site becomes light and gains freedom of space like air. In other words, it is 'airy topography'. The crack of inner site is a frame taking changes of scenery inside. The crack of outer site makes linear crack for lighting at night and it changes the site to be glow. Visitors experience different scenery from the mound. They experience 'Change of scenery' maintaining even though their location changes according to moving sequences through indoor and outdoor space. Transformation of numerous frames and passages is transformed in movement of mound. Created passage and mound is the exhibition space where provides endlessly changing scenery.

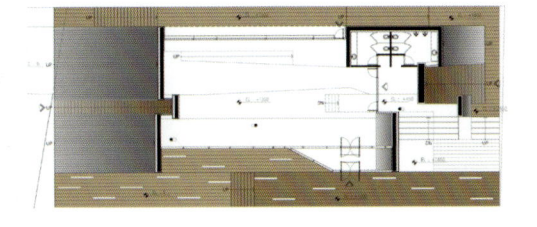

SITE PLAN

Korea Town Complex
Accumulating Korean Memory Boxes, Newyork

Architects Jang Yoon Gyoo, Yoon Jung Hyun

COMPOUND BODY 589

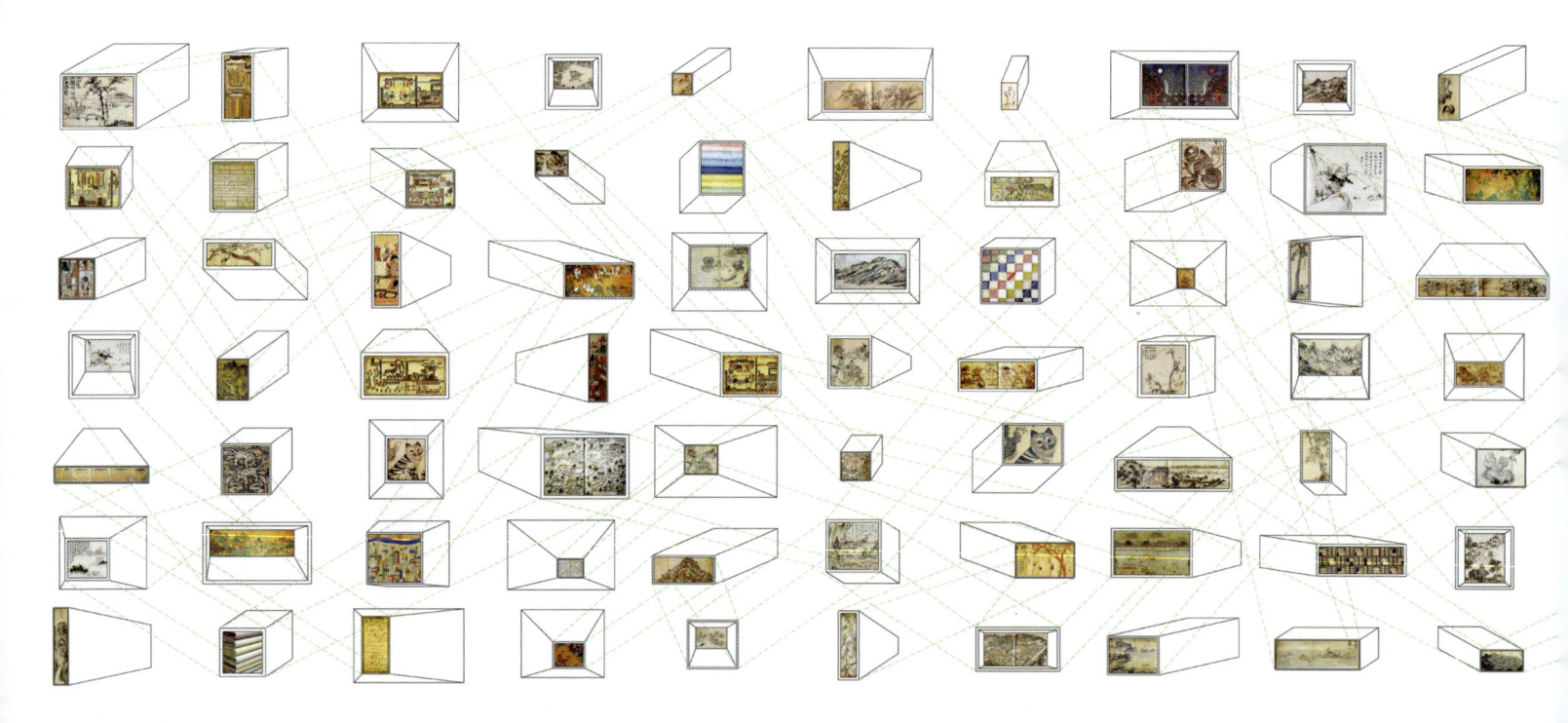

MEMORY ACCUMULATION THRESHOLD

At the site rolling as the gate of Korean Town on 32th street in Manhattan, we suggest a tower accumulating memory. This tower works as threshold locating on the entrance. And it also has a meaning of lying on the center of the eastern and western culture as an intermediate installation. The main concept for landmark is that the accumulation of Korean identity expresses at the gate of Korean Town. The box visualizing Korean history, memory and image are stacked horizontally for the new urban landmark. Furthermore, it works as a point of contact for western and oriental culture inserting the interactive box and space.

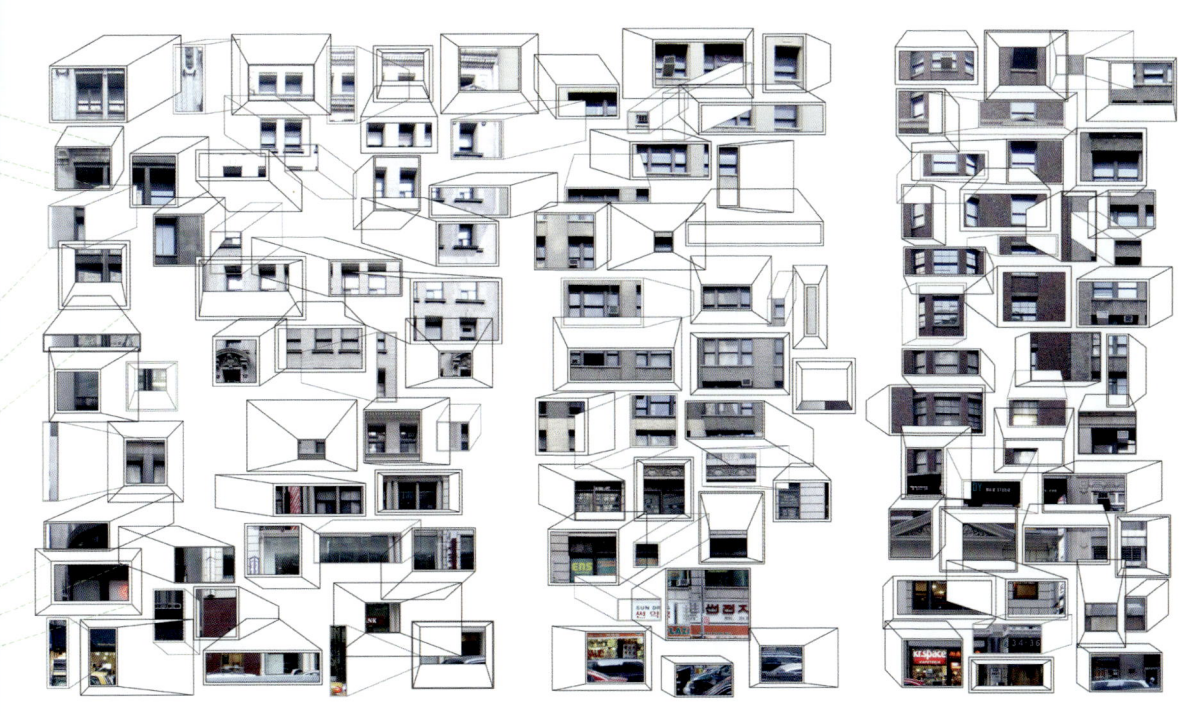

COMPOUND BODY 591

// Situation
The Gate, which is located at the end of a boundary in any urban or architectural context, was a very monumental and symbolic architectural object, which controlled various movements such as human and vehicles functionally. In particular, it has been one of the important physical elements in major architectural space in East Asia and is also identified as a binary element which has a neutral reaction between inner and outer space.

In present, as the site is growing more and more, the boundary of the city is destroyed and may be obscured in urban area, which means its limit or role is changes, at least in the metropolitan cities. The meaning of the gate is isolated, wrecked, and loses its original contents and formality. Actually it needs to be given new role and function in new environmental situation.

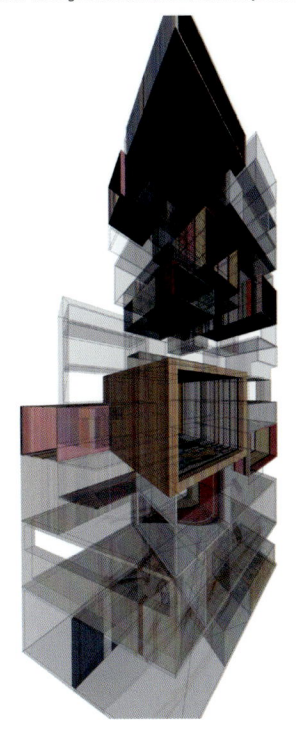

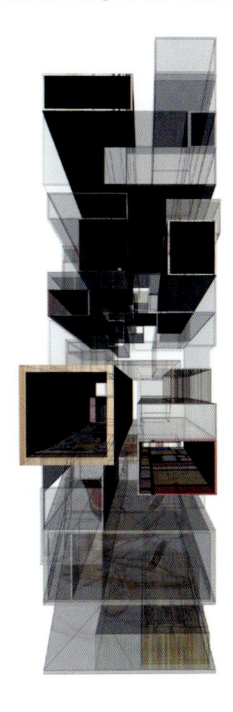

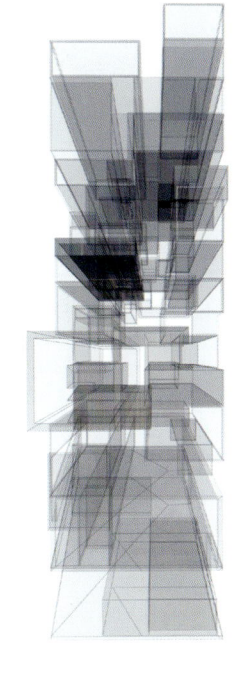

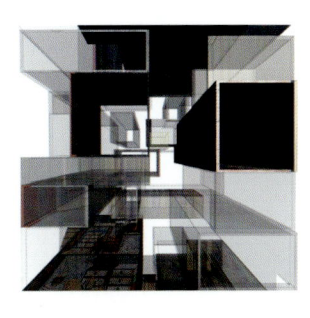

Memory Accumulation & Urban Threshold
In this proposal, the memory accumulation Device as an urban threshold is defined, not as a peripheral subsistence out of the center but an essential part of the center, furthermore the center, itself. The relation of each boxes links to images and memories of Korea town and its value. And it makes an enormous networking system from New York City, where many Korean immigrants are living, to the homeland, Korea. This new threshold addresses what Korea town needs, howit is shown, and contains its urban identity, potential and possibility, and Korean culture as well.

Korean Identity & Interactive Boxes
The tower as a landmark of Korea Town will create new memories of the city and is working as a threshold in between western and eastern culture. It is representing Korea, itself by the accumulating its memory boxes vertically, which are including the history, images, and characters of Korea. Furthermore, it can be combined with the interactive boxes and vertical space, which is called urban crack, to be in new boundary of western and eastern culture. We know that we all have a nexus system, not just one thing, with various element and function. The tower and new manipulated park, two binary elements are also in a special networking system to bridge visible or invisible urban factors and spiritual structures.

Space wall

Wall Garden

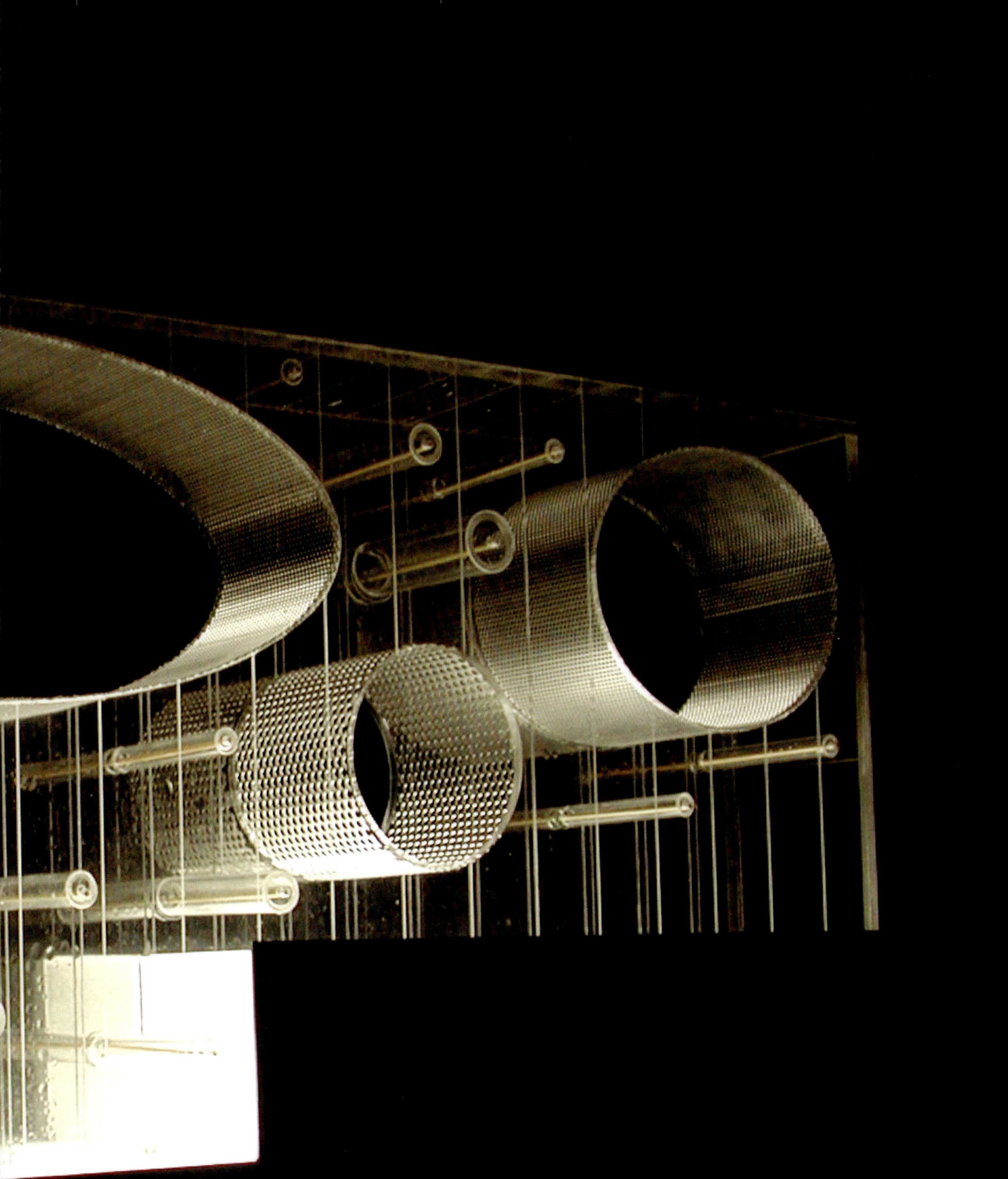

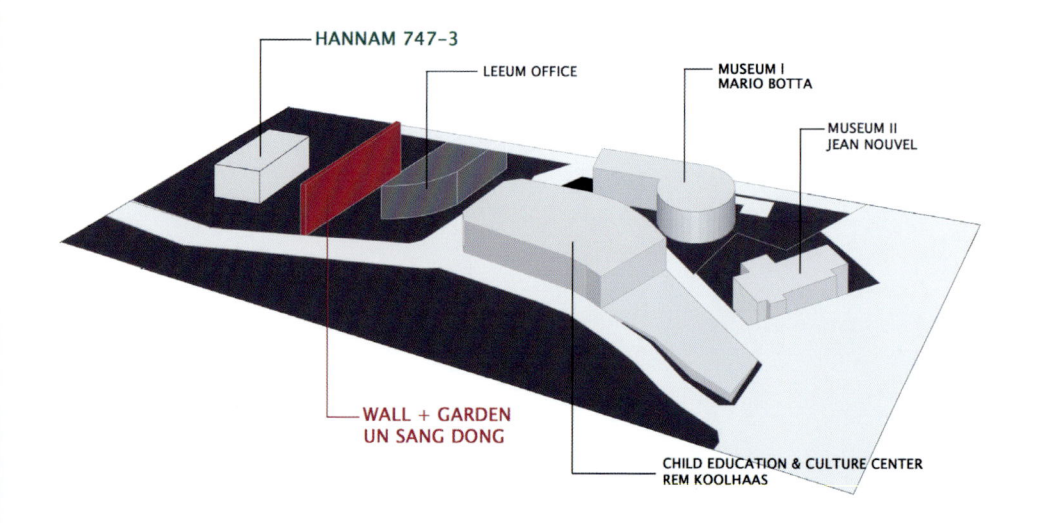

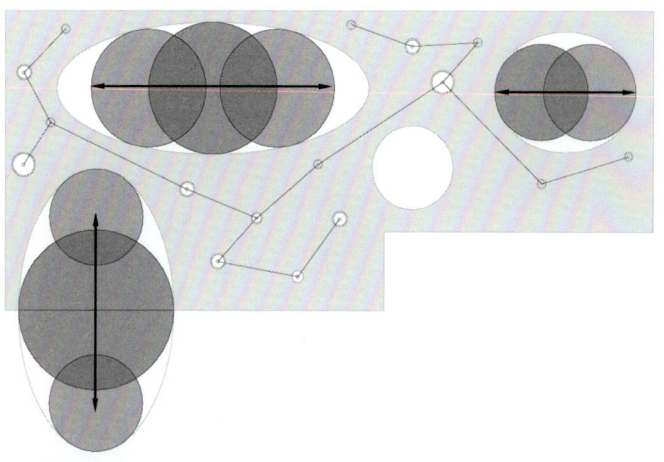

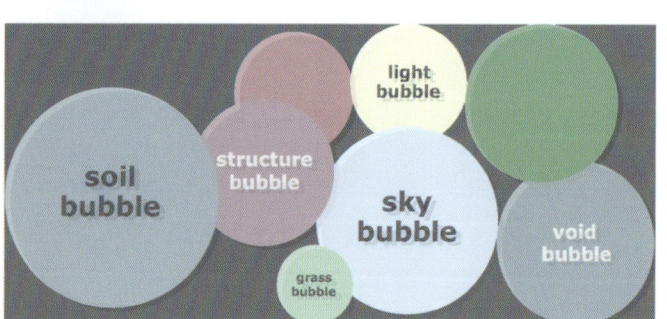

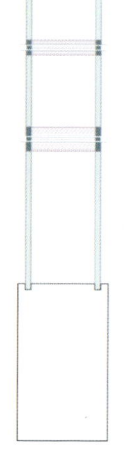

PROGRAM WALL

Wall Garden is program wall suggested for repairing a wall of the house next to Samsung Leeum Museum in Hanam, Seoul. Existing role of fence in house as background of garden and public property of the site with independent territory are adopted. Role of the program wall is secure of house territory primarily, peculiarity of art museum and providing diverse information and new circumstance. Program wall is a part of landscape, scenery moving installation and characteristic light.
It is complex and active installation of change participating in public culture rather than simple factor of garden.

Phenomenon

Materials consisting of program wall are defined by program. Principle of the main material is manipulation of scenery and non-scenery. Inner garden is space expanding infinitely using reflecting glass, transparent glass and light. It is phenomenon of personal perception beyond recognition of general experiences. At the boundary of house and museum, this mechanic installation reacts the time, the climate and visual point.

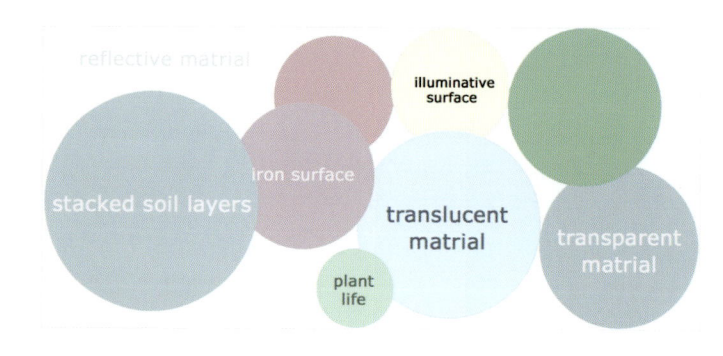

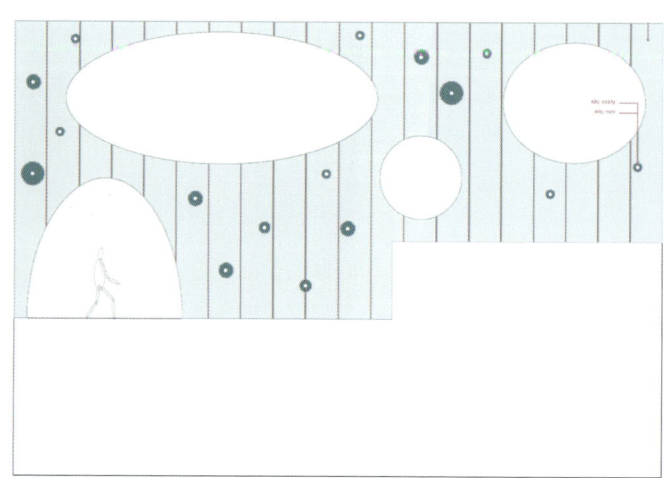

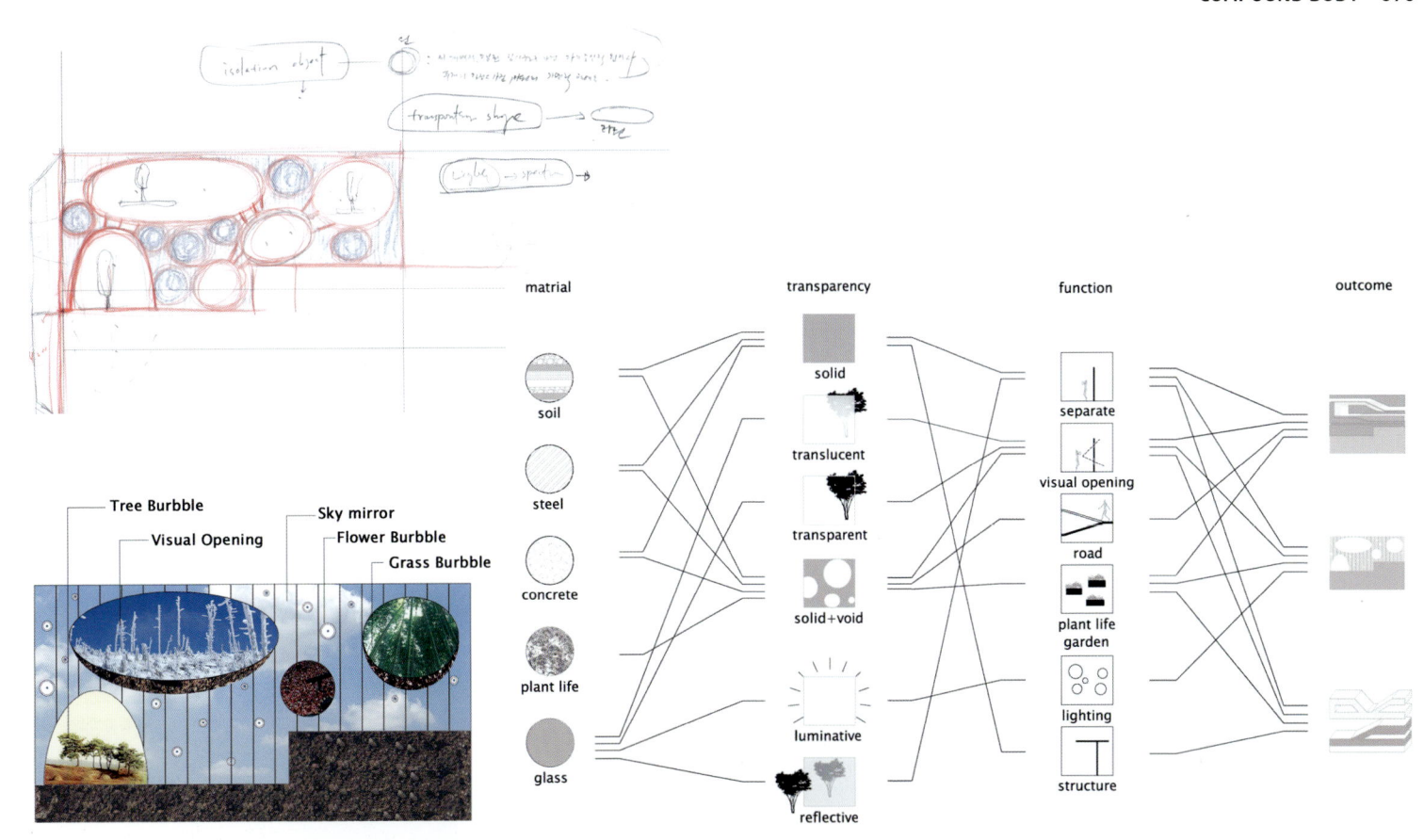

COMPOUND BODY

matrial	transparency	function	outcome
soil	solid	separate	
steel	translucent	visual opening	
concrete	transparent	road	
plant life	solid+void	plant life garden	
glass	luminative	lighting	
	reflective	structure	

Tree Burbble
Visual Opening
Sky mirror
Flower Burbble
Grass Burbble

Stacking
program

Office of UNSANGDONG
Architects Cooperation
to be continue...

Architects Jang Yoon Gyoo, Shin Chang Hoon, Kim Min Tae COMPOUND BODY 597

598

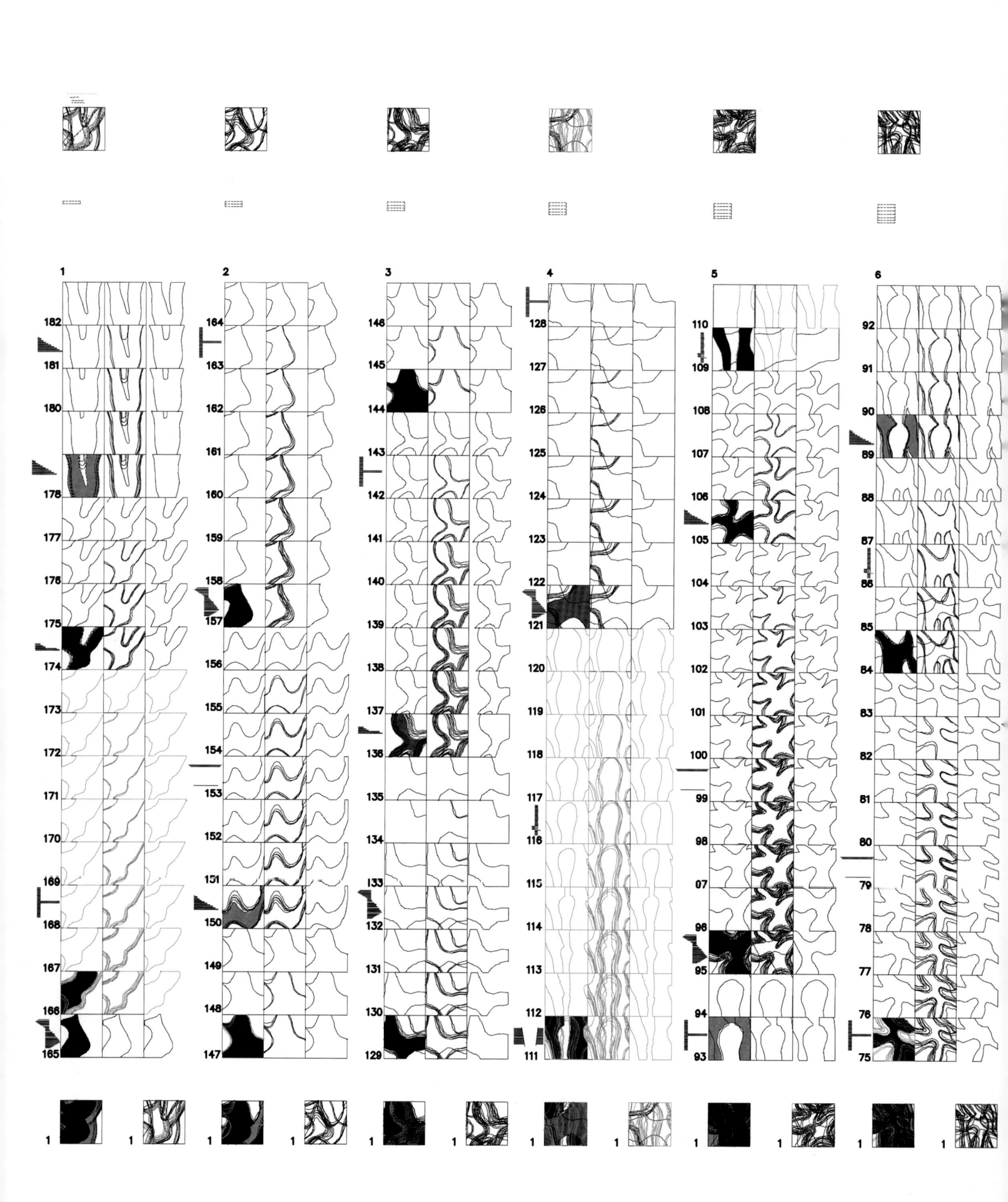

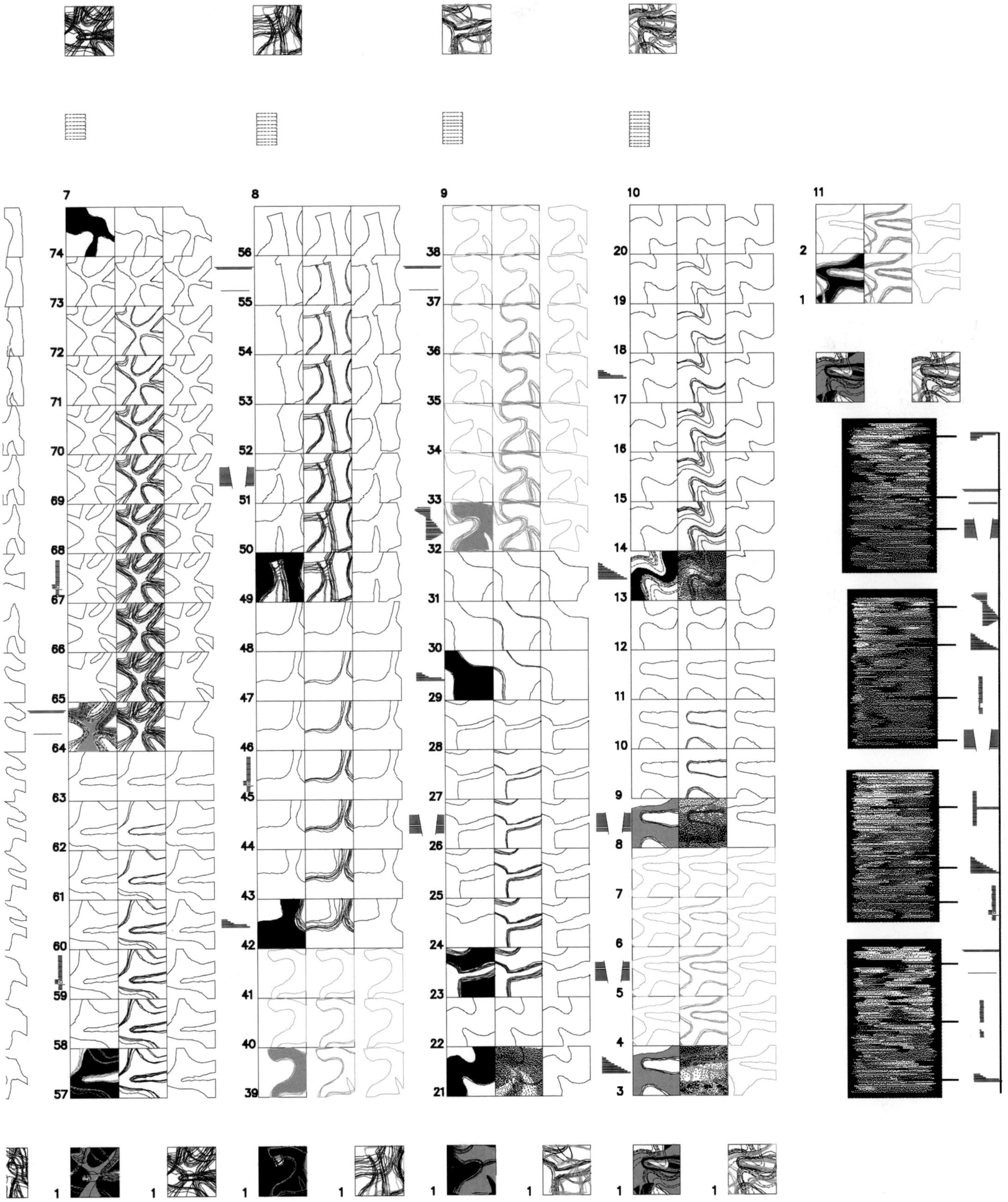
7
74 73 72 71 70 69 68 67 66 65 64 63 62 61 60 59 58 57
8
56 55 54 53 52 51 50 49 48 47 46 45 44 43 42 41 40 39
9
38 37 36 35 34 33 32 31 30 29 28 27 26 25 24 23 22 21
10
20 19 18 17 16 15 14 13 12 11 10 9 8 7 6 5 4 3
11
2 1
1 1 1 1 1 1 1 1

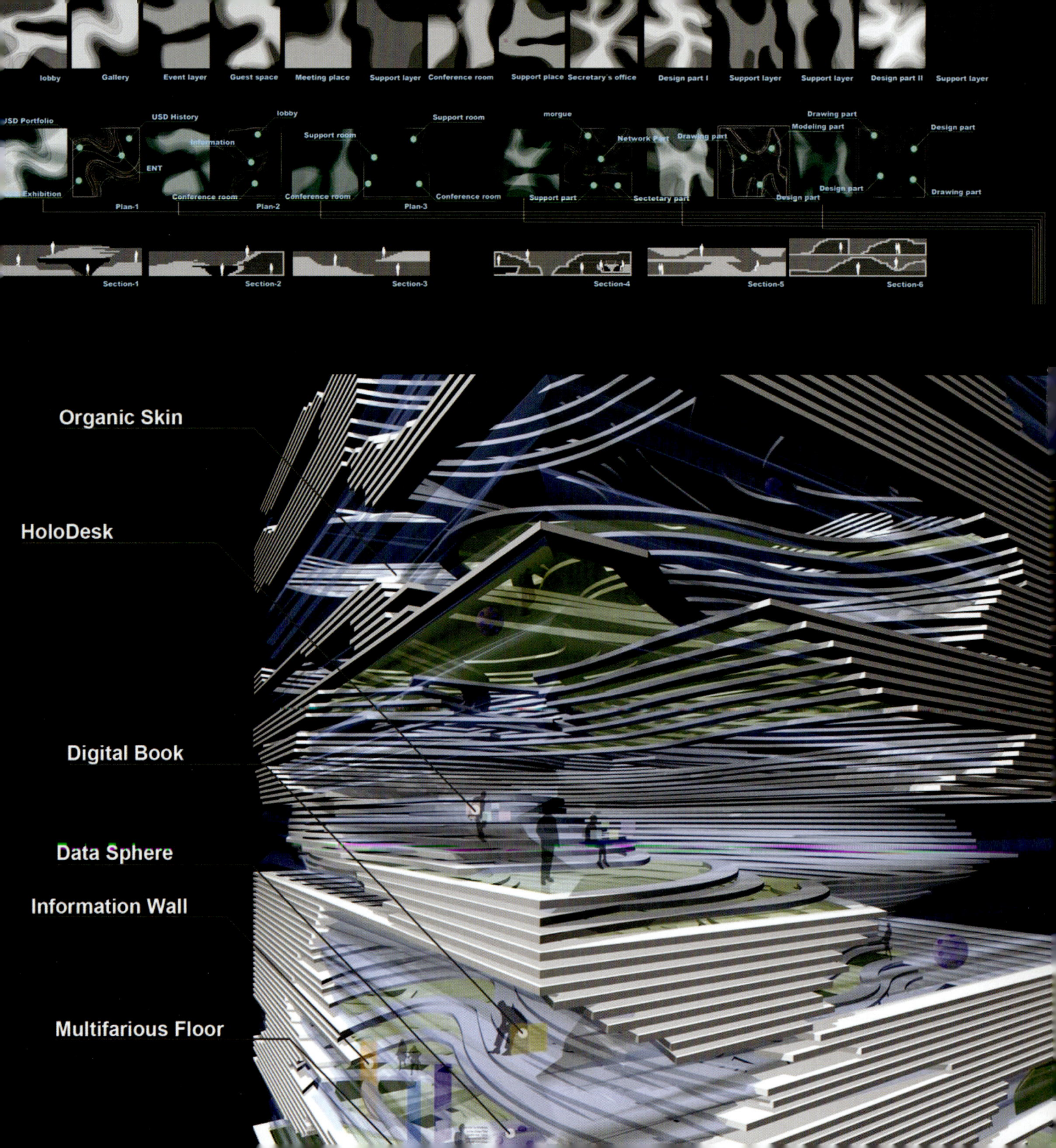

| lobby | Gallery | Event layer | Guest space | Meeting place | Support layer | Conference room | Support place | Secretary's office | Design part I | Support layer | Support layer | Design part II | Support layer |

USD Portfolio | USD History | lobby | Support room | Support room | morgue | Network Part | Drawing part | Drawing part | Modeling part | Design part | Drawing part
Information | ENT | Conference room | Conference room | Conference room | Support part | Sectetary part | Design part | Design part

Plan-1 | Plan-2 | Plan-3

Section-1 | Section-2 | Section-3 | Section-4 | Section-5 | Section-6

- Organic Skin
- HoloDesk
- Digital Book
- Data Sphere
- Information Wall
- Multifarious Floor

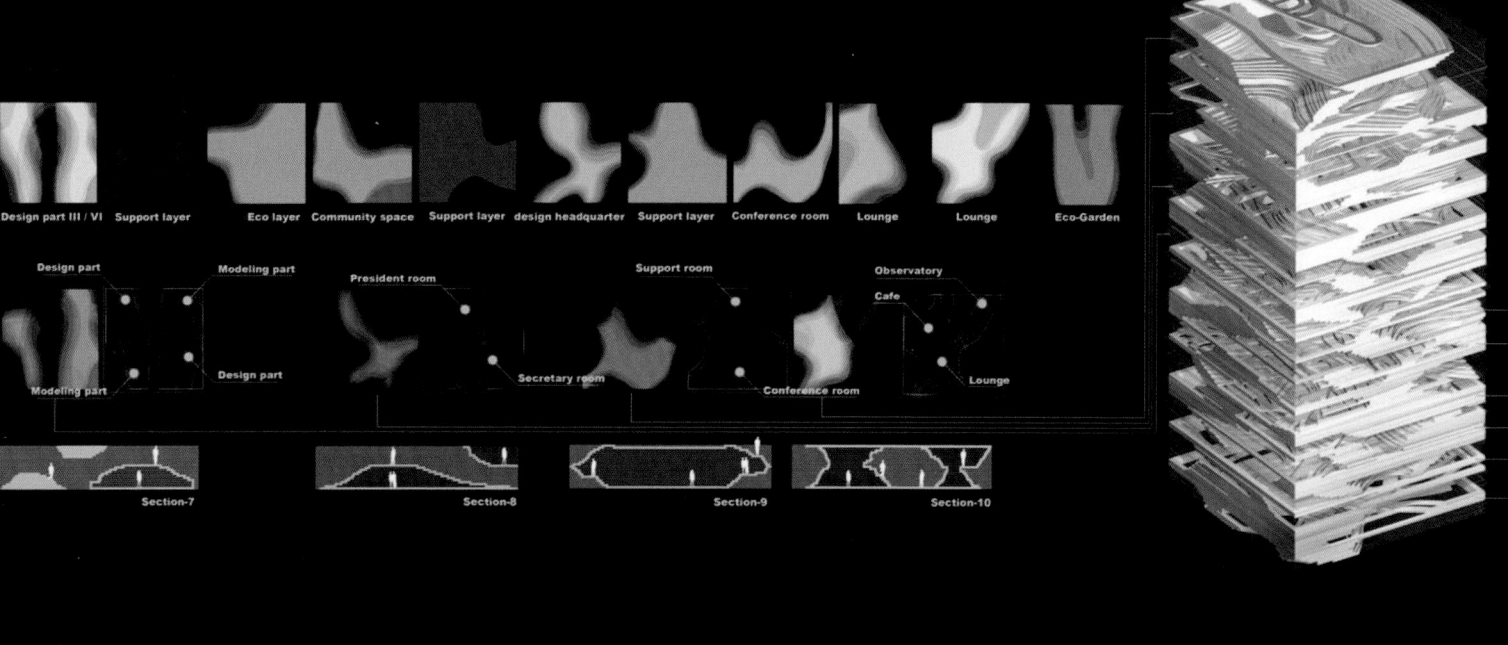

| Design part III / VI | Support layer | Eco layer | Community space | Support layer | design headquarter | Support layer | Conference room | Lounge | Lounge | Eco-Garden |

- Design part — Modeling part
- Modeling part — Design part
- President room — Secretary room
- Support room — Conference room
- Observatory — Cafe — Lounge

Section-7 Section-8 Section-9 Section-10

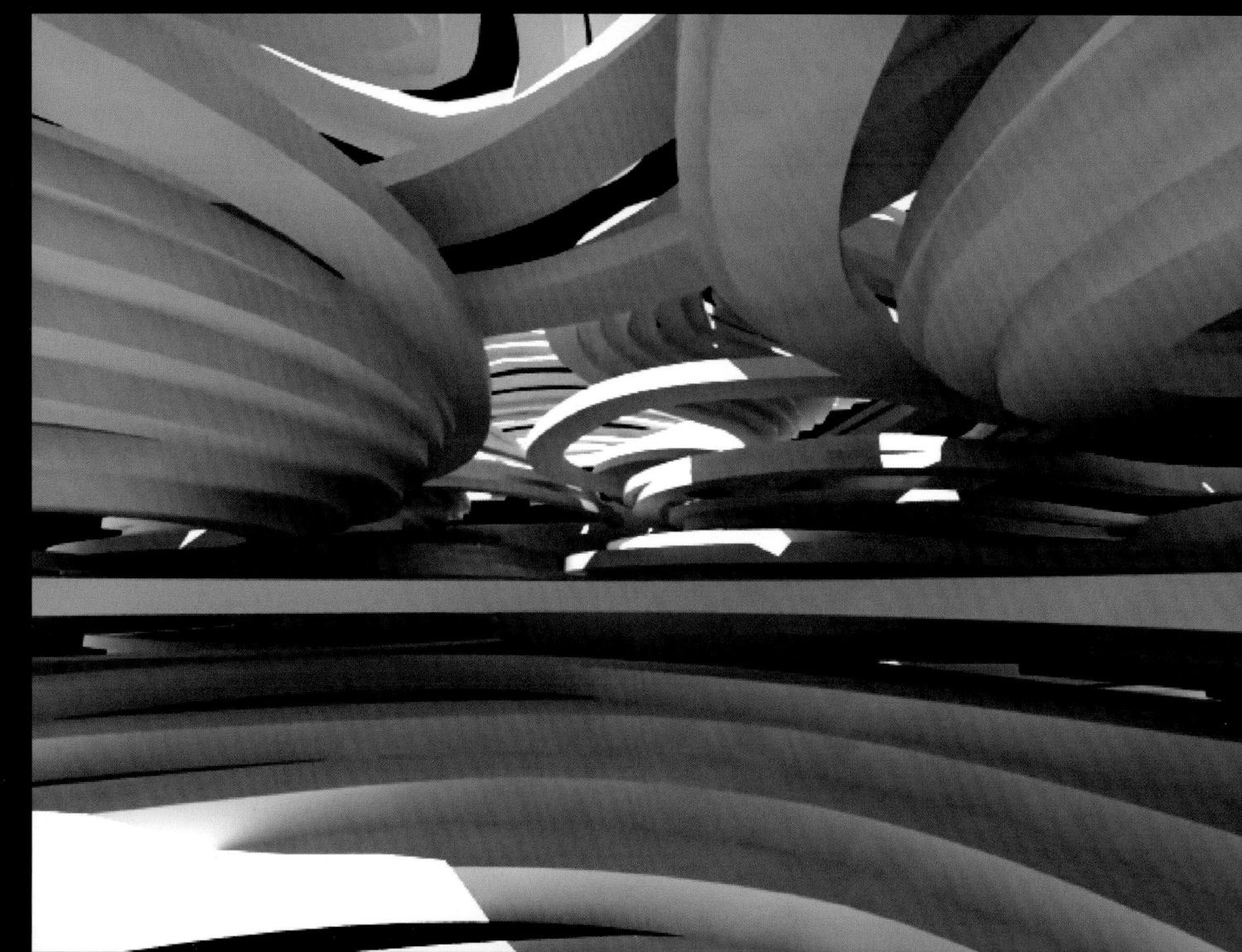

Credits

KRING
Location Seoul, South Korea
Type Mixed Use
Client Kumho Engineering & Construction
Architect Jang Yoon Gyoo, Shin Chang Hoon, Kim Kyung Tae
Team Kim Sung Min, Moon Sang Ho, Kim Se Jin, Kim Bong Kyun, Kang Seong Hyun, Seo Hye Lim, Go Young Dong, Yi Na Ra
Structural Engineers Harmony Structural Engineering
Services Engineers Mecend Engineering, Jihwa Engineering, O Yi Gong Yi Design, Forte Line Interiors
C.G ST201
Photography Sergio Pirrone

Gallery YEH
Location Seoul, South Korea
Type Culture
Client Lee Sook Young
Architect Jang Yoon Gyoo, Shin Chang Hoon, Kim Youn Soo
Team Kim Soo Young, Park Byung Gyu, Kim Hak Soo
Structural Engineers Joong-ang Engineering
Services Engineers Young Dong Engineering, Gujin Industrial Construction, Jeehwa Engineer Group
Photography Kim Yong Kwan

Yeosu Expo Thematic Pavillion
Location Yeosu, Jeollanam-do, South Korea
Type Culture
Client Yeosu City
Architect Jang Yoon Gyoo, Shin Chang Hoon
Team Kim Woo Young, Kang Seung Hyun, Kim Bong Kyun, Lee Mi Young
Structural Engineers the Kujo Engineering
Services Engineers Hanil MEC
C.G ST201

Asian Culture Complex
Location Kwang ju, South Korea
Type Culture
Client The Executive Agency for Culture Cities
Architect Jang Yoon Gyoo, Shin Chang Hoon, Kim Woo Il, Kim Woo Young
Team Kim Sung Min, Kim Youn Soo, Yeon Kyung Hee
Co-Architect Co-op Architects

Outdoor Amphitheater for Youth, Nodeul Island
Location Seoul, South Korea
Type Culture
Client Seoul City
Architect Jang Yoon Gyoo, Shin Chang Hoon
Team Kim Woo Young, Kim Youn Soo, Kim Sung Min
C.G Seo Hye Lim
Photography Kim Jae Kyung

KT&G Complex Center
Location Suwon, Kyunggi-do, South Korea
Type Mixed Use
Client KTNG Corp.
Architect Jang Yoon Gyoo, Shin Chang Hoon, Kim Woo Young
Team Choi Jae Hyuk, Park Joo Hoon
Co-Architect To Moon Architects (Choi Ki Cheol, Han Nam Soo)
C.G ST201, Lay-Us
Photography Kim Jae Kyung

Design Center in GwangJu
Loation Gwangju, South Korea
Type Culture
Client GwangJu City
Architect Jang Yoon Gyoo, Kim Woo Il, To Moon Architects(Choi Ki Cheol, Han Nam Soo), You Top Engineering(O Geum Yeol)
Team Gong Sung Geun, Jo Dong Ho, Choi Yoon Sang, Kim Hyoung Soo, Kim Chang Oh, Kim Young Cheol
Structural Engineers CS Engineering
Services Engineers Hanil MEC, Daeil E&C, Seo Ahn Landscape, Ace All Civil Engineering, AandD Interiors, Bitzro Lighting Design, Shinhwa Engineering
Construction Daewoo Enginnering & Construction, Woo Mi Construction
C.G ST201, Lay-Us
Photography Lee Ki Hwan

Flagship Tower
Location Seoul, South Korea
Type Mixed Use
Architect Jang Yoon Gyoo, Shin Chang Hoon, Kim Youn Soo
Team Seo Hye Lim, Go Young Dong, Choi Young Eun, Kim Bong Kyun, Kim Min Tae
C.G ST201
Photography Kim Jae Kyung

Life & Power Press in PaJu Book City
Location Paju Book City, Kyunggi-do, South Korea
Type Office
Client Kim Seung Ki
Architect Jang Yoon Gyoo, Shin Chang Hoon, Kim Youn Soo
Team Kim Sung Min, Kim Se Jin, Yeon Kyung Hee
Structural Engineers Joong-ang Engineering
Services Engineers Young Dong Engineering, Dong Nyuk Construction, Jeehwa Engineer Group
Photography Namgoong Sun

Theater Contour
Location Ahn Sung, Kyunggi-do, South Korea
Type Culture
Client Ahn Sung City
Architect Jang Yoon Gyoo, Shin Chang Hoon
Team Kim Woo Young, Kim Sung Min, Moon Sang Ho,

Kim Min Tae, Kang Seung Hyun, Kim Bong Kyun
Structural Engineers Harmony Engineering,
Services Engineers Jihwa Engineering, Young Dong Engineering, OSD
C.G ST201
Photography Kim Jae Kyung

Prehistoric Museum
Loation Kyunggi-do, South Korea
Type Culture
Client Kyunggi-do
Architect Jang Yoon Gyoo, Shin Chang Hoon, Kim Woo Young
Team Kim Youn Soo, Kim Sung Min, Choi Hye Jin, Kwon Woo Seok, Jung Bok Ju
C.G Kim Min Tae, ST201
Photography Kim Jae Kyung

Shanghai EXPO Industrial Pavillion
Location Shanghai, China
Type Culture
Client The Korea International Trade Association
Architect Jang Yoon Gyoo, Shin Chang Hoon
Team Kim Sung Min, Go Young Dong, Ahn Boo Young, Kim Won Il, Seo Hye Lim
Structural Engineers CSSE Engineering,
Services Engineers Hanil MEC,
Consultant G.L. Associates
C.G ST201

Gallery 303
Location Gwang Ju, South Korea
Type Culture
Client Lim Kwang Taek, AMJ Development
Architect Jang Yoon Gyoo, Shin Chang Hoon, Kim Sung Min
Team Kim Se Jin, Kim Min Tae, Kang Seung Hyun
Structural Engineers the Kujo Engineering,
Consultants Kukbo Design Co. Ltd
Photography Namgoong Sun

Gallery The Hill
Location Seoul, South Korea
Type Mixed Use
Client Han's Jaram AMC Co. Ltd
Architect Jang Yoon Gyoo, Shin Chang Hoon, Kim Kyung Tae
Team Ahn Boo Young, Shin Hye Jin
Structural Engineers the Kujo Structural Engineering
C.G Iworks
Photography Namgoong Sun

Gallery of Housing Culture in ChungJu
Location CheongJu, Chungchongbuk-do, South Korea
Type Mixed Use
Client IDEA Development & Construction
Architect Jang Yoon Gyoo, Shin Chang Hoon
Team Yi Soon Pyo, Kim Sung Min
Structural Engineers Kwang Lim Engineering

Consultants Jeehwa Engineering, Young Dong Engineering, OPUS Born Co. Ltd,
Photography Lee Cheol Hee, Namgoong Sun

Dream Art Hall In Seong Dong
Location Seoul, South Korea
Type Mixed use
Client Municipality of Seong Dong-gu
Architect Jang Yoon Gyoo, Shin Chang Hoon, Kim Sung Min
Team Kim Min Tae, Seo Hye Lim, Ryu Sam Yeol, Ahn Hye Joon, Kim Won Il, Ahn Boo Young, Kim Mi Jung, Jo Eun Chong
Structural Engineers the Kujo Structural Engineering
Services Engineers Hanil MEC, OSD, Yool Hyun Engineering
Landscape Consultants Sol To Landscape
C.G ST201
Photography Kim Jae Kyung

Museum for NamJune Paik
Location Kyunggi-do, South Korea
Type Culture
Client Kyunggi Cultural Foundation
Architect Jang Yoon Gyoo, Shin Chang Hoon
Team Park Byung Gyu, Lee Mi Young
Co-Architect Seo Su Kyoung
Photography Kim Yong Kwan

Pusan Tower
Loation Busan, South Korea
Type Culture
Client Busan City
Architect Jang Yoon Gyoo, Park Byung Gyu, Lee Mi Young
Photography Unsangdong Architects Cooperation

City Tower in ChungLa
Location Incheon, Kyunggi-do, South Korea
Type Culture
Client Korea Land & Housing Corporation
Architect Jang Yoon Gyoo, Shin Chang Hoon, Kim Sung Min
Team Kim Min Tae, Kim Se Jin, Seo Hye Lim, Kang Seung Hyun, Kim Bong Kyun, Go Young Dong, Yi Na Ra
Structural Engineers Hub Engineering
C.G Seo Hye Lim, Kim Min Tae

ChiChi Memorial
Location Nantou County, ChiChi, Taiwan
Type Culture
Architect Jang Yoon Gyoo, Shin Chang Hoon, Kim Woo Il
Team Kim Woo Young, Seo Soo Kyung
Photography Unsangdong Architects Cooperation

Thousand Palace
Location Seoul, South Korea
Type Culture
Client Seoul City

Architect Jang Yoon Gyoo, Shin Chang Hoon
Team Kim Sung Min, Kim Min Tae, Seo Hye Lim, Go Young Dong
Structural Engineers the Kujo Engineering
Consultants Mak Max Korea
Photography Sergio Pirrone

Design of Exhibition Space in GwangJu Biennale
Loation Gwang Ju, South Korea
Type Culture
Client Kyunggi-do
Architect Jang Yoon Gyoo, Shin Chang Hoon
Team Kim Youn Soo, Park Byung Gyu, Kim Hak Soo, Lee Mi Young, Yang Seon Ah, Hyun bong Shil, Jung Hoon
Photography Jin Hyo Sook

Paris Olympic Memorial
Loation Paris, France
Type Culture
Client Paris Olympic Committee
Architect Jang Yoon Gyoo, Shin Chang Hoon
Team Kim Youn Soo, Kim Hak Soo, Seo Soo Kyoung
C.G ST201, Choi Sun Young
Photography Unsangdong Architects Cooperation

Gallery JUNGMISO
Loation Seoul, South Korea
Type Culture
Client Gallery Jungmiso, Yoon Seok Hwa
Architect Jang Yoon Gyoo, Shin Chang Hoon
Team Kim Woo Young, Kim Youn Soo, Kim Sung Min
Consultants Joo Yeon Geon Jang, Choi Kwan Jae, Han Woo Lim, Won Jae Seon
Photography Song Jae Young

Actress 〈YOONSUKHWA〉 Space for Performance
Loation Seoul, South Korea
Type Culture
Client Yoon Seok Hwa
Architect Jang Yoon Gyoo
Co-Artist Jang Yoon Sung
Team Park Byung Gyu, Lee Mi Young, O Young Suk, Kim Beon Jun
Consultants Joo Yeon Geon Jang, Choi Kwan Jae, Han Woo Lim, Won Jae Seon
Photography Moon Jung Sik

Gallery JUNSOOCHUN
Loation Ilsan, Kyunggi-do, South Korea
Type Culture
Client Jeon Soo Cheon
Architect Jang Yoon Gyoo, Kim Min Tae
Photography Unsangdong Architects Cooperation

Plaza of GwangJu Biennale

Loation Gwangju, South Korea
Type Culture
Client Gwang Ju Biennale Foundation
Architect Jang Yoon Gyoo, Shin Chang Hoon
Team Kim Woo Young, Seo Soo Kyung, Park Byung Gyu,
Lee Mi Young
Consultants Joo Yeon Geon Jang, Choi Kwan Jae
Photography Unsangdong Architects Cooperation

Ravin Peace Plaza Vertical Interaction
Loation Israel
Type Civic
Architect Jang Yoon Gyoo, Lee Mi Young
Photography Unsangdong Architects Cooperation

Dancing Apartment
Loation Seoul, South Korea
Type Culture
Architect Jang Yoon Gyoo, Seo Hye Lim
C.G Seo Hye Lim
Photography Unsangdong Architects Cooperation

Kolon Theme Housing
Type Residence
Client Kolon Enginnering & Construction
Architect Jang Yoon Gyoo, Shin Chang Hoon
Team Kim Sung Min, Kim Min Tae, Kim Bong Kyun,
Lim Yi Hyun
Structural Engineers the Kujo Engineering
Photography Kim Bong Kyun

Prugio Labotega Officetel
Type Residence
Client Daewoo Enginnering & Construction
Architect Jang Yoon Gyoo, Shin Chang Hoon
Team Kim Sung Min, Kim Min Tae, Kang Seung Hyun,
Jang Chol Min
Construction Daewoo Enginnering & Construction
C.G ST201

Headquarter Office of SK Networks
Location Seoul, South Korea
Type Office
Client SK Networks
Architect Jang Yoon Gyoo, Shin Chang Hoon, Junglim
Architects(Kim Bok Su, Baik Seung Yong)
Team Kim Bong Kyun, Shim Hyung Sun, Kim Ho Jin, Shim
Jae Hyun, Choi Jin Kyu
Co-Architect Junglim Architects(Kim Min Sung, Jeon
Seong Ryul, Baik Woo Heum, O Seung Tae,
Jeong Su Young, Kim Seon Ju, Choi Kwang
Heon)
Structural Engineers Cross Structural Engineering
Services Engineers Jeong Do Engineering, Yu Won Enc,
Se Kwang Engineering,
Landscape Consultants Poong Gyung Landscape
C.G 3D focus, Wmass

Headquater Office of Evervill
Location SungNam, Kyunggi-do, South Korea
Type Office
Client HyunJin Evervill
Architect Jang Yoon Gyoo, Shin Chang Hoon, Kim Woo Il
Team Kim Woo Young, Kim Youn Soo, Kim Sung Min,
Kim Dong Chan, Ryu Sam Yeol
Photography Kim Jae Kyung

Campus Complex, University of Seoul
Location Seoul, South Korea
Type Education
Client University of Seoul
Architect Jang Yoon Gyoo, Shin Chang Hoon, Kim Woo Il
Team Jung Won Chan, Park Mi Jin, Kim Woo Young,
Kim Youn Soo, Kim Sung Min, Kim Dong Chan,
Lee Ho Seon
Structural Engineers Hankook Structural Engineering
Consultants Kuk Dong Munhwa Engineering, Hanil MEC
Construction Daedo Construction
Co-Architect Co-op Architects
Photography Kim Jong Oh

School of Architecture,
Seoul National University
Loation Seoul, South Korea
Type Education
Client Seoul National University
Architect Jang Yoon Gyoo, Moon Jin Ho,
Baik Moon Gi(Jung Lim Architects),
Han Sang Wook(Kachi Architects)
Team Kim Woo Young, Seo Soo Kyung, Kim Bok Soo,
Yoon Gyu Seop, Kim Young Geun, Kwak Ji Young,
Lee Jeong Wan, Choi Sung Yoon, You Hee Jin, Seo
Hyun Jung, Choi Young Sik, Park Moo Ryong, Jang
Myong Yong
Structural Engineers Archipronet Engineering
Services Engineers Namu Engineering, Daeil Engineering,
Seoul National University, Hankook
Engineering, Acemol Engineering
Landscape Consultants Group Han
Construction Doosan Engineering & Construction,
Tae Young Engineering & Construction,
Photography Kim Jong Oh

Cheong Shim Elementary School
Location Gapyoung, Kyunggi-do, South Korea
Type Education
Client Cheong Shim
Architect Jang Yoon Gyoo, Shin Chang Hoon
Team Kim Kyung Tae, Ryu Sam Yeol, Seo Hye Lim, Kim
Min Tae, Ahn Boo Young, Go Young Dong, Jo In
Kyoung, Jo Eun Chong
Structural Engineers Dae Sung A&C
Services Engineers Hanil MEC, Yool Hyun Engineering
Landscape Consultants Poong Gyung Landscape
C.G ST201
Photography Kim Bong Kyun

Province Hall of ChungNam
Location Hongsung, Chungchongnam-do, South Korea
Type Civic
Client Chungchongnam-do
Architect Jang Yoon Gyoo, Shin Chang Hoon,
To Moon Architects(Choi Ki Cheol, Yi Soo Yeol)
Team Kim Sung Min, Go Young Dong, Jin Jung Eun,
Co-Architect To Moon Architects(Hong Chang Sung, Bae Chang Min, Bae Kyung sik, Yi Hyun Soo, O Jung Woon, Choi Jung Suk, Gu Min Beom, Park Yoo Jung, Jin Jae Ho, Choi Seong Ah, Ha Yoon Ho, Yi Woo Jun)
Structural Engineers Hyng Sang Structural Engineering
Services Engineers Hanil MEC, Il Sin E&C, Dong Woo Engineering,
Construction Gujin Industrial Construction
C.G 3D Focus

Kaleidoscope Gallery
Location Wonju, Gangwon-do, South Korea
Type Culture
Client Jeong Geum Sook
Architect Jang Yoon Gyoo, Shin Chang Hoon
Team Kim Sung Min, Kim Min Tae, Kang Seung Hyun
Structural Engineers the Kujo Engineering,
Services Engineers Jihwa Engineering, Young Dong Engineering
Photography Kim Jae Kyung

Atelier For Ceramic Artist
Location Yeo Ju, Kyunggi-do, South Korea
Type Residence/Studio
Client Lee Jung Suk, Ko Hee Sook
Architect Jang Yoon Gyoo, Shin Chang Hoon
Team Lee Soon Pyo, Kim Min Tae
Structural Engineers Harmony Engineering
Photography Namgoong Sun

Eco Frame House
Loation Kyunggi-do, South Korea
Type Residence
Architect Jang Yoon Gyoo, Shin Chang Hoon,
Lee Mi Young
Team Kim Woo Young, Yeon Kyung Hee, Kwon Woo Seok, Jung Bok Ju, Choi Hye Jin
Photography Unsangdong Architects Cooperation

Kolon E+Green Home
Location Yongin, Kyunggi-do, South Korea
Type Residence/Education
Client Kolon Engineering & Construction
Architect Jang Yoon Gyoo, Shin Chang Hoon,
Kim Youn Soo
Team Choi Young Eun, Ahn Hye Joon, Kim Ho Jin, Seo Yu Lim, Kim Ji Hye,
Structural Engineers the Kujo Engineering
Services Engineers Fraunhofer GMBH, Hanil MEC, CVNET
Photography Kim Jae Kyung

Eco Deck House
Loation Kyunggi-do, South Korea
Type Residence
Architect Jang Yoon Gyoo, Shin Chang Hoon,
Lee Mi Young
Team Kim Woo Young, Yeon Kyung Hee, Kwon Woo Seok, Jung Bok Ju, Choi Hye Jin
Photography Unsangdong Architects Cooperation

Gallery CAMELLIA HILL
Location Jeju, South Korea
Type Residence
Client Yang Eon Bo
Architect Jang Yoon Gyoo, Shin Chang Hoon
Team Kim Youn Soo, Kim Woo Young, Park byung Gyu, Lee Mi Young, Seo Soo Kyung

Wall Garden
Loation Seoul, South Korea
Type Culture
Architect Jang Yoon Gyoo, Shin Chang Hoon
Team Kim Youn Soo
Photography Unsangdong Architects Cooperation

Office of UNSANGDONG Architects Cooperation
Loation Seoul, South Korea
Type Office
Architect Jang Yoon Gyoo, Shin Chang Hoon,
Kim Min Tae
Photography Unsangdong Architects Cooperation

Published by
UNSANGDONG Publishing Co.

Edited by
Jang Yoon Gyoo ygjang@hananet.net
Shin Chang Hoon chshin12@naver.com

Documentation
UNSANGDONG Architects

Texts
Jang Yoon Gyoo, Sergio Pirrone, Benjamin Budde, Mathias Remmele

Book Design
Yellowrabbit / hyelim + bj

Translations
**Helen Choi Hae Jung, Professor, Kookmin University
Choi Young Eun, Kim Mi Jung**

Photographer
**Sergio Pirrone, Kim Yong Kwan, Kim Jae Kyung,
Namgoong Sun, Kim Jong Oh, Jin Hyu Sook,
Lee Ki Hwan, Kim Bong Kyun, Song Jae Young,
Moon Jung Sik**

Production
UNSANGDONG Architects
163-43, HaeHwa-Dong, JongNo-Gu, Seoul, South Korea
T +82. 2 764 8401
F +82. 2 764 8403
M usdspace@hanmail.net
www.usdspace.com

Printing
Pandacom Printing Co., Ltd, Korea
57-1, Chungmuro 3ga, Jung-Gu, Seoul, Korea
T +82. 2 2278 3167
F +82. 2 2268 0726
www.pandacom.co.kr

© of the edition UNSANGDONG
© of the texts their authors
© of the photographs their authors

All rights reserved

ISBN 978-89-965136-9-8